THE LONGMAN HANDBOOK OF
MODERN IRISH HISTORY
Since 1800

THE LONGMAN HANDBOOK OF
MODERN IRISH HISTORY
Since 1800

N. C. Fleming and Alan O'Day

PEARSON
Longman

Harlow, England • London • New York • Boston • San Francisco • Toronto • Sydney • Singapore • Hong Kong
Tokyo • Seoul • Taipei • New Delhi • Cape Town • Madrid • Mexico City • Amsterdam • Munich • Paris • Milan

PEARSON EDUCATION LIMITED

Edinburgh Gate
Harlow CM20 2JE
United Kingdom
Tel: +44 (0)1279 623623
Fax: +44 (0)1279 431059
Website: www.pearsoned.co.uk

First edition published in Great Britain in 2005

© Pearson Education Limited 2005

The rights of N. C. Fleming and Alan O'Day to be identified
as authors of this work have been asserted by them in accordance
with the Copyright, Designs and Patents Act 1988.

ISBN 0 582 08102 5

British Library Cataloguing in Publication Data
A CIP catalogue record for this book can be obtained from the British Library

Library of Congress Cataloging in Publication Data
O'Day, Alan.
    The Longman handbook of modern Irish history since 1800 / Alan O'Day and N.C.
Fleming.
        p. cm.
    Includes bibliographical references and index.
    ISBN 0–582–08102–5 (pbk.)
    1. Ireland—History—19th century—Handbooks, manuals, etc. 2. Ireland—History—
20th century—Handbooks, manuals, etc. I. Fleming, N. C. (Nicholas Coit) II. Title.

DA950.O34 2005
941.508—dc22

                                                                            2004057337

10 9 8 7 6 5 4 3 2 1
09 08 07 06 05

Set by 35 in 10/12pt ITC New Baskerville
Printed and bound in Malaysia.

The Publishers' policy is to use paper manufactured from sustainable forests.

CONTENTS

INTRODUCTION

The rationale for this book originated with easing the difficulty encountered by all scholars of modern Irish history, namely the time-consuming chore of collecting political, social and economic data for the last two centuries. This book is therefore the first one-stop volume of Irish historical facts and figures, a book that will, we hope, assist scholars, students, journalists, civil servants, and general readers to avoid endless hours of rummaging through obscure and hard-to-find files and publications.

Choosing what to include in a publication such as this can often be the most difficult task. In deciding, we have had to consider relevance, accuracy, reliability, availability and completeness. This is no easy task, especially when it is accompanied by the perennial constraints of academic publishing, namely space, deadlines and teaching commitments. Nevertheless, the team at Pearson Education have been unstinting in their encouragement and support. Our work colleagues have also been generous, both in supplying encouragement and, in many cases, informed corroboration. In view of the help we have received, it might be wise to reaffirm that the final responsibility for the accuracy of this book lies with the authors. In doing so, we acknowledge the possibility for human error, and the problems inherent in certain sources. It is partly for that reason that we have striven to include sources. But their inclusion will also allow readers to follow up the information contained herein should they chose to do so.

Two sources in particular deserve special mention: the annual yearbooks published by the Central Statistics Office (CSO) of Ireland, Dublin, and by the Northern Ireland Statistics and Research Agency (NIAAS), Belfast. There are, of course, many other sources, institutions, and people who have helped us at various stages, including: Ark: Northern Ireland Political and Social Archive; Bodleian Library, Oxford; British Academy; Garda Museum and Archives; Greyfriars, University of Oxford; Honourable Society of King's Inns, Dublin; Institute of Historical Research, University of London; Institute of Irish Studies, Queen's University Belfast; Law Society of Ireland; Linen Hall Library, Belfast; Main Library, Queen's University Belfast; Northern Ireland Court Service; Nuffield Foundation; Presbyterian Historical Society; St Patrick's College, Maynooth; Trinity College, Dublin and the Wesley Historical Archive, Belfast. Among those who have given us much appreciated assistance have been Walter Arnstein, Paul Bew, Timothy Bowman, D. George Boyce, Miles Bradbury, Mike Bromley, Dominic Bryan, Melanie Carter, Chris Cook, Myra Dowling, David Fitzpatrick, Barbara Gauntt, Gordon Gillespie, S. W. Gilley, A. C. Hepburn, Bronach Kane, Liam Kennedy, Michael Kennedy, Barbara King, Carla King, Donal Lowry, Gillian McIntosh, Val McLeish, Donald McRaild, Fiona Markham, Patrick Maume, Sarah Morgan, Marc Mulholland,

Janet Nolan, Frances Nugent, Col. Helen E. O'Day, Mary O'Dowd, Rich Palser, Senia Păseta, W. S. Peterson, Roland Quinault, Carmel Quinlan, Revd Robert Roddie, Christopher Shepard, John Stevenson, Roger Swift, F. M. L. Thompson, Diane Urquhart, W. E. Vaughan, Brian M. Walker, Jon Wakelyn, Margaret Ward and Fr Tom Weinandy.

N.C.F. and A.O'D
Belfast and Oxford
November 2004

Publisher's acknowledgements

We are grateful to the following for permission to reproduce copyright material:

Cambridge University Press for extracts of data from *Abstracts of British Historical Statistics* (1962); Four Courts Press for an extract adapted from *The Law Society of Ireland, 1852–2002: Portrait of a Profession* by Eamonn G. Hall and Daire Hogan; Lilliput Press for an extract published in *The Cost of Living in Ireland* by David Dickson and Cormac O'Grada (2003); Oxford University Press for an extract published in *The Oxford Companion to Law* by David Walker (1980); Palgrave Macmillan for an extract published in *Land, Politics, and Nationalism* by Phillip Bull © Bull, Phillip; and Taylor Francis for an extract published in *The Irish in Britain* by John Archer Jackson (1963).

In some instances we have been unable to trace the owners of copyright material, and we would appreciate any information that would enable us to do so.

POLITICAL HISTORY

CHRONOLOGY

1801

1 Jan. Act of Union took effect.
3 Feb. William Pitt announced intention to resign as Prime Minister because King George III refused to countenance Catholic Emancipation (*see* 14 Mar.).
14 Mar. Pitt resigned (*see* 3 Feb.).
17 Mar. Henry Addington appointed Prime Minister.
21 May Viscount Castlereagh resigned as Chief Secretary.
25 May Philip Yorke, Earl of Harwicke, sworn in as Lord Lieutenant; Charles Abbott appointed Chief Secretary.
2 July Copyright Act (41 Geo. III, c. 107). Trinity College received entitlement to a copy of every book published in the United Kingdom and Ireland.

1802

13 Feb. William Wickham appointed Chief Secretary.
13 Mar. John Freeman Mitford appointed Lord Chancellor of Ireland.
27 Mar. Peace of Amiens ended war with France.
30 June United Irishmen released from imprisonment at Fort George, Inverness-shire, Scotland, on condition of going into exile.
12–31 July In UK general election Henry Addington retained his majority.

1803

Jan. Influenza epidemic began and continued until June.
21 Feb. Edward Despart hanged for conspiracy to overthrow the government.
18 May UK declaration of war on France.
9 June Edmund Ignatius Rice opened first Christian Brothers' School in Waterford (*see* 15 Aug. 1808).
1 July General synod of Ulster accepted government scheme for augmentation and redistribution of *regium donum.*
23 July Robert Emmet's rebellion in Dublin.
24 July Thomas Russell issued proclamation for a northern rising.
29 July Habeas corpus suspended; Act for suppression of rebellion.
25 Aug. Emmet arrested.
9 Sept. Russell arrested.
19 Sept. Emmet tried and convicted in Dublin of high treason.
20 Sept. Emmet hanged and decapitated.
20 Oct. Russell tried and convicted in Downpatrick of high treason.
21 Oct. Russell executed.
14 Dec. Bank of Ireland took over Parliament House in College Green.

1804

14 Jan. Cow-pock Institution opened for vaccination on Edward Jenner's principle against smallpox.

6 Feb. Sir Evan Napean appointed Chief Secretary.

10 May Pitt appointed Prime Minister (*see* 23 Jan. 1806).

1805

23 Mar. Nicholas Vansittart appointed Chief Secretary.

25 Mar. Catholic petition presented to parliament.

9 Apr. Pope Pius VII confirmed rules and granted final approval of the community of the Presentation Sisters at Cork founded by Namo Negle.

13–14 May Catholic petition debated in the House of Commons.

10 July Act allowing grand juries to fund maintenance of dispensaries.

25 Sept. Sir John Newport appointed Chancellor of the Irish Exchequer.

21 Oct. Battle of Trafalgar.

1806

23 Jan. Death of Prime Minister Pitt (*see* 10 May 1804).

11 Feb. 'Ministry of all the Talents' formed under Lord Grenville as Prime Minister.

17 Mar. Foundation stone laid for College of Surgeons, Dublin.

28 Mar. John Russell, Duke of Bedford, sworn in as Lord Lieutenant; William Elliot appointed Chief Secretary.

21 July Act gave Lord Lieutenant authority to appoint commission to inquire into education.

c. **Sept.** Peasant movement, the Thrashers, began disturbances in north-west (*see* 5 Dec.).

10 Nov. Hibernian Bible Society formed.

Nov. – Dec. General election: Grenville gained supporters and retained premiership.

5 Dec. Seven Threshers executed (*see* Sept.).

1807

19 Jan. First meeting of Gaelic Society of Dublin.

1 Feb. Order of Sisters of St Brigid founded at Tullow, Co. Carlow.

15 Feb. Foundation stone laid of chapel, later Chapel Royal, at Dublin Castle.

24 Mar. Fall of Grenville ministry over bill extending right of Catholics to hold commissions in the army.

31 Mar. Duke of Portland appointed Prime Minister.

19 Apr. Charles Lennox, Duke of Richmond, sworn in as Lord Lieutenant; Sir Arthur Wellesley appointed Chief Secretary.

13 May/6 June UK general election, termed 'no popery' election, had the outcome of Portland remaining Prime Minister.

21 May William Saurin appointed Attorney-General.

1 Aug. Insurrection Act.

13 Aug. Act empowering Lord Lieutenant to appoint commissioners to carry out paving, cleansing and lighting of Dublin's streets. Possessions of Arms Act.

1808

5 Jan. Start of progressive reduction of duties on calicoes, muslins, cotton yarn, and cotton twist imported from Great Britain under the terms of the Act of Union.

30 Jan. Commencement of construction of Viscount Nelson's Pillar on Sackville Street, Dublin (*see* 8 Mar. 1966).

25 May Henry Grattan's motion to consider Catholic petition defeated (281–128). It marked the beginning of the 'veto' controversy.

3 June Dublin Police Magistrates Act placed police under control of 18 magistrates (6 elected by Corporation, 12 appointed by the Lord Lieutenant).

15 Aug. Edmund Rice founded Irish Christian Brothers in Waterford (*see* 9 June 1803).

14–15 Sept. Catholic bishops rejected royal veto of episcopal appointments.

1809

7 Mar. Belfast Harp Society formed to teach harping to the sightless (abandoned 1813).

13 Apr. Robert Dundas appointed Chief Secretary.

24 May Re-establishment in Dublin of General Committee of the Catholics of Ireland to seek Emancipation.

30 May Defeat of motion for inquiry into tithe collection.

15 June Drainage of Bogs Act.

4 Oct. Spencer Perceval appointed Prime Minister (*see* 11 May 1812).

18 Oct. William Wellesley-Pole appointed Chief Secretary.

7 Nov. Sir Patrick Dun's Hospital in Dublin opened.

Nov. Sunday School Society for Ireland founded.

1810

Mar. Richmond National Institution for the Instruction of the Industrious Blind in Dublin opened.

15 June Act to incorporate the Belfast Academical Institution.

20 June Unlawful Oaths Act extended powers against oath-bound secret societies (*see* 1 Aug. 1807).

3 July Foundation stone laid for Belfast Academical Institution (Royal Belfast Academical Institution from 1831).

10 July Grand Orange Lodge adopted new rules omitting secret articles.

1 Sept. Commission appointed to inquire into the state of Irish records.

18 Sept. Dublin freemen and freeholders aggregate meeting resolved to prepare petition for Repeal of the Union.

1811

5 Feb. George Augustus Frederick, Prince of Wales, became Regent.

12 Feb. Chief Secretary, William Wellesley-Pole, issued circular to sheriffs and magistrates to proceed under the Convention Act against Catholics involved in appointment of delegates to the Catholic Committee.

9 July Meeting of Catholics in Dublin established committee to manage petitions for the repeal of the remaining penal laws.

30 July Proclamation of illegality of representatives to Catholic Committee.

2 Dec. Kildare Place Society (Society for Promoting the Education of the Poor in Ireland) founded to organise non-denominational schools.

1812

11 May Prime Minister Spencer Perceval assassinated.

20 Apr. Maurice FitzGerald, MP, presented Irish Protestant petition for Catholic relief.

8 June Earl of Liverpool appointed Prime Minister (*see* 10 Apr. 1827).

4 Aug. Robert Peel appointed Chief Secretary.

10 Oct. – 10 Nov. General election: Liverpool remained Prime Minister.

1813

30 Apr. Henry Grattan introduced Catholic Relief bill in the House of Commons (*see* 24 May).

24 May Grattan's Catholic Relief bill withdrawn after amendment excluding Catholics from sitting in parliament carried (252–247).

2 July Arms Act.

3 July General Synod of Ulster declared in favour of abolition of political distinctions on account of religious profession.

10 July Endowed Schools Act. Provided for commissioners to direct royal schools and supervise others.

12 July First sectarian disturbances in Belfast.

26 July 'Battle of Garvagh', a sectarian confrontation in Co. Londonderry, left one Catholic dead.

26 Aug. Charles, Viscount Whitworth sworn in as Lord Lieutenant.

1814

1 Feb. Belfast Academical Institution opened (prefix Royal added 1831).

11 Apr. Abdication of Napoleon.

27 May Infirmaries Act provided for appointment of apothecaries.

30 May First Peace of Paris.

3 June Catholic Board suppressed by viceregal proclamation.

14 July Clongowes Wood College (Jesuit) opened.

25 July Peace Preservation Act empowered Lord Lieutenant to appoint in disturbed areas 'a chief magistrate of police', a clerk, a chief constable and a force of sub-constables, responsible to Dublin Castle but paid from local taxation.

30 July Revised Insurrection Act (*see* 1 Aug. 1807).
12 Aug. Foundation stone laid for General Post Office, Dublin (opened 6 Jan. 1818).
1 Nov. Congress of Vienna opened.
Dec. Apprentice Boys of Londonderry Club formed.

1815
19 Jan. Daniel O'Connell at a meeting of Catholics in Dublin warned the Pope and Irish Hierarchy that the lower clergy and Catholic masses would revolt against any 'veto' arrangement.
1 Feb. Daniel O'Connell killed John D'Esterre in a duel.
28 Mar. Foundation stone for Dublin Catholic Pro-Cathedral laid.
30 May In House of Commons motion for committee on laws affecting Catholics defeated.
9 June Conclusion of the Congress of Vienna.
18 June Battle of Waterloo.
22 June Napoleon abdicated again. Richmond Lunatic Asylum Act provided for regulation of Dublin asylum.
24 Aug. Catholic bishops adopted anti-veto resolutions for transmission to Rome.
1 Sept. Mary Augustine Aikenhead appointed Superior-General of new order, Irish Sisters of Charity.
20 Nov. Second Peace of Paris.

1816
1 Feb. Pope Pius VII reaffirmed that he did not object to British government veto over Irish episcopal appointments.
13 Feb. Catholic meeting in Lord Trimleston's house adopted petition to parliament declaring that Catholics were ready to accept 'qualified' Emancipation, that is Emancipation with the veto.
18 May National Institution for the Education of Deaf and Dumb Children of the Poor founded.
26 June Act to Facilitate Recovery of Possession of Land by Landlords.
1 July Consolidated Fund Act (amalgamated Exchequers of Great Britain and Ireland).
Aug. – Oct. Potato crop failed; start of first major famine since 1742.
15 Aug. Last public executions in Belfast.
30 Sept. Horticultural Society of Ireland founded (prefix Royal adopted 1838).
Sept. – Oct. Typhus epidemic began (lasted until Dec. 1819 causing *c.* 50,000 deaths).

1817
5 Jan. Unification of Irish and British Exchequers.
9 May Henry Grattan's motion in House of Commons for Catholic Emancipation defeated.

7

16 June Poor Employment Act empowered Lord Lieutenant to appoint commissioners to direct public works financed by mortgages of rates (local taxation).

17 June Foundation stone laid for Wellington Obelisk in Phoenix Park.

11 July Act for establishment of lunatic asylums; Grand Jury Presentments Act regulated expenditure on public works.

30 Sept. National fever committee appointed to disburse government aid for victims of typhus epidemic.

9 Oct. Charles, Earl Talbot, sworn in as Lord Lieutenant.

1818

6 Jan. General Post Office in Dublin opened to the public (*see* 12 Aug. 1814).

28 Jan. Hiberno-Celtic Society founded to preserve and publish ancient Irish literature.

22 Apr. Select committee of the House of Commons appointed to inquire into fever in Ireland.

30 May Fever Hospitals Act provided for establishment of fever hospitals and extension of dispensary system.

9 June – 25 July General election: Liverpool remained Prime Minister.

30 June Revd Henry Montgomery elected Moderator of the General Synod of Ulster.

9 July Presbyterian Secession Synod formed.

10 July First meeting of the Primitive Wesleyan Methodist Conference.

3 Aug. Charles Grant appointed Chief Secretary in successor to Sir Robert Peel.

1819

6 Apr. Select committee of the House of Commons appointed to inquire into the state of disease and conditions of the poor in Ireland.

16 Apr. Irish Harp Society succeeded the Belfast Harp Society.

3 May Defeat of petition in favour of Catholic relief (243–241).

12 July Fisheries Act provided for appointment of commissioners to regulate sea fishing.

Oct. Ribbon disturbances proliferate.

1820

19 Jan. Grand Orange Lodge issued circular against unauthorised Orange 'orders'.

29 Jan. George III died; succeeded by the Regent as George IV. Revd John MacHale argued against education of Catholics and Protestants together (mixed education).

13 Mar. – 13 Apr. General election: Liverpool remained Prime Minister.

25 May Crisis of bank failures began.

4 June Henry Grattan died in London.

29 June Dublin Society adopted prefix Royal.
8 July Act for Lighting the City and Suburbs of Dublin with Gas.
5 Sept. Pope Pius VII sanctioned the Irish Christian Brothers.

1821
18 Jan. Theatre Royal opened in Dublin.
2 Apr. Bill for Catholic relief passed in House of Commons by 19 votes (*see* 17 Apr.).
17 Apr. Bill for Catholic relief defeated in House of Lords (159–120) (*see* 2 Apr.).
28 May Census of population throughout Ireland (6,801,827).
5 June Belfast Natural History Society formed (renamed Belfast Natural History and Philosophical Society, 23 Aug. 1842).
2 July Act permitted joint stock banks outside radius of 50 miles from Dublin; Bank of Ireland deprived of its monopoly.
12 Aug. – 3 Sept. King George IV visited Ireland; Dunleary is renamed Kingstown.
Sept. – Nov. Potato crop failed.
25 Oct. Begging of second non-subscription controversy in Synod of Ulster (*see* 18–20 Aug. 1829).
19 Nov. Seventeen people burned to death in a house in Tubber, Co. Tipperary, by presumed 'Rockite' gang.
29 Dec. Richard, Marquis Wellesley, sworn in as Lord Lieutenant; Henry Goulburn appointed Chief Secretary.

1822
15 Jan. William Conynham Plunket appointed Attorney-General of Ireland.
11 Feb. Insurrection Act permitted sentence of seven years transportation. (*see* 30 July 1814); Habeas Corpus Suspension Act in force until 1 Aug.
22 Mar. Act to regulate the importation of arms, gunpowder and ammunition.
30 Apr. Bill to permit Catholic peers to take seats in House of Lords passes in House of Commons.
24 May Poor Employment Act. Provided £50,000 for road construction in response to failure of potato crop.
June – Dec. Fever epidemic in west of Ireland.
22 June Bill to allow Catholic peers to be admitted to the House of Lords defeated in the Upper House (171–129).
5 July Act abolished Irish window and hearth taxes.
22 July Act (proposed by Richard 'Humanity Dick' Martin) to prevent cruel and improper treatment of cattle.
5 Aug. County Constabulary Act established police force in each county.

12 Aug. Suicide of Marquis of Londonderry (Viscount Castlereagh).
24 Oct. William Magree, Church of Ireland Archbishop of Dublin, began the 'Second Reformation'.
5 Nov. Loreto nuns began educational work in Ireland.

1823

11 Feb. Parliamentary by-election in County Dublin won by candidate supporting Catholic emancipation.
25 Apr. Daniel O'Connell and Richard Lalor Shiel presided at meeting of 20 Catholics which resolved to form an organisation to agitate for Catholic Emancipation.
2 May Customs and Excise Act consolidated Boards of Customs and of Excise of Great Britain and Ireland.
3 May Hibernian Philanthropic Society founded.
11 May Daniel Murray became Catholic Archbishop of Dublin.
12 May Catholic Association formed in Dublin.
23 May Act for lighting with gas Belfast and suburbs.
18 July Unlawful Oaths Act strengthened powers against associations bound by oaths; Excise Duty Act abolished minimum charge on stills.
19 July Irish Tithe Composition Act allowed fixed money payment in lieu of tithes.
4 Aug. Orange Order changed rules and abolished requirement for oath on admission.
5 Aug. Royal Hibernian Academic of Arts received charter.
30 Aug. Belfast gas lighting system began operation.
9 Sept. Catholic refused burial at St Kevin's Church in Dublin (*see* 17 Nov.).
17 Nov. Committee of Catholic Association recommended founding a burial committee to purchase land for Catholic burials (*see* 9 Sept. 1823, 22 Feb. 1832).

1824

1 Jan. First issue of (Belfast) *Northern Whig.*
24 Jan. Daniel O'Connell proposed to the Catholic Association the 'Catholic rent' as the means to finance the movement.
12 Apr. Act to Repeal the Duties on All Articles Manufactured in Great Britain and Ireland Respectively on their Importation into either Country from the Other.
19 May Select committee of the House of Lords began sitting (to 23 June) in investigation into faction fighting in Ireland.
2 June Report of the select committee of the House of Commons on the survey and valuation of Ireland (Ordnance Survey).
14 June Commission of inquiry into education in Ireland.
22 June Board of Ordnance directed Thomas Colby to make a cartographic survey of the country.
29 Oct. First issue of the (Dublin) *Morning Register.*

23 Dec. Day believed by many Protestants to be fixed for their massacre by Catholics ('Pastorini's prophecies').

1825
9 Mar. Unlawful Societies Act directed at Catholic Association and Orange Order.
18 Mar. Orange Order and Catholic Association dissolved.
25 Mar. Catholic Emancipation bill introduced in the House of Commons.
10 May Catholic Relief bill passed by the House of Commons.
18 May Catholic Relief bill defeated in the House of Lords (178–130).
30 May First report of the commission on Irish Education (*see* 14 June 1824, 27 Jan. 1827).
27 June Currency Act (assimilated Irish currency to British from 5 Jan. 1826); Excise Licences Act raised Irish duties to levels of Great Britain.
30 June Final report of parliamentary select committee on the state of Ireland.
13 July Daniel O'Connell founded 'new' Catholic Association.
14 Nov. Catholic Pro-Cathedral opened in Marlborough Street, Dublin.

1826
5 Jan. Irish currency assimilated with British; gallon and bushel measures standardised.
7 Mar. Motion on Catholic relief defeated in House of Commons (276–272).
12 Mar. Pope Leo XII's encyclical *Quo graviera* condemned secret societies.
5 May Act restricting sub-letting of lands and tenements.
26 May Act for uniform valuation of lands and tenements for local taxation.
12 June – 8 July General election: Liverpool remained Prime Minister. On 1 July pro-emancipation candidates won seat for Co. Waterford.
7 July Daniel O'Connell announced plan to re-institute the 'Catholic rent'.
July Fever epidemic.
30 Aug. Daniel O'Connell at Waterford inducted the first members in his 'Order of Liberators'.

1827
27 Jan. Fourth report of commissioners on Irish Education (on Belfast Academical Institution) (*see* 14 June 1824, 30 May 1825).
10 Apr. George Canning appointed Prime Minister (*see* 31 Aug.).
29 Apr. William Lamb appointed Chief Secretary.
8 Aug. George Canning died (*see* 10 Apr.).
31 Aug. Viscount Goderich appointed Prime Minister (*see* 22 Jan. 1828).
24 Sept. Catherine McAuley opened house in Dublin as school and asylum for the poor (dedicated to Our Lady of Mercy, 24 Sept. 1828; *see also* 12 Dec. 1831).
5 Nov. Sir Anthony Hart appointed Lord Chancellor of Ireland.

1828

8 Jan. Viscount Goderich resigned as Prime Minister (*see* 31 Aug. 1827).

13 Jan. 'Simultaneous Meetings' of Catholic Association in *c.* 1,600 of 2,500 parishes challenged the government on Emancipation.

22 Jan. Duke of Wellington appointed Prime Minister (*see* 16 Nov. 1830).

1 Feb. Daniel O'Connell's 'Address of the Catholic Association to the Protestant Dissenters of England' on Emancipation.

1 Mar. William Henry Paget, Marquis of Anglesey, sworn in as Lord Lieutenant.

11 Mar. Select committee of the House of Commons appointed to consider Irish education.

9 May English Test and Corporation Acts repealed, allowing Dissenters to hold public office.

12 May Motion for settlement of Catholic question passed by House of Commons (272–266).

19 May Report of select committee of House of Commons on Irish education recommended establishment of government body to control elementary schools.

21 May William Lamb resigned as Chief Secretary.

21 June Lord Francis Leveson-Gower appointed Chief Secretary.

24 June Daniel O'Connell announced intention to contest the Co. Clare parliamentary by-election.

5 July O'Connell declared victory in by-election in Co. Clare (2,057 to 982 for William Vesey-Fitzgerald).

9 July Motion for settlement of Catholic question defeated in the House of Lords.

15 July Linen and Hempen Manufactures Act abolished linen board.

25 July Act providing for lighting, cleansing and watching of Irish cities and towns.

1 Aug. Duke of Wellington advised the King that Catholic Emancipation was essential.

14 Aug. Founding of Brunswick Constitutional Club to preserve the Protestant Constitution.

15 Sept. Revival of the Orange movement.

16 Oct. General Synod of Ulster adopted remonstrance which split Synod (*see* 18–20 Aug. 1829, 25–27 May 1830).

24 Nov. First issue of *Pilot*, an O'Connellite organ.

11 Dec. Duke of Wellington's letter to Patrick Curtis, Archbishop of Armagh, on the need for a settlement to the Emancipation question.

1829

1 Jan. Marquess of Anglesey, Lord Lieutenant, recalled following publication of letter urging Catholic Emancipation.

5 Feb. King's speech announced intention to legislate on Catholic Emancipation.

5 Mar. Catholic Relief bill introduced in House of Commons by Sir Robert Peel. Act for the suppression of dangerous associations or assemblies in Ireland.

6 Mar. Hugh Percy, Duke of Northumberland, sworn in as Lord Lieutenant.

13 Apr. Roman Catholic Relief Act; Irish Parliamentary Elections Act raised property qualification for ballot from 40 shillings to £10, reducing electorate from 216,000 to 37,000.

15 May Daniel O'Connell prohibited from taking seat in House of Commons because the Emancipation Act is not retrospective.

30 July O'Connell returned for Co. Clare parliamentary by-election unopposed.

18–20 Aug. Revd Henry Montgomery and supporters seceded from Presbyterian General Synod and established the Remonstrant Synod (*see* 16 Oct. 1828, 25–27 May 1829).

1830

4 Feb. Daniel O'Connell took seat in House of Commons.

9 Feb. Catholic bishops expressed gratitude for Emancipation and counsel priests against participation in political controversies in the future.

6 Apr. Formation of Friends of Ireland of All Religious Denominations (*see* 24 Apr.).

24 Apr. Friends of Ireland of All Religious Denominations declared illegal (*see* 6 Apr.).

10 May Formation of Zoological Society of Dublin (*see* 1 Sept. 1831).

25–27 May First meeting of Remonstrant Synod (*see* 16 Oct. 1828, 18–20 Aug. 1829).

26 June King George IV died; succeeded by William IV.

16 July Arms Act to regulate for one year importation of arms and gunpowder.

17 July Sir Henry Hardinge appointed Chief Secretary.

27–29 July Revolution in Paris; abdication of Charles X.

2–24 Aug. General election; swing against the Duke of Wellington.

7 Aug. Louis-Phillippe declared king of France.

Oct. 'Tithe War', a protest against payment of tithes to Church of Ireland clergy began in Graiguenamanagh, Co. Kilkenny (*see* 3 Mar., 18 June 1831).

16 Nov. Duke of Wellington resigned as Prime Minister (*see* 22 Jan. 1828).

22 Nov. Earl Grey appointed Prime Minister (*see* 16 July 1834).

29 Nov. Edward Stanley appointed Chief Secretary.

23 Dec. Marquis of Anglesey sworn in as Lord Lieutenant.

1831

Jan. Terry Alt agrarian disturbances began.

18 Jan. Daniel O'Connell arrested on charge of conspiracy to violate and evade Lord Lieutenant's proclamation under law for the suppression of dangerous associations (*see* 5 Mar. 1829).

1 Mar. First parliamentary reform bill introduced in the House of Commons.

3 Mar. In 'Tithe War' police seize cattle in Graiguenamanagh, Co. Kilkenny (*see* Oct. 1830, 18 June).

1 May First issue of (Dublin) *Comet*, O'Connellite weekly.

4–21 May General election; Earl Grey gained an increased majority.

18 June 'Tithe Massacre' at Newtownbary, Co. Wexford (*see* Oct. 1830, 3 Mar.).

1 Sept. Zoological gardens in Phoenix Park, Dublin, opened to the public.

6 Sept. Act authorising construction of Dublin–Kingstown railway (*see* 31 July, 17 Dec. 1834).

9 Sept. Edward Stanley secured £30,000 to establish system of non-denominational national education.

15 Oct. Public Works Act to reorganise the Board of Works; Tumultuous Rising Act replaced capital punishment by transportation.

23 Oct. Richard Whately consecrated Church of Ireland Archbishop of Dublin.

31 Oct. Scheme for national system of non-denomination education outlined by Edward Stanley.

1 Nov. Belfast Museum opened.

26 Nov. Commissioners of National Education appointed.

29 Nov. Geological Society of Ireland founded.

12 Dec. Religious Sisters of Mercy established with Catherine McAuley as Superior (*see* 24 Sept. 1827).

15 Dec. Committees appointed by both Houses of Parliament to inquire into Irish tithes. Census of population.

1832

Jan. Asiatic cholera appeared in Belfast and Dublin, spreading throughout the country and lasting until 1833.

18 Jan. First meeting of Daniel O'Connell's National Council.

19 Jan. Irish parliamentary reform bill introduced in the House of Commons.

c. **Feb.** Whitefeet disturbances in midland counties.

22 Feb. First internment in Glasnevin cemetery (*see* 9 Sept., 17 Nov. 1823).

15 Mar. Asiatic cholera reached Belfast and persisted in Ireland until 1833.

9 May Earl Grey resigned as Prime Minister; reinstated when the Duke of Wellington failed to form a ministry.

31 May Select Committee of the House of Commons appointed to inquire into disturbances in Ireland (*see* 2 Aug.).

1 June Act to facilitate recovery of tithes.

30 June First issue of *Dublin Penny Journal* edited by Caesar Otway and George Petrie.

1 Aug. Arms Act, continuation for one year.

2 Aug. Report of Select Committee of House of Commons to inquire into disturbances in Ireland (*see* 31 May).

7 Aug. Irish Reform Act increased Ireland's representation from 100 to 105.
16 Aug. Party Processions Act to curb sectarian conflict; Irish Tithe Composition Act.
12 Dec. – 2 Jan. General election; Grey remained Prime Minster.
22 Dec. Sectarian rioting in Belfast.

1833

5 Jan. First issue of the *Dublin University Magazine*, founded by Isaac Butt (ran until 1877).
18 Jan. First meeting of Daniel O'Connell's 'National Council'.
11 Mar. Viscount Althorp introduced Irish Church bill in the House of Commons (withdrawn 20 Mar.; *see* 23 Apr.).
29 Mar. Sir John Cam Hobhouse appointed Chief Secretary.
2 Apr. Coercion Act for suppression of disturbances empowered Lord Lieutenant to suppress public meetings.
23 Apr. Viscount Althorp introduced a new Irish Church bill in the House of Commons (*see* 11 Mar.).
17 May Edward John Littleton appointed Chief Secretary.
20 July Appointment of commission of inquiry into Irish Municipal Corporations.
14 Aug. Church Temporalities Act abolished 10 bishoprics and provided for other reforms of the Church of Ireland.
28 Aug. Act to provide for the more impartial trial of offences.
29 Aug. Irish Tithes Arrears Act advanced £1 million for relief of tithe owners.
25 Sept. Appointment of Royal Commission of Inquiry into the Poorer Classes in Ireland with Archbishop Richard Whatley as chairman (*see* 4 May 1836).
26 Sept. Marquis Wellesley sworn in as Lord Lieutenant.
29 Dec. Sectarian rioting in Belfast.

1834

23 Jan. St Vincent's Hospital operated by the Sisters of Charity, the first hospital in the United Kingdom run by women, opened in Dublin.
28 Jan. Catholic Hierarchy secretly resolved that chapels shall not be used, as in the past, for political meetings and that clergy shall stand aloof from politics.
20 Feb. Edward Littleton, Chief Secretary, introduced in the House of Commons a resolution to commute tithes into a land tax.
22–30 Apr. Daniel O'Connell's motion to Repeal the Union debated in the House of Commons.
May Royal Dublin Society's first industrial exhibition.
4 June Royal Commission on state of religious and other instruction appointed; it undertook the first systematic enumeration of religious affiliation.

16 July William Lamb, Lord Melbourne, appointed Prime Minister (*see* 14 Nov.).

21 July John MacHale, Bishop of Killala, appointed Archbishop of Tuam. A national bank founded under O'Connell's auspices.

31 July First train in Ireland ran from Dublin to Kingstown (*see* 6 Sept. 1831, 17 Dec.).

14 Nov. King dismissed Lord Melbourne as Prime Minister (*see* 16 July).

17 Nov. Duke of Wellington appointed Prime Minister (*see* 10 Dec.).

10 Dec. Sir Robert Peel appointed Prime Minister (*see* 17 Nov., 8 Apr. 1835).

16 Dec. Sir Henry Hardinge appointed Chief Secretary.

17 Dec. Dublin–Kingstown railway opened (*see* 6 Sept. 1831, 31 July).

1835

1 Jan. First issue of Philip Barron's *Ancient Ireland* devoted to reviving and cultivating the Irish language.

5 Jan. – 9 Feb. General election. Whigs, Radicals and O'Connellites gained a majority.

6 Jan. Thomas Hamilton, Earl of Haddington, sworn in as Lord Lieutenant.

18 Feb. Lichfield House meeting between Daniel O'Connell, Whigs and Radicals (*see* 27 Feb.).

27 Feb. Daniel O'Connell offered to aid Whigs to defeat Peel's administration in return for amendment to the Irish Reform Act, and municipal and tithe reform (*see* 18 Feb.).

23 Mar. Appointment of House of Commons select committee on Orangeism (*see* 10 July).

30 Mar. Debate on the Irish Tithe bill began.

8 Apr. Sir Robert Peel resigned as Prime Minister (*see* 10 Dec. 1834).

12 Apr. William Crolly, Bishop of Down and Connor, appointed Archbishop of Armagh.

18 Apr. Lord Melbourne appointed Prime Minister (*see* 14 Nov. 1834, 30 Aug. 1841).

22 Apr. George William Frederick Howard, Viscount Morpeth, appointed Chief Secretary.

29 Apr. Michael O'Loghlen, the first Catholic to hold a law office since the seventeenth century, appointed Solicitor-General of Ireland.

11 May Constantine Phipps, Earl of Mulgrave, sworn in as Lord Lieutenant.

June Total Abstinence Society formed at Strabane, Co. Tyrone.

2 July William Sharman Crawford opened the tenant-right campaign in the House of Commons.

10 July First report of House of Commons select committee on Orangeism (*see* 23 Mar.).

25 July Earl of Mulgrave sworn in as Lord Lieutenant; Viscount Morpeth appointed Chief Secretary; Thomas Drummond became Under-Secretary of the Irish Office.

31 July Government introduced first of six Irish Municipal Reform bills.

10 Aug. Irish Constabulary bill introduced in House of Commons (*see* 26 Aug.).

26 Aug. Irish Constabulary bill rejected by the House of Lords (*see* 10 Aug.).

31 Aug. Act 'for the better prevention and more speedy punishment of offences endangering the public peace in Ireland' is last insurrection Act.

8 Oct. Adoption of new rules for Apprentice Boys of Londonderry Club.

1836

Feb. Total abstinence society formed in Belfast.

14 Apr. Grand Orange Lodge of Ireland decided to dissolve.

4 May House of Commons debated reports of the Royal Commission on the Irish Poor Law (*see* 25 Sept. 1833).

17 May First meeting of Petition Committee for Corporate Reform and Settlement of the Tithe Question (*see* 2 July).

19 May Act for construction of railway between Belfast and Armagh city (*see* 12 Aug. 1839).

20 May Constabulary Act to consolidate the laws relating to the constabulary force.

2 July National Association for Municipal Reform (General Association of Ireland) founded by Daniel O'Connell (*see* 17 May).

4 July Dublin Police Act established metropolitan police force.

13 July Act for Dublin to Drogheda railway (*see* 24 May 1844).

20 Aug. Grand Jury Act.

20 Oct. Royal Commission on construction of railways in Ireland appointed (*see* 13 July 1838).

Nov. Total Abstinence Society formed in Dublin.

1837

20 June King William IV died; Victoria succeeded to the throne.

31 July – 17 Aug. General election; Lord Melbourne remained Prime Minister.

18 Nov. First issue of Fergus O'Connor's (Leeds) *Northern Star*.

1 Dec. Lord John Russell introduced Irish Poor Law bill in the House of Commons.

1838

10 Apr. Fr Theobald Mathew founded temperance movement in Cork City.

5 July Trinity College established a Chair of Irish.

11 July First Catholic in modern era, Stephen Woulfe, appointed Chief Baron of the Irish Exchequer.

13 July Final report of the Irish railway commissioners (*see* 20 Oct. 1836).

31 July Poor Relief Act extended English Poor Law to Ireland creating 130 Unions (*see* 10 Aug. 1872).

17

15 Aug. Tithe Rent Charge Act converted tithe to a rent charge and laid own scales payable.

1 Sept. George Nicholls appointed Poor Law Commissioner for Ireland.

1839

6–7 Jan. 'Night of the Big Wind'.

c. **Feb.** Church Education Society for Ireland formed to provide and maintain schools of Established Church outside national system.

12 Mar. Letter from Prefect of Propaganda, exhorting clergy to eschew politics.

21 Mar. Select Committee of House of Lords (Roden Committee) appointed to inquire into crime and outrage in Ireland since 1835.

3 Apr. Viscount Ebrington (Hugh Fortescue) sworn in as Lord Lieutenant.

8 Apr. Irish Poor Law Unions (130) came into existence.

29 May Irish Medical Association founded.

12 Aug. Belfast to Lisburn section of Ulster Railway opened (*see* 19 May 1836, 12 Sept. 1842).

19 Aug. Act for the Improvement of the Navigation of the River Shannon.

24 Aug. Unlawful Oaths Act directed against societies using signs or passwords.

1840

17 Mar. Irish Archaeological Society founded. Foundation stone laid for Catholic cathedral at Armagh.

15 Apr. Formation by Daniel O'Connell of National Association of Ireland (*see* 13 July).

24 Apr. First poor law union workhouse opened in Dublin.

15 May Isaac Butt defended unreformed Dublin Corporation at bar of the House of Lords.

23 June Meeting to form Ulster Constitutional Association.

10 July Union of the General Synod of Ulster and Secession Synod to form General Assembly of the Presbyterian Church in Ireland.

13 July National Association of Ireland renamed Loyal National Repeal Association under O'Connell's leadership (*see* 15 Apr.).

26 July First large meeting for repeal of the union (Castlebar, Co. Mayo).

6 Aug. First use of photography in Ireland by Francis Beatty.

10 Aug. Irish Municipal Reform Act dissolved 58 municipal corporations and reconstituted 10.

1841

c. **Mar.** Agricultural Improvement Society of Ireland formed.

Mar. – Apr. Tresham Gregg founded Dublin Protestant Operative Association to oppose O'Connell and Liberal politics.

17–19 Apr. Thomas Davis and John Blake Dillon join the Repeal Association.

5 June Melbourne government defeated in House of Commons.

6 June First thorough census of population.

17 June Society of Attorneys and Solicitors of Ireland formed.

1–19 July General election; Conservatives gained a majority.

30 Aug. Sir Robert Peel appointed Prime Minister (*see* 30 June 1846). First issue of *Cork Examiner.*

25 Oct. Election of reformed Dublin Corporation: Liberals secured 49 of 60 seats.

1 Nov. Daniel O'Connell elected Lord Mayor of Dublin.

1842

10 June First issue of James MacKnight's (Belfast) *Banner of Ulster.*

18 June Capital Punishment Act abolishes death penalty for numerous offences in Ireland.

5 Aug. Drainage Act.

10 Aug. Fisheries Act.

12 Aug. Act confirmed validity of marriages celebrated by dissenting clergy.

6 Sept. Edward, Lord Eliot, appointed Chief Secretary.

12 Sept. Lisburn to Portadown section of Ulster Railway opened (*see* 19 May 1836, 12 Aug. 1839, 1 Mar. 1848).

15 Sept. Thomas, Earl de Grey, sworn in as Lord Lieutenant.

15 Oct. First issue of the *Nation* (*see* 5 June 1897).

18 Oct. All Hallows College Dublin opened.

10 Nov. Papal rescript allowed each bishop to decide attitude towards Board of National Education.

10 Nov. Passenger Act introduces regulation of general conditions of ships.

1843

25–28 Feb. Daniel O'Connell's motion on Repeal debated in Dublin Corporation carried (45–15). Isaac Butt spoke against the motion.

9 Mar. Repeal monster meeting in Trim, Co. Meath.

9 May Peel announced that he would not shrink at asking parliament for powers to deal with the Repeal campaign.

11 June At Repeal meeting at Mallow, Co. Cork, Daniel O'Connell issued his 'Mallow Defiance'.

15 Aug. Largest Repeal meeting with an estimated attendance of 750,000 held at Hill of Tara, Co. Meath (*see* 8 Oct.).

22 Aug. Arms Act amends law 'relative to the registering of arms and the importation, manufacture and sale of arms, gunpowder and ammunition'.

7 Oct. Lord Lieutenant proclaimed proposed Repeal meeting at Clontarf (*see* 8 Oct.).

8 Oct. O'Connell cancelled the demonstration scheduled for Clontarf (*see* 7 Oct.).

14 Oct. O'Connell arrested on charge of conspiracy (*see* 10 Feb., 30 May, 4, 13 Sept. 1844).

16 Oct. Sir William Rowan Hamilton discovered his formula for multiplication of quarternions.

20 Oct. William Smith O'Brien joined Repeal Association (*see* 30 May 1844).

20 Nov. Royal Commission (Devon Commission) appointed to inquire into occupation of land (*see* 14 Feb. 1845).

1844

10 Feb. O'Connell and others convicted; he received 12-month prison sentence (*see* 14 Oct. 1843, 30 May, 4, 13 Sept.).

24 May Lord Lieutenant opened the Dublin to Drogheda railway (*see* 13 July 1836, 15 Feb. 1849).

30 May O'Connell began term of imprisonment (*see* 14 Oct. 1843, 10 Feb., 4, 13 Sept.); William Smith O'Brien assumed leadership of Repeal Association (*see* 20 Oct. 1843).

19 July Nonconformist Chapels Act.

29 July William A'Court, Lord Heytesbury, sworn in as Lord Lieutenant.

6 Aug. Act authorising construction of railway from Dublin to Cashel and Carlow (*see* 4 Aug. 1846).

9 Aug. Marriages Act required to keep record of all non-Catholic marriages; Charitable Donations and Bequests Act established religiously mixed bequests board.

4 Sept. House of Lords overturned the convictions of O'Connell and others (*see* 14 Oct. 1843, 10 Feb., 30 May, 13 Sept.).

13 Sept. O'Connell and associates released from prison (*see* 14 Oct. 1843, 10 Feb., 30 May, 4 Sept.).

15 Oct. Letter from Prefect of Propaganda to Archbishop Crolly, prescribing that clergy eschew politics, and urging him to reprove those who refuse to do so.

Dec. Society of St Vincent de Paul introduced to Ireland.

1845

1 Feb. Sir Thomas Francis Freemantle appointed Chief Secretary.

14 Feb. Devon Commission reported (*see* 20 Nov. 1843).

15 Feb. Earl of Rosse's telescope at Birr castle came into operation.

12, 26 May O'Connell and Thomas Davis differed over Academic Colleges bill at meetings of Repeal Association.

23 May Twenty-one Irish Catholic bishops adopted resolution on the Academic Colleges bill, withholding their approbation.

1 June Party Processions Act lapsed.

30 June Maynooth College Act provided for capital grant of £30,000 and increased annual grant from £8,928 to £26,360.

21 July Act for the appointment of additional constables for keeping the peace near public works. Midland Great Western Railway of Ireland Act empowered construction of railway from Dublin to Mullingar and Longford.

31 July Colleges Act established Queen's Colleges at Belfast, Cork and Galway.

8 Aug. Central Criminal Lunatic Asylum Act provided for construction of asylum for criminal lunatics.

12, 27 Aug. Meetings at Enniskillen to revive Orange institution.

Aug. Initial reports of potato crop failure.

9 Sept. Arrival of potato blight in Ireland reported in *Dublin Evening Post.*

16 Sept. Constabulary directed to report weekly on local crops and to estimate extent of loss. Thomas Davis died.

17 Oct. Lord Lieutenant reported general failure of potato crop.

31 Oct. Mansion House Committee formed to examine extent of potato losses and to suggest remedies.

c. **9–10 Nov.** Sir Robert Peel, on his own responsibility, ordered purchase in America of £100,000 of Indian corn for shipment to Ireland.

18 Nov. Appointment of relief commission to administer scheme of relief supplementary to that provided under Poor Relief Act, 1938 (*see* 31 July 1838). Catholic bishops divide on attitude to Queen's Colleges.

20 Nov. First meeting of the Relief Commission on Ireland.

12 Dec. Visitors of Trinity College, Dublin, dismiss appeal over refusal to elect a Catholic to a scholarship on the grounds that his religion disqualified him from being a member of the body corporate. Celtic Society founded.

1846

14 Feb. Henry Pelham-Clinton, Earl of Lincoln, appointed Chief Secretary.

5 Mar. Public Works Act authorises county relief works under the administration of the Board of Works; Act to encourage sea fisheries by grants for the construction of piers, harbours and other works; Drainage Act.

13 Mar. Three hundred people evicted from village of Ballinglass, Co. Galway.

24 Mar. Irish Public Health Act to deal with fever.

28 Mar. Depots open for the sale of food being distributed by relief committee.

26 June Importation of Corn Act virtually abolished duties on imported corn, grain, meal and flour.

29 June Sir Robert Peel resigned as Prime Minister (*see* 30 Aug. 1841).

30 June Lord John Russell appointed Prime Minister (*see* 21 Feb. 1852).

6 July Henry Labouchere appointed Chief Secretary.

9 July John O'Connell sought repudiation of physical force from all members of the Repeal Association (*see* 28 July).

11 July John Ponsonby, Earl of Bessborough, sworn in as Lord Lieutenant; Thomas Redington appointed as the first Catholic Under-Secretary.

13 July Congregation in Rome decides against Catholic involvement in the new Queen's Colleges.

14 July Reappearance of potato disease reported by Sir Randolph Routh to Charles Trevelyan.

28 July Young Ireland group seceded from Repeal Association over principle of physical force (*see* 9 July).

1 Aug. Charles Trevelyan memorandum detailed defects of previous relief scheme and outlined a new plan to meet the coming crisis.

4 Aug. Great Southern and Western Railway between Dublin (Kingstown) and Carlow opened (*see* 6 Aug. 1844).

18 Aug. Act for regulating the gauge of railways fixed it in Ireland at 5 feet, 3 inches.

28 Aug. Constabulary Act removed financial charge from counties and enlarged the reserve; Poor Employment Act empowered Board of Works to execute relief works by means of treasury loans.

30 Aug. Discovery of new species of potato fungus.

31 Aug. Irish Public Health Act (Fever Act) expired (*see* 24 Mar.).

6 Sept. Lord Lieutenant authorised restarting relief works uncompleted on 15 August.

Nov. Beginning of severe winter.

13 Nov. Irish Quakers establish Central Relief Committee of the Society of Friends.

28 Dec. Authorisation of opening of western food depots.

1847

1 Jan. British Association for the Relief of Extreme Distress formed.

11 Jan. Beginning of series of letters in the *Nation* by James Fintan Lalor on the land question and political independence.

13 Jan. Irish Confederation established under leadership of William Smith O'Brien.

14 Jan. Outbreak of typhus and 'relapsing fever'.

26 Jan. Duties on corn imports suspended until 1 Sept.

8 Feb. O'Connell made his last appearance in the House of Commons.

26 Feb. Destitute Poor Act ('Soup Kitchen Act') permitted relief commissioners to administer outdoor relief.

27 Apr. Irish Fever Act amended and continued Irish Public Health Act.

4 May Breakdown of efforts to reunite Loyal National Repeal Association and Irish Confederation.

15 May O'Connell died at Genoa (*see* 5 Aug.).

26 May George Villiers, Earl of Clarendon, sworn in as Lord Lieutenant. Ulster Tenant Right Association formed at Londonderry.

c. June First collection of agricultural statistics, undertaken by constabulary.

8 June Poor Relief Act empowered boards of guardians to grant outdoor relief to specified classes of people (*see* 7 Aug. 1862).

16 June William Sharman Crawford's bill to legalise 'Ulster Custom' refused a second reading by the House of Commons (112–25).

22 July Sir William Meredyth Somerville appointed Chief Secretary. Poor Relief Act created separate Poor Law Commission for Ireland.

31 July – 18 Aug. General election; Russell retained office.

5 Aug. O'Connell's funeral in Dublin; burial in Glasnevin Cemetery (*see* 15 May).

19 Sept. Meeting of tenant farmers at Holycross, Co. Tipperary, convened by James Fintan Lalor to form a tenant league.

1 Oct. Soup kitchens close.

23 Nov. Dublin Statistical Society founded.

Dec. John Mitchel broke with the *Nation*.

20 Dec. Crime and Outrage Act.

1848

3 Jan. Pius IX rescript urging Irish bishops to forbid clerical political involvement.

5 Feb. John Mitchel withdrew from the Irish Confederation.

12 Feb. First issue of the *United Irishman* edited by Mitchel.

1 Mar. Portadown–Armagh section of Ulster Railway opened (*see* 19 May 1836, 12 Aug. 1839, 12 Sept. 1842).

7 Mar. William Sharman Crawford reintroduced tenant-right bill in the House of Commons (*see* 5 Apr.).

15 Mar. At meeting of Irish Confederation in Dublin, William Smith O'Brien and Thomas Francis Meagher advocated physical force.

21 Mar. Information sworn against Smith O'Brien, Mitchel and Meagher (*see* 13, 16 May).

5 Apr. Sharman Crawford's tenant-right bill refused a second reading (145–22) (*see* 7 Mar.).

22 Apr. Treason Felony Act for the better security of the crown and government.

9 May First meeting of Protestant Repeal Association.

13 May Mitchel arrested (*see* 21 Mar.).

16 May Jury disagreed and Smith O'Brien acquitted on sedition charges (*see* 21 Mar.).

26 May Mitchel convicted (*see* 21 Mar., 13, 16 May, 1 June).

27 May Mitchel sentenced to 14 years' transportation (*see* 21 Mar., 13, 26 May, 1 June).

1 June Mitchel transported to Australia (*see* 21 Mar., 13, 26, 27 May).

9 June Alien Act to remove aliens from the realm.

12 June Agreement between Loyal National Repeal Association and Irish Confederation to unite as Irish League.

21 June Council of Irish Confederation decision to dissolve.

24 June First issue of the *Irish Felon* edited by John Martin (*see* 22, 28 July).

July–Sept. General failure of potato crop.

8 July Charles Gavan Duffy arrested. Anne Elgee and Margaret Callan run the *Nation* after the arrest (*see* 1 Sept. 1849).

22 July *Irish Felon* seized by police (*see* 24 June, 28 July).

25 July Habeas corpus suspended (until March 1849).

27 July James Fintan Lalor arrested.

28 July Police arrested 10 members of the *Nation*'s staff and seized machinery.

29 July Approximately 100 Confederates, including Smith O'Brien, engaged about 40 police at Boulagh Commons, near Ballingarry, Co. Tipperary, in the 'Battle of Widow McCormack's cabbage patch' (*see* 5 Aug.).

1 Aug. Inauguration of regular mail service by rail between London and Ireland via Holyhead and Kingstown.

5 Aug. Smith O'Brien arrested (*see* 29 July, 28 Sept. – 23 Oct., 9, 23 Oct.).

14 Aug. Encumbered Estates Act to facilitate sale of encumbered properties (*see* 28 July 1849).

31 Aug. Unlawful Oaths Act.

4 Sept. Acts prohibited importation of animals from diseased districts of Ireland into Great Britain.

28 Sept. – 23 Oct. Smith O'Brien, Thomas Francis Meagher, Terence Bellew McManus and Patrick O'Donohoe tried on treason charges (*see* 29 July, 5 Aug., 9, 23 Oct.).

9 Oct. O'Brien sentenced to be hanged, drawn and quartered (*see* 29 July, 5 Aug., 28 Sept. – 23 Oct., 5 June, 9 July 1849).

23 Oct. Meagher, McManus and O'Donohoe also sentenced to be hanged, drawn and quartered (*see* 29 July, 5 Aug., 28 Sept. – 23 Oct., 5, June, 9 July 1849).

Nov. Cholera returned.

1849

6 Jan. First issue of Joseph Brennan's *Irishman*.

15 Feb. Drogheda–Dundalk and Dundalk–Castleblayney railways opened (*see* 24 May 1844, 10 June 1852).

19 Feb. Kilkenny Archaeological Society founded (renamed Royal Society of Antiquaries of Ireland) (*see* 14 Jan. 1890).

29 Mar. Society for Irish Church Missions to Roman Catholics formed.

6 Apr. Archbishop William Crolly died of cholera.

May New rules of Loyal Orange Institution of Ireland adopted.

5 June Sentences of O'Brien, Meagher, McManus and O'Donohoe commuted to transportation for life (*see* 29 July, 5 Aug., 28 Sept. – 23 Oct., 9, 23 Oct. 1848).

26 June Passenger Act; Act to remove doubts about punishment of treason by transportation.

9 July O'Brien, Meagher, McManus and O'Donoghue transported to Van Diemen's Land (*see* 29 July, 5 Aug., 28 Sept. – 23 Oct., 9, 23 Oct. 1848, 5 June).

12 July Sectarian affray in which *c.* 20 Catholics were killed at Dolly's Brae, near Castlewellan, Co. Down.

28 July Encumbered Estates Act superseded previous Act and provided for appointment of 'encumbered estates court' (*see* 14 Aug. 1848).

1 Aug. Dublin Improvement Act abolished Wide Streets Commission and Paving Board and vested their powers in Dublin Corporation.

3–12 Aug. Queen Victoria and Prince Albert visited Cork, Dublin and Belfast.

1 Sept. Revival of the *Nation* newspaper (*see* 8 July 1848).

16 Sept. Attack on Cappoquin police barracks, instigated by James Fintan Lalor.

14 Oct. Formation of Tenant Protection Society at Callan, Co. Kilkenny.

18 Oct. Formal opening of Great Southern and Western Railway extension from Mallow to Cork.

Oct. Queen's Colleges at Belfast, Cork and Galway opened to students.

27 Dec. James Fintan Lalor died.

1850

5 Jan. First issue of the *Tablet* edited by Frederick Lucas published in Dublin.

18 Feb. Sir William Somerville, Chief Secretary, introduced the Landlord and Tenant bill in the House of Commons.

24 Feb. Paul Cullen consecrated Catholic Archbishop of Armagh and Primate of All Ireland.

12 Mar. Party Processions Act provided for confiscation of emblems and arms (*see* 28 Aug. 1860, 27 June 1872).

3 July General Assembly of the Presbyterian Church in Ireland adopted petition to parliament in favour of the statutory recognition of tenant right.

4 July Temperance committee of Presbyterian ministers formed in Belfast marked revival of temperance cause among Ulster Protestants.

6–9 Aug. Tenant-right conference held in Dublin.

9 Aug. Tenant League founded (*see* 8–9 Sept. 1852).

14 Aug. Representation of the People Act trebled county electorate but reduced borough electorate by one-fourth.

22 Aug. – 19 Sept. Synod of Catholic bishops at Thurles declared opposition to Catholics attending the Queen's Colleges (*see* 1 Jan. 1852).

3 Sept. Charter established Queen's University in Ireland.

29 Sept. Pope Pius IX re-established Catholic episcopal hierarchy in England and Wales (*see* 4 Nov.).

4 Nov. Prime Minister Russell denounced papal brief to re-establish hierarchy (*see* 29 Sept.).

1851

7 Feb. Lord John Russell's motion to bring in the Ecclesiastical Titles bill debated in the House of Commons (*see* 1 Aug.).

1 March the *Tablet* coined the phrase 'Irish Brigade' for the Irish opponents of the Ecclesiastical Titles bill. It was sometimes known also as 'the Pope's Brass Band'.

30 Mar. Census of population; first to take account of number of Irish speakers.

5 June Terence Bellow McManus escaped from Van Diemen's Land and fled to the United States where he settled in San Francisco.

1 Aug. Ecclesiastical Titles Act prohibited assumption in United Kingdom of territorial titles by Catholic archbishops, bishops and deans (*see* 7 Feb., 29 Sept.).

7 Aug. Poor Relief Act provided for establishment of dispensaries.

19 Aug. Meeting held in Dublin to oppose the Ecclesiastical Titles Act led to the formation of the Catholic Defence Association of Great Britain and Ireland.

29 Sept. Ecclesiastical Titles Act became law (*see* 1 Aug.).

1852

1 Jan. Decrees of Synod of Thurles promulgated in all Catholic chapels in Ireland (*see* 22 Aug. – 19 Sept. 1850).

21 Feb. Lord John Russell resigned as Prime Minster (*see* 30 June 1846).

23 Feb. Earl of Derby appointed Prime Minister (*see* 19 Dec.).

1 Mar. Richard Southwell Bourke, Lord Naas, appointed Chief Secretary.

10 Mar. Archibald Montgomerie, Earl of Eglinton, sworn in as Lord Lieutenant.

17 Mar. St Patrick's Day demonstration held in New York City; first such celebration.

3 May Archbishop Paul Cullen translated to Dublin.

8 May Isaac Butt won Harwich parliamentary by-election and entered House of Commons for the first time.

10 May Revd John Henry Newman gives his first lecture on university education in Dublin.

1 June Holyhead and Howth linked by telegraph cable.

10 June Portadown–Dundalk railway opened; connected Belfast and Dublin except for crossing of Boyne (*see* 15 Feb. 1849, 22 June 1853) National Exhibition opened in Cork.

30 June Act for valuation of rateable property, 'Griffith's Valuation', provided for uniform valuation of the whole country on the basis of tenements.

9–29 July General election: Earl of Derby retained office.

8–9 Sept. National conference of Tenant League adopted policy of independent opposition to any government which did not take up tenant right (*see* 6–9 Aug. 1850).

10 Sept. Friends of Religious Freedom and Equality formed.

13 Dec. Thirty-six Irish Liberal MPs met and formed the Independent Irish Party.

16 Dec. Lord Derby's government defeated over the budget in the House of Commons.

23 Dec. Derby resigned as Prime Minister (*see* 23 Feb.).

19 Dec. Earl of Aberdeen formed ministry with inclusion of William Keogh and John Sadleir from Independent Irish Party (*see* 1 Feb. 1855).

1853
6 Jan. Edward Eliot, Earl of St Germans, sworn in as Lord Lieutenant; Sir John Young appointed Chief Secretary.
17 Mar. Ossianic Society founded to promote early Irish literature.
12 May – 31 Oct. Irish Industrial Exhibition in Dublin.
18 June Act to extend the income tax to Ireland.
19 July John Mitchel escaped from Van Diemen's Land for the USA.
22 June Completion of viaduct over Boyne opened rail link between Belfast and Dublin (*see* 10 June 1852).
28 June Income tax extended to Ireland.
20 Aug. Act to Substitute in Certain Cases Other Punishments in Lieu of Transportation.
29 Aug. – 4 Sept. Queen Victoria visited Ireland to attend the Irish Industrial Exhibition in Dublin.
1 Nov. First meeting of the Irish Institution in Dublin.
23 Nov. Northcote–Trevelyan report on the civil service; advocated examination for entry and promotion based on merit.
5 Dec. Assembly's College, Belfast, opened for the theological training of the Presbyterian clergy. Yard opened in Belfast for the construction of iron ships.

1854
14 Jan. First instalment of John Mitchel's 'Jail Journal'.
26 Feb. William Smith O'Brien received pardon (*see* 9 Oct. 1848, 5 June 1849, 8 July 1856).
28 Mar. Beginning of Crimean War.
18 May Catholic Synod issues instructions regarding the political conduct of the clergy.
4 June Revd John Henry Newman installed as Rector of the Catholic University.
10 Aug. Statutory provision for the establishing of a National Gallery of Painting, Sculpture and Fine Art in Dublin. Town Improvement Act provided for election of town commissioners to administer towns with over 1,500 population.
19 Aug. Londonderry–Enniskillen railway opened.
21–26 Aug. Donnybrook Fair held for the last time.
3 Nov. Catholic University of Ireland opened; Revd J. H. Newman first rector.
29 Nov. Board of Trinity College established 16 non-foundation scholarships open to candidates of all religious denominations.
Dec. Edward J. Harland arrived in Belfast to become manager of Queen's Island shipyard.

1855
c. **Feb.** Emmet Monument Association formed in New York.
1 Feb. Lord Aberdeen resigned as Prime Minister (*see* 19 Dec. 1852).

6 Feb. Lord Palmerston appointed Prime Minister (*see* 20 Feb. 1858).

1 Mar. Edward Horsman appointed Chief Secretary.

13 Mar. George Howard, Earl of Carlisle, sworn in as Lord Lieutenant.

5 Apr. Completion of Dublin–Belfast railway.

26 June Public Libraries (Ireland) Act promoted establishment of free libraries by town councils.

22 Aug. Catholic Cathedral at Kilkenny consecrated: Augustus Pugin architect.

2 Nov. Cecilia Street School of Medicine opened as part of Catholic University.

6 Nov. Charles Gavan Duffy departed for Australia.

1856

Jan. Irish Academy of Music founded.

16 Jan. End of Crimean War.

13 Feb. Collapse of Tipperary Bank owned in part by John Sadleir (*see* 17 Feb.).

17 Feb. Suicide of Sadleir (*see* 13 Feb.).

1 May Catholic University Church, St Stephen's Green, opened; John Hungerford Pollen architect.

30 June Peace Preservation Act (*see* 20 Dec. 1847).

8 July William Smith O'Brien returned to Ireland (*see* 9 Oct. 1848, 5 June 1849, 26 Feb. 1854).

Dec. Jeremiah O'Donavan (O'Donovan Rossa) established Phoenix Society at Skibbereen, Co. Cork.

1857

3 Mar. Lord Palmerston's government defeated in House of Commons.

20 Mar. – 16 Apr. General election; Palmerston returned with increased majority.

27 May Henry Arthur Herbert appointed Chief Secretary.

13–19 July Sectarian rioting in Belfast.

17 Aug. Illicit Distillation (Ireland) Act transferred duties of revenue police to constabulary.

6 Sept. Sectarian rioting in Belfast provoked by Revd 'Roaring' Hugh Hanna.

10 Sept. Commission appointed to inquire into Belfast riots.

20 Nov. Commission on Belfast rioting reported.

1858

20 Feb. Palmerston resigned as Prime Minister (*see* 6 Feb. 1855).

26 Feb. Lord Derby appointed Prime Minister (*see* 12 June 1859).

4 Mar. Lord Naas appointed Chief Secretary.

12 Mar. Earl of Eglinton sworn in as Lord Lieutenant.

17 Mar. Irish Republican Brotherhood (IRB) founded by James Stephens.

5 Apr. Portadown–Dungannon section of Ulster Railway opened.

May O'Donovan Rossa's Phoenix National and Literary Society incorporated into the IRB.

17 July First issue of Denis Holland's *Irishman*.

2 Aug. Act to Facilitate Sale and Transfer of Land consolidated Acts dealing with encumbered estates and altered title of court of Land Estates Court. Medical Act provided for creation of General Medical Council to maintain standards in medical education in United Kingdom and for registration of medical practitioners. Irish Reformatory Schools Act provided for inspection and maintenance of schools for juvenile offenders run by denomination bodies.

10 Aug. Society for Promotion and Cultivation of the Irish Language began.

20 Aug. First official transatlantic telegraph message transmitted.

23 Aug. – 17 Sept. Cardinal Wiseman's visit to Ireland made him the first cardinal to set foot in the country for 200 years.

Sept. Irish Temperance League formed in Belfast by businessmen and Presbyterian clergy.

29 Sept. Irish auxiliary of the United Kingdom Alliance (temperance) formed in Dublin.

8 Dec. Arrest in County Cork of 15 members of the Phoenix Society.

9 Dec. James Stephens granted supreme control over the IRB.

Dec. Edward Harland purchased Robert Hickson's shipyard at Queen's Island, Belfast.

1859

29 Jan. Foundation stone for the National Gallery of Painting and Sculpture laid; Charles Lanyon and Francis Fowke architects (*see* 30 Jan. 1864).

2 Feb. Castleblayney–Enniskillen Railway opened.

29 Mar. *Irish Times* commenced publication.

31 Mar. Lord Derby's ministry defeated. Independent Irish Party split.

Apr. John O'Mahony reconstituted the Emmet Monument Association in New York as the Fenian Brotherhood.

30 Apr. – 20 May General election.

12 June Lord Palmerston appointed Prime Minister (*see* 18 Oct. 1865).

24 June Edward Cardwell appointed Chief Secretary.

29 June Meeting in Belfast marked the height of the Protestant religious revival in Ulster.

13 July Earl of Carlisle sworn in as Lord Lieutenant.

18 July Tralee and Killarney Railway opened.

5 Aug. Joint Pastoral of Catholic bishops stated grievances concerning education and provision of chaplains in the military.

1860

15 May Land Improvement Act authorised loans for erection of dwellings for labourers.

16 May In order to deter recruitment in Ireland for the Irish Papal Brigade, the Lord Lieutenant issued a proclamation pointing to penalties under the Foreign Enlistment Act.

3 June Archbishop Cullen letter condemned emigration and mixed education.

28 Aug. Refreshment Houses Act facilitated issue of wine licences. Party Processions Act strengthened powers against provocative behaviour (*see* 12 Mar. 1850). Land Property Improvement Act, 'Napier's Law'.

5 Sept. Blackrock College opened (originally named French College of the Immaculate Heart of Mary).

11 Sept. Papal states in Italy invaded by troops from Piedmont-Sardinia.

1861

22 Feb. Select committee of the House of Commons appointed to inquire into the administration of the relief of the poor in Ireland.

18 Mar. Foundation of the National Brotherhood of St Patrick, a republican organisation.

7 Apr. Census of population.

8–10 Apr. Derryveagh evictions in Co. Donegal.

29 July Sir Robert Peel (Jr) appointed Chief Secretary.

21–30 Aug. Queen Victoria visited Ireland.

2 Sept. Dungannon–Omagh section of Ulster Railway opened.

Sept.–Dec. Thomas Francis Meagher formed the Irish Brigade in New York for service in the American Civil War.

24 Sept. Mater Misericordiae Hospital, Dublin, opened by Sisters of Mercy.

10 Nov. Terence Bellow McManus funeral in Dublin.

1862

1 Jan. Partnership of Harland & Wolff formed (*see* 1 July 1874).

5 July Lord Palmerston rejected request by Catholic University for a charter.

7 Aug. Poor Relief Act extended provision for outdoor relief, abolishing 'quarter acre restriction' (*see* 8 June 1847).

22 Oct. Dublin United Trades' Association formed.

1863

Feb. First issue *Irish Temperance League Journal* (Belfast).

20 Apr. Registration of British and Deaths Act.

28 July Registration of Marriages Act. Salmon Fisher Act.

Aug. Brotherhood of St Patrick condemned by Catholic Hierarchy.

13 Nov. St Stephen's Green, Dublin, opened to the public.

28 Nov. First issue of *Irish People* edited by John O'Leary (*see* 16 Sept. 1865).

1864

1 Jan. Compulsory vaccination of babies introduced. Richard Chenevix Trench consecrated Church of Ireland Archbishop of Dublin.

21 Jan. John Martin and Daniel O'Donoghue founded Irish National League.

30 Jan. National Gallery of Ireland formally opened (*see* 29 Jan. 1859).

7 Mar. Archbishop Cullen's pastoral letter denounced Fenianism.
11 Apr. Select committee of House of Commons to inquire into scientific institutions of Dublin.
15 Apr. First Dublin Horse Show.
30 June Beerhouses Act facilitated establishment of beerhouses.
5 July First meeting of the Royal College of Physicians.
29 July Contagious Diseases Prevention Act provided for medical inspection and control of prostitutes (*see* 11 June 1866).
8 Aug. Foundation stone of O'Connell Monument laid in Dublin. It led to two weeks of sectarian rioting in Belfast (8–19 Aug.).
8 Nov. John, Lord Wodehouse, sworn in as Lord Lieutenant.
8 Dec. Pope Pius IX issued 'Syllabus of Errors' condemning socialism, liberalism and freemasonry.
29 Dec. National Association of Ireland established with support of Archbishop Cullen.

1865
23 Jan. Archbishop Cullen issued pastoral to his clergy, calling for their co-operation in the National Association of Ireland.
20 Feb. First meeting of National Association (*see* 29 Dec. 1864).
24 Feb. St Patrick's Cathedral, Dublin, reopened after restoration at expense of Sir Benjamin Lee Guinness.
9 May Dublin International Exhibition in Earlsfort Terrace opened.
June Richard Pigott, manager of *Irishman*, secured its ownership.
29 June Act abolished town police force of Belfast and transferred duties to Constabulary of Ireland (*see* 9 Aug. 1870).
12–24 July General election; Palmerston retained office.
24 Aug. Foundation stone laid of Methodist College, Belfast.
15 Sept. Arrest of Fenian leaders (*see* 11, 27 Nov., 6, 16 Dec.).
16 Sept. Last issue of *Irish People* (*see* 28 Nov. 1863).
10 Oct. Magee College, Londonderry, opened.
18 Oct. Death of Prime Minster Palmerston (*see* 12 June 1859).
29 Oct. Earl Russell appointed Prime Minister (*see* 28 June 1866).
5 Nov. Bishop Thomas Nulty and his clergy withdrew from National Association and formed Meath Tenant Right Society.
11 Nov. Arrests of more leading Fenians, including Charles J. Kickham and James Stephens (*see* 24–25 Nov., 5 Jan. 1866).
24–25 Nov. James Stephens escaped from Richmond Prison, Dublin.
27 Nov. Thomas Clarke Luby sentenced to 20 years' imprisonment (*see* 15 Sept.).
2 Dec. Fenian Brotherhood split.
5–6 Dec. Irish independent MPs met in Dublin to consider their position towards government policy, bringing about an apparent reunification of the Independent Irish Party.
6 Dec. John O'Leary sentenced to 20 years' imprisonment (*see* 15 Sept.).

7 Dec. Chichester Fortescue appointed Chief Secretary.

16 Dec. Jeremiah O'Donovan Rossa sentenced to 20 years' imprisonment (*see* 15 Sept.).

1866

5 Jan. Charles J. Kickham sentenced to 14 years' transportation (*see* 11 Nov. 1865).

24 Jan. Castlebar–Westport extension of Great Northern & Western Railway opened.

18 Feb. Habeas Corpus Suspension Act.

23 Feb. John Devoy arrested.

6 Mar. Cattle Disease Act.

19 Apr. First Fenian attempt on Canada foiled.

27 Apr. Independent Irish opposition MPs split on the Reform bill.

30 Apr. Parliamentary Oaths Act.

31 May – 3 June Second Fenian invasion of Canada.

11 June Contagious Diseases Act (*see* 29 July 1864, 11 Aug. 1869).

22 June Paul Cullen made Ireland's first cardinal.

28 June Earl of Derby appointed Prime Minister.

9 July John Boyle O'Reilly sentenced to be shot for recruiting for the Fenians while serving in the British army. Sentence commuted to 20 years' transportation.

10 July Lord Naas appointed Chief Secretary.

20 July James Hamilton, Marquis of Abercorn, sworn in as Lord Lieutenant.

11 Oct. Alexandra College for young ladies opened in Dublin.

17 Dec. James Stephens deposed as Head Centre of Fenian Brotherhood in USA.

20 Dec. Irish Association for the Closing of Public Houses on Sunday founded in Dublin.

1867

11 Feb. Planned Fenian attack on Chester Castle thwarted.

11–12 Feb. Fenians attacked Kells, Co. Meath, and were dispersed.

17 Feb. Catholic Bishop David Moriarty denounced Fenians.

26 Feb. Suspension of Habeas Corpus Act.

5–6 Mar. Fenian rising; outbreaks in Counties Dublin, Clare, Cork, Limerick, Louth, Tipperary and Wicklow.

5 Apr. School of Physic (Ireland) Amendment Act abolished religious tests for some professorships in the University of Dublin.

13 May Government commission began investigation into treatment of Fenian prisoners.

31 May Act to continue suspension of habeas corpus to 1 Mar. 1868.

17 June Dublin Port Act established Dublin port and dock board and commissioners of Irish lights.

20 June Clan na Gael founded in New York by Jerome J. Collins.

12 July William Johnston of Ballykilbeg led large Orange procession in protest against Party Processions Act.

12 Aug. Public Records Act provided for establishment and regulation of Public Record Office at Four Courts, Dublin, and regulation of State Paper Office at Dublin Castle.

17 Aug. Col. Thomas J. Kelly became Head Centre of IRB.

11 Sept. Kelly and Captain Thomas Deasy captured in Manchester.

12 Sept. Irish Constabulary granted the prefix 'Royal' in recognition of its role in suppressing Fenian rising.

18 Sept. Fenians attempted rescue of Kelly and Deasy in Manchester; killing of Sergeant Charles Brett (*see* 23 Nov.).

1–3 Oct. Catholic bishops rejected principle of state endowment of the church.

Oct. Classes began at Royal College of Science.

23 Nov. Executions of William Philip Allen, Michael Larkin and Michael O'Brien convicted of Brett's murder (*see* 18 Sept.).

7 Dec. Publication of 'God Save Ireland' by T. D. Sullivan; anthem of national movement until 1916.

12 Dec. Viceregal proclamation declared funeral processions for 'Manchester martyrs' illegal (*see* 23 Nov.).

13 Dec. Attempted Fenian rescue in Clerkenwell ended with 12 civilians being killed and 50 injured (*see* 26 May 1868).

23 Dec. Dean Richard O'Brien and group of Limerick priests issued declaration in favour of repeal of the Union.

1868

14 Jan. Royal Commission (Earl of Powis chairman) established to inquire into primary education (*see* 21 May 1870).

27 Feb. Benjamin Disraeli appointed Prime Minister (*see* 3 Dec.).

5 Mar. First meeting of Protestant Defence Association to uphold the established status of the Church of Ireland.

10 Mar. Chief Secretary announced that the Catholic University was to be granted a charter.

19 Mar. Earl of Mayo introduced Irish Reform bill in the House of Commons.

21 Mar. Fenian, Captain William Mackey (alias Lomasney) sentenced to 12 years' penal servitude for treason felony.

23 Mar. William E. Gladstone advocated that the Church of Ireland be disestablished.

10–11 May 'Murphy riots' at Ashton-under-Lyme, Lancashire.

26 May In the last public execution in the British Isles, Michael Barrett was hanged for the deaths resulting from the explosion at Clerkenwell (*see* 13 Dec. 1867).

13 July Representation of the People Act reduced rated occupier franchise from £8 to £4 and introduced lodger franchise in parliamentary boroughs.

31 July Promissory Oaths Act reduced number of persons required to take the oaths in Ireland, but still included the Lord Lieutenant, Lord Chancellor and Commander-in-Chief of the army.

3 Aug. Amnesty resolutions in Cork City Council marked beginnings of clemency campaign on behalf of Fenian prisoners.

15 Aug Foundation of Irish National Teachers' Organisation (INTO).

29 Sept. John Wilson-Patten appointed Chief Secretary.

5 Nov. Initiation of organisation to secure the release of the Fenian prisoners, the Irish Liberation Society.

17 Nov. – 2 Dec. General election.

3 Dec. William Ewart Gladstone appointed Prime Minister.

18 Dec. Thomas O'Hagan appointed first Catholic Lord Chancellor of Ireland since the seventeenth century.

23 Dec. John, Earl Spencer, sworn in as Lord Lieutenant; Chichester Fortescue appointed Chief Secretary.

1869

26 Jan. Irish Permissive Bill Association founded in Dublin to support local option.

22 Feb. Announcement that 49 (of 81) non-military Fenian prisoners would be released.

1 Mar. Irish Church bill introduced in the House of Commons.

6 Mar. *Irishman* claimed that Fenian prisoners were subjected to ill-treatment.

28 Apr. Sectarian rioting at Londonderry during visit of Prince Arthur.

29 June Amnesty Association founded; Isaac Butt selected as president.

26 July Irish Church Act disestablished Church of Ireland and ended annual grants to Maynooth College and *regium donum* for training Presbyterian ministry.

11 Aug. Contagious Diseases Act (*see* 29 July 1864, 11 June 1866).

18 Aug. IRB's supreme council adopted 'Constitution of the Irish Republic'.

28 Sept. Irish Tenant League inaugurated, Isaac Butt as its head.

19 Nov. Route Tenants' Defence Association formed in Antrim, first of its type in Ulster.

27 Nov. Jeremiah O'Donovan Rossa, an imprisoned Fenian, won the County Tipperary parliamentary by-election in a low poll (*see* 10 Feb. 1870).

8 Dec. Vatican Council opened in Rome.

1870

12 Jan. Papal condemnation of Fenians.

2–3 Feb. Land Conference in Dublin.

10 Feb. Rossa, an undischarged felon, disqualified from sitting in the House of Commons (*see* 27 Nov. 1869).

15 Feb. Irish Land bill introduced in the House of Commons.

28 Feb. Denis Caulfield Heron defeated the ex-Fenian prisoner Charles J. Kickham (1,668–1,664) at second County Tipperary parliamentary by-election.

4 Apr. Peace Preservation Act amended Act of 1856 (*see* 30 June 1856).
19 May Meeting of supporters of home government in the Bilton Hotel, Dublin.
21 May Report of Powis Commission on primary education (*see* 14 Jan. 1868).
25 May Abortive Fenian invasion of Canada.
18 July Dogma of papal infallibility promulgated. Michael Davitt sentenced to 15 years' imprisonment.
July John Boyle O'Reilly became editor of Boston *Pilot.*
1 Aug. Landlord and Tenant Act.
9 Aug. Act abolishing city police force of Londonderry, with its duties transferred to the Royal Irish Constabulary (*see* 29 June 1865).
10 Aug. Glebe Loans Act authorised Commissioners of Public Works to grant loans for two-thirds of the cost of purchase of glebes.
27 Aug. The *Oceanic* built in Belfast by Harland & Wolff launched.
1 Sept. First public meeting of the Home Government Association in Dublin. First issue of *Irish World* published by Patrick Ford in New York. First issue of the *Belfast Evening Telegraph.*
20 Sept. Fall of Rome; end of the temporal rule of the Pope.
15 Oct. Charter incorporating Representative Church Body (*see* 26 July 1869).
26 Dec. William Smith O'Brien monument unveiled in Dublin.

1871

1 Jan. Irish Church Act comes into effect; Church of Ireland becomes a voluntary body (*see* 26 July 1869).
12 Jan. Spencer Compton Cavendish, Marquis of Hartington, appointed Chief Secretary.
17 Jan. John Martin scored first home rule victory at by-election in Meath (1,140–684).
Jan. Thirty-three Fenians released from prison.
2 Apr. Census of population.
16 June Protection of Life and Property in Certain Parts of Ireland Act (Westmeath Act) allowed detention without trial for agrarian offences.
18 July Dublin Corporation pledged itself to the home rule movement.
20 Sept. Isaac Butt returned unopposed at the Limerick City parliamentary by-election.
5 Oct. Fenian attack in Manitoba, Canada.
27 Nov. Gaiety Theatre, Dublin, opened.
30 Nov. Consecration of St Finbarre's Cathedral, Cork.

1872

1 Feb. First tramcars run in Dublin (*see* 28 Aug.).
8 Feb. J. P. Nolan wins County Galway parliamentary by-election in the home rule interest (2,823–658).
12 Feb. County Kerry parliamentary by-election won by home rule candidate, R. P. Blennerhassett (2,237–1,398).

15 Feb. First convention of Dungannon by Ulster Volunteers called for an Irish parliament.

1 Apr. – 27 May Galway election petition tried before Judge William Keogh; J. P. Nolan unseated. Keogh made unflattering references to the influence of the Catholic clergy in the election contest (27 May).

23 Apr. Commissioners of national education dismissed Revd Robert O'Keefe as manager of Callan National Schools.

3 June Select committee of House of Lords (Lord Chelmsford chairman) appointed to inquire into the operation of the Land Act of 1870.

27 June Party Processions Acts of 1850 and 1860 repealed (*see* 12 Mar. 1850, 28 Aug. 1860).

18 July Ballot Act instituted secret voting.

10 Aug. Local Government Board Act established local government board which assumed functions of Poor Law Commission (*see* 31 July 1838).

15–20 Aug. Sectarian rioting in Belfast.

28 Aug. First tramcars run in Belfast (*see* 1 Feb.).

26 Nov. Catholic Union founded.

1873

8 Jan. Meeting of Irish in Manchester to form Home Rule Confederation of Great Britain.

8 Feb. Catholic bishops expressed disapproval of Gladstone's University bill.

12 Mar. Irish University bill defeated (287–284) in the House of Commons.

17 Mar. IRB adopted new constitution.

26 May University of Dublin Tests Act abolished religious tests in Trinity College.

July First issue of *Irish Monthly* edited by Revd Matthew Russell, S.J.

15 Aug. National Agricultural Labourers' Union founded.

7 Sept. Beginning of renewed campaign for release of the Fenian prisoners by the Amnesty Association.

18–21 Nov. National Conference founded Home Rule League.

1874

31 Jan. – 12 Feb. General election; Conservatives triumphed but 60 candidates standing as home rulers were successful.

20 Feb. Disraeli appointed Prime Minister (created Earl of Beaconsfield, 21 Aug. 1876).

27 Feb. Sir Michael Hicks Beach appointed Chief Secretary.

3 Mar. Home Rule Party formed with Isaac Butt as chairman.

18 Mar. Charles Stewart Parnell defeated in County Dublin parliamentary by-election (2,183–1,235).

30 June – 2 July Motion to go into committee of the House of Commons to consider relations between Great Britain and Ireland (home rule) rejected (458–61).

1 July William James Pirrie and Walter H. Wilson taken into partnership by Harland & Wolff (*see* 1 Jan. 1862).

30 July Joseph Biggar employed 'obstruction' on the Expiring Laws Continuance bill in the House of Commons and was criticised by Butt.

7 Aug. Licensing Act aided the drink trade.

7 Nov. Publication of Gladstone's pamphlet, 'The Vatican Decrees in their Bearing on Civil Allegiance'.

1 Dec. Plan for creation of denominational teacher training colleges adopted by the board of commissioners.

14 Dec. Irish Football Union (Irish Rugby Football Union, 5 Feb. 1880) formed in Dublin.

1875

13 Jan. Gladstone announced retirement as leader of the Liberal Party.

20–21 Jan. Tenant Right Conference in Dublin.

3 Feb. Marquess of Hartington became Liberal Party leader in the House of Commons.

16 Feb. John Mitchel returned unopposed at Co. Tipperary parliamentary by-election (*see* 18 Feb.).

18 Feb. As an undischarged Felon Mitchel's election was invalidated by the House of Commons (*see* 16 Feb.).

19 Feb. First Irish international rugby match (versus England) ended in English victory.

12 Mar. Mitchel elected a second time but the seat was awarded to his Conservative opponent, Stephen Moore.

19 Apr. Charles Stewart Parnell returned in the Meath by-election (*see* 22 Apr.).

22 Apr. Parnell took his seat in the House of Commons (*see* 19 Apr.) Joseph Biggar spearheaded obstruction on the Peace Preservation bill in the House of Commons.

26 Apr. Parnell's maiden speech in the House of Commons.

28 May Peace Preservation Act amended and continued Peace Preservation Act, 1870 (*see* 4 Apr. 1870).

5–7 Aug. O'Connell centenary celebrations in Dublin.

11 Aug. Irish Pharmacy Act instituted and incorporated Pharmaceutical Society of Ireland.

30 Aug – 20 Sept. National synod of Catholic bishops repeated condemnation of the Queen's Colleges and extended this to Trinity College Dublin.

1876

Mar. Jeremiah O'Donovan Rossa established 'skirmishing fund' in the United States.

1 Apr. Amalgamation of Dublin and Drogheda, Dublin and Belfast Junction, Irish North-Western and Ulster railways created Great Northern Railway.

17–18 Apr. Clan na Gael rescue of six Fenian prisoners from Western Australia.

24 Apr. Church of Ireland synod recommended establishment of temperance societies.

12 May House of Commons passed resolution in favour of Sunday closing of public houses in Ireland.

30 June – 1 July Debate on home rule in House of Commons; motion defeated (291–61).

8–15 Aug. Decision taken at Clan na Gael convention at Philadelphia to form joint directory of Clan na Gael and IRB (*see* 5 Mar. 1877).

15 Aug. Sectarian disturbances in Belfast.

20 Aug. IRB Supreme Council withdrew neutrality towards Home Rule Party; MPs who belong to the movement directed to give up their seats by 5 March 1878.

15 Nov. T. D. Sullivan replaced his younger brother A. M. Sullivan as proprietor of the *Nation*.

12 Dec. John Winston Spencer Churchill, Duke of Marlborough, sworn in as Lord Lieutenant.

29 Dec. Society for the Preservation of the Irish Language founded in Dublin.

1877

28 Jan. John O'Mahony resigned as Head Centre of Fenian Brotherhood.

2 Feb. Jeremiah O'Donovan Rossa becomes Head Centre of the Fenian Brotherhood in New York.

12 Feb. Select committee (House of Commons) on Irish Sunday Closing bill appointed (*see* 9 May).

5 Mar. Supreme Council of IRB enforced decision that MPs who belonged to organisation must resign their parliamentary seats. Joseph Biggar and John O'Connor Power refused (*see* 8–15 Aug. 1876).

23 Mar. Beer Licences Regulation (Ireland) Act.

Mar. Clan na Gael gained control of 'skirmishing fund'.

1 May Commission appointed by House of Commons under chairmanship of George John Shaw-Lefevre to inquire into the land purchase clauses of the Land Act of 1870 (*see* 27 June 1878).

9 May Select committee on Sunday closing reported in favour of total Sunday closing.

21 June Ten Molly Maguires executed in Pennsylvania.

27 July – 1 Aug. Obstruction of House of Commons business by a small section of the Home Rule Party.

14 Aug. General Prisons (Ireland) Act; Supreme Court of Judicature Act; Dublin Science and Art Museum Act.

27–28 Aug. Home Rule Confederation of Great Britain annual convention; C. S. Parnell chosen as president for the coming year.

9 Oct. General Prisons Board of Ireland came into operation (*see* 14 Aug.).

17 Oct. – 12 Nov. Gladstone visited Ireland where he received freedom of city of Dublin on 7 Nov.

19 Dec. Michael Davitt released from Dartmour prison on parole.

27 Dec. Beginning of series of articles by William O'Brien on conditions in the Galtree.

1878

14–15 Jan. Home Rule conference for purpose of considering parliamentary tactics.

15 Feb. James Lowther appointed Chief Secretary.

27 June Report of the Commission appointed to consider land purchase clauses of the Land Act of 1870 (*see* 1 May 1877).

8 Aug. Public Health Act.

16 Aug. Intermediate Education Act; Sale of Liquors on Sunday (Ireland) Act.

16 Sept. Davitt began lecture tour in the United States (concluded 8 Dec.).

13 Oct. Davitt and John Devoy at Brooklyn called for a new policy for the Fenian movement (*see* 27 Oct., 27 Dec., 19–26 Jan. 1879).

21–22 Oct. C. S. Parnell re-elected president of the Home Rule Confederation of Great Britain at its annual convention.

26 Oct. Mayo Tenants' Defence Association founded by J. J. Louden and James Daly.

27 Oct. Davitt–Devoy proposals first described as 'an Irish new departure'; Devoy offered Parnell the support of the Fenians (*see* 13 Oct., 27 Dec., 19–26 Jan. 1879).

8 Nov. Irish Association for the Prevention of Intemperance formed in Dublin.

27 Dec. Publication of Devoy's letter on 'new departure' in *Freeman's Journal* (*see* 13, 27 Oct., 19–26 Jan. 1879).

1879

19–26 Jan. Supreme Council of IRA rejected 'new departure' (*see* 13, 27 Oct., 27 Dec. 1878).

4 Feb. Last attendance of Isaac Butt at the Home Rule League in Dublin.

28 Feb. Outbreak of disturbances in Connemara which arose through conflict between Catholics and teachers of Society for Irish Church Missions to Roman Catholics.

7–9 Mar. Parnell met Devoy, John O'Leary and Davitt in Boulogne to discuss 'new departure'.

20 Apr. Tenant Right Association demonstration in Irishtown, Co. Mayo.

22 May Following Butt's death, William Shaw elected sessional chairman of the Home Rule Party.

1 June Parnell, Devoy and Davitt met to consider the 'new departure'.

8 June Parnell addressed land meeting at Westport, Co. Mayo.

21 July Irish Convention Act (1793) repealed.

26 July James Lysaght Finigan, supported by Parnell, returned in the Ennis borough parliamentary by-election (83–77).

14 Aug. Commission to inquire into condition of agriculture in United Kingdom appointed (Richmond Commission) (*see* 14 Jan. 1881, 11 July 1882).

15 Aug. University Education Act provided for the formation of the Royal University.

16 Aug. National Land League of Mayo founded at Castlebar.

21 Aug. Apparition of the Virgin Mary at Knock, Co. Mayo.

29 Sept. Parnell and Davitt issued 'Appeal to the Irish Race' calling for Irish overseas to aid the new land agitation.

21 Oct. Irish National Land League founded in Dublin with Parnell as president.

19 Nov. Arrest of Davitt, James Daly and James Bryce Killen on charge of sedition.

Dec. Duchess of Marlborough, wife of Lord Lieutenant, established fund for relief of the distressed tenantry.

21 Dec. Parnell and John Dillon sailed for the United States to raise money for the Irish National Land League and for the relief of the distressed tenantry (*see* 2 Jan. 1880).

1880

2 Jan. Mansion House Fund for relief of distressed tenantry established. Parnell and Dillon arrived in New York (*see* 21 Dec. 1879).

2 Feb. Parnell addressed the United States House of Representatives.

5 Feb. Irish Rugby Football Union formed.

20 Feb. Parnell at Cincinnati was alleged to have called for the destruction of 'the last link' between Great Britain and Ireland. He subsequently denied using the phrase.

1 Mar. Seed Supply Act empowered boards of guardians to supply seed potatoes to impoverished tenants.

8 Mar. Government dissolved parliament and called a general election.

11 Mar. Irish National Land and Industrial League of the United States founded by Parnell in New York.

15 Mar. Relief of Distress Act extended power of Local Government Board to grant outdoor relief.

21 Mar. Parnell arrived at Queenstown (Cork) on his return from America.

30 Mar. – 13 Apr. General election; Liberals returned to office.

c. Mar. Gaelic Union for the Preservation and Cultivation of the Irish Language founded.

23 Apr. W. E. Gladstone appointed Prime Minister for the second time.

27 Apr. Royal University of Ireland chartered.

29 Apr. National Convention on land reform held in Dublin.

30 Apr. William Edward Forster appointed Chief Secretary.

Apr. Workman Clark shipyard established.

4 May Salvation Army began mission in Sandy Row, Belfast. Francis, Earl Cowper, sworn in as Lord Lieutenant.

17 May Parnell defeated William Shaw for the sessional chairmanship of the Irish Party (23–18).

28 May John O'Connor Power introduced Land bill in the House of Commons.

1 June Peace Preservation Act, 1875, expired (*see* 28 May 1875).

19 June Government introduced the Compensation for Disturbances bill in the House of Commons (*see* 4 Aug.).

28–30 June Jeremiah O'Donovan Rossa established United Irishmen of America.

27 July St Stephen's Green, Dublin, opened to the public.

29 July Royal Commission (Bessborough Commission) to inquire into the workings of the 1870 Land Act appointed (*see* 4 Jan. 1881).

30 July Parnell met Mrs Katherine O'Shea, wife of Captain William Henry O'Shea, MP for Country Clare for the first time.

2 Aug. Relief of Distress Act.

4 Aug. Compensation for Disturbances bill defeated in the House of Lords (282–51) (*see* 19 June).

19 Sept. Parnell outlined policy known as 'boycotting' at Ennis.

24 Sept. – 26 Nov. Ostracism of Captain Boycott in Mayo.

14 Oct. Parnell's declaration at Galway that he would not have 'taken off my coat' if he did not believe the present agitation would lead to 'our legislative independence'.

24 Oct. First meeting of Ladies' Land League in New York.

2 Nov. Parnell and 13 others charged with conspiracy to prevent the payment of rent (*see* 28 Dec., 25 Jan. 1881).

18 Nov. Irish Football Association founded.

11–26 Nov. Orange labourers harvested crops on estate where Captain Boycott is the agent.

27 Dec. Meeting of Irish Parliamentary Party resolved to sit in opposition permanently.

28 Dec. Opening of trial of Parnell and others (*see* 2 Nov., 25 Jan. 1881).

Dec. Orange Emergency Committee, to resist the Land League, formed by the Grand Orange Lodge; Irish landlords form the Property Defence Association.

1881

4 Jan. Bessborough Commission reported (*see* 29 July 1880).

14 Jan. Richmond Commission preliminary report (*see* 14 Aug. 1879, 11 July 1882).

Fenian dynamiters set off explosions at Salford military barracks in Lancashire.

16–17 Jan. William Shaw and a number of MPs withdraw from the Irish Party.

24 Jan. Protection of Person and Property bill introduced in the House of Commons.

25 Jan. Trial of Parnell and other Land League leaders collapsed in Dublin when the jury failed to agree (*see* 2 Nov., 28 Dec. 1880).

26 Jan. Ladies' Land League headed by Anna Parnell given sanction of Land League executive (*see* 31 Jan.).

41

31 Jan. Ladies' Land League launched (*see* 26 Jan.).

31 Jan. – 2 Feb. Irish Party obstruction in the House of Commons of the Protection of Person and Property bill.

3 Feb. Davitt's parole revoked and he was returned to prison.

2 Mar. Protection of Person and Property Act.

12 Mar. Catholic Archbishop of Dublin, Edward McCabe, denounced Ladies' Land League in pastoral letter.

21 Mar. Peace Preservation Act to restrict the carrying and possession of arms.

3 Apr. Census of population.

7 Apr. Land bill introduced in the House of Commons.

2 May John Dillon arrested (*see* 8 Aug.).

24 May First priest, Fr Eugene Sheehy, arrested under Protection of Person and Property Act.

2 Aug. Richard Pigott sold his newspapers to Irish National Publishing Company (Parnell chairman).

8 Aug. Dillon released from prison due to ill health (*see* 2 May).

13 Aug. First issue of *United Ireland* edited by William O'Brien.

22 Aug. Land Law Act; Royal University of Ireland Act endowed it with £20,000 per annum from Church Surplus Fund.

7 Sept. T. A. Dickson, Liberal, returned at Co. Tyrone parliamentary by-election against the Land League candidate.

15–17 Sept. Land League Convention in Dublin; accepted Parnell's advice to 'test' the new land legislation.

3 Oct. Irish Liberal MP, George Errington, accorded quasi-official recognition for his mission to the Vatican.

13 Oct. Parnell detained in Kilmainham jail.

14–16 Oct. Arrest of Thomas Sexton, J. P. Quinn, William O'Brien, J. J. O'Kelly, Dillon and other Land League leaders.

18 Oct. No-Rent Manifesto issued by the Land League prisoners from Kilmainham gaol.

19 Oct. No-Rent Manifesto denounced by Catholic Archbishop Thomas Croke.

20 Oct. Land League proclaimed. Land Commission Court held first session.

29 Oct. Belfast United Trades' Council formed.

16 Dec. First 'special resident' magistrates appointed.

1882

27 Mar. Edward McCabe, Catholic Archbishop of Dublin, created cardinal.

31 Mar. 'Tuke Committee' formed; purpose to fund emigration.

10–24 Apr. Parnell free on parole.

28 Apr. Lord Cowper resigned as Lord Lieutenant; succeeded by 5th Earl Spencer.

2 May Parnell and other Land League leaders released under terms of 'Kilmainham Treaty'; W. E. Forster resigned in protest.

6 May Earl Spencer sworn in as Lord Lieutenant; Davitt released; Lord Frederick Cavendish and T. H. Burke assassinated in Phoenix Park, Dublin.
9 May George Otto Trevelyan appointed Chief Secretary.
11 May Prevention of Crime bill introduced in the House of Commons (*see* 12 July).
15 May Arrears bill introduced in the House of Commons (*see* 18 Aug.).
6 June Davitt advocated 'Land Nationalisation'.
30 June – 1 July Irish Party obstruction of the House of Commons in protest at the Prevention of Crime bill (*see* 11 May, 12 July).
11 July Richmond Commission final report (*see* 14 Aug., 1879, 14 Jan. 1881).
12 July Prevention of Crime Act (Crimes Act) to provide special powers (*see* 11 May).
July Land Corporation to counteract intimidation of persons occupying holdings from which tenants had been evicted.
Aug. Agitation in RIC over pay and conditions; strike among Limerick city force; Lord Lieutenant appointed committee to investigate grievances.
15 Aug. Exhibition of Irish Arts and Manufactures opened in Rotunda hospital gardens, Dublin.
16 Aug. Parnell received freedom of the city of Dublin.
17 Aug. Maamtrasna murders in Co. Galway 'Joyce country'.
18 Aug. Arrears of Rent Act (*see* 15 May); Labourers' Cottages and Allotments Act; Ancient Monuments Protection Act provided for Commissioners of Works to undertake maintenance of ancient monuments including 18 in Ireland (*see* 27 June 1892).
21 Aug. Irish Labour and Industrial Union established in Dublin.
26 Aug. – 8 Sept. Section of Dublin Metropolitan Police demanded treatment similar to that of RIC.
3 Oct. Catholic University renamed University College (*see* 26 Oct. 1883).
17 Oct. National Conference formed the Irish National League.

1883
13 Jan. Arrest of members of the Invincibles for the murders of Burke and Cavendish (*see* 6 May 1882).
26 Jan. Ulster Land Committee formed at Belfast as central body representing tenant-right groups of Ulster.
3 Mar. National tribute begun for Parnell who faced foreclosure on his estate, Avondale, for unpaid debt.
5 Apr. Dynamite conspirators, including Thomas Clarke, arrested in London and Birmingham.
9 Apr. Beginning of trials of Invincibles on charges connected with Phoenix Park murders (*see* 6 May 1882, 13 Jan.).
11 May Parnell tribute condemned by Vatican.
14 May – 9 June Executions of Phoenix Park murderers (*see* 13 Jan., 9 Apr.).
30 June T. M. Healy won the Co. Monaghan parliamentary by-election (2,376–2,001).

4 July Parnell received the freedom of Cork City.

17 July William H. K. Redmond won Wexford borough parliamentary by-election over The O'Conor Don (307–126).

29 July James Carey, who informed on the Invincibles, murdered by Patrick O'Donnell (*see* 17 Nov.).

25 Aug. Labourers Act enabled local authorities to borrow money to erect dwellings for agricultural labourers; Corrupt and Illegal Practices Act.

26 Sept. Beginning of 'invasion of Ulster' by National League.

28 Sept. Formal opening of Portrush–Bushmills electric railway.

30 Sept. Irish National League of Great Britain founded; T. P. O'Connor chosen as president.

2–17 Oct. Sir Stafford Northcote visited Ulster.

16 Oct. Narrow avoidance of collision between Nationalists and Orangemen at Rosslea, Co. Fermanagh.

24 Nov. Lord Rossmore suspended from magistracy.

26 Oct. University College transferred to the Jesuits (*see* 3 Oct. 1882).

26 Oct. Tramways and Light Railways Act.

17 Nov. Execution of O'Donnell for the murder of Carey (*see* 29 July).

11 Dec. Parnell presented with cheque for more than £37,000 from the National Tribute.

1884

1 Oct. Catholic Hierarchy asked Irish Party to represent its education interests in the House of Commons.

22 Oct. First women to receive a degree in Ireland from the Royal University.

23 Oct. Sir Henry Campbell-Bannerman appointed Chief Secretary.

1 Nov. Gaelic Athletic Association (GAA) founded in Thurles, Co. Tipperary.

1 Dec. Redistribution bill introduced in the House of Commons (*see* 25 June 1885).

6 Dec. Representation of the People Act extended franchise and equalised requirements across the United Kingdom.

13 Dec. William Mackey Lomasney killed while trying to blow up London Bridge.

18 Dec. Archbishop Croke became patron of GAA (*see* 1 Nov.).

1885

9 Jan. Parnell received freedom of Clonmel, Co. Cork.

21 Jan. Parnell at Cork declared that 'no man has the right to fix the boundary to the march of a nation'.

24 Jan. American Fenian dynamite campaign caused explosions in the Tower of London, Westminster Hall and the House of Commons.

21 Feb. Irish Amateur Athletic Association founded.

10 Apr. Foundation stone for the Science and Art Museum and the National Library of Ireland laid by the Prince and Princess of Wales.

1 May Irish Loyal and Patriotic Union founded.

9 June Gladstone's ministry defeated in the House of Commons.

16 June Inaugural meeting of Dublin Hermetic Society (W. B. Yeats in the chair).

23 June William Walsh, president of St Patrick's College, Maynooth, succeeded to the Catholic archbishopric of Dublin. Marquis of Salisbury appointed Prime Minister of a minority government (*see* 9 June).

25 June Sir William Hart Dyke appointed Chief Secretary. Redistribution of Seats Act abolished all but nine Irish parliamentary boroughs (*see* 1 Dec. 1884).

27 June Edward Gibson as Baron Ashbourne became Lord Chancellor of Ireland.

30 June Henry Herbert, Earl of Carnarvon, sworn in as Lord Lieutenant.

14 July Collapse of Munster Bank (William Shaw a major shareholder).

17 July Irish Land Purchase bill introduced in the House of Lords (*see* 14 Aug.).

1 Aug. Secret meeting between Parnell and Carnarvon in London.

14 Aug. Purchase of Land Act; Labourers Act; Education Endowments Act.

25 Aug. Parnell made major pronouncement on forthcoming general election.

1 Sept. Parnell defined the Irish Party platform as having 'a single plank' of self-government.

5 Oct. First National League convention to select parliamentary candidates held in Wicklow with Parnell in the chair.

30 Oct. Katharine O'Shea sent Gladstone draft of home rule constitution.

21 Nov. Manifesto to Irish of Great Britain to vote against Liberals and Radicals.

22–24 Nov. Parnell campaigned in Liverpool on behalf of candidacy of Captain William Henry O'Shea.

23 Nov. – 9 Dec. General election; Irish Party won 86 seats.

17 Dec. Herbert Gladstone announced that his father was converted to home rule, 'Hawarden Kite'.

28 Dec. Irish Defence Union (protection of landlords) founded.

1886

8 Jan. Ulster Loyalist Anti-Repeal Union formed from demonstration in Belfast against home rule.

12 Jan. Parliament opened; Lord Carnarvon resigned.

23 Jan. William Henry Smith appointed Chief Secretary.

25 Jan. Irish Unionist Party founded; Col. Edward J. Saunderson chosen as leader.

26 Jan. Salisbury ministry defeated in House of Commons (329–250).

28 Jan. Salisbury resigned.

1 Feb. Gladstone appointed Prime Minister for third time.

1–10 Feb. Galway by-election; Parnell imposed Captain O'Shea on the constituency.

6 Feb. John Morley appointed Chief Secretary.

10 Feb. John Gordon, Earl of Aberdeen, sworn in as Lord Lieutenant.

16 Feb. Catholic bishops expressed approval of home rule; published on 22 Feb.

22 Feb. Lord Randolph Churchill in Belfast 'played the Orange Card'.

28 Feb. Dublin United Trades' Council formed.

27 Mar. Joseph Chamberlain and Sir G. O. Trevelyan resigned from the cabinet.

8 Apr. Gladstone introduced Government of Ireland bill.

16 Apr. Contagious Diseases Acts, 1866 to 1869 repealed.

17 Apr. Land Purchase bill introduced in the House of Commons.

Irish Protestant Home Rule Association founded.

3–4 June Sectarian rioting on Belfast docks began summer of disturbances.

4 June Ulster Liberal Unionist Committee formed.

8 June Government of Ireland bill defeated on its second reading (341–311).

26 June Parliament dissolved.

1–17 July General election; Irish Party won 85 seats.

25 July Salisbury appointed Prime Minister for second time.

5 Aug. Charles Vane-Tempest-Stewart, sixth Marquess of Londonderry, sworn in as Lord Lieutenant; Sir Michael Hicks Beach appointed Chief Secretary.

18 Aug. General Sir Redvers Buller appointed as temporary Special Commissioner for Kerry and Clare.

25 Aug. Commission to inquire into Belfast riots appointed.

20 Sept. Parnell's Tenants' Relief bill defeated in the House of Commons.

29 Sept. Royal Commission under Lord Cowper established to inquire into operation of the Land Acts of 1881 and 1885 (*see* 21 Feb. 1887).

16 Oct. Royal Commission under James Abernethy appointed to inquire into Irish Public Works.

23 Oct. Plan of Campaign published in *United Ireland.*

25 Oct. Guinness Brewery became public limited liability company.

2 Dec. Archbishop William Walsh endorsed the Plan of Campaign.

18 Dec. Government declared Plan of Campaign illegal.

1887

21 Feb. Cowper Commission reported (*see* 29 Sept. 1886).

7 Mar. Arthur James Balfour appointed Chief Secretary.

7, 10, 14 Mar. *The Times* publication of series 'Parnellism and Crime' (*see* 18 Apr., 13 May).

28 Mar. Criminal Law and Procedure bill introduced in the House of Commons.

31 Mar. Irish Land bill introduced in the House of Lords.

15 Apr. William O'Brien, Plan of Campaign leader, arrested.

17 Apr. John Dillon arrested.

18 Apr. *The Times* published facsimile letter of Charles Stewart Parnells condoning the murder of T. H. Burke in 1882 (*see* 7, 10, 14 Mar., 13 May).

13 May Resumption of 'Parnellism and Crime' series (*see* 7, 10, 14 Mar., 18 Apr.).

7 July Arrival of Archbishop Ignatius Persico, envoy from the Vatican, to report on the state of the country.
19 July Criminal Law and Procedure Act for the prevention and punishment of crime.
20 July Parnell at the National Liberal Club lauded Gladstone.
19 Aug. National League proclaimed as a dangerous association.
23 Aug. Land Law Act gave land courts power to fix rents of leaseholders and to revise rents determined judicially between 1881 and 1885.
9 Sept. Shooting of civilians at Mitchelstown, Co. Cork; three killed when police opened fire.
15 Oct. Sir Joseph West Ridgeway appointed Under-Secretary.
1 Dec. Conclusion of series 'Parnellism and Crime' in *The Times* (*see* 7, 10, 14 Mar., 18 Apr.).

1888
1 Apr. First All-Ireland Hurling Championship final.
20 Apr. Papal rescript condemns Plan of Campaign and boycotting.
29 Apr. First All-Ireland Football Championship final.
5 May First issue of *Irish Catholic*.
8 May Parnell at the Liberal Eighty Club dissociated himself and the Irish Party from the Plan of Campaign.
14 May Royal charter founding Institute of Chartered Accountants in Ireland.
20 May Meeting in Phoenix Park, Dublin, rejected the papal rescript on the Plan of Campaign.
24 June Pope Leo XIII's letter to Irish Hierarchy repeated condemnation of boycotting and the Plan of Campaign.
5 July Verdict against F. H. O'Donnell in suit against *The Times* over the articles 'Parnellism and Crime'.
17 July Government introduced bill to establish special commission to inquire into all charges made against Irish MPs and others.
20 July Parnell at the National Liberal Club upheld the Nationalist-Liberal alliance.
13 Aug. Special Commission Act.
17 Sept. – 22 Nov. 1889 Special Commission, Parnellism and Crime met (*see* 13 Feb. 1890).
5 Nov. Charter created borough of Belfast a city (*see* 20 May 1892).
24 Dec. Land Purchase Act.

1889
5 Feb. Major Henri Le Caron (Thomas Bealis Beach), government operative, gave evidence before Special Commission (*see* 17 Sept. 1888).
20–22 Feb. Richard Pigott exposed as forger of facsimile letters published in *The Times*; committed suicide in Madrid on 21 Feb. (*see* 7, 10, 14 Mar., 18 Apr., 13 May 1887).

Feb. 'Syndicate' formed secretly by Balfour to protect Ponsonby estate at Youghal against Plan of Campaign.

22 Apr. – 8 May Parnell testimony before Special Commission (*see* 17 Sept. 1888).

4 May Irish Federated Trade and Labour Union first conference in Dublin.

8 May Parnell received in triumph at the National Liberal Club.

June Total Abstinence League of the Sacred Heart founded (later Pioneer League).

14 June Irish Society for the Prevention of Cruelty to Children founded.

30 Aug. Light Railways Act; Technical Instruction Act.

5 Oct. Lawrence Dundas, Earl of Zetland, sworn in as Lord Lieutenant.

25 Oct. Tenants' Defence Association launched in Dublin.

22 Nov. Final session of the Special Commission (*see* 17 July, 13 Aug., 17 Sept. 1888, 13 Feb. 1890).

2 Dec. 152 tenants on A. H. Smith-Barry estate in Tipperary town evicted.

18–19 Dec. Parnell visited Gladstone at Hawarden to discuss the shape of the next home rule bill.

24 Dec. Captain W. H. O'Shea filed for divorce, naming Parnell as co-respondent (*see* 15, 17 Nov. 1890).

1890

14 Jan. Royal Society of Antiquaries of Ireland founded.

21 Jan. Irish Democratic Trade and Labour Federation formed at Cork.

13 Feb. Report of the Special Commission on Parnellism and Crime (*see* 17 July, 13 Aug., 17 Sept. 1888, 22 Nov. 1889).

12 Apr. 'New Tipperary' opened by the leaders of the Plan of Campaign.

30 July Mary Hannon first female graduate of an Irish medical school registered as a medical practitioner.

29 Aug. Science and Art Museum and National Library of Ireland opened.

18 Sept. Dillon and William O'Brien break bail and flee abroad (*see* 12 Feb. 1891).

21 Sept. First issue of *Labour World* (London) edited by Michael Davitt.

15, 17 Nov. Trial of O'Shea divorce petition in high court, London; O'Shea awarded decree nisi (*see* June 1891).

20 Nov. Meeting of Nationalists in Leinster Hall, Dublin, upheld Parnell's leadership.

25 Nov. Parnell unanimously re-elected chairman of the Irish Party.

26 Nov. Gladstone's letter declaring that if Parnell remained Irish leader his own leadership would be 'almost a nullity' published.

29 Nov. Under increasing pressure to withdraw, Parnell's defiant Manifesto to the Irish People published in support of his continuing leadership.

1–6 Dec. Irish Party met in Committee Room 15 of the House of Commons; session ends when Justin McCarthy and a majority withdrew and met separately.

3 Dec. Standing Episcopal Committee of the Irish Catholic Hierarchy repudiated Parnell's leadership.

10 Dec. Parnell received a hero's welcome on arrival in Dublin; he replaced Matthew Bodkin with Edmund Leamy as editor of *United Ireland.*

22 Dec. Sir John Pope-Hennessy returned at Kilkenny North by-election for the anti-Parnellites (2,527–1,362).

30–31 Dec. Initial meetings between Parnell, Dillon and O'Brien in Boulogne, 'Boulogne Negotiations' on the leadership (*see* 11 Feb. 1891).

1891

11 Feb. Unsuccessful close of the 'Boulogne Negotiations' (*see* 30–31 Dec. 1890).

12 Feb. Dillon and O'Brien returned to Great Britain and were immediately rearrested and imprisoned in Galway jail (*see* 18 Sept. 1890).

7 Mar. *National Press* launched as an anti-Parnell organ under the control of T. M. Healy.

10 Mar. National Federation, an anti-Parnellite body, founded in Dublin.

14 Mar. Irish Labour League formed.

2 Apr. Bernard Collery, Anti-Parnellite, defeated Parnellite Valentine Dillon at Sligo North parliamentary by-election (3,261–2,493).

5 Apr. Census of population.

6 Apr. Irish Unionist Alliance formed from Irish Loyal and Patriotic Union.

1 May 'Loop Line' connected Dublin railway termini.

June W. H. O'Shea's divorce decree made absolute (*see* 15, 17 Nov. 1890).

25 June Parnell and Katharine O'Shea married in Sussex.

8 July John Hammond, Anti-Parnellite, returned in the Carlow parliamentary by-election (3,755–1,539).

30 July Dillon and O'Brien released from prison and rejected Parnell's leadership.

5 Aug. Purchase of Land Act increased facilities for purchase and established Congested Districts Board.

21 Sept. *Freeman's Journal* deserted Parnell.

25 Sept. James Stephens, founder of the IRB, who had lived in exile since 1866, returned to Ireland.

27 Sept. Parnell's last public speech at Creggs, Co. Roscommon.

1–2 Oct. National Liberal Federation conference at Newcastle-upon-Tyne adopted the 'Newcastle Programme' which downgraded the central position of home rule.

6 Oct. Parnell died at Brighton.

11 Oct. Parnell's funeral and burial in Glasnevin attended by 100,000.

9 Nov. William L. Jackson appointed Chief Secretary.

18 Dec. First issue of a new Parnellite organ, the *Irish Daily Independent.*

24 Dec. John Redmond standing as a Parnellite returned at the Waterford City parliamentary by-election over Michael Davitt (Anti-Parnellite) (1,775–1,229).

28 Dec. Irish Literary Society founded in London at the home of W. B. Yeats.

Dec. Workman Clark start their own engine works at Queen's Island, Belfast.

1892

Jan. First issue of journal of the *Cork Historical and Archaeological Society.*

23 Jan. Amnesty Association of Great Britain and Ireland founded in London by Dr Mark Ryan.

22 Feb. Irish Education bill for compulsory school attendance introduced in the House of Commons.

28 Mar. *Freeman's Journal* and *National Press* merged as single newspaper.

20 May First Lord Mayor of Belfast (*see* 5 Nov. 1888).

17 June Ulster Unionist Convention in Botanic Gardens, Belfast, resolved to have nothing to do with a home rule parliament.

23 June Southern Unionists Convention.

27 June Irish Education Act abolished fees in National Schools and made attendance compulsory for children between age 6 and 14 (*see* 22 Feb.); Ancient Monuments Protection Act.

12–26 June General election; Liberals largest party, Nationalists return 81.

15 Aug. W. E. Gladstone appointed Prime Minister for the fourth time.

16 Aug. National Literary Society founded in Dublin by W. B. Yeats.

22 Aug. Robert Milnes, Baron Houghton, sworn in as Lord Lieutenant; John Morley appointed Chief Secretary.

23 Sept. Electricity station, owned by Dublin Corporation, began operation.

29 Sept. Belfast Labour Party formed; first labour party in Ireland.

14 Oct. Commission under Sir James Charles Mathew appointed to inquire into estates where tenants had been evicted (*see* 25 Feb. 1893).

25 Nov. Douglas Hyde's presidential address to the National Literary Society on the need to de-anglicise Ireland.

1893

19 Jan. Michael Logue, Archbishop of Armagh, created cardinal.

13 Feb. Gladstone introduced second home rule bill in the House of Commons (*see* 2, 9 Sept.).

25 Feb. Report of the Evicted Tenants Commission (*see* 14 Oct. 1892).

21–22 Apr. Disturbances in Belfast following second reading of home rule bill.

16 May Electric tramways began operation from Haddington Road to Dalkey.

23–30 May Salisbury visited Ulster.

27 July Act enabling Belfast Water Commissioners to build reservoirs.

31 July Gaelic League inaugurated by Douglas Hyde, Eoin MacNéill and others, with Hyde its first president.

2 Sept. Home rule bill passed in House of Commons (301–267) (*see* 13 Feb., 9 Sept.).

9 Sept. Home rule bill defeated in the House of Lords (419–41) (*see* 13 Feb., 2 Sept.).

1894

3 Mar. W. E. Gladstone resigned as Prime Minister.

5 Mar. Lord Rosebery appointed Prime Minister (*see* 25 June 1895).

12 Mar. Rosebery, in the House of Lords, stated that home rule would only pass when the 'predominant partner', England, approved it.

18 Apr. Irish Agricultural Organisation Society founded by Sir Horace Plunkett.

19 Apr. Evicted Tenants bill introduced in the House of Commons (*see* 14 Aug.).

27–28 Apr. First meeting of the Irish Trade Union Congress.

12 May T. M. Healy attacked any attempt at reunification of the Irish Party.

26 May Royal Commission under H. C. E. Childers appointed to examine financial relations between Ireland and Great Britain (*see* 28 Mar. 1895, 5 Sept. 1896).

14 Aug. Evicted Tenants bill defeated in the House of Commons (249–30) (*see* 19 Apr.).

23 Oct. 'Paris Fund' handed over to Justin McCarthy.

7 Nov. Reunification of the Northern Presbytery with the Antrim Presbytery.

1895

23 Jan. Electricity station owned by Belfast Corporation began operation.

9 Mar. First issue of the *Irish Homestead* edited by George Russell, known as AE, as an organ of the Irish Agricultural Organisation Society.

28 Mar. First report of the Commission on Financial Relations Between Ireland and Great Britain (*see* 26 May 1894, 5 Sept. 1896).

25 May Oscar Wilde sentenced to two years' imprisonment with hard labour for homosexual offences.

21 June Liberal ministry defeated in House of Commons.

23 June Rosebery resigned as Prime Minister.

25 June Salisbury appointed Prime Minister for third time.

4 July Gerald Balfour appointed Chief Secretary.

8 July Earl of Cadogan sworn in as Lord Lieutenant.

12–26 July General election; Salisbury retained office and 82 Nationalists returned.

27 Aug. Sir Horace Plunkett proposed formation of the Recess Committee.

11 Oct. Strike by engineers at Harland & Wolff shipyard in Belfast (*see* 27 Jan. 1896).

7 Nov. T. M. Healy expelled from the Irish National League of Great Britain.

13 Nov. Healy expelled from the executive of the Irish National Federation.

1896

27 Jan. Harland & Wolff shipyard reopened following strike (*see* 11 Oct. 1895).

2 Feb. Justin McCarthy resigned from chairmanship of Anti-Parnellites.

18 Feb. John Dillon elected chairman of Anti-Parnellites (31–21) (*see* 7 Feb. 1899).

13 Mar. Pope Leo XIII empowered St Patrick's College, Maynooth, to grant degrees of pontifical university.

31 Mar. Poor Law Guardians Act enabled women to be elected as Poor Law Guardians.

20 Apr. First screening of a film in Ireland in Dublin.

29 May Irish Socialist Republican Party founded by James Connolly and others.

1 Aug. Recess Committee report (*see* 27 Aug. 1895).

14 Aug. Locomotives on Highways Act removed restrictions on power-driven vehicles on public roads; Land Law Act.

1–3 Sept. Irish Race Convention at Leinster Hall, Dublin.

5 Sept. Publication of the report of Royal Commission on the Financial Relations Between Ireland and Great Britain (*see* 26 May 1894, 28 Mar. 1895).

6 Oct. Rosebery resigned Liberal Party leadership.

1897

12 Jan. People's Rights Association founded by T. M. Healy.

17 May First Oireachtas (Irish Literary Festival) held in Dublin.

18–22 May First Feis Ceoil (Irish Music Festival).

5 June *Nation* ceased publication (*see* 15 Oct. 1842).

1898

23 Jan. United Irish League founded by William O'Brien.

21 Feb. Local Government bill introduced in the House of Commons.

20 Mar. First *feis* organised by Gaelic League.

29 Mar. Registration Act gave women and peers the local government franchise.

Mar. Celebrations of centenary of the rising of the United Irishmen.

30 May Viceregal Commission under Christopher Palles appointed to inquire into intermediate education (*see* 22 Dec., 11 Aug. 1899, 6 Aug. 1900).

12 Aug. Local Government Act provided for elected county and district councils (*see* 21 Feb., 22 Dec.).

13 Aug. First issue of *Workers' World* edited by James Connolly.

29 Sept. Thomas J. Clarke released from Portland prison (*see* 5 Apr. 1883, 3 May 1916).

22 Dec. First report of Palles Commission (*see* 30 May, 11 Aug. 1899, 6 Aug. 1900). Lord Lieutenant declared that women were qualified to sit on district councils and be town commissioners (*see* 12 Aug.).

27 Dec. League of the Sacred Heart founded (total abstinence society for women; men admitted Feb. 1901).

1899

Jan. First local government elections.

7 Feb. Dillon resigned chairmanship of Anti-Parnellites (*see* 18 Feb. 1896).

4 Mar. First issue of *United Irishman* edited by Arthur Griffith.

18 Mar. First issue of *An Claidheamh Soluis*, organ of the Gaelic League edited by Eoin MacNeill

4 Apr. Meeting to attempt reunification of home rule factions.

29 Apr. Griffith outlined constitutional position of Hungary in *United Irishman.*

8 May Irish Literary Theatre staged W. B. Yeat's, *Countess Cathleen.*

20 June Catholic Truth Society founded.

9 Aug. Agricultural and Technical Instruction Act established Department of Agriculture and Technical Instruction.

11 Aug. Final report of the Palles Commission (*see* 30 May 1898, 22 Dec. 1898, 6 Aug. 1900).

11 Oct. Boer War began.

25 Oct. Davitt withdrew from the House of Commons in protest against the Boer War.

1900

30 Jan. Reunification of Irish Party (*see* 6 Feb.).

6 Feb. John Redmond elected chairman of united Irish Party (*see* 30 Jan.).

3–26 Apr. Queen Victoria visited Ireland.

22 May Commissioners of National Education ended system of payment by results.

19–20 June United Irish League recognised as official organisation of the Irish Party; John Redmond elected president.

20 July Debate on the Irish language in the House of Commons.

6 Aug. Intermediate Education Act (*see* 30 May 1898, 22 Dec. 1898, 11 Aug. 1899, 22 May).

1 Sept. First issue of the *Leader* edited by D. P. Moran.

29 Sept. – 12 Oct. General election; Conservatives gained increased majority, Nationalist returned 82 MPs.

30 Sept. Cumann na nGaedheal founded by Arthur Griffith.

9 Nov. George Wyndham appointed Chief Secretary.

11 Dec. T. M. Healy expelled from Irish Party.

1901

22 Jan. Death of Queen Victoria; succession of Edward VII.

14 Mar. Society of Incorporated Accountants in Ireland formed.

31 Mar. Census of population.

5 June Ulster Farmers' and Labourers' Union and Compulsory Purchase Association founded by T. W. Russell.

1 July Royal Commission on University Education in Ireland under Lord Robertson appointed (*see* 20 Feb. 1903).

30 Sept. Classes commenced at Municipal Technical Institute, Belfast.

4 Dec. United Irish League of American founded in New York.

1902

14 Feb. Rosebery at Liverpool cast doubt on the utility of home rule.

4 Mar. Ancient Order of Hibernians achieved unity in Ireland under Board of Erin.

2 Apr. First performance of W. B. Yeat's *Cathleen ni Houlihan.*

31 May Treaty of Vereeniging ended Boer War.

11 July Salisbury resigned as Prime Minister.

12 July Arthur Balfour appointed Prime Minister.

31 July Sale of Intoxicating Liquors (Licences) Act reduced numbers of drink licences.

16 Aug. Earl of Dudley sworn in as Lord Lieutenant.

18 Aug. T. H. Sloan, shipyard worker, Independent Unionist and member of the Belfast Protestant Association, won the parliamentary by-election for Belfast South.

3 Sept. Captain John Shawe-Taylor calls for a land conference in a letter published in *The Times* (*see* 20 Dec.).

8 Nov. Sir Antony MacDonnell appointed Under-Secretary (*see* 14 July 1908).

Nov. Emergence of Ulster branch of Irish Literary Theatre.

20 Dec. Land Conference convened in Dublin (*see* 3 Sept., 3 Jan. 1903).

1903

3 Jan. Report of the Land Conference recommended tenant purchase financed by treasury loans (*see* 20 Dec. 1902).

1 Feb. Irish Literary Theatre became Irish National Theatre Society.

20 Feb. Fourth and final report of the Royal Commission on University Education in Ireland (*see* 1 July 1901).

2 Mar. Patrick Pearse became editor of Gaelic League newspaper, *An Claidheamh Soluis.*

25 Mar. Land bill (Wyndham bill) introduced in the House of Commons (*see* 3 Jan.).

27 Mar. Bank Holiday Act. St Patrick's Day designated a bank holiday.

12 May Viceregal Commission on Poor Law Reform in Ireland appointed (*see* 10 Oct. 1906).

6 June First meeting of National Council founded by Arthur Griffith protested against the royal visit by Edward VII.

11 June Independent Orange Order founded in Belfast by T. H. Sloan.

2 July First road race for cars in United Kingdom between Carlow and Kildare.

21 July – 1 Aug. Edward VII visited Ireland.

14 Aug. Wyndham Land Act (Irish Land Act) largest piece of land purchase legislation.

25 Aug. Dillon at Swinford, Co. Mayo, expressed 'no faith in the doctrine of conciliation'.

18 Sept. James Connolly emigrated to America.

8 Oct. First performance of John Millington Synge's *In the Shadow of the Glen,* in Molesworth Hall, Dublin.

9 Oct. David Sheehy won parliamentary by-election for Meath South over John Howard Parnell, brother of Charles (2,245–1,031).

4 Nov. William O'Brien announced withdrawal from public life.

6 Nov. O'Brien resigned from Irish Party.

1904

2 Jan. Commencement of series 'The Resurrection of Hungary' by Arthur Griffith in the *United Irishmen.*

Jan. Pogrom against Jews incited by Redemptorist priest in Limerick.

25 Feb. First public performance of Synge's *Riders to the Sea*, at Molesworth Hall, Dublin.

26 Apr. – 5 May King Edward VII visited Ireland.

28 Apr. King laid foundation stone for new buildings of Royal College of Science in Upper Merrion Street, Dublin.

4 July First college (Coláiste na Mumhan) to train teachers of Irish opened in Ballingeary, Co. Cork.

25 Aug. Land Conference dissolved (*see* 3 Sept., 20 Dec. 1902, 3 Jan. 1903).

26 Aug. Irish Reform Association founded by William O'Brien and Dunraven and the latter's scheme of devolved government published.

27 Sept. Wyndham's letter in *The Times* repudiated Irish Reform Association plan.

1 Nov. First public performance of George Bernard Shaw's *John Bull's Other Island* in London.

Nov. Publication of first issue of *Uladh*, review of Ulster literary theatre.

2 Dec. Unionist conference in Belfast called for vigilance and resistance to devolution.

27 Dec. Abbey Theatre in Dublin opened with plays by Lady Gregory and Yeats.

1905

2 Jan. First issue of *Irish Independent* founded by William Martin Murphy.

4 Feb. First public performance of Synge's *The Well of the Saints* in the Abbey Theatre.

3 Mar. Ulster Unionist Council formed.

5 Mar. George Wyndham resigned as Chief Secretary.

8 Mar. Dungannon Clubs founded in Belfast by Bulmer Hobson.

12 Mar. Walter Long appointed Chief Secretary.

9 June First public performance of Padraic Colum's *The Land*, at the Abbey Theatre.

13 July Independent Orange Order issued 'Magheramore Manifesto'.

12 Sept. Carnegie Free Library opened in Cork.

15 Oct. Capuchin Order inaugurated temperance crusade.

11 Nov. Dr Douglas Hyde departed for lecture tour of the United States ($64,000 raised).

28 Nov. At annual convention of National Council name Sinn Féin given to Arthur Griffith's policy.

4 Dec. Royal Commission under Lord George Hamilton as chairman to inquire into Poor Law in the United Kingdom appointed (*see* 14 Apr. 1909). Arthur Balfour resigned as Prime Minister.

5 Dec. Sir Henry Campbell-Bannerman appointed Prime Minister. Electric tramways began operation in Belfast.

14 Dec. Earl of Aberdeen sworn in as Lord Lieutenant; James Bryce appointed Chief Secretary.

1906
13–27 Jan. General election; Campbell-Bannerman retained office, Nationalists returned 83 MPs.
Apr. Ulster Liberal Association founded.
1 May Catholic Episcopal Standing Committee urged Irish Party to oppose English and Welsh education bill (*see* 2 May).
2 May Irish Party agreed to opposed education bill (*see* 1 May).
5 May First issue of *Sinn Féin* founded and edited by Arthur Griffith.
2 June Appointment of Royal Commission under Sir Edward Fry on Trinity College and University College Dublin (*see* 31 Aug., 12 Jan. 1907).
18 July Viceregal Commission under Sir Charles Scotter appointed to inquire into Irish railways (*see* 4 July 1910).
20 July Royal Commission under Earl of Dudley on congestion in Ireland appointed (*see* 14 Nov., 5 May 1908).
1 Aug. Belfast City Hall opened (architect Alfred Bramwell-Thomas).
4 Aug. Labourers Act provided additional finance for labourers' cottages.
30 Aug. Waterford–Rosslare–Fishguard rail route opened. Last major railway extension.
31 Aug. First Report of Fry Commission (*see* 2 June, 12 Jan. 1907).
10 Oct. Report of Viceregal Commission on Poor Law (*see* 12 May 1903).
14 Oct. Laurence Ginnell denounced grazing system and advocated 'cattle-driving'.
20 Oct. First public performance of Lady Gregory's *The Gaol Gate* at the Abbey Theatre.
1 Nov. Walter Long elected leader of the Unionist Parliamentary Party.
14 Nov. First report of Dudley Commission (*see* 20 July, 5 May 1908).
31 Dec. Expiration of the Peace Preservation Act, 1881.

1907
Jan. James Larkin arrived in Belfast as organiser for the National Union of Dock Labourers.
12 Jan. Report of the Fry Commission (*see* 2 June, 31 Aug. 1906).
28–30 Jan. J. M. Synge's *The Playboy of the Western World* opened at the Abbey Theatre, causing rioting.
29 Jan. Augustine Birrell appointed Chief Secretary.
9 Mar. First public performance of Lady Gregory's *The Rising of the Moon* at the Abbey Theatre.
21 Apr. Sinn Féin League formed from the Dungannon Clubs and Cumann na nGaedheal.
4 May – 9 Nov. Irish International Exhibition opened at Ballsbridge, Dublin.
6 May – late Nov. Dock strike in Belfast under the leadership of James Larkin (*see* 24 July).

7 May Birrell introduced Irish Council bill in the House of Commons (*see* 21 May, 3 June).

21 May National Convention chaired by John Redmond condemned Irish Councils bill (*see* 7 May, 3 June).

3 June Campbell-Bannerman announced withdrawal of Irish Councils bill (*see* 7, 21 May).

4 July Irish Tobacco Act permitted tobacco growing.

6 July Discovery of theft of Irish State Jewels from Dublin Castle.

24 July Mutiny in support of strikers by the Royal Irish Constabulary in Belfast (*see* 6 May).

2 Aug. *Ne temere decree* affecting marriage between Catholics and non-Catholics issued by Pope Pius X.

11 Aug. James Larkin formed branch of the National Union of Dock Labours in Dublin.

12 Aug. Sectarian rioting in Falls Road, West Belfast; army killed four people.

28 Aug. Evicted Tenants Act empowered Estate Commissioners to purchase land compulsorily for evicted tenants.

5 Sept. National Council absorbed into Sinn Féin League.

Oct. First issue of *Irish Educational Review.*

Dec. Thomas J. Clarke returned to Ireland (*see* 5 Apr. 1883, 29 Sept. 1898, 3 May 1916).

16 Oct. Marconi's wireless telegraph opened at Clifden, Co. Galway, for transatlantic press telegrams.

13 Dec. William O'Brien and John Redmond discussed O'Brien's return to the Irish Party.

19 Dec. Joint Committee of Unionist Associations of Ireland founded.

1908

17 Jan. William O'Brien and T. M. Healy rejoined the Irish Party. Sinn Féin won 15 seats in Dublin Municipal Council elections.

20 Jan. Dublin Municipal Art Gallery opened, first gallery dedicated to modern art in the United Kingdom.

10 Feb. Hugh Lane received freedom of the City of Dublin.

21 Feb. Sinn Féin candidate, Charles J. Dolan, at the Leitrim North parliamentary by-election defeated by the Irish Party nominee (3,103–1,157).

3 Apr. Sir Henry Campbell-Bannerman, near death, resigned as Prime Minister.

8 Apr. Henry Herbert Asquith appointed Liberal Prime Minister.

5 May Final report of Dudley Commission (*see* 20 July, 14 Nov. 1906).

19–20 May Lindsay Crawford expelled from Independent Orange Order.

July Sir Antony MacDonnell resigned as Under-Secretary (*see* 8 Nov. 1902).

14 July Sir James Dougherty appointed Under-Secretary.

1 Aug. Irish Universities Act replaced Royal University with National University of Ireland and Queen's University of Belfast; Old Age Pensions Act created pensions for people over 70.

8 Sept. Patrick Pearse opened Scoil Eanna (St Enda's school) in Rathmines.
9–12 Nov. Strike of dockers and carters at Cork, organised by James Larkin and James Fearon of National Union of Dock Labourers.
11 Nov. Irish Women's Franchise League founded by Hanna Sheehy-Skeffington and Margaret Cousins.
21 Dec. Housing of the Working Classes Act increased powers of local authorities to build houses; Children's Act reformed law affecting children and adolescents.
29 Dec. James Larkin formed Irish Transport Workers' Union, forerunner of Irish Transport and General Workers' Union, with himself as general secretary.
31 Dec. Tuberculosis Prevention Act.

1909

9–10 Feb. United Irish League Convention; William O'Brien and John Dillon shouted down on separate issues.
1 Apr. Carnegie Library opened in Great Brunswick Street, Dublin.
14 Apr. Report on Ireland of the Royal Commission to inquire into Poor Law in United Kingdom (*see* 4 Dec. 1905).
29 Apr. 'People's Budget' introduced by David Lloyd George in the House of Commons.
16 Aug. Fianna Éireann founded by Constance, Countess Markievicz and Bulmer Hobson.
25 Aug. G. B. Shaw's, *The Shewing-up of Blanco Posnet* performed at the Abbey Theatre.
20 Sept. Labour Exchanges Act.
25 Sept. Health Resorts and Watering-Places Act first legislation related to tourism.
30 Nov. Lloyd George's budget rejected by House of Lords.
3 Dec. Irish Land Act increased power of purchase and gave authority for compulsory purchase to Congested Districts Board (9 Edw. VII, c. 42).
10 Dec. Herbert Asquith at the Albert Hall in London endorsed home rule as a Liberal policy intention for the next parliament.
20 Dec. First purpose-built cinema opened in Dublin.
31 Dec. Harry Ferguson made first aeroplane flight from Ireland at Old Park, Hillsborough, Co. Down.

1910

15–28 Jan. General election; Asquith retained office, Nationalists returned 82 MPs.
21 Feb. Sir Edward Carson elected leader of Unionist Party (*see* 4 Feb. 1921).
31 Mar. All-for-Ireland League founded in Cork City by William O'Brien.
29 Apr. Finance Act (1909–10) established a more stringent system of liquor licences.
5 May First public performance of Padraic Colum's *Thomas Muskerry* at the Abbey Theatre.

6 May King Edward VII died; succeeded by George V.

7 May Failure of Abbey Theatre to close in mourning for king caused withdrawal of financial support of Miss A. E. F. Horniman.

11 June General Assembly of Presbyterian Church decided to co-operate with Church of Ireland and other evangelical churches (*see* 15 Oct. 1911).

June–Nov. Constitutional Conference; Irish Party not invited to participate.

23 June Senate of the National University of Ireland made Gaelic a requirement for matriculation from 1913.

4 July Publication of final report of Viceregal Commission on Irish Railways (*see* 18 July 1906).

26 July James Connolly returned to Ireland from the United States.

Nov. First issue of *Irish Freedom* and Irish Republican Brotherhood journal.

10 Nov. Failure of the Constitutional Conference announced.

3 Dec. – 13 Jan. 1911 General election; Asquith retained office, Nationalists returned 84 MPs.

1911

23 Jan. Ulster Women's Unionist Council founded.

22 Feb. Parliament bill introduced in the House of Commons.

Mar. First issue of *Irish Review.*

1 Apr. *Titanic* launched in Belfast (*see* 14–15 Apr. 1912).

2 Apr. Census of population.

27 May First issue of the *Irish Worker* edited by James Larkin.

30 June Dublin Employers' Federation founded; William Martin Murphy the first president.

7–12 July King George V visited Ireland.

18 Aug. Parliament Act restricted power of House of Lords.

21 Aug. Irish Women's Suffrage Federation founded.

26 Aug. Lock-out of foundrymen at Wexford because of their determination to join Irish Transport and General Workers' Union.

5 Sept. Irish Women Workers' Union founded by Delia Larkin.

23 Sept. Orange Order and Unionist Clubs rally at Craigavon House, near Belfast, and addressed by Sir Edward Carson.

1 Oct. Parnell Monument by Augustus Saint-Gaudens in Upper Sackville Street, Dublin, unveiled by John Redmond.

15 Oct. Joint Committee of Presbyterian Church and Church of Ireland met for the first time (*see* 11 June 1910).

17 Oct. Report of committee chaired by Sir Henry Primrose on the finances of a future home rule government.

8 Nov. Arthur Balfour resigned as leader of the Conservative Party.

13 Nov. Andrew Bonar Law chosen leader of Conservative Party.

16 Dec. Local Authorities (Qualification of Women) Act enabled women to become members of county and borough councils; National Insurance Act established state heath and employment insurance.

1912

8 Feb. Winston Churchill spoke at Celtic Park, Belfast.

Mar. First issue of *Studies: An Irish Quarterly Review.*

9 Apr. Bonar Law at Balmoral, near Belfast, pledged support of British Unionists for Ulster Unionist resistance to home rule.

11 Apr. Asquith introduced third Home Rule bill in House of Commons (*see* 16, 30 Jan., 7, 15 July 1913).

14–15 Apr. *Titanic* sank on maiden voyage (*see* 1 Apr. 1911).

2 May T. C. Agar-Roberts proposed in the House of Commons exclusion of four Ulster counties from Home Rule (*see* 11, 13, 18 June).

11, 13, 18 June Debate in House of Commons on Agar-Roberts motion for four-county exclusion. Amendment defeated (*see* 2 May).

28 June Irish Labour Party founded.

29 June Protestant Sunday school excursion at Castledawson, Co. Londonderry, attached by Ancient Order of Hibernians procession (*see* 2 July).

2 July Protestant shipyard workers in Belfast expelled Catholics from yards in reprisal for Castledawson attack (*see* 29 June).

18–20 July Asquith visited Dublin.

27 July Speaking at Unionist rally at Blenheim Palace, Bonar Law stated there 'are things higher than parliamentary majorities'.

14 Sept. Riot between supporters of Belfast football clubs, Celtic (Catholic) and Linfield (Protestant).

18 Sept. 'Ulster Day' with signing of Ulster's Solemn League and Covenant.

30 Dec. Second American tour of Abbey Theatre opened.

1913

1 Jan. Sir Edward Carson's amendment to Home Rule bill for the exclusion of Ulster from its operation debated and defeated.

16 Jan. Home Rule bill passed in House of Commons (367–257) (*see* 11 Apr. 1912, 30 Jan. 1913, 25 May 1914).

30 Jan. Home Rule bill defeated in House of Lords (326–69) (*see* 16 Jan.).

31 Jan. Ulster Volunteer Force (UVF) formed.

7 Mar. Trade Union Act regulated political activities of unions.

7 July Home Rule bill passed in House of Commons (352–243) (*see* 11 Apr. 1912, 16, 30 Jan., 15 July, 25 May 1914).

15 July Home Rule bill defeated in House of Lords (302–64) (*see* 11 Apr. 1912, 16, 30 Jan., 7 July).

18 Aug. William Martin Murphy led employers' lock-out.

26 Aug. James Larkin called general strike; he and four others arrested for 'seditious conspiracy' (*see* 18 Jan. 1914).

30 Aug. James Connolly sentenced to three months' imprisonment.

30 Aug. – 1 Sept. Disturbances in Dublin from labour unrest.

3 Sept. Dublin Employers' Federation imposed pledge not to belong to Irish Transport and General Workers' Union (*see* 18 Jan. 1914).

17 Sept. Carson at Newry indicated the formation of a provisional Ulster government in the event home rule including Ulster was implemented.

24 Sept. Standing Committee of Ulster Unionist Council approved establishment of a provisional government in the event of home rule.

6 Oct. Irish Women's Suffrage Federation welcomed Carson's promise that women would be granted vote under provisional Ulster government; report of the court of inquiry into the lock-out.

14 Oct. First secret talk between Asquith and Bonar Law on the home rule crisis.

21 Oct. Archbishop Walsh denounced evacuation of children of locked-out workers to Britain.

27 Oct. James Larkin sentenced to seven months' imprisonment for seditious language.

1 Nov. Eoin MacNeill, in *An Claidheamh Soluis,* advocated formation of National Volunteer Force (*see* 11, 25 Nov.).

6 Nov. Second secret talk between Asquith and Bonar Law on the crisis.

11 Nov. First meeting of steering committee to form Irish Volunteers (*see* 1, 25 Nov.).

19 Nov. Irish Citizen Army formed.

25 Nov. Irish Volunteers formed (*see* 1, 11 Nov.).

4 Dec. Royal proclamation prohibiting importation into Ireland of military arms and ammunition.

10 Dec. Last secret talk between Asquith and Bonar Law on the home rule crisis.

1914

15 Jan. Bonar Law announced the end of meetings with Asquith.

18 Jan. Irish Transport and General Workers' Union advised members to return to work if not obliged to take 'pledge' not to join the Union (*see* 26 Aug., 3 Sept. 1913).

31 Jan. Agreement between Builders' Association and Builders' Labourers' Union to exclude Irish Transport and General Workers' Union members and to resume normal working.

7 Feb. Report on working-class housing in Dublin by Department Committee of Local Government Board. First issue of the *Irish Volunteer.*

4 Mar. British Anti-Home Rule Covenant launched.

9 Mar. Asquith announced in the House of Commons that the third Home Rule bill would be amended (*see* 12 May, 23 June).

20–25 Mar. Curragh incident when 57 officers stated unwillingness to coerce north into home rule.

2 Apr. Cumann na mBan founded as women's counterpart of Irish Volunteers (*see* 25 Nov. 1913).

24–25 Apr. Larne gunrunning by UVF.

12 May Asquith announced an amending bill on home rule to be brought forward (*see* 9 Mar., 23 June).

25 May Home Rule bill passed in House of Commons for the third time (*see* 16 Jan., 7 July 1913).

10 June John Redmond called for 25 nominees of the Irish Party to be placed on the Provisional Committee of the Irish Volunteers (*see* 16 June).

15 June Publication of James Joyce's *Dubliners.*

16 June Provisional Committee of the Irish Volunteers accepted Redmond's demand (*see* 10 June).

21–24 June Buckingham Palace Conference to resolve the home rule impasse ended in failure.

23 June Government of Ireland (Amendment) bill introduced to provide temporary exclusion of parts of Ulster by county option from home rule scheme (*see* 9 Mar., 12 May, 8 July).

28 June Austrian Archduke Franz Ferdinand and his wife assassinated in Sarajevo.

8 July Amendment bill altered by the House of Lords to enable permanent exclusion of Ulster from home rule (*see* 23 June).

10 July Provisional Government of Ulster met in Belfast.

26 July Irish Volunteers land rifles at Howth, Co. Dublin; later in the day troops fired on crowd at Bachelor's Walk, Dublin; 4 killed and 30 wounded.

1–2 Aug. Gunrunning for Irish Volunteers at Kilcoole, Co. Wicklow.

3 Aug. Germany declared war on France. In the event of the United Kingdom entering the conflict, Redmond announced his support and proposed the Irish and Ulster Volunteers be employed in defence of Ireland.

4 Aug. Belgium invaded by Germany; United Kingdom declared war on Germany.

8 Aug. Defence of the Realm Act.

10 Aug. Education (Provision of Meals) Act enabled local authorities to provide meals for school children.

15 Aug. Press censorship introduced.

Aug. Establishment of 36th (Ulster) Division in part based on the UVF.

9 Sept. Conference in Dublin of revolutionary leaders to discuss opportunity for insurrection.

15 Sept. Suspending Act delayed implementation of home rule for one year or the duration of the war.

18 Sept. Government of Ireland Act.

20 Sept. John Redmond at Woodenbridge, Co. Wicklow, called on the Irish Volunteers to fight for Britain in the war, causing it to split (*see* 24 Sept.).

24 Sept. Eoin MacNeill and others repudiated John Redmond's role in the Irish Volunteers (*see* 20 Sept.).

25–26 Sept. Asquith visited Dublin and with Redmond addressed recruiting meeting in Mansion House.

28 Sept. Irish Neutrality League established (James Connolly president).

1 Oct. Report of Royal Commission of inquiry on landing of arms at Howth (*see* 26 July).

12 Oct. Sir Matthew Nathan appointed Under-Secretary.

17 Oct. First issue of *National Volunteer.*

24 Oct. James Larkin departed for America; succeeded as acting general secretary of the Irish Transport and General Workers' Union by James Connolly.

2–4 Dec. Suppression of the newspapers *Sinn Féin*, *Irish Freedom* and *Irish Volunteer*.

5 Dec. Intermediate Education Act.

27 Dec. Sir Roger Casement signed a 'treaty' in Berlin for the establishment of an Irish brigade in German service.

1915

5 Jan. William T. Cosgrave, Sinn Féin, returned unopposed to the Dublin Corporation.

7 Feb. First issue of *Spark*, a militant nationalist periodical.

18 Feb. Ivor Churchill Guest, Baron Wimborne, sworn in as Lord Lieutenant.

18 Mar. Defence of the Realm Amendment Act.

7 May *Lusitania* torpedoed near Kinsale.

25 May Coalition government formed; Asquith remained Prime Minster and Sir Edward Carson joined the cabinet as Attorney-General for England.

c. **late May** Supreme Council of IRA established military committee or council, consisting of Patrick Pearse, Joseph Mary Plunkett and Eamonn Ceannt.

19 June First issue of *Nationality*, edited by Arthur Griffith.

29 June Following a dispute, Douglas Hyde resigned presidency of the Gaelic League and was succeeded by Eoin MacNéill.

1 Aug. Funeral of Jeremiah O'Donovan Rossa; Pearse delivered graveside oration.

Dec. Military Council of IRB formed.

mid-Dec. 16th (Irish) Division departed for France.

1916

Jan. Supreme Council of IRB decided to begin insurrection at earliest opportunity.

19–22 Jan. Connolly conferred with IRB Military Council at Dolphin's Barn, Dublin.

10 Feb. Redmond and Lord Wimborne addressed recruiting meeting at Mansion House, Dublin.

4 Mar. Irish Race Convention held in New York.

3 Apr. Pearse, as director of organisation, issued orders to Irish Volunteers for three-day march and field manoeuvres throughout Ireland, to begin on Easter Sunday (23 Apr.) (*see* 22 Apr.).

20 Apr. Arrival of *Aud* in Tralee Bay with cargo of arms for Irish Volunteers (*see* 21 Apr.).

21 Apr. *Aud* intercepted by British naval patrol and scuttled off Queenstown. Sir Roger Casement captured, Co. Kerry (*see* 20 Apr., 26–29 June, 3 Aug.).

22 Apr. Eoin MacNeill cancelled Irish Volunteer manoeuvres scheduled to begin on Easter Monday (*see* 3 Apr.).

23 Apr. Military Council of Irish Volunteers decided to begin rebellion the next day (*see* 24 Apr.).

24 Apr. (Monday) Easter Rising began. General Post Office and other buildings in Dublin seized by Irish Volunteers and Citizen Army. Proclamation of Irish Republic. Arrival in Dublin of British troops stationed at the Curragh, Co. Kildare.

25 Apr. Martial law declared throughout Dublin city and county (*see* 29 Apr.).

26 Apr. Francis Sheehy-Skeffington and two others summarily executed at Portobello military barracks on orders of Capt. J. C. Bowen-Colthurst (*see* 6–7 June). Proclamation suspending in Ireland operation of sect. 1 of Defence of the Realm Act.

27 Apr. Birrell and General Sir John Maxwell arrived in Dublin, the latter to assume command of the military operation.

29 Apr. Pearse, Connolly and Thomas MacDonagh surrendered, ending the Rising (*see* 24 Apr.). Martial law declared throughout the country (*see* 25 Apr.).

1 May First internees reached Great Britain.

3 May After secret courts martial, Pearse, Clarke and MacDonagh executed (*see* 4, 5, 8, 9, 12 May). Birrell resigned as Chief Secretary; Asquith assumed the duties of the office in addition to remaining Prime Minister.

4 May Joseph Mary Plunkett, Edward Daly, Michael O'Hanrahan and William Pearse executed (*see* 3, 5, 8, 9, 12 May).

5 May John MacBride executed (*see* 3, 4, 8, 9, 12 May).

8 May Con Colbert, Eamonn Ceannt, Michael Mallin and Sean Heuston executed (*see* 3, 4, 5, 9, 12 May). Redmond warned that executions were alienating many 'who have not the slightest sympathy with the insurrection'.

9 May Thomas Kent executed in Cork (*see* 3, 4, 5, 8, 12 May).

10 May Asquith announced appointment of a Royal Commission under Lord Hardinage to inquire into the Irish disturbances (*see* 18 May, 3 July).

11 May Dillon urged cessation of executions.

12 May Connolly and Sean MacDermott were the last to be executed (*see* 3, 4, 5, 8, 9 May).

12–18 May Asquith visited Ireland to learn about events at first hand.

18 May Commission to Inquire into the Disturbances opened (*see* 10 May, 3 July).

23 May David Lloyd George given task of negotiating settlement of Irish question.

25 May Asquith in the House of Commons announced that old system of government in Ireland had broken down.

29 May Proposals for Irish settlement by Lloyd George shown to Sir Edward Carson and Viscount Middleton (*see* 12 June).

6–7 June Court martial found Bowen-Colthurst guilty of murder while insane (*see* 26 Apr.).

12 June Ulster Unionist Council accepted home rule with Ulster exclusion (*see* 23, 29 May).

23 June Convention of Ulster nationalists accepted Ulster exclusion from home rule (*see* 23 May).

26–29 June Trial and conviction of Casement for high treason (*see* 21 Apr., 3 Aug.).

July *Catholic Bulletin* began series extolling Catholic piety of rebels.

1 July Battle of the Somme began with 36th (Ulster) Division sustaining heavy losses throughout offensive (*see* 13 Nov.).

3 July Report of Royal Commission on the Disturbances in Ireland (*see* 10, 18 May).

20 July Meeting in Londonderry against partition led to formation of Anti-Partition League (later Irish Nation League).

22 July George Bernard Shaw's letter 'Shall Roger Casement Hang?' published in *Manchester Guardian.*

3 Aug. Casement executed at Pentonville prison, London (*see* 21 Apr., 26–29 June); Henry Edward Duke appointed Chief Secretary.

17–18 Aug. Irish Trade Union congress and Labour Party convention at Sligo held neutral attitude to rebellion.

23 Aug. Act extended Greenwich Mean Time to Ireland.

15 Sept. Yeats's poem 'Easter 1916' published.

4 Nov. Lt-Gen. Sir Bryan Mahon replaced Maxwell as commander-in-chief of the British military in Ireland.

13 Nov. Somme offensive ended (*see* 1 July).

6 Dec. Asquith resigned as Prime Minster.

7 Dec. Lloyd George appointed Prime Minister (*see* 19 Oct. 1922).

13 Dec. First public performance of Lennox Robinson's *The White-Headed Boy* at the Abbey Theatre.

22–23 Dec. 600 internees released from Frongoch and Reading jails and returned to Ireland.

29 Dec. Publication of James Joyce's *A Portrait of the Artist as a Young Man.*

1917

5 Feb. Sinn-Féin-endorsed candidate, George Noble Count Plunkett, won Roscommon North parliamentary by-election over Irish Party nominee (3,022–1,708).

17 Feb. Resumption of publication of *Nationality* edited by Arthur Griffith.

6 Apr. The United States declared war on Germany.

19 Apr. Sinn Féin National Council established.

Apr. Ford Motor Co. began construction of a factory at Cork.

8 May Declaration against partition, signed by 16 Catholic and 3 Protestant bishops, published.

9 May Sinn Féin candidate defeated Irish Party nominee at the Longford South parliamentary by-election (1,493–1,461).

16 May John Redmond accepted Lloyd George's proposal for an Irish Convention (*see* 21 May).

21 May Announcement of a Convention of Irishmen of all Parties for the purpose of producing a scheme of Irish self-government (*see* 16, 28 May, 25 July, 5, 12 Apr. 1918).

28 May Sinn Féin declined to participate in the proposed Irish Convention (*see* 21 May).

16 June Remaining prisoners released.

10 July Eamon de Valera, Sinn Féin nominee, in the Clare East parliamentary by-election, defeated the Irish Party candidate (5,010–2,035).

25 July Irish Convention met at Trinity College; Sir Horace Plunkett elected chairman (*see* 21 May, 5 Apr. 1918, 12 Apr. 1918).

c. **July** IRB adopted new constitution.

10 Aug. W. T. Cosgrave, Sinn Féin, defeated the Irish Party candidate in the Kilkenny City parliamentary by-election (772–392).

25 Sept. Thomas Ashe died in Mountjoy jail while on hunger strike.

25–26 Oct. De Valera elected president of Sinn Féin.

27 Oct. De Valera elected president of Irish Volunteers.

25 Nov. Southern Unionist proposed a compromise to end Irish Convention deadlock.

11 Dec. First public performance of Oliver St John Gogarty's *Blight* at the Abbey Theatre.

1918

15 Jan. Bishop O'Donnell opposed surrender of Irish control of economy questions; nationalists split on issue in the Irish Convention.

2 Feb. Irish Party candidate defeated Sinn Féin opponent and the Independent Unionist in the Armagh South parliamentary by-election (2,324–1,305).

6 Feb. Representation of the People Act enfranchised all men over 21 and some women over 30; Redistribution of Seats Act made constituencies of approximately equal population.

20 Feb. Southern Unionist Committee formed.

6 Mar. Redmond died.

12 Mar. Dillon elected chairman of the Irish Party (*see* 6 Mar.).

22 Mar. Captain William Archer Redmond, son of John, captured his father's vacated seat against Sinn Féin in the Waterford City parliamentary by-election (1,242–745).

3 Apr. Irish Party nominee defeated Sinn Féin candidate in the Tyrone East parliamentary by-election (1,802–1,222).

5 Apr. Last meeting of the Irish Convention (*see* 21 May, 25 July 1917, 12 Apr.).

9 Apr. Lloyd George introduced the Military Services bill extending conscription to Ireland. Standing Episcopal Committee protested against conscription proposal (*see* 18 Apr.).

12 Apr. Publication of report of the Irish Convention (*see* 21 May, 25 July 1917, 5 Apr.).

18 Apr. Military Service Act (*see* 9 Apr.). Mansion House Conference opposed conscription.

19 Apr. Sinn Féin candidate returned unopposed in the King's County parliamentary by-election.

21 Apr. Nationalists of all varieties signed anti-conscription pledge.

23 Apr. One-day general strike outside Ulster sponsored by Nationalists in protest against conscription.

4 May Edward Shortt appointed Chief Secretary.

5 May Dillon and de Valera spoke from same platform at anti-conscription meeting in Ballaghadereen, Co. Mayo.

11 May John, Viscount French, sworn in as Lord Lieutenant.

17–18 May Arrest of approximately 200 members of Sinn Féin for conspiracy to aid Germany in the war.

15 June Lord Lieutenant French imposed martial law throughout most of the south and west of the country.

20 June Conscription and home rule plans abandoned. Arthur Griffith of Sinn Féin defeated Irish Party candidate in the Cavan East parliamentary by-election (3,795–2,581).

June Ulster Unionist Labour Associated founded.

3 July Many Nationalist organisations banned, including Irish Volunteers and Sinn Féin.

5 July Order proscribing meetings, assemblies or processions in public places.

15 Aug. First issue of *An tÓglach*, organ of Irish Volunteers.

10 Oct. Irish mail-boat *Leinster* sunk by German submarine, with loss of *c.* 500 lives.

1 Nov. Irish Labour Party withdrew from the forthcoming general election.

2 Nov. Lloyd George declared intention to introduce partition.

2 Nov. Irish Labour Party and Trades Union Congress adopted new constitution.

11 Nov. Armistice ended war.

21 Nov. Parliament (Qualification of Women) Act entitled women to sit and vote in the House of Commons.

2–3 Dec. Dillon, MacNeill and Lord Mayor of Dublin sought to distribute candidates in eight Ulster constituencies in order to maximise Catholic vote. The final allocation made by Cardinal Logue on 4 Dec.

4 Dec. Nomination day for general election; 25 Sinn Féin candidates returned unopposed.

14–28 Dec. General election; Sinn Féin won 73 seats with Countess Markievicz the first woman elected to the House of Commons.

1919

13 Jan. James Ian Macpherson appointed Chief Secretary.

15 Jan. First use of proportional representation in Sligo municipal elections.

21 Jan. Irish Republican Army unit killed two policemen in Soloheadbeg, Co. Tipperary. This act regarded as opening the Anglo-Irish War.

21 Jan. Dáil Éireann formed at Mansion House, Dublin.

22 Jan. Cathal Brugha elected acting President of Dáil Éireann (*see* 21 Jan.).

24 Jan. Irish Unionist Alliance split; Unionist Anti-Partition League begun.

25 Jan. Strike by Federation of Engineering and Shipbuilding Trades in Belfast.

3 Feb. De Valera escaped from Lincoln jail.

22 Feb. Irish Race Convention met at Philadelphia.

6–10 Mar. Remaining Sinn Féin prisoners released.

1 Apr. Second session of Dáil Éireann opened; de Valera elected President.

4 Apr. Dáil Éireann authorised issue of 'republican bonds'.

8 Apr. De Valera re-elected president of Sinn Féin.

14–25 Apr. General strike at Limerick led to establishment of Limerick Soviet.

3 May Delegates from Irish-American 'Friends of Irish Freedom' arrived in Ireland to investigate political situation.

13 May Two policemen killed during rescue of Seán Hogan at Knocklong railway station, Co. Limerick.

29 May Public Health Act provided for medical care of elementary school children.

3 June Local Government (Ireland) Act; provided for proportional representation at local authority elections.

11 June De Valera arrived in New York.

18 June Dáil Éireann established arbitration courts.

19 June Dáil Éireann approved National Loan prospectus.

23 June RIC district inspector shot dead by IRA in Thurles, Co. Tipperary.

28 June Versailles Treaty.

4 July Proclamation suppressed Sinn Féin, Irish Volunteers, Cumann na mBan and Gaelic League in Co. Tipperary.

31 July Detective in G Division of Dublin Metropolitan Police shot dead by IRA in Dublin.

19 Aug. Dáil Éireann resolved that clergymen be ex-officio justices in arbitration courts. Widespread IRA activity in Co. Clare.

20 Aug. Dáil Éireann resolved that Irish Volunteers and its own members and officials must swear allegiance to the Irish Republic and to the Dáil.

1 Sept. Last substantial railway branch line opened at Castlecomer, Co. Kilkenny.

7 Sept. North Cork Brigade of IRA attacked troops in Fermony, Co. Cork, killed one soldier; in evening first reprisal incident.

12 Sept. Dáil Éireann declared illegal.

17 Sept. Police and military enter *Cork Examiner* and dismantled machinery.

20 Sept. Republican newspapers suppressed.

7 Oct. British Cabinet Committee appointed to consider Irish self-government.

15 Oct. Proclamation outlawed Sinn Féin, Irish Republican Army and other organisations.

10 Nov. Patrick Street, Cork, sacked and looted by crown forces.

11 Nov. First issue of Sinn Féin and Dáil newspaper, *Irish Bulletin.*

15 Dec. Police seized type and plant for production of *Freeman's Journal.*

19 Dec. Unsuccessful attempt to assassinate the Lord Lieutenant, Viscount French, near Phoenix Park.
21 Dec. IRA destroyed *Irish Independent* offices and production plant.

1920
2 Jan. Black and Tans formed.
15 Jan. Local government elections held under proportional representation (Sinn Féin, other nationalists and Labour won control of 172 of 206 borough and urban district councils).
30 Jan. Mayoral elections; Unionist elected for Belfast, Nationalist in Londonderry, Labour at Wexford and Sinn Féin candidates in eight boroughs.
Jan. Dáil Éireann floats external loan.
20 Feb. Imposition of curfew, midnight to 5 a.m., in Dublin Metropolitan Police District.
25 Feb. Better Government of Ireland bill introduced in House of Commons (*see* 23 Dec.).
10 Mar. Ulster Unionist Council accepted Better Government of Ireland bill. Six Republican prisoners executed in Dublin.
20 Mar. Lord Mayor of Cork and Commandant of 1st Cork Brigade of IRA, Tomás Mac Curtáin, shot dead by RIC.
26 Mar. Magistrate investigating Sinn Féin and Dáil Éireann funds shot dead in Dublin.
12 Apr. Sir Hamar Greenwood appointed Chief Secretary. Cattle-drive in Rockview, Co. Westmeath, began policy of cattle-driving and enforced land redistribution.
27 Apr. IRA attacked police barracks at Ballylanders, Co. Limerick.
8 May De Valera repudiated right of British Ambassador to Washington to represent Ireland.
16–19 May Soviet established at central creamery, Knocklong, Co. Limerick.
23 May Beatification by Pope of Archbishop Oliver Plunkett. 'Munitions strike' by railwaymen at Kingstown, Co. Dublin (*see* 21 Dec.).
28 May IRA attack on police barracks at Kilmallock, Co. Limerick.
12 June County council and rural district council elections resulted in successes for Sinn Féin which in Ulster gained control of 36 of the 55 rural district councils.
14 June Mount Shannon, largest house in Co. Limerick, burnt out by IRA.
24 June Decision to revive the Ulster Volunteer Force (UVF).
28 June Connacht Rangers' mutiny in India.
29 June Dáil Éireann assembled for first time since Oct. 1919.
17 July Divisional commander of RIC in Munster shot dead by IRA at Cork.
19 July Sectarian violence lasting four days erupted in Londonderry resulting in 19 deaths.
21–24 July Sectarian disturbances in Belfast resulted in more than a dozen deaths and the expulsion of Catholic workers from shipyards.
27 July Auxiliary Division of the Royal Irish Constabulary formed.

69

6 Aug. Dáil Éireann sanctioned boycott of goods from Protestant firms in Belfast (*see* 21, 24 Jan. 1922).

9 Aug. Restoration of Order in Ireland Act.

13 Aug. Anti-Partition League called for settlement on Dominion lines.

22 Aug. Murder of district inspector at Lisburn precipitated attack on Sinn Féin members and their property. IRA destroyed creamery owned by Southern Unionist at Knocklong, Co. Limerick.

23 Aug. Six constables shot in ambush at Macroom, Co. Cork.

23–31 Aug. Disturbances in Belfast caused *c.* 30 deaths; curfew imposed on 31 Aug.

2 Sept. Sir James Craig's demand for a constabulary for Northern Ireland conceded by the British government (*see* 1 Nov.).

20 Sept. Black and Tan raid on Balbriggan, Co. Dublin.

28 Sept. IRA captured military barracks in Mallow, Co. Cork, the only military barracks captured during the Anglo-Irish War.

14 Oct. Seán Treacy of the 3rd Tipperary Brigade killed in gun battle in Talbot Street, Dublin.

24 Oct. Patrick McCartan, Dáil envoy in Washington, sent formal protest to the American State Department, detailing British atrocities in Ireland.

25 Oct. Death in Brixton prison of Terence MacSwiney, Lord Mayor of Cork, after 74 days on hunger strike.

1 Nov. Kevin Barry executed in Mountjoy prison. Enrolment of recruits began in Ulster for Special Constabulary Force (*see* 2 Sept.).

2 Nov. Military raid on University College Dublin.

2–9 Nov. 'Battle of Ballinalee' led by Seán Mac Eoin, 'Blacksmith of Ballinalee'.

16 Nov. American Association for the Recognition of the Irish Republic launched in the United States by de Valera.

21 Nov. IRA squad assassinated 14 British secret service agents; later in the day a unit of Black and Tans killed 12 during a Gaelic football fixture at Croke Park in Dublin.

27 Nov. IRA arson attack in Liverpool.

28 Nov. Auxiliary policy patrol destroyed by IRA at Kilmichael, Co. Cork.

10 Dec. Proclamation of martial law in Cork, Kerry, Limerick and Tipperary.

11–12 Dec. Black and Tans and Auxiliaries sack Cork.

21 Dec. Railwaymen agreed to resume normal handling of government traffic (*see* 23 May).

23 Dec. Better Government of Ireland Act provided for two Irish parliaments and a Council of Ireland, and permitted Catholics to hold office of Lord Lieutenant (*see* 2 May 1921). De Valera arrived secretly in Dublin from America.

26 Dec. RIC shot dead five people at a dance at Bruff, Co. Limerick.

1921

1 Jan. Beginning of government sanctioned reprisals.

1 Feb. White Cross founded by Sinn Féin.

4 Feb. Sir James Craig replaced Sir Edward Carson as leader of Ulster Unionist Party.

19 Feb. Commandant of Auxiliaries, unable to curb excesses of his troops, resigned.

28 Feb. Six Republican prisoners executed in Cork and six British soldiers killed in Cork City.

7 Mar. Mayor and former Mayor of Limerick shot dead.

14 Mar. Six Republican prisoners executed in Dublin.

21 Apr. Secret meeting in Dublin between the Earl of Derby and de Valera.

2 May Viscount FitzAlan, a Catholic, sworn in as Lord Lieutenant (*see* 23 Dec. 1920).

5 May Craig and de Valera had a secret meeting in Dublin.

13 May Nominations closed for elections to parliaments of Northern Ireland and Southern Ireland (*see* 24 May).

24 May Elections to the two parliaments; 124 Sinn Féin candidates returned for Southern Ireland (*see* 13 May).

25 May Custom House, Dublin, burned by IRA.

7 June Northern Ireland parliament met and cabinet appointed with Craig as Prime Minster.

22 June King George V formally opened the parliament of Northern Ireland.

28 June Southern Ireland parliament opened and held its only session before being adjourned.

4–8 July De Valera and Arthur Griffith met Lord Midleton, representing Southern Unionists, at Mansion House, Dublin.

9–15 July Sectarian disturbances in Belfast after disclosure of draft terms of truce left more than 20 dead.

11 July Truce between Republican and British forces.

14–21 July Three meetings in London between Lloyd George and de Valera.

16 Aug. Second Dáil Éireann convened at Mansion House, Dublin. Delegates composed of Sinn Féin members elected to parliament of Southern Ireland.

19 Aug. Cardinal Logue, Archbishop of Armagh, rejected invitation by Northern Ireland Minister of Education, Lord Londonderry, to nominate members of the proposed Commission on Education.

7 Sept. Our Lady of Mercy (renamed Legion of Mary on 15 Nov. 1925) founded by Frank McDuff and others.

14 Sept. Dáil Éireann sanctioned appointment of republican delegates to meet representatives of the British government in London.

29 Sept. Lloyd George offered de Valera formula for discussions (*see* 30 Sept.).

30 Sept. De Valera accepted Lloyd George's framework for discussions (*see* 29 Sept.).

11 Oct. – 6 Dec. Anglo-Irish conference in London.

18 Oct. William O'Brien and Cathal O'Shannon expelled from the Socialist Party of Ireland on grounds of 'reformism'.

Nov. Communist Party of Ireland formed.

10 Nov. Lloyd George and Craig conferred in London.

13 Nov. Arthur Griffith signed document agreeing that Northern Ireland could remain outside a united Ireland if a Boundary Commission was accepted.

15–16 Nov. Southern Unionist representatives consulted by British government and then by Griffith.

17–18 Nov. National Unionist Association conference in Liverpool approved of the Anglo-Irish negotiations.

19–25 Nov. Sectarian rioting in Belfast caused 27 deaths.

22 Nov. Northern Ireland government invested with control of Royal Irish Constabulary and responsibility for law and order (*see* 5 Dec.).

5 Dec. Craig announced expansion of Northern Ireland Special Constabulary (*see* 22 Nov.).

6 Dec. Articles of Agreement for a Treaty.

7 Dec. Treaty signed (*see* 7 Jan., 31 Mar. 1922).

8 Dec. Eamon de Valera denounced the Treaty.

9 Dec. British released interned IRA members.

12 Dec. Dublin Committee of the Anti-Partition League accepted the Treaty.

14 Dec. Carson attacked the Treaty in the House of Lords. Dáil Éireann debate on the Treaty began. Local Government (Emergency Powers) Act (Northern Ireland) allowed dissolution of uncooperative local councils.

14–16 Dec. Westminster parliament ratified the Treaty.

15 Dec. De Valera produced an alternative formula in the Dáil: 'Document No. 2'.

19 Dec. Griffith introduced motion in Dáil to approve the Treaty.

22 Dec. Dáil adjourned for Christmas (*see* 2 Jan. 1922).

1922

2 Jan. Dáil Éireann reconvened (*see* 22 Dec. 1921).

5 Jan. First issue of *The Republic of Ireland*, an anti-Treaty organ edited by Erskine Childers.

7 Jan. Dáil Éireann approved the Anglo-Irish Treaty (64–58) (*see* 7 Dec. 1921, 31 Mar.).

9 Jan. De Valera resigned as President of Dáil Éireann.

10 Jan. Griffith elected President of Dáil Éireann, defeating de Valera.

14 Jan. Meeting of members elected to the House of Commons of Southern Ireland chose Provisional Government for the Irish Free State (Michael Collins, chairman) and approved the Treaty. The session boycotted by anti-Treaty TDs.

16 Jan. Michael Collins took formal control of Dublin Castle from Lord Lieutenant FitzAlan. Evacuation of British troops and disbanding of the RIC proceeded.

21 Jan. Craig–Collins discussions ended Belfast Boycott and guaranteed position of Belfast Catholics (*see* 6 Aug. 1920).

24 Jan. Provisional Government ended the 'Belfast Boycott' (*see* 6 Aug. 1920, 21 Jan.).

31 Jan. Free State army took possession of headquarters at Beggars' Bush Barracks, Dublin.

1 Feb. Date set for final transfer of duties to seven government departments in Northern Ireland.

2 Feb. Publication in Paris of *Ulysses* by James Joyce.

5 Feb. Cumann na mBan rejected the Treaty.

6 Feb. Achille Ratti elected Pope (Pius XI).

12–15 Feb. Violence by IRA began in Belfast in which 27 people were killed.

21 Feb. Enlistment began into police force of the Provisional Government (Civil Guard).

18 Mar. Anti-Treaty group formed Cumann na Poblachta under the leadership of de Valera.

26–27 Mar. Anti-Treaty representatives of 49 IRA brigades established executive council headed by Oscar Traynor.

28 Mar. Rory O'Connor, on behalf of 'Irregulars', the anti-Treaty IRA, repudiated the authority of Dáil Éireann.

29 Mar. 'B' Specials shot dead Catholic politician Owen McMahon in Austin Road, Belfast. Anti-Treaty supporters destroyed print machine of the *Freeman's Journal*.

30 Mar. Craig–Collins Pact signed in London. Craig agreed to recruit Catholics into the Special Constabulary and to reinstate them in their shipyard jobs; Collins agreed to act against IRA units operating against the North from the Free State.

31 Mar. Irish Free State (Agreement) Act gave force of law to Treaty (*see* 7 Dec. 1921, 7 Jan.).

1 Apr. Transfer of power from Great Britain to Ireland officially signed.

7 Apr. Civil Authorities (Special Powers) Act (Northern Ireland).

9 Apr. Anti-Treaty IRA Executive appointed Army Council; Liam Lynch appointed Chief of Staff.

13–14 Apr. Rory O'Connor led anti-Treaty IRA seizure of the Four Courts in Dublin (*see* 27, 28 June).

24 Apr. General strike in Free State against 'militarism' called for by the Labour Party.

26 Apr. Catholic Hierarchy announced acceptance of the Treaty.

20 May Collins–de Valera Pact provided for Sinn Féin panel of candidates for the general election. Shane's Castle, Co. Antrim, attacked and burned by IRA.

20–22 May Further violence in Belfast in which 14 killed, including one Stormont MP.

23 May Northern Ireland government declared IRA, Irish Volunteers, IRB, Cumann na mBan and Fianna illegal organisations.

27 May Draft Constitution of the Free State presented to the British government.

31 May Constabulary Act (Northern Ireland) establishes the Royal Ulster Constabulary.

8 June Last meeting of the second Dáil Éireann.

14 June Collins repudiated electoral pact made with de Valera.

15 June Draft Constitution of the Free State issued to the press.

16 June General election for Dáil Éireann; Pro-Treaty, 58; Anti-Treaty, 36; Labour, 17; Farmers, 7; Independents, 6, University of Dublin, 4.

22 June Assassination of Gen. Sir Henry Wilson in London.

27 June Members of anti-Treaty force in Four Courts kidnapped pro-Treaty Gen. J. J. 'Ginger' O'Connell (*see* 13–14 Apr.).

28 June Beginning of civil war with the bombardment of the Four Courts (*see* 13–14 Apr., 27, 30 June).

30 June Four Courts and Public Record Office in Dublin destroyed (*see* 13–14 Apr., 27, 28 June).

30 June – 5 July Government troops attacked anti-Treaty headquarters in O'Connell St., Dublin; Cathal Brugha wounded and captured. He died on 7 July.

6 July Provisional Government issued call to arms.

12 July Michael Collins appointed Commander-in-Chief of Free State War Council.

20 July Limerick and Waterford captured by government troops.

4 Aug. Constabulary (Ireland) Act provided for disbanding of the Royal Irish Constabulary.

11 Aug. Cork captured by government troops; anti-Treaty forces evacuated Fermoy, Co. Cork, the last town under their control.

12 Aug. Griffith died.

22 Aug. Collins assassinated in Co. Cork.

25 Aug. William T. Cosgrave appointed chairman of Provisional Government.

9 Sept. Third Dáil Éireann convened; W. T. Cosgrave elected President.

11 Sept. Local Government (Northern Ireland) Act abolished proportional representation for local elections and required declaration of allegiance from persons elected to or working for local authorities (12 & 13 Geo. V, c. 15).

18 Sept. Constitution bill introduced.

28 Sept. Army Emergency Powers resolution approved by Dáil Éireann; established military courts with power to impose death penalty.

10 Oct. Catholic Hierarchy issued pastoral condemning republican resistance to the Free State.

16 Oct. Army Emergency Powers order became effective.

19 Oct. Lloyd George resigned as United Kingdom Prime Minister (*see* 7 Dec. 1916).

23 Oct. Andrew Bonar Law appointed United Kingdom Prime Minister (*see* 20 May 1923).

25 Oct. Constitution of the Irish Free State (Saorstát Éireann) enacted.

27 Oct. District and parish courts established outside Dublin City.

2 Nov. Local Authorities (Election and Constitution) Act (Northern Ireland) postponed local government elections.

15 Nov. General election in the United Kingdom; Bonar Law remained Prime Minster.

17 Nov. Beginning of executions of IRA 'irregulars' (*see* 2 May 1923).

24 Nov. Erskine Childers executed by the Free State.

5 Dec. Irish Free State Constitution and Consequential Provisions Acts received royal assent.

6 Dec. T. M. Healy sworn in as Governor-General of the Free State; Dáil approved nominations to executive council.

7 Dec. Northern Ireland exercised right to opt out of the Free State.

8 Dec. Rory O'Connor, Liam Mellows and two other Irregulars executed without trial as reprisal for assassination of pro-Treaty deputy, Sean Hales. Powers of Lord Lieutenant lapsed in Northern Ireland.

11 Dec. First meeting of the Free State Senate.

12 Dec. Duke of Abercorn sworn in as the first Governor-General of Northern Ireland.

20 Dec. Adaptation of Enactments Act (IFS), adapted British Acts in force on 6 Dec. 1922 to circumstances of Free State.

18 Dec. Commission on Agriculture established in the Free State under James MacNeill.

1923

23 Jan. First meeting of the United Council of Christian Churches and Religious Communions in Ireland (Protestant body).

29 Jan. House of Senator Sir Horace Plunkett at Foxrock, Co. Dublin, burned by Irregular IRA.

8 Feb. Governments offered amnesty to anyone who surrendered with arms on or before 18 Feb.

12 Feb. Anglo-Irish financial agreement signed; Free State agreed to pay land annuities to British treasury.

6 Mar. Report of the (Ernest) Blythe Commission on administrative reform in the Free State.

22 Mar. Members of Association of our Lady of Mercy began rehabilitation work among prostitutes in Bentley Place district of Dublin.

28 Mar. Double Taxation (Relief) Act granted relief where there was liability to both IFS and British tax. Local Government (Temporary Provisions) Act abolished workhouse system in the Free State.

31 Mar. – 1 Apr. Separation of Free State fiscal system from the United Kingdom; customs barriers between Free State and United Kingdom came into effect.

10 Apr. Liam Lynch, chief of Irregular IRA, wounded in engagement with government forces in Comeragh mountains, Co. Waterford.

12 Apr. First performance of Seán O'Casey's *The Shadow of a Gunman* at the Abbey Theatre.

27 Apr. De Valera announced that offensive operations were suspended (Frank Aiken issued similar order for Irregular IRA Council).

30 Apr. James Larkin returned to Ireland from the United States.

8 May Free State Civil Service Commission appointed.

20 May Andrew Bonar Law resigned as British Prime Minister (*see* 23 Oct. 1922).

23 May Stanley Baldwin appointed British Prime Minister.

24 May End of the Civil War.

3 June Larkin attacked William O'Brien, precipitating a split in the labour movement.

8 June Board of Commissioners of Intermediate Education dissolved.

15 June Larkin formed the Workers' Union of Ireland (WUI). Intoxicating Liquor (NI) Act extended Sunday closing to Belfast.

22 June Public Record (NI) Office Act established Public Record Office of Northern Ireland. Education (NI) Act restructured primary and secondary education, creating non-denominational schools under local authorities.

16 July Censorship of Films Act.

24 July Land Law (Commission) Act dissolved the Congested Districts Board and transferred its functions to the Land Commission.

1 Aug. Public Safety (Emergency Powers) Act enabled government to continue to detain people without trial.

3 Aug. Indemnity Act.

8 Aug. Act to establish a police force to be called the 'Gárda Siochána'.

9 Aug. Land Act empowered commission to take over untenanted land (Hogan Act).

15 Aug. De Valera arrested in Ennis, Co. Clare, and detained without trial until 16 Aug. 1924.

27 Aug. General election in IFS; Cumann na nGaedheal retained office.

Aug. First issue of *Dublin Magazine* edited by Seamas O'Sullivan.

10 Sept. IFS admitted to the League of Nations.

19 Sept. Meeting of fourth Dáil Éireann; Cosgrave elected President of the Executive Council.

14 Oct. – 23 Nov. Hunger strike by several hundred detainees in IFS.

11 Nov. W. B. Yeats became first Irish person to win the Nobel Prize for Literature.

6 Dec. General election in United Kingdom.

1924

16 Jan. Renewal of Public Safety Act (*see* 1 Aug. 1923).

22 Jan. James Ramsay MacDonald appointed British Prime Minister.

18 Feb. Announcement of reorganisation of the Free State army; proposed reduction in numbers.

Feb. Agreement between IFS government and Siemens-Schuckert of Berlin for hydroelectric scheme on Shannon river (*see* 4 July 1925).

3 Mar. O'Casey's *Juno and the Paycock* opened at the Abbey Theatre.

6–12 Mar. Army mutiny in the Free State.

7 Mar. Joseph McGrath, IFS Minster for Industry and Commerce, resigned in protest at the handling of army problems.

10 Mar. Gen. Eoin O'Duffy, Chief Commissioner of the Civic Guard, appointed to command IFS defence forces.

15 Mar. Committee of Inquiry into Army Mutiny appointed under Eoin MacNeill, chairman.

18 Mar. Troops laid siege to a public house in Parnell Street, Dublin, occupied by persons implicated in mutiny (*see* 19 Mar.).

19 Mar. Executive Council expressed disapproval of military action taken on 18 Mar. Richard Mulcahy, Minister for Defence, resigned.

12 Apr. Courts of Justice Act reorganised judiciary.

21 Apr. Ministers and Secretaries Act regulated government departments and allowed parliamentary secretaries to be appointed.

26 Apr. Free State government requested that in conformity with the Treaty a Boundary Commission be established.

10 May Craig refused to nominate NI representative to the Boundary Commission (*see* 4 Aug.).

20 May Executive Council dissolved the Dublin Corporation.

29 May Public Libraries (NI) Act empowered county councils to provide public library service.

1 June Free State Department of Education assumed control over all education.

5 June Old Age Pensions Act reduced pension by one shilling per week.

11 July Free State registered Anglo-Irish Treaty with the League of Nations.

23 July Railway Act amalgamated 17 railway companies into a single corporation (*see* 1 Jan. 1925).

2–17 Aug. Tailteann (Gaelic) games in Croke Park, Dublin.

4 Aug. Cosgrave and MacDonald agreed to introduce legislation empowering British government to appoint NI member of Boundary Commission (*see* 10 May).

5 Aug. Military Pensions Act provided pensions for those who served in government forces 1922–23, Irish Volunteers and IRA, 1916–21.

12 Aug. Under Anglo-Irish agreement the British government agreed to pay £900,000 to the Free State for damage to property prior to the Truce.

14 Aug. Free State government received Leinster House from Royal Dublin Society.

15 Sept. British Broadcasting Company opened in Belfast.

29 Oct. General election in United Kingdom.

4 Nov. Stanley Baldwin appointed British Prime Minster (*see* 5 June 1929).

6 Nov. First meeting of the Boundary Commission in London.

8 Nov. Free State government declared amnesty for offences committed between 6 Dec. 1921 and 12 May 1923.

13 Nov. First public performance of Hamilton Harty's 'Irish Symphony' in Manchester.

19 Nov. Publication of the last issue of the *Freeman's Journal* (established 10 Sept. 1763).

1925

1 Jan. Great Southern Railways Co. formed from amalgation of 27 railway companies (*see* 23 July 1924).

27 Jan. Coimisiún na Gaeltachta established to inquire into the preservation of Irish-speaking areas.

11 Feb. William T. Cosgrave carried motion in Dáil Éireann urging Senate to consent to standing order prohibiting introduction of private bills for divorce, effectively ending divorce within the jurisdiction of the Free State.

26 Mar. Local Government Act (IFS).

2 Apr. Act for amalgamation of the Dublin Metropolitan Police with the Garda Síochána.

3 Apr. General election in Northern Ireland.

28 Apr. Joseph Devlin and T. S. MacAllister first Nationalists to take their seats in the parliament of Northern Ireland.

28 May Northern Ireland Land Act.

4 July Shannon Electricity Act.

7 Nov. *Morning Post* (London) 'leaked' findings of the Boundary Commission.

14 Nov. IRA Convention withdrew its allegiance from the 'Republican government' of Eamon de Valera and established its own supreme authority, the Army Council.

20 Nov. Eoin MacNeill resigned from Boundary Commission; resigned as Minster for Education on 24 Nov.

3 Dec. Agreement signed by Craig, Cosgrave and Baldwin shelved the Boundary Commission report.

1926

1 Jan. Radio 2RN opened in Dublin (later Radio Éireann).

8 Mar. Free State Banking Commission appointed.

9–11 Mar. Sinn Féin Ard-Fheis; Eamon de Valera resigned presidency.

19 Mar. Ultimate Financial Agreement signed between British and Free State governments.

18 Apr. Census of population in Free State and Northern Ireland.

4–12 May General strike in Great Britain.

16 May De Valera inaugurated the Fianna Fáil Party.

27 May School Attendance Act (IFS).

29 May Enforcement of Court Order Act (IFS).

1 June Ancient Monuments Act (NI).

28 July Local Authorities (Officers and Employees) Act (IFS); Local Appointments Commission established.

Sept. National League Party launched by Capt. William Redmond.

2 Oct. Royal College of Science, Dublin, merged with University College Dublin.

19 Oct. – 23 Nov. Imperial Conference in London.

11 Nov. George Bernard Shaw awarded the Nobel Prize for Literature.

19 Nov. Public Safety (Emergency Powers) Act.

2 Dec. Tariff Commission appointed.

1927

1 Jan. Compulsory attendance at school for children between the ages of 6 and 14 came into effect.

21 Apr. Ernest Blythe announced the establishment of the Economy Committee.

20 May Intoxicating Liquor Act, 1917 (IFS).

23 May Dáil Éireann dissolved.

28 May Agricultural Credit and Electricity (Supply) Acts (IFS).

9 June General election in the Free State.

22 June Fifth Dáil Éireann met; W. T. Cosgrave re-elected President of the Executive Council. Fianna Fáil TDs decline to take the oath.

10 July Kevin O'Higgins, Minister of Justice, assassinated by Republicans.

11 Aug. Public Safety Act (IFS). Eamon de Valera and Fianna Fáil deputies take their seats in Dáil Éireann after signing parliamentary oath.

20 Aug. Currency Act (establishing separate currency for the Free State).

25 Aug. Dáil Éireann dissolved.

15 Sept. General election in the Free State.

11 Oct. Sixth Dáil Éireann met; W. T. Cosgrave re-elected President of the Executive Council.

9 Nov. Election (Amendment No. 2) Act (IFS) required candidates before nomination to declare their intention of taking the oath if elected.

1928

May Joseph Devlin formed the National League of the North.

12 July Constitution (Amendment No. 10) Act, 1928 (IFS) (abolished the right to referendum).

10 Oct. Irish Manuscripts Commission established; chairman Eoin MacNéill.

14 Oct. Dublin Gate Theatre Studio founded by Michaeál Mac Liammóir and Hilton Edwards.

12 Oct. Issue of new Free State currency.

28 Oct. Library Association of Ireland founded.

26 Dec. Public Safety Act, 1928 (IFS); repealed 1917 act.

1929

23 Feb. Cork City Management Act, 1929 (IFS) established managerial system of local government.

27 Feb. Closure of Kilmainham jail.

16 Apr. House of Commons (Method of Voting and Redistribution of Seats) Act (NI); abolished proportional representation.

22 May General election in Northern Ireland; Viscount Craigavon continued as Prime Minster.

30 May General election in United Kingdom.

5 June J. Ramsay MacDonald appointed United Kingdom Prime Minster.

16 June Beginning of celebration of centenary of Catholic Emancipation.

28 June Legal Practitioners (Qualification) Act, 1929 (IFS), required future law students to pass examination in the Irish language.

16 July Censorship of Publications Act (IFS).

14 Sept. IFS signed Article 36 of the Permanent Court of International Justice at Geneva.

29 Oct. 'Black Tuesday' – Wall Street Crash.

20 Dec. Housing (Gaeltach) Act (IFS); grants and loans for housing in Gaeltacht.

1930

26 Feb. National Monuments Act (IFS).

Mar. First issue of *Analecta Hibernica* published by the Irish Manuscripts Commission.

1 Apr. Irish Trade Union Congress and Labour Party split.

4 June Public Charitable Hospitals (Temporary Provisions) Act, 1930 (IFS); inaugurated hospital sweepstakes.

17 June Education Act (Northern Ireland).

17 July Local Government (Dublin) Act (IFS) extended administrative area of the city.

21 July Vocational Education Act (IFS).

5 Aug. National exhibition of Irish manufactures opened in Dublin.

17 Sept. Free State elected to Council of League of Nations.

Nov. Free State imposed duty on imported butter.

31 Dec. Minster for Local Government dissolved Mayo County Council for rejecting appointment of a Protestant as county librarian.

1931

7 May Foundation of Óige, Irish hostelling movement.

24 Aug. J. Ramsay MacDonald's government resigned.

5 Sept. First issue of the *Irish Press*, founded by Eamon de Valera.

21 Sept. The United Kingdom abandoned the Gold Standard.

17 Oct. Constitution (Amendment No. 17) Act (IFS) established a five-member military tribunal to deal with political crime.

18 Oct. Pastoral of Catholic Hierarchy condemned IRA and denounced Saor Éire.

20 Oct. Constitutional (Declaration of Unlawful Associations) Order outlawed the IRA, Saor Éire and other organisations.

27 Oct. General election in United Kingdom; MacDonald remained Prime Minister.

6 Nov. Custom Duties (Provisional Imposition) Act (IFS) allowed imposition or variation of duties to prevent dumping of goods.

11 Dec. Statute of Westminster, 1931; empowered Dominion parliaments to repeal or amend any Act of the United Kingdom parliament.

22 Dec. Landlord and Tenant Act, 1931 (IFS), gives greater security to tenants in urban areas.

1932

29 Jan. Dáil Éireann dissolved.

9 Feb. Army Comrades' Association founded.

16 Feb. General election in the Free State.

29 Feb. United Kingdom Import Duties Act introduced general tariffs.

9 Mar. Seventh Dáil Éireann meets; Eamon de Valera becomes President of the Executive Council. Fianna Fáil government.

10 Mar. Government releases 20 political prisoners.

17 Mar. Society of St Patrick for Foreign Missions (later St Patrick's Missionary Society) formed.

18 Mar. Order suspended military tribunal, and order declaring the IRA illegal lapsed.

22–26 June 31st Eucharistic Congress in Dublin.

30 June Payment of land annuities to Britain withheld; beginning of the economic war.

11 July Irish Free State (Special Duties) Act (UK); imposed 20 per cent duty on *c.* two-thirds of Free State exports to the UK.

21 June – 20 Aug. Imperial Economic Conference, Ottawa, Canada.

23 July Emergency Imposition of Duties Act (IFS) empowered Executive Council to vary rates and to limit imports from particular countries.

3 Aug. Housing (Financial and Miscellaneous Provisions) Act (IFS) provided government grants to local authority housing schemes.

18 Sept. Announcement of formation of Irish Academy of Letters.

6 Oct. Farmers' organisation formed on 13 Sept. became the National Farmers' and Ratepayers' League.

29 Oct. Control of Manufactures Act (IFS); required that majority of shares in any new manufacturing business must be owned by Free State nationals.

16 Nov. Prince of Wales opened Stormont, new home of the parliament of Northern Ireland.

1 Nov. James MacNeill's appointment as Governor-General of Free State terminated.

26 Nov. Domhnall Ua Buachalla became Governor-General (IFS).

Dec. Federation of Irish Industry became the Confederation of Irish Industry.

1933

2 Jan. Dáil Éireann dissolved.

4 Jan. Agreement between Frank MacDermot, leader of National Farmers' and Ratepayers' League, and James Dillon, Independent, to form Centre Party.

24 Jan. General election in Free State; Eamon de Valera remained chairman of the Executive Council.

8 Feb. Eighth Dáil Éireann meets.

22 Feb. Gen. Eoin O'Duffy dismissed as Chief Commander of Civic Guard.

24 Mar. Army Comrades Association adopted distinctive dress code and became known as Blueshirts.

30 Mar. Land (Purchase Annuity Fund) Act (IFS).

3 May Constitution (Removal of Oath) Act (IFS).

4 May Agricultural Produce (Cereals) Act (IFS).

9 May Civil Authorities (Special Powers) Act (NI).

11 June Communist Party of Ireland re-established by the Revolutionary Workers' Group and the Workers' Party of Ireland.

20 July O'Duffy elected leader of the Army Comrades Association which adopted name of National Guard.

31 July Industrial Credit Act (IFS).

22 Aug. National Guard proclaimed an unlawful association.

23 Aug. Sugar Manufacture Act (IFS); established Comhlucht Siúicre Éireann Teo.

2 Sept. Union of Cumann na nGaedheal, National Centre Party and Blueshirts to form United Ireland Party (O'Duffy leader). Subsequently it became Fine Gael.

13 Oct. Land Act, 1933 (IFS); reduced land annuity payments by half.

2 Nov. Constitution (Amendments Nos. 20 and 21) Acts (IFS).

16 Nov. Constitution (Amendment No. 22), abolished rights of appeal to Privy Council in London Act (IFS); Unemployment Assistance Act.

30 Nov. General election in Northern Ireland; Craigavon remained Prime Minister.

8 Dec. Government order declared Young Ireland Association an unlawful organisation.

14 Dec. League of Young replaced Young Ireland Association.

1934

18 Jan. T. J. Campbell on Joseph Devlin's death became leader of the Nationalist Party in Northern Ireland.

5 May First issue of *Republican Congress*.

29 May Town and Regional Planning Act (IFS).

5 June Representation of the People Act (NI); extended residence qualification for voting from three to seven years and candidates at nomination had to declare intention of taking their seats.

13 Sept. Military Service Pensions Act and Industrial Alcohol Act (IFS).

21 Sept. Eoin O'Duffy resigned presidency of the United Ireland Party and League of Youth.

Nov. Commission appointed by Minister for Finance (IFS) to inquire into banking, currency and credit.

12 Dec. Geographical Society of Ireland founded.

22 Dec. Anglo-Irish 'Cattle and Coal' Agreement.

1935

19 Feb. Public Dance Halls Act (IFS).

28 Feb. Criminal Law Amendment Act (IFS) forbade importation of contraceptives and raised age of consent to 17.

21 Mar. W. T. Cosgrave elected chairman of the United Ireland Party.

10 Apr. Irish Nationality and Citizenship and Aliens Acts (IFS).

7 June Ramsay MacDonald resigned as United Kingdom Prime Minster; he was succeed by Stanley Baldwin.

8 June League of Youth renamed the National Corporative Party.

20 June Pigs and Bacon Act established marketing boards (IFS).

12–21 July Sectarian rioting in Belfast.

16 July Summary Jurisdiction and Criminal Justice Act; Road and Railway Transport Act (NI).

2 Aug. Widows' and Orphans' Pension Act (IFS).

14 Nov. General election in United Kingdom; Stanley Baldwin remained Prime Minster.

1936

20 Jan. Death of King George V; succeeded by Edward VIII.

17 Feb. Anglo-Irish Coal-Cattle Pact renewed.

24 Feb. Ulster Society for Irish Historical Studies founded.

24 Apr. Constitution (Amendment No. 23) Act (IFS) ended university representation in Dáil Éireann.

26 Apr. Census of population (IFS).

19 May Final meeting of Free State Senate.

29 May Senate of the IFS abolished (Constitution (Amendment No. 24) Act).

18 June IFS government declared the IRA an illegal organisation.

July Patrick Belton's Irish Christian Front formed.

3 Nov. Irish Historical Society founded.

28 Nov. Agricultural Wages Act; minimum rates for farm workers; Liffey Reservoir Act (IFS).

10 Dec. Abdication of Edward VIII; succeeded by George VI.

11 Dec. Constitution (Amendment No. 27) Act (FS) removed king from the constitution and abolished the office of Governor-General.

12 Dec. Executive Authority (External Relations) Act (IFS).

1937

24 Feb. Spanish Civil War (Non-intervention) Act (IFS).

28 Feb. Census of population (NI).

1 May Draft constitution of Éire published.

28 May Stanley Baldwin resigned as United Kingdom Prime Minister; succeeded by Neville Chamberlain.

8 June Executive Powers (Consequential Provision) Act (IFS) transferred to Executive Council all functions of crown representative.

14 June New constitution approved by Dáil Éireann which was then dissolved.

1 July General election and referendum in the Free State on the new constitution: for the constitution, 685,105; against, 526,945.

28–29 July George VI visited Northern Ireland.

29 Dec. New Constitution (IFS) came into effect.

1938

9 Feb. General election in Northern Ireland: Craigavon remained Prime Minister.

1 Mar. First issue of *Irish Historical Studies.*

24 Mar. Irish Committee for Historical Sciences founded.

25 Apr. Anglo-Irish agreements on Treaty ports, finance and trade ended the Economic War.

26 Apr. Craigavon announced UK government agreement to find means to maintain Northern Ireland social services at UK level if NI revenue proved insufficient.

27 Apr. Initial meeting of Seanad Éireann (replaced Senate, dissolved 29 May 1936).

16 May Finance (Agreement with UK) Act (É).

17 May Éire (Confirmation of Agreements) Act (É).

27 May Dáil Éireann dissolved.

17 June General election in Éire.

25 June Dr Douglas Hyde inaugurated as first President of Éire.

11 July Cork harbour defences transferred to Irish government.

15 Aug. Clann na Talmhan formed.

12 Sept. Eamon de Valera elected President of the Assembly of the League of Nations.

17 Oct. De Valera offered Northern Ireland retention of its existing status (subject to 'fair' treatment of its minority), with transfer to Dublin of powers reserved to Westminster.

22 Dec. NI instituted internment.

23 Dec. Announcement of movement to promote better understanding between the north and south of Ireland (became Irish Association for Cultural, Economic and Social Relations).

1939

10 Jan. Commission on Vocational Organisation (Bishop Browne chairman) appointed (É).

16 Jan. IRA bombing campaign in England started.

4 May Prime Minister Chamberlain announced that Northern Ireland would be excluded from British conscription bill.

30 May Treason Act (É).

14 June Offences Against the State Act (É).

23 June Unlawful Organisation (Suppression) Order (É) outlawed the IRA.

27 June Mrs Kathleen Clarke first woman to be elected Lord Mayor of Dublin.

1 July Irish Red Cross established.

4 July Matrimonial Causes Act (NI).

22 Aug. Internment invoked in Éire.

23 Aug. IRA bomb in Coventry.

2 Sept. Eamon de Valera announced Éire's intention to remain neutral in European War; first amendment of the Constitution Act that national emergency existed.

3 Sept. United Kingdom and France declared war on Germany.
Emergency Powers Act (É).

1940
3 Jan. Government of Éire introduced Emergency Powers (Amendment) bill and Offences against the State (Amendment) bill to combat the IRA.
8 Jan. Food rationing introduced in Northern Ireland.
10 May Neville Chamberlain resigned as United Kingdom Prime Minister; succeeded by Winston Churchill.
7 June Defence Forces Temporary Provisions Act (É).
19 June Institute for Advanced Studies Act (É).
Oct. Initial issue of *The Bell* edited by Seán O'Faolain.
7 Nov. De Valera stated that Éire was unwilling to lease 'Treaty ports' to Great Britain.
24 Nov. Death of James Craig, First Viscount Craigavon; succeeded by John Miller Andrews as Unionist Party leader and Prime Minister of Northern Ireland.
27 Dec. John Charles McQuaid consecrated Catholic Archbishop of Dublin.

1941
1, 2, 3 Jan. German bombs dropped on Éire.
2 Jan. United Kingdom restricted volume of shipping to ports in Éire.
16 Jan. Worst outbreak of foot-and-mouth disease began.
28 Jan. Emergency Powers Order (no. 67) provided for censorship of press messages to places outside Éire.
7–8 Apr. First German bombing of Belfast.
7 May Wages Standstill Order (É).
23 Sept. Trade Union Act (É).
7 Dec. Japan bombed Pearl Harbor; USA entered the war on 8 Dec.
11 Dec. Germany and Italy declared war on USA.

1942
26 Jan. First US troops arrived in Belfast; Eamon de Valera protested on the following day.
19 Feb. James Dillon, deputy leader of Fine Gael, resigned from party, following criticism of his support of Irish-American alliance.
25 Mar. Federated Union of Employers certified as trade union.
3, 5 Apr. IRA attacks in Northern Ireland.
26 May Referendum Act (É); procedures for referendums.
4 Nov. Central Bank Act (É) established central bank.

1943
1 Feb. Central Bank opened in Dublin; Council for the Encouragement of Music and the Arts established in Northern Ireland.
28 Apr. John Miller Andrews resigned leadership of the Unionist Party and as Prime Minster of NI; succeeded by Sir Basil Brooke on 1 May.

22 June General election in Éire.
26 Oct. Comhdháil Náisiúnta na Gaeilge formed (co-ordinating body for Irish language organisations).

1944

7 Jan. Irish Transport and General Workers' Union disaffiliated from the Labour Party.
14 Jan. National Labour Party founded.
18 Jan. W. T. Cosgrave resigned as leader of Fine Gael; succeeded by Richard Mulcahy on 26 Jan.
21 Jan. 'American Note' requested withdrawal of German and Japanese representatives in Éire.
23 Feb. Children's Allowances Act (É).
30 May General election in Éire.
8 Dec. Transport Act (É); established Córas Iompair Éireann.

1945

6 Feb. Housing Act (NI); established Northern Ireland Housing Trust.
25 Apr. Split in Irish Trade Union Congress; formation of Congress of Irish Unions (CIU).
2 May Eamon de Valera expressed official condolences on death of Hitler.
5 May Racing Board and Racecourse Act (É).
8 May European War ended.
13 May Churchill's victory speech criticised Irish neutrality.
16 May De Valera replied to Churchill defending Irish record.
14 June General election in Northern Ireland.
14 June Seán T. O'Kelly elected President of Éire.
5 July General election in the United Kingdom.
26 July Clement Attlee appointed Prime Minister of the United Kingdom.
4 Aug. National Stud Act (É).
14 Aug. Japan surrendered; end of Second World War.
6 Sept. Duke of Abercorn, Governor of Northern Ireland since 1922, resigned; succeeded by Vice-Admiral the Earl of Granville.
14 Nov. Irish Anti-Partition League formed.
13 Dec. Family Allowances Act (NI).

1946

3 Feb. Censorship of Publications Act (É).
19 Feb. National Insurance Act (NI) extended British welfare legislation to the province.
28 Feb. Public Health, Elections and Franchise Acts (NI).
12 May Census of population (É).
1 June Turf Development Act (É) established Bord na Móna.
6 July Clann naPoblachta founded by Seán McBride.

27 Aug. Industrial Relations Act (É) established Labour Court; and Industrial Research and Standards Act established Institute for Industrial Research and Standards.

15 Nov. Irish Naval Service formed.

24 Dec. Departments of Health and Social Welfare established; commencement of rural electrification scheme in Éire.

1947

27 Mar. Education Act (NI).

28 June Éire ratified Economic Co-operation Agreement.

31 July Northern Ireland Act (UK); extended powers of NI parliament.

13 Aug. Health Act (É).

7 Oct. Catholic Hierarchy expressed disapproval of parts of Health Act.

28 Oct. Éire signed European Recovery Programme agreement.

23 Dec. Safeguard of Employment Act (NI) restricted employment of persons who were not NI workers.

1948

4 Feb. General election in Éire.

10 Feb. John A. Costello (Fine Gael) elected Taoiseach and formed coalition government.

22 June Catholic bishops condemned suggestions for abolition of Sunday closing of public houses in rural areas.

7 Sept. Costello, while in Canada, announced government's intention to repeal External Relations Act, thereby establishing Ireland as a Republic.

21 Dec. Republic of Ireland Act (É).

1949

10 Feb. General election in Northern Ireland.

23 Feb. Announcement by Seán MacBride that British claim to sovereignty in Northern Ireland made it impossible for Éire to participate in the North Atlantic Treaty Organisation (NATO).

3 Apr. Irish Labour Party (NI) formed in Belfast.

18 Apr. Éire left Commonwealth on becoming a Republic.

5 May Republic a founder member of the Council of Europe; accepted jurisdiction of the European Court of Human Rights.

2 June Ireland Act (UK) recognised the Republic of Ireland.

30 July Land Reclamation Act (ROI).

10 Sept. Sterling devalued ($4.03 to $2.80).

21 Dec. Irish News Agency Act (ROI).

1950

23 Feb. General election in United Kingdom. Clement Attlee remained Prime Minster.

4 Apr. Council of Education (ROI) appointed.

6 June Unification of Labour and National Labour parties with William Nolan as leader.

13 June Erne Drainage and Development Act (ROI) gave effect to joint Republic/Northern Ireland scheme of drainage and electricity generation.

25 June Beginning of Korean War.

27 June Erne Drainage and Development Act (NI); corresponded to Republic's Act on 13 June.

11 Oct. Catholic Hierarchy objected to the proposed Mother-and-Child Scheme (*see* glossary).

20 Dec. Industrial Development Authority Act (ROI).

1951

9 Jan. Agreement between Republic and Northern Ireland on future of Great Northern Railway.

4 Apr. Catholic bishops condemned the Mother-and-Child Scheme.

8 Apr. Census of population in Republic and Northern Ireland.

11 Apr. Dr Noel Browne, Minister for Health (ROI), resigned over Mother-and-Child Scheme.

8 May Arts Act (ROI) established the Arts Council.

30 May General election in Republic.

13 June Eamon de Valera appointed Taoiseach.

18 July Abbey Theatre, Dublin, destroyed by fire.

23 Aug. Public Order Act (NI) required written notice of processions (other than customary processions).

25 Oct. General election in United Kingdom.

26 Oct. Winston S. Churchill appointed United Kingdom Prime Minister.

10 Dec. Nobel Prize for Physics for Dr. E. T. S. Walton of Trinity College, Dublin.

21 Dec. Córas Tráchtála incorporated as body for promotion of exports.

1952

6 Feb. King George VI died; succeeded by Elizabeth II.

22 Apr. Sea Fisheries Act (ROI) established Bord Iascaigh Mhara.

14 June Social Welfare Act (ROI) established co-ordinated system of social insurance.

3 July Tourist Traffic Act (ROI) established Bord Fáilte to promote tourism.

13 Dec. Adoption Act (ROI); adopters had to be of the same religion as the child.

1953

2 June Coronation of Queen Elizabeth II.

1–3 July Queen Elizabeth II visited Northern Ireland.

8 Aug. Chester Beatty Library, Dublin, opened.

22 Oct. General election in Northern Ireland.

29 Oct. Health Act (ROI) incorporated a Mother-and-Child Scheme.

1954

6 Apr. Flags and Emblems (Display) Act (NI); an offence to interfere with flying of Union Jack.

18 May General election in Republic.

2 June John A. Costello (Fine Gael) became Taoiseach in a coalition government.

12 June IRA raid on Gough military barracks, Armagh.

12 July Report of Commission on Emigration and other Republic of Ireland Population Problems.

12 Aug. Report of the Council of Education (ROI).

17 Oct. IRA attacked Omagh military barracks.

1955

6 Jan. National Farmers' Association formed (ROI).

6 Apr. Sir Anthony Eden appointed Prime Minster in succession to Winston Churchill.

26 May General election in United Kingdom; Eden remained Prime Minister.

21 July Regular television transmission began in Northern Ireland.

2 Dec. Offences Against the State Act (1939) applied in the Republic.

14 Dec. ROI admitted to the United Nations.

1956

13 Mar. Emergency Imposition of Duties Act to deal with balance-of-payments deficit (ROI).

8 Apr. Census of population (ROI).

30 May Thomas Kenneth Whitaker appointed Secretary to the Republic's Department of Finance.

17 July Irish Nationality and Citizenship Act (ROI) permitted persons born in Northern Ireland after 6 Dec. 1922 to be declared Irish citizens.

24 July Family Allowances and National Insurance Act (NI).

31 Oct. Beginning of British/French/Israel seizure of Egypt's airfields and canal.

1 Dec. Ron Delany won the gold medal in the 1,500 metres in the Olympic Games.

12 Dec. Beginning of IRA campaign against Northern Ireland.

21 Dec. Ten new security regulations introduced in Northern Ireland.

1957

9 Jan. Sir Anthony Eden resigned as United Kingdom Prime Minister.

10 Jan. Harold Macmillan appointed United Kingdom Prime Minister.

5 Mar. General election in ROI.

20 Mar. Eamon de Valera elected Taoiseach.

25 Mar. Treaty of Rome signed.

13–27 May First Dublin International Theatre Festival.

5 July Government in the Republic invoked Offences Against the State Act (1940) to deal with IRA campaign against Northern Ireland.
18 Dec. Gaeltacht Industries Act (ROI); established Gaeltarra Éireann to run small industries in Irish-speaking districts. Republic became member of the International Monetary Fund (IMF) and joined the World Bank.

1958
19 Feb. Agriculture Act (ROI) established An Foras Talúntais (Agricultural Research Institute).
20 Mar. General election in Northern Ireland.
21 May Yeats Society formed.
10 June Ulster Folk Museum Act (NI).
2 July Industrial Development (Encouragement of External Investment) Act (ROI) removed restrictions on foreign ownership in manufacturing industry.
16 July Appointment of Commission to advise on measures to hasten restoration of Irish language.
11 Nov. Programme for Economic Expansion presented to Dáil.
Dec. Publication of *Economic Development* (by T. K. Whittaker and others).

1959
10 Feb. Congress of Irish Unions and Irish Trade Union Congress voted to unify in Irish Congress of Trade Unions (ICTU).
17 June Eamon de Valera elected President of the Republic.
23 June Seán Lemass became leader of Fianna Fáil and Taoiseach.
8 Oct. General election in United Kingdom; Harold Macmillan remained Prime Minister.
21 Oct. James Dillon succeeded Richard Mulcahy as leader of Fine Gael.
24 Nov. Funds of Suitors Act (ROI) authorised payment for rebuilding of the Abbey Theatre, Dublin.

1960
7 Feb. Credit Union League of Ireland formed.
3 Mar. Brendan Corish succeeded William Norton as leader of the Labour Party (ROI).
12 Apr. Broadcasting Authority Act (ROI) established new Radio Éireann authority.
20 Sept. Frederick H. Boland (ROI) elected president of the General Assembly of the United Nations.
30 Nov. *Belfast Telegraph* acquired by Roy Thomson.

1961
16 Jan. Dairy Produce Marketing Act (ROI) established Bord Bainne (Milk Board).
8 Feb. Committee (Lord Robbins chairman) to review higher education in Great Britain.

9 Apr. Census of population (ROI).

23 Apr. Census of population in Northern Ireland.

25 Apr. Last IRA internees in the Republic released.

1 Aug. Republic applied for full membership of the European Economic Community.

3 Oct. ROI joined UNESCO.

4 Oct. General election in Republic: Seán Lemass remained Taoiseach in a minority government.

31 Dec. Television service commenced in the Republic.

1962

26 Feb. IRA announced end of campaign against Northern Ireland.

25 Apr. Publication of *Report of the Council of Education* (ROI) (secondary school curriculum).

31 May General election in Northern Ireland.

6 July Gay Byrne hosted his first *Late Late Show*.

11 Oct. Second Vatican Council opens.

23 Oct. Publication of report of joint working party on economy of Northern Ireland.

1963

25 Mar. Lord Brookeborough retired as Prime Minister of Northern Ireland and leader of the Unionist Party; succeeded by Capt. Terence O'Neill.

20 May Minister for Education (ROI) announced plans for comprehensive secondary schools and regional technological colleges.

4 June Revd Ian Paisley led march to Belfast City Hall to protest at tributes to the late Pope.

26–29 June US President John F. Kennedy visited Republic.

22 Aug. Publication of Second Programme for Economic Expansion (ROI).

10 Sept. William Conway appointed Catholic Archbishop of Armagh.

9 Oct. First meeting of National Industrial Economic Council (ROI).

19 Oct. Harold Macmillan resigned as United Kingdom Prime Minister; succeeded by Earl of Home (Sir Alec Douglas-Home).

Oct. Publication of Robbins Committee report on higher education in Great Britain.

20 Nov. In view of Robbins Report a committee (Sir John Lockwood chairman) was appointed to review facilities for higher education in Northern Ireland.

22 Nov. President Kennedy assassinated in Dallas, Texas.

1964

10 Jan. Publication of final report of commission on restoration of Irish language; recommended increased use.

Jan. Campaign for Social Justice founded in Dungannon, Co. Tyrone.

2 June Eddie McAteer elected leader of the Nationalist Party at Stormont.

July Publication of Second Programme for Economic Expansion (ROI).

28 Sept. – 3 Oct. Sectarian rioting in Belfast.

15 Oct. United Kingdom general election.

16 Oct. Harold Wilson appointed United Kingdom Prime Minister.

18 Dec. Submission of Wilson report on economic development in Northern Ireland.

1965

14 Jan. Taoiseach Seán Lemass and Prime Minister Terence O'Neill met at Stormont.

16 Jan. White paper *Athbheochan na Gaeilge: The Restoration of the Irish Language* set out 10-year plan for restoration of Irish as general medium of communication.

2 Feb. Nationalist Party in Northern Ireland accepted role as official opposition at Stormont.

9 Feb. O'Neill and Lemass met in Dublin.

10 Feb. Publication of Lockwood Committee report on higher education in Northern Ireland.

15 Feb. First meeting of Northern Ireland Economic Council.

1 Mar. Roger Casement reinterred in Glasnevin cemetery.

7 Apr. General election in Republic; Lemass remained Taoiseach.

21 Apr. Liam Cosgrave succeeded James Dillon as leader of Fine Gael.

24 June New Towns Act (NI).

15 Aug. Cathedral of Our Lady Assumed into Heaven and St Nicholas, Galway, consecrated.

16 Sept. Dissolution of Clann na Poblachta.

25 Nov. General election in Northern Ireland.

14 Dec. Anglo-Irish Free Trade Area Agreement took effect 1 July 1966.

22 Dec. Succession Act (ROI) pertained to inheritance rights of wife and children.

23 Dec. Publication of Investment in Education: Report of the Survey Team appointed by the (ROI) Minister for Education in Oct. 1962.

1966

4 Mar. Capital punishment abolished in Northern Ireland except for political murders.

8 Mar. Nelson's Pillar in O'Connell Street, Dublin, destroyed.

31 Mar. General election in United Kingdom: Harold Wilson remained Prime Minister.

10 Apr. Beginning of commemoration of the Easter Rising of 1916.

17 Apr. Census of population (ROI).

21 June Catholic bishops announed proposal to develop St Patrick's College, Maynooth, into 'an open centre of higher studies'.

28 June Ulster Volunteer Force banned in Northern Ireland.

18 July Abbey Theatre reopened.

19 July Revd Ian Paisley convicted of unlawful assembly and breach of the peace (NI).

22 Aug. Announcement of amalgamation of Munster and Leinster Bank, Provincial Bank of Ireland, and Royal Bank of Ireland as Allied Irish Banks.
10 Sept. Minister for Education (ROI) promised free post-primary education in Sept. 1967.
9 Oct. Census of population (NI).
4 Nov. United Council of Christian Churches and Religious Communions in Ireland renamed Irish Council of Churches.
8 Nov. Seán Lemass announced resignation as leader of Fianna Fáil and Taoiseach.
10 Nov. Jack Lynch elected Taoiseach.

1967
1 Feb. Northern Ireland Civil Rights Association founded; stated its objectives on 6 Feb.
21 Feb. Landlord and Tenant (Ground Rents) Act (ROI).
7 Mar. Industrial Training Act (ROI) established An Chomhairle Oiliúna (AnCO), an industrial training organisation.
11 May Republic's application for membership in EEC failed.
22 Mar. Publication of Commission on Higher Education 1960–67, Presentation and Summary of Report.
11 May ROI and UK reapplied for membership of the EEC.
11 July Censorship of Publications Amendment Act (ROI); over 5,000 works removed from banned list.
24 Aug. Publication Commission on Higher Education, 1960–67 Report, Vol. I (ROI).
18 Nov. Statue of Wolfe Tone in St Stephen's Green, Dublin, unveiled.
11 Dec. Taoiseach Lynch visited Prime Minister Terence O'Neill at Stormont.

1968
8 Jan. Prime Minister O'Neill visited Taoiseach Lynch in Dublin.
26 Mar. Education (Amendment) Act (NI) increased grants to voluntary schools.
10 June First women elected Fellows of Trinity College Dublin.
15 Aug. Establishment of Higher Education Authority (ROI).
24 Aug. Northern Ireland Civil Rights Association march.
14 Sept. St Patrick's College, Maynooth, admitted its first lay students for degree courses.
1 Oct. Opening of the New University of Ulster, Coleraine (renamed University of Ulster).
3–5 Oct. Violence followed Northern Ireland Civil Rights Association march which had been banned by William Craig, Minister of Home Affairs.
9 Oct. Students at the Queen's University of Belfast formed 'People's Democracy'; Londonderry Citizens' Action Committee formed.
15 Oct. Nationalist Party withdrew as official opposition at Stormont.
5 Nov. United Kingdom Prime Minister Harold Wilson demanded reforms in Northern Ireland.

22 Nov. NI Prime Minister Terence O'Neill announced a series of reforms.

28 Nov. Electoral Law Act (NI) abolished university constituency, redistributed seats and provided for permanent boundary commission.

3 Dec. Lord Grey of Naunton sworn in as Governor of NI.

1969

1–4 Jan. People's Democracy marchers ambushed.

8 Jan. Ulster Defence Force (UDF) founded to protect Protestant lives and property.

5 Feb. New Ulster Movement formed to support Prime Minister O'Neill.

24 Feb. General election in Northern Ireland: O'Neill remained Prime Minister.

3 Mar. Commission under Lord Cameron appointed to investigate the causes of recent outbreaks of violence in Northern Ireland.

Mar. Publication of Third Programme, Economic and Social Development, 1969–72.

26 Mar. Electoral Amendment Act (ROI) increased size of Dáil from 138 to 142.

17 Apr. Bernadette Devlin elected Westminster MP for Mid-Ulster (maiden speech on 22 Apr.).

25 Apr. 500 British troops arrived in Northern Ireland.

28 Apr. Captain Terence O'Neill resigned as UUP leader and Prime Minister.

1 May Major James Chichester-Clark became Prime Minister of Northern Ireland.

6 May Amnesty announced for all offences connected with demonstrations in Northern Ireland since 5 Oct. 1968.

18 June General election in Republic: Jack Lynch remained Taoiseach.

2 July *The Reshaping of Local Government: Further Proposals,* white paper (ROI).

12–16 July Sectarian rioting in Londonderry.

20 July Londonderry Citizens' Defence Association replaced Londonderry Citizens' Action Committee.

2–5 Aug. Sectarian disturbances in Belfast.

12–15 Aug. Widespread rioting in NI.

14 Aug. Deployment of British troops in NI.

19 Aug. 'Downing Street Declaration' issued by British and Northern Ireland governments.

26 Aug. Review body under Lord Hunt to inquire into the Royal Ulster Constabulary and the Special Constabulary.

27 Aug. Tribunal established under Sir Leslie Scarman to inquire into recent disturbances in Northern Ireland.

12 Sept. Report of the Cameron Commission.

10 Oct. Report of the Hunt Commission.

23 Oct. Samuel Beckett awarded the Nobel Prize for Literature.

25 Nov. Electoral Law Act (NI) lowered qualifying age for franchise to 18, extended local government franchise to all parliamentary electors, and postponed triennial local government elections to 1971.

28 Nov. First issue of *Loyalist News*.

17 Dec. Review body on reorganisation of local government in Northern Ireland appointed under Patrick Macrory.

18 Dec. Ulster Defence Regiment Act (UK) established part-time security force under army control.

1970

11 Jan. Split in Sinn Féin results in two wings, Officials and Provisionals.

24 Feb. Health Act (ROI).

15 Mar. Communist Parties in Republic and Northern Ireland united to form the Community Party of Ireland with Michael O'Riordan as General Secretary.

26 Mar. Police Act (NI) established police authority, police association, police advisory board and Royal Ulster Constabulary reserve.

31 Mar. – 1 Apr. Beginning of phased disbanding of the 'B' Special Constabulary in Northern Ireland.

21 Apr. Alliance Party formed in Northern Ireland.

30 Apr. 'B' Specials disbanded and duties transferred to Ulster Defence Regiment.

3 May Irish Council of Churches and Catholic Church established a joint group on social problems.

6 May Lynch dismissed Charles Haughey and Neil T. Blaney from the cabinet over allegations of illegal arms importation; Kevin Boland then resigned. Lynch then survived a vote of confidence in the Dáil.

28 May Haughey, Blaney and two others charged in a Dublin court with conspiracy to illegally import arms for use by the IRA. They denied any involvement.

29 May Macrory report on major services in Northern Ireland.

18 June General election in United Kingdom.

19 June Edward Heath appointed United Kingdom Prime Minister.

25 June Catholic Hierarchy removes restrictions on Catholics attending Trinity College Dublin.

2 July Blaney was found not guilty of illegal arms importation by a Dublin jury (*see* 28 May, 23 Oct.).

21 Aug. Social Democratic and Labour Party (SDLP) formed in Northern Ireland.

16 Sept. National Institute for High Education, Limerick opens (renamed University of Limerick, 1989).

5 Oct. American President, Richard M. Nixon, visited the Republic.

23 Oct. Haughey and two others were found not guilty of illegal arms importation by a Dublin jury (*see* 6, 28 May, 2 July).

9 Nov. Irish School of Ecumenics inaugurated.

9 Dec. Irish Society for Archives founded.

17 Dec. Government of Northern Ireland announced general acceptance of Macrory report.

1971

17 Jan. Official Sinn Féin ended abstention policy from Dáil, Stormont and Westminster.

25 Feb. Housing Executive Act (NI) concentrated authority in one executive which replaced functions of local authorities and the Northern Ireland Housing Trust.

20 Mar. Major James Chichester-Clark resigned as Northern Ireland Prime Minister.

23 Mar. Brian Faulkner appointed Northern Ireland Prime Minister. Local Government (Boundaries) Act (NI).

1 Apr. Northern Ireland Polytechnic at Jordanstown opened.

11 Apr. Gaelic Athletic Association (GAA) removed the ban on 'foreign games'.

18 Apr. Census of population (ROI).

25 Apr. Census of population (NI).

28 July Central Bank Act (ROI).

9–10 Aug. Internment introduced in Northern Ireland.

20 Aug. Publication of White Paper, *A Record of Constructive Change* (NI).

31 Aug. Radio Free Londonderry began transmission.

Committee (Sir Edmund Compton chairman) appointed to investigate allegations of physical brutality committed against persons arrested on 9 August.

14 Sept. Democratic Unionist Party formed by Revd Ian Paisley and Desmond Boal.

19 Sept. Aontacht Eireann (Unity of Ireland) Party founded by Kevin Boland.

1 Oct. Order restraining RTE from reporting activities associated with illegal organisations.

16 Nov. Compton Committee reported that detainees were ill-treated.

1972

1 Jan. Irish Farmers' Association (IFA) formed from farmers' organisations in the Republic.

4 Jan. Archbishop McQuaid resigned; succeeded by Fr Dermot Ryan.

22 Jan. Treaty of accession to EEC signed by Republic and United Kingdom.

31 Jan. Following the shootings in Londonderry (Bloody Sunday), the government announced that it had recalled its ambassador to the United Kingdom and Lynch announced a day of national mourning for 2 Feb.

2 Feb. British Embassy in Dublin burned.

Lord Widgery appointed to lead tribunal of inquiry into events in Londonderry.

24 Feb. Northern Ireland Act (UK).

2 Mar. Publication of report of the Parker Committee; described methods of interrogation in Northern Ireland.

23 Mar. Local Government Act (NI); composition of district councils.

24 Mar. Suspension of Northern Ireland government; direct rule from Westminster and William Whitelaw appointed Secretary of State for Northern Ireland.

30 Mar. Northern Ireland (Temporary Provisions) Act (UK) suspended Stormont for one year.

2 Apr. Radio na Gaeltachta opens.

6 Apr. Report of the Scarman tribunal.

19 Apr. Report of the Widgery tribunal.

10 May Referendum in Republic on membership of EEC.

26 May Government of the Republic announced establishment of Special Criminal Court re-instituted to deal with crimes arising out of the Northern Ireland conflict. Trial by jury was suspended.

29 May Official IRA suspended operations in Northern Ireland.

20 June NI Secretary of State, William Whitelaw, announced special category status for certain prisoners.

1 July School-leaving age in the Republic raised from 14 to 15.

7 July Whitelaw met Provisional IRA leaders in London.

31 July Operation Motorman removed barricades in Belfast and Londonderry.

14 Aug. Education and Libraries (Northern Ireland) Order (UK).

20 Sept. SDLP's *Towards a New Ireland* published.

29 Sept. Commission (Lord Diplock chairman) to consider legal procedures for dealing more effectively with terrorist activities in Northern Ireland established.

6 Oct. Lynch closed the Sinn Féin office in Dublin.

30 Oct. Publication of British government paper on future of Northern Ireland. Contained guarantee of constitutional position but introduced 'Irish' dimension.

2 Nov. In Dáil a bill passed authorising a referendum to remove the special position of the Catholic Church from the constitution.

19 Nov. Seán MacStiofáin, leader of the IRA, was arrested in Dublin (He was subsequently sentenced to six months' imprisonment in the Republic.)

1 Dec. Two people were killed by an IRA bomb in Dublin.

3 Dec. Offences against the State (Amendment) Act (ROI) enabled Garda's belief that a person belonged to an illegal organisation to be used as evidence.

6 Dec. Whitelaw announced establishment of special task force of military and police to deal with sectarian murders.

7 Dec. Referendum in the Republic lowered voting age from 21 to 18.

13 Dec. Owners of Bewley's Cafés Ltd, Dublin, transferred to Bewley Community (employees).

20 Dec. Publication of the report of the Diplock Commission.

29 Dec. Ruairi Ó Bradaigh, President of Sinn Féin, arrested and held under new legislation.

31 Dec. Martin McGuinness was arrested and held under the new legislation.

1973

Jan. UK and ROI joined the EEC.

20 Jan. Loyalist paramilitary car bomb in Sackville Place, Dublin, killed one person and injured 17 others.

5 Feb. Dissolution of Dáil.

26 Feb. Publication of the report of the Commission on Status of Women (ROI).

28 Feb. General election in Republic.

14 Mar. Liam Cosgrave elected Taoiseach of a coalition government.

20 Mar. British government published white paper proposing new assembly for Northern Ireland elected by proportional representation.

28 Mar. *Claudia* intercepted off the Waterford coast and found laden with 5 tonnes of weapons on route to the IRA.

30 Mar. Vanguard Unionist Progressive Party (VUPP) founded by William Craig.

3 May Northern Ireland Assembly Act (UK); established assembly of 78 members.

30 May District council elections in Northern Ireland held under proportional representation for the first time since 1922.

Erskine Hamilton Childers elected President of the Republic.

28 June General election to NI Assembly.

18 July Northern Ireland Constitution Act (UK) abolished Northern Ireland parliament.

25 July Northern Ireland (Emergency Provisions) Act (UK) repealed the Special Powers Act and provided for 'terrorist-type' offences to be tried by a single judge.

31 July First meeting of Northern Ireland Assembly; dissolved in disorder. Act (ROI) abolishing bar against continued employment of women civil servants who married while in post.

6 Aug. Kenneth Littlejohn, one of two brothers arrested during a bank robbery, claimed during his trial in Dublin that he had been working for British intelligence (MI6) in an attempt to infiltrate the Official IRA.

17 Sept. Edward Heath visited the Republic; first United Kingdom Prime Minister to travel there since independence.

31 Oct. IRA used a hijacked helicopter to free three of their members, including Séamus Twomey, Chief of Staff of the IRA, from the exercise yard of Mountjoy Prison, Dublin.

12 Nov. Ulster Freedom Fighters and Red Hand Commandos declared illegal.

21 Nov. Agreement reached on power-sharing Assembly.

22 Nov. Unionist Party, SDLP and Alliance Party agreed to form power-sharing Executive for Northern Ireland.

2 Dec. Francis Pym succeeded William Whitelaw as Secretary of State for Northern Ireland.

6 Dec. United Ulster Unionist Council formed; opposed to power-sharing.

6–9 Dec. Sunningdale Conference.

1974

1 Jan. Northern Ireland Executive took office.

4 Jan. Sunningdale Agreement repudiated by UUUC.

7 Jan. Brian Faulkner resigned as Ulster Unionist Party leader.

23 Jan. Official Unionists, Vanguard Unionist Progressive Party, and Democratic Unionist Party withdrew from Northern Ireland Assembly in protest against the Executive.

28 Feb. General election in UK.

4 Mar. Harold Wilson appointed United Kingdom Prime Minister.

5 Mar. Merlyn Rees succeeded Francis Pym as Secretary of State for Northern Ireland.

13 Mar. Taoiseach Liam Cosgrave accepted status of Northern Ireland as unalterable except by decision of a majority of the people of Northern Ireland.

14–28 May Ulster Workers' Council general strike against the Sunningdale Agreement.

17 May Loyalist bombs killed 33 people in the Republic.

23 May Report of the Anglo-Irish Law Enforcement Commission recommended that extra-territorial jurisdiction be conferred on courts in both parts of Ireland.

28 May Executive of Northern Ireland collapses.

29 May Northern Ireland Prorogation Order reinstates direct rule from Westminster.

4 July British government white paper, *The Northern Ireland Constitution*, announced the setting up of an elected constitutional convention to seek a political settlement.

16 July Taoiseach Liam Cosgrave voted, as a matter of conscience, against his own government's contraception bill.

17 July Northern Ireland Act (UK) provided for constitutional convention.

8 Oct. Seán MacBride awarded Nobel Prize for Peace.

10 Oct. General election in the United Kingdom: Wilson remained Prime Minister.

7 Nov. Republic's government announced that Irish would no longer be obligatory for entry into the civil service.

21 Nov. Two bombs in Birmingham killed 21 people.

Nov. Provisional IRA declared illegal in Great Britain.

28 Nov. The government introduced legislation which would allow people to be tried for offences committed outside the jurisdiction of the Republic.

29 Nov. Prevention of Terrorism Act (UK) provided for deportation from, and prohibition of entry to, Great Britain.

3 Dec. Cearbhall Ó Dálaigh elected President of the Republic.

8 Dec. Irish Republican Socialist Party (IRSP) and Irish National Liberation Army (INLA) formed.

16 Dec. Minister for Education (ROI) announced plans for higher education.

1975

1 Jan. ROI assumed presidency of EEC for six months.

31 Jan. Gardiner Report recommended continuation of internment and abolition of 'special category' or political status for convicted prisoners.

17 Mar. IRA prisoner shot dead by the Irish army during an attempted escape from Portlaoise Prison, Co. Laois.

26 Mar. Harland & Wolff's shipyard in Belfast to be nationalised.

10 Apr. Prevention of Terrorism Act (UK) renewed for six months.

1 May General election to Northern Ireland Constitutional Convention.

8 May First meeting of the Northern Ireland Constitution Convention.

5 June Referendum in United Kingdom on remaining in EEC.

7 Aug. Prevention of Terrorism Act (UK) applied to Northern Ireland.

29 Aug. Eamon de Valera died at the age of 92.

8 Sept. UUUC convention rejected power-sharing; William Craig resigned leadership of Vanguard Unionist Progressive Party.

3 Oct. Ulster Volunteer Force declared illegal. Tiede Herrema, a Dutch industrialist living and working in the Republic, was abducted and held hostage in Co. Kildare. On 21 Oct. Gardaí surrounded the house and a siege began which lasted until his release on 6 Nov.

12 Oct. Blessed Oliver Plunkett canonised (first Irish saint since 1226).

5 Dec. Internment ended in Northern Ireland.

19 Dec. Red Hand Commandos' car bomb killed two men in Dundalk, Co. Louth.

1976

2 Mar. Juries Act (ROI) made electoral roll basis for jury service instead of property qualification.

9 Mar. Northern Ireland Constitution Convention dissolved.

10 Mar. Republic referred case alleging torture of prisoners in Northern Ireland to the European Court of Human Rights.

26 Mar. Merlyn Rees announced abolition of special category status in Northern Ireland prisons from 31 March.

5 Apr. Prime Minister Harold Wilson resigned; succeeded by James Callaghan.

12 Apr. Committee established under W. G. H. Quigley to inquire into the economy of Northern Ireland.

6 May Eight members of the SAS who claimed to have made a map-reading error and crossed the border were arrested in the Republic.

13 July Adoption Act (ROI) allowed adoption in which adoptive and natural parents were not of the same religious denomination.

21 July Christopher Ewart-Biggs, British Ambassador to ROI, and his secretary killed in a landmine explosion.

22 July Fair Employment (Northern Ireland) Act (UK) established agency to promote 'equality of opportunity'.

12 Aug. Women demonstrated in favour of peace in West Belfast; start of Peace People.

18 Aug. Brian Faulkner announced his retirement from politics.

1 Sept. The government declared that a state of emergency existed which allowed the police to hold people for seven days without having to bring a charge against them (ROI).

2 Sept. European Court of Human Rights found the United Kingdom guilty of torture of republican prisoners in Northern Ireland.

10 Sept. Roy Mason appointed Secretary of State for Northern Ireland.

15 Sept. Mrs Anne Letitia Dickson elected leader of the Unionist Party of Northern Ireland; first woman to lead a political party in Ireland.

15 Oct. Publication of Quigley report on economy of Northern Ireland; recommended capital investment.

16 Oct. A member of the Garda was killed by an IRA booby-trap bomb near Portlaoise, Co. Laois.

22 Oct. ROI President Ó Dálaigh resigned.

9 Nov. Dr Patrick Hillery elected ROI President.

30 Nov. Máiréad Corrigan and Betty Williams, founders of the Peace People, awarded the Nobel Prize for Peace.

3 Dec. Hillery becomes ROI President.

1977

4 Apr. Workers' Participation (State Enterprises) Act (ROI).

6 Apr. Unfair Dismissals Act (ROI).

17 Apr. Cardinal William Conway, Catholic Primate of All Ireland, died in Armagh.

16 June General election in the Republic; Fianna Fáil had a majority of 20 seats.

23 June Liam Cosgrave resigned leadership of Fine Gael.

1 July Dr Garret FitzGerald became leader of Fine Gael; Brendan Corish resigned leadership of the Labour Party and was succeeded by Frank Cluskey.

1 July Employment Equality Agency established (ROI).

5 July Jack Lynch elected Taoiseach.

28 Sept. James Callaghan, British Prime Minister, and Lynch held a meeting in Downing St, London, where they discussed cross-border economic co-operation.

14 Oct. Tomás Ó Fiaich was appointed as the new Catholic Archbishop of Armagh and Primate of All Ireland.

26 Nov. William Craig announced disbanding of Vanguard organisation.

1978

8 Jan. Lynch called for a British declaration of intent to withdraw from Northern Ireland.

18 Jan. European Court of Human Rights ruled that interrogation methods of internees in Northern Ireland were inhumane and degrading but not torture.

24 Sept. Ian Paisley held a religious service in Dublin, at the Mansion House, for the first time.

Dec. Dublin Institute of Technology established.

101

1979

13 Mar. Republic joined European Monetary System (EMS).

30 Mar. Airey Neave, Conservative spokesman on Northern Ireland, assassinated by the INLA.

3 May General election in the United Kingdom.

4 May Margaret Thatcher appointed United Kingdom Prime Minister.

5 May Humphrey Atkins appointed Secretary of State for Northern Ireland.

7 June Elections to the European parliament.

30 June Archbishop of Armagh, Tomás Ó Fiaich, created cardinal.

7 Aug. Civilian in the Republic of Ireland was shot dead by the IRA during a bank robbery in Tramore, Co. Waterford.

27 Aug. Earl Mountbatten killed by IRA bomb.

5 Sept. Thatcher and Lynch met in London to discuss security matters.

29 Sept. First papal visit to Ireland.

2 Oct. Provisional IRA rejected the Pope's call for peace.

5 Oct. The British and Irish governments agreed to strengthen the drive against paramilitary groups.

15 Oct. The Economic and Social Research Institute (ROI) published the results of an opinion poll that had been carried out between July and September 1978, revealing that 21 per cent of people in the Republic expressed some level of support for the IRA.

1–2 Nov. Irish Republic security forces seized a quantity of arms at Dublin docks which were believed to have originated in the USA and to be bound for the IRA. The shipment totalled 156 weapons and included the M-60 machine gun, and were worth an estimated £500,000. Lynch stated that he believed that the conflict in Northern Ireland continued to be 'as intractable as at any stage in the last ten years'.

22 Nov. Gerry Fitt resigned as SDLP leader.

28 Nov. John Hume elected leader of the SDLP.

7 Dec. Charles J. Haughey elected leader of Fianna Fáil.

11 Dec. Haughey elected Taoiseach.

1980

7 Jan. Constitutional conference opened at Stormont; boycotted by Unionists.

16 Feb. At the Fianna Fáil (FF) conference in Dublin, Charles Haughey, the Taoiseach, called for a joint initiative, on behalf of the British and Irish governments, to try to find a political solution to the conflict in Northern Ireland.

24 Mar. Constitutional conference adjourned indefinitely.

15 Apr. Humphrey Atkins, Secretary of State for Northern Ireland, met in Dublin with Haughey and members of the Irish government.

25 Apr. Electoral commission (ROI) recommendation that Dáil representation be increased by 18 seats was accepted.

21 May Meeting of Margaret Thatcher and Charles Haughey concluded with a communiqué on the 'unique relationship'.

9 June Haughey argued on the BBC television programme *Panorama* that it was in the best interests of both Britain and Ireland for Britain to withdraw from Northern Ireland. He indicated that some form of federation could be possible in the event of a British withdrawal.

19 June European Commission on Human Rights criticised Great Britain's handling of the H-Block protest.

27 Oct. Seven Republican prisoners in the Maze start hunger strike.

8 Dec. Thatcher and Haughey met in Dublin and agreed to establish an Anglo-Irish Committee and conduct joint studies on a wide range of subjects. This was the first visit to Dublin by a British Prime Minister since the Treaty in 1921. The phrase 'totality of relationships' was first used at this meeting.

18 Dec. Maze prison hunger strike called off.

1981

1 Mar. Start of hunger strike for restoration of political status began in the Maze prison.

17 Mar. 'Friends of Ireland' launched by some members of the American Congress.

22 Mar. Brian Lenihan, then Republic Foreign Minister, said that the on-going talks between the British and Irish governments could lead to a United Ireland in ten years.

9 Apr. Bobby Sands, on hunger strike, elected MP for Fermanagh and South Tyrone in by-election.

5 May Sands died on hunger strike and this sparked widespread rioting.

20 May Local elections in Northern Ireland; major gains for the DUP and republican candidates.

11 June General election in the Republic; when counting was completed a minority government was formed between a coalition of Fine Gael and Labour (*see* 30 June). Two H-Block prisoners were elected to the Dáil. Frank Cluskey resigned as leader of the Labour Party and was succeeded by Michael O'Leary.

30 June Dr Garret FitzGerald elected Taoiseach and formed a coalition government.

14 July The Irish government asked the United States government to use its influence with Britain on the issue of the hunger strike.

20 Aug. Last death of a hunger striker.

13 Sept. James Prior appointed NI Secretary of State.

Sept. FitzGerald on Radio Telefís Éireann set out his vision for a new Republic in what became know as his 'constitutional crusade' – to make the Republic a society where the majority ethos would be expressed in a way so as not to alienate Protestants living in NI.

3 Oct. Provisional IRA called off the hunger strike.

6 Oct. Announcement that all prisoners would be allowed to wear their own clothing.

6 Nov. Margaret Thatcher and Garret FitzGerald met in London where they agreed to establish the Intergovernmental Council.

14 Nov. Loyalist 'Day of Action' in protest at security policy.

1982

27 Jan. The coalition government (ROI) collapsed when independent TDs voted against proposed tax increases on items such as petrol, alcohol and tobacco.

1 Feb. Corporal punishment banned in Republic's schools.

18 Feb. General election in Republic.

20 Feb. An officer in the Garda Síochána was shot dead by the Irish National Liberation Army when he went to a house in Tallaght, Dublin.

21 Feb. Ireland won rugby Triple Crown.

9 Mar. Charles J. Haughey elected Taoiseach.

17 Mar. Haughey visited the USA for St Patrick's Day celebrations where he called on the American government to put more pressure on Britain to consider the possibility of Irish unity.

25 Mar. British government support for plan of 'rolling devolution'.

13 May European parliament called for ban on plastic bullets.

13 July First conviction in Republic of Irish citizen for crime committed outside the jurisdiction.

16 Sept. New Ireland Group founded by John Robb.

6 Oct. Des O'Malley, the Irish Minister from Trade, Commerce and Tourism, resigned from the government because of disagreements with Haughey on Northern Ireland and the economy. O'Malley later formed the Progressive Democrats.

20 Oct. General election to Northern Ireland Assembly.

28 Oct. Michael O'Leary resigned leadership of Labour Party and joined Fine Gael; he was succeeded by Dick Spring.

4 Nov. The coalition government (ROI) was defeated in a vote of confidence in the Dáil.

28 Nov. General election in the Republic; a new coalition government of Fine Gael and the Irish Labour Party was elected.

Dec. Garret FitzGerald elected Taoiseach and formed a coalition cabinet.

7 Dec. The Supreme Court made a ruling which opened up the possibility of extradition between the Republic and the UK when it rejected the claim that paramilitary offences were politically motivated.

1983

5 Jan. INLA proscribed in the Republic.

28 Jan. The government in the Republic of Ireland announced that it would introduce legislation to give full voting rights to approximately 20,000 British citizens.

8 Feb. Shergar, the Derby winner in 1981, kidnapped and never found.

11 Mar. The Republic's government announced that it was establishing a forum, which became known as the New Ireland Forum, which had been first proposed by the Northern Ireland SDLP (*see* 2 May 1984).

21 Mar. Irish (ROI) punt devalued by *c.* 5 per cent.

27 Apr. The Fianna Fáil opposition in the Dáil managed to have an anti-abortion amendment to the Irish constitution carried by 87 votes to 13 (*see* 7 Sept.).

30 May First meeting of New Ireland Forum in Dublin Castle.

9 June General election in the United Kingdom: Margaret Thatcher remained Prime Minister.

7 Sept. 'Pro-life' amendment to the constitution carried in referendum (*see* 27 Apr.).

7 Nov. First meeting of Anglo-Irish Intergovernmental Council.

13 Nov. ROI army participated for the first time in Remembrance Day ceremony in Dublin.

13 Nov. Gerry Adams became president of Sinn Féin.

24 Nov. Don Tidey, an American supermarket executive, was kidnapped by the IRA, Co. Dublin (*see* 16 Dec.).

16 Dec. Security forces rescued Tidey at Ballinamore, Co. Leitrim, but during the gun battle a soldier and a Garda Síochána cadet were killed (*see* 24 Nov.).

17 Dec. IRA bomb outside Harrods in London killed five people.

1984

17 Jan. Ford factory in Cork announced closure.

15 Mar. FitzGerald addressed the United States Congress and called on Americans to urge the British to accept the proposals that were emerging from the New Ireland Forum.

18 Mar. Dominic McGlinchey became the first republican to be extradited from the Republic to Northern Ireland.

4 Apr. The British government issued an apology to the Irish government over undercover operations by the Royal Ulster Constabulary in the territory of the Republic in December 1982.

2 May Publication of report of the New Ireland Forum.

1–4 June US President Ronald Reagan visited ROI; he addressed a joint session of the Dáil and Senate where he stated that US policy was not to interfere in matters relating to Northern Ireland, but he criticised violence in the region and supported the New Ireland Forum.

June General election for the European parliament; referendum on constitution; extending voting rights to non-citizens approved.

10 Sept. Douglas Hurd appointed Secretary of State for Northern Ireland.

12 Oct. IRA bomb exploded at Grand Hotel, Brighton, during the Conservative Party conference.

19 Nov. FitzGerald met Thatcher in England. Following the meeting Thatcher ruled out the three options proposed in the report of the New Ireland Forum: 'A united Ireland was one solution. That is out. A second solution was confederation of the two states. That is out. A third solution was joint authority. That is out.'

1985

19 Feb. ROI government introduced legislation that allowed it to freeze the bank accounts of people believed to be holding funds on behalf of paramilitary organisations.

25 Feb. Des O'Malley, Fianna Fáil TD, was expelled from the party for refusing to vote against a bill to liberalise contraceptive legislation.

30 Mar. Ireland won rugby Triple Crown.

27 June The INLA shot dead a member of the Garda Síochána during an armed robbery at a post office in Ardee, Co. Louth.

13 July Live Aid organised by Bob Geldof.

2 Sept. Tom King appointed NI Secretary of State.

15 Nov. Republic and UK sign Anglo-Irish Agreement.

21 Nov. The Anglo-Irish Agreement passed in the Dáil by 88 votes to 75.

11 Dec. First meeting of the Anglo-Irish Intergovernmental Conference at Stormont Castle.

17 Dec. All 15 Unionist MPs resigned their seats in the House of Commons in protest at the Anglo-Irish Agreement.

21 Dec. Progressive Democrat Party founded by Desmond O'Malley.

1986

23 Jan. 14 of 15 Unionists who resigned in protest against Anglo-Irish Agreement won re-election.

24 Feb. The government signed the European Convention on the Suppression of Terrorism.

26 June Constitutional Referendum on Divorce was rejected by 63.5 per cent to 36.5 per cent.

23 July Northern Ireland Assembly dissolved.

2 Aug. Punt (ROI) devalued by *c.* 8 per cent.

2 Nov. Sinn Féin voted to end policy of abstention from the Dáil.

8 Nov. The UFF planted four bombs in the centre of Dublin.

1987

20 Jan. The coalition government ended after the Labour Party withdrew its support.

7 Feb. The UFF exploded incendiary devices in Co. Donegal and in Dublin.

14 Feb. General election in the Republic.

10 Mar. Charles J. Haughey elected Taoiseach and formed a minority government.

11 Mar. Dr Garret FitzGerald resigned as leader of Fine Gael.

21 Mar. Alan Dukes was elected as leader of Fine Gael.

26 May Referendum in Republic on Single European Act carried.

12 June General election in the United Kingdom; Margaret Thatcher remained Prime Minister.

14 Sept. Ian Paisley and James Molyneaux ended 19-month boycott of meetings with British government ministers.

16 Sept. European Commission of Human Rights held that provisions of Prevention of Terrorism Act must be changed.

8 Nov. IRA bomb killed 11 in Enniskillen during Remembrance Day commemoration.

30 Nov. Law altered (ROI) requiring prima facie evidence of a case before someone could be extradited.

1988

11 Jan. John Hume and Gerry Adams met in Belfast.

27 Jan. Garda Síochána uncovered one of the largest stores of IRA weapons near Malin Head, Co. Donegal.

6 Mar. Three members of IRA killed in Gibraltar by SAS (*see* 6 Sept. 1993).

19 Oct. UK Home Secretary Douglas Hurd announced a ban on direct statements on radio and television by organisations advocating the use of violence.

29 Nov. European Court of Human Rights ruled against detention without trial beyond four days.

1989

15 June General election in the Republic. Although Fianna Fáil gained the largest number of seats, it did not win sufficient support to form a government.

29 June Dáil assembled and failed to elect a Taoiseach.

12 July Charles J. Haughey elected Taoiseach and headed a coalition cabinet with the Progressive Democrats.

28 July Peter Brooke appointed NI Secretary of State.

14 Sept. Inauguration of University of Limerick.

1990

1 Jan. Amalgamation of the Irish Transport and General Workers' Union and the Federated Workers' Union of Ireland; Republic of Ireland took the presidency of the European Union for six months.

1 Mar. An appeal to the Supreme Court by Chris and Michael McGimpsey on the issue of Articles 2 and 3 of the Irish constitution was rejected. The court ruled that Articles 2 and 3 were a 'claim of legal right' over the 'national territory'. The court stated that the articles represented a 'constitutional imperative' rather than merely an aspiration.

13 Mar. The Supreme Court upheld the appeal of Dermot Finucane and James Clarke, who had escaped from the Maze prison in Sept. 1983, against extradition to Northern Ireland.

8 May Cardinal Tomás Ó Fiaich, Catholic Primate of All Ireland, died aged 66.

30 July Conservative MP Ian Gow, a supporter of Ulster Unionists, was killed by the IRA.

6 Nov. Cahal Daly was announced as the new Catholic Primate of All Ireland.

9 Nov. Mary Robinson was elected as ROI President having won on the second count.

13 Nov. Alan Dukes resigned as leader of Fine Gael.

20 Nov. John Bruton was elected as the new leader of Fine Gael.

21 Nov. Margaret Thatcher announced intention to resign as United Kingdom Prime Minister.

28 Nov. John Major appointed UK Prime Minister.

1991

14 Feb. Charges against Desmond Ellis, who had been extradited from the Republic to Britain, were changed when he appeared in court. This contravened Irish law and the incident sparked a row between the two countries.

14 Mar. Six men convicted of Birmingham pub bombings (1974) released by the Appeal Court.

6 Apr. The Irish Supreme Court rejected an application for the extradition of Owen Carron who had been charged with a firearms offence in NI but had fled to the Republic before his trial.

11 Apr. Haughey made the first official visit to NI by a Taoiseach since Seán Lemass in 1965.

30 Apr. Bilateral party talks on Northern Ireland began at Stormont.

26 June Convictions of Guilford four and Maguire seven for bombings in 1974 quashed by the Court of Appeal.

28 June Cahal Daly, Archbishop of Armagh, was elevated by the Pope to cardinal.

19 July A civilian from Dundalk was shot dead by the IRA who claimed that he had been a Garda Síochána informer, a claim denied by the Gardaí.

28 July The Ulster Freedom Fighters exploded seven incendiary devices in shops in the Republic.

4 Dec. John Major met Haughey in Dublin; it was the first visit by a British Prime Minister since 1980. The two leaders agreed to hold biannual meetings.

1992

20 Jan. In ROI Des Geraghy was to replace Proinsias De Rossa as Workers' Park MEP from Feb.

30 Jan. Haughey announced his resignation as both Taoiseach and leader of Fianna Fáil.

3 Feb. Robinson first ROI President to pay official visit to NI.

6 Feb. Albert Reynolds won leadership vote to head Fianna Fáil.

7 Feb. Maastricht Treaty signed.

11 Feb. Reynolds became Taoiseach (*see* 6 Feb.).

22 Feb. De Rossa together with five other Workers' Party TDs walked out of a party meeting in Dublin. They later announced that they were forming a new organisation. Initially the new party was called New Agenda. The split occurred when De Rossa failed to get an assurance from the Workers' Party that the organisation had ended its links with the Official Irish Republican Army (*see* 29 Mar.).

26 Feb. ROI Supreme Court lifted abortion injunction; Taoiseach met Major.

6 Mar. New round of all-party talks in NI announced.

11 Mar. Major announced UK general election for 9 Apr.

23 Mar. Adams handed in letter to Downing St, enclosing Sinn Féin policy document 'Towards a Lasting Peace in Ireland'.

29 Mar. New Agenda renamed Democratic Left (*see* 22 Feb.).

9 Apr. General election in the UK; John Major remained Prime Minister. IRA bomb in City of London killed three, injured 90.

11 Apr. Sir Patrick Mayhew appointed Secretary of State for Northern Ireland.

21 May ROI government impounded copies of *Guardian* newspaper containing advertisement for Marie Stopes clinics.

4 June Appeal Court in London quashed conviction of Judith Ward for M62 bombing in 1974.

18 June ROI referendum approved Maastricht Treaty.

1 July NI Royal Irish Regiment resulted from merger of Ulster Defence Regiment and Royal Irish Rangers.

10 Aug. UDA added to list of banned organisations in Northern Ireland.

16, 17 Sept. UK left Exchange Rate Mechanism.

21, 22 Sept. Molyneaux led a delegation from the UUP to talks in Dublin Castle, Dublin, with the Irish government. The topics discussed included constitutional matters, security co-operation, channels of communication between the two states, and identity and allegiance. The DUP did not attend. These were the first formal discussions by Unionists in Dublin since 1922.

6 Nov. The coalition government of ROI fell; a general election was called for 25 Nov.

10 Nov. NI political talks ended at Stormont.

25 Nov. ROI general election (*see* 6 Nov.).

7 Dec. Major visited Albert Reynolds in Dublin.

1993

12 Jan. ROI Albert Reynolds became Taoiseach in a Fianna Fáil–Labour coalition government. In NI UDA announced intention to target 'pan-nationalist front'.

19 Jan. In NI Opsahl Commission began public hearings.

17 Jan. ROI government established a new committee to monitor Northern Ireland policy.

30 Jan. ROI punt devalued by 10 per cent.

1, 2 Feb. In ROI Seanad election count.

20 Mar. Two IRA bombs in Warrington, England.

Apr. Neil Jordan awarded an Oscar for his screenplay *The Crying Game.*

20 Apr. In NI Molyneaux presented Major with UUP's 'Blueprint for Stability'.

24 Apr. Massive IRA bomb in the City of London.

19 May NI local elections.

27 May In the first official contact between an Irish president and a British monarch, Robinson travelled to London to attend a meeting with the Queen at Buckingham Palace.

3 June Bill making condoms freely available passed in Dáil by one vote.

9 June In NI Opsahl Commission report published.

10 June Jean Kennedy Smith, sister of the late president John F. Kennedy, the next American Ambassador to ROI.

18 June Robinson visited NI and shook hands with community leaders including Gerry Adams.

23 June ROI National Economic and Social Forum launched.

8 Aug. First nationalist parade allowed through centre of Belfast.

16 Aug. In ROI UN Human Rights Committee report identified Section 31 of the Broadcasting Act, treatment of travellers, Special Criminal Court and lack of availability of divorce as problems.

24 Aug. UK TV *Cook Report* named Martin McGuinness as an IRA leader; 25th anniversary of first civil rights march in NI.

1 Sept. Belfast City Council ban on Mary Robinson from any city-owned premises.

6 Sept. European Commission on Human Rights inquiry into Gibraltar killings of IRA operatives found that UK authorities had case to answer (*see* 6 Mar. 1988).

Sept. First participation of Irish military in UN peacekeeping action (Somalia).

5 Oct. In ROI Des O'Malley retired as president of Progressive Democrats.

11 Oct. ROI government launched National Plan to creat 200,000 new jobs.

12 Oct. In ROI Mary Harney elected PD leader (*see* 5 Oct.).

1 Nov. Maastricht Treaty came into force.

2 Nov. UK government published NI Structural Funds Plan.

10 Nov. In ROI FM 104 broadcast first condom advertisement.

11 Nov. In NI DUP published *Breaking the Logjam.*

14 Nov. In ROI Robinson attended ecumenical service of remembrance in St Patrick's Cathedral, Dublin.

15 Dec. Downing Street Declaration by UK/ROI governments.

1994

1 Jan. IRA bombed Linenhall Library, Belfast.

11 Jan. ROI government announced that order banning Sinn Féin from radio and TV would not be renewed from midnight 19 Jan.

16 Jan. UDA published plan that included transfer of three counties to ROI and removal of Catholics from remaining parts of NI.

19 Jan. First radio interview of Gerry Adams in ROI.

26 Jan. ROI budget introduced residential property tax.

30 Jan. Adams granted 48-hour visa to visit the USA.

11 Feb. UUP won parliamentary by-election in Belfast Victoria.

26 Feb. Alan Dukes and Michael Noon resigned from Fine Gael front bench.

23 Feb. Amalgamation of IDATU, INUVG and ATA (see glossary) to form new trade union.

25 Feb. In ROI High Court allowed extradition of Joseph Magee to face trial for murder of a British soldier.

28 Feb. UUP launched *Blueprint for Stability.*

9 Mar. House of Commons voted to set up a select committee on Northern Ireland affairs. IRA fired five mortar bombs at Heathrow Airport.

28 Mar. UK government released Roger Casement's diaries.

20 Apr. In UK Paul Hill's conviction for murder of a British soldier quashed by court of appeal.

19 May In response to Sinn Féin requests, the Northern Ireland Office issued a commentary on the Downing Street Declaration.

2 June Helicopter carrying 25 anti-terrorist experts crashed in Scotland killing all on board.

9 June European parliament and ROI local elections.

30 June ROI publication of NESF report, *Ending Long-term Unemployment.*

21 July Tony Blair elected leader of Labour Party in UK.

1 Aug. US Congress voted $19 million for Fund for Ireland.

31 Aug. IRA announced a 'complete cessation of military operations'.

14 Sept. IRA prisoners in letter in *Irish News* supported ceasefire and unarmed strategy.

16 Sept. UK ban on broadcast interviews with Sinn Féin lifted.

3 Oct. US government lifted ban on contacts with Sinn Féin.

4 Oct. Ken Maginnis and Gerry Adams appeared on *Larry King Live* in US.

13 Oct. The Combined Loyalist Military Council (CLMC) announced that it would cease all operational hostilities.

20 Oct. Marjorie (Mo) Mowlem became UK Labour Party spokesperson on NI.

21 Oct. British government lifted exclusion orders on Gerry Adams and Martin McGuiness which had barred them from entering Great Britain.

26 Oct. Forum for Peace and Reconciliation opened in Dublin Castle.

11 Nov. ROI by-elections won by Fine Gael and Democratic Left.

16 Nov. ROI Labour ministers resigned from government.

17 Nov. ROI government resigned.

20 Nov. Fianna Fáil elected Bertie Ahern party leader.

1 Dec. US President Clinton appointed former Senate majority leader George Mitchell special economic adviser on Ireland.

13 Dec. ROI Minister for Finance said public finances in surplus for the first time since 1967; Major launched Economic Forum in Belfast.

15 Dec. ROI coalition government formed from Fine Gael, Labour Party and Democratic Left. John Bruton, leader of Fine Gael, elected Taoiseach.

1995

2 Jan. Stormont debating chamber destroyed by fire.

15 Jan. Down GAA county convention voted to lift ban on members of RUC and British Army; first NI county to do so.

23 Jan. Respective heads of Catholic Church and Church of Ireland preached together in Canterbury.

27 Jan. ROI Taoiseach and Táaiste had first formal meeting with Sinn Féin president.

2 Feb. UUS won a parliamentary by-election in Newtownabbey, Co. Antrim.

7 Feb. ROI Dáil agreed to end the state of emergency declared in 1938 and renewed in 1976.

20 Feb. DUP issued *DUP Formula for Political Progress.*

21 Feb. UUP issued *A Practical Approach to Problem Solving in NI.*

22 Feb. ROI and UK governments published *Frameworks for the Future.*

9 Mar. US dropped ban on Adams raising money for Sinn Féin; Queen visited Belfast.

10 Mar. UUP rejected 'Frameworks' document.

14 Mar. Adams opened Sinn Féin office in Washington.

16 Mar. President Clinton shook hands with Adams in Washington.

24 Mar. NI troop patrols ceased from midnight.

25 Apr. In NI INLA stated it had operated ceasefire since July 1994.

12 May ROI President signed Abortion Information Act after Supreme Court found it constitutional.

31 May Prince Charles arrived in Dublin for two-day official visit.

1 June *Irish Press* board announced company would go into liquidation.

12 June UK Prevention of Terrorism Act renewed.

15 June Robert McCartney won North Down parliamentary by-election.

30 June Mildred Fox, daughter of late TD Johnny Fox, won Wicklow by-election as an Independent in ROI.

3 July UK Private Lee Clegg, sentenced to life imprisonment for the shooting of a joyrider, was released, resulting in widespread rioting in nationalist areas.

27 July ROI High Court found withholding tax unconstitutional.

28 Aug. In NI Molyneaux resigned as leader of the UUP.

8 Sept. In NI David Trimble elected leader of the UUP.

25 Sept. ROI censorship board lifted ban on *Playboy* magazine.

27 Sept. European Court of Human Rights ruled that the shooting of three unarmed IRA members on active service in Gibraltar in March 1988 breached the Human Rights Convention.

11 Oct. Cardinal Daly said Catholic Church would report all reasonable suspicions of child abuse to Garda.

26 Oct. Catholic bishops reiterated opposition to divorce.

27 Oct. The Queen and President Robinson shared their first public engagement, celebrating the 150th anniversary of the foundation of the Queen's University Belfast, University College Cork and University College Galway.

Oct. Seamus Heaney awarded the Nobel Prize for Literature.

26 Nov. ROI referendum on divorce carried.

28 Nov. Major and Taoiseach issue 12-point joint communiqué in Downing St.

10 Nov. – 1 Dec. Clinton visited both parts of Ireland.

12 Dec. ROI voted in UN General Assembly to condemn all nuclear testing.

13 Dec. Council of Europe report criticised treatment of prisoners by ROI.

21 Dec. Jack Charlton resigned as national football manager.

1996

23 Jan. Mitchell report on decommissioning released.

2 Feb. Report of the Forum for Peace and Reconciliation.

6 Feb. IRA bomb at Canary Wharf in London.

7 Feb. IRA ended ceasefire.

10 Feb. Bruton announced that the Irish government was breaking off ministerial contact with Sinn Féin in the light of the IRA bombing in London.

16 Feb. IRA bomb on bus in London.

28 Feb. Following meeting between Major and Bruton it was announced that all-party talks would begin on 10 June.

24 Mar. Dr Donal Murray installed as the Catholic Bishop of Limerick.

2 Apr. British government introduced legislation to widen powers of the Prevention of Terrorism Act.

3 Apr. Cecila Keaveney and Brian Leniham, Fianna Fáil, won by-elections in Donegal North East and Dublin West.

15 May Northern Ireland Forum to have 110 seats, 90 filled from the 18 parliamentary constituencies, each with five delegates. The remaining 20 seats to be distributed to the 10 parties (two each) with the highest total number of votes.

20 May Adams announced Sinn Féin would support Mitchell document.

30 May General election for the Northern Ireland Forum.

4 June Robinson began the first official state visit to Britain by an Irish head of state.

10 June Launch of negotiations for the peace process in NI.

15 June IRA bomb destroyed a shopping arcade in Manchester city centre.

20 June An IRA 'bomb factory' found by Gardí near Clonasee, Co. Laois. The government ended all contacts with Sinn Féin.

26 June Veronica Guerin, a Dublin journalist, murdered.

1 July ROI assumed EU presidency for six months.

13 July Seventeen people killed by bomb at Enniskillen.

29 July Multi-party talks in NI recessed until 9 Sept.

9 Sept. Multi-party talks resumed.

11 Sept. Bruton addressed a joint session of the US Congress.

13 Sept. On a trip to Belfast Robinson shook hands with Gerry Adams.

1 Oct. Cardinal Daly retired as Catholic Archbishop of Armagh (*see* 3 Nov.).

6 Oct. Beatification of Edmund Ignatius Rice, founder of the Christian Brothers and the Presentation Brothers.

31 Oct. Teilifís na Gaeilge, new Irish language television service, launched.

3 Nov. Sean Brady became Catholic Archbishop of Armagh and Primate of All Ireland (*see* 1 Oct.).

8 Nov. High Court in Belfast ruled that citizens of the ROI were eligible for appointments in the NI civil service.

8 Dec. Revd Martin Smyth resigned as Grand Master of the Orange Order, a post he had held since 1972.

1997

3 Jan. ROI government recorded revenue surplus of £3,000m.

26 Jan. Divorce became legal in ROI.

29 Jan. Announcement of new judicial body to review 'Bloody Sunday' (*see* 31 Jan., 19 Apr. 1972).

12 Mar. ROI President Mary Robinson announced that she would not be seeking a second term.

26 Mar. In NI the Parades Commission established to adjudicate on disputed marches.

1 May General election in UK; Labour victory.

2 May Tony Blair appointed Prime Minister.

3 May Mo Mowlam appointed Secretary of State for Northern Ireland.

16 May Taoiseach dissolved Dáil and called general election (*see* 6 June).

23 May Unionists lost control of Belfast City Council for first time.

1 June Blair apologised for Britain's failure to tackle the Irish potato famine of the 1840s.

6 June ROI general election; ruling coalition government of Fine Gael, Labour and Democratic Left obtained 77 seats but was defeated by a coalition of Fianna Fáil, Progressive Democrats, and a number of Independents, who obtained 81 seats. Sinn Féin won its first seat in the Dáil since its decision in 1986 to end its policy of abstentionism. The incoming government was led by Bertie Ahern (*see* 26 June).

12 June Robinson nominated United Nations High Commissioner for Human Rights.

26 June Ahern elected Taoseach.

19 July IRA announced it was restoring the 1994 ceasefire.

9 Aug. ROI government won clear majority in Seanad elections.

12 Aug. Adams received a visa to enter the USA.

26 Aug. UK and ROI governments signed agreement establishing an independent international commission on decommissioning in NI.

29 Aug. Mo Mowlam accepted the 'veracity' of the IRA ceasefire and invited Sinn Féin to join the multi-party talks in September.

2 Sept. ROI government declared that flags on all public buildings should be flown at half mast during the funeral of Princess Diana.

9 Sept. Sinn Féin formally signed the Mitchell principles on non-violence.

12 Sept. Robinson stepped down as President and became High Commissioner for Human Rights at the United Nations.

24 Sept. General John de Chastelain appointed chair of the independent commission on decommissioning.

29 Oct. A Labour Force Survey showed that the workforce stood at 1.3 million which was the highest level in the history of the ROI.

30, 31 Oct. Mary McAleese elected President of ROI.

5 Nov. IR Dick Spring resigned as leader of the Labour Party of ROI.

11 Nov. McAleese inaugurated as President (*see* 30, 31 Oct.).

13 Nov. Ruairi Quinn elected as the leader of the Labour Party.

1 Dec. Mo Mowlam announced RUC recruits no longer required to swear service to the Queen.

7 Dec. McAleese broke new ecumenical ground but caused controversy within the Catholic Hierarchy when she took communion at a Church of Ireland service in Christ Church Cathedral, Dublin.

11 Dec. Adams and Sinn Féin delegation visited Downing Street, the first such visit since December 1921.

27 Dec. Loyalist Volunteer Force (LVF) leader Billy Wright killed by the INLA inside the Maze prison.

1998

6 Jan. ROI economy in 1997 reported in surplus.

7 Jan. Mowlam visited the Maze prison to meet republican and loyalist prisoners in an attempt to prevent the collapse of the loyalist ceasefire and of the peace talks.

26 Jan. UUP left the peace talks.

30 Jan. Blair announced a new judicial inquiry into 'Bloody Sunday' (*see* 30 Jan., 19 Apr. 1972).

8 Feb. ROI government announced largest package of road funding.

19 Feb. Sinn Féin expelled from the peace talks.

7 Mar. ROI government confirmed intention to alter Articles 2 and 3 claiming sovereignty over the whole island in the 1937 constitution.

11 Mar. ROI by-elections in Limerick East and Dublin North returned Labour candidates Jan. O'Sullivan and Sean Ryan.

13 Mar. Adams outlined 'A Bridge to the Future', the Sinn Féin approach to multi-party talks.

19 Mar. EU Commission unveiled details of 'Agenda 2000' proposals for internal reform ahead of enlargement.

23 Mar. Sinn Féin returned to the peace talks.

29 Mar. Christian Brothers apologise to anyone ill-treated while in their care.

11 Apr. Belfast or Good Friday Agreement.

21 Apr. ROI Freedom of Information Act, which allowed access to personal information held by public bodies, came into effect.

27 Apr. ROI government announced that it would create a consultative committee on racism and inter-culturalism.

1 May Seamus Heaney was appointed Saoi of Aosdana, the highest award Ireland can bestow on an artist.

12 May UK Chancellor of the Exchequer announced 'A Framework for Prosperity' to boost NI economy.

19 May Hume and Trimble appeared on the same platform for the first time in support of a yes vote in the referendum on the Belfast Agreement.

22 May There was a huge turnout (NI 81.10 per cent, Yes 71.12 per cent, No 28.88 per cent; Republic 56.26 per cent, Yes 94.39 per cent, No 5.61 per cent) in the first all-Ireland poll since 1920 voted on the Good Friday Agreement.

In ROI the Amsterdam Treaty was ratified in a referendum: Yes 62 per cent, No 38 per cent.

25 June Elections to the new Northern Ireland Assembly.

1 July Trimble elected First Minister of NI Assembly; Seamus Mallon, SDLP, elected Deputy First Minister.

11 July Largest sporting event ever staged in Ireland, the Tour de France began in Dublin. The Tour was brought to Ireland because of the French link in the 1798 Rising by the United Irishmen.

6 Aug. Thomas McMahon, convicted of the murder of Earl Mountbatten and three other people in 1979, released from prison.

8, 9 Aug. LVF declared an 'absolute utter finish' to its paramilitary campaign.

15 Aug. Bomb exploded in Omagh (NI); the largest single death toll in any incident during the troubles.

19 Aug. Ahern announced the government's intention to introduce tough anti-terrorist measures to include seizure of land or other property which has been used for storing weapons or making bombs and that a suspect's right to silence would be withdrawn.

22 Aug. INLA announced ceasefire.

2 Sept. Dáil met to impose emergency measures consequent upon the Omagh bombing.

3 Sept. ROI anti-terrorism measures became law.

3, 4 Sept. President Clinton visited.

7 Sept. Real IRA declared a ceasefire.

9 Sept. Trimble and Adams met for the first time face to face.

10 Sept. First group of republican and loyalist prisoners from the Maze prison released under the Belfast Agreement.

19, 20 Sept. TV3, first commercial station in ROI, launched.

21 Sept. Michael Bell resigned as chairman of Labour parliamentary party.

16 Oct. Hume and Trimble awarded Noble Peace Prize (*see* 10 Dec.).

23 Oct. Simon Coveney, Fine Gael, won by-election to Dáil for Cork South Central.

29 Nov. Ruairi Quinn and Proinsias De Rossa agreed to merger of Labour and Democratic Left parties (*see* 12, 13 Dec.).

23 Nov. Ahern said that he believed a united Ireland was inevitable within 20 years.

26 Nov. Blair became the first British Prime Minister to address both houses of the Oireachtas (the Irish parliament) the Dáil and the Seanad.

30 Nov. ROI Central Statistical Office estimated that population was the highest in the history of the state.

1 Dec. Telecom Eireann's monopoly on voice transmission ended.

10 Dec. Hume and Trimble received Noble Peace Prize (*see* 16 Oct.).

12, 13 Dec. ROI Labour Party and Democratic Left agreed to merge.

18 Dec. First decommissioning of arms with destruction of some LVF weapons.

1999

1 Jan. Euro became the official currency of the ROI.

27 Jan. IRA informer, Eamon Collins, killed at Newry.

12–13 Mar. British army Private Lee Clegg cleared of murder, resulting in widespread disturbances in nationalist areas (NI). On 18 June, Clegg was sentenced to four years' and having already served these, was released from prison.

15 Mar. Solicitor representing Garvaghy Road residents, Rosemary Nelson, killed by car bomb.

1 Apr. Twenty hours of inter-party and intergovernmental talks at Hillsborough ended in deadlock on the issue of decommissioning.

28 Apr. ROI Justice Minister, John O'Donoghue, and Mo Mowlam established an Independent Commission for the Locations of Victims' Remains to search for bodies of IRA victims and grant criminal immunity. Sale of ROI company Cablelink suspended by High Court following allegations of insider dealing. It was announced that a committee was to be set up to deal with complaints against the ROI judiciary.

29 Apr. ROI Central Bank warned banks and building societies that they were lending too much to mortgage borrowers.

2–4 May Public tension between Taoiseach and Tánaiste over Philip Sheedy affair.

3 May Taoiseach met PLO leader Yasser Arafat in Dublin.

6 May Cablelink sold to NTL for £535m (ROI).

1 June First Sinn Féin councillor, Marie Moore, elected Deputy Mayor of Belfast.

12 June ROI local elections witnessed increase in Sinn Féin vote from 2.1 per cent to 3.5 per cent.

17 June An IRA informer in England, Martin McGartland, survived assassination attempt.

23 June ROI Education Minister, Michael Martin, announced that secondary school teachers who did not use Gaelic no longer needed to pass an exam in the language.

1–21 July Further attempts at breaking NI talks deadlock.

22 Aug. Allegations of government corruption levelled by Labour concerning the building of a new terminal at Dublin airport.

9 Sept. Chris Patten's Report on Policing in NI officially released.

30 Sept. Ian Paisley met Ahern in Dublin concerning sectarian attacks on Free Presbyterian churches in the Republic.

5 Oct. Peter Mandelson succeeded Mo Mowlam as NI Secretary of State.

18 Oct. For first time, ROI nurses held a national strike.

20 Oct. Jack Lynch died.

18 Nov. Following ten weeks of inter-party talks, George Mitchell released his final report on political progress.

23 Nov. RUC collectively awarded George Cross.

29 Nov. NI Assembly elected a 10-person power-sharing Executive; David Trimble as First Minister and Seamus Mallon as Deputy First Minister.

3 Dec. Twenty-seven years of direct rule ended as the NI Executive met for the first time at Stormont. North–South Ministerial Council met at Armagh.
16 Dec. McAleese in Oireaschas called for an 'inclusive Ireland' which was extended to immigrants as well.
17 Dec. British–Irish Council launched in London with ministers attending from ROI, NI, UK, Scotland, Wales, Channel Islands and Isle of Man.

2000

14 Jan. ROI government to establish judicial inquiry to investigate child abuse in state and religious primary and secondary schools.
22 Jan. David Andrews resigned as ROI Minister for Foreign Affairs.
31 Jan. Independent International Commission on Decommissioning reported that while IRA did not threaten peace process no decommissioning had taken place.
8, 9 Feb. Westminster House of Commons debated and passed Northern Ireland bill allowing implementation of direct rule.
11 Feb. Mandelson suspended NI Assembly.
12 Feb. Direct rule from London reimposed.
27 Mar. Saville Inquiry into Bloody Sunday began receiving oral evidence in Londonderry.
6 May Blair and Ahern issued joint statement committing British government to restoration of Assembly and Executive by 22 May.
29 May Power returned to devolved bodies in NI.
1 June Real IRA bomb at Hammersmith Bridge in London.
5 June Cathal Crumley elected first Sinn Féin mayor of Londonderry.
13 June Taoiseach promised to review budgetary increases in social welfare and to prevent profiteering in food, drink, petrol and housing prices.
23 June ROI High Court ruling gave prisoners right to vote.
1 Aug. ROI government approved development of a £4.3 billion metro system for Dublin.
6 Sept. Inquest into Omagh bomb began.
21 Sept. William McCrea (DUP) won South Antrim parliamentary by-election.
2 Oct. European Convention of Human Rights came into force in UK.
24 Oct. Mandelson used reserved powers to order the flying of Union Jack over seven government buildings on 17 designated days.
23 Nov. John Bruton defeated challenge to his leadership of Fine Gael.
1 Dec. Disqualifications bill which allowed members of Dáil to stand for election to the NI Assembly and Westminster parliament passed in UK parliament.
12 Dec. President Clinton made his third visit to Ireland.
16 Dec. UDA and UVF agreed truce in loyalist feud.

2001

25 Jan. Mandelson resigned as Secretary of State for NI.
30 Jan. Trimble's ban on Sinn Féin ministers attending North–South meetings declared unlawful by High Court judge in Belfast.

4 Mar. Catholic Primate, Archbishop Seán Brady, called for progress on decommissioning in NI.

8 Mar. IRA issued statement of intention to enter discussions with decommissioning body.

9 Apr. ROI Foreign Affairs Minister pledged IR£372,625 for 45 organisations in NI involved in cross-community activities.

12 Apr. Real IRA vowed to step up its campaign of violence.

30 May Disclosed that IRA had opened up two arms dumps for further inspection.

7 June NI general election and local government election. SF and DUP made gains at expense of SDLP and UUP.

20 June IRA announced that it would not bow to Unionists or British government on decommissioning.

1 July Trimble resigned as First Minister.

10 July UFF confirmed that ceasefire remained but withdrew support for Belfast Agreement.

12 July Orange Order parades ended in violence and riots.

1 Aug. Pro-Agreement parties received non-negotiable proposals from British and ROI governments.

13 Aug. Three IRA members arrested in Colombia for training anti-government guerrillas.

1 Sept. Pupils at Holy Cross Catholic Girls' Primary School run loyalist gauntlet on the first day of the new school year.

10 Sept. NI Assembly temporarily suspended.

11 Sept. Attacks on World Trade Center in New York and Pentagon in Washington.

12 Sept. Ahern announced that Friday would be a national day of mourning (ROI) for the victims of the terrorist attacks in the USA.

14 Sept. National day of mourning for the victims of the terrorist attacks in the USA. Ahern and McAleese led the mourning (ROI) at an ecumenical service in Dublin.

17 Sept. Hume announced that he was stepping down as leader of the SDLP (*see* 28 Sept.).

22 Sept. Secretary of State Reid announced further one-day suspension of NI Assembly.

28 Sept. Mark Durkan became leader of SDLP (*see* 17 Sept.).

14 Oct. Ten IRA men, including Kevin Barry, who had been executed by British authorities during the War of Independence reburied in Glasnevin cemetery following a mass at the Pro-Cathedral.

21 Oct. Adams called for IRA to move on decommissioning.

5 Nov. Police Service of Northern Ireland formally came into existence, replacing RUC.

6 Nov. Trimble re-elected First Minister; Durkin elected Deputy First Minister.

18 Nov. GAA rule 21 banning police and members of British army from playing football and hurling abolished.

ELECTIONS

Electorate and votes at general elections

NB Electorate and votes recorded in thousands

Ireland (Westminster)

	Total electorate	Electorate in contested seats	Votes recorded	Seats contested	Unopposed returns
1832	90	65	89	69	34
1835	98	56	60	56	47
1837	122	64	65	50	53
1841	94	44	49	34	69
1847	125	59	32	41	62
1852	164	109	132	71	32
1857	191	118	142	58	45
1859	200	66	93	41	62
1865	203	83	93	48	55
1868	223	74	93	36	67
1874	223	183	225	83	18
1880	229	194	251	86	15
1885	738	592	451	80	21
1886	738	245	195	32	69
1892	741	569	393	81	20
1895	732	289	221	42	59
1900	758	233	149	32	69
1906	687	164	135	21	80
1910 Jan.	684	263	221	40	63
1910 Dec.	684	264	208	41	62
1918	1,926	1,451	1,039	76	25

Irish Free State/Éire/Republic of Ireland (Dáil Éireann)

NB Until 1937 the figures exclude university electors and seats

	Electorate	Votes recorded
1927 June	1,725	1,775
1927 Sept.	1,725	1,991
1932	1,688	1,292
1933	1,720	1,397
1937	1,775	1,352
1938	1,770	1,302
1943	1,816	1,348
1944	1,816	1,230
1948	1,800	1,337
1951	1,785	1,344
1954	1,763	1,348
1957	1,738	1,239
1961	1,671	1,180
1965	1,683	1,264
1969	1,735	1,335
1973	1,784	1,366
1977	2,119	1,617
1981	2,275	1,734
1982 Feb.	2,275	1,680
1982 Nov.	2,335	1,701
1987	2,446	1,794
1989	2,449	1,678
1992	2,557	1,751
1997	2,741	1,807
2002	3,002	1,879

Source: *Dáil Éireann 29th Dáil Election, May 2002: Election Results and Transfer of Votes* (Dublin, 2003), p. 56; available online: <www.irlgov.ie/oireachtas/a-misc/ELEC02%20-%2001.PDF>.

Northern Ireland (Westminster)

	Total electorate	Electorate in contested seats	Votes recorded	Seats contested	Unopposed returns
1922	609	161	208	3	9
1923	615	210	242	4	8
1924	610	522	519	10	2
1929	772	573	510	9	3
1931	773	252	282	4	8
1935	805	401	451	6	6
1945	836	767	720	11	1
1950	865	725	561	10	2
1951	872	580	463	8	4
1955	873		647	12	–

	Total electorate	Electorate in contested seats	Votes recorded	Seats contested	Unopposed returns
1959	875		576	12	–
1964	891		638	12	–
1966	902		596	12	–
1970	1,017		779	12	–
1974 Feb.	1,027		718	12	–
1974 Oct.	1,037		702	12	–
1979	1,027		696	12	–
1983	1,049		765	17	–
1987	–		730	17	–
1992	–		785	17	–
1997	1,175		791	18	–
2001	1,191		810	18	–

Dáil elections, 1918–2002

Parties that formed the new government in bold

1st Dáil (1918)	70 SF	(no vote totals – see below)					
2nd Dáil (1921)	125 SF	(no vote totals – see below)					
3rd Dáil (1922)	**58 pro-Treaty***	35 anti-Treaty*	17 Lab	7 Fmr	11 oth*		
	38.5%	21.3%	21.4%	7.9%			
4th Dáil (1923)	**63 CnaG**	44 Republicans	15 Fmr	14 Lab	17 oth**		
	39.0%	27.4%	12.1%	10.6%			
5th Dáil (June 1927)	**47 CnaG**	44 FF	22 Lab	11 Fmr	8 NL	5 SF	16 oth
	27.4%	26.2%	12.6%	8.9%	7.3%	3.6%	
6th Dáil (Sept. 1927)	**62 CnaG**	57 FF	13 Lab	6 Fmr	2 NL	13 oth**	
	38.6%	35.2%	9.1%	6.4%	1.6%		
7th Dáil (1932)	**72 FF**	57 CnaG	7 Lab	4 Fmr	13 oth**		
	44.5%	35.2%	7.7%	2.0%			
8th Dáil (1933)	**77 FF**	48 CnaG	11 NCP	8 Lab	9 oth**		
	49.7%	30.4%	9.2%	5.7%			
9th Dáil (1937)	**69 FF**	48 FG	13 Lab	8 oth			
	45.2%	34.8%	10.3%				
10th Dáil (1938)	**77 FF*****	45 FG***	9 Lab	7 oth			
	51.9%	33.3%	10.0%				
11th Dáil (1943)	**67 FF**	32 FG	17 Lab	13 CnaT	9 Inds		
	41.8%	23.1%	15.7%	9.0%			
12th Dáil (1944)	**76 FF**	30 FG	11 CnaT	8 Lab	4 Nat Lab	9 Inds	
	48.9%	20.5%	10.8%	8.7%	2.7%		
13th Dáil (1948)	68 FF	**31 FG**	**14 Lab**	**10 CnaP**	**7 CnaT**	**5 Nat Lab**	12 Inds
	41.9%	**19.8%**	**8.7%**	**13.3%**	**5.5%**	**2.6%**	
14th Dáil (1951)	**69 FF**	40 FG	16 Lab	6 CnaT	2 CnaP	14 Inds	
	46.3%	25.8%	11.4%	2.9%	4.1%		
15th Dáil (1954)	65 FF	**50 FG**	**19 Lab**	**5 CnaT**	3 CnaP	5 Inds	
	43.4%	**32.0%**	**12.1%**	**3.1%**	3.8%		
16th Dáil (1957)	**78 FF**	40 FG	13 Lab	4 SF	3 CnaT	1 CnaP	8 Inds
	48.3%	26.6%	9.1%	5.4%	2.4%	1.7%	
17th Dáil (1961)	**70 FF**	47 FG	16 Lab	2 CnaT	2 NPD	1 CnaP	6 oth
	43.8%	32.0%	11.7%	1.5%	1.0%	1.1%	
18th Dáil (1965)	**72 FF**	47 FG	22 Lab	1 CnaP	2 Inds		
	47.7%	34.1%	15.4%	0.8%			

19th Dáil (1969)	**75 FF**	50 FG	18 Lab	1 Ind			
	44.6%	33.3%	16.6%				
20th Dáil (1973)	69 FF	**54 FG**	**19 Lab**	2 Inds			
	46.2%	**35.1%**	**13.7%**				
21st Dáil (1977)	**84 FF**	43 FG	17 Lab	4 Inds			
	50.6%	30.6%	11.6%				
22nd Dáil (1981)	78 FF	**65 FG**	**15 Lab**	2 H-Blocks	1 SFWP	5 Inds	
	45.3%	**36.5%**	**9.9%**	3.1%	1.7%		
23rd Dáil	**81 FF**	63 FG	15 Lab	3 SFWP	4 Inds		
(Feb. 1982)	**47.3%**	37.3%	9.1%	2.2%			
24th Dáil	75 FF	**70 FG**	**16 Lab**	2 WP	3 Inds		
(Nov. 1982)	45.2%	**39.2%**	**9.4%**	3.3%			
25th Dáil (1987)	**81 FF**	51 FG	14 PD	12 Lab	4 WP	4 oth	
	44.2%	27.1%	11.9%	6.5%	3.8%		
26th Dáil (1989)	**77 FF**	55 FG	15 Lab	7 WP	**6 PD**	1 Gr	5 Inds
	44.2%	29.3%	9.5%	5.0%	**5.5%**	1.5%	
27th Dáil (1992)	**68 FF******	45 FG****	**33 Lab******	10 PD	4 DL****	1 Gr	5 Inds
	39.1%	24.5%	**19.5%**	4.7%	2.8%	1.4%	
28th Dáil (1997)	**76 FF**	55 FG	17 Lab	**4 PD**	4 DL	2 Gr	1 SF 7 oth
	39.3%	27.9%	10.4%	**4.7%**	2.5%	2.8%	2.5%
29th Dáil (2002)	**81 FF**	31 FG	22 Lab	**8 PD**	6 Gr	5 SF	14 oth
	41.5%	22.5%	10.8%	**4.0%**	3.8%	6.5%	

* 1922: 17 pro-Treaty, 16 anti-Treaty and 4 independent TDs were elected unopposed.

** 1923: September 1927, 1932, and 1933, 3 independent TDs were elected unopposed (representing Dublin University).

*** 1938: 4 Fianna Fail and 2 Fine Gael TDs were elected unopposed.

**** 1994: the Fianna Fail/Labour coalition broke down and was replaced by a Fine Gael/Labour/Democratic Left coalition.

Source: <www.ark.ac.uk/elections>

Key:

SF	Sinn Féin
FF	Fianna Fail
FG	Fine Gael
Lab	Labour
Fmr	Farmers' Party
CnaG	Cumann na nGaedheal
NL	National League
Oth	Others
CnaT	Clann na Talmhan
Nat Lab	National Labour Party
NCP	National Centre Party
Inds	Independents
SFWP	Sinn Féin the Workers' Party
CnaP	Clann na Poblachta
NPD	National Progressive Democrats
PD	Progressive Democrats
H-Blocks	H-Block Prisoners
Gr	Green Party
WP	Workers' Party
DL	Democratic Left

123

Presidential elections

1938

Dr Douglas Hyde was the only nomination and was duly declared elected. He was inaugurated as President on 25 June 1938.

1945

This three-way contest took place on 14 June 1945 and was won by Sean T. O'Kelly on the second count. He was inaugurated as President on 25 June 1945.

Electorate	Percentage poll	Total poll	Quota
1,803,463	63.02	1,136,625	543,170

Candidate	1st preference	%	Transfer of McCartan's vote	%	Result	%
Patrick McCartan (Ind.)	212,834	19.59	−212,834			
Sean MacEoin (FG)	335,539	30.89	+117,886	55.39	453,425	44.50
Sean T. O'Kelly (FF)	537,965	49.52	+27,200	12.78	565,165	55.49
Non-Transferable Papers			67,748	31.83		
Total	1,086,338	100		100	1,018,590	

1952

President O'Kelly was the only candidate and was duly declared elected. He was inaugurated as President on 25 June 1952.

1959

This two-way contest took place on 17 June 1959. Eamon de Valera was the winner and he was inaugurated as President on 25 June 1959.

Electorate	Turnout	Total poll	Quota
1,678,450	58.37	979,628	477,770

Candidate	Votes	%
Eamon de Valera (FF)	538,003	56.30
Sean MacEoin (FG)	417,536	43.70
Total	955,539	100

1966

This two-way contest took place on 1 June 1966 and was won by Eamon de Valera. He was inaugurated as President on 25 June 1966.

Electorate	Turnout	Total poll	Quota
1,709,161	65.35	1,116,915	553,503

Candidate	Votes	%
Eamon de Valera (FF)	558,861	50.48
Thomas F. O'Higgins (FG)	548,144	49.52
Total	1,107,005	100

1973

Two candidates contested this election which took place on 30 May 1973. Erskine Childers was the victor and he was inaugurated as President on 25 June 1973.

Electorate	Turnout	Total poll	Quota
1,977,817	62.22	1,230,584	611,820

Candidate	Votes	%
Erskine Childers (FF)	635,867	51.97
Thomas F. O' Higgins (FG)	587,771	48.03
Total	1,230,584	100

1974

The election was brought about by the death of President Childers on 17 June 1974. Cearbhall O'Dalaigh was the only nomination for President and was duly declared elected. He was inaugurated as President on 19 December 1974.

1976

President O'Dalaigh resigned on 22 October 1976. Dr Patrick Hillery was the only nomination for the election and was duly declared elected. He was inaugurated as President on 3 December 1976.

1983

President Hillery was elected unopposed. He was inaugurated as President on 3 December 1983.

1990

In a three-way contest, Mary Robinson won the election on the second count. She was inaugurated as President on 3 December 1990.

Electorate	Turnout	Total poll	Quota
2,471,308	64.10	1,584,095	787,326

Candidate	1st preference	%	Transfer of Currie's vote	%	Result	%
Austin Currie (FG)	267,902	17.01	−267,902			
Brian Lenihan (FF)	694,484	44.10	+36,789	13.73	731,273	47.21
Mary Robinson (Ind.)	612,265	38.89	+205,565	76.73	817,830	52.79
Non-transferable votes			25,548	9.54		
Total	1,574,651	100		100	1,549,103	100

1997

This election was contested by a record five candidates and was won by Mary McAleese on the second count. She was inaugurated as President on 11 November 1997.

Electorate	Turnout	Total poll	Quota
2,471,308	64.10	1,574,651	787,326

Candidate	1st preference	%	Transfer of Nally, Roche and Scallon's votes	%	Result	%
Mary Banotti (FG)	372,002	29.30	+125,514	38.81	497,516	41.35
Mary McAleese (FF)	574,424	45.24	+131,835	40.76	706,259	58.67
Derek Nally (Ind.)	59,529	4.69	−59,529			
Adi Roche (Ind.)	88,423	6.96	−88,423			
Dana Rosemary Scallon (Ind.)	175,458	13.82	−175,458			
Non-transferable votes			66,061	20.43		
Total	1,269,836	100		100	1,203,775	100

Index of parliamentary candidates, 1801–1921

The names of all candidates are listed, along with the names of the constituencies they contested. For a successful candidate the dates between which the seat was held are given; for an unsuccessful candidate the date of the contest. Where a member subsequently lost his seat, this is indicated by '(def.)' after the year of his defeat, and where a member was elected at a by-election in the year of a general election this is marked by '(by)' after the date; '(by)' is also used to signify a candidate defeated in similar circumstances. Where membership ends in death, this is shown by '(d.)' after the final date.

Abbott, William, Cork City, 1868
Abraham, William, Limerick West, 1885–92; Cork North-East, 1893–1910(Jan.) (def.); Dublin Harbour, 1910(by)–15 (d.)
Acheson, Viscount (Archibald Acheson), Armagh Co., 1801–7, 1830–47
Acton, Lt Col. William, Wicklow Co., 1832, 1837, 1841–8
Adair, Charles, Carrickfergus, 1830
Adair, Sir R. S., bt, Antrim Co., 1869
Adams, A. A., Down North, 1906
Adams, P. F., Kings Co. (Tullamore), 1914
Agar-Ellis, Hon. L. G. F., Kilkenny Co., 1852, 1857–74 (def.)
Ahern, Jeremiah, Cork South-East, 1910(Dec.)
Aird, J. J., Queen's Co. (Ossory), 1916
Alcock, W. C., Waterford City, 1801–2 (unseated on petition); Wexford Co., 1806(by), 1807–12
Alexander, Henry, Londonderry City, 1801–20
Alexander, Viscount (J. D. Alexander), Tyrone Co., 1835, 1837–9
Alexander, John, Carlow, 1853–9 (def.)
Alexander, Leslie, Coleraine, 1837
Alexander, Nathaniel, Antrim Co., 1841(by)–52
Alexander, R. J., Londonderry Co., 1874
Alexander, S. M., Londonderry Co., 1878, 1880
Alexander, W. H., Belfast (St Anne's), 1918
Allanson-Winn, R. G., Kerry South, 1892
Allen, Lt Col. W. J., Armagh North, 1917–22
Allman, R. L., Bandon, 1880, 1880(by)–5
Ambrose, Dr Daniel, Louth South, 1892–6 (d.)
Ambrose, Dr Robert, Mayo West, 1893–1910(Jan.)
Anderson, H. A., Londonderry North, 1918–19
Anderson, Sir RN, Londonderry City, 1918
Andrews, Charles, QC, Kinsale, 1874
Andrews, W. D., LL D, QC, Down Co., 1878
Annesley, Lt Col. Hon. Hugh, Cavan Co., 1857–74
Anstey, T. C., Youghal, 1847–52
Archbold, Robert, Kildare Co., 1837–47
Archdale, Lt E. M., Fermanagh North, 1898–1903, 1916–22

Archdale, W. H., Fermanagh Co., 1874–85; Fermanagh North, 1886
Archdall, Mervyn (sen.), Fermanagh Co., 1801–2
Archdall, Lt Gen. Mervyn, Fermanagh Co., 1802–34
Archdall, Capt. M. E., Fermanagh Co., 1834–74
Archdall, Richard, Kilkenny City, 1801 (by)–2; Dundalk, 1802–6
Armstrong, Sir Andrew, bt, King's Co., 1841 (by)–52
Armstrong, H. B., Armagh Mid, 1921–2
Armstrong, Richard, Sligo, 1865–8
Arnold-Forster, H. O., Belfast West, 1892–1906
Arnott, D. T., Youghal, 1880
Arnott, Sir John, Kinsale, 1859–63
Arundel and Surrey, Earl of (H. G. F. Howard), Limerick City, 1851–2
Atkinson, Rt Hon. John, QC, Londonderry North, 1895–1906
Attwood, M. W., Kinsale, 1841
Austin, Michael, Limerick West, 1892–1900

Bagenal, Philip, Carlow, 1837
Bagenal, Walter, Carlow Co., 1802–6, 1812
Bagenal, William, Carlow Co., 1806–12
Bagwell, Lt Col. John, Cashel, 1801–2
Bagwell, John, Tipperary Co., 1801–6 1807, 1812
Bagwell, John, Clonmel, 1832, 1835, 1857 (by)–74 (def.)
Bagwell, Richard, Cashel, 1801–1
Bagwell, Col. Rt Hon. William, Clonmel, 1801 (by)–19; Tipperary Co., 1819 (by)–26
Baillie, J. E., Tralee, 1813 (by)–18
Baldwin, Dr Herbert, Cork City, 1830, 1832–7
Ball, Francis, Drogheda, 1832
Ball, F. E., Dublin Co. South, 1900
Ball, John, Sligo, 1848; Carlow Co., 1852–7; Sligo Co., 1857; Limerick City, 1858
Ball, Rt Hon., J. T., LL D, QC, Dublin University, 1865, 1868–75
Ball, Nicholas, Clonmel, 1836–9
Bambridge, Capt. J. H., RN, Cork City, 1885
Barbour, J. D., Lisburn, 1863 (unseated on petition), 1865; Antrim South, 1885
Barbour, Robert, Lisburn, 1863
Barclay, Charles, Dundalk, 1826–30
Barker, W. P., Tipperary Co., 1837
Barnes, Dermot, Belfast (St Anne's), 1918
Barnett, W. D., Portarlington, 1874
Barrett-Hamilton, Capt. Samuel, Wexford South, 1892
Barrie, H. T., Londonderry North, 1906–18, 1919–22 (d.)
Barrington, John, Waterford City, 1865
Barrington, Jonah, Dublin City, 1802
Barron, Sir H. W., bt, Waterford City, 1832–47 (def.), 1848–52 (def.), 1857, 1859, 1865–8 (def.), 1869 (elected but unseated on petition)

Barron, Lt John, Waterford Co., 1830(by)

Barron, P. G., Dungarvan, 1834, 1834

Barry, C. R., QC, Dungarvan, 1865–8 (def.)

Barry, Edward, Cork South, 1892–1940(Dec.) (def.)

Barry, G. R., Cork Co., 1865–7 (d.)

Barry, Q. S., Cork Co., 1832–41

Barry, J. R., Bandon, 1835

Barry, John, Wexford Co., 1880–5; Wexford South, 1885–93

Barry, Michael, Cork North, 1910(Jan.)

Barry, R. J., KC, Tyrone North, 1907–11

Barton, Capt. C. R., Fermanagh Co., 1874

Barton, Lt Col., Christopher, Tipperary South, 1885

Barton, D. P., QC, Armagh Mid, 1891–1900

Barton, R. C., Wicklow West, 1918–22

Barton, S. W., Tipperary Co., 1838

Barton, T. H., Clonmel, 1852

Barton, T. J., Roscommon Co., 1835

Barton, William, Tipperary Co., 1818

Bateman, John, Kerry Co., 1830; Tralee, 1837 (elected but unseated on petition)

Battersby, T. S. F., KC, Fermanagh South, 1900, 1910(Jan.)

Bateson, Sir Robert, bt, Londonderry Co., 1830–42

Bateson, Robert, Londonderry Co., 1842–4 (d.)

Bateson, Thomas, Londonderry Co., 1844–57

Baxter, Robert, Londonderry City, 1870

Baxter, Sir W. J., Antrim North, 1910(Jan.)

Bayley, R. P., Athlone, 1859, 1868

Bayley, W. M., Kilkenny City, 1830

Beamish, F. B., Cork City, 1837–41, 1853–65

Beaslai, Pierce, Kerry East, 1918–22

Beattie, Andrew, Down West, 1907, 1908

Beattie, A. J., Down West, 1905

Becher, R. H., Cork Co., 1832

Becher, W. W., Mallow, 1818–26

Bective, Earl of (Thomas Taylor), Meath Co., 1812–30

Beddoes, Major H. R., Antrim East, 1906

Belfast, Earl of (G. H. Chichester), Carrickfergus, 1818–20; Belfast, 1820–30; Antrim Co., 1830–7; Belfast, 1837 (elected but unseated on petition); Belfast, 1841

Bellew, Hon. C. B., Kilkenny North, 1885

Bellew, Sir Patrick, bt, Louth Co., 1831(by)–2, 1834–7

Bellew, R. M., Louth Co., 1830, 1832–52, 1857, 1859–65

Bellew, Capt. T. A., Galway Co., 1852–7 (def.)

Bellingham, A. H., Louth Co., 1880(by)–5

Bennet, Capt. R. H. A., RN, Enniskillen, 1807(by)–7

Bennett, J. H., Belfast (Pottinger), 1918

Bennett, T. W. W., Limerick East, 1910(Jan.)

Bent, John, Sligo, 1818–20

Beresford, Lord Charles, Waterford Co., 1874–80 (def.)

Beresford, D. W. P., Carlow Co., 1862–8

Beresford, G. de la P., Athlone, 1841 (elected but unseated on petition), 1843

Beresford, Capt. G. de la P., Armagh City, 1875–85

Beresford, Lord G. T., Londonderry Co., 1802–12; Coleraine, 1812–14; Waterford Co., 1814(by)–26 (def.), 1830(by)–1

Beresford, Rt Hon. John, Waterford Co., 1801–6 (d.); Enniskillen, 1802 (elected to sit for Waterford Co.)

Beresford, J. B., Londonderry Co., 1874

Beresford, J. C., Dublin City, 1801–4; Waterford Co., 1806(by)–11

Beresford, Sir J. P., bt, Coleraine, 1809–12, 1814–23, 1832 (elected but unseated on petition)

Beresford, Major William, Waterford City, 1837

Beresford, Field Marshal Sir W. C., Waterford Co., 1811(by)–14

Bernard, Viscount (Francis Bernard), Bandon, 1831(by)–31(by) (def.); Cork Co., 1832, 1835; Bandon, 1842–57

Bernard, Col. Hon. H. B., Bandon, 1863–8 (def.)

Bernard, Viscount (James Bernard), Youghal, 1806–7, 1818–20; Cork Co., 1807–18; Bandon, 1820–6, 1830–1

Bernard, Viscount (J. F. Bernard), Bandon, 1874

Bernard, Capt. P. B., Bandon, 1880–80(by)

Bernard, Hon. R. B., Bandon, 1812–15

Bernard, Capt. Thomas, King's Co., 1841(by), 1852

Bernard, Col. Thomas, King's Co., 1802–32 (def.)

Bernard, Capt. T. S. W., King's Co. (Birr), 1885, 1886

Bernard, Lt Col. Hon. W. S., Bandon, 1832–5, 1857–63

Best, R. D., Armagh South, 1909

Biggar, J. G., Londonderry City, 1872; Cavan Co., 1874–85; Cavan West, 1885–90 (d.)

Biggs, Jacob, Bandon, 1832

Binden, Burton, Clare Co., 1830

Bingham, Lord (George Bingham), Mayo Co., 1865–74

Bingham, Lord G. C., Mayo Co., 1826–30

Black, Samuel, Antrim Co., 1880

Blackall, Major S. W., Longford Co., 1847–51

Blacker, St I. T., Armagh Co., 1880

Blackney, Walter, Carlow Co., 1832–5

Blane, Alexander, Armagh South, 1885–92 (def.); Westmeath North, 1892

Blake, Hon. Edward, QC, Longford South, 1892–1907

Blake, J. A., Waterford City, 1857–69; Waterford Co., 1880–4; Carlow Co., 1886(by)–7 (d.)

Blake, J. C., Cork City, 1895, 1900

Blake, Mark, Mayo Co., 1840–6

130

Blake, M. J., Galway, 1832(def. but elected on petition)–57

Blake, Sir Valentine, bt, Galway, 1812(elected after petition)–20 (def.), 1830, 1838, 1841–7 (d.)

Blake, V. O'C., Roscommon, 1847

Blake, Col. Xaverius, Galway Co., 1832

Blakiston-Houston, John, Down North, 1898–1900

Bland, L. H., QC, King's Co., 1852–9 (def.)

Blayney, Hon. C. D., Monaghan Co., 1830–4

Blennerhassett, Arthur, Kerry Co., 1837–41 (def.)

Blennerhassett, Sir Rowland, bt, Galway, 1865–74; Kerry Co., 1880–5; Dublin (Harbour), 1885

Blennerhassett, R. P., Kerry Co., 1872–85

Bligh, Hon. J. D., Meath Co., 1831(by)

Bligh, Thomas, Meath Co., 1802–12

Bloomfield, F. G., Waterford City, 1885

Bloomfield, J. C., Fermanagh North, 1885

Blunden, Lt Col. Overington, Kilkenny City, 1812–14

Blythe, Ernest, Armagh North, 1918; Monaghan North, 1918–22

Boddington, Samuel, Tralee, 1807(by)–1807

Bodkin, J. J., Galway, 1831–2; Galway Co., 1835–47

Bodkin, M. McD., Roscommon North, 1892–5

Boland, H. J., Roscommon South, 1918–22

Boland, J. P., Kerry South, 1900–18

Bolton, Cornelius, Waterford Co., 1806; Waterford City, 1807

Bond, J. W. McG., Armagh City, 1855–7 (def.), 1859–65

Bowman, Alexander, Belfast North, 1885

Bowyer, Sir George, bt, Dundalk, 1852–68 (def.); Wexford Co., 1874–80

Bourke, Hon. H. L., Meath Co., 1880

Bourke, R. S. (afterwards Lord Naas), Kildare Co., 1847–52(by)

Bourne, James, Wexford, 1841

Bourne, W. S., Bandon, 1815–18

Boyd, John, LL D, Coleraine, 1843–52(by), 1857–62 (d.)

Boyd, RN, Tyrone South, 1910(Dec.)

Boyle, Capt. Hon. Courtenay, RN, Bandon, 1806–7

Boyle, Daniel, Mayo North, 1910(Jan.)–18 (def.)

Boyle, Viscount (Henry Boyle), Cork Co., 1801–7; Bandon, 1807; Youghal, 1807 (elected for both but succeeded as Lord Carleton and Earl of Bandon)

Boyle, James, Donegal West, 1900–2

Boyle, J. A., Tyrone Co., 1839

Boyle, Hon. John, Cork Co., 1827–30; Cork City, 1830–2 (def.)

Boyle, Viscount (Richard Boyle), Cork Co., 1830–2

Boyle, Hon. Robert, Cork Co., 1868

Brabazon, Lord (W. C. Brabazon), Dublin Co., 1830–2, 1837–41 (def.)

Brabazon, Sir W. J., bt., Mayo Co., 1832, 1835–40 (d.)

Brady, D. C., Newry, 1835–7 (def.)

Brady, F. W., Dublin City, 1857, 1859
Brady, James, Dublin Harbour, 1910(Dec.)
Brady, Dr John, Leitrim Co., 1852–80
Brady, P. J., Dublin (St Stephen's Green), 1910(Jan.)–18 (def.)
Brazier-Creagh, Capt. K. A. A., Mallow, 1874
Brewster, R. A. F., Portarlington, 1883–5
Bridgeman, Hewitt, Ennis, 1832, 1835–47
Bridgeman, Hewitt, jnr., Ennis, 1832
Brine, Capt. Frederick, Kinsale, 1859
Briscoe, J. C., Dublin (College Green), 1918
Brodigan, Francis, Drogheda, 1857, 1865, 1868
Brooke, Sir A. B., bt, Fermanagh Co., 1840–54 (d.)
Brooke, Sir A. D., bt, Fermanagh South, 1895
Brooke, Frank, Fermanagh South, 1885, 1886
Brooke, Sir Henry, bt, Fermanagh Co., 1806, 1807, 1812, 1823, 1830
Brooke, H. V., Donegal Co., 1801–2, 1806–8 (d.)
Brooke, Richard, Fermanagh Co., 1806
Brooke, Thomas, Fermanagh Co., 1830
Brooks, Maurice, Dublin City, 1874–85
Brown, J. S., Belfast, 1880, Down Co., 1885(by); Down North, 1885
Brown, T. W., KC, Down North, 1918–22(by)
Brown, W. H., Londonderry North, 1910(Dec.)
Browne, Arthur, Roscommon, 1835
Browne, Rt Hon. Denis, Mayo Co., 1801–18; Kilkenny City, 1820–6
Browne, Dominick, Mayo Co., 1814–26, 1830–6
Browne, G. E., Mayo Co., 1870–8 (def.)
Browne, James, Mayo Co., 1818–31
Browne, John, Mayo Co., 1831–5 (def.), 1836
Browne, J. D., Mayo Co., 1847
Browne, Sir J. E., bt, Mayo Co., 1806
Browne, Lord J. T., Mayo Co., 1857(by)–68
Browne, R. C., Carlow, 1852
Browne, R. D., Mayo Co., 1836–50 (d.)
Browne, Hon. William, Kerry Co., 1830–1, 1841–7
Brownlow, Charles, Armagh Co., 1818–32
Brownlow, William, Armagh Co., 1807(by)–15 (d.)
Bruce, Sir H. H., bt, Coleraine, 1843, 1847, 1862–74 (def.), 1880–5; Londonderry Co., 1857
Bruce, P. C., Dundalk, 1807(by)–8
Bruen, Francis, Carlow, 1832, 1835–7 (def.), 1839 (elected but unseated on petition)
Bruen, Col. Henry, Carlow Co., 1812–31, 1832, 1835–7 (def.), 1840–53 (d.)
Bruen, Henry, Carlow Co., 1857–80 (def.)
Brugha, Cathal, Waterford Co., 1918–22
Brunskill, G. F., Tyrone Mid, 1910(Jan.)–1910(Dec.) (def.)
Bryan, Major George, Kilkenny Co., 1837–43(d.)

Bryan, G. L., Kilkenny Co., 1865–80

Brydges, Sir J. W. H., Coleraine, 1823–31 (unseated on petition); Armagh City, 1831(by)–2

Buckley, Daniel, Kildare North, 1918–22

Bunbury, Thomas, Carlow Co., 1837(by), 1837, 1841–6 (d.)

Burgess, J. Y., Armagh Co., 1826

Burgh, Sir U. B., Carlow Co., 1818–26

Burke, Viscount (H. G. de Burgh-Canning), Galway Co., 1867–71

Burke, J. M., Cork South-East, 1910(Jan.)

Burke, Sir John, bt, Galway Co., 1830–2 (def.)

Burke, Robert, Galway, 1837; Kildare Co., 1837

Burke, S. A., Tipperary Mid, 1918–22

Burke, Sir T. J., bt, Galway Co., 1847(by)–65

Burn, T. H., Belfast (St Anne's), 1918–22

Burroughs, William, Enniskillen, 1802(by)–6

Burrowes, Robert, Cavan Co., 1855–7

Burton, Hon. F. N., Clare Co., 1801–8

Burton, F. N. V., Clare Co., 1877

Burton, William, Carlow Co., 1801–2 (def.)

Butler, Augustine, Clare Co., 1832

Butler (afterwards Butler Clarke), Hon. C. H., Kilkenny City, 1802–9, 1814–20; Kilkenny Co., 1820(by)–30

Butler, Col. H. T., Carlow, 1880

Butler, Lord J. A. W. F., Kilkenny Co., 1880

Butler, Hon. J. W., Kilkenny Co., 1801–20(by)

Butler, Lord J. W., Kilkenny Co., 1852

Butler, Lt Col. Hon. Pierce, Kilkenny Co., 1826, 1831(by), 1832–46 (d.)

Butler, P. S., Kilkenny City, 1828; Kilkenny Co., 1843–52

Butler, Sir Richard, bt, Carlow Co., 1801–2 (def.)

Butler, Richard, Tipperary Co., 1874

Butler, Sir T. P., bt, Carlow Co., 1885

Butt, Isaac, QC, Mayo Co., 1850; Youghal, 1852–65 (def.); Monaghan Co., 1871; Limerick City, 1871–9 (d.)

Byng, Sir John, Londonderry Co., 1831

Byrne, Alfred, Dublin (Harbour), 1915–18 (def.)

Byrne, G. M., Wexford Co., 1880–3; Wicklow West, 1885–92

Caher, Viscount (Richard Butler), Tipperary Co., 1818–19 (succeeded as Earl of Glengall)

Cairns, Rt Hon., Sir H. McC., QC, Belfast, 1852–66

Calcutt, F. M., Clare Co., 1857–9 (def.), 1860–3 (d.)

Caldbeck, Capt. Richard, Queen's Co. (Ossory), 1885

Callaghan, Daniel, Cork City, 1830(by)–49 (d.), (1835, defeated but elected on petition)

Callaghan, Gerrard, Cork City, 1820, 1826(by), 1829 (elected but on petition election declared void)

Callan, Philip, Dundalk, 1868–80 (def.); Louth Co., 1874 (elected but chose to sit for Dundalk); Louth Co., 1880–5; Louth North, 1885, 1892; Louth South, 1896

Campbell, Bernard, Down West, 1918; Belfast (Pottinger), 1918

Campbell, Henry, Fermanagh South, 1885–92

Campbell, Col. James, Sligo South, 1895

Campbell, J. H. M., QC, Dublin (St Stephen's Green), 1898–1900 (def.); Dublin University, 1903–17

Campbell, John, Armagh South, 1900–6

Campbell, T. J., KC, Monaghan South, 1918

Campden, Viscount (C. G. Noel), Cork Co., 1860

Canning, Rt Hon., George, Tralee, 1802–6; Sligo, 1812 (elected but chose to sit for Liverpool)

Canning, Col. George, Sligo, 1806(by)–12

Cantwell, J. MacN., Louth Co., 1854; Dundalk, 1857

Carden, John, Cashel, 1859

Carew, J. L., Kildare North, 1885–92 (def.), 1895; Dublin (College Green), 1896–1900 (def.); Meath South, 1900–3 (d.)

Carew, R. S., Wexford Co., 1812–30, 1831(by)–4

Carew, Hon. R. S., Waterford Co., 1840–7; Wexford Co., 1852

Carlisle, A. M., Belfast West, 1906

Carmichael, J. C. McO., Kinsale, 1880

Carney, Miss Winifred, Belfast (Victoria), 1918

Carolan, Michael, Belfast (Shankill), 1918

Carpenter, J. P. B., Belfast West, 1910(Jan.)

Carroll, Barcroft, Cork City, 1859

Carroll, John, New Ross, 1818–21

Carroll, Patrick, Limerick Co., 1847

Carson, Rt Hon. Sir E. H., KC, Dublin University, 1892–1918; Belfast (Duncairn), 1918–21

Carvill, P. G. H., Newry, 1880, 1892–1906 (def.)

Casey, J. S., Tipperary Co., 1877–80

Cassidy, Robert, Queen's Co., 1835

Castlereagh, Viscount (F. W. R. Stewart), Down Co., 1832–52

Castlereagh, Viscount (Robert Stewart), Down Co., 1801–5 (def.), 1812–21

Castlereagh, Viscount (C. S. Vane-Tempest), Down Co., 1878–84

Castlerosse, Rt Hon. Viscount (V. A. Browne), Kerry Co., 1852–72

Caulfeild, Hon. Henry, Armagh Co., 1802–7, 1815–18 (def.) 1820–30

Caulfeild, Lt Col. J. M., Armagh Co., 1847–57 (def.)

Cavendish, Hon. C. C., Youghal, 1841–7

Cavendish, Capt. Hon. W. G., Bandon, 1837

Chaine, James, Antrim Co., 1874–85 (d.)

Chambers, James, KC, Belfast South, 1910–17 (d.)

Chance, P. A., Kilkenny South, 1885–94

Chapman, B. J., Westmeath Co., 1841–7

Chapman, Sir M. L., bt, Westmeath Co., 1832–41

Charley, Sir W. T., QC, Belfast East, 1892(by)

Chatterton, Rt Hon. H. E., Dublin University, 1867

Chatterton, Col. J. C., Cork City, 1835 (elected but unseated on petition), 1837, 1841, 1852, 1853

Chester, Henry, Louth Co., 1837–40

Chichester, Sir Arthur, bt, Carrickfergus, 1812–18; Belfast, 1818–20; Carrickfergus, 1820–30 (def.); Belfast, 1830–2; Carrickfergus, 1832

Chichester, Lt Col. Arthur, Wexford Co., 1830–1

Chichester, Lord Arthur, Donegal Co., 1831; Belfast, 1832–5 (def.)

Chichester, Lord H. F., Donegal Co., 1832; Belfast, 1842

Chichester, Lord J. L., Belfast, 1845–52

Chichester, Lt Col. R. P. D. S., Londonderry South, 1921–2 (d.)

Chichester, Lord S. S., Carrickfergus, 1802–7(by)

Chinnery, Sir Broderick, bt, Bandon, 1801–6

Christmas, William, Waterford City, 1832–5 (def.), 1841 (elected but unseated on petition), 1852

Clancy, J. J., KC, Dublin North, 1885–1918 (def.)

Clancy, J. J., Sligo North, 1918–22

Clark, G. S., Belfast North, 1907–10(Jan.)

Clarke, J. J., Londonderry Co., 1857(by)–9

Clarke, Thomas, Dublin Co. South, 1918

Clay, R. K., Portarlington, 1880

Clements, Hon. C. S., Leitrim Co., 1847–52 (def.)

Clements, Col. H. J., Leitrim Co., 1805–18 (def.); Cavan Co., 1840–3 (d.)

Clements, H. J. B., Cavan East, 1892

Clements, Lt Col. J. M., Leitrim Co., 1820–6, 1830–2 (def.)

Clements, Viscount (Nathaniel Clements), Leitrim Co., 1801–5

Clements, Viscount (R. B. Clements), Leitrim Co., 1826–30 (def.), 1832–9 (d.)

Clements, Viscount (W. S. Clements), Leitrim Co., 1839(by)–47

Cliffe, Anthony, Wexford Co., 1835

Clifford, Capt. Sir A. W. J., RN, Bandon, 1818–20; Dungarvan, 1820–2; Bandon, 1831(by)–2

Clinton, Lord R. P., Kinsale, 1848

Close, M. C., Armagh Co., 1857–64, 1874–85

Clow, W. M., Antrim South, 1910(Dec.)

Cochrane, G. C., Armagh City, 1874

Cochrane, Sir Henry, Dublin (College Green), 1892

Cogan, D. J., Wicklow East, 1900–7, 1918

Cogan, Rt Hon. W. H. F., Kildare Co., 1852(by)–80

Colclough, Caesar, Wexford Co., 1806(by)–6, 1818–20

Colclough, John, Wexford Co., 1806–7 (def.)

Cole, Hon. A. H., Enniskillen, 1828–44

Cole, Col. A. L., Enniskillen, 1865, 1868

Cole, Lt Gen. Hon. G. L., Fermanagh Co., 1803–23

Cole, Hon. H. A., Enniskillen, 1844–51; Fermanagh, 1854–80

Cole, Hon. J. L., Enniskillen, 1859(by)–68
Cole, Viscount (J. W. Cole), Fermanagh Co., 1801–3
Cole, Viscount (L. E. Cole), Enniskillen, 1880–5
Cole, Viscount (W. W. Cole), Fermanagh Co., 1831–40
Coote, Charles, Cavan Co., 1818, 1826, 1831–40
Coote, Sir C. H., bt, Queen's Co., 1818, 1820, 1821(by)–47, 1852–9
Coote, C. H., Queen's Co., 1801–2
Coote, C. H. jun., Queen's Co., 1837
Coote, Major Gen. Sir Eyre, Queen's Co., 1802–6
Coote, Eyre, Clonmel, 1830(by)–2
Coote, William, Tyrone South, 1916–22
Collery, Bernard, Sligo North, 1891–1900(by)
Colles, William, Kilkenny City, 1812
Collett, E. J., Cashel, 1819–30
Collett, John, Athlone, 1843–7
Collett, W. R., Tipperary Co., 1869
Collins, Cornelius, Limerick West, 1918–22
Collins, Eugene, Kinsale, 1865, 1874–85
Collins, Michael, Cork South, 1918–22
Collis, John, Kinsale, 1812
Collivet, Michael, Limerick City, 1918–22
Collum, Capt. A. P. T., Fermanagh North, 1910
Collum, John, Enniskillen, 1851(by), 1852(by), 1859(by), 1865, 1868
Collum, Capt. L. J., Enniskillen, 1874
Collum, Capt. William, Enniskillen, 1880
Colthurst, Lt Col. D. La T., Cork Co., 1879–85
Colthurst, Sir G. C., bt, Kinsale, 1863–74
Colthurst, Sir George, bt, Cork Co., 1879
Colthurst, Sir N. C., bt, Cork City, 1812–29 (d.)
Commins, Andrew, LL D, Roscommon Co., 1880–5; Roscommon South,
    1885–92 (def.), Cork South-East, 1893–1900
Condon, T. J., Tipperary East, 1885–1918 (def.), Roscommon North, 1895
Connor, C. C., Antrim North, 1892–5
Connolly, Joseph, Antrim Mid, 1918
Connolly, Laurence, Longford South, 1885–8
Connor, F. McC., Cork South, 1885
Connor, H. D., KC, Dublin (St Stephen's Green), 1910(Jan.)
Conolly, Lt Col. E. M., Donegal Co., 1831–49 (d.)
Conolly, Thomas, Donegal Co., 1849–76 (d.)
Conway, Prof. A. W., National University of Ireland, 1918
Conway, Michael, Leitrim North, 1885–92; Tipperary Mid, 1892
Conyngham, Lord F. N., Clare Co., 1857–9, 1874–80
Cooke, J. F., QC, Donegal East, 1900
Cooper, Capt. B. R., Dublin Co. South, 1910(Jan.)–1910(Dec.) (def.)
Cooper, C. W., Sligo Co., 1859–65
Cooper, Lt Col. E. H., Sligo Co., 1865–8 (def.)

Cooper, E. J., Sligo Co., 1832–41, 1857–9
Cooper, E. S., Sligo Co., 1806–30
Cooper, James, Fermanagh South, 1918
Cooper, J. E., Sligo Co., 1801–6
Coote, Charles, Cavan Co., 1818, 1826
Coote, Sir C. H., bt, Queen's Co., 1818, 1820, 1821(by)–47, 1852–9
Coote, C. H., Queen's Co., 1801–2
Coote, C. H. jun., Queen's Co., 1837
Coote, Major Gen. Sir Eyre, Queen's Co., 1802–6
Coote, Eyre, Clonmel, 1830(by)–2
Coote, William, Tyrone South, 1916–22
Cope, R. C., Armagh Co., 1801–2
Copeland, W. T., Coleraine, 1831–3 (defeated but elected following petition),
    1833–7
Coppinger, T. S., Cork Co., 1832
Corbally, M. E., Meath Co., 1840–1, 1842–71 (d.)
Corbet, W. J., Wicklow Co., 1880–5, Wicklow East, 1885–92 (def.), 1895–1900
Corbett, T. L., Tyrone East, 1892, 1895; Down North, 1898, 1900–10 (d.)
Corbitt, R. S., Down South, 1886
Corcoran, Timothy, Cork Mid, 1910(Dec.)
Corrigan, Sir D. J., bt, Dublin City, 1868, 1870–4
Corry, Viscount (Armar Lowry Corry), Fermanagh Co., 1823–31
Corry, Rt Hon. Isaac, Dundalk, 1801(by)–2; Newry, 1802–6 (def.), 1807
Corry, Sir J. P., bt, Belfast, 1874–85; Belfast East, 1885; Armagh Mid, 1886(by)–
    91 (d.)
Corry, Viscount (Somerset Lowry Corry), Tyrone Co., 1801–2 (succeeded as
    Earl of Belmore)
Corry, T. C. S., Monaghan Co., 1807(by)–12, 1813–18
Cosbie, George, Cork City, 1909
Cosby, Lt Col. R. A. G., Queen's Co., 1880; Queen's Co. (Leix), 1885, 1886,
    1892
Cosgrave, James, Galway East, 1914–18
Cosgrave, W. T., Kilkenny City, 1917–18; Kilkenny South, 1918–22
Costello, Marcus, Dublin City, 1832(by)
Costello, Patrick, Waterford City, 1848
Cotter, J. L., Mallow, 1812–18
Cotton, W. F., Dublin Co. South, 1910(Dec.)–17 (d.)
Cotton, Capt. Hon. W. H. S., Carrickfergus, 1847–57
Counsell, E. P. S., Dublin University, 1886
Coussmaker, George, Kinsale, 1813–21(d.)
Cox, J. R., Clare East, 1885–92 (def.)
Cradock, Lt Col. Hon. J. H., Dundalk, 1830–1
Craig, C. C., Antrim South, 1903–22
Craig, James, Carrickfergus, 1807(by)–12. (def.)
Craig, Sir James, bt, Fermanagh North, 1903; Down East, 1906–18; Down
    Mid, 1918–21

Craig, J. W., QC, Down South, 1892

Crampton, P. C., Dublin University, 1831, 1832; Dungarvan, 1834

Craven, Capt. Augustus, Dublin Co., 1852

Crawford, Lindsay, Armagh North, 1906(by)

Crean, Eugene, Queen's Co. (Ossory), 1892–1900; Cork South-East, 1900–18

Crichton, Hon. C. F., Enniskillen, 1868

Crichton, Viscount (J. H. Crichton), Enniskillen, 1868–80; Fermanagh Co., 1880–5

Crilly, Daniel, Mayo North, 1885–1900

Crofton, Sir Malby, bt, Sligo North, 1895

Crofts, Christopher, Cork City, 1868

Croker, Rt Hon. J. W., LL D, Downpatrick, 1806, 1807–12 (def.); Athlone, 1812–18; Dublin University, 1818, 1827–30 (def.)

Cromie, John, Antrim Co., 1833

Cronin, T. B., Kerry South, 1910(Dec.)

Crosbie, James, Kerry Co., 1801–6, 1807, 1812–26 (def.)

Crosbie, Major Pierce, Kerry Co., 1830

Crowley, James, Kerry North, 1918–22

Crowley, Dr John, Mayo North, 1918–22

Crumley, Patrick, Fermanagh South, 1910(Dec.)–18 (def.)

Cuffe, James, Tralee, 1819(by)–28 (d.)

Cullinan, John, Tipperary South, 1900–18 (def.)

Cummins, John, Wexford South, 1910(Dec.)

Curran, J. P., Newry, 1812

Curran, Thomas, Sligo South, 1892–1900

Curran, T. B., Kilkenny City, 1892–5; Donegal North, 1895–1900

Curry, William, Armagh City, 1837–40

Cusack, Dr Bryan, Galway North, 1918–22

Cusack, John Newry, 1910(Jan.)

Cusack, Dr P. J., Meath North, 1918

Cuthbert, John, Kinsale, 1832

Dalberg-Acton, Sir J. E. E., bt, Carlow, 1859–65

Dalton, J. J., Donegal West, 1890–92; Meath South, 1892, 1893

Dalway, M. R., Carrickfergus, 1868–80 (def.); Antrim East, 1885

Dalway, Noah, Carrickfergus, 1801–2

Daly, Denis, Galway, 1837

Daly, Rt Hon. D. B., King's Co., 1801–2; Galway, 1802–05; Galway Co., 1805–18 (def.)

Daly, James, Galway, 1805–11; Galway Co., 1812–30 (def.), 1832–5

Daly, James, Monaghan South, 1895–1902

Daly, John, Tralee, 1874

Daly, John, Cork City, 1876, 1880–4

Daly, John, Limerick City, 1895 (elected but declared ineligible)

Daly, St George, Galway, 1801–1

Damer, Lt Col. Hon. G. L. D., Portarlington, 1832, 1835–47

Damer, Hon. L. S W. D., Portarlington, 1857–65 (def.), 1868–80

Dane, Paul, Enniskillen, 1859(by)

Dane, R. M., Fermanagh North, 1892–8

D'Arcy, Hyacinth, Galway Co., 1874

D'Arcy, John, Galway Co., 1830, 1835

D'Arcy, M. P., Wexford Co., 1868–74 (def.)

Dare, R. W. H., Wexford Co., 1874

Daunt, W. J. O'N., Mallow, 1832 (elected but unseated on petition)

Davey, Major W. H., Belfast (Duncairn), 1918; Londonderry City, 1918

Davidson, J. A., Down North, 1918

Davis, James, Dundalk, 1880

Davis, R. G., Youghal, 1832

Davison, Richard, Belfast, 1852–60

Davitt, Michael, Meath Co., 1882 (elected but disqualified); Waterford City, 1891; Meath North, 1892 (elected but unseated on petition); Cork North-East, 1893–3 (res.); Kerry East, 1895 (elected but chose to sit for Mayo South); Mayo South, 1895–1900(by)

Dawson, Alexander, Louth Co., 1826–31 (d.)

Dawson, Charles, Carlow, 1880–5

Dawson, Rt Hon. G. R., Londonderry Co., 1815(by)–30; Londonderry City, 1832, 1837

Dawson, J. H. M., Clonmel, 1820–30; Limerick Co., 1830(by)(defeated but elected on petition)–30

Dawson, Lionel, Tipperary Co., 1826

Dawson, Richard, Monaghan Co., 1801–7 (d.)

Dawson, R. P., Londonderry Co., 1859–74

Dawson, R. T., Monaghan Co., 1812–13

Dawson, Hon. T. V., Louth Co., 1841–7; Monaghan Co., 1847–52

Dawson, Hon. Vesey (afterwards Viscount Cremorne), Monaghan Co., 1865–8

Deane, Gerald, Westmeath Co., 1830

Dease, Edmund, Queen's Co., 1870–80

Dease, J. A., Kerry Co., 1872

Dease, M. O'R., Cavan Co., 1857; Louth Co., 1868–74 (def.)

Deasy, John, Cork City, 1884–5; Mayo West, 1885–93

Deasy, Rt Hon. Rickard, QC, Cork Co., 1855–61

de Cobain, E. S. W., Belfast East, 1885–92 (expelled from Commons)

Delahunty, James, Waterford City, 1868, 1874; Waterford Co., 1877–80

Delany, George, New Ross, 1878

Delany, William, Queen's Co. (Ossory), 1900–16 (d.)

de la Poer, Edmond, Waterford Co., 1866–73

de la Poer, Raymond, Kilkenny South, 1885, 1892

de la Poer, Capt. W. G., Waterford East, 1885

de Markievicz, Mme Constance, Dublin (St Patrick's), 1918–22

Dempsey, C. J., Londonderry Co., 1881; Belfast North, 1886

139

Dempsey, Patrick, Belfast West, 1903
Dennehy, Dr P. R., Tipperary East, 1892
Denny, Sir Edward, bt, Tralee, 1818–19, 1832
Denny, Sir Edward, bt, Tralee, 1828(by)–9
Denny, William, Tralee, 1835, 1852
Dering, Sir E. C., Wexford, 1829(by)–31 (elected in 1829 and 1830 after petition)
de Robeck, Baron (J. H. Fock), Kildare North, 1885
de Robeck, Baron (J. H. M. Fock), Queen's Co., 1837
de Roiste, Liam, Cork City, 1918–22
de Valera, Eamon, Clare East, 1917–22; Belfast (Falls), 1918; Down South, 1918; Mayo East, 1918 (elected)
De Vere, S. E., Limerick Co., 1854–9
Devereux, F. H., Kilkenny City, 1857
Devereux, J. T., Wexford, 1847–59
Devereux, R. J., Wexford, 1865–72
Devine, T. J., Roscommon North, 1917
Devlin, C. R., Galway, 1903–6
Devlin, Joseph, Kilkenny North, 1902(by)–6 (elected but chose to sit for Belfast West); Belfast West, 1906–18; Belfast (Falls), 1918–22
Diamond, Charles, Monaghan North, 1892–5
Dick, Quinton, Cashel, 1807–9
Dickson, J. R., Leitrim Co., 1847
Dickson, Samuel, Limerick City, 1830, 1832; Limerick Co., 1849–50 (d.)
Dickson, Lt Col. S. A., Limerick Co., 1850, 1859–65
Dickson, Thomas, Kinsale, 1835
Dickson, Rt Hon. T. A., Dungannon, 1874–80 (elected but unseated on petition); Tyrone Co., 1881–5; Antrim Mid, 1885; Armagh Mid, 1886(by); Dublin (St Stephen's Green), 1888–92; Tyrone South, 1892
Digby, K. T., Queen's Co., 1868–80 (def.)
Dignan, Patrick, Roscommon Co., 1859
Dillon, Hon. H. A., Mayo Co., 1802–14 (succeeded as Viscount Dillon)
Dillon, John, Tipperary Co., 1880–3
Dillon, John, Tyrone North, 1885; Mayo East, 1885–1918 (def.); Roscommon South, 1895
Dillon, J. B., Tipperary Co., 1865–6 (d.)
Dillon, V. B., Sligo North, 1891
Dixon, Rt Hon. Sir Daniel, bt, Belfast North, 1905–7 (d.)
Dixon, Capt. Herbert, Belfast (Pottinger), 1918–22
Dobbin, Leonard, Armagh City, 1832–7
Dobbs, C. R., Carrickfergus, 1832 (elected but on petition election declared void and writ suspended)
Dobbs, W. C., Carrickfergus, 1857–9
Dobbyn, J. J., Belfast (Ormeau), 1918
Dockrell, Sir M. E., Dublin (St Patrick's), 1885; Dublin Co. (Rathmines), 1918–22

Dodd, W. H., KC, Antrim North, 1892; Londonderry South, 1895; Tyrone North, 1906

Doherty, John, LL D, KC, New Ross, 1824–6; Kilkenny, 1826–30

Doherty, W. J., Kilkenny, 1880

Dolan, C. J., Leitrim North, 1906(by)–8, 1908 (stood again but was defeated)

Dolan, J. N., Leitrim Co., 1918–22

Dolan, S. B., Queen's University of Belfast, 1918

Domvile, Sir Compton, bt, Dublin Co., 1823

Domvile, Sir C. C. W., bt, Dublin Co., 1857

Don, The O'Conor (Denis O'Conor), Roscommon, 1831(by)–47

Don, The O'Conor (Owen O'Conor), Roscommon Co., 1830–1 (d.)

Donald, Thompson, Belfast (Victoria), 1918–22

Donelan, Capt. A. J. C., Cork East, 1892–1910(Dec.) (elected but unseated on petition); Wicklow East, 1911–18

Donnelly, Patrick, Armagh South, 1918(by)–22

Donovan, J. T., Wicklow West, 1914–18; Donegal South, 1918

Doogan, P. C., Tyrone East, 1895–1906 (d.)

Doris, William, Mayo West, 1910(Jan.)–18 (def.)

Dougherty, Rt Hon. Sir J. B., Tyrone North, 1892; Londonderry, 1914–18

Downing, McCarthy, Cork Co., 1868–79 (d.)

Dowse, Richard, QC, Londonderry, 1868–72

Doyle, Sir J. M., Carlow Co., 1831; Newry, 1841

Doyle, Martin, Wexford, 1832

Duckett, S. J. C., Carlow Co., 1895

Duffy, C. G., New Ross, 1852–6

Duffy, C. G., Dublin Co. South, 1918–22

Duffy, W. J., Galway South, 1900–18 (def.)

Duggan, E. J., Meath South, 1918–22

Duigenan, Patrick, LL D, Armagh City, 1801–16 (d.)

Dumigan, Daniel, Antrim East, 1918

Dunbar, George, Belfast, 1835(by)–41

Dunbar, John, New Ross, 1874–8 (d.)

Dunbar-Buller, C. W., Belfast South, 1902

Duncannon, Viscount (J. W. Ponsonby), Bandon, 1826 (elected to sit for Kilkenny Co.); Kilkenny Co., 1826–32

Dunglas, Lord (C. A. Home), Downpatrick, 1831

Dunkellin, Lord (U. C. de Burgh), Galway, 1852, 1859–65; Galway Co., 1865–7

Dunlo, Viscount (R. le P. Trench), Galway Co., 1801–5

Dunlo, Viscount (W. T. le P. Trench), Galway Co., 1859

Dunne, Lt Gen. Edward, Queen's Co., 1818, 1820

Dunne, Edward, Queen's Co., 1832

Dunne, Col. Rt Hon. F. P., Portarlington, 1837, 1847–57 (def.); Queen's Co., 1859–68.

Dunne, Major Gen. George, Queen's Co., 1874

Dunne, Michael, Queen's Co., 1852–65

Eccles, Charles, Tyrone Co., 1835
Eeliott-Palmer, Capt. Richard, Kerry West, 1892
Egan, Bernard, Mayo North, 1892, 1895, 1910(Jan.)
Ellard, J. D., Mayo Co., 1835
Elliott, William, Portarlington, 1801(by)–2
Ellis, Hercules, Cavan Co., 1852
Ellis, John, Newry, 1837–41
Ellis, Thomas, Dublin City, 1820(by)–6
Ellison-Macartney, J. W., Tyrone Co., 1873, 1874–85
Ellison-Macartney, W. G., Antrim South, 1885–1903
Engledow, C. J., Kildare North, 1895–1900 (def.)
Ennis, Sir J. J., bt, Athlone, 1856, 1857–65 (def.), 1868–74 (def.), 1880–4 (d.)
Ennis, Nicholas, Meath Co., 1874–80
Ennismore, Viscount (Richard Hare), Cork Co., 1826–7 (d.)
Ennismore, Lord (William Hare), Cork Co., 1855
Errington, George, Longford Co., 1874–85
Esmonde, Sir John, bt, Waterford Co., 1852–77 (d.)
Esmonde, Dr John, Tipperary North, 1910(Dec.)–15 (d.)
Esmonde, Lt J. L., Tipperary North, 1915–18
Esmonde, Sir Thomas, bt, Wexford, 1841–7
Esmonde, Sir T. H. G., bt, Dublin Co. South, 1885–92 (def.); Kerry West, 1892–1900, Wexford North, 1900–18 (def.)
Etchingham, Sean, Wicklow East, 1918–22
Eustace, Capt. C. S., Mallow, 1852
Eustace, Henry, Tipperary North, 1885
Evans, George, Dublin Co., 1832–41 (def.)
Evans, G. F., Cork City, 1807
Evans, Capt. Henry, RN (later Rear Admiral), Wexford, 1819(by)–20, 1826–9
Evelyn, Lyndon, Dundalk, 1813–18
Everard, Major N. T., Cavan West, 1892
Ewart, William, Kilkenny City, 1837
Ewart, William, Belfast, 1878–85; Belfast North, 1885–9 (d.)
Eyre, Giles, Galway Co., 1805, 1806, 1812

Fagan, James, Wexford Co., 1847–52
Fagan, Capt. W. A., Carlow, 1868–74
Fagan, W. T., Cork City, 1847–59 (d.)
Fahy, Frank, Galway South, 1918–22
Falconer, J. B., LL D, Wexford North, 1895
Falkiner, C. L., QC, Armagh South, 1892
Falkiner, F.J., Dublin Co., 1801–7 (def.); Carlow, 1812–18
Fallon, William, Cork Mid, 1910(Jan.)
Falls, John, Dungannon, 1841

142

Farrell, D. H., Athlone, 1841

Farrell, Gerald, Leitrim Co., 1918

Farrell, J. J., Dubun Harbour, 1915

Farrell, J. P., Kilkenny City, 1895; Cavan West, 1895(by)–1900; Longford North, 1900–18; Longford Co., 1918

Farrell, T. J., Waterford City, 1895; Kerry South, 1895(by)–1900

Farren, Thomas, Dublin (College Green), 1915

Farrington, Thomas, Cork City, 1918

Farquhar, James, Portarlington, 1824(by)–30

Fay, C. J., Cavan Co., 1874–85

Ferguson, J. F., Belfast, 1857

Ferguson, Sir R. A., bt, Londonderry City, 1830–60 (d.)

Ferrand, Walker, Tralee, 1831–2

Fetherston, Sir G. R., bt, Longford Co., 1819(by)–30

Fetherston, Sir Thomas, bt, Longford Co., 1801–19 (d.)

Fetherstonhaugh, Godfrey, KC, Fermanagh North, 1906–16

ffolliott, John, Sligo Co., 1841(by)–50

ffolliott, Col. John, Sligo North, 1885; Sligo South, 1892

ffrench, Peter, Wexford South, 1893–1918 (def.)

Field, William, Dublin (St. Patrick's), 1892–1918 (def.)

Findlater, William, Monaghan Co., 1880–5; Londonderry South, 1885

Finigan, J. L., Ennis, 1879–82

Finn, W. F., Kilkenny Co., 1832–7

Finucane, John, Limerick East, 1885–1900

Finucane, Michael, Ennis, 1832, 1835

Fish, Vice-Admiral John, Wexford, 1813–14

Fisher, Alexander, Down South, 1918

Fitzgerald, Major-Gen, Sir Augustine, bt, Clare Co., 1808–18; Ennis, 1832(by)

Fitzgerald, Sir Edward, bt, Cork City, 1910(Jan.)

Fitzgerald, Dr Gubbins, Louth South, 1895

Fitzgerald, Lord Henry, Kildare Co., 1807–13

Fitzgerald, Rt Hon. James, Ennis, 1802–8, 1812–13

Fitzgerald, Lt Gen. Sir J. F., Clare Co., 1852 (elected but unseated on petition), 1853(by)–7 (def.)

Fitzgerald, J. G., Longford South, 1888–92

Fitzgerald, Rt Hon., J. D., QC, Ennis, 1852–60

Fitzgerald, Rt. Hon. Lord O. A., Kildare Co., 1865–74 (def.)

Fitzgerald, R. A., Tipperary Co., 1845–7

Fitzgerald, Lord R. S., Kildare Co., 1802–7

Fitzgerald, R. U., Cork Co., 1801–6

Fitzgerald, Thomas, Louth Co., 1832–4 (d.)

Fitzgerald, Thomas, Tralee, 1853

Fitzgerald, Thomas, Dublin Co. (Pembroke), 1918–22

Fitzgerald, Lord W. C. O'B., Kildare Co., 1813–31

Fitzgerald, W. H. W., Ennis, 1879

Fitzgerald (afterwards Vesey-Fitzgerald), Rt Hon. W. V., Ennis, 1808–12, Clare Co., 1812; Ennis, 1813–18; Clare Co., 1818–28 (def.); Ennis, 1831–2(by)

Fitzgibbon, John, Mayo East, 1892

Fitzgibbon, John, Mayo South, 1910(Dec.)–18

Fitzgibbon, Col. Hon. R. H., Limerick Co., 1818–41

Fitzgibbon, V. B., Kinsale, 1863

Fitzpatrick, Hon. B. E. B., Portarlington, 1880–3

Fitzpatrick, J. L., Queen's Co. (Ossory), 1916–18

Fitzpatrick, Rt Hon. J. W., Queen's Co., 1837–41, 1847–52, 1857, 1865–70

Fitzsimon, Christopher, Dublin Co., 1832–7

FitzSimon, Nicholas, King's Co., 1833–41

Fitzwilliam, Hon. W. H. W., Wicklow Co., 1868–74 (def.)

Flanagan, Capt. J. W., Sligo, 1868

Flavin, Martin, Cork City, 1891–2

Flavin, M. J., Kerry North, 1896–1918

Fletcher, William, Kilkenny City, 1820,

Flood, Sir Frederick, bt, Wexford Co., 1812–18

Flynn, J. C., Cork North, 1885–1910(Jan.)

Foley, J. W., New Ross, 1880–1

Foley, P. J., Galway (Connemara), 1885–95

Forbes, Viscount (G. J. Forbes), Longford Co., 1806–36 (d.)

Forbes, Capt. Hon. W. F., Longford Co., 1857

Forde, Mathew, Down Co., 1821–6, 1830

Forde, Lt Col. W. B., Down Co., 1857–74 (def.)

Forster, Sir George, bt, Monaghan Co., 1852–65 (def.)

Fortescue, Rt Hon. C. S., Louth Co., 1847–74 (def.)

Fortescue, Hon. J. W., Youghal, 1852

Fortescue, Matthew, Louth Co., 1826

Fortescue, Thomas, Louth Co., 1840–1

Fortescue, W. C., Louth Co., 1801–6

Foster, A. H. W., Donegal South, 1885

Foster, Hon. C. T. S., Louth Co., 1835

Foster, F. J., Louth Co., 1859, 1865

Foster, Rt Hon. John, Louth Co., 1801–22

Foster, J. L., Dublin University, 1806, 1807–12; Lisburn, 1818 (elected but chose to sit for Armagh City); Armagh City, 1818–20; Louth Co., 1824–30

Foulkes, Evan, Tralee, 1807(by)–8

Fox, Charles, Longford Co., 1836, 1837

Fox, Edward, Dublin City, 1874

Fox, J. F., King's Co. (Tullamore), 1885

Fox, R. M., Longford Co., 1847–56 (d.)

Fraser, Alexander, Downpatrick, 1880

Freeland, James, Belfast (Cromac), 1918

French, Arthur, Roscommon Co., 1801–21 (d.)

French, Arthur, Roscommon Co., 1821–32

French, Hon. Charles, Roscommon Co., 1873–80

French, Col. Rt Hon. FitzStephen, Sligo Co., 1830; Roscommon Co., 1832–73 (d.)

French, John, Belfast, 1835

French, Lt Col. T. P., Galway, 1857, 1859

Freemantle, W. H., Enniskillen, 1806(by)–06

Frewen, Moreton, Cork Co., 1852(by)

Frewen, Moreton, Cork North-East, 1910(Dec.)–11

Frith, Lt Col. Hon. W. H. L., Carrickfergus, 1852

Fulham, Patrick, Meath South, 1892 (elected but unseated on petition)

Gabbett, D. F., Limerick City, 1879–85

Gageby, Robert, Belfast North, 1910(Jan.)

Gale, Peter, Queen's Co., 1832

Galligan, P. P., Cavan West, 1918–22

Galwey, J. M., Dungarvan, 1832; Waterford Co., 1832–5, 1835(by), 1835(by)

Gardner, R. R., Armagh Mid, 1886

Gavin, Major George, Limerick City, 1858 (elected but unseated on petition); 1859–74

Gayer, A. E., LL D, QC, Dublin University, 1858

George, John, QC, Wexford Co., 1852–7 (def.), 1859–66

Getty, S. G., Belfast, 1860–8

Gibbon, J. G., Wexford Co., 1880

Gibney, James, Meath North, 1893–1900 (def.)

Gibson, Rt Hon. Edward, QC, Waterford City, 1874; Dublin University, 1875–85

Gibson, James, Belfast, 1837 (elected but unseated on petition)

Gilhooly, James, Cork West, 1885–1916 (d.)

Gill, H. J., Westmeath Co., 1880–3; Limerick City, 1885–8

Gill, Peter, Tipperary Co., 1865(by), 1865

Gill, R. P., Tipperary North, 1915

Gill, T. P., Louth South, 1885–92

Ginnell, Laurence, Westmeath North, 1900, 1906–18; Westmeath Co., 1918–22

Gisborne, Thomas, Carlow, 1839–41

Givan, John, Monaghan Co., 1880–3

Gladstone, Thomas, Portarlington, 1832–5

Glendinning, R. G., Antrim North, 1906–10(Jan.)

Glentworth, Lord (H. H. Pery), Limerick City, 1812; Mallow, 1826

Glerawley, Viscount (W. R. Annesley), Downpatrick, 1815–20

Godley, J. R., Leitrim Co., 1847

Goff, Capt. T. W., Roscommon Co., 1859 (elected but unseated on petition)

Good, J. P., Dublin Co. (Pembroke), 1918

Goold, Wyndham, Limerick Co., 1850–4 (d.)

Gordon, Lt J. E., KC, Dundalk, 1831–2

Gordon, John, Athlone, 1818–20

Gordon, John, KC, Armagh Mid, 1900(by); Londonderry South, 1900–16
Gore, Hon. Robert, New Ross, 1841–7
Gore, W. R. O., Sligo Co., 1841–52 (def.)
Gore Booth, Sir Robert, Sligo Co., 1850–77 (d.)
Gorges, Hamilton, Meath Co., 1801–2
Goulburn, Rt Hon. Henry, Armagh City, 1826–31
Goulding, William, Cork City, 1874, 1876–80 (def.), 1884
Gowing, V. A., King's Co., 1874
Gowing, W. A., Westmeath Co., 1880
Grace, O. D. J., Roscommon Co., 1847–59
Grady, H. D., Limerick City, 1801–2
Graham, E. J., King's Co. (Tullamore), 1914–18 (d.)
Grattan, Rt Hon. Henry, Dublin City, 1806–20 (d.)
Grattan, Henry, Dublin City, 1820(by), 1826–30 (def.); Meath Co., 1831, 1831(by)–52 (def.)
Grattan, James, Wicklow Co., 1821(by)–41 (def.)
Graves, R. S., New Ross, 1857
Gray, E. D., Kilkenny City, 1875; Tipperary Co., 1877–80; Carlow Co., 1880–5 (elected but chose to sit for Dublin (St Stephen's Green); Dublin (St Stephen's Green), 1885–8 (d.)
Gray, Dr John, Monaghan Co., 1852
Gray, Sir John, Kilkenny City, 1865–75 (d.)
Gray, William, Monaghan Co., 1868
Green, Charles, Youghal, 1869
Greene, John, Kilkenny Co., 1847–65 (def.)
Greene, William, Dungarvan, 1802–6
Greer, S. M., Londonderry Co., 1852, 1857(by)–9, (def.); Londonderry City, 1860, 1865
Greer, Thomas, Carrickfergus, 1880–5
Greer, Dr Thomas, Londonderry North, 1892
Gregory, W. H., Dublin City, 1842–7 (def.); Dungarvan, 1853; Galway Co., 1857–72
Greville Capt. Hon. A. W. F., Westmeath Co., 1865–74 (def.)
Greville, Col. F. S. (afterwards Greville-Nugent), Longford Co., 1852–69
Greville-Nugent, Hon. G. F. N., Longford Co., 1870–4
Greville-Nugent, Capt. Hon. R. J. M., Longford Co., 1869 (elected but unseated on petition)
Griffith, Arthur, Cavan East, 1918(by)–18; Cavan West, 1918–22 (d.); Tyrone North-West, 1918–22 (d.)
Grogan, Sir Edward, bt, Dublin City, 1841–65; Dublin University, 1868
Guest, M. J., Youghal, 1869–74
Guiney, John, Cork North, 1913–18
Guiney, Patrick, Cork North, 1910(Jan.)–13 (d.); Kerry East, 1910(Dec.)
Guinness, Sir A. E., bt, Dublin City, 1868(by) (elected but unseated on petition); 1874–80 (def.)
Guinness, Sir B. L., bt, Dublin City, 1865–8 (d.)

Guinness, Sir E. C., bt, Dublin (St Stephen's Green), 1885
Guinness, R. S., Kinsale, 1847 (elected but unseated on petition)
Guinness, T. H., Dublin Co., 1883
Gun-Cunninghame, Col. R. C., Wicklow Co., 1880
Gwynn, Capt. S. L., Galway, 1906(by)–18; Dublin University, 1918

Hackett, John, Tipperary Mid, 1910(Jan.)
Hall, Dr. J. C., Monaghan North, 1886
Hall, S. C., Wexford Co., 1841
Hallett, T. G. P., Galway, 1885
Hallewell, E. G., Newry, 1851–2 (def.)
Halpin, James, Clare West, 1906–9 (d.)
Hamill Bernard, Louth North, 1916
Hamilton, Hon. A. C., Enniskillen, 1801–2
Hamilton, Lord A. J., Tyrone North, 1910(Dec.)
Hamilton, Sir Charles, bt, Dungannon, 1801(by)–2, 1803–6
Hamilton, Rt Hon. Lord Claud, Tyrone Co., 1835–7, 1839–74 (def.), 1880
Hamilton, Lord C. J., Londonderry City, 1865–8 (def.)
Hamilton, Lord Claude, Dungannon, 1807–9 (d.)
Hamilton, Lord E. W., Tyrone North, 1885–92
Hamilton, Lord F. S., Tyrone North, 1892–5
Hamilton, G. A., Dublin Co., 1826, 1830, 1832; Dublin City, 1835 (defeated
  but elected on petition)–7 (def.); Dublin University, 1843–59(by)
Hamilton, Hans, Dublin Co., 1801–23 (d.)
Hamilton, I. T., Dublin Co., 1863–85, Dublin Co. South, 1885
Hamilton, Viscount (James Hamilton), Dungannon, 1807(by)–7
Hamilton, Viscount (James Hamilton) Donegal Co., 1860–80 (def.) (later
  Marquis of Hamilton)
Hamilton, Marquis of (J. A. E. Hamilton), Londonderry City, 1900–13
Hamilton, J. H., Dublin Co., 1835, 1841–63
Hammond, John, Carlow Co., 1891–1909 (d.)
Handcock, Hon. George, Athlone, 1865
Handcock, Capt. Hon. Henry, Athlone, 1856–7 (def.)
Handcock, Richard, Athlone, 1826–32 (def.); Westmeath Co., 1837
Handcock, William, Athlone, 1801–3
Hanna, G. B., Antrim East, 1919
Hanna, Henry, KC, Dublin (St Stephen's Green), 1918
Harbinson, T. J. S., Tyrone East, 1918(by); Tyrone North-East, 1918–22
Hardinge, Hon. C. S., Downpatrick, 1851–7(by)
Hardman, Edward, Drogheda, 1801–6
Hare, Hon. Richard, Cork Co., 1812–26
Hare, Hon. William, Kerry Co., 1826–30
Harland, Sir E. J., bt, Belfast North, 1889–96 (d.)
Harrington, Edward, Kerry West, 1885–92 (def.)
Harrington, T. C., Dublin (Harbour), 1885–1910 (d.)
Harrington, Timothy, Westmeath Co., 1883–5

Harris, A. W., Kildare Co., 1880

Harris, Matthew, Galway East, 1885–90 (d.)

Harrison, Henry, Tipperary Mid, 1890–2, Limerick West, 1892; Sligo North, 1895

Harrison, Thomas, Belfast North, 1900

Harrison, Thomas, Donegal East, 1910(Jan.)

Hart, Gen. G. V., Donegal Co., 1808

Hart, Capt. John, Londonderry City, 1830, 1831(by); Londonderry Co., 1831

Hart, Sir J. W., bt, Kildare Co., 1831–2 (def.)

Hartley, James, 1848

Hartopp, G. H. W. F., Dundalk, 1820(by)–24 (d.)

Hany, Robert, Dublin City, 1831 (elected but unseated on petition)

Harvey, Charles (afterwards Harvey-Savill-Onley), Carlow, 1818–26

Haskin, Robert, Belfast (Woodvale), 1918

Haslett, Sir J. H., Belfast West, 1885–6 (def.); Belfast North, 1896–1905 (d.)

Hassard, M. D., Waterford City, 1857–65

Hatchell, John, Wexford Co., 1857–9 (def.)

Hatton, George, Lisburn, 1801–2

Hatton, Capt. V. F., Wexford Co., 1841–7

Haviland Burke, Edmund, Kerry North, 1892; Dublin Co. South, 1895; King's Co. (Tullamore), 1900–14 (d.); Louth North, 1900

Hawes, Benjamin, Kinsale, 1848–52(by)

Hawthorne, C. S., Downpatrick, 1802–6, 1812–15

Hay, Lord John, Belfast, 1865

Hayden, J. P., Roscommon South, 1897–1918 (def.)

Hayden, L. P., Leitrim South, 1885–92; Roscommon South, 1892–7 (d.)

Hayes, Sir E. S., bt, Donegal Co., 1831–60 (d.)

Hayes, Hugh, Down West, 1922(by)

Hayes, Dr Richard, Limerick West, 1918–22

Hayes, Roger, Waterford City, 1832

Hayes, Sean, Cork West, 1918–22

Hazleton, Richard, Dublin Co. South, 1906; Galway North, 1906(by)–14 (resigned but stood again); Louth North, 1910(Jan.), 1910(Dec.) (elected but unseated on petition); Galway North, 1914–18 (def.)

Healy, F. J., Cork West, 1916

Healy, Maurice, Cork City, 1885–1900 (def.), 1909–10(Jan.) (def.); Cork North East, 1910(by)(Dec.); Cork City, 1910(Dec.)–18

Healy, Maurice, Waterford West, 1910(Dec.)

Healy, T. J., Wexford North, 1892(by)–1900 (def.)

Healy, T. M., KC, Wexford, 1880(by)–83; Monaghan Co., 1883–5; Monaghan North, 1885 (elected but chose to sit for Londonderry South); Londonderry South, 1885–6 (def.); Longford North, 1887–92; Louth North, 1892–1910(Jan.) (def.); Cork North-East, 1911–18

Heard, J. I., Kinsale, 1852(by)–9

Hearn, M. L., Dublin Co. South, 1917–18

Heaton-Armstrong, W. C., Tipperary Mid, 1892

Hely, Charles, Kilkenny Co., 1847

Hely-Hutchinson, Hon. Christopher, Cork City, 1802(by)–12 (def.), 1818–26(by) (d.)

Hely-Hutchinson, Major Gen. Hon. John, Cork City, 1801–2

Hely-Hutchinson, John, Cork City, 1826(by)–30

Hely-Hutchinson, Hon. John, Tipperary Co., 1826–30 (def.), 1831–2

Hely-Hutchinson, Hon. Richard, Clonmel, 1837; Waterford Co., 1852

Hemphill, Rt Hon. C. H., KC, Cashel, 1857, 1859; Tyrone North, 1895–1906

Henchy, D. O'C., Kildare Co., 1852–9

Hennessy, J. P., King's Co., 1859–65 (def.); Wexford Co., 1866

Henry, D. S., KC, Tyrone North, 1906, 1907; Londonderry South, 1916–21

Henry, Mitchell, Galway Co., 1871–85

Herbert, H. A., Kerry Co., 1806–12; Tralee, 1812–13 (res.)

Herbert, Rt Hon. H. A., Kerry Co., 1847–66 (d.)

Herbert, H. A., Kerry Co., 1866–80

Herbert, Lord Reginald, Dublin (St Stephen's Green), 1910(Dec.)

Herdman, Emerson, Londonderry City, 1899

Herdman, E. C., Tyrone North, 1910(Jan.), 1911

Herdman, E. T., Donegal East, 1892, 1895

Heron, D. C., QC, Tipperary Co., 1869, 1870–4

Hervey, William, Wexford Co., 1834

Heygate, Sir F. W., bt, Londonderry Co., 1859–74

Hickey, M. C., Cork South-East, 1900

Hickson, S. M., Kerry Co., 1837

Higgins, Capt. B. H., Tyrone Co., 1852

Higgins, G. G. O., Mayo Co., 1850–7 (def.)

Higgins, Thomas, Galway North, 1906–6 (d.)

Hill, Capt. Arthur, Down West, 1898–1905

Hill, Lord A. E. (afterwards Hill-Trevor), Down Co., 1845–80

Hill, Lord A. M. C., Newry, 1832–5

Hill, Lord A. M. W., Down Co., 1817–36

Hill, Lord A. W., Down Co., 1880–5, Down West, 1885–98; Belfast South, 1906; Down West, 1907–8

Hill, Rt Hon. Lord George, Carrickfergus, 1826

Hill, Lord G. A., 1830–2

Hill, Rt Hon. Sir G. F., bt, Londonderry Co., 1801(by)–2; Londonderry City, 1802–30; Coleraine, 1806 (elected to sit for Londonderry City)

Hill, Lord Marcus, Carrickfergus, 1830

Hillsborough, Earl of (A. T. B. W. S. Hill), Down Co., 1836–45

Hinds, J. T., Meath Co., 1868, 1875

Hoctor, Patrick, Tipperary North, 1915

Hogan, J. F., Tipperary Mid, 1893–1900

Hogan, Michael, Tipperary North, 1906–10(Dec.)

Hogg, Adam, Londonderry City, 1880

Hogg, D. C., Londonderry City, 1913–14 (d.)

Hogg, Lt Col. J. MacN. McG., Lisburn, 1857

Holford, G. P., Dungannon, 1812–18
Holmes, Rt Hon. Hugh, QC, Dublin University, 1885(by)–7
Holmes, William, Dungannon, 1852
Hooper, John, Cork South-East, 1885–9
Horgan, Daniel, Cork City, 1892
Horner, A. L., KC, Tyrone South, 1906, 1910(Jan.)–16 (d.)
Houston, Arthur, QC, Londonderry North, 1895
Houston, King, Tyrone North-East, 1918
Howard, F. J., Youghal, 1837–41
Howard, Hon. H. M., Wicklow East, 1910(Dec.)
Howard, Sir Ralph, bt, Wicklow Co., 1829(by)–47, 1848–52
Howard, Major R. J., Tyrone South, 1900
Hudson, W. E., Monaghan Co., 1835
Hughes, Sir Frederick, Wexford, 1874, 1880
Hughes, H. G., QC, Cavan Co., 1855; Longford Co., 1856–7
Hughes, Thomas, Dundalk, 1808–12 (d.)
Humble, Sir J. N., Dungarvan, 1857
Hume, Joseph, Kilkenny City, 1837–41
Hume, W. H., Wicklow Co., 1801–16 (d.)
Hume (later Dick, 1864), W. W. F., Wicklow Co., 1852–80 (def.); Wicklow
    West, 1885, 1886
Hume-Rochfort, Gustavus, Westmeath Co., 1801–24 (d.)
Humphreys, Major, Tyrone Co., 1839
Humphreys, Major John, Wicklow Co., 1832, 1837
Hunt, Sir A. de V., Limerick Co., 1820
Hunter, Thomas, Cork North-East, 1918–22
Hussey, S. M., Tralee, 1880
Hutton, Robert, Dublin City, 1837–41 (def.)
Hyde, John, Youghal, 1820–6

Ingestre, Viscount (H. J. C. Talbot), Armagh City, 1831(by); Dublin City,
    1832(by)
Inglis, Rt Hon. John, Lisburn, 1852(by)
Inglis, Sir R. H., bt, Dundalk, 1824–6
Innes, A. C., Newry, 1865–8
Ireland, William, Dublin (St Stephen's Green), 1906
Irving, John, Antrim Co., 1837–45 (d.)

Jackson, George, Mayo Co., 1801–2
Jackson, G. V., Mayo Co., 1830
Jackson, H. V., King's Co., 1880
Jackson, H. W., Monaghan North, 1892
Jackson, Rt Hon. J. D., Bandon, 1835–42; Dublin University, 1842–3
Jackson, R. W., Armagh City, 1835
Jacob, Ebenezer, Dungarvan, 1834 (elected but unseated on petition)
Jameson, Major J. E., Clare West, 1895–1906

Jellett, W. M., K. C., Dublin University, 1918, 1919–22

Jephson, C. D. O. (after 1835 Jephson Norreys, bt, from 1838), Mallow, 1820, 1826–59 (def.)

Jephson, Denham, Mallow, 1802–12

Jephson, L. H., Tipperary Co., 1852

Jocelyn, Hon. John, Louth Co., 1807–10

Jocelyn, Hon. John, Dundalk, 1832

Jocelyn, Viscount (Robert Jocelyn), Louth Co., 1806–7, 1810–20

Johnson, W. G., Belfast, 1841 (elected but unseated on petition)

Johnson, W. M., QC, Mallow, 1874

Johnston, H. H., Dublin University, 1886

Johnston, James, Dublin Co., 1826

Johnston, John, Dublin Co., 1835

Johnston, J. A. W., Down South, 1910(Dec.), 1918

Johnston, M. J., Down East, 1918

Johnston, P. F. C., Donegal Co., 1852

Johnston, Robert, Newry, 1892

Johnston, William, Downpatrick, 1857; Belfast, 1868–78; Belfast South, 1885–1902 (d.)

Johnston, W. J., Londonderry South, 1910(Dec.)

Jones, D. J., Sligo Co., 1837

Jones, Robert, Sligo, 1832

Jones, Capt. Theobald, RN, Londonderry Co., 1830–57

Jones, Rt Hon. Theophilus, Leitrim Co., 1801–2 (def.)

Jones, T. T., Athlone, 1803–6

Jones, Walter, Coleraine, 1801–6, 1807(by)–9

Jordan, Jeremiah, Clare West, 1885–92; Fermanagh North, 1892; Meath South, 1893–5 (def.); Fermanagh South, 1895–1910(Dec.)

Joyce, J. H., Galway (Connemara), 1892

Joyce, Michael, Limerick City, 1900–18

Joyce, Pierce, Galway, 1874(by)

Julian, J. E. J., Kerry West, 1900

Kavanagh, A. McM., Wexford Co., 1866–8; Carlow Co., 1868–80 (def.)

Kavanagh, Thomas, Carlow Co., 1826(by)–31, 1832, 1835 (elected but unseated on petition), 1835(by)–7 (d.)

Kavanagh, W. McM., Kilkenny North, 1892; Armagh South, 1895; Carlow Co., 1908–10(Jan.)

Kaye, W. S. B., LL D, QC, Armagh City, 1875

Keane, Sir John, bt, Youghal, 1801–6

Keane, Sir Richard, bt, Dungarvan, 1807; Waterford Co., 1832–5

Keane, Sir R. F., bt, Waterford West, 1885

Keamey, F. E., LL D, Limerick City, 1900

Keating, Matthew, Kilkenny South, 1909–18 (def.)

Keating, Maurice, Kildare Co., 1801–2

Keating, Robert, Waterford Co., 1847–52

Keene, A. P., Wicklow East, 1918

Keightley, S. R., LL D, Antrim South, 1993; Londonderry South, 1906, 1910(Dec.)

Keily, Richard, New Ross, 1847

Kelly, A. I., Armagh City, 1832

Kelly, Bernard, Donegal South, 1885–7 (d.)

Kelly, E. J., Donegal East, 1910(Jan.)–22

Kelly, J. J., Limerick Co., 1874

Kelly, J. J., Dublin (St Patrick's), 1918

Kelly, J. S., Dublin (St James's), 1918

Kelly, James, Limerick City, 1844–7

Kelly, R. W., Mallow, 1880(by)

Kelly, Thomas, Dublin (St Stephen's Green), 1918–22

Kelly, T. B., Queen's Co., 1831

Kennedy, E. J., Sligo South, 1887–8

Kennedy, Sir Edward, bt, Kildare Co., 1852

Kennedy, Dr Evory, Donegal Co., 1874

Kennedy, P. J., Kildare North, 1892–5; Westmeath North, 1900–6

Kennedy, Tristram, Louth Co., 1852–7 (def.); King's Co., 1859; Louth Co., 1865(by)–8; Donegal Co., 1874

Kennedy, V. P., Cavan West, 1904–18

Kenny, Dr J. E., Cork South, 1885–92; Dublin (College Green), 1892–6

Kenny, M. J., Ennis, 1882–5; Tyrone Mid, 1885–95

Kenny, Peter, Newry, 1841

Kenny, William, QC, Dublin (St Stephen's Green), 1892–8

Kent, D. R., Cork East, 1918–22

Keogh, C. A., Sligo Co., 1868

Keogh, Capt. J. H., Carlow Co., 1852

Keogh, Rt Hon. William, QC, Athlone, 1847–56

Keown, John, Downpatrick, 1837

Keown, William, Downpatrick, 1867–74

Ker, David, Athlone, 1820(by)–26; Downpatrick, 1835–41

Ker, D. S., Downpatrick, 1841–7; Down Co., 1852–7 (def.); Downpatrick, 1859–67

Ker, Lord Mark, Antrim Co., 1830

Ker, Richard, Downpatrick, 1847–51, 1857(by)–9

Ker, R. W., Down Co., 1884–5

Ker, Capt. R. W. B., Down East, 1885–90

Kerr, S. P., Fermanagh North, 1910(Jan.)

Kerr-Smiley, P. K., Down South, 1906; Antrim North, 1910(Jan.)–22

Kerry, Knight of (Rt Hon. Maurice Fitzgerald), Kerry Co., 1801–31; Tralee, 1806 (elected but chose to sit for Kerry Co.); Kerry Co., 1835

Kertland, William, Drogheda, 1859

Kettle, A. J., Cork Co., 1880; Carlow Co., 1891

Kettle, T. M., Tyrone East, 1906(by)–10(Dec.)

Kickham, C. J., Tipperary Co., 1870

Kidd, Joseph, Armagh City, 1837

Kiely, John, Clonmel, 1819–20

Kilbride, Denis, Kerry South, 1887–95 (elected but chose to sit for Galway North); Galway North, 1895–1900; Kildare South, 1903–18 (def.)

Kildare, Marquis of (C. W. Fitzgerald), Kildare Co., 1847–52

Killeen, Lord (Arthur Plunket), Meath Co., 1830(by)–32

Kinderley, G. H., Tralee, 1852

King, Hon. Edward, Roscommon Co., 1802–6

King, Hon. Henry, Sligo Co., 1826–31 (def.)

King, Hon. James, Cork Co., 1837

King, John, Enniskillen, 1806(by)–6

King, J. G., King's Co., 1865–8

King, Hon. Robert, Roscommon Co., 1826–30

King, Hon. Robert, Cork Co., 1826–32 (def.)

King-Harman, Capt. E. R., Londord Co., 1870; Dublin City, 1870; Sligo Co., 1877–80 (def.); Dublin Co., 1883–5

King-Harman, Hon. L. H., Londord Co., 1847, 1852

King-Kerr, Dr James, Antrim East, 1900

Kingsborough, Viscount (Edward King), Cork Co., 1818–26

Kinnear, Rev John, DD, Donegal Co., 1880–5

Kirk, G. H., Louth Co., 1874(by)–80 (def.)

Kirk, Peter, Carrickfergus, 1835–47

Kirk, William, Newry, 1852–9 (def.); Armagh City, 1865; Newry, 1868–71 (d.)

Kirk, W. M., Newry, 1865

Kirwan, John, Galway Co., 1826

Kirwan, Martin, Mayo Co., 1814

Kisbey, W. H., QC, Down South, 1885

Knight, M. E., Monaghan North, 1910(Jan.), 1910(Dec.), 1918

Knox, E. F. V., Cavan West, 1890–5 (elected but chose to sit for Londonderry City); Londonderry City, 1895–9

Knox, Hon. George, LL D, Dublin University, 1801–7; Dungannon, 1802 (elected but chose to sit for Dublin University), 1806 (elected but chose to sit for Dublin University)

Knox, Major Gen. Hon. John, Dungannon, 1801(d.)

Knox, Hon. J. H., Newry, 1826–32

Knox, Lt Col., Hon. J. J., Dungannon, 1831–7

Knox, Major L. E., Sligo, 1868 (on petition election declared void and constituency disfranchised, 1870); Mallow (by Feb.) 1870, (by May) 1870

Knox, Hon. Thomas, Tyrone Co., 1806–12

Knox, Hon. Thomas (afterwards Viscount Northland), Tyrone Co., 1812–18; Dungannon, 1818–31, 1837–8 (res.)

Knox, Hon. Thomas (afterwards Viscount Northland), Dungannon, 1838–51

Knox, Col. Hon., W. S., Dungannon, 1851–74 (def.), 1880, 1880(by); Tyrone Co., 1881

Kyle, Samuel, Belfast (Shankill), 1918 (d.)

Lamb, Hon. William, Portarlington, 1807–12
Lambert, Gustavus, Westmeath Co., 1832; Meath Co., 1835
Lambert, Henry, Wexford Co., 1830, 1832–5; New Ross, 1852
Lambert, J. S., Galway Co., 1826(elected after petition)–32
Lane, Denny, Cork City, 1876
Lane, W. J., Cork East, 1885–92
Langston, John, Portarlington, 1806(by)
Lanigan, John, Cashel, 1857, 1859–65 (def.)
Lanyon, Sir Charles, Belfast, 1866–8 (def.)
Lalor, Patrick, Queen's Co., 1832–5 (def.)
Lalor, Richard, Queen's Co., 1880–5; Queen's Co. (Leix), 1885–92
Lamb, Hon. George, Dungarvan, 1822–34
Lardner, J. C. R., Monaghan North, 1907–18
La Touche, Col. David, Carlow Co., 1802–16 (d.)
La Touche, D. C., Dublin City, 1832(by)
La Touche, John, Kildare Co., 1801–2
La Touche, John, Dublin City, 1802–6 (def.); Leitrim Co., 1807–20
La Touche, Peter, Leitrim Co., 1802–6
La Touche, Robert, Kildare Co., 1802–30
La Touche, Robert, Carlow Co., 1816–18
Laverty, Charles, Monaghan South, 1910(Jan.)
Law, Hugh, Rt Hon., QC, Londonderry Co., 1874–81
Law, H. A., Donegal West, 1902–18
Lawder, J. O., Leitrim South, 1885
Lawes, R. B., Athlone, 1852
Lawless, Hon. C. J., Clonmel, 1846–53 (d.)
Lawless, F. J., Dublin Co. North, 1918–22
Lawson, Rt Hon. J. A., QC, LL D, Dublin University, 1857; Portarlington, 1865–8 (def.)
Lawther, Samuel, Antrim South, 1900
Layard, Major B. V., Carlow, 1841–7 (def.)
Lea, Sir Thomas, bt, Donegal Co., 1876, 1879–85; Donegal East, 1885; Londonderry South, 1886–1900
Leader, N. P., Cork Co., 1812; Kilkenny City, 1830–2
Leader, N. P., Cork, 1841, 1847(by), 1861–8
Leahy, James, Kildare Co., 1880–5; Kildare South, 1885–92 (def.)
Leamy, Edmund, Waterford City, 1880–5; Armagh Mid, 1885; Cork North-East, 1885–7; Sligo South, 1888–92, Waterford East, 1892; Galway, 1895, 1900; Kildare North, 1900–5 (d.)
Lecky, Conolly, Londonderry City, 1831
Lecky, Rt Hon. W. E. H., Dublin University, 1895(by)–1903
Lee, Edward, Dungarvan, 1801–2; Waterford Co., 1802–6 (def.)
Leeper, Dr G. R., Fermanagh North, 1895
Lefroy, Anthony, Longford Co., 1830–7 (def.), 1842(elected after petition)–7 (def.); Dublin University, 1858–70
Lefroy, A. G., Kildare Co., 1837

Lefroy, Rt Hon. T. L., LL D, Dublin University, 1827, 1830–42

Legg, C. McF., Antrim East, 1919

Lehmann, Frederick, Waterford Co., 1877

Leigh, Major Charles, New Ross, 1806–7, 1812–18

Leigh, Francis, Wexford, 1801–1, 1821–4

Leigh, Robert, New Ross, 1801–2

Lennon, James, Carlow Co., 1918–22

Lentaigne, John, Dublin Co., 1852

Leslie, C. P., Monaghan Co., 1801(by)–26 (def.); New Ross, 1830–1

Leslie, Col. C. P., Monaghan Co., 1843–71 (d.)

Leslie, David, Monaghan Co., 1835

Leslie, Sir John, bt, Monaghan Co., 1871–80 (def.); Monaghan North, 1885, 1886

Leslie, S. R., Londonderry City, 1910(Jan.), 1910(Dec.)

Lever, J. O., Galway City, 1859(by)–65 (def.), 1880–5

Levinge, Sir R. G. A., bt, Westmeath Co., 1837, 1847, 1852, 1857–65, 1874

Lewis, A. G., Monaghan Co., 1830

Lewis, Sir C. E., bt, Londonderry City, 1872–85, 1885–6 (elected but unseated on petition); Antrim North, 1887–92

Lewis, H. O., Carlow, 1874–80

Lewis, T. F., Ennis, 1826–8

Leycester, Joseph, Cork City, 1835 (elected but unseated on petition), 1837

Liddell, Henry, Down West, 1905–7

Lindsay, W. A., Belfast South, 1917–18; Belfast (Cromac), 1918–22

Little, P. J., Dublin Co. (Rathmines), 1918

Litton, Edward, QC, Coleraine, 1837–43

Litton, E. F., QC, Tyrone Co., 1880–1

Lloyd, Hardress, King's Co., 1807–18

Lloyd, Thomas, Limerick Co., 1826–30(by) (d.)

Lloyd, W., Roscommon Co., 1831

Loftus, Viscount (J. L. Loftus), Wexford Co., 1801–6 (succeeded as Marquis of Ely)

Long, Rt Hon. W. H., Dublin Co. South, 1906–10(Jan.)

Longbottom, A. P., Waterford Co., 1874

Longfield, John, Mallow, 1801–2

Longfield, Col. Mountifort, Cork City, 1801–18 (def.)

Longfield, Richard, Cork Co., 1835 (defeated but elected on petition), 1835–7 (def.); Mallow, 1841

Longfield, Robert, QC, Mallow, 1859–65

Lonsdale, J. R., Armagh Mid, 1918(by)–21 (d.)

Lonsdale, Sir J. B., bt, Armagh Mid, 1900(by)–18

Loonan, William, Limerick East, 1892

Lowry, Col. J. C. J., Dublin University, 1892

Lowry Corry, Rt Hon. H. T., Tyrone Co., 1825(by)–73 (d.)

Lowry Corry, Capt. Hon. H. W., Tyrone Co., 1873–80

Lowther, Viscount (William Lowther), 1831(by)

Lucas, Edward, Monaghan Co., 1834(def. but elected on petition)–41
Lucas, Frederick, Meath Co., 1852–5 (d.)
Lundon, Thomas, Limerick East, 1909–18 (def.)
Lundon, William, Limerick East, 1900–9 (d.)
Lyle, Samuel, Londonderry Co., 1806
Lynam, James, Galway East, 1892
Lynch, Arthur, Galway, 1901–3
Lynch, Col. A. A., Galway, 1892; Galway North, 1901–6; Clare West, 1909–
   18
Lynch, A. H., Galway City, 1832–41
Lynch, D. C., Cork South-East, 1918–22
Lynch, Finian, Kerry South, 1918–22
Lynch, M. A., Galway, 1886(by)
Lynch, Nicholas, Sligo Co., 1883–5
Lynch, Patrick, KC, Clare East, 1917
Lynn, R. J., Belfast (Woodvale), 1918–22
Lyons, Dr Frands, Cork City, 1859(by)–65(by)
Lyons, Dr R. S. D., Dublin City, 1880–5

Macafee, William, Antrim North, 1910(Dec.)
Macaleese, David, Monaghan North, 1895–1900 (d.)
McAlpine, Lt Col. James, Mayo Co., 1852
Macartan, Dr Patrick, Armagh South, 1918(by)
Macartney, George, Antrim Co., 1852–9
Macartney, J. W. E., Tyrone Co., 1873, 1874–85
Macassey, Lynden, Down South, 1910(Jan.)
McBlain, F. W., LL D, Newry, 1859; Armagh Co., 1874
McBride, Major John, Mayo South, 1900(by)
McBride, Joseph, Mayo West, 1918–22
McCabe, Alex, Sligo South, 1918–22
McCalmont, Col. Hugh, Londonderry South, 1885; Antrim North, 1895–9
McCalmont, Capt. James, Longford Co., 1874
McCalmont, Col. J. M., Antrim East, 1885–1913 (d.)
McCalmont, Robert, Belfast East, 1886
McCalmont, Lt Col. R. C. A., Antrim East, 1913–19
McCance, John, Belfast, 1835(by) (d.)
McCann, James, Drogheda, 1852–65
McCann, James, QC, Dublin (St Stephen's Green), 1900–4 (d.)
McCann, Pierce, Tipperary East, 1918–22
McCarry, Patrick, Antrim North, 1918
McCartan, Michael, Down South, 1886–1902
McCartan, Dr Patrick, King's Co. (Tullamore), 1918(by); King's Co.,
   1918–22
McCarthy, Alexander, Limerick Co., 1832; Cork City, 1846–7 (def.) 1849;
   Cork Co., 1855, 1857–9; Dublin City, 1859
McCarthy, John, Tipperary Mid, 1892–3 (d.)

MacCarthy, J. G., Mallow, 1872, 1874–80

McCarthy, J. P., Galway South, 1892

McCarthy, Justin, Longford Co., 1879–85; Londonderry City, 1885; Longford North, 1885–6 (elected but chose to sit for Londonderry City); Londonderry City, 1886–92 (def.); Longford North, 1892–1900

McCarthy, J. H., Athlone, 1884–5; Newry, 1885–92

MacCaw, W. J. MacG., Tyrone East, 1906, 1906(by); Down West, 1908–18

McClean, J. R., Belfast, 1857

McClintock, Sir F. L., Drogheda, 1868

McClintock, John, Athlone, 1820–20; Louth Co., 1830–1

McClintock, John, Louth Co., 1841, 1852, 1857–9 (def.), 1865

McClintock (afterwards Bunbury McClintock), Capt. W. B., RN, Carlow Co., 1846–52 (def.), 1853–62

McClure, Sir Thomas, bt, Belfast, 1857, 1868–74 (def.); Londonderry Co., 1878–85

McCoan, J. C., Drogheda, 1880(by); Wicklow Co., 1880–5

McConnell, T. E., Belfast (Duneairn), 1921–2

McCorkell, Bartholomew, Londonderry City, 1872, 1874

McCorkell, D. B., Donegal Co., 1879; Donegal North, 1892

McCormick, William, Londonderry City, 1860–5

McCullagh, Denis, Tyrone South, 1918

McCullagh, James, LL D, Dublin University, 1847

McCullagh, W. T., Dundalk, 1847(def. but elected on petition)–52

McDermott, C. J., Sligo Co., 1837

McDermott, Patrick, Kilkenny North, 1891–1902

MacDonagh, Joseph, Tipperary North, 1918–22

McDonald, Capt. Patrick, Queen's Co., 1865

McDonald, Peter, Sligo North, 1885–91 (d.)

McDonald, W. A., Queen's Co. (Ossory), 1886–92, 1895

McDonnell, Edmund, Antrim Co., 1830, 1833

McDonnell, James, Dublin Harbour, 1892

Macdonnell, John, Clare Co., 1832

MacDonnell, J. M., Mayo Co., 1830, 1831, 1846–7 (def.)

MacDonnell, Dr M. A., Queen's Co. (Leix), 1892–1906

McDonnell, Thadeus, Limerick City, 1852

MacDonogh, Francis, QC, Carrickfergus, 1857; Sligo, 1860–5

McElroy, S. C., Antrim North, 1886, 1887

MacEntee, S. F., Monaghan South, 1918–22

McErlean, Andrew, Belfast South, 1886

McEvoy, Edward, Meath Co., 1855–74

McFadden, Edward, Donegal East, 1900–6

MacFarlane, D. H., Carlow Co., 1880–5

McGarel, Charles, Cashel, 1852

McGhee, Richard, Louth South, 1896–1900 (def.); Tyrone Mid, 1910(Dec.)–18

McGilligan, Patrick, Femmanagh South, 1892–5

McGilligan, Patrick, Londonderry North, 1918, 1919
McGillycuddy, Capt. John, Kerry East, 1892, 1896
McGovern, Thomas, Cavan West, 1900–4 (d.)
McGowan, Charles, Leitrim Co., 1876
McGrath, Henry, Down East, 1886
McGrath, Joseph, Dublin (St James's), 1918–22
McGuffin, Samuel, Belfast (Shankill), 1918–22
McGuinness, Joseph, Longford South, 1917–18; Longford Co., 1918–22
McHugh, Edward, Armagh South, 1892–1900
McHugh, J. B., Down West, 1886
McHugh, P. A., Leitrim North, 1892–1906 (elected but chose to sit for Sligo North); Clare East, 1895; Sligo North, 1906–9 (d.)
McKane, Prof. John, Armagh Mid, 1885–6 (d.)
McKean, John, Monaghan South, 1902–18
McKee, Dr J. T., Armagh South, 1918
McKelvey, J. H., Antrim Mid, 1886
McKenna, Sir J. N., New Ross, 1859, 1863; Tralee, 1865(by); Youghal, 1865–8, 1874–85; Monaghan South, 1885–92
McKenna, Patrick, Westmeath North, 1910(Jan.); Longford South, 1917
McKillop, William, Sligo North, 1900–6; Armagh South, 1906–7 (def.)
MacLachlan, Lachlan, Galway City, 1832 (elected but defeated on petition)
MacMahon, Edward, Dublin Co., 1883; Limerick City, 1883–5
MacMahon, Patrick, Wexford Co., 1852–65 (def.); New Ross, 1868–74
McMahon, R. M., Carlow Co., 1892
McMechan, William, Carrickfergus, 1859; Belfast, 1866
McMenamin, Daniel, Donegal West, 1918
McMordie, R. J., Belfast East, 1910(Dec.)–14 (d.)
McNabb, Richard, Down North, 1886
McNabb, Dr Russell, Down East, 1918; Belfast (Duncaim), 1918
MacNaghten, Edward, QC, Antrim Co., 1880–5; Antrim North, 1885–7
MacNaghten, E. A., Antrim Co., 1801–12, 1826–30
MacNaghten, Sir E. C. W., bt, Antrim Co., 1847–52
McNamara, Francis, Ennis, 1832–5
MacNamara, Major W. N., Clare Co., 1830–52
MacNeill, Prof. Eoin, D.Litt., National University of Ireland, 1918–22; Londonderry City, 1918–22
MacNeill, J. G. S., QC, Donegal South, 1887–1918
McSwiney, P. P., Dublin Co., 1868
McSwiney, T. J., Cork Mid, 1918–20 (d.)
MacTavish, C. C., Dundalk, 1847 (elected but unseated on petition)
MacVeagh, Jeremiah, Down South, 1902–22
McVeigh, Charles, Donegal East, 1906–10(Jan.)

Macklin, T. T., Dublin University, 1807
Madden, D. H., Dublin University, 1887–92

Madden, John, Monaghan Co., 1874

Magan, W. H., Westmeath Co., 1847–59

Magee, John, Drogheda, 1852

Magee, P. J., Belfast West, 1910(Jan.)

Magenis, Eiver, Down South, 1892

Magennis, John, Kilkenny City, 1917

Magennis, Richard, Enniskillen, 1812–28

Magrath, Col. J. R., Wexford North, 1892

Maguire, Denis, Newry, 1831, 1832

Maguire, J. F., Dungarvan, 1847, 1851, 1852–65; Cork City, 1865–72 (d.)

Maguire, J. R., Donegal North, 1890–2; Clare West, 1892–5 (def.)

Maher, John, Wexford Co., 1835–41

Maher, Nicholas, Tipperary Co., 1844–52

Maher, Valentine, Tipperary Co., 1841–4 (d.)

Mahon, J. L., Dublin Harbour, 1906

Mahon, Sir Ross, bt, Ennis, 1820–20(by)

Mahon, Major Gen. Hon. Stephen, Roscommon Co., 1806–26

Mahon, Hon. Thomas, Roscommon Co., 1801–2

Mahon, W. R., Clare Co., 1830, 1831

Mahon, The O'Gorman (J. P. O'Gorman Mahon), Clare Co., 1830 (unseated on petition), 1831

Mahony, David, Wicklow Co., 1880

Mahony, J. H., Kerry Co., 1841

Mahony, Pierce, Kinsale, 1837 (elected but unseated on petition)

Mahony, Pierce, Meath North, 1886–92 (def.), 1893; Dublin (St Stephen's Green), 1895

Mains, John, Donegal North, 1892–5

Malley, G. O., QC, Mayo South, 1885

Malone, Richard, Westmeath Co., 1826

Mandeville, Francis, Tipperary South, 1892–1900

Mapother, T. A. P., Roscommon Co., 1880

Manin, G. C., Sligo, 1832

Martin, Henry, Kinsale, 1806(by)–18

Martin, John, Sligo, 1832–7 (def.)

Martin, John, Longford Co., 1869; Meath Co., 1871–5 (d.)

Martin, P. L., QC, Kilkenny Co., 1874–85

Martin, Richard, Galway Co., 1801–12, 1818–26 (elected but unseated on petition)

Martin, T. B., Galway Co., 1832–47 (d.)

Marum, E. P. M., Kilkenny City, 1875; Kilkenny Co., 1880–5; Kilkenny North, 1885–90 (d.)

Massey, Godfrey, Limerick Co., 1832

Massey, H. D., Clare Co., 1801–2

Matheson, C. L., KC, Dublin (St Stephen's Green), 1904–6

Mathew, Viscount (Francis Mathew), Tipperary Co., 1802–6

Mathew, Viscount (John Mathew), Tipperary Co., 1801–2

Mathew, Major Gen. Hon. M. J., Tipperary Co., 1806–19 (d.)

Mathews, Henry, QC, Dungarvan, 1868–74 (def.), 1877, 1880

Matthew, Capt. G. B., Athlone, 1835–7

Maude, Hon. Cornwallis, Tipperary Co., 1841

Maule, W. H., Carlow, 1837–9

Maxwell, Henry, Cavan Co., 1824–39

Maxwell, Lt Col. Hon. J. P., Cavan Co., 1843–65

Maxwell, J. W., Downpatrick, 1820–30, 1832–5

Maxwell, Capt. S. H., Cavan Co., 1880; Tyrone South, 1885

Maxwell, Hon. S. R., Cavan Co., 1839–40

Maxwell-Barry, Col. John, Cavan Co., 1806–24

May, Sir Edward, bt, Belfast, 1801–14 (d.); Carrickfergus, 1807(by), 1807

May, G. A. C., QC, Carrickfergus, 1874

May, Sir Stephen, bt, Belfast, 1814–16 (d.)

Mayne, Thomas, Portarlington, 1883; Tipperary Co., 1883–5; Tipperary Mid, 1885–90

Meade, Hon. John, Down Co., 1805–17

Meade, J. M., LL D, Dublin (St Stephen's Green), 1892

Meagher, Michael, Kilkenny North, 1906(by)–18

Meagher, Thomas, Waterford City, 1847–57

Meagher, T. F., Waterford City, 1848

Meagher, William, Meath Co., 1884–5

Meehan, F. E., Leitrim North, 1908–18 (def.)

Meehan, P. A., Queen's Co. (Leix), 1906–13 (d.)

Meehan, P. J., Queen's Co. (Leix), 1913–18

Megaw, M. G., Tyrone East, 1886

Meldon, C. H., Kildare Co., 1874–85

Mellows, L. J., Galway East, 1918–22; Meath North, 1918–22

Meredyth, Henry, Meath Co., 1855

Metcalfe, Henry, Drogheda, 1820–2 (d.)

Metge, John, Dundalk, 1806–7, 1812–13, 1820 (by)

Metge, R. H., Meath Co., 1880–4

Meynell, Capt. Henry, RN, Lisburn, 1826–47

Middleton, Capt. C. M., Drogheda, 1859

Miller, A. E., QC, Dublin University, 1875

Miller, G. H., Longford South, 1892

Miller, S. B., QC, Armagh City, 1857–9 (def.), 1865–7

Miller, T. B., Armagh City, 1855

Miller, W. T., Tyrone North-West, 1918

Milroy, Sean, Tyrone East, 1918(by); Tyrone North-East, 1918

Milton, Viscount (W. T. S. W. Fitzwilliam), Wicklow Co., 1847–58

Minch, M. J., Kildare South, 1892–1903

Mitchell, John, Cork City, 1874

Mitchell, Edward, Fermanagh North, 1903–6 (def.)

Mitchell, John, Tipperary Co., 1874, 1875 (elected but disqualified), 1875 (elected but disqualified)

Mitchell-Thomson, William, Down North, 1910(by)–18

Moles, Thomas, Belfast (Ormeau), 1918–22

Molloy, B. C., King's Co., 1874; Louth Co., 1874(by); King's Co., 1880–5, King's Co. (Birr), 1885–1900 (def.)

Molloy, Michael, Carlow Co., 1910(Jan.)–18

Moloney, P. J., Tipperary South, 1918–22

Molony, C. B., Ennis, 1865

Molony, James, Clare Co., 1841

Molony, John, Limerick East, 1909

Monahan, Rt Hon. J. H., QC, Clonmel, 1847; Galway City, 1847(by Feb.)–47, 1874(by)

Monck, Hon. C. S., Wicklow, 1848

Monck, Capt. Hon. Richard, Wicklow Co., 1857

Monsell, Rt Hon. William, Limerick City, 1837; Limerick Co., 1847–74

Monsell, W. T., Limerick Co., 1806, 1807, 1811

Montagu, Rt Hon. Lord Robert, Westmeath Co., 1874–80

Montgomery, Sir H. C., bt, Donegal Co., 1808–12

Montgomery, H. L., Leitrim Co., 1852–8

Montgomery, John, Londonderry City, 1830

Moonan, G. A., Dublin Co. (Rathmines), 1918

Mooney, J. J., Dublin Co. South, 1900–6; Newry, 1906–18

Mooney, Joseph, Dublin North, 1892

Moore, Arthur, Tralee, 1801–2

Moore, Count Arthur J., Clonmel, 1874–85; Tipperary South, 1895; Londonderry City, 1899–1900 (def.)

Moore, Charles, Tipperary Co., 1865(by)–9 (d.)

Moore, George, LL D, Dublin City, 1826–31 (def.)

Moore, G. H., Mayo Co., 1846, 1847–57 (elected but unseated on petition); Kilkenny Co., 1859, 1868–70 (d.)

Moore, H. H., Tyrone Mid, 1885, 1886

Moore, Lord H. S., Lisburn, 1812–18

Moore, John, Newry, 1801–2

Moore, John, QC, Monaghan Co., 1883

Moore, Major R. L., Donegal East, 1918

Moore, R. S., Armagh City, 1852–5 (d.)

Moore, Stephen, Tipperary Co., 1837

Moore, Stephen, Tipperary Co., 1875–80; Clonmel, 1880–5

Moore, William, KC, Antrim North, 1899–1906 (def.); Armagh North, 1906(by)–17

Moore, Major W. A., Antrim East, 1919

Morgan, Capt. H. F., Kildare Co., 1874

Morgan, H. K. G., Wexford Co., 1841, 1847–52 (def.)

Morpeth, Lord (G. W. F. Howard), Dublin City, 1842

Morris, Abraham, Cork Co., 1832

Morris, George, Galway City, 1867–8

Morris, George, Galway, 1874–80

Morris, James, Cork City, 1841
Morris, Rt Hon. Michael, QC, Galway City, 1865–7
Morris, Hon. M. H. F., Galway, 1895, 1900–1
Morris, Samuel, Kilkenny South, 1894–1900
Morrogh, John, Cork South-East, 1889–93
Mosley, Sir Oswald, bt, Portarlington, 1806–7
Mostyn, Hon. G. C., Kilkenny Co., 1857
Mountcharles, Earl of (F. N. Conyngham) Donegal Co., 1825–31
Mountcharles, Earl of (H. J. Conyngham), Donegal Co., 1818–25 (d.)
Moynagh, S. H., Armagh South, 1910(Dec.)
Mulcahy, E. J., Dublin (Clontarf), 1918–22
Muldoon, John, Donegal North, 1905–6; Wicklow East, 1907–11; Cork East, 1911–18
Mulholland, H. L., Londonderry North, 1885–95
Mulholland, John, Belfast, 1868; Downpatrick, 1874–85
Mullany, Patrick, Roscommon North, 1885
Mullen, Dr St L. F., Dublin Co. South, 1892
Mullins, F. W. B., Kerry Co., 1831–7 (def.)
Mullins, J. D., Longford Co., 1831
Munster, Henry, Cashel, 1868; Mallow, 1870 (elected but unseated on petition); Donegal South, 1887
Munster, W. F., Mallow, 1872–4
Murnaghan, George, Tyrone Mid, 1895–1910(Jan.) (def.)
Murphy, F. S., Cork City, 1841–6, 1851–3
Murphy, John, Kerry East, 1900–10(Jan.) (def.)
Murphy, M. J., Waterford East, 1913–18
Murphy, N. D., Cork City, 1865(by)–80 (def.)
Murphy, N. J., Kilkenny South, 1907–9, 1910(Dec.)
Murphy, William, Cork City, 1910(Jan.)
Murphy, W. M., Dublin (St Patrick's), 1885–92 (def.); Kerry South, 1895(by); Mayo North, 1900
Murray, P. J., Clonmel, 1857(by)
Murray, R. W., Belfast East, 1885
Murray, T. L., Drogheda, 1847
Musgrave, Sir Richard, bt, Waterford Co., 1831–2, 1835–7

Naas, Rt Hon. Lord (R. S. Bourke), Coleraine, 1852(by)–7
Nagle, D. A., Mallow, 1874
Naggle, Sir Richard, bt, Westmeath Co., 1832–41
Naish, John, QC, Mallow, 1883
Nannetti, J. P., Dublin (College Green), 1900–15 (d.)
Naper, J. L., Meath, 1874, 1875
Naper, J. L. W., Meath Co., 1831
Napier, Rt Hon. Joseph, QC, Dublin University, 1847, 1848–58
Needham, Gen. Hon. Francis, Newry, 1806–19 (succeeded as Viscount Kilmorey)

Needham, Hon. F. J., Newry, 1819–26 (Viscount Newry from 1822)

Nelson, Revd Isaac, Leitrim, 1880; Mayo Co., 1880(by)–5

Nevill, Richard, Wexford, 1802–6, 1810, 1811(by)–13 (res.), 1814(by)– 19

Newcomen, Hon. T. G., Longford Co., 1802–6

Newcomen, Sir W. G., bt, Longford Co., 1801–2

Newport, Sir John, bt (afterwards Rt Hon.), Waterford City, 1802–32

Newry and Morne, Viscount (F. C. Needham), Newry, 1868, 1871–4 (def.)

Newry and Morne, Viscount (F. J. Needham), Newry, 1841–51 (d.)

Nicol, William, Youghal, 1837

Nolan, Joseph, Louth North, 1885–92; Louth South, 1892; Louth North, 1895; Louth South, 1900–18

Nolan, Col. J. P., Galway Co., 1872 (elected but unseated on petition), 1874–85; Galway North, 1885–95 (def.); Lough South, 1896; Galway North, 1900–6 (def.)

North, J. H., Dublin University, 1827, 1830; Drogheda, 1830–1(by) (d.)

Northland, Viscount (Thomas Knox), Dungannon, 1837–8

Norton, Thomas Athlone, 1853

Nugent, J. D., Dublin (College Green), 1915–18 (def.)

Nugent, Sir P. F., bt, Westmeath Co., 1847–52

Nugent, Hon. R. A., Galway East, 1885

Nugent, Sir W. R., bt, Westmeath South, 1907–18 (def.)

Nunn, E. W., Wexford Co., 1852

O'Beirne, Major Francis, Leitrim Co., 1874, 1876–85

O'Beirne, J. L., Cashel, 1865–70 (constituency disfranchised)

O'Beirne, J. L. M., Athlone, 1847

O'Brien, A. S., Limerick Co., 1837

O'Brien, Cornelius, Clare Co., 1832–47 (def.), 1852 (elected but unseated on petition), 1853–7

O'Brien, Sir Edward, bt, Clare Co., 1802–26

O'Brien, James, QC, Limerick City, 1852, 1854–8

O'Brien, J. F. X., Mayo South, 1885–95; Cork City, 1895(by)–1905 (d.)

O'Brien, John, Limerick City, 1841–52

O'Brien, K. E., Tipperary Mid, 1900–10(Jan.)

O'Brien, Prof. Liam, Armagh Mid, 1918

O'Brien, Sir Lucius, bt, Clare Co., 1826–30 (def.), 1835, 1847–52

O'Brien, Hon. L. W., Clare East, 1885

O'Brien, Sir Patrick, bt, King's Co., 1852–85

O'Brien, Patrick, Monaghan North, 1886(by)–92; Limerick City, 1892; Kilkenny City, 1895–1917 (d.)

O'Brien, P. J., Tipperary North, 1885–1906

O'Brien, Peter, Clare Co., 1979(by)

O'Brien, Robert, Leitrim South, 1892

O'Brien, Sir Timothy, bt, Cashel, 1846–59

O'Brien, William, QC, Ennis, 1879, 1880

O'Brien, William, Mallow, 1883(by)–5; Tyronne South, 1885–6 (def.); Cork North-East, 1887(by)–92 (elected but chose to sit for Cork City); Cork City, 1892–5, 1900–4 (resigned but re-elected), 1904–9, 1910(Jan.)–14 (resigned but re-elected), 1914–18; Cork North-East, 1910(Jan.) (elected but chose to sit for Cork City); Cork East, 1910(Dec.), Cork West, 1910(Dec.)

O'Brien, W. S., Ennis, 1828–31; Limerick Co., 1835–49

O'Bryen, Capt. Hon. James, Clare Co., 1808

O'Bryne, W. R., Wicklow Co., 1874–80

O'Callaghan, Hon. Cornelius, Tipperary Co., 1832–5; Dungarvan, 1837–41

O'Callaghan, Hon. W. F. O., Tipperary Co., 1874–7 (d.)

O'Clery, Keyes, Wexford Co., 1874–80 (def.)

O'Connell, Charles, Kerry Co., 1832–5

O'Connell, Daniel, Clare Co., 1828 (election declared void), 1829–30; Waterford Co., 1830–1; Kerry Co., 1831–2; Dublin City, 1832–5 (elected but unseated on petition); Kilkenny City, 1836–7 (def.); Dublin City, 1837–41 (def.); Cork Co., 1841–7 (d.); Meath Co., 1841 (elected but chose to sit for Cork Co.)

O'Connell Daniel (jun.), Carlow Co., 1841; Dundalk, 1846–7; Waterford City, 1847–8; Tralee, 1853–63

O'Connell, Daniel, Kerry South, 1885

O'Connell, G. J., Limerick Co., 1847

O'Connell, John, Youghal, 1832–7; Athlone, 1837–41; Kilkenny City, 1841–7; Limerick City, 1947–51; Clonmel, 1853–7

O'Connell, Maurice, Clare Co., 1831(by)–2; Tralee, 1832–53 (d.)

O'Connell, M. J., Kerry Co., 1835–52

O'Connor, Art, Kildare South, 1918–22

O'Connor Arthur, QC, Queen's Co., 1880–5; Queen's Co. (Ossory), 1885 (elected but chose to sit for Donegal East); Donegal East, 1885–1900; Donegal North

O'Connor, Dr Bernard, Clare West, 1892

O'Connor, Feargus, Cork Co., 1832–5 (elected but unseated on petition)

O'Connor, Major G. B., Dublin (College Green), 1910(Jan.)

O Connor, H. M, Limerick East, 1910(Dec.)

O'Connor, James Wicklow West, 1892–1910 (d.)

O'Connor, John, Kerry South, 1885–7

O'Connor, John, Tipperary Co., 1885(by)–5; Tipperary South, 1885–92 (def.); Kilkenny City, 1892 (def.); Kildare North, 1905–18 (def.)

O'Connor, T. P., Galway, 1880–5 (elected but chose to sit for Liverpool, Scotland div.) 1885–1929 (d.)

O'Conor, D. M., Sligo Co., 1868–83 (d.)

O'Conor Don, The (C. O. O'Conor), Roscommon Co., 1860–80 (def.); Wexford, 1883 (def.)

O'Conor Don, The (Denis O'Conor), Roscommon Co., 1831–47

O'Conor Don, The (Owen O'Conor), Roscommon Co., 1830–1 (d.)

Odell, Lt Col. William, Limerick Co., 1801–18

O'Doherty, J. E., Donegal North, 1885–90

O'Doherty, Joseph, Donegal North, 1918–22

O'Doherty, Dr K. I., Meath North, 1885–6

O'Doherty, Philip, Donegal North, 1906–18 (def.)

O'Doherty, William, Donegal North, 1900–5 (d.)

O'Donnell, F. H., Galway, 1874, 1874(by) (elected but unseated on petition); Dungarvan, 1877–85

O'Donnell, John, Mayo South, 1900(by)–10(Dec.)

O'Donnell, Matthew, Kilkenny City, 1859

O'Donnell, Thomas, Kerry West, 1900–18

O'Donoghue, Charles, Westmeath South, 1892

O'Donoghue, The (Daniel O'Donoghue), Tipperary Co., 1857(by)–65(by); Tralee, 1865(by)–85

O'Donoghue, T. P., Meath South, 1918

O'Dowd, John, Sligo North, 1900(by)–18 (def.)

O'Driscoll, Florence, Monaghan South, 1892–95; Tipperary Mid, 1900

O'Dwyer, Martin, Tipperary Mid, 1910(Dec.)

O'Ferrall, Rt Hon. R. M., Kildare Co., 1830–47; Longford, 1851–2; Kildare Co., 1859–65, 1880 (def.)

O'Flaherty, Anthony, Galway, 1847(by), 1847–57 (elected but unseated on petition)

O'Flaherty, Edmund, Dungarvan, 1852

O'Flaherty, M. J., Galway, 1868

O'Flaherty, Sean, Donegal East, 1918

Ogle, Vice-Admiral Sir Charles, bt, Portarlington, 1831

Ogle, Rt Hon. George, Dublin City, 1801–2 (def.)

Ogle, H. M., Drogheda, 1802, 1806–7 (def.), 1812–20

O'Gorman, Major Purcell, Waterford City, 1874–80 (def.)

O'Gorman, Richard, Limerick City, 1847

O'Gorman Mahon, Col. The (J. P. O'Gorman Mahon), Clare Co., 1830–1; Ennis, 1847–52 (def.), 1874 (def.); Clare Co., 1877 (def.), 1879(by)–85; Carlow, 1887–91 (d.)

O'Grady, Lt Col. Standish, Limerick Co., 1818, 1820–6 (def.), 1830(by) (elected but unseated on petition), 1830–5

O'Grady, Walter, Limerick Co., 1820

O'Hagan, Rt Hon. Thomas, Tralee, 1863–5

O'Hanlon, J. F., Cavan East, 1918(by)

O'Hanlon, Thomas, Cavan East, 1885–92

O'Hara, Charles, Sligo Co., 1801–22 (d.)

O'Hara, F. K., Sligo Co., 1883

O'Hara, H. H. H., Antrim Co., 1857

O'Hara, James, Galway, 1826–31

O'Hara, Capt. James, Galway, 1868

O'Hare, Patrick, Monaghan North, 1906–7

O'Hea, Patrick, Donegal West, 1885–90

O'Higgins, Brian, Clare West, 1918–22

O'Higgins, KC, Queen's Co., 1918–22

O'Keefe, F. A., Limerick City, 1888–95; Wicklow East, 1895; Limerick City, 1895(by)–1900

O'Keefe, John, Dungarvan, 1874–7 (d.)

O'Keefe, Patrick, Cork North, 1918–22

O'Kelly, Conor, Mayo North, 1900–10(Jan.); Mayo South, 1910(Jan.)

O'Kelly, E. P., Wicklow East, 1895(by)–95; Wicklow West, 1910(by)–14 (d.)

O'Kelly, James, Roscommon, 1880–5; Roscommon North, 1885–92 (def.), 1895–1917 (d.)

O'Kelly, J. J., Louth Co., 1918–22

O'Kelly, S. T., Dublin (College Green), 1918–22

O'Leary, Daniel, Cork West, 1910(Jan.), 1910(Dec.), 1916–18

O'Leary, Dr W. H., Drogheda, 1874–80 (d.)

Oliver, C. S., Limerick Co., 1802–6

O'Loghlen, Sir Bryan, bt, Clare Co., 1877–80

O'Loghlen, Sir C. M., bt, QC, Clare Co., 1863–77 (d.)

O'Loghlen, Rt Hon. Michael, Dublin City, 1832(by), Dungarvan, 1835–7(by)

O'Mahony, The (P. C. de L. O'Mahony), Wicklow West, 1918

O'Mahony, The (Pierce O'Mahony), Dublin Harbour, 1915

O'Mahony, Sean, Fermanagh South, 1918–22

O'Maille, Padraic, Galway (Connemara), 1918–22

O'Malley, Sir Samuel, bt, Mayo Co., 1814

O'Malley, William, Galway (Connemara), 1895–1918 (def.)

O'Mara, James, Kilkenny South, 1900–7, 1918–22

O'Mara, Stephen, Queen's Co. (Ossory), 1886(by)–86

O'Neill, Capt. Hon. A. E. B., Antrim Mid, 1910(Jan.)–15 (d.)

O'Neill, Dr Charles, Armagh South, 1900, 1909–18 (d.)

O'Neill, C. P., Dublin Co. (Pembroke), 1918

O'Neill, Hon. Edward, Antrim Co., 1863–80

O'Neill, J. A., Kildare Co., 1847

O'Neill, Major Gen. J. B. R., Antrim Co., 1802–41(by)

O'Neill, Hon. R. T., Antrim Co., 1885; Antrim Mid, 1885–1910(Jan.)

O'Neill, R. W. A., Antrim Mid, 1915–22

O'Reilly, J. T., Waterford City, 1837

O'Reilly, Major M. W., Longford Co., 1862–79

O'Reilly, William, Dundalk, 1832–5

Ormsby, C. M., Carlow, 1801(by)–6

Ormsby-Gore, William, Leitrim Co., 1806–7

Ormsby-Gore, W. R., Leitrim Co., 1858–76

Orr, James, Armagh North, 1900

Osborne, R. B., Waterford City, 1869, 1870–4 (def.)

O'Shaughnessy, P. J., Limerick West, 1900–18

O'Shaughnessy, Richard, Limerick City, 1874–83 (res.)

O'Shea, Capt. W. H., Clare Co., 1880–5; Galway City, 1886(by)

O'Shee, J. J., Waterford City, 1918

O'Shiel, K. R., Antrim South, 1918; Fermanagh North, 1918
Ossory, Earl of (John Butler), Kilkenny Co., 1830–2
O'Sullivan, Eugene, Kerry East, 1906, 1910(Jan.)–10(Dec.)
O'Sullivan, R. L., Cork City, 1918
O'Sullivan, Timothy, Kerry East, 1910(Dec.)–18
O'Sullivan, W. H., Limerick Co., 1874–85
Otway, Capt. R. J., Tipperary Co., 1852
Otway Cave, Hon. Robert, Tipperary Co., 1832(by)–32, 1835–45 (d.)
Oxmantown, Lord (William Parsons), King's Co., 1821–35

Pakenham, Capt. E. W., Antrim Co., 1852–4 (d.)
Pakenham, Lt Col. H. A., Londonderry City, 1913
Pakenham, Hon. H. R., Westmeath Co., 1808(by)–26
Pakenham, Lt Col. T. H., Antrim Co., 1854–65
Pallas, Rt Hon. Christopher, Londonderry City, 1872
Palliser, Major William, Dungarvan, 1865
Palliser, Wray, Waterford Co., 1814(by)
Palmer, Capt. R. W. H., Mayo Co., 1857–65
Parker, Capt. Peter, RN, Waterford, 1810(by)–11 (res.)
Parnell, C. S., Dublin Co., 1874(by); Meath Co., 1875–80 (elected but chose
  to sit for Cork City); Mayo Co., 1880 (elected but chose to sit for Cork
  City); Cork City, 1880–91 (d.)
Parnell, Sir H. B., bt, Queen's Co., 1802(by)–2; Portarlington, 1802(by);
  Queen's Co., 1806(by)–32
Parnell, Sir John, bt, Queen's Co., 1801 (d.)
Parnell, J. H., Wicklow Co., 1874; Wicklow West, 1892; Meath South, 1895–
  1900, 1903
Parnell, W. H., Wicklow Co., 1817(by)–21 (d.)
Parsons, John, King's Co., 1818–21
Parsons, Sir Lawrence, bt, King's Co., 1801–7
Parsons, Hon. R. C., Dublin University, 1887
Patton, A. St G., Cork Mid, 1885; Fermanagh South, 1892
Payne, J. W., Bandon, 1880(by); Cork West, 1885
Payne, Somers, Cork West, 1892
Pearson, W. L., Dublin (St Stephen's Green), 1892
Peel, Robert, Cashel, 1809–12
Pennefather, Kingsmill, Tipperary Co., 1807
Pennefather, Mathew, Cashel, 1830–2(by), 1835
Pennefather, Richard, Cashel, 1818–19
Penrose-Fitzgerald, R. U., Youghal, 1874
Penland, Robert, Drogheda, 1822
Perceval, Lt Col. Alexander, Sligo Co., 1822(by), 1831–47
Perceval, Alexander, Sligo South, 1885
Perceval, Spencer, Ennis, 1818–20
Perfse, Dudley, Galway, 1826
Perrier, W. L., Cork City, 1852

Perrin, Louis, Dublin City, 1831 (elected but unseated on petition); Monaghan Co., 1832–5; Cashel, 1835(by)

Phillips, John, Longford South, 1907(by)–17 (d.)

Pigot, Rt Hon. D. R., Clonmel, 1839–46

Pigott, Richard, Limerick City, 1868

Pike, Joseph, Cork City, 1885

Pim, J. E., Cork City, 1872, 1874

Pim, Jonathan, Dublin City, 1865–74 (def.)

Pim, J. T., Dublin Co. South, 1886

Pinkerton, John, Antrim North, 1885; Galway, 1886–1900

Plunket, Rt Hon. D. R., LL D, QC, Dublin City, 1868; Dublin University, 1870–95 (created Lord Rathmore)

Plunket, Rt Hon. W. C., LL D, Dublin University, 1802, 1812–27

Plunkett, Hon. G. J., Meath Co., 1871–4

Plunkett, Count G. N., Tyrone Mid, 1892; Dublin (St Stephen's Green), 1895, 1898; Roscommon North, 1917(by)–22

Plunkett, Hon. H. C., Dublin Co. South, 1892–1900 (def.); Galway, 1901

Plunkett, Hon. Randal, Meath Co., 1835

Pochin, Charles, Enniskillen, 1807–12

Poe, Lt Col. W. H., Queen's Co. (Ossory), 1895

Ponsonby, Capt. A. E. V., Carlow, 1857

Ponsonby, Hon. C. F. A. C., Dungarvan, 1851–2

Ponsonby, Hon. Frederick, Galway, 1811–12 (elected but unseated on petition)

Ponsonby, Hon. Frederick, Kildare Co., 1835; Carlow Co., 1840

Ponsonby, Hon. F. C., Kilkenny Co., 1806–26

Ponsonby, Hon. George, Kilkenny Co., 1806(by)–6; Cork Co., 1806–12 (def.); Youghal, 1826–32; Dublin University, 1832

Ponsonby, Rt. Hon. George, Wicklow Co., 1801(by)–6; 1816(by)–17 (d.)

Ponsonby, J. B., Galway, 1802(by)–2

Ponsonby, Thomas, Kerry Co., 1835

Ponsonby, Col. Hon. William, Londonderry Co., 1806, 1812–15 (d.)

Ponsonby, Hon. William, Youghal, 1847

Ponsonby, Rt. Hon. W. B., Kilkenny Co., 1801–6

Ponsonby, Hon. W. F. S., Youghal, 1812

Pope-Hennessy, Sir John, Kilkenny North, 1890(by)–1

Porcher, J. D., Dundalk, 1807(by)

Porter, Rt Hon. A. M., QC, Londonderry Co., 1881–4 (res.)

Porter, J. G. V., Fermanagh Co., 1874, 1880

Porter, S. C., Belfast (Pottinger), 1918

Potter, Robert, Limerick City, 1852–4 (d.)

Pottinger, Eldred, Down Co., 1812

Powell, Caleb, Limerick Co., 1841–7 (def.)

Power, Sir James, bt, Wexford Co., 1835–47, 1865–8

Power, John, Dungarvan, 1837(by); Waterford Co., 1837–40

Power, J. O'C., Mayo Co., 1874(by)–85; Mayo West, 1892

Power, J. T., Wexford Co., 1868–74 (def.)

Power, Dr Maurice, Cork Co., 1874(by)–52(by)
Power, N. M., Waterford Co., 1847–59
Power, Patrick, Waterford Co., 1835–5 (d.)
Power, P. J., Waterford Co., 1884(by)–5; Waterford East, 1885–1913 (d.)
Power, Richard, Waterford Co., 1801–2, 1806–14 (d.)
Power, Richard, Waterford Co., 1814(by)–30
Power, Richard, Waterford City, 1874–85, 1885–91 (d.)
Power, Robert, Dungarvan, 1807
Power, Robert, Waterford Co., 1831–2 (def.)
Prendergast, M. G., Galway, 1818, 1820–6
Primrose, Viscount (A. J. Primrose), Cashel, 1806–7
Pringle, Henry, Monaghan Co., 1883
Prittie, Hon. F. A., Carlow, 1801(by)–1; Tipperary Co., 1806–18 (def.), 1819(by)–31
Prittie, H. S., Carlow, 1801(by)
Proby, Hon. G. L., Wicklow Co., 1816(by)–29 (res.)
Proby, Rt Hon. Lord (G. L. Proby), Wicklow Co., 1858–68
Proby, Lord W. A., Wicklow Co., 1801(by)
Puerfoy, Capt. E. B., Clonmel, 1857(by)
Pusey, Philip, Cashel, 1831(by)–2
Pyne, J. D., Waterford West, 1885–90 (d.)

Quin (Wyndham-Quin from 1815), Hon. W. H., Limerick Co., 1806–20
Quinn, Thomas, Leitrim Co., 1880; Kilkenny City, 1886–92

Rae, Sir William, bt, Portarlington, 1831–2
Ram, Abel, Wexford Co., 1801–6, 1807–12
Raphael, Alexander, Carlow Co., 1835(by) (elected but unseated on petition)
Rawdon, Col. J. D., Armagh City, 1840–52
Rea, John, Belfast, 1874
Reade, W. M., Kilkenny City, 1830; Waterford City, 1835, 1841 (elected but unseated on petition)
Rearden, D. J., Athlone, 1865–8
Redington, Sir T. N., Dundalk, 1837–46; New Ross, 1856
Redmond, J. E., Wexford, 1859–65 (def.)
Redmond, J. E., New Ross, 1881–5; Wexford North, 1885–91; Cork City, 1891; Waterford City, 1891–1918 (d.)
Redmond, P. W., Wexford Co., 1835
Redmond, W. A., Wexford, 1872–80 (d.)
Redmond, Capt. W. A., Tyrone East, 1910(Dec.)–18; Waterford City, 1918(by)–22
Redmond, Walter, Wexford, 1872
Redmond, W. H. K., Wexford, 1883–5; Fermanagh North, 1885–92; Cork City, 1892; Clare East, 1892–1917 (d.); Cork City, 1910(Dec.)
Reddy, Michael, King's Co. (Birr), 1900–18
Reeves, R. W. C., Clare Co., 1877; Ennis, 1882; Clare West, 1885

Reid, D. D., Tyrone East, 1910(Dec.); Down East, 1918–22
Reilly, John, Sligo, 1860
Rennie, M. B., Carrickfergus, 1837
Rentoul, J. A., QC, Down East, 1890–1902
Reynolds, John, Dublin City, 1847–52 (def.), 1857
Reynolds, W. J., Tyrone East, 1885–95
Ricardo, David, Portarlington, 1819(by)–24 (d.)
Rice, J. H., Limerick City, 1910(Jan.), 1910(Dec.)
Rice, T. S., Limerick City, 1818, 1820(defeated at general election but elected on petition)–32
Rich, Sir George, Dublin City, 1832
Richardson, Henry, Coleraine, 1835
Richardson, J. J., Lisburn, 1853–7, 1863
Richardson, J. N., Armagh Co., 1880–5
Richardson, Jonathan, Lisburn, 1857–63
Richardson, T. W., Armagh South, 1918(by)
Richardson, William, Armagh Co., 1818–20
Roberts, Cramer, Kildare Co., 1830
Robertson, Lt Col. Caleb, Roscommon North, 1885
Robertson, C. H. de G., Kerry East, 1885
Robinson, Hon. F. J., Carlow, 1806–7
Robinson, Joseph, Down Mid, 1918
Robinson, Sir T. W., Dublin Co. South, 1918
Robson, William, Dundalk, 1868
Roche, Augustine, Cork City, 1895(by), 1895, 1905–10(Dec.); Louth North, 1911–16 (d.)
Roche, Sir D. V., bt, Limerick City, 1832–44
Roche, Col. Edmund, Cork Co., 1861
Roche, E. B., Cork Co., 1837–55
Roche, John, Galway East, 1890–1914 (d.)
Roche, Hon. J. B. B., Kerry East, 1896–1900
Roche, William, Limerick City, 1832–41
Rochfort, Lt Col. Gustavus, Westmeath Co., 1826–32 (def.)
Rochfort, Horace, Carlow Co., 1830
Rochfort, Col. Horace, Carlow, 1865, 1868
Roe, George, Tipperary Co., 1874
Roe, James, Tipperary Co., 1826; Cashel, 1832–5
Ronayne, Dominick, Dungarvan, 1830; Clonmel, 1832–6 (d.)
Ronayne, J. P., Cork City, 1872–6 (d.)
Roper-Caldbeck, Capt. W. C., Dublin North, 1885
Rorke, J. H., Longford, 1832 (elected but unseated on petition)
Ross, David, Mallow, 1847
Ross, D. R., Belfast, 1841, 1842–7
Ross, John, QC, Londonderry City, 1892–5 (def.)
Rossa, J. O'D., Tipperary Co., 1869 (elected but disqualified)
Rowan, Dr Thomas, Down South, 1895

Rowan, Lt Col. William, Kerry West, 1885

Rowe, John, Wexford Co., 1830, 1832

Rowley, Clotworthy, Downpatrick, 1801(by)

Rowley, Rear Adm. Sir Josias, bt, Kinsale, 1821–6

Rowley, Hon. R. T., Meath Co., 1831

Rowley, S. C., Downpatrick, 1801(by)–2, Kinsale, 1802–6

Rowley, William, Kinsale, 1801–2

Russell, Charles, QC, Dundalk, 1868, 1874, 1880–5

Russell, F. W., Limerick City, 1852–71 (d.)

Russell, John, Kinsale, 1826–32

Russell, Lord John, Bandon, 1826(by)–30

Russell, Rt Hon. T. W., Tyrone South, 1886–1910(Jan.) (def.); Tyrone North, 1911–18

Rutherford, M. M. A., Monaghan South, 1892

Ruthven, Edward, Kildare Co., 1832–7 (def.)

Ruthven, E. S., Downpatrick, 1806–7 (def.), 1815, 1818, 1820, 1830–2; Dublin City, 1832–5 (elected but unseated on petition)

Ryan, E. A., Waterford West, 1910(Jan.)

Ryan, F. W., King's Co. (Birr), 1910

Ryan, G. E., Tipperary Mid, 1885

Ryan, Dr James, Wexford South, 1918–22

Ryan, Michael, Limerick Co., 1850

Rylett, Revd Harold, Tyrone Co., 1881

Sadleir, James, Tipperary Co., 1852–7 (expelled from Commons)

Sadleir, John, Carlow, 1847–53 (def.); Sligo, 1853–6 (d.)

St George, Christopher, Galway Co., 1847–52

St Lawrence, Viscount (W. U. Tristram), Galway, 1868–74(by)

Samuels, Rt Hon. A. W., KC, Dublin University, 1903, 1917–19

Sandwith, Lt Col. J. L., Tyrone East, 1900

Sarsfield, Capt. D. R. P., Cork City, 1891

Saunders, R. C., Newry, 1886

Saunders, Capt. R. J. P., Wicklow West, 1892

Saunderson, Alexander, Cavan Co., 1826–31

Saunderson, A. D., Tyrone East, 1910(Jan.)

Saunderson, Col. Rt Hon. E. J., Cavan Co., 1865–74 (def.); Armagh North, 1885–1906 (d.)

Saunderson, Francis, Cavan Co., 1801–6

Saunderson, Samuel, Cavan West, 1885

Savage, Archibald, Belfast (Cromac), 1918

Savage, Francis, Down Co., 1801–12(by)

Saxton, Sir Charles, bt, Cashel, 1812–18

Scanlan, Thomas, Sligo North, 1909–18 (def.)

Scott, Claude, Dungannon, 1809–12

Scully, Francis, Tipperary Co., 1847–57

Scully, Vincent, QC, Cork Co., 1852(by)–7 (def.), 1859–65 (def.)

Scully, Vincent, Kilkenny North, 1890
Sears, William, Mayo South, 1918–22
Seaward, Josh, Limerick City, 1865
Seeds, Roben, LL D, QC, Belfast, 1878, 1880; Belfast South, 1885
Sexton, Robert, Dublin (St Stephen's Green), 1888
Sexton, Thomas, Sligo Co., 1880–5; Belfast West, 1885; Sligo South, 1885–6
   (elected but chose to sit for Belfast West); Belfast West, 1886–92 (def.);
   Kerry North, 1892–6
Seymour, Rear Admiral, G. H., Antrim Co., 1865–9 (d.)
Seymour, Sir H. B., Lisburn, 1819(by)–26; Antrim Co., 1845–7; Lisburn,
   1847–52 (d.)
Seymour, Capt. H. de G. (afterwards Earl of Yarmouth), Antrim Co., 1869–
   74
Seymour, H. H. J., Antrim Co., 1818–22 (d.)
Shakespeare, Arthur, Portarlington, 1812–16
Shanahan, Philip, Dublin Harbour, 1918–22
Sharman Crawford, Arthur, Down Co., 1884
Sharman Crawford, James, Down Co., 1874–8 (d.)
Sharman Crawford, Major John, Down Co., 1880
Sharman Crawford, Col. R. G., Down North, 1900; Belfast East, 1914–18;
   Down Mid, 1921–2
Sharman Crawford, William, Down Co., 1831; Belfast, 1832; Dundalk, 1835–
   7; Down Co., 1852
Sharp, Richard, Portarlington, 1816(by)–19(by)
Shaw, Rt Hon. Frederick, Dublin City, 1830–1 (def.) (new election on peti-
   tion), 1832(by); Dublin University, 1832–48
Shaw, Robert, Dublin City, 1804–26
Shaw, William, Bandon, 1857(by), 1868–74; Cork Co., 1874–85
Shawe-Taylor, Capt. John, Galway, 1906(by)
Sheares, J. W. P., Cork South-East, 1892
Shee (afterwards O'Shee), J. J., Waterford West, 1895(by)–1918
Shee, William, Kilkenny Co., 1852–7 (def.), 1859
Sheehan, DD, Cork Mid, 1901–18; Limerick West, 1910(Dec.)
Sheehan, J. D., Kerry East, 1885–95
Sheehy, David, Galway South, 1885–1900; Waterford City, 1892; Meath South,
   1903–18
Sheil, Edward, Athlone, 1874–80 (def.); Meath Co., 1882–5; Meath South,
   1885–92
Sheil, Rt Hon. R. L., Louth Co., 1830, 1831–2; Tipperary Co., 1832–41;
   Dungarvan, 1841–51
Sheridan, R. B., Waterford Co., 1807
Sherlock, David, QC, King's Co., 1868–80; Dublin (College Green), 1885
Shillington, Thomas, Armagh North, 1885; Tyrone South, 1895
Shirley, E. J., Monaghan Co., 1826–31
Shirley, E. P., Monaghan Co., 1841–7

Shirley, S. E., Monaghan Co., 1868–80 (def.); Monaghan South, 1885
Shortall, Sir Patrick, Dublin (Clontarf), 1918
Sinclair, W. P., Antrim Co., 1885(by); Antrim North, 1885
Singleton, C. J., Leitrim North, 1900
Singleton, H. C., Meath Co., 1847
Skeffington, John, Tyrone South, 1918
Skeffington, T. H., Louth Co., 1822(by)–4 (succeeded as Viscount Ferrall)
Skipton, George, Londonderry City, 1860
Slater, G. G., Longford Co., 1874
Sleator, G. W. W., Longford Co., 1851
Slipsey, Dr M. B., Cork West, 1916
Sloan, T. H., Belfast South, 1902–10(Jan.) (def.), 1910(Dec.)
Sloyan, Thomas, Galway North, 1918
Small, J. F., Wexford Co., 1883–5; Down South, 1885–6
Smiley, Sir J. R., bt, Belfast West, 1906, 1910(Dec.)
Smith, H. S., Westmeath Co., 1885
Smith, R. V., Tralee, 1829(by)–31
Smith, T. B. C., Youghal, 1835
Smith-Barry, A. H., Cork Co., 1867–74
Smithwick, J. F., Kilkenny City, 1880(by)–6
Smithwick, Richard, Kilkenny Co., 1846–7
Smyth, P. J., Waterford City, 1870; Westmeath Co., 1871–80; Tipperary Co., 1880–5
Smyth, Richard, Youghal, 1830
Smyth, Prof. Richard, Londonderry Co., 1874–8 (d.)
Smyth, Robert, Westmeath Co., 1824(by)–6 (def.)
Smyth, R. J., Lisburn, 1852(by)–3 (d.)
Smyth, T. F., Leitrim South, 1906–18
Smyth, William, Westmeath Co., 1801–8 (res.)
Smyth, W. M., Drogheda, 1822–6 (def.)
Smythe, Col. J. R., Youghal, 1859
Sneyd, Nathaniel, Cavan Co., 1801–26; Enniskillen, 1806 (elected but chose to sit for Cavan)
Somers, J. P., Sligo, 1837–47 (elected but unseated on petition), 1848, 1848–52 (def.), 1853, 1856, 1857 (elected but unseated on petition), 1859, 1860
Somerville, Sir Marcus, bt, Meath Co., 1801–31 (d.)
Somerville, Rt Hon. Sir W. M., bt, Drogheda, 1837–52 (def.)
Southwell, R. H., Cavan Co., 1826, 1831
Spaight, James, Limerick City, 1858–9 (def.), 1865, 1874, 1879, 1880, 1883, 1885
Spencer, Lt Gen. Sir Brent, Sligo, 1815(by)–18
Spencer, Joshua, Sligo, 1813–15
Stacpoole, William, Ennis, 1860–79 (d.)
Stack, Austin, Kerry West, 1918–22

Stack, John, Kerry North, 1885–92
Stack, T. N., Kerry North, 1910(Jan.)
Stackpoole, William, Clare Co., 1852
Staines, Michael, Dublin (St Michan's), 1918–22
Staniforth, John, Athlone, 1868
Stanley, E. J., Monaghan Co., 1865
Staples, Rt Hon. John, Antrim Co., 1801–2
Staples, Robert, Queen's Co. (Ossory), 1892
Staples, Sir Thomas, bt, Newry, 1835
Stawell, Lt Col. Sampson, Kinsale, 1832–5
Stephen, James, Tralee, 1808(by)–12
Stewart, A. R., Londonderry Co., 1814(by)–30
Stewart, Lt Col. Hon. C. W., Londonderry Co., 1801–14(by)
Stewart, Lt Col. H. H. A., Donegal North, 1885, 1886
Stewart, Sir Hugh, bt, Tyrone Co., 1830–5
Stewart, James, Tyrone Co., 1801–12
Stewart, Sir James, bt, Donegal Co., 1802–18
Stewart, Rt Hon. Sir John, bt, Tyrone Co., 1802(by)–6, 1812–25 (d.)
Stewart, John, Down Co., 1826
Stewart, William, Tyrone Co., 1818–30
Stewart, W. J., Belfast (Ormeau), 1918
Stewart, Capt. W. V., Waterford Co., 1835(by)–47
Stirling, James, Dublin City, 1880
Stock, Joseph, LL D, Dublin University, 1837; Cashel, 1838–46
Stock, T. O., Carlow, 1865–8
Stoney, R. V., Mayo West, 1885
Stoney, Capt. T. B., Donegal East, 1886
Stopford, Viscount (James Stopford), Wexford Co., 1818, 1820–30
Stopford, Viscount (J. W. M. Stopford), Wexford North, 1885
Strahan, Andrew, 1807–12
Stronge, Col. Sir J. M., bt, Armagh Co., 1864–74
Stuart, H. V., Waterford Co., 1826–30
Stuart, Hon. H. W. V., Waterford Co., 1873–4, 1880–5
Stuart, J. M., Tyrone East, 1885
Stuart, William, Armagh City, 1820–6
Stubber, Nicholas, Galway, 1865, 1866
Stubbs, Henry, Donegal South, 1892, 1895
Style, Sir T. C., bt, Donegal Co., 1831
Sudley, Viscount (A. S. Gore), Donegal Co., 1801–6
Suffern, George, Belfast, 1847
Sullivan, A. M., Louth Co., 1874–80 (elected but declined the seat); Meath
    Co., 1880(by)–2
Sullivan, Donal, Westmeath South, 1885–1907 (d.)
Sullivan, Rt Hon. Edward, QC, Mallow, 1865–70
Sullivan, Sir Edward, bt, Dublin (St Stephen's Green), 1886
Sullivan, Michael, Kilkenny City, 1847(by)–65

Sullivan, Richard, Kilkenny City, 1832–6
Sullivan, T. D., Westmeath Co., 1880–5; Dublin (College Green), 1885–92 (def.); Donegal West, 1892–1900
Sullivan, T. K., Bandon, 1863
Swanston, Alexander, Bandon, 1874–80
Sweeney, J. A., Donegal West, 1918–22
Sweetman, John, Wicklow East, 1892–5(by) (resigned but stood again), 1895 (def.); Meath North, 1895
Sweetman, R. M., Wexford North, 1918–22
Swift, Richard, Sligo Co., 1852–7 (def.)
Symes, Lt Col. Michael, Carlow, 1806(by)
Synan, E. J., Limerick Co., 1859, 1859–85

Taaffe, John, Sligo Co., 1852
Tait, Sir Peter, Limerick City, 1868, 1874
Talbot, Darcy, Wexford Co., 1831
Talbot, James, Athlone, 1830, 1831, 1832–5 (def.)
Talbot, J. H., New Ross, 1832–41, 1847–52
Talbot, Col. R. W., Dublin Co., 1802, 1807–30 (def.)
Talbot, William, Kilkenny City, 1801–1
Talbot, Hon. W. C., Waterford Co., 1859–65, 1866
Talbot, W. J., Roscommon South, 1885
Talbot-Crosbie, Maurice, Cork City, 1918
Tanner, Dr C. K. D., Cork City, 1885–1901 (d.); Galway North, 1892
Tarpey, Hugh, Galway, 1880
Taylor, Daniel, Coleraine, 1874–80 (def.)
Taylor, Rt Hon. Col. T. E., Dublin Co., 1841–83 (d.)
Taylor, Walter, Monaghan Co., 1826
Tenison, E. K., Leitrim Co., 1847–52, 1857; Roscommon Co., 1859; Leitrim Co., 1865
Tenison, Major William, Monaghan South, 1895
Tennent, Sir J. E., Belfast, 1832–41 (elected; defeated on petition but re-elected at new election), 1842–5; Lisburn, 1852(by)
Tennent, R. J., Belfast, 1832, 1835(by), 1847–52 (def.)
Thomas, Lt Col. Henry, Kinsale, 1835–41
Thompson, Dr E. C., Tyrone Mid, 1892, 1895; Fermanagh North, 1898; Tyrone South, 1900; Monaghan North, 1900(by)–6
Thompson, Robert, Downpatrick, 1837
Thompson, Robert, Belfast North, 1910(Jan.)–18
Thompson, Skeffington, Meath Co., 1802
Thomson, Henry, Newry, 1880–5, 1892, 1895
Tierney, Rt Hon. George, Athlone, 1806–7; Bandon, 1807(by)–12
Tighe, R. M., Westmeath Co., 1812
Tighe, R. S., Westmeath Co., 1812
Tighe, Thomas, Mayo Co., 1874 (elected but unseated on petition), 1874(by)
Tighe, William, Wicklow Co., 1806(by)–16 (d.)

Torrens, Robert, Carrickfergus, 1859–68 (def.)

Tottenham, A. L., Leitrim Co., 1876, 1880–5

Tottenham, Charles, New Ross, 1802–5 (res.)

Tottenham, Charles, New Ross, 1831(by), 1835, 1856–63

Tottenham, Lt Col. C. G., New Ross, 1863–8, 1874, 1878–80 (def.); Wicklow East, 1885, 1886, 1895(by), 1895

Tottenham, G. L., Leitrim North, 1885

Tottenham, Ponsonby, Wexford, 1801(by)–2; New Ross, 1805–6

Towneley, Charles, Sligo, 1848 (elected but unseated on petition), 1852 (elected but unseated on petition)

Traill, Anthony, LL D, Dublin University, 1875

Traill, W. A., Antrim North, 1887

Trant, Major Fitzgibbon, Tipperary East, 1885

Trench, Hon. C. G., Tipperary North, 1892

Trench, Frederick, Portarlington, 1801 (created Lord Ashtown)

Trench, Major F. W., Dundalk, 1812(by)

Trench, Capt. Hon. W. Le P., Galway Co., 1872(defeated but elected on petition)–4

Trench, W. T., King's Co. (Birr), 1892

Treston, L. A., Sligo, 1859

Tuite, H. M., Westmeath Co., 1826–30 (def.), 1841–7

Tuite, James, Westmeath North, 1885–1900

Tullamore, Lord (C. W. Bury), Carlow, 1826–32

Tully, Jasper, Leitrim South, 1892–1906; Roscommon North, 1917

Turley, J. J., Monaghan North, 1918

Turnbull, Dr Arthur, Londonderry South, 1916

Turner, Adam, Belfast North, 1896

Turner, J. F., Athlone, 1807(by)–12

Tuthill, John, Limerick City, 1817

Tyrone, Earl of (J. H. de la P. Beresford), Waterford Co., 1865–6

Tyrwhitt, Thomas, Portarlington, 1802(by)–6 (res.)

Upton, Hon. F. G., Downpatrick, 1802

Upton, Major Gen. Hon. G. F., Antrim Co., 1859–63

Urquhart, W. P., Westrneath Co., 1852–7, 1859–71 (d.)

Valentia, Viscount (G. A. Annesley), Wexford Co., 1818; 1830–1 (def.)

Valentine, John, Tyrone Mid, 1910(Jan.)

Vance, John, Dublin City, 1852–65 (def.); Armagh City, 1867–73 (d.)

Vandeleur, Col. C. M., Clare Co., 1841, 1852, 1853, 1859–74 (def.)

Vandeleur, Capt. H. S., Clare Co., 1879, 1880

Vandeleur, J. O., Ennis, 1801–2

Van Homrigh, Peter, Drogheda, 1826–30

Vereker, Rt Hon. Col. Charles, Limerick City, 1802–17

Vereker, Col. Hon. C. S., Limerick City, 1874

Vereker, John (jun.), Limerick City, 1832

Vereker, Hon. J. P., Limerick City, 1817–20 (elected but unseated on petition)

Verner, E. W., Lisburn, 1863(by), 1863–73; Armagh Co., 1873–80

Verner, Thomas, Carrickfergus, 1812

Verner, Lt Col. Sir William, bt, Armagh Co., 1826, 1832–68

Verner, William, Armagh Co., 1868–73 (d.)

Verner, Sir W. E. H., bt, Armagh Co., 1880

Verschoyle, Col. J. H., Antrim Mid, 1906

Vesey, Hon. Thomas, Queen's Co., 1835–7 (def.), 1841–52

Vigors, N. A., Carlow, 1832–5 (def.); Carlow Co., 1835(by) (elected but unseated on petition), 1837(by)–40 (d.)

Villiers-Stuart, Henry, Cork East, 1885

Waddy, Cadwallader, Waterford Co., 1832, 1834–5

Waldron, Laurence, Tipperary Co., 1857(by), 1857–65, 1866

Waldron, L. A., Dublin (St Stephen's Green), 1904–10(Jan.)

Walker, C. A., Wexford, 1831–41

Walker, Rt Hon. Samuel, QC, Londonderry Co., 1884–5; Londonderry North, 1885; Londonderry South, 1892

Walker, William, Belfast North, 1905, 1906, 1907

Wallace, Sir Richard, bt, Lisburn, 1873–85

Wallace, Col. R. H., Down East, 1902

Wallace, Thomas, LL D, KC, Drogheda, 1818, 1820, 1826, 1831, 1831–2; Carlow Co., 1832–5

Wallace, T. B., Down West, 1921–2(by)

Waller, John, Limerick Co., 1801–2

Walpole, Gen. Hon. George, Dungarvan, 1806–20

Walsh, J. J., Cork City, 1918–22

Walsh, John, Cork South, 1910(Dec.)–18

Walsh, Rt Hon. J. E., LL D, Dublin University, 1866–7

Walsh, Louis, Londonderry South, 1918

Walsh, Thomas, Cork North, 1885

Walsh, W. H., King's Co. (Tullamore), 1885

Wanklyn, J. L., Galway, 1910(Dec.)

Ward, M. F., Galway, 1874(by)–80

Ward, P. J., Donegal South, 1918–22

Ward, Robert, Down Co., 1812(by)

Waring, Major Henry, Newry, 1857

Waring, Col. Thomas, Down North, 1885–98 (d.)

Warren, Sir A. R., bt, Cork South-East, 1885

Warren, Sir Augustus, bt., Cork City, 1829

Waters, George, QC, Mallow, 1870–2

Watson, W. H., Kinsale, 1841–7 (def.)

Waugh, Robert, Belfast (Victoria), 1918

Webb, Alfred, Waterford West, 1890–5 (res.)

Webb, Robert, Mallow, 1880

Webb, T. E., LL D, Dublin University, 1868
Webber, D. W., Armagh City, 1816–18
Weguelin, Christopher, Youghal, 1868 (elected but unseated on petition)
Welch, P. R., Kilkenny Co., 1847
Wellesley, Sir Arthur, Tralee, 1807 (elected to sit for Newport, Isle of Wight)
Wellesley, Hon. Henry, Athlone, 1807 (by)
Wellesley, Richard, Ennis, 1820 (by)–6
Wellesley-Pole, Rt Hon. William, Queen's, 1801 (by)–21 (unseated), 1830 (unseated)
West, J. B., Dublin City, 1832, 1835 (defeated but elected on petition)–7 (def.), 1841–2 (d.)
Westenra, Hon. H. R., Monaghan Co., 1818–30 (def.), 1831–2 (def.), 1834 (elected but unseated on petition), 1835–43 (succeeded as Lord Rossmore)
Westenra, Lt Col. Hon. J. C., Monaghan, 1830; King's Co., 1831
Westenra, Lt Col. Hon. J. C., King's Co., 1835–52
Westenra, Hon. P. C., Monaghan South, 1886; Monaghan North, 1895
Westropp, Ralph, Limerick City, 1832
Weymes, P. H., Westmeath Co., 1918
White, A. H., Londonderry North, 1906
White, Capt. Charles, Clare Co., 1860
White, Lt Col. Hon. C. W., Dublin Co., 1865; Tipperary Co., 1866–75
White, Col. Henry, Dublin Co., 1823–32; Longford Co., 1835, 1837–47, 1857–61
White, Luke, Dublin Co., 1806
White, Luke, Leitrim Co., 1812, 1818–24 (d.)
White, Luke, Longford Co., 1819 (elected but unseated on petition), 1835, 1836, 1837–41 (def.)
White, Lt Col. Hon. Luke, Clare Co., 1857, 1859 (elected but unseated on petition); Longford Co., 1861–2 (def.). Carrickfergus, 1865
White, Patrick, Meath North, 1900–18
White, Lt Col. Samuel, Leitrim Co., 1824–47
White, Thomas, Leitrim Co., 1806
White, Col. Thomas, Dublin Co., 1818, 1820
White, Dr V. J., Waterford City, 1918 (by), 1918
Whiteside, Rt Hon. James, QC, Enniskillen, 1851–9; Dublin University, 1859 (by)–66
Whitla, Sir William, Queen's University of Belfast, 1918–22
Whitty, P. J., Louth North, 1916–18
Whitworth, Benjamin, Drogheda, 1865–8 (elected but unseated on petition), 1874; Kilkenny City, 1875–80; Drogheda, 1880 (by)–5
Whitworth, Thomas, Drogheda, 1869–74
Whitworth, William, Newry, 1874–80
Whyte, J. C., Downpatrick, 1837
Wickham, Rt Hon. William, Cashel, 1802–6

Wigram, Sir Robert, bt, Wexford, 1806–7
Wigram, Sir Robert, Wexford, 1829(by) (unseated), 1830 (unseated)
Wigram, William, New Ross, 1807–12
Wigram, William, Wexford, 1820–6
Wigram, William, New Ross, 1826–30, 1831(by)–2
Williams, Daniel, Cork City, 1918
Williams, Robert, Kilkenny City, 1809–12
Williamson, James, Armagh North, 1886; Down East, 1910(Dec.)
Wills, James, Carrickfergus, 1832
Wilson, Charles, Antrim Co., 1874, 1880
Wilson, D. J., Dublin North, 1895; Tyrone North, 1900
Wilson, D. M., KC, Down West, 1918–21
Wilson, E. D., Carrickfergus, 1802, 1812
Wilson, Field-Marshal, Sir H. H., bt, Down North, 1922(by)2 (d.)
Wilson, James, Longford South, 1885
Wilson, J. M., Longford North, 1885, 1892
Wilson, John, Westmeath North, 1885
Wilson, John, Dublin University, 1857
Wilson, Sir Samuel, Londonderry Co., 1881
Wilson, Thomas, Limerick City, 1837
Wilson, William, Donegal Co., 1876–9 (d.)
Wilson, William, Tyrone North, 1895
Wolff, G. W., Belfast East, 1892(by)–1910(Dec.)
Wood, Lt Col. A. J., Cork City, 1859
Woods, E. H., Dublin North, 1892
Woods, Sir R. H., Dublin University, 1917, 1918–22
Workman, John, Belfast South, 1885
Woulfe Rt Hon. Stephen, Cashel, 1835(by)–8
Wright, George, QC, Dublin University, 1895(by)
Wyndham-Quin, Hon. W. H., Limerick Co., 1806–20
Wynne, John, Sligo, 1830–2 (def.)
Wynne, Rt Hon. J. A., Sligo, 1856–60
Wynne, Owen, Sligo, 1801–6 (res.), 1820–30
Wynne, Owen, Sligo North, 1892
Wylie, J. O., Tyrone North, 1886
Wyse, Thomas, Tipperary Co., 1830–2; Waterford City, 1832, 1835–47 (def.)

Yarmouth, Earl of (F. C. Seymour-Conway), Lisburn, 1802–12; Antrim Co., 1812–18
Yarmouth, Earl of (Richard Seymour-Conway), Antrim Co., 1822–6 (when first elected, Viscount Beauchamp)
Yates, J. A., Carlow Co., 1837–41 (def.)
Young, Rt Hon. Sir John, bt, Cavan Co., 1831–55
Young, Samuel, Cavan East, 1892–1918 (d.)
Young, Sir William, bt, Cavan Co., 1830

Index of parliamentary candidates, post-1921

Key
Name of candidate, constituency
Northern Ireland Parliament (1921–72); Assembly (1973–86); Constitutional Convention (1975) = italics
Northern Ireland candidates for Westminster Parliament = (w)
European Parliament = capitals
Successful candidate = dates between which the seat was held. Loss of seat at a subsequent general election is indicated by '(def.)' after the relevant date; death is shown by '(d.)'.
Unsuccessful candidate = date of the contest
By-elections are indicated by '(by)'

Abbey of the Holy Cross, *see* Fitzsimon
Abbott, H. J. J., Longford-Westmeath, 1977, 1987–9 (def.)
Able-O'Reilly, Patrick, Dún Laoghaire, 1987
Acheson, Caroline (Carrie), Tipperary South, 1981–2(Feb.) (def.)
Acheson, P. N., *Fermanagh-Tyrone South,* 1979
Adams, Alexander, *Down,* 1921: *Ards,* 1929
Adams, Gerard, *Belfast West,* 1982–; Belfast West (w), 1983–
Adams, Owen, *Belfast East,* 1973
Agnew, Fraser, *Antrim South,* 1982–6
Agnew, Iris, *Antrim North,* 1974(by), 1975
Agnew, Norman, *Belfast East,* 1973–5 (def.); Belfast East (w), 1979
Agnew, Patrick, *Armagh South,* 1938–45 (def.)
Agnew, Patrick, Louth, 1981–2(Feb.)
Agnew. T. B., *Londonderry South,* 1949; *Londonderry Mid,* 1953
Ahern, Bertie, Dublin (Finglas), 1977–81; Dublin Central, 1981–
Ahern, Dennot, Louth, 1987–
Ahern, George, Meath, 1948
Ahem, Joseph, Cork East, 1948
Ahern, Kathleen (Kit), Kerry North, 1965, 1969, 1973, 1977–81 (def.)
Ahern, Liam, Cork North-East, 1969, 1973–4 (d.)
Ahern, Michael, Cork East, 1982(Nov.)
Ahern, Michael, Kerry South, 1987
Ahern, Therese, Tipperary South, 1989
Aherne, Chrissie, Cork South-Central, 1981
Aherne, Patrick, Limerick West, 1955(by)
Aiken, Frank, Louth, 1987, 1989
Aiken, Frank T., Louth 1923–73; *Armagh,* 1921
Aird, W. P., Leix-Offaly, 1927(Sept.)–32
Alderdice, J. T., Belfast East (w), 1987; NORTHERN IRELAND, 1989
Alexander, R. B., *Belfast (Victoria),* 1945–53

Allen, Bernard, Cork North-Central, 1981–

Allen, Brendan W., Galway West, 1944

Allen, Cecil, *Belfast (Cromac)*, 1962, 1962(by)

Allen, David, Cork Borough, 1948

Allen, David, *Antrim North*, 1975–6

Allen, Denis, Wexford, 1927(June), 1927(Sept.)–33 (def.), 1936(by)–61

Allen, Edward, Cork East, 1981

Allen, George, Longford-Westmeath, 1957

Allen, J. A., *Londonderry*, 1982–6

Allen, Lorcan, Wexford, 1961–82(Nov.) (def.), 1987, 1989

Allen, S. J., Cork City North-West, 1969, 1973; Cork City, 1977

Allen, Thomas, *Belfast (Cromac)*, 1953

Allen, William, *Down North*, 1973

Allen, William B., Galway North, 1948

Allen, William E. D., Fermanagh-Tyrone (w), 1922; Belfast West (w), 1929–31

Allen, Lt Col. Sir William J., Armagh (w), 1922–47 (d.)

Allister, James Hugh, *Antrim North*, 1982–6; Antrim East (w), 1983

Allman, Daniel T., Kerry South, 1943

Alton, Prof. Ernest Henry, Dublin University, 1921–37

Ambrose, Thomas, Tipperary South, 1982(Nov.)

Anderson, Commander A. W., *Londonderry City*, 1968(by)–73

Anderson, Sir RN, *Londonderry*, 1921–9

Anderson, Thomas, Cavan, 1969

Andrews, David, Dún Laoghaire and Rathdown, 1965–77; Dún Laoghaire, 1977–

Andrews, J. L. O., *Down Mid*, 1953–64

Andrews, J. M., *Down*, 1921–9; *Down Mid*, 1929–53

Andrews, Niall, Dublin Co. South, 1977–81; Dublin South, 1981–7; DUBLIN, 1984–

Andrews, Patrick, Meath, 1987

Annesley, Allen, *Antrim South*, 1973

Annesley, G. F., Down South (w), 1951

Annett, William, *Down South*, 1973

Annon, W. T., *Belfast East*, 1973; *Belfast North*, 1975–6

Anthony, R. S., Cork Borough, 1923, 1927(June)–38 (def.), 1943–8 (def.), 1951

Appleton, Ronald, *Queen's University Belfast*, 1953

Archdale, D. T., *Enniskillen*, 1969

Archdale, Sir E. M., *Fermanagh North, Fermanagh-Tyrone*, 1921–9; *Enniskillen*, 1929–38

Archer, Peter, Meath, 1987

Ardill, Capt. R. A., *Carrick*, 1965–9; *Antrim South*, 1973–6

Armstrong, C. W., Armagh (w), 1954(by)–9

Armstrong, H. B., *Armagh Mid*, 1921(by)–2

Armstrong, Leo, Donegal South-West, 1983(by); Dublin Central, 1983(by)
Armstrong, M. H., *Armagh,* 1975–6
Armstrong, T. F., Leitrim-Sligo, 1932
Ashe, J. S., Dublin Co., 1923
Ashe, M. A., Galway West, 1943, 1944, 1948
Ashe, Séamus, Dublin South-Central, 1981
Aspell, Patrick, Kildare, 1982(Nov.)
Atkins, Donal, Wicklow, 1987
Austin, Joseph, *Belfast North,* 1982; Belfast North (w), 1983
Aylward, Edward, Carlow-Kilkenny, 1921–2 (def.)
Aylward, Liam, Carlow-Kilkenny. 1977–
Aylward, Robert (Bob), Carlow-Kilkenny, 1965, 1969, 1973

Babington, A. B., *Belfast South,* 1925(Nov.)(by)–9; *Belfast (Cromac),* 1929–38
Babington, R. J., *Down North,* 1969–73
Bailey, J. E., *Down West,* 1938–62
Bailie, R. J., *Newtownabbey,* 1969–73
Bailie, Thomas, *Down North,* 1941(by)–53 (def.)
Baillie, W. J., *Belfast North,* 1973
Baine, J. R., *Belfast (Ballynafeigh),* 1945
Baird, E. A., *Fermanagh-Tyrone South,* 1973–76, 1982; Fermanagh-Tyrone South (w), 1979
Baird, James, *Belfast South,* 1921
Baird, James, Waterford, 1923
Banahan, Thomas, Dublin South-East, 1969
Bannister, Grace, *Belfast South,* 1973
Bannister, John, *Belfast (Pottinger),* 1965
Banotti, Mary, Dublin Central, 1983(by); DUBLIN 1984–
Barbour, Sir John Milne, *Antrim,* 1921–9; *Antrim South,* 1929–51 (d.)
Barbour, W. P., *Fermanagh-Tyrone South,* 1975
Barkley, J. H., Belfast South (w), 1964; *Belfast (Cromac),* 1965, 1969
Barlow, Hannah, Dublin (Artane), 1977; Dublin North-Central, 1981
Barnes, Dermot, *Belfast South,* 1921
Barnes, J. A., Monaghan, 1923
Barnes, Monica, LEINSTER, 1979; Dún Laoghaire, 1981, 1982(Feb.), 1982(Nov.)–
Barr, Albert Glenn, *Londonderry,* 1973–6
Barr, Andrew, *Belfast (Bloomfield),* 1953, 1965
Barr, Arthur E. S., Londonderry (w), 1979
Barr, Frank, Dublin North-West, 1981, 1982(Feb.)
Barr, I. C., *Mid-Ulster,* 1973, 1975
Barr, J. W. S., *Londonderry North,* 1969
Barrett, Frank, Clare, 1923
Barrett, Frank, Clare, 1987
Barrett, Garrett, Cork North, 1951
Barrett, Michael, Dublin North-West, 1981–

Barrett, Seán, Dublin Co. South, 1977; Dún Laoghaire, 1981–

Barrett, Stephen D., Cork Borough, 1948, 1951, 1954(Mar.)(by)–69

Barrett, Sylvester, Clare, 1968(by)–87; MUNSTER, 1984–9

Barron, Joseph, Dublin South-Central, 1948, 1951, 1954, 1957, 1961–5 (def.)

Barry, Anthony, Cork Borough, 1954–7 (def.), 1961–5 (def.)

Barry, Brereton, Wexford, 1923

Barry, Cornelius, Cork South-West, 1989

Barry, Daniel, Kerry South, 1969, 1973

Barry, David, Dublin Co., 1923

Barry, David, Cork South-East, 1944

Barry, John, Cork East, 1927(June), 1927(Sept.)

Barry, John, Donegal West, 1957

Barry, Kevin, Kerry North, 1961

Barry, M. J., Carlow-Kilkenny, 1948

Barry, Michael, Carlow-Kilkenny, 1923, 1925(by)

Barry, Michael P., Cork North. 1927(June)

Barry, Myra, Cork North-East, 1979(by)–81; Cork East, 1981–7

Barry, Peter, Cork City South-East, 1969–77; Cork City, 1977–81; Cork South-Central, 1981–

Barry, Peter (pseud.), Antrim North (w), 1986(by); Antrim South (w), 1986(by); Londonderry East (w), 1986(by); Strangford (w), 1986(by)

Barry, Philip H., Cork East, 1927(Sept.)

Barry, Ralph Brereton, Wicklow, 1943

Barry, Richard, Cork East, 1951, 1953(by)–61; Cork North-East, 1961–81

Barry, T. B., Cork Borough, 1946(by)

Bartley, Gerald, Galway, 1932–7; Galway West, 1937–65

Bartley, Gerald, Galway West, 1982(Nov.)

Barton, B. F., Kildare, 1933

Barton, R. C., Kildare-Wicklow, 1921–3; Wicklow 1923

Bates, Sir Richard Dawson, *Belfast East*, 1921–9; *Belfast (Victoria)*, 1929–45

Batterberry, Richard, Dublin South-West, 1948, 1951

Battersby, William, Meath, 1989

Baxter, J. L., *Antrim North*, 1973–5

Baxter, Patrick F., Cavan 1922, 1923–7(Sept.) (def.), 1932; Clare, 1933; Cavan, 1943

Baxter, Paul E., *Londonderry*, 1982

Baxter, Philip, Cavan, 1925(by)

Beamish, R. H., Cork Borough, 1922, 1923–7(June)

Béaslaí, Piaras, Kerry-Limerick West, 1921–3

Beattie, Sir Andrew, Dublin South, 1923

Beattie, Charles, Mid-Ulster (w), 1955, 1955(by) (declared elected but disqualified)

Beattie, John, *Belfast East*, 1925–9; *Belfast (Pottinger)*, 1929–49 (def.); *Belfast Central*, 1953; Belfast West (w), 1943(by)–50 (def.), 1950(by), 1951–5 (def.)

Beattie, William, *Belfast (Woodvale)*, 1929

Beattie, Revd William J., *Antrim South*, 1969, 1970(by)–76, 1982–6; Belfast North (w), 1970; Lagan Valley (w), 1983

Beausang, Seán, Cork South-Central, 1987

Beckett, J. W., Dublin South, 1927(June)–37 (def.), 1938–9 (d.)

Beegan, Patrick, Galway, 1932–7; Galway East, 1937–48; Galway South, 1948–58 (d.)

Beggs, Andrew, *Antrim Mid*, 1938

Beggs, J. R. (Roy), *Antrim North*, 1982–6; Antrim East (w), 1983–5, 1986(by)

Begley, Michael, Kerry South, 1965, 1966(by), 1969–89 (def.)

Begley, Patrick, Dún Laoghaire and Rathdown, 1957

Begley, Seán, Mid-Ulster (w), 1987

Behal, Richard, MUNSTER, 1984

Behan, John, Laoighis-Offaly, 1961

Beirne, John (sen.), Roscommon, 1943–8

Beirne, John (jun.), Roscommon, 1948–61 (def.)

Beirne, W. H., Dublin South, 1943, 1944

Bell, B. O., Dublin (Clontarf), 1977

Bell, Daniel, Dublin (Finglas), 1977

Bell, Desmond, Dublin North-East, 1954, 1957

Bell, Edward, *Belfast (Bloomfield)*, 1958; Down North (w), 1964; *Ards*, 1965

Bell, Edward S., Monaghan, 1948

Bell, M., Dublin North-East, 1943

Bell, Michael, Louth, 1981, 1982(Feb.), 1982(Nov.)–; LEINSTER, 1989

Bell, R. L., *Belfast (Woodvale)*, 1969

Bell, W. B., *Belfast North*, 1975–6; *Antrim South*, 1982–96

Bellew, James, Louth, 1977

Bellew, Thomas, Louth, 1981, 1982(Feb.–Nov.) (def.), 1987

Belton, John (Jack), Dublin North-East, 1948–63 (d.)

Belton, Louis, Longford-Westmeath, 1989–

Belton, Luke, Dublin North-Central, 1961, 1965–77; Dublin (Finglas), 1977–81; Dublin Central, 1981, 1982(Feb.), 1987

Belton, Patrick, Longford-Westmeath, 1922, Leix-Offaly, 1923; Dublin Co., 1926(by), 1927(June–Sept.) (def.); Dublin North, 1932, 1933–7; Dublin Co., 1937, 1938–43 (def.), 1944

Belton, Patrick, Dublin North-East, 1963(by)–77; Dublin (Artane), 1977; Dublin North-Central, 1981

Belton, Robert, Longford-Westmeath, 1927(June), 1933

Bennett, G. C., Limerick, 1927(June)–48; Limerick East, 1948, 1951

Bennett, James, Longford-Westmeath, 1969, 1977, 1981

Bennett, Liam M. M. W., Limerick West, 1954

Bennett, Louisa, Dublin Co., 1944

Bennett, Olga, Dublin West, 1987, 1989

Benson, E. E., Dublin Townships, 1937–44 (def.)

Benson, T. H., *Antrim North*, 1982

Bergin, James C., Kildare, 1927(June)

Bergin, John J., Kildare-Wicklow, 1922; Kildare, 1927(June)

Bergin, Patrick, Carlow-Kilkenny, 1948

Berkery, Thomas, Tipperary North, 1981, 1982(Feb.), 1982(Nov.), 1989

Bermingham, John, Cork Borough, 1954, 1957

Bermingham, Joseph, Kildare, 1969, 1970(by), 1973–87

Bermingham, Patrick J., Leix-Offaly, 1923

Bermingham, Patrick Joseph, Leix-Offaly 1943, 1944

Bermingham, Patrick Joseph, Dublin South-East, 1957

Bernardo, Henry, Dublin Mid, 1922

Best, Richard, *Armagh,* 1921–5(Nov.)

Bewley, Charles, Mayo South, 1923

Biggane, William, Cork North, 1954

Bingham, R. McF., *Belfast (Bloomfield),* 1961(by), 1962

Binnie, Robert, *North Antrim,* 1973

Bird, John, Meath, 1989

Birmingham, G. M., Dublin North-Central, 1981–9 (def.)

Black, Alister, *Armagh,* 1975–6, 1982

Black, Arthur, *Belfast South,* 1925–9; *Belfast (Willowfield),* 1929–41

Black, Christopher, Meath, 1927(Sept.)

Black, Maureen, Cork City, 1977

Black, Norman, *Belfast (Victoria),* 1945

Black, Patrick (Paud), Cork North-Central, 1987

Black, Richard, Cavan, 1969

Black, W. B., Dublin Townships, 1938

Blair, John, MUNSTER, 1979; Cork North-Central, 1981

Blake, William, *Enniskillen,* 1949

Blakely, John, *Antrim South,* 1973

Blakiston-Houston, Maj. Charles, *Belfast (Dock),* 1929–33 (def.)

Blakiston-Houston, Lt Col. J. M., Fermanagh-Tyrone (w), 1935; Down (w), 1945

Blaney, Neil, Donegal, 1927(June)–37; Donegal East, 1937–8 (def.), 1943–8(Nov.) (d.)

Blaney, Neil T. C., Donegal East, 1948(Dec.)(by)–61; Donegal North-East, 1961–77; Donegal, 1977–81; Donegal North-East, 1981; CONNACHT-ULSTER, 1979–84 (def.), 1989–

Blaney, Raymond, *Down South,* 1975

Bleakes, W. G., *Down North,* 1982–6

Bleakley, D. W., *Belfast (Victoria),* 1949, 1953, 1958–65 (def.); *Belfast East,* 1973–6; Belfast East (w), 1970, 1974(Feb.), 1974(Oct.); NORTHERN IRELAND, 1979

Blease, W. J., *Belfast (Oldpark),* 1953

Blease, W. V., *Belfast (St Anne's),* 1965

Blennerhassett, John, Kerry North, 1969, 1973, 1977

Blevins, Alexander, *Tyrone Mid, 1958–62* (def.); *Tyrone East,* 1964(by)

Blevins, Samuel, *Armagh North,* 1958

Blood, D. J., Louth, 1932

Blowick, Joseph, Mayo South, 1943–65

Blythe, Ernest, Monaghan, 1921–33 (def.)

Boal, D. N. O., *Belfast (Shankill)*, 1960(by)–73

Bogan, P. J., Mid-Ulster (w), 1987

Boggs, Bertie, Donegal North-East, 1969, 1973

Bobbett, E. F., Dublin Co., 1943; Wicklow, 1953(by)

Bohan, Séamus, Dún Laoghaire and Rathdown, 1961

Boland, D. T., Kildare, 1948

Boland, Gerald, Roscommon, 1923–61 (def.)

Boland, Harry J., Mayo South-Roscommon South, 1921–2(Aug.) (d.)

Boland, Hazel, Dún Laoghaire, 1981

Boland, J. A., Tipperary, 1944

Boland, John, Dublin Co. North, 1969, 1973, 1977–l; Dublin North, 1981–9 (def.)

Boland, Kevin, Dublin Co., 1951, 1954, 1957–69; Dublin Co. South, 1969–70, 1973; Dublin South-West, 1976(by), 1981; LEINSTER, 1989

Boland, P. J., Leix-Offaly, 1927(June)–54

Boland, Thomas, Dublin West, 1981

Boles, Edward, Leitrim, 1943

Bolger, Deirdre, LEINSTER, 1984

Bolger, John, Carlow-Kilkenny, 1977

Bolger, Thomas, Carlow-Kilkenny, 1923, 1925(by)–7(June), 1932

Bolingbrook, John, Mayo East, 1981, 1982(Feb.), 1982(Nov.)

Boomer, C. J., *Belfast West*, 1982; Lagan Valley (w), 1983

Booth, Lionel, Dún Laoghaire and Rathdown, 1954, 1957–69

Boran, Nicholas, Kilkenny, 1943

Boswell, Bernard, Belfast East, 1959

Boucher, Dermot, Dún Laoghaire, 1981

Bourke, Daniel, Limerick, 1927(June), 1927(Sept.)–48; Limerick East, 1948–52 (d.)

Bourke, Denis E., Tipperary, 1943

Bourke, John (Jack), Limerick East, 1982 (Nov.)

Bourke, S. A., Tipperary Mid/North/South, 1921–3; Tipperary, 1923–38 (def.), 1943

Bourke, Thomas, Tipperary, 1943, 1944

Bourke, Thomas P., Dublin South, 1944

Bourne, J. J., Wicklow, 1943

Bowe, J. J., Wexford, 1937, 1943, 1948, 1951, 1954

Bowers, Mary, Dublin South-Central, 1989

Bowers, Thomas, Meath, 1933

Bowes, Michael, Cork North-Central, 1989

Bowles, James, Leix-Offaly, 1932

Boyce, Eamonn, Belfast West (w), 1955

Boyd, Brian, *Belfast (Willowfield)*, 1969

Boyd, Herbert, Belfast East (w), 1983

Boyd, James, *Ards*, 1929

Boyd, R. N., *Antrim North*, 1929, 1938; Antrim (w), 1929

Boyd, T. W., *Belfast (Victoria)*, 1938; *Belfast (Bloomfield)*, 1949; *Belfast (Pottinger)*, 1953, 1958–69; Belfast East (w), 1945, 1950, 1951, 1955

Boyd, W. R., *Belfast (Woodvale)*, 1953, 1955(by), 1958–65 (def.), 1969; *Belfast West*, 1973; *Belfast North*, 1975, 1982; Belfast North (w), 1955; Belfast West (w), 1964, 1974(Feb.)

Boylan, Andrew, Cavan-Monaghan, 1987–

Boylan, Terence, Kildare, 1964(by)–73 (def.)

Boylan, Terence, Dublin Co. West, 1977

Boyle, Daniel, Mayo North, 1910(Jan.)–18 (def.)

Boyle, Daniel C., Donegal West, 1943, 1948

Boyle, E. J., Dublin South-Central, 1969

Boyle, Gerald, Mayo East, 1969

Boyle, J. M., *Mourne*, 1929

Boyle, Rita, Dublin North-West, 1982(Feb.)

Brack, Anthony, Dublin North-West, 1944

Bracken, Evelyn, Kildare, 1981

Bracken, Michael, Meath-Westmeath, 1944

Bradford, H. E., *Down North*, 1982

Bradford, Paul, Cork East, 1987, 1989–

Bradford, Robert, *Belfast (Oldpark)*, 1938

Bradford, Revd Robert J., *Antrim South*, 1973; Belfast South (w), 1974(Feb.)–81 (d.)

Bradford, Roy H., *Belfast (Victoria)*, 1965–73; *Belfast East*, 1973–5 (def.); Down North (w), 1974(Feb.)

Bradley, Michael, Cork Mid/South/North/South-East/West, 1922–3

Bradley, P. J., Cork Borough, 1927(June)

Brady, B. M., Donegal, 1932–7; Donegal West, 1937–49 (d.)

Brady, Edward, Monaghan, 1927(June), 1932

Brady, Gerard, Dublin Central, 1969

Brady, Gerard, Dublin (Rathmines West), 1977–81; Dublin South-East, 1981–

Brady, Gerard, Kildare, 1981, 1982(Feb.– Nov.) (def.), 1987

Brady, John (Jack), Dublin South-Central, 1948

Brady, John, Belfast West, 1974(Feb.)

Brady, John G., *Belfast (Pottinger)*, 1953

Brady, John G., *Belfast West*, 1975

Brady, Kathleen, Carlow-Kilkenny, 1961

Brady, Laurence, Leix-Offaly, 1923–7(June), 1933, 1937

Brady, Laurence, W., Leix-Offaly, 1943

Brady, Michael, Kildare, 1969

Brady, Michael, Longford-Westmeath, 1969

Brady, Peter R. C., Fermanagh-Tyrone South (w), 1966

Brady, Philip A., Dublin South-Central, 1951–4 (def.), 1957–77

Brady, Richard, Dublin North-West, 1982(Nov.)

Brady, Robert, Longford-Westmeath, 1982(Feb.), 1982(Nov.)

Brady, Rory, Longford-Westmeath, 1957–61 (def.)

Brady, Seán, Dublin Co., 1927(June), 1927(Sept.)–48; Dún Laoghaire and Rathdown, 1948–65 (def.)

Brady, Seán, Clare, 1948

Brady, Vincent, Dublin North-Central, 1977–

Brady, William (Bill), Dublin (Ballyfermot), 1977

Branigan, Richard (Dick), Louth, 1981

Brasier, B. W., Cork East, 1927(June), 1927(Sept.), 1932–3 (def.); Cork South-East, 1937–43

Breathnach, Bhaltar, Dublin North-West, 1951, 1954

Breathnach, Cormac, Dublin North, 1932–7; Dublin North-West, 1937–54

Breathnach, Fionán, Dublin North-Central, 1948, 1951, 1954

Breathnach, Fursa, see Walsh Breathnach, Osgur, Dún Laoghaire, 1982(Feb.)

Brennock, Michael, Waterford, 1923

Bree, Declan, Sligo-Leitrim, 1977, 1981, 1982(Feb.), 1982(Nov.), 1987, 1989

Breen, Daniel, Waterford-Tipperary East, 1922, Tipperary, 1923–7(June) (def.), 1932–48; Tipperary South, 1948–65

Breen, E. J., Leix-Offaly, 1937, 1938, 1943

Breen, John, Dublin North-West, 1945(by), 1951

Breen, Kate, Kerry, 1927(June)

Breen, M. I., *Londonderry*, 1982

Brennan, Austin, Clare, 1948

Brennan, Bernard, M., Sigo-Leitrim, 1973

Brennan, Brian, Belfast West (w), 1979; NORTHERN IRELAND, 1979

Brennan, Conal, Dublin South-West, 1981, 1982(Nov.)

Brennan, Edward (Ned), Dublin North-East, 1981, 1982(Feb–Nov.) (def.), 1987

Brennan, Francis, Longford-Westmeath, 1957

Brennan, Gerry, Dublin South-East, 1987

Brennan, J. J., Monaghan, 1948, 1954, 1957

Brennan, John, Belfast West (w), 1959

Brennan, John, Dún Laoghaire and Rathdown, 1961

Brennan, John (Jack), Dublin North-East, 1981

Brennan, John J., *Belfast (Falls)*, 1962; *Belfast (Central)*, 1965–9 (def.)

Brennan, Joseph, Donegal West, 1949(by), 1951–61; Donegal South-West, 1961–9; Donegal-Leitrim, 1969–77; Donegal, 1977–80 (d.)

Brennan, Joseph, Galway East, 1982(Feb.)

Brennan, Joseph P., Dún Laoghaire and Rathdown, 1948–51 (def.), 1954

Brennan, Lawrence, Tipperary North, 1954

Brennan, Martin, Sligo, 1938–48

Brennan, Matthew, Sligo-Leitrim, 1981, 1982(Feb.)–

Brennan, Michael, Roscommon, 1923, 1927(June) 1932 (def.), 1933–43 (def.), 1944, 1948, 1951

Brennan, Michael, Sligo, 1937

Brennan, Michael, Dublin West, 1982(Nov.)

Brennan, Patrick, Clare, 1921–3

Brennan, Patrick (Paudge), Wicklow, 1953(by), 1954–73 (def.), 1981–2(Feb.)
  (def.), 1982(Nov.)–87
Brennan, Patrick, Limerick West, 1987
Brennan, Patrick J., Kildare, 1948
Brennan, Robert, Dublin Co., 1927(June), 1927(by), 1927(Sept.)
Brennan, Séamus, Dublin South, 1981–
Brennan, Thomas, Wicklow, 1943, 1944–53 (d.)
Brennan, Thomas, Waterford, 1969, 1982(Nov.)
Brennan, Thomas, Dublin North-East, 1981
Brennan, Thomas, Clare, 1987
Brennan, Victor, Belfast South, 1979
Breslin, Cormac, Donegal West, 1937–61; Donegal South-West, 1961–9;
  Donegal-Leitrim, 1969–77
Bresnihan, Richard, Limerick West, 1951
Brett, P, J., Longford-Westmeath, 1927(June)
Brick, James, Galway West, 1981, 1982(Feb.), 1982(Nov.), 1987, 1989;
  CONNAUGHT-ULSTER, 1984, 1989
Brien, David, *Fermanagh-Tyrone South*, 1973
Briody, Patrick, Leitrim-Sligo, 1927(June)
Briscoe, Ben, Dublin South-West, 1965–9; Dublin South-Central, 1969–77;
  Dublin (Rathmires West) 1977–81; Dublin South-Central, 1981–
Briscoe, Coghlan, Dublin North, 1927(June)
Briscoe, Robert, Dublin South, 1927(June), 1927(by), 1927(Sept.)–48;
  Dublin South-West, 1948–65
Broadhurst, Brig. R. J. C., *Down South*, 1973–5 (def.)
Broderick, Henry, Longford-Westmeath, 1927(June)–32 (def.), 1933;
  Athlone-Longford, 1937, 1943
Broderick, Michael, Cork North-East, 1973, 1974(by), 1977
Broderick, Seán, Galway, 1923–37; Galway East, 1937–43 (def.)
Broderick, Seán, Limerick West, 1977, 1982(Feb.)
Broderick, W. J., Cork East, 1932–7; Cork South-East, 1937; Waterford, 1938–
  43; Cork South-East, 1943–8
Broggy, Aidan, Dublin South-Central, 1982(Feb.)
Brommel, Anthony (Tony), Limerick East, 1989
Brooke, Sir B. S., *see* Brookeborough, 1st Viscount
Brooke, Capt. Hon. J. W., *see* Brookeborough, 2nd Viscount
Brookeborough, 1st Viscount (B. S. Brooke), *Lisnaskea*, 1929–68
Brookeborough, 2nd Viscount (Capt. J. W. Brooke), *Lisnaskea*, 1968(by)–73;
  Down North, 1973–6
Brooks, M. A. B., *Belfast East*, 1973; Donegal North-East, 1987
Brophy, Eileen, Carlow-Kilkenny, 1982(Feb.), 1982(Nov.)
Brosnan, Con (Cornelius), Kerry, 1933
Brosnan, Denis, Kerry, 1923
Brosnan, John, Cork North-East, 1979(by); Cork East, 1981
Brosnan, Seán, Cork North-East 1965, 1969–73 (def.), 1974(by)–9 (d.);
  IRELAND, 1977–9

Brosnan, Timothy, Cork North-Central, 1989
Broughan, E. J., Carlow-Kilkenny, 1923
Broughan, Thomas, Dublin North-East, 1989
Brown, Brian, Londonderry, 1973
Brown, C. J., Antrim North, 1982
Brown, Edward, Antrim South (w), 1950; Belfast South (w), 1955
Brown, H. R., *Queen's University Belfast*, 1962
Brown James, *Down South*, 1938–45, 1958; *Mourne*, 1945; Down (w), 1945, 1946(by)
Brown, William, *Down South*, 1982–6
Browne, Capt. A. C., Belfast West (w), 1931–42 (d.)
Browne, Francis, Louth, 1982(Feb.)
Browne, H. I., Fermanagh-Tyrone South (w), 1974(Feb.)
Browne, Jeremiah P., Cork South, 1948
Browne, John, Carlow-Kilkenny, 1981, 1987, 1989–
Browne, John, Wexford, 1982(Nov.)–
Browne, Joseph, Dublin Townships, 1943
Browne, Michael (Miko), Mayo North, 1961–5 (def.); Mayo East, 1969
Browne, N. C., Dublin South-East, 1948–54 (def.), 1957–65 (def.), 1969–73; Dublin (Artane), 1977–81; Dublin North-Central, 1981–2(Feb.)
Browne, Patrick, Mayo North, 1937–54 (def.), 1957
Browne, Patrick, Waterford, 1966(by)–73 (def.)
Browne, Seán, Wexford, 1951, 1954, 1957–61 (def.), 1965, 1969–81 (def.), 1982(Feb.–Nov.)
Browne, W. F., Leitrim-Sligo, 1927(Sept.), 1932–7; Sligo, 1937
Brownlow, Maj. W. S., *Down North*, 1973–5 (def.); Down North (w), 1974(Oct.)
Brugha, Caitlín, Waterford, 1923–7(Sept.)
Brugha, Cathal, Waterford-Tipperary East, 1921–2(July) (d.)
Brugha, Ruairí; Waterford, 1948; Dublin Co. South, 1969, 1973–7 (def.); Dublin South, 1982(Nov.); IRELAND, 1977–9; DUBLIN, 1979
Brush, Lt Col. E. H. (Peter), *Down South*, 1975–6
Bruton, Barry, *Belfast South*, 1982
Bruton, John, Meath, 1969–
Bruton, Richard, Dublin North-Central, 1982(Feb.)–
Bryan, C. J., Cork West, 1948, 1951
Buchanan, Gerard, Dublin South-West, 1965; Dublin South-Central, 1973
Buckley, Daniel G., Cork Borough, 1943
Buckley, Donal, Kildare-Wicklow, 1921–2 (def.); Kildare, 1923, 1927(June)–32 (def.)
Buckley, Frank, Dublin South, 1981, 1982(Nov.)
Buckley, Seán, Cork West, 1923–7(June) (def.), 1938–48; Cork South, 1948–54
Buggle, Deirdre, Dublin South-Central, 1987
Bugler, Patrick, Clare, 1968(by); Clare-Galway South, 1969, 1973
Bulbulia, Katherine, Waterford, 1981, 1982(Nov.), 1989
Bulfin, Francis, Leix-Offaly, 1921–7(June) (def.)

Buller, A. W., *Down West*, 1969

Bunting, Maj. R. T., *Belfast (Victoria)*, 1969

Burchill, D. J. M., *Belfast South*, 1975–6; *Belfast East*, 1982–6; Antrim North (w), 1979; Belfast East (w), 1983

Burges, Capt. Y. A., Fermanagh-Tyrone (w), 1931

Burgess, Roland, Dublin Co., 1954, 1957

Burke, Charles, Clare, 1948

Burke, Christopher, Dublin Central, 1982(Feb.), 1983(by), 1987, 1989

Burke, Colm, Cork North-Central, 1982(Nov.)

Burke, David, Carlow-Kilkenny, 1948

Burke, Denis, Tipperary South, 1961, 1965

Burke, Hubert, Tipperary South, 1977

Burke, J. J., Roscommon, 1954–64 (d.)

Burke, J. M., Cork West, 1933–7

Burke, Joan, T., Roscommon, 1964(by)–9; Roscommon-Leitrim, 1969–81

Burke, Joseph, Athlone-Longford, 1937

Burke, Joseph, Galway East, 1981, 1982(Nov.), 1987

Burke, Joseph J., Roscommon, 1927(Sept.)

Burke, Liam, Cork Borough, 1967(by); Cork City North-West, 1969–77; Cork City, 1977, 1979(by)–81; Cork North-Central, 1981–9 (def.)

Burke, Malachi K., Dublin Co. South, 1973

Burke, Michael, Cork East, 1948

Burke, Michael C., Limerick, 1938

Burke, Patrick, Clare, 1927(Sept.), 1932–45 (d.)

Burke, Patrick John, Cork West, 1948

Burke, Patrick Joseph, Dublin Co., 1944–69; Dublin Co. North, 1969–73

Burke, Raphael P., Dublin Co. North, 1973–81; Dublin North, 1981–

Burke, Richard (Dick), Dublin Co. South, 1969–77; Dublin West, 1981–2(Mar.)

Burke, Robert M., Galway, 1933; Galway East, 1937, 1938, 1943; Galway North, 1948

Burke, Stanislaus, Clare, 1943

Burke, Thomas, Clare, 1948

Burke, Thomas P., Leitrim, 1943

Burke, Thomas T., Clare, 1937–51 (def.)

Burke, U. R., Galway East, 1981, 1982(Feb.), 1982(by), 1982(Nov.), 1987

Burke, William, Galway North, 1951

Burke, William, Galway North-East, 1969

Burn, T. H., Belfast West, 1921–5 (def.)

Burns, A. W. J., *Down North*, 1962

Burns, Joseph, *Londonderry North*, 1960(by)–73

Burns, T. E., *Belfast South*, 1973–6

Burnside, D. W. B., *Antrim North*, 1973, 1982

Burton, Joan, Dublin Central, 1989

Burton, Philip, Cork North-East, 1961–9; Cork Mid, 1969–73 (def.)

Butler, Bernard, Dublin Townships, 1937, 1943–8; Dublin South-West, 1948–59 (d.)

Butler, E. G., Dublin South-East, 1948

Butler, George, Dublin South-West, 1969

Butler, John, Waterford-Tipperary East, 1922–3; Waterford, 1923–7(June) (def.), 1927(Sept.), 1937, 1943

Butler, Joseph, Carlow-Kilkenny, 1987

Butler (Ní Scolláin), Nóirín, Dublin North-Central, 1973

Butterfield, John, Laoighis-Offaly, 1973, 1981, 1982(Feb.)

Butterley, Anthony, Dublin Co. North, 1969

Byrne, Alfred, Dublin Mid, 1922–3; Dublin North, 1923–8, 1932–7; Dublin North-East, 1937–56 (d.)

Byrne, Alfred P., Dublin North-West, 1937–44 (def.), 1948–52 (d.)

Byrne, Andrew, Leix-Offaly, 1923

Byrne, Brendan, Dublin South-West, 1981

Byrne, Christopher M., Kildare-Wicklow 1921–3; Wicklow, 1923–7(June) (def.), 1927(Sept.), 1932, 1937, 1943–4 (def.), 1948

Byrne, Conor, Longford-Westmeath, 1923–7(June) (def.), 1948

Byrne, Daniel J., Waterford-Tipperary East, 1922–3

Byrne, David, Dublin Co., 1948, 1951

Byrne, Deirdre, *Antrim South*, 1973

Byrne, Denis, Dublin Co., 1927(June)

Byrne, Edward, Wicklow, 1944

Byrne, Eric J., Dublin (Rathmines West), 1977; Dublin South-Central, 1981, 1982(Feb.), 1982(Nov.), 1987, 1989

Byrne, Frank, Leix-Offaly, 1957

Byrne, Gus, Wexford, 1981, 1982(Feb.), 1982(Nov.)

Byrne, Henry, Laoighis-Offaly, 1961, 1965–9, 1973

Byrne, Henry J., Wicklow, 1944

Byrne, Hugh, Dublin North-West, 1969–77; Dublin (Cabra), 1977–81; Dublin North-West, 1981–2(Feb.) (def.), 1982(Nov.)

Byrne, Hugh, Wexford, 1981–9 (def.)

Byrne, James, Down South, 1938

Byrne, James, Dún Laoghaire and Rathdown, 1969

Byrne, Joan, Dublin North-West, 1989

Byrne, John J., Dublin North, 1927(June)–33 (def.); Dublin North-West, 1937

Byrne, Kevin, Dublin North-Central, 1977

Byrne, Laurence, Laoighis-Offaly, 1973

Byrne, Mary, Galway West, 1969

Byrne, Mary, Dublin North-Central, 1981, 1982(Feb.)

Byrne, Matthew, Carlow-Kilkenny, 1965

Byrne, Michael, Dublin South, 1937, 1944

Byrne, Patrick, Dublin North-East, 1956(by)–69

Byrne, Patrick J., *Armagh South*, 1969

Byrne, Patrick L., Dublin South, 1923

Byrne, Richard, *Belfast West*, 1921; *Belfast (Falls)*, 1929–42 (d.)
Byrne, Seán, Tipperary South, 1977, 1981, 1982(Feb.)–87 (def.)
Byrne, Shane, Dublin Central, 1987
Byrne, Thomas, Wexford, 1944
Byrne, Thomas, Wicklow, 1973
Byrne, Thomas N. J., Dublin North-West 1952(by)–61 (def.)
Byrne, Toddie, Clare-Galway South, 1969, 1973; Galway West, 1977

Cafferky, Dominick, Mayo South, 1943–8 (def.), 1951–4 (def.), 1957, 1961
Caffrey, Ernest, Mayo East, 1989
Caffrey, J. H., Cavan, 1969
Caffrey, Thomas, Dublin North, 1982(Nov.)
Caffrey, W. J., Sligo, 1937
Cahalane, J. J., Cork South-West, 1969
Cahill, Aileen, Cavan-Monaghan, 1982(Nov.)
Cahill, Francis, Dublin North, 1923–4
Cahill, John, Dublin North-West, 1944
Cahill, Martin, Clare, 1973
Cahill, Michael, Cork East, 1927(June)
Cahill, Michael, Leix-Offaly, 1927(June)
Cahill, P. J., Kerry-Limerick West, 1921–3; Kerry, 1923–7(June)
Cahill, P. J., Dublin South, 1939(by), 1943; Dublin South-Central, 1948
Cahill, T. J., Dublin South-Central, 1987; DUBLIN, 1989
Cahill, W. A., Galway West, 1969
Cairns, J. F., *Belfast Central*, 1953; *Belfast (Oldpark)*, 1969
Caldwell, Robert, *Belfast (Bloomfield)*, 1965, 1969
Caldwell, T. H., *Belfast (Willowfield)*, 1969–73; Antrim South (w), 1970
Callaghan, Hugh, Donegal West, 1943
Callaghan, Patrick, Kerry South, 1973
Callaghan, V. C., Cork South-West, 1977
Callan, J. B., Louth, 1943
Callan, Paul, Louth, 1969, 1973
Callan, Thomas, Roscommon, 1982(Nov.)
Callanan, Gerry, Dublin, South-East, 1957
Callanan, John, Clare-Galway South, 1973–7; Galway East, 1977–82(June) (d.)
Callanan, Peter, Cork South-West, 1981
Calleary, P. A., Mayo North, 1952(by)–69
Calleary, Seán, Mayo East, 1973–
Callely, Ivor, Dublin North-Central, 1987, 1989–
Callwell, William, Carrick, 1943(by), 1945(by), 1945
Calnan, Michael, Cork South-West, 1982(Feb.)
Calvert, D. N., Fermanagh-*Tynone South*, 1975; Armagh (w), 1979; *Armagh*, 1982–6
Calvert, L. I. M., *Queen's University Belfast*, 1944(by), 1945–53
Calvert, S. E. B., *Mourne*, 1958

Campbell, Sir D. C., *Belfast South*, 1952(by)–63 (d.)

Campbell, Gerry, *Belfast West*, 1973

Campbell, Gregory L., *Londonderry*, 1982–6; Foyle (w), 1983, 1987

Campbell, Harold, Galway East, 1977

Campbell, Sir John, *Queen's University Belfast*, 1921–9

Campbell, John, Belfast East (w), 1931

Campbell, John D., *Carrick*, 1943(by)–5(Jan.) (d.); Antrim (w), 1943(by)–5(Jan.) (d.)

Campbell, Joseph, Louth, 1954(by), 1954

Campbell, Joseph, Down North (w), 1955, 1959

Campbell, Lloyd, *Belfast North*, 1921–9

Campbell, Mathew, Louth, 1927(June)

Campbell, P. C. D., *Londonderry City*, 1969

Campbell, R. A., *Tyrone Mid*, 1949

Campbell, R. V., *Bangor*, 1969; *Down North*, 1973–5 (def.)

Campbell, Seán P., Dublin South, 1927(June)

Campbell, Sheena, Upper Bann (w), 1990(by)

Campbell, Thomas, Belfast North (w), 1987

Campbell, Thomas J., *Belfast East*, 1921; *Belfast West*, 1931; *Belfast Central*, 1934(by)–46

Campion, Michael, Dublin South-Central, 1977

Canavan, Ivor, *Londonderry*, 1975

Canavan, M. W. E., *Londonderry*, 1973–6

Canning, Alphonsus, Donegal West, 1949(by)

Canning, Manus, Londonderry (w), 1955, 1959

Caraher, J. B. (Ben), *Belfast South*, 1973, 1975, 1982; Belfast South (w), 1974(Feb.), 1974(Oct.)

Caraher, Thomas, Monaghan, 1948

Cardwell, Joshua, *Belfast (Pottinger)*, 1969–73; *Belfast East*, 1973–6

Carew, John, Limerick East, 1952(by)–61 (def.)

Carey, Cornelius, Cork North-East, 1965

Carey, Donal, Clare, 1977, 1982(Feb.–)

Carey, Eamonn, Mayo West, 1969

Carey, Edmond, Cork East, 1927(June), 1927(Sept.)–32 (def.); Cork South-East, 1938, 1943

Carey, J. N., Mayo West, 1982(Feb.)

Carey, Malachy, *Lisnaskea*, 1969

Carey, Patrick, Dublin North-West, 1987

Carey, Patrick J., Leitrim, 1943

Carey, William, Meath, 1969

Carlin, Andrew, *Belfast (Clifton)*, 1945

Carney, Frank, Donegal, 1927(June)–33

Carney, Frank, Louth, 1977

Carney, Martin, Mayo South, 1954

Carolan, Michael, *Belfast North*, 1921

Carpenter, Patrick, Carlow-Kilkenny, 1977, 1981, 1982(Feb.)

Carr, A. V., *Londonderry*, 1975; Belfast North (w), 1979

Carr, Gerard, *Belfast South*, 1982; Belfast South (w), 1983, 1986(by), 1987

Carrigy, James, Longford-Westmeath, 1923

Carroll, Edmund J., Clare, 1938

Carroll, Edward, Dublin North, 1927(June)

Carroll, Gerard, Cork City South-East, 1973

Carroll, James, Dublin South-West, 1954, 1957–65 (def.)

Carroll, John, LEINSTER, 1984; Laoighis-Offaly, 1987

Carroll, Michael, Dún Laoghaire and Rathdown, 1969, 1973; Dún Laoghaire, 1977

Carroll, Patrick, Dublin (Cabra), 1977; Dublin Central, 1981

Carroll, Seán, Limerick, 1923–7(June); Limerick East, 1948

Carroll, Stephen, Carlow-Kilkenny, 1948

Carron, John, *Lisnaskea*, 1949; *Fermanagh South*, 1965–73

Carron, O. G., Fermanagh-Tyrone South (w), 1981(by)–3 (def.), 1986(by); *Fermanagh-Tyrone South*, 1982–6

Carson, John, Belfast North (w), 1974(Feb.)–9; *Belfast North*, 1982–6

Carson, P. V., Wexford, 1948

Carson, T. D., *Armagh*, 1973–6

Carter, Frank, Longford-Westmeath, 1951–7 (def.), 1961–77

Carter, Michael, Leitrim-Sligo, 1927(June–Sept.) (def.), 1932

Carter, Thomas, Leitrim-Roscommon North, 1921–3; Leitrim-Sligo, 1923–4

Carter, Thomas, Athlone-Longford, 1943–8; Longford-Westmeath, 1948–51

Carton, Victor, Dublin North-East, 1954, 1961, 1965; Dublin North-Central, 1957(Nov.)(by)

Carty, F. J., Sligo-Mayo East. 1921–3; Leitrim-Sligo, 1923–37; Sligo, 1937–43

Carty, J. W., Limerick, 1933

Carty, Leo, Wexford, 1969

Carty, Michael, Galway South, 1957–61; Galway East, 1961–9; Clare-Galway South, 1969–73

Casey, Daniel, Cork North-East, 1961, 1969

Casey, O. B., Cork South-Central, 1982(Nov.)

Casey, Patrick, Kerry, 1923, 1927(June); Kerry North, 1937

Casey, Seán, Cork Borough, 1948, 1951, 1954(by), 1954–67 (d.)

Cashman, Daniel, Cork East, 1948

Cashman, Griff, Dublin Central, 1969, 1973

Cass, Breda, Dublin South-West, 1987

Cassidy, A. J., Donegal, 1927(June), 1927(Sept.)–32 (def.), 1933

Cassidy, M. J., Mayo South, 1951; Mayo North, 1961

Castlereagh, Viscount (E. C. S. R. Vane Tempest-Stewart), *Down*, 1931–45

Cathcart, G. A., *Fermanagh-Tyrone South*, 1975

Caughey. John, Antrim North (w), 1964

Caul, B. P., Belfast South (w), 1982(by); NORTHERN IRELAND, 1989

Cavanagh, D. J., Londonderry (w), 1945

Cawley, James, Dublin Townships, 1943

Cawley, Patrick, Galway, 1933; Galway East, 1937, 1938, 1943; Galway South, 1948, 1951–4 (def.)

Cawley, Patrick J., Sligo-Leitrim, 1982(Feb.)

Chambers, Charles, Kildare, 1961,1965

Chambers, G. H., Belfast East (w), 1979

Charles, Peter, Roscommon, 1961

Chichester, Debra, *see* Parker

Chichester-Clark, Maj. J. D., *Londonderry South,* 1960(by)–73

Chichester-Clark, Capt. J. L.-C., *Londonderry South,* 1929–33(Jan.) (d.)

Chichester-Clark, Robin, Londonderry (w), 1955–74(Feb.)

Childers, E. H., Athlone-Longford, 1938–48; Longford-Westmeath, 1948–61; Monaghan, 1961–73(June)

Childers, E. R., Kildare-Wicklow, 1921–2 (def.)

Christie, D. H., *Londonderry North,* 1933–8

Christie, Joseph, Dublin South-West, 1961, 1965

Clancy, Daniel, Limerick, 1932

Clancy, John, Clare, 1943

Clancy, Patrick, Limerick, 1923–32 (def.)

Clancy, Patrick, Limerick East, 1969

Clark, Capt. G. A., *Belfast (Dock),* 1938–45 (def.)

Clark, H. M., Antrim North (w), 1959–70 (def.)

Clark, J. H., Dublin North, 1923

Clarke, Anthony (Tony), Dún Laoghaire, 1982(Nov.)

Clarke, Frank, Galway South, 1958(by)

Clarke, James, Leix-Offaly, 1944

Clarke, John, Mayo North, 1948

Clarke, John, Dublin South-Central, 1969

Clarke, Kathleen, Dublin Mid, 1921–2 (def.); Dublin North 1927(June-Sept.) (def.), 1928(by); Dublin North-East, 1948

Clarke, Laurence, Meath, 1982(Nov.)

Clarke, Patrick, Dublin South-East, 1987

Clarke, Philip C., Fermanagh-Tyrone South (w), 1955 (elected but disqualified)

Clarke, Thomas, Limerick East, 1952(by)

Clarke, William, *Enniskillen,* 1938

Clarke, William, Wicklow, 1944, 1948, 1953(by)

Clarkin, A. S., Dublin South, 1944; Dublin North-West, 1952(by)

Clear, Kevin, DUBLIN, 1979

Cleary, M. R., Limerick, 1923

Cleary, R. G., Longford-Westmeath, 1927(June)

Cleere, W. J., Carlow-Kilkenny, 1948

Cleland, Arthur, *Belfast (Willowfield),* 1938

Clenaghan, J. C., *Antrim South,* 1982

Clerkin, Andrew, Dublin South, 1927(Sept.)

Clery, Prof. A. E., National University of Ireland, 1927(June–Sept.)

Clery, Michael, Mayo North, 1927(June), 1927(Sept.)–37; Mayo South, 1937–45

Cline, Edward, Roscommon, 1923

Clinton, M. A., Dublin Co., 1961–9; Dublin Co. North, 1969–77; Dublin Co. West, 1977–81; LEINSTER, 1979–89

Clinton, Thomas, Meath, 1923

Clohessy, Patrick, Limerick East, 1954, 1957–69, 1973, 1977

Clohessy, Peadar, Limerick East, 1981–2(Feb.) (del.), 1987–

Close, S. A., Fermanagh-Tyrone South (w), 1981(by); *Antrim South*, 1982–6; Lagan Valley (w), 1983, 1987

Clow, E. M., *Belfast (St Anne's)*, 1929

Clulow, William, *Belfast South*, 1982

Clune, W. E., Clare, 1943

Cluskey, Frank, Dublin South-Central, 1958(by), 1961, 1965–9; Dublin Central, 1969–77; Dublin South-Central, 1977–81 (def.), 1982(Feb.)–89(Apr.) (d.); DUBLIN, 1981–3, 1984

Cobbe, W. H. M., Leix-Offaly, 1927(June)

Coburn, George, Louth, 1954(Mar.)(by)–61

Coburn, James, Monaghan, 1923; Louth, 1927(June)–53 (d.)

Codd, P. J., Wexford, 1977

Coffey, Anthony (Tony), Galway West, 1977, 1981; CONNACHT-ULSTER, 1979

Coffey, Elizabeth (Betty), Dún Laoghaire, 1989

Cogan, Barry, Cork Mid, 1977–81; Cork South-Central, 1981, 1982(Nov.), 1987, 1989

Cogan, Patrick, Wicklow, 1937, 1938–54 (def.)

Coghlan, P. J., Dublin South-West, 1961

Colbert, James, Limerick, 1923–33 (def.)

Colbert, Michael, Limerick, 1937–8 (def.), 1944–8; Limerick West, 1955(by)–7 (def.)

Cole, John (Jack) C., Cavan, 1951, 1954, 1957

Cole, John J., Cavan, 1923–7(June) (def.), 1927(Sept.)–32 (def.), 1933, 1937–44 (def.), 1948

Cole, T. L., *Belfast (Pottinger)*, 1933, 1938; Belfast East (w), 1945–50; *Belfast (Dock)*, 1949–53 (def.)

Cole, W. L., Cavan, 1922–3 (def.)

Coleman, Donal, Cork South-Central, 1982(Feb.)

Coleman, John, Limerick, 1927(June)

Coleman, John (Jack), Longford-Westmeath, 1970(by), 1973

Coleman, John K., Cork South-Central, 1989

Colgan, John, Dublin Central, 1982(Nov.)

Colgan, John B. M., Dublin South-West, 1954, 1957

Colgan, M. J., Dublin North-East, 1944

Colivet, M. P., Limerick City-Limerick East, 1921–3; Limerick, 1923

Colleran, Luke, Sligo-Leitrim, 1957

Colley, Anne, Dublin South, 1987–9 (def.)

Colley, George, Dublin North-East, 1961–9; Dublin North-Central, 1969–77; Dublin (Clontarf), 1977–81; Dublin Central, 1981–3 (d.)

Colley, Henry (Harry), Dublin North-East, 1943, 1944–57 (def.)

Collier, M. P., Leix-Offaly, 1938, 1944

Collins, Conor (Cornelius), Kerry-Limerick West, 1921–3

Collins, D. P., Dublin North-Central, 1961

Collins, Edward, Waterford, 1966(by), 1969–87 (del.)

Collins, Gerard, Limerick West, 1967(by)–

Collins, James, *Belfast (Dock)*, 1938; *Belfast (Falls)*, 1945

Collins, James J., Limerick West, 1948–67 (d.)

Collins, Capt. Jeremiah, Cork Borough, 1923

Collins, John H., *Armagh*, 1925–9; *Down South*, 1929–33

Collins, Leo, Meath, 1959(by)

Collins, Martin, Tipperary North, 1957

Collins, Michael, Cork Mid/North/Soutb/South-East/West 1921–2(Aug.) (d.); *Armagh*, 1921–2 (d.)

Collins, Michael, Dublin South-Central, 1973; Dublin (Rathmines West), 1977; Dublin South Central, 1981

Collins, Noel, Cork North-East, 1973, 1977

Collins, Noel, *Down South*, 1973

Collins, Patrick, Galway North, 1948

Collins, Seán, Cork West, 1948–57 (def.); Cork South-West, 1961–9 (def.)

Collins-O'Driscoll, Margaret, Dublin North, 1923–33 (def.)

Colohan, Hugh, Kildare-Wicklow, 1922–3; Kildare, 1923–31 (d.)

Colton, Adrian, Mid-Ulster (w), 1986(by)

Colton, E. J. Leix-Offaly, 1948

Comerford, Henry, Galway West, 1981

Comiskey, Owen, Meath-Westmeath, 1944

Commons, Bernard, Mayo South, 1943, 1944, 1945(by)–51 (def.) 1954

Comyn, Michael, Clare, 1923

Conaghan, Hugh, Donegal North-East, 1976(by); Donegal, 1977–81; Donegal North-East, 1981–9 (def.)

Conaghan, Michael, Dublin West, 1982(May)(by), 1982(Nov.), 1987, 1989

Conaty, Thomas, *Belfast West*, 1975

Concannon, Helena, National University of Ireland, 1933–7

Concannon, Patrick, Roscommon, 1957

Condon, Thomas Joseph, Tipperary, 1927(June)

Condon, William, Limerick, 1927(June)

Condron, John, Leis-Offaly, 1943

Condron, Joseph, Dublin West, 1982(May)(by)

Condy, Catherine, *Belfast East*, 1973, 1975

Conlan, John, Kildare, 1923–7(June) (def.), 1927(Sept.)

Conlan, John F., Monaghan, 1969–77; Cavan-Monaghan, 1977–87 (def.)

Conlan, Patrick, Monaghan, 1927(June)

Conlon, Malachy, *Armagh South*, 1945–50 (d.)
Conlon, Martin, Roscommon, 1925(by)–33 (def.), 1948
Conn, S. E., *Londonderry*, 1973–6
Connaughton, Joseph, Roscommon, 1957
Connaughton, Paul, Galway North-East, 1975(by); Galway East, 1977, 1981–
Connell, George, Leix-Offaly, 1943, 1944
Connellan, Joseph, *Armagh South*, 1929–33; *Down South*, 1949–67 (d.)
Connolly, Cornelius, Cork West, 1923–7(June)
Connolly, Cornelius, Cork Borough, 1944
Connolly, D. N., Wicklow, 1981, 1982(Nov.)
Connolly, Enda, Dublin Central, 1989
Connolly, G. C., Laoighis-Offaly, 1969–
Connolly, James J., Dublin North-East, 1982(Feb.)
Connolly, Jeremiah R., Cork Borough, 1944
Connolly, Joseph, *Antrim*, 1921
Connolly, Joseph, Dublin Co. North, 1969; Dublin Co. West, 1977
Connolly, M. E., *Armagh*, 1973, 1975
Connolly, M. J., Longford-Westmeath, 1927(June), 1927(Sept.)–32
Connolly, P. M., Longford-Westmeath, 1932
Connolly, R. J., Louth, 1943–4 (def.), 1948–51 (def.), 1954(by), 1954;
    Dublin South-Central, 1957
Connolly, Thomas, Galway West, 1961
Connor, David, Cork West, 1923
Connor, John, Kerry North, 1948, 1951, 1954–5 (d.)
Connor, John, Louth, 1981
Connor, John, Roscommon, 1981–2(Feb,) (def). 1982(Nov.), 1987, 1989–
Connor, Michael, Louth, 1927(June)
Connor, Patrick, Kerry South, 1961–9 (def.)
Connor-Scarteen, Michael, Kerry South, 1977, 1982(Feb.)
Conroy, P. D., Galway, 1923
Conroy, Richard, Dublin Co. Mid., 1977; Dublin South-West, 1981, 1982(Feb.),
    1982(Nov.); Dún Laoghaire, 1987
Considine, M., Clare, 1951
Conway, Andrew, Leitrim-Sligo, 1933
Conway, Prof. Arthur, National University of Ireland, 1922
Conway, Declan, Waterford, 1927(June)
Conway, Seán, Meath, 1981, 1982(Feb.), 1982(Nov.)
Conway, Timothy, Kildare, 1989
Coogan, Eamonn, Kilkenny, 1944–8 (nominated but d. before election)
Coogan, Fintan, Galway West, 1951, 1954–77 (def.), 1982(Feb.), 1982(Nov.)–
    7 (def.), 1989
Coogan, Thomas, Carlow-Kilkenny, 1973, 1977
Cook, D. S., Belfast South (w), 1974(Feb.), 1982(by), 1983, 1986(by), 1987;
    Belfast South, 1982–6; NORTHERN IRELAND, 1984
Cook, M. F. A., Upper Bann (w), 1987
Cooke, M. J., Galway, 1932

Cooney, Eamonn, Dublin North, 1927(June), 1927(Sept.)–37; Dublin North-West, 1937, 1938–43, 1944

Cooney, Joseph, Meath-Westmeath, 1943

Cooney, P. M., Longford-Westmeath, 1961, 1965, 1969, 1970(by)–7 (def.), 1981–9; CONNACHT-ULSTER, 1979; LEINSTER, 1989–

Cooper, Maj. B. R., Dublin Co., 1923–30 (d.)

Cooper, D. H. H., *Mid-Ulster*, 1975

Cooper, I. A., *Londonderry Mid*, 1969–73; *Mid-Ulster*, 1973–6; Mid-Ulster (w), 1974(Feb.), 1974(Oct.)

Cooper, James, *Fermanagh-Tyrone*, 1921–9

Cooper, N. A., Fermanagh-Tyrone (w), 1945

Cooper, R. G. (Bob), *Belfast West*, 1973–6

Coote, William, *Fermanagh-Tyrone*, 1921–5

Corbett, Eamonn, Galway, 1935(by)–7; Galway West, 1937, 1943–4

Corbett, Mary, Tipperary, 1943

Corcoran, Bernard, Leix-Offaly, 1957, 1961

Corcoran, Helen, Louth, 1982(Feb.)

Corcoran, James A., Cork North-Central, 1982(Feb.)

Corcoran, John W., Mayo North, 1933

Corcoran, Laurence, Dublin South-West, 1969, 1970(by); Dublin (Ballyfermot), 1977; Dublin South-Central, 1982(Nov.)

Corcoran, Timothy, Cork Borough, 1923, 1927(June)

Corcoran, W. M., Wexford, 1948

Corish, Brendan, Wexford, 1943(by)–82(Feb.)

Corish, Desmond, Wexford, 1982(Feb.)

Corish, Richard, Wexford, 1921–45 (d.)

Corkery, Daniel, Cork Mid/North/South/South East/West, 1921–3; Cork North. 1923–32 (def.), 1933–7; Cork West, 1937

Corkey, D. E., *Antrim South*, 1970(by)

Corkey, Revd Prof. Robert, *Queen's University Belfast*, 1929–43(June) (res.)

Corley, Michael, Clare, 1973

Corr, James, Cork South-Central, 1981, 1982(Feb.–Nov.), 1989

Corr, John, Dublin Co., 1937

Corr, Seán, Dublin West, 1982(Feb.)

Corrigan, P. E., Fermanagh-Tyrone South (w), 1987

Corrigan, Thomas, Fermanagh-Tyrone (w), 1924

Corrigan, Thomas, Mayo North, 1965

Corry, John, Dublin Co. North, 1977

Corry, M. J., Cork East, 1927(June)–37; Cork South-East, 1937–48; Cork East 1948–61; Cork North-East, 1961–9

Corvin, H. C., Belfast North (w), 1924; Belfast West (w), 1943(by)

Cosgrave, James, Galway, 1923–7(June) (def.), 1927(Sept.)

Cosgrave, Liam, Dublin Co., 1943–8; Dún Laoghaire and Rathdown, 1948–77; Dún Laoghaire, 1977–81

Cosgrave, Liam T., Dún Laoghaire, 1981–7 (def.), 1989

Cosgrave, M. J., Dublin (Clontarf), 1977–81; Dublin North-East, 1981–

Cosgrave, P. B. J., Dublin North-West, 1921–3; Dublin South, 1923–4 (d.)

Cosgrave, Thomas, Dublin North-East, 1961

Cosgrave, W. T., Kilkenny North, 1918–22; Carlow-Kilkenny, 1921–7(Sept.) (elected but chose to sit for Cork Borough); Cork Borough, 1927 (Sept.)–44

Cosgrove, Paraic, Mayo West, 1982(Feb.), 1982(Nov.), 1987, 1989

Cosgrove, Peter J., *Fermanagh South*, 1969

Costello, Declan D., Dublin North-West, 1951–69; Dublin South-West, 1973–7

Costello, Dudley, Roscommon, 1937, 1938

Costello, John A., Dublin Co., 1933–7; Dublin Townships, 1937–48; Dublin South-East, 1948–69

Costello, Joseph, Dublin Central, 1987, 1989

Costello, Séamus, Wicklow, 1968(by), 1973, 1977

Costelloe, Patrick, Limerick, 1943

Costelloe, W. J., Dublin Co., 1943

Cott, Gerard, Cork North-East, 1969–73

Cotter, Edward, Cork West, 1949(by), 1954–61; Cork South-West, 1961–9

Cotter, S. P., Cork Mid, 1965(by), 1965

Cotter, William, Tipperary, 1943

Cotter, William (Bill), Cavan-Monaghan, 1989–

Cotterell, Andrew, Carlow-Kilkenny, 1989

Cotterell, William, Carlow-Kilkenny, 1957

Coughlan, Cathal, Donegal South-West, 1983(by)–6 (d.)

Coughlan, Clement, Donegal, 1980(by)–1; Donegal South-West, 1981–3 (d.)

Coughlan, Mary, Donegal South-West, 1987–

Coughlan, Stephen, Limerick East, 1954, 1957, 1961–77 (def.)

Coulter, Robert J., Antrim North (w), 1983

Coulter, Rose J., *Belfast West*, 1973–6

Coulter, W. A., *Down South*, 1982

Coulthard, John, *Antrim South*, 1968(by); *Belfast (Victoria)*, 1969; Belfast South (w), 1970; *Belfast East*, 1973

Counihan, Marcus, Kerry South, 1987

Counihan, W. J., Clare, 1943

Courtney, Edward, *Belfast (Bloomfield)*, 1958

Courtney, James, Kerry South, 1965

Courtney, P. B., Down South (w), 1979

Cousins, J. E., *Antrim South*, 1975; Belfast West (w), 1979

Cousley, C. J., *Antrim North*, 1982–6

Coveney, Hugh, Cork South-Central, 1981–2(Feb.) (def.), 1982(Nov.)–7 (def.)

Cowan, Peadar, Meath-Westmeath, 1937, 1938, 1943, 1944; Dublin North-East, 1948–54 (def.), 1961

Cowan, Rory, Dublin North-East, 1965

Cowen, Bernard, Laoighis-Offaly, 1969–73 (def.), 1977–84 (d.)

Cowen, Brian, Laoighis-Offaly, 1984(by)–
Cox, Agnes, Dublin North-West, 1987
Cox, James, Galway West, 1961
Cox, Patrick, MUNSTER, 1989–
Coyle, Henry, Mayo North, 1923–4 (disqualified)
Craig, Capt. C. C., *Antrim South*, 1903(by)–22; Antrim (w), 1922–9
Craig, Sir James, *see* Craigavon, Viscount
Craig, Prof. Sir James, Dublin University, 1921–33(July) (d.)
Craig, James, *Carrick*, 1969; *Antrim North*, 1973–5
Craig, William, *Belfast Central*, 1958; *Larne*, 1960(by)–73; *Antrim North*, 1973–
   5; *Belfast East*, 1975–6, 1982; Belfast East (w), 1974(Feb.)–79 (def.)
Craigavon, Viscount James (James Craig), *Down*, 1921–9; *Down North*, 1929–
   40 (d.)
Crawford, Randall, *Londonderry*, 1975
Crawford, (Robert), *Antrim*, 1921–9; *Antrim Mid*, 1929–38
Crawford, Col. Robert G. Sharman, *see* Sharman Crawford
Crawford, W. E., Dublin Co., 1932
Cree, Samuel, *Belfast (Shankill)*, 1958, 1960(by)
Creed, Donal, Cork Mid, 1965(by), 1965–81; Cork North-West, 1981–9;
   IRELAND, 1973–7
Creed, Michael, Cork North-West, 1989–
Cregan, D. D., Cork South-Central, 1981, 1982(Feb.)
Cregan, Eamonn, Limerick East, 1981
Cregan, James, Kildare, 1927(June)
Crilly, Thomas, Dublin South-East, 1987, 1989
Crinion, Brendan, Kildare, 1961–9; Meath, 1969, 1973–82(Feb.)
Croly, W. J., Dublin South-West, 1948, 1954
Cronin, Capt. Denis, Cork West, 1943
Cronin, E. J., Cork East, 1933; Cork North, 1937
Cronin, Jeremiah, Cork North-East, 1965–81; MUNSTER, 1979–84(May)
Cronin, John, Cork North, 1927(June)
Cronin, John, Tipperary, 1927(June)
Cronin, M. P., Tipperary North, 1948, 1954
Cronin, William (Billy), Cork East, 1982(Feb.)
Crosbie, James, Cork Borough, 1944
Crothers, D. S. F., *Antrim South*, 1973–5
Crotty, John, Cork North, 1943
Crotty, Kieran, Carlow-Kilkenny, 1969–89
Crotty, Patrick, Waterford, 1977
Crotty, Patrick J., Carlow-Kilkenny, 1948–69
Crotty, Raymond, DUBLIN, 1989
Crowe, F. E., *Armagh*, 1973
Crowe, John (Jack), Tipperary South, 1981, 1987
Crowe, M. B., Limerick East, 1968(by), 1977; MUNSTER, 1979
Crowe, Patrick, Tipperary South, 1948, 1951–7 (def.)
Crowe, Seán, Dublin South-West, 1989

Crowley, Bartholomew, Clare, 1937

Crowley, Desmond, Clare, 1981

Crowley, Ellen, Cork Borough, 1943

Crowlcy, Florence, Cork Mid, 1965(by), 1965–9; Cork South-West, 1969–77 (def.), 1981–2(Feb.) (def.), 1982(Nov.)

Crowley, Frank, Cork Mid, 1977; Cork North-West, 1981–

Crowley, Frederick H., Kerry, 1927(June), 1927(Sept.)–37; Kerry South, 1937–45 (d.)

Crowley, H. M., Kerry South, 1945(by)–66 (d.)

Crowley, James, Kerry-Limerick West, 1921–3; Kerry, 1923–32 (def.)

Crowley, John, Mayo North/West, 1921–3; Mayo North, 1923–7(June)

Crowley, Patrick, Cork West, 1943

Crowley, Tadhg (Timothy), Limerick, 1924(by), 1927(June)–37 (def.), 1938–44 (def.); Limerick East, 1948, 1951–7

Cruise-O'Brien, Conor, Dublin North-East, 1969–77; Dublin (Clontarf), 1977; IRELAND, 1972–3

Crumley, Charles, *Londonderry*, 1982

Cudden, James, Meath, 1982(Feb.)

Cuffe, J. P., Dublin Co., 1932

Cuív, Eamon, *see* Ó Cuív

Cullen, Denis, Leix-Offaly, 1923; Dublin North, 1925(by), 1927(June-Sept.) (def.), 1932

Cullen, F. J., *Belfast East*, 1982; Belfast East (w), 1983, 1986(by), 1987

Cullen, Martin, Waterford, 1987–9 (def.)

Cullen, Matthew, Meath, 1954

Cullen, Matthew J., Dún Laoghaire and Rathdown, 1948, 1951, 1954

Culleton, Christopher, Wexford, 1943

Cullimore, Séamus, Wexford, 1989–

Cullimore, Thomas, Wexford, 1948

Culliton, T. J., Laoighis-Offaly, 1969, 1973

Cumiskey, Dublin North-Central, 1969, 1973, 1977

Cummings, Edward, NORTHERN IRELAND, 1979

Cummins, Camella, Meath, 1987

Cummins, Charles B., Carlow-Kilkenny, 1965

Cummins, John, Wexford, 1923

Cummins, P. J., Dublin South-Central, 1958(by)–65 (def.); Dublin South-East, 1969, 1973

Cummins, William, Kerry North, 1938

Cunning, W. A., Antrim East, 1983

Cunningham, Angela, Cork North-East, 1974(by)

Cunningham, Francis, Donegal-Leitrim, 1973

Cunningham, Gearóid, Dublin North-West, 1943, 1944

Cunningham, Liam, Donegal East, 1951–61; Donegal North-East, 1961–76 (d.)

Cunningham, Michael, Kildare, 1948

Cunningham, Michael, Mid-Ulster (w), 1970

Cunningham, Patrick, Fermanagh-Tyrone (w), 1935–50
Cunningham, Patrick, Galway North-East, 1969
Cunningham, Sir S. Knox, Belfast West (w), 1943(by), 1945; Antrim South (w), 1955–70
Cunningham, W. F., *Down South*, 1929
Curley, Desmond, Roscommon-Leitrim, 1977
Curley, John, Dublin North-Central, 1981, 1982(Feb.)
Curley, Patrick, Galway, 1923
Curran, B. P., Upper Bann (w), 1983, 1987
Curran, Charles, Waterford, 1973
Curran, Dermot, Down North (w), 1974(Feb.)
Curran, E. R., *Tyrone East*, 1969
Curran, J. F., Dublin South-Central, 1982(Feb.)
Curran, Maj. L. E., Carrick (w), 1945(Apr.)(by)–9
Curran, P. J., Dublin Co., 1927(June). 1932–3 (def.)
Curran, Richard, Tipperary, 1933–7 (def.), 1938–43 (def.)
Currie, G. B. H., Down North, 1955–70
Currie, J. Austin, *Tyrone East*, 1964(by)–73; *Fermanagh-Tyrone South*, 1973–6, 1982–6; Fermanagh-Tyrone South (w), 1979, 1986(by); Dublin West, 1989–
Curristan, Eunan, Donegal-Leitrim, 1969
Curry, James, Strangford (w), 1983
Curtin, Owen, Cork South-Central, 1987
Curton, John, Kildare, 1931(by)
Cusack, Bryan, Galway, 1921–3, 1927(June)
Cusack, Thomas, Queen's University Belfast (w), 1945
Cushinan, H. J., Antrim, South (w), 1987
Cushley, W. H., *Belfast (Oldpark)*, 1962
Cushnahan, J. W., Belfast North (w), 1979; *Down North*, 1982–6; Down North (w), 1983, 1986(by), 1987; MUNSTER, 1989–

Dalton, L. J., Tipperary, 1923–7(June)
Dalton, Thomas, Dublin South-West, 1973
Daly, Brendan, Clare, 1973–
Daly, Denis, Kerry, 1933–7
Daly, Donal J., Cork Borough, 1954, 1957, 1961
Daly, Edward, Meath, 1961
Daly, F. J., Cork Borough, 1922, 1927(June), 1943–4
Daly, James, Waterford, 1927(June)
Daly, James, Meath-Westmeath, 1937
Daly, John, Cork East, 1923–33
Daly, May, Kerry North, 1957
Daly, Patrick, Cork East, 1933–73; Cork North, 1937–43 (def.), 1944
Daly, Patrick T., Dublin North, 1923
Daly, Thomas, Donegal, 1924(by)
Daly, Thomas A., *Fermanagh-Tyrone South*, 1973–7

Dalzell, Alexander, *Belfast (Woodvale)*, 1933
Danaher, B. G., Limerick West, 1965, 1969, 1973, 1982(Nov.)
Darby, Brigid, Kildare, 1933; Carlow-Kildare, 1937
D'Arcy, M. J., Wexford, 1973, 1977–87 (def.), 1989–
Darcy, Thomas, Longford-Westmeath, 1951, 1954, 1961
Dardis, John, LEINSTER, 1989
Darmody, Terence, Tipperary South, 1973, 1981, 1982(Feb.)
Davern, Donal, Tipperary South, 1965–9
Davern, M. C. Noel, Tipperary South, 1969–81, 1987–; MUNSTER, 1979–84
   (def.)
Davern, M. J., Tipperary South, 1948–65
Davey, John, Londonderry East (w), 1983, 1987
Davies, S. G., Cork South-West, 1987
Davin, J. J., Tipperary, 1932
Davin, Michael, Leix-Offaly, 1956(by)
Davin, Séamus, Dublin North-West, 1943
Davin, William, Leix-Offaly, 1922–56 (d.)
Davis, Gerald, Roscommon, 1923
Davis, Ivan, *Antrim South*, 1982–6
Davis, Matthew, Athlone-Longford, 1937–8 (def.); Roscommon, 1948
Davis, Michael, Mayo North, 1927(June)–37
Davis, S. P., Dublin South-Central, 1954; Mayo North, 1965
Davison, John C., *Armagh*, 1925(Nov.)(by)–9; *Armagh Mid*, 1929–31(Aug.)
   (res.)
Davison, Sir Joseph, *Belfast West*, 1923(by)
Davitt, R. E., Meath, 1933–7
Davy, E. O'D., Dublin South 1932
Dawson, Edward, Waterford, 1948
Day, Robert, Cork Borough 1922–3 (def.)
Deane, R. E., Fermanagh-Tyrone, 1935
Dearle, Seoirse, Dublin South-West, 1957; Dublin North-Central, 1973
Deasy, Joseph, Dublin South-West, 1948
Deasy, M. Austin, Waterford 1969, 1973, 1977–
Deasy, Richard, Dublin South-West, 1951, 1954
Deasy, Rickard, Tipperary North, 1969
de Blacam, Aodh, Louth, 1948
de Burca, Máirín, Dublin North-Central, 1973
de Courcy Ireland, John, Dún Laoghaire, 1982(Nov.); DUBLIN, 1984
Dee, Eamon, Waterford-Tipperary East, 1921–2 (def.)
Deegan, J. T., Dún Laoghaire and Rathdown, 1965; Dublin Co. South,
   1970(by)
Deegan, Seán, Tipperary North, 1987
Deenihan, James, Kerry North, 1982(Nov.), 1987–
Deering, Mark, Wicklow, 1951, 1953(by)–7 (def.), 1965
Deering, Michael, Carlow-Kilkenny, 1982(Feb.)
De Groot, Cornelius, LEINSTER, 1989

Delaney, Charles, Leix-Offaly, 1943
Delaney, Conor, Dublin South-West, 1989
Delaney, James, Dublin West, 1987
Delaney, Joseph, Leix-Offaly, 1923
Delaney, Michael, Carlow-Kilkenny, 1927(Sept.)
Delaney, V. S., Longford-Westmeath, 1930(by)
Delap, P. C., Donegal-Leitrim, 1970(by)–3 (def.); Donegal, 1977
de Loughry, Peter, Carlow-Kilkenny, 1927(Sept.)–32
de Loughry, T. F., Kilkenny, 1943
Dempsey, M. G., Dublin North-East, 1957
Dempsey, Noel, Meath, 1987–
Dennehy, John, Cork Mid, 1977; Cork City, 1979(by); Cork South-Central, 1987–
Dennehy, Thomas, Kerry, 1923, 1927(June)
Dennehy, William, Kerry South, 1954
Denning, Lord Tom [pseud.; Enda O'Callaghan], Dublin North-Central, 1989
Depew, Henry, Leitrim-Sligo, 1923
Derham, M. J., Dublin Co., 1921–4 (d.)
de Roiste, Liam, Cork Borough, 1921–3, 1927(June)
de Rossa, Proinsias, Dublin (Finglas), 1977; Dublin North-West, 1981, 1982(Feb.)–
DUBLIN, 1989–92(Jan.) (res.)
Derrig, Thomas, Mayo North/West, 1921–3; Mayo South, 1923; Mayo North, 1925(by); Carlow-Kilkenny, 1927(June)–37; Kilkenny, 1937–48; Carlow-Kilkenny, 1948–56 (d.)
de Siúin, Liam, Wicklow, 1982(Nov.), 1987
Desmond, Barry, Dún Laoghaire and Rathdown, 1969–77; Dún Laoghaire, 1977–89; DUBLIN, 1989–
Desmond, Cornelius, Cork Borough, 1956(by)
Desmond, Daniel, Cork South-East, 1944; Cork South, 1948–61; Cork Mid, 1961–4 (d.)
Desmond, Eileen, Cork Mid, 1965(Mar.)(by)–9 (def.), 1972(by), 1973–81; Cork South-Central, 1981–7; MUNSTER. 1979–81, 1984, 1989
Desmond, T. N., Cork Mid, 1961
Desmond, William, Cork Borough, 1932–7 (def.)
de Stacpoole, Duc George, Meath, 1933
de Valera, Eamon, Clare, 1921–59; *Down*, 1921–9; *Down South*, 1933–8
de Valera, Síle, Dublin Co. Mid. 1977–81; Dublin South, 1981, 1982(Feb.); Clare, 1982(Nov.), 1987–; DUBLIN, 1979–84
de Valera, Vivion, Dublin North-West, 1945(by)–8; Dublin North-Central, 1948–69; Dublin Central, 1969–77; Dublin (Cabra), 1977–81
Devane, Michael, Cork East, 1957
Devanny, Frank, Mayo North, 1952(by)
Devereux, R. J., Wicklow, 1932
Devine, Patrick, *Londonderry*, 1982

Devins, James, Sligo-Mayo East, 1921–3
Devitt, J. M., Dublin Co., 1932
Devlin, Joseph, *Antrim*, 1921–5; *Belfast West*, 1921–9; *Belfast Central*, 1929–34 (d.); Fermanagh-Tyrone (w), 1929–34 (d.)
Devlin, J., Bernadette, *see* McAliskey
Devlin, P. J., *Belfast (Falls)*, 1969–73; *Belfast West*, 1973–6; NORTHERN IRELAND, 1979
Devlin-McAliskey, *see* McAliskey
Devoy, Herbert, Carlow-Kilkenny, 1956(by), 1957
Diamond, Harry, *Belfast Central*, 1934(by); *Belfast (Falls)*, 1945–69 (def.); Belfast West (w), 1964
Dickson, A. L., Carrick, 1969–73; *Antrim South*, 1973–6; Belfast North (w), 1979
Dickson, J. W., *Belfast (Woodvale)*, 1938
Dickson, Dr N. S., *Queen's University Belfast*, 1949(Nov.)(by)
Dickson, Robert, *Belfast West*, 1925
Dickson, William, Belfast West (w), 1979; *Belfast West*, 1982
Dillon, Andrew, Dublin North-Central, 1981, 1982(Nov.)
Dillon, James M., Donegal, 1932–7; Monaghan, 1938–69
Dillon, Patrick, Meath, 1954
Dillon, Thomas, Galway, 1923
Dillon-Byrne, Jane, DUBLIN, 1979; Dún Laoghaire, 1981, 1989
Dillon-Leetch, Thomas, Mayo East, 1973
Dineen, John, Cork East/North-East, 1922–3; Cork East, 1923–7(June) (def.)
Dineen, Patrick, Cork South, 1957
Diskin, K. M., Donegal-Leitrim, 1973
Diver, Hugh, Donegal East, 1948
Dixon, Beatrice, Dublin South-West, 1957
Dixon, Herbert, *see* Glentoran, 1st and 2nd Barons
Dobbs, Frank, Sligo-Leitrim, 1987
Dobson, John, *Down West*, 1965(June)(by)–73
Docherty, J. B., *Belfast (Woodvale)*, 1953
Dockrell, H. M., Dublin Co., 1932–48; Dún Laoghaire and Rathdown, 1948
Dockrell, H. P., Dún Laoghaire and Rathdown, 1951–7 (def.), 1961–77; Dún Laoghaire, 1977
Dockrell, M. E., Dublin South, 1943–8; Dublin South-Central, 1948–9; Dublin Central, 1969–77; Dublin South-Central, 1977
Dodd, Gerald, Roscommon-Leitrim, 1973
Doherty, Arthur, Londonderry East, 1983, 1987
Doherty, Eugene, Donegal, 1923–33 (def.)
Doherty, Hugh, Donegal, 1932, 1933–7
Doherty, James, Roscommon, 1961
Doherty, James N., Donegal East, 1948
Doherty, Joseph, Donegal West, 1943
Doherty, Kieran, Cavan-Monaghan, 1981(June–Aug.) (d.)
Doherty, Patrick, Tipperary, 1923

Doherty, Patrick, Donegal North-East, 1989; CONNACHT-ULSTER, 1989
Doherty, Patrick H., Donegal, 1932
Doherty, Patrick J., Donegal East, 1957
Doherty, Patrick Joseph, *Belfast West*, 1973
Doherty, Patrick Joseph, *Down North*, 1982
Doherty, Seán, Mayo North, 1957–61
Doherty, Sean, Roscommon-Leitrim, 1977–81; Roscommon, 1981–9 (def.); CONNACHT-ULSTER, 1989
Doherty, Tomás, Dublin North-Central, 1957
Doherty, Vincent, Dublin North-Central, 1981
Dolan, James N., Leitrim-Roscommon North, 1921–3; Leitrim-Sligo, 1923–32 (def.), 1933–7; Leitrim, 1937
Dolan, John (Seán) B., *Queen's University Belfast*, 1921
Dolan, Owen, Sligo-Leitrim, 1948
Dolan, Owen J., Longford-Westmeath, 1927(Sept.)
Dolan, Séamus, Cavan, 1954, 1957, 1961–5, 1969, 1973
Dolan, Thomas, Laoighis-Offaly, 1973
Dolly, William, Galway, 1923
Dolphin, Francis, Cavan, 1948
Donald, Thompson, *Belfast East*, 1921–5 (def.)
Donaldson, A. E., *Down North*, 1973
Donaldson, Denis, Belfast East (w), 1983
Donaldson, G. M., *Belfast South*, 1925(Nov.)(by)
Donaldson, J. H., *Down South*, 1985(by)–6
Donaldson, W. J., *Belfast (St Anne's)*, 1933
Donegan, Bartholomew (Batt), Cork North, 1954, 1957–61; Cork North-East, 1961; Cork Mid, 1969
Donegan, Maurice, Cork West, 1923
Donegan, Michael, Cork North-West, 1982(Feb.)
Donegan, Patrick, Limerick East, 1948, 1957
Donegan, Patrick S., Louth, 1954–7 (def.), 1961–81
Donegan, Thomas, Louth, 1982(Nov.)
Donnellan, J. F., Galway East, 1964(by)–9; Galway North-East, 1969–77; Galway East, 1977–81; Galway West, 1981–9
Donnellan, Michael, Galway West, 1940(by); Galway East, 1943–8; Galway North, 1948–61; Galway East, 1961–4 (d.)
Donnelly, A. E., *Fermanagh-Tyrone*, 1925–9; *Tyrone West*, 1929–49
Donnelly, Brendan, Wicklow, 1954, 1957
Donnelly, Desmond L., Down (w), 1946(by)
Donnelly, Don, Dublin North-Central, 1989
Donnelly, Eamon, *Armagh*, 1925–9; Monaghan, 1927(Sept.); Leitrim-Sligo, 1929(by); Leix-Offaly, 1932, 1933–7; *Belfast (Falls)*, 1942(by)–5
Donnelly, Francis, Mid-Ulster (w), 1974(Oct.), 1979; *Mid-Ulster*, 1975, 1982; Londonderry East (w), 1983, 1987; NORTHERN IRELAND, 1979
Donnelly, James A., *Belfast (Cromac)*, 1949
Donnelly, James J., Fermanagh-Tyrone South (w), 1966

Donnelly, John J., Dublin North, 1927(June)
Donnelly, K. Philomena, Dublin North-West, 1987
Donnelly, Michael, Dublin South-East, 1969, 1981, 1982(Feb.), 1987
Donnelly, Niall, Dublin North-West, 1987
Donnelly, P. J., *Armagh South*(Feb.)1918(by)–22
Donnelly, P. J., *Armagh South*, 1929
Donnelly, R. J., *Belfast West*, 1973
Donnelly, Simon, Dublin South, 1943
Donnelly, Thomas, *Belfast North*, 1973, 1975; Belfast North (w), 1974(Feb.), 1974(Oct.)
Donoghue, T. A., Monaghan, 1969
Donohoe, Martin, Dún Laoghaire, 1982(Feb.)
Donohue, P. A., Cavan, 1948
Donohoe, W. P., Dublin North-West, 1948
Donovan, Con, Cork City South-East, 1969
Donovan, John (Jack), Limerick East, 1987
Donovan, M. D., Dublin South-East, 1982(Feb.)
Doolan, Gerard, Dublin North-West, 1987, 1989
Dooley, Patrick, Kildare, 1954, 1957–65 (def.), 1973
Doolin, James, CONNACHT-ULSTER, 1979
Dooney, Triona, Dublin North-Central, 1987, 1989
Doorley, F. A., Leix-Offaly, 1923
Doran, Arthur, *Down South*, 1973
Doran, John, Wexford, 1954
Doran, John J., Roscommon, 1927(June), 1927(Sept.), 1943
Doran, Peter, Upper Bann (w), 1990(by)
Doran, William, Dublin North-Central, 1977
Dore, M. J. K., Limerick West, 1948
Dorgan, James, Meath, 1977
Dorr, P. M., Roscommon, 1923
Dougan, George, Armagh Central, 1941(by)–55 (d.)
Dougan, John, Antrim North (w), 1955, 1959
Douglas, J. H., Dublin South-East, 1948, 1951
Douglas, W. A. B., *Londonderry*, 1973–6, 1982–6
Dowd, Benny, Laoighis-Offaly, 1977
Dowdall, T. P., Cork Borough, 1932–43
Dowling, Joseph, Dublin South-West, 1959(by), 1961, 1965–77; Dublin (Ballyfermot), 1977; Dublin South-Central, 1982(Feb.)
Dowling, Joseph, Cork East, 1981
Dowling, Richard (Dick), Carlow-Kilkenny, 1981, 1982(Feb.), 1982(Nov.)–7
Dowling, Samuel W., *Down South*, 1973
Dowling, Seán, Dublin South, 1943
Dowling, William, *Belfast (Windsor)*, 1937(by)–45
Downey, Hugh, *Belfast (Dock)*, 1945–9 (def.)
Downey, James, Dublin Central, 1969
Doyle, Andrew, Wexford, 1969, 1973

Doyle, Avril, Wexford, 1982(Nov.)–9 (def.)
Doyle, Edward, Carlow-Kilkenny, 1923–32 (def.)
Doyle, Gerald, Wexford, 1987
Doyle, John, Tipperary North, 1969, 1973
Doyle, Joseph, Dublin South-East, 1981, 1982(Feb.), 1982(Nov.)–7 (def.), 1989–
Doyle, Michael, Wexford, 1922–7(Sept.) (def.), 1932, 1933
Doyle, Patrick J., Leix-Offaly, 1932, 1933, 1937, 1948
Doyle, Peadar S., Dublin South, 1923–48; Dublin South-West, 1948–56 (d.)
Doyle, Peigín, Dublin South-Central, 1973
Doyle, Samuel, *Belfast North*, 1982
Doyle, Séamus, Wexford, 1921–3
Doyle, Seán, Meath-Westmeath, 1943; Meath, 1948
Doyle, Seán, Wexford, 1982(Feb.)
Doyle, Stephen, Kerry South, 1982(Feb.), 1982(Nov.)
Driscoll, Michael, Cork Borough, 1938
Drohan, Frank, Waterford-Tipperary East, 1921–2
Drury, John, Roscommon, 1923
Duchon, Mairéad, Dublin South, 1987
Dudgeon, Jeffrey, Belfast South (w), 1979
Duff, A. H., *Iveagh*, 1958
Duff, J. A., *Belfast East*, 1921–5 (def.); *Belfast (Pottinger)*, 1929
Duffy, G. Gavan, Dublin Co., 1921–3 (def.)
Duffy, John, Kerry South, 1943
Duffy, Joseph, Cavan-Monaghan, 1989
Duffy, L. J., Cork Borough, 1927(Sept.)
Duffy, Mary, Galway West, 1987
Duffy, Michael, Longford-Westmeath, 1930(by)
Duffy, Pádraig M. S., Cavan-Monaghan, 1987
Duffy, Patrick, Monaghan, 1923–7(June) (def.), 1927(Sept.)
Duffy, Patrick, Mayo South, 1954, 1957
Duffy, Patrick, Cavan, 1957, 1961
Duffy, Patrick A., *Mid-Ulster*, 1973–6; Mid-Ulster (w), 1979
Duffy, Séamus, Roscommon, 1927(June)
Duffy, Seán, Athlone-Longford, 1937
Duffy, Thomas, Dublin North-East, 1961, 1969; Dublin (Clontarf), 1977
Duffy, W. J., Galway, 1927(June–Sept.)
Duggan, Cornelius, Cork Borough, 1933
Duggan, E. J., Louth-Meath, 1921–3; Meath, 1923–33
Duggan, Hugh, Donegal West, 1948
Duggan, Liam, Cork North-East, 1977
Duggan, M. A., Cork North-East, 1979(by); Cork East, 1981, 1982(Nov.)
Duigan, Charles, Roscommon, 1981
Duignan, Peadar, Galway West, 1951–4
Duke, Richard, Dublin Co., 1932
Dukes, A. M., MUNSTER, 1979; Kildare, 1981–

Dunbar, Martin, Wexford, 1948, 1965

Dundon, Edward, Carlow-Kilkenny, 1933; Wexford, 1938

Dungan, Seán, Dublin Co. North, 1973

Dunleath, Baron (C. E. H. J. Mulholland), *Down North*, 1973–6, 1982–6

Dunlop, Dorothy, *Belfast East*, 1982–6

Dunlop, John, *Mid-Ulster*, 1973–5, 1982; Mid-Ulster (w), 1974(Feb.)–83

Dunlop, S. J., *Antrim South*, 1975–6

Dunlop, Victoria, *Belfast (Clifton)*, 1959(by)

Dunn, Alistair, Upper Bann (w), 1990(by)

Dunne, Christopher, Dublin South-West, 1987

Dunne, Cora, Dublin South-West, 1970(by)

Dunne, Francis, Laoighis-Offaly, 1981

Dunne, Joseph, Laoighis-Offaly, 1989

Dunne, Morgan, Wexford, 1961

Dunne, Patrick, Dublin North, 1981

Dunne, Patrick J., Dublin North-East, 1965, 1969, 1973; Dublin (Artane),
    1977; Dublin North-West, 1981, 1982(Feb.)

Dunne, Patrick J., Dublin South-Central, 1969

Dunne, Seán, Dublin Co., 1947(by), 1948–57, 1961–9; Dublin South-West,
    1969 (18–25 June) (d.)

Dunne, Thomas, Waterford, 1927(June)

Dunne, Thomas, Tipperary North, 1957, 1961–77 (def.); IRELAND, 1973–7

Dunphy, Kevin, LEINSTER, 1989

Dunphy, Mary, Cork South-Central, 1987

Dunphy, Michael, MUNSTER, 1979

Durack, Séamus, Clare, 1982(Nov.)

Durcan, Frank, Mayo West, 1989

Durcan, J. J., Mayo South, 1948

Durcan, Patrick, Mayo West, 1981, 1982(Feb.), 1982(Nov.), 1987

Durkan, B. J., Kildare, 1981–2(Feb.) (def.), 1982(Nov.)–

Dwan, Frank, Tipperary North, 1987

Dwyer, Edward, Limerick West, 1965, 1967(by), 1969, 1977

Dwyer, James, LEINSTER, 1984

Dwyer, James J., Dublin Co., 1921–2 (def.); Leix-Offaly, 1926(by)–32 (def.)

Dwyer, Kevin, Galway East, 1982(Feb.), 1982(by), 1982(Nov.)

Dwyer, Liam, Cork West, 1948

Dwyer, Martin, Tipperary, 1923

Dwyer, Ubi, Dún Laoghaire, 1981, 1982(Feb.)

Dwyer, William, Cork Borough, 1943, 1944–6; Cork East, 1948

Dyar, Patrick, Roscommon, 1923

Eager, G. A., Louth, 1973

Eakins, T. G. E., *Tyrone South*, 1969

Egan, Barry M., Cork Borough, 1927(June)–32, 1933

Egan, Bowes, *Enniskillen*, 1969

Egan, K. P., Leix (Laoighis)-Offaly, 1956(by)–65 (def.)

Egan, Martin M., Galway, 1923
Egan, Michael, Cork Borough, 1924(by)–7(June) (def.)
Egan, Nicholas, Leix (Laoighis)-Offaly, 1951, 1954–69
Egan, P. J., Leix-Offaly, 1923–7(June) (def.)
Egan, William, Dublin South-East, 1987
Elder, Nelson, *Belfast South*, 1973–5
Eley, Rod, Dublin West, 1982(Feb.)
Elliott, Áine, Dún Laoghaire, 1981
Elliott, J. F. B., Armagh North, 1965
Elliott, Rowley, *Fermanagh-Tyrone*, 1925–9; *Tyrone South*, 1929–44 (d.)
Elliott, Thomas, *Tyrone North*, 1938
Elliott, W. H., *Belfast East*, 1975
Ellis, John, Roscommon-Leitrim, 1977; Sligo-Leitrim, 1981–2(Nov.) (def.),
    1987–
Ellis, Richard, Roscommon, 1961
Ellis, Robert, Dublin South-East, 1969
Elmore, T. F., Louth, 1969
Emerson, Peter, *Belfast North*, 1982
Empey, R. N. M., *Belfast East*, 1975–6, 1982
English, Dr Ada, National University of Ireland, 1921–2 (def.)
English, B. T., *Armagh*, 1975
English, Seán, Kildare, 1989; LEINSTER, 1989
Ennis, J. T., Dublin Co., 1932, 1933, 1937
Ennis, Mary, Dublin Co., 1943
Enright, Michael, Wexford, 1987, 1989; LEINSTER, 1989
Enright, T. W., Laoighis-Offaly, 1969–
Ervine, William, *Bannside*, 1929
Erwin, A. H., *Antrim North*, 1975
Esmonde, Sir A. C., Tipperary, 1943; Wexford, 1951–73; IRELAND,
    1972–3
Esmonde, J. Grattan, Wexford, 1973–7 (def.)
Esmonde, Sir J. L., Wexford, 1936(by), 1937–44 (def.), 1948–51
Esmonde, O. Grattan, Wexford, 1923–7(June), 1927(Sept.)–36 (d.)
Esmonde, William, Wexford, 1961
Etchingham, Seán, Wexford, 1921–2 (def.)
Evans, A. J., Fermanagh-Tyrone South (w), 1974(Oct.)
Everett, James, Kildare-Wicklow, 1922–3; Wicklow, 1923–67 (d.)
Ewart, S.D., Armagh (w), 1964

Fagan, Charles, Longford-Westmeath, 1933–7; Meath-Westmeath, 1937–48;
    Longford-Westmeath, 1948–61
Fahey, Francis, Galway West, 1981, 1982(Feb.)–
Fahey, John, Carlow-Kilkenny, 1957, 1961
Fahey, John (Jackie), Tipperary South, 1961, 1965–77; Waterford, 1977–;
    MUNSTER, 1989
Fahey, P.J., Galway East, 1965

Fahy, Frank, Galway, 1921–37; Galway East, 1937–48; Galway South, 1948–53 (d.)
Fahy, John, Clare, 1943
Fahy, Michael (the Stroke), Galway West, 1987
Fahy, P.J., Mid-Ulster (w), 1979
Fahy, W. J., Cork East, 1923
Fallon, Anthony, Galway, 1923
Fallon, Connie, Roscommon-Leitrim, 1977
Fallon, John (Jack), Dublin North-West, 1969
Fallon, John, Sligo-Leitrim, 1969
Fallon, Michael, Roscommon, 1965
Fallon, Seán, Longford-Westmeath, 1973, 1977, 1981
Fallon, Thomas, Sligo-Leitrim, 1954
Fallon, William, Meath, 1927(June)
Falls, Sir C. F., Fermanagh-Tyrone (w), 1923, 1924–9
Falvey, James, Kerry South, 1987
Falvey, Thomas, Clare, 1927(June–Sept.) (def.), 1933
Fanning, John, Tipperary North, 1951–69
Fanning, P. J., Wexford, 1927(June)
Fardy, Michael, Wexford, 1957
Farr, Barkley, *Down South*, 1973
Farrell, Denis, Dublin Co. North, 1973
Farrell, Eamonn, Dublin North-West, 1981
Farrell, Joseph, Louth, 1973–81
Farrell, Liam C., Dublin South-West, 1969
Farrell, Louise, Tipperary South, 1981
Farrell, Mairéad, Cork North-Central, 1981
Farrell, Michael, *Bannside*, 1969
Farrell, Patrick, Cavan, 1937, 1943
Farrell, Patrick, Longford-Westmeath, 1948, 1951
Farrell, Peter, Roscommon, 1944
Farrell, Peter, Roscommon, 1948
Farrell, Seán, Leitrim-Sligo, 1923–7(June) (def.)
Farrell, Thomas, Dublin North-West, 1987, 1989
Farrell, W. P., Sligo-Leitrim, 1951, 1961(Mar.) (by); Roscommon, 1965
Farrelly, Denis, Meath, 1954, 1959(by), 1961–9 (def.), 1973
Farrelly, J. J., Dublin South, 1923
Farrelly, J. V., Meath, 1981–
Farrelly, P. L., Cavan, 1923
Farren, S. N., Antrim North (w), 1979, 1983, 1987; *Antrim North*, 1982–6
Farrington, Thomas, Cork City, 1918
Faulkner, Alfred, Longford-Westmeath, 1954
Faulkner, A. Brian D., *Down East*, 1949–73; *Down South*, 1973–6
Faulkner, Neil, Donegal, 1923
Faulkner, Pádraig, Louth, 1954(Mar.) (by), 1957–87
Fausset, Robert, Cavan-Monaghan, 1981, 1982(Feb.)

Fawcett, John (Jack), *Antrim North*, 1974(by)

Fawsitt, S. Mac D., Cork South, 1954, 1957

Fay, Andrew, Leix-Offaly, 1927(Sept.)

Fay, B. C., Cavan, 1937, 1944

Fay, James, Dublin West, 1987

Fay, Ray, Dublin North-East, 1969; Dublin North-Central, 1977

Feehan, M. M., Dublin North-West, 1948, 1951, 1954

Feely, Frank, *Down South*, 1973–6, 1982–6

Feeney, Brian, Belfast North (w), 1983

Feeney, Seán, Waterford, 1947(by)

Feery, Francis, Laoighis-Offaly, 1961, 1965, 1969

Fegan, William (Bill), Dublin North-West, 1982(Nov.)

Fennell, Nuala, Dublin Co. South, 1977; Dublin South, 1981–7 (def.), 1989–; DUBLIN, 1979

Fennessy, J. J., Cork Borough, 1948

Fennessy, William (Billy), Cork North-East, 1973

Ferguson, Desmond, Meath, 1973

Ferguson, E. C., Enniskillen, 1938–49(July)

Ferguson, James P., Iveagh, 1949

Ferguson, John, *Belfast (Oldpark)*, 1965; *Belfast North*, 1973–5 (def.); Belfast North (w), 1974(Oct.)

Ferguson, Richard, *Antrim South*, 1968(by)–70

Ferguson, W. Raymond, Fermanagh-Tyrone South (w), 1979; *Fermanagh-Tyrone South*, 1982–6

Fernandez, Joseph, Meath, 1989

Ferran, F. P., Sligo-Mayo East, 1921–3

Ferris, Michael, Tipperary South, 1977, 1987, 1989–; MUNSTER, 1989

Ferris, Capt. Andrew, *Larne*, 1937(by)

Ferron, Thompson, *Armagh North*, 1945

Fettes, Christopher, DUBLIN, 1984

ffrench-O'Carroll, Michael, Dublin South-West, 1951–4 (def.), 1957

Fielding, Thomas, Carlow-Kilkenny, 1951, 1954, 1956(by)

Figgis, Darrell, Dublin Co., 1922–5 (d.)

Filgate, Edward, Louth, 1977–82(Nov.)

Finan, James, Sligo-Leitrim, 1982(Nov.)

Finan, John, Roscommon, 1948, 1951–4 (def.)

Finlay, Flight Lt., G. I., *Belfast (Willowfield)*, 1945

Finlay, H. J., Roscommon, 1923–4

Finlay, John, Leix-Offaly, 1933–8 (def.)

Finlay, T. A. (Sen.), Dublin Co., 1930(by)–3

Finlay, T. A. (jun.), Dublin South-Central, 1954–7 (def.)

Finn, J. J., Meath, 1961

Finn, Martin, Mayo South, 1961, 1965; Mayo East, 1969–77 (def.), 1981

Finn, Michael, Cork West, 1954, 1957; Cork South-West, 1961, 1965

Finnan, Séamus, Longford-Westmeath, 1969, 1982(Nov.), 1987

Finnegan, Matthew, Dublin North-East, 1969

Finnegan, Michael, Dublin West, 1981

Finnegan, Patrick, Galway East, 1989

Finnerty, Martin, Galway, 1923

Finnerty, Michael, Galway East, 1989

Finnerty, W. J., Longford-Westmeath, 1927(June); Athlone-Longford, 1937, 1938, 1943; Longford-Westmeath, 1948

Finnery, J. U., Down West, 1933

Finucane, Declan, Kerry North, 1987

Finucane, Michael, Kerry North, 1969

Finucane, Michael, Limerick West, 1987, 1989–

Finucane, Patrick, Kerry North, 1943–69

Fisher, John, Down South, 1967(by)

Fisher, Joseph, *Mourne*, 1953

Fitt, Gerard, *Belfast (Dock)*, 1958, 1962–73; *Belfast North*, 1973–6; Belfast West (w), 1966–83 (def.)

Fitzgerald, Alexis, Dublin Central, 1973; Dublin South-Central, 1977; Dublin South, 1981; Dublin South-East, 1982(Feb.–Nov.) (def.)

Fitzgerald, Brian, Meath, 1982(Nov.), 1989

FitzGerald, Desmond, Dublin Co., 1921–32; Carlow-Kilkenny, 1932–7; Kilkenny, 1937; Dublin Co., 1944

Fitzgerald, Edward, Cork Borough, 1927(June)

Fitzgerald, Eithne, Dublin South, 1981, 1982(Nov.), 1987, 1989

FitzGerald, Garret M. D., Dublin South-East, 1969–

Fitzgerald, Gene, Cork Mid, 1972(by)–81; Cork South-Central, 1981–7; MUNSTER, 1984–

Fitzgerald, John (Jack), Meath-Westmeath, 1943; Meath, 1948, 1969

Fitzgerald, John, Dún Laoghaire and Rathdown, 1957, 1961, 1965

Fitzgerald, L. J., Dublin North-East, 1981–2(Feb.) (def.), 1982(Nov.)–

Fitzgerald, Michael, Tipperary, 1947(by); Tipperary South, 1948, 1961

Fitzgerald, Michael, Tipperary South, 1982(Feb.), 1982(Nov.)

Fitzgerald, Nicholas, Waterford-Tipperary East, 1922

Fitzgerald, Séamus (James), Cork East/North-East, 1921–2 (def.); Cork East, 1923, 1927(Sept.)

Fitzgerald, Séamus, Cork Borough, 1943–4 (def.), 1954(Mar.)(by)

Fitzgerald, Thomas, Kerry South, 1982(Feb.)

Fitzgerald-Kenney, James, Mayo South, 1927(June)–48

Fitzgibbon, Gerald, Dublin University, 1921–3

Fitzgibbon, H. M., Roscommon, 1923

Fitzherbert, G. E., Fermanagh-Tyrone South (w), 1964

Fitzpatrick, Dermot, Dublin Central, 1987–

Fitzpatrick, J. B., Monaghan, 1954

Fitzpatrick, K. B., Dún Laoghaire, 1987, 1989

Fitzpatrick, Michael, Dublin North-West, 1948–51 (def.)

Fitzpatrick, Séan, Dublin Co. South, 1969

Fitzpatrick, T. J., Dublin South-Central, 1961, 1965–9; Dublin Central, 1969–77; Dublin South-Central, 1977–82(Nov.) (def.)

Fitzpatrick, T. J., Cavan, 1965–77; Cavan-Monaghan, 1977–89
Fitzsimmons, P. D., *Down South*, 1983
Fitzsimmons, W. K., *Belfast (Duncairn)*, 1956(by)–73
Fitzsimon, William (Abbey of the Holy Cross), Dublin South-East, 1981, 1982(Feb.), 1982(Nov.); Tipperary South, 1982(Feb.); Cork East, 1989; Cork North-Central, 1989; Cork North-West, 1989; Cork South-Central, 1989; Tipperary North, 1989; Tipperary South, 1989; MUNSTER, 1989
Fitzsimons, Eoghan, Dublin (Clontarf), 1977
Fitzsimons, James N., Meath, 1977–87; LEINSTER, 1984–
Fitzsimons, John, Dublin Co., 1923
Fitzsimons, Michael, Kildare, 1932
Fitzsimons, Patrick, Limerick, 1943, 1944; Limerick West, 1948
Fitzsimons, Sylvester, Roscommon, 1961
Flaherty, Mary, Dublin North-West, 1981–
Flanagan, Charles, Laoighis-Offaly, 1987–
Flanagan, James, Roscommon, 1927(June)
Flanagan, James, Sligo-Leitrim, 1961
Flanagan, James, Laoighis-Offaly, 1969, 1977
Flanagan, James J., Leix-Offaly, 1948, 1951
Flanagan, O. J., Leix (Laoighis)-Offaly, 1943–87
Flanagan, Robert P., Sligo-Leitrim, 1948
Flanagan, Rosemary, Fermanagh-Tyrone South (w), 1983, 1987
Flanagan, Seán, Mayo South, 1951–69; Mayo East, 1969–77 (def.); CONNACHT-ULSTER, 1979–89
Flannery, John, Mayo East, 1982(Feb.)
Flavin, Garrett, Waterford, 1923
Fleming, B. A., Dublin Co. West, 1977; Dublin West, 1981–2(Nov.) (def.), 1987
Fleming, Harry, Dublin North-West, 1987, 1989
Fleming, Pádraic, Dublin North, 1927(Sept.)
Fleming, T. A., *Londonderry*, 1982
Flinn, H. V., Cork Borough, 1927(Sept.)–43
Flood, Christopher, Dublin South-West, 1987–
Flynn, Anthony, Louth, 1938
Flynn, Charles, Mayo North, 1923
Flynn, James, Sligo-Leitrim, 1948
Flynn, John, Kerry, 1932–7; Kerry South, 1937–43, 1948–57 (def.)
Flynn, Pádraig, Mayo West, 1977–
Flynn, Patrick J., Roscommon, 1951
Flynn, Seán P., *Belfast South*, 1973
Flynn, Stephen, Leitrim-Sligo, 1932–7; Leitrim, 1937–48; Sligo-Leitrim, 1948–60 (d.)
Flynn, T., Waterford, 1951
Fogarty, Andrew, Tipperary, 1927(June)–48; Tipperary North, 1948
Fogarty, P. J., Dublin Co., 1937–47 (d.)
Foley, Daniel J., Waterford, 1932, 1937

216

Foley, Denis, Kerry North, 1977, 1981–9 (def.)
Foley, Denis, Kerry North, 1982(Feb.)
Foley, Desmond, Dublin Co., 1965–9; Dublin Co. North, 1969–73 (def.)
Foley, Frank. Dublin North-West, 1943, 1944; Dublin South-Central, 1948
Foley, Gerald, Sligo-Leitrim, 1957, 1961, 1965
Foley, M. J., Dublin South-Central, 1989
Foley, W. A., Dublin Central, 1983(by)
Foran, William, Waterford, 1961
Ford, Patricia, Down North (w), 1953(by)–5
Forde, Daniel P., Cork North, 1927(June)
Forde, David, Cork North, 1943
Forde, Dermot J., Meath, 1977, 1981, 1982(Feb.)
Forde, James, Mayo North, 1948
Forde, K. A. Y., *Mourne*, 1965
Forde, Malachi, Mayo South, 1937
Forde, Patrick, Cork Mid, 1965, 1969–72 (d.)
Forde, Patrick M.D., Down South (w), 1979, 1983; *Down South*, 1982
Forrest, Anna, Mid-Ulster (w), 1969(by)
Forrest, George, Mid-Ulster (w), 1965(by)–8 (d); *Tyrone East*, 1958
Forsythe, Clifford, *Antrim South*, 1982–6; Antrim South (w), 1983–5, 1986(by)–
Foster, Revd Ivan, *Fermanagh-Tyrone South*, 1982–6
Foster, R. J., Londonderry (w), 1974(Feb.), 1974(Oct.)
Fox, C. Joseph, Dublin Co. North, 1977–81; Dublin North, 1981; DUBLIN, 1979
Fox, Desmond, Dublin (Artane), 1977
Fox, John, Wicklow, 1982(Nov.)
Fox, Michael, Laoighis-Offaly, 1982(Nov.), 1987
Fox, Patrick, *Londonderry (Foyle)*, 1945
Fox, W. D. H. (Billy), Monaghan, 1965, 1969–73 (def.)
Foxe, Thomas, Roscommon, 1989–
Fraher, Liam, Limerick, 1937
Frawley, John, Limerick East, 1981, 1982(Feb.)
Frayne, Patrick, Carlow-Kildare, 1944
Freehill, Mary, Dublin South-East, 1977, 1981; Dublin Central, 1987
Freeman, Michael, Dublin North-West, 1965
French, Peter, *see* ffrench
French, Seán, Cork Borough, 1924(by), 1927(June)–32, 1933
French, Seán, Cork Borough, 1967(by)–9; Cork City North-West, 1969–77; Cork City, 1977–81; Cork North-Central, 1981–2(Nov.) (def.); MUNSTER, 1979
French, Thomas, *Armagh*, 1982, 1983(by); Upper Bann (w), 1983, 1986(by), 1987, 1990(by)
French-O'Carroll, *see* ffrench-O'Carroll
Friel, John, Donegal East, 1937–51 (def.)
Fryar, Samuel, *Down West*, 1933–8

Fullam, Patrick, Meath, 1957, 1965
Fuller, Stephen, Kerry North, 1937–43 (def.)
Fullerton, Edward, CONNACHT-ULSTER, 1984; Donegal North-East, 1987
Fullerton, N. B., *Belfast (Shankill)*, 1953
Fulton, J. N., *Belfast (Shankill)*, 1933, 1938
Furlong, George, Tipperary South, 1951
Furlong, Walter, Cork Borough, 1943, 1944–8 (def.), 1951
Fyffe, J. C., *Tyrone West*, 1962
Fyffe, W. S., *Tyrone North*, 1969–73

Gabbey, Robert, *Down North*, 1982
Gaffney, Patrick, Carlow-Kilkenny, 1922–3 (def.)
Gage, Lt Col. H. Conolly, Belfast South (w), 1945–52
Galbraith, R. H., *Antrim Mid*, 1969
Gallagher, Christopher, Donegal West, 1948; Donegal South-West, 1961
Gallagher, Colm, Dublin North-Central, 1948, 1951–4 (def.), 1957(Mar.–June) (d.)
Gallagher, Denis, Mayo North, 1954; Mayo West, 1969, 1973–89
Gallagher, Gerry, Dublin West, 1987
Gallagher, James, Sligo-Leitrim, 1961–73, 1977–81
Gallagher, Joan, Sligo-Leitrim, 1969
Gallagher, Michael, Mayo South, 1943
Gallagher, Patrick, Waterford, 1977, 1981, 1982(Feb.–Nov.) (def.), 1987, 1989
Gallagher, Patrick (the Cope), Donegal South-West, 1981–
Gallagher, Patrick, Laoighis-Offaly, 1989
Gallagher, W. F., Mayo South, 1938, 1943
Gallen, Edward, Donegal, 1923
Galt, W. H. C., Londonderry, 1924
Galvin, James, Wexford, 1951
Galvin, Jeremiah, Cork West, 1932, 1933
Galvin, John, Cork Borough, 1954, 1956(by)–63 (d.)
Galvin, John J., Laoighis-Offaly, 1969
Galvin, Sheila, Cork Borough, 1964(by)–5
Gamble, B. W., Fermanagh-Tyrone South (w), 1964
Gamble, J. F., *Tyrone North*, 1930(by)–43 (d.)
Gamble, W. J., *Belfast North*, 1973
Gannon, Bernard, Kerry North, 1982(Nov.)
Gannon, Francis, Sligo-Leitrim, 1948
Gannon, Michael, Dublin Co., 1961, 1965; Dublin Co. North, 1969, 1973; Dublin West, 1982(Feb.)
Garahan, Hugh, Longford-Westmeath, 1923, 1927(June–Sept.) (def.)
Gardiner, James, Tipperary, 1944
Gardiner, Robert, Donegal West, 1957
Gardner, J. S., Belfast East (w), 1959(by), 1959; *Down Mid*, 1964(by)
Garland, R. T., Dublin South, 1982(Nov.), 1987, 1989–
Garland, Seán, Dublin North-Central, 1957(Nov.)(by)

Garrett, John (Jack), Mayo North, 1954, 1961; Mayo East, 1969

Garvey, J. G., Dublin South-West, 1981

Garvey, M. J., Roscommon, 1954

Gaston, James A., *Antrim Mid*, 1929

Gaston, Joseph A., *Antrim North*, 1982–6

Gaul, V. G., Dublin North, 1987, 1989

Gaule, Charles, Wicklow, 1923

Gault, W. H. S., *Belfast North*, 1982; Belfast North (w), 1983

Gavin, John, Longford-Westmeath, 1923

Gavin, Pádraic, Mayo East, 1987

Gavin, Patrick, Mayo South, 1951

Gawn, William, *Antrim South*, 1973

Gaynor, Seán, Tipperary, 1938

Geoghegan, James, Longford-Westmeath, 1930(by)–7

Geoghegan, John, Galway West, 1954–75 (d.)

Geoghegan-Quinn, Máire, Galway West, 1975(by)–

Geraghty, Desmond, DUBLIN, 1984

Geraghty-Bowler, Susan, Dublin North-Central, 1965

Gergood, Robert, Antrim (w), 1943(by); *Belfast (Oldpark)*, 1945–9 (def.)

Gibb, Andrew, *Antrim South*, 1982

Gibbons, Hugh, Roscommon, 1964(by), 1965–9; Roscommon-Leitrim, 1969–77

Gibbons, James M., Carlow-Kilkenny, 1957–81 (def.), 1982(Feb.–Nov.) (def.); IRELAND, 1973–7

Gibbons, John, Mayo West, 1982(Feb.)

Gibbons, M. P., Carlow-Kilkenny, 1987–9 (def.)

Gibbons, Patrick, Mayo South, 1948, 1951

Gibbons, S. F., Carlow-Kilkenny, 1923–4, 1932–7; Kilkenny, 1937

Gibson, H. J. S., *Down North*, 1982–6; Strangford (w), 1983

Gibson, Peter, Dublin South-East, 1977, 1982(Nov.)

Gibson, S. McK., Belfast West (w), 1974(Oct.)

Gibson, W. K., *Belfast (Ballynafeigh)*, 1929

Gilbride, Eugene (sen.), Leitrim-Sligo, 1927(June), 1932

Gilbride, Eugene (jun.), Sligo-Leitrim, 1948–69

Gilbride, Seán, Dublin North, 1987, 1989

Giles, Capt. Patrick, Meath-Westmeath, 1937–48; Meath, 1948–61

Gilbawley, Eugene, Sligo-Leitrim, 1961–9 (def.), 1973–81

Gilhooly, James, Leitrim, 1943

Gill, Anthony (Tony), Donegal North-East, 1976(by)

Gill, J. F., Leix-Offaly, 1926(by), 1927(June–Sept.) (def.), 1932

Gill, Séamus, Donegal, 1977

Gillen, Joseph P., *Fermanagh-Tyrone*, 1921

Gillespie, A. J., *Bannside*, 1945

Gillespie, D. F., *Belfast West*, 1973–5 (def.); Belfast East (w), 1974(Feb.)

Gillespie, John (Jack), Monaghan, 1938

Gillespie, Neil, Londonderry (w), 1966

Gilligan, James, Leitrim-Sligo, 1923, 1927(June), 1927(Sept.)
Gilligan, John, Limerick East, 1982(Feb.)
Gilmartin, Charles, Mayo South, 1945(by)
Gilmartin, Maeve, Donegal-Leitrim, 1969, 1970(by)
Gilmore, Eamon, Dún Laoghaire, 1982(Nov.), 1987, 1989–
Gilmore, G. J., Dublin Co., 1938
Ginnell, Eamon, Meath, 1948
Ginnell, Laurence, Longford-Westmeath, 1921–3
Ginnelly, James, Mayo North, 1948, 1954
Glackin, Edward, Dublin Central, 1983(by)
Glasgow, S. A., *Mid-Ulster*, 1982
Glass, John, *Belfast (Falls)*, 1938, 1942(by)
Glass, John B. C., *Belfast South*, 1973–6, 1982; Belfast South (w), 1974(Oct.),
    1979
Glass, R. C. W., *Antrim North*, 1982
Gleasure, Robert, Kerry North, 1961
Gleeson, Carmel, Dún Laoghaire and Rathdown, 1969
Gleeson, E. J., Kerry, 1923
Gleeson, Michael, Dublin North-East, 1973
Gleeson, Patrick, Carlow-Kilkenny, 1948, 1951
Gleeson, Seán, Tipperary, 1927(June), 1927(Sept.)
Gleeson, William, Tipperary, 1923
Glendenning, William, *Belfast West*, 1982–6
Glendinning, R. J., *Mid-Ulster*, 1973; Armagh (w), 1974(Feb.)
Glenn, Alice, Dublin North-Central, 1973; Dublin (Finglas), 1977; Dublin
    Central, 1981–2(Feb.) (def.), 1982(Nov.)–7 (def.)
Glentoran, 1st Baron (Capt. Herbert Dixon), *Belfast East*, 1921–9; Belfast
    East (w), 1922–39; *Belfast (Bloomfield)*, 1929–50 (d.)
Glentoran, 2nd Baron (Herbert Dixon), *Belfast (Bloomfield)*, 1950(by)–61
Glynn, B. M., Galway South, 1953(by), 1954–7
Glynn, Hugh, Sligo-Leitrim, 1989
Glynn, Peadar, Sligo, 1943
Glynn, Seán, Galway North, 1948, 1951
Godfrey, Frank, Louth, 1977, 1981, 1982(Feb.), 1982(Nov.); Meath, 1977
Gogan, R. P. (Dick), Dublin North-West, 1948, 1951, 1954–77; Dublin (Cabra),
    1977
Golding, H. J., Down South (w), 1970, 1974(Feb.)
Goligher, E. R., *Belfast West*, 1975
Good, Herman, Dublin Townships, 1944
Good, J. P., Dublin Co., 1923–37
Good, Matthew, Dublin Co., 1924(by)
Gordon, Lt Col. A. R. G., *Down East*, 1929–49
Gordon, Dawson, *Belfast (Dock)*, 1929
Gordon, F. P., Clare, 1959(by), 1961, 1965
Gordon, J. F., *Antrim*, 1921–9; *Carrick*, 1929–43
Gordon, M. W., Londonderry (w), 1945

Gordon, Maj. N. F., *Mourne*, 1949

Gorey, D. J., Carlow-Kilkenny, 1922–7(Sept.) (def.) 1927(by)–33 (def.); Kilkenny, 1937–43

Gorey, Richard, Kilkenny, 1943

Gorman, Christopher, Meath, 1989

Gorman, Noel (Flukie), Sligo-Leitrim, 1982(Nov.), 1987

Gormley, Francis, Longford-Westmeath, 1932–3 (def.)

Gormley, John, Meath, 1982(Feb.); Dublin South-East, 1989

Gormley, P. J., *Londonderry Mid.*, 1953–69 (def.); Londonderry (w), 1966

Gormley, Seán, Meath, 1987

Gormley, T. C., *Tyrone Mid*, 1958, 1962–73; *Mid-Ulster*, 1973

Gormley, William, Sligo, 1943

Gorry, P. J., Leix-Offaly, 1923, 1927(June), 1927 (Sept.13)–33 (def.), 1937–51 (def.)

Goulding, Seán, Waterford, 1927(Sept.)–37 (def.), 1938, 1943, 1944

Goulding, Lady Valerie, Dún Laoghaire, 1982(Nov.)

Gourley, Desmond, *Mid-Ulster*, 1973

Gourley, Thomas, *Down North*, 1982

Governey, Desmond, Carlow-Kilkenny, 1960(by), 1961–77 (def.), 1981–2(Nov.)

Gowdy, M. J., *Belfast South*, 1973

Grace, Jean, Clare, 1968(by)

Graham, Archibald, *Tyrone South*, 1938

Graham, E. S. D., *Belfast South*, 1982–3 (d.)

Graham, George, *Down South*, 1982–6

Graham, Jean M., *Belfast South*, 1973

Graham, John, *Antrim [town]*, 1938

Graham, William, *Antrim [town]*, 1929

Grant, Ferga, Limerick East, 1987

Grant, William, *Belfast North*, 1921–9; *Belfast (Duncairn)*, 1929–49(Aug.) (d.)

Grealy, John, Mayo South, 1948

Greaney, P. J., Roscommon, 1981

Green, D. G. R., *Down North*, 1973, 1975–6, 1982

Green, Martin, Fermanagh-Tyrone South (w), 1981(by)

Greene, Ita, Dublin North-Central, 1982(Feb.), 1982(Nov.)

Greer, A. H. C., *Armagh*, 1973

Gregg, W. J., *Antrim [town]*, 1949

Gregory, Anthony (Tony), Dublin Central, 1981, 1982(Feb.)

Grehan, Frances, Roscommon-Leitrim, 1973

Grenham, John, Longford-Westmeath, 1933

Griffin, Brendan, Tipperary South, 1969, 1973–89 (def.)

Griffin, Gerard, Clare, 1954

Griffin, James, Meath, 1957–9 (d.)

Griffin, John, Waterford, 1952(by), 1966(by)

Griffin, Laurence, Clare, 1981

Griffin, Matthew, Limerick, 1927(June), 1927(Sept.)

Griffin, Patricia, Dún Laoghaire, 1989

Griffin, W. J., Cork North, 1938
Griffith, Arthur, Cavan, 1921–2(Aug.) (d.)
Groarke, Thomas, Longford-Westmeath, 1923
Grogan, Laurence, Louth, 1957, 1961
Grogan, M. H., Roscommon, 1932
Groome, Joseph, Wicklow, 1951
Groome, Terence, Kildare, 1961
Grosvenor, Col. R. G., Fermanagh-Tyrone South (w), 1955–64
Grúgain, Labhrás, *see* Grogan, Laurence
Guerin, Michael, Clare, 1989
Guinan, J. J., Dún Laoghaire and Rathdown, 1965, 1969; Laoighis-Offaly, 1977
Guinevan, John, Cork East, 1987
Guinness, M. N., Dublin Co., 1927(June)
Guiry, Jerome, Waterford, 1943
Gunning, William, *Belfast East,* 1973
Guy, Dermot, CONNACHT-ULSTER, 1989
Gyle, J. W., *Belfast East,* 1925–9; *Belfast (Dock),* 1929

Hacket Pain, Brig. Gen. Sir William, Londonderry South (w), 1922 (Jan.(by)–Nov.)
Hackett, B. C., Dublin North, 1927(June)
Hackett, John, Tipperary, 1927(June)
Haffey, G. A., Belfast West (w), 1983
Hagan, Thomas, *Londonderry,* 1973
Hale, R. J., *Down West,* 1938
Hales, Seán, Cork Mid/North/South/South-East/West, 1921–2(Dec.) (d.)
Hales, Thomas, Cork West, 1933–7 (def.) 1944; Cork South, 1948
Hales, William, Cork West, 1923
Hall, David, Meath, 1923–7(Sept.)
Hall, Frank, Dublin (Cabra), 1977
Hall, Hugh, Cork East, 1987
Hall-Raleigh, Simon, Fermanagh-Tyrone South (w), 1981 (by); Belfast South (w), 1982(by); *Belfast South,* 1982
Hall-Thompson, Maj. R. L., *Belfast (Clifton),* 1969–73; *Belfast North,* 1973–6
Hall-Thompson, Lt Col. S. H., *Belfast (Clifton),* 1929–53 (def.)
Halley, Victor, *Belfast Central,* 1945(by)
Halliden, P. J., Cork North, 1943–51
Halligan, Brendan, Dublin South-West, 1976(by)–7; Dublin (Finglas), 1977; Dublin North-West, 1981, 1982(Nov.); DUBLIN, 1983–4
Halpin, Cormac, Clare, 1943
Halpin, Eamonn, Dublin South-Central, 1954
Hamill, John, *Londonderry,* 1973
Hamilton, Albert, Belfast South (w), 1963(by); *Armagh Mid,* 1965
Hamilton, Marquess of (James Hamilton), Fermanagh-Tyrone South (w), 1964–70 (def.)

Hammond, Owen, Dún Laoghaire, 1982(Nov.)

Hanafin, Desmond, Tipperary North, 1977, 1981

Hanafin, Jane (Binkie), Tipperary North, 1982(Feb.)

Hanafin, Mary, Dublin South-East, 1989

Hand, Thomas, Dublin Co. South, 1977; Dublin South, 1981, 1982(Feb.), 1982(Nov.)

Hanley, Gus, Longford-Westmeath, 1981, 1982(Feb.)

Hanley, M. J., Sligo, 1943

Hanly, D. J., Waterford, 1944

Hanna, Francis, *Belfast Central*, 1946(by)–65

Hanna, G. B. (sen.), *Antrim*, 1921–9; Larne (w), 1929–37

Hanna, G. B. (jun.), *Belfast (Duncairn)*, 1949(Nov.)(by)–56

Hanna, J. A., *Belfast West*, 1921

Hanniffy, Constance, Laoighis-Offaly, 1977

Hannigan, Christopher, Dublin Co., 1943

Hannigan, Joseph, Dublin South, 1937–43 (def.), 1944

Hannon, Edward, Leitrim-Sligo, 1927(Sept.)

Harbison, T. J. S., *Fermanagh-Tyrone*, 1921–9; Fermanagh-Tyrone (w), 1922–4, 1929–30 (d.)

Harcourt, R. J. R., *Down South*, 1949; *Belfast (Woodvale)*, 1950(by)–5

Harden, Maj. J. R. E., Armagh (w), 1948(by)–54

Hardy, M. J., Mayo North, 1943, 1948

Hargadon, William, Sligo-Leitrim, 1948

Harkin, Daniel, Donegal South-West, 1982(Feb.)

Harkin, F. P., *Belfast North*, 1921

Harkin, Gerard, Leix-Offaly, 1948

Harkin, John, Donegal North-East, 1973

Harkin, Manus, Donegal East, 1943

Harland, H. P., Belfast East (w), 1940(by)–5

Harney, Geraldine, Dublin Central, 1989

Harney, Mary, Dublin South-East, 1977; Dublin South-West, 1981–; DUBLIN, 1989

Harrington, John (Jack), Cork Borough, 1965

Harrington, Joseph, Limerick East, 1977, 1981, 1982(Feb.)

Harrington, T. J., Cork West, 1944

Harrington, Win, Limerick East, 1977, 1982(Feb.)

Harris, Thomas, Kildare, 1923, 1931(by)–7; Carlow-Kildare, 1937–48; Kildare, 1948–57 (def.)

Harrison, Henry, Dublin Co., 1927(June)

Hart, Michael, Wexford, 1969

Harte, Laurence, Sligo-Leitrim, 1948

Harte, P. D., Donegal North-East, 1961–77; Donegal, 1977–81; Donegal North-East, 1981–; CONNACHT-ULSTER, 1989

Hartland, V. A. E., Cork East, 1951; Cork City South-East, 1973

Hartnett, Noel, Dún Laoghaire and Rathdown, 1948; Dublin South-Central, 1958(by)

Hartney, Seán, Limerick, 1943
Harty, Fionán, Kerry North, 1981
Harty, Florence, Kerry, 1927(June)
Harvey, Cecil, *Down South*, 1973–6; Down South (w), 1983
Harvey, W. J., Dún Laoghaire, 1981
Harwood, P. A., Cavan-Monaghan, 1977
Haskins, D. H., Wicklow, 1933
Haslett, Alexander, Monaghan, 1927(June)–32 (def.), 1933–7 (def.), 1943
Haslett, James L., Monaghan, 1951, 1954
Haslett, John T., *Fermanagh-Tyrone South*, 1982; Fermanagh-Tyrone South (w), 1987
Hassard, John (Jack), *Tyrone South*, 1965; *Fermanagh-Tyrone South*, 1973
Hassett, J. J., Tipperary, 1927(June)–33
Haughey, C. J., Dublin North-East, 1951, 1954, 1956(by), 1957–77; Dublin (Artane), 1977–81; Dublin North-Central, 1981–
Haughey, P. D., Fermanagh-Tyrone South (w), 1974(Feb.); *Antrim North*, 1975; *Mid-Ulster*, 1982–6; Mid-Ulster (w), 1983, 1987
Haughey, Seán, Dublin North-East, 1987, 1989
Haughton, Maj. S. G., Antrim (w), 1945–50
Haverty, James, Galway, 1923
Hawthorne, I. G., *Armagh South*, 1949; *Armagh Central*, 1955(by)–69
Hayden, John, Meath-Westmeath, 1937
Hayden, Laurence, Leitrim-Sligo, 1923
Hayden, Thomas, Carlow-Kildare, 1943, 1944; Carlow-Kilkenny, 1951
Hayes, Edmond, Kerry North, 1965
Hayes, Gerard, Limerick West, 1954
Hayes, Hugh, *Down West*, 1922(Feb.(by)–Nov.)
Hayes, James, Wexford, 1981, 1982(Feb.), 1982(Nov.)
Hayes, John, Limerick East, 1952(by)
Hayes, Liam, Dublin North-West, 1969
Hayes, Michael, National University of Ireland, 1921–33 (def.); Dublin South, 1923 (elected but chose to sit for National University)
Hayes, R. F., Limerick City-Limerick East, 1921–3; Limerick, 1923–4
Hayes, Seán, Cork Mid/North/South/South-East/West, 1921–3
Hayes, Seán, Tipperary, 1927(June)–37 (def.), 1943, 1947(by)
Hayes, Séan, Limerick, 1943
Hayes, Stephen, Wexford, 1936(by)
Hayes, William, Limerick City-Limerick East, 1921–3
Hazard, F. D., *Belfast (Ballynafeigh)*, 1962
Hazlett, J. J., *Tyrone South*, 1929
Healy, A. A. (Gus), Cork Borough, 1957–61 (def.), 1965–9; Cork City South-East, 1969–77
Healy, Alexander M., Cork Borough, 1927(Sept.), 1932

Healy, Cahir, *Fermanagh-Tyrone*, 1925–9; *Fermanagh South*, 1929–65; Fermanagh-Tyrone, 1922–4 (w), 1931(Mar.)(by)–35; Fermanagh-Tyrone South (w), 1950–5

Healy, Denis, Clare, 1927(June), 1944

Healy, Denis D., Dublin South, 1927(June), 1933, 1937

Healy, John B., Kerry South, 1943–8 (def.)

Healy, Michael, Wicklow, 1987

Healy, Patrick, Dublin North-East, 1981, 1987, 1989

Healy, Séamus (Shay), Tipperary South, 1987, 1989

Healy, Séan, Tipperary South, 1969

Healy, Séan B., Dublin Co., 1923

Healy, Thomas, Dublin North-East, 1954

Healy, Thomas F., Dublin Co., 1926(by)

Heath, S. R., Strangford (w), 1983

Heavey, Michael, Longford-Westmeath, 1954

Hedigan, John, Dublin North-Central, 1954

Heenan, T. A., Belfast West (w), 1959

Heery, J. D., Dublin South-West, 1948

Heffernan, Michael R., Tipperary, 1923–32 (def.), 1933

Heffernan, Myles, Dublin South-West, 1954

Hefferon, M. J., Mayo North, 1948

Hegarty, D. J., Cork East, 1923

Hegarty, John, Dublin South-Central, 1958(by), 1961

Hegarty, Patrick, Cork North-East, 1973–81; Cork East, 1981–9 (def.)

Hehir, Michael, Clare, 1923

Henderson, George, *Antrim*, 1925–9; *Bannside*, 1929; Antrim (w), 1929

Henderson, George, Kildare, 1927(June)

Henderson, J. D. A., *Lisnaskea*, 1969

Henderson, Capt. O. W. J., *Belfast (Victoria)*, 1953–8 (def.)

Henderson, S. J., *Londonderry North*, 1953

Henderson, T. G., Belfast North (w), 1923, 1929; *Belfast North*, 1925–9; *Belfast (Shankill)*, 1929–53 (def.)

Hendron, James, *Belfast South*, 1975–6

Hendron, Joseph G., *Belfast West*, 1975–6, 1982–6; Belfast West (w), 1983, 1987

Henehan, P. J., Tipperary, 1932

Hennessy, Charles, Cork South-Central, 1987

Hennessy, Louise, Wexford, 1981, 1982(Feb.)

Hennessy, M. J., Cork East/North-East, 1922–3; Cork East, 1923–32 (def.)

Hennessy, Philip, Kildare, 1977

Hennessy, Richard, Dublin South, 1932

Hennessy, T. P., Dublin South, 1925(by)–7(June), 1927(Aug.)(by)–33 (def.)

Hennigan, John, Sligo-Mayo East, 1922; Leitrim-Sligo, 1923–33 (def.); Leitrim, 1937

Henry, Bernard, Meath, 1948

Henry, Mark, Mayo North, 1927(June)–32
Herbert, Michael, Limerick East, 1965, 1969–81, 1982(Nov.); IRELAND, 1972–9; MUNSTER, 1979
Herlihy, Thomas, Dublin North-Central, 1954, 1957(Nov.)(by), 1961, 1965
Heron, Archibald, Mayo North, 1923; Dublin Co., 1924(by); Leitrim-Sligo, 1927(June), 1927(Sept.); Dublin Co., 1933; Dublin North-West, 1937–8 (def.); Dublin North-East, 1948
Herron, D. S., *Down South*, 1973, 1975
Herron, G. L., *Antrim South*, 1982
Herron, Thomas, *Belfast East*, 1973
Heskin, Denis, Waterford, 1943–8 (def.); Cork East, 1954
Heslip, H. J., *Down South*, 1973–6
Hession, J. M., Galway North, 1951–7 (def.)
Hewat, William, Dublin North, 1923–7(June)
Hewson, Gilbert, Limerick, 1927(June–Sept.) (def.), 1932
Hickey, Dr E. M., *Queen's University Belfast*, 1948(by), 1949–58
Hickey, James, Cork Borough, 1937, 1938–43 (def.), 1948–54 (def.)
Hickey, James, Limerick East, 1965
Hickey, Liam, Limerick East, 1969
Hickey, P. J., Dublin Co., 1943
Higgins, F. W., Sligo-Leitrim, 1948, 1961
Higgins, James, Longford-Westmeath, 1927(June), 1927(Sept.)
Higgins, James, Mayo East, 1981, 1982(Feb.), 1982(Nov.), 1987–
Higgins, M. D., Galway West, 1969, 1973, 1975(by), 1977, 1981–2(Nov.) (def.), 1987–; CONNACHT-ULSTER, 1979, 1984
Higgins, Terence, Clare, 1969
Higgins, Thomas I., Sligo-Leitrim, 1969, 1973, 1977
Higgins, W. P., Galway West, 1943
Hill, Robert, *Belfast (Duncairn)*, 1933, 1938; *Belfast (Woodvale)*, 1950(by)
Hill, Seán, Tipperary South, 1987
Hillery, B. J., Dublin South-Central, 1981; Dún Laoghaire, 1989–
Hillery, P. J., Clare, 1951–73
Hilliard, James, Meath, 1948
Hilliard, C. M., Meath, 1982(Feb.)
Hilliard, Michael, Meath-Westmeath, 1943–8; Meath, 1948–73 (def.); IRELAND, 1972–3
Hinchin, Daniel, Cork North, 1927(June), 1927(Sept.), 1932, 1933
Hinds, W. S., *Belfast (Willowfield)*, 1958–69 (def.)
Hiney, James, Dublin South-Central, 1969
Hipwell, Richard, Leix-Offaly, 1927(June), 1944
Hoban, J. J., Galway, 1923
Hoban, Mona, Cavan-Monaghan, 1981
Hobbs, Anthony (Tony), Cork East, 1987, 1989
Hoey, Christopher, Dublin North-East, 1973
Hoey, E. D., Dublin South, 1943
Hoey, J. J., Longford-Westmeath, 1948

Hogan, Brigid, *see* Hogan-O'Higgins
Hogan, Conor, Clare, 1923–7 (June)
Hogan, Daniel (sen.), Leix-Offaly, 1937
Hogan, Daniel (jun.), Leix-Offaly, 1938–43 (def.), 1948, 1951, 1954
Hogan, James, Galway, 1936 (by)
Hogan, Patrick, Clare, 1923–38 (def.), 1943–4 (def.), 1948–69 (Jan.) (d.)
Hogan, Patrick, Tipperary South, 1961–73
Hogan, Patrick J., Galway, 1921–36 (d.)
Hogan, Patrick Joseph, Longford-Westmeath, 1951
Hogan, Patrick K., Limerick, 1923–7 (June)
Hogan, Philip, Carlow-Kilkenny, 1987, 1989–
Hogan, Seán, Clare, 1943
Hogan, Thomas, Carlow-Kilkenny, 1969
Hogan-O'Higgins, Brigid (formerly Hogan), Galway South, 1957–61; Galway East, 1961–9; Clare-Galway South, 1969–77; Galway East, 1977
Hollywood, Seán, Down South (w), 1974 (Feb.), 1974 (Oct.); *Down North*, 1975
Holman, N. P., Dublin North-East, 1987
Holmes, Andrew, *Belfast (St Anne's)*, 1962
Holmes, E. J., *Belfast (Ballynafeigh)*, 1965, 1969; Belfast South (w), 1966
Holmes, Henry, Antrim (2), 1945
Holmes, Henry, *Belfast (Shankill)*, 1953–9
Holmes, J. E., Armagh (w), 1970; *Belfast South*, 1973, 1975; Belfast South (w), 1974 (Feb.), 1974 (Oct.); Upper Bann (w), 1990 (by)
Holohan, Joseph, Dublin North, 1981
Holohan, Richard, Carlow-Kilkenny, 1927 (June)–32 (def.), 1933–7; Kilkenny, 1937
Holt, S. E., Leitrim-Sligo, 1925 (by)–9 (d.)
Honan, Catherine, Laoighis-Offaly, 1987, 1989
Honan, Flan, Clare, 1968 (by), 1969
Honan, T. V., Clare, 1923
Hopper, Michael, Dublin North-West, 1969
Horan, Benjamin, *Belfast East*, 1982
Horan, Eamon, Kerry, 1927 (June)
Horan, Edmund, Kerry North, 1943; Kerry South, 1944, 1944 (by), 1945 (by)
Horan, P. D., Laoighis-Offaly, 1984 (by)
Horgan, John, Cork Borough, 1927 (June–Sept.) (def.), 1932, 1933
Horgan, John, Dublin Co. South, 1977–81; Dublin South, 1981, 1982 (Feb.); DUBLIN, 1981–3
Hosey, E. D., Dublin South-Central, 1957
Houlahan, Patrick, *Armagh*, 1975
Houlihan, James, Limerick West, 1987
Houlihan, James W., Laoighis-Offaly, 1969, 1973
Houlihan, Patrick, Clare, 1927 (June)–32 (def.), 1933–7 (def.)
Hourigan, R. V., Limerick East, 1981
Houston, Denis, Donegal, 1923, 1927 (June)

Houston, John, *Belfast South*, 1975

Houston, Robert, Monaghan, 1957

Howard, Michael, Clare, 1969, 1973, 1981

Howlin, Brendan, Wexford, 1982(Nov.), 1987–

Hughes, C. F., *Belfast (Oldpark)*, 1953

Hughes, Hector, Wexford, 1923

Hughes, James, Carlow-Kilkenny, 1932; Carlow-Kildare, 1938–48

Hughes, Joseph, Carlow-Kilkenny, 1948–60 (d.)

Hughes, Joseph, Dublin South-Central, 1948

Hughes, Joseph P., Clare, 1943

Hughes, Michael, Dublin North-Central, 1948

Hughes, Owen, Mayo South, 1948

Hughes, Peter, Louth-Meath, 1921–3; Louth, 1923–7(June) (def.), 1927(Sept.), 1932

Hughes, Sarah, *Belfast East*, 1973

Hughes, Séamus J., Dublin North, 1923; Dublin South, 1924(by)

Hull, Charles, *Belfast (Woodvale)*, 1950(by)

Hull, William (Billy), *Belfast North*, 1973

Hume, John, *Londonderry (Foyle)*, 1969–73; *Londonderry*, 1973–6, 1982–6; Londonderry (w), 1974(Oct.); Foyle, 1983–; NORTHERN IRELAND, 1979–

Humphreys, Francis, Carlow-Kilkenny, 1932–3 (def.); Carlow-Kildare, 1937–48; Carlow-Kilkenny, 1948, 1951–4 (def.), 1957–61

Hungerford, Sir A. W., *Belfast (Oldpark)*, 1929–45 (def.)

Hunt, H. J., Clare, 1927(June), 1932

Hunter, Alexander, *Carrick*, 1950(by)–65

Hunter, George, Donegal-Leitrim, 1969

Hunter, Ivan, *Antrim South*, 1982

Hunter, Thomas, Cork East/North-East, 1921–2 (def.)

Hurley, Donal, Cork Borough, 1964(by)

Hurley, Jeremiah, Cork Borough, 1932, 1933; Cork South-East, 1937–43

Hurley, John, Cork South-East, 1943

Hurley, Kevin, Cork City South-East, 1969

Hurley, Liam, Cork North-East, 1974(by)

Hurson, Martin, Longford-Westmeath, 1981

Hussey, Gemma, Wicklow, 1981, 1982(Feb.)–9

Hussey, Thomas, Galway East, 1964(by), 1965; Galway North-East, 1969, 1973–7; Galway East, 1977–81 (def.), 1982(Feb.), 1982(Nov.), 1987

Huston, Robert, *Belfast (Cromac)*, 1962(Dec.)(by)

Hutchieson, I. C. W., *Down South*, 1965

Hutchinson, Douglas, *Armagh*, 1973–6, 1982

Hyde, H. M., Belfast North (w), 1950–9

Hyland, Barbara M., Dublin Central, 1987; Dublin North, 1987; Dublin North-Central, 1987; Dublin North-East, 1987; Dublin North-West, 1987; Dublin South, 1987; Dublin South-Central, 1987; Dublin South-East, 1987; Dublin South-West, 1987; Dublin West, 1987; Dún Laoghaire, 1987; Louth, 1987; Wicklow, 1987, 1989; Kerry South, 1989

Hyland, Brendan, Wicklow, 1948
Hyland, Liam, Laoighis-Offaly, 1977, 1981–
Hyland, Patrick, Kildare, 1977
Hynds, I.E., Strangford (w), 1987
Hynes, Desmond, Dublin South-East, 1982(Feb.)
Hynes, Gus, Galway East, 1965
Hynes, Owen, Dublin South, 1943

Ireland, Capt. Denis, Belfast East (w), 1929
Ireland, J. de C., *see* de Courcy Ireland
Irwin, H. M., *Fermanagh-Tyrone*, 1931
Irwin, Sir S. T., *Queen's University Belfast*, 1948(by)–61 (d.)
Irwin, W. A., *Londonderry City*, 1945, 1947(by)

Jackman, Mary, Limerick East, 1989
Jacob, Joseph, Wicklow, 1987–
Jago, Gerry, Dublin South-West, 1987
Jago, Val, Cork South-Central, 1982(Nov.)
Jeffers, Frank, Louth, 1943, 1944
Jeffrey, W. H., *Armagh*, 1982; Newry and Amagh (w), 1987
Jenkins, James, Wexford, 1969
Jennings, Gerard, Longford-Westmeath, 1951
Jennings, Michael, Dublin Central, 1987, 1989
Jess, H. G., *Down North*, 1973
Jinks, John, Leitrim-Sligo, 1927(June–Sept.) (def.)
Johnson, James, Monaghan, 1937
Johnson, Thomas, Dublin Co., 1922–7(Sept.) (def.)
Johnston, Bert, *Fermanagh-Tyrone South*, 1982
Johnston, David, *Down East*, 1929; Down (w), 1929
Johnston, Francis, Louth, 1969
Johnston, H. M., Meath, 1957, 1959(by)–61 (def.)
Johnston, James, Monaghan, 1923
Johnston, John, *Armagh North*, 1929–45
Johnston, Robert, Antrim South (w), 1970; *Antrim South*, 1973
Johnstone, H. A., *Belfast East*, 1982
Johnstone, Prof. R. J., *Queen's University Belfast*, 1921–38(Oct.) (d.)
Jones, Colette, Upper Bann (w), 1990(by)
Jones, D. F., Limerick West, 1955(by), 1957–77
Jones, E. W., *Londonderry City*, 1951(by)–68
Jones, G. A., Wicklow, 1981, 1989
Jones, K. T., *Belfast North*, 1973; Down North (w), 1974(Oct.), 1979; *Down North*, 1975
Jones, Patrick, Kerry South, 1948
Jones, Patrick, Carlow-Kilkenny, 1982(Nov.)
Jones, William, Waterford, 1937
Jones-Cassidy, Ailish, Limerick West, 1977

Jordan, Michael, Wexford, 1922, 1923, 1927(June), 1927(Sept.)–32 (def.)
Jordan, Raymond, *Belfast South*, 1975
Jordan, Stephen, Galway, 1927(June), 1927(Sept.)–37; Galway East, 1937, 1943
Jordan, Timothy, Mayo North, 1938
Joyce, Ann (Nan), Dublin South-West, 1982(Nov.)
Joyce, Bernard, Mayo South, 1954
Joyce, Carey, Cork North-East, 1977; Cork East, 1981–2(Feb.) (def.)
Joyce, E. E., Cork East, 1927(June)
Joyce, Michael, Limerick, 1927(June)
Joyce, P. D., Galway West, 1965, 1973

Kane, A. J., *Mid-Ulster*, 1982–6
Kane, Eamon, Kildare, 1970(by)
Kane, Pamela, Dublin North-East, 1987
Kavanagh, Bernard, Dublin Co., 1923
Kavanagh, John, Kerry, 1927(June)
Kavanagh, Laurence, Laoighis-Offaly, 1982(Feb.)
Kavanagh, Liam, Wicklow, 1968(by), 1969–; IRELAND, 1973–9; LEINSTER, 1979–81
Kavanagh, P. J., Leix-Offaly, 1944
Kavanagh, Thomas, Longford-Westmeath, 1951
Kealey, P. J. D., *Londonderry*, 1975
Kealy, Donal, Tipperary North, 1987
Keane, Bartley, Galway West, 1943
Keane, J. J., Galway West, 1940(by)–3 (def.), 1944, 1948
Keane, J. J., Mayo South, 1965
Keane, O. J., *Belfast (Clifton)*, 1949
Keane, Peter, Kildare, 1951
Keane, Peter, Mayo West, 1977; Mayo East, 1982(Feb.)
Keane, R. H., Waterford, 1923, 1927(June)
Keane, Seán (sen.), Cork North, 1943; Cork East, 1948–53 (d.)
Keane, Seán (jun.), Cork East, 1953(by), 1954
Keaney, T. J., Dublin North-West, 1961
Kearney, Joseph, Leix-Offaly, 1943
Kearney, Patrick, Belfast South (w), 1955
Kearns, M. G., Carlow-Kilkenny, 1987
Keating, Bernard, Wicklow, 1977
Keating, C. E., Wicklow, 1977
Keating, John, Wexford, 1927(June–Sept.) (def.), 1932–43 (def.), 1944–8 (def.)
Keating, Justin, Dublin Co. North, 1969–77; Dublin Co. West, 1977; IRELAND, 1972–3; LEINSTER, 1984(Feb–June) (def.)
Keating, Michael, Dublin Central, 1973; Dublin North-Central, 1977–81; Dublin Central, 1981–9
Keating, Michael J., Cavan, 1938, 1943

Keating, Peter, Dublin Central, 1969

Keaveney, John, Roscommon, 1927(June), 1927(Sept.)

Keaveney, Michael, Mayo North, 1923

Keaveney, Patrick, Donegal North-East, 1976(by)–7; Donegal, 1977

Keeble, Cecilia, Dublin South-West, 1961

Keeffe, James, Carlow-Kilkenny, 1969

Keegan, John, Kildare, 1961

Keegan, Seán, Longford-Westmeath, 1965, 1970(by), 1973, 1977–82(Nov.) (def.)

Keegan, William (Billy), Dublin (Finglas), 1977; Dublin North-West, 1981, 1982(Feb.), 1982(Nov.)

Keeley, May, Laoighis-Offaly, 1987

Keely, Fergus, Dublin North-West, 1973

Keely, S. P., Galway, 1927(Sept.), 1933–7; Clare, 1937

Keenan, Thomas, Laoighis-Offaly, 1973, 1982(Feb.)

Keery, Neville, Dún Laoghaire and Rathdown, 1969, 1973

Kehoe, Anthony (Tony), Tipperary South, 1982(Nov.), 1987

Kehoe, Patrick, Wexford, 1932, 1933–7, 1943

Kelleher, Humphrey, Cork Borough, 1932

Kelleher, John, Cork North-Central, 1982(Nov.), 1987, 1989

Kelleher, Liam, Roscommon, 1923

Kelleher, Seán, Cork South-West, 1981

Kelly, A. K., *Antrim South*, 1982; Antrim East (w), 1983, 1987

Kelly, C. J., Cork North-East, 1973

Kelly, Douglas, Mayo South, 1957

Kelly, Edward, Monaghan, 1954–7 (def.), 1961

Kelly, Edward J., Donegal, 1927(Sept.)

Kelly, Frank, Galway, 1932

Kelly, James, Laoighis-Offaly, 1969, 1977

Kelly, James A., Dublin North-East, 1969, 1973

Kelly, James I., Cavan, 1973; Cavan-Monaghan, 1977, 1982(Feb.)

Kelly, James P., Meath, 1927(June), 1927(Sept.), 1932–7; Meath-Westmeath, 1937–43 (def.), 1944

Kelly, Jeremiah, Dublin North-East, 1954

Kelly, John, Wexford, 1944

Kelly, John, Kerry South, 1989

Kelly, John J., Kerry North, 1943

Kelly, John M., Dublin South-Central, 1969, 1973–7; Dublin Co. South, 1977–81; Dublin South, 1981–9

Kelly, John W. B., *Down Mid*, 1964(by)–73

Kelly, Joseph, Mayo North, 1923

Kelly, Laurence, Cork North-West, 1989–

Kelly, Mary, Cork South-Central, 1982(Feb.)

Kelly, Michael, Dublin North-Central, 1969

Kelly, Michael A., Roscommon, 1948, 1951; Dublin North-East, 1954

Kelly, Patricia, Dublin North-East, 1981

Kelly, Patrick, Dublin South-Central, 1969
Kelly, Patrick, Donegal, 1980(by); Donegal South-West, 1981, 1982(Feb.)
Kelly, Patrick M., Clare, 1923, 1927(June)–32 (def.)
Kelly, Peter, Galway West, 1937, 1938
Kelly, Peter, Dublin South-East, 1977
Kelly, Philip (Philo), Longford-Westmeath, 1977
Kelly, Robert, Cork West, 1923
Kelly, Seán, Leix-Offaly, 1923
Kelly, Seán, Dublin (Rathmines West), 1977
Kelly, Thomas, Dublin South, 1921–3, 1933–43
Kelly, Thomas, Meath, 1982(Nov.)
Kelly, Thomas J., *Down South*, 1953, 1958
Kelly, Thomas W., Mayo South, 1927(June)
Kelly, William, *Tyrone Mid*, 1953–8
Kelly, William J., *Antrim North*, 1973
Kemmy, James, Limerick East, 1977, 1981–2(Nov.) (def.), 1987–
Kenneally, Brendan, Waterford, 1989–
Kenneally, James, Cork North-Central, 1981, 1982(Feb.), 1982(Nov.)
Kenneally, William, Cork Borough, 1923
Kenneally, William, Waterford, 1952(by)–61 (def.), 1965–82(Feb.) (def.)
Kennedy, A. Laurence, NORTHERN IRELAND, 1989
Kennedy, Adrian J., *Armagh North*, 1969
Kennedy, Daniel, Leix-Offaly, 1923, 1932
Kennedy, Daniel, Tipperary, 1932, 1937, 1943
Kennedy, Daniel, Tipperary North, 1957
Kennedy David G., *Tyrone East*, 1938
Kennedy, Geraldine, Dún Laoghaire, 1987–9 (def.)
Kennedy, Hugh, Dublin South, 1923(Oct.)(by)–4
Kennedy, James, *Belfast (Windsor)*, 1945
Kennedy, James J., Wexford, 1965–9
Kennedy, John P., Dublin South-East, 1969
Kennedy, John W., *Belfast (Cromac)*, 1962(Dec.)(by)–73
Kennedy, Marion, Dún Laoghaire, 1982(Feb.)
Kennedy, Michael, Tipperary, 1927(June)
Kennedy, Michael, J., Longford-Westmeath, 1927(June)–37; Meath-
    Westmeath, 1937–48; Longford-Westmeath, 1948–65
Kennedy, Patrick, *Belfast Central*, 1969–73; *Belfast West*, 1973
Kennedy, Patrick C., Limerick East, 1969, 1973, 1977, 1982(Feb.)
Kennedy, Seán, Donegal West, 1951, 1954, 1957
Kennedy, Thomas, Donegal South-West, 1989
Kennedy, William, *Belfast (Ballynafeigh)*, 1945
Kennelly, Séamus, Sligo-Leitrim, 1982(Feb.)
Kenny, Enda, Mayo West, 1975(by)–
Kenny, Henry, Mayo South, 1954–69; Mayo West, 1969–75 (d.)
Kenny, John, Dublin North-Central, 1973
Kenny, K. J., Dublin North, 1923

Kenny, Michael, Dublin North-West, 1981
Kenny, Seán, Dublin North-East, 1981, 1982(Feb.), 1982(Nov.), 1987, 1989
Kent, D. Rice, Cork East/North-East, 1921–3; Cork East, 1923–7(Sept.)
Kent, William, Cork South, 1951
Kent, William Rice, Cork East, 1927(Sept.)–32 (def.), 1933–7
Keogan, James, Cavan, 1943
Keogh, Helen, Dún Laoghaire, 1987
Keogh, Michael, Dublin North-West, 1943
Keogh, Michael J., *Down South*, 1967(by)–73
Keogh, Myles, Dublin South, 1922–33 (def.), 1937–8 (def.), 1943
Keohane, Joseph, Kerry North, 1973
Kerin, Redmond, Leix-Offaly, 1951, 1954
Kerins, P. D. P., Belfast West (w), 1974(Oct.); *Belfast West*, 1975
Kerlin, Frank, Dublin South, 1927(Sept.)–32
Kerr, J. F., *Belfast (Woodvale)*, 1962
Kerr, Val, Monaghan, 1973
Kerrigan, Andrew, Roscommon, 1989
Kerrigan, Patrick, Cork Borough, 1967(by); Cork City North-West, 1969, 1973;
    Cork City, 1977–9 (d.)
Kettyles, D. A., Fermanagh-Tyrone South (w), 1983, 1986(by), 1987
Keyes, Christopher, Limerick East, 1957
Keyes, M. J., Limerick, 1923, 1927(June–Sept.) (def.), 1932, 1933–48;
    Limerick East, 1948–57
Keyes, R. P., Cork West, 1927(Sept.), 1932–3 (def.)
Kidd, R. J. (Bob), *Carrick*, 1962, 1965; *Antrim South*, 1973, 1982; Antrim South
    (w), 1974(Feb.), 1979
Kidney, John, Cork North-East, 1977
Kiely, Daniel, Kerry North, 1982(Feb.), 1982(Nov.), 1987
Kiely, Rory, Limerick West, 1969
Kiernan, June, Longford-Westmeath, 1989
Kieman, M. M., Cavan-Monaghan, 1989
Kiernan, P. G., Sligo-Leitrim, 1948
Kiersey, John, Waterford, 1932–3 (def.)
Kilbane, Patrick J., Mayo West, 1981
Kilbride, Thomas, Longford-Westmeath, 1969, 1973
Kilfedder, J. A., Belfast West (w), 1964–6 (def.); Down North (w), 1970–85,
    1986(by)–; *Down North*, 1973–6, 1982–6; NORTHERN IRELAND, 1979,
    1984
Kilkelly, Michael, Tipperary South, 1951, 1954
Killane, J. J., Longford-Westmeath, 1923–7(June) (def.), 1927(Sept.)–30 (d.)
Killean, J. J., Longford-Westmeath, 1948
Killeen, Timothy, Dublin North-East, 1969, 1973; Dublin (Artane), 1977–81;
    Dublin North-West, 1981, 1982(Feb.), 1982(Nov.)
Killian, Michael, Roscommon, 1927(June)
Killilea, Mark (sen.), Galway, 1927(June)–32 (def.), 1933–7; Galway East,
    1937–48; Galway North, 1948–61; Galway East, 1961

Killilea, Mark (jun.), Galway North-East, 1973; Galway East, 1977–81; Galway West, 1981–2(Feb.) (def.), 1982(Nov.), 1987; CONNACHT-ULSTER, 1987–

Killion, Patrick, Athlone-Longford, 1937

Kilroy, James, Mayo North, 1943–51 (def.)

Kilroy, Michael, Mayo South, 1923–37; Mayo North, 1937; Mayo South, 1944; Mayo North, 1954

Kilroy, Thomas, Roscommon-Leitrim, 1969

Kinahan, C. H. G., Antrim South (w), 1974(Feb.), 1974(Oct.), 1979; *Antrim South*, 1975–6

Kinahan, R. G. C., *Belfast (Clifton)*, 1958–9

Kinane, Patrick, Tipperary, 1947(by)–8; Tipperary North, 1948–51 (def.), 1954

King, Frank, Waterford, 1977

King, Irene, Galway West, 1973

King, John, Meath, 1989

King, Thomas, Galway North, 1954

King, W. G., *Antrim South*, 1973

Kingston, D. J., Cork West, 1948

Kinsella, Patrick, Wexford, 1945(by)

Kinsella, Vera, Dublin South-Central, 1977

Kirby, John, Limerick East, 1961

Kirk, H. V., *Belfast (Windsor)*, 1956(by)–73; *Belfast South*, 1973–5

Kirk, Owen, Cavan-Monaghan, 1977

Kirk, Séamus, Louth, 1982(Nov.)–

Kirkland, E. T., *Antrim South*, 1982

Kirkpatrick, T. J., *Belfast South*, 1982–6

Kirrane, M. J., Sligo-Leitrim, 1954

Kirwan, Oscar, Dublin North, 1932

Kirwan, P. W. (Billy), Waterford, 1977

Kissane, Eamon, Kerry, 1932–7; Kerry North, 1937–51 (def.), 1954

Kitt, M. F., Galway North, 1948–51 (def.), 1954, 1957–61; Galway East, 1961–9; Galway North-East, 1969–74 (d.)

Kitt, M. P., Galway North-East, 1975(by)–7; Galway East, 1977, 1981–

Kitt, Thomas, Dublin South, 1981, 1982(Feb.), 1982(Nov.), 1987–

Kyle, Samuel, *Belfast North*, 1925–9; *Belfast (Oldpark)*, 1929

Kyne, Séamus, Galway West, 1973

Kyne, T. A., Waterford, 1947(by), 1948–69 (def.), 1973–7

Kyne, William (Billy), Waterford, 1981

Lacy, Michael, Tipperary South, 1954

Lacy, Richard (Dick), Dublin North-East, 1969; Sligo-Leitrim, 1981

Laffan, Bartholomew, Limerick, 1923

Lagan, J. A., *Mid-Ulster*, 1975, 1982; Mid-Ulster (w), 1979, 1983

Lahiffe, Robert, Galway South, 1948–51 (def.), 1953(by)–7 (def.)

Laing, G. E. S., Dublin Co. Mid, 1977; Dublin South-West, 1981, 1982(Feb.)

Laird, J. D., *Belfast (St Anne's)*, 1970(by)–3; *Belfast West*, 1973–6
Laird, N. D., *Belfast (St Anne's)*, 1969–70 (d.)
Laird, S. E., Down South (w), 1987
Lalor, Anthony, Dublin South-Central, 1951
Lalor, P. J., Laoighis-Offaly, 1961–81; LEINSTER, 1979–
Lambert, Joseph, Galway South, 1957
Lambert, Patrick, Galway, 1927(June), 1932
Lambert, Robert, Wexford, 1923–7(June)
Lane, James, Cork North-Central, 1982(Feb.); Cork South-Central, 1982(Nov.)
Lane, Patrick, MUNSTER, 1989–
Lane, Patrick J., Kerry South, 1951
Langan, Patrick, Limerick West, 1948
Langhammer, M. F., NORTHERN IRELAND, 1989
Lanigan, John, Waterford, 1987
Lanigan, Michael, Carlow-Kilkenny, 1977, 1981, 1982(Nov.)
Larkin, Aidan J., Mid-Ulster, 1973–5 (def.)
Larkin, Alison M., Dublin North-West, 1987, 1989
Larkin, Denis, Dublin North-East, 1951, 1954–61 (def.), 1963(by), 1965–9
Larkin, Hilda, Dublin South-West, 1959(by), 1961
Larkin, James (sen.), Dublin North, 1927(Sept.) (elected but disqualified), 1928(by), 1932, 1933; Dublin North-East, 1937–8 (def.), 1943–4 (def.)
Larkin, James (jun.), Dublin Co., 1927(Sept.); Dublin South, 1932, 1943–8; Dublin South-Central, 1948–57
Larkin, John (Jack), Kerry North, 1973
Larkin, Joseph, Dublin Co., 1957
Larkin, Thomas, *Fermanagh-Tyrone*, 1925
Larkin, Thomas, Roscommon, 1927(June)
Larkin, W. J., Limerick, 1923; Dublin North, 1927(June), 1927(Sept.)
Larmour, Samuel, *Antrim South*, 1982
Laverty, May, Dublin South-West, 1948
Laverty, S. H., *Antrim South*, 1983
Lavery, Cecil, Dublin Co., 1935(by)–8 (def.)
Lavery, F. J., *Belfast (Willowfield)*, 1941(by)
Lavery, G. M., *Belfast (St Anne's)*, 1970(by)
Lavery, Patrick, *Down*, 1921
Lavery, T. R., *Down*, 1921–9
Lavery, William (Bill), *Belfast North*, 1975, 1982
Lavin, Andrew, Leitrim-Roscommon North, 1921–3; Roscommon, 1923–7(June) (def.), 1927(Sept.)
Lavin, Thomas, Sligo-Leitrim, 1982(Nov.), 1987
Law, H. A., Donegal, 1923, 1927(June)–32 (def.)
Lawler Thomas, Kildare, 1923
Lawless, F. J., Dublin Co., 1921–2
Lawless, William, Wicklow, 1953(by)
Lawless William A., Wicklow, 1969

Lawlor John, Dublin North, 1923; Dublin South, 1927(Sept.)

Lawlor, Liam Dublin Co. West, 1977–81; Dublin West, 1981, 1982(Feb.–Nov.) (def.), 1987–

Lawlor, Maurice, Kerry, 1927(Sept.)

Lawlor, Maurice, Kerry North, 1954

Lawlor, Patrick (Patsy), Kildare, 1981, 1982(Feb.)

Lawlor, Thomas, Dublin South, 1925(by), 1927(June–Sept.) (def.), 1932, 1937–8 (def.)

Lawlor, Thomas, Carlow-Kildare, 1943

Leahy, Daniel, Waterford, 1948, 1951, 1954

Leahy, M., Cork South-East, 1937

Leahy, Patrick (Pakie), Tipperary South, 1977

Leahy, T. P., Cork Borough, 1965; Cork City North-West, 1969

Leavy, Daniel, Longford-Westmeath, 1965

Leavy, Frederick, Kildare, 1987

Leckey, K. H., *Down North*, 1973

Ledden, James, Limerick, 1923–7(June)

Leddin, Declan, Limerick East, 1989

Leddy, C. E., Belfast West (w), 1935

Ledwidge, J., Wicklow, 1951

Ledwidge, Mary, Wicklow, 1954

Lee, John, Tipperary, 1943

Lee, Patrick, Dublin Central, 1987, 1989–

Leeburn, W. J., *Tyrone South*, 1945(Apr.)(by); Belfast North (w), 1945, 1950; *Belfast (Willowfield)*, 1949

Leeke, George, *Londonderry*, 1921–9; *Londonderry Mid*, 1929–45

Leen, William (Billy), Kerry North, 1987

Lehane, Con, Dublin South-Central, 1948–51 (def.)

Lehane, Cornelius, Leix-Offaly, 1948

Lehane, Denis, Cork West, 1943

Lehane, John, Cork West, 1923

Lehane, Neil, Cork Mid, 1969

Lehane, P. D., Cork South-East, 1943, 1944; Cork South, 1948–54 (def.)

Lemass, Eileen, Dublin South-West, 1976(by); Dublin (Ballyfermot), 1977–81; Dublin West, 1981–2(Feb.) (def.), 1982(by), 1982(Nov.)–7; DUBLIN, 1984–9 (def.)

Lemass, N. T., Dublin South-West, 1956(by)–76 (d.)

Lemass, S. F., Dublin South, 1924(by), 1924(by)–48; Dublin South-Central, 1948–69

Leneghan, J. R., Mayo North, 1944, 1951, 1961–5 (def.); Mayo West, 1969–73 (def.)

Lenihan, Brian, Longford-Westmeath, 1954; Roscommon, 1957, 1961–9; Roscommon-Leitrim, 1969–73 (def.); Dublin Co. West, 1977–81; Dublin West, 1981–; IRELAND, 1973–7

Lenihan, Charles, Kerry North, 1957, 1961

Lenihan, Patrick, Roscommon, 1981

Lenihan, Patrick J., Longford-Westmeath, 1961, 1965–70 (d.)

Lennon, James, Carlow-Kilkenny, 1921–2 (def.)

Lennon, James G., *Armagh South*, 1933

Lennon, Joseph, Louth, 1977, 1987

Leonard, Clare, Dublin South-West, 1989

Leonard, E. P., Dún Laoghaire and Rathdown, 1973

Leonard, James, Monaghan, 1973–7; Cavan-Monaghan, 1977–81 (def.), 1982(Feb.)–

Leonard, John, Sligo-Leitrim, 1948

Leonard, Patrick, Dublin North, 1925(by)–7(June) (def.), 1927(Sept.)–32 (def.)

Leonard, Thomas, Dublin Central, 1969, 1973; Dublin (Cabra), 1977–81; Dublin Central, 1981, 1982(Feb.), 1982(Nov.), 1983(by)–7

L'Estrange, Gerald, Meath-Westmeath, 1944; Longford-Westmeath, 1948, 1961, 1965–87; IRELAND, 1977–9

Lewis, Hugh, Armagh (w), 1970, 1974(Feb.)

Leyden, Terence, Roscommon-Leitrim, 1977–81; Roscommon, 1981–

Liddy, S. J., Clare, 1921–3

Lillis, Thomas, Clare, 1948

Lindsay, Capt. D. C., *Belfast Central*, 1929

Lindsay, J. Kennedy, *Antrim South*, 1973–6, 1982

Lindsay, P. J., Mayo North, 1937, 1938, 1943, 1948, 1952(by), 1954–61 (def.), 1965–9; Dublin North-Central, 1969, 1973

Linehan, C. F., *Down North*, 1973

Linehan, M. P., Monaghan, 1943

Linehan, Timothy, Cork North, 1937–44 (def.)

Lipper, Michael, Limerick East, 1968(by), 1969, 1973, 1977–81 (def.), 1982(Feb.)

Liston, P. T., Limerick West, 1948

Liston, Seán, Limerick West, 1989

Little, D. J., *Down West*, 1962–5(May)

Little, Revd James, Down (w), 1939(by)–46 (d.)

Little, James H., Down (w), 1946(by)

Little, P. J., Waterford, 1927(June)–54

Lloyd, T. E., Limerick, 1937

Lloyd-Dodd, Prof. F. T., *Queen's University Belfast*, 1949(Nov.)(by)–62

Lodge, Jeremiah, Laoighis-Offaly, 1981, 1982(Feb.), 1982(Nov.), 1987

Loftus, Eithne, Dublin West, 1987

Loftus, S. D., Dublin North-East, 1961, 1963(by), 1965, 1969; Dublin North-Central, 1973; Dublin (Clontarf), 1977; Dublin North-East, 1981–2(Feb.) (def.), 1982(Nov.); Dublin North-Central, 1982(Feb.), 1987, 1989; DUBLIN, 1979, 1984

Logan, E. M., *Belfast East*, 1973

Logan, J. S., *Antrim South*, 1975

Logue, G. K., *Mid-Ulster*, 1973

Logue, H. A., *Londonderry*, 1973–6, 1982–6; Londonderry (w), 1974(Feb.), 1979

Lohan, Lawrence, Dún Laoghaire, 1987

Lombard, Patrick, Cork Mid, 1969

Lonergan, Patrick, Monaghan, 1943

Lonergan, Thomas, Tipperary South, 1987, 1989

Long, C. V., Donegal, 1977

Long, James, Cork North-West, 1982(Nov.)

Long, Capt. W. J., *Ards*, 1962–73

Looney, T. D., Cork South-East, 1943–4 (def.)

Loughlin, Gerard, Lagan Valley, 1983

Loughman, Francis, Tipperary South, 1938–48; Tipperary South, 1948, 1951, 1957–61 (def.)

Loughnane, William (Billy), Clare, 1989

Loughnane, William (Bill) A., Clare-Galway South, 1969–77; Galway West, 1977–81; Clare, 1981–2(Nov.) (def.)

Loughran, John (Jack), Dún Laoghaire, 1977

Loughrey, J. A., Donegal North-East, 1976(by), 1982(Feb.), 1982(Nov.), 1987, 1989

Love, Michael, Dublin North-West, 1943

Lovett, G. M., Cavan, 1951

Lowden, Joseph, *Belfast (St Anne's)*, 1945

Lowe, C. M., *Belfast (Duncairn)*, 1938

Lowe, Harry, Dublin South-West, 1969

Lowry, Andrew, Donegal, 1923

Lowry, Donal, Dublin Co. South, 1973

Lowry, J. T., Lagan Valley (w), 1986(by), 1987

Lowry, Michael, Tipperary North, 1987–

Lowry, William, *Londonderry City*, 1939(by)–47

Lucey, Con, Cork Borough, 1923, 1927(June), 1927(Sept.)

Lundon, Thomas, Limerick East, 1909(by)–18 (def.)

Lupton, Angela, CONNACHT-ULSTER, 1989

Lydon, M. F., Galway West, 1944–51 (def.), 1954, 1957

Lyle, Dr William, *Queen's University Belfast*, 1942(by)–5 (def.), 1949(Feb.–Aug.) (d.)

Lynch, Bernard, Clare, 1957

Lynch, Celia, Dublin South-Central, 1954–61; Dublin North-Central, 1961–77

Lynch, D. C., Cork South-East, 1918–20

Lynch, Eamonn, Cork East, 1927(Sept.), 1932; Dublin South, 1938

Lynch, Fionán, Kerry-Limerick West, 1921–3; Kerry, 1923–37; Kerry South, 1937–44(Oct.)

Lynch, Gerard, Kerry North, 1969–77 (def.), 1981

Lynch, Gilbert, Galway, 1927(June–Sept.) (def.); Dublin Co., 1944

Lynch, James B., Dublin South, 1932–7, 1938–48; Dublin South-Central, 1948, 1951

Lynch, John, Cork North, 1923

Lynch, John, Leitrim-Sligo, 1923

Lynch, John (Jack), Cork Borough, 1948–69; Cork City North-West, 1969–77; Cork City, 1977–81

Lynch, John, Limerick West, 1948

Lynch, John, Kerry North, 1951–4 (def.), 1957

Lynch, John, Armagh (w), 1959, 1964

Lynch, John (Jack), Clare, 1969

Lynch, Joseph P., Leix-Offaly, 1921–3

Lynch, Kathleen, Cork South-Central, 1987, 1989

Lynch, Kevin, Waterford, 1981

Lynch, Michael, Meath, 1977, 1981, 1982(Feb.–Nov.) (def.), 1987–9 (def.)

Lynch, Patrick, Donegal East, 1938

Lynch, Peter T., Roscommon, 1948, 1954

Lynch, Ralph, Dublin South, 1937

Lynch, Séamus, *Belfast North*, 1973, 1975, 1982; Belfast North (w), 1979, 1983, 1986(by), 1987; NORTHERN IRELAND, 1984, 1989

Lynch, Seán, Longford-Westmeath, 1982(Feb.)

Lynch, Seán F., Athlone-Longford, 1937; Longford-Westmeath, 1948

Lynch, Thaddeus, Waterford, 1952(by), 1954–66 (d.)

Lynch, Thomas N., Limerick West, 1969

Lynchehaun, Seán, Mayo North, 1944, 1948, 1957

Lynn, Kathleen, Dublin Co., 1923–7(June) (def.), 1927(Aug.)(by)

Lynn, Sir R. J., Belfast West (w), 1922–9; *Belfast West*, 1921–9; *Antrim North*, 1929–45(Aug.) (d.)

Lyons, Denis, Cork North-Central, 1981–

Lyons, George, Dublin South, 1923

Lyons, John, Longford-Westmeath, 1922–7(June), 1927(Sept.)

Lyons, M. D., Mayo South, 1954, 1957, 1961, 1965–9

Lyons, Seán, Dublin West, 1987

Lyons, Thomas, *Tyrone North*, 1943(by)–69; Fermanagh-Tyrone (w), 1945

Lyttle, Eugene, *Fermanagh-Tyrone South*, 1975

Lyttle, Thomas, *Belfast North*, 1973

McAteer, H. K., *Tyrone Mid*, 1929–41 (d.)

McAleese, Mary, Dublin South-East, 1987

McAlinden, John, *Armagh North*, 1949

McAlinden, Leo, Sligo-Leitrim, 1954, 1957

McAliskey, J. Bernadette (formerly Devlin), *Londonderry South*, 1969; Mid-Ulster (w), 1969(by)–74(Feb.) (def.); NORTHERN IRELAND, 1979; Dublin North-Central, 1982(Feb.), 1982(Nov.)

McAlister, Mary, Antrim North (w), 1974(Feb.), 1984 (Oct.)

MacAllister, D. J., Antrim South (w), 1970

McAllister, James, *Armagh*, 1982–6; Newry and Armagh (w), 1983, 1986(by), 1987

McAllister, Thomas, Clare, 1981

McAllister, Thomas S., *Antrim*, 1925–9

McAndrew, Pádraig, Mayo North, 1943

Mac an Iomaire, Peadar, Galway West, 1969

MacAnthony, Joseph, Dublin Co. South, 1970(by)

McAnulty, J. G., *Belfast West*, 1982

Mac Aonghusa, Proinsias, Louth, 1965; Dún Laoghaire and Rathdown, 1969

McArdle, James, Louth, 1981

McArdle, P. J., Monaghan, 1943, 1944

McAteer, E. G., *Londonderry Mid*, 1945–53; *Londonderry (Foyle)*, 1953–69 (def.); Londonderry (w), 1970; *Londonderry*, 1973

McAteer, Fergus, Londonderry (w), 1979

McAteer, H. J., Londonderry (w), 1950, 1964

Macaulay, Gordon, Dublin North-East, 1965

McAuley, J. J., Longford-Westmeath, 1948, 1957

McAuley, Richard, Lagan Valley (w), 1983

McAuliffe, H. L., Wicklow, 1961

McAuliffe, Patrick, Cork North, 1943, 1944–61; Cork North-East, 1961–9 (def.)

McAuliffe, Timothy, Longford-Westmeath, 1965, 1969

McAuliffe-Ennis, Helena, Longford-Westmeath, 1987

McBennett, Eoin, Kildare, 1987

McBirney, R. M., *Belfast (Willowfield)*, 1965; *Belfast East*, 1966; *Belfast (Pottinger)*, 1969

McBride, B. V., *Tyrone North*, 1949

McBride, J. M., Mayo North/West, 1921–3; Mayo South, 1923–7(June) (def.)

McBride, Robert, *Down*, 1921–9; *Down West*, 1929–33

MacBride, Seán, Dublin Co., 1947(by)–8; Dublin South-West, 1948–57 (def.), 1959(by), 1961; Dublin South-Central, 1958(by)

McBrien, Ronald, Dublin South-Central, 1987, 1989

McBrinn, Robert, *Belfast (Willowfield)*, 1945; Belfast South (w), 1951

McCabe, Alexander, Sligo-Mayo East, 1921–3; Leitrim-Sligo, 1923–4

McCabe, F. F., Cork East, 1927(June)

McCabe, John, Dublin South, 1937

McCabe, John P., Dublin Co., 1922, 1923, 1927(June)

McCabe, Nicholas, Louth, 1981

McCabe, William, Dublin South, 1923

McCammick, S. J., *Armagh*, 1973

McCann, E. J., *Londonderry (Foyle)*, 1969; Londonderry (w), 1970

McCann, John, Dublin South, 1937, 1938, 1939(by)–48; Dublin South-Central, 1948–54 (def.)

McCann, John, Dublin West, 1989

McCann, Joseph M., Tipperary, 1933

McCann, Sidney, Dublin Co., 1961

McCarroll, F. E., *Londonderry City*, 1949

McCarroll, J. J., *Londonderry (Foyle)*, 1929–37 (d.)

McCarron, Daniel, Donegal North-East, 1973

McCarron, Daniel, Dublin South-Central, 1981

McCarry, Kate, Donegal, 1927(Sept.)
McCartan, Michael, Fermanagh-Tyrone (w), 1924
McCartan, Patrick, Tullamore, Leix-Offaly, 1921–2 (def.); Cork Borough, 1948; Dublin South-East, 1951; Dublin North-East, 1957
McCartan, Patrick, Dublin North-East, 1981, 1982(Feb.), 1982(Nov.), 1987–
McCarthy, Agnes P., Clare, 1977, 1981, 1982(Feb.), 1982(Nov.)
McCarthy, Andrew, Dublin Co., 1938
McCarthy, Con, Dublin South-West, 1982(Feb.)
McCarthy, Daniel, Dublin South, 1921–4
McCarthy, Daniel, Cork West, 1923
McCarthy, David, Antrim North, 1973(June–July) (d.)
McCarthy, Edward (Ted), Cork Mid, 1965
McCarthy, Eugene, Cork West, 1932, 1933
McCarthy, Jeremiah, Cork West, 1927(June)
McCarthy, John, Mayo South, 1948
McCarthy, John C., Cork South-West, 1981, 1982(Feb.)
McCarthy, Joseph, Cork North-Central, 1987
MacCarthy, Joseph A., Cork West, 1927(June)
McCarthy, Kieran, Cork East, 1987
McCarthy, Martin, Cork North-West, 1982(Nov.)
MacCarthy, Seán, Cork South-East, 1943, 1944–8; Cork Borough, 1948, 1951–4; Cork South. 1954–61; Cork Mid, 1961–5
McCarthy, Seán, Tipperary South, 1981–9 (def.)
McCarthy, Thomas, Wexford, 1923, 1927(June)
McCarthy-Morrogh, F. D., Cork Borough, 1943
McCartin, J. J., Sligo-Leitrim, 1981–2(Feb.) (def.), 1982(Nov.)–97 (def.); CONNACHT-ULSTER, 1979–
McCartney, R. L. Down North, 1982; Down North (w), 1983, 1987
McCarvill, Patrick, Monaghan, 1922–7(Sept.), 1948
McCauley, Dominick, Donegal North-East, 1965
McCauley, Hugh, Donegal East, 1954
McCausland, Nelson, Belfast North, 1982
McClay, Thomas, Tyrone West, 1949
McClean, P. J., Mid-Ulster (w), 1987
McCleery, Sir W. V., Antrim North, 1945(Oct.)(by)–58
McClelland, S. D., Antrim South (w), 1987
McClements, J. E., Antrim North, 1975
McCloskey, E. V., Antrim South, 1973–6
McClure, Dr H. I., Queen's University Belfast, 1962–9
McClure, K. M., Down North, 1973
McClure, W. J., Londonderry, 1975–6, 1982–6; Londonderry East (w), 1983
McCollum, Charles, Monaghan, 1969
McCollum, W. P., Belfast South, 1973
McConaghy, A. P., Antrim North, 1982
McConnell, Alexander, Belfast (Willowfield), 1929
McConnell, David, Belfast East (w), 1964

McConnell, Francis, *Tyrone Mid,* 1958
McConnell, Sir Joseph, Antrim (w), 1929–42 (d.)
McConnell, R. D., *Bangor,* 1969–73; *Down North,* 1973–6
McConnell, R. W. B., *Antrim South,* 1951(by)–68(Aug.) (res.)
McConnell, T. E., Belfast (Duncairn) (w), 1921(by)–2; Belfast North (w), 1922–9
McConville, John, *Belfast West,* 1925
McCool, Seán (John), *Londonderry (Foyle),* 1933; Donegal East, 1943, 1948
MacCormac, S. L., Meath, 1957
McCormack, James, Donegal East, 1944
McCormack, Joseph, Laoighis-Offaly, 1981, 1982(Feb.), 1982(Nov.), 1984(by), 1987, 1989
McCormack, Nial, Mayo North, 1943
McCormack, Pádraic, Galway West, 1977, 1981, 1982(Feb.), 1989–
McCormack, Peter, Carlow-Kilkenny, 1982(Feb.)
Mac Cormaic, C. P., Dublin North-Central, 1987
McCormick, Maj. J. H., *Belfast (St Anne's),* 1929–38
McCormick, Patrick, Antrim (w), 1924
McCoy, Austin, Dublin North-Central, 1987
McCoy, Bernard, *Belfast South,* 1921
McCoy, J. S., Limerick West, 1987–9
McCoy, W. F., *Tyrone South,* 1945(Apr.)(by)–65
McCracken, W. J., *Iveagh,* 1953
McCrann, P. J., Longford-Westmeath, 1927(June)
McCrann, T. V., Roscommon-Leitrim, 1973
McCrea, J. J., Wicklow, 1948, 1953(by)
McCrea, Raymond S., *Belfast South,* 1982–6; Belfast South (w), 1983
McCrea, Revd Robert T. William, Belfast South (w), 1982(by); *Mid-Ulster,* 1982–6; Mid-Ulster (w), 1983–5, 1986(by)–
McCreevy, Charles, Kildare, 1977–
McCrossan, Dominick, Fermanagh-Tyrone (w), 1934(by)
McCullagh, Sir Crawford, *Belfast South,* 1921–5 (def.)
McCullagh, E. V., *Tyrone Mid,* 1948(by)–53 (def.)
McCullough, Denis, *Belfast West,* 1921; Donegal, 1924(by)–7(June)
McCullough, Raymond, *Down South,* 1982–5 (d.)
McCullough, W. H., *Belfast (Bloomfield),* 1945, 1949
MacCurtain, Tomás, Armagh (w), 1955
McCurtin, Seán (John) P., Tipperary, 1923–7(June), 1932, 1933
McCusker, J. Harold, Armagh (w), 1974(Feb.)–83; Upper Bann (w), 1983–5, 1986(by)–90 (d.); *Armagh,* 1982–6
McCusker, Patrick, *Newry and Armagh,* 1986(by)
McDaid, James, *Fermanagh-Tyrone South,* 1973
McDaid, James, Donegal North-East, 1989–
MacDermot, Frank, Belfast West (w), 1929; Roscommon, 1932–7
McDermott, Frank, Meath, 1981, 1982(Feb.)
MacDermott, J. C., *Queen's University Belfast,* 1938–44

McDevitt, H. A., Donegal East, 1937, 1938–43
McDevitt, Joseph, Donegal West, 1948
Mac Domhnaill, Aindrias, Tipperary North, 1957
McDonagh, Bernard, *Belfast West*, 1975
MacDonagh, Joseph, Tipperary Mid/North/South, 1921–3
McDonagh, Michael, Sligo-Leitrim, 1948, 1951, 1957
McDonagh, Séamus, Meath, 1987
Mac Donagh, T. J., Tipperary North, 1948
McDonald, C. B., Laoighis-Offaly, 1969, 1973–7 (def.), 1981, 1982(Feb.),
    1982(Nov.), 1987; IRELAND, 1972–9; LEINSTER, 1979, 1989
McDonald, Edward, Carlow-Kilkenny, 1927(June)
McDonald, Edward, Dún Laoghaire, 1987
McDonald, James, *Antrim South*, 1975, 1982–6; Upper Bann (w), 1983
McDonald, Patrick, Wexford, 1969
McDonald, Patrick J., *Tyrone Mid*, 1969
McDonnell, Alasdair, Antrim North (w), 1970; Belfast South (w), 1979,
    1982(by), 1983, 1987
McDonnell, James, Galway, 1927(June)
McDonnell, Joseph, Sligo-Leitrim, 1981
McDonnell, Patrick, Dublin North-West, 1965, 1969, 1973
McDonnell, Patrick J., Dublin South-East, 1989
McDonnell, R. J., Meath, 1927(Sept.)
McDonnell, William (Billy), *Antrim South*, 1982; Lagan Valley (w), 1987
McDonogh, Frederick, Galway, 1932, 1933
McDonogh, Martin, Galway, 1927(June)–35 (d.)
McDonogh, Thomas, Galway, 1935(by)
McDowell, Derek, Dublin North-Central, 1989
McDowell, H. F., Down South (w), 1986(by)
McDowell, J. W., *Ards*, 1953; *Belfast (Duncairn)*, 1956(by), 1962, 1965; Belfast
    North (w), 1959, 1964; *Newtownabbey*, 1969
McDowell, Kathleen, Dublin North-West, 1948
McDowell, M. A., Dublin South-East, 1987–9 (def.)
MacDowell, Vincent, Dublin South-East, 1954
McDowell, Vincent, Dún Laoghaire and Rathdown, 1973
McEleney, James, Donegal East, 1951, 1954
McElgunn, Farrell, Roscommon-Leitrim, 1969, 1973; IRELAND, 1972–3
McElhinney, John, Donegal East, 1943
McElhinney, John, Galway West, 1948, 1951
McElligott, William, Kerry, 1927(June)
McEllistrim, Thomas (sen.), Kerry, 1923–37; Kerry North, 1937–69
McEllistrim, Thomas (jun.), Kerry North, 1969–7 (def.), 1989–
McElroy, Revd A. H., *Ards*, 1945; Down North (w), 1950, 1951, 1964; *Queen's
    University Belfast*, 1958, 1966(by); *Ards*, 1962; *Enniskillen*, 1965
McElroy, F. E., *Mid-Ulster*, 1975, 1982
McElvaney, Hugh, Cavan-Monaghan, 1982(Nov.)
McElwaine, Séamus, Monaghan, 1961; Cavan-Monaghan, 1982(Feb.)

McElwee, F. B., *Mid-Ulster*, 1982

McEniff, Seán, CONNACHT-ULSTER, 1979

MacEntee, S. F., Monaghan, 1921–2; *Belfast West*, 1921; *Fermanagh-Tyrone*, 1921; Dublin Co., 1923, 1923(by), 1927(June)–37; Dublin Townships, 1937–48; Dublin South-East, 1948–69

Mac Eoin, Gen. Seán, Longford-Westmeath, 1921–3; Leitrim-Sligo, 1929(by)–32; Longford-Westmeath, 1932–7; Athlone-Longford, 1937–48; Longford-Westmeath, 1948–65 (def.)

McEvoy, James, Kildare, 1973

McEvoy, Michael, Dublin North-West, 1969, 1973

McEvoy, Sean, Mayo East, 1977, 1982(Nov.)

McFadden, Brendan, Longford-Westmeath, 1989

McFadden, Michael Óg, Donegal, 1927(June)–32 (def.), 1933–7; Donegal West, 1937–51 (def.)

McFadden, Patrick, Donegal, 1923–7(June) (def.)

McFarland, Walter, *Belfast East*, 1973, 1975

McFaul, K. I., *Antrim North*, 1975–6, 1982

Mac Feorais, Martin, Dublin South, 1987

McGahey, John, Monaghan, 1937

McGahon, Brendan, Louth, 1981, 1982(Feb.), 1982(Nov.)

McGahon, Hugh, Louth, 1977

McGarry, James, Dublin South-Central, 1961

McGarry, Seán, Dublin Mid, 1921–3; Dublin North, 1923–4

McGarry, Thomas, Roscommon, 1981

McGarvey, Ian, Donegal North-East, 1982(Feb.)

McGarvey, P. J., Mid-Ulster (w), 1964

Mac Gearailt, Breandán, Kerry South, 1987

McGee, Patrick, Louth, 1923

McGeough, Pearse, LEINSTER, 1989

McGettigan, Martin, Dublin North-East, 1987

McGill, Patricia, Dublin Co. North, 1977; Dublin North, 1982(Feb.)

McGill, Patrick, *Mid-Ulster*, 1973

McGilligan, Michael, Donegal, 1933

McGilligan, P. J., National University of Ireland, 1923(Nov.)(by)–37; Dublin North-West, 1937–48; Dublin North-Central, 1948–65 (def.)

McGing, James, Mayo South, 1933, 1937

McGing, Mary, CONNACHT-ULSTER, 1984

McGinley, Denis, Donegal, 1980(by); Donegal South-West, 1981, 1982(Feb.)–

McGinley, J. P., Donegal, 1921–3

McGinley, J. P., Donegal East, 1948(Dec.)(by)

McGinley, P. J., Donegal, 1927(Sept.)

Mac Giolla, Tomas, Tipperary North, 1961; Dublin South-West, 1976(by); Dublin (Ballyfermot), 1977; Dublin West, 1981, 1982(Feb.), 1982(by), 1982(Nov.)–; DUBLIN, 1979

McGirl, J. J., Sligo-Leitrim, 1957–61 (def.), 1982(Feb.), 1987

McGivern, John, *Antrim (town)*, 1965

McGladdery, J. R., Down North (w), 1970

McGlade, Francis, Belfast North (w), 1955, 1959, 1964

McGlade, John, *Belfast (Falls)*, 1945

McGleenan, C. E., *Armagh South*, 1950(by)–8; Armagh (w), 1935, 1966

McGlinchey, Bernard, Donegal North-East, 1973; Donegal, 1977; Donegal North-East, 1981, 1982(Nov.)

McGlinchey, Daniel, Donegal East, 1943, 1944

McGoldrick, Ann, Dún Laoghaire, 1987, 1980

McGoldrick, P. J., Donegal, 1921–7(June) (def.), 1927(Sept.)

McGoldrick, T. J., Sligo, 1943

McGoldrick, T. R., Sligo-Leitrim, 1965

McGonagle, Christopher, Dublin Co., 1948

McGonagle, Stephen, *Londonderry (Foyle)*, 1958, 1962

McGorry, John, Cavan, 1938

Macgougan, John, *Belfast (Oldpark)*, 1938; Down South (w), 1950; *Belfast (Falls)*, 1953

McGourran, G. J., *Belfast (Falls)*, 1942(by)

McGovern, J. F., Cavan, 1954, 1957, 1961

McGovern, P. G., Cavan, 1933–44

McGowan, A. W., *Antrim South*, 1973

McGowan, G. L., Dublin Co., 1937–8

McGowan, Henry, Donegal, 1923

McGowan, James, Sligo-Mayo East, 1922; Leitrim-Sligo, 1927(June)

McGowan, Martin B., Leitrim-Sligo, 1923–7(June); Sligo-Leitrim, 1951, 1954

McGowan, Michael, Leitrim, 1943; Sligo-Leitrim, 1948

McGowan, P. J., Londonderry East (w), 1987

McGrady, E. K., *Down East*, 1949, 1969; *Down South*, 1973–6, 1982–6; Down South (w), 1979, 1983, 1986(by), 1987–

McGran, R. P., Dublin North-Central, 1977

McGrath, D.C., Cork Mid, 1961

McGrath, Frank, Tipperary, 1927(June)

McGrath, Joseph, Dublin North-West, 1921–3; Mayo North, 1923–4

McGrath, Martha T., Londonderry East (w), 1983

McGrath, Martin J., Mayo North, 1948, 1951, 1952(by), 1954

McGrath, Patrick (Pa), Cork Borough, 1946(by)–56 (d.)

McGrath, Paul, Longford-Westmeath, 1989–

McGrath, T. G., *Down South*, 1933

McGrattan, P. J., Down North (w), 1964

McGreal, M. J., Mayo West, 1975(by)

McGuckin, Basil, *Londonderry*, 1925–9

McGuffin, Samuel, *Belfast (North)*, 1921–5; *Belfast (Shankill)*, 1929

McGuigan, M. C. J., NORTHERN IRELAND, 1984

McGuinness, Bernard, Donegal North-East, 1981

McGuinness, Francis, Longford-Westmeath, 1922–3 (def.)

McGuinness, James M., *Londonderry*, 1982–6; Foyle (w), 1983, 1987

McGuinness, John, Leix-Offaly, 1923–5 (disqualified)

McGuinness, John, Carlow-Kilkenny, 1982(Feb.)
McGuinness, Joseph, Longford-Westmeath, 1921–2
McGuinness, Mairéad, Dublin North-East, 1957
McGuinness, Michael J., Carlow-Kilkenny, 1961
McGuinness, P. A., Roscommon, 1961; Roscommon-Leitrim, 1969
McGuinness, Séamus, Dublin South-West, 1961
McGuire, George, Mayo South, 1961
McGuire, Gerry, Laoighis-Offaly, 1981, 1982(Feb.)
McGuire, J, I., Dublin South, 1933–7 (def.)
McGuire, W. J., Roscommon, 1957
McGurk, Charles, Meath-Westmeath, 1943
McGurk, Michael, *Tyrone Mid*, 1941(by)–8 (d.)
McGurran, Malachy, Armagh, 1974(Oct.); *Armagh*, 1975
McHale, Joseph, Mayo East, 1987
McHenry, Maurice, *Antrim North*, 1975
McHenry, P. J., *Down North*, 1973
McHugh, James, Leitrim, 1943
McHugh, John, *Fermanagh-Tyrone*, 1925–9
McHugh, P. J., Bannside (w), 1970(by); Antrim North (w), 1970; *Antrim North*, 1973
McHugh, Thomas, Monaghan, 1922
McHugh, Vincent, Clare, 1951, 1954
McIntyre, Gerard, Dublin (Artane), 1977
McIntyre, P. F., Dublin North, 1923
McIvor, E. G., *Londonderry*, 1973
McIvor, W. B., *Larkfield*, 1969–73; *Belfast South*, 1973–5
Mack, J. J., Dublin south-West, 1961
McKay, John, Dublin (Cabra), 1977
McKay, John A., *Fermanagh-Tyrone South*, 1975–6
McKeague, John, Galway, 1927(June)
McKeague, John D., Belfast North (w), 1970
MacKeamey, J. G., *Armagh South*, 1950(by); *Belfast (Falls)*, 1953, 1958
McKeaveney, William, *Belfast Central*, 1934(by)
McKee, James T., Armagh (w), 1924
McKee, John (Jack), *Antrim North*, 1982–6
McKee, Sir W. Cecil, *Belfast (St Anne's)*, 1969
McKeever, Edward, Meath, 1977
McKeigue, Thomas, Laoighis-Offaly, 1989
Macken, C. A., Dublin North-West, 1943; Dublin North-Central, 1948; Dublin North-West, 1954, 1957, 1961
McKenna, James, J., Dublin (Ballyfermot), 1977
McKenna, John, Cavan-Monaghan, 1977
McKenna, John, Dublin South-East, 1982(Nov.)
McKenna, Justin C., Louth-Meath, 1921–2 (def.)
McKenna, Laurence, Louth, 1927(June), 1927(Sept.)
McKenna, Patrick, Meath-Westmeath, 1943, 1944

McKenna, Patrick, Kerry North, 1944
McKenna, Patrick J., Longford-Westmeath, 1923–7(June) (def.), 1927(Sept.)
McKenna, Patrick J., Meath, 1965
McKenna, Seán, Kerry North, 1981
McKenna, Stephen, *Mid-Ulster*, 1973, 1975
McKenna, T. P., Cavan, 1923
McKeown, Ciarán, Dublin South-West, 1969
McKeown, J. G., *Belfast East*, 1973
McKeown, Michael, *Belfast (Clifton)*, 1969
McKeown, R. J., *Belfast North*, 1921–5
McKernan, J. F., Belfast South (w), 1950
Mackey, Anthony, Limerick, 1923
McKibbin, A. J., Belfast East (w), 1950–8 (d.)
McKiernan, Patrick, Cavan-Monaghan, 1987
Macklin, Oliver, Roscommon, 1964(by)
McKnight, Robert, Belfast South (w), 1964
McKnight, Seán, Belfast South (w), 1983, 1987
McLachlan, P. J., *Antrim South*, 1973–5 (def.); Belfast East (w), 1974(Oct.)
McLaughlin, Daniel, *Tyrone North*, 1969
McLaughlin, F. P A., Belfast West (w), 1955–64
McLaughlin, Seán, Donegal North-East, 1961, 1965
McLeavey, Kevin, Wicklow, 1968(by)
MacLogan, P. J., *Armagh South*, 1933–8
McLoughlin, Anthony (Tony), Sligo-Leitrim, 1981
McLoughlin, Frank, Meath, 1977, 1981, 1982(Nov.)–7 (def.)
McLoughlin, George, Dublin South-Central, 1961, 1965
McLoughlin, John, Donegal East, 1937, 1948
McLoughlin, Joseph, Sligo-Leitrim, 1961(Mar.)(by)–77 (def.)
McLoughlin, K. F., Mayo East, 1969
McMahon, Bernadette, Meath, 1987
McMahon, James, Dublin Co., 1961, 1965; Dublin South-West, 1969
McMahon, John, Leix-Offaly, 1938
McMahon, Lawrence, Dublin Co South, 1970(by)–7; Dublin Co. Mid, 1977–
    81; Dublin South-West, 1981–2(Nov.) (def.), 1987, 1989
McMahon, Mary, *Belfast West*, 1982; Belfast West (w), 1983, 1987
McMahon, Patrick, Meath-Westmeath, 1943
McMahon, Patrick C., Clare, 1943
McMahon, Pearse, Antrim North (w), 1983
McManamy, John, Carlow-Kilkenny, 1969, 1973
MacManaway, Revd J. G., *Londonderry City*, 1947(by)–51; Belfast West (w),
    1950 (elected but disqualified)
McManus, Elizabeth (Liz), LEINSTER, 1984
McManus, F. J., Fermanagh-Tyrone South (w), 1970–4(Feb.) (def.)
McManus, J. U., Wicklow, 1977, 1981, 1982(Feb.), 1982(Nov.), 1987
McManus, Michael, Kildare, 1982(Nov.)
McManus, Patrick, Belfast North, 1987

McManus, Seán, Sligo-Leitrim, 1977, 1989
McManus, Thomas, Longford-Westmeath, 1948
McMaster, B. J. H., Belfast West (w), 1970
McMaster, Joseph, *Belfast (Victoria)*, 1938
McMaster, S. R., Belfast East (w), 1959(Mar.)(by)–74(Feb.) (def.); Belfast South (w), 1974(Oct.)
McMenamin, Daniel, Donegal, 1923, 1927(June–Sept.), 1932–7; Donegal East, 1937–61
McMenamy, B. P., Dublin West, 1987
McMichael, Gary, Upper Bann (w), 1990(by)
McMichael, John, Belfast South (w), 1982(by)
McMillan, William, *Belfast (Ballynafeigh)*, 1938
McMillan, William, Belfast West (w), 1964
McMordie, Julia, *Belfast South*, 1921–5
McMullan, T. W., *Down*, 1921–9
McMullan, William, *Belfast West*, 1925–9; *Belfast (Falls)*, 1929; *Belfast Central*, 1934(by)
McMurrough Kavanagh, Arthur, Carlow-Kilkenny, 1927(June)
McNabb, Dinah, *Armagh North*, 1945–69
Macnaghten, Capt. E. L., Londonderry (w), 1922
Macnaghten, Sir M. M., Londonderry North (w), 1922(June(by)–Nov.); Londonderry (w), 1922–8
McNally, H. G., *Armagh*, 1973
McNally, John, Galway, 1923
McNally, John, Carlow-Kilkenny, 1977
McNamara, Bernard, Clare, 1981
MacNamara, J. J., Limerick, 1943
MacNamara, P. J., Clare, 1923
MacNamara, Thomas, Galway South, 1953(by)
McNamee, Séamus, Longford-Westmeath, 1987
McNarry, D. M., *Belfast East*, 1973, 1975; *Down North*, 1982
McNeice, R. J., *Belfast South*, 1975
Mac Néill, Prof. Eoin, *Londonderry*, 1921–5; National University of Ireland, 1921–3 (elected but chooses to sit for Clare), 1927(June); Clare, 1923–7(June)
McNeill, RN, *Queen's University Belfast*, 1929–35
McNelis, Michael, Donegal, 1923
Maconachie, Elizabeth (Bessie) H., *Queen's University Belfast*, 1953–69
McParland, James, *Armagh South*, 1958
McPhillips, Ivan, CONNACHT-ULSTER, 1989
McQuade, John, *Belfast (Woodvale)*, 1965–73; *Belfast North*, 1973–5; Belfast West (w), 1974(Feb.), 1974(Oct.); Belfast North (w), 1979–83
McQuaid, Patrick, Cavan, 1923
McQuaid, W. G., *Mid-Ulster*, 1982
McQuillan, D. F., *Fermanagh-Tyrone South*, 1973, 1982
McQuillan, John, Roscommon, 1948–65 (def.)

Mac Raghnaill, Donnchadha, Louth, 1973, 1977, 1981, 1982(Feb.), 1982(Nov.), 1987; LEINSTER, 1979

McRoberts, B. J. H., *Armagh South*, 1962

McShane, Michael, Dublin South-Central, 1969, 1973

McShane, P. R., *Down South*, 1973

MacSharry, Raymond, Sligo-Leitrim, 1969–89(May) (res.); CONNACHT-ULSTER, 1984–7

McSorley, Dr Frederick, *Queen's University Belfast*, 1933, 1938, 1945–8 (d.)

McSorley, M. K., *Mid-Ulster*, 1982–6

McSorley, Peter, *Armagh South*, 1965

McSparran, James, *Mourne*, 1945–58

McStay, Anne, Dublin West, 1981

McSweeney, Jeremiah, Kerry, 1923

MacSwiney, Mary, Cork Borough, 1921–7(June) (def.)

MacSwiney, Seán, Cork Mid/North/South/South-East/West, 1921–2 (def.)

McTigue, F. K., Clare, 1982(Feb.)

Mac Ualtair, Murchadh, Galway South, 1957, 1958(by)

McVea, V. S., *Belfast (Ballynafeigh)*, 1953, 1958

McVeagh, Jeremiah, *Down South*, 1922(by), Monaghan, 1927(June)

McWey, Michael, Kildare, 1969

MacWhinney, Charles, Londonderry (w), 1924; *Londonderry*, 1925

McWilliam, H. R., Monaghan, 1957

Madden, D. J., Limerick, 1932, 1944; Limerick West, 1948–55 (d.)

Madden, J. A., Mayo North, 1924(by)–7(Sept.)

Madden, William, Limerick West, 1967(by)

Magee, Brian, Monaghan, 1954

Magee, Margaret T., Down South (w), 1983

Magee, Michael J., Cavan, 1943

Magee, R. A. E., *Belfast South*, 1973–5 (def.)

Magee, S. D., Down South (w), 1986(by)

Magee, Thomas, *Larkfield*, 1969

Magennis, Carlow-Kilkenny, 1927(June)

Magennis, Prof. William, National University of Ireland, 1922–7(June) (def.)

Magill, William, *Belfast South*, 1925; *Belfast (Windsor)*, 1929

Maginess, W. B., *Iveagh*, 1938–64

Maginness, Alban, *Belfast East*, 1975; *Belfast North*, 1982; Antrim South (w), 1983; Belfast North (w), 1987

Maginnis, J. F., Armagh (w), 1959–74(Feb.); *Armagh*, 1975

Maginnis, Kenneth, Fermanagh-Tyrone South, 1982–6; Fermanagh-Tyrone South (w), 1981(by), 1983–5, 1986(by)–

Magowan, J. I., *Armagh Mid*, 1969

Magowan, Samuel, *Iveagh*, 1964(by)–73

Maguire, B. J., Leitrim-Sligo, 1927(June), 1927(Sept.)–37; Leitrim, 1937–48; Sligo-Leitrim, 1948–51 (def.), 1954–7 (def.)

Maguire, C. A., National University of Ireland, 1927(Sept.); Dublin Co., 1930(by); National University of Ireland, 1932–7

Maguire, Daniel, Carlow-Kilkenny, 1954
Maguire, Francis, Dublin North-West, 1982(Nov.)
Maguire, G. C., Mayo South, 1932, 1933
Maguire, Hugh, Monaghan, 1923
Maguire, Joseph, *Fermanagh-Tyrone South*, 1982
Maguire, L. J., Dublin South-Central, 1969, 1973
Maguire, M. Francis, Fermanagh-Tyrone South (w), 1974(Oct.)–81 (d.)
Maguire, Patrick, Limerick East, 1957
Maguire, Patrick J., Monaghan, 1948–54
Maguire, Paul, *Belfast North*, 1982–6; Belfast North (w), 1983, 1986(by)
Maguire, Thomas, Mayo South-Roscommon South, 1921–3; Mayo South, 1923–7(June)
Maher, Bryan, Meath, 1987
Maher, James, Dublin North-Central, 1961, 1965
Maher, Martin, Tipperary, 1927(June)
Maher, Peadar, Leix-Offaly, 1951–61
Maher, T. J., MUNSTER, 1979– ; Tipperary South, 1981
Mahoney, James, Wexford, 1969
Mahony, Philip, Kilkenny, 1943–4 (def.)
Maitland, S. E., *Down West*, 1945
Makowski, Brigid, Clare, 1982(Feb.), 1987
Mallon, S. F., *Armagh*, 1973–6; 1982 (elected but disqualified); Armagh (w), 1974(Oct.), 1979; Newry and Armagh (w), 1983, 1986(by)–
Malone, Bernard, Dublin North-East, 1981, 1982(Feb.); Dublin North, 1982(Nov.), 1987
Malone, James, Monaghan, 1969
Malone, John, Dublin (Clontarf), 1977
Malone, Pádraig, Limerick East, 1987
Malone, Patrick, Kildare, 1964(by), 1970(by)–7 (def.)
Malone, Simon, Kildare, 1923
Malone, Thomas, Tipperary, 1943
Malone, Thomas, Limerick East, 1948
Maloney, Eamonn, Dublin South-West, 1987
Mandeville, J. P., Waterford-Tipperary East, 1922
Manley, Tadhg (Timothy), Cork South, 1951, 1954–61; Cork Borough, 1964(by)
Manning, Joseph, Carlow-Kilkenny, 1982(Nov.)
Manning, Maurice, DUBLIN, 1979; Dublin North-East, 1981, 1982(Feb.)–7 (def.), 1989
Manning, Vincent, Dublin (Clontarf), 1977; Dublin North-East, 1982(Nov.)
Mannion, Brian, Galway West, 1987
Mannion, John, Galway West, 1951–4 (def.), 1957, 1965
Mannion, John M., Galway West, 1969, 1973, 1975(by), 1977–81
Mannion, Michael, Galway North, 1948
Mansfield, Michael, Waterford, 1932, 1933

Mark, J. M., *Londonderry*, 1921–9; *Londonderry North*, 1929–33

Markey, Bernard, Monaghan, 1969, 1973; Louth, 1977, 1981–92(Nov.) (def.), 1989

Markey, J. E., Down South (w), 1979

Markievicz, C. G. de, Dublin South, 1921–2 (def.), 1923–7(July) (d.)

Marks, J. C., *Down North*, 1965, 1973

Marrinan, D. P., *Belfast Central*, 1958

Marry, Gerard, Meath, 1965, 1969

Marry, Gerard, Meath, 1987

Marsh, Arnold, Dún Laoghaire and Rathdown, 1948

Marsh, Philip, Dublin (Artane), 1977

Martin, James H., Fermanagh-Tyrone South (w), 1959

Martin, James J., Leix (Laoighis)-Offaly, 1957, 1961, 1965

Martin, John W. N., *Belfast (Woodvale)*, 1955(by)–8 (def.)

Martin, Leo, Dublin Central, 1982(Feb.)

Martin, Michael, Dublin North-Central, 1981

Martin, Mícheál, Cork South-Central, 1987, 1989–

Martin, Thomas, *Armagh Central*, 1945

Martin, W. J., *Down South*, 1973, 1982

Maskey, Alexander, *Belfast West*, 1982

Mason, R. L., *Belfast East*, 1973

Masterson, Frank, Kildare, 1987

Matthews, A. P., Meath, 1927(Sept.)–32 (def.)

Matthews, Christopher, Meath, 1923, 1927(June)

Matthews, Damien, Cavan-Monaghan, 1989

Matthews, George, *Belfast (Victoria)*, 1945

Matthews, William, *Londonderry*, 1975, 1982

Mawhinney, Gordon, *Antrim South*, 1982–6; Antrim South (w), 1983, 1987

Maxwell, Patrick, *Londonderry (Foyle)*, 1937(by)–53 (def.)

May, W. M., *Ards*, 1949–62(Mar.) (d.)

Meagher, Martin, Tipperary, 1923

Meagher, Michael A., Dublin North-West, 1982(Nov.)

Meagher, Thomas, Tipperary, 1943

Meaney, Cornelius (Con), Cork North, 1937–43 (def.), 1944, 1948, 1951; Cork Mid, 1961–5

Meaney, Michael, Carlow-Kilkenny, 1982(Nov.)

Meaney, T. J., Clare, 1987, 1989

Meaney, T. J. V., Cork Mid, 1965–81; Cork North-West, 1981–2(Nov.)

Medlar, Martin, Carlow-Kilkenny, 1956(by)–65 (def.)

Medlar, P.C., Dublin South, 1923, 1932, 1937

Mee, John, Mayo West, 1982(Nov.)

Meegan, P. O., Meath, 1951

Meehan, F. J., Galway, 1932

Meighan, J. J., Roscommon 1943–4 (def.)

Megaw, R. D., *Antrim*, 1921–5 (def.)

Megraw, S. L., *Belfast (Woodvale)*, 1945
Melaugh, Eamonn, Londonderry, 1979; *Londonderry*, 1982; Foyle (w), 1983, 1987
Melia, D. C., Dublin (Clontarf), 1977
Mellows, H. C., Galway, 1923–7(June) (def.)
Mellows, L. J., Galway, 1921–2 (def.)
Melvin, Hugh, Clare-Galway South, 1973
Merrigan, Matthew, Dublin South-West, 1954, 1970(by); Dublin (Finglas), 1977; Dublin North-West, 1981; Dublin West, 1982(May)(by)
Midgley, H. C., *Belfast East*, 1921; Belfast West (w), 1923, 1924; *Belfast (Dock)*, 1933–8 (def.); *Belfast (Willowfield)*, 1941(by)–58; Belfast South (w), 1945
Miley, James, Wicklow, 1969, 1973, 1977
Miley, Martin, Kildare, 1977, 1981
Millar, A. G., Galway South, 1958(by)–6l; Galway East, 1961–9
Millar, C. G., *Londonderry City*, 1933
Millar, Frank (sen.), *Belfast North*, 1973–6, 1982–6
Millar, Frank (jun.), *Antrim South*, 1982; *Belfast South*, 1984(by)–6; Belfast West (w), 1987
Millar, Gerard, Clare-Galway South, 1969
Millea, Patrick, Carlow-Kilkenny, 1987, 1989
Miller, Alexander, Cork Borough, 1965
Miller, J. B., *Antrim North*, 1973
Miller, Samuel, *Tyrone East*, 1949
Miller, W. T., *Fermanagh-Tyrone*, 1921–9; *Tyrone North*, 1929–30 (d.)
Mills, W. S., Belfast North (w), 1959–74(Feb.)
Milne Barbour, *see* Barbour
Milner, W. H., Leix-Offaly, 1948
Milroy, Seán, *Fermanagh-Tyrone*, 1921–4; Cavan, 1921–5; Dublin North, 1925(by); Cavan, 1927(June) Minch, Capt. S. B., Kildare, 1932–7; Carlow-Kildare, 1937–8 (def.)
Minford, Hugh, *Antrim (town)*, 1929–50 (d.)
Minford, N. O., *Antrim (town)*, 1951(by)–73; *Antrim South*, 1973–5
Minford, T. F. B., *Bannside*, 1970(by)
Minihan, Eoin, Wexford, 1987
Minihane, Daniel, Cork West, 1923
Mistéil, Bhaltar, Leix-Offaly, 1957
Mistéil, Tomás, *see* Mitchell, T. J.
Mitchell, Lt. Col. Dr A. B., *Queen's University Belfast*, 1929, 1935(by)–42 (d.)
Mitchell, Gabriel (Gay), Dublin South-Central, 1981–
Mitchell, James, Dublin South-West, 1970(by), 1973, 1976(by); Dublin (Ballyfermot), 1977–81; Dublin West, 1981–
Mitchell, M. T., Galway North-East, 1973
Mitchell, Olivia, Dublin South, 1989
Mitchell, P. G., Dublin North-West, 1982(Nov.)
Mitchell, Maj. R. J., *Armagh North*, 1969–73; *Armagh*, 1973

Mitchell, T. J., Mid-Ulster (w), 1955 (elected but disqualified), 1955(by) (elected but disqualified), 1956(by), 1959, 1964, 1966; Dublin North-East, 1957, 1961

Mitchell, William, *Fermanagh-Tyrone South*, 1973

Moane, Edward, Mayo South, 1927(June), 1927(Sept.), 1932–8 (def.)

Moclair, T. S., Mayo South, 1927(June), 1932

Mockler, Frank, Cork Borough, 1965

Moher, J. W., Cork East, 1951, 1953(by), 1954–61; Cork North-East, 1961–5 (def.)

Molan, Cornelius, Cork East, 1923

Moles, P. G., *Belfast South*, 1982

Moles, Thomas, Belfast South (w), 1922–9; *Belfast South*, 1921–9; *Belfast (Ballynafeigh)*, 1929–37 (d.)

Molloy, Aloysius, Fermanagh-Tyrone South (w), 1964

Molloy, F. J., *Fermanagh-Tyrone South*, 1982

Molloy, Robert, Galway West, 1965–; CONNACHT-ULSTER, 1989

Moloney, D. J., Kerry North, 1956(by), 1957–61 (def.)

Moloney, Patrick J., Tipperary Mid/North/South, 1921–3

Moloney, Peter P., Tipperary, 1923

Molony, David, Tipperary North, 1982(Feb.)–7

Molyneaux, J. H., Antrim South (w), 1970–83; Lagan Valley (w), 1983–5, 1986(by)–; *Antrim South*, 1982–6

Monaghan, Brian, Donegal, 1923

Monaghan, Eamonn, Donegal South-West, 1987

Monaghan, K. A., Donegal North-East, 1987

Monaghan, Séamus, Donegal, 1927(June)

Monahan, Edward, Clare, 1945(by), 1948

Mongan, J. W., Galway, 1927(June), 1927(Sept.)–33 (def.); Galway West, 1937–51

Montague, Richard, *Belfast (Duncairn)*, 1962

Montgomery, A. H., Monaghan, 1948

Montgomery, John, Dublin (Ballyfermot), 1977; Dublin West, 1981, 1982(Feb.), 1982(Nov.), 1987, 1989

Montgomery, M. J., Londonderry (w), 1974(Feb.), 1974(Oct.)

Moody, Phoebe, *Belfast (Bloomfield)*, 1938

Mooney, A. J., Leitrim-Sligo, 1925(by), 1927(June), 1932; Leitrim, 1938

Mooney, James, Dublin South-Central, 1961; Dublin Central, 1969, 1973

Mooney, Joseph M., Leitrim, 1943; Sligo-Leitrim, 1954, 1961, 1969, 1973

Mooney, Mary, Dublin South-Central, 1987–9 (def.)

Mooney, Patrick, Monaghan, 1948, 1954–69 (def.), 1973, 1973(by)

Moore, Anne, Kildare, 1969

Moore, John, Kerry, 1932

Moore, Col. Joseph S., Wicklow, 1923

Moore, M. P., Leix-Offaly, 1948

Moore, Patrick, Limerick East, 1982(Nov.)

Moore, Patrick M., *Down*, 1921

Moore, Peter, Louth, 1961

Moore, Richard G., Antrim North (w), 1966, 1970

Moore, Revd Robert, *Londonderry North*, 1938–60 (d.)

Moore, Séamus, Wicklow, 1927(June)–43

Moore, Seán, Dublin South-East, 1957, 1961, 1965–82(Feb.) (def.), 1982(Nov.)

Moore, Terence, LEINSTER, 1989

Moore, Thomas O., Armagh (w), 1974(Feb.), 1979; *Armagh*, 1975; Fermanagh-Tyrone South (w), 1981(by); *Down South*, 1982; Newry and Armagh (w), 1983

Morahan, B. A., Mayo West, 1975(by), 1977

Morahan, J. T., Mayo South, 1943

Morahan, O. P., Mayo South, 1957, 1965

Moran, Brendan, Dublin South-Central, 1982(Nov.)

Moran, Frank, Mayo North, 1951

Moran, James, Roscommon, 1923

Moran, John, Dublin South-West, 1948

Moran, Martin T., Mayo South, 1932

Moran, Michael, Mayo South, 1937, 1938–69; Mayo West, 1969–73 (def.); Galway West, 1977

Moran, Noel, Clare, 1989

Moran, Robert, Wexford, 1938, 1944, 1945(by)

Morgan, Arthur, Louth, 1987, 1989

Morgan, J. W., *Belfast (Cromac)*, 1953–62

Morgan, Murtagh, *Belfast (Dock)*, 1953–8

Morgan, Norman, Clare-Galway South, 1969, 1973; Galway North-East, 1975(by); Galway East, 1977, 1982(July)(by)

Morgan, Patrick, Dublin South, 1927(June)

Morgan, S. M., Belfast South, 1973

Morgan, W. J., *Belfast (Oldpark)*, 1949–58 (def.); *Belfast (Clifton)*, 1959(by)–69 (def.); *Antrim South*, 1970(by); *Belfast North*, 1973–6

Moriarty, John, Carlow-Kilkenny, 1957, 1961, 1965

Morley, P. J., Mayo East, 1973, 1977–

Moroney, Anthony, Dublin South-Central, 1957

Moroney, Terence, Waterford, 1982(Nov.)

Moroney, William (Bill), Wexford, 1982(Feb.)

Morrell, L. J., *Londonderry*, 1973–5 (def.)

Morris, Christopher, CONNACHT-ULSTER, 1979

Morris, Frank, Donegal East, 1957

Morris, J. F., Dublin Co., 1927(June)

Morris, Patrick, Tipperary, 1927(June)

Morris, Patrick, Galway West, 1943

Morris, Pearse, Dublin Co. South, 1969

Morrison, D. G., *Mid-Ulster*, 1982–6; Mid-Ulster (w), 1983, 1986(by); NORTHERN IRELAND, 1984, 1989

Morrison, George, *Antrim South*, 1975–6

Morrison, Dr H. S., *Queen's University Belfast*, 1921–9

Morrisroe, James, Mayo North, 1933–7; Mayo South, 1937

Morrissey, Daniel, Tipperary Mid/North/South, 1922–3; Tipperary, 1923–48; Tipperary North, 1948–57

Morrissey, John, Tipperary South, 1948, 1951, 1954, 1957

Morrissey, John, *Belfast West,* 1975

Morrissey, Michael, Waterford, 1937–47 (d.)

Morrow, A. J., *Belfast East,* 1982–6; Strangford (w), 1983, 1987

Morrow, James, *Belfast (Duncairn),* 1945, 1949, 1949(by); *Belfast South,* 1945, 1951

Mortell, Charles, Cork East, 1981

Mortished, R. J. P., Dublin North, 1927(June)

Moylan, Patrick, Galway North-East, 1969; Roscommon, 1981

Moylan, Seán, Cork Mid/North/South/South-East/West, 1921–3; Cork North, 1932–57 (def.)

Moynihan, Donal, Cork North-West, 1981, 1982(Feb.), 1982(Nov.)–9 (def.)

Moynihan, James, Cork West, 1951

Moynihan, Michael, Kerry South, 1954, 1961, 1965, 1966(by), 1973, 1977, 1981–7 (def.), 1989–

Mulcahy, D. A., Leitrim-Sligo, 1923

Mulcahy, Liam, Belfast East (w), 1955

Mulcahy, Noel, Dublin North-Central, 1977

Mulcahy, Gen. R. J., Dublin North-West, 1921–3; Dublin North, 1923–37; Dublin North-East, 1937, 1938–43 (def.); Tipperary, 1944–8; Tipperary South, 1948–61

Muldoon, Mary, *Belfast West,* 1982

Muldowney, Patrick, Leix-Offaly, 1948

Mulhern, Paul, Dublin Co. Mid, 1977

Mulholland, Capt. Hon. H. G. H., *Down,* 1921–9; *Ards,* 1929–45

Mulholland, Patrick, Louth, 1969

Mullan, C. H., *Down South,* 1945; Down (w), 1946(by)–50

Mullarney, Máire, Dublin South-East, 1982(Nov.), 1987; Dublin North-East, 1989

Mullen, Eugene, Mayo South, 1927(June–Sept.) (def.)

Mullen, Frederick, Dublin North-Central, 1957

Mullen, Michael, Dublin North-Central, 1951; Dublin North-West, 1957, 1961–9; Dublin (Cabra), 1977

Mullen, Thomas, Dublin Co., 1933, 1935(by), 1938–43

Mulligan, Angela, Dublin North-East, 1989

Mullins, Thomas, Cork West, 1927(June)–32

Mullins, Thomas L., Carlow-Kildare, 1943, 1944; Dublin Co., 1947(by)

Mullins, William, Kilkenny, 1943

Mulroy, James, Louth, 1987

Mulvany, P. J., Meath, 1923–7(June)

Mulvey, Anthony, Fermanagh-Tyrone (w), 1935–50; Mid-Ulster (w), 1950–1

Munden, P. J., Dublin South, 1923

Munnelly, John, Mayo North, 1927(Sept.), 1932, 1933, 1937–43

Munro, James, Dublin (Artane), 1977

Murnaghan, S. M., Belfast South (w), 1959; *Queen's University Belfast*, 1961 (by)–9; *Down North*, 1969; *Belfast South*, 1973; Down North (w), 1966

Murney, Michael, Down (w), 1924

Murnoy, Peter, *Down South*, 1945–9

Murphy, Aidan, Wicklow, 1987

Murphy, Bernard, Cork North-Central, 1987; Cork South-Central, 1987

Murphy, Catherine, Kildare, 1969; LEINSTER, 1989

Murphy, Charles, Dublin South, 1921–2 (def.), 1923–7 (June) (def.), 1927 (Aug.) (by)

Murphy, Ciarán P., Wicklow, 1973–82 (Nov.) (def.), 1989

Murphy, Conn, Dublin Co., 1923; Dublin North, 1927 (June)

Murphy, Declan, Cork South-Central, 1982 (Feb.)

Murphy, E. S., *Londonderry City*, 1929–39

Murphy, G. C., Dublin North-Central, 1965

Murphy, James, Carlow-Kilkenny, 1933

Murphy, James, *Londonderry North*, 1945

Murphy, James, Louth, 1957

Murphy, James, Dublin Co. South, 1969, 1970 (by), 1973, 1977

Murphy, James E., Louth-Meath, 1921–3; Louth, 1923–37 (def.)

Murphy, John, Tipperary North, 1948

Murphy, John, Dublin South-Central, 1957–8

Murphy, John D., *Belfast (St Anne's)*, 1969

Murphy, Joseph X., Dublin Co., 1927 (Sept.)–32 (def.)

Murphy, Liam, Carlow-Kilkenny, 1973

Murphy, Matthew J., Limerick, 1923, 1927 (June)

Murphy, Michael, Wexford, 1936 (by)

Murphy, Michael, Limerick West, 1969

Murphy, Michael F., Cork North-Central, 1987, 1989; Cork South-Central, 1987

Murphy, Michael P., Cork West, 1951–61; Cork South-West, 1961–81

Murphy, Noel, Dublin Co. Mid, 1977

Murphy, Noel, Dublin South-West, 1982 (Nov.)

Murphy, Noel, Cork North-Central, 1987, 1989

Murphy, Patrick, Cork East, 1927 (June)

Murphy, Patrick S., Cork East, 1932–7; Cork North, 1937

Murphy, Patrick T., Dublin Co., 1957, 1961; Dublin Co. North, 1969, 1977

Murphy, Peter, Longford-Westmeath, 1987

Murphy, Philip, Cork South-West, 1981

Murphy, Robert J., Wexford, 1945 (by), 1948

Murphy, Robert R., *Armagh*, 1973

Murphy, Ronald, Cork Borough, 1965

Murphy, Samuel, *Antrim North*, 1975

Murphy, Séamus, Dublin North-East, 1954

Murphy, Thomas, Kildare, 1927 (Sept.)

Murphy, Thomas, Leix-Offaly, 1948

Murphy, Timothy J., Cork West, 1923–49 (d.)
Murphy, William, Clare, 1937
Murphy, William, Clare, 1951–67 (d.)
Murphy, William J., Cork West, 1949(by)–51
Murphy, William M., Dublin North-East, 1951
Murray, Aidan, Cavan-Monaghan, 1981
Murray, Brian, Dublin (Artane), 1977
Murray, Damien, Dublin Co. South, 1973
Murray, Fintan, Dublin North-West, 1973
Murray, Frederick, Cork Borough, 1923
Murray, James, NORTHERN IRELAND, 1979
Murray, John A., Tipperary South, 1948
Murray, Patrick, Dublin North-West, 1943
Murray, Patrick, Dublin South-Central, 1989
Murray, Thomas, Athlone-Longford, 1943
Murray, Thomas, *Fermanagh-Tyrone South*, 1975
Murrin, Joseph, CONNACHT-ULSTER, 1984
Mussen, George, Down South (w), 1964, 1966
Myers, William, Kerry South, 1943
Myles, Maj. J. S., Donegal, 1923–37; Donegal East, 1937–43 (def.), 1944
Mylotte, Martin, Galway West, 1951

Nagle, M. J., Cork Borough, 1927(Sept.)
Nagle, Thomas, Dublin South, 1927(June)
Nagle, Thomas A., Cork Mid/North/South/South-East/West, 1922–3; Cork
    North, 1923–7(June)
Nagle, Thomas J., Cork East, 1989
Nally, M. M., Mayo South, 1923–43 (def.)
Napier, O.J., *Belfast East*, 1973–6, 1982–6; Belfast East (w), 1979, 1983,
    1986(by); NORTHERN IRELAND, 1979
Napier, Samuel, *Down North*, 1949; Belfast South (w), 1952(by); *Queen's
    University Belfast*, 1953
Narain, Jagat, Belfast South (w), 1982(by)
Nash, Patrick, Belfast West (w), 1924
Naughten, Liam, Roscommon-Leitrim, 1977; Roscommon, 1981, 1982(Feb.)–
    99 (def.)
Naughton, William, Dublin South-Central, 1948
Naughton, William, Dublin Central, 1969
Nealon, Donal, Tipperary North, 1965
Nealon, Edward (Ted), Dublin (Clontarf), 1977; Sligo-Leitrim, 1981–
Nealon, John, Dublin Central, 1969
Nealon, Leo, Dublin North-Central, 1965
Neary, J. P., Dublin North, 1927(June)
Neeson, Seán, *Antrim North*, 1982–6; Antrim East (w), 1983, 1986(by), 1987
Neilan, Martin, Galway, 1936(by)–7
Neill, Maj. Ivan, *Belfast (Ballynafeigh)*, 1949–73

257

Neill, S. D., *Antrim South*, 1982
Neill, W. F., Belfast North (w), 1945–50
Nelson, T. C., *Enniskillen*, 1949(Oct.)(by)–58
Nestor, J. J., Galway, 1927(June), 1927(Sept.)
Neville, Daniel, Limerick West, 1987
Neville, Edward, Cork North, 1923
Neville, Laurence, Cork Borough, 1954
Nevin, Michael, Sligo, 1943, 1944; Sligo-Leitrim, 1951
Newcombe, Cahal, *Londonderry*, 1975
Newell, Cecil, *Mourne*, 1969
Newell, Martin, Galway South, 1948
Newell, Thomas, *Armagh Central*, 1962; *Armagh*, 1973
News, Hugh, *Armagh*, 1973–6; 1982–6
Ní Chinnéide, Bláithnaid, Dublin South-West, 1976(by)
Ní Chionnaith, Ite, Dublin South-West, 1976(by)
Nicholson, J. F., *Armagh*, 1982–6; Newry and Armagh (w), 1983–5 1986(by), 1987; NORTHERN IRELAND 1989–
Nicolls, George, Galway 1921–7(June)
Ní Dhubhghaill Ní Dhuinn, M. M., Dublin Central, 1989
Ní Ghidhir, Áine Louth, 1982(Nov.)
Ní Scolláin Nóirín, *see* Butler
Nix, G. M., Clare, 1981
Nixon, J. W., *Belfast North*, 1925; *Belfast (Woodvale)*, 1929–49 (d.)
Nixon, R. S., *Down North*, 1953–69; Down North (w), 1970
Noble, Cecil, *Fermanagh-Tyrone South*, 1982
Noctor, John, Wexford, 1932
Nohilly, John, Galway North, 1948
Nolan, I. A., Dublin West, 1981
Nolan, James, Roscommon-Leitrim, 1969
Nolan, James, Tipperary North, 1987
Nolan, Jeremiah P., Kerry North, 1948
Nolan, John P. Carlow-Kilkenny, 1927(June)
Nolan, John T., Limerick, 1923–7(June) (def.), 1927(Sept.)–32 (def.), 1933
Nolan, M. J., Carlow-Kilkenny, 1982(Nov.)
Nolan, Michael G., Kildare, 1948, 1951
Nolan, Patrick, Carlow-Kildare, 1937
Nolan, Samuel, Dublin Central, 1969
Nolan, Seán, Cork Mid/North/South/South-East/West 1921–2 (def.)
Nolan, Thomas, Carlow-Kilkenny, 1961, 1965–82(Feb.) (def.); IRELAND, 1972–9; LEINSTER, 1979
Nolan, William, Carlow-Kilkenny, 1954
Nolan, William (Bill), Cork North-Central, 1982(Nov.)
Noonan, Elizabeth (Liz), Dublin South-East, 1981, 1982(Feb.), 1982(Nov.)
Noonan, John, DUBLIN, 1984; Dublin South-West, 1987
Noonan, Joseph, MUNSTER, 1989

Noonan, Mary, Cork East, 1981
Noonan, Michael, Limerick East, 1981–
Noonan, Michael J., Limerick West, 1969–
Noonan, Michael K., Cork East, 1924(by)–7(June) (def.)
Norris, Walter, Waterford, 1943
Norris, William A., *Londonderry*, 1982
Norris, Denis, Wexford 1977, 1981
Norton, Patrick, Kildare, 1964(by), 1965–9 (def.)
Norton, Patrick, Dublin South-East, 1973
Norton, William, Dublin Co., 1926(by)–7(June) (def.); Kildare, 1931(by),
    1932–7; Carlow-Kildare, 1937–48; Kildare, 1948–63 (d.)
Nugent, John D., Dublin South-Central, 1965
Nugent, John Dillon, *Armagh*, 1921–5 (def.)
Nugent, John J., Donegal East, 1954
Nugent, Martin, Limerick East, 1987
Nugent, P. J., Dublin North-West, 1937

O Baoill, Cathal, Down North (w), 1983
O'Beirne, Francis, Leitrim-Sligo, 1925(by)
O'Beirne, Frank, Sligo, 1944
Ó Brádaigh, Ruairí, *see* Brady, Rory
Ó Briain, Donnchadh, Limerick, 1932, 1933–48; Limerick West, 1948–69
Ó Briain, Liam, *see* O'Brien
O'Brien, C. Cruise, *see* Cruise-O'Brien
O'Brien, Derek, Belfast West (w), 1979
O'Brien, D. J., Cork Borough, 1961
O'Brien, Eamonn, Dublin Co. North, 1977
O'Brien, Eugene P., Leix-Offaly, 1932–3 (def.)
O'Brien, Fergus, Dublin South-East, 1969, 1973–7; Dublin South-Central,
    1977–8(Feb.) (def.), 1982(Nov.)–
O'Brien, Francis, Carlow-Kilkenny, 1961
O'Brien, Hugh, Clare, 1977, 1981
O'Brien, Hugh, Longford-Westmeath, 1989
O'Brien, James, Limerick, 1923
O'Brien, James, Longford-Westmeath, 1969
O'Brien, Michael, Galway, 1923
O'Brien, Michael, Waterford, 1927(June)
O'Brien, Patrick, Cork East, 1933
O'Brien, Patrick, Meath, 1961
O'Brien, Patrick, Tipperary South, 1969
O'Brien, Patrick J., Cork South-East, 1943; Cork Borough, 1944; Cork East,
    1948
O'Brien, Ria, Waterford, 1977
O'Brien, Seán, Meath, 1982(Feb.); Laoighis-Offaly, 1984(by)
O'Brien, Stan, Dublin North-East, 1961, 1963(by), 1965
O'Brien, Thomas, Dublin Co. South, 1969

O'Brien, William, Dublin South, 1922–3 (def.); Tipperary, 1927(June–Sept.) (def.), 1933, 1937–8 (def.)

O'Brien, William, Limerick West, 1969, 1973, 1977–87

O'Brien, William H., Limerick, 1923

O'Byrne, J. J., Wexford, 1922

O'Byrne, P. J., Count, Tipperary, Mid/North/South, 1921–2 (def.)

O'Byrne, T. M., Dublin South, 1938

O'Byrne-Cregan, John, Dublin North-Central, 1957(Nov.)(by)

O'Callaghan, Daniel, Wexford, 1922–3 (def.)

O'Callaghan, Donal, Cork Borough, 1921–2 (def.)

O'Callaghan, Enda, see Denning

O'Callaghan, Joseph, Cork North-Central, 1987

O'Callaghan, Katherine, Limerick City-Limerick East, 1921–3; Limerick, 1923

O'Callaghan, Kevin C., Cork North, 1951

O'Callaghan, Patrick, Cork Mid, 1972(by)

Ó Caoláin, Caoimhghín, CONNACHT-ULSTER, 1984, 1989; Cavan-Monaghan, 1987, 1989

O'Carroll, Edward, Dublin North, 1923

O'Carroll, Harry, Sligo-Leitrim, 1965

O'Carroll, Maureen, Dublin North-Central, 1954–7 (def.)

O'Carroll, Richard, Wicklow, 1981

O Ceallaigh, Pádraig, Galway North, 1957; Galway East, 1961, 1964(by), 1965, 1989; Roscommon, 1964(by)

Ó Ceallaigh, Seán, Clare, 1959(by)–69

Ó Cinnéide, Pilib, Tipperary South, 1961

Ó Cinnéide, Seán, see Kennedy

O'Cleary, Michael, *Antrim North*, 1982; Antrim East (w), 1983

Ó Cléirigh, Pádraic, Dublin North-Central, 1961, 1965

Ó Coigligh, Eoin, Louth, 1943, 1944

Ó Conaill, Dáithí, Cork Borough, 1961

Ó Conaill, Tomás, Cork East, 1982(Feb.), 1982(Nov.)

O'Connell, Anthony (Tony), Roscommon-Leitrim, 1973

O'Connell, Con, Cork North-Central, 1987

O'Connell, Donal, Cork North-Central, 1982(Nov.)

O'Connell, Eoin, Kerry South, 1944(Nov.)(by)

O'Connell, Jeremiah A., Leitrim-Sligo, 1923

O'Connell, John, Galway West, 1954

O'Connell, John F., Dublin South-West, 1965–77; Dublin (Ballyfermot), 1977–81; Dublin South-Central, 1981–7 (def.), 1989–; DUBLIN, 1979–81

O'Connell, Sir John R., Dublin South, 1922

O'Connell, Joseph, Clare, 1982(Feb.)

O'Connell, Maurice, Dublin South-Central, 1969

O'Connell, Michael, Kerry South, 1981

O'Connell, Michael L., Kerry North, 1938

O'Connell, Richard, Limerick, 1924(by)–32 (def.), 1933

O'Connell, Thomas, Kerry North, 1937

O'Connell, Thomas J., Galway, 1922–7(June); Mayo South, 1927(June)–32 (def.)

O'Connell, Timothy, Limerick, 1937, 1943; Limerick West, 1948

O'Connell, V. W., Cork City North-West, 1969, 1973

O'Connor, Art, Kildare-Wicklow, 1921–2 (def.); Kildare, 1923, 1927(June); Leix-Offaly, 1926(by)

O'Connor, Bartholomew (Batt), Dublin Co., 1923, 1924(by)–35 (d.)

O'Connor, Brídín, Dublin West, 1987, 1989

O'Connor, Denis, Cork North-East, 1961

O'Connor, Denis J., Dublin South, 1981, 1982(Nov.)

O'Connor, Donal J., Dublin North, 1925(by)

O'Connor, Edmond, Kerry, 1933

O'Connor, Elizabeth, Dublin South, 1938

O'Connor, James, Waterford, 1943

O'Connor, James, Leix-Offaly, 1948

O'Connor, James, Limerick West, 1948

O'Connor, James P., Dublin South-East, 1965

O'Connor, John, Dún Laoghaire, 1977

O'Connor, John P., Dublin Co., 1932, 1933

O'Connor, John S., Dublin North-West, 1943, 1944–8; Dublin North-Central, 1948

O'Connor, John W., Mayo South, 1944

O'Connor, Joseph, Dublin North-East, 1973

O'Connor, Joseph, Tipperary North, 1981

O'Connor, Kathleen, Kerry North, 1956(by)–7

O'Connor, L. J., Dublin Co., 1948

O'Connor, Matthew, Kildare, 1965

O'Connor, Michael, Louth, 1938

O'Connor, Michael, Dublin South-West, 1961

O'Connor, Michael (Scarteen), see Connor-Scarteen

O'Connor, Michael J., Mayo South, 1923

O'Connor, N. P., Galway West, 1981, 1982(Feb.)

O'Connor, O. J., Mayo North, 1923

O'Connor, Patrick (Paudie), Kerry South, 1981

O'Connor, Patrick (Scarteen), see Connor

O'Connor, Paul O., Galway West, 1989

O'Connor, Philip, Dublin North-Central, 1982(Nov.), 1987

O'Connor, R. H., *Tyrone West*, 1949–73

O'Connor, Seán, Clare, 1954

O'Connor, Thomas, Cavan, 1969

O'Connor, Thomas O., Kerry North, 1948, 1951

O'Connor, Timothy, Kerry South, 1961–81 (def.); MUNSTER, 1979

O'Connor, William, Limerick West, 1951, 1954

Ó Cosgarda, Pádraig, Galway West, 1948

Ó Cuinnegáin, Gearóid, see Cunningham

Ó Cuív, Eamon, Galway West, 1987, 1989
Ó Dálaigh, Cearbhall, *see* O'Daly, Carroll
O'Daly, Carroll, Dublin South-West, 1948, 1951
O'Daly, Séamus, Dublin South-East, 1982(Feb.), 1982(Nov.); Dublin West, 1982(May)(by)
O'Dea, L. E., Galway, 1923–7(June); Galway West, 1938
O'Dea, Seán, Clare, 1927(Sept.)
O'Dea, W. G., Limerick East, 1981, 1982(Feb.)–
Ó Dochartaigh, Tomás, Waterford, 1943; Tipperary, 1944
O'Doherty, Joseph, Donegal, 1921–7(June) (def.), 1933–7
O'Donnell, Colm, Tipperary South, 1951
O'Donnell, Colum, Donegal North-East, 1969
O'Donnell, Desmond, *Belfast West*, 1973
O'Donnell, F. H., Dublin South, 1932
O'Donnell, Hugh, Leitrim-Sligo, 1932
O'Donnell, James, Donegal East, 1948(Dec.)(by)
O'Donnell, James, Limerick West, 1961
O'Donnell, John, Donegal West, 1937
O'Donnell, Joseph, Belfast East (w), 1987
O'Donnell, Michael A., Kerry, 1927(June), 1927(Sept.)
O'Donnell, Mícheál, Louth, 1973, 1982(Nov.)
O'Donnell, Patrick, Mayo South, 1927(June), 1927(Sept.), 1933
O'Donnell, Patrick, Donegal West, 1949(by) 61; Donegal South-West, 1961–9; Donegal-Leitrim, 1969–70 (d.)
O'Donnell, Peadar, Donegal, 1923–7(June)
O'Donnell, Thomas, Sligo-Mayo East, 1921–3; Leitrim-Sligo, 1923
O'Donnell, Thomas, Kerry, 1923
O'Donnell, Thomas, Clare, 1927(June); Dublin Co., 1932
O'Donnell, Thomas, Roscommon, 1943
O'Donnell, Thomas G., Limerick East, 1961–87 (def.); MUNSTER, 1979–89
O'Donnell, W. F., Tipperary, 1943–7 (d.)
O'Donoghue, Dáithí, Dublin North, 1923
O'Donoghue, Donal, Dublin South-East, 1948
O'Donoghue, Donal J., Kerry South, 1944(Nov.)(by)–8 (def.)
O'Donoghue, Francis, Cavan-Monaghan, 1982(Feb.)
O'Donoghue, H. B., Cavan, 1943
O'Donoghue, John, Kerry South, 1981, 1982(Feb.), 1982(Nov.), 1987–
O'Donoghue, Martin, Dún Laoghaire, 1977–82(Nov.) (def.)
O'Donoghue, Michael N., Dublin North-East, 1981, 1982(Feb.)
O'Donoghue, Pádraig, Kerry South, 1948
O'Donoghue, Patrick, Down South, 1973–6, 1982–6
O'Donoghue, Thomas, Kerry-Limerick West, 1921–3; Kerry, 1923–7(June)
O'Donoghue, Timothy, Tipperary South, 1965
O'Donovan, Cornelius, Cork West, 1927(June)
O'Donovan, Cornelius, Cork South-Central, 1987
O'Donovan, Denis, Cork South-West, 1987, 1989

O'Donovan, John, Dublin South-East, 1954–7 (def.), 1961
O'Donovan, John, Dublin South-West, 1965; Dublin South-Central, 1969–73 (def.)
O'Donovan, Thomas H., Cork West, 1927(June)
O'Donovan, Timothy J., Cork West, 1923–44 (def.)
O'Dowd, Fergus, Louth, 1977, 1987
O'Dowd, John, Sligo South, 1900(Mar.)(by)–18 (def.)
O'Dowd, John, Louth, 1933
O'Dowd, P. J., Roscommon, 1927(June)–32 (def.), 1933–7 (def.)
O'Driscoll, Denis J., Tipperary, 1943; Tipperary South, 1948
O'Driscoll, Donal, Cork North-East, 1969
O'Driscoll, Michael, Cork Borough, 1946(by); Cork South, 1948
O'Driscoll, P. F., Cork West, 1943–8
O'Driscoll, T. F., Dublin North, 1927(Sept.)
O'Droighneáin, Oisín, Dublin Co., 1944
O'Dubhghaill, Seán, Cork Borough, 1943, 1944, 1948
O'Dubhghaill, Tomás, Dublin South-Central, 1957, 1961; Dublin South-West, 1959(by)
Ó Dubhthaigh, Pádraig, see Duffy, Patrick
O'Duffy, Gen. Eoin, Monaghan, 1921–2(Dec.)
O'Dwyer, John, Clare, 1927(June)
O'Farrell, John J., Dublin North-West, 1922
O'Farrell, John T., Dublin Co., 1943
O'Farrell, Seán, Longford-Westmeath, 1923
O'Farrell, Sylvester, Dublin North, 1932
O'Farrelly, Prof. Agnes, National University of Ireland, 1923, 1927(June)
Ó Fearghail, Seán, Kildare, 1987, 1989
O'Flaherty, Anthony (Tony), Dublin Central, 1989
O'Flaherty, John, Donegal, 1927(Sept.)
O'Flaherty, Richard, Limerick East, 1987
O'Flaherty, Samuel, Donegal, 1921–3 (def.)
O'Flanagan, Diarmuid, Dublin South-West, 1987
O'Flynn, James, Clare, 1927(June)
O'Foighil, Pól, Galway West, 1975(by), 1981, 1982(Nov.); CONNACHT-ULSTER, 1984
O'Gallachóir, Eamon, Donegal South-West, 1983(by)
O'Gaora, Colm, Galway, 1923
O'Gorman, D. L., Cork East, 1923, 1927(June–Sept.) (def.), 1932
O'Gorman, P. J., Cork East, 1945–54 (def.), 1957
O'Gorman, Seán, Wexford, 1969, 1973
O'Gowan, Brig. F. D., Cavan, 1951
O'Grady, Gerard, Foyle (w), 1983
O'Grady, Seán, Clare, 1927(June), 1932–51 (def.), 1957
O'Grady, Seán, Kerry South, 1982(Nov.), 1987
O'Hagan, Desmond, Down South (w), 1979, 1987
O'Hagan, E. F., *Down South*, 1973

O'Hagan, John J., *Antrim North*, 1973–5

O'Hagan, Joseph B., *Armagh*, 1982

O'Hagan, P. F., Down (w), 1935

O'Hagan, Raymond, *Belfast West*, 1973

O'Halloran, John, Dublin West, 1982(May)(by)

O'Halloran, Michael, Dublin (Artane), 1977; Dublin North-Central, 1981, 1982(Feb.), 1989

O'Hanlon, G. O., Down South (w), 1974(Oct.); *Down South*, 1975; Newry and Armagh (w), 1987

O'Hanlon, Jeremiah G., Cork North-East, 1969

O'Hanlon, John F., Cavan, 1925(by), 1927(June)–33 (def.)

O'Hanlon, P. M., *Armagh South*, 1969–73; *Armagh*, 1973–5 (def.), 1982; Armagh (w), 1974(Feb.)

O'Hanlon, Rory, Monaghan, 1973(Nov.)(by); Cavan-Monaghan, 1977–

O'Hanlon, Thomas, Louth, 1927(June)

O'Hanlon, Thomas, Wexford, 1948

Ó hAnnluain, Eineachán, Monaghan, 1957–61

O'Hanrahan, Henry, Dublin North, 1923

O'Hanrahan, James, Dublin North-Central, 1987

O'Hanrahan, Peter, Carlow-Kilkenny, 1977

O'Hara, Anthony (Tony), Dublin West, 1981, 1982(Feb.)

O'Hara, Anthony N., Dublin North-Central, 1982(Feb.)

O'Hara, M. H., Mayo North, 1937

O'Hara, Patrick, Mayo North, 1923, 1927(June), 1932–3

O'Hara, Thomas, Mayo North, 1943, 1944, 1951–7 (def.), 1961, 1965–9; Mayo East, 1969–73 (def.)

O'Hara, W. J., Dublin North, 1927(Sept.)

O'Hare, Fergus, *Belfast North*, 1982

O'Hare, G. L., *Larkfield*, 1969

O'Hare, John, *Belfast West*, 1973

O'Hare, Paschal J., *Belfast West*, 1975; Belfast North (w), 1979; *Belfast North*, 1982–6

O'Hare, Patrick J., Louth, 1961, 1965

O hÉigeartaigh, Seán, Cork Borough, 1957

O'Higgins, Brian, Clare, 1921–7(June) (def.)

O'Higgins, J. F., Limerick East, 1968(by)

O'Higgins, KC, Leix-Offaly, 1921–3; Dublin Co., 1923–7(July) (d.)

O'Higgins, M. J., Dublin South-West, 1948–51 (def.), 1954–61; Wicklow, 1961–9 (def.)

O'Higgins, T. F. (sen.), Dublin North, 1929(by)–32; Leix-Offaly, 1932–48; Cork Borough, 1948–53 (d.)

O'Higgins, T. F. (jun), Dublin South, 1943; Leix (Laoighis)-Offaly, 1948–69; Dublin Co. South, 1969–73

O'Higgins-O'Malley, Una, Dún Laoghaire, 1977

O'Hourihan, Peadar, Cork Mid/North/South/South-East/West, 1922

O'Hurley, Seán, Longford-Westmeath, 1927(June)

264

O'Kane, James, *Londonderry Mid*, 1969

O'Kane, Kathleen (Kitty), Belfast West (w), 1974(Oct.)

O'Kane, L. T., *Tyrone North*, 1965, 1969

O'Keeffe, Bartholomew (Batt), Cork South-Central, 1987–9 (def.)

O'Keeffe, D. G., Clare, 1987, 1989

O'Keeffe, Edmond (Ned), Cork East, 1982(Nov.)–

O'Keeffe, James, Cork South-West, 1977–; MUNSTER, 1979

O'Keeffe, James J., Dublin South-West, 1951, 1957, 1961–5 (def.), 1969; Dublin (Rathmines West), 1977

O'Keeffe, Patrick, Cork Mid/North/South/South/East/West, 1921–2 (def.)

O'Kelly, E. J., Dublin South, 1923

O'Kelly, F. J., Donegal South-West, 1982(Nov.), 1987, 1989

O'Kelly, H. J., Donegal, 1923

O'Kelly, John J., Louth-Meath, 1921–3; Meath, 1923; Roscommon, 1925(by)

O'Kelly, Joseph, Roscommon, 1944

O'Kelly, Peter, Dublin Co., 1922

O'Kelly, Seán D., Galway East, 1943

O'Kelly, Seán T., Dublin Mid, 1921–3; Dublin North, 1923–37; Dublin North-West. 1937–45

O'Kennedy, Michael, Tipperary North, 1965, 1969–81(Jan.), 1982(Feb.)–

O'Kennedy, Seán, Wexford, 1927(June)

O'Leary, Cornelius (Con), Cork North-Central, 1989

O'Leary, Daniel, Cork West, 1923

O'Leary, Daniel A., Cork North, 1927(Sept.)–37; Cork West, 1937–8 (def.), 1943, 1944

O'Leary, Daniel, Cork Mid, 1973

O'Leary, Diarmuid J., Kerry, 1927(June)

O'Leary, Don, Cork North-Central, 1987

O'Leary, John, Wexford, 1943–57 (def.)

O'Leary, John, Kerry South, 1966(by)

O'Leary, John J., Kerry South, 1951, 1954

O'Leary, Michael, Dublin North-Central, 1965–81; Dublin Central, 1981–2(Nov.); Dublin South-West, 1982(Nov.)–7; DUBLIN, 1979–81

O'Leary, Seán, Cork Borough, 1927(June), 1932

O'Leary, Seán, Cork Borough, 1965; Cork City South-East, 1969, 1973; Cork Mid, 1977

O'Leary, William, Kerry, 1927(June)–32

O'Lehane, Declan, Limerick East, 1987

Ó Liatháin, E. E., Dublin South, 1987, 1989

Oliver, N. C., *Down North*, 1975

Oliver, William, *Belfast (Dock)*, 1958–62 (def.), 1965

O'Loghlen, P. J., Clare, 1938–43 (def.), 1944–8

O'Loughlin, Peter, Clare, 1923

O'Loughlin, Peter, Clare, 1948

O'Loughlin, Thaddeus, Wexford, 1961

O'Mahoney, John (Seán), *Fermanagh-Tyrone*, 1921–5 (def.)

O'Mahony, D. G. (The O'Mahony), Wicklow, 1927(June)–38 (def.)

O'Mahony, Eithne, Cork South-West, 1981

O'Mahony, Eoin, Cork South-East, 1938; Wexford, 1957; Cork Borough, 1967(by)

O'Mahony, Florence, Dún Laoghaire and Rathdown, 1969, 1973; Dublin North-Central, 1982(Nov.), 1987; Dún Laoghaire, 1989; DUBLIN, 1983–4

O'Mahony, John J., Limerick, 1927(June)

O'Mahony, Joseph, Cork West, 1923

O'Mahony, Patrick J., Dublin South-West, 1973

O'Mahony, T. C. G., Dublin North-Central, 1982(Feb.)

O'Mahony, Thomas, Cork East, 1923–4 (d.)

O'Mahony, Una, Dublin North-Central, 1989

Ó Máille, Pádraic, Galway, 1921–7(June) (def.), 1927(Sept.)

Ó Máille, Pádraig, Dublin Co., 1932

O'Malley, C. G., DUBLIN, 1986–9 (def.)

O'Malley, Desmond J., Limerick East, 1968(by)–

O'Malley, Donogh B., Limerick Fast, 1954–68 (d.)

O'Malley, Ernest, Dublin North, 1923–7(June)

O'Malley, Hilda, Limerick East, 1969

O'Malley, John, Galway West, 1987

O'Malley, P. J., Mayo South, 1923

O'Malley, Patrick, Dublin West, 1987–9 (def.)

Ó Maoláin, Michael, Galway West, 1943

Ó Maolcathaigh, Pádraig, Limerick East, 1957

Ó Mathghamhna, Eoin, see O'Mahony

Ó Méalóid, Clare, Dún Laoghaire, 1982(Feb.)

O'Meara, James, Dublin South, 1924(by)–7(June)

O'Meara, John, Tipperary, 1923

O'Meara, M. J., Athlone-Longford, 1944

O'Meara, Thomas, Clare, 1954

Ó Mochlóir, Liam, Cork East, 1957

O'Moore, Seán, Dublin North-East, 1948

O Moráin, Mícheál, see Moran, Michael

Ó Muireagáin, Mícheál, Dublin South-Central, 1987, 1989

O'Mullane, M. J., Dublin South, 1923, 1923(by), 1925(by), 1927(June)

O'Mulloy, Séamus, Galway, 1927(June)

Ó Murchú, E. M., Laoighis-Offaly, 1984(by)

Ó Murchú, Liam, Cork North-Central, 1982(Feb.)

O'Neill, Bernard, Armagh South, 1933

O'Neill, Eamonn, Cork West, 1927(Sept.), 1932–43 (def.), 1944–8; Cork South, 1948

O'Neill, John, Kerry, 1923

O'Neill, John, Dublin South, 1924(by), 1927(June)

O'Neill, Joseph A., Dublin Co., 1927(Sept.)

O'Neill, Laurence, Dublin Mid, 1922–3; Dublin North, 1927(Sept.)

O'Neill, Lucia, Dublin North-West, 1989

O'Neill, Michael, Mid-Ulster (w), 1951–5, 1956(by)

O'Neill, Michael, Galway West, 1987

O'Neill, Nancy, Wicklow, 1965, 1968(by)

O'Neill, Pádraig, Dublin South, 1987

O'Neill, Patrick, *Down*, 1921–9; *Mourne*, 1929–38

O'Neill, Patrick J., Leitrim-Sligo, 1923

O'Neill, Phelim F., Mid-Ulster (w), 1970

O'Neill, Hon. Phelim R. H., Antrim North (w), 1952(by)–9; *Antrim North*, 1958–73 (def.)

O'Neill, Raymond, Cork South-West, 1987

O'Neill, Sir Robert W. H., Antrim (w), 1922–52; *Antrim*, 1921–9

O'Neill, Séamus, Wexford, 1948, 1951

O'Neill, Stephen, Cork South-West, 1989

O'Neill, Capt. Hon. T. M., *Bannside*, 1946(by)–70

Ó Néill, Mac Gabhann, S. O., Cavan-Monaghan, 1982(Nov.)

O'Rahilly, Alfred, Cork Borough, 1923–4

O'Rahilly, Eoghan, Dublin South, 1932

O'Rahilly, R. MacE, (The O'Rahilly), Dublin Co., 1951; Dublin North-West, 1952(by)

O'Regan, James, Clare, 1923

O'Regan, Maurice, Leitrim-Sligo, 1933

O'Reilly, Brendan, Belfast South (w), 1959

O'Reilly, Henry, Cavan, 1923

O'Reilly, Ignatius, Dublin South-East, 1973

O'Reilly, James, Cavan, 1943

O'Reilly, James, Armagh (w), 1948(by); *Mourne*, 1958–73; *Down South*, 1973

O'Reilly, John J., Cavan, 1925(by)–37 (def.)

O'Reilly, Joseph, Cavan-Monaghan, 1989

O'Reilly, Kevin, Louth, 1932

O'Reilly, Matthew, Meath, 1927(June)–37; Meath-Westmeath, 1937–48; Meath, 1948–54 (def.)

O'Reilly, Michael W., Dublin Co., 1923

O'Reilly, Patrick (Castlepoles), Cavan, 1948–51 (def.), 1954

O'Reilly, Patrick (Murmod), Cavan, 1943–8, 1951–65 (def.), 1969–73 (def.)

O'Reilly, Patrick Able, *see* Able-O'Reilly

O'Reilly, Peter P., Wicklow, 1943

O'Reilly, Richard, Dublin South-West, 1982(Nov.)

O'Reilly, T. J., Mayo North, 1927(June), 1927(Sept.), 1932

O'Reilly, Thomas, Kerry, 1927(June)–33

O'Reilly, Thomas, Dublin North, 1927(Sept.)

O'Reilly, Thomas, Dublin North-East, 1937, 1938

O'Reilly, Thomas, Cavan-Monaghan, 1982(Feb.)

O'Reilly, Thomas F., Wicklow, 1948

O'Reilly, Thomas P., Cavan, 1944–8 (def.)

Ó Riain, Alfonsus, Waterford, 1961

O'Riordan, Jeremiah, Kerry South, 1951

O'Riordan, Michael, Cork Borough, 1946(by); Dublin South-West, 1951, 1954; Dublin South-Central, 1961, 1965; Dublin Central, 1973

O'Riordan, Seán, Cork North-West, 1987

Ormonde, Ann, Dublin South, 1987, 1989

Ormonde, Donal, Waterford, 1982(Feb.), 1982(Nov.)–7 (def.)

Ormonde, John, Waterford, 1947(by)–65 (def.)

O'Rourke, Brian, Monaghan, 1937

O'Rourke, Bridget, Louth, 1973

O'Rourke, C. J., Waterford, 1938

O'Rourke, Daniel, Mayo South-Roscommon South, 1921–3; Roscommon, 1927(Sept.), 1932–3 (def.), 1937–43 (def.), 1944–51 (def.), 1954, 1957

O'Rourke, Dermot F., Dublin South-Central, 1969, 1973

O'Rourke, James, Leitrim-Sligo, 1923

O'Rourke, John, Cavan, 1965

O'Rourke, John, Clare, 1987

O'Rourke, Kevin, Down South (w), 1955, 1959

O'Rourke, Mary, Longford-Westmeath, 1982(Feb.), 1982(Nov.)–

O'Rourke, Michael, Dublin Co., 1943, 1944

O'Rourke, P. V., Sligo-Leitrim, 1969

O'Rourke-Glynn, Leonore, Kildare, 1982(Feb.)

Orr, Capt. L. P. S., Down South (w), 1950–74(Oct.)

O'Ryan, Michael, Waterford, 1927(June)

O'Shannon, Cathal, Louth-Meath, 1922–3; Louth, 1923; Meath, 1927(Sept.)

O'Shaughnessy, Andrew, Cork Borough, 1923–7(June)

O'Shaughnessy, John A., Cork North-East, 1965

O'Shaughnessy, John J., Limerick, 1932–3 (def.), 1937–8 (def.)

O'Shaughnessy, Thomas, Clare, 1987

O'Shea, Brian, Waterford, 1982(Feb.), 1982(Nov.), 1987, 1989–

O'Shea, Joseph, Kerry South, 1982(Nov.)

O'Shea, M. J., *Down South*, 1973

O'Shea, Neil, Roscommon-Leitrim, 1969; Longford-Westmeath, 1981

O'Shea, Patrick, Kerry, 1927(June), 1927(Sept.)

O'Shea, Patrick J., Kerry South, 1937, 1948

O'Shea, W., MUNSTER, 1989

O'Shea-Leamy, Lillie, Dublin North, 1927(June); Dublin North-East, 1954

O'Shee, J. J., Waterford West, 1895(Sept.)(by)–1918; Waterford Co., 1918

O'Shiel, K. R., *Fermanagh-Tyrone*, 1921

Ó Síocháin, P. A., Clare, 1965

Ó Snodaigh, Aengus, Dublin South-East, 1987

O'Sullivan, Brendan, Dublin, 1982(May)(by)

O'Sullivan, Colm, Kerry South, 1982(Nov.)

O'Sullivan, Cornelius D., Limerick, 1927(June), 1927(Sept.)

O'Sullivan, D. F., Cork South-West, 1982(Feb.)

O'Sullivan, Daniel, Longford-Westmeath, 1987

O'Sullivan, Denis, Tipperary, 1947(by); Tipperary South, 1948
O'Sullivan, Denis J., Cork North, 1948, 1951–61; Cork Mid, 1961–9, 1972(by)
O'Sullivan, Dominick, Cork North, 1933
O'Sullivan, Donal, Dublin Co. South, 1969, 1970(by)
O'Sullivan, Edward (Ned), Kerry North, 1989
O'Sullivan, Eugene, Kerry, 1927(June)
O'Sullivan, Eugene, Cork West, 1938
O'Sullivan, Garry, Cork South-Central, 1982(Nov.)
O'Sullivan, Gearóid, Carlow-Kilkenny, 1921–3; Dublin Co., 1927(Aug.)(by)–
  37 (def.)
O'Sullivan, Gerry, Cork North-Central, 1987, 1989–
O'Sullivan, Jeremiah, Cork West, 1927(June)
O'Sullivan, John, Limerick East, 1982(Nov.)
O'Sullivan, John L., Cork West, 1937, 1954; Cork South, 1951; Cork South-
  West, 1961, 1965, 1969–77 (def.)
O'Sullivan, John L., Cork South-West, 1982(Nov.)
O'Sullivan, John M., Kerry, 1923–37; Kerry North, 1937–43 (def.)
O'Sullivan, Martin, Dublin North, 1932, 1933; Dublin Co., 1938; Dublin
  North-West, 1943–8; Dublin North-Central, 1948–51 (def.)
O'Sullivan, Michael, Galway West, 1938
O'Sullivan, Michael, Kerry South, 1961
O'Sullivan, Tadhg, Kerry South, 1969
O'Sullivan, Thomas, Cork Mid, 1965
O'Sullivan, Timothy J., Mayo North, 1923
O'Sullivan, Timothy Joseph, Belfast Central, 1953
O'Sullivan, Timothy Joseph, Cork City South-East, 1973
O'Sullivan, Timothy T. (Ted), Cork West, 1937–54
O'Sullivan, Toddy, Cork City, 1979(by); Cork North-Central, 1981–7; Cork
  South-Central, 1987–
O'Sullivan, William, Kerry South, 1937
O'Toole, James (Séamus), Wicklow, 1957–61 (def.)
O'Toole, Laurence, Wicklow, 1932
O'Toole, M. J., Mayo West, 1989–
O'Toole, Patrick, Mayo East, 1973, 1977–87 (def.)
O'Toole, Vincent, Waterford, 1982(Feb.)
Ó Tuairisg, Seosamh, Galway West, 1973
Ó Tuathail, Peadar, Galway West, 1987
Overend, D. A., *Belfast (Shankill)*, 1965, 1969; Belfast North (w), 1966
Overend, Robert, *Mid-Ulster*, 1975–6, 1982
Owen, Nora, Dublin North, 1981–7 (def.), 1989–
Owens, George, Louth, 1948
Owens, Gerard, Dublin Co., 1943
Owens, T. A., *Fermanagh-Tyrone South*, 1982; Mid-Ulster (w), 1983, 1986(by)

Pain, see Hacket Pain
Paisley, E. E., *Belfast East*, 1973–6

Paisley, Revd I. R. K., *Bannside*, 1969, 1970(by)–3; *Antrim North*, 1973–6, 1982–6; Antrim North (w), 1970–85, 1986(by)–; NORTHERN IRELAND, 1979–

Palmer, P. W., Kerry South, 1948–61

Panter, Maj. G. W., *Mourne*, 1938–45

Parker, Brian, Galway East, 1982(July)(by), 1982(Nov.)

Parker, Dame Debra (formerly Chichester), *Londonderry*, 1921–9; *Londonderry South*, 1933(Mar.)(by)–60

Parkes, M. R., Limerick East, 1987

Passmore, Thomas, Belfast West (w), 1979, 1983; *Belfast West*, 1982–6

Patrick, Capt. John, *Antrim Mid*, 1938–45

Patrick, M. W., *Bannside*, 1939(by)–46 (d.)

Patten, A. S., Wicklow, 1927(June)

Patterson, F. G., *Fermanagh South*, 1949; Fermanagh-Tyrone South (w), 1951; *Lisnaskea*, 1968(by)

Pattison, J. P., Carlow-Kilkenny, 1932, 1933–7; Kilkenny, 1937–48; Carlow-Kilkenny, 1948–51 (def.), 1954–7 (def.)

Pattison, Séamus, Carlow-Kilkenny, 1960(by), 1961–; LEINSTER, 1981–3

Pearse, Margaret, Dublin Co., 1921–2 (def.)

Pearse, Margaret M., Dublin Co., 1933–7 (def.)

Peers, Noel, Dublin North-East, 1989

Pentland, J. W., *Down North*, 1982–6

Perceval-Maxwell, Capt. J. R., *Ards*, 1945–9

Perceval-Price, Col. M. C., *Mourne*, 1962

Pettit, Michael, Leix-Offaly, 1957

Phelan, Basil, Wicklow, 1969, 1973

Phelan, James, Dublin North-West, 1965

Phelan, John J., Dublin North-East, 1948

Phelan, Nicholas, Waterford-Tipperary East, 1922–3

Phelan, Patrick, Kildare-Wicklow, 1922

Phelan, Thomas, Laoighis-Offaly, 1987

Phelan, W. J., Dublin South-Central, 1954

Phillips, Francis, Longford-Westmeath, 1923

Phillips, M. A., Tipperary, 1943

Pierse, Robert, Keny North, 1982(Feb.)

Pilkington, Joseph, Sligo-Leitrim, 1954

Pilkington, William (Liam), Leitrim-Sligo, 1923

Plummer, Alan, Dublin South-West, 1989

Plunkett, G. N., Count, Roscommon North 1917(by)–22; Leitrim-Roscommon North, 1921–3; Roscommon, 1923–7(June) (def.); Galway, 1936(by)

Pollock, George, Monaghan, 1948

Pollock, H. MacD., *Belfast South*, 1921–9; *Belfast (Windsor)*, 1929–37 (d.)

Pollock, R. D., Down (w), 1929

Pollock, T. D., *Mid-Ulster*, 1973–5 (def.)

Poots, C. B., *Iveagh*, 1969; *Down North*, 1973–6, 1982

Pope, Frederick, Dublin South-West, 1965

Porter, Norman, *Belfast (Clifton)*, 1953–8 (def.), 1959(by); *Belfast (Duncairn)*, 1969

Porter, R. W., *Queen's University Belfast*, 1966(by)–9; *Lagan Valley*, 1969–73

Pounder, R. J., Belfast South (w), 1963(by)–74(Feb.) (def.); NORTHERN IRELAND, 1972–4

Powell, J. Enoch, Down South (w), 1974(Oct.)–85, 1986(by)–7 (def.)

Powell, Joubert, Tipperary North, 1948

Powell, P. J., Tipperary South, 1969

Powell, T. P., Galway, 1927(June)–33 (def.); Galway West, 1961

Power, Edmond, Dublin South-West, 1956(by), 1957

Power, Noel, Cork South-Central, 1982(Nov.)

Power, Patrick, Kildare, 1969–89; IRELAND, 1977–9; LEINSTER, 1979

Power, Richard, Limerick East, 1982(Nov.)

Power, Seán, Kildare, 1989–

Powers, Frank, Laoighis-Offaly, 1969

Pratschke, Anthony (Tony), Limerick East, 1969

Prendergast, Frank, Limerick East, 1981, 1982(Nov.)–7 (def.)

Prendergast, Peter, Dublin South-East, 1973, 1977

Prendergast, Renée, Galway West, 1975(by)

Prendiville, P. M., *Belfast East*, 1982; Belfast East (w), 1983

Press, R. H., *Belfast (Windsor)*, 1938; *Antrim*, 1943(by)

Price, Albert, Belfast West (w), 1974(Feb.)

Price, James, *Belfast (Victoria)*, 1929

Price, W. J., *Down East*, 1938

Pringle, J. A., Fermanagh-Tyrone (w), 1922, 1923, 1924–9; *Larne*, 1929

Prior, John, Cork West, 1923–7(June) (def.)

Proctor, Frederick, *Belfast North*, 1973

Proctor, Maj. O. N., *Armagh Mid*, 1938

Purcell, Colm, Kildare, 1987

Purcell, Seán, Galway East, 1961, 1965

Quaid, John, Limerick, 1923

Quigley, J. O., Mayo South, 1938, 1943

Quigley, Liam, Carlow-Kilkenny, 1989

Quigley, Nicholas, Tipperary South, 1987

Quill, Mairín, Cork City, 1977; Cork North-Central, 1981, 1987–

Quill, Timothy, Cork North, 1927(June–Sept.) (def.), 1937, 1938

Quillinan, M. J., Limerick, 1927(June)

Quin, Herbert, *Queen's University Belfast*, 1944(by)–9

Quinn, Alphonso, Sligo-Leitrim, 1954

Quinn, Eithne, Roscommon, 1987

Quinn, James, Dublin North-Central, 1969

Quinn, John, Galway, 1923

Quinn, John, Meath, 1927(June)

Quinn, John G., Down South (w), 1966, 1970

Quinn, Ruairí; Dublin South-East, 1973, 1977–81 (def.), 1982(Feb.)–

Quinn, Séamus C., *Londonderry (Foyle)*, 1965
Quinn, Seán, Limerick, 1938
Quinn, T. J., Mayo West, 1977, 1981
Quinn, Ursula, Dublin West, 1989
Quirke, James, Waterford, 1957
Quirke, William, Tipperary, 1923
Quish, D. P., Limerick, 1943; Limerick East, 1954

Rabbitte, Patrick, Dublin South-West, 1982(Nov.), 1987, 1989–
Rackard, William, Wexford, 1965
Raftery, Thomas, MUNSTER, 1984–9 (def.)
Rainey, W. A., *Antrim North*, 1975
Ramsey, W. W., Armagh (w), 1979; Upper Bann (w), 1990(by)
Randles, Thomas, Kerry South, 1982(Nov.)
Ratigan, Séamus, Dublin South-Central, 1982(Nov.)
Rea, Thomas, *Belfast South*, 1973
Reade, James, Carlow-Kilkenny, 1927(Sept.)
Reagan, Seán, Antrim North (w), 1987
Reck, Patrick (Padge), Wexford, 1987
Reddin, Kerry, Dublin South-Central, 1951
Reddington, James, Galway, 1927(June)
Redmond, B. M., Waterford, 1933–52 (d.)
Redmond, Pierce, Dublin South-West, 1969
Redmond, Thomas, Wexford, 1937
Redmond, Thomas J., Longford-Westmeath, 1923
Redmond, Capt. W. A., Waterford, 1923–32(Apr.) (d.)
Regan, James J., Roscommon, 1957
Regan, John P., Mayo East, 1982(Nov.)
Regan, Martin, Galway East, 1938
Regan, Michael A., Meath, 1977
Regan, Patrick, Mayo South, 1948
Reid, D. D., Down, 1922–39 (d)
Reid, Ernest, *Queen's University Belfast*, 1949(Nov.)(by)
Reid, Frank, Donegal South-West, 1965
Reid, J. J., Donegal South-West, 1982(Feb.), 1983(by)
Reid, James, *Belfast (Cromac)*, 1929
Reid, Richard, *Mid-Ulster*, 1975–6
Reidy, James, Limerick, 1932–7 (def.), 1938–48; Limerick East, 1948–54 (def.)
Reidy, John W., Cork Borough, 1954, 1956(by)
Reihill, Patrick, *Fermanagh-Tyrone South*, 1973
Reilly, Hugh, Dublin North, 1981, 1982(Feb.)
Reilly, John, Mayo North, 1961
Reilly, Joseph, Meath, 1987, 1989
Reilly, Michael, Mayo West, 1969
Renshaw, J. W., *Queen's University Belfast*, 1943(by)–5
Reynolds, Albert, Longford-Westmeath, 1977–

Reynolds, F. F., Limerick East, 1977

Reynolds, Gerry, Sligo-Leitrim, 1989–

Reynolds, James, Leitrim, 1944

Reynolds, James, Roscommon-Leitrim, 1977

Reynolds, Mary, Leitrim-Sligo, 1932–3 (def.); Leitrim, 1937–48; Sligo-Leitrim, 1948–61

Reynolds, Patrick J., Roscommon, 1961–9; Roscommon-Leitrim, 1969, 1973–7 (def.)

Reynolds, Patrick T., Leitrim-Sligo, 1927(Sept.)–32 (nominated but d. before election)

Reynolds, Thomas, Dublin South-West, 1951

Rice, B. M., Monaghan, 1938–54

Rice, Daniel, *Down East*, 1965

Rice, Eamonn, Monaghan, 1932–7 (d.)

Rice, F. G., Down South (w), 1979

Rice, H. J., Longford-Westmeath, 1957

Rice, John J., Kerry South, 1957–61 (def.)

Rice, Joseph, Kilkenny, 1938; Carlow-Kilkenny, 1948

Rice, P. J., Lagan Valley (w), 1987

Rice, R P., Cork City South-East, 1973

Rice, Vincent, Dublin South, 1927(June-Sept.) (def.) Dublin North, 1928(by), 1932, 1933–7, Dublin North-West, 1937; Dublin South, 1943

Richardson, E. G., Anoagh South, 1958–69 (def.)

Richardson, Lt Col. H. S. C., Fermanagh-Tyrone South (w), 1950

Ridge, Joseph, Galway West, 1943, 1961

Ridge, Therese, Dublin South-West, 1987

Riordan, D. G., Limerick East, 1987

Ritchie, Geraldine, Down South (w), 1987

Ritchie, Patrick, *Antrim South*, 1982

Ritchie, William, *Belfast (St Anne's)*, 1970(by)

Robb, J. H., *Queen's University Belfast*, 1921–38

Robbins, Eugene, Meath-Westmeath, 1937

Robbins, Frank, Dublin North-East, 1944, 1948

Robbins, Laurence, Longford-Westmeath, 1921–2 (def.)

Robinson, A. J., Leitrim-Sligo, 1927(Sept.)

Robinson, E. R., Leitrim-Sligo, 1927(June)

Robinson, Maj. H. C., *Larne*, 1937(by)–44 (d.)

Robinson, James, *Belfast North*, 1975

Robinson, Mary, Dublin (Rathmines West), 1977; Dublin West 1981

Robinson, Peter, *Belfast East*, 1975, 1982–6; Belfast East (w), 1979–85, 1986(by)–

Robinson, Séamus, Waterford-Tipperary East, 1921–2 (def.)

Robinson, Sir T. W., Dublin Co. South, 1918

Robinson, William, Belfast North (w), 1974(Oct.)

Roche, Charles, Kerry, 1927(June)

Roche, Edmond, Kerry-Limerick West, 1921–3

Roche, Garrett, Cork East, 1948
Roche, Jean, Dublin West, 1987
Roche, John (Jack), Cork North-West, 1982(Nov.), 1987
Roche, John, Wexford, 1982(Nov.)
Roche, John M., Wexford, 1927(June)
Roche, Richard (Dick), Wicklow, 1987–
Roddy, Joseph, Sligo-Leitrim, 1948–57 (def.)
Roddy, Martin, Leitrim-Sligo, 1923, 1925(by)–37; Sligo, 1937–8 (def.), 1943–8
Rodgers, Bríd, Upper Bann (w), 1987, 1990(by)
Rodgers, James, *Belfast East*, 1973
Rodgers, Dr Samuel, *Belfast (Pottinger)*, 1945, 1949–58 (def.); *Queen's University Belfast*, 1961(by)
Rodgers, Séumus, Donegal South-West, 1961; Donegal-Leitrim, 1973; Donegal, 1977, 1980(by); Donegal South-West, 1982(Feb.), 1982(Nov.), 1983(by), 1987, 1989; CONNACHT-ULSTER, 1979, 1989
Roe, P. J., Louth, 1938; Dublin Co., 1943
Roe, T. F., Louth, 1948, 1951
Rogers, Oliver, Cavan-Monaghan, 1987
Rogers, P. J., Leitrim-Sligo, 1933–7; Sligo, 1937–48; Sligo-Leitrim, 1948, 1951–4 (def.), 1957–61
Ronaldson, J. W., Galway, 1927(June)
Ronan, P. A., Wexford, 1973
Rooney, Eamonn, Dublin Co., 1947(by), 1948–65 (def.); Dublin Co. North, 1969
Rooney, James J. Dublin Co., 1933
Rooney, John, Dublin Co., 1922–3 (def.), 1927(June)
Rosenfield, J. B., *Belfast (Ballynafeigh)*, 1962; Belfast South (w), 1964
Ross, Charles, Louth, 1987
Ross, George, Cork West, 1927(June)
Ross, Hugh, Upper Bann (w), 1990(by)
Ross, Maj. Sir R. D., Londonderry (w), 1929(Jan.)(by)–51(Mar.)
Ross, Shane, DUBLIN, 1984
Ross, William, Londonderry (w), 1974(Feb.)–83; Londonderry East (w), 1983–5, 1986(by)–
Rossiter, William, Wexford, 1977
Rowan, P.J., Antrim South (w), 1974(Feb.), 1974(Oct.), 1979
Rowan-Hamilton, Lt Col. D. A., *Down East*, 1969; *Down South*, 1973, 1975
Rowlette, Dr R. J., Dublin University, 1933(Oct.)(by)–7
Roycroft, Thomas, Cork West, 1948
Roycroft, W. J., Cork West, 1937
Ruane, J. T., Mayo North, 1923; Mayo South, 1948, 1951
Russell, Edward (Ted), Limerick East, 1973, 1977
Russell, G. E., Limerick East, 1948, 1951, 1952(by), 1957–61 (def.), 1965
Ruttle, James, Wicklow, 1981
Ruttledge, P.J., Mayo North/West, 1921–3; Mayo North, 1923–52 (d.)

Ryall, J. G. W., Cork East, 1951

Ryan, A. G. (Tony), Dublin Central, 1983(by)

Ryan, Con, Limerick, 1943

Ryan, Denis, Tipperary North, 1987

Ryan, Dermot A., Dublin North-Central, 1969

Ryan, Eoin, Dublin South-East, 1987, 1989

Ryan, Frank, Dublin South, 1937

Ryan, Ger, Tipperary North, 1981

Ryan, Prof. Hugh, National University of Ireland, 1923

Ryan, James, Wexford, 1921–2 (def.), 1923–65

Ryan, James G., Dublin North-West, 1948

Ryan, Col. Jeremiah, Tipperary, 1927(Sept.) 1933, 1937–44, 1947(by); Tipperary North, 1951

Ryan, John J., Tipperary North, 1969, 1973–87 (def.), 1989

Ryan, Martin, Tipperary, 1932, 1933–43(July) (d.)

Ryan, Mary B., Tipperary, 1944–8; Tipperary North 1948–61 (def.)

Ryan, Michael, Galway North-East, 1969

Ryan, Noel, Waterford, 1987

Ryan, Paschal, J., Tipperary South, 1977

Ryan, Patrick, Clare, 1923

Ryan, Patrick, Tipperary, 1923–7(June)

Ryan, Patrick, Tipperary South, 1987

Ryan, Revd Patrick, MUNSTER, 1989

Ryan, Patrick L., Tipperary, 1923, 1927(June)

Ryan, Philip, Dublin Co., 1923

Ryan, Richie, Dublin South-West, 1959(by)–69; Dublin South-Central, 1969–77; Dublin (Rathmines West), 1977–81; Dublin South-East, 1981–2(Feb.); IRELAND, 1972–3, 1977–9; DUBLIN, 1979–86

Ryan, Robert, Limerick, 1927(June), 1927(Sept.), 1932–48; Limerick East, 1948–51 (def.)

Ryan, Seán, Dublin Co. North, 1977; Dublin North, 1981, 1982(Nov.), 1987, 1989–

Ryan, Thomas, Waterford, 1933

Ryan, Thomas, Cork North-Central, 1981

Ryan, Tomás, Cork North-Central, 1982(Feb.); Cork South-Central, 1982(Nov.)

Ryan, William, Tipperary South, 1965, 1969, 1973

Ryder, E. I., Cork South-West, 1982(Nov.)

Sabhat, Seámus, Clare, 1959(by), 1961

St Leger, Michael, Kildare, 1969

Salter-Townshend, George, MUNSTER, 1989

Samuel, M. H., *Antrim North*, 1982; Antrim North (w), 1983; Londonderry East (w), 1987; NORTHERN IRELAND, 1989

Sands, Robert (Bobby) G., Fermanagh-Tyrone South (w), 1981(by) (Apr.–May) (d)

Sargent, Trevor, Dublin North, 1987, 1989; DUBLIN, 1989

Sarsfield, J. J., Louth, 1973

Savage, Archibald, *Belfast East*, 1921

Savory, Prof. D. L., Queen's University of Belfas t(w), 1940(by)–50; Antrim South (w), 1950–5

Sayers, W. E., *Mid-Ulster*, 1973

Scannell, Michael, Kerry North, 1969

Scott, Alexander (Sandy), *Antrim South*, 1973; Belfast North (w), 1974(Feb.); *Belfast East*, 1975

Scott, James, *Belfast South*, 1982

Scott, John F., Roscommon, 1954

Scott, Sir John H., Cork Borough, 1923, 1927(June), 1927(Sept.)

Scott, Seán, Roscommon, 1957

Scott, Walter, *Belfast (Bloomfield)*, 1961(by)–73; *Belfast East*, 1973

Scully, M. F., Cork West, 1923

Searight, Norman, *Belfast (Willowfield)*, 1953, 1958, 1962; Belfast South (w), 1959, 1963(by)

Sears, William, Mayo South-Roscommon South, 1921–3; Mayo South, 1923–7(June) (def.)

Seawright, George, *Belfast North*, 1982–6; Belfast North (w), 1983, 1987

Semple, Samuel, *Antrim South*, 1975

Sexton, Martin, Clare, 1927(Sept.)–33 (def.), 1938

Seymour, John, Tipperary, 1927(June)

Seymour, Thomas, *Antrim North*, 1973

Shalloo, Thomas, Clare, 1937

Shanahan, Patrick, Clare, 1945(by)–8 (def.)

Shanahan, Philip, Dublin Mid, 1921–2 (def.)

Shanahan, Thomas, Tipperary North, 1969

Shanks, James, Dublin South, 1923

Shanley, Dermot, Galway West, 1987, 1989

Shanley, Patrick, Mayo South, 1951

Shannon, James, Wexford, 1923, 1927(June–Sept.) (def.), 1932

Shannon, Rose, Roscommon, 1961

Sharkey, John (Jack), Belfast North (w), 1970

Sharkey, Martin, LEINSTER, 1984

Sharkey, Thomas, Dublin South, 1987

Sharman Crawford, Col. R. G., Down Mid (w), 1921(by)–2

Shatter, Alan, Dublin South, 1981–

Shaw, A. W., *Belfast (Willowfield)*, 1958

Shaw, Daniel, Sligo-Leitrim, 1961, 1965

Shaw, P. W., Longford-Westmeath, 1923–33

Sheahan, Denis, Kerry South, 1987

Sheahan, Thomas, Cork East, 1981, 1982(Nov.)

Shearer, J. M., Mid-Ulster (w), 1950, 1951

Shee, J. J., *see* O'Shee

Sheedy, J. J., Dublin Co., 1948

Sheehan, Charles, Carlow-Kilkenny, 1948

Sheehan, Donal, Limerick West, 1981

Sheehan, Michael (Ballintemple), Cork Borough, 1948–51 (def.), 1956(by)

Sheehan, Michael (Blackrock), Cork Borough, 1948

Sheehan, Nicholas, Waterford, 1947(by), 1948

Sheehan, P. J., Cork South-West, 1969, 1973, 1977, 1981–

Sheehan, Seán, Laoighis-Offaly, 1982(Nov.)

Sheehy, Michael, Cork West, 1944

Sheehy, Timothy, Cork West, 1927(June)–32 (def.)

Sheehy, Timothy, Tipperary, 1927(June), 1927(Sept.)–33 (def.), 1937, 1943

Sheehy-Skeffington, Hanna, Dublin South, 1943

Sheldon, W. A. W., Donegal East, 1943–61

Sheppard, J. F., Dublin North-West, 1943

Sheridan, D. J., Dublin North-East, 1948

Sheridan, J. M., Longford-Westmeath, 1951, 1954, 1957, 1961–81

Sheridan, Michael, Cavan, 1927(June), 1927(Sept.), 1932–61

Sheridan, Patrick, Cavan, 1923

Sherlock, Joseph, Cork North-East, 1973, 1974(by), 1977, 1979(by); Cork East, 1981–2(Nov.) (def.), 1987–; MUNSTER, 1984, 1989

Sherrard, Ailish, Meath, 1989

Sherry, T. A., *Larkfield*, 1969

Sherwin, Frank, Dublin North-Central, 1957, 1957(by)–65 (def.); Dublin Central, 1969; Dublin (Cabra), 1977

Sherwin, Seán, Dublin South-West, 1969, 1970(by)–3 (def.); Dublin West, 1982(Nov.)

Shields, B. F., Dublin South, 1923

Shields, H. W., *Londonderry*, 1921

Shields, R. W., *Londonderry Mid*, 1969

Shields, V. P., Galway South, 1948, 1951, 1953(by), 1954

Shillington, Maj. D. G., *Armagh*, 1921–9; *Armagh Central*, 1929–41

Shortall, Sir Patrick, Dublin (Clontarf), 1918

Simmonds-Gooding, Hamilton, Down South (w), 1964

Simms, Very Revd J. M., Down North (w), 1922(July(by)–Nov.); Down (w), 1922–31

Simms, Dr Samuel, *Queen's University Belfast*, 1938, 1945

Simpson, F. V., *Larne*, 1945(by), 1945; *Carrick*, 1953; *Belfast (Oldpark)*, 1958–73; *Belfast North*, 1973

Simpson, Mary, *Armagh*, 1982–6

Simpson, N. D., Dublin South, 1981

Simpson, Robert, *Antrim Mid*, 1953–73

Sinclair, Betty, *Belfast (Cromac)*, 1945

Sinclair, Maj. J. M., *Mourne*, 1933; *Belfast (Cromac)*, 1938–53(Jan.) (d.)

Sinclair, Col. Thomas, Queen's University Belfast (w), 1923–40

Sinnott, James, Wexford, 1951

Skehan, Bartholomew (Batt), Clare, 1923

Skelly, Liam, Dublin West, 1982(May)(by)–7 (def.)

Skelly, Michael, Carlow-Kilkenny, 1923–7(June) (def.), 1927(Nov.)(by)

Skinner, L. B., Cork North, 1943–8; Cork East, 1948

Slattery, Harry, Carlow-Kilkenny, 1982(Nov.)

Slattery, M. A., Dún Laoghaire and Rathdown, 1961

Slattery, N. M., Dublin (Rathmines West), 1977

Slattery, Thomas, Kerry, 1927(Sept.)

Slattery, William, Limerick East, 1961

Slein, James, Dublin North-West, 1957

Slevin, Hugh, Sligo-Leitrim, 1989

Slevin, James, *Tyrone South*, 1949

Sloyan, Thomas, Galway, 1923

Smiles, Lt Col. Sir W. D., Down (w), 1945–50; Down North (w), 1950–3 (d)

Smith, Andrew, Dublin South-East, 1973; Dublin South-Central, 1977; Dublin South-East, 1981, 1982(Feb.), 1982(Nov.), 1987

Smith, F. J., *Belfast North*, 1973

Smith, H. E., *Belfast (Dock)*, 1969

Smith, James, *Antrim South*, 1975, 1982

Smith, James J., Cavan, 1937

Smith, John A., Limerick, 1923, 1927(June)

Smith, Matthew, Dún Laoghaire and Rathdown, 1951

Smith, Michael, Tipperary North, 1969–73 (def.), 1977–82(Feb.) (def.), 1982(Nov.), 1987–

Smith, Michael, Cavan-Monaghan, 1977, 1981, 1982(Feb.), 1982(Nov.)

Smith, Michael, Cork North-West, 1981, 1982(Feb.)

Smith, Patrick, Cavan, 1923–77

Smith, Peter, *Belfast North*, 1982

Smith, Rodney A. M., Antrim South (w), 1970

Smith, Ronald P., Louth, 1987, 1989

Smith, W. W., *Armagh*, 1982

Smithers, John, Dublin North-East, 1948, 1951

Smyth, A. Clifford, *Antrim North*, 1973, 1974(by)–6; Down North (w), 1979

Smyth, Colm, Longford-Westmeath, 1987

Smyth, D. W., Belfast North (w), 1974(Feb.)

Smyth, E. M., *Down South*, 1982, 1985(by)

Smyth, Frank, Dún Laoghaire, 1981

Smyth, Hugh, *Belfast West*, 1973–6, 1982

Smyth, J.J., Roscommon, 1951

Smyth, K. A., *Antrim South*, 1975, 1982; Antrim South (w), 1979, 1983

Smyth, Maureen C., *Belfast West*, 1973

Smyth, Michael, Kildare, 1923, 1927(June), 1927(Sept.)

Smyth, Michael, Galway West, 1965

Smyth, Michael, Tipperary South, 1973

Smyth, Samuel, *Belfast East*, 1973

Smyth, T. L., *Belfast East*, 1973

Smyth, Revd W. M., *Belfast South*, 1975–6, 1982–6; Belfast South (w), 1982(by)–85; 1986–
Smythe, Timothy, Clare, 1948
Snoddy, W. J., *Antrim South*, 1973
Somers, James, Dublin North-West, 1973; Dublin Central, 1981, 1982(Nov.), 1983(by)
Somerset, Thomas, Belfast North (w), 1929–45
Somerset, W, C., *Antrim South*, 1975
Sommerville, J. O., *Belfast South*, 1973
Speed, Anne, DUBLIN, 1989
Speers, J. A., *Armagh*, 1982, 1983(by)–6
Spence, William, *Belfast (Bloomfield)*, 1969; *Belfast West*, 1973
Spooner, James, Dublin South-West, 1973
Spring, Daniel, Kerry North, 1943–81
Spring, Richard (Dick), Kerry North, 1981–
Stack, Austin, Kerry-Limerick West, 1921–3; Kerry, 1923–7(Sept.)
Stack, Liam, Cork Borough, 1948
Stafford, James J., Wexford, 1927(June)
Stafford, John, Dublin Central, 1987–
Stafford, Matthew, Dublin North, 1933
Stafford, Thomas, Dublin North-East, 1957; Dublin North-Central, 1961, 1969
Stagg, Emmet, Kildare, 1981, 1987–
Staines, Michael, Dublin North-West, 1921–3, 1937, 1938, 1943
Stakelum, J. P., Tipperary, 1944
Stankard, Edward, Galway East, 1944
Stanley, S. F., Clare-Galway South, 1969
Stapleton, Richard, Tipperary, 1932, 1943–4 (def.); Tipperary South, 1948
Staunton, Andrew, Galway, 1927(Sept.)
Staunton, Myles, Mayo West, 1969, 1973–7 (def.), 1989; CONNAUGHT-ULSTER, 1979
Steele, James, Belfast West (w), 1950
Steele, S. A., *Antrim North*, 1973
Stein, F. E., Dún Laoghaire, 1977
Stevenson, G. D., *Londonderry*, 1973
Stevenson, Dr Howard, *Queen's University Belfast*, 1938(Dec.)(by)–49 (def.)
Stewart, Alexander, *Antrim North*, 1945
Stewart, Alexander, *Tyrone West*, 1958
Stewart, Charles, *Queen's University Belfast*, 1958–66
Stewart, James, *Belfast West*, 1973
Stewart, Revd John, *Belfast North*, 1973, 1975
Stewart, Joseph F., *Tyrone East*, 1929–64 (d); Fermanagh-Tyrone (w), 1934(by)–5
Stewart, Leslie, *Belfast (Victoria)*, 1962
Stewart, Robert, *Belfast South*, 1973
Stewart, S. A., Antrim South (w), 1964, 1966; *Antrim South*, 1965
Stewart, W. J., Belfast South (w), 1929–45; *Belfast (Cromac)*, 1938

Stockley, Prof. W. F. P., National University of Ireland, 1921–3 (def.), 1923(by)
Stokes, M. J., Dublin South-Central, 1982(Nov.)
Strain, Trevor, *Antrim North*, 1973
Stronge, Sir C. Norman L., *Armagh Mid*, 1938(Sept.)(by)–69
Stronge, Maj. Hon. J. M., *Armagh Mid*, 1969–73; *Armagh*, 1973–5
Sullivan, J. B., Cork North, 1948
Sullivan, James P., *Belfast West*, 1975
Sullivan, Redmond, Kerry South, 1977
Sullivan, Terence, Cork South-West, 1973
Sutherland, Peter, Dublin North-West, 1973
Swann, George, *Antrim South*, 1973
Swanton, Kathleen, Dublin North-Central, 1957
Sweeney, Charles, Donegal, 1932
Sweeney, J. A., Donegal, 1921–3
Sweeney, Margaret, Galway West, 1987
Sweeney, Michael J., Meath-Weatmeath, 1937, 1938, 1943
Sweeney, Pádraig (Paidí), Waterford, 1987, 1989
Sweeney, Patrick, Dublin South-West, 1973
Sweeney, Ronan, Donegal North-East, 1987
Sweetman, Edmund, Wicklow, 1944, 1948
Sweetman, Gerard, Carlow-Kildare, 1937, 1943; Kildare, 1948–70 (d.)
Sweetman, James, Dublin North-East, 1948
Sweetman, Michael, Dublin North-West, 1969
Swift, Brian, Waterford, 1981, 1982(Nov.), 1987–9 (def.)

Taggart, J. A., *Londonderry*, 1973
Tallon, James, Wicklow, 1981, 1982(Feb.); Dublin West, 1982(May)(by); Donegal South-West, 1983(by); Dublin Central, 1983(by); Laoighis-Offaly, 1984(by); Wexford, 1987
Tang, Muriel, Belfast East (w), 1983
Taylor, Francis, Clare, 1969–81
Taylor, J. D., *Tyrone South*, 1965–73; *Fermanagh-Tyrone South*, 1973–5; *Down North*, 1975–6, 1982–6; Strangford (w), 1983–5, 1986(by); NORTHERN IRELAND, 1979–89
Taylor, Madeleine, *see* Taylor-Quinn
Taylor, Mervyn, Dublin Co. South, 1973; Dublin Co. Mid, 1977; Dublin South-West, 1981–
Taylor-Quinn, Madeleine (formerly Taylor), Clare, 1981–2(Feb.) (def.), 1982(Nov.)–
Teehan, John, Wexford, 1981
Teehan, P. J., Carlow-Kilkenny, 1957, 1959(by)–61 (def.)
Teevan, Denis, Wicklow, 1982(Feb.)
Teevan, Thomas, Dublin South-West, 1948
Teevan, Thomas L., Belfast West (w), 1950(Nov.)(by)–1 (def.)
Tench, Gerald, Dublin Co., 1927(June)
Thompson, Francis H. E., *Mid-Ulster*, 1975–6

Thompson, Frederick, *Belfast (Ballynafeigh)*, 1937(by)–49
Thompson, J. Y., *Down South*, 1953
Thompson, Norman, *Belfast (Clifton)*, 1962, 1965, 1969
Thompson, Robert S., *Belfast (St Anne's)*, 1949; *Belfast (Bloomfield)*, 1950(by)
Thompson, Roy, *Antrim South*, 1982–6; Antrim South (w), 1983
Thompson, Samuel, Down South (w), 1964
Thompson, Seán, Kildare, 1982(Nov.)
Thompson, W. J., *Mid-Ulster*, 1973–6, 1982–6; Mid-Ulster (w), 1983
Thornbury, P. J., *Belfast Central*, 1933
Thornley, David, Dublin North-West, 1969–77; Dublin (Cabra), 1977; IRELAND, 1973–7
Thornton, Edward, Cavan, 1948
Thornton, Thomas, Mayo South, 1961
Thornton, W. N. J., Mid-Ulster (w), 1970, 1974(Feb.)
Thrift, Prof. W. E., Dublin University, 1921–37
Tiernan, Carol, Kildare, 1989
Tierney, Martin, Monaghan, 1965
Tierney, Prof. Michael, Galway, 1923; Mayo North, 1924(by), 1925(by)–7(June); National University of Ireland, 1927(Sept.)–32 (def.)
Tierney, Myles, Dublin Co. South, 1977
Tierney, Patrick, Tipperary, 1943; Tipperary North, 1951, 1954, 1957–69
Tierney, Thomas, Galway West, 1969
Timlin, M. J., Athlone-Longford, 1938, 1943, 1944
Timmins, Godfrey, Wicklow, 1961, 1968(by)–87 (def.), 1989–
Timmons, Eugene, Dublin North-East, 1948, 1951, 1954, 1961–5 (def.), 1969–77; Dublin (Artane), 1977; Dublin North-Central, 1981
Timoney, James, Tipperary, 1937
Timoney, John J., Tipperary South, 1948–51 (def.)
Toal, Brendan, Monaghan, 1973(Nov.)(by)–7; Cavan-Monaghan, 1977
Tobin, Denis A., Cork North-Central, 1987
Tobin, Dermot, Wicklow, 1989
Tobin, Laurence, Tipperary, 1927(Sept.)
Todd, W. R., *Armagh*, 1925(Nov.)(by); *Armagh Mid*, 1929; Armagh (w), 1929
Tolan, W. J., Leitrim-Sligo, 1927(June)
Toman, Cyril, *Armagh Mid*, 1969; *Down South*, 1982
Tomlin, J. C., *Antrim South*, 1973, 1982
Toner, Joseph, Dublin South-Central, 1948
Toomey, W. C., Cork North, 1948
Topping, W. W. B., *Larne*, 1945(Apr.)(by)–59
Tormey, William (Bill), Dublin North-West, 1987, 1989
Townsend, James, Carlow-Kilkenny, 1981
Tracey, M.D., Dublin South-East, 1982(Feb.)
Trainor, J. P., Dublin North-East, 1944, 1948, 1951
Trainor, Malachy, *Armagh South*, 1958, 1962
Trant, Patrick, Kerry, 1932

Travers, John, Leitrim, 1937
Traynor, Michael, Antrim South (w), 1955, 1959
Traynor, Oscar, Dublin North, 1925(by)–7(Sept.), 1929(by), 1932–7; Dublin North-East, 1937–61
Treacy, Andrew, Roscommon, 1954
Treacy, Noel, Galway East, 1982(July)(by)–
Treacy, Peter, Tipperary North, 1982(Feb.)
Treacy, Seán, Tipperary South, 1957, 1961–; MUNSTER, 1981–4
Trecey, Richard, Tipperary, 1927(Sept.)
Trench, R. P., Kildare, 1927(June)
Trimble, Noel, *Belfast North*, 1975
Trimble, Raymond, *Belfast North*, 1982
Trimble, W. D., *Down North*, 1973; *Belfast South*, 1975–6; Upper Bann (w), 1990(by)–
Troy, Joseph, Dublin North, 1932
Tubman, Patrick, Leitrim, 1937
Tubridy, Seán, Galway, 1927(June)–32 (def.); 1933; Galway West, 1937–40 (d.)
Tucker, Edward, Dublin South, 1923
Tuffy, Eamon, Dublin West, 1981, 1987, 1989
Tully, James, Meath, 1951, 1954–7 (def.), 1959(by), 1961–82(Feb.)
Tully, Jasper, Roscommon, 1923
Tully, John, Cavan, 1948–61 (def.), 1965–9 (def.)
Tunney, James, Dublin Co., 1943–4 (def.); Dublin North-West, 1948
Tunney, James C., Dublin North-West, 1965, 1969–77; Dublin (Finglas), 1977–81; Dublin North-West, 1981–; DUBLIN, 1984
Tuohy, P. F., Mayo South, 1923, 1927(June)
Turley, P. V., Monaghan, 1973
Turner, P.O., Dublin South-West, 1965
Turnly, J. F., *Antrim North*, 1973, 1974(by), 1975–6; Antrim North (w), 1979
Twaddell, W. J., *Belfast West*, 1921–2 (d)
Twomey, Michael, Cork West, 1943
Twomey, S. P., Cork Borough, 1954, 1956(by), 1961
Twomey, S. P., Cork South-Central, 1981
Tynan, Edward (Ted), Cork City, 1977, 1979(by); Cork North-Central, 1981, 1982(Feb.)
Tynan, Robert, Dublin Co., 1932
Tynan, Thomas, Leix-Offaly, 1927(June–Sept.) (def.)
Tynan, W. A., Carlow-Kildare, 1938

Upton, Patrick, Dublin South-Central, 1989
Utley, T. E., Antrim North (w), 1974(Feb.)

Vaughan, Daniel, Cork Mid/North/South/South-East/West, 1922–3; Cork North, 1923–33 (def.)
Vaughan, Robert, *Tyrone East*, 1962

Victory, James, Longford-Westmeath, 1923, 1927(June–Sept.) (def.), 1932, 1933–7; Athlone-Longford, 1937–43 (def.), 1944

Vipond, D. H., Monaghan, 1973(Nov.)(by); Down South, 1974(Oct.)

Vitty, Denis, *Belfast East*, 1982–6

Wade, Edward, Limerick East, 1989

Waldron, Terence, Mayo North, 1927(June)

Walker, A. Cecil, *Belfast North*, 1973; Belfast North (w), 1979, 1983–5, 1986(by)–

Walker, D. H., *Belfast (Woodvale)*, 1950(by)

Walker, Herbert, *Belfast (Pottinger)*, 1962

Wall, E. J., Carlow-Kilkenny, 1927(June)

Wall, Mark, Galway North, 1948

Wall, Michael, Carlow-Kilkenny, 1973

Wall, Michael, Dublin South-Central, 1987

Wall, Nicholas, Waterford, 1923–7(June) (def.), 1927(Sept.), 1933–8 (def.)

Wallace, Daniel, Cork North-Central, 1981, 1982(Feb.), 1982(Nov.)–

Wallace, E. B., *Queen's University Belfast*, 1945, 1949

Wallace, Revd J. B., *Belfast North*, 1921

Wallace, J. D., *Belfast (St Anne's)*, 1938

Wallace, Kevin, Cork North-Central, 1989

Wallace, Mary, Meath, 1987, 1989–

Wallace, T. B., Down West (w), 1921(by)–2(Jan.)

Waller, B. C., Dublin University, 1927(June)

Walsh, Anthony (Tonie), Dublin South-East, 1989

Walsh, Cormac, Kerry, 1923

Walsh, Eamonn, Dublin South-West, 1987

Walsh, Fursa, Galway West, 1951, 1954

Walsh, James E., Wexford, 1933

Walsh, James J., Cork Borough, 1921–7(Sept.)

Walsh, John, *Londonderry*, 1921

Walsh, John, Kerry North, 1948

Walsh, Joseph, Cork South-West, 1977–81 (def.), 1982(Feb.)–

Walsh, Laurence J., Louth, 1937–43 (def.), 1944–8 (def.), 1951–4 (def.)

Walsh, Liam, Waterford, 1944

Walsh, Louis J., *Antrim*, 1921

Walsh, Máire, Dublin Co. North, 1973

Walsh, Mary, Wicklow, 1973

Walsh, Maud, Dublin Townships, 1937

Walsh, Michael, Cork East, 1924(by)

Walsh, Michael, Galway West, 1965

Walsh, Norman, Waterford, 1954, 1957

Walsh, Patrick, Tipperary South, 1951, 1954

Walsh, Patrick K., Limerick, 1923

Walsh, Richard, Mayo South, 1927(June), 1927(Sept.)–43 (def.), 1944–51

Walsh, Richard, Waterford, 1965

Walsh, Samuel H., *Belfast (Shankill)*, 1969

Walsh, Seán, Dublin Co., 1961, 1965; Dublin Co. North, 1969, 1973–7; Dublin Co. Mid., 1977–81; Dublin South-West, 1981–9 (def.)

Walsh, Seán, Carlow-Kilkenny, 1977, 1981, 1982(Feb.), 1982(Nov.); LEINSTER, 1979

Walsh, Thomas, Kilkenny, 1943, 1944; Carlow-Kilkenny, 1948–56 (d.)

Walsh, William (Ballinrobe), Mayo South, 1943

Walsh, William (Kiltimagh), Mayo South, 1943

Walton, Simon, Kilkenny, 1938

Ward, C. F., Monaghan, 1927(June), 1927(Sept.)–48

Ward, Edward, Dublin North-West, 1948

Ward, F. C., Monaghan, 1961

Ward, Martin, Limerick West, 1957

Ward, Michael J., Dublin Central, 1982(Feb.)

Ward, P. J., Donegal, 1921–4

Warden, M. I., *Belfast South*, 1982

Waring, M. A., *Iveagh*, 1929–33

Warnock, J. E., *Belfast (St Anne's)*, 1938–69

Waters, Frank, Longford-Westmeath, 1948, 1951

Watkins, Thomas, Dublin Co., 1943, 1948

Watt, S. J., *Queen's University Belfast*, 1958; Belfast East (w), 1964

Watt, T. D., Dublin North-West, 1969

Watton, W. C., *Larne*, 1962

Webster, William (Bill), Londonderry (w), 1979

Wells, J. H., *Down South*, 1982–6; Upper Bann (w), 1983

Wellwood, William, Londonderry (w), 1951(May)(by)–5

West, H. W., *Enniskillen*, 1958–73; *Fermanagh-Tyrone South*, 1973–6; Fermanagh-Tyrone South (w), 1974(Feb.–Oct.) (def.), 1981(by); NORTHERN IRELAND, 1979

Weymes, P. H., Westmeath, 1918

Whelan, James, Dublin North, 1923

Whelan, Patrick, Longford-Westmeath, 1989

Whelan, Séamus, Wexford, 1977

Whelan, Seán, Waterford, 1969, 1977

Whelehan, Joseph, Galway, 1921–3

Whitaker, H. T., *Belfast North*, 1925

Whitby, Adrian, *Antrim South*, 1970(by)

White, James, Donegal South-West, 1965; Donegal-Leitrim, 1970(by), 1973–7; Donegal, 1977–81; Donegal South-West, 1981–2(Feb.)

White, John, Donegal, 1923–33

White, Michael, Dublin Central, 1981, 1982(Feb.), 1982(Nov.), 1983(by)

White, Patrick, Meath, 1923

White, Peter, Dublin South, 1943

White, V. J., Waterford-Tipperary East, 1921–3; Waterford, 1923, 1927(June)–32 (def.), 1933

Whitla, Sir William, Queen's University Belfast (w), 1918–23

Whitten, Herbert, *Armagh Central*, 1969–73; *Armagh*, 1973–6

Whyte, Ann, Cork North-Central, 1987
Whyte, Liam, Tipperary North, 1961, 1969, 1973, 1977
Whyte, Martin, Clare, 1954
Wiegleb, Edward, *Belfast (Cromac)*, 1969
Wilcock, J. V., *Londonderry City*, 1968(by)
Wiley, Colm, Clare, 1982(Nov.)
Wilkinson, Anne, Donegal North-East, 1981, 1982(Feb.), 1982(Nov.), 1989
Willey, T. G., *Armagh*, 1973
Williams, Gareth, Antrim North, 1987
Williams, Richard, Dublin Co., 1951
Williamson, Anthony, *Down South*, 1973, 1975
Williamson, Gerald, Meath-Westmeath, 1937
Williamson, John, *Londonderry*, 1975
Willoughby, William, Wexford, 1989
Wilson, A. F., *Belfast (Windsor)*, 1945–56
Wilson, B. A. S., *Down North*, 1982
Wilson, C. G., *Belfast South*, 1982
Wilson, David, Belfast North (w), 1929
Wilson, Field Marshal Sir Henry H., Down North, 1922(Feb.(by)–June) (d.)
Wilson, Hubert J. C., Longford-Westmeath, 1923; Athlone-Longford, 1937;
    Longford-Westmeath, 1954
Wilson, Hugh, *Larne*, 1969; *Antrim North*, 1973–6; Antrim North (w),
    1974(Oct.), 1979
Wilson, John C., *Iveagh*, 1933–8
Wilson, John P., Cavan, 1973–7; Cavan-Monaghan, 1977–
Wilson, L. F., Antrim South (w), 1964
Wilson, Marcus, Dublin North-East, 1969
Wilson, Richard, Kildare-Wicklow, 1922–3; Wicklow, 1923–7(June) (def.),
    1927(Sept.)
Wilson, Robert N., *Antrim Mid*, 1945–53
Wilson, Samuel, *Belfast East*, 1982
Wilson, W. I., *Iveagh*, 1929, 1938
Wilton, C. J., *Londonderry City*, 1965, 1969
Wilton, W. McC., *Belfast (Oldpark)*, 1933; *Belfast (Clifton)*, 1938; *Belfast West*,
    1943(by)
Wolahan, Seán, Wicklow, 1987, 1989
Wolfe, George, Kildare, 1923–32
Wolfe, J. T., Cork West, 1927(June)–33
Woodburn, John, Antrim Mid (w), 1933
Woods, F. N., *Down South*, 1969
Woods, M. J., Dublin (Clontarf), 1977–1; Dublin North-East, 1981–
Woods, Lt Col. P. J., *Belfast West*, 1923(by)–9; *Belfast South*, 1925 (elected but
    chooses to sit for Belfast West); *Belfast (St Anne's)*, 1929; Belfast South (w),
    1929
Workman, Maj. Robert, *Down North*, 1941(by)
Wright, Anthony (Tony), Waterford, 1987

Wright, G. V., Dublin North, 1987–9 (def.)
Wright, Patrick, Kildare, 1987
Wright, Thomas, *Belfast South*, 1973
Wright, Thomas, Dublin North, 1982(Feb.), 1982(Nov.)
Wright, Verdun, *Mid-Ulster*, 1973
Wright, W. T., *Antrim North*, 1975–6
Wycherley, Florence, Cork West, 1954, 1957–61; Cork South-West, 1961
Wylie, David, *Belfast (Oldpark)*, 1945
Wylie, John, *Antrim North*, 1969
Wynne, Stanley, *Lisnaskea*, 1968(by)
Wyse, Pearse, Cork Borough, 1965–9; Cork City South-East, 1969–77; Cork
    City, 1977–81; Cork South-Central, 1981–

Yates, Ivan, Wexford, 1981–
Yeates, Padraig, Dublin North-Central, 1982(Nov.)
Yeats, M. B., Dublin South-East, 1948, 1951; IRELAND, 1972–9; DUBLIN,
    1979
Young, G. C. G., *Bannside*, 1929–39 (d.)
Young, Kenneth, Down North (w), 1970; *Down North*, 1973

Zammitt, E. A., Foyle (w), 1987

Source: Brian M. Walker (ed.), *Parliamentary Elections Results in Ireland,
1918–92* (Dublin and Belfast, 1992).

HEADS OF STATE

United Kingdom of Great Britain and Ireland/Northern Ireland

Sovereigns

	Reign
George III	25 Oct. 1760 – 19 July 1821
George IV	Prince Regent from 5 Feb. 1811
	29 Jan. 1820 – 26 June 1830
William IV	26 June 1830 – 20 June 1837
Victoria	20 June 1837 – 22 Jan. 1901
Edward VII	22 Jan. 1901 – 6 May 1910
George V	6 May 1910 – 20 Jan. 1936
Edward VIII	20 Jan. 1936 – 11 Dec. 1936 (d. 1972)
George VI	11 Dec. 1936 – 6 Feb. 1952
Elizabeth II	6 Feb. 1952

Lord Lieutenants (Viceroy)

	Appointed
Philip Yorke, 3rd Earl of Hardwicke	17 Mar. 1801
Edward Clive, 1st Earl of Powis	21 Nov. 1802
John Russell, 6th Duke of Bedford	12 Feb. 1806
Charles Lennox, 4th Duke of Richmond	1 Apr. 1807
Charles Whilworth, 1st Baron Whilworth (cr. Viscount Whilworth, 14 June 1813; Earl of Whilworth, 28 Nov. 1815)	14 June 1813
Charles Chetwynd Talbot, 2nd Earl Talbot	17 Sept. 1817
Richard Wellesley, 1st Marquis Wellesley	10 Dec. 1821
Henry William Paget, 1st Marquis of Anglesey	27 Feb. 1828
Hugh Percy, 3rd Duke of Northumberland	2 Feb. 1829
Henry William Paget, 1st Marquis of Anglesey	22 Nov. 1830
Richard Wellesley, 1st Marquis of Anglesey	11 Sept. 1833
Thomas Hamilton, 9th Earl of Haddington	29 Dec. 1834
Constantine Henry Phipps, 6th Earl of Mulgrave (cr. Marquis of Normanby, 25 June 1838)	23 Apr. 1835
Hugh Fortescue, Viscount Ebrington (cr. 2nd Earl Fortescue, 16 June 1841)	1 Mar. 1839
Thomas Philip de Grey, 2nd Earl de Grey	3 Sept. 1841
William A'Court, 1st Baron Hertesbury	10 July 1844
John William Ponsonby, 4th Earl of Bessborough	6 July 1846
George William Frederick Villirs, 4th Earl of Clarendon	20 May 1847

Archibald William Montgomerie, 13th Earl of Eglinton	27 Feb. 1852
Edward Granville Eliot, 3rd Earl of St Germans	4 Jan. 1853
George William Frederick Howard, 7th Earl of Carlisle	28 Feb. 1855
Archibald William Montgomerie, 13th Earl of Eglinton (cr. Earl of Winton, 17 June 1859)	26 Feb. 1858
George William Frederick Howard, 7th Earl of Carlisle	18 June 1859
John Woodhouse, 3rd Baron Woodhouse (cr. Earl of Kimberley, 1 June 1866)	1 Nov. 1864
James Hamilton, 2nd Marquis of Abercorn (cr. Duke of Abercorn, 10 Aug. 1868)	6 July 1866
John Poyntz Spencer, 5th Earl Spencer	12 Dec. 1868
James Hamilton, Duke of Abercorn	2 Mar. 1874
John Winston Spencer Churchill, 7th Duke of Marlborough	28 Nov. 1876
Francis Thomas de Grey Cowper, 7th Earl Cowper	3 May 1880
John Poyntz Spencer, 5th Earl Spencer	3 May 1882
Henry Howard Molyneux Herbert, 4th Earl of Carnarvon	27 June 1885
John Campbell Hamilton Gordon, 7th Earl of Aberdeen	6 Feb. 1886
Charles Stewart Vane-Tempest Stewart, 6th Marquis of Londonderry	3 Aug. 1886
Lawrence Dundas, 3rd Earl of Zetland	30 July 1889
Robert Offley Ashbourton Milnes, 2nd Baron Houghton (assumed surname Crewe-Milner, 8 June 1894)	18 Aug. 1892
George Henry Cadogan, 6th Earl Cadogan	29 June 1895
William Humble Ward, 3rd Earl of Dudley	11 Aug. 1902
John Campbell Hamilton Gordon, 7th Earl of Aberdeen	11 Dec. 1905
Ivor Churchill Guest, 2nd Baron Wimborne	16 Feb. 1915
John Denton Pinkstone French (1st Viscount French of Ypres and of High Lake)	7 May 1918
Lord Edmund Bernard Talbot (cr. Viscount Fitzlan of Derwent, 28 Apr. 1921; resumed paternal surname, Fitzlan-Howard, 9 June 1921)	22 Apr. 1921

Governors of Northern Ireland

(Office abolished in 1973)

	Appointed
James Albert Edward Hamilton, 3rd Duke of Abercorn	11 Dec. 1922
William Spencer Levenson Gower, 4th Earl Granville	7 Sept. 1945
John de Vere Loder, 2nd Baron Wakehurst	1 Dec. 1952
John Maxwell Eskine, 1st Baron Erskine of Ressick	1 Dec. 1964
Ralph Francis Alnwick Grey, Baron Grey of Naunton	2 Dec. 1968

Irish Free State/Éire/Republic of Ireland

Governor Generals of the Irish Free State, 1922–1938

	Appointed
Timothy Michael Healy	6 Dec. 1922
James MacNeill	15 Dec. 1927
Domhnall Ua Buachalla	26 Nov. 1933

Uachtarán na hÉireann (President), 1938–

	Elected
Douglas Hyde	4 May 1938
Seán Thomas O'Kelly	18 June 1945
Eamon de Valera	18 June 1959
Erskine Hamilton Childers	31 May 1973
Cearbhall Ó Dálaigh	3 Dec. 1974
Patrick John Hillery	9 Nov. 1976
Mary Robinson	9 Nov. 1990
Mary McAleese	30 Oct. 1997

THE HOUSE OF LORDS

The United Kingdom House of Lords

Composition

The Act of Union (1800) specified that four Lords spiritual of Ireland, by rotation of sessions, and 28 Lords temporal of Ireland, elected for life by the peers of Ireland, should be the number to sit and vote on the part of Ireland in the House of Lords of the parliament of the United Kingdom. Any person holding an Irish peerage would not be disqualified from being elected to serve for any constituency in the House of Commons of the United Kingdom, unless he was previously elected to sit in the House of Lords of the United Kingdom.

Irish peers holding English, Great Britain or United Kingdom titles held seats in their own right in the House of Lords. Twenty-eight representative peers were elected from among the Irish peers to sit in the House of Lords for life. No representative peer was elected to fill a vacancy after creation of the Irish Free State. The last representative peer died in 1961.

Irish spiritual and representative peers

	Prelates	Representative peers	Entitled to vote
1820	4	28	372
1830	4	28	399
1837	4	28	421
1840	16	28	448
1850	4	28	441
1860	4	28	443
1870	–	28	462
1880	–	28	500
1890	–	28	539
1900	–	28	577
1910	–	28	622
1920	–	27	716
1930	–	18	753
1939	–	13	785
1950	–	6	847
1960	–	1	908
1970	–	–	1,057
1980	–	–	1,171
1990	–	–	1,186

The original 28 Irish representative peers

Elected 2 Aug 1800

John Thomas	13th Earl of Clanricarde
George Frederick	7th Earl of Westmeath
Thomas	2nd Earl of Bective
Robert	2nd Earl of Roden
John Denis	3rd Earl of Altamont
John	2nd Earl of Glendore
Thomas	2nd Earl of Longford
John	1st Earl of Erne
Otway	1st Earl of Desart
Robert	1st Earl of Leitrim
Richard	2nd Earl of Lucan
Robert	1st Earl of Londonderry
Henry	1st Earl Conyngham
Francis	2nd Earl of Llandaff
Robert	2nd Viscount Wicklow
Thomas	1st Viscount Northland
Laurence	Viscount Oxmantown
Charles Henry	2nd Viscount O'Neill
Francis	1st Viscount Bandon
Richard Hely	1st Viscount Donoughmore
Hugh	1st Viscount Carleton
Richard	11th Baron Calier
Edmund Henry	2nd Baron Callen
Charles	Lord Somerton
Richard	1st Viscount Longueville
Robert	1st Baron Rossmore
James	Baron Tyrawly

Elections on vacancy of Irish representative peers

New peer	Title	Replacing	Date of election	Died
Bury, Charles William	1st E of Charleville	B Rosemore	2 Nov. 01	31 Oct. 35
Cole, John Willoughby	2nd E of Enniskillen	E of Desart	15 Oct. 04	32 Mar. 40
Du Pré, Alexander	2nd E of Caledon	E of Leitrim	26 Nov. 04	8 Apr. 39
Caulfeild, Francis William	2nd E of Charlemont	E of Llandaff	22 Nov. 06	25 Dec. 63
King, George	3rd E of Kingston	E of Rosse	11 July 07	18 Oct. 39
Trench, Richard Le Poer	2nd E of Clancarty	E of Clanricarde	16 Dec. 08	24 Nov. 37
Gardiner, Charles John	E of Blessington	M of Sligo	15 Apr. 09	25 May 29
Parsons, Lawrence	2nd E of Rosse	E of Normanton	21 Oct. 09	24 Feb. 41
Acheson, Archibald	2nd E of Gosford	V Longeville	19 Aug. 11	27 Mar. 40
Moore, Stephen	2nd E Mountcashell	E of Westmeath	24 Mar. 15	27 Oct. 22
Maxwell, John James	2nd E of Farnham	E of Glandore	3 Mar. 16	23 July 23

291

New peer	Title	Replacing	Date of election	Died
O'Brien, William	2nd M of Thomand	B Callan	3 Mar. 16	21 Aug. 46
Bourke, John	4th E of Mayo	E of Wicklow	3 Mar. 16	23 May 49
Butler, Somerset Richard	3rd E of Carrick	V Northland	13 Mar. 19	4 Feb. 38
Corry, Somerset Lowry	2nd E Belmore	E of Glengall	1 May 1819	18 Apr. 41
Blackwood, J. S.	2nd B Dufferin and Clandeboye	E of Roden	7 Oct. 1820	8 Aug. 36
Wingfield, Richard	5th V Powerscourt	M of Londonderry	3 Aug. 21	9 Aug. 23
Howard, William	3rd E of Wicklow	Baron Tyrawley	10 Nov. 21	22 Mar. 69
King, Robert Edward	1st V Lorton	E of Mountcashell	5 Feb. 23	20 Nov. 54
Freke, John Evans	6th B Carbery	E of Farnham	25 Oct. 23	12 May 45
Vereker, Charles	2nd V Gort	V Powerscourt	5 Dec. 23	11 Nov. 42
Barry, John Maxwell	5th B Farnham	E of Donoughmore	18 Dec. 25	20 Sept. 38
Moore, Stephen	3rd E of Mountcashell	V Carleton	2 July 26	10 Oct. 83
Prittie, Henry	2nd B Dunalley	E of Erne	18 Dec. 28	10 Oct. 54
Buttler, Richard	2nd E of Glengall	E of Blessington	1 Sept. 29	22 June 58
St Leger, Hayes	3rd V Doneralle	M of Headfort	15 Mar. 30	27 Mar. 54
Nugent, George T. J.	M of Westmeath	E of Bandon	25 Feb. 31	5 May 71
De Burgh, Ulysses	2nd B Downes	M Conyngham	29 Mar. 33	28 July 63
Bernard, James	2nd E of Bandon	E of Longford	31 July 35	31 Oct. 58
Plunkett, Edward Wadding	14th B Dunsany	E of Charleville	18 Jan. 36	11 Dec. 48
Cornwallis, Maude	3rd V Hawarden	B Dufferin	31 Oct. 36	12 Oct. 56
Dillon, Robert	3rd B Clonbrock	E of Clancarty	20 Feb. 38	4 Dec. 93
Bury, Charles William	2nd E of Charleville	E of Carrick	13 Apr. 38	14 July 51
Vessey, John	2nd V De Vesci	B Farnham	19 Jan. 39	19 Oct. 55
Maxwell, Henry	7th B Farnham	E of Caledon	2 July 39	20 Aug. 68
Henry, Windham	2nd E of Dunraven	E of Lucan	22 Sept. 39	6 Aug. 50
Crofton, Edward	2nd B Crofton	E of Kingston	20 Jan. 40	17 Dec. 69
Bingham, George Charles	3rd E of Lucan	E of Enniskillen	22 Jun. 40	10 Nov. 88
Du Pré, James	3rd E of Caledon	E of Rosse	7 May 41	30 June 55
Blayney, Cadwallader D.	12th B Blayney	E O'Neill	12 June 41	18 Jan. 74
Handcock, Richard	3rd B Castlemaine	E of Belmore	6 July 41	4 July 69
O'Neill, John B. R.	3rd V O'Neill	V Gort	13 Feb. 43	12 Feb. 55
Parsons, William	3rd E of Rosse	E of Limerick	23 Feb. 45	31 Oct. 67
Crichton, John	3rd E Erne	B Carbery	24 July 45	2 Oct. 85
Cuffe, Johyn Otway O'Connor	3rd E of Desart	M of Thomand	11 Dec. 46	1 Apr. 65
Massy, Eyre	3rd B Clarina	B Dunsany	16 Apr. 49	18 Nov. 72
Browne, John Davendish	3rd B Kilmaine	E of Gosford	22 June 49	12 Jan. 73
Danvers, George J. D. B.	5th E of Lanesborough	E of Mayo	14 Aug. 49	7 July 66
Plunkett, Randall, Edward	15th B Dunsany	E of Dunraven	19 Nov. 50	7 Apr. 52
Daly, Denis St G.	2nd B Dunsandle and Clanconal	E of Charlesville	23 Sept. 51	12 Jan. 93
Bourke, Robert	5th E of Mayo	B Dunsany	22 June 52	12 Aug. 67
White, Richard	2nd E of Bantry	V Doneralle	1 July 54	16 July 68
Ward, Edward	4th V Bangor	B Dunalley	9 Jan. 1855	14 Sept. 81
Damer, Henry J. R. D.	3rd E of Portarlington	V Lorton	24 Feb. 55	1 Mar. 89
St Leger, Hayes	4th V Doneralle	V O'Neill	2 May 55	26 Aug. 87
Trevor, Arthur Hill	3rd V Dungannon	E of Caledon	11 Sept. 55	11 Aug. 63

New peer	Title	Replacing	Date of election	Died
Hewitt, James	4th V Lifford	V De Vesci	23 Jan. 56	20 Nov. 87
Vessey, Thomas	3rd V De Vesci	V Harwarden	10 Jan. 57	23 Dec. 75
Cory, Somerset Richard Lowry	4th E of Belmore	E of Bandon	13 Jan. 57	6 Apr. 13
Bernard, Francis	3rd E Bandon	E of Glengall	21 Aug. 58	17 Feb. 77
Maude, C.	4th V Hawarden (E de Montalt)	V Dungannon	2 Dec. 62	9 Jan. 05
O'Brien, Lucius	13th B Inchiquin	B Downes	20 Oct. 63	22 Mar. 72
Plunkett, Edward	16th B Dunsany	E of Charlemont	8 Mar. 64	22 Feb. 89
Verker, John Prendergast	3rd V Gort	E of Desart	12 June 65	20 Oct. 65
Wingfield, Mervyn	7th V Powerscourt	V Gort	26 Dec. 65	5 June 04
Upton, George Frederick	3rd V Templetown	E of Lanesborough	14 Sept. 66	4 Jan. 90
Annesley, William Richard	4th E Annesley	E of Mayo	15 Oct. 67	10 Aug. 74
Butler, Theobald Fitzwalter	14th B Dunboyne	E of Rosse	11 Jan. 68	22 Mar. 81
Winn, Charles Allanson	3rd B Headley	E of Bantry	26 Sept. 68	20 July 77
Parsons, Laurence	4th E of Rosse	B Farnham	22 Dec. 68	30 Aug. 08
White, William Henry Hare Hedges	3rd E of Bantry	E of Wicklow	6 July 69	15 Jan. 84
Guthrie, G. D. A. F.	2nd B Oranmore and Browne	B Castlemaine	6 Sept. 69	15 Nov. 00
Butler, John V. D.	6th E of Lanesborough	B Crofton	5 Apr. 70	12 Sept. 05
De Moleyns, Darvolics Blakeney	5th B Ventry	M of Westmeath	10 July 71	8 Feb. 14
Howard, Charles Francis Arnold	5th E of Wicklow	B Inchiquin	19 June 72	21 June 91
Crofton, Edward Henry Churchill	3rd B Crofton	B Clarina	11 Feb. 73	22 Sept. 12
O'Brien, Edward Donough	14th B Inchiquin	B Kilmaine	5 Apr. 73	9 Apr. 00
Handcock, Richard	4th B Castlemaine	B Blayney	9 May 74	26 Apr. 92
Scott, John Henry Reginald	4th E of Clonmell	E Annesley	10 Nov. 74	22 June 91
Massy, John Thomas William	6th B Massy	V De Vesci	14 Mar. 76	28 Nov. 15
Annesley, Hugh	5th E Annesley	E of Bandon	28 Apr. 77	15 Dec. 08
Alexander, James	5th E of Caledon	B Headley	20 Oct. 77	28 Apr. 98
Bernard, James Francis	4th E of Bandon	B Dunboyna	6 June 81	18 May 24
Leeson, Edward Nugent	6th E of Miltown	E of Wicklow	23 Aug. 81	30 May 90
Needham, Francis Charles	3rd E of Kilmorey	V Bangor	31 Dec. 81	28 July 15
Winn, Charles Mark Allason	4th B Headley	E Mountcashel	20 Dec. 83	13 Jan. 13
Rowley, Hercules Edward	4th B Langford	E of Bantry	14 Mar. 84	29 Oct. 19
Ward, Henry William Crosbie	5th V Bangor	E of Erne	27 Nov. 85	23 Feb. 11
King-Tenison, Henry E. N.	8th E of Kingston	V Doneralle	24 Oct. 87	13 Jan. 96
Howard, Cecil Ralph	6th E of Wicklow	V Lifford	24 Jan. 88	24 July 91
Massy, Eyre Challoner Henry	4th B Clarina	E of Lucan	21 Dec. 88	16 Dec. 97
Bunbury, Thomas K. McC.	2nd B Rathdonnel	B Dunsany	8 Apr. 89	23 May 29
Bingham, George	4th E of Lucan	E of Portarlington	19 Apr. 89	5 June 14
Browne, Francis William	4th B Kilmaine	V Templetown	21 Feb. 90	9 Nov. 07
Bourke, Dermot Robert Wyndham	7th E of Mayo	E of Miltown	14 July 90	31 Dec. 27
Freke, William Charles Evans	8th B Carbary	E of Clonmell	3 Aug. 91	7 Nov. 94
Pritte, Henry O'Callaghan	4th B Dunalley	E of Wicklow	9 Oct. 91	5 Aug. 27

293

New peer	Title	Replacing	Date of election	Died
Deane-Morgan, Hamilton M. Fitzmaurice	4th B Muskerry	B Castlemaine	19 June 92	5 June 29
Plunkett, John William	17th B Dunsany	B Dunsandle	6 Mar. 93	16 Jan. 99
Upton, Henry Edward	4th V Templetown	B Clonbrock	29 Jan. 94	2 Oct. 39
Dillon, Luke Gerald	4th B Clonbrock	B Carbery	23 Jan. 95	12 May 17
Damer, Lionel George Henry Seymour Dawson	5th E of Portarlington	E of Kingston	20 Mar. 96	31 Aug. 00
Handcock, Albert Edward	5th B Castlemaine	B Clarina	Mar. 98	7 July 37
Maxwell, Somerset Henry	10th B Farnham	E of Caledon	22 July 98	22 Nov. 00
Ponsonby, William Moore	9th E of Drogheda	B Dunsany	6 Apr. 99	28 Oct. 08
Raymond, Harvey De Montmorency	3rd V Franfort De Montmorncey	B Inchiquin	30 May 00	7 May 02
O'Brien, Lucius William	15th B Inchiquin	E of Portarlington	23 Nov. 00	10 Dec. 29
Butler, Robert St John Fitzwalter	16th B Dunboyne	B Oramore and Browne	4 Jan. 01	29 Aug. 13
Nugent, Anthony Francis	11th E of Westmeath	B Farnham	5 Feb. 01	12 Dec. 33
Browne-Guthrie, George Henry Brown	3rd B Oramore and Browne	V Frankfort De Montmorency	11 July 02	30 June 27
Bellew, Charles Bertram	3rd B Bellew	V Powerscourt	1 Aug. 04	15 July 11
Bligh, Ivo Francis Walter	8th E of Darnley	E de Montalt	9 Mar. 05	10 Apr. 27
Howard, Ralph Francis	7th E of Wicklow	E of Lanesborough	28 Nov. 05	11 Oct. 46
Curzon, George N.	1st B Curzon of Kedleston	B Kilmaine	21 Jan. 08	20 Mar. 25
Oliver, Frederick	3rd B Ashtown	E of Rosse	4 Nov. 08	Vac Nov. 13
Maxwell, Arthur Kenilis	11th B Farnham	E of Drogheda	18 Dec. 08	5 Feb. 57
Vessey, Richard	5th V De Vesci	E Annesley	10 Feb. 09	16 Aug. 58
Browne, John Edward Deane	5th B Kilmaine	V Bangor	14 Apr. 11	28 Aug. 46
Parsons, William Edward	5th E of Rosse	B Bellew	10 Oct. 11	10 Jun. 18
Horsely-Beresford, John Graham Hope Delapoer	5th B Decles	B Crofton	19 Nov. 12	31 Jan. 44
Ward, Maxwell Richard Crosbie	6th V Bangor	B Headley	7 Mar. 13	17 Nov. 50
Butler, Charles J. Brinsely	7th E Lanesborough	E of Belmore	6 June 13	18 Aug. 29
Moore, Henry C. Ponsonby	10th E of Drogheda	B Dunboyne	21 Nov. 13	22 Nov. 57
Bryan, George Leopold	4th B Bellew	B Ventry	21 Apr. 14	14 June 35
Bingham, George Charles	5th E of Lucan	E of Lucan	11 Aug. 14	20 Apr. 49
Lambert, Frederick Rudolph	10th E of Cavan	E of Kilmorey	14 Sept. 15	27 Aug. 46
Crofton, Arthur Edward Lowther	4th B Crofton	B Ashtown	10 Jan. 16	15 June 46
Needham, Francis Charles Adelbert Henry	4th E of Kilmorey	B Massy	14 Feb. 16	11 Jan. 61
King-Tenison, Henry Edwin	9th E of Kingston	B Clonbrock	10 July 17	11 Jan. 46
Caulfeild, James Edward	8th V Charlemont	E of Rosse	19 Aug. 18	30 Aug. 49
Jocelyn, Robert Soame	8th E of Roden	B Langford	22 Dec. 19	11 Aug. 49

B = Baron
D = Duke
E = Earl
M = Marquess
V = Viscount

Lords Chancellors of Great Britain

Chairman/speaker of the House of Lords

	Appointed
1st Baron Brougham and Vaux	22 Nov. 1830
Baron Lyndhurst	21 Nov. 1834
The seal in commission	23 Apr. 1835
Baron Cottenham	16 Jan. 1836
Baron Lyndhurst	3 Sept. 1841
1st Baron Cottenham (cr. Viscount Crowhurst and Earl of Cottenham 1850)	6 July 1846
In commission	19 June 1850
Lord Truro	15 July 1850
1st Baron St Leonards	27 Feb. 1852
Lord Cranworth	28 Dec. 1852
1st Baron Chelmsford	26 Feb. 1858
Baron Campbell	15 June 1859
1st Baron Westbury	26 June 1861
Lord Cranworth	7 July 1865
1st Baron Chelmsford	6 July 1866
Lord Cairns of Garmoyle	29 Feb. 1868
Lord Hatherley	9 Dec. 1868
1st Earl of Selborne	15 Oct. 1872
Lord Cairns (cr. Viscount Garmoyle and 1st Earl Cairns 1878)	21 Feb. 1874
1st Earl of Selborne	28 Apr. 1880
1st Earl of Halsbury	24 June 1885
1st Baron Herschell	6 Feb. 1886
1st Earl of Halsbury	3 Aug. 1886
1st Baron Herschell	18 Aug. 1892
1st Earl of Halsbury	29 June 1895
Lord Loreburn	10 Dec. 1905
1st Viscount Haldane	10 June 1912
Lord Buckmaster	25 May 1915
Lord Finlay	10 Dec. 1916
1st Earl of Birkenhead	10 Jan. 1919
Lord Cave	24 Oct. 1922
1st Viscount Haldane	22 Jan. 1924
Lord Cave	6 Nov. 1924
1st Viscount Hailsham	28 Mar. 1928
Lord Sankey	7 June 1929
1st Viscount Hailsham	7 June 1935
Lord Maugham	3 Mar. 1938
Lord Caldecote	3 Sept. 1939
Lord Simon	12 May 1940
Lord Jowitt	27 July 1945

	Appointed
Lord Simonds	30 Oct. 1951
Lord Kilmuir	18 Oct. 1954
Lord Dilhorne	13 July 1962
Lord Gardiner	16 Oct. 1964
Lord Hailsham of St Marylebone (formerly 2nd Viscount Hailsham, cr. Baron 1970)	20 June 1970
Lord Elwyn-Jones	5 Mar. 1974
Lord Hailsham of St Marylebone	5 May 1979
Lord Havers	13 June 1987
Lord Mackay of Clashfern	26 Oct. 1987
Lord Irvine of Lairg	2 May 1997
Lord Falconer of Thoroton	12 June 2003

The Southern Irish Senate of 1920

Created by the Better Government of Ireland Act (1920). Only met three times in 1921. To consist of the Lord Chancellor of Ireland, as chairman; 15 peers of the realm (Southern Ireland), elected by their peers; eight Privy Councillors, elected by Privy Councillors; two representatives of the Church of Ireland; two representatives of the Catholic Church (which declined to nominate); 16 individuals nominated by the Lord Lieutenant, including two who wereto be nominated after consultation with the Labour movement (which also declined to be involved); and 17 elected by county councils. In total there were to be 39 senators excluding the Lord Chancellor.

Members of the (1921) Senate of Southern Ireland

Sir John Ross, Lord Chancellor of Ireland and Chairman of the Senate

Peers resident in Southern Ireland elected by their peers

Baron Cloncurry
Baron de Freyne
Earl of Desart
Earl of Donoughmore
Earl of Dunraven and Mount-Earl*
Baron HolmPatrick
Baron Inchiquin
Earl of Kenmore
Earl of Mayo*
Earl of Midleton
Baron Oranmore and Brown
Viscount Powerscourt
Baron Rathdonnell
Marquess of Sligo
Earl of Wicklow*

Privy Councillors to be elected by Privy Councillors

Sir William Goulding, bt
Earl of Granard*
W. McMurrough Kavanagh
Sir Bryan Mahon*
Earl of Meath
Sir Thomas Stafford, bt
L. A. Waldron (resigned before the first meeting of the Senate)
Earl of Westmeath

Representatives of the Church of Ireland

Archbishop C. F. D'Arcy
J. A. F. Gregg

Representatives of Catholic Church not nominated by the Church

Appointed by the Lord Lieutenant

A. Jameson*
Sir Andrew Beattie
Sir John Arnott, bt
E. H. Andrews
H. S. Guinness*
H. P. Glynn
J. W. R. Campbell
F. F. Denning
C. G. Gamble
Sir John Moore
Sir William Taylor
Sir John Purser Griffith*
G. O'Callaghan Westropp
Sir Nugent Everard, bt*

*Became members of the first Irish Free State Senate in 1922.
Source <www.ark.ac.uk>.

LOCAL GOVERNMENT

Lords Mayor of Dublin

	Appointed
Charles Thorp	1800
Richard Manders	1801
Jacob Poole	1802
Henry Hutton	1803
Meredith Jenkins	1804
James Vance	1805
Joseph Pemberton	1806
Hugh Trevor	1807
Frederick Darley	1808
Sir William Stamer, bt	1809
Nathaniel Horne	1810
William Henry Archer	1811
Abraham Bradley King	1812
John Cash	1813
John Claudius Beresford	1814
Robert Shaw	1815
Mark Bloxham	1816
John Alley	1817
Sir Thomas McKenny	1818
Sir William Stamer, bt	1819
Sir Abraham Bradley King	1820
Sir John Kingston James, bt	1821
John Smith Fleming	1822
Richard Smyth	1823
Drury James	1824
Thomas Abbott	1825
Samuel Wilkinson Tyndall	1826
Sir Edmund Nugent	1827
Alexander Montgomery	1828
Jacob West	1829
Sir Robert Way, bt	1830
Sir Thomas Whelan	1831
Charles Palmer Archer	1832
Sir George Whiteford	1833
Arthur Perrin	1834
Arthur Morison	1835
William Hodges	1836

Samuel Warren	1837
George Hoyte	1838
Sir Nicholas William Brady	1839
Sir John Kingston James, bt	1840
Daniel O'Connell	1841
George Row	1842 and 1843
Sir Timothy O'Brien, bt	1844
John L. Arabin	1845
John Keshan	1846
Michael Staunton	1847
Jeremiah Dunne	1848
Sir Timothy O'Brien, bt	1849
John Reynolds	1850
Benjamin Lee Guinness	1851
John D'Arcy	1852
Robert Henry Kinaham	1853
Sir Edward McDowell	1854
Joseph Boyce	1855
Fergus Farrell	1856
Richard Akinson	1857
John Campbell	1858
James Lambert	1859
Redmond Carroll	1860
Richard Akinson	1861
Denis Moylan	1862
John Prendergast Vereker	1863
Peter Paul McSwiney	1864
Sir John Barrington	1865
James William Mackey	1866
William Lane Joynt	1867
Sir Joseph Carroll	1868 and 1869
Edward Purdon	1870
Patrick Bulfin	1871 (died 12/13 June)
John Campbell	1871
Robert Garde Durdin	1872
Sir James William Mackey	1873
Maurice Brooks	1874
Peter Paul McSwiney	1875
Sir George Bolstger Owens, bt	1876
Hugh Tarpey	1877 and 1878
Sir John Barrington	1879
Edmund Dwyer Gray	1880
George Moyers	1881
Charles Dawson	1882 and 1883
William Meagher	1884
John O'Connor	1885

Timothy Daniel Sullivan	1886 and 1887
Thomas Sexton	1888 and 1889
Edward Joseph Kennedy	1890
Joseph Michael Meade	1891 and 1892
James Shanks	1893
Valentine Blake Dillon	1894 and 1895
Richard F. McCoy	1896
Daniel Tallon	1897, 1898 and 1899
Sir Thomas Devereux Pile, bt	1900 and 1901
Timothy Charles Harrington	1902 and 1903
Joseph Hutchinson	1904 and 1905
Joseph Patrick Nannatti	1906 and 1907
Gerald O'Reilly	1908
William Coffey	1909
Michael Doyle	1910
John J. Farrell	1911
Lorcan G. Sherlock	1912 through 1915
James Mitchell Gallagher	1915 and 1916
Laurence O'Neill	1917 through 1923
Mayoralty dissolved	1924 through 1929
Alfred Byrne	1830 through 1938
Caitlín Bean Ui Chléarigh	1939 and 1940
Peader Seán Ua Dubhghaill	1941 and 1942
Martin O'Sullivan	1943 and 1944
Peader Seán Ua Dubhghaill	1945
John McCann	1946
Patrick Joseph Cahill	1947
John Breen	1948
Cormac Breathnach	1949
John Belton	1950
Andrew S. Clarkin	1951 and 1952
Bernard Butler	1953
Alfred Byrne	1954
Denis Larkin	1955
Robert Briscoe	1956
James Carroll	1957
Catherine Byrne	1958
Philip A. Brady	1959
Maurice Edward Dockrill	1960
Robert Briscoe	1961
James O'Keefe	1962
Seán Moore	1963
John McCann	1964
Eugene Timmons	1965 and 1966
Thomas Strafford	1967
Frank Cluskey	1968

Office suspended	1969 through 1973
James O'Keefe	1974
Patrick Dunne	1975
James Mitchell	1976
Michael Collins	1977
Patrick Belton	1978
William Cumiskey	1979
Fergus O'Brien	1980
Alexis Fitzgerald	1981
Daniel Browne	1982
Michael Keating	1983
Michael O'Halloran	1984
Jim Tunney	1985
Bertie Ahern	1986
Carmencita Hederman	1987 (first woman mayor)
Ben Briscoe	1988
Seán Haughey	1989
Michael Donnelly	1990
Seán Kenny	1991
Gay Mitchell	1992
Tomás MacGiolla	1993
John Gormley	1994
Seán D. Loftus	1995
Brendan Lynch	1996
John Stafford	1997
Joe Doyle	1998
Mary Freehill	1999
Maurice Ahern	2000
Michael Malcahy	2001
Dermot Lacey	2002
Royston Brady	2003

Honorary freemen of the City of Dublin

Municipal Privileges Ireland Act (1876) (39 and 40 Vic., c. 76) conferred the right to elect and admit individuals to the Honorary Freedom of the City.

	Date of resolution	Date of signature
Isaac Butt	4 Sept. 1876	16 Oct. 1876
William E. Gladstone	1 Nov. 1877	7 Nov. 1877
Ulyssess S. Grant	30 Dec. 1878	3 Jan. 1879
Capt. Edward E. Potter	26 Apr. 1880	4 May 1880
Charles Stewart Parnell	3 Jan. 1882	16 Aug. 1882
John Dillon	3 Jan. 1882	16 Aug. 1882
Kevin Izod O'Doherty	10 Aug. 1885	1 Sept. 1885

	Date of resolution	Date of signature
Patrick A. Collins	22 July 1887	2 Aug. 1887
William O'Brien	22 July 1887	2 Aug. 1887
Timothy Daniel Sullivan	10 Dec. 1887	24 Oct. 1893
Thomas Sexton	28 Dec. 1887	Did not sign roll
Marquess of Ripon	16 Jan. 1888	2 Feb. 1888
John Morley	16 Jan. 1888	2 Feb. 1888
Patrick F. Cardinal Moran	1 Oct. 1888	4 Oct. 1888
Margaret, Lady Sandhurst	19 Sept. 1889	20 Sept. 1889
James Stansfeld	19 Sept. 1889	20 Sept. 1889
George Salmon	14 Mar. 1892	30 June 1892
Stuart Knill	23 Dec. 1892	2 Jan. 1893
John E. Redmond	18 Dec. 1901	3 Apr. 1902
Patrick A. McHugh	30 Oct. 1901	3 Apr. 1902
An Craoibhin Aoibhin (Douglas Hyde)	29 June 1906	7 Apr. 1907
Spencer Harty	2 Sept. 1907	Did not sign roll
Sir Hugh Lane	10 Feb. 1909	Did not sign roll
Richard Croker	1 July 1907	24 Aug. 1908
E. O'Meagher Condon	28 Sept. 1909	6 Oct. 1909
Charles A. Cameron	30 Sept. 1910	20 Feb. 1911
Dr Duno Meyer	18 July 1911	22 Apr. 1912
An Canoach (Peadar Ua Laoghaire)	18 July 1911	22 Apr. 1912
Daniel Mannix (RC Archbishop of Melbourne)	5 Aug. 1920	Did not sign roll
John Count McCormack	23 Sept. 1923	6 Sept. 1923
Ehrenfried Gunther (Baron Von Hunefeld)	20 June 1928	3 July 1928
Capt. Hermann Keohl	30 June 1928	1928
Maj. James Fitzmaurice	30 June 1928	3 July 1928
Frank B. Kellogg	25 Aug. 1928	30 Aug. 1928
Lorenzo Cardinal Lauri	2 May 1932	1932
Sir John Lavery	12 Aug. 1935	17 Sept. 1935
John Purser Griffith	4 May 1936	8 June 1936
George Bernard Shaw	4 Mar. 1936	28 Aug. 1946
Richard Cardinal Cushing	16 Sept. 1949	16 Sept. 1949
Paul A. Dever	16 Sept. 1949	16 Sept. 1949
Seán T. Ó Ceallaigh (Seán T. O'Kelly)	4 May 1953	2 June 1953
John Cardinal D'Alton	4 May 1953	2 June 1953
Gerald P. O'Hara	12 June 1954	27 July 1954
Sir Alfred Chester Beatty	7 Nov. 1955	26 July 1956
G. P. Cardinal Agagianian	1 May 1961	22 June 1961
Michael Cardinal Browne	16 July 1962	23 Aug. 1962
John Fitzgerald Kennedy	27 May 1963	28 June 1963
Hilton R. H. Edwards	11 June 1973	22 June 1973
Michael Mac Liammoir	11 June 1973	22 June 1973
Eamon de Valera	3 Feb. 1975	7 Mar. 1975
John A. Costello	3 Feb. 1975	7 Mar. 1975
Pope John Paul II	24 Sept. 1979	28 Sept. 1978
Noel Purcell	22 June 1984	28 June 1984

	Date of resolution	Date of signature
Maureen Potter O'Leary	22 June 1984	28 June 1985
Akihito, Crown Prince of Japan	20 Feb. 1985	4 Mar. 1985
Michiko, Crown Princess of Japan	20 Feb. 1985	4 Mar. 1985
Stephen Roche	28 Sept. 1987	29 Sept. 1987
Nelson F. Mandela	18 July 1988	1 July 1990
Patrick J. Hillery	4 Mar. 1991	22 Apr. 1991
Mother M. Teresa	1 Feb. 1993	2 June 1993
Jack Charlton	11 Apr. 1994	26 May 1994
William J. Clinton	6 Nov. 1995	1 Dec. 1995
Gabriel M. Byrne	12 Apr. 1999	11 May 1999
Aug San Suu Ryi	1 Nov. 1999	Under house arrest Burma
Paul McGuinness	1 Nov. 1999	18 Mar. 2000
The Edge	1 Nov. 1999	18 Mar. 2000
Larry Mullen, jun.	1 Nov. 1999	18 Mar. 2000
A. Clayton	1 Nov. 1999	18 Mar. 2000
Bono	1 Nov. 1999	18 Mar. 2000
Mikhail Gorbachev	3 Dec. 2001	9 Jan. 2002

Mayors/Lords Mayor of Belfast

Mayors

	Appointed
George Dunbar	1842 and 43
John Clarke	1844
Andrew Mulholland	1845
John Kane	1846
John Harrison	1847
George Suffern	1848
William Gilliland Johnson	1849
James Sterling	1850 and 1851
Samuel Graeme Fenton	1852
William McGee	1853
Frederick Harry Lewis	1854
Thomas Verner	1855
Samuel Gibson Getty	1856, 1857 and 1858
William Ewart, jun.	1859 and 1860
Edward Coey	1861
Charles Lanyon	1862
John Lyttle	1863, 1864 and 1865
William Mullan	1866
David Taylor	1867
Samuel McCausland	1868

	Appointed
Frederick Harry Lewis	1869
Samuel Browne	1870
Philip Johnson	1871
John Savage	1872
James Alex Henderson	1873 and 1874
Thomas Graham Lindsay	1875
Robert Boag	1876
John Preston	1877 and 1878
John Browne	1879 and 1880
Edward Porter Cowan	1881
Sir Edward Cowan	1882
Sir David Taylor	1883 and 1884
Edward J. Harland	1885
Sir Edward J. Harland, bt	1886
James Horner Haslett	1887 and 1888
Charles C. Conor	1889 and 1891

Lords Mayor (charter granted 1892)

Daniel Dixon	1892 and 1893
William McCammond	1894 and 1895
William J. Pirrie	1896 and 1897
James Henderson	1898
Otto Jaffe	1899
R. J. McConnell	1900
Sir Daniel Dixon	1901, 1902 and 1903
Sir Otto Jaffe	1904
Rt Hon. Sir Daniel Dixon, bt	1905 and 1906
Rt Hon. the Earl of Shaftesbury	1907
Sir Robert Anderson	1908 and 1909
R. J. McMordie	1910 through 1913 (died 25 Mar. 1914)
Sir Robert Anderson	1914 (temporary appointment 27 Mar.)
Crawford McCullagh	1914, 1915 and 1916 (elected 1 Apr. 1914)
James Johnston	1917 and 1918
John C. White	1919
William Frederick Coates	1921 and 1922
William George Turner	1924 through 1928
Sir William Frederick Coates	1929 and 1930
Sir Crawford McCullagh	1931 through 1941
George R. Black	1942 (22 May–28 Dec.)
Rt Hon. Sir Crawford McCullagh	1943, 1944 and 1945
William Frederick Neill	1946, 1957 and 1948
William Ernest George Johnston	1949 and 1950

	Appointed
James Henry Norritt	1951 and 1952
Percival Brown	1953 and 1954
Robert John Rolston Harcourt	1955 and 1956
Major William Cecil McKee	1957 and 1958
Robert George Caldwell Kinahan	1959 and 1960
Martin Kelso Wallace	1961 and 1962
William Jenkins	1963, 1964 and 1965
William Duncan Geddis	1966, 1967 and 1968
Joseph Foster Cairns	1969, 1970 and 1971
William Christie	1972, 1973 and 1974
Myles Humphreys	1975 and 1976
James Stewart	1977
David Cook	1978
William Bell	1979
John Carson	1980
Grace Bannister	1981
Thomas William Sanderson Patton	1982
A. Ferguson	1983 and 1984
John Carson	1985
Samuel Wilson	1986
John J. D. Gilmore	1987
Nigel A. Dodds	1988
Reginald Empey	1989
Fred Cobain	1990
Nigel A. Dodds	1991
Herbert Ditty	1992
Reginald Empey	1993
Hugh Smyth	1994
Eric Smyth	1995
Ian Adamson	1996
Alban Maginness	1997
David Alderdice	1998
Robert Stoker	1999
Samuel Wilson	2000
James Rodgers	2001
Alex Maskey	2002
Martin Morgan	2003

Mayors/Lords Mayor of Cork

Mayors

	Appointed
Michael Robert Westropp	1801 and 1802
Richard Lane	1803
Thomas Wagget	1804

305

	Appointed
Charles Evanson	1805
Rowland Morrison	1806
John Day	1807
Thomas Harding	1808
John Foster	1809
Noblett Johnson	1810
Paul Maylor	1811
Thomas Dorman	1812
Peter Dumas	1813
Sir David Perrier	1814
Henry Sadlier	1815
John George Newsom	1816
Edward Allen	1817
Thomas Gibbings	1818
Richard Digby	1819
Isaac Jones	1820
Sir Anthony Perrier	1821
Edward Newsom	1822
Henry Bagnell	1823
Bartholomew Gibbings	1824
John N. Wrixon	1825
Thomas Harrison	1826
Richard N. Parker	1827
Thomas Dunscombe	1828
Thomas Pope	1829
George Knapp	1830
Joseph Garde	1831
John Besnard	1832
Joseph Leycester	1833
Charles Perry	1834
Andrew Spearing	1835
Peter Besnard	1836
John Saunders	1837
John Bagnell	1838
Lionel J. Westropp	1839
James Lane	1840
Julius Besnard	1841
William Lyons	1842
Francis B. Beamish	1843
William Fagan	1844
Richard Dowden	1845
Andrew F. Roche	1846
Edward Hackett	1847 (died July)
Andrew Roche	1847 (elected to replace Hackett)
William Lyons	1848 and 1849

	Appointed
John Shea	1850
James Lambkin	1851
William Hackett	1852
John Francis Maguire	1853
John N. Murphy	1854
Sir John Gordon	1855
William Fitzgibbon	1856 and 1857
Daniel Donegan	1858
John Arnott	1859, 1860 and 1861
John Francis Maguire	1862, 1863 and 1864
Charles J. Cantillon	1865
Francis Lyons	1866, 1867 and 1868
Daniel V. O'Sullivan	1869
William Hegarty	1870
John Daly	1871, 1872 and 1873
Daniel A. Nagle	1874 and 1875
George Penrose	1876
Barry J. Sheehan	1877
William V. Greeg	1878
Patrick Kennedy	1879 and 1880
Sir Daniel V. O'Sullivan	1881
Daniel J. Galvin	1882, 1883 and 1884 (to June)
Barry J. Sheehan	1884 (from June)
Paul J. Madden	1885 and 1886
John O'Brien	1887 and 1888
Daniel Ryan	1889
Daniel Horgan	1890, 1891 and 1892
Augustine Roche	1893 and 1894
Patrick H. Meade	1895
Sir John Scon	1896
Patrick H. Meade	1897 and 1898
Eugene Crean	1899

Lords Mayor (charter granted 1900)

Daniel J. Hegarty	1900
Edward Fitzgerald	1901, 1902 and 1903
Augustine Roche	1904
Joseph Barrett	1905, 1906 and 1907
Richard Cronin	1907
Thomas Donovan	1908, 1909, and 1910 (unseated by writ, 20 Dec. 1910)
Henry O'Shea	1911 (14–23 Jan.)
James Simcox	1911 and 1912 (resigned 12 Apr.)

307

	Appointed
Henry O'Shea	1912 through 1915 (elected 19 Apr. 1912)
Tomás C. Butterfield	1916, 1917 and 1918
William F. O'Connor	1919
Tomás MacCurtain	1920 (killed by British forces, 20 Mar.)
Terence MacSwiney	1920 (elected 30 Mar.; died on hunger strike, 25 Oct.)
Domhnall Ó Ceallachain	1920 through 1923 (elected 4 Nov. 1920)
Seán French	1924 through 1929
Francis J. Daly	1930 and 1931
Seán French	1932 and 1937 (died 12 Sept.)
James Hickey	1937, 1938 and 1939 (elected, 21 Sept. 1937)
William Desmond	1940
John Horgan	1941
James Allen	1942
Richard S. Anthony	1942 (elected 29 Aug.)
James Hickey	1943
Seán Cronin	1944
Michael Sheehan	1945 through 1948
Seán MacCarthy	1949 and 1950
Walter Furlong	1951
Patrick McGrath	1952 through 1955
Seán Casey	1956
Richard V. Jago	1957
Seán MacCarthy	1958
Jane Dowdall	1959 (first woman to hold office)
Stephen D. Barrett	1960
Anthony Barry	1961
Seán Casey	1962
Seán MacCarthy	1963
Augustine A. Healy	1964
Cornelius Desmond	1965
Seán Casey	1966 (died 29 Apr.)
Seán MacCarthy	1966 (elected 9 May)
Pearse Wyse	1967 (elected 8 July)
John Bermingham	1968
Thomas Pearse Leahy	1969
Peter Barry	1970
Timothy J. O'Sullivan	1971
Seán O'Leary	1972
Patrick Kerrigan	1973
Pearse Wyse	1974

	Appointed
Augustine A. Healy	1975
Seán French	1976
Gerald Y. Goldberg	1977
Brian C. Sloane	1978
James A. Corr	1979
Toddy O'Sullivan	1980
Paud Black	1981
Hugh Coveney	1982
John Dennehy	1983
Liam Burke	1984
Dan Wallace	1985
Gerry O'Sullivan	1986
Thomas Brosnan	1987
Bernard Allen	1988
Chrissie Aherne	1989
Frank Nash	1990
Denis Cregan	1991
Micheál Martin	1992
John Murray	1993
Tim Falvey	1994
Joe O'Callaghan	1995
James A. Corr	1996
Dave McCarthy	1997
Joe O'Flynn	1998
Damian Wallace	1999
P. J. Hourican	2000
Tom O'Driscoll	2001
John Kelleher	2002
Colm Burke	2003

PARLIAMENT AND GOVERNMENT

The United Kingdom House of Commons
The Irish composition of the House of Commons in 1800–1832

Constituencies	MPs
Irish boroughs	
Armagh	1
Athlone	1
Bandon Bridge	1
Belfast	1
Carlow	1
Carrickfergus	1
Cashel	1
Clonmel	1
Cork	1
Downpatrick	1
Drogheda	1
Dublin	2
Dundalk	1
Dungannon	1
Dungarvan	1
Ennis	1
Enniskillen	1
Galway	1
Kilkenny	1
Kinsale	1
Limerick	1
Lisburn	1
Londonderry	1
Mallow	1
New Ross	1
Newry	1
Portarlington	1
Sligo	1
Tralee	1
Waterford	1
Wexford	1
Youghal	1
Irish counties	
Antrim	2
Armagh	2

Constituencies	MPs
Carlow	2
Cavan	2
Clare	2
Cork	2
Donegal	2
Down	2
Dublin	2
Fermanagh	2
Galway	2
Kerry	2
Kildare	2
Kilkenny	2
King's County	2
Leitrim	2
Limerick	2
Londonderry	2
Longford	2
Louth	2
Mayo	2
Meath	2
Monaghan	2
Queen's County	2
Roscommon	2
Sligo	2
Tipperary	2
Tyrone	2
Waterford	2
Westmeath	2
Wexford	2
Wicklow	2

Irish University

University of Dublin	2

Irish representation in the House of Commons

	Ireland	United Kingdom total
1801–26	100	658
1826–32	100	658
1832–67	105	658
1868–85	105	658
1885–1918	103	670
1918–22	105	707
	N.I.	
1922–45	13	615
1945–50	13	640
1950–55	12	625
1955–74	12	630
1974–83	17	635
1983–97	17	651
1997–	18	659

Voters

Estimated numbers of electors in Ireland, 1831–1886

	Counties	Boroughs	Total	Increase
1831	52,162	23,798	75,960	
1833	60,607	31,545	92,152	16,192
1866	172,010	31,545	204,665	
1869	176,825	45,625	222,450	17,785
1883	165,997	58,021	224,018	
1886	631,651	106,314	737,965	513,947

Voters as a proportion of the adult male population of the UK

	England and Wales	Scotland	Ireland
1833	1 in 5	1 in 8	1 in 20
1869	1 in 3	1 in 3	1 in 6
1886	2 in 3	3 in 5	1 in 2

Parliamentary reform and Ireland, 1800–2000

1800 Act of Union passed by Irish and British parliaments.

1801 Act of Union takes effect, adds 100 members for Ireland to the House of Commons.

1825 Catholic Emancipation Bill rejected in House of Lords.

1829 Catholic Emancipation Act. Catholics can enter parliament and hold civil and military offices. Irish Parliamentary Elections Act raises franchise from 40-shilling freeholders to £10 freeholders. To balance Emancipation Daniel O'Connell agrees to raise county franchise to £10.

1832 Reform Act redistributes seats and creates a single qualification for all United Kingdom boroughs. Counties: £10 freeholders; leaseholders for life and copyholders of estates of £10; 60-year leaseholders and their assignees of estates of the same value; 14-year leaseholder of £20 estates. Cities and boroughs: £10 occupiers and resident freemen if by birth or servitude or admitted before March 1831. Ireland given five extra seats – Belfast, Dublin University, Galway, Limerick and Waterford (net increase 18).

1850 Irish Franchise Act reduces borough franchise to £8. County franchise set at £12, linked with occupation instead of ownership or leasehold. Irish electorate trebles.

1868 Borough franchise reduced to £4 by Irish Reform Act. Lodgers occupying property valued at £10 or more enfranchised. Leaves number of seats unchanged.

1869 Two Irish boroughs disenfranchised for bribery, Cashel and Sligo.

1884 The Representation of the People Act (1884) creates a uniform householder and lodger franchise in every borough and county in the United Kingdom, based on the franchise created for the English boroughs in 1867. It also provides for an occupation franchise for those with lands or tenements worth £10 a year.

1885 Reform Act reorganises and harmonises United Kingdom constituencies. In Ireland 22 boroughs returning one member each are disenfranchised. Also, three boroughs returning two members each deprived of one member. Twenty-one seats reallocated to Irish counties, and four seats to Belfast and Dublin.

1918 Representation of the People Act. Vote given to all men over 21 and to women over 30 if they are ratepayers or wives of ratepayers.

1919 Seventy-three Sinn Féin MPs boycott Westminster to form the first Dáil Éireann.

1920	Better Government of Ireland Act establishes bicameral parliaments in Northern Ireland (NI) and Southern Ireland. Only the former properly established. Representation to Westminster continues with 13 seats for Northern Ireland. Sinn Féin MPs continue to boycott Westminster.
1921	Sinn Féin use Better Government of Ireland Act elections to form a second Dáil Éireann with 125 deputies. NI general election to 52-seat House of Commons. Commons elected 24 of the 26 members of the Senate for eight-year terms, the mayors of Belfast and Londonderry ex officio.
1922	Anglo-Irish Treaty approved by Dáil Éireann. Dublin Castle and its functions transferred to the Provisional Government of new Irish Free State (IFS). According to IFS constitution voting in general elections to be by proportional representation, constituencies to be revised every 12 years, should not be more than one TD per 30,000 population and not less than one per 20,000. Maximum parliamentary term seven years. Upper chamber a 60-member Senate, half the membership elected by Dáil for three- or nine-year terms (chosen by lot), the other half nominated by President of Executive Council (Prime Minister) for either six- or 12-year terms. Northern Ireland parliament abolishes proportional representation for local elections.
1923	IFS grants vote to women over the age of 21.
1925	Elections for 19 vacancies in IFS Senate. Only all-IFS constituency election until 1945 presidential election.
1928	UK grants vote to women over the age of 21. Elections to IFS Senate reformed to include only TDs and Senators.
1929	NI parliament abolishes proportional representation for Westminster elections.
1936	IFS Senate abolished.
1937	New Irish constitution grants representation to the University of Dublin and the National University of Ireland. Senate revived with 60 members: 49 elected, 11 nominated by the Taoiseach (Prime Minister).
1948	Representation of the People Act abolishes plural voting in the UK – the practice of having one vote in the constituency of the place of residence, and also in the place of business or university where educated. Permanent Boundary Commissioners set up to report every seven years.
1950	Number of NI seats at Westminster reduced to 12.
1958	Redistribution of Seats Act modifies UK rules governing Boundary Commissioners and requests reports every 10–15 years.
1963	Maximum term of Dáil reduced to five years.

1968	The Queen's University of Belfast constituency of the NI parliament abolished.
1969	Representation of the People Act reduced UK minimum age of voting from 21 to 18 years.
1973	Proportional representation restored for NI local and Westminster elections.
1982	Dáil Éireann expanded to 166 seats. Seanad seats remain at 60.
1983	Number of NI seats at Westminster increased to 17.
1979	UK Euro-constituencies created for direct elections to European parliament.
1997	New Westminster seat created for NI (West Tyrone).
1998	108 members returned to the new NI assembly: six assembly seats per Westminster seat.

Further reading: see Sidney Elliot, 'The Northern Ireland Electoral System: A Vehicle for Disputation', in Patrick J. Roche and Brian Barton (eds), *The Northern Ireland Question: Nationalism, Unionism and Partition* (Aldershot: Ashgate, 1999).

Effects of the Reform Acts

Estimated electorate in 1831	75,950
Percentage increase, 1831–3	
Counties	16
Boroughs	33
Total	21
Percentage increase 1833–66	122
Percentage increase 1866–9	
Counties	3
Boroughs	31
Total	8
Electorate in 1869	220,155
Percentage increase 1869–83	1
Percentage increase 1883–6	
Counties	282
Boroughs	83
Total	229

Composition of the House of Commons

Period	Eng.	Wales	Scot.	Ire.	Co.	Bor.	Univ.	Total
1707–1800	489	24	45	–	122	432	4	558
1801–26	489	24	45	100	186	467	5	658
1826–32	489	24	45	100	188	465	5	658
1832–67	471	29	53	105	253	399	6	658
1868–85	463	30	60	105	283	366	9	658
1885–1918	465	30	72	103	377	284	9	670
1918–22	498	30	74	105	372	320	15	707
1922	492	36	74	13	300	303	12	615

The House of Commons miscellaneous

Speakers of the House of Commons

Date of election	Name
11 Feb. 1801	Sir John Mitford
10 Feb. 1802	Charles Abbott
2 June 1817	Charles Manners-Sutton
19 Feb. 1835	James Abercromby
27 May 1839	Charles Shaw-Lefevre
30 Apr. 1857	John Evelyn Denison
9 Feb. 1872	Henry Bouverie Brand
26 Feb. 1884	Arthur Wellesley Peel
10 Apr. 1895	William Court Gully
20 June 1905	James Lowther
28 Apr. 1921	J. Whitley
21 June 1928	E. Fitzroy
9 Mar. 1943	D. Clifton Brown
1 Nov. 1951	W. Morrison
21 Oct. 1959	Sir H. Hylton-Foster
16 Oct. 1965	H. King
21 Jan. 1971	Selwyn Lloyd
3 Feb. 1976	George Thomas
15 Jan. 1983	Bernard Weatherill
17 Apr. 1992	Betty Boothroyd
23 Oct. 2000	Michael Martin

Irish seats forfeited

MPs left or expelled from the House before or after their conviction and imprisonment on criminal charges:

2 Mar. 1903   Arthur Lynch (Nationalist)   Galway

Irish Members who forfeited seats as a result of being adjudged bankrupt:

17 Sept. 1903   P. McHugh (Nationalist)   North Leitrim (re-elected)
15 July 1909   N. Murphy (Nationalist)   South Kilkenny

Payment of MPs (from 1911 when salary introduced)

	Basic pay p.a.
1911	£400
1931	£360
1934	£380
1935	£400
1936	£600
1954	£1,250
1964	£3,250
1969	£3,250
1972	£4,500
1974	£4,500
1975	£5,750
1976	£5,750
1977	£6,270
1978	£6,897
1979	£9,450
1980	£11,750
1981	£13,950
1982	£14,510
1983	£15,308
1984	£16,106
1985	£16,904
1986	£17,702
1987	£18,500
1988	£22,548
1989	£24,107
1990	£26,701
1991	£28,970
1992	£30,854
1993	£30,854
1994	£31,687
1995	£33,189
1996	£43,000
1997	£43,860
1998	£45,066
1999	£47,008
2000	£48,371

Parliamentary sessions

Date summoned	Date of dissolution
22 Jan. 1801	29 June 1802
31 Aug. 1802	24 Oct. 1806
13 Dec. 1806	29 Apr. 1807
22 June 1807	29 Sept. 1812
24 Nov. 1812	10 June 1818
4 Aug. 1818	29 Feb. 1820
21 Apr. 1820	2 June 1826
25 July 1826	24 July 1830
14 Sept. 1830	23 Apr. 1831

Parliamentary hours of sitting

In 1831 the House met at 4 p.m., the usual hour since about 1760. In 1833 and 1834 the House met at noon, and adjourned between 3 p.m. and 5 p.m., when it met again. The early sitting was mostly devoted to petitions, which then occupied much time. Between 1835 and 1888 the House usually met at 4 p.m., except on Wednesdays after 9 Aug. 1843 when it met occasionally at noon, a practice established by resolution on 26 Jan. 1846, and by standing order, 25 June 1852. Between 1867 and 1888, on Tuesdays and Fridays before and after Whitsuntide, the House often met at 2 p.m., the sitting being suspended between 7 p.m. and 9 p.m., at which hour it was resumed; these sittings were termed morning and evening sittings respectively. From 27 Feb. 1888 until 2 May 1902 the House usually met at 3 p.m.

Public petitions

A feature of the work of the House of Commons during the early part of the nineteenth century was public petitions which occupied a great part of the time of the House of Commons. It was not until 1839 that these debates were discontinued and their place was gradually taken by questions to ministers.

Session	Petitions presented
1801	298
1812–13	1,699
1827	3,635
1833	10,394
1843	33,898

Parliament/Dáil of Southern Ireland/Irish Free State/Éire/Republic of Ireland

At the UK general election held in December 1918, 73 Sinn Féin candidates were returned. Refusing to take their seats at Westminster, they formed the

First Dáil Éireann on 21 Jan. 1919. The Better Government of Ireland Act (1920) created the separate jurisdictions of Northern and Southern Ireland. The Southern parliament had 128 seats. Elections to both were held but as all seats were left uncontested in Southern Ireland on nomination day, 24 May 1921, there was no poll. Sinn Féin members declined to sit in the Southern parliament, constituting themselves as the Second Dáil. Following the Anglo-Irish Treaty, 6 Dec. 1921, elections to the Third Dáil were held on 16 June 1922.

Seats in Dáil Éireann, 1922–2001

1922	128
1923	153
1937	138
1948	147
1961	144
1977	148
1981–	166

Ceann Comhairle (Chairman) of the Dáil

Seán T. O'Kelly	1919–21
Eoin MacNeill	1921–22
Michael Hayes	1922–32
Frank Fahey	1932–51
Patrick Hogan	1951–67
Cormac Breslin	1967–73
Seán Treacy	1973–77
Joseph Brennan	1977–80
Pádraig Faulkner	1980–81
John O'Connell	1981–82
Tom Fitzpatrick	1982–87
Seán Treacy	1987–97
Séamus Pattison	1997–

Cathaoirleach (Chairman) of the Seanad

	Year appointed
Lord Glenavy	1922
Thomas Westropp Bennett	1928
No appointment	1936–8
Seán Gibbons	1938
Seán Goulding	1943
Timothy J. O'Donovan	1948
Liam O Buachalla	1951
Patrick F. Baxter	1954
Liam Ó Buachalla	1957
Micheál Yeats	1969

	Year appointed
James Dooge	1973
Seámus Dolan	1977
Charles McDonald	1981
Tras Honan	1982
Patrick J. Reynolds	1983
Tras Honan	1987
Seán Doherty	1989
Seán Fallon	1992
Liam Naughton	1995
Brian Mullooly	1997–

In 1967 there were 144 members of the Dáil and 60 members of the Seanad. The Dáil was expanded in 1982 (22nd Dáil) to 166 seats. The number of Seanad seats remained at 60.

(Source: *Institute of Public Administration Yearbook and Directory*)

United Kingdom government reports and commissions
Vice-Regal commissions

Title	Chair	Size	Appointed	Reported	Commission no.
Irish Inland Fisheries	S. Walker	7	Aug. 1899	Jan. 1901	488
Poor Law Reform in Ireland	M. L. Micks	3	May 1903	Oct. 1906	3202
Trinity College Dublin, Estates Commission	G. Fitzgibbon	3	June 1904	Apr. 1905	2526
Arterial Drainage (Ire)	A. Binnie	5	Sept. 1905	Feb. 1907	3374
Irish Railways, Inc. Light Railways	C. Scotter	7	July 1906	July 1910	5247
Circumstances of the Loss of the Regalia of the Order of St Partick	J. Shaw	3	Jan. 1908	Jan. 1908	3936
Irish Milk Supply	P. O'Neill	9	Nov. 1911	Oct. 1913	7129
Primary Education (Ire) System of Inspection	S. Dill	8	Jan. 1913	Jan. 1914	7235
Dublin Disturbances	D. Henry	2	Dec. 1913	Feb. 1914	7269
Primary Education (Ire) 1918	Ld Killanin	17	Aug. 1918	Feb. 1919	60
Intermediate Education (Ire)	T. Molony	14	Aug. 1918	Mar. 1919	66
Under Sheriffs and Bailiffs (Ire)	T. O'Shaughnessy	5	Oct. 1918	May 1919	190
Reorganisation and Pay of the Irish Police Forces	J. Ross	6	Oct. 1919	Dec. 1919	603
Clerk of the Crown and Peace, etc. (Ire)	J. Wakely	7	Oct. 1919	Jun. 1920	805

Key Acts of Parliament (UK), official government reports, papers and reports commissioned by the Northern Ireland Office and agreements relating to the Northern Ireland crisis

Legislation of UK and NI parliaments

Civil Authorities (Special Powers) Act (NI) 1922 (7 Apr.)
Flags and Emblems (Display) Act (NI) 1954
Electoral Law Act (NI) 1968 (28 Nov.)
Parliamentary Commissioner Act (NI) 1969 (24 June)
Community Relations Act (NI) 1969 (11 Nov.)
Commissioner for Complaints Act (NI) 1969 (25 Nov.)
Police Act (NI) 1971 (26 Mar.)
Criminal Justice (Temporary Provisions) Act (NI) 1970 (1 July)
Prevention of Incitement to Hate Act (NI) 1970 (2 July)
Local Government (Boundaries) Act (NI) 1971 (23 Mar.)
Housing Executive Act (NI) 1971 (25 Feb.)
NI (Temporary Provisions) Act 1972 (Mar.)
Prevention of Terrorism (Temporary Provisions) Act 1974 (29 Nov.)
Fair Employment (NI) Act 1976 (22 July)
Northern Ireland Act 1982 (23 July)
Police (NI) Act 1988 (July)
NI Act 1988 (Nov.)

UK Government Commissions (Parliament Command Paper number in parenthesis)

Disturbances in Northern Ireland. September 1969 (Cmnd. 532) [Cameron Report]

Report of the Advisory Committee on Police in Northern Ireland. October 1969 (Cmnd. 535) [Hunt Report]

Local Government in Northern Ireland. 29 May 1970 (Cmnd. 546) [Macrory Report]

Report of the Inquiry into Allegations Against the Security Forces of Physical Brutality in Northern Ireland Arising Out of Events on the 9th August 1971. November 1971 (Cmnd. 4832) [Compton Report]

Report of the Committee of Privy Counsellors Appointed to Consider Authorised Procedures for the Interrogation of Persons Suspected of Terrorism. March 1972 (Cmnd. 4901) [Parker Report]

Violence and Civil Disturbances in Northern Ireland in 1969. April 1972 (Cmnd. 566) [Scarman Report]

Report of the Tribunal Appointed to Inquire into the Events on Sunday, 30th January 1972. 18 April 1972 (HC 220) [Widgery Report]

Report of the Commission to Consider Legal Procedures to Deal with Terrorist Activities in Northern Ireland. 20 December 1972 (Cmnd. 5185) [Diplock Report]

321

Report of a Committee to Consider, in the Context of Civil Liberties and
  Human Rights, Measures to Deal with Terrorism in Northern Ireland.
  30 January 1975 (Cmnd. 5847) [Gardiner Report]
Report of the Committee of Inquiry into Police Interrogation Procedures in
  Northern Ireland. 16 March 1979 (Cmnd. 7497) [Bennett Report]
Review of the Northern Ireland (Emergency Provisions) Acts 1978 and 1987.
  1990 (Cmnd. 1115) [Colville Report]

Reports and papers commissioned by the Northern Ireland Office

The Future of Northern Ireland: A Paper for Discussion. 1972
Northern Ireland Constitutional Proposals. 20 March 1973 (Cmnd. 5259)
The Northern Ireland Constitution. 4 July 1974 (Cmnd. 5675)
Constitutional Convention, Procedure. 1974
The Government of Northern Ireland: A Society Divided. 5 February 1975
[Standing Advisory Commission on Human Rights]. The Protection of
  Human Rights by Law in Northern Ireland. 1977 (Cmnd. 7009)
The Government of Northern Ireland: A Working Paper for a Conference.
  20 November 1979 (Cmnd. 7763)
The Government of Northern Ireland: Proposals for Further Discussion.
  2 July 1980 (Cmnd. 7950)
Northern Ireland: A Framework for Devolution. 5 April 1982 (Cmnd. 8541)
Police Complaints and Discipline: a Consultative Paper. 1985
[Standing Advisory Commission on Human Rights]. Religious and Political
  Discrimination and Equality of Opportunity in Northern Ireland: Report
  on Fair Employment. 1987 (Cmnd. 237)
Fair Employment in Northern Ireland. May 1988 (Cmnd. 380)
[Standing Advisory Commission on Human Rights]. Religious and Political
  Discrimination and Equality of Opportunity in Northern Ireland, Second
  Report. June 1990 (Cmnd. 1107)
Northern Ireland: Ground Rules for Substantive All-Party Negotiations. 1996
  (Cm. 3232)

POLITICAL PARTIES

Glossary of major political parties

See also the glossary on pp. 737–88.

Alliance Party (NI) Established Apr. 1970 with the intention of attracting both Protestant and Catholic support. It pursues a middle ground with the main strength being among the middle classes in the suburbs. The party has never obtained more than 20 per cent of votes at an election.

Clann na Poblachta (É/ROI) ('party of the Republic') Founded in 1946, by Séan McBride among others, advocating policies of social reform; it was part of the first inter-party government, 1948–51 but was dissolved in 1965.

Clann na Talmhan (É/ROI) ('party of the land') Founded on 29 June 1939 in order to advance the interests of small farmers; it contested elections until 1961, gaining a place in the first two inter-party governments, but disappeared in 1965, with supporters generally transferring to Fine Gael.

Commonwealth Labour Party (NI) Founded by Harry Midgley in Dec. 1942, it contested six seats in 1945 and won 8 per cent of the vote. It disappeared after Midgley joined the Ulster Unionists in 1947.

Communist Party (IFS/É/ROI) Founded in Oct. 1921 and dissolved in 1924 when James Larkin's Irish Workers' League subsumed it. The party was re-established in 1933 but dissolved in 1941 to be revived in 1948 as the Irish Workers' League, becoming the Communist Party of Ireland in 1970. It has not enjoyed significant electoral success.

Cumann na nGaedheal (IFS/É/ROI) ('party of the Irish') Pro-treaty founded on 8 Apr. 1923. It held the reins of government until losing the general election in Feb. 1932. In Sept. 1933 it joined with the National Centre Party and National Guard to form Fine Gael. Generally the party was conservative on social and economic policy.

Democratic Left (ROI) Established in 1992 by former members of the Workers' Party; it has participated in coalition government 1993–7.

Democratic Unionist Party (DUP/Ulster Democratic Unionist Party) (NI) Founded Sept. 1971 by Ian Paisley and Desmond Boal as a successor to the Protestant Unionist Party. Sometimes socially progressive, it appeals to militant unionists and less well-off Protestants. In 2003 it become the largest party in the elections to the Northern Ireland Assembly.

Fianna Fáil (IFS/É/ROI) ('soldiers of Ireland') Founded on 16 May 1926 by Eamon de Valera among others from a section of Sinn Féin. Since 1932 it

323

has usually been the party with the largest number of seats in the Dáil. Until 1989 it was able to form governments without the aid of other parties. Traditionally, it has been a more nationalist and social radical group than its main rivals.

Fine Gael (IFS/É/ROI) ('kindred of the Irish') Founded on 8 Sept. 1933 from a merger of Cumann na nGaedheal, the National Party and the National Guard, it was the largest group in the inter-party governments. It is more moderate on the national question and generally more conservative than Fianna Fáil.

Green Party (ROI) Formed in 1981 as part of the ecology movement, it gained increased support after 1989.

Independent Opposition Party (Independent Irish Party) Formed in 1851 from Catholic MPs opposed to the Ecclesiastical Titles Act and the Irish Tenant League (founded 1850), it won a considerable number of parliamentary seats initially but gradually lost impetus and disappeared in 1859.

Irish Party (Home Rule Party, Nationalist Party) (Ireland/IFS) Formed in 1874 it was the largest national party until the general election of 1918 when it was supplanted by Sinn Féin and survived in skeletal form into the 1920s.

Irish Socialist Republican Party (ISRP) Established by James Connolly in 1896 as an avowedly socialist organisation, it collapsed after his departure for the United States in 1903.

Labour Party (Ireland/IFS/É/ROI) In 1912 the Irish Trade Union Congress agreed to form the party. Its electoral strength has been in Munster and Leinster; the party has been part of several Fine Gael and Fianna Fáil-led governments.

National Labour Party (É/ROI) Founded in 1944 by deputies expelled from the Labour Party. It rejoined the Labour Party in 1950.

National League (IFS/É/ROI) Founded on 12 Sept. 1926 by William Archer Redmond among others; it was conservative on social issues and supported the Anglo-Irish Treaty. After initial success, support dwindled and it dissolved in 1931.

Nationalist Party (NI) Formed in Northern Ireland as the successor to the Irish Party, it contested elections from 1921 and was the main opposition group at Stormont until being supplanted by the Social Democratic and Labour Party after 1970.

Northern Ireland Labour Party (NILP) (NI) Founded in 1924 it functioned mainly in Belfast and tried to act as a bridge between Catholics and Protestants by taking no position on the national question. Although struggling on into the 1980s its support disappeared with the beginning of the Troubles in 1968.

Progressive Democrats (ROI) Formed in 1985 it participated with Fianna Fáil in the coalition government 1989–92 and again from 1997. A generally conservative party, it advocates some left-of-centre social policies.

Repeal Party (Ireland) Operated from the early 1830s until the 1850s, it was a vehicle for Daniel O'Connell and his sons, advocating the repeal of the Union. It enjoyed its greatest electoral successes in the 1830s.

Saor Éire (IFS/É) Found by the Irish Republican Army (IRA) in 1931 to forward republican-socialist principles. It was declared illegal in October 1931.

Sinn Féin ('Ourselves') (Ireland/IFS/É/ROI/NI) A radical nationalist party founded by Arthur Griffith and Bulmer Hobson in 1905, it advocated abstention from the Westminster parliament. In spite of occasional successes, it only became a major force at the general election of 1918 when it took on the mantle of the largest nationalist party. This position was soon lost but the party has been revived, especially since 1981, and by the beginning of the twenty-first century it was the largest Catholic party in Northern Ireland and commanded electoral support in the Republic.

Social Democratic and Labour Party (SDLP) (NI) Formed in 1970 on moderate nationalist and social democratic principles, it was the largest party representing Catholics in Northern Ireland until being overtaken by Sinn Féin after 2000.

Ulster Liberal Party (Ireland/NI) A considerable electoral force until 1886, it enjoyed a brief revival between 1906 and 1914 and had a final curtain call from 1958 to 1969.

Ulster Unionist Party (Ireland/NI) Evolved from the threat of home rule in 1885–6, it was the largest party in Northern Ireland from 1921 until 2003 and formed all Stormont governments until the parliament was suspended in 1972. It sought to encompass all Protestants and unionists in Northern Ireland, though this claim became increasingly fragile after 1969.

Unionist Party of Northern Ireland (NI) Founded by Brian Faulkner in Sept. 1974 in order to support the Sunningdale proposals for a power-sharing Executive in Northern Ireland. It disappeared in 1981.

Workers' Party (ROI/NI) Founded in 1982 before which it was known as Sinn Féin Workers' Party, it advocated radical social policies; the party lost most of its members to the Democratic Left in 1992.

Party leaders

Party   *Year appointed*

Clann na Poblacta
Seán MacBride   1946–57

Cumann na nGaedheal
William T. Cosgrave   1922–32
(Major partner in creation of Fine Gael)

Democratic Unionist Party
Ian Paisley   1971–

Fianna Fáil
Eamon de Valera   1926
Seán Lemass   1959
Jack Lynch   1966
Charles Haughey   1979
Albert Reynolds   1992
Bertie Ahern   1994

Fine Gael
Eoin O'Duffy   1933
William T. Cosgrave   1934
Richard Mulcachy   1944
James Dillon   1959
Liam Cosgrave   1965
Garret Fitzgerald   1977
Alan Dukes   1987
John Bruton   1990
Michael Noonon   2001
Enda Kenny   2002

Labour Party
Thomas Johnson   1918
T. J. O'Connell   1927
William Norton   1932
Brendan Corish   1960
Frank Cluskey   1977
Michael O'Leary   1981
Dick Spring   1982
Ruairi Quinn   1997
(Merger with Democratic Left 1999)
Pat Rabbitte   2002

Party	*Year appointed*

Progressive Democrats

Desmond O'Malley	1985
Mary Harney	1993

Sinn Féin (Provisional)

Ruairi Ó Bradaigh	1970
Gerry Adams	1983–

Social Democratic and Labour Party

Gerry Fitt	1970
John Hume	1979
Mark Durkan	2001

Ulster Unionist Party

Edward Saunderson	1886
Walter Long	1906
Sir Edward Carson	1910
Sir James Craig	1921
John Miller Andrews	1940
Sir Basil Brooke	1943
Terence O'Neill	1963
James Chichester-Clark	1969
Brian Faulkner	1971
Harry West	1974
James Molyneaux	1979
David Trimble	1995

PRINCIPAL MINISTERS

United Kingdom of Great Britain and Ireland/Northern Ireland
Prime Ministers

	Appointed
William Pitt	19 Dec. 1783
Henry Addington	17 Mar. 1801
William Pitt	10 May 1804
Lord William Wyndham Grenville	11 Feb. 1806
3rd Duke of Portland	31 Mar. 1807
Spencer Perceval	4 Oct. 1809
2nd Earl of Liverpool	8 June 1812
(resumed office on accession of George IV)	29 Jan. 1820
George Canning	10 Apr. 1827
Viscount Goderich	31 Aug. 1827
1st Duke of Wellington	22 Jan. 1828
2nd Earl Grey	22 Nov. 1830
2nd Viscount Melbourne	16 July 1834
1st Duke of Wellington	17 Nov. 1834
Sir Robert Peel	10 Dec. 1834
2nd Viscount Melbourne	18 Apr. 1835
(resumed office on accession of Victoria)	20 June 1837
Sir Robert Peel	30 Aug. 1841
Lord John Russell (cr. Earl Russell 1864)	20 June 1846
23rd Earl of Derby	23 Feb. 1852
4th Earl of Aberdeen	19 Dec. 1852
3rd Viscount Palmerston	6 Feb. 1855
23rd Earl of Derby	20 Feb. 1858
3rd Viscount Palmerston	12 June 1859
1st Earl Russell	29 Oct. 1865
23rd Earl of Derby	28 June 1866
Benjamin Disraeli (cr. Earl of Beaconsfield 1876)	27 Feb. 1868
William Ewart Gladstone	3 Dec. 1868
1st Earl of Beaconsfield	20 Feb. 1874
William Ewart Gladstone	23 Apr. 1880
3rd Marquess of Salisbury	23 June 1885
William Ewart Gladstone	1 Feb. 1886
3rd Marquess of Salisbury	25 July 1886
William Ewart Gladstone	15 Aug. 1892
5th Earl of Rosebery	5 Mar. 1894

	Appointed
3rd Marquess of Salisbury	25 June 1895
(resumed office on the accession of Edward VII)	23 Jan. 1901
Arthur James Balfour	12 July 1902
Sir Henry Campbell-Bannerman	5 Dec. 1905
Herbert Henry Asquith	7 Apr. 1908
(resumed office on accession of George V)	8 May 1910
David Lloyd George	7 Dec. 1916
Andrew Bonar Law	23 Oct. 1922
Stanley Baldwin	22 May 1923
James Ramsay MacDonald	22 Jan. 1924
Stanley Baldwin	4 Nov. 1924
James Ramsay MacDonald	5 June 1929
Stanley Baldwin	7 June 1935
(resumed office on accession of Edward VIII)	31 Jan. 1936
(resumed office on accession of George VI)	11 Dec. 1936
(Arthur) Neville Chamberlain	28 May 1937
Winston Leonard Spencer Churchill	10 May 1940
Clement Richard Attlee	26 July 1945
Winston Leonard Spencer Churchill	26 Oct. 1951
Winston Leonard Spencer Churchill (resumed office on accession of Elizabeth II) (cr. KG 1953)	7 Feb. 1952
Sir (Robert) Anthony Eden	6 April 1955
(Maurice) Harold Macmillan	10 Jan. 1957
Sir Alec Douglas-Home (formerly 14th Earl of Home)	19 Oct. 1963
(James) Harold Wilson	16 Oct. 1964
Edward Heath	19 June 1970
(James) Harold Wilson	4 Mar. 1974
(Leonard) James Callaghan	5 Apr. 1976
Margaret Hilda Thatcher	4 May 1979
John Major	29 Nov. 1990
Tony Blair	2 May 1997

Chancellors of the Exchequer

	Appointed
William Pitt	27 Dec. 1783
Henry Addington	20 Mar. 1801
William Pitt	13 May 1803
Lord Henry Petty	5 Feb. 1806
Spencer Perceval	26 Mar. 1807
Nicholas Vansittart	9 June 1812
Viscount Goderich	31 Jan. 1823
George Canning	20 Apr. 1827
John Charles Herries	3 Sept. 1827
Henry Goulburn	22 Jan. 1828

329

	Appointed
J. C. Spencer, Viscount Althrop	22 Nov. 1830
Sir Robert Peel	10 Dec. 1834
Thomas Spring Rice	18 Apr. 1835
Sir Francis Thornhill Baring	26 Aug. 1839
Henry Goulburn	3 Sept. 1841
Sir Charles Wood	6 July 1846
Benjamin Disraeli	27 Feb. 1852
William Ewart Gladstone	28 Dec. 1852
Sir George Cornewall Lewis	28 Feb. 1855
Benjamin Disraeli	26 Feb. 1858
William Ewart Gladstone	18 June 1859
Benjamin Disraeli	6 July 1866
George Ward Hunt	29 Feb. 1868
Robert Lowe	9 Dec. 1868
William Ewart Gladstone	30 Aug. 1873
Sir Stafford Northcote	21 Feb. 1874
William Ewart Gladstone	28 Apr. 1880
Hugh Culling Eardley Childers	16 Dec. 1882
Sir Michael Hicks Beach	24 June 1885
Sir William Harcourt	6 Feb. 1886
Lord Randolph Churchill	3 Aug. 1886
George Joachim Goschen	14 Jan. 1887
Sir William Harcourt	18 Aug. 1892
Sir Michael Hicks Beach	29 June 1895
Charles Thomson Richie	12 July 1902
Joseph Austen Chamberlain	9 Oct. 1903
Herbert Henry Asquith	11 Dec. 1905
David Lloyd George	16 Apr. 1908
Reginald McKenna	27 May 1915
Andrew Bonar Law	11 Dec. 1916
Austen Chamberlain	14 Jan. 1919
Sir Robert Stevenson Horne	5 Apr. 1921
Stanley Baldwin	25 Oct. 1922
Neville Chamberlain	11 Oct. 1923
Philip Snowden	23 Jan. 1924
Winston L. S. Churchill	7 Nov. 1924
Philip Snowden	8 June 1929
Neville Chamberlain	9 Nov. 1931
Sir John Simon	28 May 1937
Sir Howard Kingsley Wood	13 May 1940
Sir John Anderson	28 Sept. 1943
Hugh J. N. Dalton	28 July 1945
Sir R. Stafford Cripps	17 Nov. 1947
Hugh T. N. Gaitskell	25 Oct. 1950
Richard Austen Butler	27 Oct. 1951

	Appointed
Harold Macmillan	22 Dec. 1955
George Edward Peter Thorneycroft	14 Jan. 1957
Derick Heathcoat Amory	7 Jan. 1958
John Selwyn Brooke Lloyd	27 July 1960
Reginald Maudling	13 July 1962
James Callaghan	16 Oct. 1964
Roy Harris Jenkins	30 Nov. 1967
Iain Norman Macleod	20 June 1970
Anthony Perrinott Lysberg Barber	25 July 1970
Denis Winston Healey	5 Mar. 1974
Geoffrey Howe	5 May 1979
Nigel Lawson	9 June 1983
John Major	26 Oct. 1989
Norman Lamont	28 Nov. 1990
Kenneth Clarke	27 May 1993
Gordon Brown	2 May 1997

Secretaries of State for the Home Department

	Appointed
William Henry Cavendish-Bentinck, 3rd Duke of Portland	11 July 1794
Thomas Pelham (cr. 1st Lord Pelham 1801)	30 July 1801
Charles Philip Yorke	17 Aug. 1803
Robert Banks Jenkinson (summoned to parliament as Lord Hawkesbury 1803)	12 May 1804
G. J. Spencer, 2nd Earl Spencer	5 Feb. 1806
Lord Hawkesbury	25 Mar. 1807
Richard Ryder	1 Nov. 1809
Henry Addington, 1st Viscount Sidmouth	11 June 1812
Sir Robert Peel	17 Jan. 1822
William Sturges-Bourne	30 Apr. 1827
Henry Petty-FitzMaurice, 3rd Marquess of Lansdowne	16 July 1827
Sir Robert Peel	26 Jan. 1828
William Lamb, 2nd Viscount Melbourne [Irish] and 2nd Lord Melbourne [UK]	22 Nov. 1830
John William Ponsonby, 1st Lord Duncannon 1834 (4th Earl of Bessborough [Irish] 1844)	19 July 1834
Henry Goulburn	15 Dec. 1834
John Russell, commonly called Lord John Russell (1st Earl Russell 1861)	18 Apr. 1835
Constantine Henry Philpps, 1st Marquess of Normanby	30 Aug. 1839
Sir James Robert George Graham, bt	6 Sept. 1841
Sir George Grey, bt	6 July 1846
Spencer Horatio Walpole	27 Feb. 1852
Henry John Temple, 3rd Viscount Palmerston [Irish]	28 Dec. 1852
Sir George Grey, bt	8 Feb. 1855

	Appointed
Spencer Horatio Walpole	26 Feb. 1858
Thomas Henry Sutton Sotheron Estcourt	3 Mar. 1859
Sir George Cornewall Lewis, bt	18 June 1859
Sir George Grey	25 July 1861
Spencer Horatio Walpole	6 July 1866
Gathorne Hardy (1st Earl of Cranbrook 1892)	17 May 1867
Henry Austin Bruce (1st Lord Aberdare 1873)	9 Dec. 1868
Robert Lowe (1st Viscount Sherbrooke 1880)	9 Aug. 1873
Sir Richard Assheton Cross (Viscount Cross)	21 Feb. 1874
Sir William George Granville Venables Vernon Harcourt	28 Apr. 1880
Sir Richard Assheton Cross (Viscount Cross)	24 June 1885
Hugh Culling Eardley Childers	6 Feb. 1886
Henry Matthews (1st Viscount Llandaff 1895)	3 Aug. 1886
Herbert Henry Asquith (1st Earl of Oxford and Asquith 1925)	18 Aug. 1892
Sir Matthew White Ridley (1st Viscount Ridley 1900)	29 June 1895
Charles Thomson Ritchie (1st Viscount Ritchie 1905)	12 Nov. 1900
Aretas Akers-Douglas (1st Viscount Chilston 1911)	12 July 1902
Herbert John Gladstone (1st Viscount Gladstone 1910)	11 Dec. 1905
Winston Leonard Spencer Churchill (Sir) (KG 1953)	19 Feb. 1910
Reginald McKenna	24 Oct. 1911
Sir John Allsebrook Simon (1st Viscount Simon 1940)	27 May 1915
Herbert Louis Samuel (Sir) (1st Viscount Samuel 1937)	12 Jan. 1916
Sir George Cave (1st Viscount Cave 1918)	11 Dec. 1916
Edward Shortt	14 Jan. 1919
William Clive Bridgeman (1st Viscount Bridgeman 1929)	25 Oct. 1922
Arthur Henderson	23 Jan. 1924
Sir William Joynson-Hicks (1st Viscount Brentford 1929)	7 Nov. 1924
John Robert Clynes	8 June 1929
Sir Herbert Samuel (1st Viscount Samuel 1937)	26 Aug. 1931
Sir John Gilmour	1 Oct. 1932
Sir John Allsebrook Simon (1st Viscount Simon 1940)	7 June 1935
Sir Samuel John Gurney Hoare, bt (1st Viscount Templewood 1944)	28 May 1937
Sir John Anderson (1st Viscount Waverley 1952)	3 Sept. 1939
Herbert Stanley Morrison (Baron Morrison of Lambeth)	3 Oct. 1940
Sir Donald Bradley Somervell (Lord Somervell of Harrow 1954)	25 May 1945
James Chuter Ede (Baron Chuter-Ede)	3 Aug. 1945
Sir David Maxwell Fyfe (1st Viscount Kilmuir 1954)	28 Oct. 1951
Gwilym Lloyd-George (1st Lord Tenby 1957)	18 Oct. 1954
Richard Austen Butler (Baron Butler of Saffron Walden)	13 Jan. 1957
Henry Brooke (Baron Brooke of Cumnor)	13 July 1962
Sir Frank Soskice (Baron Stow Hill)	18 Oct. 1964
Roy Harris Jenkins (Lord Jenkins)	23 Dec. 1965

	Appointed
(Leonard) James Callaghan (Lord Callaghan)	30 Nov. 1967
Reginald Maudling	20 June 1970
(Leonard) Robert Carr (Baron Carr of Hadley)	19 July 1972
Roy Harris Jenkins (Lord Jenkins)	5 Mar. 1974
Merlyn Rees (Lord Rees)	10 Sept. 1976
William Stephen Ian Whitelaw (1st Viscount Whitelaw 1983)	5 May 1979
Leon Brittan (Sir)	10 June 1983
Douglas Richard Hurd	2 Sept. 1985
David Waddington (Lord Waddington)	26 Oct. 1989
Kenneth Baker	28 Nov. 1990
Kenneth Clarke	11 Apr. 1992
Michael Howard	27 May 1993
Jack Straw	2 May 1997
David Blunkett	8 June 2001

Secretaries of State for the Colonies, 1921–1925/Dominion Affairs, 1925–1947/Commonwealth Relations, 1947–1950

	Appointed
Winston Leonard Spencer Churchill	14 Feb. 1921
Victor Christian William Cavendish, 9th Duke of Devonshire	25 Oct. 1922
James Henry Thomas	23 Jan. 1924
Leopold Charles Maurice Stennett Amery	7 Nov. 1924
Sidney James Webb	8 June 1929
James Henry Thomas	13 June 1930
Malcolm MacDonald	27 Nov. 1935
Edward Montagu Cavendish Stanley, Lord Stanley	16 May 1938
Malcolm MacDonald	4 Nov. 1938
Sir Thomas Walker Hobart Inskip (cr. Viscount Caldecote, 6 September 1939)	5 Feb. 1939
(Robert) Anthony Eden	4 Sept. 1939
Viscount Caldecote	15 May 1940
Robert Arthur James Gascoyne-Cecil, Viscount Cranborne	4 Oct. 1940
Clement Richard Attlee	23 Feb 1942
Viscount Cranborne	28 Sept 1943
Christopher Addison, Viscount Addison	3 Aug. 1945
Philip John Noel-Baker	14 Oct. 1947

For **Lord Chancellor** *see* Peerage

Ireland, 1801–1922

Chancellors and Keepers of the Great Seal

	Appointed
John Fitzgibbon (cr. Baron Fitzgibbon, 6 July 1789; Viscount Fitzgibbon, 6 Dec. 1793; Earl of Clare, 12 June 1795)	29 June 1789

	Appointed
John Mitford, Baron Redesdale	15 Mar. 1802
George Ponsonby	25 Mar. 1806
Thomas Manners-Sutton, Baron Manners	1 May 1807
Sir Anthony Hart	5 Nov. 1827
William Conynham Plunket, Baron Plunket	23 Dec. 1830
Sir Edward Burtenshaw Sugden	13 Jan. 1835
William Conynham Plunket, Baron Plunket	30 Apr. 1835
Sir John Campbell (cr. Baron Campbell, 30 June 1841)	28 June 1841
Sir Edward Burtenshaw Sugden	28 Sept. 1841
Maziere Brady	16 July 1846
Francis Blackburne	10 Mar. 1852
Maziere Brady	13 Jan. 1853
Joseph Napier	10 Mar. 1858
Maziere Brady	27 June 1859
Francis Blackburne	24 July 1866
Abraham Brewster	29 Mar. 1867
Thomas O'Hagan (cr. Baron O'Hagan, 14 January 1870)	18 Dec. 1868
Joseph Napier, James Lewis, William Broome	11 Mar. 1874 (in commission)
John Thomas Ball	1 Jan. 1875
Lord O'Hagan	10 May 1880
Hugh Law	11 Nov. 1881
Sir Edward O'Sullivan, bt	11 Dec. 1883
John Naish	23 May 1885
Edward Gibson (cr. Baron Ashbourne, 4 July 1885)	1 July 1885
John Naish	11 Feb. 1886
Baron Ashbourne	5 Aug. 1886
Samuel Walker	22 Aug. 1892
Baron Ashbourne	8 July 1895
Samuel Walker (bt, 12 July 1906)	14 Dec. 1905
Redmond John Barry	5 Sept. 1911
Ignatius John O'Brien (bt, 15 Jan. 1916) (cr. Baron Shandon, 1 July 1918)	26 Mar. 1913
Sir James Henry Mussen Campbell, bt (cr. Baron Glenavy, 1 July 1921)	19 June 1918
Sir John Ross, bt	27 Jan. 1921

Chief Secretaries of the Irish Office

	Appointed
Robert Stewart, Viscount Castlereagh	3 Nov. 1798
Charles Abbot	25 May 1801
William Wickham	11 Feb. 1802
Sir Evan Napean	6 Feb. 1804
Nicholas Vansittart	23 Mar. 1805

	Appointed
Charles Long	21 Sept. 1805
William Elliot	28 Mar. 1806
Sir Arthur Wellesley	19 Apr. 1807
Robert Dundas	13 Apr. 1809
William Wellesley-Pole	18 Oct. 1809
Sir Robert Peel	4 Aug. 1812
Charles Grant	3 Aug. 1818
Henry Goulburn	29 Dec. 1821
William Lamb	29 Apr. 1827
Lord Francis Levenson-Gower	21 June 1828
Sir Henry Hardinge	17 July 1830
Edward George Geoffrey Smith Stanley	29 Nov. 1830
Sir John Cam Hobhouse	29 Mar. 1833
Edward John Littleton	17 May 1833
Sir Henry Hardinge	16 Dec. 1834
George William Frederick Howard, Viscount Morpeth	22 Apr. 1835
Edward Granville Eliot, Lord Eliot	6 Sept. 1841
Sir Thomas Francis Freemantle	1 Feb. 1845
Henry Pelham Pelham-Clinton, Earl of Lincoln	14 Feb. 1846
Henry Labouchere	6 July 1846
Sir William Meredyth Somerville	22 July 1847
Richard Southwell Bourke, Lord Naas	1 Mar. 1852
Sir John Young	1 Mar. 1853
Edward Horsman	1 Mar. 1855
Henry Arthur Herbert	27 May 1857
Richard Southwell Bourke, Lord Naas	4 Mar. 1858
Edward Cardwell	24 June 1859
Sir Robert Peel (younger)	29 July 1861
Chichester Samuel Parkinson-Fortescue	7 Dec. 1865
Richard Southwell Bourke, Lord Naas (6th Earl of Mayo, 12 Aug. 1867)	10 July 1866
John Wilson-Patten	29 Sept. 1868
Chichester Samuel Parkinson-Fortescue	23 Dec. 1868
Spencer Compton Cavendish, Marquis of Hartington	12 June 1871
Sir Michael Hicks Beach	27 Feb. 1874
James Lowther	15 Feb. 1878
William Edward Foster	30 Apr. 1880
Lord Frederick Charles Cavendish	6 May 1882
George Otto Trevelyan	9 May 1882
Sir Henry Campbell-Bannerman	23 Oct. 1884
Sir William Hart Dyke	23 June 1885
William Henry Smith	23 Jan. 1886
John Morley	6 Feb. 1886
Sir Michael Hicks Beach	5 Aug. 1886
Arthur James Balfour	7 Mar. 1887

	Appointed
William Lewies Jackson	9 Nov. 1891
John Morley	22 Aug. 1892
Gerald William Balfour	4 July 1895
George Wyndham	9 Nov. 1900
Walter Hume Long	12 Mar. 1905
James Bryce	14 Dec. 1905
Augustine Birrell	29 Jan. 1907
Henry Edward Duke	3 Aug. 1916
Edward Shortt	4 May 1918
James Ian Macpherson	13 Jan. 1919
Sir Hamar Greenwood	12 Apr. 1920

Attorneys General

	Appointed
John Stewart	23 Dec. 1800
Standish O'Grady	8 June 1803
William Conyngham Plunket	23 Oct. 1803
William Saurin	21 May 1807
William Conyngham Plunket	22 Jan. 1822
Henry Joy	18 June 1827
Francis Blackburne	11 Jan. 1831
Louis Perin	29 Apr. 1835
Michael O'Loghlen	31 Aug. 1835
John Richards	10 Nov. 1836
Stephen Woulfe	3 Feb. 1837
Nicholas Ball	11 July 1839
Maziere Brady	23 Feb. 1839
David Richard Pigot	14 Aug. 1840
Francis Blackburne	28 Sept. 1841
Thomas Brady Cusack Smith	4 Nov. 1842
Richard Wilson Greene	2 Feb. 1846
Richard Moore	16 July 1846
James Henry Monaghan	24 Dec. 1847
John Hatchell	22 Oct. 1850
Joseph Napier	12 Mar. 1852
Abraham Brewster	13 Jan. 1853
William Nicholas Keogh	2 Mar. 1855
John David Fitzgerald	10 Apr. 1856
James Whiteside	1 Mar. 1856
John David Fitzgerald	27 June 1859
Richard Deasy	22 Feb. 1860
Thomas O'Hagan	14 Feb. 1861
James Anthony Lawson	3 Feb. 1865
John Edward Walsh	23 July 1865
Michael Morris	1 Nov. 1866

	Appointed
Hedges Eyre Chatterton	29 Mar. 1867
Robert Richard Warren	23 Aug. 1867
John Thomas Ball	7 Dec. 1868
Edward Sullivan	21 Dec. 1868
Charles Robert Barry	26 Jan. 1870
Richard Dowse	13 Jan. 1872
Christopher Palles	5 Nov. 1872
John T. Ball	12 Mar. 1874
Henry Ormsby	21 Jan. 1875
George Augustus Chichester May	27 Nov. 1875
Edward Gibson	15 Feb. 1877
Hugh Law	10 May 1880
William Moore Johnson	17 Nov. 1881
Andrew Marshall Porter	13 Jan. 1883
John Naish	19 Dec. 1883
Samuel Walker	3 June 1885
Hugh Holmes	2 July 1885
Samuel Walker	12 Feb. 1886
Hugh Holmes	9 Aug. 1886
John George Gibson	30 July 1887
Peter O'Brien	19 Jan. 1888
Dodson Hamilton Madden	6 Dec. 1889
John Akinson	1 July 1892
Hugh Hyacinth O'Rorke MacDermot (The MacDermot)	24 Aug. 1892
John Akinson	8 July 1895
James Henry Mussen Campbell	4 Dec. 1905
Richard Robert Cherry	20 Dec. 1905
Redmond John Barry	2 Dec. 1909
Charles Andrew O'Connor	26 Sept. 1911
Ignatius John O'Brien	24 June 1912
Timothy Francis Molony	10 Apr. 1913
John Francis Moriarty	20 June 1913
Jonathan Pim	1 July 1914
John Gordon	8 June 1915
James H. M. Campbell	9 Apr. 1916
James O'Connor	8 Jan. 1917
Arthur Warren Samuels	7 Apr. 1918
Denis Stanislaus Henry	6 July 1919
Thomas Watters Brown	5 Aug. 1920

Solicitors-General, 1800–1921

	Appointed
William Cusack Smith	23 Dec. 1800
James McClelland	9 Jan. 1902
William Conyngham Plunket	5 Nov. 1803

337

	Appointed
Charles Kendal Bushe	24 Oct. 1805
Henry Toy	1 Mar. 1822
John Doherty	18 June 1827
Philip Cecil Crampton	23 Dec. 1830
Michael O'Loghlen	21 Oct. 1834
Edward Pennefather	27 Jan. 1835
Michael O'Loghlen	29 Apr. 1835
John Richards	21 Sept. 1835
Stephen Woulfe	10 Nov. 1836
Maziere Brady	3 Feb. 1837
David Richard Pigot	11 Feb. 1839
Richard Moore	14 Aug. 1840
Edward Pennefather	18 Sept. 1841
Joseph Devonsher Jackson	11 Nov. 1841
Thomas Barry Cusack Smith	22 Sept. 1842
Richard Wilson Green	4 Nov. 1842
Abraham Brewster	3 Feb. 1846
James Henry Monaghan	16 July 1846
John Hatchell	24 Dec. 1847
Henry George Hughes	22 Oct. 1850
James Whiteside	12 Mar. 1852
William Nicholas Keogh	13 Jan. 1853
John David Fitzgerald	2 Mar. 1855
Jonathan Christian	15 Apr. 1856
Henry George Hughes	26 Jan. 1858
Edmund Hayes	31 Mar. 1858
John George	8 Feb. 1859
Richard Deasy	14 July 1859
Thomas O'Hagan	22 Feb. 1860
James Anthony Lawson	14 Feb. 1861
Edward Sullivan	10 Feb. 1865
Michael Morris	3 Aug. 1866
Hedges Eyre Chatterton	8 Nov. 1866
Robert Richard Warren	4 Apr. 1867
Michael Harrison	19 Sept. 1867
John Thomas Ball	4 Nov. 1868
Henry Ormsby	7 Dec. 1868
Charles Robert Barry	21 Dec. 1868
Richard Dowse	14 Feb. 1870
Christopher Palles	6 Feb. 1872
Hugh Law	18 Nov. 1872
Henry Ormsby	12 Mar. 1874
Hon. David Robert Plunket	29 Jan. 1875
Gerald Fitzgibbon	3 Mar. 1877
Hugh Holmes	14 Dec. 1878

	Appointed
William Moore Johnson	24 May 1880
Andrew Marshall Porter	17 Nov. 1881
John Naish	9 Jan. 1881
Samuel Walker	19 Dec. 1883
Hugh Hyacinth O'Rorke MacDermot (The MacDermot)	June 1885
John Monroe	3 July 1885
John George Gibson	5 Dec. 1885
Hugh Hyacinth O'Rorke MacDermot (The MacDermot)	12 Feb. 1886
John George Gibson	9 Aug. 1886
Peter O'Brien	11 July 1887
Dodgson Hamilton Madden	19 Jan. 1888
John Akinson	6 Dec. 1889
Edward Carson	1 July 1892
Charles Hare Hemphill	24 Aug. 1892
William Kenny	28 Aug. 1895
Dunbar Plunket Barton	1 Jan. 1898
George Wright	30 Jan. 1900
James Henry Mussen Campbell	8 Jan. 1903
Redmond John Barry	20 Dec. 1904
Charles Andrew O'Connor	2 Dec. 1909
Ignatius John O'Brien	19 Oct. 1911
Thomas Francis Molony	24 June 1912
John Francis Moriarty	25 Apr. 1913
Jonathan Pim	20 June 1913
James O'Connor	1 July 1914
J. Chambers	19 Mar. 1917
Arthur Warren Samuels	12 Sept. 1917
John Blake Powell	7 Apr. 1918
Denis Stanislaus Henry	27 Nov. 1918
Daniel Martin Wilson	6 July 1919
Thomas Watters Brown	2 June 1921
	(post vacant 5 Aug. 1921)

Prime or First Sergeants

	Appointed
St George Daly	28 Jan. 1799
Edmund Stanley	1 July 1801
Arthur Browne	29 Dec. 1802
Arthur Moore	25 July 1805
William Johnson	25 July 1816
Henry Joy	28 Oct. 1817
Thomas Langlois Lefroy	13 May 1822
Thomas Goold	Apr. 1830
Edward Pennefather	Feb. 1832
Louis Perrin	Feb. 1835

	Appointed
Richard Wilson Greene	23 May 1835
Joseph Stock	4 Nov. 1842
John Howley (Kt 14 August 1865)	10 June 1851
Richard Armstrong	13 Feb. 1866
David Sherlock	25 Oct. 1880
James Robinson	25 May 1884
Charles Hare Hemphill	19 July 1885
William Bennet Campion	17 Nov. 1892
Charles Andrew O'Connor	5 Dec. 1907
John Francis Moriarty	15 Mar. 1910
Charles Louis Matheson	1 July 1913
Alexander Martin Sullivan	29 Oct. 1919

Secretaries of State for Ireland and Keepers of the Signet or Privy Seal

	Appointed
Robert Stewart, Viscount Castlereagh	24 July 1797
Charles Abbot (cr. Baron Colchester, 3 June 1817)	12 June 1801

Under-Secretaries

	Appointed
Edward Cooke	6 June 1796
Alexander Marsden	21 Oct. 1801
James Trail	8 Sept. 1806
Charles Saxton (succ. as bt, 11 November 1808)	6 Sept. 1801
William Gregory	5 Oct. 1812
Lt. Col. Sir William Gosset	1 Jan. 1831
Thomas Drummond	25 July 1835
Norman Hilton MacDonald	28 May 1840
Edward Lucas	15 Sept. 1841
Richard Pennefather	Aug. 1845
Thomas Nicholas Redington	11 July 1846
John Arthur Wynne	Mar. 1852
Major Thomas Aistrew Larcon (Major General, 1 April 1858)	Jan. 1853
Sir Edward Robert Wetherall	1 Dec. 1868
Thomas Henry Burke	20 May 1869
Robert George Crookshank Hamilton	9 May 1882
Maj. Gen. Sir Redvers Henry Buller	10 Dec. 1886
Col. Sir Joseph Ridgeway	15 Oct. 1887
David Harrell (Kt 19 January 1893)	12 Jan. 1893
Sir Antony Patrick MacDonnell	8 Nov. 1902
Sir James Brown Dougherty	14 July 1908
Lt. Col. Sir Matthew Nathan	12 Oct. 1914
Sir Robert Chalmers	6 May 1916
Sir William Patrick Byrne	23 Oct. 1916

	Appointed
James MacMahon	15 July 1918
Sir John Anderson	28 May 1920

Dáil Éireann, 1919–1922

Heads of Irish government

		Appointed
Cathal Brugha	President of the Ministry *pro tem*	22 Jan. 1919
Eamon de Valera	President of Dáil Éireann	1 Apr. 1919
Arthur Griffith	President of Dáil Éireann	10 Jan. 1922
Michael Collins	Chairman, Provisional Government	14 Jan. 1922
William T. Cosgrave	Chairman, Provisional Government	15 Aug. 1922

Irish Free State/Éire/Republic of Ireland

Cumann na nGaedheal (Sept. 1922 to Mar. 1932)

Office	
President of Executive Council	William T. Cosgrave
Finance	William T. Cosgrave (until Sept. 1923)
	Ernest Blythe
Justice (called Home Affairs until 1924)	Kevin O'Higgins (until July 1927)
	J. Fitzgerald Kenny
External Affairs	Desmond Fitzgerald (until June 1927)
	Kevin O'Higgins (until Oct. 1927)
	P. McGilligan
Defence	Richard Mulcahy (until Mar. 1924)
	William T. Cosgrave
	P. Hughes
	Desmond Fitzgerald
Agriculture (called Lands and Agriculture 1924 to 1928)	P. Hogan
Education	Eoin MacNeill (until Nov. 1924)
	J. M. O'Sullivan
Industry and Commerce	J. McGrath (until March 1924)
	P. McGilligan
Posts and Telegraph	J. J. Walsh (until Oct. 1927)
	Ernest Blythe
Fisheries	F. Lynch
Local Government and Public Health (called Local Government until 1924)	Ernest Blythe (until Sept. 1925)
	J. A. Burke (until June 1927)
	Richard Mulcahy
Attorney-General	H. Kennedy (until June 1924)
	J. O'Byrne (until Jan. 1926)
	J. A. Costello

Fianna Fáil (Mar. 1932 to Feb. 1948)

Office

President of Executive Council (called Taoiseach from Dec. 1927)	Eamon de Valera
Finance	Seán MacEntee (until June 1939)
	Sean T. Ó Ceallaigh
Justice	J. Geoghegan (until June 1938)
	Patrick J. Ruttledge (until Aug. 1939)
	Gerry Boland
External Affairs	Eamon de Valera
Defence	Frank Aiken (until Aug. 1939)
	Oliver Traynor
Agriculture	J. Ryan (until Jan. 1947)
	P. Smith
Education	T. Derrig (until September 1939)
	Sean T. Ó Cealliagh (until Sept. 1939)
	Eamon de Valera (until June 1940)
	T. Derrig
Industry and Commerce	Seán Lemass (until June 1939)
	Seán MacEntee (until Aug. 1941)
	Seán Lemass
Posts and Telegraphs	J. Connolly (until Feb. 1935)
	Gerry Boland (until Nov. 1936)
	Oliver Traynor (until Sept. 1939)
	T. Derrig (until Sept. 1939)
	Patrick J. Little
Lands (called Lands and Fisheries until 1934)	P. J. Ruttledge (until Feb. 1935)
	J. Connolly (until May 1936)
	Frank Aiken (until Nov. 1936)
	Gerry Boland (until Sept. 1939)
	Sean Moylan
Local Government and Public Health (called Local Government after 1947)	Sean T. Ó Ceallaigh (until September 1939)
	P. Ruttledge (until August 1941)
	Seán MacEntee
Health (from 1947)	J. Ryan
Social Welfare (from 1947)	J. Ryan
Co-ordination of Defensive Measures (1939–45)	Eamon de Valera
Supplies (1939–45)	Seán Lemass
Attorney-General	C. A. Maguire (until Nov. 1936)
	J. Geoghegan (until Dec. 1936)
	P. Lynch (until Mar. 1940)
	K. Haugh (until Oct. 1942)
	K. Dixon (until Apr. 1946)
	C. Ó Dalaigh

Inter-party (Feb. 1948 to June 1951)

Office	
Taoiseach	John A. Costello (C. na P)
Finance	P. McGilligan (FG)
Justice	Seán MacEoin (until Mar. 1951)
	D. Morrissey
External Affairs	Seán MacBride
Defence	T. F. O'Higgins (until Mar. 1951)
	Seán MacEoin
Agriculture	James Dillon
Education	Richard Mulcahy
Industry and Commerce	D. Morrissey (until Mar. 1951)
	T. F. O'Higgins
Posts and Telegraphs	J. Everett
Lands	J. Blowick
Local Government	T. J. Murphy (until Apr. 1949)
	M. Keyes
Health	Noel Browne (until Apr. 1951)
	John A. Costello
Social Welfare	W. Norton (Tánaiste)
Attorney-General	C. Lavery (until Apr. 1950)
	C. F. Casey

Fianna Fáil (June 1951 to June 1954)

Office	
Taoiseach	Eamon de Valera
Finance	Seán MacEntee
Justice	Gerry Boland
External Affairs	Frank Aiken
Defence	Oliver Traynor
Agriculture	Thomas Walsh
Education	Seán Moylan
Industry and Commerce	Seán Lemass (Tánaiste)
Posts and Telegraphs	Erskine Childers
Lands	Thomas Derrig
Local Government	Patrick Smith
Health	John Ryan
Social Welfare	John Ryan
Attorney-General	Cearbhall Ó Dalaigh
	T. Teevan

343

Inter-party (June 1954 to Mar. 1957)

Office

Taoiseach	John A. Costello (FG)
Finance	Gerry Sweetman
Justice	James Everett
External Affairs	Liam Cosgrave
Defence	Seán MacEoin
Agriculture	James Dillon
Education	Richard Mulcahy
Industry and Commerce	William Norton (Tánaiste, Lab.)
Posts and Telegraphs	M. Keyes
Lands	J. Blowick (until July 1956)
	Richard Mulcahy (until Oct. 1956)
	P. J. Lindsay
Gaeltacht (from July 1956)	Richard Mulcahy (until October 1956)
	P. J. Lindsay
Local Government	P. O'Donnell
Health	Tom O'Higgins
Social Welfare	Brendan Corish (Lab.)
Attorney-General	P. McGilligan

Fianna Fáil (Mar. 1957 to Mar. 1973)

Office

Taoiseach	Eamon de Valera (until June 1959)
	Seán Lemass (until Nov. 1966)
	Jack Lynch
Finance	John Ryan (until Apr. 1965)
	Jack Lynch (until Nov. 1966)
	Charles Haughey (until May 1970)
	George Colley
Justice	Seán Lemass (until 1959)
	Oliver Traynor (until October 1961)
	Charles Haughey (until 1964)
	Brian Lenihan (until Mar. 1968)
	Michael O'Morain (until 1970)
	Dessie O'Malley
External Affairs	Frank Aiken (until 1969)
	Patrick Hillery (until 1973)
	Brian Lenihan
Defence	Kevin Boland (until Oct. 1961)
	Gerald Bartley (until Apr. 1965)
	Michael Hilliard (until 1969)
	James Gibbons (until 1970)
	Jeremiah Cronin (until 1973)

Office

Agriculture (called Agriculture and Fisheries from July 1965)	Frank Aiken (until May 1957)
	S. Moylon (until Nov. 1957)
	Patrick Smith (until Aug. 1964)
	Charles Haughey (until Nov. 1966)
	Neil Blaney (until May 1970)
	James Gibbons
Education	Jack Lynch (until June 1959)
	Patrick Hillery (until April 1965)
	George Colley (until July 1966)
	Donogh O'Malley (until 1968)
	Jack Lynch (until 1968)
	Brian Lenihan (until 1969)
	Padraig Faulkner
Industry and Commerce	Sean Lemass (Tánaiste)
	Jack Lynch (until April 1965)
	Patrick Hillery (until July 1966)
	George Colley (until 1970)
	P. J. Lalor
Posts and Telegraphs	Neil Blaney (until April 1957)
	J. Ormonde (until June 1959)
	Michael Hilliard (until April 1965)
	Joseph Brennan (until November 1966)
	Erskine Childers (until 1969)
	P. J. Lalor (until 1970)
	Gerry Collins
Lands	Erskine Childers (until July 1959)
	Michael O'Morain (until Mar. 1968)
	Padraig Faulkner (until 1969)
	Seán Flanagan
Gaeltacht	Jack Lynch (until June 1957)
	Michael O'Morain (until July 1959)
	Gerald Bartley (until 1961)
	Michael O'Morain (until 1968)
	Padraig Faulkner (until 1969)
	George Colley
Local Government	P. Smith (until November 1957)
	Neil Blaney (until 1966)
	Kevin Boland (until 1970)
	Bobby Molloy
Health	Seán MacEntee (Tánaiste from June 1959)
	Donogh O'Malley (until July 1966)
	Seàn Flanagan (until 1969)
	Erskine Childers

345

Office

Social Welfare	P. Smith (until November 1957)
	Seán MacEntee (until October 1961)
	Kevin Boland (until November 1966)
	Joseph Brennan (until 1969)
	Kevin Boland (until May 1970)
	Joseph Brennan
Transport and Power	Erskine Childers (until 1969)
(from July 1959)	Brian Lenihan (until 1973)
	Michael O'Kennedy
Labour (from July 1966)	Patrick Hillery (until 1969)
	Joseph Brennan
Attorney-General	A. Ó Caoimh (until Mar. 1965)
	C. Condon

Inter-party (Mar. 1973 to July 1977)

Office	(Fine Gael unless otherwise stated)
Taoiseach	Liam Cosgrave
Finance	Richie Ryan
Justice	Patrick Cooney
Foreign Affairs	Garret Fitzgerald
Defence	Patrick Donegan (until 1976)
	Liam Cosgrave
Agriculture and Fisheries	Mark Clinton
Education	Dick Burke (until 1976)
	Peter Barry
Industry and Commerce	Justin Keating (Lab.)
Posts and Telegraphs	Conor Cruise O'Brien (Lab.)
Lands	Thomas J. Fitzpatrick (until 1976)
	Patrick Donegan
Gaeltacht	Thomas O'Donnell
Local Government	James Tully (Lab.)
Health	Brendan Corish (Lab.)
Social Welfare	Brendan Corish (Lab.)
Transport and Power	Peter Barry (until 1976)
	Thomas Fitzpatrick
Labour	Michael O'Leary (Lab.)
Marine	Patrick Donegan
Attorney-General	Declan Costello

Fianna Fáil (July 1977 to June 1981)

Office

Taoiseach	Jack Lynch (until Dec. 1979)
	Charles Haughey
Finance	George Colley (until Dec. 1979 Tánaiste)
	Michael O'Kennedy

Office

Justice	Gerry Collins
Foreign Affairs	Michael O'Kennedy (until Dec. 1979)
	Gerry Collins
Defence	Bobby Molloy (until Dec. 1979)
	Padraig Faulkner
Agriculture	James Gibbons (until Dec. 1979)
	Ray MacSharry
Education	John Wilson
Industry, Commerce and Energy (created in 1977, changed to Industry, Commerce and Tourism in Dec. 1979)	Des O'Malley
Energy (created in 1979)	George Colley
Posts and Telegraphs	Padraig Faulkner (until Dec. 1979)
	Albert Reynolds
Marine	Brian Lenihan (until Dec. 1979)
	Patrick Power
Gaeltacht	Dennis Gallagher (until Dec. 1979)
	Maire Geoghegan-Quinn
Environment	Sylvester Barrett
Health	Charles J. Haughey (until Dec. 1979)
	Michael Woods
Social Welfare	Charles J. Haughey (until Dec. 1979)
	Michael Woods
Transport and Power (renamed Tourism and Transport in 1977)	Padraig Faulkner
Labour	Gene Fitzgerald
Public Services	George Colley (until Dec. 1979)
	Gene Fitzgerald
Attorney-General	A. J. Hederman

Coalition (June 1981 to Mar. 1982)

Office	(Fine Gael unless otherwise stated)
Taoiseach	Garret Fitzgerald
Finance	John Bruton
Justice	Jim Mitchell
Foreign Affairs	John Kelly (until Oct.)
	James Dooge (from Oct.)
Defence	James Tully (Lab.)
Agriculture	Alan Dukes
Education	John Boland
Industry and Energy	Michael O'Leary (Lab.) (Tánaiste)
Trade, Commerce and Tourism	John Kelly
Posts and Telegraphs	Patrick Mark Cooney
Marine (Fisheries and Forestry)	Tom Fitzpatrick

347

Office	(Fine Gael unless otherwise stated)
Gaeltacht	Paddy O'Toole
Environment	Peter Barry
Health	Eileen Desmond (Lab.)
Social Welfare	Eileen Desmond (Lab.)
Transport and Power (renamed Tourism and Transport in 1977)	Patrick Cooney
Labour	Liam Kavanagh (Lab.)
Attorney-General	Peter Sutherland

Fianna Fáil (Mar. to Dec. 1982)

Office	
Taoiseach	Charles Haughey
Finance	Ray McSharry
Justice	Seán Doherty
Foreign Affairs	Gerry Collins
Defence	Patrick Power
Agriculture	Brian Lenihan (Tánaiste)
Education	Martin O'Donohue (until Oct. 1982)
	Gerard Brady
Industry, Commerce and Tourism	Desmond O'Malley
Industry and Energy	Albert Reynolds
Posts and Telegraphs	John Wilson
Marine	Brendan Daly
Gaeltacht	Padraig Flynn (until Oct. 1982)
	Martin J. O'Toole
Environment	Ray Burke
Health	Michael Woods
Social Welfare	Michael Woods
Transport	John Wilson
Labour	Gene Fitzgerald
Public Services	Gene Fitzgerald
Attorney-General	P. Connolly

Coalition (Dec. 1982 to Mar. 1987)

Office	(Fine Gael unless otherwise stated)
Taoiseach	Garret Fitzgerald
Finance	Alan Dukes (until 1986)
	John Bruton
Justice	Michael Noonan (until 1986)
	Alan Dukes
Foreign Affairs	Peter Barry (Tánaiste from January 1987)
Defence	Patrick Cooney (until 1986)
	Patrick O'Toole
Agriculture	Austin Deasy

Office

Education	Gemma Hussey (until 1986)
	Patrick Cooney
Industry and Energy (title changed to Energy in 1983)	John Bruton (until 1983)
Energy	Dick Spring (1983–7, Lab., Tánaiste)
Posts and Telegraphs (title changed in 1984 to Communications, Posts and Telegraphs)	Jim Mitchell
Marine, Fisheries and Forestry	Patrick O'Toole (until 1986)
	Liam Kavanagh (Lab.)
Environment	Dick Spring (until 1984, Lab.)
	Tánaiste until January 1993.
	Liam Kavanagh (until 1986, Lab.)
	John Boland
Health and Social Welfare	Barry Desmond (until 1986, Lab.)
	Gemma Hussey
Transport	Jim Mitchell (until 1984)
Trade, Commerce and Tourism	Frank Cluskey (Lab.)
Labour	Liam Kavanagh (until 1984, Lab.)
	Ruairi Quinn (Lab.)
Public Services (abolished in January 1987)	Ruairi Quinn (until January 1987, Lab.)
Attorney-General	Peter Sutherland (until 1986)
	John Rogers

Fianna Fáil (Mar. 1987 to July 1989)

Office

Taoiseach	Charles Haughey
Finance	Ray McSharry
Justice	Gerry Collins
Foreign Affairs	Brian Lenihan (Tánaiste)
Defence	Michael Noonan
Agriculture and Food	Michael O'Kennedy
Education	Mary O'Rourke
Energy and Commerce	Ray Burke
Communications	Ray Burke
Marine	Brendan Daly
Gaeltacht	Charles Haughey
Environment	Padraig Flynn
Health	Rory O'Hanlon
Social Welfare	Michael Woods
Tourism and Transport	John Wilson
Labour	Bertie Ahern
Attorney-General	John Murray

Coalition Fianna Fáil/Progressive Democrats (July 1989 to Jan. 1993)

Office	(Fianna Fáil unless otherwise stated)
Taoiseach	Charles Haughey (until Feb. 1992)
	Albert Reynolds
Finance	Albert Reynolds (until Nov. 1991)
	Bertie Ahern
Justice	Ray Burke (until February 1992)
	Padraig Flynn
Foreign Affairs	Gerry Collins (until Dec. 1992)
	David Andrews
Defence	Brian Lenihan (until December 1990, Tánaiste)
	Brendan Daly
Agriculture	Michael O'Kennedy (until February 1992)
	Joe Walsh
Education	Mary O'Rourke (until Feb. 1992)
	Seamus Brennan
Industry and Commerce	Dessie O'Malley (until November 1992, PD)
	Bertie Ahern
Energy	Bobby Molloy (until Nov. 1992, PD)
Communications	Ray Burke (until 1991)
	Seamus Brennan
Marine	John Wilson (until Dec. 1992)
	David Andrews
Gaeltacht	Charles Haughey (until Feb. 1992)
	John Wilson
Environment	Padraig Flynn (until Feb. 1992)
	Michael Smith
Health	Rory O'Hanlon (until Feb. 1992)
	John O'Connell
Social Welfare	Michael Woods (until Feb. 1992)
	Charlie McCreevy (until Jan. 1993)
	Michael Woods
Tourism and Transport	Seamus Brennan (until Feb. 1992)
Tourism and Trade (created in January 1993)	Charlie McCreevy
Labour	Bertie Ahern (until Feb. 1992)
	Brian Cowan
Attorney-General	John Murray (until Feb. 1992)
	Harry Whelehan

Coalition Fianna Fáil/Labour (Jan. 1993 to Dec. 1994)

Office	(Fianna Fáil unless otherwise stated)
Taoiseach	Albert Reynolds
Finance	Bertie Ahern
Justice	Maire Geoghegan-Quinn
Foreign Affairs	Dick Spring (Lab., Tánaiste)
Defence and Marine	David Andrews
Agriculture, Food and Forestry	Joe Walsh
Education	Niamh Breathnach (Lab.)
Enterprise and Employment	Ruairi Quinn (Lab.)
Transport, Energy and Communications	Brian Cowen
Arts, Culture and the Gaeltacht	Michael D. Higgins
Environment	Michael Smith
Health	Brendan Howlin
Social Welfare	Michael Woods (until Feb. 1993) Charlie McCreevy (until Jan. 1994) Michael Woods
Tourism and Trade	Charlie McCreevy
Equality and Law Reform	Mervyn Taylor
Attorney-General	Harry Whelehan

Coalition Fine Gael, Labour and Democratic Left (Dec. 1994 to June 1997)

Office	(Fine Gael unless otherwise stated)
Taoiseach	John Bruton
Finance	Ruairi Quinn (Lab.)
Justice	Nora Owen
Foreign Affairs	Dick Spring (Lab., Tánaiste)
Defence and Marine	Hugh Coveney
Agriculture, Food and Forestry	Ivan Yates
Education	Niamh Bhreathnach
Enterprise and Employment	Richard Bruton
Transport, Energy and Communications	Michael Lowry
Arts, Culture and the Gaeltacht	Michael D. Higgins (Lab.)
Environment	Brendan Howlin (Lab.)
Health	Michael Noonan
Social Welfare	Proinsias De Rossa (DL)
Tourism and Trade	Enda Kenny
Equality and Law Reform	Mervyn Taylor (Lab.)
Attorney-General	Dermot Gleeson

Coalition Fianna Fáil/Progressive Democrats (June 1997–June 2002)

Office	(Fianna Fáil unless otherwise stated)
Taoiseach	Bertie Ahern
Finance	Charlie McCreevy
Justice, Equality and Law Reform	John O'Donoghue
Foreign Affairs	Ray Burke (until 7 Oct. 1997)
	David Andrews (until 26 Jan. 2000)
	Brian Cowen
Defence	Michael Smith
Agriculture, Food and Rural Development	Joe Walsh
Education and Science	Joe Walsh (until Jan. 2000)
	Michael Woods
Enterprise, Trade and Employment	Mary Harney (PD, Tánaiste)
Public Enterprise	Mary O'Rourke
Arts, Heritage, Gaeltacht and the Islands	Síle de Valera
Environment and Local Government	Noel Dempsey
Health and Children	Barry Cowen (until 27 Jan. 2000)
	Micheál Martin
Social, Community and Family Affairs	Dermot Ahern
Tourism, Sport and Recreation	Jim McDaid
Marine and National Resources	Michael Woods (to Jan. 2000)
	Frank Fahey
Attorney-General	David Byrne (to 17 July 1999)
	Michael McDowell

Coalition Fianna Fáil/Progressive Democrats (June 2002–)

Office	(Fianna Fáil unless otherwise stated)
Taoiseach	Bertie Ahern
Finance	Charlie McCreevy
Justice, Equality and Law Reform	Michael McDowell
Foreign Affairs	Brian Cowen
Defence	Michael Smith
Agriculture, Food and Rural Development (to be renamed Agriculture and Food)	Joe Walsh
Education and Science	Noel Dempsey
Enterprise, Trade and Employment	Mary Harney (PD, Tánaiste)
Public Enterprise (to be renamed Transport)	Seamus Brennan
Arts, Heritage, Gaeltacht and the Islands (to be renamed Community, Rural and Family Affairs)	Eamon Ó Cuiv

Office	(Fine Gael unless otherwise stated)
Environment and Local Government	Martin Cullen
Health and Children	Micheál Martin
Social, Community and Family Affairs (to be renamed Social and Family Affairs)	Mary Coughlan
Tourism, Sport and Recreation (to be renamed Arts, Sport and Tourism)	John O'Donoghue
Marine and National Resources (to be renamed Communications and Natural Resources)	Dermot Ahern
Attorney-General	Rory Brady

Northern Ireland, 1920–2003

Government of Sir James Craig (UUP), 1921–1940

Office	
Prime Minister	Sir James Craig (cr. Viscount Craigavon)
Finance	Henry Pollock John Andrews (from 1937)
Home Affairs	Robert Bates
Education	Marquess of Londonderry Lord Charlemont (from 1927) J. H. Robb (from 1933)
Agriculture	Edward Archdale Sir Basil Brooke (from 1933)
Labour	John Andrews D. G. Shillington (from 1937) J. F. Gordon (from 1939)
Commerce (cr. in 1925)	J. M. Barbour

Government of John Andrews (UUP), 1940–1943

Office	
Prime Minister	John Andrews
Finance	J. M. Barbour
Home Affairs	Robert Bates
Education	J. H. Robb
Agriculture	Lord Glentoran
Labour	J. F. Gordan
Commerce	Sir Basil Brooke
Public Security (created in 1941)	William Grant Harry Midgley (from 1942)

Government of Sir Basil Brooke (UUP), 1943–1963

Office

Prime Minister	Sir Basil Brooke (cr. Viscount Brookeborough)
Finance	J. M. Sinclair
	Brian Maginnes (from 1953)
	G. B. Hanna (from 1956)
	Terence O'Neill (from 1956)
Home Affairs	W. Lowry
	J. E. Warnock (from 1944)
	Brian Maginnes (from 1945)
	George Hanna (from 1953)
	Terence O'Neill (from 1956)
Education	Revd R. Corkey
	S. H. Hall-Thompson (from 1944)
	Harry Midgley (from 1952)
	W. M. May (from 1957)
	Ivan Neill (from 1962)
Agriculture	R. Moore
	Harry West (from 1960)
Labour	William Grant
	Brian Maginnes
	Harry Midgley (from 1949)
	Ivan Neill (from 1951)
	H. V. Kirk (from 1962)
Commerce	Sir R. T. Nugent
	W. V. McCleery (from 1949)
	Lord Glentoran (from 1953)
	Jack Andrews
Health (from 1944)	William Grant
	Dame Dera Parker (from 1949)
	Jack Andrews (from 1957)
	William Morgan (from 1961)

Government of Capt. Terence O'Neill (UUP), 1963–1969

Office

Prime Minister	Terence O'Neill
Finance	Jack Andrews
	Herbie Kirk
Home Affairs	William Craig
	R. W. McConnell (from 1964)
	William Craig (from 1966)
	Walter Long (from 1968)
Education	Ivan Neill
	Herbert Kirk (from 1964)

Office	
Education	William Long (from 1966)
	William Fitzsimmons
Agriculture	Harry West
	Major James Chichester-Clark (from 1967)
Labour	William Morgan
Commerce	Brain Faulkner
Health	William Morgan
	William Craig (from 1964)
	William Morgan
Development (created in 1965)	William Craig
	William Fitzsimmons (from 1966)
	Ivan Neill (from 1968)

Government of Maj. James Chichester-Clark (UUP), 1969–1971

Office	
Prime Minister	James Chichester-Clark
Finance	Herbie Kirk
Home Affairs	Robert Porter
Education	Phelim O'Neill
	Walter Long (1969)
Agriculture	Phelim O'Neill
	Roy Bradford (1969)
Labour	William Morgan
Commerce	Brian Faulkner
Health	Robert Porter
	Walter Fitzsimmons (1969)
Development	Walter Long
	Brian Faulkner (1969)

Government of Brian Faulkner (Ulster Unionist Party), 1971–1972

Office	
Prime Minister	Brian Faulkner
Finance	Herbert Kirk
Home Affairs	Robert Porter
Education	Walter Long
Agriculture	Phelim O'Neill
Labour	William Morgan
Commerce	Robin Bailie
Health	Walter Fitzsimmons
Development	Roy Bradford
Community Relations (created in 1971)	David Bleakley
	Basil McIvor (1971)

Northern Ireland Executive (Coalition), 1974

Office

Chief Executive	Brian Faulkner (UUP)
Deputy Chief Executive	Gerry Fitt (SDLP)
Legal	Oliver Napier (Alliance)
Education	Basil McIvor (UUP)
Finance	Herbert Kirk
Labour	William Morgan
Commerce	John Hume (SDLP)
Environment	Roy Bradford
Health and Social Services	Paddy Devlin
Agriculture	Leslie Morrell (UUP)
Information	John L. Baxter

The Northern Ireland Executive (Coalition), 1999–2003

The Executive was elected on 29 November 1999 and comprises a First Minister, Deputy First Minister and 10 other ministers, each of whom has responsibility for one of the 10 departments. Two junior ministers were subsequently appointed to the Office of the First and Deputy First Minister. There are also committees of 11 Assembly members to 'advise and assist' the ministers. The committees will provide a system of checks and balances and allow Assembly members to question ministers on policy matters. The two most senior figures in each committee are the chair and the deputy chair. The Assembly was suspended on 14 October 2002 and dissolved on 28 April 2003. Assembly elections were held on 26 November 2003.

First Minister	David Trimble (UUP) [resigned 1 July 2001, re-elected 6 Nov. 2001]
Deputy First Minister	Seamus Mallon (until Nov. 2001, SDLP); Mark Durkan (SDLP) [elected 6 Nov. 2001]
Junior ministers to the Office of the First and Deputy First Minister's Office	Denis Haughey (SDLP) Dermot Nesbitt (UUP) [moved to Environment, Feb. 2002] James Leslie (UUP)
Agriculture and Rural Development Minister	Brid Rodgers (SDLP)
Committee Chair	Revd Ian Paisley (DUP)
Deputy Chair	George Savage (UUP)
Culture, Arts and Leisure Minister	Michael McGimpsey (UUP) [ceased to hold office 19 Oct. 2001; appointed again from 24 Oct. 2001]

Chair	Eamon O'Neill (SDLP)
Deputy Chair	Mary Nelis (SF)
Education Minister	Martin McGuinness (SF)
Chairman	Danny Kennedy (UUP)
Deputy Chair	Sammy Wilson (DUP)
Enterprise, Trade and Investment Minister	Sir Reg Empey (UUP) [ceased to hold office 19 Oct. 2001; appointed again from 24 Oct. 2001]
Chair	Pat Doherty (SF)
Deputy Chair	Seán Neeson (APNI)
Environment Minister	Sam Foster (UUP) [ceased to hold office 19 Oct. 2001; appointed again from 24 Oct. 2001, resigned Feb. 2002]
	Dermot Nesbitt (UUP)
Chair	Revd William McCrea (DUP)
Deputy Chair	Carmel Hanna (SDLP)
Finance and Personnel Minister	Mark Durkan (SDLP)/Seán Farren (SDLP) (from 14 Dec. 2001)
Chair	Francie Molloy (SF)
Deputy Chair	James Leslie (UUP)
Health, Social Services and Public Safety Minister	Bairbre de Brún (SF)
Chair	Dr Joe Hendron (SDLP)
Deputy Chair	Tommy Gallagher (SDLP)
Higher and Further Education, Training and Employment Minister	Sean Farren (SDLP)/Carmel Hanna (SDLP) (from 14 Dec. 2001)
Chair	Dr Esmond Birnie (UUP)
Deputy Chair	Mervyn Carrick (DUP)
Regional Development Minister	Peter Robinson (DUP) (ceased to hold office 27 July 2000)/Geogory Campbell (DUP) (ceased to hold office 19 Oct. 2001; appointed from 24 Oct. 2001)/Peter Robinson reappointed.
Chair	Dennis Haughey (SDLP)
Deputy Chair	Alan McFarland (UUP)
Social Development Minister	Nigel Dodds (DUP) (ceased to hold office 27 July 2000; appointed 24 Oct. 2001)/Maurice Morrow (27 July 2000–19 Oct. 2001)/Nigel Dodds reappointed.
Chair	Fred Cobain (UUP)
Deputy Chair	Michelle Gildernew (SF)

Secretaries of State for Northern Ireland, 1972–2004

	Appointed
William S. I. Whitelaw	14 Mar. 1972
Francis Leslie Pym	5 Dec. 1973
Merlyn Rees	5 Mar. 1974
Roy Mason	10 Sept. 1976
Humphrey E. Atkins	5 May 1979
James Prior	14 Sept. 1981
Douglas Hurd	11 Sept. 1984
Thomas King	3 Sept. 1985
Peter Brooke	24 July 1989
Sir Patrick Mayhew	11 Apr. 1992
Marjorie (Mo) Mowlam	3 May 1997
Peter Mandleson	11 Oct. 1999
John Reid	24 Jan. 2001
Paul Murphy	4 Oct. 2002

SOCIAL AND RELIGIOUS HISTORY

COMMUNICATIONS

Major periodicals

Achill Missionary Herald and Western Witness (1837–1850s)
Founded on 31 July 1837 by the Revd Edward Nangle to further evangelical views in Connacht. It ceased publication in the early 1850s.

Anglo-Celt (Cavan) (1846 to date)
Weekly 1851 Thursday; 1872 Saturday. 1851 Neutral; 1866 Liberal, 1880s Nationalist, circulating counties Cavan, Meath, Westmeath, Monaghan, Leitrim, Longford and Fermanagh.
Proprietors: 1857 Zechariah Wallace; 1858 Joseph Wallace; 1866 P. Brady; 1867 Philip Fitzpatrick; 1868 John F. O'Hanlon; 1888 Mrs O'Hanlon.

Armagh Guardian (1844–1982)
Weekly Friday. Conservative, Church of Ireland, circulating Armagh and a 10-mile radius, partially through other parts of Ireland and North America. Articles on agriculture and commerce with some literary content.
Proprietors: 1851 John Thompson; 1881 W. C. B. Thompson; 1893 Sam Delmege Trimble.

Armagh Observer (Dungannon) (1930 to date)

Armagh Standard (1879–1909)
Weekly Friday. 1885 Conservative; 1888 Constitutional; 1889 Conservative, circulating Armagh and district. Local and district news with correspondence, tales and miscellanies. Incorporated into the *Ulster Gazette*.
Proprietor (1889 and editor): John Young.

Athlone Sentinel (1834–61)
Weekly Friday. 1851 Conservative; 1857 Liberal, Catholic, with a wide circulation in the west and midlands. Contained items of general and local content.
Proprietor: John Daly.

Athlone Times (1877–1902)
Weekly Saturday. Independent, circulating town and district. Local events, social, political and religious, summaries of home and foreign news.
Proprietors: 1877 Henry McClenaghan; 1888 S. J. McClenaghan.

Ballina Chronicle (1849–51)
Weekly Wednesday. Independent, circulating Mayo and local counties.
Proprietor: Thomas Ham.

Ballina Herald (1844–1962)
Weekly. Neutral, circulating Mayo, Sligo, and adjoining counties.
Proprietors: R. W. Joynt and J. Duncan.

Ballina Journal (1880–95)
Weekly Monday. Liberal, circulating Ballina, Mayo and Connacht generally.
Proprietors: 1881 W. R. Armstrong; 1888 J. T. Armstrong.

Ballina National Times (July 1866)
Weekly. Independent, circulating in Ballina and district. Articles on all
tyranny and injustice.
Proprietor: John Bourns.

Ballinrobe Chronicle (1866–1903)
Weekly Saturday. Independent, circulating Ballinrobe and Mayo. Articles on
agriculture, commerce, politics and general literature.
Proprietors: 1867 Gore Kelly; 1892 Miss Gore Kelly.

Ballymena Advertiser (1866–92)
Weekly Saturday. Liberal, circulating Ballymena and district.
Proprietor: M. Edwin.

Ballymena Observer (1855–1985)
Weekly 1857 Saturday; 1889 Friday. Liberal-Conservative, Unionist.
Proprietors: 1857 George White; 1877 John Weir.

*Ballymena Weekly Telegraph/*1966 *Ballymena Times* (1867–1970)
Weekly Friday. Neutral. Local reports, markets, North of Ireland news. Serial
tales, joke columns and competitions.
Proprietor: J. Laughlin.

Ballymoney Free Press (1863–1934)
Weekly Thursday. Liberal, circulating Ballymoney and towns of Ulster. Local
and general news.
Proprietor: S. C. McElroy.

*Ballyshannon Herald and North Western Advertiser/*1884 *Donegal Independent*
    (10 June 1831–?12 Apr. 1884)
Weekly 1851 Friday; 1868 Saturday. 1864 Conservative; 1884 Independent-
Conservative; 1886 Independent, Church of England, circulating through-
out Connacht and Ulster and partial circulation throughout UK.
Proprietors: 1857 David Carter; 1858 Andrew Green; 1884 Sam Delmege
Trimble.

Banbridge Chronicle (Banbridge, Co. Down) (1880) *Banbridge Chronicle and
    Downshire Standard* (1870–1985)
1876 Weekly Saturday; 1888 bi-weekly Wednesday and Saturday. Independent, tenant right.
Proprietor: J. E. Emerson.

Banner of Ulster (Belfast) (1842–69)
1851 bi-weekly Tuesday and Friday; 1857 tri-weekly Tuesday, Thursday and Saturday. Liberal, circulating throughout Ulster, organ of the General Assembly of the Presbyterian Church and in great measure represented the opinions of all the Evangelical Protestant Dissenters of Ireland.
Proprietors: 1851 John Prenter; 1857 McCormick and Dunlop; 1866 Samuel E. McCormick.

Belfast Daily Post/1884 *Belfast Weekly Post* (1882–84)
Daily. Liberal, non-sectarian, advocating tenant rights, maintenance of the Union and the interests of the British Empire. Circulation in Belfast and North of Ireland.
Proprietors: 1882 P. Stirling; 1884 J. Clarence Newsome.

Belfast Evening Telegraph 1918/*Belfast Telegraph* (1870 to date)
Daily. Conservative, circulating Belfast and Ulster.

Belfast Mercury (1854) *Belfast Daily Mercury* (1851–61)
1854 tri-weekly Tuesday, Thursday and Saturday; 1857 daily.
Liberal/Radical circulating Belfast and Ulster and generally throughout Ireland.
Proprietors: 1851 James Simms; 1857 James Simms and Frederick Farrer; 1860 Ulster Printing Co.

Belfast Morning News/1880 *Ulster Weekly News*/1883 *Belfast Morning News* (1855–92)
1857 tri-weekly Monday, Wednesday and Friday; 1872 daily; 1880 weekly. 1857 Neutral; 1883 Independent; 1885 Home Rule; 1888 Nationalist, circulating Belfast and main towns in north and north-west of Ireland.
Proprietors: 1851 R. and D. Read; 1884 F. W. Bell; 1888 E. Dwyer Gray; 1889 G. H. Page; 1889 Mrs Dwyer Gray; 1892 The Morning News Co Ltd; 1885 The organ of the Home Rule Party in the North of Ireland.

Belfast Morning News (1855–92)
Tri-weekly Tuesday, Thursday and Saturday. A cheap vehicle of local news circulating Belfast and neighbourhood. Went Parnellite in 1890, hence its demise and incorporation into the *Irish News* in 1892.

Belfast News-Letter (1737 to date)
Founded by Francis Joy on 1 September 1737, it is the oldest daily newspaper in Ireland and second only to *Lloyd's List* in the British Isles. It became a tri-weekly in 1851 and a daily in 1855. Protestant and Conservative circulating in counties Antrim and Down, generally throughout Ulster, partially in England and Scotland.
Proprietors: 1851 James Alexander Henderson; 1885 Henderson and Co.

Belfast Times (1872)
Daily. Conservative, circulating Belfast, Ulster, generally in Ireland, Scotland and England.
Proprietors: D. and J. Allen. Also the name of a tabloid that ran for one week in Jan. 1979.

Belfast Weekly News (1855–1942)
Saturday. 1885 Organ of the Orange Institution, circulating Belfast and district.
Proprietors: 1857 J. A. Henderson; 1885 Henderson and Co.

Belfast Weekly Press (1858–85)
Family paper covering agriculture and trade.
Proprietors: 1864 McCormick and Dunlop; 1866 Samuel E. McCormick.
(Not entered in *Newspaper Press Directory* after 1885.)

Belfast Weekly Telegraph (1873–1964)
Saturday. Recognised organ of the Orange Society in Ulster and abroad.
Proprietors: W. and G. Baird.

Ballymoney Free Press (Antrim) (1863–1934)
Incorporated into the *Coleraine Chronicle* in 1934.

Bell (1940–54)
Founded by Seán O'Faolain in 1940, it was the leading Irish literary journal, publishing fiction, poetry and articles on national and international affairs. It opposed censorship. It ceased publication in April 1948 but reappeared in November 1950, running until 1955.

Bray Gazette/1871 *Bray and Kingston Gazette*/1877 *Bray Herald* (1861–72)
Weekly Saturday. Neutral, circulating Bray and district. Local news and a list of visitors. Proprietor and editor 1864 G. R. Powell; 1879 proprietor William McPhail.

Bray People (Bray, Co. Wicklow) (1920 to date)

Capuchin Annual (1930–77)
Published by the Capuchin Friary in Dublin from 1930 to 1977, it published fiction and verse along with articles on theology, history, literature and art.

Carlow Nationalist/1888 *Nationalist and Leinster Times* (1883 to date)
Weekly Saturday. Nationalist, circulating counties Carlow, Kildare, Wicklow and Queen's/Laois. 1884 contains full reports of National League meetings, agricultural and general news and military news of Curragh Camp.
Proprietor: P. J. Conlan.

Carlow Post (1853–78)
Weekly Saturday. Liberal/Nationalist, Catholic, circulating Carlow and Leinster generally. News and political content.
Proprietor: 1857 Thomas Price; 1868 Louisa Price.

Carlow Sentinel (Carlow) (1830–1920)
Weekly Saturday. Conservative, Churches of England and Ireland, circulating Co. Carlow and Leinster generally. Agricultural, commercial, political and literary content.
Proprietors: 1851 T. A. Carroll; 1857 Mrs Sarah Carroll.

Carlow Weekly News (1855–63)
Weekly Saturday. Neutral, circulating Carlow and district. Local news.
Proprietor: T. Edwards.

Carrickfergus Advertiser and County Gazette (Antrim) (1883–1946)
Weekly Friday. Conservative, Protestant, circulating town of Carrickfergus and County Antrim. Local and county news.
Publisher: 1885 A. W. Wheeler; 1891 William Ritchie.

Carrickfergus Freeman (1865–66)
Weekly Saturday. Independent, circulating Carrickfergus and neighbourhood. Local topics.
Publisher: John Henderson.

Carrick's Morning Post (1812–32)
Daily newspaper founded by Richard Lonergan in 1812, it was purchased and amalgamated into the *Dublin Times* in 1832.

*Cashel Gazette/*1872 *Cashel Gazette, Tipperary Reporter and Weekly Advertiser* (1864–93)
Weekly Saturday. Neutral, circulating Cashel and district. Original literature and antiquarian articles. 1883–6 occasional articles in Irish language.
Proprietor: H. Davis White.

Cashel Sentinel (1885–1914)
Weekly Saturday. Nationalist, Home Rule, circulating Cashel and district. Local and general news.
Proprietor: T. Walsh.

Castlebar Telegraph or *Connacht Ranger/*1877 *Connacht Telegraph* (1830 to date)
Weekly Wednesday. Liberal, Catholic, circulating throughout Connacht, UK and abroad. All proceedings in parliament, foreign and domestic news and reports of local meetings.
Proprietors: 1864 Charlotte Macdonnell; 1877 O'Hea and Daly; 1880 James Daly.

Catholic Bulletin (Dublin) (1911–39)
Monthly. Edited by J. J. O'Kelly until 1921, then anonymously by Thomas Corcoran SJ thereafter.
Publisher: M. H. Gill and Co.

Cavan Observer (1857–64)
Weekly Saturday. Conservative, circulating Armagh and Co. Cavan. Agricultural and commercial interests of the county.
Proprietor: Charlotte Bourns.

365

Cavan Weekly News (1864–1909)
Weekly Friday. 1868 Independent; 1869 Protestant-Conservative; 1874 Protestant; 1888 Liberal-Conservative, circulating Cavan and county. Local news.
Proprietor: John Fegan.

Celt (Waterford) (1876–7)
Weekly Saturday. Neutral.
Proprietor: M. Hayes; 1879 taken over by the *Munster News.*

Champion or Sligo News/1868 *Sligo Champion* (1836 to date)
Weekly 1851 Saturday; 1857 Monday. 1851 Radical; 1857 Liberal, later Catholic, Nationalist. Circulated Sligo County and Leitrim, Mayo, Roscommon and Donegal.
Proprietors: 1851 Edward Howard Verdon; 1864 Edward O'Farrell; 1879 Edward Gayer; 1886 P. A. McHugh.

Christian Advocate/1923 *Irish Christian Advocate*/1972 *Conference News*/1973
   Methodist Newsletter (Belfast) (1883 to date)
Weekly, evangelical, circulated among Methodists. The monthly *Irish Evangelist* its forerunner (1859–1883). Dublin editions were published of the British *Methodist Magazine* (1801–22) and the *Primitive Wesleyan Magazine* (1823–78).

Citizen/1881 *Citizen and County News*/1886 *Waterford Citizen* (Waterford) (1859–
   1906)
1864 weekly Friday; 1870 bi-weekly Tuesday and Friday. 1864 Independent; 1881 Liberal, Catholic, Repeal, circulating Waterford and district.
Proprietor: James Harnett McGrath.

City Week (Belfast) (1964–70)

City Wide News (Philsboro, Dublin) (1994 to date)

Clare Advertiser (Kilrush) (1856)
Weekly Saturday. Neutral, reformist, circulating Clare, Limerick and Cork.
Proprietor: John A. Carroll.

Clare Champion (Ennis) (1903 to date)

Clare Examiner (Ennis) (1878–87)
Weekly Saturday. 1880 Nationalist; 1882 Constitutional, circulating Ennis and counties Clare and Limerick. Local and county news.
Proprietor: Thomas Maguire.

Clare Freeman (Ennis) (1853–84)
1857 weekly Saturday; 1877 bi-weekly Wednesday and Saturday. Liberal, circulating Clare, Limerick, Galway and generally south and west of Ireland. Local and general news from UK and abroad, as well as some literary content.
Proprietors: 1857 James Knox Walker; 1868 Mrs M. Laing Walker; 1879 C. L. Nono.

*Clare Independent/*1882 *Independent and Muster Advertiser* (Ennis) (1875–85)
Weekly Saturday. 1878 Catholic; 1881 Liberal; 1885 Nationalist, circulating Ennis, Clare and Tipperary.
Proprietor: T. S. Cleary.

*Clare Journal/*1879 *Clare Journal and Ennis Advertiser* (Ennis) (1776–1917)
Bi-weekly Monday and Thursday. Conservative, Church of England, circulating Ennis, Clare and through Ireland generally. Advocated interests of agriculture and commerce.
Proprietors: 1857 John B. Knox; 1865 John B. Knox and Son.

Clare Weekly News (Ennis) (1878–80)
Weekly Saturday. Liberal-Conservative, circulating Ennis and county.
Proprietor: John B. Knox and Son.

Clonmel Chronicle (Tipperary)/1888 *Clonmel Chronicle and Waterford Advertiser* (1848–1935)
Bi-weekly Wednesday and Saturday. Conservative, circulating Tipperary, King's County/Offaly, Antrim, Dublin. Commercial and agricultural content.
Proprietor: Edmond Woods.

Coleraine Chronicle (Co. Londonderry) (1844–1967)
Weekly Saturday. 1851 Conservative; 1864 Liberal, circulating Ulster, UK and US. Presbyterian paper with agricultural, commercial, political and family content.
Publishers: 1851 Robert Huey; 1857 John McCombie.
Proprietors: 1851 H. Boyde Mackey; 1868 John McCombie.

Coleraine Constitution (Co. Londonderry) (1875–1908)
Weekly Saturday. Conservative, Unionist, circulating Londonderry and Antrim and through the provinces.
Publisher: J. Hamilton Simms; 1884 J. M. Russell.

Connacht Sentinel (Galway City) (1925 to date)

Connacht Tribune (Galway City) (1909 to date)

*Connaught Champion/*1908 *Connacht Champion* (Galway City) (1904–11)
Weekly. Nationalist, O'Brienite, circulating in Connacht generally.
Proprietor: O'Donnell and Co. Ltd.

Connaught Patriot (Tuam) (1859–69)
Weekly Saturday. Nationalist, tenant right, Catholic, circulating Tuam and Connacht.
Publisher: Martin A. O'Brennan.

Connaught People (Ballina) (1883–6)
Weekly Saturday. Nationalist, circulating Galway, Roscommon, Mayo and King's County. Political content but also attends to agricultural and commercial interests of community.
Proprietor: A. G. Scott.

Connaught Telegraph (Castlebar, Co. Mayo) (1828 to date)
Weekly. National, circulating Connacht, UK, France, USA, India.
Proprietor: R. A. Gillespie.

Connaught Watchman (Ballina) (1851–63)
Weekly Wednesday. Conservative, Protestant, circulating Mayo, Sligo, Leitrim,
Galway and Roscommon. Some literary content.
Proprietor: Thomas Ham.

Connaught Witness (Roscommon) (1870)
Weekly Saturday. Conservative, circulating Roscommon and district.
Proprietor: L. W. Lennon.
(Not entered in *Newspaper Press Directory* after 1871.)

Cookstown News (Dungannon, Tyrone) (1896–1916)
Weekly. Non-political, circulating Dungannon and surrounding area.
Proprietor: Tyrone Printing Co.

Cork Constitution (Cork City) (1822–1924)
1822 tri-weekly Tuesday, Thursday, Saturday; 1872 daily. Conservative, Church
of England, circulating Cork County and towns and principal towns in Kerry,
Limerick, Waterford and Tipperary. Aristocratic tone.
Proprietors: 1851 Anthony Savage, George Edwards, George Savage; 1857
Messrs A. Savage and G. E. Savage; 1871 Cork Constitutional Co Ltd.

Cork County Eagle (Cork City) (1857–1928)
Weekly. Independent nationalist, circulating Co. Cork and throughout
Munster. Ceased publication during Civil War after presses destroyed by
irregular forces.
Proprietor: F. P. E. Potter.

Cork Daily Southern Reporter/1871 *Irish Daily Telegraph* (1807–73)
1851 Tuesday, Thursday, Saturday; later daily. 1851 Liberal. Circulated Cork
and Munster generally. Only organ of constitutional liberalism in the south
of Ireland.

County of Wexford Express/1878 *Kilkenny and Wexford Express*/1878 *Wexford and
    Kilkenny Express* (1875–1907)
Weekly Wednesday. Nationalist. Favours peasant proprietorship.
Proprietor: J. Fisher.

Cork Evening Echo (Cork City) (1892)
Daily evening. Independent, circulating city and county of Cork. Foreign
and domestic news.
Proprietors: D. Gillman and F. P. E. Potter.
(Not entered in *Newsplan Press Directory* after 1873.)

Cork Examiner (1841 to date)
Daily newspaper founded in 1841 by John Francis Maguire. The publishers
also issue the *Cork Evening Echo* and the *Weekly Examiner*.

Cork Herald/1864 *Daily Herald and Cork Weekly Herald* (1856–1901)
Weekly Saturday; 1864 Daily. Began as a Liberal paper; by 1889 a Nationalist paper, circulating Cork and surrounding towns.
Proprietors: 1851 Patrick Dennehy; 1857 Felix Mullan; 1869 Bryan Hennessy; 1870 Daniel Gillman; 1872 D. Gillman and Frederick P. E. Potter.

Cork Weekly Examiner (Cork City) (1850–1981)
Weekly. National, printed Sinn Féin notes, circulating city and Co. Cork, counties Kerry, Limerick, Clare, Tipperary, Dublin and England.
Proprietor: Thomas Crosbie and Co. Ltd.

Cork Weekly News (Cork City) (1883–1925)
Weekly. Conservative, circulating city and Co. Cork, counties Kerry, Limerick, Waterford and Tipperary.
Proprietor: News and Sons Ltd.

County Down Spectator (1904 to date)
Weekly. Conservative, circulating throughout Ulster.
Proprietor: D. E. Alexander.

County Tipperary Independent (Nenagh) (June 1879)
Weekly Thursday. Independent, circulating Nenagh and Co. Tipperary.
Proprietor: J. Fisher.

County Wexford Express/1871 *Wexford Express* (1875–1907)
1871 weekly Wednesday; 1874 bi-weekly Wednesday and Saturday. Independent, circulating Wexford and New Ross and supplying county news.
Proprietors: 1871 J. Fisher; 1883 W. G. Fisher; 1891 H. D. Fisher.

Daily Express (Dublin) (1851–1960)
Daily. Unionist and Protestant, circulating throughout Ireland, London.
Proprietor: Dublin Express and Mail Ltd.

Derry Journal (1772 to date)
Three times weekly. Originally Conservative; 1820s Liberal; 1830s Nationalist, circulating Londonderry, Donegal and throughout Ulster.
Proprietors: McCarroll family; Derry Journal Ltd.

Derry Weekly News (1892–1956)
Weekly. Independent, circulating Londonderry and district.
Proprietors: John McAdam; North of Ireland Publishing Co.

Derry People (Omagh) (1902 to date)

Donegal Democrat (Ballyshannon, Co. Donegal) (1919 to date)
Weekly. Nationalist, circulating Ballyshannon.
Editor: John Downey.

Donegal Independent (Ballyshannon) (1831–1927)
Twice weekly. Independent, circulating Co. Donegal and adjoining counties.
Proprietor: P. A. Mooney.

369

Donegal People's Press (Sligo town) (1931 to date)

Donegal Vindicator (Ballyshannon) (1889–1956)
Weekly Friday. Nationalist, circulating north-west. Local and district news.
Proprietor: John McAdam.

Down Independent (Downpatrick) (1878–82)
Weekly Saturday. Liberal, circulating Downpatrick and district.
Publisher: 1878 A. J. Matthews; 1881 Down Independent Co. Ltd.

*Downpatrick Recorder/*1879 *Down Recorder* (1836 to date)
Weekly Saturday. Conservative, Church of Ireland, circulating every town in
Co. Down. Political, religious and literary journal, representing interests of
agriculture.
Proprietor: 1851 Conway Pilson; 1877 J. S. Clarke.

Downshire Protestant (Downpatrick) (1855–62)
Weekly Friday. Protestant, circulating principal towns of Downshire. Information on Protestant societies in UK and information of agriculture, manufactures and local matters.
Proprietor: William Johnston.

Drogheda Advertiser (Louth) (1896–1929)
Weekly. Conservative independent, circulated counties Meath, Louth and
Dublin.
Proprietor: A. McDougall.

Drogheda Argus (Louth) (1835 to date)
Weekly Saturday. Liberal, circulating north Leinster. Information on agricultural, commercial and manufacturing matters. Political, religious and some
literary content.
Proprietors: 1851 Patrick Kelly; 1858 Anne Kennedy; 1868 John Hughes;
1888 A. Hughes.

Drogheda Conservative (1837–1908)
Weekly Saturday. Conservative, Protestant, circulating locally. Agricultural
and commercial matters, some literary content.
Proprietors: 1851 John Apperson; 1857 Alexander McDougall; 1870 James
Willcock; 1874 John McDougall; 1888 A. McDougall. Incorporated into
Drogheda Advertiser.

Drogheda Independent (1884 to date)
Weekly Saturday. Nationalist, circulating Drogheda and surrounding counties.
Local news.
Proprietor: Drogheda Independent Co.

Drogheda Leader (Drogheda, Co. Louth) (1995 to date)

Dromore Weekly Times (Co. Down) (1900–52)
Weekly. No editorial policy, circulated in Lisburn and district.
Proprietor: R. J. Hunter. Incorporated into *Mourne Observer.*

Dublin Evening Mail (1823–1962)
Daily. Independent, unionist, circulating Dublin, Ireland, and Britain. Originally founded to oppose Catholic Emancipation.
Proprietor: Maunsell and Co; Sir Horace Plunkett; *c.* 1900 Baron Ardilaun.

Dublin Morning Register (1824–43)
Liberal newspaper founded by Michael Staunton.

Dublin Morning Star (1824–5)
Founded by J. T. Haydn as an anti-Catholic periodical.

Dublin Opinion (1922–72)
Monthly. Founded as a satirical magazine and briefly revived in the late 1970s.

Dublin People (Dublin) (1987 to date)

Dublin Saturday Post (1910–20)

Dublin Times (1832–3)
Founded with the support of Dublin Castle, it was free.

Dublin University Magazine (1833–77)
Editors included Isaac Butt, Charles Lever and Mortimer O'Sullivan.

Dundalk Democrat (Co. Louth) / and *People's Journal* (1849 to date)
Weekly Saturday. 1851 Ultra-Liberal; 1884 National circulating north-east.
Proprietors: 1851 Joseph Cartan; 1873 Thomas Roe.

Dundalk Express (1860–70)
Weekly Saturday. Independent, circulating Dundalk and Co. of Louth.
Proprietor: Gerard McCarthy.

Dundalk Herald (1868–1921)
Weekly Saturday. Independent-Conservative, circulating Dundalk, Louth, Monaghan.
Proprietor: Edward Carlton.

Dungannon News (Cookstown, Co. Tyrone) (1893–1916)
Weekly. Independent, circulating in Dungannon and Co. Tyrone.
Publishers: J. and H. L. Glasgow Ltd.

Dungannon Democrat (Dungannon, Co. Tyrone) (1913–24)

Dungannon Observer (Dungannon, Co. Tyrone) (1930)

Dungarvan Leader and Southern Democrat (Dungarvan, Co. Waterford) (1938 to date)

Dungarvan Observer (Waterford City) / and *Munster Industrial Advocate* (1912 to date)
Weekly. National.

East Galway Democrat (Ballinasloe, Co. Galway) (1910–49)
Weekly. Nationalist, circulating throughout the district.
Proprietors: Nicholas and M. D. O'Carroll.

371

Echo (Tallaght) (1980 to date)

Echo and South Leinster Advertiser (Enniscorthy, Co. Wexford) (1903 to date)
Weekly. Independent nationalist, one of the earliest newspapers to embrace
Sinn Féin, circulated Co. Wexford. Since 1988 it has been published under
four different mastheads: *Enniscorthy Echo, Wexford Echo, Gorey Echo* and *New
Ross Echo.*
Proprietor: North Wexford Printing Co.

Enniscorthy Guardian (Co. Wexford) (1889–1971)
Weekly Saturday. Nationalist, circulating Wexford, Carlow and Wicklow.
Local news.
Proprietor: E. Walsh.

Enniscorthy News (1856–1912)
Weekly Saturday. Neutral, circulating Enniscorthy and district. News of
Enniscorthy, general news and biographies of eminent men.
Proprietor: George Griffiths.

Enniskillen Advertiser (1864–77)
Weekly Thursday. 1865 neutral; 1867 Liberal but not partisan, circulating
Enniskillen and district. Local news.
Proprietor: J. Hamilton.

Evening Echo (Cork City) (1892 to date)
Daily. National, circulating in city and county of Cork, counties Kerry, Limer-
ick, Clare, Tipperary, Dublin and England.
Publisher: Thomas Crosbie and Co. Ltd.

Evening Herald/1814 Sentinel (1805–15)
Liberal newspaper founded by John Magee jun. in 1805; it became the
Sentinel in 1814 but disappeared in 1815.

Evening Herald (Dublin) (1891 to date)
Daily. Independent nationalist, circulating throughout Ireland.
Evening edition of the *Irish Independent.*

Evening Irish Times (Dublin) (1858–1921)

Evening News (Waterford City) (1898–1957)
Daily. National, circulating in Waterford, counties Tipperary, Kilkenny,
Wexford and south-east Ireland.
Proprietor: News Printing Works.

Evening Press (Dublin) (1954–95)

Evening Telegraph (Dublin), 1870 *News* (Enniscorthy, Co. Wexford) (1856–
1912)
Weekly Saturday. Neutral, circulating Enniscorthy and county of Wexford.
Mostly local news.
Proprietors: 1857 John Pilkington; 1869 James Owens; 1884 R. and W. Owen.

Fermanagh Herald (Enniskillen, Co. Fermanagh) (1902 to date)
Weekly. Nationalist, pro-IPP, circulating in Co. Fermanagh.
Proprietor: Northwest of Ireland Printing Co.

Fermanagh Mail (1808–93)
Weekly Thursday; 1869 Monday. Independent, circulating through county of
Fermanagh and partially in neighbouring counties.
Proprietor: T. R. J. Polson.

Fermanagh News (1907–1930)

Fermanagh News (1967 to date)

*Fermanagh Reporter/*1874 *Impartial Reporter* (Enniskillen) (1826 to date)
1851 Weekly Thursday; 1888 bi-weekly Wednesday and Saturday. Conservative,
Protestant, pro-land reform, circulating Enniskillen, county of Fermanagh
and neighbouring counties.
Proprietor: 1851 William Trimble; 1888 W. and W. C. Trimble; 1889 W.
Trimble; E. Trimble.

Fermanagh Times (Enniskillen) (1870–1949)
Weekly Thursday. Conservative, Protestant, circulating Enniskillen and
Co. Fermanagh. Local and county news.
Publisher: 1885 A. W. Wheeler; 1891 William Ritchie.

Flag of Ireland (1868–74)
An Irish republican newspaper.
Proprietor: Richard Piggot.

Freeman's Journal (Dublin) (1763–1923)
Founded in Dublin, it was once the country's leading and then nationalist
daily newspaper. Taken over by Irish Parliamentary Party in 1891 but ceased
publication in 1923 and was absorbed into the *Irish Independent*

Free Press (Wexford) (1888)
Weekly Saturday. Nationalist, circulating principal towns and villages of Co.
Wexford. Local and district news.
Proprietor: W. Corcoran.

Frontier Sentinel (Newry, Co. Down) (1904–72)
Weekly. Nationalist, circulating in counties Down, Armagh and Louth.
Proprietor: Northwest Printing and Publishing Co.

Gaelic-American (1903–27)
Founded by John Devoy in New York as a Clan na Gael vehicle, the first
edition appeared on 13 September 1903 and it ran until 1927.

Galway American (1862–3)
Weekly Saturday. Liberal, circulating Galway and neighbouring counties.
Publisher: James Daly.

Galway Express (Galway City) (1853–1920)
Weekly Saturday. Conservative, circulating Galway, Mayo, Roscommon, Clare, Limerick and partially throughout United Kingdom.
Proprietors: John and Alexander McDougall.

Galway Mercury (1844–60)
Weekly Saturday. Liberal, circulating Connacht and Munster, Dublin and many important towns in England.
Proprietors: 1851 James Davis; 1857 J. C. O'Shaughnessy and John Mahon; 1858 Michael Winter and John Mahon.

Galway Observer (Galway City) (1881–1966)
Weekly Saturday. 1881 National; 1883 Liberal; 1884 Independent; 1888 National, circulating Galway and neighbourhood.
Proprietor: A. G. Scott.

Galway Vindicator (1841–99)
Bi-weekly Wednesday and Saturday. 1857 Liberal; 1868 Liberal-Independent, Catholic, circulating Galway, Mayo, Roscommon, Clare, Limerick and Cork and extensively in London and Dublin.
Proprietors: 1851 J. P. Blake; 1857 John Francis Blake (died 1864); 1865 Lewis L. Ferdinand.

General Advertiser (Dublin) (1837–1924)
Weekly. Neutral, circulating throughout Ireland.
Publisher: General Advertiser Ltd.

Gorey Correspondent/1878 *Gorey Correspondent and Arklow Standard* (1855–92)
Weekly Saturday. Neutral, circulating Gorey and Co. Wexford. Local and miscellaneous news.
Proprietor: 1864 Samuel Clarke; 1877 Clarke and Son.

Guardian (Nenagh) (1838 to date)
Twice weekly. Liberal-Conservative, circulating in Nenagh and surrounding area.
Proprietors: Gabriel Prior, Nenagh Guardian Co.

Guardian (Wexford town) (1847–56)

Herald and Western Advertiser (Tuam, Co. Galway) (1837 to date)
Weekly. National-Liberal, circulating counties Galway, Mayo, Sligo, Roscommon, Dublin, and USA.
Proprietor: Richard J. Kelly.

Hibernia (1937–75)
Founded as a review covering current, literary and economic affairs, it was published monthly until Oct. 1968 when it became a fortnightly until Sept. 1975 from which time it was a weekly.

Impartial Reporter (Enniskillen, Co. Fermanagh) (1825 to date)
Weekly. Independent-Protestant, circulating in Ulster.
Proprietor: W. C. Trimble.

Indiu (Dublin) (1943–1984)
Gaelic-language newspaper.

Ireland's Own (1902–present)
Founded by Edward O'Cullen as a weekly magazine, it was popular with the Irish abroad.

Ireland's Saturday Night (Belfast) (1894 to date)
Weekly. Sports news, circulating in Belfast and Dublin.
Proprietor: W. and G. Baird Ltd.

Iris Oifigiuil (*Irish State Gazette*) (Dublin) (1922 to date)

Irish Bulletin (1919–21)
Periodical published by Dáil Éireann during the Anglo-Irish War, it first appeared on 11 Nov. 1919 and ran until 1921.

Irish Daily Telegraph (Londonderry) (1904–18)
Daily. Neutral, circulating Belfast and Dublin.
Proprietor: W. and G. Baird Ltd.

Irish Freedom (1910–14)
Published by the Irish Republican Brotherhood.

Irish Homestead (1895–1923)
Founded in 1895 as a vehicle of the Co-operative Movement, it was edited by George W. ('AE') Russell. It merged with the *Irish Statesman* in 1923.

Irish Independent (Dublin) (1891 to date)
Founded as the *Irish Daily Independent* by Charles Stewart Parnell, the first issue appeared on 18 Dec. 1891. In 1900 it merged with the *Daily Nation* controlled by William Martin Murphy and became the *Irish Independent* in 1905. In 1906 the *Sunday Independent* began publication.

Irish Monthly (Dublin) (1873–1954)
Catholic and literary, contributors included many of the leaders of the literary revival.
Publisher: M' Glashan and Gill.

Irish News (Belfast) (1855 to date)
Daily. Catholic-nationalist, circulating Ulster and throughout Ireland.
Proprietor: Irish News Ltd.

Irish News Agency (1949–57)
Established by Seán MacBride in 1949 to publicise Ireland abroad. It published *Eire-Ireland*, which was abolished in 1957.

Irish Peasant/1906 *Peasant*/1907 *Peasant and Irish Ireland*/1909 *Irish Nation and Irish Peasant* (1905–10)
Founded by James McCann in 1905, it came to play a role in the Irish-Ireland movement.

Irish People (1973 to date)
Founded by James Stephens in Nov. 1863 as the official organ of the Irish Republican Brotherhood, it was suppressed in Sept. 1865.

Irish People (1899–1908)
Weekly newspaper founded by William O'Brien on 16 Sept. 1899 as an organ of the United Irish League, it ceased publication in 1908.

The Irish People (Dublin) (1973 to date)

Irish Post (Belfast) (1910–?)

Irish Press (Dublin) (1931–95)
Daily newspaper founded in September 1931 by Eamon de Valera to provide a forum for Fianna Fáil. The company also published the *Sunday Press* (1949) and the *Evening Press* (Sept. 1954).

Irish Press Agency (1886–90)
Founded in Oct. 1886 under the management of J. J. Clancy, it distributed information in England on Irish affairs. Briefly resurrected by Stephen Gwynn c. 1906.

Irish Statesman (1919–30)
Weekly review established in 1919 with the aid of Sir Horace Plunkett, it absorbed the *Irish Homestead* in 1923, ceasing publication in 1930.

Irish Times (Dublin) (1859 to date)
Daily newspaper founded by Major Laurence E. Knox in 1859. Originally Ascendancy and Unionist, it is now an organ fostering liberal views.

Irish Weekly (Belfast) (1891–1982)
Weekly. National, circulating Belfast and Ulster.
Proprietor: Irish News Ltd.

Irish Weekly Independent (Dublin) (1893–1960)

Irish Worker (1911–32)
Founded by James Larkin in May 1911 as a weekly newspaper to forward the trade union and labour movement. It was suppressed during the First World War but revived by Larkin in October 1930, ceasing publication in March 1932.

Irish World (1870–1980)
Founded by Patrick Ford in 1870 in New York, it was noted for its nationalist views in the nineteenth century. After 1914 it took a separatist stance.

Kerry Champion (Tralee, Kerry) (1928–58)
Proprietor: M. P. Ryle.

Kerry Evening Post (Tralee, Co. Kerry) (1774–1917)
Bi-weekly Wednesday and Saturday. Conservative, Protestant, circulating Co. Kerry and south of Ireland. Full local information.
Proprietors: 1851 John and Jeffery Eagar; 1864 George Raymond; 1882 George and Alexander Raymond; 1884 George Raymond.

Kerry Evening Star (Tralee, Co. Kerry) (1902–14)
Twice weekly. Nationalist, circulating in Tralee and Co. Kerry.
Publisher: M. P. Ryle.

Kerry Examiner (Tralee) (1840–56)
Bi-weekly Tuesday and Friday. Liberal, Catholic, circulating Cork, Limerick, Clare, Tipperary, Waterford and Wexford. Religious, political and literary journal.
Proprietor: Patrick O'Loughlin Byrne.

Kerry Independent (Tralee) (1880–4)
Bi-weekly Monday and Thursday. Nationalist, Catholic, circulating all the towns of Co. Kerry.
Proprietor: Henry Brassill.

Kerry News (Tralee, Co. Kerry) (1894–1941)
Twice weekly. Nationalist, circulating counties Kerry, Cork, Limerick and Clare.
Proprietor: John B. Quinnell and Sons.

Kerry People (Tralee, Co. Kerry) (1902–28)
Weekly. Nationalist, circulating Co. Kerry.
Proprietors: M. P. Ryle; 1921, Davis Ryle.

Kerry Sentinel (Tralee) (1878–1918)
1878 Weekly Friday; 1885 bi-weekly Tuesday and Friday. Independent, Nationalist, Catholic, circulating Tralee and County Kerry. Mainly local news.
Proprietors: 1878 T. Harrington; 1888 E. Harrington.

Kerry Star (1861–3)
Bi-weekly Tuesday and Friday. Independent, circulating Kerry and neighbouring counties.
Proprietor: T. J. O. Kane.

Kerry Vindicator (Tralee) (1876)
Weekly Saturday. Nationalist, circulating Tralee, Kerry and Munster. County and provincial news.
Proprietor: James Joseph Long.

Kerry Weekly Reporter (Tralee) (1883–1936)
Weekly Saturday. 1885 Nationalist; 1888 Liberal, circulating Tralee and county of Kerry. Local and general news, with tales, sketches and miscellanies.
Proprietor: J. Quinnell.

Kerryman (Tralee) (1904 to date)
Weekly. Nationalist, circulating in Co. Kerry.
Proprietor: Kerryman Ltd.

Kildare Observer (Naas, Co. Kildare) (1879–1935)
Weekly Saturday. Independent, circulating Naas, Co. Kildare, and other eastern counties. Local news.
Proprietor: William S. Gray.

Kilkenny Journal (Kilkenny) (1767 as *Finn's Leinster Journal.* Under present title 1830–1935)
Bi-weekly Wednesday and Saturday. 1851 Liberal; 1892 Nationalist, circulating county and city of Kilkenny and subscribers in other parts of Ireland and England.
Proprietors: 1851 Cornelius Maxwell; 1858 Mary Anne Maxwell; 1882 Representatives of Mary Anne Maxwell.

Kilkenny Moderator (Kilkenny) (1814–1925)
Bi-weekly Wednesday and Saturday. Conservative, Church of Ireland, circulating Kilkenny, Carlow, Waterford, Wexford, Clonmel, Cork. Political and literary journal addressing agriculture, commercial and manufacturing interests.
Proprietors: 1851 Abraham Denroche; 1857 John G. A. Prim; 1877 M. W. Lalor; Standish O'Grady.

Kilkenny People (Kilkenny) (1893–1926) incorporated with *Kilkenny Post* (1926)

Kilkenny Post (Kilkenny) (1925–28 Dec. 1960)

Killarney Echo (Tralee, Co. Kerry) (1899–1920)
Weekly. Nationalist, circulating Tralee and south Co. Kerry.
Proprietor: John B. Quinnell and Sons.

Kilrush Herald (Kilrush, Co. Clare) (1877–1922)
Weekly 1878 Thursday; 1885 Saturday. 1879 Independent; 1880 Liberal and Independent, circulating counties Clare, Limerick, Kerry, Galway, Tipperary and Dublin, England, America and the colonies. Local and county news.
Proprietor: P. J. Boyle.

King's County Chronicle (Birr) (1845–1963)
Weekly Wednesday; 1873 Thursday. Conservative, Church of Ireland, circulating midlands. 1867 editions are published for Roscrea and Tullamore under the titles of *Midland Counties Advertiser* and *Leinster Reporter.*
Proprietors: 1851 Francis H. Shields; 1873 John Wright.

Kingstown and Bray Observer (1870–1)
Weekly Saturday. Independent, circulating Kingstown area.
Publisher: W. Reid.

Kingstown Courier (1856)
Weekly Saturday. Neutral, circulating Dublin, Kingstown and county.
Publisher: Robert Chamney.

Kingstown Journal (1863)
Neutral, circulating Kingstown and district.
Publisher: P. Kelly.

Larne Weekly Recorder (1881–5)
Weekly Saturday. Independent, circulating Larne and district. Local and general news.
Publishers: 1881 John H. McLean; 1885 P. O'C. Patman.

Larne (Weekly) Reporter (1865–1904)
Weekly Saturday. Liberal, circulating Larne and district. Local news.
Proprietor: 1867 J. Read and Son; 1877 S. A. Read and Sons; 1882 John S. McAlmont.

Larne Times (Larne, Co. Antrim) (1892 to date)
Weekly. Conservative, circulating Fairhead, Antrim to suburbs of Belfast. Known as the *East Antrim Times* between 1962 and 1983.
Proprietor: W. and G. Baird Ltd.

Leader (1906–73)
Irish-Ireland, founded by D. P. Moran, editor until 1936, followed by Nuala Moran.

Leader (Dromore, Co. Down) (1916 to date)
Weekly. Circulating Dromore.

Leinster Express (Maryborough, Queen's Co.) (1831 to date)
Weekly Saturday. Independent, circulating midland counties. Advocates development of industrial resources of Ireland.
Proprietors: 1857 Henry W. Talbot, Kingstown, Co Dublin; 1868 J. W. Talbot; 1874 Geo. W. Talbot; 1889 Michael Carey.

Leinster Independent (Maryborough) (1869–75)
Weekly Saturday. Independent, Catholic, circulating throughout province.
Proprietor: J. T. Quigley.

Leinster Leader (Naas, Co. Kildare) (1880 to date)
Weekly Saturday. Nationalist, circulating Naas, Kildare, Carlow and Queen's County.
Publisher: S. J. Fletcher.

Leinster Reporter and Central Weekly Times (Tullamore) (1858–1930)
Weekly 1864 Wednesday; 1874 Thursday. Neutral, circulating Tullamore and district. Local news.
Proprietors: 1864 Francis H. Shields; 1873 John Wright.

Leinster Reporter and County Kildare Herald (Naas) (1859)
Weekly Friday for Saturday. Progressive-Conservative, circulating Kildare and generally in Munster. Local and provincial news, literature and sporting topics.
Proprietor: Richard Bull.
(Not entered in *Newspaper Press Directory* after 1879.)

Leitrim Gazette/1868 *Leitrim and Longford Advertiser*/1870 *Leitrim Advertiser* (Mohill) (1856–1924)
Weekly 1857 Saturday; 1872 Thursday. 1858 Liberal; 1864 Liberal-Conservative; 1865 Conservative; 1869 Independent, circulating Leitrim and Connacht. News of Ireland, England and abroad, with tales and varieties.
Proprietors: 1857 Robert J. Turner; 1880 E. Turner; 1881 Representatives of late R. Turner.

Leitrim Journal (Carrick-on-Shannon) (1850–72)
Weekly Saturday. Independent, circulating Carrick-on-Shannon. Local news.
Proprietor: William Trimble.

Leitrim Observer (Carrick-on-Shannon) (1889 to date)
Weekly Saturday. Nationalist, circulating Leitrim and surrounding counties.
Proprietor: F. Mulvey.

Liberator (Tralee, Kerry) (1915–39)
Nationalist, circulating locally.
Managing director: Maurice Griffin.

Limerick and Clare Examiner (1846–55)
Bi-weekly Wednesday and Saturday. Liberal, Repeal, circulating counties
Limerick and Clare. Reports of public meetings.
Proprietor: R. Goggin.

Limerick Chronicle (Limerick City) (1766 to date)
1851 bi-weekly Wednesday and Saturday; 1864 tri-weekly Tuesday, Thursday
and Saturday. Founded by John Ferar in 1766, it is the oldest newspaper in
the Republic of Ireland. 1857 Neutral; 1867 Moderate-Conservative, circulating
Ireland, England, Scotland and partially in the colonies. Literary newspaper.
Proprietors: 1857 Henry Watson; 1864 William Hosford and Sarah Bassett;
1875 William Hosford.

Limerick Echo (Limerick City) (1897–47)
Weekly, later twice weekly. Nationalist, circulating counties Limerick,
Tipperary, Clare and Kerry.
Proprietor: 1921, C. O'Sullivan.

Limerick Leader (Limerick City) (1889 to date)
Tri-weekly Monday, Wednesday and Friday. Nationalist, circulating Limerick,
Clare and Tipperary.
Proprietor: John McEnery.

Limerick Observer (Limerick City) (1856–7)
Tri-weekly Tuesday, Thursday and Saturday. Neutral, circulating Limerick,
Dublin and Cork.
Proprietor: Patrick Lynch.

Limerick Reporter/1850 and *Tipperary Vindicator* (1839–96)
Bi-weekly 1851 Tuesday and Friday; 1857 Wednesday and Saturday. Liberal,
circulating Tipperary, Limerick, King's County, Queen's County, Kerry, Clare,
Galway, Cork, etc.
Proprietor: Maurice Lenihan.

Limerick Weekly News (1888)
Weekly Saturday. Nationalist, circulating Limerick City and district. General
and local news, National League meetings fully reported.

Publisher: E. Asbie.
(Not entered in *Newspaper Press Directory* after 1890.)

Lisburn Herald (Lisburn, Co. Antrim) (1891–1961)
Weekly. Unionist, circulating Lisburn, counties Antrim and Down.
Proprietor: Robert McMullan.

Lisburn Standard (Lisburn, Co. Antrim) (1877–1959)
Weekly Saturday. 1885 Neutral; 1888 Conservative, circulating Lisburn and
neighbourhood. Local and district and some general news.
Proprietors: 1885 W. Honston; 1888 J. E. Reilly.

Londonderry Guardian (1857–71)
Weekly Wednesday paper. Conservative, Protestant, circulating Londonderry
and Ulster. General news and literary content.
Proprietor: George Alleyn O'Driscoll.

*Londonderry Journal/*1877 *Derry Journal* (1772 to date)
Weekly 1857 Wednesday; bi-weekly 1865 Wednesday and Saturday; tri-weekly
1872 Monday, Wednesday and Friday. 1851 Liberal; 1868 Independent-
Liberal; 1888 Independent; 1892 Nationalist, circulating generally in Ulster.
Political, non-sectarian journal providing general and local news.
Proprietors: 1857 Arthur McCorkell; 1864 Thomas McCarter.

Londonderry Sentinel (Londonderry City) (1829 to date)
Bi-weekly Tuesday and Friday; tri-weekly 1873 Tuesday, Thursday and Friday;
1880 Tuesday, Thursday and Saturday. Conservative, circulating counties
Londonderry, Donegal, Tyrone, Fermanagh.
Proprietors: 1851 Mrs Barbara Hamilton Wallen (Mrs William Wallen); 1858
John Montgomery Johnston; 1864 Thomas Chambers and James Calhoun;
1879 James Calhoun.

*Londonderry Standard/*1889 *Derry Standard* (1836–1964)
1851 weekly Thursday; 1869 bi-weekly Wednesday and Saturday; 1888 tri-
weekly Monday, Wednesday and Friday. 1851 Conservative; 1858 Liberal-
Conservative; 1880 Liberal; 1889 Liberal-Unionist, Presbyterian, circulating
Londonderry and county, Dublin, towns in Scotland and England. Supported
tenant right.
Proprietors: 1851 James Macpherson and Thomas McCarter; 1868 James
Macpherson; 1879 William Glendinning; James McKnight.

Longford Chronicle (1855)
Weekly Saturday. Neutral, circulating locally. London compendium of news
to which local news of Longford added.
Proprietor: M. G. Parker.
(Not entered in *Newspaper Press Directory* after 1857.)

Longford Independent (Longford town) (1868–1925)
Weekly Saturday. Liberal; 1872 Liberal-Independent; 1877 Independent,
circulating Longford and midland counties.

381

Proprietors: 1869 R. Turner; 1880 E. Turner; 1888 Representatives of the late R. Turner.

Longford Journal (Longford town) (1839–1937)
Weekly Saturday. Conservative, Church of England, circulating Co. Longford. News of agriculture and commerce.
Proprietors: 1851 John Dwyer; 1869 W. T. Dann; 1871 Edward Dann; 1877 W. T. Dann.

Longford Leader (Longford town) (1897 to date)
Weekly. Circulating counties Cavan, Leitrim, Roscommon, and Westmeath. Founded by J. P. Farrell.
Proprietor: Longford Printing and Publishing Co. Ltd.

Longford News (Longford town) (1938 to date)
Proprietors: Mr Gill; Albert Reynolds TD.

Loughrae Guardian (Ballinasloe, Co. Galway) (1893–1912)

Lurgan and Portadown Examiner (Lurgan, Co. Armagh) (1934 to date)

Lurgan Gazette (Co. Armagh)/1871 *Lurgan Watchman and Gazette*/1878 *Lurgan Watchman* (1856–74)
Weekly Saturday. Conservative, circulating Lurgan and Ulster. Local news.
Proprietor: G. W. McCutcheon.

Lurgan Mail (Co. Armagh) (1890 to date)
Weekly. Conservative, circulating Lurgan, and in counties Armagh, Down and Antrim.
Proprietor: Louis Richardson.

Lurgan Times (Co. Armagh) (1875–1915)
Weekly Saturday. Independent, circulating Lurgan, surrounding towns and counties of Armagh, Antrim, Down, Londonderry, Tyrone and Louth. Local news and miscellanies.
Proprietor (1889 and editor): William White.

Mayo Constitution (Castlebar) (1851–72)
Weekly 1851 Tuesday; 1872 Saturday. Conservative, 1872 Church of Ireland, circulating Mayo, Sligo, and in Dublin, London, etc.
Proprietors: 1851 Alexander Bole; 1864 John Bole; 1870 Norman Bole.

Mayo Examiner (Castlebar) (1868–1903)
Weekly Monday. 1868 Liberal; 1888 Nationalist, Catholic, circulating Castlebar, county of Mayo and west of Ireland. Advocates tenant right and the interests of Catholics.
Proprietors: A. H. Sheridan; 1877 M. and A. H. Sheridan; 1882 Martin Sheridan.

Mayo News (Westport, Co. Mayo) (1892 to date)
Weekly. Nationalist, Sinn Féin, circulating throughout Co. Mayo.
Proprietors: William and P. J. Doris.

Meath Chronicle (Kells/Navan, Co. Meath) (1891 to date)
Weekly. Nationalist, circulating in counties Meath, Westmeath and Cavan.
Proprietors: Thomas Daly; J. David and Sons Ltd.

Meath Herald (Kells, Co. Meath) (1845–1936)
Weekly Saturday. Independent, circulating Kells, Meath Westmeath, Louth,
Cavan and Kildare.
Proprietors: 1857 Thomas Kelly Henderson; 1866 George and John
Henderson; 1880 James B. Henderson; 1892 John G. Henderson.

Meath People (Naas) (1857–63)
Weekly Saturday. 1858 Liberal; 1864 Anti-Whig, Catholic, circulating Cavan,
Meath and Westmeath.
Proprietor: James O'Reilly.

Meath Reporter (Trim) (1870–1901)
Weekly Saturday. Neutral, circulating Trim. News of the town and county.
Proprietor: T. K. Henderson.

Mid-Ulster Mail (Cookstown, Co. Tyrone) (1891 to date)
Weekly Saturday. Conservative, circulating south Londonderry, East and South
Tyrone and Mid-Ulster generally. Local and district paper.
Proprietor: H. L. Glasgow.

Mid-Ulster Observer (Cookstown, Co. Tyrone) (1950 to date)

Midland Counties Advertiser (Roscrea) (1854–1948)
Weekly 1857 Saturday; 1864 Thursday. Independent, circulating Roscrea.
Proprietors: 1857 Francis H. Shields; 1873 John Wright.

Midland Counties Gazette (Longford) (1852–63)
Weekly Saturday. Liberal, circulating Longford, Westmeath, Roscommon and
King's County.
Publisher: B. Casserly.

Midland Herald (Mullingar, Co. Westmeath) (1948–57)

Midland News (Roscrea) (1880–4)
Neutral, circulating Tipperary, King's County, Queen's County and Kilkenny.
Local news.
Proprietor and publisher: James Gray jun.
(Not entered in *Newspaper Press Directory* after 1884.)

Midland Reporter/Westmeath Nationalist (Mullingar, Co. Westmeath) (1891–
    1939)
Twice weekly. Nationalist, circulating town and Co. Westmeath.
Proprietor: George W. Tully.

Midland Tribune (Birr) (1881 to date)
Weekly Thursday. Nationalist, circulating King's County, Queen's County,
Tipperary, Galway, Roscommon, Clare and Westmeath.
Proprietors: 1881 The Midland Tribune Joint Stock Co.; 1889 John Powell.

Monaghan Democrat and People's Journal (Monaghan) (1906)
Nationalist, a local version of the *Dundalk Democrat.*
Proprietors: Executors of Thomas Roe deceased.

Mourne Observer and Dromore Weekly Times (Newcastle, Co. Down) (1949 to date)

Munster Express/1859 *Munster Express* and *The Celt* (Waterford) (1860 to date)
Weekly Saturday. 1864 Neutral; 1889 Nationalist, circulating Waterford and
Munster. General news.
Proprietors: 1864 Joseph Fisher; 1883 W. G. Fisher; 1891 H. D. Fisher.

Morning Mail (Dublin) (1869–1912)
Daily. Independent, circulating Dublin, Ireland and British Isles.
Proprietor: Maunsell and Co.

Munster News (Limerick City) (1851–1935)
Bi-weekly Wednesday and Saturday. Liberal, circulating Limerick and Munster generally.
Proprietors: Francis Counihan; 1869 Francis Counihan and Son.

Nation (1842–91, 1897–1900)
Founded by Charles Gavan Duffy, the initial issue appeared on 15 October
1842. It was an organ of Young Ireland. Early editors were Thomas Davis and
John Mitchel. Duffy sold the journal to A. M. Sullivan in 1855 and then it
passed to his older brother, T. D. Sullivan, in 1877 and was sold outside the
family in 1887. It was anti-Parnellite during the split and ceased publication
in 1891. Re-emerged in late 1890s as a Healeyite organ.

Nationalist (Clonmel, Tipperary)/and *Munster Advertiser* (1886 to date)
Four times a week. Nationalist, circulating in the district of Clonmel.
Proprietor: Nationalist Newspapers Co. Ltd.

Nationalist and Leinster Times (Carlow) (1883 to date)
Weekly. Nationalist, circulating in counties Carlow, Kildare, Wicklow, Queen's
and Kilkenny.
Proprietor: Annie F. Reddy.

Nationality (1915–19)
Founded by Arthur Griffith.

Nenagh Guardian (Nenagh, Co. Tipperary) (1838 to date)
Bi-weekly Wednesday and Saturday. Conservative, Church of Ireland, circulating locally.
Proprietors: 1851 Charles W. Kempston; 1858 George Prior; 1866 Adam
Prior; 1892 Margaret Prior.

Nenagh News (Nenagh, Co. Tipperary) (1893–1926)
Weekly. Nationalist, circulating Nenagh, Thurles, Templemore, Roscrea and
district. Incorporated into the *Nenagh Guardian* in 1926.

New Ireland Review (1893–1911)
Published by the staff of University College Dublin.

New Irish Library (1893–present)
A series of books issued by Sir Charles Gavan Duffy after he settled in London.

New Ross Reporter (Waterford City) (1871–1910)
Bi-weekly Wednesday and Saturday; 1877 weekly Saturday. Neutral, circulating New Ross and counties of Wexford, Waterford, Kilkenny and Carlow.
Proprietor: 1871 Ward and Longmire; 1877 W. R. Ward.

New Ross Standard (1879–99)
Weekly Saturday. Nationalist, Catholic, circulating New Ross, Wexford, Kilkenny, Carlow and district.
Proprietors: 1880 W. Corcoran; 1881 E. Walsh.

News and Star (Waterford City) (1848 to date)
Weekly. Nationalist, circulated locally.
Proprietor: News Printing Works.

Newry Commercial Telegraph/Newry Telegraph (1812–1970)
Tri-weekly Tuesday, Thursday and Saturday. Conservative, Protestant, circulating counties Down, Armagh, Tyrone, Londonderry.
Proprietors: 1851 James Henderson; 1864 Henry G. Henderson; 1877 J. Henderson and Co.

*Newry Examiner and Louth Advertiser/*1880 *Dundalk Examiner and Louth Advertiser* (1830–1960)
Bi-weekly 1851 Wednesday and Saturday; 1880 weekly Saturday. 1851 Liberal; 1880 Nationalist, circulating Louth, Meath, Dublin, Westmeath, Sligo, Donegal, Fermanagh, Tyrone, Armagh, Antrim, Down, Leitrim and Londonderry and (1889) America. National news.
Proprietors: 1851 P. Dowdall; 1857 Patrick Dowdall; 1865 P. Dowdall and Son; 1866 P. Dowdall; 1880 John Matthews (died 1883).

Newry Herald (1858–64)
Tri-weekly Tuesday, Thursday and Saturday. 1858 Liberal; 1864 Liberal and Independent.
Proprietors: 1858 Walter Burns; 1864 proprietor and publisher: William Hutchison.

Newry Reporter (Newry, Co. Down) (1837 to date)
Bi-weekly 1868 Wednesday and Saturday; 1872 Thursday and Saturday; 1873 Tuesday and Saturday. 1868 Independent; 1873 Liberal, circulating Newry. News of county.
Proprietor: James Burns.

*Newry Standard/*1883 *Belfast and Newry Standard* (1879–99)
Independent, circulating Newry and district. Local and general news.
Published: Bank Parade Newry.

385

News (Enniscorthy, Co. Wexford) (1856–1912)
Weekly Saturday. Neutral, circulating Enniscorthy and county of Wexford.
Mostly local news.
Proprietors: 1857 John Pilkington; 1869 James Owens; 1884 R. and W. Owen.

Newtownards Chronicle (Newtownards, Co. Down) (1873–present)
Weekly Saturday. 1873 Liberal Conservative and (1879) Independent Tenant
Right; 1883 Liberal-Conservative, circulating local and county.
Publisher: William Henry.

Newtownards Spectator (Newtownards, Co. Down) (1904 to date)
Weekly. Conservative, in town and County Down.
Proprietors: G. Craig; D. E. Alexander.

North Antrim Standard (Ballymoney) (1710–1922)
Weekly. Unionist, circulating Ballymoney and north Antrim.
Proprietors: J. M. Russell; North Constitution Ltd., Coleraine.

Northern Constitution (Coleraine, Co. Londonderry) (1874 to date)
Weekly. Unionist, circulating counties Londonderry and Antrim.
Proprietor: Coleraine Constitutional Newspaper Co. Ltd.

Northern Standard (Monaghan) (1839 to date)
Weekly. Conservative, circulated throughout Ulster.
Proprietors: William Swan; 1921 Philip C. McMinn.

North Down Herald (1871)/*North Down Herald and Bangor Gazette* (Bangor)
(1880–1952)
Weekly 1880 Saturday; 1888 Friday. 1880 Independent; 1892 Liberal, circulating North Down and district. Non-political journal.
Proprietor: W. G. Lyttle.

Northern Herald (Ballymoney) (1860–3)
Weekly Independent, circulating counties Antrim, Londonderry, Donegal
and Tyrone. Local reports, meetings, etc.
Proprietor: James W. Lithgow.

Northern Herald (Londonderry) (1879)
Tri-weekly Tuesday, Thursday and Saturday. Liberal, Catholic, circulating
Londonderry and throughout north-west of Ireland.
Publisher: J. Coghlan.
(Not entered in *Newspaper Press Directory* after 1881.)

Northern Standard (Monaghan) (1839 to date)
Weekly 1851 Saturday; 1877 Friday; 1891 Saturday. 1851 High Tory; 1857
Conservative, Protestant, circulating north midland counties, Belfast, Dublin,
America and colonies.

Proprietors: Arthur Wellington Holmes; 1857 John Holmes; 1871 William Swan.

Northern Star (Belfast) (1868–72)
Tri-weekly Tuesday, Thursday and Saturday. Liberal, Catholic, circulating Belfast. Political and literary journal.
Proprietors: 1869 A. J. McKenna; 1871 J. McVeagh.

Northern Whig (Belfast) (1824–1963)
Daily. Liberal, circulating throughout Ulster, generally in Leinster, Munster, Connacht, in Britain and abroad.
Proprietor: Northern Whig Ltd.

Omagh News (1862–72)
Weekly Saturday. 1865 Liberal; 1866 Independent, circulating Omagh and the county. Mainly local news.
Proprietor: S. D. Montgomery.

Outlook (Rathfriland, Co. Down) (1968)

People (Wexford) (1853 to date)
Weekly Saturday. 1857 Liberal; 1865 Independent; 1881 Nationalist, Catholic, circulating town and district. Local and county news.
Proprietors: 1857 James A. Johnson and William Power; 1858 William Power; 1858 took over Wexford Guardian; 1864 M. J. Sutton and R. A. Fitzgerald; 1871 E. Walsh.

People's Advocate (Monaghan) (1876–1906)
Weekly Saturday. Nationalist, Catholic, circulating counties Monaghan, Fermanagh, Tyrone, etc.
Publisher: D. MacAleese.

People's Press/Donegal People's Press (Lifford, Co. Donegal) (1931 to date)

Pilot (1829–49)
Founded and edited by Richard Barrett in 1829 to support Daniel O'Connell's fight for Catholic Emancipation.

Post (Kilkenny) (1925–60)

Portadown Express (Portadown, Co. Armagh) (1906–20)
Weekly. Unionist, circulation local.
Proprietor: A. C. Shannon; Portadown Printing Co. Ltd.

Portadown Times (Lurgan, Co. Armagh) (1922 to date)

Portadown Weekly News/1873 Portadown and Lurgan News (1859–1982)
Weekly Saturday. Conservative; 1892 Unionist, circulating locally and Ulster.
Proprietors: 1864 John H. Farrell; 1877 Trustees of Mrs Farrell; 1880 Mrs Farrell; 1882 S. Farrell; 1892 John Young.

Protestant Watchman (Lurgan) (1856–68)
Weekly Saturday. Conservative, Protestant, circulating Lurgan and district. Local news of the town and neighbourhood with general news and historical notes.
Proprietor: 1864 Richard J. Evans; 1868 George F. Evans.
(Not entered in *Newspaper Press Directory* after 1868.)

Roscommon Champion (Roscommon) (1935 to date)

Roscommon Constitutionalist (Boyle) (1885–91)
Weekly Saturday. 1885 Constitutionalist; 1892 Independent, circulating Roscommon and an extensive district. Local and district news.
Publisher: 1885 C. Dell Smith; 1891 Thomas Stuart; 1892 J. C. Anderson.

Roscommon (1858 and Leitrim) *Gazette* (Boyle) (1822–82)
Weekly Saturday. Conservative, circulating Boyle of Co. Roscommon, Carrick-on-Shannon, counties Mayo, Sligo, etc.
Proprietors: 1851 J. Bromell; 1864 E. C. Bromell; 1872 A. W. Bromell; 1877 G. C. Bromell.

Roscommon Herald (Boyle) (1859 to date)
Weekly Saturday. 1864 Liberal; 1891 Nationalist, Catholic.
Proprietors: 1864 George M. Tully; 1866 Honoria J. Tully; 1891 Jasper Tully.

Roscommon Journal (Roscommon town) (1827–1927)
Weekly Saturday. 1851 Liberal; 1864 Independent, circulating locally.
Proprietors: 1851 Charles Tully; 1864 Mrs Anna Tully; 1877 William Tully.

Roscommon Messenger (Roscommon town) (1848–1935)
Weekly. Independent-nationalist, circulating in Co. Roscommon and adjacent counties.
Proprietor: John Hayden.

Roscommon Reporter (1850–60)
Neutral, circulating Co. Roscommon County and counties Longford, Galway and Leitrim.
Proprietor: Landon W. Lennox.

Roscommon Weekly Messenger (1848–73, revived 1892–1935)
Weekly Saturday. Liberal, circulating local counties. After 1892 Independent.
Proprietors: Alexander O'Connor Eccles; after 1892 L. P. Hayden.

Roscrea Review (Tipperary) (1927–9)
Weekly. Circulating counties Tipperary, Offaly and Laois. Publisher: Francis Fany.

Sinn Féin (1906–14)
Founded and edited by Arthur Griffith as the organ of Sinn Féin.

Skibbereen and West Carbery Eagle/1868 *West Cork and Carbery Eagle*/1891 *Eagle and County Cork Advertiser* (Skibbereen) (1857–1928)
Weekly Saturday. 1864 Neutral; 1878 Independent, circulating throughout Cork. General newspaper with scientific and literary intelligence.

388

Proprietors: 1864 Potter Bros; 1866 F. P. E. Potter; 1871 Potter and Son; 1872 Potter and Robertson; 1873 J. W. Potter; 1882 Peel Eldon; 1886 F. P. E Potter.

Sligo Advertiser (1885–91)
Weekly Wednesday. Nationalist, circulating Sligo and district. Local and district news with some general intelligence.
Proprietor: J. Tiernan.

Sligo Champion (Sligo town) (1836 to date)
Weekly. Nationalist, circulating in counties Sligo, Leitrim, Fermanagh, Cavan, Mayo, Roscommon, Galway and Donegal.
Proprietors: Charles McHugh; P. A. McHugh; Mrs P. A. McHugh.

Sligo Chronicle (1850–93)
Weekly Saturday. Conservative, circulating locally and in Connacht. Family journal with literary news and miscellany.
Proprietors: 1851 Charles Sedley; 1864 James W. Sedley.

Sligo Gazette (1887–91)
Weekly Friday. Nationalist, circulating throughout Sligo, Leitrim, Mayo and Roscommon.
Local and regional news, public proceedings, market intelligence, etc.
Proprietor: J. Stinson.

Sligo Independent (1855–1961)
Weekly Saturday. 1857 Neutral; 1858 Conservative, circulating local counties.
Proprietors: 1857 William Gillmor; 1858 Alexander Gillmor; 1881 Miss Jane Gillmor.

Sligo Journal (1752–1866)
Weekly Friday. Conservative, Church of Ireland, circulating locally.
Proprietor: 1851 Anne Bolton.

Sligo Nationalist (Sligo town) (1910–20)
Weekly. Nationalist, circulating locally.
Editor: James MacGowan.

Sligo Times (Sligo town) (1909–14)
Weekly. Conservative, circulating County Sligo and town.
Publisher: R. Smyllie.

*Southern Chronicle/*1872 *Limerick Southern Chronicle/*1873 *Bassett's Daily Chronicle/* 1884 *Bassett's Southern Advertiser/*1888 *Bassett's Daily Advertiser* (Limerick) (1863–85)
Bi-weekly Wednesday and Saturday. 1864 Conservative; 1888 Neutral, circulating Limerick and south of Ireland.
Proprietors: 1864 G. W. Bassett; 1885 W. Guest Bassett; 1886 Bassett and Lochhead.

389

Southern Democrat (Newcastle West, Co. Limerick) (1917–19)
Weekly, Labour; Sinn Féin, circulating Newcastle and district.
Proprietor: Eagle Printing Co.

Standard/Catholic Standard/Catholic Herald (Dublin) (1928 to date)
From 1978 published in London.

*Standard and Waterford Conservative Gazette/*1884 *Waterford Standard* (1863–
  1953)
Bi-weekly Wednesday and Saturday. Conservative, Churches of England and
Ireland, circulating Waterford, Dublin, Kilkenny, Wexford, Tipperary, among
nobility and clergy.
Proprietors: 1864 Waterford Publishing Company Ltd; 1868 Robert Whalley
(who also ran *Waterford News Letter* devoted to shipping movements).

Saturday Record (Ennis, Co. Clare) (1885–1917)
Weekly Saturday. Neutral, circulating Ennis and neighbourhood. Local
news.
Proprietor: John B. Knox and Son.

Southern Star (Skibbereen, Co. Cork) (1890 to date)
Weekly. Nationalist, circulating in Co. Cork and surrounding area.
Proprietor: Southern Star Co. Ltd.

Star (Dublin) (1824–5)
Proprietor: J. T. Haydn.

Strabane Chronicle (Co. Tyrone) (1896 to date)
Weekly. Independent, circulating in counties Tyrone, Donegal and London-
derry.
Proprietors: Frank McMenamin; Mrs F. McMenamin; Northwest of Ireland
Printing and Publishing Co.

Strabane Weekly News (Omagh, Co. Tyrone) (1908 to date)
Weekly. Unionist, circulating in Strabane and Co. Tyrone.
Proprietor: Tyrone Constitution Ltd.

Strokestown Democrat (Strokestown, Co. Roscommon) (1913–48)
Weekly. Irish-Ireland nationalist, circulating in town and district.
Proprietors: Patrick Monahan; Owen Monahan.

Sunday Independent (Dublin) (1905 to date)
Weekly. Independent nationalist, circulated in Ireland and Britain.
Proprietor: Independent Newspapers Ltd.

Sunday News (Belfast) (1965–93)

Sunday Press (Dublin) (1949–95)

Thom's Directory (1752–1842)
Begun as the *Dublin Directory* in 1752, it became the property of Alexander
Thom in 1842 and was then renamed.

390

Times Pictorial (Dublin) (1941–53)

Tipperary/ 1883 *Tipperary Leader* (Thurles) (1881–1926)
Bi-weekly Wednesday and Saturday. 1882 Nationalist; 1884 Neutral; 1885
Nationalist, circulating Limerick, Waterford, Kilkenny, Queen's and King's
County, Galway, Clare, Kerry and Dublin.
Proprietors: 1881 Thomas P. Gill; 1885 W. G. Fisher.

Tipperary Advocate (Nenagh) (1881–1926)
Weekly Saturday. 1858 Liberal; 1864 Independent; 1871 Republican, Catho-
lic, circulating Nenagh and Roscrea.
Proprietor: P. B. Gill.

Tipperary and Clare Independent (Nenagh) (1867–69)
Advocates tenant right, independent, local and county news.
Proprietor: John O'Shea.

Tipperary Champion (Waterford City) (1899–1910)

Tipperary Chronicle (Clonmel) (1839)
Bi-weekly Wednesday and Saturday. Conservative, circulating Clonmel, Carrick-
on-Suir, Tipperary, Thurles, Fethard.
Proprietor: Edmond Woods.

Tipperary Free Press (Clonmel) (1826–81)
Bi-weekly 1851 Wednesday and Saturday; 1864 Tuesday and Friday. Radical,
circulating counties Tipperary, Waterford, Cork, Limerick and Kilkenny.
Proprietors: 1851 John Hackett; 1864 Hackett Brothers; 1877 E. C. Hackett;
1883 taken over by the *Tipperary Independent.*

Tipperary Independent (Clonmel) (1882–1906)
Neutral, circulating counties Tipperary, Limerick and Kilkenny.
Proprietors: 1881 J. Fisher; 1883 W. G. Fisher; 1891 H. D. Fisher.

Tipperary Nationalist (Clonmel) (1889–90)
Bi-weekly Wednesday and Saturday. Nationalist.
Proprietor: Nationalist Newspaper Co. Ltd.

Tipperary News (Clonmel) (1891)
Weekly Saturday. Nationalist, circulating Clonmel, Co. Tipperary and district.
Local and district news.

Tipperary People (Clonmel) (1865–1921)
Weekly Saturday. Independent, circulating Clonmel and Co. Tipperary.
Local and district intelligence.
Publisher: O'Connel Hacket.

Tipperary Star (Thurles, Co. Tipperary) (1909 to date)

Tipperary Weekly News (Clonmel) (1858)
Weekly Saturday. Independent, circulating counties Tipperary and Limerick.
Proprietor: Edmond Woods.

Tralee Chronicle (1843–81)
1851 Saturday; 1865 Tuesday and Friday. 1851 Neutral; 1865 Independent; 1867 Liberal, circulating Kerry and south of Ireland.
Proprietors: 1851 James Raymond Eagar; 1867 John William Weekes; 1874 Mrs Blanche Weekes and J. J. Long; 1877 Mrs Blanche Weekes.

Tuam Herald (Tuam, Co. Galway) (1837 to date)
Weekly Saturday. 1851 Liberal; 1883 National-Independent, Catholic, Fianna Fail, circulating counties Galway and Mayo.
Proprietors: 1851 Richard John Kelly; 1864 Jasper Kelly; 1868 Richard J. Kelly; 1930s Burke family.

Tuam News (1871–1904)
Weekly Friday. Independent, Catholic, circulating Tuam and Connacht.
Proprietors: 1870 E. Byrne; 1877 John McPherson; 1879 John McPhilpin.

Tullamore Tribune (Tullamore, Co. Offaly) (1978 to date)
A variant of the *Midland Tribune.*

Tyrawley Herald/1872 *Ballina Herald* (Ballina) (1844–70)
Weekly Thursday. 1851 Neutral; 1888 Nationalist; 1889 Neutral, circulating Ballina, Castlebar, Boyle, etc.
Proprietors: 1851 William Richey; 1864 R. W. Joynt.

Tyrone Constitution (Omagh, Co. Tyrone) (1844 to date)
Weekly Friday. Conservative, Protestant, circulating locally and in Londonderry and Dublin.
Proprietors: 1851 John Nelis; 1864 George W. McCutcheon; 1868 Nathaniel Carson.

Tyrone Courier (Dungannon) (1880 to date)
Weekly Saturday. 1880 Liberal-Conservative; 1885 Conservative, circulating county and Ulster generally. Information on local trades.
Proprietor: 1880 A. J. Mathews; 1891 J. D. Crockett.

Tyrone Democrat (Dungannon, Co. Tyrone) (1966 to date)

Ulster Echo (Belfast) (1874–1916)
Daily. 1874 Neutral; 1879 Liberal; 1889 Liberal Unionist.
Publisher: A. G. McMonagle (publisher of *Witness,* a Presbyterian church newsletter).

Ulster Examiner (Belfast) (1868–82)
1869 tri-weekly Tuesday, Thursday and Saturday; 1871 Daily. Liberal, Catholic, circulating Ulster.
Proprietors: 1869 Kerr and Fitzpatrick; 1871 J. Serridge.

Ulster Guardian (Belfast) (1903–20)
Weekly. Liberal, circulating in Belfast and Ulster.
Proprietor: Ulster Guardian Ltd.

Ulster Herald (Omagh, Co. Tyrone) (1901 to date)
Weekly. Nationalist, circulating throughout Ulster.
Proprietor: Northwest Printing and Publishing Co. Ltd.

Ulster Observer (Belfast) (1862–8)
Tri-weekly Tuesday, Thursday and Saturday. Liberal, Catholic, circulating
Belfast and Ulster.
Proprietor: The Ulster Catholic Publishing Co. Ltd.

Ulster Gazette (Armagh) (1844–68)
1851 Saturday; 1870 Tuesday and Friday; 1872 Wednesday and Saturday;
1873 Saturday. 1851 Neutral; 1857 Conservative, Church of Ireland, circulating city and county of Armagh, towns of Newry, Monaghan, Dungannon,
Dundalk, Lurgan, Loughgall, Moy, Markethill.
Proprietors: 1851 Matthew Small; 1857 E. Darlington; 1866 J. Heatley
(bankrupt); 1874 Thomas White; 1884 McClelland and Peel (bankrupt).

Ulster Star (Lisburn, Co. Antrim) (1957 to date)

Ulsterman (Belfast) (1852–9)
Bi-weekly Wednesday and Saturday. Liberal, Catholic, circulating Belfast and
Ulster.
Proprietor: D. Holland.

United Ireland (1881–91)
First issued on 12 Aug. 1881 and edited by William O'Brien, it supported the
Irish Party under the leadership of Charles Stewart Parnell, ceasing publica-
tion in 1898.

United Irishman (1847–8)
Founded by John Mitchel in 1847, it was suppressed in 1848. Between 1899 and
1906 Arthur Griffith run another newspaper with the same logo. Since 1948 a
third newspaper bearing the same title has been an organ of the Irish Republican Army. After the IRA split in 1970 the title was used by Official Sinn Féin.

Voice of Labour (1922–7)
Organ of the Labour Party and trade union movement.

Warden/1909 *Irish Weekly Mail* (Dublin) (1821–39)
Weekly. Unionist, circulating generally throughout Ireland, British cities and
India.
Manager: J. T. Robson.

Watchman (Enniscorthy) (1869–86)
Weekly Saturday. 1865 Neutral; 1881 Nationalist, circulating Enniscorthy and
Wexford County. Local news and advertisements.
Proprietor: George Griffiths.

Waterford Chronicle and (1768) *New Ross Reporter* (1866–1910)
1851 bi-weekly Wednesday and Saturday; 1871 Tuesday and Friday; 1873
weekly Wednesday; 1874 Saturday. 1851 Liberal; 1884 Independent-Liberal,
Nationalist, Catholic.

Proprietors: 1851 H. M. Flynn; 1857 Patrick Flynn; 1858 P. Flynn and Co.; 1864 Patrick Curran; 1867 W. R. Ward and James Longmire; 1877 W. R. Ward.

Waterford Evening Star/Evening Star (Waterford) (1917–40)
Daily. Nationalist, circulating Waterford and district.
Proprietor: Cornelius O'Mahony.

Waterford Mail/1871 Waterford Daily Mail (1823–1908)
Bi-weekly Wednesday and Saturday. 1851 Conservative; 1882 National, Protestant, circulating locally. General discussions and literary content.
Proprietors: 1851 R. Henderson; 1857 Joseph Fisher; 1883 W. G. Fisher; 1891 J. D. Fisher.

Waterford Mirror/1800 Waterford Mirror and Tramore Visitor (1860–1910)
Weekly Wednesday. Circulating Waterford, Tramore and district. News, markets, timetables.
Proprietors: 1871 John S. Palmer; 1877 Ward Bros.

Waterford News (1848 to date)
Weekly Friday. Liberal, Catholic, circulating locally and in England and America.
Proprietors: 1851 Cornelius Redmond; 1857 Edward S. Kenney; 1888 C. P. Redmond; News Printing Works.

Waterford News-Letter (Waterford City) (1800–1917)

Waterford Standard (Waterford City) (1882–1953)
Twice weekly. Unionist, circulating in city and county of Waterford, counties Dublin, Kilkenny, Limerick, Wexford, Tipperary and others.

Waterford Star (Waterford City) (1892–1959)
Weekly. Nationalist, circulating in the city and county of Waterford.
Proprietor: Cornelius O'Mahony.

Weekly Examiner (Belfast) (1870–92)
Home Rule, 1889 Nationalist, circulating Belfast and throughout Ulster. Also a large circulation in Scotland. News of week with articles, serial tales, etc.
Proprietor: 1885 E. Dwyer Gray MP; 1892 Morning News Co. Ltd.

Weekly Freeman (Dublin) (1871–1924)
Weekly. Nationalist, circulating throughout Ireland and in large British towns.
Proprietor: Freeman's Journal Ltd.

Weekly Irish Times/Times Pictorial (Dublin) (1875–1958)
Weekly. Independent, non-political, circulating throughout Ireland and Britain.
Publisher: Irish Times Co. Ltd.

Weekly Saturday
Nationalist, Catholic, circulating Ballinasloe and district. Leading articles on political and local subjects with general local news.
Publisher: 1877 John Callanan; 1889 Michael O'Brien.

Western Nationalist (Roscommon town) (1907–20)

Western News (Ballinasloe) (1876–1926)
Weekly. Neutral, circulating in counties Galway, Mayo, Roscommon and King's.
Proprietors: Albert Hastings; William Hastings.

Weekly Northern Whig (Belfast) (1858–1940)
Weekly. Liberal-Unionist, circulating in Belfast, Ulster and throughout Ireland.
Proprietor: Northern Whig Co. Ltd.

Weekly Observer (Newcastle West, Co. Limerick) (1917–27)
Weekly, Irish-Ireland, Sinn Féin, circulating Newcastle and district.
Proprietor: Mrs M. M. Byrnes.

Western People (Ballina, Co. Galway) (1883 to date)
Weekly. National, circulating in Ballina, counties Mayo, Sligo and Roscommon.
Proprietor: T. A. Walsh.

Western People (Ballina) (1883 to date)
Weekly Saturday. Nationalist. Popular local paper. Local intelligence.
Proprietor: 1883 P. J. Smyth; 1889 Western People Co. Ltd.

Western Star (Ballinasloe) (1845–1902)
Weekly Saturday. 1851 Neutral; 1857 Conservative; 1870 Liberal-Conservative; 1873 Independent, Protestant, circulating Galway, Roscommon, Mayo, etc.
Proprietors: 1851 Thomas French; 1857 Robert Hood Smythe; 1870 Henry McClenaghan; 1888 S. J. McClenaghan.

Westmeath Examiner (Mullingar, Co. Westmeath) (1882 to date)
Weekly Saturday. Independent, circulating Westmeath, Longford and Meath.
Local and district news.
Proprietor: L. P. Hayden.

Westmeath Guardian/1877 *Westmeath Guardian and Longford Newsletter* (Mullingar) (1851–1928)
Weekly 1851 Thursday; 1885 Saturday. Conservative, Unionist, Church of Ireland, circulating locally.
Proprietor: 1851 J. Siggins; 1875 S. Wallis.

Westmeath/Offaly Independent (Athlone) (1848–1906)
Weekly Saturday. 1851 Independent; 1857 Conservative; 1877 Liberal; 1885 Nationalist, circulating Athlone and adjoining counties. News, politics, literary and miscellaneous articles.
Proprietors: 1851 James Martin; 1871 William N. Martin; 1873 P. S. Walsh; 1883 M. Walsh; 1885 Chapman and Co.; 1888 T. Chapman.

Wexford Constitution (1858–87)
1864 Weekly Saturday; 1871 bi-weekly Wednesday and Saturday. Conservative, Protestant, circulating counties Wexford, Wicklow, Carlow, Kilkenny and Waterford.
Proprietors: 1864 Alexander Mackay; 1884 Isabella Mackay.

Wexford Guardian (1847)
Weekly Saturday. Liberal, Catholic, tenant right, circulating locally. Political and literary content.
Proprietors: 1851 Thomas Roche; 1857 Robert Pitt. Taken over by the *People,* Jan. 1857.

Wexford Herald (1787–1865)
Weekly Saturday. Neutral, circulating Wexford district. Local and general news, novelettes, varieties, etc.
Proprietor: 1858 James Anglin.

Wexford Independent (1869–1906)
Bi-weekly Wednesday and Saturday. Liberal; 1891 Liberal-Unionist, circulating locally and in south of Ireland.
Proprietors: 1851 John Greene; 1868 John Greene.

Wexford Recorder (1880)
Weekly Friday. Conservative, circulating Wexford and district.
Proprietor: Albert Hastings.
(Not entered in *Newspaper Press Directory* after 1882.)

Wexford Standard (1879)
Weekly Saturday. Nationalist, Catholic.
Proprietor: E. Walsh.
(Not entered in *Newspaper Press Directory* after 1887.)

Whitehead News (Carrickfergus, Co. Antrim) (1926–31)

Wicklow News Letter (1857–1927)
Weekly Saturday. Neutral, circulating Wicklow neighbourhood. News of the week, with tales, varieties, etc.
Proprietor: William McPhail; 1877 William McPhail and Sons.

Wicklow People (1882 to date)
Weekly Saturday. Nationalist, circulating Wicklow, Dublin Carlow and Kildare. Political and commercial intelligence, book reviews, etc.
Proprietor: E. Walsh.

Wicklow Press (Wexford town) (1905–16)
Weekly. Nationalist, circulating in principal towns and villages of Wicklow and adjoining counties.
Proprietor: Mary A. Corcoran.

Witness (Belfast) (1874–1941)
Weekly, Presbyterian, circulating in Ulster and Ireland generally.
Publisher: A. McMonagle.

Sources: *Newspaper Press Directory; Willings Press Guide*; Virginia E. Glandon, *Arthur Griffith and the Advanced-Nationalist Press Ireland, 1900–1922* (New York, 1985); James O'Toole and Sara Smyth, *Newsplan: Report of the Newsplan Project in Ireland* (2nd edn, London, 1998); Brian Inglis, *The Freedom of the Press in Ireland, 1784–1841* (London, 1954); Tom Clyde, *Irish Literary Magazines: An Outline History and Descriptive Bibliography* (Dublin, 2003).

Mail and telecommunications

Irish Free State/Éire/Republic of Ireland, 1924–2001

Note: from 1975 the statistics exclude inward international calls.

Key:
N&P   Newspapers and packets
Parcl. Parcels
Telegr. Telegrams

Millions unless indicated

	Letters	Post-cards	N&P	Parcl.	Telegr. ('000)	Phone calls (trunk)(local)		Licences ('000) Radio	TV
1924	135	10	59	16	3,760	16		1.0	–
1925	130	9	59	5	3,506	15		1.5	–
1926	130	9	62	5	3,283	19		7.7	–
1927	124	9	64	5	3,083	20		19	–
1928	128	11	65	5	2,999	21		24	–
1929	125	11	66	5	2,472	21		26	–
1930	125	11	66	5	2,131	22		26	–
1931	125	10	71	5	1,998	22		26	–
1932	125	10	71	5	1,778	23		29	–
1933	120	8	65	5	1,675	25		33	–
1934	117	9	65	5	1,552	26		51	–
1935	–	–	–	5	1,481	27		66	–
1936	131	9	67	5	1,502	29		88	–
1937	139	10	70	5	1,531	31		105	–
1938	–	–	–	–	1,513	35		140	–
1939	141	10	74	6	1,508	37		155	–
1940	138	10	73	5	1,502	39		170	–
1941	–	–	–	–	1,441	41		184	–
1942	124	8	54	6	1,672	44		176	–
1943	–	–	–	–	1,876	45		171	–
1944	–	–	–	–	2,061	48		173	–
1945	151	11	67	8	2,167	53		173	–
1946	–	–	–	–	2,494	58		176	–
1947	–	–	–	–	2,814	62		179	–
1948	–	–	–	–	2,895	8	56	195	–
1949	178	7	87	10	2,648	8	60	271	–
1950	180	7	89	9	2,611	9	65	289	–
1951	181	7	88	9	2,705	10	72	311	–
1952	182	7	97	9	2,597	10	76	374	–
1953	177	8	107	9	2,447	11	78	400	–
1954	193	8	117	9	2,367	12	81	399	–
1955	196	9	127	9	2,323	13	83	431	–
1956	–	–	–	–	1,919	14	87	462	–
1957	192	9	113	8	1,441	14	92	473	–

	Letters	Post-cards	N&P	Parcl.	Telegr. ('000)	Phone calls (trunk)	(local)	Licences ('000) Radio	TV
1958	194	8	124	8	1,331	15	98	474	–
1959	–	–	–	–	1,235	16	107	487	–
1960	–	–	–	–	1,174	14	121	493	–
1961	216	8	128	8	1,110	13	136	490	–
1962	–	–	–	–	1,100	15	144	419	93
1963	222	8	130	8	1,048	17	153	363	150
1964	218	7	125	8	1,022	18	164	314	222
1965	220	7	130	7	911	21	178	269	255
1966	216	7	135	7	847	23	198	240	288
1967	220	8	136	7	812	25	212	217	308
1968	225	8	139	7	792	28	234	197	376
1969	215	13	150	9	812	33	260	172	394
1970	220	13	154	9	804	38	263	150	416
1971	218	13	152	9	747	42	287	130	433
1972	218	13	152	9	710	47	320	115	476
1973	219	13	133	9	726	623		–	496
1974	226	13	143	9	730	711		–	527
1975	236	12	139	8	671	809		–	565
1976	239	12	139	8	614	863		–	590
1977	250	11	147	8	561	1,023		–	617
1978	250	8	148	8	573	1,161		–	616
1979	144	6	92	4	354	1,467		–	693
1980	246	12	146	6	523	1,657		–	667
1981	259	12	–	5	498	1,729		–	648
1982	242	12	–	5	435	1,730		–	660
1983	249	12	–	6	303	2,004		–	677
1984	415.0*				268	2,228		–	704
1985	434.0				223	2,312		–	717
1986	447.0				122	2,579		–	752
1987	445.9				–	2,806		–	788
1988	464.7				–	–		–	760
1989	471.7				–	–		–	782
1990	482.0				–	3,753		–	806
1991	494.1				–	4,016		–	829
1992	483.5				–	4,333		–	849
1993	518.1				–	4,408		–	857
1994	551.7				–	5,041		–	867
1995	559.8				–	5,348		–	878
1996	578.0				–	6,059		–	889
1997	646.6				–	7,858		–	990
1998	669.8				–	–		–	1,016
1999	705.4				–	–		–	1,038
2000	733.6				–	–		–	1,057
2001	779.8				–	–		–	1,097

* Combined classification in the millions of 'letter post: items delivered'.
Sources: B. R. Mitchell and Phyllis Deane, *Abstract of British Historical Statistics* (Cambridge, 1962), and CSO, Chapter 12.

Broadcasting: chronology of main events

1924	British Broadcasting Company begins radio broadcasting in Northern Ireland.
1926	1 Jan. Ireland's first radio station, the state-controlled Dublin Broadcasting Station, sometimes called 2RN, begins transmitting.
1927	A second radio station set up at Cork, broadcasting local programmes and 2RN. Royal charter establishes the British Broadcasting Corporation, the world's first public broadcasting organisation.
1930	Cork station closes.
1933	6 Feb. 2RN superseded by Radio Athlone, covering a greater area.
1936	New transmitter outside Lisburn, Co. Antrim, allows BBC radio transmissions to cover 50-mile radius around Belfast. BBC in London begins world's first regular television broadcasts; cease at outbreak of Second World War in 1939.
1937	Radio Athlone becomes known as Radio Éireann, although this is not the official name until 1960.
1938	139,000 radio licences issued in Eire following drive to curb evasion.
1939	In Northern Ireland 124,000 radio licences issued, suggesting that one in two NI families have a radio compared with one in four in Eire.
1946	BBC television resumes broadcasting from London.
1948	261,000 radio licences issued following drive to curb evasion.
1955	BBC television begins transmitting in NI; funded by licences.
1956	BBC monopoly of UK television ends with introduction of independent television, funded by advertising.
1959	Ulster Television (independent) begins transmitting in NI, funded by advertising.
1960	ROI Broadcasting Act (1960) creates Radio Éireann Authority. Many homes in east of Ireland receiving British television transmissions from either Northern Ireland or Great Britain without paying licences.
1961	502,000 radio licences issued in ROI. 31 Dec. Public service television broadcasting commences in ROI, funded by advertising and licences.
1964	Second BBC television channel launched, BBC2.
1966	ROI government-appointed body, Radio Telefís Éireann Authority (RTE), established to oversee public broadcasting.
1972	BBC monopoly of UK radio ends with introduction of commercial stations. In ROI Raidió na Gaeltachta, a Gaelic-language station, is launched.

1972	Entire RTE Authority dismissed by ROI government for sanctioning an interview with an IRA spokesman. Restrictions lifted in 1994.
1978	In ROI a second public television station launched, RTE 2.
1982	Second UK independent channel, Channel 4, launched.
1989	In UK the first satellite television station launched, Sky TV.
1996	In ROI Teilifís na Gaeilge (now TG4), a Gaelic-language television station, is launched.
1998	In UK digital television transmissions begin. RTE's monopoly on TV broadcasting in ROI ended with the launch of the commercial channel TV3.

EDUCATION

Chronology of main events

1806	(–1812) Reports from the Commissioners of the Board of Education.
1811	Kildare Place Society founded (parliamentary grant to train teachers, 1814).
1817	School for Catholic laity at Maynooth College closed (Maynooth founded in 1795 for training Catholic priests).
1820	First inspector of schools appointed.
1824	(–1827) Reports of the Commissioners of Irish Education Inquiry. Kildare Place Society begins training of women.
1828	Report from the Select Committee on Education in Ireland HC 1828 (80) IV, 223.
1829	Establishment of National Schools system under the Education Board. Grants to Kildare Place Society ceased.
1833	National Board trains National School teachers.
1837	(–1838) Report for the Select Committee on Foundation Schools, etc., HC 1837 (701) VII, 345 (Wyse).
1844	National Board's charter of incorporation.
1845	Colleges (Ireland) Act (1845) creates Queen's Colleges at Belfast, Cork and Galway.
1850	The Queen's University of Ireland incorporated to award degrees at the Queen's Colleges.
1853	Presbyterian College, Belfast, founded to provide theological training.
1854	Catholic University founded in Dublin.
1859	Reconstitution of National Board giving Catholics half of representation.
1860	Catholic ban on model schools.
1861	Magee College, in Londonderry, founded as a Presbyterian college with faculties of arts and theology.
1868	(–1870) Reports of Commission of Inquiry (Powis), HC 1870 (C.6) XXVIII.
1872	Payment by results made nationwide.
1873	Teacher contracts of employment.

1878	Intermediate Education (Ireland) Act.
1879	Teacher superannuation scheme.
1882	Royal University of Ireland (RUI) established as new examining body in place of the Queen's University of Ireland. Catholic University students also allowed to take RUI degrees.
1883	Catholic University renamed University College, Dublin. State support for denominational training colleges.
1898	Report of Commission on Manual and Practical Instructions (Belmore), HC 1898 (C. 8923), XLIII, 405.
1900	Revised programme for primary schools abolishing results fees. Intermediate Education Amendment Act.
1904	Bilingual programme. Dale Report, HC 1904 (Cd. 1981), XX, 947.
1908	Irish Universities Act (1908) creates two new universities, the National University of Ireland (NUI) and the Queen's University of Belfast. NUI a federal body of University Colleges consisting of the former Queen's Colleges at Cork and Galway and University College, Dublin.
1913	Report of Vice-Regal Committee of Inquiry into Primary Education (Dill), HC 1914 (Cd. 7235), XXVIII, 1081.
1919	Report of Vice-Regal Committee of Inquiry (Killanin), HC 1919 (Cmd. 60), XXI, 741.
1921	NI: establishment of Ministry of Education.
1921	(–1922) IFS: Report of National Programme Conference.
1922	IFS: new national school programme.
1923	NI: Education Act allows creation of non-denominational primary schools; Catholic sector refuse to join the scheme.
1924	IFS: establishment of Department of Education.
1925	NI: Amendment Act strengthens Protestant character of state schools.
1925	(–1926) IFS: report and programme of National Conference.
1926	IFS: compulsory attendance legislation. IFS: founding of the preparatory colleges.
1927	NI: Education Act brings Northern Ireland into line with the rest of UK education reforms.
1966	ROI: Ireland creates new education system in line with the UK.
1968	New University of Ulster established at Coleraine, Co. Antrim.
1970	A National Institute of Higher Education founded at Limerick.
1971	Ulster Polytechnic established at Jordanstown, Co. Antrim.
1976	A National Institute of Higher Education founded at Dublin.

1984	Merger of Ulster Polytechnic, New University of Ulster, and Belfast Art College creates the University of Ulster.
1989	National Institutes of Higher Education at Limerick and Dublin gain full university status as the University of Limerick and Dublin City University respectively.
1992	400-year anniversary of the founding of Trinity College, Dublin (University of Dublin).
1996	Constituent colleges of National University of Ireland gain independence.

Primary schools

Ireland, 1833–1920

	No. of schools	Pupils on rolls ('000)	Average no. attending ('000)	No. of teachers ('000)
1833	789	107	–	–
1835	1,106	146	–	–
1836	1,181	154	–	–
1837	1,300	167	–	–
1838	1,384	170	–	–
1839	1,581	193	–	–
1840	1,978	233	–	–
1841	2,337	282	–	–
1842	2,721	320	–	–
1843	2,912	355	–	–
1844	3,153	396	–	–
1845	3,426	433	–	–
1846	3,637	456	–	–
1847	3,825	403	–	–
1848	4,109	507	–	–
1849	4,321	481	–	–
1850	4,547	511	–	–
1851	4,704	520	–	4.6
1852	4,875	545	280	–
1853	5,023	551	271	4.9
1854	5,178	551	267	5.1
1855	5,124	536	252	5.0
1856	5,245	560	258	5.4
1857	5,337	776	268	5.5
1858	5,408	804	266	5.6
1859	5,496	807	269	5.6
1860	5,632	804	263	6.0
1861	5,830	803	285	6.4
1862	6,010	813	285	7.0
1863	6,163	841	297	7.2

	No. of schools	Pupils on rolls ('000)	Average no. attending ('000)	No. of teachers ('000)
1864	6,263	870	315	7.5
1865	6,372	922	321	7.8
1866	6,453	911	316	7.8
1867	6,520	913	322	8.0
1868	6,586	968	355	8.3
1869	6,707	991	359	8.6
1870	6,806	999	359	8.8
1871	6,914	1,022	364	9.0
1872	7,050	1,010	356	9.4
1873	7,160	1,020	373	9.5
1874	7,257	1,007	395	9.9
1875	7,267	1,012	390	10.1
1876	7,334	1,032	417	10.3
1877	7,370	1,024	418	10.5
1878	7,443	1,037	437	10.7
1879	7,522	1,032	435	10.8
1880	7,590	1,083	469	10.7
1881	7,648	1,066	454	10.6
1882	7,705	1,083	469	10.5
1883	7,752	1,081	468	10.6
1884	7,832	1,089	493	10.7
1885	7,936	1,076	502	11.0
1886	8,024	1,072	490	11.0
1887	8,112	1,072	515	11.2
1888	8,196	1,061	494	11.1
1889	8,251	1,053	508	11.2
1890	8,298	1,037	489	11.1
1891	8,346	1,022	506	11.3
1892	8,403	1,020	495	11.4
1893	8,459	1,032	527	11.6
1894	8,505	1,028	526	11.8
1895	8,557	1,018	520	11.9
1896	8,606	809	535	12.0
1897	8,631	799	521	12.0
1898	8,651	795	519	12.0
1899	8,670	785	514	12.1
1900	8,684	746	478	11.9
1901	8,692	741	482	11.9
1902	8,712	737	487	12.0
1903	8,720	727	482	12.0
1904	8,710	730	484	12.3
1905	8,659	738	500	12.5
1906	8,602	728	494	12.6
1907	8,538	675	486	12.7
1908	8,468	689	495	12.7
1909	8,401	679	501	12.8

	No. of schools	Pupils on rolls ('000)	Average no. attending ('000)	No. of teachers ('000)
1910	8,337	679	496	12.8
1911	8,289	685	513	13.0
1912	8,255	669	499	13.2
1913	8,229	682	503	13.3
1914	8,207	680	508	13.5
1915	8,163	679	500	13.5
1916	8,118	678	494	13.4
1917	8,060	684	489	13.4
1918	8,002	689	488	13.4
1919	7,947	683	488	13.3
1920	7,898	692	482	–

Source: B. R. Mitchell and Phyllis Deane, *Abstract of British Historical Statistics* (Cambridge, 1962), p. 802.

Irish Free State/Éire/Republic of Ireland, 1921–2001

	No. of schools	Pupils on rolls ('000)	Average no. attending ('000)	No. of teachers ('000)
1921	5,746	498	365	–
1922	5,696	496	356	–
1923	5,684	497	369	–
1924	5,636	493	363	–
1925	–	–	–	11.4
1926	5,648	522	399	13.2
1927	5,641	524	413	13.3
1928	5,555	517	424	13.6
1929	5,447	515	420	13.7
1930	5,401	512	421	13.6
1931	5,378	509	417	13.7
1932	5,361	508	417	13.6
1933	5,334	513	422	13.6
1934	5,306	505	422	13.7
1935	5,280	496	413	13.6
1936	5,243	489	405	13.5
1937	5,212	482	393	13.4
1938	5,166	474	393	13.4
1939	5,127	470	385	13.3
1940	5,114	471	389	13.3
1941	5,076	472	381	13.1
1942	5,034	466	382	13.1
1943	5,064	465	381	13.1
1944	5,032	464	373	12.9
1945	5,009	463	375	12.8
1946	4,957	458	371	12.8

	No. of schools	Pupils on rolls ('000)	Average no. attending ('000)	No. of teachers ('000)
1947	4,946	453	355	12.8
1948	4,922	457	374	12.6
1949	4,896	459	377	12.7
1950	4,886	464	382	12.9
1951	4,878	468	377	12.8
1952	4,876	476	393	12.9
1953	4,880	484	401	13.0
1954	4,874	490	405	13.1
1955	4,872	495	405	13.2
1956	4,871	501	419	13.3
1957	4,869	503	424	13.4
1958	4,869	504	420	13.6
1959	4,878	505	425	13.8
1960	4,882	506	431	13.9
1961	4,880	503	428	14.0
1962	4,867	501	421	13.1
1963	4,864	502	428	14.2
1964	4,848	476	435	14.3
1965	4,847	473	449	14.5
1966	4,797	476	434	14.6
1967	4,685	481	447	14.7
1968	4,450	494	444	14.8
1969	4,295	500	445	14.7
1970	4,117	506	453	14.9
1971	4,012	511	458	15.1
1972	3,879	517	463	15.4
1973	3,776	523	464	15.6
1974	3,688	522	465	16.1
1975	3,585	530	474	16.7
1976	3,508	538	481	17.1
1977	3,468	543	488	17.3
1978	3,449	546	496	17.6
1979	3,432	548	497	18.4
1980	3,415	552	503	18.8
1981	3,402	556	508	19.4
1982	3,397	559	512	19.9
1983	3,393	565	515	20.0
1984	3,387	567	519	–
1985	3,382	577	–	20.9
1986	3,448	577	–	21.1
1987	3,450	576	–	21.2
1988	3,447	574	–	21.2
1989	3,427	568	–	20.3
1990	3,428	552	–	20.3
1991	3,437	544	–	20.4
1992	3,425	534	–	20.7

	No. of schools	Pupils on rolls ('000)	Average no. attending ('000)	No. of teachers ('000)
1993	3,405	529	–	20.7
1994	3,391	514	–	20.7
1995	3,387	466	–	20.9
1996	3,381	476	–	21.1
1997	–	467	–	21.0
1998	–	458	–	21.1
1999	–	451	–	22.0
2000	3,340	445	–	21.9
2001	3,323	–	–	22.9

Sources: B. R. Mitchell and Phyllis Deane, *Abstract of British Historical Statistics* (Cambridge, 1962), p. 804, and CSO.

Northern Ireland, 1922–2002/3

	No. of schools	Pupils on rolls ('000)	Average no. attending ('000)	No. of teachers ('000)
1922	2,066	153	153	4.2
1923	2,054	156	156	4.3
1924	2,041	157	157	4.3
1925	2,006	165	165	4.3
1926	1,970	170	170	4.4(g)
1927	1,948	169	169	5.3
1928	1,933	169	169	5.3
1929	1,920	168	168	5.4
1930	1,893	172	172	5.3
1931	1,868	174	174	5.4
1932	1,837	177	177	5.4
1933	1,814	177	177	5.5
1934	1,790	174	174	5.4
1935	1,775	172	172	5.4
1936	1,753	171	171	5.3
1937	1,727	167	167	5.3
1938	1,700	166	166	5.3
1939	–	–	–	–
1940	–	–	–	–
1941	–	–	–	–
1942	–	–	–	–
1943	–	–	–	–
1944	–	–	–	–
1945	–	185	–	4.9
1946	1,649	187	–	4.9
1947	1,642(h)	185	–	5.4
1948	1,651	183(h)	–	5.7

407

	No. of schools	Pupils on rolls ('000)	Average no. attending ('000)	No. of teachers ('000)
1949	1,650	187	–	5.7
1950	1,665	189	–	5.8
1951	1,665	194	–	5.9
1952	1,662	200	–	6.1
1953	1,655	204	–	6.1
1954	1,641	205	–	6.3
1955	1,635	207	–	6.3
1956	1,635	208	–	6.5
1957	1,615	206	–	6.4
1958	1,597	203	–	6.4
1959	1,584	197	–	6.4
1960	1,568	196	–	6.4
1961	1,550	192	–	6.4
1962	1,526	192	–	6.4
1963	1,505	193	–	6.4
1964	1,484	192	–	6.5
1965	1,443	194	–	6.7
1966	1,411	197	–	6.9
1967	1,376	202	–	7.1
1968	1,335	207	–	7.2
1969	1,302	211	–	7.4
1970	1,266	215	–	7.6
1971	1,250	218	–	7.8
1972	1,209	217	–	7.9
1973	1,190	217	–	8.1
1974	1,176	216	–	8.2
1975	1,176	216	–	8.3
1976	1,164	213	–	8.6
1977	1,165	210	–	8.9
1978	1,163	207	–	8.8
1979	1,151	202	–	8.6
1980	1,161	199	–	8.5
1981	1,153	198	–	8.5
1981/2*	1,149	194	–	8.3
1982/3	1,140	189	–	8.2
1983/4	1,126	189	–	8.1
1984/5	1,121	188	–	8.1
1985/6	1,109	188	–	8.1
1986/7	1,101	189	–	8.2
1987/8	1,117	191	–	8.4
1988/9	1,109	193	–	8.4
1989/90	1,104	194	–	8.5
1990/1	1,104	191	–	8.6
1991/2	1,098	191	–	8.7
1992/3**	957	187	–	8.0
1993/4	951	187	–	8.2

	No. of schools	Pupils on rolls ('000)	Average no. attending ('000)	No. of teachers ('000)
1994/5	938	187	–	8.4
1995/6	923	187	–	8.4
1996/7	920	187	–	8.4
1997/8	920	184	–	8.3
1998/9	916	182	–	8.1
1999/2000	917	179	–	8.0
2000/1	902	178	–	7.9
2001/2	899	176	–	7.9
2002/3	897	174	–	7.8

(g) statistics to 1926 relate to teachers receiving personal salaries from the Ministry of Education.
(h) Subsequently including state-maintained nursery and special needs.
* CSO; statistics include all first-level schools except hospital schools. Source prior to this is R. B. Mitchell and Phyllis Deane, *British Historical Statistics* (Cambridge, 1962).
** From 1992/3 only grant-aided schools are included and special schools and preparatory departments of grammar schools are excluded.
Source: Mitchell and Deane, *Abstract of British Historical Statistics*, p. 803; NIAAS, Chapter 5.

Secondary schools
Irish Free State/Éire/Republic of Ireland, 1943–2001

	No. of schools	No. of pupils ('000)	No. of full-time teachers ('000)
1943	377	40	3.4
1944	379	41	3.5
1945	385	42	3.5
1946	393	43	3.6
1947	404	44	3.7
1948	409	45	3.7
1949	416	47	3.9
1950	424	49	3.8
1951	434	50	3.9
1952	441	52	4.0
1953	447	54	4.2
1954	458	56	4.1
1955	474	59	4.4
1956	480	62	4.6
1957	489	66	4.8
1958	494	70	4.9
1959	512	73	5.0
1960	526	77	5.2
1961	542	80	5.3

	No. of schools	No. of pupils ('000)	No. of full-time teachers ('000)
1962	557	85	5.6
1963	569	89	5.9
1964	573	93	6.2
1965	585	99	6.5
1966	588	104	6.7
1967	595	119	7.2
1968	598	134	8.1
1969	600	144	9.1
1970	599	151	9.6
1971	593	157	10.2
1972	574	162	10.7
1973	554	167	11.3
1974	541	173	12.1
1975	539	183	11.8
1976	537	189	12.2
1977	532	193	12.7
1978	531	197	13.3
1979	527	199	13.4
1980	524	201	13.5
1981	520	201	13.8
1982	516	204	14.1
1983	511	206	14.1
1984*	–	–	19.2
1985	814	329	19.0
1986	811	335	14.5
1987	816	341	19.5
1988	817	343	–
1989	812	342	18.9
1990	808	339	18.7
1991	794	342	18.8
1992	791	349	19.3
1993	804	368	19.8
1994	809	371	20.4
1995	–	370	20.9
1996	768	371	21.0
1997	–	368	21.1
1998	–	362	20.8
1999	–	354	21.1
2000	782	349	21.4
2001	780	345	–

* From 1984 the figures include all second-level schools.
Sources: B. R. Mitchell and Phyllis Deane, *Abstract of British Historical Statistics* (Cambridge, 1962); and CSO.

Northern Ireland, 1972/3–2002/3

Funding and control of Northern Ireland secondary schools was varied and not a simple division of Catholic schools and state schools. The statistical measurement for secondary education therefore changed over time. Below is a record of all controlled, voluntary maintained, voluntary schools, and grant-aided schools. The definitions of these can change and overlap over time. The table begins in 1972/3 as that is when technical intermediate schools were not separately classified and instead included with secondary intermediate schools. Most fluctuations occur in the non-grammar sector. The very small number of independent schools and grammar school preparatory departments are not included.

	No. of schools	No. of pupils ('000)	No. of teachers
1972/3	259	–	7.8
1973/4	259	–	8.5
1974/5	261	149	8.5
1975/6	262	152	8.7
1976/7	262	155	9.3
1977/8	261	157	9.8
1978/9	261	158	10.1
1979/80	262	159	10.2
1980/1	262	159	10.1
1981/2	261	160	10.1
1982/3	261	159	10.2
1983/4	261	158	10.1
1984/5	260	156	10.1
1985/6	254	153	10.0
1986/7	251	149	9.9
1987/8	249	145	9.7
1988/9	245	143	9.7
1989/90	240	140	9.5
1990/1	239	142	9.4
1991/2	236	143	9.3
1992/3	234	146	9.5
1993/4	232	148	9.6
1994/5	232	150	9.8
1995/6	236	152	9.9
1996/7	238	153	10.0
1997/8	238	153	9.9
1998/9	237	155	9.9
1999/2000	238	155	9.9
2000/1	238	156	10.2
2001/2	235	156	10.1
2002/3	235	156	10.1

Source: NIAAS, Chapter 5.

411

Full-time students at Irish universities/third-level education

Ireland

	No. of students
1909/10	2,254
1910/1	2,531
1911/2	2,638
1912/3	2,751
1913/4	2,507
1914/5	2,362
1915/6	2,321
1916/7	2,431
1917/8	2,725
1918/9	3,383
1919/20	3,647
1920/1	3,658
1921/2	3,492

Irish Free State/Éire/Republic of Ireland

1922/3	3,446
1923/4	3,322
1924/5	3,249
1925/6	3,159
1926/7	3,037
1927/8	3,171
1928/9	3,532
1929/30	3,896
1930/1	4,311
1931/2	4,639
1932/3	4,954
1933/4	4,965
1934/5	5,054
1935/6	5,011
1936/7	5,163
1937/8	5,336
1938/9	5,370
1939/40	5,425
1940/1	5,430
1941/2	5,549
1942/3	5,758
1943/4	5,938
1944/5	6,341
1945/6	6,620
1946/7	7,022
1947/8	6,985

1948/9	7,319
1949/50	7,458
1950/1	7,231
1951/2	6,794
1952/3	6,917
1953/4	7,011
1954/5	7,284
1955/6	7,278
1956/7	7,669
1957/8	8,019
1958/9	8,676
1959/60	9,155
1960/1	10,021
1961/2	10,297
1962/3	11,119
1963/4	12,085
1964/5	13,006
1965/6	14,147
1966/7	15,278
1967/8	15,838
1968/9	16,908
1969/70	18,045
1970/1	18,793
1971/2	19,686
1972/3	20,178
1973/4	20,435
1974/5	20,771
1975/6	20,276
1976/7	21,001
1977/8	21,706
1978/9	21,759
1979/80	21,934
1980/1	22,266
1981/2	22,952
1982/3	23,469
1983/4	24,069
1984/5*	55,088
1985/6	55,088
1986/7	56,579
1987/8	59,490
1988/9	62,970
1989/90	65,949
1990/1	69,988
1991/2	76,809
1992/3	84,140
1993/4	92,595
1994/5	–
1995/6	102,662
1996/7	107,501
1997/8	–

1998/9	–
1999/2000	122,626
2000/1	126,300
2001/2	131,812

* From 1984/5 figures include all third-level institutions including teacher training, aided and non-aided institutions. Previously only the University of Dublin and the National University of Ireland (excluding Maynooth College) are included.

Northern Ireland, 1974–2002

Full-time students at universities and polytechnics in Northern Ireland from 1974/5. Prior to this the statistics only record new entrants and degrees/subjects taken.

1974/5	7,101
1975/6	7,438
1976/7	7,511
1977/8	7,560
1978/9	7,509
1979/80	7,828
1980/1	7,971
1981/2	8,238
1982/3	8,621
1983/4	8,909
1984/5	14,395 (University of Ulster triples its intake)
1985/6	14,622
1986/7	14,973
1987/8	15,505
1988/9	15,976
1989/90	16,503
1990/1	17,703
1991/2	19,245
1992/3	20,821
1993/4	22,750
1994/5*	27,244
1995/6	28,972
1996/7	29,422
1997/8	31,836
1998/9	31,574
1999/2000	32,484
2000/1	32,880
2001/2	34,386

* Defined as full-time students living in Northern Ireland in university-level education in Northern Ireland.
Sources: CSO; NIAAS.

LANGUAGE

Irish speakers

Year	Total	Leinster	Munster	Connaught	Ulster (part of)
All ages					
1861	1,077,087	35,704	545,531	409,482	86,370
1871	804,547	16,247	386,494	330,211	71,595
1881	924,781	27,452	445,766	366,191	85,372
1891	664,387	13,677	307,633	274,783	68,294
1901	619,710	26,436	276,268	245,580	71,426
1910	553,717	40,225	228,694	217,087	67,711
1926	543,511	101,474	198,221	175,209	68,607
3 years and over					
1926	540,802	101,102	197,625	174,234	67,841
1936	666,601	183,378	224,805	183,082	74,336
1946	588,725	180,755	189,395	154,187	64,388
1961	716,420	274,644	228,726	148,708	64,342
1971	789,429	341,702	252,805	137,372	57,550
1981	1,018,413	473,225	323,704	155,134	66,350
1986	1,042,701	480,227	337,043	158,386	67,045
1991	1,095,830	511,639	352,177	162,680	69,334

LAW, ORDER AND DEFENCE

Police chiefs

Inspectors-General of the Constabulary, 1836–1922

Lt Gen. Sir James Shaw Kennedy	1836
Maj. Duncan Warburton	1838
Gen. Sir Duncan McGregor	1838
Sir Henry Brownrigg	1858
Col. Sir John Stewart Wood	1865
Lt Col. George Hillier	1876
Col. Robert Bruce	1882
Sir Andrew Reed	1885
Col. Sir Neville Chamberlain	1900
Brig. Gen. Sir Joseph Byrne	1916
Sir Thomas J. Smith	1920

Inspectors-General/Chief Constables of the Royal Ulster Constabulary, later the Police Service of Northern Ireland, 1922–2003

Sir Thomas J. Smith	1922
Lt Gen. Sir Charles Wickham	1922
Sir Richard Pim	1945
Sir Albert Kennedy	1965
J. A. Peacock	1969
Sir Arthur Young (first 'Chief Constable')	1969
Sir Graham Shillington	1970
Sir James Flanagan	1973
Sir Kenneth Newman	1976
Sir John Hermon	1980
Sir Hugh Annesley	1989
Sir Ronnie Flanagan	1996
Hugh Orde	2002

Commissioners of An Garda Síochána, 1922–2003

Alderman Michael Staines	Feb. 1922
Gen. Eoin O'Duffy	Sept. 1922
Col. Eamon Broy	1933
Michael Kinnane	1938
Daniel Costigan	1952
William Quinn	1965
Michael Wymes	1968
Patrick Malone	1973
Edmund Garvey	1975
Patrick McLaughlin	1978
Laurence Wren	1983
Eamonn Doherty	1987
Eugene Crowley	1988
Patrick Culligan	1991
Patrick Byrne	1996
Noel Conroy	2003

The judiciary

Irish courts were established on the English model of King's Bench, Common Pleas, Exchequer and Chancery. Under the Irish Judicature Act (1877) these were amalgamated into the High Court and Court of Appeal. Under the 1922 Constitution new courts, the Supreme Court and the High Court, were created, and the office of Lord Chancellor abolished. In Northern Ireland the superior court is the Supreme Court of Judicature, consisting of the High Court of Justice, divided into Queen's Bench, Chancery and Family Divisions; the Court of Appeal; and the Crown Court.

Lords Chancellor of Ireland

Appointed

1789	Lord Fitzgibbon
1802	John Mitford
1806	George Ponsonby
1807	Thomas Maurice Sutton
1827	Anthony Hart
1830	William Conyngham Plunket
1834	Edward Burtenshaw Sugden
1835	William Conyngham Plunket
1841	John Campbell
1841	Edward Burtenshaw Sugden
1846	Maziere Brady
1852	Francis Blackburne
1852	Maziere Brady

417

1858	Joseph Napier
1859	Maziere Brady
1866	Francis Blackburne
1867	Abraham Brewster
1868	Thomas O'Hagan
1874	Seal in commission
1875	John Thomas Ball
1880	Thomas O'Hagan
1881	Hugh Law
1883	Edward Sullivan
1885	John Naish
1885	Lord Ashbourne
1886	Edward Sullivan
1886	Lord Ashbourne
1892	Samuel Walker
1895	Lord Ashbourne
1905	Samuel Walker
1911	Redmond John Barry
1913	Ignatius John O'Brien
1918	James H. Mussen Campbell
1921	John Ross

Masters of the Rolls

1801	Michael Smith
1802	John Philpot Curran
1803	William MacMahon
1804	Francis Blackburne
1805	Thomas Berry Cusack Smith
1806	John Edward Walsh
1807	Edward Sullivan
1808	Andrew Marshall Porter
1809	Richard Edmund Meredith
1912–24	Charles Andrew O'Connor

Vice-Chancellor

1867	Hedges Eyre Chatterton

Lords Justice of Appeal

1856	Francis Blackburne
1857	Abraham Brewster
1858	Jonathan Christian
1859	Richard Deasy
1860	Gerald Fitzgibbon
1861	Charles Robert Barry
1862	Hugh Holmes

1863	Richard Robert Cherry
1864	John Francis Moriarty
1865	Stephen Ronan
1866	Thomas Francis Molony
1867	James O'Connor

Chief Justices of the Upper Bench or King's (or Queen's) Bench, after 1887 also Lord Chief Justice of Ireland

1798	Viscount Kilwarden
1803	William Downes
1822	Charles Kendal Bushe
1841	Edward Pennefather
1846	Francis Blackburne
1852	Thomas Langlois Lefroy
1866	James Whiteside
1877	George Augustus Chichester May
1887	Michael Morris
1889	Peter O'Brien
1913	Richard Robert Cherry
1916	James Henry Mussen Campbell
1918–24	Thomas Francis Molony

Chief Justices of the Common Bench or Common Pleas

1800	John Toler
1827	William Conyngham Plunket
1830	John Doherty
1850	James Henry Monahan
1876	Michael Morris

(Court merged with Court of Queen's Bench, 1887.)

Chief Barons of the Exchequer

1783	Viscount Avonmore
1805	Standish O'Grady
1831	Henry Joy
1838	Stephen Woulfe
1840	Maziere Brady
1846	David Richard Pigot
1874	Christopher Palles

(Court merged in the Queen's Bench Division, 1898.)

Chief Justices of Irish Free State/Éire/Republic of Ireland

1924	Hugh Kennedy
1936	Timothy Sullivan
1946	Conar Alexander Maguire
1961	Cearbhall O'Dalaigh

419

1973	William O. B. Fitzgerald
1974	Thomas F. O'Higgins
1985	Thomas A. Finlay
1994	Liam Hamilton
2000	Ronan C. Keane

Lord Chief Justice of Northern Ireland, 1922–

1922	Sir Denis Stanislaus Henry
1925	Sir William Moore
1937	Sir James Andrews
1951	Lord MacDermott
1971	Robert Lynd Erskine Lowry
1988	Sir Brian Hutton
1997	Sir Robert Carswell

Sources: F. Elrington Ball, *The Judges in Ireland, 1221–1921*, 2 vols (London, 1926), vol. 2, pp. 326–30; David M. Walker, *The Oxford Companion to Law* (Oxford, 1980).

Crime

Indictable offences known to the police, Ireland, 1864–1919

	Total	Against the person	Against property with violence	Against property without violence
1864	10,865	1,701	547	6,501
1865	9,766	1,585	483	5,592
1866	9,082	1,701	424	5,135
1867	9,260	1,306	532	5,624
1968	9,090	1,399	521	5,748
1869	9,178	1,406	623	5,459
1870	9,517	1,448	657	5,515
1871	8,155	1,469	497	4,801
1872	7,716	1,757	446	4,326
1873	6,942	1,370	432	4,143
1874	6,662	1,329	388	4,149
1875	6,598	1,635	354	3,935
1876	6,261			3,549
		1,627	376	
	9,175			6,463
1877	9,674	1,625	361	6,804
1878	10,933	1,578	485	7,814
1879	12,432	1,457	592	8,454
1880	12,779	1,369	584	7,235
1881	15,550	1,475	754	7,683
1882	13,966	1,503	560	7,464
1883	10,585	1,197	416	7,348

	Total	Against the person	Against property with violence	Against property without violence
1884	10,593	1,392	329	7,285
1885	10,453	1,294	359	6,944
1886	10,544	1,458	535	6,364
1887	9,876	1,274	355	6,372
1888	9,544	1,224	347	6,428
1889	9,221	1,089	308	6,364
1890	8,603	1,073	389	5,733
1891	8,689	1,013	294	6,030
1892	8,468	986	326	5,758
1893	8,935	1,066	386	5,933
1894	8,374	1,110	374	6,069
1895	7,471	776	382	5,087
1896	8,801	876	456	6,285
1897	9,464	803	544	6,911
1898	9,988	877	537	7,217
1899	9,144	803	480	6,485
1900	8,972	681	456	6,548
1901	9,003	651	630	6,518
1902	8,736	650	719	6,347
1903	9,137	614	693	6,900
1904	9,617	622	771	7,270
1905	9,728	583	756	7,310
1906	9,465	526	783	7,152
1907	9,418	526	769	6,949
1908	10,266	627	828	7,393
1909	9,873	523	913	7,134
1910	9,870	574	732	7,064
1911	9,831	580	867	6,878
1912	9,931	544	960	7,196
1913	9,241	672	831	6,525
1914	8,504	587	709	6,067
1915	7,873	457	646	5,841
1916	7,397	375	735	5,417
1917	7,401	329	800	5,281
1918	7,547	338	735	4,758
1919	8,130	507	1,115	4,166

For 1876 the figures relate to the year ending 30 Sept. The 'Total' column includes crimes not recorded in the other three columns.

Indictable offences known to the police, NI, 1928–2002

Hybrid offences, which become indictable only if tried on indictment, are included.

	Total	Against the person	Against property with violence	Against property without violence
1928	2,402	104	507	1,625
1929	2,324	126	559	1,462
1930	2,471	95	505	1,665
1931	2,753	97	491	1,794
1932	3,587	155	774	2,009
1933	3,105	118	733	1,963
1934	3,710	132	772	2,336
1935	4,350	219	762	2,190
1936	3,642	109	877	2,367
1937	3,016	133	764	1,794
1938	2,818	108	606	1,739
1939	2,579	(Analysis of breakdown not continued after 1938)		
1940	2,990			
1941	3,586			
1942	4,307			
1943	4,566			
1944	5,123			
1945	5,709			
1946	6,112			
1947	6,894			
1948	7,581			
1949	6,241			
1950	7,475			
1951	8,048			
1952	7,498			
1953	6,890			
1954	6,428			
1955	6,049			
1956	6,427			
1957	6,555			
1958	7,594			
1959	7,606			
1960	8,460			
1961	9,850			
1962	10,286			
1963	10,859			
1964	10,428			
1965	12,846			
1966	14,673			
1967	15,404			
1968	16,294			
1969	20,303			

	Total	Against the person	Against property with violence	Against property without violence
1970	24,810			
1971	30,828			
1972	35,884			
1973	32,057			
1974	33,314			
1975	37,482			
1976	39,779			
1977	45,335			
1978	45,335			
1979	54,208			
1980	56,316			
1981	62,496			
1982	62,020			
1983	63,984			
1984	62,352			
1985	63,025			
1986	66,284			
1987	61,779			
1988	55,890			
1989	55,147			
1990	57,198			
1991	63,492			
1992	67,532			
1993	66,228			
1994	67,886			
1995	68,808			
1996	68,549			
1997	62,222			
1998	109,053			
1999	119,111			
2000	119,912			
2001	139,786			
2002	142,496			

Sources: Mitchell and Deane, *Abstract of British Historical Statistics*; NIAAS.

Indictable offences known to the police, IFS/É/ROI, 1927–2001

	Total	Against the person	Against property with violence	Against property without violence
1927	7,091	504	908	4,574
1928	6,061	499	810	3,881
1929	5,877	426	759	3,956
1930	6,000	430	695	4,099
1931	6,341	490	884	4,188
1932	6,390	410	980	4,296
1933	6,954	548	968	4,478
1934	7,229	565	1,047	4,244
1935	6,538	507	1,032	4,144
1936	6,484	548	1,197	4,197
1937	6,232	518	1,000	4,292
1938	6,769	453	1,102	4,850
1939	8,202	387	1,186	6,186
		401	1,407	6,771
1940	9,014	(rearrangement of the classification in 1940)		
		442	1,658	6,748
1941	13,180	459	2,179	10,391
1942	17,213	505	2,858	13,649
1943	17,305	545	2,879	13,714
1944	15,863	571	2,497	12,593
1945	16,786	639	2,732	13,227
1946	15,078	638	2,077	11,782
1947	15,329	436	2,727	12,004
1948	14,949	535	2,883	11,354
1949	12,171	496	2,407	9,130
1950	12,231	499	2,445	9,157
1951	14,127	446	2,996	10,513
1952	14,720	465	2,728	11,301
1953	15,602	531	3,032	11,813
1954	11,917	455	2,538	8,753
1955	11,531	525	2,325	8,555
1956	12,782	542	2,695	9,365
1957	14,037	473	3,061	10,339
1958	16,567	558	3,645	12,219
1959	17,865	587	3,824	13,270
1960	15,375	675	2,982	11,470
1961	14,818	701	3,186	10,623
1962	15,307	885	3,466	10,666
1963	16,203	1,047	4,006	10,823
1964	17,700	1,045	4,282	11,972
1965	16,736	1,113	4,213	11,014
1966	19,029	1,132	4,957	12,631
1967	20,558	1,149	5,575	13,452
1968	23,104	1,151	6,469	15,091

	Total	Against the person	Against property with violence	Against property without violence
1969	25,972	1,170	7,563	16,764
1970	30,756	1,142	9,577	19,557
1971	37,781	1,256	10,654	24,929
1972	39,237	1,321	11,600	25,568
1973	38,022	1,655	11,800	23,567
1974	40,096	1,709	12,973	24,345
1975	48,387	1,456	16,432	30,335
1976	54,382	1,714	20,903	31,540
1977	62,946	2,063	23,154	37,465
1978	62,000	2,266	21,119	38,397
1979	64,057	2,326	21,535	39,980
1980	72,782	2,351	24,878	45,298
1981	89,400	(breakdown changes format)		
1982	97,616			
1983	102,387			
1984	99,727			
1985	91,285			
1986	86,574			
1987	85,358			
1988	89,544			
1989	86,792			
1990	87,658			
1991	94,406			
1992	95,391			
1993	98,979			
1994	101,036			
1995	102,484			
1996	100,785			
1997	90,875			
1998	85,627			
1999	81,274			
2000	73,276			
2001	86,621			

Source: CSO.

Military

Commanders of the forces in Ireland, 1801–1922

Gen. Sir William Meadows	1801
Lt Gen. Sir Henry Fox	1803
Gen. Sir William Cathcart	1803
Gen. Charles, Earl of Harrington	1805
Gen. Sir John Hope	1812

Gen. Sir George Hewett	1813
Gen. Sir George Beckwith	1816
Gen. Sir David Baird	1820
Lt Gen. Sir Samuel Achmuty	1822
F. M. Viscount Combermere	1822
Lt Gen. Sir George Murray	1825
Lt Gen. Sir John Byng	1828
Lt Gen. Sir Richard Hussey Vivian	1831
F. M. Sir Edward Blakeney	1835
F. M. Lord Seaton	1855
Gen. Sir George Brown	1860
Gen. Sir Hugh Rose (Lord Strathnairn from 1866)	1865
Gen. Lord Sandhurst	1870
Gen. Sir John Michel	1875
Gen. Sir Thomas Steele	1880
Gen. Prince Edward of Saxe-Weimar	1885
F. M. Viscount Wolseley	1890
F. M. Earl Roberts	1895
F. M. the Duke of Connaught	1900
F. M. Lord Grenfall	1904
Gen. Sir Neville Lyttleton	1908
Lt Gen. Sir A. H. Paget	1912
Maj. Gen. Lovick Friend	1914
Lt Gen. Sir John Maxwell	1916
Lt Gen. Sir Frederick Shaw	1918
Gen. Sir Nevil Macready	1920

Total numbers in defence forces (permanent and reserve), Republic of Ireland

	Permanent	*Reserve*
1960	8,965	24,569
1965	8,199	21,946
1970	8,574	20,253
1975	12,059	17,221
1980	13,383	19,249
1985	13,778	16,358
1990	13,233	15,982
1995	12,742	16,188
1997	11,536	15,166
2001	10,675	13,076

LEADERS OF RELIGIOUS DENOMINATIONS

Key: trs. translated to another See
      d.   died in office
      res. resigned

Note: date of appointment taken as either date of election or consecration

(Roman) Catholic Church (in Ireland)
Popes

	Elected	Died
Pius VII	14 Mar. 1800	20 Aug. 1823
Leo XII	28 Sept. 1823	10 Feb. 1829
Pius VIII	21 Mar. 1829	30 Nov. 1830
Gregory XVI	2 Feb. 1831	1 Jan. 1846
Pius IX	16 June 1846	7 Feb. 1878
Leo XIII	20 Feb. 1878	20 July 1903
Pius X	4 Aug. 1903	20 Aug. 1914
Benedict XV	3 Sept. 1914	22 Jan. 1922
Pius XI	6 Feb. 1922	10 Feb. 1939
Pius XII	2 Mar. 1939	9 Oct. 1958
John XXIII	28 Oct. 1958	3 June 1963
Paul VI	21 June 1963	6 Aug. 1978
John Paul I	26 Aug. 1978	28 Sept. 1978
John Paul II	16 Oct. 1978	2 Apr. 2005

Cardinals

	Date of creation
Paul Cullen	22 June 1866
Edward McCabe	27 Mar. 1882
Michael Logue	16 Jan. 1893
Patrick O'Donnell	14 Dec. 1925
Joseph McRory	12 Dec. 1929
John D'Alton	12 Jan. 1953
William Conway	22 Feb. 1965
Tomás Séamus Ó Fiaich	30 June 1979
Cahal Brendan Daly	28 June 1991
Desmond Connell	21 Feb. 2001

Archbishops

	Appointed	Termination of office
Armagh		
Richard O'Reilly	11 Nov. 1787	31 Jan. 1818
Patrick Curtis	28 Oct. 1819	26 July 1832
Thomas Kelly	26 July 1832	13 Jan. 1835
William Crolly	12 Apr. 1835	6 Apr. 1849
Paul Cullen	24 Feb. 1850	trs. Dublin 1 May 1852
Joseph Dixon	21 Nov. 1852	29 Apr. 1866
Michael Kieran	3 Feb. 1867	15 Sept. 1869
Daniel MacGettigan	11 May 1870	3 Dec. 1887
Michael Logue	3 Dec. 1887	19 Nov. 1924
Patrick O'Donnell	19 Nov. 1924	22 Oct. 1927
Joseph McRory	22 June 1928	13 Oct. 1945
John D'Alton	25 Apr. 1946	1 Feb. 1963
William Conway	10 Sept. 1963	17 Apr. 1977
Tomás Séamus Ó'Faich	18 Aug. 1977	8 May 1990
Cahal Brendan Daly	6 Nov. 1990	1 Oct. 1996
Seán Brady	1 Oct. 1996	
Cashel		
Thomas Bray	14 Oct. 1792	15 Dec. 1820
Patrick Everard	15 Dec. 1820	1822
Robert Laffan	18 Mar. 1823	1833
Michael Slattery	24 Feb. 1834	4 Feb. 1857
Patrick Leahy	29 June 1857	26 Jan. 1875
Thomas William Croke	24 June 1875	22 July 1902
Thomas Fennelly	27 July 1902	res. 7 Mar. 1913
John Harty	18 Jan. 1914	11 Sept. 1946
Jeremiah Kinanne	11 Sept. 1946	18 Feb. 1959
Thomas Morris	21 Dec. 1959	res. 12 Sept. 1998
Dermott Clifford	12 Sept. 1988	
Dublin		
John Thomas Troy	3 Dec. 1786	11 May 1823
Daniel Murray	11 May 1823	26 Feb. 1852
Paul Cullen	3 May 1852	24 Oct. 1878
Edward M'Cabe	25 July 1879	11 Feb. 1885
William Walsh	2 Aug. 1885	9 Apr. 1921
Edward Byrne	9 Apr. 1921	9 Feb. 1940
John Charles McQuaid	27 Dec. 1940	res. 4 Jan. 1972
Dermot Ryan	13 Feb. 1972	trs. Roman Curia 1984
Kevin McNamara	20 Jan. 1985	8 Apr. 1987
Desmond Connell	21 Jan. 1988	

Tuam

Edward Dillon	19 Nov. 1798	13 Aug. 1809
Oliver O'Kelly	12 Mar. 1815	18 Apr. 1834
John MacHale	26 Aug. 1834	7 Nov. 1881
John MacEvilly	7 Nov. 1881	26 Nov. 1902
John Healy	13 Feb. 1903	16 Mar. 1918
Thomas Gilmartin	10 July 1918	14 Oct. 1939
Joseph Walsh	16 Jan. 1940	res. 31 Jan. 1969
Joseph Cunnane	17 Mar. 1969	res. 11 July 1987
Joseph Cassidy	22 Aug. 1987	res. 28 June 1994
Michael Neary	17 Jan. 1995	

Bishops by province

Armagh Province

	Appointed	Termination of office
Ardagh		
John Cruise	17 Aug. 1788	18 June 1812
James Magauran	12 Mar. 1815	3 June 1829
William O'Higgins	30 Nov. 1829	3 Jan. 1853
John Kilduff	29 June 1853	21 June 1867
Neale MacCabe	2 Feb. 1868	22 July 1870
George Michael Conroy	11 Apr. 1871	4 Aug. 1878
Bartholomew Woodlock	1 June 1879	res. 1894
Joseph Hoare	19 Mar. 1895	14 Apr. 1927
James Joseph MacNamee	31 July 1927	24 Apr. 1966
Cahal Brendan Daly	16 July 1967	trs. Down and Connor 24 Aug. 1982
Colm O'Reilly	10 Apr. 1983	
Clogher		
Hugh O'Reilly	24 Mar. 1778	3 Nov. 1801
James Murphy	3 Nov. 1801	19 Nov. 1824
Edward Kerman	19 Nov. 1824	20 Feb. 1844
Charles MacNally	20 Feb. 1844	20 Nov. 1864
James Donnelly	26 Feb. 1865	29 Dec. 1893
Richard Owens	16 Aug. 1894	3 Mar. 1909
Patrick MacKenna	10 Oct. 1909	7 Feb. 1942
Eugene O'Callaghan	4 Apr. 1943	res. 3 Dec. 1969
Patrick Mulligan	18 Jan. 1970	res. 3 Sept. 1979
Joseph Duffy	7 Sept. 1979	
Down and Connor		
Patrick MacMullan	8 Oct. 1794	25 Oct. 1824
William Crolly	1 May 1825	trs. Armagh Apr. 1835
Cornelius Denvir	22 Nov. 1835	res. 5 May 1865

429

Patrick Dorrian	4 May 1865	3 Nov. 1885
Patrick MacAlister	28 Mar. 1886	26 Mar. 1895
Henry Henry	22 Sept. 1895	8 Mar. 1908
John Tohill	20 Sept. 1908	4 July 1914
Joseph MacRory	14 Nov. 1915	trs. Armagh, 22 June 1928
Daniel Magreean	25 Aug. 1929	18 Jan. 1962
William Philbin	5 June 1962	res. 24 Aug. 1982
Cahal Brendan Daly	17 Oct. 1982	trs. Armagh 6 Nov. 1990
Patrick Joseph Walsh	18 Mar. 1991	

Dromore

Matthew Lennan	20 Apr. 1770	22 Jan. 1801
Edmund Derry	19 July 1801	29 Oct. 1819
Hugh O'Kelly	16 Apr. 1820	14 Aug. 1825
Thomas Kelly	27 Aug. 1826	trs. to Armagh as coadj. 1 Dec. 1828; retained Dromore until Mar. 1833
Michael Blake	17 Mar. 1833	res. 27 Feb. 1860
John Pius Leahy	27 Feb. 1860	6 Sept. 1890
Thomas MacGivern	6 Sept. 1890	24 Nov. 1900
Henry O'Neill	7 July 1901	9 Oct. 1915
Edward Mulhern	30 Apr. 1916	12 Aug. 1943
Eugene O'Doherty	28 May 1944	res. 22 Nov. 1975
Francis Gerard Brooks	25 Jan. 1976	res. 4 June 1999
John McAreavey	4 June 1999	

Kilmore

James Dillon	10 Aug. 1800	1806
Farrell O'Reilly	24 Aug. 1807	30 Apr. 1829
James Browne	30 Apr. 1829	11 Apr. 1865
Nicholas Conaty	11 Apr. 1865	17 Jan. 1886
Bernard Finegan	13 June 1886	11 Nov. 1887
Edward MacGennis	15 Apr. 1888	15 May 1906
Andrew Boylan	19 May 1907	25 Mar. 1910
Patrick Finegan	11 Sept. 1910	25 Jan. 1937
Patrick Lyons	3 Oct. 1937	27 Apr. 1949
Austin Quinn	10 Sept. 1950	res. 10 Oct. 1972
Francis Joseph McKiernan	10 Dec. 1972	res. 16 Oct. 1998
Philip Leo O'Reilly	16 Oct. 1998	

Derry

Charles O'Donnell	24 Nov. 1797	19 July 1824
Peter MacLaughlin	11 May 1824	18 Aug. 1840
John MacLaughlin	18 Aug. 1824	res. 18 Aug. 1864
Francis Kelly	18 June 1864	1 Sept. 1889
John Keys O'Doherty	2 Mar. 1890	25 Feb. 1907
Charles MacHugh	20 Sept. 1907	12 Feb. 1926
Bernard O'Kane	26 Sept. 1926	5 Jan. 1939
Neil Farren	1 Oct. 1939	res. 14 Apr. 1973

Edward Daly	31 Mar. 1974	res. 26 Oct. 1993
Séamus Hegarty	1 Oct. 1994	

Meath

Patrick Joseph Plunkett	28 Feb. 1779	11 Jan. 1827
Robert Logan	11 Jan. 1827	22 Apr. 1830
John Cantwell	21 Sept. 1830	11 Dec. 1866
Thomas Nulty	11 Dec. 1866	24 Dec. 1898
Matthew Gaffney	25 June 1890	res. 1906
Laurence Gaughran	24 June 1906	14 June 1928
Thomas Mulvany	30 June 1929	16 June 1943
John D'Alton	16 June 1943	trs. Armagh 25 Apr. 1946
John Kyne	29 June 1947	23 Dec. 1966
John McCormack	10 Mar. 1968	res. 16 May 1990
Michael Smith	16 May 1990	

Raphoe

Anthony Coyle	1782	21 Jan. 1801
Peter MacLaughlin	24 Aug. 1802	res. 12 Jan. 1819
Patrick MacGettigan	17 Sept. 1820	1 May 1861
Daniel MacGettigan	1 May 1861	trs. Armagh 7 Mar. 1870
James MacDevitt	30 Apr. 1871	5 Jan. 1879
Michael Logue	20 July 1879	trs. Armagh as coadj. 30 Apr. 1887
Patrick O'Donnell	3 Apr. 1888	trs. Armagh as coadj. 14 Feb. 1922
William McNeely	22 July 1923	11 Dec. 1963
Anthony McFeely	27 June 1865	res. 16 Feb. 1982
Séamus Hegarty	28 Mar. 1982	trs. Derry, 1 Oct. 1994
Philip Boyce	29 June 1995	

Dublin Province

Ferns

James Caulfied	19 Oct. 1786	14 Jan. 1814
Patrick Ryan	14 Jan. 1814	9 Mar. 1819
James Keatinge	21 Mar. 1819	7 Sept. 1849
Myles Murphy	10 Mar. 1850	13 Aug. 1856
Thomas Furlong	22 Mar. 1857	12 Nov. 1875
Michael Warren	7 May 1876	22 Apr. 1884
James Browne	14 Sept. 1884	21 June 1917
William Codd	25 Feb. 1918	12 Mar. 1938
James Staunton	5 Feb. 1939	26 June 1963
Donal Herlihy	15 Nov. 1964	2 Apr. 1983
Brendan Comiskey	11 Apr. 1984	res. 6 Apr. 2002

Kildare and Leighlin

Daniel Delany	18 Sept. 1787	9 July 1814

Michael Corcoran	21 Sept. 1815	22 Feb. 1819
James Doyle	14 Nov. 1819	15 June 1834
Edward Nolan	28 Oct. 1834	14 Oct. 1837
Francis Haly	25 Mar. 1838	19 Aug. 1855
James Walshe	30 Mar. 1856	5 Mar. 1888
James Lynch	5 Mar. 1888	19 Dec. 1896
Patrick Foley	19 Dec. 1896	24 July 1926
Mathew Cullen	5 June 1927	2 Jan. 1936
Thomas Keogh	18 Oct. 1936	res. 25 Sept. 1967
Patrick Lennon	25 Sept. 1967	res. 10 Dec. 1987
Laurence Ryan	10 Dec. 1987	res. 4 June 2002
James Moriarty	4 June 2002	

Ossory

James Lanigan	21 Sept. 1789	11 Feb. 1812
Kyran Marum	5 Mar. 1815	22 Dec. 1827
William Kinsella	26 July 1829	12 Dec. 1845
Edward Walsh	26 July 1846	11 Aug. 1872
Patrick Francis Moran	11 Aug. 1872	trs. Sydney 14 Mar. 1884
Abraham Brownrigg	14 Dec. 1884	1 Oct. 1928
Patrick Collier	1 Oct. 1928	10 Jan. 1964
Peter Birch	10 Jan. 1964	7 Mar. 1981
Laurence Forristal	10 June 1981	

Cashel Province

Cloyne and Ross (separated into Cloyne and Ross, 24 Nov. 1850)

William Coppinger	4 June 1791	9 Aug. 1831
Michael Collins	9 Aug. 1831	8 Dec. 1831
Bartholomew Crotty	11 June 1833	3 Oct. 1846
David Walsh	2 May 1847	19 Jan. 1849
Timothy Murphy	16 Sept. 1849	4 Dec. 1856

Cloyne (from 1857)

William Keane	5 May 1857	15 Jan. 1874
James MacCarthy	28 Oct. 1874	9 Dec. 1893
Robert Browne	19 Aug. 1894	23 Mar. 1935
James Roche	23 Mar. 1935	31 Aug. 1956
John Ahern	9 June 1957	

Ross (from 1857, united with Cork, 19 Apr. 1958)

William Keane	2 Feb. 1851	trs. Cloyne 5 May 1857
Michael O'Hea	7 Feb. 1858	18 Dec. 1876
William Fitzgerald	11 Nov. 1877	24 Nov. 1877
Denis Kelly	9 May 1897	18 Apr. 1924
James Roche	30 May 1926	trs. Cloyne as coadj. 26 June 1931
Patrick Casey	15 Sept. 1935	19 Sept. 1940

Denis Moynihan	21 Sept. 1941	trs. Kerry 10 Feb. 1953

Cork

Francis Moylan	19 June 1787	10 Feb. 1815
John Murphy	23 Apr. 1815	1 Apr. 1847
William Delany	15 Aug. 1847	14 Nov. 1886
Thomas A. O'Callaghan	13 Nov. 1886	14 June 1916
Daniel Cohalan	29 Aug. 1916	24 Aug. 1952
Cornelius Lucey	24 Aug. 1952	res. 23 Aug. 1980
Michael Murphy	23 Aug. 1980	d. 7 Oct. 1996
John Buckley	19 Dec. 1997	

Kerry

Charles Sughre	11 June 1798	29 Sept. 1824
Cornelius Egan	29 Sept. 1824	22 July 1856
David Moriarty	22 July 1856	1 Oct. 1877
Daniel M'Carthy	25 Aug. 1878	23 July 1881
Andrew Higgins	5 Feb. 1882	1 May 1889
John Coffey	10 Nov. 1889	14 Apr. 1904
John Mangan	18 Sept. 1904	1 July 1917
Charles O'Sullivan	27 Jan. 1918	29 Jan. 1927
Michael O'Brien	24 July 1927	4 Oct. 1952
Denis Moynihan	10 Feb. 1953	res. 17 July 1969
Eammon Casey	9 Nov. 1969	trs. Galway 21 July 1976
Kevin McNamara	22 Aug. 1976	trs. to Dublin 15 Nov. 1984
Diarmaid O'Súilleabháin	29 Mar. 1985	d. 27 Aug. 1994
William Murphy	17 June 1995	

Killaloe

Michael Peter MacMahon	4 Aug. 1765	20 Feb. 1807
James O'Shaughnessy	20 Feb. 1807	5 Aug. 1829
Patrick MacMahon	5 Aug. 1829	7 June 1836
Patrick Kennedy	7 June 1836	19 Nov. 1850
Daniel Vaughan	8 June 1851	29 July 1859
Michael Flannery	29 July 1859	19 June 1891
Thomas MacRedmond	19 June 1891	5 Apr. 1904
Michael Fogarty	4 Sept. 1904	25 Oct. 1955
Joseph Rodgers	25 Oct. 1955	10 July 1966
Michael Harty	19 Nov. 1967	d. 2 Oct. 1994
William Walsh	2 Oct. 1994	

Limerick

John Young	19 June 1796	22 Sept. 1813
Charles Tuohy	23 Apr. 1815	17 Mar. 1828
John Ryan	17 Mar. 1828	6 June 1864
George Buttler	6 June 1864	3 Feb. 1886
Edward Thomas O'Dwyer	29 June 1886	19 Aug. 1917
Denis Hallinan	2 Mar. 1918	2 July 1923

433

David Keane	2 Mar. 1924	12 Mar. 1945
Patrick O'Neill	24 Feb. 1946	26 Mar. 1958
Henry Murphy	31 Aug. 1958	8 Oct. 1973
Jeremiah Newman	14 July 1974	d. 3 Apr. 1995
Donal Brendan Murray	10 Oct. 1996	

Waterford and Lismore

Thomas Hussey	26 Feb. 1797	11 July 1803
John Power	25 Apr. 1804	27 Jan. 1816
Robert Walsh	4 July 1817	1 Oct. 1821
Patrick Kelly	9 Feb. 1822	8 Oct. 1829
William Abraham	12 Jan. 1830	23 Jan. 1837
Nicholas Foran	24 Aug. 1837	11 May 1855
Dominic O'Brien	30 Sept. 1855	12 June 1873
John Egan	19 Jan. 1890	10 June 1891
Richard Alphonsus Sheehan	31 Jan. 1892	14 Oct. 1915
Bernard Hackett	19 Mar. 1916	1 June 1932
Jeremiah Kinane	29 June 1933	trs. Cashel as coadj. 4 Feb. 1942
Daniel Cohalan	4 Apr. 1943	27 Jan. 1965
Michael Russell	19 Dec. 1965	res. 27 May 1993
William Lee	27 May 1993	

Tuam Province

Achonry

Thomas O'Connor	Apr. 1788	18 Feb. 1803
Charles Lynagh	29 Apr. 1803	Apr./May 1808
John O'Flynn	12 Nov. 1809	17 May 1817
Patrick MacNicholas	17 May 1818	11 Feb. 1852
Patrick Durcan	30 Nov. 1852	1 May 1875
Francis MacCormack	1 May 1875	trs. Galway 26 Apr. 1887
John Lyster	8 Apr. 1888	17 Jan. 1911
Patrick Morrisroe	3 Sept. 1911	27 May 1946
James Fergus	4 May 1947	res. 17 Mar. 1976
Thomas Flynn	20 Feb. 1977	

Clonfert

Thomas Costello	30 June 1786	8 Oct. 1831
Thomas Coen	8 Oct. 1831	25 Apr. 1847
John Derry	21 Sept. 1847	28 June 1870
Patrick Duggan	14 Jan. 1872	15 Aug. 1896
John Healy	15 Aug. 1896	trs. Tuam 12 Feb. 1903
Thomas O'Dea	30 Aug. 1903	trs. Galway 29 Apr. 1909
Thomas Gilmartin	13 Feb. 1910	trs. Galway 13 July 1918
Thomas O'Doherty	14 Sept. 1919	trs. Galway 13 July 1923
John Dignan	1 June 1924	12 Apr. 1953
William Philbin	14 Mar. 1954	trs. to Down and Connor 5 June 1962

Thomas Ryan	16 June 1963	res. 1 May 1982
Joseph Cassidy	1 May 1982	trs. Tuam 22 Aug. 1987
John Kirby	18 Feb. 1988	

Elphin

Edward French	prov. 13 Feb. 1787	29 Apr. 1810
George Thomas Plunket	24 Feb. 1815	8 May 1827
Patrick Burke	8 May 1827	16 Sept. 1843
George Joseph Plunkett Browne	26 Mar. 1844	1 Dec. 1858
Laurence Gillooly, C. M.	1 Dec. 1858	15 Jan. 1895
John Clancy	24 Mar. 1895	19 Oct. 1912
Bernard Coyne	30 Mar. 1913	17 July 1929
Edward Doorly	17 July 1926	4 Apr. 1950
Vincent Hanly	24 Sept. 1950	9 Nov. 1970
Dominic Joseph Conway	1 May 1971	res. 24 May 1994
Christopher Jones	24 May 1994	

Galway

George Joseph Plunket	23 Oct. 1831	trs. Elphin 26 Mar. 1844
Laurence O'Donnell	28 Oct. 1844	29 June 1855
John MacEvilly	22 Mar. 1857	trs. Tuam as coadj. 2 Feb. 1878

Galway, Kilmacduagh and Kilfenora

Thomas Carr	26 Aug. 1883	trs. Melbourne Sept. 1886
Francis MacCormack	26 Apr. 1887	res. 21 Oct. 1908
Thomas O'Dea	29 Apr. 1909	9 Apr. 1923
Thomas O'Doherty	13 July 1923	15 Dec. 1936
Michael Browne	10 Oct. 1937	res. 21 July 1976 d. 7 Feb. 1979
Eamonn Casey	21 July 1976	res. 6 May 1992
James McLoughlin	10 Feb. 1993	

Kilmacduagh and Kilfenora (joined with Galway)

Nicholas Joseph Archdeacon	12 Oct. 1800	27 Nov. 1823
Edmund French	13 Mar. 1825	20 July 1852
Patrick Fallon	26 Jan. 1853	res. 31 Aug. 1866

Killala

Dominic Bellew	1780	c. 1812
Peter Waldron	24 Feb. 1815	20 May 1834
John MacHale	20 May 1834	trs. Tuam 26 Aug. 1834
Francis Joesph O'Finan	Mar. 1835	Dec. 1847
Thomas Feeny	11 Jan. 1848	9 June 1873
Hugh Conway	9 June 1873	23 Apr. 1893
John Conmy	23 Apr. 1893	26 Aug. 1911
James Naughton	7 Jan. 1912	16 Feb. 1950
Patrick O'Boyle	25 Feb. 1951	res. 12 Oct. 1970

435

Thomas McDonnell	13 Dec. 1970	res. 21 Jan. 1987
Thomas A. Finnegan	3 May 1987	res. 19 Feb. 2002
John Fleming	19 Feb. 2002	

Presidents of St Patrick's College, Maynooth

	Appointed
Thomas Hussey	25 June 1795
Peter Flood	17 Jan. 1798
Andrew Dunne	24 Feb. 1803
Patrick Byrne	17 June 1807
Patrick Everard	29 June 1810
Daniel Murray	29 June 1812
Bartholomew Crotty	13 Nov. 1813
Michael Slattery	19 June 1832
Michael Montague	25 June 1834
Charles W. Russell	25 June 1845
William J. Walsh	22 June 1880
Robert Browne	7 Oct. 1885
Denis Gargan	9 Oct. 1894
Daniel Mannix	13 Oct. 1903
John F. Hogan	8 Oct. 1912
James MacCaffrey	8 Oct. 1918
John D'Alton	23 June 1936
Edward Kissance	23 June 1942
Gerard Mitchell	23 June 1967
Patrick Corrish	23 Nov. 1967
Jeremiah Newman	8 Oct. 1968
Tomás Ó Fiaich	12 June 1974
Michael Olden	26 Sept. 1977
Míceál Ledwith	1 Jan. 1985
Matthew O'Donnell	22 June 1994
Dermot Farrell	9 Dec. 1996

Church of Ireland (Anglican)

Archbishops and bishops

Archbishops of Armagh

	Appointed	*Termination of office*
William Stuart	22 Nov. 1800	6 May 1822
Lord John George Beresford	17 June 1822	18 July 1862
Marcus Gervais Beresford	15 Oct. 1862	26 Dec. 1885
Robert Bent Know	11 May 1886	23 Oct. 1893
Robert Samuel Gregg	14 Dec. 1893	10 Jan. 1896
William Alexander	25 Feb. 1896	res. 1 Feb. 1911
John Baptist Crozier	2 Feb. 1911	11 Apr. 1920

Charles Fredrick D'Arcy	17 June 1920	1 Feb. 1938
John Godfrey Fitzmaurice Gregg	15 Dec. 1938	res. 18 Feb. 1959
James McCann	19 Feb. 1959	res. 16 July 1969
George Otto Simms	17 July 1969	res. 11 Feb. 1980
John Ward Armstrong	25 Feb. 1980	res. 1 Feb. 1986
Robert Eames	21 Apr. 1986	

Archbishops of Dublin

	Appointed	Termination of office
Robert Fowler	8 Jan. 1779	10 Oct. 1801
Viscount Somerton		
(Earl of Normanton, 1806)	7 Dec. 1801	14 July 1809
Euseby Cleaver	25 Aug. 1809	Dec. 1819
Lord John George Beresford	21 Apr. 1820	trs. Armagh 17 June 1822
William Magee	24 June 1822	18 Aug. 1835
Richard Whately	23 Oct. 1831	8 Oct. 1868
Richard Chenevix Trench	1 Jan. 1864	res. 28 Nov. 1884
Baron Plunkett	23 Dec. 1884	d. 1 Apr. 1897
John Ferguson Peacocke	19 May 1897	res. 3 Sept. 1915
John Henry Bernard	7 Oct. 1915	res. 30 June 1919
Charles Frederick D'Arcy	15 Oct. 1919	trs. Armagh 17 June 1920
John Allen Fitzgerald Gregg	10 Sept. 1920	trs. Armagh 1 Jan. 1939
Arthur William Barton	15 Feb. 1939	res. 15 Nov. 1956
George Otto Simms	11 Dec. 1956	trs. Armagh 17 July 1969
Alan Alexander Buchanan	14 Oct. 1969	res. 10 Apr. 1977
Henry Robert McAdoo	19 Apr. 1977	1985
Donald A. R. Caird	1985	1996
Walton N. F. Empey	26 Apr. 1996	2002
John Robert Winder Neill	29 Aug. 2002	

Archbishops/Bishops of Tuam (ceased to be archbishopric 25 Mar. 1839; thereafter bishopric united to Armagh)

	Appointed	Termination of office
William Beresford		
(Baron Decies 1812)	10 Oct. 1794	8 Sept. 1819
Power Le Poer Trench	10 Nov. 1819	25 Mar. 1839
(Killala united to Tuam from 13 Apr. 1834)		
Thomas Plunket		
(Baron Plunket 1854)	14 Apr. 1839	19 Oct. 1866
Charles Brodrick Bernard	30 Jan. 1867	31 Jan. 1890
James O'Sullivan	15 May 1890	res. Feb. 1913
Benjamin John Plunket	10 May 1913	trs. Meath 15 Oct. 1919
Arthur Edwin Ross	24 Feb. 1920	24 May 1923
John Orr	6 Aug. 1923	trs. Meath 15 Nov. 1927
John Mason Harden	6 Jan. 1928	2 Oct. 1931
William Hardy Holmes	2 Feb. 1939	trs. Meath 19 Oct. 1938
John Winthrop Crozier	2 Feb. 1939	res. 31 Dec. 1957

Arthur Hamilton Butler	27 May 1958	trs. Connor 14 Oct. 1969
John Coote Duggan	2 Feb. 1970	res. 1985
John Neill	6 Jan. 1986	trs. Cashel 1987
Richard Henderson	27 Nov. 1997	

Archbishops/Bishops of Cashel (ceased to be archbishopric 28 Dec. 1838; thereafter bishopric united to Dublin)

	Appointed	*Termination of office*
Charles Agar	6 Aug. 1779	trs. Dublin, 7 Dec. 1801
Charles Brodrick	9 Dec. 1801	6 May 1822
Richard Laurence	21 July 1822	28 Dec. 1838
Stephen Creagh Sandes	Feb. 1839	13 Nov. 1842
Robert Daly	29 Jan. 1843	16 Feb. 1872
Maurice Fitzgerald Day	14 Apr. 1872	res. 30 Sept. 1899
Henry Stewart O'Hara	24 Feb. 1900	res. 31 Mar. 1919
John Frederick McNeice	24 June 1931	trs. Down 13 Dec. 1934
Thomas Arnold Harvey	25 Mar. 1935	res. 15 May 1958
William Cecil de Pauley	29 Sept. 1958	30 Mar. 1968
John Ward Armstrong	21 Sept. 1968	trs. Armagh 25 Feb. 1980
Noel Vincent Willoughby	28 Mar. 1980	1997
J. R. W. Neill	23 Apr. 1997	

Bishops of Cork (Dublin Province)

Hon. Thomas Stopford	29 June 1794	24 Jan. 1805
Lord John George Beresford	24 Mar. 1805	trs. Raphoe 10 Aug. 1807
Hon. Thomas St Lawrence	27 Sept. 1807	10 Feb. 1831
Samuel Kyle	27 Mar. 1831	10 May 1848
(Cloyne united to Cork from 14 Sept. 1835)		
James Wilson	30 July 1848	5 Jan. 1857
William Fitzgerald	8 Mar. 1857	trs. Killaloe 3 Feb. 1862
John Gregg	16 Feb. 1862	26 May 1878
Robert Samuel Gregg	4 July 1878	trs. Armagh 14 Dec. 1893
William Edward Meade	6 Jan. 1894	12 Oct. 1912
Charles Benjamin Dowse	23 Dec. 1912	res. 15 Sept. 1933
William Edward Flewett	30 Nov. 1933	5 Aug. 1938
Robert Thomas Hearn	13 Nov. 1938	14 July 1952
George Otto Simms	28 Oct. 1952	trs. Dublin 11 Dec. 1956
Richard Gordon Perdue	10 Feb. 1957	res. 20 May 1978
Samuel Greenfield Poyntz	17 Sept. 1978	trs. Connor 1987
R. A. Warke	23 Nov. 1987	1999
W. P. Colton	29 Jan. 1999	

Bishops of Ferns (Dublin Province)

Euseby Cleaver	13 June 1789	trs. Dublin 25 Aug. 1809
Percy Jocelyn	13 Sept. 1809	trs. Cloger 3 Apr. 1820
Lord Robert Ponsonby Tottenham Loftus	5 May 1820	trs. Clogher 21 Dec. 1822
Thomas Elrington	21 Dec. 1822	12 July 1835
(united to Ossory)		

Bishops of Kildare (Dublin Province)

George Lewis Jones	5 June 1890	9 Mar. 1804
Charles Lindsay	14 May 1804	8 Aug. 1846

(united to Dublin; in 1876 separated from Dublin and united to Meath)

Bishiops of Killaloe (Cashel Province to 1833 then Dublin Province)

William Knox	21 Sept. 1794	trs. Derry 9 Sept. 1803
Charles Dalrymple Lindsay	13 Nov. 1803	trs. Kildare 14 May 1804
Nathaniel Alexander	22 May 1804	trs. Down 21 Nov. 1804
Lord Robert Ponsonby Tottenham Loftus	16 Dec. 1804	trs. Ferns 5 May 1820
Richard Mant	7 May 1820	trs. Down 23 Mar. 1823
Alexander Arbuthnot	11 May 1823	9 Jan. 1828
Richard Ponsonby	16 Mar. 1828	trs. Derry 21 Sept. 1831
Edmund Knox	9 Oct. 1831	trs. Limerick 29 Jan. 1834
Charles Butson	29 Jan. 1834	23 Mar. 1836
Stephen Creagh Sandes	12 June 1836	trs. Cashel 23 Jan. 1839
L. Tonson (Baron Riversdale, 1848)	17 Feb. 1839	13 Dec. 1861
William Fitzgerald	3 Feb. 1862	24 Nov. 1883
William Bennett Chester	24 Feb. 1884	27 Aug. 1893
Frederick Richard Wynne	10 Dec. 1893	3 Nov. 1896
Mervyn Archdall	2 Feb. 1897	res. 31 Mar. 1912
Charles Benjamin Dowse	11 June 1912	trs. Cork 23 Dec. 1912
Thomas Sterling Berry	25 Mar. 1913	res. 6 Mar. 1924
Henry Edmund Patton	1 May 1924	28 Apr. 1943
Robert M'Neil Boyd	21 Sept. 1943	trs. Derry 20 Mar. 1945
Hedley Webster	25 July 1945	res. 30 Sept. 1953
Richard Gordon Perdue	2 Feb. 1954	trs. Cork 19 Feb. 1957
Henry Arthur Stanistreet	11 June 1957	res. 2 Nov. 1971
Edwin Owen	25 Jan. 1972	

(united to Limerick in 1976)

Bishops of Limerick (Cashel Province; Dublin Province from 1833)

Thomas Barnard	12 Sept. 1794	7 June 1806
Charles Mongan Warburton	12 July 1806	trs. Cloyne 18 Sept. 1820
Thomas Elrington	8 Oct. 1820	trs. Ferns 21 Dec. 1822
John Jebb	12 Jan. 1823	9 Dec. 1833
Edmund Knox	29 Jan. 1834	3 May 1849
William Higgin	15 July 1849	trs. Derry 7 Dec. 1853
Henry Griffin	1 Jan. 1854	5 Apr. 1866
Charles Graves	29 June 1866	17 July 1899
Thomas Bunbury	1 Nov. 1899	19 Jan. 1907

Raymond D'Audemar Orpen	2 Apr. 1907	res. 31 Dec. 1920
Harry Vere White	18 Oct. 1921	res. 31 Oct. 1931
Charles King Irwin	2 Feb. 1934	trs. Down 6 Aug. 1942
Evelyn Charles Hodges	2 Feb. 1942	res. 30 Sept. 1960
Robert Wyse Jackson	6 Jan. 1961	res. 12 July 1970
Donald A. R. Caird	29 Sept. 1970	trs. Meath and Kildare 9 Sept. 1976

(See then united with Killaloe)

Edwin Owen	5 Dec. 1976	res. 6 Jan. 1981
Walton N. F. Empey	25 Mar. 1981	trs. Dublin 26 Apr. 1996
E. F. Darling	9 Sept. 1985	2000
M. H. G. Mayes	8 Sept. 2000	

Bishops of Meath (Armagh Province; Dublin Province from 1876)

Thomas Lewis O'Beirne	18 Dec. 1798	17 Feb. 1823
Nathaniel Alexander	21 Mar. 1823	21 Oct. 1840
Charles Dickinson	27 Dec. 1840	12 July 1842
Edward Stopford	6 Nov. 1842	17 Sept. 1850
Thomas Stewart Townsend	1 Nov. 1850	1 Sept. 1852
Joseph Henderson Singer	28 Nov. 1852	16 July 1866
Samuel Butcher	14 Oct. 1866	29 July 1876
W. Conyngham, Baron Plunket	10 Dec. 1876	trs. Dublin 23 Dec. 1884
Charles Parsons Reichel	29 Sept. 1885	29 Mar. 1894
Joseph Ferguson Peacocke	11 June 1894	trs. Dublin 19 May 1897
James Bennett Keene	17 Oct. 1897	5 Aug. 1919
Hon. Benjamin John Plunket	15 Oct. 1919	res. 31 Mar. 1925
Thomas G. G. Collins	17 Mar. 1926	3 July 1927
John Orr	15 Nov. 1927	21 July 1938
William Hardy Holmes	19 Oct. 1938	res. 31 May 1945
James McCann	24 Aug. 1945	trs. Armagh 19 Feb. 1959
Robert Bonsall Pike	19 May 1959	27 Dec. 1973
Donald A. R. Caird	14 Sept. 1976	1985
Walton Empey	22 July 1985	1996
R. L. Clarke	7 June 1996	

Bishops of Ossory (Dublin Province)

Hugh Hamilton	24 Jan. 1799	1 Dec. 1805
John Kearney	2 Feb. 1806	22 May 1813
Robert Fowler	20 June 1813	31 Dec. 1841

(Ferns united to Ossory 12 July 1835)

James Thomas O'Brien	20 Mar. 1842	12 Dec. 1874
Robert Samuel Gregg	30 Mar. 1875	trs. Cork 4 July 1878
William Pakenham Walsh	29 Sept. 1878	res. 30 Sept. 1897
John Baptist Crozier	30 Nov. 1897	trs. Down 26 Sept. 1907
Charles Frederick D'Arcy	5 Nov. 1907	trs. Down 29 Mar. 1911
John Henry Bernard	25 July 1911	trs. Dublin 7 Oct. 1915
John A. Fitzgerald Gregg	28 Dec. 1915	trs. Dublin 10 Sept. 1920
John G. Fitmaurice Day	1 Nov. 1920	trs. Armagh 27 Apr. 1938
Forde Tichborne	24 June 1938	18 Feb. 1940
John Percy Phair	11 June 1940	res. 31 Dec. 1961
Henry Robert McAdoo	11 Mar. 1962	trs. Dublin Apr. 1977

(See then united to Cashel)

Bishops of Clogher (Armagh Province)

John Porter	30 Dec. 1797	27 July 1819
Lord John George Beresford	3 Apr. 1820	trs. Dublin 21 Apr. 1820
Percy Jocelyn	3 Apr. 1820	depr. 21 Oct. 1822
Lord Robert Ponsonby		
Tottenham Loftus	21 Dec. 1822	26 Sept. 1850
(See united to Armagh 1850–86)		
Charles Maurice Stack	29 June 1886	res. 13 Dec. 1902
Charles Frederick D'Arcy	24 Feb. 1903	trs. Ossory 6 Nov. 1907
Maurice Day	25 Jan. 1908	27 May 1923
James MacManaway	6 Aug. 1923	res. 30 Sept. 1943
Richard Tyner	6 Jan. 1944	6 Apr. 1958
Alan Alexander Buchanan	30 Sept. 1958	trs. Dublin 22 Nov. 1969
Richard Patrick Crosland Hanson	17 Mar. 1970	res. 31 Mar. 1973
Robert William Heavener	29 June 1973	res. 31 May 1980
George McMullan	7 Sept. 1980	1986
B. D. A. Hannon	7 May 1986	2001
M. G. St A. Jackson	21 Nov. 2001	

Bishops of Connor (Armagh Province)

Charles King Irwin	1 Jan. 1945	res. 32 May 1956
Robert C. H. Glover Elliott	21 Sept. 1956	res. 31 Aug. 1960
A. H. Butler	16 Sept. 1969	1981
William John McCappin	30 Nov. 1981	1987
Samuel Greenfield Poyntz	15 Oct. 1987	1995
J. E. Moore	31 Mar. 1995	

Bishops of Derry (Armagh Province)

Frederick August Hervey		
(Earl of Bristol 1779)	18 Feb. 1768	8 July 1803
Hon. William Knox	9 Sept. 1803	10 July 1831
Hon. Richard Ponsonby	21 Sept. 1831	27 Oct. 1853
(Raphoe united to Derry from 5 Sept. 1834)		
William Higgin	7 Dec. 1853	12 July 1867
William Alexander	6 Oct. 1867	trs. Armagh 25 Feb. 1896
George A. Chadwick	25 Mar. 1896	res. 31 Jan. 1916
Joseph Irvine Peacocke	25 Apr. 1916	res. 31 Dec. 1944
Robert M'Neill Boyd	20 Mar. 1945	1 July 1958
Charles John Tyndall	14 Oct. 1958	res. 30 Sept. 1969
Cuthbert Irvine Peacocke	6 Jan. 1970	res. 31 Mar. 1975
Robert Henry Alexander Eames	9 June 1975	trs. Down 20 May 1980
James Mchaffey	7 Sept. 1980	2002
K. R. Good	13 Mar. 2002	

Bishops of Down (Armagh Province)

William Dickson	1 Feb. 1784	19 Sept. 1804
Nathaniel Alexander	21 Nov. 1804	trs. Meath Mar. 1823

441

Richard Mant	23 Mar. 1823	2 Nov. 1848
Robert Bent Knox	1 May 1849	trs. Armagh 11 May 1886
William Reeves	1 May 1849	12 Jan. 1892
Thomas James Welland	25 Mar. 1892	29 July 1907
John Baptist Crozier	26 Sept. 1907	trs. Armagh 2 Feb. 1911
Charles Frederick D'Arcy	29 Mar. 1911	trs. Dublin 15 Oct. 1919
Charles T. P. Grierson	28 Oct. 1919	res. 30 Nov. 1934
John Frederick McNeice	12 Dec. 1934	14 Apr. 1942
Charles King Irwin	17 Nov. 1942	res. 1 Jan. 1945
William Shaw Kerr	25 Jan. 1945	res. 31 July 1955
Frederick Julian Mitchell	18 Oct. 1945	res. 7 Nov. 1969
Robert Eames	20 May 1980	1986
G. McMullan	7 Mar. 1986	1997
H. C. Miller	18 Feb. 1997	

Bishops of Dromore (Armagh Province)

Thomas Percy	26 May 1782	30 Sept. 1811
George Hall	17 Nov. 1811	23 Nov. 1811
John Leslie	26 Jan. 1812	trs. Elphin 16 Nov. 1819
James Saurin	19 Dec. 1819	9 Apr. 1842
	(See united to Down)	

Bishops of Kilmore (Armagh Province)

Charles Broderick	19 Jan. 1796	trs. Cashel 9 Dec. 1801
George de la Poer Beresford	1 Mar. 1802	15 Oct. 1841
John Leslie	15 Oct. 1841	22 July 1854
Marcus Gervais Beresford	24 Sept. 1854	trs. to Armagh 16 Oct. 1862
Hamilton Verschoyle	26 Oct. 1862	28 Jan. 1870
Charles Leslie	24 Apr. 1870	8 July 1870
Thomas Carson	2 Oct. 1870	7 July 1874
John Richard Darley	25 Oct. 1874	20 Jan. 1884
Samuel Shone	25 Apr. 1884	res. 1 Sept. 1897
Alfred George Elliott	17 Oct. 1897	28 Sept. 1915
William Richard Moore	30 Nov. 1915	23 Feb. 1930
Arthur William Barton	1 May 1930	trs. Dublin 15 Feb. 1939
Albert Edward Hughes	25 Apr. 1939	res. 12 May 1950
Frederick Julian Mitchell	21 Sept. 1950	trs. Down 18 Oct. 1955
Charles John Tyndall	2 Feb. 1956	trs. Derry 14 Oct. 1958
Edward Francis Butler Moore	6 Jan. 1959	res. 31 May 1981
William Gilbert Wilson	21 Sept. 1981	1993
M. H. G. Mayes	29 Apr. 1993	

Bishops of Raphoe (Armagh Province)

James Hawkins	1 Apr. 1780	23 June 1807
Lord John George Beresford	10 Aug. 1807	trs. Clogher 25 Sept. 1819
William Magee	24 Oct. 1819	trs. Dublin 24 June 1822
William Bissett	21 July 1822	5 Sept. 1834
	(See united to Derry)	

442

Bishops of Cloyne (Cashel Province)

William Bennett	27 June 1794	16 July 1820
Charles Mongan Warburton	18 Sept. 1820	9 Aug. 1826
John Brinkley	8 Oct. 1826	14 Sept. 1835
	(See united to Cork)	

Bishops of Waterford and Lismore (Cashel Province)

Richard Marlay	21 Mar. 1795	1 July 1802
Hon. Power Le Poer Trench	21 Nov. 1802	trs. Elphin 30 Apr. 1810
Joseph Stock	1 May 1810	14 Aug. 1813
Hon. Richard Bourke	10 Oct. 1813	15 Nov. 1832
	(See united to Cashel)	

Bishops of Clonfert (Tuam Province)

Matthew Young	3 Feb. 1799	28 Nov. 1800
George de la Poer Beresford	1 Feb. 1801	trs. Kilmore 1 Mar. 1802
Nathaniel Alexander	21 Mar. 1802	trs. Killaloe 22 May 1804
Christopher Burtson	29 July 1804	22 Mar. 1836

Bishops of Elphin (Tuam Province)

John Law	27 Mar. 1795	19 Mar. 1810
Hon. Power Le Poer Trench	30 Apr. 1810	trs. Tuam 10 Nov. 1819
John Leslie	16 Nov. 1819	22 July 1854

Bishops of Killala (Tuam Province)

Joseph Stock	28 Jan. 1798	trs. Waterford 1 May 1810
James Verschoyle	6 May 1810	13 Apr. 1834
	(See united to Tuam)	

Presbyterian Church in Ireland

Moderators of the Presbyterian Synod of Ulster to 1840

Joseph Hay	1801
Nathaniel Shaw	1802
Thomas Henry	1803
James Horner	1804
Robert Rentoul	1805
William Neilson	1806
Henry Henry	1807
Joseph Denham	1808
Samuel Hanna	1809
William Dunlop	1810
James Banhead	1811
Thomas McKay	1812

James Morrell	1813
George Hay	1814
John McCance	1815
Robert Stewart	1816
Nathaniel Alexander	1817
Henry Montgomery	1818
Alexander Patterson	1819
Andrew George Malcolm	1820
Edward Reid	1821
John Mitchel	1822
Robert Hogg	1823
Henry Cooke	1824
James Carlile	1825
William Wright	1826
James Seaton Reid	1827
Patrick White	1828
Robert Park	1829
Robert Winning	1830
James Morgan	1831
John Brown	1832
Moses Finlay	1833
William McClure	1834
John Barnett	1835
Hugh Walker Rodgers	1836
William Craig	1837
Henry Wallace	1838
James Denham	1839
James Elder	1840

Moderators of the General Assembly of the Presbyterian Church from 1840

Samuel Hanna	1840
Henry Cooke	1841
John Edgar	1842
Robert Stewart	1843
John Brown	1844
James Carlile	1845
James Morgan	1846
William McClure	1847
Henry Jackson Dobbin	1848
John Barnett	1849
William Bailey Kirkpatrick	1850
John Coulter	1851
John Bleckley	1852
Henry William Molyneaux	1853
David Hamilton	1854

Robert Allen	1855
Robert Wilson	1856
Alexander Porter Gowdy	1857
John Johnson	1858
William Gibson	1859
Samuel Marcus Dill	1860
John MacNaughton	1861
Henry Cooke	1862
John Rogers	1863 and 1864
David Wilson	1865 and 1866
Robert Montgomery	1867
Charles Lucas Morrell	1868
Richard Smyth	1869 and 1870
Lowry Edmonds Berkeley	1871
William Johnston	1872 and 1873
William Magill	1874
Josias Leslie Porter	1875
John Meneely	1876
George Bellis	1877
Thomas Witherow	1878
Robert Watts	1879
Jackson Smyth	1880
William Fleming Stevenson	1881
Thomas Yong Killen	1882
Hamilton Brown Wilson	1883
James Maxwell Rogers	1884
James Weir Whigham	1885
Robert Ross	1886
John Henry	1887
Robert John Lynd	1888
William Clarke	1889
William Park	1890
Nathaniel Macauley Brown	1891
Robert McChenye Edgar	1892
William Todd Martin	1893 and 1894
George Raphael Buick	1895
Henry McLlroy Williamson	1896
Matthew Leitch	1897
William Barry	1898
David Alexander Taylor	1899
John McCurdy Hamilton	1900
James Heron	1901
John Edgar Henry	1902
John MacDermott	1903
Samuel Prenter	1904
William McMordie	1905

William McKean	1906
John Davidson	1907
John McIlveen	1908
John Courtenay Clarke	1909
John Howard Murphy	1910
John Macmillan	1911
Henry Montgomery	1912
William John Macauley	1913
James Bingham	1914
Thomas Macafee Hamill	1915
Thomas West	1916
John Irwin	1917
James McGranahan	1918
John Morrow Simms	1919
Henry Patterson Glenn	1920
William James Lowe	1921
William Gordon Straham	1922
George Thompson	1923
Robert Wilson Hamilton	1924
Thomas Haslett	1925
Robert Kennedy Hanna	1926
James Thompson	1927
Thomas Alexander Smyth	1928
John Lowe Morrow	1929
Edward Clarke	1930
James Gilbert Paton	1931 and 1932
William Corkey	1933
Thomas McGimpsey Johnstone	1934
Andrew Frederick Moody	1935
Frederick William Scott O'Neill	1936
John Waddell	1937
William John Currie	1938
James Haire	1939
James Barkley Woodburn	1940
William Alexander Watson	1941
Wilson Moreland Kennedy	1942
Phineas McKee	1943
Andrew Gibson	1944
Robert Corkey	1945
Thomas Byers	1946
Robert Boyde	1947
Alfred William Neill	1948
Gordon Douglas Erskine	1949
Joseph Hugh Rush Gibson	1950
Hugh McKlroy	1951
John Knox Lelie McKean	1952

446

James Ernest Davey	1953
John Knowles	1954
James Carlile Breakley	1955
Thomas McCurdy Barker	1956
Robert John Wilson	1957
William McAdam	1958
Thomas Alexander Byers Smith	1959
Austin Alfred Fulton	1960
William Alexander Albert Park	1961
John Higginson Davey	1962
William Alexander Montgomery	1963
James Dunlop	1964
Samuel James Park	1965
Alfred Martin	1966
William Boyd	1967
John Herbert Withers	1968
John Talbot Carson	1969
James Loughbridge Mitchell Haire	1970
Frederick Rupert Gibson	1971
Robert Victor Alexander Lymas	1972
John Whiteford Orr	1973
George Temple Lundie	1974
George Frederick Hayston Wynne	1975
Andrew John Weir	1976
Thomas Algeo Patterson	1977
David Burke	1978
William Magee Craig	1979
Ronald Gavin Craig	1980
James Girvan	1981
Eric Paul Gardner	1982
T. J. Simpson	1983
Howard Cromie	1984
Robert Dickson	1985
John Thompson	1986
William Fleming	1987
A. G. Brown	1988
James Matthews	1989
R. F. G. Holmes	1990
Rodney Sterritt	1991
John Dunlop	1992
Andrew R. Rodgers	1993
David J. McGaughey	1994
John Rees	1995
Harry Allen	1996
Samuel Hutchinson	1997
Samuel John Dixon	1998

John Lockington	1999
Trevor Morrow	2000
Alistair Dunlop	2001
Russell Birney	2002
Ivan McKay	2003

The Methodist Church of Ireland

Vice-President of the Conference and President of the Methodist Church in Ireland from 1868

(The President of the British Conference presides at the annual Irish Conference.)

Henry Price	1868
James Tobias	1869
Joseph W. McKay	1870
Robinson Scott	1871
William P. Applebe	1872
George Vance	1873
Wallace McMullen	1874
Gibson McMillen	1875
Joseph W. McKay	1876
James Tobias	1877
Wallace McMullen	1878
William Guard Price	1879
William P. Applebe	1880
James Tobias	1881
Oliver McCutcheon	1882
William Crook	1883
James Donnelly	1884
Thomas A. McKee	1885
Joseph W. McKay	1886
John Donor Powell	1887
Wallace McMullen	1888
William G. Price	1889
Oliver McCutcheon	1890
John Woods Ballard	1891
William Gorman	1892
Wesley Guard	1893
William Nicholas	1894
Wallace McMullen	1895
William Crook	1896
James Robertson	1897
R. Crawford Johnson	1898
William Crawford	1900
John O. Park	1901

Wesley Guard	1902
William Nicholas	1903
Thomas Knox	1904
George R. Wedgewood	1905
James R. Robertson	1906
William Crawford	1907
James D. Lamont	1908
Joseph W. R. Campbell	1909
John O. Park	1910
Wesley Guard	1911
George R. Westwood	1912
Samuel T. Boyd	1913
William R. Budd	1914
John O. Price	1915
Pierce Martin	1916
William Maguire	1917
Hugh McKeag	1918
James Kirkwood	1919
Henry Shire	1920
William H. Smyth	1921
James M. Alley	1922
James W. Parkhill	1923
William Corrigan	1924
Edward B. Cullen	1925
Robert M. Ker	1926
William H. Smyth	1927
Randall C. Phillips	1928
John C. Robertson	1929
William Moore	1930
Frederick E. Harte	1931
John A. Duke	1932
R. Lee Cole	1933
John A. Watson	1934
Thomas J. Irwin	1935
William H. Massey	1936
C. Henry Crookshank	1937
Thomas T. Allen	1938
Alexander McCrea	1939
Hugh M. Watson	1940
John N. Spence	1941
Beresford S. Lyons	1942
George A. Joynt	1943
Limmilan L. Northridge	1944
Edward Whittaker	1945
Robert H. Gallagher	1946
John England	1947

W. E. Morley Thompson	1948
John W. Stutt	1949
J. R. Wesley Roddie	1950
Henry N. Medd	1951
John Montgomery	1952
Richard M. L. Waugh	1953
Ernest Shaw	1954
Albert Holland	1955
Samuel E. McCaffrey	1956
J. Wesley McKinney	1957
Robert J. Good	1958
R. Ernest Ker	1959
Robert W. McVeigh	1960
Charles W. Ranson	1961
James Wicheart	1962
Frederick E. Hill	1963
Samuel H. Baxter	1964
Robert A. Nelson	1965
Samuel J. Johnson	1966
Robert D. E. Gallagher	1967
Gerald G. Myles	1968
George E. Good	1969
James Davison	1970
Charles H. Bain	1971
Edward R. Lindsay	1972
Harold Sloan	1973
R. Desmond Morris	1974
Hedley Washington Plunkett	1975
Richard Greenwood	1976
Robert G. Livingstone	1977
John Turner	1978
Vincent Parkin	1979
W. Sydney Callaghan	1980
Ernest W. Gallagher	1981
Charles G. Eyre	1982
Cecil A. Newall	1983
Paul Kingston	1984
Hamilton Skillen	1985
Sydney Frame	1986
William I. Hamilton	1987
T. Stanley Whittington	1988
George R. Morrison	1989
William T. Buchanan	1990
J. Winston Good	1991
J. Derek H. Richie	1992
Richard H. Taylor	1993

450

Edmund T. I. Mawhinney	1994
Charles G. Walpole	1995
Kenneth Best	1996
Norman W. Taggart	1997
David J. Kerr	1998
Kenneth A. Wilson	1999
Kenneth Todd	2000
Harold Good	2001
Winston Graham	2002
James Rea	2003
Brian Fletcher	2004

MEMBERSHIP OF RELIGIOUS DENOMINATIONS

Ireland during the union

Figures in these two tables have been drawn from different sources.

Denominations of total population of Ireland, 1834–1911

	RC	%	C of I	%	Presbyterians	%
1834	6,427,712	80.9	852,064	10.7	642,356	8.1
1861	4,505,265	77.7	693,357	12.0	523,291	9.0
1871	4,150,867	76.7	667,998	12.3	497,548	9.2
1881	3,960,891	76.5	639,574	12.4	470,734	9.1
1891	3,547,307	75.4	600,103	12.8	444,974	9.5
1901	3,308,661	74.2	581,089	13.0	443,276	9.9
1911	3,242,670	73.9	576,611	13.1	440,525	10.0

Denominations of total population of Ireland, 1861–1911

Figures in square brackets are religious denominations as percentages of the population.

Year	RC	C of I	Presb	Method	Others	Non-RC total
1861	4,505,263	693,357	523,291	45,399	31,655	1,293,702
	[77.69]	[11.96]	[9.02]	[0.79]	[0.54]	[22.31]
1871	4,150,867	667,998	497,648	43,441	52,423	1,261,510
	[76.69]	[12.34]	[9.20]	[0.80]	[0.97]	[23.31]
1881	3,960,891	639,574	470,734	48,839	54,798	1,213,945
	[76.54]	[12.36]	[9.10]	[0.94]	[1.06]	[23.46]
1891	3,547,307	600,103	444,974	55,500	56,866	1,157,443
	[75.40]	[12.75]	[9.46]	[1.18]	[1.21]	[24.60]
1901	3,308,661	581,089	443,276	62,006	63,743	1,150,114
	[74.21]	[13.03]	[9.94]	[1.39]	[1.43]	[25.79]
1911	3,242,670	576,611	440,523	62,382	68,031	1,147,549
	[73.86]	[13.13]	[10.04]	[1.42]	[1.55]	[26.14]

452

Denominations in province of Leinster, 1861–1911

Year	RC	C of I	Presb	Method	Others
Leinster					
1861	1,252,553	180,587	12,355	3,290	5,850
	[85.9]	[12.4]	[0.9]	[0.4]	[0.4]
1871	1,145,104	164,586	12,556	6,530	10,675
	[85.5]	[12.3]	[0.9]	[0.5]	[0.8]
1881	1,094,825	157,522	12,059	7,006	7,577
	[85.6]	[12.3]	[0.9]	[0.6]	[0.6]
1891	1,012,007	147,520	12,460	7,770	8,003
	[85.2]	[12.4]	[1.0]	[0.7]	[0.7]
1901	981,768	141,615	11,987	7,977	9,482
	[85.16]	[12.29]	[1.04]	[0.60]	[0.82]
1911	990,043	140,182	12,866	8,068	10,883
	[85.20]	[12.06]	[11.11]	[0.69]	[0.94]
County Carlow					
1861	50,539	6,229	106	182	81
	[88.4]	[10.9]	[0.2]	[0.3]	[0.2]
1871	45,621	5,656	132	136	85
	[88.3]	[10.9]	[0.3]	[0.3]	[0.2]
1881	41,223	5,048	81	129	87
	[88.5]	[10.8]	[0.2]	[0.3]	[0.2]
1891	36,139	4,454	118	163	62
	[88.3]	[10.9]	[0.3]	[0.4]	[0.2]
1901	33,399	3,946	164	197	42
	[88.48]	[10.45]	[0.44]	[0.52]	[0.11]
1911	32,317	3,600	122	157	56
	[89.15]	[9.93]	[0.34]	[0.43]	[0.15]
Drogheda Town					
1861	13,342	1,031	207	144	16
	[90.5]	[7.0]	[1.4]	[1.0]	[0.1]
1871	12,381	854	152	82	43
	[91.7]	[6.3]	[1.1]	[0.6]	[0.3]
1881	11,313	746	131	98	9
	[92.0]	[6.1]	[1.0]	[0.8]	[0.1]
1891	10,966	653	126	114	14
	[92.4]	[5.5]	[1.1]	[0.9]	[0.1]
County Dublin					
1861	83,556	18,914	936	402	1,151
	[79.6]	[18.0]	[0.9]	[0.4]	[1.1]
1871	111,964	39,289	2,995	1,434	3,254
	[70.5]	[24.7]	[1.9]	[0.9]	[2.0]
1881	119,741	41,282	3,350	1,802	3,133
	[70.7]	[24.4]	[2.0]	[1.1]	[1.8]

Year	RC	C of I	Presb	Method	Others
1891	121,404	42,771	4,232	2,421	3,387
	[69.7]	[24.6]	[2.4]	[1.4]	[1.9]
1901	110,879	37,674	3,585	2,322	3,108
	[70.37]	[23.91]	[2.27]	[1.47]	[1.98]
1911	122,372	39,323	4,400	2,709	3,590
	[70.99]	[22.81]	[2.55]	[1.57]	[2.08]
Dublin City					
1861	196,549	49,251	4,875	1,897	2,236
	[77.1]	[19.3]	[2.0]	[0.8]	[.08]
1871	195,180	39,878	4,517	1,828	4,904
	[79.2]	[16.2]	[1.8]	[0.8]	[2.0]
1881	200,774	39,565	4,463	1,932	2,868
	[80.4]	[15.9]	[1.8]	[0.8]	[1.1]
1891	201,418	35,125	3,492	1,708	3,258
	[82.2]	[14.4]	[1.4]	[0.7]	[1.3]
1901*	237,645	41,663	4,074	2,342	4,914
	[81.73]	[14.34]	[1.40]	[0.80]	[1.69]
1911	253,370	39,359	4,217	2,322	5,536
	[83.13]	[12.91]	[1.38]	[0.76]	[1.82]
Dublin Suburbs					
1861	29,639	17,668	1,724	380	874
	[58.4]	[35.2]	[3.4]	[1.2]	[1.8]
County Kildare					
1861	79,121	10,439	876	375	135
	[87.0]	[11.5]	[1.0]	[1.0]	[0.4]
1871	71,879	19,038	969	500	228
	[86.0]	[12.0]	[1.1]	[0.6]	[0.3]
1881	65,935	8,503	770	392	204
	[87.0]	[11.2]	[1.0]	[0.1]	[0.3]
1891	59,034	9,096	1,310	573	193
	[84.1]	[12.9]	[1.9]	[0.8]	[0.3]
1901	54,863	7,393	688	419	204
	[86.31]	[11.63]	[1.08]	[0.66]	[1.98]
1911	54,684	10,498	611	576	258
	[82.7]	[15.76]	[0.92]	[0.86]	[0.38]
County Kilkenny					
1861	105,356	4,750	127	72	36
	[95.5]	[4.3]	[0.1]	[0.1]	[–]
1871	91,955	4,385	127	82	120
	[95.1]	[4.6]	[0.1]	[0.1]	[0.1]
1881	83,198	3,761	122	81	70
	[95.4]	[4.3]	[0.1]	[0.1]	[0.1]
1891	72,836	3,112	121	82	62
	[95.6]	[4.2]	[2.4]	[0.1]	[0.1]

Year	RC	C of I	Presb	Method	Others
1901	74,830	3,978	170	114	67
	[94.53]	[5.03]	[0.21]	[0.14]	[0.09]
1911	71,193	3,357	214	72	126
	[94.97]	[4.48]	[0.28]	[0.10]	[0.17]

Kilkenny Town

Year	RC	C of I	Presb	Method	Others
1861	12,769	1,242	97	42	24
	[89.7]	[9.0]	[0.7]	[0.3]	[0.3]
1871	11,369	1,181	80	64	16
	[89.5]	[9.3]	[0.6]	[0.5]	[0.1]
1881	10,952	1,195	84	62	7
	[89.0]	[9.7]	[0.7]	[0.5]	[0.1]
1891	9,896	1,032	49	50	21
	[89.6]	[9.3]	[0.4]	[0.5]	[0.2]

King's County

Year	RC	C of I	Presb	Method	Others
1861	79,955	9,109	327	409	243
	[88.8]	[10.1]	[0.4]	[0.5]	[0.2]
1871	67,411	7,479	281	411	318
	[88.9]	[9.9]	[0.4]	[0.5]	[0.4]
1881	65,040	6,883	290	426	213
	[89.3]	[9.4]	[0.4]	[0.6]	[0.3]
1891	58,264	6,432	291	463	123
	[88.9]	[9.8]	[0.4]	[0.7]	[0.2]
1901	53,806	5,513	353	392	123
	[89.40]	[9.16]	[0.50]	[0.65]	[0.20]
1911	51,178	4,906	353	270	125
	[90.05]	[8.63]	[0.62]	[0.48]	[0.22]

County Longford

Year	RC	C of I	Presb	Method	Others
1861	64,801	6,196	560	95	42
	[90.4]	[8.6]	[0.8]	[0.1]	[0.1]
1871	58,138	5,215	659	124	365
	[90.1]	[8.1]	[1.0]	[0.2]	[0.6]
1881	55,501	4,887	396	189	34
	[91.0]	[8.0]	[0.7]	[0.3]	[–]
1891	48,071	4,033	279	211	53
	[91.3]	[7.7]	[0.5]	[0.4]	[0.1]
1901	42,742	3,403	256	203	68
	[91.58]	[7.29]	[0.55]	[0.43]	[0.15]
1911	40,297	3,081	230	163	49
	[91.96]	[7.03]	[0.54]	[0.37]	[0.11]

County Louth

Year	RC	C of I	Presb	Method	Others
1861	69,678	5,203	937	139	16
	[91.7]	[6.9]	[1.2]	[0.2]	[–]

Year	RC	C of I	Presb	Method	Others
1871	64,367	4,878	1,001	126	139
	[91.3]	[6.9]	[1.4]	[0.2]	[0.2]
1881	59,806	4,424	874	152	71
	[91.6]	[6.8]	[1.3]	[0.2]	[0.1]
1891	53,897	4,179	821	174	94
	[91.1]	[7.1]	[1.4]	[0.3]	[0.1]
1901	60,171	4,218	980	296	155
	[91.42]	[6.40]	[1.49]	[0.45]	[0.24]
1911	58,303	4,043	934	232	153
	[91.58]	[6.33]	[1.47]	[0.36]	[0.24]

County Meath

1861	103,327	6,492	428	106	20
	[93.6]	[5.9]	[0.4]	[0.1]	[−]
1871	89,140	5,826	369	127	96
	[93.3]	[6.1]	[0.4]	[0.1]	[0.1]
1881	81,743	5,293	323	65	45
	[93.45]	[6.05]	[0.37]	[0.08]	[0.05]
1891	71,690	4,815	367	69	46
	[93.12]	[6.25]	[0.48]	[0.09]	[0.06]
1901	62,643	4,394	330	66	64
	[92.81]	[6.51]	[0.49]	[0.10]	[0.09]
1911	60,660	3,945	350	35	81
	[93.19]	[6.06]	[0.54]	[0.09]	[0.12]

Queen's County

1861	80,025	9,683	240	492	210
	[88.3]	[10.7]	[0.3]	[0.5]	[0.2]
1871	70,186	8,652	307	394	252
	[88.0]	[10.8]	[0.4]	[0.5]	[0.3]
1881	64,315	7,899	290	399	221
	[88.0]	[10.8]	[0.4]	[0.5]	[0.3]
1891	56,913	6,954	292	524	195
	[87.7]	[10.7]	[0.5]	[0.8]	[0.3]
1901	50,599	5,950	295	419	154
	[88.13]	[10.36]	[0.51]	[0.73]	[0.27]
1911	48,480	5,307	282	369	191
	[88.74]	[9.71]	[0.52]	[0.68]	[0.35]

County Westmeath

1861	83,749	6,336	343	156	205
	[92.1]	[7.0]	[0.4]	[0.2]	[0.3]
1871	71,765	5,997	302	157	211
	[91.5]	[7.7]	[0.4]	[0.2]	[0.2]
1881	66,201	4,971	319	195	112
	[92.2]	[6.9]	[0.4]	[0.3]	[0.2]

Year	RC	C of I	Presb	Method	Others
1891	60,049	4,482	283	207	88
	[92.23]	[6.88]	[0.43]	[0.32]	[0.14]
1901	56,673	4,271	319	251	115
	[91.96]	[6.93]	[0.52]	[0.41]	[0.18]
1911	54,779	4,550	342	203	112
	[91.32]	[7.58]	[0.57]	[0.34]	[0.19]

County Wexford

Year	RC	C of I	Presb	Method	Others
1861	130,103	12,759	287	482	323
	[90.4]	[8.7]	[0.2]	[0.3]	[0.2]
1871	120,356	11,296	360	367	287
	[90.7]	[8.5]	[0.3]	[0.3]	[0.2]
1881	112,794	10,177	288	391	204
	[91.1]	[8.2]	[0.2]	[0.3]	[0.2]
1891	102,180	8,779	250	369	200
	[91.4]	[7.9]	[0.2]	[0.3]	[0.2]
1901	95,435	7,859	271	342	197
	[91.67]	[7.55]	[0.26]	[0.33]	[0.19]
1911	94,413	7,050	254	234	222
	[92.31]	[6.89]	[2.25]	[0.33]	[0.22]

County Wicklow

Year	RC	C of I	Presb	Method	Others
1861	70,044	15,285	285	717	148
	[81.0]	[17.7]	[0.3]	[0.8]	[0.2]
1871	63,392	13,963	305	680	357
	[80.6]	[17.7]	[0.4]	[0.9]	[0.4]
1881	56,230	12,888	276	693	299
	[79.9]	[18.3]	[0.4]	[1.0]	[0.4]
1891	49,250	11,598	429	642	217
	[79.3]	[18.7]	[0.7]	[1.0]	[0.3]
1901	48,085	11,354	502	614	271
	[79.05]	[18.66]	[0.83]	[1.01]	[0.43]
1911	47,999	11,165	557	606	384
	[79.06]	[18.39]	[0.92]	[1.00]	[0.63]

Denominations in province of Munster, 1861–1911

Year	RC	C of I	Presb	Method	Others
Munster					
1861	1,420,076	80,860	4,013	4,436	4,173
	[93.8]	[5.3]	[0.3]	[0.3]	[0.3]
1871	1,304,684	74,213	4,091	4,758	5,739
	[93.6]	[5.3]	[0.3]	[0.4]	[0.4]
1881	1,249,384	70,128	3,987	4,769	2,847
	[93.8]	[5.3]	[0.3]	[0.4]	[0.21]

457

Year	RC	C of I	Presb	Method	Others
1891	1,098,072	62,722	3,646	5,221	2,741
	[93.7]	[5.4]	[0.3]	[0.4]	[0.2]
1901	1,007,876	56,671	3,426	4,974	3,241
	[93.65]	[5.27]	[0.32]	[0.46]	[0.30]
1911	973,805	50,646	4,180	4,175	2,689
	[94.04]	[4.89]	[0.41]	[0.40]	[0.26]

County Clare

Year	RC	C of I	Presb	Method	Others
1861	162,612	3,323	228	89	53
	[97.8]	[2.0]	[0.1]	[0.1]	[–]
1871	144,440	3,027	220	64	113
	[97.7]	[2.0]	[0.2]	[–]	[0.1]
1881	138,508	2,669	165	65	50
	[97.9]	[1.9]	[0.1]	[0.1]	[–]
1891	122,047	2,246	106	53	31
	[98.04]	[1.8]	[0.1]	[0.04]	[0.02]
1901	110,062	2,036	157	48	31
	[97.98]	[1.81]	[0.14]	[0.04]	[0.02]
1911	102,300	1,709	166	38	19
	[98.14]	[1.64]	[0.16]	[0.04]	[0.02]

County Cork, east riding

Year	RC	C of I	Presb	Method	Others
1861	264,754	18,279	899	461	2,003
	[92.4]	[6.4]	[0.3]	[0.2]	[0.7]

County Cork, west riding

Year	RC	C of I	Presb	Method	Others
1861	162,140	14,543	219	1,299	100
	[90.9]	[8.2]	[0.1]	[0.7]	[0.1]

County Cork

Year	RC	C of I	Presb	Method	Others
1871	400,905	31,297	1,216	2,228	2,788
	[91.3]	[7.1]	[0.3]	[0.5]	[0.6]
1881	381,217	29,773	1,491	2,057	945
	[91.7]	[7.2]	[0.4]	[0.5]	[0.2]
1891	331,613	26,787	1,381	2,426	880
	[91.3]	[7.4]	[0.4]	[0.7]	[0.2]
1901	299,973	24,025	1,102	2,221	1,168
	[91.32]	[7.31]	[0.33]	[0.68]	[0.36]
1911	288,455	22,992	1,038	2,047	899
	[91.45]	[7.29]	[0.33]	[0.63]	[0.28]

Cork City

Year	RC	C of I	Presb	Method	Others
1861	61,148	10,632	881	893	567
	[83.9]	[13.2]	[1.1]	[1.1]	[0.7]
1871	66,716	9,196	1,028	718	984
	[84.8]	[11.7]	[1.3]	[0.9]	[1.3]

Year	RC	C of I	Presb	Method	Others
1881	68,655	9,221	889	867	492
	[85.7]	[11.5]	[1.1]	[1.1]	[0.6]
1891	64,361	8,620	749	867	548
	[85.7]	[11.4]	[1.0]	[1.2]	[0.7]

County Borough*
1901	65,751	7,996	728	841	806
	[86.38]	[10.50]	[0.96]	[1.01]	[1.06]
1911	67,814	6,576	912	641	728
	[88.44]	[8.58]	[1.19]	[0.84]	[0.95]

County Kerry
1861	195,159	6,200	243	161	57
	[96.7]	[3.1]	[0.1]	[0.1]	[−]
1871	190,332	5,592	206	213	243
	[96.8]	[2.9]	[0.1]	[0.1]	[0.1]
1881	194,283	5,897	213	350	296
	[96.6]	[2.9]	[0.1]	[0.2]	[0.2]
1891	173,195	5,077	210	399	255
	[96.7]	[2.8]	[0.1]	[0.2]	[0.2]
1901	160,511	4,431	220	355	209
	[96.85]	[2.67]	[0.13]	[0.22]	[0.13]
1911	155,322	3,725	265	265	114
	[97.26]	[2.33]	[0.17]	[0.17]	[0.07]

County Limerick
1861	166,604	5,648	148	301	100
	[96.4]	[3.3]	[0.1]	[0.2]	[−]
1871	147,389	4,729	118	249	98
	[96.6]	[3.1]	[0.1]	[0.2]	[−]
1881	137,574	4,027	105	261	103
	[96.6]	[2.8]	[0.1]	[0.2]	[0.1]
1891	117,895	3,379	111	298	74
	[96.8]	[2.8]	[0.1]	[0.2]	[0.1]
1901	104,714	2,743	111	290	89
	[97.01]	[2.54]	[0.10]	[0.27]	[0.08]
1911	101,502	2,550	136	273	90
	[97.08]	[2.44]	[0.13]	[0.26]	[0.09]

Limerick City
1861	39,124	4,238	418	344	352
	[87.9]	[9.6]	[1.0]	[0.8]	[0.7]
1871	34,836	3,427	316	267	507
	[88.5]	[8.7]	[0.8]	[0.7]	[1.3]
1881	33,891	3,781	300	300	290
	[87.9]	[9.8]	[0.8]	[0.8]	[0.7]

Year	RC	C of I	Presb	Method	Others
1891	32,894	3,294	315	331	321
	[88.5]	[8.9]	[0.8]	[0.9]	[0.9]

County Borough

Year	RC	C of I	Presb	Method	Others
1901	33,977	3,055	320	436	356
	[89.06]	[8.0]	[0.84]	[1.14]	[0.96]
1911	34,865	2,316	847	213	277
	[90.52]	[6.01]	[2.20]	[0.55]	[0.72]

County Tipperary, north riding

Year	RC	C of I	Presb	Method	Others
1861	101,171	7,359	194	397	99
	[92.6]	[6.7]	[0.2]	[0.4]	[0.1]

County Tipperary, south riding

Year	RC	C of I	Presb	Method	Others
1861	133,710	5,441	304	175	256
	[95.6]	[3.9]	[0.2]	[0.1]	[0.2]

County Tipperary

Year	RC	C of I	Presb	Method	Others
1871	203,227	11,855	607	641	382
	[93.8]	[5.4]	[0.3]	[0.3]	[0.2]
1881	188,115	10,211	487	574	225
	[94.2]	[5.1]	[0.3]	[0.3]	[0.1]
1891	162,871	9,126	468	558	165
	[94.0]	[5.3]	[0.3]	[0.3]	[0.1]
1901	150,332	8,702	465	560	173
	[93.82]	[5.43]	[0.29]	[0.35]	[0.11]
1911	144,156	7,221	432	435	189
	[94.57]	[4.74]	[0.28]	[0.29]	[0.12]

County Waterford

Year	RC	C of I	Presb	Method	Others
1861	107,225	3,208	245	50	231
	[96.6]	[2.9]	[0.2]	[0.1]	[0.2]
1871	96,235	3,229	145	92	260
	[96.3]	[3.2]	[0.1]	[0.1]	[0.3]
1881	86,870	2,979	165	90	207
	[96.2]	[3.3]	[0.2]	[0.1]	[0.2]
1891	74,186	2,791	121	96	205
	[95.8]	[3.6]	[0.2]	[0.1]	[0.3]
1901*	57,985	2,120	142	88	83
	[95.97]	[3.50]	[0.24]	[0.15]	[0.14]
1911	54,060	2,027	201	122	92
	[95.68]	[3.59]	[0.35]	[0.22]	[0.16]

*Amendment of boundaries to incorporate areas previously part of the county into the county borough.

Year	RC	C of I	Presb	Method	Others
Watford City					
1861	20,429	1,989	234	266	375
	[87.7]	[8.5]	[1.0]	[1.2]	[1.6]
1871	20,604	1,861	235	285	364
	[88.2]	[8.0]	[1.0]	[1.2]	[1.61]
1881	20,271	1,570	172	205	239
	[90.3]	[7.0]	[0.8]	[0.9]	[1.0]
1891	18,810	1,402	185	193	262
	[90.2]	[6.7]	[0.9]	[0.9]	[1.3]
County Borough*					
1901	24,571	1,565	181	135	317
	[91.79]	[5.85]	[0.68]	[0.50]	[1.18]
1911	25,331	1,530	183	139	281
	[90.23]	[5.57]	[0.67]	[0.51]	[1.02]

*Extension of boundaries to incorporate areas previously part of the county.

Denominations in province of Ulster, 1861–1911

Year	RC	C of I	Presb	Method	Others
Ulster					
1861	966,613	391,315	503,835	32,090	20,443
	[50.5]	[20.4]	[26.3]	[1.7]	[1.1]
1871	897,230	393,268	477,729	29,903	35,098
	[48.9]	[21.5]	[26.1]	[1.6]	[1.9]
1881	833,566	379,402	451,629	34,825	43,653
	[47.8]	[21.8]	[25.9]	[2.0]	[2.5]
1891	744,859	362,791	426,245	40,528	45,391
	[46.0]	[22.4]	[26.3]	[2.5]	[2.8]
1901	699,202	360,373	425,526	47,372	50,353
	[44.18]	[22.77]	[26.88]	[2.99]	[3.18]
1911	690,816	366,773	421,410	48,816	33,881
	[43.67]	[23.19]	[26.64]	[3.09]	[3.41]
County Antrim					
1861	61,639	45,275	131,687	4,014	5,219
	[24.8]	[18.3]	[53.2]	[1.6]	[2.1]
1871	55,640	45,670	122,918	3,287	8,846
	[23.5]	[19.3]	[52.0]	[1.4]	[3.8]
1881	51,590	45,212	116,813	3,427	10,687
	[22.7]	[19.8]	[51.3]	[1.5]	[4.7]
1891	44,960	42,178	105,299	3,623	10,246
	[21.8]	[20.4]	[51.0]	[1.8]	[5.0]
1901	40,381	40,983	99,552	3,739	11,435
	[20.59]	[20.90]	[50.77]	[1.91]	[5.83]
1911	39,751	42,118	97,198	3,813	10,984
	[20.50]	[21.72]	[50.14]	[1.97]	[5.67]

461

Year	RC	C of I	Presb	Method	Others
County Armagh					
1861	92,760	58,735	30,746	6,086	1,759
	[48.8]	[30.9]	[16.2]	[3.2]	[0.9]
1871	55,640	45,670	122,918	3,287	8,846
	[23.5]	[19.3]	[52.0]	[1.4]	[3.6]
1881	75,709	53,390	26,077	4,884	3,117
	[46.4]	[32.7]	[16.0]	[3.0]	[1.9]
1891	66,004	46,135	22,919	5,339	2,892
	[46.1]	[32.2]	[16.0]	[3.7]	[2.0]
1901	56,652	49,922	20,097	5,098	2,623
	[45.18]	[32.64]	[16.02]	[4.07]	[2.09]
1911	54,526	39,037	18,969	5,056	2,703
	[45.33]	[32.45]	[15.77]	[4.20]	[2.25]
Belfast City					
1861	41,406	30,080	42,604	4,946	2,566
	[33.9]	[24.6]	[33.2]	[4.1]	[2.2]
1871	55,575	46,423	60,249	6,775	5,390
	[31.9]	[26.6]	[34.5]	[3.9]	[3.1]
1881	59,975	58,410	71,521	9,141	9,075
	[28.8]	[28.1]	[34.4]	[4.4]	[4.3]
1891	67,378	75,522	87,234	13,747	12,069
	[26.3]	[29.5]	[34.1]	[5.4]	[4.7]
1901	84,992	102,991	120,269	21,506	19,422
	[24.34]	[29.50]	[34.44]	[6.16]	[5.56]
1911	93,243	118,173	130,575	23,782	21,174
	[24.10]	[30.54]	[33.74]	[6.15]	[5.47]
Carrickfergus Town					
1861	1,046	1,821	5,582	292	681
	[11.1]	[19.3]	[50.2]	[3.1]	[7.3]
1871	995	1,623	5,455	366	958
	[10.6]	[17.3]	[58.0]	[3.9]	[10.2]
1881	1,169	1,746	5,525	435	1,134
	[11.7]	[17.4]	[55.2]	[4.4]	[11.3]
1891	822	1,781	4,761	404	1,155
	[9.2]	[20.0]	[53.4]	[4.5]	[12.9]*
County Cavan					
1861	123,942	23,017	5,352	1,318	277
	[80.5]	[15.0]	[3.5]	[0.9]	[0.1]
1871	113,174	21,223	5,004	1,056	278
	[80.4]	[15.1]	[3.6]	[0.7]	[0.2]
1881	104,685	10,022	4,396	1,088	285
	[80.9]	[14.7]	[3.4]	[0.8]	[0.2]
1891	90,508	16,361	3,809	1,046	193
	[80.9]	[14.6]	[3.4]	[0.9]	[0.2]
1901	79,026	14,112	3,220	987	196
	[81.02]	[14.47]	[3.30]	[1.01]	[0.20]

Year	RC	C of I	Presb	Method	Others
1911	74,271	12,052	2,843	781	326
	[81.46]	[14.20]	[3.12]	[0.86]	[0.36]

County Donegal

Year	RC	C of I	Presb	Method	Others
1861	178,182	29,943	26,215	2,354	701
	[75.1]	[12.6]	[11.0]	[1.0]	[0.3]
1871	162,270	27,125	23,080	1,818	1,041
	[75.7]	[12.4]	[10.6]	[0.8]	[0.5]
1881	157,608	24,750	20,784	2,014	870
	[76.5]	[12.0]	[10.1]	[1.0]	[0.4]
1891	142,893	21,884	18,055	2,006	797
	[77.0]	[11.8]	[9.7]	[1.1]	[0.4]
1901	135,029	19,908	16,212	1,828	745
	[77.73]	[11.46]	[9.33]	[1.05]	[0.43]
1911	133,021	18,020	15,016	1,698	782
	[78.93]	[10.69]	[8.91]	[1.01]	[0.46]

County Down

Year	RC	C of I	Presb	Method	Others
1861	97,240	60,657	133,421	4,233	3,751
	[32.5]	[20.3]	[44.6]	[1.4]	[1.2]
1871	88,003	60,868	116,017	3,663	8,743
	[31.7]	[21.9]	[41.9]	[1.3]	[3.2]
1881	76,690	56,514	99,301	3,894	11,791
	[30.9]	[22.8]	[40.0]	[1.6]	[4.7]
1891	66,640	52,002	89,427	4,713	11,226
	[29.8]	[23.2]	[39.9]	[2.1]	[5.0]
1901	64,467	47,130	80,024	4,390	9,878
	[31.31]	[22.89]	[38.87]	[2.13]	[4.80]
1911	64,485	47,063	77,583	4,461	10,711
	[31.56]	[23.04]	[37.98]	[2.18]	[5.24]

County Fermanagh

Year	RC	C of I	Presb	Method	Others
1861	59,751	40,608	1,909	3,455	45
	[56.5]	[38.4]	[1.8]	[3.3]	[–]
1871	51,876	35,072	1,813	3,794	239
	[55.9]	[37.8]	[1.9]	[4.1]	[0.3]
1881	47,359	30,874	1,708	4,863	75
	[55.6]	[36.4]	[2.0]	[5.7]	[0.1]
1891	41,102	26,869	1,312	4,779	108
	[55.4]	[36.2]	[1.8]	[6.4]	[0.2]
1901	36,198	23,099	1,282	4,744	107
	[55.32]	[35.30]	[1.96]	[7.25]	[0.17]
1911	34,740	21,123	1,264	4,028	681
	[56.18]	[34.16]	[2.05]	[6.51]	[1.10]

County Londonderry

Year	RC	C of I	Presb	Method	Others
1861	83,402	31,218	64,602	1,136	3,851
	[45.3]	[16.9]	[35.1]	[0.6]	[2.1]

463

Year	RC	C of I	Presb	Method	Others
1871	77,358	32,079	58,779	957	4,733
	[44.4]	[18.5]	[33.8]	[0.6]	[2.7]
1881	73,274	31,596	54,727	938	4,456
	[44.4]	[19.1]	[33.2]	[0.6]	[2.7]
1891	67,748	29,730	48,936	990	4,605
	[44.6]	[19.6]	[32.2]	[0.6]	[3.0]
County					
1901	43,274	20,528	36,701	745	3,264
	[41.41]	[19.64]	[35.10]	[0.71]	[3.14]
1911	41,478	20,028	34,236	756	5,347
	[41.54]	[20.06]	[34.29]	[0.76]	[3.35]
Borough					
1901	22,022	7,276	8,981	701	912
	[55.21]	[18.22]	[22.49]	[1.76]	[2.32]
1911	22,923	7,248	8,700	1,183	826
	[56.21]	[17.53]	[21.33]	[2.90]	[2.03]
County Monaghan					
1861	92,799	17,721	15,149	439	374
	[73.4]	[14.0]	[12.0]	[0.03]	[0.03]
1871	84,345	15,641	13,914	493	576
	[76.4]	[13.6]	[12.1]	[0.4]	[0.5]
1881	75,714	13,623	12,213	544	654
	[73.7]	[13.3]	[11.9]	[0.5]	[0.6]
1891	63,154	11,247	10,876	489	440
	[73.3]	[13.0]	[12.6]	[0.6]	[0.5]
1901	54,757	9,528	9,532	423	371
	[73.39]	[12.77]	[12.78]	[0.56]	[0.50]
1911	53,369	8,725	8,512	395	460
	[74.68]	[12.21]	[11.91]	[0.55]	[0.65]
County Tyrone					
1861	134,716	52,240	46,568	3,757	1,219
	[56.5]	[21.9]	[19.5]	[1.6]	[0.5]
1871	119,937	49,201	42,156	3,115	1,357
	[55.6]	[22.8]	[19.5]	[1.5]	[0.6]
1881	109,793	44,256	38,564	3,597	1,509
	[55.5]	[22.4]	[19.5]	[1.8]	[0.8]
1891	93,650	39,082	33,617	3,392	1,660
	[54.6]	[22.8]	[19.6]	[2.0]	[1.0]
1901	82,404	33,896	29,656	3,211	1,400
	[54.73]	[22.51]	[19.70]	[2.13]	[0.93]
1911	79,015	32,386	26,514	2,863	1,887
	[55.39]	[22.70]	[18.58]	[2.01]	[1.32]

Denominations in province of Connacht, 1861–1911

Year	RC	C of I	Presb	Method	Others
Connacht					
1861	866,023	40,595	3,088	2,643	786
	[94.8]	[4.5]	[0.3]	[0.3]	[0.1]
1871	803,849	35,931	3,272	2,250	911
	[95.0]	[4.2]	[0.4]	[0.3]	[0.1]
1881	783,116	32,522	3,059	2,239	721
	[95.3]	[3.9]	[0.4]	[0.3]	[0.1]
1891	692,369	27,070	2,623	1,981	731
	[95.5]	[3.7]	[0.4]	[0.3]	[0.1]
1901	619,815	22,430	2,337	1,683	667
	[95.81]	[3.47]	[0.36]	[0.26]	[0.10]
1911	588,004	19,010	2,069	1,323	578
	[96.24]	[3.11]	[0.34]	[0.22]	[0.09]
County Galway					
1861	246,330	7,365	392	279	145
	[96.8]	[2.9]	[0.2]	[0.1]	[−]
1871*	222,575	6,552	443	222	85
	[96.8]	[2.9]	[0.2]	[0.1]	[−]
1881	216,635	5,568	399	200	32
	[97.2]	[2.5]	[0.2]	[0.1]	[−]
1891	192,884	4,310	361	151	47
	[97.5]	[2.2]	[0.2]	[0.1]	[−]
1901**	187,220	4,402	616	188	123
	[97.23]	[2.29]	[0.32]	[0.10]	[0.06]
1911	177,920	3,544	495	152	113
	[97.64]	[1.95]	[0.27]	[0.06]	[0.06]

*Includes parish of Innishbofin transferred from Leitrim in 1873.
**Includes Galway City.

Galway City					
1861	15,621	837	189	127	193
	[91.9]	[5.0]	[1.2]	[0.8]	[1.1]
1871	18,586	915	172	97	73
	[93.6]	[4.6]	[0.9]	[0.5]	[0.4]
1881	17,453	1,294	250	124	50
	[91.0]	[6.8]	[1.3]	[0.6]	[0.3]
1891	15,480	1,030	267	120	62
	[91.3]	[6.1]	[1.6]	[0.7]	[0.3]

Included in Galway County thereafter.

465

Year	RC	CI	Presb	Method	Others
County Leitrim					
1861	94,006	9,488	338	879	33
	[89.8]	[9.1]	[0.3]	[0.8]	[–]
1871*	85,974	8,385	364	786	53
	[90.0]	[8.8]	[0.3]	[0.8]	[0.1]
1881	81,470	7,735	297	833	37
	[90.2]	[8.6]	[0.3]	[0.9]	[–]
1891	71,098	6,447	246	784	43
	[90.4]	[8.2]	[0.3]	[1.0]	[0.1]
1901	62,860	5,550	218	694	21
	[90.65]	[8.0]	[0.32]	[1.00]	[0.03]
1911	58,159	4,694	186	510	33
	[91.47]	[7.99]	[0.29]	[0.80]	[0.05]

*Excludes parish of Innishbofin transferred to Galway County in 1873.

Year	RC	CI	Presb	Method	Others
County Mayo					
1861	246,583	6,739	961	418	95
	[96.8]	[2.6]	[0.4]	[0.2]	[–]
1871	237,060	6,093	1,079	316	226
	[96.8]	[2.5]	[0.4]	[0.1]	[0.1]
1881	238,262	5,575	925	275	175
	[97.1]	[2.3]	[0.4]	[0.1]	[0.1]
1891	213,602	4,351	722	218	141
	[97.5]	[2.0]	[0.3]	[0.1]	[0.1]
1901	194,504	3,790	591	181	98
	[97.66]	[1.9]	[0.30]	[0.09]	[0.05]
1911	188,069	3,380	515	141	72
	[97.86]	[1.76]	[0.27]	[0.07]	[0.04]
County Rosscommon					
1861	151,047	5,728	277	162	48
	[96.1]	[3.6]	[0.2]	[0.1]	[–]
1871	135,223	4,801	356	149	139
	[96.1]	[3.4]	[0.3]	[0.1]	[0.1]
1881	127,813	4,137	307	165	68
	[96.5]	[3.1]	[0.2]	[0.1]	[0.1]
1891	110,290	3,543	336	128	100
	[96.4]	[3.1]	[0.3]	[0.1]	[0.1]
1901	99,085	2,273	250	100	83
	[97.34]	[2.23]	[0.25]	[0.10]	[0.08]
1911	91,731	1,887	195	64	79
	[97.63]	[2.01]	[0.21]	[0.07]	[0.08]
County Sligo					
1861	112,436	10,438	931	778	262
	[90.1]	[8.4]	[0.7]	[0.6]	[0.2]
1871	104,429	9,185	864	680	335
	[90.4]	[8.0]	[0.7]	[0.6]	[0.3]
1881	101,483	8,213	881	642	359
	[90.9]	[7.4]	[0.8]	[0.6]	[0.3]

466

Year	RC	C of I	Presb	Method	Others
1891	89,015	7,389	691	380	338
	[90.8]	[7.3]	[0.7]	[0.6]	[0.4]
1901	76,146	6,415	662	518	342
	[90.56]	[7.69]	[0.79]	[0.61]	[0.41]
1911	94,413	7,050	254	234	222
	[92.31]	[6.89]	[2.25]	[0.33]	[0.22]

Irish Free State/Éire/Republic of Ireland, 1926–1971

The figures in square brackets are religious denominations as percentages of the population.

Year	RC	C of I	Presb	Method	Jews	Bapt	Others	Total
1926	2,751,269	164,215	32,429	10,663	3,686	717	9,013	220,723
	[92.6]	[5.5]	[1.1]	[0.4]	[0.1]	[–]	[0.3]	[7.4]
1936	2,773,920	145,030	28,067	9,649	3,749	715	7,290	194,500
	[93.4]	[4.9]	[0.9]	[0.3]	[0.1]	[–]	[0.2]	[6.6]
1946	2,786,033	124,829	23,870	8,355	3,907	462	7,651	169,074
	[94.3]	[4.2]	[0.8]	[0.3]	[0.1]	[–]	[0.3]	[5.7]
1961	2,673,473	104,016	18,953	6,676	3,255	481	11,487	144,868
	[94.9]	[3.7]	[0.7]	[0.2]	[0.1]	[–]	[0.4]	[5.1]
1971	2,795,596	97,741	16,054	5,646	2,635	591	59,985	182,652
	[93.87]	[3.28]	[0.54]	[0.19]	[0.09]	[0.02]	[2.01]	[6.13]
1991	3,228,327	82,840	13,199	5,037	1,581	–	38,743	3,525,719

Ulster/Northern Ireland since 1926

Denominations in nine-county Ulster since 1926

The figures in square brackets are religious denominations as percentages of the population. Statistics on religious denominations in 1971 do not include those whose usual addresses were outside Northern Ireland or members of the armed forces. The total enumerated was 1,519,640.

Year	RC	C of I	Presb	Method	Others
1926	665,882	369,009	414,637	51,518	55,606
	[42.78]	[23.71]	[26.64]	[3.31]	[3.57]
1936/7	662,431	370,840	409,140	56,773	60,830
	[42.46]	[23.77]	[26.23]	[3.64]	[3.90]
1961	686,186	360,053	424,918	72,918	98,491
	[41.79]	[21.92]	[25.87]	[4.44]	[6.00]
1971	657,948	348,051	415,623	72,125	233,097
	[38.1]	[20.2]	[24.1]	[4.2]	[13.5]

Denominations in Northern Ireland since 1926

Year	RC	C of I	Presb	Method	Others	Total Protestants
1926	420,428	393,374	338,724	49,554	54,481	836,133
	[33.5]	[31.3]	[27.0]	[3.9]	[4.3]	[66.5]
1937	428,290	390,931	345,474	55,135	59,915	851,455
	[33.5]	[30.5]	[27.0]	[4.3]	[4.7]	[66.5]
1951	471,460	410,215	353,245	66,639	69,362	899,461
	[34.4]	[29.9]	[25.8]	[4.9]	[5.0]	[65.6]
1961	497,547	413,113	344,800	71,865	97,917	927,495
	[34.9]	[29.0]	[24.2]	[5.0]	[6.9]	[65.1]
1971	477,921	405,717	334,318	71,235	230,449	1,041,719
	[31.4]	[26.7]	[22.0]	[4.7]	[15.2]	[68.6]
1981	414,532	281,472	339,818	58,731		
	[28.0]	[19.0]	[22.9]	[4.0]		
1991	605,639	279,280	336,891	59,517		
	[38.4]	[17.7]	[21.4]	[3.8]		

The increase in others in 1971 is mainly explained by the large number of people who refused to state their religion, the final official figures showing that 142,511 or 9.4 per cent of the total population so refused. The remaining 87,938 were composed of many small groups, the largest of which were the Baptists (16,563), the Brethren (16,480), the Congregational Church (10,072) and the Free Presbyterians (7,337).

OCCUPATIONS

Occupations at censuses

Ireland, 1871–1911 (males)

	(in thousands)				
	1871	1881	1891	1901	1911
Public administration[a]	25	27	27	30	32
Armed forces	37	40	38	32	34
Professional occupations and their subordinate services[b]	30	31	31	31	38
Domestic offices and personal services[c]	60	40	41	33	32
Commercial occupations	21	22	28	35	39
Transport and communications	53	48	53	58	62
Agriculture, horticulture and forestry	879	891	834	780	713
Fishing	9	11	11	10	9
Mining and quarrying	4	3	2	3	2
Metal manufacture, machines, implements, vehicles, precious metals, etc.	42	39	42	47	52
Building and construction	50	49	47	54	52
Wood, furniture, fittings and decorations	15	13	12	11	10
Bricks, cement, pottery and glass	1	1	1	1	1
Chemicals, oils, soap, resin, etc.	–	1	2	2	3
Skins, leather, hair and feathers	1	2	2	1	1
Paper, printing, books and stationery	6	7	7	7	8
Textiles	60	48	46	38	37
Clothing	48	43	38	32	30
Food, drink and tobacco	42	46	46	46	43
Gas and water supply	1	1	1	2	2
All others occupied	265	169	150	155	180
Total occupied	1,635	1,572	1,504	1,414	1,387
Total unoccupied	78[e]	961	815	786	805

Ireland, 1871–1911 (females)

	(*in thousands*)				
	1871	*1881*	*1891*	*1901*	*1911*
Public administration[a]	1	1	3	4	3
Armed forces	–	–	–	–	–
Professional occupations and their subordinate services[b]	17	20	23	25	34
Domestic offices and personal services[c]	363	241	226	199	150
Commercial occupations	1	1	2	5	9
Transport and communications	1	1	1	1	1
Agriculture, horticulture and forestry	98	96	91	86	59
Fishing	–	–	–	–	–
Mining and quarrying	–	–	–	–	–
Metal manufacture, machines, implements, vehicles, precious metals, etc.	1	–	1	–	–
Building and construction	–	–	–	–	–
Wood, furniture, fittings and decorations	1	1	1	1	1
Bricks, cement, pottery and glass	–	–	–	–	–
Chemicals, oils, soap, resin, etc.	–	–	–	–	–
Skins, leather, hair and feathers	1	3	1	–	–
Paper, printing, books and stationery	2	3	4	4	4
Textiles	134	82	84	72	68
Clothing	128	118	116	106	66
Food, drink and tobacco	14	13	13	12	10
Gas and water supply	–	–	–	–	–
All others occupied	77	39	28	31	24
Total occupied	1,242[d]	815	641	550	430
Total unoccupied	213[d]	1,827[e]	1,744	1,709	1,768

[a] including naval personnel
[b] including persons engaged in recreational activities but excluding unspecified students
[c] including the catering trades
[d] including wives as occupied
[e] over 16 years old only.

IFS/É/ROI, 1926–1971 (males)

For this and the following table 1951 is recorded twice due to a change in the inclusion of proprietors, managers and foremen in the industrial categories.

	(*in thousands*)						
	1926	*1936*	*1946*	*1951*	*1951*	*1961*	*1971*
Agriculture, horticulture and forestry	550	537	512	445	445	348	261
Fishing	6	4	4	3	3	2	3
Mining and quarrying	3	3	3	4	4	6	5
Treatment of non-metalliferous mining products other than coal	1	1	1	2	1[b]	1[b]	2[b]
Gas, coke and chemical manufacture	2	1	1	1	–	1	2
Metal manufacture, engineering and allied trades	28	27	28	34	40	35	49
Electrical goods	3	4	5	8	7	9	18
Textiles	3	3	4	5	4	5	3
Leatherworking	8	9	8	9	8	6	4
Clothing other than footwear	8	8	7	8	7	5	9
Food, drink and tobacco	18	11	13	13	10	11	15
Woodworking	24	24	21	25	25	17	22
Paper and printing	4	4	4	5	4	5	6
Other manufactures	2	2	2	2	2	3	6
Building	48	62	54	75	71	49	16
Painting and decorating	5	5	5	7	6	7	8
Transport and communications	64	67	58	68	65	55	58
Commercial, finance and insurance occupations (excluding clerical staff)	57	63	56	73	74	66	73
Public administration	18	19	21	28	–	–	–
Armed forces	15	7	14	8	8	9	9
Drivers of stationary engines, cranes, etc.	2	2	3	4	4	5	8
Warehousemen, storekeepers, packers, bottlers, etc.	5	11	6	9	9	12	15
Professional and technical occupations	20	29	34	36	37	38	53
Services, sport, recreation	22	24	26	19	27	25	31
Clerical workers	17	18	20	22	30	32	36
Administrative, executive, management, etc.	–	–	–	–	12	12	17
Foremen and supervisors of manual workers	–	–	–	–	6	7	13
Others occupied	26	47	55	46	46	49	92
Total population aged 14 and over[a]	1,157[a]	1,133	1,102	1,097	1,097	997	1,050
Total unoccupied aged 14 and over	193[a]	146	138	150	150	176	218

IFS/É/ROI, 1926–1971 (females)

	(*in thousands*)						
	1926	*1936*	*1946*	*1951*	*1951*	*1961*	*1971*
Agriculture, horticulture and forestry	112	107	82	68	68	42	25
Fishing	–	–	–	–	–	–	–
Mining and quarrying	–	–	–	–	–	–	–
Treatment of non-metalliferous mining products other than coal	–	–	–	–	–	–	–
Gas, coke and chemical manufacture	–	–	–	–	–	–	–
Metal manufacture, engineering and allied trades	–	–	1	1	1	1	1
Electrical goods	–	–	–	–	–	1	3
Textiles	5	5	5	8	8	9	25
Leatherworking	1	2	2	3	3	3	3
Clothing other than footwear	18	21	19	22	22	16	23
Food, drink and tobacco	5	4	4	6	6	5	5
Woodworking	1	1	1	–	–	–	–
Paper and printing	2	2	2	3	3	3	3
Other manufactures	–	1	1	1	1	2	2
Building	–	–	–	–	–	–	–
Painting and decorating	–	–	–	–	–	–	–
Transport and communications	1	1	1	5	4	2	4
Commercial, finance and insurance occupations (excluding clerical staff)	28	31	32	40	40	39	36
Public administration	4	4	8	5	–	–	–
Armed forces	–	–	–	–	–	–	–
Drivers of stationary engines, cranes, etc.	–	–	–	–	–	–	–
Warehousemen, storekeepers, packers, bottlers, etc.	2	4	5	7	7	9	8
Professional and technical occupations	30	33	37	39	39	41	51
Services, sport, recreation	110	110	103	80	79	62	50
Clerical workers	13	19	24	31	35	46	67
Administrative, executive, management, etc.	–	–	–	–	2	1	1
Foremen and supervisors of manual workers	–	–	–	–	1	1	1
Others occupied	1	4	8	4	4	3	2
Total population aged 14 and over[a]	1,127	1,072	1,081	1,062	1,062	1,001	1,056
Total unoccupied aged 14 and over	783	721	746	737	737	715	768

[a] aged 12 and over in 1926
[b] glass and ceramics only.

IFS/É/ROI, 1981–1991 (males)

	(*in thousands*)	
	1981	*1991*
Agriculture and forestry workers and fishermen	186	149
Mining, quarrying and turf	5	3
Electrical and electronics	32	31
Engineering and related trades	66	63
Woodworkers	26	26
Leather and leather substitute	3	1
Textile and clothing	12	7
Food, beverage and tobacco	21	18
Paper and printing	7	7
Workers in other products	16	14
Building and construction	25	23
Printers and decorators	9	10
Operators of cranes, etc.	12	10
Foremen and supervisors	17	9
Transport and communication	62	58
Warehouse and despatch clerks, packers and bottlers	18	18
Clerical	39	43
Commerce, insurance and finance	89	99
Service workers	42	54
Labourers and unskilled	73	77
Administrative, executive and managerial	31	41
Professional and technical	79	91
Armed forces	14	11
Employed but not stated	15	25
Total population aged 15 and over	1,194	1,271
Total unoccupied aged 15 and over	281	359

Source: Central Statistics Office, Chapter 2.

IFS/É/ROI, 1981–1991 (females)

Only when female employment is below 1,000 is the figure given as a decimal fraction.

	(*in thousands*)	
	1981	*1991*
Agriculture and forestry workers and fishermen	12	16
Mining, quarrying and turf	0.01	0.1
Electrical and electronics	7	9
Engineering and related trades	4	4
Woodworkers	0.3	0.4

473

	(*in thousands*)	
	1981	*1991*
Leather and leather substitute	2	0.8
Textile and clothing	18	17
Food, beverage and tobacco	6	6
Paper and printing	3	3
Workers in other products	4	6
Building and construction	0.02	0.09
Printers and decorators	0.07	0.4
Operators of cranes, etc.	0.004	0.04
Foremen and supervisors	1	1
Transport and communication	7	4
Warehouse and despatch clerks, packers and bottlers	5	5
Clerical	101	122
Commerce, insurance and finance	43	61
Service workers	52	71
Labourers and unskilled	0.6	7
Administrative, executive and managerial	4	12
Professional and technical	75	100
Armed forces	0.016	0.1
Employed but not stated		13
Total population aged 15 and over		1,315
Total unoccupied aged 15 and over		842

Source: CSO.

Persons aged 15 years and over in employment classified by NACE economic sector, 1997–2002

	(*in thousands*)			
Economic sector	*1997*	*1999*	*2001*	*2002*
Broad economic sector				
Agriculture	141.5	135.9	120.1	120.7
Industry	398.8	450.9	497.3	484.0
Services	839.6	1,004.3	1,099.3	1,145.1
Economic sector (NACE Revd 1)				
Males				
Agriculture, forestry and fishing	125.5	120.4	107.2	108.4
Other production industries	200.4	215.7	222.3	213.1
Construction	104.4	135.9	172.0	172.3
Wholesale and retail trade	108.8	118.8	130.7	125.0
Hotels and restaurants	32.7	41.8	43.1	44.7
Transport, storage and communication	51.4	72.0	80.9	81.4

Economic sector	(in thousands)			
	1997	1999	2001	2002
Financial and other business services	71.4	99.2	110.5	114.0
Public administration and defence	45.0	45.1	45.4	48.2
Education	33.4	32.6	32.3	33.8
Health	27.1	24.9	27.4	31.2
Other services	40.4	41.5	42.1	45.1
TOTAL	840.3	947.3	1,013.9	1,017.2
Females				
Agriculture, forestry and fishing	16.1	15.5	12.9	12.4
Other production industries	88.1	93.2	94.8	89.8
Construction	6.0	6.1	8.2	8.8
Wholesale and retail trade	84.5	105.1	117.1	120.8
Hotels and restaurants	43.7	60.8	61.6	60.1
Transport, storage and communication	13.6	23.9	29.5	28.8
Financial and other business services	63.3	96.6	107.8	115.1
Public administration and defence	27.2	29.3	35.0	41.0
Education	59.8	67.9	70.4	76.2
Health	92.6	95.1	115.1	125.8
Other services	44.8	50.3	50.1	53.9
TOTAL	539.7	643.9	702.5	732.7
All persons				
Agriculture, forestry and fishing	141.5	135.9	120.1	120.7
Other production industries	288.5	308.9	317.1	302.9
Construction	110.4	142.1	180.2	181.1
Wholesale and retail trade	193.3	223.3	247.8	245.9
Hotels and restaurants	76.4	102.6	104.8	104.8
Transport, storage and communication	65.0	96.0	110.4	110.2
Financial and other business services	134.7	195.8	218.3	229.1
Public administration and defence	77.2	74.4	80.4	89.2
Education	93.2	100.5	102.7	110.0
Health	119.7	119.9	142.6	157.0
Other services	85.1	91.8	92.3	99.0
TOTAL	1,379.9	1,591.1	1,716.5	1,749.9

Source: CSO.

Heads of major professional bodies

Presidents of the Royal College of Physicians of Ireland

Founded 1667; assumed present title in 1890; previously the King and Queen's College of Physicians in Ireland. The College is a wide-ranging fellowship of medical specialists. Presidential term begins on St Luke's Day, 18 October, each year.

475

Appointed

1800	Patrick Plunkett
1801	Edward Hill
1802	William Harvey
1803	Francis Hopkins
1804	Alexander Pellisier
1805	James Cleghorn
1807	Daniel Mills
1808	Edward Hill
1809	William Harvey
1810	Francis Hopkins
1811	James Cleghorn
1812	Thomas Herbert Orpen
1813	Edward Hill
1814	William Harvey
1815	Francis Hopkins
1816	James Cleghorn
1817	Anthony Gilholy
1818	Thomas Herbert Orpen
1819	Hugh Ferguson
1820	James Callenan
1821	George Francis Todderick
1822	Robert Bredin
1823	Samuel Litton
1824	John O'Brien
1825	James John Leary (resigned 28 Jan.)
1826	William Brooke (elected 20 Feb.; re-elected St Luke's Day)
1827	Hugh Ferguson
1828	Charles Richard A. Lendrick
(Biennial presidency)	
1829	Samuel Litton
1831	Hugh Ferguson
1834	Jonathan Osborne
1836	Charles Philip Croker
1838	George Alexander Kennedy
1841	Sir Henry Marsh, Bart.
1843	Robert James Graves
1845	Sir Henry Marsh
1847	Robert Collins
1849	William Stokes
1851	William Fetherston-Haugh Montgomery
1853	Evory Kennedy
1855	John Mollan
1857	Sir Henry Marsh
1859	Dominic John Corrigan
1864	Thomas Edward Beatty

Appointed

1866	William Stokes
1867	Fleetwood Churchill
1869	John Thomas Banks
1871	Alfred Hudson
1873	James Foulis Duncan
1875	Samuel Gordon
1878	Henry Haswell Head
1880	George Johnston
1882	William Moore
1884	Francis Richard Cruise
1886	James Little
1888	Lombe Atthill
1890	John Magee Finny
1892	Walter George Smith
1895	Thomas Wrigley Grimshaw
1896	Sir George Duffey
1898	John William Moore
1900	Sir Christopher J. Nixon
1902	Sir Arthur Vernon Macan
1904	Sir William Josiah Smyly
1906	Joseph Michael Redmond
1908	Andrew John Horne
1910	J. Hawtrey Benson
1912	Charles Edward FitzGerald
1914	Ephraim MacDowel Cosgrave
1916	Joseph Francis O'Carroll
1919	Sir James Craig
1922	Michael Francis Cox
1924	Sir William John Thompson
1925	Henry Thomas Wilson
(triennial presidency)	
1927	William Arthur Winter
1930	Thomas Gilman Moorhead
1933	Francis Carmichael Purser (died in office; Moorhead acted as President until St Luke's Day)
1934	John Agar Matson
1937	William Boxswell
1940	Robert James Rowlette
1943	William Geoffrey Harvey
1946	Bethel Solomons
1949	Leonard Abrahamson
1952	Edward Thomas Freeman
1956	Francis Joseph O'Connell
1959	Patrick Theodore Joseph O'Farrell
1960	Robert Elsworth Steen

Appointed

1963	Robert Brian Pringle
1966	Alan Herbert Thompson
1969	David Michael Mitchell
1972	William John Edward Jessop
1974	Bryan Gerard Alton
1977	Alan Proctor Grant CBE
1980	Peter Dermot Joseph Holland
1983	John Gilbert Kirker
1986	Michael Drury (died in office)
1989	Ciaran Barry
1991	Stephen Doyle
1994	Stanley Roberts
1997	Joseph Brian Keogh

Presidents of the Royal College of Surgeons in Ireland

Founded 1784.

Appointed

1801	James Rivers
1802	Abraham Colles
1803	Solomon Richards
1804	Francis M'Evoy
1805	Robert Hamilton
1806	Gerard Macklin
1807	Francis M'Evoy
1808	Solomon Richards
1809	Richard Dease
1810	John Armstrong Garnett
1811	Philip Crampton
1812	John Creighton
1813	Richard Carmichael
1814	Cusack Roney
1815	Samuel Wilmot
1816	Robert Moore Pelle
1817	Andrew Johnston
1818	Solomon Richards
1819	Thomas Hewson
1820	Philip Crampton
1821	Charles Hawkes Todd
1822	James Henthorn
1823	John Kirby
1824	John Creighton
1825	Alexander Read
1826	Richard Carmichael
1827	James William Cusack

Appointed

1828	Cusack Roney
1829	William Auchinleck
1830	Abraham Colles
1831	Rawdon MacNamara
1832	Samuel Wilmot
1833	James Kerin
1834	John Kirby
1835	Alexander Read
1836	Francis White
1837	Arthur Jacob
1838	William Henry Porter
1839	Maurice Collis
1840	Robert Adams
1841	Thomas Rumley
1842	William Tagert
1843	James O'Beirne
1844	Sir Philip Crampton, bt
1845	Richard Carmichael
1846	Samuel Wilmot
1847	James William Cusack
1848	Robert Harrison
1849	Andrew Ellis
1850	Thomas Edward Beatty
1851	Leonard Trant
1852	Edward Hutton
1853	William Hargrave
1854	Charles Benson
1855	Sir Philip Crampton, bt
1856	Robert Carlisle Williams
1857	Hans Irvine
1858	James William Cusack
1859	Christopher Fleming
1860	Robert Adams
1861	William Jameson
1862	Thomas Lewis Mackesy
1863	William Colles
1864	Arthur Jacob
1865	Samuel George Wilmot
1866	Richard George Herbert Butcher
1867	Robert Adams
1868	George Hornidge Porter
1869	Rawdon MacNamara (secundus)
1870	Albert Jasper Walsh
1871	James Henry Wharton
1872	Frederick Kirkpatrick

479

Appointed

1873	John Denham
1874	Jolliffe Tufnell
1875	Edward Hamilton
1876	George Hugh Kidd
1877	Robert M'Donnell
1878	Philip Crampton Smyle
1879	Edward Dillon Mapother
1880	Alfred H. M'Clintock
1881	Samuel Chaplin
1882	John Kellock Barton
1883	William Ireland Wheeler
1884	Edward Hallaran Bennet
1885	Sir Charles Alexander Caeron
1886	Sir William Stokes
1887	Anthony Hagerty Corley
1888	Henry Fitzgibbon
1889	Austin Meldon

(Biennial presidency)

1890	Henry Gray Croly
1892	Edward Hamilton
1894	Sir William Thornley Stoker
1896	Sir William Thomson
1898	Robert LaFayette Swan
1900	Sir Thomas Myles
1902	Sir Lambert Hepenstall Ormsby
1904	Sir Arthur Chance
1906	Sir Henry Rosborough Swanzy
1908	Sir John Lentaigne
1910	Sir Robert Henry Woods
1912	Richard Dancer Purefoy
1914	Sir Frederick Conway Dwyer
1916	Sir William Taylor
1918	John Benjamin Story
1920	Edward H. Taylor
1922	Sir William Ireland De Courcey Wheeler
1924	R. Charles B. Maunsell
1926	Andrew Fullerton
1928	Thomas E. Gordon (died in office, 24 July 1929)
1930	Richard Atkinson Stoney
1932	Frank Crawley
1934	Seton Pringle
1936	Adams Andrew McConnell
1938	William Doolin
1940	Henry Stokes
1942	Thomas Ottiwell Graham

480

Appointed

1944	Edward Leo Sheridan
1946	Frederick Gill
1948	Henry Sords Meade
1950	William Pearson
1952	Michael Plunkett Burke
1954	Sir Ian Fraser
1956	Anthony Burton Clery
1958	Thomas George Wilson
1961	Nigel Alexander Kinnear
1963	Terence Millin
1966	Edward Neale McDermott
1968	Douglas Montgomery
1970	John Paul Lanigan
1972	Francis Arthur Joseph Mary Duff
1974	John McAuliffe Curtin
1976	Stanley Thomas McCollum
1978	Keith Shaw
1980	J. A. O'Connell

Registrars of the College (Clerk and Housekeeper until 1832)

1816	Joesph Humphreys
1819	Peter Ruttledge Courtney
1832	Cornelius O'Keefe
1849	James W. Boyton
1856	John Brennan
1889	George Francis Blake
1911	Alfred Miller
1938	William Norman Rae
1962	Harry O'Flanagan
1980	William Arthur Lysagt MacGowan

Treasurers of the Honourable Society of King's Inns, 1804–1979

The Society of King's Inns is the professional body for barristers. It was founded in 1541 during the reign of Henry VIII. The formal records of King's Inns, the *Black Book*, date from 1607. Initially a voluntary society, by 1634 membership was compulsory for barristers wishing to practise in the courts. From 1690 until 1792 Catholics were effectively excluded from practice by the penal laws. The running of the Inn was invested in its most senior officer, the Treasurer, until 1 October 1979 when, under new rules, the management of the Inn, other than certain reserved functions, was vested in a new Council.

Key: LCJ Lord Chief Justice   QC Queen's Counsel
          MR Master of the Rolls   SC Senior Counsel
          KC King's Counsel

Appointed

1804	Viscount Avonmore
1805	William Downes
1806	Lord Norbury
1807	S. O'Grady
1809	Mr Justice Day
1811	Mr Justice Fox
1813	W. C. Smith
1814	Charles Osborne
1815	Baron McCleland
1816	Judge Mayne
1817	Judge Fletcher
1818	Judge Moore
1819	Judge Johnson
1820	Judge Jebb
1822	Mr Justice Burton
1823	Baron Pennefather
1824	Charles Kendal Bushe, LCJ
1825	Mr Justice Vandeleur
1826	Mr Justice Torrens
1827	William MacMahon, MR
1828	Lord Plunkett
1830	S. O'Grady
1831	Sir William Smith, bt
1832	Baron Foster
1833	John Doherty
1834	Henry Joy
1835	Mr Justice Burton
1837	Mr Justice Torrens
1838	Baron Foster
1839	Judge Crampton
1840	Judge Perrin
1842	Baron Richards
1843	Nicholas Ball
1845	Thomas Lefroy
1846	Edward Pennefather, LCJ
1847	Francis Blackburn, LCJ
1848	T. B. C. Smith, MR
1849	David R. Pigot
1850	Judge Moore
1851	James Henry Monahan, LCJ of Common Pleas
1852	The Lord Chancellor
1853	Baron Greene
1854	No Treasurer
1855	Thomas Lefroy
1856	T. B. C. Smith, MR

Appointed

1858	James Henry Monahan, LCJ of Common Pleas
1859	Mr Justice Christian
1860	Mr Justice O'Brien
1861	Mr Justice Hayes
1862	Baron Fitzgerald
1864	John David Fitzgerald
1866	Baron Deasy
1866	Mr Justice O'Hagan
1867	James Whiteside, LCJ
1868	The Lord Chancellor
1870	Mr Justice Lawson
1871	George Battersby, QC
1872	Gerald FitzGibbon
1873	Baron Dowse
1874	Mr Justice Morris
1875	The Judge of the Court of Probate
1876	Hewitt Poole Jellett
1877	Mr Justice Barry
1878	James Murphy
1879	George Augustus Chichester May
1880	Edward Pennefather, QC
1881	Mr Justice Harrison
1882	Mr Sergeant Sherlock
1883	Judge Townsend
1884	Thomas de Moleyns, QC
1885	Andrew M. Porter, MR
1886	Piers F. White, QC
1887	The Lord Chief Baron of the Exchequer
1888	Arthur Stanley Jackson, QC
1889	Lord Justice Fitzgibbon
1890	John Richardson, QC
1891	Mr Justice Holmes
1892	Samuel Walker
1893	Judge Miller
1894	Charles Hare Hemphill, QC, Solicitor-General
1895	Mr Justice Johnson
1896	William Bennett Campion, QC
1897	Mr Justice O'Brien
1898	The MacDermot, QC
1899	Mr Justice Andrews
1900	John H. Twigg, QC
1901	Mr Justice Gibson
1902	Stephen Ronan
1903	Mr Justice Boyd
1904	Mr Sergeant Dodd

Appointed

1905	Mr Justice Madden
1906	James H. M. Campbell, KC, MP
1907	Mr Justice Kenny
1908	Charles L. Matheson, KC
1909	Mr Justice Wright
1910	Charles A. O'Connor, KC, Solicitor-General
1911	Mr Justice Barton
1912	John Gordon, KC
1913	Mr Justice Wylie
1914	Denis Henry, KC
1915	Gerald FitzGerald
1916	Arthur W. Samuels, KC
1917	Thomas Lopdell O'Shaughnessy
1918	Godfrey Fetherstonhaugh, KC
1919	Mr Justice Moore
1920	Robert F. Harrison
1921	Mr Justice Powell
1922	William Morgan Jellett, KC, MP
1923	Thomas Francis Molony, LCJ
1924	Samuel L. Brown, KC
1925	Mr Justice FitzGibbon
1926	Alexander F. Blood, KC
1927	Mr Justice Hanna
1928	Garrett William Walker
1929	Mr Justice Wylie
1930	Hewitt R. Poole
1931	Mr Justice Sullivan, President of the High Court
1932	Frederick W. Price
1933	Frederick W. Price
1934	Mr Justice Meredith
1935	Ernest J. Phelps, SC
1936	Mr Justice Johnson
1937	Frederick F. Denning
1938	Mr Justice Murnaghan
1939	A. Kingsbury Overend, KC
1940	Mr Justice O'Byrne
1941	Thomas S. McCann, KC
1942	Conor A. Maguire, President of the High Court
1943	Patrick Lynch, KC
1944	Judge Geoghegan
1945	J. M. FitzGerald, SC
1946	Mr Justice Davitt
1947	J. A. Costello
1948	Judge Gavin Duffy
1949	R. G. L. Leonard, KC

Appointed

1950	Mr Justice Shannon
1951	Vincent Rice, SC
1952	Mr Justice Lavery
1953	Frank FitzGibbon, QC
1954	Mr Justice M. C. Maguire
1955	Mr Carson
1956	Mr Justice Haugh
1957	P. McCarthy
1958	Mr Justice Kingsmill Moore
1959	Henry J. Molony
1960	Mr Justice O'Daly
1961	Richard McGonigal, SC
1962	Mr Justice Budd
1963	Thomas F. Bacon
1964	Mr Justice Murnaghan
1965	Mr Campbell
1966	Mr Justice McLoughlin
1967	Denis Pringle
1968	Mr Justice FitzGerald
1969	C. Micks
1970	Mr Justice Teevan
1971	T. K. Liston, SC
1972	Mr Justice O'Caoimh
1973	Thomas B. Hannin
1974	Mr Justice Walsh
1975	Ernest M. Wood
1976	Mr Justice Kenny
1977	Oliver D. Gogarty, SC
1978	Mr Justice Henchy
1979	Thomas Vincent Davy, SC

Source: Library of the Honourable Society of King's Inns.

Presidents of the Law Society of Ireland, 1842–2003

The Law Society of Ireland is the professional body for solicitors. It dates back to 1773 when a statute was enacted to regulate the moral and educational qualifications of solicitors seeking admission as attorneys. This in turn led to the formation of the Society of Attorneys in 1774 and then the Law Club of Ireland in 1791. This became the Law Society of Ireland in 1830. In 1841 the name Society of Attorneys and Solicitors was adopted and its first Royal Charter was obtained from Queen Victoria in 1852. The organisation formally adopted the title 'Incorporated Law Society of Ireland' in 1888, the event being formally noted by a supplemental charter, again granted by Queen Victoria.

	Term of office
Josias Dunn	1842–48
William Goddard	1848–60
Sir Richard J. T. Orpen	1860–76
Edward Reeves	1876
William Roche	1876–7
Sir William Findlater	1877–8
William Read	1878–9
Henry A. Dillon	1879–80
John H. Nunn	1880–1
Henry J. P. West	1881–2
Henry T. Dix	1882–3
William D'Alton	1883–4
John Galloway	1884–5
Henry L. Keily	1885–6
Sir Patrick Maxwell	1886–7
Richard S. Reeves	1887–8
John MacSheehy	1888–9
W. Burroughs Stanley	1889–90
Francis R. M. Crozier	1890–1
Thomas C. Franks	1891–2
Edward Fitzgerald	1892–3
John Alexander French	1893–4
Trevor T. L. Overend	1894–5
Sir William Fry	1895–6
Sir William Findlater	1896–7
William Henry Dunne	1897–8
Hugh Stuart Moore	1898–9
Richard S. Reeves	1899–1900
James Goff	1900–1
Sir George Roche*	
Charles A. Stanuell	1901–2
Sir Augustine F. Baker	1902–3
Robert Keating Clay*	
Edward D. MacLaughlin*	
Edward D. MacLaughlin	1904–5
Sir John P. Lynch	1905–6
William S. Hayes	1906–7
George H. Lyster	1907–8
William J. Shannon	1908–9
Richard A. MacNamara	1909–10
Frederick W. Meredith	1910–11
Gerald Byrne	1911–12
James Henry	1912–13
Henry J. Synott	1913–14
Arthur E. Bradley	1914–15

	Term of office
Charles St George Orpen	1915–16
John W. Richards	1916–17
William V. Seddall	1917–18
Richard Blair White	1918–19
Robert G. Warren	1919–20
Charles G. Gamble	1920–1
Patrick J. Brady	1921–2
Joseph E. MacDermott	1922–3
James Moore	1923–4
Arthur H. S. Orpen	1924–5
Thomas G. Quirke	1925–6
William T. Sheridan	1926–7
Basil Thompson	1927–8
Edward H. Burne	1928–9
Peter Seales	1929–30
Alexander D. Orr	1930–1
Laurence J. Ryan	1931–2
W. Gordon Bradley	1932–3
James J. Lynch	1933–4
Charles Laverty	1934–5
Michael E. Knight	1935–6
John J. Duggan	1936–7
Thomas W. Delaney	1937–8
Daniel J. Reilly	1938–9
Henry P. Mayne	1939–40
J. Travers Wolfe	1940–1
G. Acheson Overend	1941–2
John B. Hamill	1942–3
Louis E. O'Dea	1943–4
Patrick F. O'Reilly	1944–5
Daniel O'Connell	1945–6
H. St J. Blake	1946–7
Seán Ó hUadhaigh	1947–8
Patrick R. Boyd	1948–9
William J. Norman	1949–50
Roger Green	1950–1
Arthur Cox	1951–2
James R. Quirke	1952–3
Joseph Barrett	1953–4
Thomas A. O'Reilly	1954–5
Dermot P. Shaw	1955–6
Niall S. Gaffney	1956–7
John Carrigan	1957–8
John R. Halpin	1958–9
John J. Nash	1959–60
Ralph J. Walker	1960–1

	Term of office
George G. Overend	1961–2
Francis J. Lanigan	1962–3
Desmond J. Collins	1963–4
John Maher	1964–5
Robert McD. Taylor	1965–6
Patrick O'Donnell, TD	1966–7
Patrick Noonan	1967–8
Eunan McCarron	1968–9
James R. C. Green	1969–70
Brendan A. McGrath	1970–1
James W. O'Donovan	1971–2
Thomas V. O'Connor	1972–3
Peter D. M. Prentice	1973–4
William A. Osborne	1974–5
Patrick C. Moore	1975–6
Bruce St John Blake	1976–7
Joseph L. Dundon	1977–8
Gerald Hickey	1978–9
Walter Beatty	1979–80
Moya Quinlan	1980–1
Brendan W. Allen	1981–2
Michael P. Houlihan	1982–3
Frank O'Donnell	1983–4
Anthony E. Collins	1984–5
Laurence Cullen	1985–6
David R. Pigot	1986–7
Thomas D. Shaw	1987–8
Maurice R. Curran	1988–9
Ernest Margetson	1989–90
Donal G. Binchy	1990–1
Adrian P. Bourke	1991–2
Raymond T. Monahan	1992–3
Michael V. O'Mahony	1993–4
Patrick A. Glynn	1994–5
Andrew F. Smyth	1995–6
Francis D. Daly	1996–7
Laurence K. Shields	1997–8
Patrick O'Connor	1998–9
Anthony H. Ensor	1999–2000
Ward McEllin	2000–1
Elma Lynch	2001–2
Geraldine M. Clarke	2002–3

Note: *Served during the planned term of the previous incumbent.
Source: Eamonn G. Hall and Daire Hogan (eds), *The Law Society of Ireland, 1852–2002: Portrait of a Profession* (Dublin, 2002), appendix 2.

POPULATION AND EMIGRATION

Ireland

Population of Ireland

Population	Total	% increase/decrease
1800	3,800,000	
1813	5,937,836	
1821	6,801,827	
1831	7,767,401	+14.19
1841	8,175,124	+5.25
1851	6,663,385	−19.85
1861	5,798,967	−11.50
1871	5,412,377	−6.67
1881	5,174,836	−4.39
1891	4,704,750	−9.08
1901	4,458,775	−5.23
1911	4,390,219	−1.54

	IFS/É/ROI	NI	Total
1926	2,971,992	1,256,561	4,228,553
1936	2,968,420	(1937) 1,279,745	4,248,165
1946	2,955,107		
1947	2,960,593	1,370,921	4,331,514
1948	2,818,341	1,425,042	4,243,383
1949	2,884,002	1,484,775	4,368,777
1950	2,978,248	1,536,065	4,514,313
1951	3,368,217		
1952	3,443,405	1,532,196*	4,975,601
1953	3,540,643		
1991	3,525,719	1,577,836	5,103,555
1996	3,626,087	−	−
2002	3,917,300	−	−

*Arising from difficulties during the enumeration stages of the 1981 census a number of house-
holds were not enumerated. These figures contain the estimated element of non-enumeration.
Source: CSO (1998–9), p. 26, table 2.1; and p. 374, table 2; and W. E. Vaughan and A. J.
Fitzpatrick (eds), *Irish Historical Statistics: Population, 1821–1971* (Dublin, 1978), p.3.

Population in the provinces (in thousands)

	Leinster	*Munster*
1821	1,757.7	1,935.6
1831	1,909.7	2,227.2
1841	1,973.7	2,396.2
1851	1,672.7	1,857.7
1861	1,457.6	1,513.6
1871	1,339.5	1,393.5
1881	1,279.0	1,331.1
1891	1,187.8	1,172.4
1901	1,152.8	1,076.9
1911	1,162.0	1,035.5
1926	1,149.1	969.9
1936	1,220.4	942.3
1946	1,281.1	917.3
1951	1,336.6	898.9
1956	1,338.9	877.2
1961	1,332.1	849.2
1966	1,414.4	859.3
1971	1,498.1	882.0
1979	1,743.9	979.8
1981	1,790.5	998.3
1986	1,852.6	1,020.6
1991	1,860.9	1,009.5
1996	1,924.7	1,033.9
2002	2,105.4	1,101.3

	Ulster	*Connacht*
1821	1,998.5	1,110.2
1831	2,286.6	1,343.9
1841	2,386.4	1,418.9
1851	2,011.9	1,010.0
1861	1,914.2	913.1
1871	1,833.2	846.2
1881	1,743.1	821.7
1891	1,619.8	724.8
1901	1,582.8	646.9
1911	1,581.7	611.0
1926	300.1*	552.9
1936	280.3	525.5
1946	263.9	492.8
1951	253.3	471.9
1956	235.9	446.2
1961	217.5	419.5

	Ulster	Connacht
1966	208.3	402.0
1971	207.2	390.9
1979	226.0	418.5
1981	230.2	424.4
1986	236.0	431.4
1991	232.2	423.0
1996	234.3	433.2
2002	246.6	464.1

* From 1926 the census details for Ulster exclude the population of Northern Ireland.
Source: CSO.

Population of the six largest cities, 1813–1911

	Dublin	Belfast	Cork	Waterford	Galway	Londonderry
1813	176,610	64,394	25,467	24,684		
1821	185,881	37,277	100,658	28,679	27,775	9,313
1831	204,155	53,287	107,016	28,821	33,120	19,620
1841	232,726	75,308	80,720	23,216	17,275	15,196
1851	246,679	97,784	82,625	22,979	20,055	19,727
1861	246,465	119,393	79,594	22,869	16,448	20,519
1871	246,326	174,412	78,642	23,349	15,597	25,242
1881	249,602	208,122	80,124	22,457	15,471	29,162
1891	245,001	255,950	75,345	20,852	13,800	33,200
1901	290,638	349,180	76,122	26,769	13,426	39,892
1911	304,802	386,947	76,673	27,464	13,225	40,780

Urban population, percentage of total by province, 1841–1911

	Leinster	Munster	Ulster	Connacht	Total
1841	22.43	16.15	9.46	5.65	13.89
1851	26.88	18.48	12.60	6.89	17.03
1861	31.83	21.00	14.46	7.02	19.36
1871	36.00	21.88	19.29	7.16	22.20
1881	38.38	21.97	22.91	7.66	24.07
1891	40.07	22.44	27.62	7.31	26.44
1901	44.47	25.37	34.76	7.59	31.06
1911	47.25	25.58	38.38	8.13	33.50

Source: Vaughan and Fitzpatrick, *Irish Historical Statistics: Population, 1821–1971* (Dublin, 1978) pp. 28–41.

491

Marriages, 1830–1920

		Per thousand of population
1830	41,840	
1831	41,223	
1832	41,899	
1833	42,990	
1834	46,007	
1835	46,751	
1836	44,283	
1837	42,984	
1838	48,342	
1839	46,707	
1840	40,004	
1841	38,868	
1842	33,015	
1843	33,515	
1844	34,385	
1845	36,323	
1846	34,433	
1847	25,906	
1848	29,112	
1849	29,304	
1850	30,666	
1864	27,406	4.86
1865	30,802	5.51
1866	30,121	5.45
1867	29,742	5.42
1868	27,699	5.07
1869	26,277	5.01
1870	28,667	5.29
1871	28,960	5.37
1872	26,943	5.02
1873	25,730	4.82
1874	24,481	4.61
1875	24,037	4.53
1876	26,388	4.96
1877	24,722	4.63
1878	25,284	4.73
1879	23,254	4.34
1880	20,363	3.92
1881	21,826	4.24
1882	22,029	4.32
1883	21,368	4.25
1884	22,585	4.54
1885	21,177	4.29
1886	20,594	4.20
1887	20,945	4.31
1888	20,060	4.18

1889	21,521	4.52
1890	20,990	4.45
1891	21,475	4.59
1892	21,530	4.65
1893	21,714	4.71
1894	21,602	4.71
1895	23,120	5.07
1896	23,055	5.08
1897	22,891	5.05
1898	22,580	5.00
1899	22,311	4.96
1900	21,330	4.77
1901	22,564	5.08
1902	22,949	5.18
1903	22,992	5.21
1904	22,961	5.21
1905	23,078	5.25
1906	22,662	5.16
1907	22,509	5.14
1908	22,734	5.19
1909	22,650	5.17
1910	22,112	5.05
1911	23,473	5.37
1912	23,283	5.31
1913	22,266	5.08
1914	23,695	5.41
1915	24,154	5.57
1916	22,245	5.09
1917	21,073	4.81
1918	22,570	5.13
1919	27,193	6.09
1920	26,826	5.98

Source: Vaughan and Fitzpatrick, *Irish Historical Statistics*, pp. 242, 246.

Number of marriages registered and average annual marriage rate per 1,000 population for each intercensal period since 1881

| Period | IFS/É/OI | | Year | NI | |
	No. of marriages	Rate		No. of marriages	Rate
1881–91	145,976	4.0			
1891–1901	148,134	4.4			
1901–11	153,674	4.8			
1911–26	230,525	5.0			
1926–36	136,699	4.6			
1936–46	159,426	5.4			
1946–51	80,868	5.5			
1951–6	79,541	5.4			

Period	IFS/É/OI No. of marriages	Rate	Year	NI No. of marriages	Rate
1956–61	76,669	5.4			
1961–6	80,754	5.7			
1966–71	95,662	6.5			
1971–9	171,705	6.8			
1979–81	42,728	6.3			
1981–6	95,648	5.5			
1986–91	91,141	5.2			
1991–6	82,804	4.6	1991	9,221	5.8
			1992	9,392	5.8
			1993	9,045	5.5
			1994	8,683	5.3
			1995	8,576	5.2
			1996	8,297	5.0

Source: CSO.

Births, 1832–1920

1832	245,624			
1833	265,462			
1834	265,950			
1835	265,111			
1836	262,957			
1837	265,305			
1838	259,533			
1839	268,376			
1840	249,538			
	Males	Females	Total	Births per 1,000 population
1864	70,075	66,339	136,414	24.2
1865	74,386	70,584	144,970	25.9
1866	75,095	70,995	146,090	26.5
1867	74,332	70,056	144,388	26.3
1868	75,172	70,879	146,051	26.7
1869	74,921	70,738	145,659	26.7
1870	76,792	73,054	149,846	27.7
1871	77,314	74,041	151,355	28.1
1872	76,904	72,374	149,278	27.8
1873	74,229	70,148	144,377	27.1
1874	72,516	68,772	141,288	26.6
1875	71,118	67,202	138,320	26.1
1876	72,160	68,309	140,469	26.4
1877	71,704	67,955	139,659	26.2
1878	68,549	65,568	134,117	25.1
1879	69,860	65,468	135,328	25.2
1880	66,004	62,082	128,086	24.7
1881	64,793	61,054	125,847	24.5

1882	63,039	59,609	122,648	24.0
1883	60,695	57,468	118,163	23.5
1884	61,152	57,723	118,875	23.9
1885	59,482	56,469	115,951	23.5
1886	58,898	55,029	113,927	23.2
1887	57,810	54,590	112,400	23.1
1888	56,186	53,371	109,557	22.8
1889	55,177	52,664	107,841	22.7
1890	54,250	51,004	105,254	22.3
1891	55,476	52,640	108,116	23.1
1892	53,571	50,663	104,234	22.5
1893	54,323	51,759	106,082	23.0
1894	53,922	51,432	105,354	23.0
1895	54,658	51,455	106,113	23.3
1896	55,329	52,312	107,641	23.7
1897	54,679	51,985	106,664	23.5
1898	54,254	51,203	105,459	23.3
1899	53,351	50,549	103,900	23.1
1900	52,234	49,225	101,459	22.7
1901	51,984	48,992	100,976	22.7
1902	52,568	49,295	101,863	23.0
1903	52,173	49,658	101,831	23.1
1904	53,155	50,656	103,811	23.6
1905	52,509	50,323	102,832	23.4
1906	53,386	50,150	103,536	23.6
1907	52,171	49,571	101,742	23.2
1908	52,396	49,643	102,039	23.3
1909	52,726	50,033	102,759	23.5
1910	52,103	49,860	101,963	23.3
1911	52,448	49,310	101,758	23.3
1912	51,700	49,335	101,035	23.0
1913	51,158	48,936	100,094	22.8
1914	50,659	48,147	98,806	22.6
1915	49,272	46,311	95,583	22.0
1916	47,161	44,276	91,437	20.9
1917	44,277	42,093	86,370	19.7
1918	44,652	42,652	87,304	19.8
1919	46,202	43,123	89,325	20.0
1920	51,275	48,261	99,536	22.2

Source: Vaughan and Fitzpatrick, *Irish Historical Statistics*, pp. 241, 244–5.

Number of births registered in each intercensal period and birth rate per 1,000 population since 1881

Year	IFS/É/ROI births registered	Rate	Year	NI Births registered	Rate
1881–91	835,072	22.8			
1891–1901	737,934	22.1			
1901–11	713,709	22.4			
1911–26	968,742	21.1			
1926–36	583,502	19.6			
1936–46	602,095	20.3			
1946–51	329,270	22.3			
1951–6	312,517	21.3			
1956–61	302,816	21.2			
1961–6	312,709	21.9			
1966–71	312,796	21.3			
1971–9	548,413	21.6			
1979–81	146,224	21.5			
1981–6	333,457	19.1			
1986–91	277,546	15.7			
1991–6	249,455	14.0	1991	26,265	16.5
			1992	25,572	15.9
			1993	24,909	15.3
			1994	24,289	14.8
			1995	23,860	14.5
			1996	24,582	14.8

Source: CSO.

Deaths, 1833–1920

1833	94,713
1834	96,623
1835	101,961
1836	123,114
1837	141,688
1838	130,222
1839	140,239
1840	141,536
1841	85,646
1842	68,732
1843	70,499
1844	75,055
1845	86,900
1846	122,889
1847	249,335
1848	208,252
1849	240,797
1850	164,093

	Males	Females	Total	Deaths per 1,000 population
1851	96,798			
1852	80,112			
1853	79,883			
1854	78,563			
1855	80,416			
1856	77,834			
1857	77,104			
1858	82,005			
1859	85,264			
1860	94,349			
1861	58,235			
1862	64,415			
1863	70,771			
1864	46,346	46,798	93,144	16.5
1865	46,246	46,908	93,154	16.7
1866	46,140	46,887	93,027	16.8
1867	46,945	46,558	93,503	17.0
1868	43,359	42,826	86,185	15.8
1869	45,012	44,581	89,593	16.4
1870	45,501	44,961	90,462	16.7
1871	44,233	44,115	88,348	16.4
1872	48,991	48,303	97,294	18.1
1873	48,956	48,581	97,537	18.3
1874	46,474	45,487	91,961	17.3
1875	48,923	49,190	98,114	18.5
1876	46,108	46,216	92,324	17.3
1877	47,182	46,361	93,543	17.5
1878	50,116	49,513	99,629	18.6
1879	52,268	52,821	105,089	19.6
1880	51,640	51,266	102,906	19.8
1881	45,064	44,971	90,035	17.5
1882	43,633	44,867	88,500	17.3
1883	47,567	48,661	96,228	19.2
1884	43,389	43,765	87,154	17.5
1885	45,089	45,623	90,712	18.4
1886	43,493	43,799	87,292	17.8
1887	43,911	44,674	88,585	18.2
1888	42,474	43,418	85,892	17.9
1889	41,089	41,819	82,908	17.4
1890	42,140	43,710	85,850	18.2
1891	42,090	43,909	85,999	18.4
1892	44,009	46,035	90,044	19.4
1893	49,788	42,033	82,821	18.0
1894	41,377	42,151	83,528	18.2
1895	41,764	42,631	84,395	18.5
1896	37,364	38,336	75,700	16.7
1897	41,582	42,257	83,839	18.5
1898	49,738	41,666	82,404	18.2
1899	39,699	40,000	79,699	17.7
1900	42,953	44,653	87,606	19.6
1901	39,341	39,778	79,119	17.8

497

	Males	*Females*	*Total*	*Deaths per 1,000 population*
1902	38,569	39,107	77,676	17.5
1903	38,308	39,050	77,358	17.5
1904	39,330	40,183	79,513	18.0
1905	37,278	37,793	75,071	17.1
1906	37,131	37,296	74,427	16.9
1907	38,618	38,716	77,334	17.6
1908	38,219	38,672	76,891	17.6
1909	37,108	37,865	74,973	17.1
1910	37,052	37,842	74,894	17.1
1911	36,198	36,277	72,475	16.6
1912	35,986	36,201	72,187	16.5
1913	37,512	37,182	74,694	17.1
1914	35,812	35,533	71,345	16.3
1915	38,136	38,015	76,151	17.6
1916	35,975	35,416	71,391	16.3
1917	36,288	36,436	72,724	16.6
1918	39,236	39,459	78,695	17.9
1919	39,019	39,593	78,612	17.6
1920	33,141	33,397	66,538	14.8

Sources: Vaughan and Fitzpatrick, *Irish Historical Statistics*, pp. 78–81, 243, 247–8.

Number of deaths registered and death rate per 1,000 of the population in each intercensal period since 1881

Year	IFS/É/ROI	Rate	Year	NI	Rate
1881–91	639,073	17.4			
1891–1901	588,391	17.6			
1901–11	534,305	16.8			
1911–26	731,409	16.0			
1926–36	420,323	14.2			
1936–46	428,297	14.5			
1946–51	201,295	13.6			
1951–6	178,083	12.2			
1956–61	170,736	11.9			
1961–6	166,443	11.7			
1966–71	164,644	11.2			
1971–9	267,378	10.5			
1979–81	65,991	9.7			
1981–6	164,336	9.4			
1986–91	158,300	9.0			
1991–6	157,389	8.8	1991	15,096	9.5
			1992	14,988	9.3
			1993	15,633	9.6
			1994	15,114	9.2
			1995	15,310	9.3
			1996	15,218	9.1

Emigration, 1842–1920

	Total no.	Per 1,000	Males	Females
1842	89,686			
1843	37,509			
1844	54,289			
1845	74,969			
1846	105,955			
1947	215,444			
1848	178,159			
1849	214,425			
1850	209,054			
1851	249,721			
1852	190,322	30.0		
1853	173,148	27.9		
1854	140,555	23.1		
1855	91,914	15.3		
1856	90,781	15.2		
1857	95,081	16.1		
1858	64,337	10.9		
1859	80,599	13.8		
1860	84,621	14.5		
1861	64,292	11.1		
1862	70,117	12.1		
1863	117,229	20.5		
1864	114,169	20.2		
1865	101,497	18.1		
1866	99,467	18.0		
1867	80,624	14.7		
1868	61,018	11.2		
1869	66,568	12.2		
1870	74,855	13.8		
1871	71,240	13.2		
1872	78,102	14.5		
1873	90,149	16.9		
1874	73,184	13.8		
1875	51,462	9.7		
1876	37,587	7.1		
1877	38,503	7.2	20,847	17,656
1878	41,124	7.7	20,916	20,208
1879	47,065	8.8	25,807	21,258
1880	95,517	17.6	49,906	45,558
1881	78,417	15.2	40,106	38,311
1882	89,136	17.5	46,978	42,158
1883	108,724	21.6	55,264	53,460
1884	75,863	15.2	38,054	37,809
1885	62,034	12.6	30,873	31,161
1886	63,135	12.9	31,950	31,185

499

		Per 1,000	Males	Females
1887	82,923	17.1	43,176	39,747
1888	78,684	16.4	41,310	37,374
1889	70,477	14.8	36,226	34,251
1890	61,313	13.0	31,361	29,952
1891	59,623	12.7	30,046	29,577
1892	50,867	11.0	25,495	25,372
1893	48,147	10.4	23,044	25,103
1894	35,895	7.8	15,318	20,577
1895	48,703	10.7	21,398	27,305
1896	38,995	8.6	17,751	21,244
1897	32,535	7.2	13,966	18,569
1898	32,241	7.1	14,030	18,211
1899	41,232	9.2	18,621	22,611
1900	45,288	10.1	21,901	23,387
1901	39,613	8.9	18,127	21,486
1902	40,190	9.1	18,765	21,425
1903	39,789	9.0	18,671	21,047
1904	36,902	8.4	17,165	19,737
1905	30,676	7.0	16,082	14,594
1906	35,344	8.0	19,230	16,114
1907	39,082	8.9	21,124	17,958
1908	23,295	5.3	10,480	12,815
1909	28,676	6.5	14,916	13,760
1910	32,457	7.4	17,737	14,720
1911	30,573	7.0	16,671	13,902
1912	29,344	6.7	15,325	14,019
1913	30,967	7.1	16,452	14,515
1914	20,314	4.6	10,660	9,654
1915	10,659	2.4	6,567	4,092
1916	7,302	1.7	1,743	5,559
1917	2,111	0.5	838	1,273
1918	980	0.2	442	538
1919	2,975	0.7	1,137	1,838
1920	15,531	3.5	6,044	9,487

Source: Vaughan and Fitzpatrick, *Irish Historical Statistics*, pp. 260–3.

Irish in Great Britain, 1876–1951

Settled in Great Britain

	England and Wales	Scotland	Total
1876	7,980	8,807	16,787
1877	11,573	8,698	20,271
1878	10,965	7,683	18,648
1879	9,107	6,391	15,498
1880	7,741	5,808	13,549
1881	5,713	4,910	10,623
1882	4,984	5,672	10,656
1883	5,334	4,764	10,101
1884	5,506	3,481	8,990
1885	3,633	2,196	5,829
1886	4,072	1,245	5,318
1887	3,925	1,137	5,062
1888	4,282	1,414	5,696
1889	2,893	1,146	4,039
1890	2,998	1,474	4,472
1891	2,528	1,614	4,142
1892	1,007	923	1,930
1893	783	569	1,352
1894	944	643	1,587
1895	1,107	648	1,755
1896	1,272	642	1,914
1897	1,454	827	2,281
1898	1,667	1,142	2,809
1899	2,633	1,508	4,141
1900	4,123	1,927	6,050
1901	4,077	2,187	6,264
1902	2,690	2,028	4,718
1903	1,839	1,808	3,647
1904	2,011	1,457	3,468
1905	1,950	1,537	3,487
1906	2,247	1,818	4,065
1907	2,344	1,618	3,962
1908	1,874	1,032	2,906
1909	1,924	607	2,531
1910	1,656	440	2,096
1911	1,604	411	2,015
1912	1,421	446	1,867
1913	911	238	1,149
1914	914	133	1,047
1915	1,954	944	2,898
1916	1,724	722	2,446
1917	996	912	1,908
1918	605	274	879
1919	843	230	1,073
1920	469	113	582

Source: John Archer Jackson, *The Irish in Britain* (London: Routledge & Kegan Paul, 1963), table VII, p. 191.

Irish born in England and Wales, and Scotland as a percentage of total population, 1841–1951

	England and Wales Irish born	%	Scotland Irish born	%
1841	289,404	1.8	126,321	4.8
1851	519,959	2.9	207,367	7.2
1861	601,634	3.0	204,083	6.7
1871	566,540	2.5	207,770	6.2
1881	562,374	2.2	218,745	5.9
1891	458,315	1.6	194,807	4.8
1901	426,565	1.3	205,064	4.6
1911	375,325	1.0	174,715	3.7
1921	364,747	1.0	159,020	3.3
1931	381,089	0.9	124,296	2.6
1951	627,021	1.4	89,007	1.7

Sources: Jackson, *The Irish in Britain*, p. 11; maps of distribution in GB, 1841, p. 8; 1861, p. 12; 1891, p. 16; 1951, p. 20; table of Irish-born, place of residence, D. H. Akenson, *The Irish Diaspora: A Primer* (Belfast, 1996), p. 54; table 8, emigrants' religion, Akenson, p. 46; table 7 age distribution p. 44; destinations of emigrants, Vaughan and Fitzpatrick, p. 259, 264–5; emigration by province, Vaughan and Fitzpatrick, pp. 341–53.

Irish Free State/Éire/Republic of Ireland

Percentages of urban population and in Dublin, 1911–1991

This measurement is not found in CSO abstracts post-1991.

	Population	Urban population %	Dublin population %
1911	3,139,688	29.7	12.3
1926	2,971,992	31.8	13.7
1936	2,968,420	35.5	15.9
1946	2,955,107	39.3	17.1
1961	2,818,341	46.4	19.1
1971	2,978,248	52.2	26.9
1981	3,443,405	55.6	29.1
1991	3,523,401	57.0	29.1

Emigration, 1911–1991

Period	Net emigration	Annual average
1911–26	405,029	27,002
1926–36	166,751	16,675
1936–46	187,111	18,711
1946–61	528,334	35,222
1961–71	134,511	13,451
1971–81	−104,000	−10,400
1981–91	64,617	6,462

Births, 1921–2001

	Males	Females	Total	Births per 1,000 population
1921	31,333	29,677	61,010	19.7
1922	30,344	28,505	58,849	19.5
1923	31,808	29,882	61,690	20.5
1924	32,713	30,689	63,402	20.1
1925	31,818	30,251	62,069	20.8
1926	31,382	29,794	61,176	20.6
1927	30,606	29,448	60,054	20.3
1928	30,327	28,849	59,176	20.1
1929	29,583	28,697	58,280	19.8
1930	29,913	28,440	58,353	19.8
1931	29,409	27,677	57,086	19.3
1932	28,842	27,398	56,240	19.1
1933	29,381	27,983	57,364	19.4
1934	29,825	28,072	57,897	19.5
1935	29,898	28,368	58,266	19.6
1936	29,602	28,513	58,115	19.6
1937	28,893	27,595	56,488	19.2
1938	29,108	27,817	56,925	19.4
1939	28,804	27,266	56,070	19.1
1940	29,029	27,565	56,594	19.1
1941	29,198	27,582	56,780	19.0
1942	34,013	32,104	66,117	22.3
1943	33,241	31,134	64,375	21.9
1944	33,637	31,788	65,425	22.2
1945	34,336	32,525	66,861	22.7
1946	35,120	32,802	67,922	22.9
1947	35,674	33,304	68,978	23.2
1948	33,993	31,937	65,930	22.0
1949	32,880	31,273	64,153	21.5
1950	32,867	30,698	63,565	21.4
1951	32,303	30,575	62,878	21.2
1952	33,026	31,605	64,631	21.9
1953	32,241	30,317	62,558	21.2
1954	32,087	30,447	62,534	21.3

503

	Males	Females	Total	Births per 1,000 population
1955	31,483	30,139	61,622	21.1
1956	31,257	29,483	60,740	21.0
1957	31,335	29,907	61,242	21.2
1958	30,498	29,012	59,510	20.9
1959	30,685	29,503	60,188	21.2
1960	31,141	29,594	60,735	21.5
1961	30,687	29,138	59,825	21.2
1962	31,650	30,132	61,782	21.8
1963	32,486	30,760	63,246	22.2
1964	32,759	31,313	64,072	22.4
1965	32,438	31,087	63,525	22.1
1966	32,173	30,042	62,215	21.6
1967	31,642	29,665	61,307	21.1
1968	31,469	29,535	61,004	21.0
1969	32,143	30,769	62,912	21.5
1970	33,086	31,198	64,284	21.9
1971	34,751	32,800	67,551	22.7
1972	35,375	33,152	68,527	22.7
1973	35,304	33,409	68,713	22.5
1974	35,432	33,475	68,907	22.3
1975	34,532	32,646	67,178	21.2
1976	34,849	32,869	67,718	21.0
1977	35,518	33,374	68,892	21.1
1978	35,766	34,533	70,299	21.2
1979	37,355	35,184	72,539	21.5
1980	38,267	35,797	74,064	21.9
1981	37,075	35,083	72,158	21.0
1982	36,256	34,587	70,843	20.4
1983	34,642	32,475	67,117	19.2
1984	33,222	30,840	64,062	18.2
1985	32,068	30,320	62,388	17.6
1986	31,875	29,745	61,620	17.4
1987	29,931	28,502	58,433	16.5
1988	28,083	26,517	54,600	15.4
1989	26,754	25,264	52,018	14.8
1990	27,559	25,485	53,044	15.1
1991	27,122	25,596	52,718	15.0
1992	26,307	24,782	51,089	14.4
1993	25,359	23,945	49,304	13.8
1994	24,744	23,184	47,928	13.4
1995	25,135	23,643	48,787	13.5
1996	26,350	24,305	50,655	14.0
1997	27,061	25,714	52,775	14.4
1998	29,848	26,121	53,969	14.6
1999	27,817	26,107	53,924	14.4
2000	27,896	26,343	54,239	14.3
2001	29,753	28,129	57,882	15.1

Marriages, 1921–2001

	Marriages	*Per 1,000 population*
1921	15,102	4.88
1922	15,141	5.01
1923	15,632	5.19
1924	14,822	4.93
1925	13,820	4.63
1926	13,570	4.57
1927	13,418	4.54
1928	13,716	4.65
1929	13,593	4.61
1930	13,631	4.63
1931	13,133	4.44
1932	13,029	4.42
1933	13,992	4.72
1934	14,251	4.8
1935	14,336	4.83
1936	14,763	4.98
1937	14,780	5.01
1938	14,803	5.07
1939	15,204	5.18
1940	15,212	5.14
1941	15,021	5.02
1942	17,470	5.9
1943	17,328	5.88
1944	16,772	5.7
1945	17,301	5.86
1946	17,525	5.91
1947	16,290	5.49
1948	16,115	5.38
1949	16,009	5.36
1950	16,018	5.4
1951	16,017	5.41
1952	15,876	5.38
1953	15,888	5.39
1954	15,831	5.38
1955	16,443	5.63
1956	16,761	5.78
1957	14,657	5.08
1958	15,061	5.28
1959	15,420	5.42
1960	15,465	5.46
1961	15,329	5.44
1962	15,627	5.5
1963	15,556	5.5
1964	16,128	5.6
1965	16,946	5.9
1966	16,849	5.8

	Marriages	Per 1,000 population
1967	17,788	6.1
1968	18,993	6.5
1969	20,304	6.0
1970	20,778	7.1
1971	22,014	7.4
1972	22,302	7.4
1973	22,816	7.5
1974	22,833	7.4
1975	21,280	6.7
1976	20,580	6.4
1977	20,016	6.1
1978	21,184	6.4
1979	20,806	6.2
1980	21,792	6.4
1981	20,612	6.0
1982	20,224	5.8
1983	19,467	5.6
1984	18,513	5.2
1985	18,791	5.3
1986	18,573	5.2
1987	18,309	5.2
1988	18,382	5.2
1989	17,769	5.1
1990	17,838	5.1
1991	17,441	4.9
1992	16,636	4.7
1993	16,824	4.7
1994	16,297	4.5
1995	15,604	4.3
1996	16,174	4.5
1997	15,631	4.3
1998	16,783	4.5
1999	18,526	4.9
2000	19,168	5.1
2001	19,246	5.0

Source: CSO.

Deaths, 1921–2001

	Males	Females	Total	Deaths per 1,000 population
1921	22,038	21,499	44,537	14.39
1922	22,748	21,799	44,547	14.74
1923	21,561	20,656	42,217	14.01
1924	22,821	22,359	45,180	15.03
1925	22,118	21,532	43,650	14.62

	Males	Females	Total	Deaths per 1,000 population
1926	20,844	20,896	41,740	14.06
1927	21,812	21,865	43,677	14.77
1928	20,933	20,859	41,792	14.17
1929	21,547	21,444	42,991	14.59
1930	21,075	20,627	41,702	14.16
1931	21,754	21,193	42,947	14.52
1932	21,801	21,183	42,984	14.58
1933	20,610	19,929	40,539	13.69
1934	19,920	19,163	39,083	13.15
1935	21,541	20,992	41,543	13.98
1936	21,920	20,666	42,586	14.35
1937	23,331	21,755	45,086	15.29
1938	20,637	19,404	40,041	13.63
1939	21,567	20,150	41,717	14.22
1940	21,611	20,274	41,885	14.16
1941	22,642	21,155	43,787	14.63
1942	21,868	19,772	41,640	14.05
1943	22,663	20,831	43,494	14.76
1944	23,477	21,651	45,128	15.33
1945	22,266	20,496	42,762	14.49
1946	21,863	19,594	41,457	13.98
1947	23,461	20,600	44,061	14.84
1948	19,117	17,240	36,357	12.13
1949	19,876	18,186	38,062	12.73
1950	20,026	17,715	37,741	12.71
1951	22,476	19,906	42,382	14.32
1952	18,918	16,187	35,105	11.89
1953	18,420	16,171	34,591	11.73
1954	19,199	16,336	35,535	12.08
1955	19,773	16,988	36,761	12.59
1956	18,269	15,641	33,910	11.70
1957	18,355	15,956	34,311	11.89
1958	18,495	15,753	34,248	12.00
1959	18,603	15,640	34,243	12.03
1960	17,484	15,176	32,660	11.54
1961	18,750	16,013	34,763	12.33
1962	18,335	15,483	33,838	12.0
1963	18,199	15,596	33,795	11.9
1964	17,630	15,000	32,630	11.4
1965	17,965	15,057	33,022	11.5
1966	19,148	15,965	35,113	12.2
1967	17,035	14,465	31,400	10.8
1968	18,031	15,126	33,157	11.4
1969	18,340	15,394	33,734	11.6
1970	18,755	15,536	34,291	11.4
1971	17,357	14,533	31,890	10.7
1972	18,731	15,650	34,381	11.4

	Males	Females	Total	Deaths per 1,000 population
1973	18,689	15,503	34,192	11.2
1974	18,923	15,998	34,921	11.3
1975	18,077	15,096	33,173	10.4
1976	18,465	15,578	34,043	10.6
1977	18,297	15,335	33,632	10.3
1978	18,442	15,352	33,794	10.2
1979	18,693	15,078	33,771	10.0
1980	18,230	15,242	33,472	9.8
1981	18,068	14,861	32,929	9.6
1982	17,755	14,702	32,457	9.3
1983	18,026	14,950	32,976	9.4
1984	17,485	14,951	32,076	9.1
1985	18,190	15,006	33,196	9.4
1986	18,313	15,317	33,630	9.5
1987	17,002	14,411	31,413	8.9
1988	16,980	14,600	31,580	8.9
1989	17,058	15,053	32,111	9.1
1990	16,828	14,542	31,370	9.0
1991	16,603	14,702	31,305	8.9
1992	16,516	14,415	30,931	8.7
1993	17,053	15,113	32,148	9.0
1994	16,286	14,590	30,876	8.6
1995	17,075	15,184	32,259	9.0
1996	16,672	15,051	31,723	8.7
1997	16,501	15,680	31,581	8.6
1998	16,553	15,010	31,563	8.5
1999	16,961	15,647	32,608	8.7
2000	15,930	15,185	31,115	8.2
2001	15,408	14,404	29,812	7.8

Source: CSO.

Northern Ireland

Population of Northern Ireland, 1926–1991

	Males	Females	Total	Percentage change
1926	608,088	648,473	1,256,361	+0.5
1937	623,154	656,591	1,279,745	+1.8
1951	667,819	703,102	1,370,921	+7.1
1961	694,224	730,818	1,425,042	+3.9
1966	723,884	760,891	1,484,775	+4.2
1971	754,676	781,389	1,536,065	+3.5
1981	749,480	782,716	1,532,196	
1991	769,071	808,765	1,577,836	
2001	821,449	863,818	1,685,267	

Major urban centres of population, 1926–1991

	Belfast	Londonderry	Newtownabbey	Bangor	Lisburn
1926	415,151	45,159		13,311	12,406
1937	438,086	47,813		15,769	13,042
1951	443,671	50,092	20,215	20,610	14,781
1961	415,856	53,762	37,448	23,862	17,700
1966	398,405	55,694	47,384	26,921	21,522
1971	416,679	66,545	58,114	35,260	31,836
1981*	314,360	89,126	72,266	66,283	84,022
1991	283,746	94,918	73,832	70,308	99,162

*From 1981 census the figures are based on council areas.

Births in Northern Ireland, 1921–2002

	Males	Females	Total	Births per 1,000 population
1921	15,184	14,526	29,710	23.6
1922	15,098	14,433	29,531	23.3
1923	15,332	14,763	30,900	23.9
1924	14,800	13,696	28,496	22.7
1925	14,185	13,501	27,686	22.0
1926	14,576	13,586	28,162	22.5
1927	13,693	12,983	26,676	21.7
1928	13,441	12,522	25,963	20.8
1929	13,048	12,362	25,410	20.4
1930	13,178	12,701	25,879	20.8
1931	13,162	12,511	25,673	20.5
1932	12,874	12,233	25,107	20.1
1933	12,648	11,953	24,601	19.6
1934	13,165	12,200	25,365	20.1
1935	12,780	11,962	24,742	19.5
1936	13,278	12,631	25,909	20.3
1937	13,008	12,404	25,412	19.8
1938	13,196	12,546	25,742	20.0
1939	12,890	12,350	25,240	19.5
1940	13,180	12,183	25,363	19.6
1941	14,059	12,828	26,887	20.9
1942	15,252	14,393	29,645	22.9
1943	16,337	15,184	31,521	24.2
1944	15,840	15,060	30,900	23.5
1945	14,945	14,062	29,007	22.0
1946	15,475	14,659	30,134	22.6
1947	16,011	15,243	31,254	23.3
1948	15,263	14,269	29,532	21.9
1949	15,027	14,079	29,106	21.4
1950	14,903	13,891	28,794	21.0
1951	14,639	13,838	28,477	20.7

509

	Males	Females	Total	Births per 1,000 population
1952	14,846	13,914	28,760	20.9
1953	15,039	13,945	28,984	20.9
1954	14,817	13,986	28,803	20.8
1955	15,085	13,880	28,965	20.8
1956	15,100	14,389	29,489	21.1
1957	15,490	14,618	30,108	21.5
1958	15,700	14,601	30,301	21.6
1959	15,877	14,932	30,809	21.9
1960	16,609	15,380	31,989	22.5
1961	16,404	15,511	31,915	22.4
1962	16,810	15,755	32,565	22.7
1963	17,323	16,091	33,414	23.1
1964	17,615	16,730	34,345	23.6
1965	17,702	16,188	33,890	23.1
1966	17,333	15,895	33,228	22.5
1967	17,168	16,247	33,415	22.4
1968	17,151	16,022	33,173	22.1
1969	16,600	15,828	32,428	21.4
1970	16,539	15,547	32,086	21.1
1971	16,504	15,261	31,765	20.7
1972			29,994	19.4
1973			29,200	18.9
1974			27,160	17.6
1975			26,130	17.0
1976			26,361	17.1
1977			25,437	16.5
1978			26,239	17.1
1979			28,178	18.2
1980			28,582	18.5
1981			27,302	17.8
1982			27,028	17.6
1983			27,255	17.7
1984			27,693	17.9
1985			27,635	17.7
1986			28,152	18.0
1987			27,865	17.7
1988			27,767	17.6
1989			26,080	16.5
1990			26,499	16.7
1991			26,265	16.5
1992			25,572	15.9
1993			24,909	15.3
1994			24,098	14.8
1995			23,860	14.5
1996			24,382	14.6
1997			24,087	14.3
1998			23,668	14.0

	Males	Females	Total	Births per 1,000 population
1999			22,957	13.6
2000			21,512	12.8
2001			21,962	13.0
2002			21,385	12.6

Source: CSO Appendix.

Marriages in Northern Ireland, 1921–2001

Year	Marriages	Per 1,000 population
1921	8,121	6.46
1922	8,072	6.36
1923	7,974	6.33
1924	7,514	5.97
1925	7,682	6.11
1926	7,228	5.76
1927	7,175	5.74
1928	7,264	5.81
1929	7,426	5.96
1930	7,547	6.07
1931	7,369	5.89
1932	6,959	5.56
1933	7,630	6.07
1934	8,230	6.51
1935	8,844	6.96
1936	9,144	7.17
1937	8,623	6.73
1938	8,617	6.7
1939	9,185	7.09
1940	9,795	7.56
1941	11,966	9.29
1942	11,673	9.01
1943	10,155	7.79
1944	9,508	7.24
1945	10,452	7.92
1946	9,801	7.4
1947	9,517	7.1
1948	9,360	6.9
1949	9,216	6.8
1950	9,080	6.6
1951	9,410	6.9
1952	9,300	6.8
1953	9,416	6.8
1954	9,154	6.6
1955	9,513	6.8
1956	9,359	6.7

Year	Marriages	Per 1,000 population
1957	9,391	6.7
1958	9,257	6.6
1959	9,610	6.8
1960	9,881	7.0
1961	9,861	6.9
1962	9,832	6.9
1963	10,155	7.0
1964	10,614	7.3
1965	10,452	7.1
1966	10,735	7.3
1967	10,924	7.3
1968	11,240	7.5
1969	11,587	7.7
1970	12,297	8.1
1971	12,152	7.9
1972	11,905	7.7
1973	11,212	7.2
1974	10,783	7.0
1975	10,867	7.1
1976	9,914	6.4
1977	9,696	6.3
1978	10,304	6.7
1979	10,214	6.6
1980	9,923	6.4
1981	9,636	6.2
1982	9,913	6.4
1983	9,990	6.5
1984	10,361	6.7
1985	10,343	6.6
1986	10,224	6.5
1987	10,363	6.6
1988	9,960	6.3
1989	10,019	6.3
1990	9,588	6.0
1991	9,221	5.8
1992	9,392	5.8
1993	9,045	5.5
1994	8,683	5.3
1995	8,576	5.2
1996	8,297	5.0
1997	8,071	4.8
1998	7,826	4.6
1999	7,628	4.5
2000	7,584	4.5
2001	7,281	4.3

Source: NIAAS.

Deaths in Northern Ireland, 1921–2002

	Males	Females	Total	Deaths per 1,000 population
1921	9,371	9,930	19,301	15.3
1922	9,484	10,311	19,795	15.6
1923	9,047	9,743	18,790	14.9
1924	9,787	10,512	20,299	16.1
1925	9,572	10,212	19,784	15.7
1926	9,161	9,666	18,827	15.0
1927	8,721	9,495	18,216	14.6
1928	8,699	9,305	18,004	14.4
1929	9,470	10,452	19,822	15.9
1930	8,391	8,757	17,148	13.8
1931	8,817	9,232	18,049	14.4
1932	8,669	9,143	17,812	14.2
1933	8,957	9,197	18,154	14.4
1934	8,727	8,794	17,521	13.9
1935	9,174	9,418	18,592	14.6
1936	9,023	9,406	18,429	14.4
1937	9,418	9,864	19,282	15.1
1938	8,736	8,913	17,649	13.7
1939	8,745	8,797	17,542	13.5
1940	9,565	9,376	18,941	14.6
1941*	9,761	9,879	19,640	15.2
1942	8,824	8,432	17,256	13.3
1943	8,812	8,625	17,437	13.4
1944	8,433	8,358	16,791	12.8
1945	8,058	8,206	16,264	12.3
1946	8,386	8,280	16,666	12.5
1947	8,590	8,323	16,913	12.6
1948	7,728	7,397	15,125	11.2
1949	7,930	7,722	15,652	11.5
1950	8,037	7,802	15,839	11.6
1951	8,888	8,740	17,608	12.8
1952	7,666	7,146	14,812	10.8
1953	7,670	7,143	14,813	10.9
1954	7,747	7,377	15,124	10.9
1955	7,861	7,546	15,407	11.2
1956	7,643	7,215	14,858	10.6
1957	7,929	7,258	15,187	10.9
1958	7,918	7,214	15,132	10.8
1959	7,979	7,424	15,403	10.9
1960	7,892	7,404	15,296	10.8
1961	8,422	7,686	16,108	11.3
1962	7,927	7,299	15,226	10.6
1963	8,339	7,560	15,899	11.0
1964	8,037	7,317	15,354	10.5
1965	8,200	7,351	15,551	10.6

513

	Males	Females	Total	Deaths per 1,000 population
1966	8,639	7,782	16,441	11.1
1967	7,729	6,941	14,671	9.8
1968	8,235	7,698	15,933	10.6
1969	8,608	7,730	16,338	10.8
1970	8,764	7,787	16,551	10.9
1971	8,593	7,609	16,202	10.6
1972			17,032	11.0
1973			17,669	11.4
1974			17,327	11.2
1975			16,511	10.7
1976			17,030	11.1
1977			16,921	11.0
1978			16,153	10.5
1979			16,811	10.9
1980			16,835	10.9
1981			16,256	10.4
1982			15,918	10.4
1983			16,039	10.4
1984			15,692	10.1
1985			15,955	10.2
1986			16,065	18.0
1987			15,334	17.7
1988			15,813	17.6
1989			15,844	16.5
1990			15,426	9.7
1991			15,096	9.5
1992			14,988	9.3
1993			15,633	9.6
1994			15,114	9.2
1995			15,310	9.3
1996			15,218	9.1
1997			14,971	8.9
1998			14,993	8.9
1999			15,663	9.3
2000			14,903	8.8
2001			14,513	8.6
2002			14,586	8.6

*Figures for 1941 are for civilian deaths only.
Source: B. R. Mitchell and Phyllis Deane, *British Historical Statistics*; CSO.

Annual emigration from Northern Ireland, 1924–63

	Emigrants
1924	8,177
1925	8,725
1926	12,859
1927	11,913
1928	10,303
1929	12,602
1930	9,217
1931	1,086
1932	610
1933	640
1934	838
1935	693
1936	655
1937	835
1938	844
No returns during Second World War	
1947	1,941
1948	3,300
1949	3,259
1950	3,370
1951	3,048
1952	4,772
1953	6,300
1954	4,988
1955	3,745
1956	5,088
1957	4,984
1958	2,946
1959	2,490
1960	2,618
1961	2,597
1962	2,717
1963	2,758

Intercensal net movement out of the Six Counties/Northern Ireland, 1881–2001

	Total nos.
1881	140,670
1891	67,738
1911	65,417
1901	107,573
1937	57,651
1951	67,267
1961	92,228
1966	37,701
1971	24,838
1981	161,660
1991	44,289
2001	−20,469

515

THE IRISH PEERAGE

Creations in the Irish peerage in use *circa* 1918

Dukes (2)

Leinster, Duke of, 1766; Marquess of Kildare and Earl of Offaly, 1761; Earl of Kildare, 1316; Baron of Offaly, 1205 (Viscount Leinster, 1847, Great Britain; Baron Kildare, 1870, United Kingdom).

Abercorn, Duke of, and Marquess of Hamilton, 1868; Viscount Strabane, 1701; Baron Strabane, 1617; and Baron Mountcastle, 1701 (Marquess of Abercorn, 1790; Viscount Hamilton, 1786, Great Britain); Earl of Abercorn, 1606; Baron of Paisley, 1587; Baron Abercorn, 1603; Baron Hamilton, Montcastle and Kilpatrick, 1606, bt, 1635, Scotland.

Marquesses (9)

Waterford, Marquess of, 1786; Earl of Tyrone, 1746; Viscount Tyrone and Baron Beresford, 1720; Baron de la Poer, 1375 (Baron Tyrone, 1786, Great Britain); bt, Great Britain, 1665.

Downshire, Marquess of, 1780; Earl of Hillsborough and Viscount Kilwarin, 1751; Viscount Hillsborough, 1717, Baron Hill, 1717; Viscount Fairford, 1772 (Baron Harwich, 1766, Great Britain).

Donegall, Marquess of, and Earl of Belfast, 1791; Earl of Donegall, 1647; Viscount Chichester and Baron Belfast, 1625 (Baron Fisherwick, 1790, Great Britain).

Headfort, Marquess of, 1800; Earl of Bective, 1736; Viscount Headford, 1762; Baron Headfort, 1760 (Baron Kenlis, 1831, United Kingdom; bt, Great Britain, 1704.

Sligo, Marquess of, 1800; Earl of Altamont, 1771; Earl of Clanricarde, 1800; Viscount Westport, 1768; Baron Monteagle, 1760 (Baron Monteagle of Westport, 1806, United Kingdom).

Ely, Marquess of, 1800; Earl of Ely, 1794; Viscount Loftus, 1789; Baron Loftus, 1785 (Baron Loftus, 1801, United Kingdom); bt, Great Britain, 1780.

Londonderry, Marquess of, 1816; Earl of Londonderry, 1790; Viscount Castlereagh, 1795; Baron Londonderry, 1789; Earl Vane and Viscount Seaham, 1823 (Baron Stewart, 1814, United Kingdom).

Conyngham, Marquess, Earl of Mount-Charles and Viscount Slane, 1816; Earl Conyngham and Viscount Mount-Charles, 1797; Viscount Conyngham, 1789; Baron Conyngham, 1781 (Baron Minster, 1821, United Kingdom).

Ormonde, Marquess of, 1825; Earl of Ormonde, 1328; Earl of Ossory, 1526; Viscount Thurles, 1535 (Baron Ormonde, 1821, United Kingdom). Hereditary Chief Butler of Ireland.

Earls (55)

Waterford, Earl of, 1446 (Earl of Shrewsbury, 1442, England; Earl Talbot and Viscount Ingestre, 1784; Baron Talbot, 1733, Great Britain). Hereditary Lord High Steward of Ireland.

Cork and Orrery, Earl of; Earl of Cork and Viscount Dungarvan, 1620; Earl of Orrery, 1660; Baron Boyle of Youghal, 1616; Baron Broghill, Viscount Kinalmeakey, and Baron of Bandon Bridge, 1628 (Baron Boyle of Marston, 1711, Great Britain).

Weathmeath, Earl of, 1621; Baron Delvin, 1486.

Desmond, Earl of, Viscount Callan and Baron Fielding, 1622 (Earl of Benbigh, 1622; Viscount Fielding and Baron Fielding, 1620; Baron St Liz, 1664, England): a Count of the Holy Roman Empire.

Meath, Earl of, 1627; Lord Brabazon, Baron of Ardee, 1616 (Baron Chaworth, 1831, United Kingdom).

Fingall, Earl of, 1628; Baron Killen, 1463 (Baron Fingall, 1831, United Kingdom).

Cavan, Earl of, and Viscount Kilcoursie, 1647; Lord Lambert, Baron of Cavan, 1617.

Drogheda, Earl of, 1661; Viscount Moore, 1621; Lord Moore, Baron of Millifonte, 1616.

Granard, Earl of, 1684; Viscount Granard and Baron of Clanehugh, 1675 (Baron Granard, 1806, United Kingdom).

Fitz-William, Earl and Viscount Milton, 1716; Lord Fitz-William, Baron of Liffer, 1620 (Earl Fitz-William and Viscount Milton, 1746; Baron Milton, 1742, Great Britain).

Kerry, Earl of, and Viscount Clanmaurice, 1722; Earl of Shelburne, 1753; Viscount Fitzmaurice and Baron Dunkeron, 1751; Baron of Kerry and Lixnaw, 1374 (Marquess of Lansdowne, Earl of Wycombe, and Viscount Calne, 1784; Baron Wycombe, 1760, Great Britain); Baron Nairne, Scotland, 1681.

Darnley, Earl of, 1725; Viscount Darnley, 1723; Baron Clifton of Rathmore, 1721.

Egmont, Earl of, 1733; Viscount Perceval, 1722; Baron Perceval, 1715; Baron Arden, 1770 (Baron Lovel and Holland, 1762, Great Britain; Baron Arden, 1802, United Kingdom); bt, England, 1661.

Bessborough, Earl of, 1739; Viscount Duncannon, 1722; Baron of Bessborough, 1721 (Baron Ponsonby, 1740, Great Britain; and Baron Duncannon, 1834, United Kingdom).

Carrick, Earl of, 1748; Viscount Ikerrin, 1629 (Baron Butler of Mount Juliet, 1912, United Kingdom).

Shannon, Earl of, Viscount Boyle, and Baron Castle Martyr, 1756 (Baron Carleton, 1786, Great Britain).

Lanesborough, Earl of, 1756; Viscount Lanesborough, 1728; Baron of Newtown-Butler, 1715.

Mornington, Earl of, and Viscount Wellesley, 1760; Baron Mornington, 1746 (Duke of Wellington and Marquess of Douro, 1814; Marquess of Wellington, 1812; Earl of Wellington, 1812; Viscount Wellington and Baron Douro, 1809, United Kingdom).

Arran, Earl of, 1762; Viscount Sudley and Baron Saunders, 1758 (Baron Sudley, 1884, United Kingdom); bt, England, 1662.

Courtown, Earl of, and Viscount Stopford, 1762; Barton Courtown, 1758 (Baron Saltersford, 1796, Great Britain).

Mexborough, Earl of, and Viscount Pollington, 1766; Baron Pollington, 1753.

Winterton, Earl, and Viscount Turnour, 1766; Baron Winterton, 1761.

Kingston, Earl of, 1763: Viscount Kingsborough, 1766; Viscount Lorton, 1806; Baron Kingston, 1764; Baron Erris, 1800; bt, Ireland, 1682.

Sefton, Earl of, 1771; Viscount Molyneux, 1628 (Baron Sefton, 1831, United Kingdom), bt, England, 1611.

Roden, Earl of, 1771; Viscount Cocelyn, 1775; Baron Newport, 1743; bt, England, 1665.

Lisburne, Earl of 1776; Viscount Lisburne and Lord Vaughan, 1695.

Clanwilliam, Earl of, 1776; Viscount Clanwilliam and Baron Gilford, 1766 (Baron Clanwilliam, 1828, United Kingdom), bt, Ireland, 1703.

Antrim, Earl of, and Viscount Dunluce, 1785.

Longford, Earl of, 1785; Baron Longford, 1756 (Baron Silchester, 1821, United Kingdom).

Portarlington, Earl of, 1785; Viscount Carlow, 1776; Baron Dawson, 1770.

Mayo, Earl of, 1785; Viscount Mayo, 1781; Baron Naas, 1766.

Annesley, Earl, 1780; Viscount Glenawly, 1766; Baron Annesley, 1758.

Enniskillen, Earl of, 1789; Viscount Ellinskillen, 1776; Baron Mountflorence, 1760 (Baron Grinstead, 1815, United Kingdom).

Erne, Earl of, 1789; Viscount Erne, 1781, and Baron Erne, 1768 (Baron Fermanagh, 1876, United Kingdom).

Desart, Earl of, and Viscount Castle-Cuffe, 1798; Viscount Besart, 1781; Baron of Desart, 1733 (Baron Desart, 1909, United Kingdom).

Wicklow, Earl of, 1793; Viscount Wicklow, 1785; Baron Clonmore, 1776.

Clonmell, Earl of, 1793; Viscount Clonmell, 1789; Baron Clonmell, 1776.

Leitrim, Earl of, 1795; Viscount Leitrim, 1793; Baron Leitrim, 1783 (Baron Clements, 1831, United Kingdom).

Lucan, Earl of, 1795; Baron Lucan, 1776; Bt. Scotland, 1634.

Belmore, Earl of, 1797; Viscount Belmore, 1789; Baron Belmore, 1781.

Bandon, Earl of, and Viscount Bernard, 1800; Viscount Bandon, 1795; Baron Bandon, 1793.

Castle-Stuart, Earl of, 1800; Viscount Stuart, 1793; Baron Castle-Stuart, 1610; bt, Scotland, 1628.

Donoughmore, Earl of 1800; Viscount Donoughmore, 1797; Baron Donoughmore, 1783 (Viscount Hutchinson, 1821, United Kingdom).

Caledon, Earl of, 1800; Viscount Caledon, 1797; Baron Caledon, 1790.

Kenmare, Earl of, and Viscount Castlerosse, 1801; Viscount Kenmare and Baron Castlerosse, 1798 (Baron Kenmare, 1856, United Kingdom); bt, Ireland, 1622.

Limerick, Earl of, 1803; Viscount Limerick, 1800; Baron Glentworth, 1790 (Baron Foxford, 1815, United Kingdom).

Clancarty, Earl of, 1803; Viscount Dunlo, 1801; Baron Kilconnel, 1797 (Viscount Clancarty, 1823, United Kingdom).

Gosford, Earl of, 1806; Viscount Gosford, 1785; Baron Gosford, 1776 (Baron Worlingham, 1835; Baron Acheson, 1847, United Kingdom); bt, Scotland, 1628.

Rosse, Earl of, 1806; Baron Oxmantown, 1792; bt, 1677.

Normanton, Earl of, 1806; Viscount Somerton, 1800; Baron of Somerton, 1795 (Baron Somerton, 1873, United Kingdom).

Kilmorey, Earl of, and Viscount Newry and Mourne, 1822; Viscount Kilmorey, 1625.

Dunraven and Mount-Earl, Earl of, and Viscount Adare, 1822; Viscount Mount-Earl, 1816; Baron Adare, 1800 (Baron Kenry, 1866, United Kingdom); bt, Great Britain, 1781.

Listowel, Earl of, 1822; Viscount Ennismore and Listowell, 1816; Baron Ennismore, 1800 (Baron Hare, 1869, United Kingdom).

Norbury, Earl of, and Viscount Gladine, 1827; Baron Norbury, 1800; Baron Norwood, 1797.

Ranfurly, Earl of, 1831; Viscount Northland, 1791; Baron Welles, 1781 (Baron Ranfurly, 1826, United Kingdom).

Viscounts (33)

Gormanston, Viscount, 1478 (Baron Gormanston, 1868, United Kingdom).

Mountgarret, Viscount, 1550 (Baron Mountgarret, 1911, United Kingdom).

Grandison, Visount, 1620 (Earl of Jersey, 1697; Viscount Villiers and Baron of Hoo, 1691, England).

Valentia, Viscount, 1621; Baron Mountnorris, 1628 (Baron Annesley, 1917, United Kingdom); bt, 1620.

Dillon, Viscount, 1622.

Lumley, Viscount, 1628 (Earl of Scarborough, 1690; Viscount Lumley, 1889; Baron Lumley, 1681, England).

Massereene, Viscount, and Baron of Loughneagh, 1660; Viscount Ferrard, 1797; Baron Oriel, 1790 (Baron Oriel, 1821, United Kingdom).

Cholmondeley, Viscount, 1661; Baron Newborough, 1715 (Marquess of Cholmondeley and Earl of Rochsavage, 1815, United Kingdom; Earl Chomondeley and Viscount Malpas, 1706; Baron Cholmondeley, 1689; Baron Newburgh, 1716, Great Britain), bt, England 1611.

Charlemont, Viscount, 1665; Baron Caulfeild, 1620.

Downe, Viscount, 1680 (Baron Dawnay, 1897); bt, England 1642.

Molesworth, Viscount, and Baron of Phillipstown, 1716.

Chetwynd, Viscount, and Baron of Rathdown, 1717.

Midleton, Viscount, 1717; Baron Brodrick, 1815 (Baron Brodrick, 1796, Great Britain).

Boyne, Viscount, 1717; Baron Hamilton, 1715 (Baron Brancepeth, 1886, United Kingdom).

Grimston, Viscount, and Baron Dunboyne, 1719 (Earl of Verulam and Viscount Grimston, 1815, United Kingdom; Baron Verulam, 1790, Great Britain); Baron Forrester, 1632, Scotland; bt, England, 1628.

Barrington, Viscount, and Baron Barrington, 1720 (Baron Shute, 1880, United Kingdom).

Gage, Viscount, and Baron Gage, 1720 (Baron Gage, 1790, Great Britain); bt, England 1622.

Galway, Viscount, and Baron of Killard, 1727 (Baron Monckton, 1887, United Kingdom).

Powerscourt, Viscount, Baron Wingfield, 1748 (Baron Powerscourt, 1885, United Kingdom).

Ashbrook, Viscount, 1751; Baron of Castle Durrow, 1732.

Mountmorres, Viscount, 1763; Baron Mountmorres, 1756; bt, 1631.

Southwell, Viscount, 1776; Baron Southwell, 1717; bt, 1662.

De Vesci, Viscount, 1776; Baron Knapton, 1750; bt, 1698.

Lifford, Viscount, 1781; Baron Lifford, 1768.

Bangor, Viscount, 1781; Baron Bangor, 1770.

Clifden, Viscount, 1781; Baron Clifden, 1776 (Baron Mendip, 1794, Great Britain; Baron Robartes, 1869, United Kingdom).

Doneraile, Viscount, 1785; Baron Doneralle, 1776.

Harberton, Viscount, 1791; Baron Harberton, 1783.

Hawarden, Viscount, 1793; Barton de Montalt, 1785; bt, 1705.

Monck, Viscount, 1801; Baron Monck, 1797 (Baron Monck, 1866, United Kingdom).

Templetown, Viscount, 1806; Baron Templetown, 1776.

Gort, Viscount, 1816; Baron Kiltarton, 1810.

Guillamore, Viscount, and Baron O'Grady, 1831.

Barons (63)

Kingsale, Baron, Baron Courcy, 1839.

Trimlestown, Baron, 1461.

Dunsany, Baron, 1490.

Dunboyne, Baron, 1541.

Louth, Baron, 1541.

Inchiquin, Baron, 1543.

Digby, Baron, 1620 (Baron Digby, 1765, Great Britain).

Sherard, Baron, 1627.

Conway, Baron, 1712 (Marquess of Hertford and Earl of Yarmouth, 1793; Earl of Hertford and Viscount Beauchamp, 1750; Baron Conway of Ragley, 1703, Great Britain).

Carbery, Baron, 1715.

Aylmer, Baron and Baron of Balrath, 1718, bt, 1662.

Farnham, Baron, 1756; bt, Scotland, 1627.

Lisle, Baron, 1758.

Clive, Baron, 1762 (Earl of Powis, Viscount Clive, Baron Herbert and Baron Powis, 1804, United Kingdom; Baron Clive, 1794, Great Britain).

Mulgrave, Baron, 1767 (Marquess of Normanby, 1838; Earl of Mulgrave and Viscount, Normanby, 1812, United Kingdom; Baron Mulgrave, 1794, Great Britain).

Newborough, Baron, 1776; bt, 1742, Great Britain.

MacDonald, Baron, 1776; bt, 1625, Scotland.

Kensington, Baron, 1776 (Baron Kensington, 1886, United Kingdom).

Westcote, Baron, 1776 (Viscount and Baron Cobham, 1718; Baron Lyletton, 1794, Great Britain), bt, 1718, England.

Massy, Baron, 1776.

Muskerry, Baron, 1781; bt, 1709.

Hood, Baron, 1782 (Viscount Hood, 1796; Baron Hood, 1795, Great Britain); bt, 1778, Great Britain.

Sheffield of Roscommon, Baron, 1783 (Baron Stanley of Alderley, 1839; Baron Eddisbury, 1848, United Kingdom); bt, 1660, England.

Auckland, Baron, 1789 (Baron Auckland, 1793, Great Britain).

Kilmaine, Baron, 1789; bt, 1632, Scotland.

Cloncurry, Baron, 1789 (Baron Cloncurry, 1831, United Kingdom); bt, Ireland, 1776.

Clonbrock, Baron, 1790.

Waterpark, Baron, 1792; bt, 1755, Great Britain.

Graves, Baron, and Baron of Gravesend, 1794.

Bridport, Baron, 1794 (Viscount Bridport, 1868, United Kingdom).

Huntingfield, Baron, 1796; bt, 1751, Great Britain.

Carrington, Baron, 1796 (Baron Carrington, 1797, Great Britain; Viscount Wendover and Earl Carrington, 1895; Marquess of Lincolnshire, 1912, United Kingdom).

Rossmore, Baron, 1796 (Baron Rossmore, 1838, United Kingdom).

Hotham, Baron, 1797; bt, 1621, England.

Cremorne, Baron, 1797 (Earl of Dartrey, 1866; Baron Dartrey, 1847, United Kingdom).

Headley, Baron and Baron Allanson and Winn, 1797; bt, 1660, England and 1776, Ireland.

Teignmouth, Baron, 1797; bt, 1792, Great Britain.

Crofton, Baron, 1797; bt, 1758.

Ffrench, Baron, 1798; bt, 1779.

Henley, Baron, 1799; (Baron Northington, 1885, United Kingdom).

Lanford, Baron, 1800.

De-Blaquiere, Baron, 1800; bt, 1784.

Dufferin and Claneboye, Baron, 1800 (Earl of Dufferin, 1871, and Baron Clandeboye, 1850, Marquess of Dufferin and Ava, and Earl of Ava, 1888, United Kingdom); bt, Ireland, 1763.

Henniker, Baron, 1800 (Baron Hartismere, 1866, United Kingdom); bt, 1765, Great Britain.

Ventry, Baron, 1800; bt, 1797.

Wallscourt, Baron, 1800.

Dunalley, Baron, 1800.

Clanmorris, Baron, 1800.

Radstock, Baron, 1800.

Ashtown, Baron, 1800.

Clarina, Baron, 1800.

Rendlesham, Baron, 1806.

Castlemaine, Baron, 1812.

Decies, Baron, 1812.

Garvagh, Baron, 1818.

Talbot of Malahide, Baron and Lord Malahide, 1831 (Baron Talbot of Malahide, 1856, United Kingdom).

Carew, Baron, 1834 (Baron Carew, 1838, United Kingdom).

Oranmore and Browne, Baron, 1836.

Bellew, Baron, 1848; bt, 1688.

Fermoy, Baron, 1856.

Athlumney, Baron, 1863 (Baron Meredyth, 1866, United Kingdom); bt, Ireland, 1748.

Rathdonnell, Baron, 1868.

Curzon of Kedleston, Baron, 1898 (Earl Curzon, Viscount Scarsdale and Baron Ravensdale, 1911, United Kingdom).

523

The Irish peerage in 1985

Rank/name	Family name	Title in House of Lords (creation)
Duke		
Leinster	Fitzgerald	Viscount Leinster (1847)
Abercorn	Hamilton	Marquess of Abercorn (1790)
Marquess		
Waterford	Beresford	Baron Tyrone (1786)
Downshire	Hill	Earl of Hillsborough (1772)
Donegall	Chichester	Baron Fisherwick (1790)
Headford	Taylour	Baron Kenlis (1831)
Sligo	Browne	Baron Monteagle (1806)
Ely	Tottenham	Baron Loftus (1801)
Londonderry	Vane-Tempest-Stewart	Earl Vane (1823)
Conyngham	Conyngham	Baron Minster (1821)
Ormonde	Butler	Baron Ormonde (1821)
Earl		
Waterford	Chetwynd-Talbot	Earl of Shrewsbury (1442)
Cork and Orrery	Boyle	Baron Boyle (1711)
Westmeath	Nugent	No
Desmond	Fielding	Earl of Denbigh (1622)
Meath	Brabazon	Baron Chaworth (1831)
Cavan	Lambert	No
Drogheda	Moore	Baron Moore (1801)
Granard	Forbes	Baron Granard (1806)
Kerry	Petty-Fitzmaurice	Marquess of Landsdowne (1784)
Darnley	Bligh	Baron Clifton (1608)
Egmont	Perceval	Baron Lovel (1762)
Bessborough	Ponsonby	Earl of Bessborough (1937)
Carrick	Butler	Baron Butler (1912)
Shannon	Boyle	Baron Carleton (1786)
Lanesborough	Butler	No
Mornington	Wellesley	Duke of Wellington (1814)
Arran	Gore	Baron Sudley (1884)
Courtown	Stopford	Baron Saltersford (1796)
Mexborough	Saville	No
Winterton	Turnour	Baron Turnour (1952)
Kingston	King-Tenison	No
Roden	Jocelyn	No
Lisburne	Vaughan	No
Clanwilliam	Meade	Baron Clanwilliam (1828)
Antrim	McDonnell	No
Longford	Pakenham	Baron Pakenham (1945)
Portarlington	Dawson Damer	No
Mayo	Annesley	No

Rank/name	Family name	Title in House of Lords (creation)
Enniskillen	Cole	Baron Grinstead (1815)
Erne	Crichton	Baron Fermanagh (1876)
Lucan	Bingham	Baron Bingham (1934)
Belmore	Lowry-Corry	No
Castle-Stewart	Stuart	No
Donoughmore	Hely-Hutchinson	Viscount Hutchinson (1821)
Caledon	Alexander	No
Limerick	Pery	Baron Foxford (1815)
Clancarty	Le Poer Trench	Viscount Clancarty (1823)
Gosford	Acheson	Baron Worlingham (1835)
Rosse	Parsons	No
Normanton	Agar	Baron Somerton (1873)
Kilmorey	Needham	No
Dunraven and Mount-Earl	Wyndham-Quin	No
Listowel	Hare	Baron Hare (1969)
Norbury	Graham-Toler	No
Ranfurly	Knox	Baron Ranfurly (1826)

Viscount

Gormanston	Preston	Baron Gormanston (1868)
Mountgarret	Butler	Baron Mountgarret (1911)
Grandison	Child-Villiers	Earl of Jersey (1697)
Dillon	Dillon	No
Lumley	Lumley	Earl of Scarborough (1690)
Valentia	Annesley	No
Massereene and Ferrard	Skeffington	Baron Oriel (1821)
Newborough	Cholmondeley	Marquess of Cholmondeley (1815)
Charlemont	Caulfeild	No
Downe	Dawnay	Baron Dawnay (1793)
Molesworth	Molesworth	No
Chetwynd	Chetwynd	No
Midleton	Brodrick	Earl of Midleton (1920)
Boyne	Hamilton-Russell	Baron Brancepeth (1886)
Grimston	Grimston	Earl of Verulam (1866)
Barrington	Barrington	Baron Shute (1880)
Galway	Monckton-Arundell	No
Powerscourt	Wingfield	Baron Powerscourt (1885)
Ashbrook	Flower	No
Southwell	Southwell	No
De Vesci	Vesey	No
Lifford	Hewitt	No
Bangor	Ward	No
Clifden	Agar-Roberts	Baron Mendip (1794)
Doneraile	St Leger	No

Rank/name	Family name	Title in House of Lords (creation)
Harberton	Pomeroy	No
Hawarden	Maude	No
Monck	Monck	Baron Monck (1866)
Gort	Vereker	No

Baron

Kingsale	De Courcy	No
Trimlestown	Barnewell	No
Dunsany	Plunkett	No
Dunboyne	Butler	No
Louth	Plunkett	No
Inchquin	O'Brien	No
Digby	Digby	Baron Digby (1765)
Conway	Seymour	Marquess of Hertford (1793)
Carbery	Evans-Freke	No
Aylmer	Aylmer	No
Farnham	Maxwell	No
Lisle	Lysaght	No
Clive	Herbert	Earl of Powis (1804)
Mulgrave	Phipps	Marquess of Normanby (1838)
Newborough	Wynn	No
MacDonald	MacDonald of Macdonald	No
Kensington	Edwardes	Baron Kensington (1886)
Westcote	Lyttelton	Viscount Cobham (1718)
Massy	Massy	No
Muskerry	Deane	No
Hood	Hood	Viscount Hood (1796)
Sheffield	Stanley	Baron Stanley of Alderley (1839)
Kilmaine	Browne	No
Auckland	Eden	Baron Auckland (1793)
Waterpark	Cavendish	No
Graves	Graves	No
Bridport	Hood	Viscount Bridport (1868)
Huntingfield	Vanneck	No
Carrington	Carrington	Baron Carrington (1797)
Rossmore	Westenra	Baron Rossmore (1838)
Hotham	Hotham	No
Headley	Allanson-Winn	No
Crofton	Crofton	No
Ffrench	Ffrench	No
Henley	Eden	Baron Northington (1885)
Dufferin and Clandeboye	Hamilton-Temple-Blackwood	Marquess of Dufferin (1888)
Langford	Rowley-Conwy	No
Henniker	Henniker-Major	Baron Hartismere (1866)

Rank/name	Family name	Title in House of Lords (creation)
Ventry	Eveleigh de Moleyns	No
Dunally	Prittie	No
Clanmorris	Bingham	No
Ashtown	Trench	No
Rendlesham	Thelluson	No
Castlemaine	Hancock	No
Decies	De la Poer Beresford	No
Garvagh	Canning	No
Talbot of Malahide	Talbot	No
Carew	Conolly-Carew	Baron Carew (1838)
Oranmore and Browne	Browne	Baron Mereworth (1926)
Bellew	Bellew	No
Fermoy	Roche	No
Rathdonnell	McClintock Bunbury	No

Source: Ronald P. Gadd, *The Peerage of Ireland* (The Irish Peers Association), 1985.

Irish peerages extinct and dormant since the Union

Created	Extinct	Title	Family name
Royal peers			
1799	1820	Dublin, HRH the Earl of	Royal family
1789	1830	Munster, HRH the Earl of	Royal family
Other peers			
1777	1875	Aldborough, Earl of	Stratford
1717	1846	Allen, Viscount	Allen
1691	1844	Athlone, Earl of	De Ginkell
1863	1929	Althlumney, Baron of	Somerville
1800	1910	Avonmore, Viscount	Yelverton
1816	1891	Bantry, Earl of	White
1628	1823	Barrymore, Earl of	Barry
1725	1802	Bateman, Viscount	Bateman
1756	1814	Belvidere, Earl of	Rochfort
1621	1874	Blayney, Baron	Blayney
1815	1829	Blessington, Earl of	Gardiner
1825	1879	Bloomfield, Baron	Bloomfield
1753	1832	Brandon, Baron	Crosbie
1643	1822	Bulkeley, Viscount	Bulkeley
1790	1815	Callan, Baron	Agar
1784	1829	Carhampton, Earl of	Luttrell
1797	1826	Carleton, Viscount	Carleton
1789	1909	Carysfort, Earl of	Proby
1800	1827	Castlecoote, Baron	Coote

Created	Extinct	Title	Family name
1822	1839	Castlemaime, Viscount	Handcock
1703	1892	Charlemont, Earl of	Caulfeild
1806	1875	Charleville, Earl of	Bury
1825	1916	Clanricarde, Marquess of	Canning
1895	1864	Clare, Earl of	FitzGibbon
1777	1806	Clermont, Earl of	Fortescue
1776	1829	Clermont, Viscount	Fortescue
1852	1898	Clermont, Baron	Fortescue
1790	1926	Clonbrock, Baron of	Dillon
1789	1929	Clonburry, Baron of	Lawless
1793	1934	Clonmel, Earl of	Scott
1761	1824	Coleraine, Baron	Hanger
1785	1813	Cremorne, Viscount	Dawson
1642	1810	Cullen, Viscount	Cockayne
1898	1925	Curzon of Kedleston, Baron	Curzon
1800	1920	De Blaquiere, Baron	De Blaquiere
1783	1809	Delaval, Baron	Delaval
1822	1863	Downes, Baron	Be Burgh
1791	1892	Drogheda, Marquess of	Moore
1766	1862	Dungannon, Viscount	Trevor
1845	1911	Dunsandle and Coanconal, Baron	Daly
1789	1824	Eardley, Baron	Eardley
1785	1823	Farnham, Earl	Maxwell
1792	1810	Fermanagh, Baroness	Verney
1759	1912	Fife, Earl	Duff
1826	1860	Fitzgerald and Vessy, Baron	Fitzgerald
1629	1833	Fitzwilliam, Viscount	Fitzwilliam
1800	1917	Frankfort de Montmorency, Viscount	de Montmorency
1800	1883	Gardner, Baron	Gardner
1776	1815	Glandore, Earl of	Crosbie
1800	1823	Glenbervie, Baron	Douglas
1816	1858	Glengall, Earl of	Butler
1831	1955	Guillamore, Viscount and Baron	O'Grady
1800	1845	Hartland, Baron	Mahon
1797	1804	Holmes, Baron	Holmes
1819	1873	Howden, Baron	Caradoe
1701	1814	Howe, Viscount	Howe
1767	1909	Howth, Earl of	St Lawrence
1797	1867	Keith, Baroness	De Fishault
1800	1952	Kenmare, Earl of	Browne
1793	1846	Kilkenny, Earl of	Butler
1646	1833	Kingsland, Viscount	Barnewell
1800	1830	Kilwarden, Viscount	Wolfe
1795	1807	Lavington, Baron	Payne
1800	1810	Lecale, Baron	Fitzgerald
1797	1833	Llandaff, Earl of	Matthew
1795	1952	Leitrim, Earl of	Clements
1806	1898	Lismore, Viscount	O'Callaghan
1800	1811	Longueville, Viscount	Longfield
1760	1842	Ludlow, Earl	Ludlow

Created	Extinct	Title	Family name
1794	1806	Macartney, Earl	Macartney
1756	1816	Massereene, Earl of	Skeffington
1780	1853	Melbourne, Viscount	Lamb
1776	1823	Mitford, Baron	Phillips
1763	1891	Millltown, Earl of	Leeson
1753	1808	Milton, Baron	Damer
1761	1808	Molra, Earl of	Rawdon-Hastings
1781	1915	Mountcashel, Earl of	Moore
1793	1844	Mountnorris, Earl of	Annesley
1660	1802	Mountrath, Earl of	Coote
1800	1846	Mountsandford, Baron	Sandfort
1622	1882	Netterville, Viscount	Netterville
1802	1825	Newcomen, Viscount	Newcomen
1800	1850	Nugent, Baron	Greville
1800	1841	O'Neill, Earl	O'Neill
1795	1855	O'Neill, Viscount	O'Neill
1776	1877	Ongley, Baron	Ongley
1816	1820	Ormonde, Marquess of	Butler
1795	1807	Oxmantown,Viscount	Parsons
1722	1865	Palmerston, Viscount	Temple
1783	1808	Pennrhyn, Baron	Pennant
1785	1806	Pery, Viscount	Pery
1795	1850	Rancliffe, Baron	Parkyns
1628	1885	Ranelagh, Viscount	Jones
1822	1849	Rathdowne, Earl of	Monck
1783	1861	Riversdale, Baron	Tonson
1777	1883	Rokeby, Baron	Robinson-Montague
1772	1802	Ross, Earl of	Gore
1662	1850	Roscommon, Earl of	Dillon
1701	1839	St Helen's, Baron	Fitzherbert
1816	1909	Sheffield, Earl of	Holroyd
1627	1931	Sherard, Baron of	Sherard
1628	1869	Strangford, Viscount	Smythe
1797	1816	Sunderlin, Baron	Malone
1800	1821	Tara, Baron	Preston
1800	1855	Thomand, Marquess of	O'Brien
1797	1821	Tyrawley, Baron	Cuffe
1761	1853	Tyrconnell, Earl	Carpenter
1751	1818	Upper Ossory, Earl of	Fitzpatrick
1800	1920	Wallscourt, Baron of	Blake
1799	1842	Wellesley, Marquis	Wellesley
1822	1871	Westmeath, Marquess of	Nugent
1800	1825	Whitworth, Baron	Whitworth

Dormant or abeyant titles in the Irish peerage

Title	Rank	Family	Use First	Last	
Imanny	Baron	Bourke	1628	1657	Dormant
Bourke	Viscount	Bourke	1628	1767	Probably dormant
Slane	Baron	Fleming	1370?	1799	Dormant, possibly extinct
Athenry	Baron	Bermingham	1307	1799	Dormant, possibly extinct
Kilkenny	Baron	Dillon	1620	1850	Possibly extinct
Clanmailer	Viscount	O'Dempsey	1631	1691	Dormant
Rosscommon	Earl	Dillon	1620	1850	Dormant
Caher	Baron	Butler	1583	1858	Dormant, possibly extinct
Gardiner	Baron	Gardiner	1800	1883	Dormant
Milltown	Earl	Leeson	1763	1891	Dormant
Russborough	Baron	Leeson	1756	1891	Dormant
Russborough	Viscount	Leeson	1760	1891	Dormant
Avonmore	Viscount	Yelverton	1800	1910	Dormant
Ballymote	Baron	Taaffe	1628	1919	Suspended under Act of 1917
Taaffe	Viscount	Taaffe	1628	1919	Suspended under Act of 1917

Old Irish titles

Old Irish titles are officially recognised and registered but not part of the Irish peerage. In the sixteenth and seventeenth centuries chieftainries were surrendered to the crown and cease to exist. About the beginning of the nineteenth century some of the representatives of the last holders of the chieftainries assumed the titles, and they became recognised by courtesy.

The O'Brien of Thomond (held by Baron Inchiquin)
The O'Callaghan
The O'Conor Don (considered first in order of preference)
The MacDermott, Prince of Coolevin
The O'Donnell of Tyreconnell
The O'Donoghue of the Glens
The O'Donovan
The McGillycuddy of the Reeks
The O'Grady of Kilballyowen
The O'Kelly of Gallagh and Tycooly
The O'Morchoe
The O'Neill of Clannaboy

Titles extinct or dormant:

The MacMurrough Kavanagh
An Sionnach (The Fox)
The O'Toole of Fer Tíre

Other Irish hereditary titles

The Knight of Glin (FitzGerald)
The Knight of Kerry (FitzGerald)
The White Knight (FitzGibbon)

The Republic of Ireland is one of a small number of states that have an official heraldic authority, the Chief Herald of Ireland. The office was originally that of Ulster King at Arms. With the authority of the Irish government the Chief Herald recognised 'chiefs of name', but this practice was abandoned in July 2003 in response to impostors abusing the system.

Order of St Patrick (KP)

The Order was founded by King George II by warrant dated 5 Feb. 1783. The 15 original knights (the Knights Founders) were nominated on 5 Feb. 1783, invested on 11 Mar. and installed on 17 Mar. (St Patrick's Day). The Earl of Ely, through ill-health, was absent from both the investiture and the installation and hence is not considered to be one of the Knights Founders. He died without being invested.

Original Knights of St Patrick (5 Feb. 1783)

	Date of death
Prince Edward (later Duke of Kent and Strathearn)	Jan. 1820
2nd Duke of Leinster	Oct. 1804
12th Earl (later Marquess) of Clanricarde	Dec. 1797
6th Earl of Antrim	July 1791
6th Earl of Westmeath	Sept. 1792
5th Earl of Inchiquin (later Marquess of Thomand)	Feb. 1808
6th Earl (later Marquess) of Drogheda	Dec. 1822
2nd Earl of Tyrone (later Marquess of Waterford)	Dec. 1800
2nd Earl of Shannon	May 1807
2nd Earl of Clanbrassil	Feb. 1798
2nd Earl of Mornington (later Marquis Wellesley)	Sept. 1842
2nd Earl of Arran	Oct. 1809
2nd Earl of Courtown	Mar. 1810
1st Earl of Charlemont	Aug. 1799
Earl of Ely	May 1783

Subsequent creations

Invested	Title	Date of death
Feb. 1784	Earl Carysfoot	Apr. 1828
Dec. 1794	Viscount Lofus (later Marquess of Ely)	Mar. 1806
Mar. 1795	Earl of Clermont	Sept. 1806
Mar. 1798	Earl of Ormond and Ossory	Aug. 1820
Mar. 1798	Viscount Dillon	Nov. 1813
Aug. 1800	Earl of Allamont (later Marquess of Sligo)	Jan. 1809
Jan. 1801	Marquess Conynham	Dec. 1822
Mar. 1806	Marquess of Waterford	July 1826
May 1806	Marquess of Headfort	Oct. 1829
Nov. 1806	Earl of Roden	June 1820
Nov. 1807	Marquess of Ely	Sept. 1845
Apr. 1808	Earl of Shannon	Apr. 1842
Feb. 1809	Earl O'Neill	Mar. 1841
Nov. 1809	Marquess of Thomand	Aug. 1846
Mar. 1810	Marquess of Sligo	Jan. 1845
Apr. 1810	Earl of Enniskillen	Mar. 1840
Dec. 1813	Earl of Longford	May 1835
Aug. 1821	Duke of Cumberland (later King of Hanover)	Nov. 1851
Aug. 1821	Marquess of Donegall	Oct. 1844
Aug. 1821	Earl of Caledon	Apr. 1839
Aug. 1821	Earl Talbot	quit for Garter 1844
Aug. 1821	Earl of Ormond and Ossory	May 1838
Aug. 1821	Earl of Meath	Mar. 1851
Aug. 1821	Earl of Fingal	July 1836
Aug. 1821	Earl of Courtown	June 1835
Aug. 1821	Earl of Roden	Mar. 1870

Irish titles used by the royal family in 2003

Royal title	Irish title
HRH The Duke of York	Baron Killyleagh
HRH The Duke of Kent	Baron Downpatrick
HRH The Duke of Gloucester	Earl of Ulster*

*Now the courtesy title of the Duke's eldest son.

TRADE UNIONS

Trade union membership (with headquarters in IFS/É/ROI), 1923–1996

	Total unions	Members ('000)
1923		131
1924		127
1925		99
1926		95
1927		89
1928		88
1929		87
1930		87
1931		87
1932		87
1933		92
1934		98
1935		97
1936		101
1937		118
1938		122
1939		135
1940		128
1941		104
1942		113
1943		115
1944		134
1945		143
1946		160
1947		185
1948		205
1949		224
1950		243
1951		257
1952		259
1953		264
1954	97	267
1955	98	272
1956	97	271
1957	101	265
1958	99	264
1959	97	272

	Total unions	*Members ('000)*
1960	104	283
1961	104	291
1962	101	300
1963	90	298
1964	95	302
1965	92	307
1966	88	302
1967	77	305
1968	84	316
1969	93	338
1970	91	338
1971	85	328
1972	85	326
1973	85	327
1974	89	367
1975	91	359
1976	90	367
1977	91	382
1978	90	369
1979	90	397
1980	91	394
1981	94	458
1982	93	455
1983	101	448
1984	100	407
1985	101	400
1986	103	367
1987	101	298
1988	100	405
1989	98	333
1990	95	369
1991	91	350
1992	89	409
1993	76	441
1994	73	428
1995	74	471
1996	74	460

Source: CSO; yearbooks do not contain this measurement post-1996.

Industrial disputes in Irish Free State/Éire/Republic of Ireland, 1923–2002

	Disputes that began during year	*Working days lost during year ('000)*
1923	131	1,209
1924	104	302
1925	86	294
1926	57	85
1927	53	64
1928	52	54
1929	53	101
1930	83	77
1931	60	310
1932	70	42
1933	88	200
1934	99	180
1935	99	288
1936	107	186
1937	145	1,755
1938	137	209
1939	99	106
1940	89	152
1941	71	77
1942	69	115
1943	81	62
1944	84	38
1945	87	244
1946	105	150
1947	194	449
1948	147	258
1949	153	273
1950	154	217
1951	138	545
1952	82	529
1953	75	82
1954	81	67
1955	96	236
1956	67	48
1957	45	92
1958	51	126
1959	58	124
1960	49	80
1861	96	377
1962	60	104
1963	70	234
1964	87	545
1965	89	552
1966	112	784

	Disputes that began during year	*Working days lost during year ('000)*
1967	79	183
1968	126	406
1969	134	936
1970	134	1,008
1971	133	274
1972	131	207
1973	182	207
1974	219	552
1975	151	296
1976	134	777
1977	175	442
1978	152	613
1979	140	1,465
1980	130	412
1981	117	434
1982	131	434
1983	154	319
1984	192	386
1985	116	418
1986	102	309
1987	80	264
1988	65	143
1989	38	50
1990	49	223
1991	54	86
1992	38	191
1993	48	61
1994	28	25
1995	34	130
1996	30	114
1997	28	74
1998	34	37
1999	32	216
2000	39	97
2001	26	115
2002	27	21

Source: CSO.

WOMEN

Chronology of women's history, 1765–2002

1765   Lady Arabella Denny founded Ireland's first Magdalen asylum.

1769   Nano Nagle founded the Presentation Sisters in Cork.

1775   Formal beginning of the Society of Charitable Instruction initiated by Nano Nagle.

1805   Canonical approval of Presentation Order (see 1775 Society of Charitable Instruction).

1814   Dublin Female Association founded as evangelical organisation.

1815   Mary Aikenhead founded Sisters of Charity.

1820   Frances Ball founded the Loreto Sisters.

1825   Publication of *Appeal of One Half of the Human Race, Women, Against the Pretensions of the Other Half, Men, To Retain Them in Political, and Thence in Civil and Domestic Slavery* by William Thompson and Anna Wheeler.

1828   Catherine McCauley founded the Sisters of Mercy (currently the second-largest religious congregation of women in the world).

1848   Anne Elgee and Margaret Callan ran the *Nation* after the arrest of the editor.

1856   Irish Ladies' Anti-Slavery Association formed.

1859   Establishment of Ladies' Collegiate School (later Victoria College) in Belfast.

1861   Establishment of the Queen's Institute in Dublin.

1864   Parliament passed the first of three Contagious Diseases Acts (the other two were passed in 1866 and 1869) providing for the compulsory examination for venereal disease of women suspected of being prostitutes.

1866   Establishment of Alexandra College in Dublin.

1867   Committee for changes in married women's property law established by Isabella Tod in Belfast.

1868   Irish National Teachers' Organisation established.

1869   Establishment of the National Association for the Repeal of the Contagious Diseases Acts. Formation of the Ladies' National Association.

1870	Irish branch of the Ladies Association for the Repeal of the Contagious Diseases Acts established. By 1871 there were branches in Belfast, Dublin and Cork.
1872	First Irish suffrage society formed in Belfast by Isabella Tod.
1873	First group organised in Belfast to campaign for the municipal franchise for women.
1874	Thomas Haslam published three issues of the *Women's Advocate*, the first attempt to print a suffrage newspaper in Ireland.
1875	King's and Queen's College of Physicians of Ireland opened its doors to women.
1876	Anna and Thomas Haslam established the first suffrage society in Dublin.
1877	Royal College of Physicians of Ireland allowed women to sit for its licentiate.
1878	Intermediate Education Act opened up intermediate examinations to boys and girls and offered government grants to both on an equal basis.
1879	Royal University Act opened up university examinations to women.
1880	24 Oct.: Ladies' Land League formed in New York by Fanny Parnell.
1881	31 Jan.: Ladies' Land League publicly launched in Ireland.
1882	Women admitted to classes at Queen's College, Belfast. Dominican convent, Eccles Street in Dublin, offered higher education for Catholic women. Married Women's Property Act: allowed women to hold property in their own name.
1884	Oct.: Nine women, the first in Ireland, received degrees from the Royal University of Ireland.
1885	Royal College of Surgeons in Ireland, an examining body only, admitted women as graduates.
1886	Isabella Tod organised a group of women to protest against the first Home Rule bill. Women admitted to classes at Queen's College, Cork.
1887	Municipal franchise granted to women ratepayers in Belfast. The Mothers' Union established in Ireland.
1888	Women admitted to classes at Queen's College, Galway.
1893	Gaelic League formed with membership open to women on equal terms with men.
1894	Women householders gain municipal vote in Dublin townships of Kingston and Blackrock.

1896	Women Poor Law Guardians (Ireland) Act passed. The *Shan Van Vocht*, a republican journal, published from Belfast by Alice Milligan and Anna Johnston; it survived until 1899.
1897	Irish Women's Centenary Union, to commemorate the 1798 rebellion, formed in the north of Ireland.
1898	Mar.: Registration (Ireland) Act conferred municipal franchise on Irish women. Aug.: Local Government (Ireland) Act allowed women to become rural district councillors and urban district councillors. It was not until 1911 that they could become county councillors.
1900	Inghinidhe na hÉireann (Daughters of Ireland) formed, with Maud Gonne as president.
1902	Women Graduates' and Candidate Graduates' Association formed, later renamed the Women Graduates' Association.
1903	In England the Pankhursts formed the militant Women's Social and Political Union to fight for suffrage.
1904	Women admitted to Trinity College, Dublin.
1907	Lady Aberdeen established Women's National Health Association to fight tuberculosis.
1908	Universities Act granted equality to women in Irish universities. Nov.: Irish Women's Franchise League (IWFL) formed by, among others, Hanna Sheehy Skeffington and Margaret Cousins. Inghinidhe na hÉireann launched their journal *Bean na hÉireann* (Woman of Ireland), the first nationalist/feminist journal to be published in Ireland; it survived until 1911.
1909	Irish branch of the Conservative and Unionist Women's Suffrage Association formed in Dublin. Irish Women's Suffrage Society organised in Belfast.
1910	Conciliation bill, which included a suffrage measure, first introduced in parliament. Society of the United Irishwomen founded (in 1935 retitled Irish Countrywomen's Association).
1911	23 Jan.: Ulster Women's Unionist Council formed. Feb.: Munster Women's Franchise League formed. 21 Aug.: Irish Women's Suffrage Federation founded as an umbrella organisation for Irish suffrage groups. 5 Sept.: Irish Women Workers' Union founded by James and Delia Larkin. Irish Women's Reform League established in Dublin, campaigning for suffrage, school meals and technical education for girls. United Irishwomen founded by Horace Plunkett and Ellice Pilkington. Local Authorities (Ireland) (Qualification of Women) Act allowed women to become county and borough councillors.
1912	May: *Irish Citizen* newspaper founded. Women's Suffrage bill defeated. 13 June: First act of militancy by members of the

IWFL. The militant Women's Social and Political Union (WSPU) formed branches in Belfast and Dublin. June/July: eight members of the IWFL imprisoned for militancy. 18–20 July: Prime Minister Asquith visited Ireland; English suffragettes made violent protests. Sept: Ulster Women's Unionist Council gathers 228,991 signatures for Ulster's Solemn League and Covenant.

1913   Jan.: The 'Cat and Mouse' Act introduced. Irish branch of the Church League for Women's Suffrage for Anglican Women established in Dublin. Major women's suffrage conference held in Dublin. Oct.: Irish Women's Suffrage Federation welcomed Carson's promise to enfranchise women under a provisional Ulster government. Members of suffrage groups provided support to the strikers during the 1913 lock-out by organising food kitchens. Irish Nurses' Association established.

1914   Mar.: WSPU declared war on Ulster Unionists and established a centre in Belfast. 17 Mar.: WSPU mounted arson attack on Abbeylands House, the headquarters of the Ulster Volunteer Force. 2 Apr.: Cumann na mBan (Irishwomen's Council) formed as a women's auxiliary to the Irish Volunteers. Aug.: First World War began. IWFL abandoned its militant campaign; WSPU withdrew from Ireland; two suffrage prisoners in Crumlin Road jail in Belfast were released.

1915   May: Inghinidhe na hÉireann joined forces with Cumann na mBan. Congress of Women held at The Hague; from this meeting was formed the Committee of Women for Permanent Peace, which in 1919 adopted the name Women's International League for Peace and Freedom; branch established in Dublin and survived until 1932. Irish Catholic Women's Suffrage Association established in Dublin.

1916   24–9 Apr.: Easter Rising in Dublin. Women participated as members of Cumann na mBan and Irish Citizen Army.

1917   League of Women Delegates formed to safeguard the political rights of Irish women; they adopted the name Cumann na dTeachaire.

1918   11 Jan.: Delegation of members of Cumann na mBan presented a petition to US President Woodroo Wilson. Representation of the People Act granted the vote to Irish women over 30 years of age. Dec.: Constance Markievicz and Winifred Carney were the only women candidates in the general election; Markievicz became the first woman elected to parliament, but did not take up her seat in Westminster. Irish Women's Suffrage and Local Government Association re-formed as the Irish Women's Citizens and Local Government Association.

1919	Dáil Éireann formed. Constance Markievicz appointed Minister for Labour. War of Independence began. St Ultan's hospital opened in Dublin, administered and staffed by women. Belfast Suffrage Society re-formed as the Women's Political League.
1920	*Irish Citizen* ceased publication.
1922	7 Jan.: Treaty accepted by Dáil Éireann. Cumann na mBan rejected the Treaty. Mar.: Cumann na Saoirse formed by those former members of Cumann na mBan who favoured the Treaty. Under the Free State Constitution all adults over the age of 21 were eligible to vote. 1 June: Two semi-official women absorbed into the RIC and given the numbers PW1 and PW2. They were not known as police officers but matrons.
1923	Irish Civil War, *c.* 400 republican women jailed.
1924	National Council of Women of Ireland formed to 'promote co-operation among women all over Ireland interested in social welfare'.
1925	Branches of Irish Women Graduates' Association amalgamated to form the Irish Federation of University Women. Civil Service Regulation Act gave the government power to ban women from certain civil service examinations. Matrimonial Act outlawed divorce (both IFS (Irish Free State)).
1927	IFS Juries Act effectively barred most women from jury service. Mary Immaculate College, Limerick, launches Mary Immaculate Modest Dress and Deportment Crusade.
1929	Publications advocating 'the unnatural prevention of conception' could be banned under the Censorship of Publications Act (IFS).
1930	Louie Bennett became first woman president of the Irish Trades Union Congress.
1932	Ban on hiring married women teachers (eventually extended to the entire civil service in the IFS in 1936).
1934	Criminal Law Amendment Act placed a complete ban on the importation of all contraceptives into the IFS. United Irishwomen change name to Irish Countrywomen's Association.
1935	Joint Committee of Women's Societies and Social Workers formed to campaign on issues relating to women. Widows and orphans pensions introduced in the IFS.
1936	Conditions of Employment Act passed, restricting the employment opportunities of women in the IFS.
1937	1 May: Draft Constitution published. Campaign launched against it. Nov.: Constitution enacted. Women's Social and Progressive League formed. Northern Ireland branch of the Nursery Schools Association of Great Britain formed.

1939	Kathleen Clarke, widow of the executed 1916 leader, Thomas J. Clarke, elected Lord Mayor of Dublin – the first woman to hold this office.
1940	Civics Institute opens first nursery school in Dublin.
1941	5 May: Housewives Petition sent to Éire government.
1942	Irish Housewives Association established. RUC started to recruit women. The first policewoman, Marian MacMillan, given the number PW4, made sergeant by Sept. 1943.
1954	Oct: The first residential college for adult women in ROI, An Grianán, opened by President Sean T. O'Kelly.
1957	Married Women's Status Act ROI gave married women control of their own property.
1958	Marriage ban (ROI) on teachers revoked.
1959	First trained policewomen appointed to the Garda Síochána. Irish Congress of Trades' Unions Women's Advisory Committee established.
1960	RUC women permitted to carry firearms; subsequently many chose not to (*see* 1942; 1995).
1964	Guardianship of Infants Act (ROI) gave women guardianship rights equal to those of men.
1965	Irish Federation of Women's Clubs formed.
1966	National Association of Widows formed.
1967	United Nations Commission on the status of women issued a directive to women's groups to examine the status of women in their respective countries. UK Abortion Act 1967 excludes Northern Ireland.
1968	Formation of an ad hoc committee of Irish women's groups to lobby for a Commission for the Status of Women in Ireland. Mainly led by the Irish Housewives Association.
1970	Equal Pay Act (Northern Ireland) required employers to give equal terms and conditions of employment to male and female workers employed in 'like work' or 'work rated as equivalent'. Irish Women's Liberation Movement established. National Commission on the Status of Women established by the government (*see* 1968). Women's Progressive Association formed to promote the participation of women in political and public life (became Women's Political Association in 1973) (*see* 1973).
1972	*Report of the Commission on the Status of Women* published. CHERISH formed to provide advice and support for single parents. AIM (Action, Information, Motivation) formed as pressure group to campaign for the rights of wives and children.

1973	Marriage bar (ROI) which excluded married women from employment in the public service was lifted. Establishment of the Council for the Status of Women (became the National Women's Council) (*see* 1970). Women permitted to join the recently formed Ulster Defence Regiment, and given the sobriquet of 'Greenfinches'.
1974	Anti-Discrimination (Pay) Act gave women in (ROI) similar equality of pay and conditions to those in the Equal Pay Act (Northern Ireland). It came into force on 31 December 1975. Irish Women United formed. Women's Aid established to provide refuge and support for victims of domestic violence.
1975	Women in ROI given the right to jury service on same basis as men. Northern Ireland Women's Rights Movement formed. Oct.: Socialist Women's Group established.
1976	Employment Equality Act. Mairead Corrigan and Betty Williams formed the peace movement in Northern Ireland. They received the Nobel Prize for Peace on 30 Nov.
1977	Employment Equality Agency established and First Rape Crisis Centre established in Dublin. Former members of Socialist Women's Group established Belfast Women's Collective (*see* 1978).
1978	Contraceptives made legally available to married couples in the Republic. Maire Geoghegan Quinn appointed Minster for the Gaeltacht to become the first women member of a cabinet in Dublin since Constance Markievicz in 1919. Aer Lingus's first woman pilot completed her initial scheduled fight. Women Against Imperialism formed in Northern Ireland. Belfast Women's Collective split, some members leaving to form Women Against Imperialism (*see* 1977).
1979	Mellia Carroll appointed as the first woman High Court judge in ROI. Two members of Women Against Imperialism jailed following protests outside Armagh prison, Northern Ireland (*see* 1978 and 1981).
1981	Maternity (Protection of Employees) Act and Family Law (Protection of Spouses and Children) Act (ROI) gave the Circuit and District Courts power to grant barring and protection orders. Beginning of Pro-Life Amendment campaign. Women Against Imperialism dissolved (*see* 1978 and 1979).
1982	Tras Honon became first woman Cathaoirleach (Chair) of Seanad. At the November general election Ann (Nan) Joyce stood for Dublin South-West and became the first Traveller woman to contest a seat in the Dáil. Nuala Fennell appointed the first Minister of State in ROI with responsibility for Women's Affairs and Law Reform.

543

1983	Referendum on the inclusion of the statutory prohibition of abortion as Article 40.3.3. of the Irish Constitution. Family Planning Act (ROI) legalised the provision of contraceptives to those over 18 years.
1984	First referendum on divorce in which the proposal to legalise divorce was rejected (ROI).
1990	Mary Robinson became the first woman president of Ireland. General Synod of the Church of Ireland voted in favour of the ordination of women.
1992	Supreme Court judgement in the 'X Case' allowed for a pregnant woman to leave ROI in order to have an abortion if her life was judged to be in danger. Referenda in ROI on the legality of the distribution of information on abortion and on a woman's right to travel abroad for an abortion. Brook Advisory Centre opened in Belfast for advice regarding contraception, abortion and related health matters.
1993	Second Commission on the Status of Women set up. Establishment of the Department of Equality and Law Reform (absorbed in 1997 into the Department of Justice) (ROI).
1994	Family Law Act (ROI) raised the legal age of marriage from 16 to 18 years.
1995	Referendum on the provision of divorce in ROI resulted in a narrow majority in favour of divorce. Maternity Protection Act passed (ROI). RUC policewomen issued with firearms in pursuance of equality measures.
1996	Family Law (Divorce) Act allowed divorce and remarriage in ROI. Northern Ireland Women's Coalition formed to put forward an agenda of 'reconciliation through dialogue, accommodation and inclusion'.
1997	Mary McAleese elected President of Ireland in succession to Mary Robinson. Dr Mo Mowlam appointed first woman Secretary of State for Northern Ireland.
1999	Green Paper on abortion published.
2002	Defeat of constitutional referendum to roll back X Case judgement which ruled that abortion was permissible if a woman's life was in danger as a result of the threat of suicide.

Women elected representatives in the Irish Free State/Éire/Republic of Ireland

Uachtarán na hÉireann (President of Ireland)

Robinson, Mary T.W. (née Bourke), b. 21 May 1944 (elected 7 Nov. 1990)
McAleese, Mary (née Leneghan), b. 27 June 1951 (elected 30 Oct. 1997)

Members of the Dáil

Westminster Parliament/First Dáil (1918) 105 Irish seats at Westminster/Dáil 69 seats consisting of the Sinn Féin MPs elected to Westminster

Markievicz, Constance Georgina de (née Gore-Booth), b. 4 Feb. 1868, d. 27 July 1927 (Sinn Féin, Dublin St Patrick's)

2nd Dáil (1921) 128 seats

Clarke, Kathleen (née Daly), b. 1878, d. 1972 (Sinn Féin, Dublin Mid)

English, Dr Adeline (Ada), b. *c.* 1878, d. 1944 (Sinn Féin, National University of Ireland)

MacSwiney, Mary, b. 27 Mar. 1872, d. 7 Mar. 1942 (Sinn Féin, Cork City)

Markievicz, Constance Georgina de (Sinn Féin, Dublin South)

O'Callaghan, Kathleen (née Murphy), b. 1888, d. 1961 (Sinn Féin, Limerick City and Limerick East)

Pearse, Margaret (née Brady), b. 1857, d. 1932 (Sinn Féin, Dublin)

3rd Dáil (1922) 128 seats

MacSwiney, Mary (Cumann na Poblachta/Republican Association, Cork City)

O'Callaghan, Kathleen (Cumann na Poblachta/Republican Association, Limerick City and Limerick East)

4th Dáil (1923) 153 seats

Brugha, Cathlin (née Kingston), b. 1879, d. 1 Dec. 1959 (Republican, County Waterford)

Collins-O'Driscoll, Margaret (née Collins), b. 1878, d. 17 June 1945 (Cumann na nGaedheal, Dublin North)

Lynn, Dr Kathleen b. 1874, d. 14 Sept. 1955 (Sinn Féin, Dublin County)

MacSwiney, Mary (Republican, Cork City)

Markievicz, Constance de (Republican, Dublin South)

5th Dáil (June 1927) 153 seats

Brugha, Cathlin (Sinn Féin, County Waterford)

Clarke, Kathleen (Fianna Fáil, Dublin City North)

Collins-O'Driscoll, Margaret (Cumann na nGaedheal, Dublin North)

Markiewicz, Constance de (Fianna Fáil, Dublin City South)

6th Dáil (Sept. 1927) 153 seats

Collins-O'Driscoll, Margaret (Cumman na nGaedheal, Dublin North)

7th Dáil (1932) 153 seats

Collins-O'Driscoll, Margaret (Cumann na nGaedheal, Dublin City North)

Reynolds, Mary, b. *c.* 1890, d. 29 Aug. 1974 (Cumann na aGaedheal, Sligo/Leitrim)

8th Dáil (1933) 153 seats

Concannon, Helena (née Walsh), b. 1878, d. 27 Feb. 1952 (Fianna Fáil, National University)

Pearse, Margaret Mary, b. 1878, d. 7 Nov. 1968 (Fianna Fáil, Dublin County) (daughter of Mary Pearse above)

Redmond, Bridget Mary (née Mallick), b. 1905, d. 3 May 1952 (Cumann na nGaedheal, Waterford)

9th Dáil (1937) 153 seats

Redmond, Bridget Mary (Fine Gael, Waterford)
Reynolds, Mary (Fine Gael, Leitrim)

10th Dáil (1938) 153 seats

Redmond, Bridget Mary (Fine Gael, Waterford)
Reynolds, Mary (Fine Gael, Leitrim)
Rice, Bridget Mary (née Henaghan), b. 1885, d. 7 Dec. 1967 (Fianna Fáil, Monaghan)

11th Dáil (1943) 138 seats

Redmond, Bridget Mary (Fine Gael, Waterford)
Reynolds, Mary (Fine Gael, Leitrim)
Rice, Bridget Mary (Fianna Fáil, Monaghan)

12th Dáil (1944) 138 seats

Redmond, Bridget Mary (Fine Gael, Waterford)
Reynolds, Mary (Fine Gael, Leitrim)
Rice, Bridget Mary (Fianna Fáil, Monaghan)
Ryan, Mary Bridget (née Carey), b. 1898, d. 8 Feb. 1981 (Fianna Fáil, Tipperary)

By-election: 4 Dec. 1945

Crowley, Honor Mary (née Boland), b. 19 Oct. 1901, d. 18 Oct. 1966 (Fianna Fáil, South Kerry)

13th Dáil (1948) 147 seats

Crowley, Honor Mary (Fianna Fáil, South Kerry)
Redmond, Bridget Mary (Fine Gael, Waterford)
Reynolds, Mary (Fine Gael, Sligo/Leitrim)
Rice, Bridget Mary (Fianna Fáil, Monaghan)
Ryan, Mary Bridget (Fianna Fáil, North Tipperary)

14th Dáil (1951) 147 seats

Crowley, Honor Mary (Fianna Fáil, South Kerry)
Redmond, Bridget Mary (Fine Gael, Waterford)
Reynolds, Mary (Fine Gael, Sligo/Leitrim)
Rice, Mary Bridget (Fianna Fáil, Monaghan)
Ryan, Mary Bridget (Fianna Fáil, South Tipperary)

15th Dáil (1954) 147 seats

Crowley, Honor Mary (Fianna Fáil, South Kerry)
Lynch, Celia (née Quinn), b. 1908, d. 16 June 1989 (Fianna Fáil, Dublin North)

O'Carroll, Maureen (née McHugh), b., 29 Mar. 1913, d. 9 May 1984 (Labour, Dublin North Central)
Reynolds, Mary (Fine Gael, Sligo/Leitrim)
Ryan, Mary Bridget (Fianna Fáil, North Kerry)

By-election, 28 Feb. 1956

O'Connor, Kathleen, b. 1935 (Clann na Poblachta, North Kerry)

16th Dáil (1957) 147 seats

Crowley, Honor May (Fianna Fáil, South Kerry)
Hogan, Brigid (later Hogan-O'Higgins), b. March 1832 (Fine Gael, South Galway)
Lynch, Celia (Fianna Fáil, Dublin South Central)
Reynolds, Mary (Fine Gael, Sligo/Leitrim)
Ryan, Mary Bridget (Fianna Fáil, North Tipperary)

17th Dáil (1961) 144 seats

Crowley, Honor Mary (Fianna Fáil, South Kerry)
Hogan-O'Higgins, Brigid (Fine Gael, East Galway)
Lynch, Celia (Fianna Fáil, Dublin North Central)

By-election, 19 Feb. 1964

Galvin, Sheila, b. 23 Feb. 1914, d. 20 Mar. 1983 (Fianna Fáil, Cork)

By-election, 8 July 1964

Burke, Joan T. (née Crowley), b. Feb. 1929 (Fine Gael, Roscommon)

By-election, 10 Mar. 1965

Desmond, Eileen (née Harrington), b. Dec. 1932 (Labour, Mid-Cork)

18th Dáil (1965) 144 seats

Burke, Joan T. (Fine Gael, Roscommon)
Crowley, Honor Mary (Fianna Fáil, South Kerry)
Desmond, Eileen (Labour, Mid Cork)
Hogan-O'Higgins, Brigid (Fine Gael, East Galway)
Lynch, Celia (Fianna Fáil, Dublin North Central)

19th Dáil (1969) 144 seats

Burke, Joan T. (Fine Gael, Roscommon/Leitrim)
Hogan-O'Higgins, Brigid (Fine Gael, Clare/South Galway)
Lynch, Celia (Fianna Fáil, Dublin North Central)

20th Dáil (1973) 144 seats

Burke, Joan T. (Fine Gael, Roscommon/Leitrim)
Desmond, Eileen (Labour, Mid-Cork)
Hogan-O'Higgins, Brigid (Fine Gael, Clare/South Galway)
Lynch, Celia (Fianna Fáil, Dublin North Central)

By-election, 4 Mar. 1975

Geoghegan-Quinn, Máire (née Geoghegan), b. 5 Sept. 1950 (Fianna Fáil, Galway West)

21st Dáil (1977) 148 seats

Ahern, Ita (Kit) (née Liston), b. 13 Jan. 1915 (Fianna Fáil, Kerry North)
Burke, Joan T. (Fine Gael, Roscommon/Leitrim)
Desmond, Eileen (Labour, Mid-Cork)
De Valera, Sile, b. Dec. 1954 (Fianna Fáil, Dublin Mid-County)
Geoghegan-Quinn, Máire (Fianna Fáil, Galway West)
Lemass, Eileen (née Delaney), b. July 1932 (Fianna Fáil, Dublin-Balleyfermot)

By-election, 7 Nov. 1979

Barry, Myra, b. June 1957 (Fine Gael, Cork North-East)

22nd Dáil (1981) 166 seats

Acheson, Carrie (née Barlow), b. Sept. 1934 (Fianna Fáil, Tipperary South)
Barry, Myra (Fine Gael, Cork East)
Desmond, Eileen (Labour, Mid-Cork)
Fennell, Nuala (née Campbell), b. Nov. 1935 (Fine Gael, Dublin South)
Flaherty, Mary, b. May 1935 (Fine Gael, Dublin North-West)
Geoghegan-Quinn, Máire (Fianna Fáil, Galway West)
Glenn, Alice, b. Dec. 1927 (Fine Gael, Dublin Central)
Harney, Mary, b. 11 Mar. 1953 (Fianna Fáil, Dublin South-West)
Lemass, Eileen (Fianna Fáil, Dublin West)
Owen, Nora (née O'Mahony), b. June 1945 (Fine Gael, Dublin North)
Taylor-Quinn, Madeleine (née Taylor), b. May 1951 (Fine Gael, Clare)

23rd Dáil (Feb. 1982) 166 seats

Barry, Myra (Fine Gael, East Cork)
Desmond, Eileen (Labour, Cork South Central)
Fennell, Nuala (Fine Gael, Dublin South)
Flaherty, Mary (Fine Gael, Dublin North-West)
Geoghegan-Quinn, Máire (Fianna Fáil, Galway West)
Harney, Mary (Fianna Fáil, Dublin South-West)
Hussey, Gemma (née Moran), b. Nov. 1938 (Fine Gael, Wicklow)
Owen, Nora (Fine Gael, Dublin North)

24th Dáil (Nov. 1982) 166 seats

Barnes, Monica (née McDermott), b. Feb. 1936 (Fine Gael, Dun Laoghaire)
Barry, Myra (Fine Gael, East Cork)
Desmond, Eileen (Labour, Cork South Central)
Doyle, Avril (née Belton), b. 18 Apr. 1949 (Fine Gael, Wexford)
Fennell, Nuala (Fine Gael, Dublin South)
Flaherty, Mary (Fine Gael, Dublin North-West)
Geoghegan-Quinn, Máire (Fianna Fáil, Galway West)

Glenn, Alice (Fine Gael, Dublin Central)
Harney, Mary (Fianna Fáil, Dublin South-West)
Hussey, Gemma (Fine Gael, Wicklow)
Lemass, Eileen (Fianna Fáil, Dublin West)
O'Rourke, Mary (née Lenihan), b. May 1937 (Fianna Fáil, Longford/ Westmeath)
Owen, Nora (Fine Gael, Dublin North)
Taylor-Quinn, Madeleine (Fine Gael, Clare)

25th Dáil (1987) 166 seats

Barnes, Monica (Fine Gael, Dun Laoghaire)
Colley, Anne, b. July 1951 (Progressive Democrats, Dublin South)
Coughlan, Mary T., b. May 1965 (Fianna Fáil, Donegal South-West)
De Valera, Sile (Fianna Fáil, Clare)
Doyle, Avril (Fine Gael, Wexford)
Flaherty, Mary (Fine Gael, Dublin North-West)
Geoghegan-Quinn, Máire (Fianna Fáil, Galway West)
Harney, Mary (Progressive Democrats, Dublin South-West)
Hussey, Gemma (Fine Gael, Wicklow)
Kennedy, Geraldine, b. Sept. 1951 (Progressive Democrats, Dun Laoghaire)
Mary Mooney, b. Dec. 1958 (Fianna Fáil, Dublin South Central)
O'Rourke, Mary (Fianna Fáil, Longford/Westmeath)
Quill, Mairín, b. 15 Sept. 1940 (Progressive Democrats, Cork North Central)
Taylor-Quinn, Madeleine (Fine Gael, Clare)

26th Dáil (1989) 166 seats

Ahearn, Theresa, b. May 1951 (Fine Gael, Tipperary South)
Barnes, Monica (Fine Gael, Dun Laoghaire)
Coughlan, Mary T. (Fianna Fáil, Donegal South-West)
De Valera, Sile (Fianna Fáil, Clare)
Fennell, Nuala (Fine Gael, Dublin South)
Flaherty, Mary (Fine Gael, Dublin North-West)
Geoghegan-Quinn, Máire (Fianna Fáil, Galway West)
Harney, Mary (Progressive Democrats, Dublin South-West)
O'Rourke, Mary (Fianna Fáil, Longford/Westmeath)
Owen, Nora (Fine Gael, Dublin North)
Quill, Máirin (Progressive Democrats, Cork North Central)
Taylor-Quinn, Madeleine (Fine Gael, Clare)
Wallace, Mary, b. June 1959 (Fianna Fáil, Meath)

27th Dáil (1992) 166 seats

Ahearn, Theresa (Fine Gael, Tipperary South)
Bhreathnach, Niamh, b. June 1945 (Labour, Dun Laoghaire)
Burton, Joan, b. Feb. 1949 (Labour, Dublin West)
Coughlan, Mary (Fianna Fáil, Donegal South-West)
De Valera, Sile (Fianna Fáil, Clare)
Doyle, Avril (Fine Gael, Wexford)

Fitzgerald, Eithne (née Ingoldsby), b. Nov. 1950 (Labour, Dublin South)
Fitzgerald, Frances, b. Aug. 1950 (Fine Gael, Dublin South-East)
Flaherty, Mary (Fine Gael, Dublin North-West)
Geoghegan-Quinn, Máire (Fianna Fáil, Galway West)
Harney, Mary (Progressive Democrats, Dublin South-West)
Keogh, Helen, b. June 1951 (Progressive Democrats, Dun Laoghaire)
McManus, Liz (née O'Driscoll), b. Mar. 1947 (Democrat Life, Wicklow)
Moynihan-Cronin, Breeda (née Moynihan), b. Mar. 1953 (Labour, Kerry South)
O'Donnell, Liz, b. July 1956 (Progressive Democrats, Westmeath)
O'Rourke, Mary (Fianna Fáil, Westmeath)
Owen, Nora (Fine Gael, Dublin North)
Quill, Mairín (Progressive Democrats, Cork North Central)
Shortall, Róisin, b. 25 Apr. 1954 (Labour, Dublin North-West)
Wallace, Mary (Fianna Fáil, Meath)

By-election, 10 Nov. 1994, 29 June 1995, 2 Apr. 1996

Lynch, Kathleen, b. 1953 (Democratic Left, Cork North Central)
Fox, Mildred, b. June 1971 (Independent, Wicklow)
Keaveney, Cecila, b. Nov. 1968 (Fianna Fáil, Donegal North-East)

28th Dáil (1997) 166 seats

Ahearn, Theresa (Fine Gael, Tipperary South)
Barnes, Monica (Fine Gael, Dun Laoghaire)
Clune, Deirdre (née Barry), b. June 1959 (Fine Gael, Cork South Central)
Cooper-Flynn, Beverley (née Flynn), b. June 1966 (Fianna Fáil, Mayo)
Coughlan, Mary (Fianna Fáil, Donegal South-West)
De Valera, Sile (Fianna Fáil, Clare)
Fitzgerald, Frances (Fine Gael, Dublin South-East)
Fox, Mildred (Independent, Wicklow)
Hanafin, Mary, b. June 1959 (Fianna Fáil, Dun Laoghaire)
Harney, Mary (Progressive Democrats, Dublin South-West)
Keaveney, Cecilia (Fianna Fáil, Donegal North-East)
McGennis, Marian, b. Nov. 1953 (Fianna Fáil, Dublin Central)
McManus, Liz (Democrat Left, Wicklow)
Mitchell, Olivia, b. July 1947 (Fine Gael, Dublin South)
Moynihan-Cronin, Breeda (Labour, Kerry South)
O'Donnell, Liz (Progressive Democrats, Dublin South)
O'Rourke, Mary (Fianna Fáil, Westmeath)
Owen, Nora (Fine Gael, Dublin North)
Shortall, Rósin (Labour, Dublin North-West)
Wallace, Mary (Fianna Fáil, Meath)

By-election, 12 Mar. 1998

O'Sullivan, Jan (née Gale), b. 6 Dec. 1950 (Labour, Limerick East) (First woman Church of Ireland member elected since Constance Markievicz (1927). She was often subjected to sectarianism when Mayor of Limerick.)

27 Oct. 1999

Upton, Mary, b. 30 May 1946 (Labour, Dublin South Central)

29th Dáil (2002) 166 seats

Clune, Deirdre (Fine Gael, Cork South Central)
Cooper-Flynn, Beverley (Fianna Fáil, Mayo)
Coughlan, Mary (Fianna Fáil, Donegal South-West)
De Valera, Sile (Fianna Fáil, Clare)
Fitzgerald, Frances (Fine Gael, Dublin South-East)
Fox, Mildred (Independent, Wicklow)
Hanafin, Mary (Fianna Fáil, Dun Laoghaire)
Harney, Mary (Progressive Democrat, Dublin Mid-West)
Keavney, Cecilia (Fianna Fáil, Donegal North-East)
McGennis, Marian (Fianna Fáil, Dublin South Central)
McManus, Liz (Labour, Wicklow)
Mitchell, Olivia (Fine Gael, Dublin South)
Moynihan Cronin, Breeda (Labour, Kerry South)
O'Donnell, Liz (Progressive Democrats, Dublin South)
O'Rourke, Mary (Fianna Fáil, Westmeath)
O'Sullivan, Jan (Labour, Limerick East)
Owen, Nora (Fine Gael, Dublin North)
Shortall, Roisin (Labour, Dublin North-West)
Upton, Mary (Labour, Dublin South Central)
Wallace, Mary (Fianna Fáil, Meath)

Members of the Senate

First triennial period (1922–5) 60 seats

Costello, Eileen (née Edith Drury), b. 1870, d. 14 Mar. 1962 (9 years) (elected by Dáil, 7 Dec. 1922)

Desart, Ellen, Countess Dowager of (Ellen Odette O'Connor, née Bischoffsheim), b. 1857, d. 29 June 1933 (12 years) (nominated by President of the Executive Council, 6 Dec. 1922)

Green, Alice Stopford (née Stopford), b. 30 May 1847, d. 28 May 1929 (9 years) (elected by Dáil, 7 Dec. 1922)

Power, Jennie Wyse (née O'Toole), b. May 1858, d. 5 Jan. 1941 (12 years) (nominated by President of the Executive Council, 6 Dec. 1922)

Second triennial period (1925–8): no women elected

Third triennial period (1828–31) 60 seats

Clarke, Kathleen Anne, b. Oct. 1878
Costello, Eileen
Desart, Countess of, Ellen
Green Alice Stopford (died 28 May 1929)
Power, Ennie Wyse
Browne, Kathleen (elected 20 June 1929 to fill vacancy caused by death of Alice Stopford Green)

Fourth triennial period (1931–34) 60 seats

Browne, Kathleen
Clarke, Kathleen
Costello, Eileen
Desart, Countess of, Ellen (died 29 June 1933)
Power, Jennie Wyse

Fifth triennial period (1934 to abolition on 29 May 1936) 60 seats

Browne, Kathleen
Clarke, Kathleen
Costello, Eileen
Power, Jennie Wyse

Senate election (Mar. 1938) 60 seats

Concannon, Helena (née Walsh), b. 1878, d. 27 Feb. 1952 (National University of Ireland)
Kearns-MacWhinney, Linda (née Kearns), b. July 1888, d. 5 June 1951 (Fianna Fáil, Panel Member, Industrial and Commercial Panel, Nominating Bodies Sub-Panel)
Kennedy, Margaret L., b. 1892 (nominated by Taoiseach, 1 Apr. 1938)
Pearse, Margaret Mary, b. 1878, d. 7 Nov. 1968 (Fianna Fáil, Panel Member, Administrative Panel, Dáil Sub-Panel)

Senate election (Aug. 1938) 60 seats

Concannon, Helena (National University of Ireland)
Kennedy, Margaret L. (nominated by Taoiseach, 22 Aug. 1938)
Pearse, Margaret (Fianna Fáil, Panel Member, Administrative Panel, Dáil Sub-Panel)

Senate election (1943) 60 seats

Concannon, Helena (National University of Ireland)
Kennedy, Margaret L. (nominated by Taoiseach, 31 Aug. 1943)
Pearse, Margaret Mary (nominated by Taoiseach, 31 Aug. 1943)

Senate election (1944) 60 seats

Concannon, Helena (National University of Ireland)
Kennedy, Margaret L. (nominated by Taoiseach, 11 Aug. 1944)
Pearse, Margaret Mary (nominated by Taoiseach, 11 Aug. 1944)

Senate election (1948) 60 seats

Butler, Eleanor J., later Clonmore Countess of Wicklow, b. c. 1915, d. Feb./Mar. 1997 (nominated by Taoiseach, 14 Apr. 1948)
Concannon, Helena (National University of Ireland)
Pearse, Margaret Mary (Fianna Fáil, Panel Member, Administrative Panel, Nominating Bodies Sub-Panel)

By-election, 16 June 1950, 60 seats

Davidson, Mary F., b. *c.* 1902, d. 29 May 1986 (Labour, Panel Member, Industrial and Commercial Panel, Oireachtas Sub-Panel)

Senate election (1951) 60 seats

Concannon, Helena (National University of Ireland), d. 27 Feb. 1952

Dowdall, Jane (née Doggett), b. 29 Sept. 1899, d. 10 Dec. 1974 (Fianna Fáil, Panel Member, Industrial and Commercial Panel, Nominating Bodies Sub-Panel)

Pearse, Margaret Mary (nominated by Taoiseach, 9 Aug. 1951)

Senate election (1954) 60 seats

Davidson, Mary F. (Labour, Panel Member, Industrial and Commercial Panel, Oireachtas Sub-Panel)

Dowdall, Jane (Fianna Fáil, Panel Member, Industrial and Commercial Panel, Nominating Bodies Sub-Panel)

Pearse, Margaret Mary (Panel Member, Administrative Panel, Oireachtas Sub-Panel)

Senate election (1957) 60 seats

Connolly-O'Brien, Nora (née Connolly), b. 1893, d. 17 June 1981 (nominated by Taoiseach, 15 May 1957)

Davidson, Mary F. (Labour, Panel Member, Industrial and Commercial Panel, Oireachtas Sub-Panel)

Dowdall, Jane (Fianna Fáil, Industrial and Commercial Panel, Nominating Bodies Sub-Panel)

Pearse, Margaret Mary (nominated by Taoiseach, 15 May 1957)

Senate election (1961) 60 seats

Connolly-O'Brien, Nora (nominated by Taoiseach, 9 Dec. 1961)

Davidson, Mary F. (Labour, Panel Member, Industrial and Commercial Panel, Oireachtas Sub-Panel)

Pearse, Margaret Mary (nominated by Taoiseach, 9 Dec. 1961)

Senate election (1965) 60 seats

Ahern, Catherine Ita (Kit) (née Liston), b. 13 Jan. 1915 (nominated by Taoiseach, 11 June 1965)

Connolly-O'Brien, Nora (nominated by Taoiseach, 11 June 1965)

Davidson, Mary F. (Labour, Panel Member, Industrial and Commercial Panel, Oireachtas Sub-Panel)

Pearse, Margaret Mary (nominated by Taoiseach, 11 June 1965)

Senate election (1969) 60 seats

Ahern, Catherine Ita (Kit) (Fianna Fáil, Panel Member, Cultural and Education Panel, Oireachtas Sub-Panel)

Bourke, Mary T. W., later Robinson, b. 21 May 1944 (University of Dublin)

553

Desmond, Eileen (née Harrington), b. Dec. 1932 (Labour, Panel Member, Industrial and Commercial Panel, Oireachtas Sub-Panel)

Farrell, Peggy, b. 15 Nov. 1920 (nominated by Taoiseach, 19 Aug. 1969)

Owens, Evelyn P., b. 22 Jan. 1931 (Labour, Panel Member, Labour Panel, Nominating Bodies Sub-Panel)

Senate election (1973) 60 seats

Ahern, Catherine Ita (Kit) (Fianna Fáil, Panel Member, Cultural and Educational Panel, Oireachtas Sub-Panel)

Bourke, Mary T. W. (University of Dublin)

Owens, Evelyn P. (Labour, Panel Member, Labour Panel, Nominating Bodies Sub-Panel)

Walsh, Mary, b. Oct. 1929 (Fine Gael, Cultural and Educational Panel, Oireachtas Sub-Panel)

Senate election (1977) 60 seats

Cassidy, Eileen (née Foreman), b. Aug. 1932 (Fianna Fáil, nominated by Taoiseach, 25 Aug. 1977)

Goulding, Lady Valerie (née Monckton), b. Sept. 1918 (Fianna Fáil, nominated by Taoiseach, 25 Aug. 1977)

Harney, Mary, b. 11 Mar. 1953 (Fianna Fáil, nominated by Taoiseach, 25 Aug. 1977)

Honan, Tras (née Barlow), b. 4 Jan. 1930 (Fianna Fáil, Panel Member, Administrative Panel, Nominating Bodies Sub-Panel)

Hussey, Gemma (née Moran), b. Nov. 1938 (Independent, National University of Ireland)

Robinson, Mary T. W. (née Bourke) (Labour, University of Dublin)

By-election, 11 Dec. 1979

McGuinness, Catherine (née Ellis), 14 Nov. 1934 (Independent, University of Dublin)

Senate election (1981) 60 seats

Bolger, Deirdre (née Boland), b. 27 July 1938 (Fine Gael, Panel Member, Industrial and Commercial Panel, Nominating Bodies Sub-Panel)

Bulbulia, Katharine (née O'Carroll), b. July 1943 (Fine Gael, Panel Member, Administrative Panel, Oireachtas Sub-Panel)

Honan, Tras (Fianna Fáil, Panel Member, Administrative Panel, Nominating Bodies Sub-Panel)

Hussey, Gemma (Fine Gael, National University of Ireland)

Kearney, Miriam, b. July 1959 (Fine Gael, nominated by Taoiseach, 19 Aug. 1981)

Lawlor, Patsy, b. Mar. 1933 (Fine Gael, Panel Member, Cultural and Education Panel, Nominating Bodies Sub-Panel)

McGuinness, Catherine (Independent, University of Dublin)

O'Rourke, Mary (née Lenihan), b. May 1937 (Fianna Fáil, Cultural and Educational Panel, Oireachtas Sub-Panel)

Robinson, Mary T. W. (Labour, University of Dublin)

Senate election (1982) 60 seats

Barnes, Monica (née McDermott), b. Feb. 1936 (Fine Gael, Panel Member, Labour Panel, Oireachtas Sub-Panel)

Bolger, Deirdre (Fine Gael, Panel Member, Industrial and Commercial Panel, Oireachtas Sub-Panel)

Bulbulia, Katharine (Fine Gael, Panel Member, Administrative Panel, Nominating Bodies Sub-Panel)

Hannon, Camilla (née Begley), b. 21 July 1936 (Fianna Fáil, nominated by Taoiseach, 10 May 1982)

Honan, Tras (Fianna Fáil, Panel Member, Administrative Panel, Nominating Bodies Sub-Panel)

O'Rourke, Mary (Fianna Fáil, Panel Member, Cultural and Educational Panel, Oireachtas Sub-Panel)

Robinson, Mary T. W. (Labour, University of Dublin)

Taylor-Quinn, Madelene (née Taylor), b. May 1951 (Fine Gael, Panel Member, Cultural and Educational Panel, Nominating Bodies Sub-Panel)

Senate election (1983) 60 seats

Bulbulia, Katharine (Fine Gael, Panel Member, Administrative Panel, Nominating Bodies Sub-Panel)

Fennell, Nuala (née Campbell), b. Nov. 1935 (Fine Gael, nominated member (casual vacancy), nominated 20 Feb. 1987)

Honan, Tras (Fianna Fáil, Panel Member, Administrative Panel, Nominating Bodies Sub-Panel)

McAuliffe-Ennis, Helen (née McAuliffe), b. 1 Apr. 1951 (Labour, Panel Member, Cultural and Educational Panel, Oireachtas Sub-Panel)

McGuinness, Catherine (Independent, University of Dublin)

Rogers, Bríd (née Stratford), b. 20 Feb. 1935 (Independent, nominated by Taoiseach, 7 Feb. 1983)

Robinson, Mary T. W. (Labour, University of Dublin)

Senate election (1987) 60 seats

Bulbulia, Katharine (Fine Gael, Panel Member, Administrative Panel, Nominating Bodies Sub-Panel)

Fennel, Nuala (Fine Gael, Panel Member, Labour Panel, Oireachtas Sub-Panel)

Honan, Tras (Fine Fianna, Panel Member, Administrative Panel, Nominating Bodies Sub-Panel)

Robinson, Mary T. W. (Labour, University of Dublin)

Wallace, Mary, b. June 1959 (Fianna Fáil, Panel Member, Administrative Panel, Oireachtas Sub-Panel)

Senate election (1989) 60 seats

Bennett, Olga, b. Oct. 1947 (Fianna Fáil, nominated by Taoiseach, 27 Oct. 1989)

Doyle, Avril (née Belton), b. 18 Apr. 1949 (Fine Gael, Panel Member, Agricultural Panel, Nominating Bodies Sub-Panel)

555

Hederman, Camecita (née Cruess-Callaghan), b. 23 Oct. 1939 (Independent, University of Dublin)

Honan, Tras (Fianna Fáil, Panel Member, Administrative Panel, Nominating Bodies Sub-Panel)

Keogh, Helen, b. June 1951 (Progressive Democrats, nominated by Taoiseach, 27 Oct. 1989)

Jackman, Mary (née Furlong), b. Apr. 1943 (Fine Gael, Panel Member, Labour Panel, Nominating Bodies Sub-Panel)

Senate election (1993) 60 seats

Gallagher, Ann, b. Mar. 1967 (Labour, Panel Member, Industrial and Commercial Panel, Oireachtas Sub-Panel)

Henry, Mary E. F., b. 11 May 1940 (Independent, University of Dublin)

Honan, Cathy (née O'Brien), b. 16 Sept. 1951 (Progressive Democrats, Panel Member, Industrial and Commercial Panel, Oireachtas Sub-Panel)

Kelly, Mary, b. May 1952 (Labour, Cultural and Educational Panel, Oireachtas Sub-Panel)

McGennis, Marian, b. Nov. 1953 (Fianna Fáil, nominated by Taoiseach, 10 Feb. 1993)

Ormonde, Ann (Fianna Fáil, Panel Member, Cultural and Educational Panel, Nominating Bodies Sub-Panel)

O'Sullivan, Jan (née Gale), b. 6 Dec. 1950 (Labour, Panel Member, Administrative Panel, Oireachtas Sub-Panel)

Taylor-Quinn, Madeleine (née Taylor), b. May 1951 (Fine Gael, Cultural and Educational Panel, Nominating Bodies Sub-Panel)

Casual vacancies

Bhreathnach, Niamh, b. June 1945 (Labour, nominated by Taoiseach, 13 June 1997)

Cosgrave, Niamh, b. 9 Oct. 1964 (nominated by Taoiseach, 12 June 1997)

Senate election (1997) 60 seats

Cox, Margaret, b. Sept. 1963 (Fianna Fáil, Panel Member, Industrial and Commercial Panel, Oireachtas Sub-Panel)

Doyle, Avril (Fine Gael, Panel Member, Agricultural Panel, Nomating Bodies Sub-Panel)

Henry, Mary (Independent, University of Dublin)

Jackman, Mary (Fine Gael, Panel Member, Labour Panel, Nominating Bodies Sub-Panel)

Keogh, Helen (Progressive Democrats, nominated by Taoiseach, 12 Sept. 1997)

Leonard, Ann, b. Jan. 1969 (Fianna Fáil, nominated by Taoiseach, 12 Sept. 1997)

O'Meara, Kathleen, b. Jan. 1960 (Labour, Panel Member, Agricultural Panel, Oireachtas Sub-Panel)

Ormonde, Ann (Fianna Fáil, Panel Member, Cultural and Educational Panel, Nominating Bodies Sub-Panel)

Quill, Máirín, b. 15 Sept. 1940 (Progressive Democrats, nominated by Taoiseach, 12 Sept. 1997)

Ridge, Therese, b. Mar. 1941 (Fine Gael, Panel Member, Labour Panel, Nominating Bodies Sub-Panel)

Taylor-Quinn, Madeleine (Fine Gael, Panel Member, Cultural and Educational Panel, Nominating Bodies Sub-Panel)

European Parliament

(1979) 15 Irish members

De Valera, Sile (Fianna Fáil, Dublin)
Desmond, Eileen (Labour, Munster)

(1984) 15 Irish members

Banotti, Mary (née O'Mahony), b. 29 May 1939 (Fine Gael, Dublin)
Lemass, Eileen (Fianna Fáil, Dublin)

(1989) 15 Irish members

Banotti, Mary (Fine Gael, Dublin)

(1994) 15 Irish members

Ahern, Nuala (née McDowell), 5 Feb. 1949 (Green Party, Leinster)
Banotti, Mary (Fine Gael, Dublin)
McKenna, Patricia, b. 13 Mar. 1957 (Green Party, Dublin)
Malone, Bernie (née O'Brien), b. 26 Mar. 1948 (Labour, Dublin)

(1999) 15 Irish members

Ahern, Nuala (Green Party, Leinster)
Banotti, Mary (Fine Gael, Dublin)
Doyle, Avril (Fine Gael, Leinster)
McKenna, Patricia (Green Party, Dublin)
Scallon, Dana (Rosemary) (née Brown), b. 30 Aug. 1950 (Independent, Connacht-Ulster)

(2004) 16 Irish members

Doyle, Avril (Fine Gael, East)
Harkin, Marian (Independent, North-West)
McDonald, Mary Lou (Sinn Féin, Dublin)
McGuinness, Mairead (Fine Gael, East)
Sinnott, Kathy (Independent, South)

Women elected representatives in Northern Ireland

Women elected to the Westminster parliament, the Northern Ireland parliament and the various Northern Ireland assemblies and elected forums.

557

Westminster parliament

No women were elected until 1953 (13 seats until 1950 then 12 seats until 1983; since then 17 seats).

By-election, 15 Apr. 1953

Ford, Patricia (née Smiles) (Unionist, North Down)

General election (1955) 12 seats

McLaughlin, Florence Patricia Alice (née Aldwell) (Unionist, Belfast West)

General election (1959) 12 seats

McLaughlin, Florence Patricia Alice (Unionist, Belfast West)

General election (1966) 12 seats

No women elected

By-election, 17 Apr. 1969

Devlin, (Josephine) Bernadette (later McAliskey) (Unity, Mid-Ulster)

General election (1970) 12 seats

Devlin, (Josephine) Bernadette (Unity, Mid-Ulster)
In the general elections held in 1974, 1979, 1983, 1987, 1992, 1997 no women were elected.

General election (2001) 17 seats

Gildernew, Michelle (Sinn Féin, Fermanagh and South Tyrone)
Hermon, Lady (Sylvia) (Ulster Unionist, North Down)
Robinson, Iris (Democratic Unionist, Strangford)

Northern Ireland parliament

General election (1921) 52 seats

Chichester, Dehra (née Kerr Fisher, later Dame Dehra Parker) (Unionist, Londonderry City and County)
McMordie, Julia (née Gray) (Unionist, Belfast South)

General election (1925) 52 seats

Chichester, Dehra (Unionist, Londonderry)

General election (1929) 52 seats

Waring, Margaret Alicia (née Parr) (Unionist, Iveagh)

By-election, 15 May 1933

Parker, Dehra (formerly Chichester) (Unionist, Londonderry South)

General election (1933) 52 seats

Parker, Dehra (Unionist, Londonderry South)

General election (1938) 52 seats

Parker, Dehra (Unionist, Londonderry South)

General election (1945) 52 seats

Calvert, Lilian Irene Mercer (née Earls) (Independent, Queen's University Belfast)
Parker, Dehra (Unionist, Londonderry South)
McNabb, Dinah (Unionist, Armagh North)

General election (1949) 52 seats

Calvert, Lilian Irene Mercer (Independent, Queen's University Belfast)
Hickey, Dr Eileen Mary (Independent, Queen's University Belfast)
Parker, Dehra (Unionist, Londonderry South)
McNabb, Dinah (Unionist, Armagh North)

General election (1953) 52 seats

Hickey, Dr Eileen Mary (Independent, Queen's University Belfast)
Parker, Dame Dehra (Unionist, Londonderry South)
McNabb, Dinah (Unionist, Armagh North)
Maconachie, Elizabeth (Bessie) Hamill (Unionist, Queen's University Belfast)

General election (1958) 52 seats

Parker, Dame Dehra (Unionist, Londonderry South)
McNabb, Dinah (Unionist, Armagh North)
Maconachie, Elizabeth (Bessie) Hamill (Unionist, Queen's University Belfast)

By-election, 22 Nov. 1961

Murnaghan, Sheelagh Mary (Liberal, Queen's University Belfast).

General election (1962) 52 seats

McNabb, Dinah (Unionist, Armagh North)
Maconachie, Elizabeth (Bessie) Hamill (Unionist, Queen's University Belfast)
Murnaghan, Sheelagh Mary (Liberal, Queen's University Belfast)

General election (1965) 52 seats

McNabb, Dinah (Unionist, Armagh North)
Maconachie, Elizabeth (Bessie) Hamill (Unionist, Queen's University Belfast)
Murnaghan, Sheelagh Mary (Liberal, Queen's University Belfast)

General election (1969) 52 seats

Devlin, (Josephine) Bernadette Devlin (later McAliskey) (People's Democracy, Londonderry South)
Dickson, Anne Lettia (née McCance) (Unionist (O'Neill), Carrick)

Northern Ireland Senate 24 seats

1950–8

Greeves, Marion Janet (née Cadbury) (Independent)

By-election (1970)

Taggart, Edith Ashover (née Hind) (Unionist)

Northern Ireland Assembly (1973) 78 seats

Conn, Shena Elizabeth (Unionist, Londonderry)
Coulter, Rose Jean (Independent Unionist (Loyalist Coalition), Belfast West)
Dickson, Anne Lettia (Independent Unionist (Unofficial Candidate), Antrim South)
Paisley, Eileen Emily (née Cassels) (Democratic Unionist Party, Belfast East)

Constitutional Convention (1975) 78 seats

Conn, Shena Elizabeth (Official Unionist Party, United Ulster Unionist Party, Londonderry)
Coulter, Rose Jean (Official Unionist Party, United Ulster Unionist Party, West Belfast)
Dickson, Anne Lettia (Unionist Party of Northern Ireland, Antrim South)
Paisley, Eileen Emily (United Ulster Unionist Party, East Belfast)

Northern Ireland Assembly (1982) 78 seats

Dunlop, Dorothy (Official Unionist Party, East Belfast)
McSorley, Mary Katherine (Social Democratic and Labour Party, Mid-Ulster)
Simpson, Mary (Official Unionist Party, Armagh)

Northern Ireland Forum (1996) 110 seats

Armstrong, Anne (Sinn Féin, West Belfast)
Beattie, May (Democratic Unionist Party, East Antrim)
Caraher, Maria (Sinn Féin, Newry and Armagh)
McGuinness, Anne (Sinn Féin, West Belfast)
O'Connor, Michelle (Sinn Féin, Upper Bann)
Parks, Joan (Democratic Unionist Party, South Belfast)
Robinson, Iris (Democratic Unionist Party, Strangford)
Rodgers, Bríd (Social Democratic and Labour Party, Upper Bann)
Ritchie, Margaret (Social Democratic and Labour Party, South Down)
Steele, Mary (Ulster Unionist Party, East Antrim)

Northern Ireland Assembly (1998) 108 seats

Armitage, Pauline (Ulster Unionist Party, Londonderry East)
De Brún, Bairbre (Sinn Féin, West Belfast)
Bell, Eileen (Alliance, North Down)
Carson, Joan (Ulster Unionist Party, Fermanagh and South Tyrone)
Gildernew, Michelle (Sinn Féin, Fermanagh and South Tyrone)
Hanna, Carmel (Social Democratic and Labour Party, Belfast South)
Lewsley, Patricia (Social Democratic and Labour Party, Lagan Valley)
McWilliams, Prof. Monica (Northern Ireland Women's Coalition, Belfast South)

Morrice, Jane (Northern Ireland Women's Coalition, North Down)
Nelis, Mary (Sinn Féin, Foyle)
Ramsey, Sue (Sinn Féin, Belfast West)
Robinson, Iris (Democratic Unionist Party, Strangford)
Rodgers, Bríd (Social Democratic and Labour Party, Upper Bann)

Northern Ireland Assembly (2002) 108 seats

The party designation used on the ballot paper is that given below.

Beare, Norah (Ulster Unionist Party, Lagan Valley)
Bell, Eileen (Alliance, North Down)
Bradley, Mary (Social Democratic and Labour Party, Foyle)
De Brún, Bairbre (Sinn Féin, Belfast West)
Dodds, Diane (Democratic Unionist Party, Belfast West)
Dougan, Geraldine (Sinn Féin, Mid Tyrone)
Foster, Arlene (Ulster Unionist Party, Fermanagh and South Tyrone)
Gildernew, Michelle (Sinn Féin, Fermanagh and South Tyrone)
Hanna, Carmel (Social Democratic and Labour Party, Belfast South)
Kelly, Dolores (Social Democratic and Labour Party, Upper Bann)
Lewsley, Patricia (Social Democratic and Labour Party, Lagan Valley)
Long, Naomi (Alliance, Belfast East)
Nelis, Mary (Sinn Féin, Foyle)
O'Rawe, Patricia (Sinn Féin, Newry and Armagh)
Ritchie, Margaret (Social Democratic and Labour Party, South Down)
Robinson, Iris (Democratic Unionist Party, Strangford)
Ruane, Catriona (Sinn Féin, South Down)
Stanton, Kathy (Sinn Féin, Belfast North)

European Parliament

Northern Ireland three seats. No women returned until 2004 with the election of Bairbe de Brún (Sinn Féin).

Sources: Maedhbh McNamara and Paschal Mooney, *Women in Parliament, Ireland: 1918–2000* (Dublin, 2000); <www.ark.ac.uk/elections>.

Section Three

ECONOMIC HISTORY

COST-OF-LIVING INDEX, 1698–1998

For the cost-of-living index a single number is taken to represent the material position of individuals or households relative to some earlier (or later) reference point in time. Ideally we would wish to collect the prices of all the goods and services purchased by the bulk of the population in each year since, say, 1698. For most of the period these would relate primarily to food and drink, fuel and rent, clothing and footwear, and perhaps some limited spending on medicines, education and religious dues. The episodic, and sometimes crippling, expenditures relating to marriages and funerals might also enter a really comprehensive index of living costs. A place might also be found for the cost of credit to the poorer social classes, as this changed greatly during the course of the nineteenth century. Social security, in the form initially of the poor law system, changed the position facing the Irish poor, sick and aged from the 1840s. Old age pensions and other welfare measures dating from the early twentieth century built on these foundations.

Excerpt from Liam Kennedy, 'The Cost of Living in Ireland, 1698–1998', in David Dickson and Cormac Ó Gráda (eds), *Refiguring Ireland: Essays in Honour of L. M. Cullen* (Dublin, 2003), pp. 249–76.

The cost of living, 1873–1913 (1890–1900 = 100)

	1873	1882	1890	1895	1900	1913
France	110	111	102	99	94	111
Germany	118	101	100	98	104	127
UK	141	118	103	96	105	118
USA	143	118	105	97	97	114
Ireland	130	108	94	81	85	111

Source: W. A. Lewis, *Growth and Fluctuations, 1870–1913* (London, 1978), p. 70.

The long view also points to the paradox of prices and affluence. Low prices and low living costs (in money terms) are not necessarily associated with either high or rising living standards. The opposite is the case for the recent historical period, not just in Ireland but in the western world more generally. Moreover, in contemporary times living costs in money terms are far higher in economically developed as compared to less-developed countries. In the case of Ireland, to take the dramatic final quarter of the twentieth century: prices coursed cumulatively upwards in a fashion that seemed extraordinary by earlier experience. Yet, in the recorded history of the island, there was no period in which the material conditions of life registered such spectacular and sustained improvement.

Excerpt from Kennedy, 'Cost of Living'.

Cost-of-living indices, 1698–1998

1730–35 = 100

	Urban	Rural
1698	120	125
1699	117	122
1700	97	98
1701	91	95
1702	81	85
1703	75	77
1704	77	81
1705	76	80
1706	61	63
1707	86	93
1708	85	88
1709	110	112
1710	99	99
1711	88	87
1712	85	83
1713	90	88
1714	99	106
1715	114	123
1716	108	116
1717	96	101
1718	92	98
1719	80	81
1720	93	96
1721	90	95
1722	84	88
1723	76	77
1724	73	74
1725	74	73
1726	93	95
1727	101	98
1728	110	104
1729	112	115
1730	106	104
1731	93	92
1732	93	93

	Urban	Rural
1733	101	104
1734	104	105
1735	102	103
1736	98	96
1737	95	97
1738	92	93
1739	102	105
1740	122	125
1741	149	155
1742	117	118
1743	99	100
1744	95	100
1745	96	101
1746	95	100
1747	100	105
1748	93	97
1749	106	112
1750	113	119
1751	119	126
1752	116	123
1753	129	136
1754	116	122
1755	108	114
1756	110	116
1757	123	129
1758	96	100
1759	88	91
1760	85	87
1761	88	91
1762	106	111
1763	120	126
1764	133	141
1765	129	136
1766	156	166
1767	161	171
1768	138	146
1769	143	150
1770	190	190
1771	192	186
1772	185	181
1773	178	170
1774	198	193
1775	166	160
1776	157	155
1777	157	150
1778	185	179
1779	168	164

567

	Urban	Rural
1780	154	149
1781	152	146
1782	122	111
1783	202	194
1784	173	165
1785	147	136
1786	183	177
1787	184	179
1788	167	160
1789	164	156
1790	167	158
1791	186	179
1792	173	163
1793	195	182
1794	202	190
1795	201	185
1796	236	223
1797	191	172
1798	229	220
1799	228	213
1800	482	459
1801	492	496
1802	211	191
1803	269	259
1804	270	261
1805	307	291
1806	280	257
1807	289	271
1808	347	330
1809	338	316
1810	336	313
1811	314	286
1812	435	412
1813	402	372
1814	297	275
1815	270	250
1816	276	254
1817	418	413
1818	304	275
1819	312	294
1820	301	296
1821	244	220
1822	249	252
1823	214	186
1824	287	284
1825	262	234
1826	286	283

	Urban	Rural
1827	309	300
1828	224	197
1829	251	221
1830	269	259
1831	282	269
1832	228	195
1833	216	179
1834	250	246
1835	225	188
1836	255	242
1837	309	321
1838	260	247
1839	296	283
1840	287	273
1841	265	253
1842	278	284
1843	215	198
1844	235	224
1845	241	220
1846	304	308
1847	496	625
1848	382	472
1849	331	396
1850	312	367
1851	282	305
1852	267	302
1853	301	356
1854	347	398
1855	354	407
1856	333	410
1857	361	416
1858	323	359
1859	318	362
1860	360	404
1861	356	402
1862	350	403
1863	359	386
1864	345	386
1865	331	399
1866	348	406
1867	384	419
1868	365	393
1869	350	410
1870	334	405
1871	335	398
1872	367	411
1873	419	460

	Urban	Rural
1874	393	468
1875	357	427
1876	359	416
1877	360	413
1878	374	401
1879	328	373
1880	382	414
1881	313	387
1882	307	382
1883	349	398
1884	285	339
1885	285	335
1886	267	320
1887	279	329
1888	263	321
1889	307	361
1890	278	333
1891	294	338
1892	289	340
1893	281	330
1894	274	317
1895	259	286
1896	247	290
1897	241	288
1898	298	340
1899	247	296
1900	264	300
1901	279	317
1902	255	315
1903	280	323
1904	280	318
1905	270	326
1906	280	338
1907	302	354
1908	320	363
1909	288	352
1910	310	380
1911	307	368
1912	317	374
1913	345	393
1914	304	382
1915	370	447
1916	439	543
1917	633	723
1918	613	799
1919	693	888
1920	847	979

	Urban	Rural
1921	611	864
1922	611	570
1923	598	558
1924	605	564
1925	618	576
1926	602	561
1927	569	530
1928	566	527
1929	572	533
1930	556	518
1931	524	488
1932	511	476
1933	491	458
1934	498	464
1935	507	473
1936	520	485
1937	553	515
1938	563	524
1939	579	539
1940	667	621
1941	735	685
1942	813	758
1943	917	855
1944	959	894
1945	959	894
1946	946	882
1947	995	927
1948	1,031	961
1949	1,031	961
1950	1,047	976
1951	1,132	1,055
1952	1,229	1,145
1953	1,294	1,206
1954	1,298	1,209
1955	1,327	1,236
1956	1,389	1,294
1957	1,447	1,349
1958	1,509	1,406
1959	1,509	1,406
1960	1,515	1,412
1961	1,558	1,452
1962	1,623	1,512
1963	1,662	1,549
1964	1,776	1,655
1965	1,863	1,736
1966	1,919	1,788
1967	1,981	1,846

	Urban	Rural
1968	2,072	1,930
1969	2,215	2,064
1970	2,410	2,246
1971	2,624	2,446
1972	2,852	2,658
1973	3,177	2,961
1974	3,717	3,464
1975	4,491	4,185
1976	5,301	4,940
1977	6,023	5,612
1978	6,481	6,040
1979	7,340	6,840
1980	8,677	8,085
1981	10,443	9,731
1982	12,231	11,397
1983	13,513	12,591
1984	14,674	13,673
1985	15,474	14,419
1986	16,052	14,958
1987	16,560	15,431
1988	16,914	15,761
1989	17,604	16,404
1990	18,192	16,952
1991	18,768	17,488
1992	19,357	18,037
1993	19,626	18,288
1994	20,088	18,719
1995	20,596	19,192
1996	20,927	19,501
1997	21,227	19,779
1998	21,740	20,258

Source: Kennedy, *Cost of Living.*

GEOGRAPHY AND TRANSPORT

Geography

(Square miles)	Total area	Land	Water	Coastline
All Ireland	32,593	31,557	1,036	1,970
Republic of Ireland	27,137	26,401	736	1,738
Northern Ireland	5,456	5,156	300	232

Climate

Situated west of Great Britain, in the Atlantic Ocean, the island of Ireland lies between latitude 51.5 and 55.5 degrees north, and longitude 5.5 and 10.5 degrees west. January and February are the coldest months of the year, averaging 4 to 7 degrees Celsius. The warmest months are July and August with an average temperature of 14–16 degrees Celsius. Average rainfall per year is between 800 and 1,200 mm.

Counties (all Ireland)

County	Population (1996)	Major city/town	Land area (square miles)	Rank by size
Antrim	562,216	Belfast	1,093	9
Armagh	141,585	Armagh	484	28
Carlow	41,616	Carlow	346	31
Cavan	52,944	Cavan	730	19
Clare	94,006	Ennis	1,262	7
Cork	473,277	Cork	2,878	1
Donegal	129,944	Letterkenny	1,876	4
Down	454,411	Bangor	945	12
Dublin	1,529,102	Dublin	352	30
Fermanagh	54,033	Enniskillen	647	25
Galway	188,976	Galway	2,350	2
Kerry	126,130	Tralee	1,815	5
Kildare	134,992	Naas	654	24
Kilkenny	75,336	Kilkenny	796	16
Laois	52,945	Portlaoise	664	23
Leitrim	25,057	Carrick-on-Shannon	614	26
Limerick	192,140	Limerick	1,030	10
Londonderry	213,035	Londonderry/Derry	798	15
Longford	30,166	Longford	403	29

County	Population (1996)	Major city/town	Land area (square miles)	Rank by size
Louth	92,166	Dundalk	318	32
Mayo	111,524	Ballina	2,159	3
Meath	109,732	Navan	905	14
Monaghan	51,266	Monaghan	500	27
Offaly	59,080	Tullamore	771	18
Roscommon	51,975	Roscommon	984	11
Sligo	55,821	Sligo	709	22
Tipperary	133,535	Clonmel	1,647	6
Tyrone	152,827	Omagh	1,211	8
Waterford	96,295	Waterford	713	20
Westmeath	92,166	Athlone	710	21
Wexford	104,371	Wexford	909	13
Wicklow	102,683	Bray	782	17

Railways

Railway track length in miles, 1848–1921

1848	363
1849	494
1850	537
1851	624
1852	708
1853	834
1854	897
1855	987
1856	1,057
1857	1,071
1858	1,188
1859	1,265
1860	1,364
1861	1,423
1862	1,598
1863	1,741
1864	1,794
1865	1,838
1866	1,909
1867	1,928
1868	[no return for that year]
1869	[1,975]
1870	[1,975]
1871	1,988
1872	2,091
1873	2,101

1874	2,127
1875	2,148
1876	2,157
1877	2,203
1878	2,259
1879	2,285
1880	2,370
1881	2,441
1882	2,465
1883	2,502
1884	2,525
1885	2,575
1886	2,632
1887	2,674
1888	2,733
1889	2,791
1890	2,792
1891	2,863
1892	2,895
1893	2,991
1894	3,044
1895	3,173
1896	3,178
1897	3,168
1898	3,176
1899	3,176
1900	3,183
1901	3,208
1902	3,214
1903	3,270
1904	3,296
1905	3,312
1906	3,363
1907	3,362
1908	3,363
1909	3,391
1910	3,401
1911	3,402
1912	3,403
1913	3,410

No return for 1914–18

1919	3,444
1920	3,444
1921	3,444

Railway track length in miles, Republic of Ireland, 1922–1980

1922	2,677
1923	2,677
1924	2,668
1925	2,674
1926	2,674
1927	2,674
1928	2,674
1929	2,674
1930	2,668
1931	2,671
1932	2,670
1933	2,654
1934	2,643
1935	2,556
1936	2,537
1937	2,511
1938	2,511
1939	2,511
1940	2,493
1941	2,492
1942	2,492
1943	2,493
1944	2,493
1945	2,481
1946	2,481
1947	2,440
1948	2,440
1949	2,440
1950	2,440
1951	2,440
1952	2,376
1953	2,348
1954	2,263
1955	2,259
1956	2,259
1957	2,221
1958	2,197
1959	2,193
1960	1,808
1961	1,747
1962	1,655
1963	1,462
1964	1,458
1965	1,458

1966	1,455
1967	1,334
1968	1,334
1969	1,333
1970	1,333
1971	1,361
1972	1,360
1973	1,361
1974	1,360
1975	1,247
1976	1,248
1977	1,246
1978	1,247
1979	1,236
1980	1,236

Railway track length in miles, Northern Ireland, 1922–1980

1922	765
1923	765
1924	765
1925	765
1926	765
1927	765
1928	754
1929	754
1930	754
1931	754
1932	754
1933	754
1934	754
1935	754
1936	754
1937	754
1938	741
1939	741
1940	741
1941	717
1942	717
1943	717
1944	672
1945	672
1946	672
1947	672
1948	672
1949	672

1950	645
1951	645
1952	633
1953	633
1954	633
1955	549
1956	549
1957	498
1958	377
1959	340
1960	297
1961	297
1962	297
1963	297
1964	297
1965	203
1966	203
1967	203
1968	203
1969	203
1970	203
1971	203
1972	203
1973	203
1974	203
1975	203
1976	204
1977	206
1978	206
1979	206
1980	206

Motor vehicles in use (in thousands), 1921–2000

	IFS/É/ROI		NI	
Year	Cars	Motor cycles	Cars	Motor cycles
1921			3	5
1922			5	6
1923	9.2		6	8
1924	13		8	9
1925	16		10	10
1926	20		12	9
1927	22		14	9

Year	IFS/É/ROI		NI	
	Cars	Motor cycles	Cars	Motor cycles
1928	26		16	9
1929	29		18	8
1930	33		19	8
1931	36		20	7
1932	36		22	6
1933	37		23	5
1934	35		25	5
1935	38		28	5
1936	41		32	5
1937	44		36	4
1938	49		40	4
1939	52		43	3
1940	50		31	3
1941	32		36	4
1942	8.0		25	4
1943	6.2		18	1
1944	6.6		18	1
1945	7.8		34	4
1946	44		37	5
1947	52		40	5
1948	60		42	6
1949	72	5.3	48	8
1950	85	5.8	50	10
1951	97	6.4	53	11
1952	105	8.0	57	13
1953	109	11	63	16
1954	118	15	73	18
1955	128	21	84	21
1956	136	27	93	23
1957	136	29	96	26
1958	144	31	102	26
1959	155	34	115	31
1960	170	41	125	33
1961	187	46	135	33
1962	208	48	150	32
1963	230	50	172	31
1964	255	52	189	31
1965	282	52	214	28
1966	297	47	234	23
1967	315	46	251	21
1968	349	44	262	19
1969	376	42	276	16
1970	390	41	287	14
1971	414	40	299	12
1972	440	39	304	11

Year	IFS/É/ROI		NI	
	Cars	Motor cycles	Cars	Motor cycles
1973	477	39	–	–
1974	489	38	309	11
1975	512	37	314	12
1976*	551	36	326	15
1977	572	34	338	17
1978	638	31	347	17
1979	682	29	358	15
1980	734	28	365	15
1981	775	28	365	15
1982	709	26	403	16
1983	719	25	422	15
1984	711	26	446	16
1985	710	26	405	12
1986	711	26	415	11
1987	737	26	–	–
1988	749	25	443	9
1989	773	24	457	9
1990	796	23	481	10
1991	837	25	498	10
1992	858	25	516	9
1993	891	24	515	9
1994	939	24	515	9
1995	990	23	522	9
1996	1,057	24	540	10
1997	1,134	24	576	11
1998	1,197	24	585	12
1999	1,269	27	608	13
2000	1,319	31	615	14

*Figures (ROI) from 1976 onward relate to private cars.
Source: CSO (2002), p. 302 and B. R. Mitchell and Phyllis Deane, *Abstract of British Historical Statistics*, pp. 559–60.

Shipping registered in Irish Free State/Éire/Republic of Ireland, 1926–1980

	Sailing ships		Steamships and motorships	
	No.	Thousand net tons	No.	Thousand net tons
1926	166	8.7	384	56.3
1927	160	8.5	396	55.7
1928	151	6.8	403	56.0
1929	142	6.7	402	56.4
1930	116	5.9	401	54.0
1931	110	5.6	406	47.7
1932	105	5.4	412	47.9
1933	100	5.3	461	46.8
1934	95	4.9	476	57.4
1935	90	4.6	472	68.7
1936	88	4.5	470	68.1
1937	92	5.0	493	69.1
1938	93	5.5	501	110.7
1939	92	5.5	468	35.2
1940	85	5.3	447	24.9
1941	73	4.9	432	32.3
1942	66	4.8	433	46.5
1943	61	4.6	415	40.6
1944	58	4.5	408	40.2
1945	54	4.5	392	42.0
1946	50	4.4	389	33.9
1947	49	4.4	384	31.2
1948	50	4.4	398	41.8
1949	46	4.3	402	38.6
1950	47	4.4	422	41.9
1951	47	4.4	439	42.5
1952	43	4.3	444	43.4
1953	42	4.3	445	45.5
1954	41	4.2	449	45.5
1955	40	4.2	457	46.3
1956	39	4.2	463	55.2
1957	39	4.2	463	66.1
1958	39	4.2	472	78.1
1959	37	4.1	496	83.1
1960	37	4.1	484	76.3
1961	37	4.1	496	83.0
1962	34	3.1	520	96.6
1963	30	3.0	553	102.4
1964	30	2.9	584	102.6
1965	32	3.1	606	85.5
1966	33	3.1	649	86.2
1967	33	3.1	699	82.4

	Sailing ships		Steamships and motorships	
	No.	*Thousand net tons*	*No.*	*Thousand net tons*
1968	34	3.3	793	88.0
1969	34	3.4	875	88.5
1970	35	3.4	958	107.7
1971	35	3.4	1,065	108.2
1972	35	3.4	1,148	106.2
1973	34	3.4	1,223	143.8
1974	24	0.7	1,320	144.1
1975	26	0.7	1,387	144.1
1976	26	0.7	1,471	135.6
1977	33	0.7	1,569	155.2
1978	33	0.7	1,646	154.1
1979	44	0.7	1,701	147.3
1980	68	1.8	1,779	148.9

Source: Mitchell and Deane, *Abstract of British Historical Statistics,* p. 539.

PRICES AND WAGES

Consumer price index (CPI), 1976–2001 (ROI)

The CPI is designed to measure change in the average level of prices (inclusive of all indirect taxes) paid for consumer goods and services by all private households in the ROI. This index includes alcohol, tobacco and mortgage interest.

Base year: mid-Nov. 1996 = 100

1976	25.1
1977	28.5
1978	30.7
1979	34.8
1980	41.1
1981	49.5
1982	58.0
1983	64.0
1984	69.5
1985	73.3
1986	76.1
1987	78.5
1988	80.1
1989	83.4
1990	86.2
1991	88.9
1992	91.7
1993	93.0
1994	95.2
1995	97.6
1996	99.3
1997	100.7
1998	103.1
1999	104.8
2000	110.7
2001	116.1

Source: CSO (2002), p. 320.

Indices of average wages, 1800–60

$1840 = 100$

1800	125
1805	139
1810	139
1816	136
1820	122
1824	120
1831	114
1840	100
1845	100
1850	100
1855	129
1860	134

Indices of hourly wages in industrial occupations, IFS/É/ROI, 1931–80

$1953 = 100$

1931	44.5
1932	44.0
1933	43.9
1934	43.9
1935	44.0
1936	44.1
1937	44.4
1938	47.1
1939	47.9
1940	48.1
1941	49.6
1942	49.6
1943	51.8
1944	54.1
1945	55.3
1946	57.0
1947	68.3
1948	74.5
1949	81.1
1950	81.3
1951	81.7
1952	91.7
1953	100
1954	100.3
1955	100.4
1956	108.4
1957	110.8

1958	112.7
1959	116.6
1960	124.4
1961	126.4
1962	145.3
1963	147.5
1964	166.8
1965	169.9
1966	173.3
1967	191.0
1968	197.2
1969	221.1
1970	252.9
1971	294.6
1972	337.0
1973	380.7
1974	439.3
1975	515.3
1976	602.2
1977	696.0
1978	811.2
1979	879.3
1980	1,017.3

Indices of hourly wages in industrial occupations, Republic of Ireland, 1986–88

1980 = 100

1986	193.7
1987	204.9
1988	216.2

Indices of hourly wages in industrial occupations, Republic of Ireland, 1989–94

1985 = 100

1989	124.9
1990	131.6
1991	139.1
1992	145.8
1993	154.4
1994	158.3

Indices of average weekly wages in agriculture, IFS/É/ROI, 1931–80

$1953 = 100$

1931	29.8
1932	28.8
1933	27.3
1934	25.8
1935	26.1
1936	26.7
1937	27.0
1938	33.4
1939	33.7
1940	37.1
1941	37.1
1942	40.8
1943	44.5
1944	49.4
1945	49.4
1946	55.5
1947	64.9
1948	69.0
1949	75.1
1950	75.1
1951	84.3
1952	90.8
1953	100
1954	104.9
1955	104.9
1956	118.7
1957	118.7
1958	118.7
1959	126.1
1960	131.0
1961	134.7
1962	150.3
1963	150.3
1964	178.2
1965	197.2
1966	212.9
1967	221.5
1968	240.2
1969	283.7
1970	320.9
1971	399.3
1972	436.1

1973	486.0
1974	608.8
1975	746.5
1976	811.5
1977	946.5
1978	1,044.7
1979	1,225.5
1980	1,514.4

TRADE AND AGRICULTURE

Trade

External trade I (base year: 1985 = 100)

	Value of trade at current prices (£000)			Annual index of the volume of trade	
	Imports	*Exports*	*Trade balance*	*Imports*	*Exports*
1930	56,776	44,945	−11,831	15.6	12.7
1931	50,461	36,341	−14,120	16.4	11.4
1932	42,574	26,310	−16,264	14.0	9.5
1933	35,789	19,021	−16,768	12.8	8.3
1934	39,122	17,925	−21,197	13.9	8.3
1935	37,348	19,920	−17,428	13.1	9.1
1936	39,913	22,506	−17,407	13.5	9.5
1937	44,108	22,849	−21,260	13.2	8.6
1938	41,414	24,240	−17,174	12.7	8.0
1939	43,415	26,890	−16,525	13.4	8.0
1940	46,790	32,966	−13,824	10.2	7.6
1941	29,530	31,829	2,299	5.2	6.1
1942	34,630	32,665	−1,965	5.0	5.6
1943	26,359	27,809	1,450	3.8	4.4
1944	28,531	29,917	1,386	4.0	4.6
1945	41,073	35,496	−5,577	5.7	5.5
1946	72,043	39,008	−33,036	10.3	5.8
1947	131,335	39,511	−91,823	15.8	5.5
1948	136,316	49,327	−86,989	16.2	5.9
1949	130,232	60,552	−69,679	16.2	7.1
1950	159,394	72,391	−87,003	18.1	8.0
1951	204,596	81,520	−123,075	19.0	7.9
1952	172,309	101,599	−70,710	15.8	9.6
1953	182,480	114,097	−68,383	17.9	10.8
1954	179,890	115,342	−64,549	17.5	11.1
1955	204,338	110,383	−93,956		
.... *New measurement*				19.3	10.3
1955	207,663	110,851	−96,812		
1956	182,849	108,127	−74,722	16.6	10.6
1957	184,172	131,341	−52,831	15.9	12.7
1958	198,957	131,293	−67,664	17.9	12.4
1959	212,647	130,607	−82,040	19.6	11.8
1960	226,228	152,703	−73,525	20.5	14.1
1961	261,403	180,473	−80,930	23.4	16.8

	Value of trade at current prices (£000)			Annual index of the volume of trade	
	Imports	Exports	Trade balance	Imports	Exports
1962	273,724	174,390	−99,334	24.5	16.1
1963	307,684	196,539	−111,144	27.1	17.9
1964	349,318	222,004	−127,314	29.4	17.5
.... New measurement					
1964	360,781	233,893	−126,888	30.3	18.4
1965	387,802	241,202	−146,600	31.8	18.8
1966	396,720	273,378	−123,342	32.6	20.9
1967	414,664	314,504	−100,160	34.3	24.1
1968	516,124	363,689	−152,435	39.4	25.9
1969	613,640	404,246	−209,393	45.0	27.2
1970	676,652	466,672	−209,981	46.5	29.4
1971	754,913	538,662	−216,251	48.9	31.6
1972	838,053	647,549	−190,505	51.9	33.5
1973	1,137,236	869,186	−268,050	62.4	36.6
1974	1,626,311	1,134,280	−492,031	61.2	38.7
1975	1,704,114	1,447,367	−256,747	53.0	41.7
1976	2,337,932	1,859,077	−478,855	61.1	43.4
1977	3,090,887	2,518,170	−572,716	68.8	50.9
1978	3,713,098	2,963,181	−749,918	78.9	56.2
1979	4,827,923	3,477,738	−1,350,185	90.2	60.8
1980	5,420,705	4,082,496	−1,338,209	86.2	65.5
1981	6,578,406	4,777,571	−1,800,836	88.0	66.0
1982	6,816,155	5,691,442	−1,124,713	84.9	70.8
1983	7,366,775	6,943,836	−422,939	87.6	79.3
1984	8,912,170	8,897,525	−14,646	96.8	93.9
1985	9,428,198	9,743,038	314,840	100.0	100.0
1986	8,621,291	9,374,310	753,019	103.0	104.0
1987	9,155,207	10,723,498	1,568,291	109.4	118.8
1988	10,214,758	12,304,848	2,090,089	114.5	127.1
1989	12,287,833	14,596,912	2,309,079	129.3	141.4

External trade II (base year: 1990 = 100)

	Period value (£ million)			Volume index	
	Imports	Exports	Trade surplus	Imports	Exports
1970	676.7	466.7	−210.0	33.6	19.2
1971	754.9	538.7	216.3	35.4	20.5
1972	838.1	647.5	−190.5	37.5	21.8
1973	1,137.2	869.1	−268.1	45.1	23.9
1974	1,627.2	1,134.3	−492.0	44.2	25.2
1975	1,704.1	1,447.4	−256.7	38.3	27.2

	Period value (£ million)			Volume index	
	Imports	Exports	Trade surplus	Imports	Exports
1976	2,337.9	1,859.1	−478.9	44.2	28.2
1977	3,090.9	2,518.2	−572.7	49.9	33.2
1978	3,713.1	2,963.2	−749.9	57.1	36.7
1979	4,827.9	3,477.7	−1,350.2	65.5	39.6
1980	5,420.7	4,082.5	−1,338.2	62.3	42.7
1981	6,578.4	4,777.6	−1,800.8	63.7	43.0
1982	6,816.2	5,691.4	−1,124.7	61.5	46.1
1983	7,366.8	6,943.8	−422.9	63.5	51.7
1984	8,912.2	8,897.5	−14.6	70.0	61.2
1985	9,428.2	9,743.0	314.8	72.3	65.2
1986	8,621.3	9,374.3	753.0	74.4	67.6
1987	9,155.2	10,723.5	1,568.3	79.1	77.4
1988	10,214.8	12,304.8	2,090.1	82.8	82.9
1989	12,287.8	14,597.0	2,312.8	93.6	92.2
1990	12,468.8	14,336.7	1,867.9	100.0	100.0
1991	12,850.8	15,018.9	2,168.1	100.8	105.6
1992	13,194.8	16,743.8	3,549.1	105.6	121.1
1993	14,884.7	19,829.7	4,945.0	113.0	133.4
1994	17,283.4	22,753.4	5,470.1	127.9	153.2
1995	20,619.1	27,824.7	7,205.6	146.3	184.0
1996	22,429.4	30,407.0	7,977.7	160.9	202.2
1997	25,885.6	35,289.4	9,403.8	184.8	232.1

Trade by commodity group: imports (£000)

	1988	1989
Food and live animals	1,066,239	1,153,931
Beverages and tobacco	125,537	139,438
Crude materials, inedible, except fuels	294,623	343,353
Minerals, fuels, lubricants and related materials	568,001	674,301
Animal and vegetable oils, fats and waxes	43,610	49,058
Chemicals and related products	1,292,151	1,524,802
Manufactured goods classified chiefly by material	1,637,605	1,847,176
Machinery and transport equipment	3,516,580	4,649,829
Miscellaneous manufactured articles	1,345,892	1,552,922
Commodities and transactions not classified elsewhere	324,519	353,021
Total imports	10,214,758	12,287,833

Trade by commodity group: imports (£ million)

	1995	1996	1997
Food and live animals	1,475.3	1,545.8	1,656.3
Beverages and tobacco	208.4	233.4	275.8
Crude materials, inedible, except fuels	408.6	407.3	448.2
Minerals, fuels, lubricants and related materials	670.2	823.7	897.6
Animal and vegetable oils, fats and waxes	81.4	82.3	83.0
Chemicals and related products	2,636.6	2,762.1	3,210.6
Manufactured goods classified chiefly by material	2,374.3	2,422.8	2,682.1
Machinery and transport equipment	8,826.2	9,468.2	11,750.5
Miscellaneous manufactured articles	2,424.8	2,862.2	3,122.8
Commodities and transactions not classified elsewhere	331.8	580.8	571.6
Unclassified estimates	1,181.4	1,240.7	1,183.5
Total imports	20,619.1	22,429.4	25,882.1

Trade by commodity group: exports (£000)

	1988	1989
Food and live animals	2,900,560	3,208,932
Beverages and tobacco	251,270	297,870
Crude materials, inedible, except fuels	551,942	629,275
Minerals, fuels, lubricants and related materials	64,548	68,656
Animal and vegetable oils, fats and waxes	11,509	12,880
Chemicals and related products	1,612,583	2,084,847
Manufactured goods classified chiefly by material	1,036,052	1,148,765
Machinery and transport equipment	3,840,390	4,652,376
Miscellaneous manufactured articles	1,606,562	1,965,651
Commodities and transactions not classified elsewhere	429,431	527,659
Total imports	12,304,848	14,596,912

Trade by commodity group: exports (£ million)

	1995	1996	1997
Food and live animals	4,850.0	4,143.2	3,624.5
Beverages and tobacco	483.3	517.8	549.6
Crude materials, inedible, except fuels	564.2	556.7	607.6
Minerals, fuels, lubricants and related materials	120.5	116.6	147.6
Animal and vegetable oils, fats and waxes	23.6	28.0	28.7
Chemicals and related products	5,272.5	6,724.3	8,933.0
Manufactured goods classified chiefly by material	1,351.2	1,358.4	1,378.2
Machinery and transport equipment	9,597.8	10,627.7	13,359.9
Miscellaneous manufactured articles	4,326.9	4,601.9	4,760.4
Commodities and transactions not classified elsewhere	729.3	1,214.5	1,462.8
Unclassified estimates	505.6	517.9	484.4
Total imports	27,824.7	30,407.0	35,336.4

Imports by country of origin (£000)

Country of origin	1984	1985	1986	1987
United Kingdom				
Great Britain	3,482,721	3,705,624	3,247,890	3,438,550
Northern Ireland	339,282	320,545	339,889	377,367
Other EC states				
France	429,307	456,201	428,213	401,238
Belgium and Luxembourg	190,573	205,809	188,412	197,489
Netherlands	335,003	356,923	331,912	338,787
Germany (FDR)	677,646	729,349	771,583	764,584
Italy	215,595	213,987	227,710	224,955
Denmark	82,254	96,743	87,561	85,158
Greece	12,951	15,019	10,979	14,039
Portugal	–	–	40,490	41,313
Spain	–	–	119,596	117,966
Other countries				
Austria	33,346	32,321	32,437	33,706
Brazil	50,985	35,684	27,154	26,020
Canada	100,052	83,851	77,334	85,841
Finland	81,039	77,229	78,676	82,958

Country of origin	1984	1985	1986	1987
Hong Kong	66,700	52,013	47,169	50,983
India	17,871	18,267	15,247	18,681
Israel	20,866	18,713	20,019	17,378
Ivory Coast	13,338	13,640	9,271	9,693
Japan	299,570	334,351	328,407	397,643
South Korea	30,205	23,842	27,740	35,409
Malaysia	24,547	20,193	13,620	16,313
Norway	34,362	38,109	36,530	53,827
Poland	57,234	63,766	57,401	51,178
Portugal	35,112	45,544	–	–
Saudi Arabia	127	3,495	661	686
Singapore	46,608	26,861	20,078	21,707
South Africa and Namibia	17,366	18,698	16,187	6,262
Spain	100,835	101,023	–	–
Sweden	145,731	149,138	139,836	139,532
Switzerland	87,036	94,872	85,479	68,374
Taiwan	34,212	35,612	46,841	75,653
USA	1,465,922	1,602,174	1,365,383	1,555,414
USSR	46,797	47,458	30,807	32,627
Other	336,977	391,145	350,777	373,875
TOTAL	8,912,170	9,428,198	8,621,291	9,155,207

Exports by country of destination (£000)

Country of origin	1984	1985	1986	1987
United Kingdom				
Great Britain	2,476,195	2,605,819	2,603,748	3,043,819
Northern Ireland	588,269	605,278	597,620	618,811
Other EC states				
France	745,785	821,653	876,615	994,372
Belgium and Luxembourg	382,589	396,366	450,201	512,829
Netherlands	621,789	663,722	555,712	778,271
Germany (FDR)	902,867	985,310	1,022,089	1,202,610
Italy	278,848	363,930	334,273	392,478
Denmark	67,672	88,353	91,505	97,650
Greece	37,790	46,806	41,000	42,829
Portugal	–	–	26,798	31,533
Spain	–	–	137,260	164,160
Other countries				
Algeria	26,224	35,571	15,586	7,559
Australia	107,664	129,939	79,991	92,334

Country of origin	1984	1985	1986	1987
Austria	48,824	57,575	61,859	65,105
Canada	150,206	171,656	118,478	110,010
Canary Islands	13,318	14,922	12,880	19,714
Egypt	95,273	109,002	86,697	70,646
Finland	45,737	54,651	57,312	59,464
Iraq	30,171	29,599	26,534	30,238
Japan	151,170	150,341	170,628	181,236
Libya	37,287	26,845	29,911	31,474
Mexico	36,699	34,139	20,880	28,595
Nigeria	55,680	105,543	33,102	41,120
Norway	79,700	106,381	96,292	123,601
Portugal	22,123	25,871	–	–
Saudi Arabia	65,639	79,350	63,299	57,243
South Africa and Namibia	38,739	29,551	30,188	40,844
Spain	94,309	111,217	–	–
Sweden	136,437	170,889	173,546	205,367
Switzerland	99,941	127,645	154,994	168,140
USA	866,003	953,927	815,799	833,806
USSR	20,552	34,075	45,113	21,158
Venezuela	18,401	20,795	11,657	33,780
Other	555,623	577,134	532,743	622,702
TOTAL	8,897,525	9,743,038	9,374,310	10,723,498

Imports by country of origin (euro million)

Country of origin	1995	1998	2001
United Kingdom			
Great Britain	8,437.7	12,393.5	19,028.7
Northern Ireland	826.8	1,073.0	1,237.5
Other EC states			
Austria	67.7	83.6	146.9
Belgium and Luxembourg	325.8	463.8	0.0
Denmark	184.5	261.7	732.3
Finland	166.1	311.7	445.4
France	998.3	1,552.3	2,810.9
Germany	1,852.6	2,466.8	3,525.6
Greece	16.6	24.9	44.3
Italy	514.4	768.3	1,160.7
Netherlands	769.9	1,233.2	1,924.7
Portugal	76.6	107.5	156.2
Spain	249.1	439.9	652.3
Sweden	288.3	392.8	507.3

Country of origin	1995	1998	2001
Other countries			
Australia	29.8	46.3	96.0
Brazil	73.4	42.4	135.6
Canada	183.5	371.1	635.5
China	277.8	639.4	1,079.2
Czech Republic	26.2	51.4	123.0
Egypt	9.8	8.1	29.7
Guinea	67.8	93.5	106.8
Hong Kong	183.7	240.2	531.6
Hungary	16.5	237.3	408.9
India	70.8	80.9	152.4
Indonesia	46.8	82.4	116.2
Israel	35.4	180.5	241.0
Japan	1,349.6	2,773.1	2,004.0
Malaysia	420.2	437.6	583.4
Mexico	43.3	75.3	242.9
Norway	354.1	450.8	942.3
Philippines	38.6	210.0	325.6
Poland	57.7	72.1	124.0
Singapore	1,025.7	1,950.6	1,357.2
South Africa	54.4	57.3	102.6
South Korea	213.5	637.6	797.4
Switzerland	170.6	321.9	481.2
Taiwan	337.7	740.4	1,073.4
Thailand	92.1	188.6	335.5
Turkey	47.8	87.8	143.8
USA	4,607.5	6,362.5	8,711.9
Other countries	447.0	548.5	1,017.4
Country unknown	103.9	66.7	119.1
Unclassified estimates	912.7	1,083.2	1,354.4
TOTAL	26,180.9	39,715.0	57,177.5

Exports by country of destination (euro million)

Country of origin	1995	1998	2001
United Kingdom			
Great Britain	8,017.2	11,413.8	20,419.7
Northern Ireland	997.1	1,503.8	1,741.2
Other EC states			
Austria	229.2	319.9	407.5
Belgium and Luxembourg	1573.9	3645.4	0.0

Country of origin	1995	1998	2001
Denmark	448.3	587.0	602.1
France	3,328.4	4,814.2	5,614.7
Finland	237.4	289.3	396.4
Germany	5,127.2	8,292.6	11,718.7
Greece	211.8	156.7	327.6
Italy	1,361.7	1,937.1	3,312.9
Netherlands	2,457.7	3,165.4	4,277.2
Portugal	144.3	233.4	279.6
Spain	862.1	1,537.0	2,276.5
Sweden	693.3	1,089.1	1,307.2
Other countries			
Australia	181.7	449.1	835.1
Brazil	70.4	145.7	225.8
Canada	265.7	346.2	592.5
China	30.0	75.3	350.2
Czech Republic	86.0	135.3	258.3
Egypt	154.6	191.4	120.5
Hong Kong	129.7	295.1	670.1
Hungary	56.2	93.6	169.3
India	29.9	48.4	107.0
Israel	114.5	231.1	344.6
Japan	1,034.8	1,486.7	3,266.2
Malaysia	275.6	324.3	1,140.2
Mexico	101.1	164.0	552.4
Norway	373.8	560.4	587.2
Philippines	65.2	288.7	769.5
Poland	108.8	243.4	319.1
Russia	277.9	245.9	240.8
Saudi Arabia	191.1	287.9	388.5
Singapore	211.9	375.9	641.3
South Africa	126.7	343.6	398.0
South Korea	125.7	362.7	695.8
Switzerland	626.9	1,156.2	2,811.9
Taiwan	87.8	147.78	377.2
Thailand	52.8	82.7	144.3
Turkey	78.2	176.3	310.4
United Arab Emirates	67.1	102.6	197.9
USA	2,887.8	7,742.6	15,695.6
Other countries	888.0	1,255.9	1,820.9
Country unknown	633.3	280.6	449.4
Unclassified estimates	312.9	640.7	840.8
TOTAL	35,330.1	57,321.8	92,523.3

Source: Central Statistics Office (2002), pp. 276–7.

Index of industrial production, IFS/É/ROI, 1926–80

$1953 = 100$

1926	35.2
1929	38.4
1931	37.6
1936	54.0
1937	54.9
1938	53.6
1939	56.2
1940	56.0
1941	52.2
1942	43.0
1943	44.1
1944	46.8
1945	53.5
1946	60.8
1947	65.2
1948	71.3
1949	80.6
1950	91.4
1951	94.0
1952	91.6
1953	100
1954	103.3
1955	107.5
1956	105.3
1957	104.5
1958	106.5
1959	117.5
1960	126.0
1961	137.4
1962	146.2
1963	153.5
1964	165.4
1965	172.2
1966	180.4
1967	195.7
1968	217.5
1969	234.8
1970	242.7
1971	252.5
1972	263.1
1973	291.1
1974	296.4
1975	277.4

1976	302.3
1977	341.2
1978	364.2
1979	386.9
1980	383.1

Source: Mitchell and Deane, *Abstract of British Historical Statistics.*

Agriculture

Ireland, 1847–1922 (in thousands of acres)

	Pasture	Total arable
1847	–	4,100
1848	–	–
1849	–	4,402
1850	–	4,558
1851	–	4,613
1852	–	4,468
1853	9,381	4,426
1854	9,501	4,313
1855	9,558	4,374
1856	9,545	4,451
1857	9,316	4,480
1858	9,354	4,458
1859	9,491	4,425
1860	9,484	4,376
1861	9,534	4,344
1862	9,700	4,201
1863	9,758	4,102
1864	9,694	4,067
1865	9,823	3,970
1866	10,004	3,944
1867	10,061	3,827
1868	9,999	3,880
1869	10,041	3,927
1870	9,967	3,886
1871	10,071	3,815
1872	10,246	3,605
1873	10,414	3,446
1874	10,472	3,374
1875	10,409	3,399
1876	10,507	3,356
1877	10,145	3,357
1878	10,116	3,278
1879	10,211	3,201
1880	10,259	3,197

	Pasture	Total arable
1881	10,075	3,214
1882	10,110	3,141
1883	10,192	3,029
1884	10,347	2,934
1885	10,251	2,941
1886	10,163	2,957
1887	10,050	2,935
1888	9,905	2,934
1889	9,998	2,881
1890	10,212	2,839
1891	10,299	2,780
1892	10,254	2,764
1893	10,321	2,732
1894	10,214	2,768
1895	10,280	2,694
1896	10,334	2,659
1897	10,462	2,589
1898	10,470	2,547
1899	10,575	2,522
1900	10,563	2,506
1901	10,577	2,463
1902	10,635	2,436
1903	10,598	2,420
1904	10,586	2,383
1905	10,598	2,371
1906	10,063	2,411
1907	9,979	2,369
1908	10,037	2,330
1909	9,997	2,304
1910	9,868	2,371
1911	9,847	2,349
1912	9,828	2,358
1913	9,861	2,348
1914	9,928	2,328
1915	9,819	2,404
1916	9,908	2,400
1917	8,784	3,038
1918	8,683	3,239
1919	–	2,806
1920	–	2,733
1921	–	2,510
1922	–	2,443

Irish Free State/Éire/Republic of Ireland, 1923–1980 (in thousands of acres)

	Pasture	Total arable
1923	–	1,669
1924	–	1,632
1925	8,411	1,571
1926	8,416	1,551
1927	8,469	1,511
1928	8,432	1,529
1929	8,204	1,521
1930	8,082	1,458
1931	7,989	1,425
1932	7,957	1,424
1933	8,004	1,455
1934	8,053	1,497
1935	7,925	1,591
1936	7,936	1,621
1937	7,951	1,592
1938	8,040	1,568
1939	8,052	1,492
1940	7,616	1,846
1941	7,336	2,236
1942	7,178	2,425
1943	7,142	2,459
1944	7,092	2,567
1945	7,130	2,474
1946	7,217	2,413
1947	7,242	2,314
1948	7,268	2,285
1949	7,680	1,904
1950	7,826	1,769
1951	7,935	1,717
1952	7,938	1,720
1953	7,945	1,753
1954	7,929	1,808
1955	8,008	1,728
1956	8,028	1,707
1957	7,997	1,757
1958	7,948	1,778
1959	8,118	1,654
1960	7,578	1,675
1961	7,780	1,599
1962	7,964	1,588
1963	7,982	1,513
1964	8,147	1,438
1965	8,270	1,395
1966	8,465	1,262
1967	8,458	1,302

Republic of Ireland, 1996–2000 (in thousands of acres)

	Crops and pasture	Rough grazing in use	Area farmed
1996	3,912.4	429.0	4,341.4
1997	3,957.6	473.9	4,431.6
1998	3,968.4	446.4	4,414.8
1999	3,953.9	464.5	4,418.4
2000	3,936.6	506.5	4,443.1

Northern Ireland, 1923–1980 (in thousands of acres)

	Rotation grasses	Permanent grasses	Total arable
1923	593	1,208	1,230
1924	638	1,215	1,249
1925	660	1,217	1,243
1926	692	1,195	1,266
1927	648	1,250	1,202
1928	666	1,214	1,232
1929	673	1,222	1,216
1930	704	1,198	1,249
1931	722	1,254	1,205
1932	672	1,293	1,162
1933	674	1,291	1,169
1934	634	1,336	1,129
1935	618	1,362	1,107
1936	646	1,353	1,123
1937	622	1,404	1,072
1938	607	1,388	1,096
1939	565	1,442	1,036
1940	483	1,188	1,143
1941	451	1,047	1,249
1942	495	955	1,323
1943	491	910	1,341
1944	497	926	1,337
1945	532	947	1,318
1946	604	696	1,305
1947	623	1,026	1,256
1948	595	1,002	1,271
1949	577	1,042	1,217
1950	604	1,085	1,196
1951	606	1,143	1,129
1952	582	1,190	1,089
1953	552	1,233	1,045
1954	543	1,228	996
1955	553	1,248	971
1956	561	1,224	993

	Rotation grasses	Permanent grasses	Total arable
1957	527	1,231	922
1958	511	1,238	881
1959	551	1,137	905
1960	578	1,129	955
1961	486	1,048	882
1962	497	1,037	890
1963	515	1,023	912
1964	617	1,002	1,001
1965	615	1,020	979
1966	633	1,083	965
1967	593	1,156	908
1968	535	1,244	821
1969	459	1,333	723
1970	492	1,313	743
1971	474	1,342	722
1972	473	1,379	692
1973	464	1,376	666
1974	457	1,400	652
1975	690	1,160	884
1976	669	1,199	865
1977	654	1,211	865
1978	684	1,210	891
1979	643	1,254	841
1980	684	–	882

Source: Mitchell and Deane, *Abstract of British Historical Statistics*, pp. 191–3.

Northern Ireland, 1979–2000 (in thousands of hectares)

	All crops and grasses	Rough grazing	Woods and plantations	Other land	Total area of agricultural holdings
1979	847.6	–	–	–	–
1980	854.7	–	–	–	–
1981	831.7	–	–	–	–
1982	837.3	–	–	–	–
1983	839.9	–	–	–	–
1984	841.9	188.4	–	–	–
1985	842.8	185.4	–	–	–
1986	841.1	183.5	–	–	–
1987	841.2	182.6	–	–	–
1988	834.6	187.0	–	–	–
1989	824.9	193.3	12.7	31.0	1,061.9
1990	822.4	189.7	13.2	29.1	1,054.4
1991	831.8	189.6	13.2	28.7	1,063.4
1992	827.3	182.0	13.4	29.2	1,052.1
1993	842.7	179.8	11.7	21.5	1,055.8
1994	835.4	179.0	11.6	21.5	1,048.0
1995	875.5	170.9	8.1	13.2	1,067.8
1996	877.5	169.0	8.2	12.9	1,067.6
1997	884.8	164.1	8.2	11.8	1,068.9
1998	889.8	159.1	8.2	11.3	1,068.4
1999	894.6	158.7	8.2	11.5	1,073.0
2000	883.5	156.5	8.6	11.8	1,060.5

Source: CSO.

PROPERTY

Irish land legislation, 1848–1992

Statutes passed by the parliament of the United Kingdom

1848 Irish Incumbered Estates Act
To enable indebted estates to be sold free of encumbrance.

1849 Incumbered Estates (Ireland) Act
Provided for appointment of Commissioners for Sale of Incumbered Estates in Ireland, to carry out the provisions of this and the previous Act in place of the High Court of Chancery.

1852 Incumbered Estates (Ireland) Act
Provided for an extension of one year to the original three-year period within which application could be made for the sale of an estate under the legislation.

1853 Incumbered Estates (Ireland) Continuance Act
Provided for a further extension of one year in which application could be made under the legislation.

1855 Incumbered Estates (Ireland) Continuance Act
Provided for a further extension of one year.

1858 Landed Estates Court (Ireland) Act
Constituted a Landed Estates Court as a permanent court for the sale and transfer of land, whether encumbered or unencumbered, and invested it with other and more extensive powers. Replaced Commissioners of Sale of Incumbered Estates.

1860 The Landed Property (Ireland) Improvement Act [or Cardwell's Act]
Provided for compensation for improvements made by tenants where prior consent of the owner had been obtained.

1860 The Landlord and Tenant Law Amendment Act (Ireland) [or Deasy's Act]
Provided that the relation of landlord and tenant in Ireland 'shall be deemed to be founded on the express or implied Contract of the Parties, and not upon Tenure or Service'.

1870 Landlord and Tenant (Ireland) Act [or Gladstone's First Land Act]
Made enforceable at law the tenant-right custom where it existed in the province of Ulster or in cases of like practices elsewhere in Ireland. Provided for compensation for disturbance by the landlord of a tenant not enjoying a

tenant-right practice. Gave compensation for improvements made by a tenant or his predecessors where the tenant was quitting his holding and was not claiming under the other provisions of this Act. Established provision for the sale of a holding by the tenant through the Landed Estates Court and with advances from the Commissioners of Public Works (the 'Bright Clauses').

1872 Landlord and Tenant (Ireland) Act
Enacted regulations for the purchase by tenants of their holdings, and enabled sale to proceed in certain cases where advances had been paid, notwithstanding forfeiture.

1881 Land Law (Ireland) Act [or Gladstone's Second Land Act]
Provided for right of tenant to sell his tenancy, and for conversion of ordinary tenancies to fixed tenancies. Gave power to civil courts to fix rent ('judicial rent'), with provision for referral to a new Land Commission.

1882 Arrears of Rent (Ireland) Act
Provided for settlement by Land Commission of arrears of rent antecedent to the 1881 Act.

1885 Purchase of Land (Ireland) Act [or Ashbourne Act]
Gave the power to the Land Commission to make advances to the tenants for the purchase of their holdings, whether directly from their landlords or from the Land Commission.

1887 Land Law (Ireland) Act
Extended the benefits of the 1881 Act to leaseholders and made changes to the procedures for the purchase of holdings.

1888 Purchase of Land (Ireland) Amendment Act
Increased the limit of advances which were permitted to be made by the Land Commission.

1888 Land Law (Ireland) Act, Amendment Act 1889
Clarified the 1888 Act with respect to certain categories of leaseholders.

1891 Purchase of Land (Ireland) Act [or Balfour Act]
Provided for payment to vendor in land stock. Established permanency of the Land Commission. Made provision to ensure that an adequate proportion of the available funds was reserved for the purchase of farms under the value of £50. Constituted a Congested Districts Board, with powers and resources to amalgamate holdings and to aid migration and emigration, agriculture and industry in the areas defined as congested.

1893 Congested Districts Board (Ireland) Act
Gave additional powers to the Board to acquire and hold property in order to achieve its purposes.

1894 Congested Districts Board (Ireland) Act
Provided for guarantee for deposits and purchaser's insurance money, and other matters relating to the Congested Districts Board.

605

1895 Purchase of Land (Ireland) Amendment Act, Session 2
Re-enacted, with modification, section 13 of the Purchase of Land (Ireland) Act 1891.

1896 Land Law (Ireland) Act
Comprised five main parts, providing for: (1) changes to the law regarding the determination of fair rents; (2) alterations to the functioning of the Land Commission; (3) changes to the provisions for land purchase; (4) amendments to the procedures for the purchase and sale of land by the Congested Districts Board; and (5) provisions for the reinstatement of, or purchase of a holding by, an evicted tenant.

1899 Congested Districts Board (Ireland) Act
An Act to amend certain provisions of the Land Law (Ireland) Act 1896.

1901 Purchase of Land (Ireland) Act
Provided for the exceeding of the specified maximum amount for an advance towards the purchase of land.

1901 Purchase of Land (Ireland) (No. 2) Act
An Act to extend the Purchase of Land (Ireland) 1888.

1901 Congested Districts Board (Ireland) Act 1901
Provided for facilitation of resale of land by the Congested Districts Board and the extension of the powers of the Board to enable it to purchase land outside the defined congested districts.

1903 Irish Land Act [or Wyndham Act]
New provisions for purchase and resale of whole estates to the occupying tenants, with substitution of cash payments for guaranteed land stock. Establishment of a Land Purchase Aid Fund for funding of Land Commission purchases. Provision for the jurisdiction, powers and duties of the Land Commission in relation to this act to be exercised and performed by three members of the Commission, designated the Estates Commissioners.

1904 Irish Land Act
An Act to amend section 48 of the Irish Land Act 1903.

1907 Irish Land Act
An Act to make provision with respect to the disposal of mining rights under section 13 of the Irish Land Act 1903, and to amend section 54 of that Act.

1907 Evicted Tenants (Ireland) Act
Gave power to the Estates Commissioners to acquire land compulsorily for evicted tenants, but excluding land held by a tenant 'cultivating the same as an ordinary farmer in accordance with proper methods of husbandry' and land being purchased under the Land Purchase Acts.

1908 Evicted Tenants (Ireland) Act
An Act to amend section 1 of the Evicted Tenants (Ireland) Act 1907 with respect to the compulsory acquisition of tenanted land.

1909 Irish Land Act [or Birrell Act]
Altered the financial provisions of the 1903 Act. Limited the amount of an advance to a non-resident occupier. Changed the definition of a congested estate. Provided for compulsory purchase of an estate where agreement could not be reached with the vendor through the processes of the 1903 Act. Gave corporate status to the Congested Districts Board and reconstituted the Board.

1919 Irish Land (Provision for Sailors and Soldiers) Act
Extension of the benefits of the Land Purchase Acts to men who had served in the forces, subject to fitness and suitability, as if they had been tenants or proprietors.

1924 Irish Free State Land Purchase (Loan Guarantee) Act
'An Act to authorise the Treasury to guarantee a loan to be raised by the Government of the Irish Free State for the purposes of Land Purchase in that State.'

1925 Northern Ireland Land Act
Altered the rate of purchase annuity, provided for automatic sale of remaining tenanted land in Northern Ireland, and abolished the power to fix judicial rents.

1929 Northern Ireland Land Act
An Act to amend the Northern Ireland Land Act 1925.

1935 Northern Ireland Land Purchase (Winding Up) Act
'An Act to make provision for the winding up of the system of land purchase in Northern Ireland established by the Land Purchase Acts and other enactments in that behalf, for the abolition of the Land Purchase Commission, Northern Ireland, and the transfer of functions exercisable under the said Acts and other enactments.'

Statutes passed by the Oireachtas (IFS/É/ROI)

1923 Land Law (Commission) Act
Reconstituted the Irish Land Commission and dissolved the Congested Districts Board, transferring its functions, funds and staff to the Land Commission.

1923 Land Act
Abolished remaining elements of dual ownership and put the machinery for making tenants owners, and for expropriating land to relieve congestion, on an entirely compulsory basis.

1925 Land Bond Act
An Act to make further and better provision of Land Bonds under the Land Act 1923.

1926 Land Act
Averted the possibility that a landlord prior to the passing of the 1923 Act could become entitled to the land by reason of the expiration of a tenancy.

1927 Land Act
Extensive procedural provisions in relation to the functioning of the Land Commission, the financial provisions for land purchase, and other aspects of managing land occupation issues.

1929 Land Act
'An Act to give the Irish Land Commission power in certain cases to appoint limited administrators to deceased persons, to fix the standard purchase annuity in respect of holdings subject to rents other than judicial rents, to explain and amend the provisions of the Land Act 1923, in relation to fisheries and fishing rights, and to give to the Irish Land Commission power to purchase certain fisheries and fishing rights.'

1931 Land Act
'An Act to make provision for the early vesting of holdings in the purchasers thereof under the Land Purchase Acts and for that and other purposes to amend those Acts and the Local Registration of Title (Ireland) Act 1891, and also to make provision in respect of the variation of certain tithe rent-charges and variable rents.'

1933 Land (Purchase Annuities Fund) Act
Allowed surpluses in the fund, not required for the Guarantee Fund, to be made available to the Exchequer as the Minister of Finance should direct.

1933 Land Bond Act
'An Act to make provision in relation to the payment of certain purchase money and the making of certain advances under the Land Act 1923, and subsequent Land Purchase Acts by means of an issue of bonds, and in relation to the creation, issue, and redemption of bonds for that purpose, and in relation to other matters connected with the matter aforesaid, and to amend in certain respects the law relating to land Purchase Finance.'

1933 Land Act
'An Act to amend generally the law, finance, and practice relating to land purchase, and in particular to make further and better provision for the execution of the functions of the judicial and lay commissioners of the Land Commission and to provide for the revision of purchase annuities and certain other annual payments and for the funding of arrears thereof, and to provide for other matters connected with the matters aforesaid.'

1934 Land Bond Act
'An Act to make further provision for the creation and issue of Land Bonds for the purpose of the payment of purchase moneys and the making of advances under the Land Purchase Acts and to provide for the payment of interest on and the redemption of such Land Bonds and for other matters connected therewith.'

1936 Land Act
'An Act to amend and extend the Land Purchase Acts in divers respects.'

1939 Land Act
'An Act to amend and extend the Land Purchase Acts in divers respects and to amend the law in relation to the application of the Increase of Rent and Mortgage Interest (Restrictions) Acts 1923 to 1930, to dwelling-houses of which the Land Commission is the landlord.'

1946 Land Act
Gave power to the Land Commission to direct purchasers to reside on their holdings.

1949 Land Reclamation Act
Extended the use of annuities as provided under the Land Purchase Acts for the purposes of this legislation.

1950 Land Act
'An Act to amend and extend the Land Purchase Acts.'

1953 Land Act
'An Act to amend and extend the Land Purchase Acts.'

1954 Land Act
The sole purpose of this Act was to amend the retirement age of Lay Commissioners of the Land Commission from 65 to 67 years.

1964 Land Bond Act
Increased the limit on the creation and issue of land bonds for land purchase from £15 million to £25 million.

1965 Land Act
Increased the limit on the creation and issue of land bonds for land purchase from £25 million to £40 million; provided that land bonds already issued and those issued in future should be in denominations of £1; transferred the registers of land bonds to the Bank of Ireland.

1975 Land Bond Act
Increased the limit on the creation and issue of land bonds for land purchase to £60 million.

1978 Land Bond Act
Increased the limit on the creation and issue of land bonds for land purchase to £80 million.

1980 Land Bond Act
Increased the limit on the creation and issue of land bonds for land purchase to £105 million.

1983 Land Bond Act
Increased the limit on the creation and issue of land bonds for land purchase to £130 million.

1984 Land Act
Excluded leases of agricultural land from certain enactments in the Land Acts of 1860, 1870, 1881, 1887 and 1896; dissolved the Irish Church Temporalities

609

Fund established under the Irish Church Act 1869; and amended section 46 of the 1923 Land Act so as to extend its application from the registered owner of a holding to a person having interest in it.

1992 Land Bond Act
Provided for the dissolution of the Land Bond Fund established under the Act of 1923 and the Guarantee Fund established under the Act of 1891, and for the redemption of land bonds.

Source: Philip Bull, *Land, Politics and Nationalism* (Dublin, 1996), pp. 193–207.

Landowners in 1872 and 2001

The following list includes the top three landowners in terms of acreage owned in 1872 and 2001. The principal address of the landowner is included, although owners with English addresses often have residential properties on their Irish estates. N/A indicates that the exact acreage is not known.

County	*Acres owned*
ANTRIM	
1872	
1. Rev Lord O'Neill of Shane's Castle, Antrim	65,919
2. Sir Richard Wallace of Antrim Castle, Antrim	58,365
3. Earl of Antrim of Glenarm Castle, Antrim	34,292
2001	
1. The 4th Baron O'Neill of Shane's Castle, Antrim	15,000
2. The 9th Earl of Antrim of Glenarm Castle	7,500
3. Dobbs Family of Castle Dobbs, Carrickfergus	5,000
ARMAGH	
1872	
1. Earl of Charlemont of The Moy, Charlemont	20,695
2. Lord Lurgan of Brownlow House, Lurgan	15,166
3. Duke of Manchester of The Castle, Tandragee	12,298
2001	
1. The Forestry Commission	8,146
2. The 7th Earl of Gosford of Gosford Castle, Markethill	3,000
3. The 7th Earl of Caledon of Caledon House, Caledon	2,000
CARLOW	
1872	
1. Mr Henry Bruen of Oak Park	16,477
2. Mr Arthur McMurrough Kavanagh of Borris House	16,051
3. Earl of Bessborough of Bessborough House, Kilkenny	10,578

County	Acres owned

2001
1. Coillte (Irish Forestry Board) — 8,922
No other landowners of record

CAVAN

1872
1. Lord Farnham of Farnham — 25,920
2. Earl of Annesley of Castlewellan, Co. Down — 24,221
3. Marquess of Headfort of Headfort House, Kells — 14,220

2001
1. The late 12th Lord Farnham — 3,000
2. Buddy Kiernan, large farm owner — 2,000
3. Mr and Mrs Brian Mills of Coothill — 900

CLARE

1872
1. Lord Leconfield of Petworth House, Sussex — 37,292
2. The Marquess of Conyngham of Bifrons, Kent — 27,613
3. Lord Inchiquin of Dromoland, Newmarket-on-Fergus — 20,321

2001
1. Coillte — 50,531
2. The 18th Baron Inchiquin, resident at Dromoland — N/A
3. Ievers Family of Mount Ievers Court — 500

CORK

1872
1. Earl of Bantry of Macroom Castle, East Ferry — 69,500
2. Earl of Bandon of Castle Bernard, Bandon — 40,941
3. Duke of Devonshire of Chatsworth, Derbyshire — 32,550

2001
1. Coillte — 104,130
2. The Shelswell-White family — 2,500
3. Liam Cashman, owner of Rathbarry Stud — N/A

DONEGAL

1872
1. The Marquess of Conyngham of Bifrons, Kent — 122,230
2. Earl of Leitrim, resident at London — 54,352
3. Mr Horatio G. Murray-Stewart, resident in Scotland — 50,818

2001
1. Coillte — 76,465
2. The McIlhenny family of Lough Veagh — 22,000
No other landowners of record

611

County	Acres owned

DOWN

1872
1. Marquess of Downshire of The Castle, Hillsborough	78,051
2. Earl of Kilmorey of Mourne Park, Newry	40,902
3. Earl of Annesley of Castlewellan	24,221

2001
1. The National Trust	13,285
2. The Forestry Commission	12,710
3. The 6th Earl of Kilmorey, resident in England	12,000

DUBLIN (excluding the City of Dublin)

1872
1. Mr Charles Cobbe of Newbridge House, Donabate	9,948
2. Earl of Howth of Howth Castle, Dublin	7,377
3. Sir Charles Compton Domville of Santry House, Dublin	6,282

2001
1. Coillte	4,052
2. The Cobbe Family of Newbridge House, Donabate	900
3. Prince and Princess Azmat Guirey of Rathbeal Hall	300

FERMANAGH

1872
1. Marquess of Ely of Ely Lodge, Enniskillen	34,879
2. Earl of Erne of Crom Castle	31,389
3. Earl of Enniskillen of Florence Court, Enniskillen	29,635

2001
1. The Forestry Commission	58,599
2. The 6th Earl of Erne of Crom Castle	15,000
3. The 8th Earl of Belmore, resident on the estate	6,500

GALWAY

1872
1. Mr Richard Berridge of Clifden Castle, Connemara	160,152
2. Marquess of Clanricarde of Portnumna Castle	56,826
3. Lord Dunsandle and Clanconal of Dunsandle	33,543

2001
1. Coillte	82,501
2. The 4th Lord Blythe	750
3. The 5th Baron Hemphill of Kiltullen	700

County	Acres owned

KERRY

1872

1. Lord Ventry of Burnham House, Dingle	93,629
2. Earl of Kenmare of Killarney House	91,080
3. Mr Henry Arthur Herbert of Muckross Abbey	47,238

2001

1. Coillte	40,047
2. Sir George P. M. Fitzgerald, resident in England	N/A
3. Sir M. MacC. O'Connell of Lakeview House, Killarney	N/A

KILDARE

1872

1. Duke of Leinster of Carton, Maynooth	71,997
2. Marquess of Drogheda of Moore Abbey, Monastrevan	16,609
3. Sir Gerald George Aylmer of The Castle, Donadea	15,396

2001

1. Coillte	8,601
2. The Irish Defence Forces	N/A
3. The 7th Baron Carew of Naas	700

KILKENNY

1872

1. Viscount Clifden of Gowran Castle, Kilkenny	35,288
2. Earl of Bessborough of Bessborough House, Piltown	23,967
3. Mr Charles Wandesforde of Castlecomer	22,232

2001

1. Coillte	21,258
2. Baron and Baroness de Breffny of Castletown, Piltown	500
3. Jim Bolger, owner of stud at Coolcullen	(estimate) 500

LAOIS (formerly Queen's County)

1872

1. Sir Charles Henry Coote of Ballyfin, Mountrath	47,451
2. Lord Castletown of Lisduff, Templemore	22,510
3. Viscount de Vesci of Abbeyleix House, Abbeyleix	15,069

2001

1. Coillte	34,230
2. Bord Na Mona	30,000
3. The 7th Viscount de Vesci, resident in England	1,800

County	Acres owned

LEITRIM

1872
1. Lord Massey of The Hermitage, Castle Connell — 24,571
2. Mr George Lane Fox of Bramham Park, Yorkshire — 18,850
3. Mr Owen Wynn of Hazlewood, Sligo — 15,436

2001
1. Coillte — 27,213
No other landowners of record

LIMERICK

1872
1. Earl of Devon of Powderham Castle, Devon — 33,026
2. Earl of Dunraven of Adare Manor, Limerick — 14,298
3. Lord Ashtown of Woodlawn, Co. Galway — 11,273

2001
1. Coillte — 26,242
2. The 11th Earl Harrington, owner of Ballingarry stud — 900
3. The 29th Knight of Glin of Glin Castle — (estimate) 700

LONDONDERRY

1872
1. The Skinners' Livery Company, London — 34,772
2. The Drapers' Livery Company, London — 27,025
3. The Mercers' Livery Company, London — 21,241

2001
1. The Forestry Commission — 29,414
2. The National Trust — 451
No other landowners of record

LONGFORD

1872
1. Mr Edward Robert King-Harman of Rockingham, Boyle — 28,779
2. Earl of Granard of Castle Forbes, Longford — 14,978
3. Lord Annaly of Woodlands, Clonsilla, Dublin — 12,978

2001
1. Coillte — 7,252
2. Michael Magan, farmer — (estimate) 500
No other landowners of record

LOUTH

1872
1. Lord Cleremont of Ravensdale Park, Newry, Co. Down — 20,369
2. Viscount Massereene and Ferrard of Oriel Temple — 7,193
3. Mr James Hugh Smith-Barry of Foaty, Cobh, Co. Cork — 6,273

614

County	Acres owned
2001	
1. Coillte	3,355
2. Mr Larry Goodman, farmer	1,000
3. The Waddington family of Beaulieu, Drogheda	750

MAYO

1872

1. Marquess of Sligo of Westport House, Mayo	114,881
2. Viscount Dillon of Dytchley Park, Charlbury, England	83,749
3. Sir Roger William Palmer of Keenagh, Crossmolina	80,749

2001

1. Coillte	74,107
2. The 11th Marquess of Sligo of Westport House, Mayo	5,000

No other landowners of record

MEATH

1872

1. Earl of Darnley of Cobham Hall, Gravesend, Kent	25,463
2. Mr James Lennox Naper of Loughcrew, Oldcastle	18,863
3. Marquess of Lansdowne of Bowood Park, Caine, Wilts	12,995

2001

1. Coillte	3,674
2. The Earl and Countess of Mount Charles	1,000
3. The 20th Baron Dunsany	900

MONAGHAN

1872

1. Mr Evelyn Shirley of Stratford-on-Avon, Warwickshire	26,386
2. Marquess of Bath of Longleat, Wiltshire	22,762
3. Earl of Dartry of Dartry House, Coothill	17,732

2001

1. Coillte	6,661
2. Sir John Norman Ide Leslie of Glasslough	N/A

No other landowners of record

OFFALY (formerly King's County)

1872

1. Lord Digby of Minterne House, Cerne, Dorset	29,722
2. Earl of Rosse of Birr Castle, Parsonstown	22,513
3. Countess of Charleville of Charleville Forest, Tullamore	20,032

2001

1. Bord Na Mona	100,000
2. Coillte	19,165
3. The 7th Earl of Rosse, resident on estate	5,000

County	Acres owned

ROSCOMMON

1872
1. Lord de Freyne of French Park — 34,400
2. Mr Robert King Harman — 29,242
3. Mr Henry Pakenham-Mahon of Strokestown House — 26,980

2001
1. Coillte — 18,799
No other landowners of record

SLIGO

1872
1. Mr Edward Henry Cooper of Markree Castle, Colloony — 34,120
2. Sir Henry Gore-Booth of Lissadell — 31,774
3. Mr Charles William O'Hara of Cooper's Hill, Ballymote — 21,070

2001
1. Coillte — 26,815
2. The Gore-Booth family of Lissadell — N/A
No other landowners of record

TIPPERARY

1872
1. Viscount Lismore of Shanbally, Clogheen — 34,945
2. Mr Charles White of Cahercorn — 23,957
3. Lord Dunalley of Kilboy, Nenagh — 21,957

2001
1. Coillte — 59,469
2. The Holy Ghost Fathers of Rockwell College — (estimate) 500
3. John Magnier and Vincent O'Brien, stud owners — N/A

TYRONE

1872
1. Duke of Abercorn of Baronscourt, Newtownstewart — 60,000
2. Earl of Castlestuart of Stuart Hill, Stuartstown — 32,615
3. Earl of Caledon of Caledon House, Caledon — 29,236

2001
1. The Forestry Commission — 45,026
2. The 5th Duke of Abercorn, resident on the estate — 15,000
3. The 7th Earl of Caledon of Caledon House, Caledon — 7,400

WATERFORD

1872
1. Marquess of Waterford of Curraghmore — 39,883
2. Mr Henry Villers-Stuart of Dromana — 30,882
3. Duke of Devonshire of Chatsworth House, Derbyshire — 27,483

County	Acres owned
2001	
1. Coillte	40,724
2. The 8th Marquess of Waterford of Curraghmore	10,000
3. The 11th Duke of Devonshire of Chatsworth House	8,000

WESTMEATH

1872	
1. Mr Geo. Rochford-Boyd of Middleton Park, Castletown	16,397
2. Earl of Longford of Pakenham Hall, Castle Pollard	15,014
3. Mr John Malone of Baronstown, Ballinacargy	13,715
2001	
1. Coillte	10,605
2. The 7th Earl of Longford of Castle Pollard	900
3. The Beaumont family	(estimate) 500

WEXFORD

1872	
1. Lord Carew of Castleborough, Enniscorthy	17,830
2. Lord Fitzgerald of Johnstown Castle, Wexford	15, 216
3. Earl of Courtown of Courtown House, Gorey	14,426
2001	
1. Coillte	19,271
2. Bert Allen, large farmer	(estimate) 1,000
No other landowners of record	

WICKLOW

1872	
1. Earl Fitzwilliam of Wentworth House, Yorkshire	89,981
2. Viscount Powerscourt of Powerscourt, Enniskerry	40,986
3. Marquess of Waterford of Curraghmore, Waterford	26,035
2001	
1. Coillte	66,296
2. The 8th Marquess of Waterford of Curraghmore	900
3. The 15th Earl of Meath of Kilruddery, Bray	800

Source: Kevin Cahill, *Who Owns Britain* (London, 2001), pp. 318–54.

Housing

Homes completed (in thousands)

	IFS/É/ROI	NI
	(thousands)	
1923	0.4	–
1924	1.5	–
1925	3.4	–
1926	3.7	–
1927	2.1	–
1928	2.7	–
1929	3.4	–
1930	3.0	–
1931	5.2	–
1932	2.2	–
1933	7.0	–
1934	13.3	1.4
1935	14.3	4.2
1936	14.4	5.5
1937	14.3	0.7
1938	17.0	1.3
1939	12.2	0.4
1940	8.4	0.4
1941	6.3	–
1942	3.7	–
1943	2.5	–
1944	1.7	–
1945	1.3	0.1
1946	1.8	0.6
1947	2.1	1.2
1948	4.2	4.8
1949	9.4	7.6
1950	15.4	7.3
1951	15.0	7.0
1952	16.6	8.4
1953	15.4	8.0
1954	15.4	6.3
1955	16.3	7.0
1956	19.1	7.0
1957	14.6	6.5
1958	12.1	4.9
1959	14.2	4.9
1960	15.5	6.4
1961	14.6	7.1
1962	16.8	8.2
1963	17.5	8.8
1964	18.3	9.5
1965	19.6	8.9

	IFS/É/ROI	NI
	(thousands)	
1966	19.2	10.5
1967	21.9	11.1
1968	22.3	12.1
1969	21.8	11.5
1970	21.7	11.8
1971	23.9	13.9
1972	30.5	11.7
1973	33.9	10.6
1974	[24.2]	10.1
1975	35.9	8.9
1976	36.8	9.6
1977	28.9	10.8
1978	35.4	8.8
1979	44.2	7.3
1980	35.6	6.5
1981	28.9	6.5
1982	26.8	7.0
1983	26.1	9.6
1984	24.9	10.4
1985	23.9	10.8
1986	22.7	10.1
1987	18.5	9.8
1988	15.7	9.9
1989	18.1	10.3
1990	19.5	7.9
1991	19.7	6.9
1992	22.5	7.7
1993	21.4	7.2
1994	26.9	7.0
1995	30.8	8.8
1996	33.7	8.6
1997	38.8	8.9
1998	42.3	10.2
1999	46.5	9.6
2000	49.8	10.4
2001	52.6	11.7

Figures in brackets denote a change in now the figures were calculated.
Sources: Mitchell and Deane, *Abstract of British Historical Statistics*; CSO; NIAAS.

UNEMPLOYMENT

Unemployed in Irish Free State/Éire/Republic of Ireland, 1923–2001 (in thousands)

	Unemployed	Labour force
1923	35.7	
1924	36.1	
1925	36.4	
1926	25.3	
1927	21.1	
1928	22.7	
1929	20.7	
1930	20.4	
1931	25.2	
1932	62.8	
1933	72.4	
1934	103.7	
1935	119.5	
1936	99.3	
1937	81.7	
1938	88.7	
1939	93.1	
1940	84.1	
1941	74.7	
1942	76.9	
1943	67.6	
1944	60.3	
1945	60.7	
1946	59.7	
1947	55.6	
1948	61.2	
1949	60.6	
1950	53.4	
1951	50.5	
1952	60.7	
1953	70.6 [Social Welfare Act (1952) came into force]	
1954	62.4	
1955	55.2	
1956	61.4	
1957	69.7	
1958	65.3	
1959	61.7	

620

	Unemployed	Labour force
1960	52.9	
1961	46.6	
1962	46.6	
1963	50.0	
1964	48.9	
1965	49.4	
1966	47.7	
1967	55.0	
1968	58.3	
1969	57.3	
1970	64.9	
1971	62.0	
1972	71.5	
1973	66.8	
1974	71.4	
1975	103.2	
1976	112.8	
1977	111.0	
1978	102.9	
1979	92.9	
1980	100.0	
1981	127.1	
1982	154.8	
1983	180.8	1,324.9
1984	204.3	1,326.2
1985	219.6	1,316.4
1986	225.5	1,320.6
1987	226.0	1,336.5
1988	217.0	1,327.7
1989	196.8	1,307.8
1990	172.4	1,332.1
1991	198.5	1,354.4
1992	206.6	1,371.8
1993	220.1	1,403.2
1994	211.0	1,431.6
1995	177.4	1,459.2
1996	179.0	1,507.5
1997	159.0	1,539.0
1998	126.6	1,621.1
1999	96.9	1,688.1
2000	74.9	1,745.6
2001	65.4	1,781.9

Source: post-1983, CSO (2002), p. 29; pre-1983 the annual average given in the 'Live Register', CSO.

Unemployed in Northern Ireland, 1926–2002 (in thousands)

	Wholly unemployed		Temporarily stopped		
	Men	Women	Men	Women	Total
1926	32.7	13.9	2.0	4.9	56.0
1927	21.3	4.5	1.0	1.8	30.6
1928	21.8	10.6	1.8	4.5	40.8
1929	20.9	8.4	1.6	2.6	36.1
1930	20.7	18.2	2.7	5.3	60.1
1931	42.0	18.7	2.4	5.0	71.3
1932	44.0	15.2	2.4	6.5	68.2
1933	44.8	14.1	2.3	3.8	65.0
1934	40.9	13.5	1.7	2.5	61.8
1935	43.6	17.1	1.7	11.8	69.7
1936	42.1	16.8	1.4	3.2	66.7
1937	48.1	17.5	1.5	3.1	72.6
1938	54.1	25.2	2.5	6.0	90.7
1939	52.3	18.7	1.5	3.7	76.3
1940	42.9	12.9	1.6	4.1	72.0
1941	16.4	20.6	1.2	3.6	41.7
1942	8.5	8.6	1.5	2.5	20.9
1943	11.0	4.0	1.6	1.0	17.5
1944	9.1	3.5	1.3	0.8	15.1
1945	14.0	4.4	1.3	0.6	20.3
1946	26.1	4.3	0.2	0.5	31.1
1947	[24.7]	[3.1]	[0.5]	[0.7]	29.9
1948	22.2	4.4	0.4	0.8	27.8
1949	21.4	6.9	0.4	1.2	30.0
1950	20.7	5.7	0.3	0.2	26.9
1951	20.5	6.6	0.3	1.1	28.5
1952	25.0	14.7	1.8	6.7	48.3
1953	26.8	9.6	0.5	1.3	38.0
1954	23.4	7.9	0.4	1.3	33.0
1955	22.3	8.1	0.5	1.3	32.3
1956	21.7	7.0	0.5	0.9	30.1
1957	24.8	7.8	0.5	0.6	34.7
1958	29.1	11.2	1.0	2.1	43.5
1959	25.4	10.3	0.4	0.8	36.9
1960	23.6	7.8	0.5	0.5	32.4
1961	25.2	9.2	0.6	1.1	36.1
1962	25.0	10.5	0.4	0.8	36.7
1963	27.4	10.2	0.8	0.7	39.0
1964	23.3	8.9	0.3	0.4	32.8
1965	21.8	8.4	0.6	0.3	30.9
1966	22.2	8.0	0.5	0.5	31.2
1967	27.0	10.9	0.5	1.3	39.6
1968	27.4	9.2	0.3	0.3	37.2

	Wholly unemployed			Temporarily stopped		
	Men	Women		Men	Women	Total
1969	28.7	8.4		0.5	0.2	37.8
1970	27.6	8.2		0.5	0.3	36.5
1971	31.3	9.5		0.6	0.5	41.5
1972	30.0	10.6		0.9	0.4	41.1
1973	22.8	8.3		0.3	0.2	31.6
1974	22.2	7.8		1.0	0.9	31.8
1975	29.7	12.1		0.9	1.0	43.9
1976	37.5	17.4		0.5	0.5	55.9
1977	41.7	19.1		2.0	0.4	63.3
1978	45.0	20.4		0.7	0.2	66.3
1979	44.3	20.6		0.7	0.1	65.7
1980	53.6	25.3		0.6	0.2	79.6
1981*	66	26		[discontinued as a measurement]		
1982	74	29				
1983	82	31				
1984	82	30				
1985	84	31				
1986	91	34				
1987	89	32				
1988	83	31				
1989	78	28				
1990	73	24				
1991	76	23				
1992	81	24				
1993	80	23				
1994	75	22				
1995	69	19				
1996	65	19				
1997	50	14				
1998	45	13				
1999	39	11				
2000	32	10				
2001	30	10				
2002	28	9				

Figures in brackets denote a change in now the figures were calculated.
*From 1981 the figures are taken from NIAAS and are an average of the monthly figures.

623

FOREIGN RELATIONS

Section Four

FOREIGN RELATIONS

IRISH OVERSEAS MISSIONS
AND EMBASSIES

Year established	*State/international organisation*
1923	United Kingdom
1924	United States of America
1929	Boston, USA (Consulate)
	Holy See, Vatican
	France
1930	New York, USA (Consulate)
1932	Belgium
1933	Chicago, USA (Consulate)
	San Francisco, USA (Consulate)
1935	Spain
1938	Italy
1939	Canada
1940	Switzerland
1941	Portugal
1946	Australia
	Sweden
1947	Argentina
1950	The Netherlands
1951	Germany
1955	Council of Europe (Strasbourg)
1956	United Nations (Permanent Mission) (New York)
1960	Nigeria
1961	Denmark
1964	India
1965	Geneva
1966	European Economic Community (Permanent Representative) (Brussels)
1973	Japan
	Luxembourg
1974	Lebanon (closed 1982)
	Union of Soviet Socialist Republics (now Russia)
	Austria
1975	Egypt
1976	Saudi Arabia
	Iran
1977	Greece

Year established	*State/international organisation*
1978	Lesotho (Consulate)
1979	Kenya (closed 1988)
	China
	Tanzania
1980	Zambia
1984	Iraq
1989	Republic of Korea (South Korea)
1990	Poland
1992	Finland
1994	Ethiopia
1995	South Africa
	Uganda
	Czechoslovakia (now Czech Republic)
	Hungary
	Malaysia
1996	Mozambique
	Israel
1998	Cardiff, UK (Consulate)
	Edinburgh, UK (Consulate)
	Turkey
1999	Mexico
2000	Sydney, Australia (Consulate)
	Shanghai, China (Consulate)
	Singapore
	Palestinian National Authority (Ramallah)
2001	Norway
	Slovakia
	Cyprus
	Slovenia
	Brazil
	Estonia

Source: <http://foreignaffairs.gov.ie/embassies>.

TREATIES, 1921–2000

The power to make treaties was a contentious issue between Commonwealth Dominions and the UK. Ireland was at the forefront of pushing for this capability. This is a list of treaties made by the Irish Free State/Éire/Republic of Ireland. It also includes the 1921 'Anglo-Irish Treaty' agreed between Sinn Féin, or the First Dáil, and the British government.

Year/no.	Treaty, place and date of agreement

Pre-1930

1921	Articles of Agreement for a Treaty between Great Britain and Ireland, London, 6 Dec. 1921
1924	Agreement supplementing Article 12 of the Articles of Agreement for a Treaty between Great Britain and Ireland, London, 4 Aug. 1924
1925	Agreement Amending and Supplementing the Articles of Agreement for a Treaty between Great Britain and Ireland, London, 3 Dec. 1925
1928	Kellogg-Briand Pact, Paris, 27 Aug. 1928
1929–30	Exchange of Notes between Irish Free State and Germany concerning Navigation between the two territories Exchange of Notes between Irish Free State and France concerning Navigation between the two territories

1930

1 of 1930	International Convention: Suppression of the Circulation of and Traffic in Obscene Publications, Geneva, 12 Sept. 1923
2 of 1930	Intentional Convention: Securing the Abolition of Slavery and the Slave Trade, Geneva, 25 Sept. 1926
3 of 1930	Protocol: Revision of the Statute of the Permanent Court of International Justice, Geneva, 14 Sept. 1939
4 of 1930	Protocol: Accession of USA to the Protocol of Signature of Statute of the Permanent Court of International Justice, Geneva, 14 Sept. 1929
5 of 1930	International Convention: Economic Statistics, 14 Dec. 1928
6 of 1930	Exchange of Notes between Irish Free State and Greece regarding Commercial Relations, Athens, 15 May 1930
7 of 1930	Protocol: Prohibition of the Use in War of Asphyxiating, Poisonous or other Gases, and of Bacteriological Warfare, Geneva, 17 June 1925

629

8 of 1930	Declaration in Conformity with Art. 36 Statute of the Permanent Court of International Justice, Geneva, 16 Dec. 1920
9 of 1930	International Treaty: Limitation and Reduction of Naval Armament, London, 22 Apr. 1930
10 of 1930	Exchange of Notes between Irish Free State and Italy concerning Reciprocal Recognition of Passenger Ships' certificates and Emigrant Ships Regulations, Rome, 10 May 1930
11 of 1930	Exchange of Notes between Irish Free State and Guatemala concerning Commercial Relations, Guatemala, 8 Feb. – 10 Apr. 1930
12 of 1930	Exchange of Notes between Irish Free State and Switzerland concerning Unemployment Insurance, Berne, 3–4 Nov. 1930
13 of 1930	Exchange of Notes between Irish Free State and Norway for Reciprocal Exemption from Taxation of Business of Shipping, Dublin, 21 Oct. 1930
14 of 1930	Exchange of Notes between Irish Free State and Egypt concerning Commercial Relations, Cairo, 25–28 July 1930
15 of 1930	Exchange of Notes between Irish Free State and Romania concerning Commercial Relations, Bucharest, 1–27 Oct. 1930
16 of 1930	Protocol: Amending the Convention for the Regulation of Aerial Navigation, Paris, 15 June 1929
17 of 1930	Protocol: Amending the Convention for the Regulation of Aerial Navigation, Paris, 11 Dec. 1929
18 of 1930	International Agreement: Facilities for Merchant Seamen for Treatment of Venereal Disease, Brussels, 1 Dec. 1924
19 of 1930	Agreement between Irish Free State and Belgium for Exchange of Money Orders, Dublin, 24 Sept. 1929

1931

1 of 1931	Exchange of Notes between Irish Free State and Egypt concerning Commercial Relations, Cairo, 14–22 Feb. 1931
2 of 1931	Treaty between Irish Free State and Portugal concerning Commerce and Navigation, Dublin, 29 Oct. 1929
3 of 1931	General Act for Pacific Settlement of International Disputes, Geneva, 26 Sept. 1928
4 of 1931	Agreement between Irish Free State and Sweden for Reciprocal Exemption from Taxation of Business of Shipping, Dublin, 8 Oct. 1931
5 of 1931	Exchange of Notes between Irish Free State and USA concerning Reciprocal Recognition of Load Line Regulations, Dublin, 21 Sept. – 18 Nov. 1931
6 of 1931	International Convention: Dangerous Drugs, Geneva, 19 Feb. 1925

7 of 1931	Exchange of Notes between Irish Free State and Brazil concerning Commercial Relations, Rio de Janeiro, 16 Oct. 1931
8 of 1931	British Commonwealth Merchant Shipping Agreement, London, 10 Dec. 1931
9 of 1931	Treaty between Irish Free State and Germany concerning Commerce and Navigation, Dublin, 12 May 1930
10 of 1931	Exchange of Notes between Irish Free State and San Salvador concerning Commercial Relations, San Salvador, 12–30 Sept. 1931

1932

1 of 1932	Exchange of Notes between Irish Free State and Egypt concerning Commercial Relations, Cairo, 23–26 Jan. 1932
2 of 1932	Trade Agreement between Irish Free State and Canada, Ottawa, 20 Aug. 1932
3 of 1932	Convention between Irish Free State and France concerning Exchange of Money Orders, Dublin, 2 Apr. 1929
4 of 1932	Exchange of Notes between Irish Free State and San Salvador prolonging the Provisional Commercial Agreement of 25–28 July 1930, Cairo, 16–19 Feb. 1933

1933

1 of 1933	Exchange of Notes between Irish Free State and Egypt prolonging the Provisional Commercial Agreement of 25–28 July 1930, Cairo, 16–19 Feb. 1933
2 of 1933	International Convention: Limiting the Manufacture of Narcotic Drugs and Regulating Distribution, Geneva, 13 July 1931
3 of 1933	Trade Agreement between Irish Free State and South Africa, Ottawa, 20 Aug. 1932
4 of 1933	Exchange of Notes between Irish Free State and San Salvador prolonging Commercial 'Modus Vivendi' of 12–30 Sept. 1931, San Salvador, 23–28 Oct. 1933
5 of 1933	International Convention: Taxation of Foreign Motor Vehicles, Geneva, 30 Mar. 1931

1934

1 of 1934	International Convention: Safety of Life at Sea, London, 31 May 1929
2 of 1934	International Load Line Convention, London, 5 July 1930
3 of 1934	Exchange of Notes between Irish Free State and Egypt prolonging the Provisional Commercial Agreement of 25–28 July 1930, Cairo, 17–19 Feb. 1934

4 of 1934	Exchange of Notes between Irish Free State and Costa Rica concerning Commercial Relations, Panama, 2 Aug. 1933, and San Jose, 2 Apr. 1934
5 of 1934	International Agreement: Suppression of White Slave Traffic, Paris, 18 May 1904; International Convention for the Suppression of the White Slave Trade, Paris, 4 May 1910
6 of 1934	International Convention: Suppression of the Traffic of Women and Children, Geneva, 30 Sept. 1921
7 of 1934	Exchange of Notes between Irish Free State and Spain concerning Commercial Relations, Dublin, 21 June 1934
8 of 1934	International Agreement: Statistics of Causes of Death, London, 19 June 1934
9 of 1934	International Convention: Facilitating the International Circulation of Films of an Educational Character, Geneva, 11 Oct. 1933
10 of 1934	International Convention and Protocol: Suppression of Counterfeiting Currency, Geneva, 20 Apr. 1929
11 of 1934	International Convention: Respecting the Salvage of Torpedoes, Paris, 12 June 1934
12 of 1934	Agreement between Irish Free State and Denmark for Reciprocal Exemption from Taxation of Business of Shipping, London, 35 Apr. 1934
13 of 1934	Exchange of Notes between Irish Free State and Germany concerning the Release of German Property in the Irish Free State, Dublin, 14 Sept. 1934
14 of 1934	Exchange of Notes between Irish Free State and San Salvador prolonging the Commercial 'Modus Vivendi' of 12–30 Sept. 1931, San Salvador, 13 Sept. and 22 Nov. 1934

1935

1 of 1935	Exchange of Notes between Irish Free State and Germany concerning Commercial Relations, Dublin, 28 Jan. 1935
2 of 1935	Exchange of Notes between Irish Free State and Belgium concerning Commercial Relations, no venue given, 15 Feb. 1935
3 of 1935	Exchange of Notes between Irish Free State and Egypt prolonging the Provisional Commercial Agreement of 25–28 July 1930, Cairo, 5–11 Feb. 1935
4 of 1935	Exchange of Notes between Irish Free State and Spain concerning Commercial Relations, Madrid, 1 Apr. 1935
5 of 1935	Agreement between Irish Free State and Poland concerning Tonnage Measurement of Ships, Dublin, 19 Oct. 1934
6 of 1935	International Convention: Protection of Literary and Artistic Works, Rome, 2 June 1928

7 of 1935   Exchange of Notes between Irish Free State and South Africa concerning Commercial Relations, Pretoria and Dublin, 31 July 1935

8 of 1935   Exchange of Notes between Irish Free State and San Salvador prolonging the Commercial 'Modus Vivendi' of 12–30 Sept. 1931, San Salvador, 10–25 Oct. 1935

9 of 1935   International Convention and Protocol: Unification of Certain Rules relating to International Carriage by Air, Warsaw, 12 Oct. 1929

1936

1 of 1936   Exchange of Notes between Irish Free State and Egypt prolonging the Provisional Commercial Agreement of 25–28 July 1930, Cairo, 15 Feb. 1936

2 of 1936   Exchange of Notes between Irish Free State and Germany extending the Commercial Agreement of 28 Jan. 1935, Dublin, 29 Apr. 1936

3 of 1936   Exchange of Notes between Irish Free State and the Netherlands concerning Commercial Relations, Dublin, 29 July 1936

4 of 1936   International Convention with Protocol: Stamp Laws in connection with Bills of Exchange and Promissory Notes, Geneva, 7 June 1930

5 of 1936   International Convention and Protocol: Stamp Laws in connection with Cheques, Geneva, 19 Mar. 1931

6 of 1936   Exchange of Notes between Irish Free State and Turkey concerning Commercial Relations, Dublin, 1 Oct. 1936

7 of 1936   *Procès-verbal* relating to Rules of Submarine Warfare in Part IV of London Naval Treaty, 1930, London, 6 Nov. 1936

8 of 1936   Exchange of Notes between Irish Free State and Germany extending Commercial Agreement of 29 Apr. 1936, 18 Dec. 1936

1937

1 of 1937   Exchange of Notes between Irish Free State and Belgium concerning Commercial Relations, Brussels, 28 Dec. 1936 and Paris, 6 Jan. 1937

2 of 1937   Exchange of Notes between Irish Free State and Egypt prolonging the Provisional Commercial Agreement of 25–28 July 1930, Cairo, 15 Feb. 1937

3 of 1937   Exchange of Notes between Irish Free State and USA concerning Air Navigation, Dublin, 29 Sept. – 4 Nov. 1937

4 of 1937   Exchange of Notes between Irish Free State and the Netherlands extending the Commercial Arrangement of 29 July 1936, Dublin, 25 Nov. 1937

5 of 1937	Exchange of Notes between Irish Free State and Belgium prolonging the Commercial Agreement of 28 Dec. 1936 – 6 Jan. 1937, Paris, 13 Dec. 1937 and Brussels, 24 Dec. 1937

1938

1 of 1938	Agreements between Ireland and the UK, London, 25 Apr. 1938
2 of 1938	International Convention: Regulation of Whaling, Geneva, 24 Sept. 1931
3 of 1938	International Agreement: Regulation of Whaling (with Final Act of the Conference), London, 8 June 1937
4 of 1938	International Convention: Use of Broadcasting in the Cause of Peace, Geneva, 23 Sept. 1936
5 of 1938	International Convention: Suppression of the Traffic of Women of Full Age, Geneva, 11 Oct. 1933
6 of 1938	Exchange of Notes between Ireland and Brazil concerning Commercial Relations, Rio de Janeiro, 24 July 1936
7 of 1938	Additional Protocol to Convention of 12 June 1934, concerning the Salvage of Torpedoes, Paris, 12 Jan. 1938
8 of 1938	Exchange of Notes between Ireland and Egypt prolonging the Provisional Commercial Agreement of 25–28 July 1930, Cairo, 15–16 Feb. 1938
9 of 1938	Exchange of Notes between Ireland and Germany prolonging the Commercial Agreement of 18 Dec. 1936, Dublin, 3 Nov. 1938

1939

1 of 1939	Exchange of Notes between Ireland and Egypt prolonging the Provisional Commercial Agreement of 25–28 July 1930, Cairo, 7–16 Mar. 1939
2 of 1939	Exchange of Notes between Ireland and the Netherlands prolonging the Commercial Arrangement of 29 July 1936
3 of 1939	*Procès-verbal* concerning the Application of Articles of the Convention of 11 Oct. 1933, for Facilitating the International Circulation of Films of an Educational Character, Geneva, 12 Sept. 1938

1940

1 of 1940	Exchange of Notes between Ireland and Egypt prolonging the Provisional Commercial Agreement of 25–28 July 1930, Cairo, 22 Apr. – 9 May 1940
2 of 1940	International Convention: Regulation of the Meshes of Fishing Nets and Size Limits of Fish, London, 23 Mar. 1937

3 of 1940   Protocol: International Agreement of 8 June 1937, for the Regulation of Whaling, London, 24 June 1938

1941

1 of 1941   Exchange of Notes between Ireland and Egypt prolonging the Provisional Commercial Agreement of 25–28 July 1930, Cairo, 16 Feb. 1941

2 of 1941   Exchange of Notes between Ireland and UK concerning Transfer and Administration of Workmen's Compensation Awards, London, 25 Feb. – 19 May 1941

1942

1 of 1942   Exchange of Notes between Ireland and Egypt prolonging the Provisional Commercial Agreement of 25–28 July 1930, Cairo, 16 Feb. – 10 Mar. 1942

1943

1 of 1943   Exchange of Notes between Ireland and South Africa concerning Transfer and Administration of Workmen's Compensation Awards, Pretoria, 16 Mar. – 4 Nov. 1942

2 of 1943   Exchange of Notes between Ireland and Egypt prolonging the Provisional Commercial Agreement of 25–28 July 1930, Cairo, 16 Feb. – 22 Mar. 1943

1944

1 of 1944   Exchange of Notes between Ireland and Egypt prolonging the Provisional Commercial Agreement of 25–28 July 1930, Cairo, 12 Feb. – 13 Mar. 1944

1945

1 of 1945   Exchange of Notes between Ireland and USA concerning Air Transport, Washington, 3 Feb. 1945

2 of 1945   Protocols regarding Amendment of Convention relating to Regulation of Air Navigation of 13 Oct. 1919, Brussels, 1 June 1935

3 of 1945   Exchange of Notes between Ireland and Egypt prolonging the Provisional Commercial Agreement of 25–28 July 1930, Cairo, 16 Feb. – 14 Mar. 1945

4 of 1945   Interim Agreement on International Civil Aviation, Chicago, 7 Dec. 1944

1946

1 of 1946   Agreement between Ireland and UK concerning Air Services to, in, and through their Respective Territories, London, 5 Apr. 1946

2 of 1946	Exchange of Notes between Ireland and Egypt prolonging the Provisional Commercial Agreement of 25–28 July 1930, Cairo, 12 Feb. – 2 Apr. 1946
3 of 1946	Agreement between Ireland and France concerning Air Transport, Dublin, 16 May 1946
4 of 1946	Exchange of Notes between Ireland and Sweden concerning Air Transport, Dublin, 29 May 1946
5 of 1946	Not issued
6 of 1946	International Civil Aviation Convention, Chicago, 7 Dec. 1944

1947

1 of 1947	Agreement between Ireland and Czechoslovakia concerning Air Services between their Territories, Dublin 29 Jan. 1947
2 of 1947	Exchange of Notes between Ireland and USA amending Air Transport Agreement concluded at Washington, 3 Feb. 1945, Washington, 2–3 June 1947
3 of 1947	Exchange of Notes between Ireland and Sweden concerning Mutual Abolition of Visas, Dublin, 19 Mar. 1947
4 of 1947	Exchange of Notes between Ireland and the Netherlands concerning Mutual Abolition of Visas, Dublin, 1 May 1947
5 of 1947	Exchange of Notes between Ireland and Denmark concerning Mutual Abolition of Visas, Copenhagen, 13 May 1947
6 of 1947	Exchange of Notes between Ireland and Switzerland concerning Mutual Abolition of Visas, Berne, 9 June 1947
7 of 1947	Agreement between Ireland and Canada for Air Services between the two countries, Dublin, 8 Aug. 1947
8 of 1947	Trade Agreement between Ireland and Spain, Dublin, 3 Sept. 1947
9 of 1947	Exchange of Notes between Ireland and France concerning Mutual Abolition of Visas, Paris, 16–22 Apr. 1947
10 of 1947	Air Transport Agreement between Ireland and Denmark concluded by Exchange of Notes, Dublin, 18 Nov. 1947
11 of 1947	Agreement between Ireland and Italy for Air Services between the two countries, Dublin, 21 Nov. 1947

1948

1 of 1948	Exchange of Notes between Ireland and Norway concerning Mutual Abolition of Visas, Oslo, 16–17 Dec. 1947
2 of 1948	Agreement relative to Preservation or Restoration of Industrial Property Rights affected by the Second World War, Neuchatel, 8 Feb. 1947

3 of 1948	Exchange of Notes between Ireland and Egypt prolonging the Provisional Commercial Agreement of 25–28 July 1930, London, 12–28 Feb. 1948
4 of 1948	Protocol amending Agreements, Conventions and Protocols on Narcotic Drugs, New York, 11 Dec. 1946
5 of 1948	Provisional Agreement relating to Air Services between Ireland and Switzerland, Dublin, 6 May 1946
6 of 1948	Air Transport Agreement between Ireland and the Netherlands, Dublin, 10 May 1948
7 of 1948	Trade Agreement between Ireland and France concluded by Exchange of Notes, Dublin, 5 June 1948
8 of 1948	Agreement between Ireland and Norway for Air Services between the two countries, London, 21 June 1948
9 of 1948	Exchange of Notes between Ireland and Belgium concerning Mutual Abolition of Visas, Brussels, 16 Apr. 1948
10 of 1948	Economic Co-operation Agreement between Ireland and USA, Dublin, 28 June 1948
11 of 1948	Exchange of Notes between Ireland and USA extending Territorial Application of Commercial Arrangements between the two countries, Dublin, 28 June 1948
12 of 1948	Trade Agreement between Ireland and UK, Dublin, 31 July 1948
13 of 1948	Protocol for dissolution of International Institute of Agriculture and transference of its functions to Food and Agriculture Organisation of the United Nations, Rome, 30 Mar. 1946
14 of 1948	Constitution of World Health Organisation, New York, 2 July 1946
15 of 1948	Protocol concerning Office of International Public Hygiene, New York, 22 July 1946
16 of 1948	Convention for European Economic Co-operation, Paris, 16 Apr. 1948
17 of 1948	Trade Agreement between Ireland and the Netherlands concluded by Exchange of Notes, 2 Sept. 1948

1949

1 of 1949	Exchange of Notes between Ireland and Luxembourg, concerning Mutual Abolition of Visas, Brussels, 1 Dec. 1948
2 of 1949	Exchange of Notes between Ireland and Egypt prolonging the Provisional Commercial Agreement of 25–28 July 1930, London, 12–24 Feb. 1949
3 of 1949	Exchange of Notes between Ireland and Switzerland concerning Exchange of Employment Facilities, Dublin, 14 Mar. 1949

4 of 1949   Agreement between Ireland and UK for Reciprocal Relief of Double Taxation in respect of Irish Corporation Profits Tax and UK Profits Tax, no venue given, 18 May 1949

5 of 1949   Exchange of Notes between Ireland and Iceland concerning Mutual Abolition of Visas, London, 19–20 May 1949

6 of 1949   Trade Agreement between Ireland and Sweden concluded by Exchange of Notes, Dublin, 25 June 1949

7 of 1949   International Wheat Agreement, Washington, 23 March 1949

8 of 1949   Exchange of Notes between Ireland and France extending Trade Agreement of 5 June 1948, Dublin, 7 July 1949

9 of 1949   Statute of Council of Europe, London, 5 May 1949

10 of 1949   Trade Agreement between Ireland and the Military Governments for the USA, UK and French Occupied Areas of Germany, Dublin, 22 July 1949

11 of 1949   Exchange of Notes between Ireland and USA concerning Reciprocal Relaxation of Visa Requirements, Dublin, 1 Aug. 1949

12 of 1949   Trade Agreement between Ireland and the Netherlands concluded by Exchange of Notes, Dublin, 25 Nov. 1949

13 of 1949   Exchange of Notes between Ireland and Italy concerning Mutual Abolition of Visas, Dublin, 29 Nov. 1949

14 of 1949   Agreement between Ireland and France concerning the admission of 'Stagiaires' to Ireland and France, Paris, 21 Nov. 1949

1950

1 of 1950   Exchange of Notes between Ireland and USA amending Economic Co-operation Agreement of 28 June 1948, Washington, 17–18 Jan. 1950

2 of 1950   Exchange of Notes between Ireland and Egypt prolonging the Provisional Commercial Agreement of 25–28 July 1930, London, 20–21 Mar. 1950

3 of 1950   Agreement on North Atlantic Ocean Weather Stations, London, 12 May 1949

4 of 1950   Agreement between Ireland and Spain concerning Mutual Aid and Exchange of Meteorological Information, Dublin, 11 May 1950

5 of 1950   Trade Agreement between Ireland and Germany (FDR), Dublin, 12 July 1950

6 of 1950   Exchange of Notes between Ireland and France extending Trade Agreement of 5 June 1948, Dublin, 31 July 1950

7 of 1950   Treaty of Friendship, Commerce and Navigation between Ireland and USA, Dublin, 21 Jan. 1950

8 of 1950	Trade Agreement between Ireland and Austria concluded by Exchange of Notes at Headquarters of Organisation for European Economic Co-operation, Paris, 6 Oct. 1950
9 of 1950	Agreement for Establishment of European Payments Union (with Annexes and Protocol), Paris, 19 Sept. 1950
10 of 1950	Trade Agreement between Ireland and Iceland concluded by Exchange of Notes, Paris, 2 Dec. 1950
11 of 1950	Exchange of Notes between Ireland and the Netherlands extending Trade Agreement of 25 Nov. 1949, Dublin, 22 Dec. 1950

1951

1 of 1951	Trade Agreement between Ireland and Finland, concluded by Exchange of Notes, Stockholm, 1 June 1951
2 of 1951	Trade Agreement between Ireland and Norway concluded by Exchange of Notes, Dublin, 2 July 1951
3 of 1951	Exchange of Notes between Ireland and France, extending Trade Agreement of 31 July 1950, Paris, 13 July 1951
4 of 1951	Trade Agreement between Ireland and Germany (FDR), Bonn, 23 July 1951
5 of 1951	Trade Agreement between Ireland and Spain, Madrid, 19 Dec. 1951
6 of 1951	Trade Agreement between Ireland and Switzerland concluded by Exchange of Notes, Berne, 26 Dec. 1951
7 of 1951	Convention between Ireland and USA for Avoidance of Double Taxation and prevention of Fiscal Evasion with respect to Taxes on Income, Dublin, 13 Sept. 1949
8 of 1951	Convention between Ireland and USA for Avoidance of Double Taxation and Prevention of Fiscal Evasion with respect to the Estates of Deceased Persons, Dublin, 13 Sept. 1949
9 of 1951	Exchange of Notes between Ireland and Egypt prolonging the Provisional Commercial Agreement of 25–28 July 1930, London, 27 Feb. 1951
10 of 1951	Amendments to Statute of Council of Europe, Strasbourg, 22 May 1951
11 of 1951	Amendment to Statute of Council of Europe, Strasbourg, 18 Dec. 1951
12 of 1951	Exchange of Notes between Ireland and USA amending Economic Co-operation Agreement of 28 June 1948, Dublin, 20 Apr. – June 1951
13 of 1951	Exchange of Notes between Ireland and Canada amending Agreement for Air Services between the two countries signed at Dublin on 8 Aug. 1947, Dublin, 9 July 1951

14 of 1951   Exchange of Notes between Ireland and the Netherlands extending Trade Agreement of 22 Dec. 1950, Dublin, 29 Oct. 1951

1952

1 of 1952   Trade Agreement between Ireland and Portugal concluded by an Exchange of Notes, Dublin, 6 Feb. 1952

2 of 1952   Protocol amending the Convention for Suppression of the Circulation and the Traffic in Obscene Publications concluded, Geneva, 12 Sept. 1923. Opened for Signature or Acceptance, New York, 12 Nov. 1947

3 of 1952   Protocol amending the Convention for Suppression of the Circulation of Obscene Publications, Paris, 4 May 1910. Opened for Signature or Acceptance, New York, on 4 May 1949

4 of 1952   Exchange of Notes between Ireland and France extending Trade Agreement of 13 July 1951, Dublin, 18 July 1952

5 of 1952   Exchange of Notes between Ireland and France amending the Air Transport Agreement concluded at Dublin on 16 May 1946, Paris, 10 July and 14 Aug. 1952

6 of 1952   Trade Agreement between Ireland and Germany (FDR), Bonn, 26 Sept. 1952

7 of 1952   Exchange of Notes between Ireland and Belgium concerning the Cattle Trade between the two territories, Dublin, 30 June – 1 July 1952

8 of 1952   Exchange of Notes between Ireland and the Netherlands prolonging Trade Agreement of 29 Oct. 1951, Dublin, 22 Aug. 1952

9 of 1952   Protocol extending period of Agreement on North Atlantic Ocean Weather Stations, London, 12 May, 1949, Montreal, 28 May 1952

10 of 1952   Protocol bringing under International Control Drugs outside the scope of the Convention of 13 July 1931 for Limiting the Manufacture and Regulating the Distribution of Narcotic Drugs as amended by the Protocol signed at New York on 11 Dec. 1946. Opened for Signature or Acceptance, Paris, 19 Nov. 1948

11 of 1952   Convention establishing a Customs Co-operation Council (with Annex), Brussels, 15 Dec. 1950

12 of 1952   Protocol concerning the European Customs Union Study Group, Brussels, 15 Dec. 1950. Irish Instrument of Ratification deposited on 23 Sept. 1952

1953

1 of 1953   Exchange of Notes between Ireland and the Netherlands prolonging Trade Agreement of 29 Oct. 1951, Dublin, 30 Jan. 1953

2 of 1953   Exchange of Notes between Ireland and France extending Trade Agreement of 18 July 1952, Paris, 2 May 1953

3 of 1953   Amendment to the Statute of Council of Europe, Strasbourg, 4 May 1953

4 of 1953   Exchange of Notes amending the Trade Agreement of 31 July 1948, between Ireland and UK, London, 17 June 1953

5 of 1953   International Convention for Regulation of the Meshes of Fishing Nets and Size Limits of Fish, London, 5 Apr. 1946, and Amending Protocol of 2 Apr. 1953. Irish Instrument of Ratification deposited on 2 Jan. 1950

6 of 1953   Trade Agreement between the Government of Ireland and Italy, Dublin, 27 July 1953

7 of 1953   Agreement Revising and Renewing the International Wheat Agreement of 23 Mar. 1949, Washington, 13 Apr. 1953. Irish Instrument of Acceptance deposited 13 July 1953

8 of 1953   Trade Agreement between Ireland and Ceylon, London, 20 Nov. 1953

9 of 1953   Supplementary Protocols amending Agreement for Establishment of a European Payments Union, Paris, 4 Aug. 1951, 11 July 1952, 30 July 1953. Irish Instruments of Ratification of Supplementary Protocol deposited on 10 Nov. 1953

10 of 1953   Convention on the Valuation of Goods for Customs Purposes (with Annexes), Brussels, 15 Dec. 1950. Irish Instrument of Accession deposited 23 Sept. 1952

11 of 1953   Exchange of Notes between Ireland and Finland concerning Trade Agreement of 1 June 1951, Stockholm, 3 Sept. 1953

12 of 1953   Convention for the Protection of Human Rights and Fundamental Freedoms, Rome, 4 Nov. 1950 (with Declarations in accordance with Arts 25 and 46 of the Convention). Irish Instrument of Ratification deposited on 25 Feb. 1953

13 of 1953   International Convention for the Safety of Life at Sea, London, 10 June 1948. Irish Instrument of Acceptance deposited 19 Aug. 1953

14 of 1953   Trade Agreement between Ireland and Germany (FDR), Dublin, 2 Dec. 1953

15 of 1953   Exchange of Notes between Ireland and France extending Trade Agreement of 2 May 1953, Paris, 29 Dec. 1953

16 of 1953   Agreement on German External Debts, London, 27 Feb. 1953. Irish Instrument of Ratification deposited 12 Nov. 1953

17 of 1953   Exchange of Notes between Ireland and Belgium extending Agreement of 30 June – 1 July 1952, concerning the Cattle Trade between the two territories, Dublin, 29–30 June 1953

1954

1 of 1954   Agreement between Ireland and UK concerning Veterinary Surgeons, London, 6 Apr. 1954

2 of 1954   European Convention on the Equivalence of Diplomas leading to Admission to Universities, Paris, 11 Dec. 1953. Irish Instrument of Ratification deposited 31 Mar. 1954

3 of 1954   Protocol to the Convention for Protection of Human Rights and Fundamental Freedoms, signed at Rome on 4 Nov. 1950, Paris, 20 Mar. 1952. Irish Instrument of Ratification deposited 25 Feb. 1953

4 of 1954   Exchange of Notes between Ireland and France extending Trade Agreement of 2 May 1953, Dublin, 29 May 1954

5 of 1954   Consular Convention between Ireland and USA, Dublin, 1 May 1950, and Supplementary Protocol, Dublin, 3 Mar. 1952. Ratification exchanged at Washington, 13 May 1954

6 of 1954   Constitution of the European Commission for the Control of Foot and Mouth Disease, Rome, 11 Dec. 1953. Irish Instrument of Acceptance deposited 16 Dec. 1953

7 of 1954   European Convention on Social and Medical Assistance and Protocol, Paris, 11 Dec. 1953 (with Declaration in accordance with Art. 1 of the Protocol). Irish Instruments of Ratification deposited on 31 Mar. 1954

8 of 1954   European Interim Agreement on Social Security, other than schemes for Old Age, Invalidity and Survivors, and Protocol, Paris, 11 Dec. 1953 (with Declarations in accordance with Art. 1 of the Protocol). Irish Instruments of Ratification deposited 31 Mar. 1954

9 of 1954   European Interim Agreement on Social Security relating to Old Age, Invalidity, and Survivors, and Protocol, Paris, 11 Dec. 1953 (with Declarations in accordance with Art. 1 of the Protocol). Irish Instruments of Ratification deposited 31 Mar. 1954

10 of 1954   Exchange of Notes between Ireland and Monaco concerning Mutual Abolition of Visas, Paris, 6 July 1954

11 of 1954   Revision of Annex 1 of International Convention for the Regulation of Meshes of Fishing Nets and the Size Limits of Fish, London, 5 Apr. 1946, London, 3–6 Nov. 1953

12 of 1954   Supplementary Protocol No. 5 amending Agreement for the Establishment of European Payments Union, Paris, 30 June 1954. Irish Instrument of Ratification deposited 27 Oct. 1954

13 of 1954   Exchange of Notes between Ireland and Belgium extending Agreement of 30 June – 1 July 1952, concerning the Cattle Trade between the two territories, Dublin, 12 Oct. 1954

14 of 1954   General Index to the Treaty Series 1930–1953

15 of 1954   Exchange of Notes between Ireland and Belgium concerning Irish Meteorological Services for Belgian Civil Aircraft, Dublin, 30 June 1954

16 of 1954   Exchange of Notes between Ireland and Germany (FDR) concerning Trade Agreement of 2 Dec. 1953, Bonn, 22 Oct. 1954

17 of 1954   Exchange of Notes between Ireland and Finland concerning Trade Agreement of 1 June 1951, Stockholm, 3 Nov. 1954

18 of 1954   Exchange of Notes between Ireland and France concerning Trade Agreement of 29 Apr. 1954, Paris, 24 Dec. 1954

19 of 1954   Revision of Art. 6 of the International Convention (signed at London, 5 Apr. 1946) for the Regulation of Meshes of Fishing Nets and the Size Limits of Fish, Copenhagen, 4–7 May 1954

20 of 1954   Protocol concerning Immunities of Bank of International Settlements, Brussels, 30 July 1936. Signed by Ireland on 19 Jan. 1954

1955

1 of 1955   Exchange of Notes between Ireland and Finland concerning Mutual Abolition of Visas, London, 1 Feb. 1955

2 of 1955   Agreement between Ireland and USA governing disposition of balance in Counterpart Special Account, Dublin, 17 June 1954. Ratification exchanged at Washington, 17 Feb. 1955

3 of 1955   Agreement between Ireland and USA (subsidiary to Agreement of 17 June 1954) respecting use of Counterpart on a Scheme for Pasteurisation of Separated Milk in Creameries, Dublin, 31 Mar. 1955

4 of 1955   Agreement between Ireland and USA (subsidiary to Agreement of 17 June 1954) respecting use of Counterpart on a Scheme for Eradication of Bovine Tuberculosis, Dublin, 31 Mar. 1955

5 of 1955   Agreement between Ireland and USA (subsidiary to Agreement of 17 June 1954) respecting use of Counterpart for defraying Delivery Costs of Ground Limestone, Dublin, 22 Mar. 1955

6 of 1955   Agreement between Ireland and Luxembourg concerning Aerial Transport between their territories, Brussels, 27 July 1954

7 of 1955   Agreement between Ireland and USA (subsidiary to Agreement of 17 June 1954) respecting use of Counterpart on a Scheme for the Provision of Additional Laboratories and Equipment for the Institute for Industrial Research and Standards, Dublin, 7 June 1955

8 of 1955   International Plant Protection Convention, Rome, 6 Dec. 1951. Irish Instrument of Ratification deposited on 31 Mar. 1955

9 of 1955   European Convention relating to Formalities required for Patent Applications, Paris, 11 Dec. 1953. Irish Instrument of Ratification deposited on 17 June 1954

10 of 1955   European Convention on the International Classification of Patents for Invention, Paris, 19 Dec. 1954. Irish Instrument of Ratification deposited on 11 Mar. 1955

11 of 1955   Agreement between Ireland and Belgium concerning Air Transport, Brussels, 10 Sept. 1955

12 of 1955   Agreement between Ireland and Norway for Avoidance of Double Taxation on Income Derived from the Business of Sea and Air Transport, Dublin, 18 Oct. 1954. Ratifications exchanged at Oslo, 31 May 1955

13 of 1955   Agreement between Ireland and Denmark for Avoidance of Double Taxation on Income Derived from the Business of Sea and Air Transport, Dublin, 18 Oct. 1954. Notes approving Agreement exchanged at Dublin, 29 June 1955

14 of 1955   Agreement on North Atlantic Ocean Stations, Paris, 25 Feb. 1954. Irish Instrument of Acceptance deposited 17 May 1955

15 of 1955   Exchange of Notes between Ireland and USA concerning participation of Ireland in US Investment Guarantee Programme, Dublin, 5 Oct. 1955

16 of 1955   Trade Agreement between Ireland and France, Paris, 7 June 1955

17 of 1955   Exchange of Notes between Ireland and Germany (FDR) concerning Trade Agreement of 2 Dec. 1953, Dublin, 31 Oct. 1955

18 of 1955   Agreement between Ireland and Canada for Avoidance of Double Taxation and the Prevention of Fiscal Evasion with respect to Taxes on Income, Ottawa, 28 Oct. 1954. Ratifications exchanged at Dublin, 20 Dec. 1955

19 of 1955   Agreement between Ireland and Canada for Avoidance of Double Taxation and Prevention of Fiscal Evasion with Respect to Duties on the Estates of Deceased Persons, Ottawa, 28 Oct. 1954. Ratifications exchanged at Dublin, 20 Dec. 1955

20 of 1955   Exchange of Notes between Ireland and Turkey concerning Mutual Abolition of Visas, The Hague, 16 Sept. 1955 and Dublin, 27 Sept. 1955

21 of 1955   Agreement between Ireland and Sweden for Avoidance of Double Taxation on Income Derived from Business of Sea and Air Transport, Dublin, 18 Oct. 1954. Ratifications exchanged at Dublin, 25 May 1955

22 of 1955   Statute of The Hague Conference on Private International Law drawn up at the Seventh Session of the Conference held at

The Hague, 9–31 Oct. 1951. Irish Instrument of Acceptance deposited on 26 Aug. 1955

23 of 1955 Exchange of Notes between Ireland and Portugal concerning Mutual Abolition of Visas, Lisbon, 29 July 1955

24 of 1955 European Cultural Convention, Paris, 19 Dec. 1954. Irish Instrument of Ratification deposited on 11 Mar. 1955

1956

1 of 1956 Agreement between Ireland and USA (subsidiary to Agreement of 17 June 1954) respecting use of Counterpart for Defraying the Costs of Programmes submitted by Muintir na Tire, Macra na Feirme and the Irish Countrywomen's Association, Dublin, 16 Jan. 1956

2 of 1956 Trade Agreement between Ireland and France (1956–7), Dublin, 7 May 1956

3 of 1956 Agreement on the Exchange of War Cripples between Member Countries of the Council of Europe with a view to Medical Treatment, Paris, 13 Dec. 1955

4 of 1956 Exchange of Notes between Ireland and Finland concerning Trade Agreement of 1 June 1951, Stockholm, 14 May 1956

5 of 1956 Exchange of Notes between Ireland and Greece concerning Mutual Abolition of Visas, London, 5 June 1956

6 of 1956 Exchange of Notes between Ireland and UK amending the Air Transport Agreement of 1946, Dublin, 31 Aug. 1956

7 of 1956 Exchange of Notes between Ireland and Germany (FDR) concerning Trade Agreement of 2 Dec. 1953, Bonn, 10 Nov. 1956

8 of 1956 Convention relating to the Status of Refugees, Geneva, 28 July 1951. Irish Instrument of Accession deposited on 29 Nov. 1956

1957

1 of 1957 Exchange of Notes between Ireland and USA concerning Agreement signed at Dublin on 16 Jan. 1956, concerning Counterpart for Defraying the Costs of Programmes submitted by Muintir na Tire, Macra na Feirme and the Irish Countrywomen's Association, Dublin, 18 Feb. and 13 Mar. 1957

2 of 1957 Renewal of the Trade Agreement between Ireland and French Monetary Area, Paris, 15 May 1957

3 of 1957 Agreement between Ireland and USA (subsidiary to Agreement of 17 June 1954) concerning Counterpart for the Establishment of a Technical Assistance Scheme, Dublin, 14 June 1957

4 of 1957 Exchange of Notes between Ireland and Finland concerning Trade Agreement of 1 June 1951, Stockholm, 6 Sept. 1957

5 of 1957   Air Transport Agreement between Ireland and Germany (FDR), Bonn, 12 June 1956. Ratifications exchanged at Dublin, 5 June 1957

6 of 1957   Articles of Agreement of International Monetary Fund formulated at Bretton Woods on 22 July 1944, Washington, 27 Dec. 1945. Irish Instrument of Acceptance deposited on 8 Aug. 1957

7 of 1957   Articles of Agreement of International Bank for Reconstruction and Development formulated at Bretton Woods on 22 July 1944, Washington, 27 Dec. 1945. Irish Instrument of Acceptance deposited on 8 Aug. 1957

8 of 1957   Exchange of Notes between Ireland and Portugal concerning Reciprocal Grant of Most Favoured Nation Treatment in matter of Shipping, Dublin, 11 Nov. 1957

9 of 1957   Agreement between Ireland and USA (subsidiary to Agreement of 17 June 1954) concerning Counterpart on a scheme for the Provision of a Scholarship Exchange Programme, Dublin, 16 Mar. 1957. Entry into force, 23 Dec. 1957

10 of 1957   Air Transport Agreement between Ireland and Australia concluded by Exchange of Notes, Dublin, 26 Nov. and 30 Dec. 1957

11 of 1957   International Air Services Transit Agreement, Chicago, 7 Dec. 1944. Irish notification of acceptance deposited 15 Nov. 1957

12 of 1957   European Convention on the Equivalence of Periods of University Study, Paris, 15 Dec. 1956. Irish Instrument of Ratification deposited on 18 Sept. 1957

13 of 1957   Exchange of Notes between Ireland and Canada concerning Air Transport Agreement of 8 Aug. 1947, Dublin, 23 Dec. 1957

14 of 1957   Exchange of Notes between Ireland and Belgium concerning Air Transport Agreement of 10 Sept. 1955, Dublin, 16 Dec. 1957

15 of 1957   Exchange of Notes between Ireland and Belgium extending Agreement of 30 June and 1 July 1952, concerning the Cattle Trade between the two territories, Dublin, 31 Dec. 1957

16 of 1957   Protocol on Arbitration Clauses, Geneva, 24 Sept. 1923. Entered into force for Ireland on 11 Apr. 1957. Convention on Execution of Foreign Arbitral Awards, Geneva, 26 Sept. 1927. Entered into force for Ireland on 10 Sept. 1957

1958

1 of 1958   Exchange of Notes relating to the Exchange of Stagiaires between Ireland and Sweden, Dublin, 5 Dec. 1957

2 of 1958   Exchange of Notes between Ireland and France concerning Air Transport Agreement of 16 May, 1946, Dublin, 21 Jan. 1958

3 of 1958   Published as No. 13 of 1958 and No. 14 of 1958

4 of 1958   Exchange of Notes between Ireland and USA relating to Air Transport Agreement of 3 Feb. 1945, Dublin, 4 Mar. 1958

5 of 1958   Exchange of Notes between Ireland and Germany (FDR) concerning Air Transport Agreement of 12 June 1956, Dublin, 24 Mar. 1958

6 of 1958   Protocol of renewal of the Franco-Irish Trade Agreement signed at Dublin on 7 May 1956, Paris, 13 May 1958

7 of 1958   Agreement between Ireland and USA (subsidiary to the Agreement of 17 June 1954) concerning Counterpart for the Establishment of an Agricultural Institute, Dublin, 16 Apr. 1958

8 of 1958   International Convention for Prevention of Pollution of the Sea by Oil, London, 12 May 1954

9 of 1958   Exchange of Notes between Ireland and Finland concerning Trade Agreement of 1 June 1951, Stockholm, 15 Apr. and 4 July 1958

10 of 1958   Convention on the Nationality of Married Women, New York, 20 Feb. 1957

11 of 1958   Exchange of Notes between Ireland and UK amending the Air Transport Agreement of 1946, Dublin, 30 June 1958

12 of 1958   Exchange of Notes between Ireland and Germany (FDR) concerning Trade Agreement of 2 Dec. 1953, Bonn, 29 May 1958

13 of 1958   International Convention for Protection of Industrial Property, London, 2 June 1934. Entry into force for Ireland 14 May 1958

14 of 1958   International Agreement regarding False Indications of Origin on Goods, London, 2 June 1934. Irish Accession took effect 14 May 1958

15 of 1958   International Sugar Agreement of 1953, amended by the Protocol opened for Signature at London on 1 Dec. 1956. Irish Instrument of Accession deposited on 13 Oct. 1958

16 of 1958   Exchange of Notes between Ireland and France concerning Air Transport Agreement of 16 May 1946, Dublin, 19 Aug. 1958

17 of 1958   Exchange of Notes between Ireland and Germany concerning Trade Agreement of 2 Dec. 1953, Bonn, 14 Nov. 1958

18 of 1958   Articles of Agreement of the International Finance Corporation and Explanatory Memorandum, Washington, 11 Apr. 1955. Irish Instrument of Acceptance deposited 11 Sept. 1958

19 of 1958   Agreement for Co-operation between Ireland and USA concerning Civil Uses of Atomic Energy, Washington, 16 Mar. 1956. Entry into force, 9 July 1958

20 of 1958   Exchange of Notes between Ireland and Belgium extending Agreement of 30 June and 1 July 1952 concerning Cattle Trade between the two territories, Dublin, 31 Dec. 1958

21 of 1958   Universal Copyright Convention, Geneva, 6 Sept. 1952. Irish Instrument of Ratification of the Convention and Protocols deposited on 20 Oct. 1958

22 of 1958   Convention on the Intergovernmental Maritime Consultative Organisation, Geneva, 6 Mar. 1948. Entry into force 17 Mar. 1958

1959

1 of 1959   Exchange of Notes between Ireland and UK modifying Air Transport Agreement of 1946, Dublin, 30 Jan. 1959

2 of 1959   European Agreement on the Exchange of Therapeutic Substances of Human Origin, Paris, 15 Dec. 1958

3 of 1959   Agreement between Ireland and UK concerning Certain Exemptions from Tax, 4 Apr. 1959

4 of 1959   International Convention revising Berne Convention for Protection of Literary and Artistic Works, signed on 9 Sept. 1886, completed at Paris, 4 May 1896, revised at Berlin, 13 Nov. 1908, completed at Berne, 20 Mar. 1914 and revised at Rome, 2 June 1928, Brussels 26 June, 1948. Irish Accession took effect on 5 July 1959

5 of 1959   International Convention to facilitate Importation of Commercial Samples and Advertising Material, Geneva, 7 Nov. 1952. Entered into force for Ireland on 23 May 1959

6 of 1959   Agreement between Ireland and the Netherlands concerning Exchange of Stagiaires between the two territories, Dublin, 28 May 1959

7 of 1959   Convention on Establishment of Security Control in the Field of Nuclear Energy (and Protocol on the Tribunal established by the Convention), Paris, 20 Dec. 1957. Entry into force, 22 July 1959

8 of 1959   Exchange of Notes between Ireland and Belgium extending Agreement of 30 June and 1 July 1952 concerning the Cattle Trade between the two territories, Dublin, 12 Sept. 1959

9 of 1959   Exchange of Notes between Ireland and Finland in connection with the Trade Agreement of 1 June 1951, Stockholm, 29 Apr. 1959

10 of 1959   Exchange of Notes between Ireland and Spain concerning Mutual Abolition of Visas Convention, Madrid, 16 and 17 Apr. 1959

11 of 1959   International Sanitary Convention for Prevention of Foot and Mouth Disease, Paris, 1 Dec. 1956. Irish Instrument of Ratification deposited on 12 June 1959

12 of 1959   Trade Agreement between Ireland and France, Paris, 10 Nov. 1959

13 of 1959   Exchange of Notes between Ireland and UK modifying Air Transport Agreement of 1946, Dublin, 15 Aug. 1959

1960

1 of 1960   Agreement on Social Security between Ireland and UK, London, 29 Mar. 1960. Entry into force, 2 May 1960

2 of 1960   Agreement concluded by Exchange of Notes between Ireland and USA concerning Acquisition of certain Nuclear Research and Training Equipment and Materials, Dublin, 24 Mar. 1960. Entry into force, 7 Apr. 1960

3 of 1960   Agreement on the Temporary Importation, Free of Duty, of Medical, Surgical and Laboratory Equipment for Use on Free Loan in Hospitals and other Medical Institutions for Purposes of Diagnosis or Treatment, Strasbourg, 28 Apr. 1960. Entry into force, 29 July 1960

4 of 1960   Trade Agreement between Ireland and UK, London, 13 Apr. 1960

5 of 1960   Exchange of Notes between Ireland and Finland concerning Trade Agreement of 1 June 1951, Stockholm, 3 June 1960

6 of 1960   Air Transport Agreement between Ireland and Portugal, Lisbon, 24 June 1960

7 of 1960   Exchange of Notes between Ireland and France concerning Trade Agreement of 10 Nov. 1959, Paris, 7 July 1960

8 of 1960   Exchange of Notes between Ireland and UK modifying Air Transport Agreement of 1946, Dublin, 21 July 1960

9 of 1960   Customs Convention regarding ECS Carnets for Commercial Samples, Brussels, 1 Mar. 1956. Irish Instrument of Ratification of the Convention deposited 28 April 1960

10 of 1960   Exchange of Notes between Ireland and Belgium extending Agreement of 30 June and 1 July 1952 concerning the Cattle Trade between the two territories, Dublin, 23 Sept. 1960

11 of 1960   Agreement between Ireland and Sweden for Avoidance of Double Taxation with Respect to Taxes on Income and Capital, Dublin, 6 Nov. 1959. Instruments of Ratification exchanged on 19 Nov. 1960

12 of 1960   Agreement between Ireland and UK concerning Certain Exemptions from Tax, 23 June 1960

13 of 1960   Agreement between Ireland and South Africa for Avoidance of Double Taxation on Income Derived from the Business of Sea and Air Transport, London, 1 May 1958. Entry into force, 26 Aug. 1960

14 of 1960   Agreement between Ireland and Switzerland concerning Taxation of Enterprises operating Ships or Aircraft, Dublin, 18 June 1958. Entered into force, 26 Aug. 1960

15 of 1960   Exchange of Notes between Ireland and Germany (FDR) concerning Trade Agreement of 2 Dec. 1953, Dublin, 2 Apr. 1960

16 of 1960   Articles of Agreement of International Development Association, Washington, 26 Jan. 1960

1961

1 of 1961   Exchange of Notes between Ireland and UK modifying the Air Transport Agreement of 1946, Dublin, 9 May 1961

2 of 1961   Exchange of Notes between Ireland and France concerning Trade Agreement of 10 Nov. 1959, Paris, 24 May 1961

3 of 1961   Amendment to Statute of Council of Europe, Strasbourg, 3 Nov. 1961

4 of 1961   Convention placing International Poplar Commission within the Framework of Food and Agriculture Organisation of United Nations, Rome, 19 Nov. 1959

5 of 1961   Exchange of Notes between Ireland and Germany (FDR) concerning Trade Agreement of 2 Dec. 1953, Bonn, 6 Apr. 1961

6 of 1961   Protocol amending Slavery Convention signed at Geneva on 25 Sept. 1926. Opened for Signature or Acceptance at New York, 7 Dec. 1953

7 of 1961   Supplementary Convention on Abolition of Slavery, Slave Trade and Institutions and Practices Similar to Slavery, Geneva, 7 Sept. 1956

8 of 1961   Protocol to amend the Convention for Suppression of Traffic in Women and Children concluded at Geneva on 30 Sept. 1921, and Convention for Suppression of Traffic in Women of Full Age concluded at Geneva on 11 Oct. 1933, New York, 12 Nov. 1947

9 of 1961   Protocol amending International Agreement for Suppression of the White Slave Traffic, signed at Paris on 18 May 1904, and International Convention for Suppression of the White Slave Traffic, signed at Paris on 4 May 1910, New York, 4 May 1949

10 of 1961   Amended Form of Annex to European Convention on the International Classification of Patents for Invention

11 of 1961   Exchange of Notes between Ireland and Finland concerning Trade Agreement of 1 June 1951, Stockholm, 9 Sept. 1961

12 of 1961   Convention on the Organisation for Economic Co-operation and Development, Paris, 14 Dec. 1960

1962

1 of 1962   Agreement between Ireland and Germany (FDR) concerning Stagiaires, Dublin, 11 May 1960

2 of 1962   European Agreement on Travel by Young Persons on Collective Passports between Member Countries of Council of Europe, Paris, 16 Dec. 1961

3 of 1962   European Agreement on Mutual Assistance in Matter of Special Medical Treatments and Climatic Facilities, Strasbourg, 14 May 1962

4 of 1962   General Index to the Treaty Series 1954–60 in continuation of Treaty Series No. 14 of 1954 and List of Treaties 1930–60

5 of 1962   Exchange of Notes between Ireland and Finland concerning Trade Agreement of 1 June 1951, Stockholm, 31 Mar. 1962

6 of 1962   Convention on the Taxation of Road Vehicles engaged in International Goods Transport, Geneva, 14 Dec. 1956

7 of 1962   Protocol relating to an amendment to the Convention on International Civil Aviation (Article 50 (a)), Montreal, 21 June 1961

8 of 1962   International Wheat Agreement, Washington, 19 Apr. – 15 May 1962

9 of 1962   Agricultural Trade Agreement between Ireland and USA, Washington, 3 May 1962

10 of 1962   Exchange of Notes between Ireland and France concerning Trade Agreement of 10 Nov. 1959, Paris, 10 May 1962

11 of 1962   International Convention for Unification of certain Rules of Law relating to Bills of Lading, Brussels, 25 Aug. 1924

12 of 1962   Convention on the Taxation of Road Vehicles engaged in International Passenger Transport, Geneva, 14 Dec. 1956

13 of 1962   Convention on the Taxation of Road Vehicles for Private Use in International Traffic, Geneva, 18 May 1956

14 of 1962   Convention on Road Traffic, Geneva, 19 Sept. 1949

1963

1 of 1963   Geneva Convention for the Amelioration of Condition of the Wounded and Sick in Armed Forces in the Field; Geneva Convention for the Amelioration of Condition of Wounded, Sick and Shipwrecked Members of Armed Forces at Sea; Geneva Convention Relative to the Treatment of Prisoners of War; Geneva Convention Relative to the Protection of Civilian Persons in Time of War, Geneva, 12 Aug. 1949

651

2 of 1963	Convention Relating to Status of Stateless Persons, New York, 28 Sept. 1954
3 of 1963	Amendment to Statute of Council of Europe, Strasbourg, 6 May 1963
4 of 1963	Protocol to Amend the Convention for Unification of Certain Rules relating to International Carriage by Air, signed at Warsaw on 12 Oct. 1929, The Hague, 28 Sept. 1955
5 of 1963	Treaty Banning Nuclear Weapon Tests in Atmosphere, Outer Space and Underwater, Moscow, 5 Aug. 1963
6 of 1963	Exchange of Notes between Ireland and France concerning Trade Agreement of 10 Nov. 1959, Paris, 10 Dec. 1963
7 of 1963	North-East Atlantic Fisheries Convention, London, 24 Jan. 1949

1964

1 of 1964	International Sugar Agreement of 1958, London, 1 Dec. 1958; Protocol for Prolongation of the International Sugar Agreement of 1958, London, 1 Aug. 1963
2 of 1964	Exchange of Notes between Ireland and USA concerning Trade in Beef and Veal between the two territories, Washington, 25 Feb. 1964
3 of 1964	Memorandum of Understanding on the Supply of Bacon to UK Market with Exchange of Notes between Ireland and UK, London, 11 Mar. 1964
4 of 1964	Amendment to Agreement for Co-operation between Ireland and USA concerning Civil Uses of Atomic Energy, Washington, 7 Aug. 1963
5 of 1964	Exchange of Notes between Ireland and UK modifying the Air Transport Agreement of 1946, Dublin, 19 Mar. 1964
6 of 1964	Exchange of Notes between Ireland and Germany (FDR) concerning Trade Agreement of 2 Dec. 1953, Dublin, 30 Apr. 1964
7 of 1964	European Agreement on Academic Recognition of University Qualifications, Strasbourg, 14 Dec. 1959
8 of 1964	Convention between Ireland and Germany (FDR) for avoidance of Double Taxation and the Prevention of Fiscal Evasion with respect to Taxes on Income and Capital and to the *Gewerbesteuer* (Trade Tax), Dublin, 17 Oct. 1962
9 of 1964	Exchange of Notes between Ireland and Germany (FDR) concerning German War Graves in Ireland, Dublin, 13 May 1964
10 of 1964	Agreement relating to Refugee Seamen, The Hague, 23 Nov. 1957
11 of 1964	Agreement between the United Nations Special Fund and Ireland concerning Assistance from the Special Fund, New York, 3 June 1964

12 of 1964   Exchange of Notes between Ireland and USA concerning Legal Liability in respect of Loss or Damage in Ireland arising from the Operation of *N.S. Savannah*, Dublin, 18 June 1964

13 of 1964   Exchange of Notes between Ireland and UK concerning changes which UK proposes to introduce in their Production and Trade Policies relating to Cereals, London, 30 June 1964

14 of 1964   Exchange of Notes between Ireland and France concerning Trade Agreement of 10 Nov. 1959, Dublin, 8 July 1964

15 of 1964   Exchange of Notes between Ireland and Finland concerning Trade Agreement of 1 June 1951, Helsinki, 14 July 1964

16 of 1964   Agreement dated 27 June 1963, between the Minister for Agriculture for Ireland and the Irish Sugar Company and the Minister for Agriculture, Fisheries and Food for the UK for the Purchase and Sale of Sugar and Revisional Agreement, dated 25 June 1964

17 of 1964   Agreement establishing Interim Arrangements for Global Commercial Communications Satellite System and Special Agreement, Washington, 20 Aug. 1964

18 of 1964   Exchange of Notes between Ireland and Vietnam (Republic of) in regard to Commercial Relations, London, 1 Dec. 1964

19 of 1964   Cultural Agreement between Ireland and Norway, Oslo, 2 Apr. 1964

1965

1 of 1965   Convention between Ireland and Denmark for Avoidance of Double Taxation and Prevention of Fiscal Evasion with respect to taxes on Income and Capital, Copenhagen, 4 Feb. 1964

2 of 1965   International Convention relating to Co-operation for Safety of Air Navigation ('Eurocontrol') with Annexes and Protocol of Signature, Brussels, 13 Dec. 1960

3 of 1965   European Social Charter, Turin, 18 Oct. 1961

4 of 1965   Exchange of Notes between Ireland and France concerning Trade Agreement of 10 Nov. 1959, Paris, 11 Feb. 1965

5 of 1965   Amendment to Statute of Council of Europe, Strasbourg, 24 May 1965

6 of 1965   European Agreement concerning Programme Exchanges by means of Television Films, Paris, 15 Dec. 1958

7 of 1965   Exchange of Notes between Ireland and UK modifying the Air Transport Agreement of 1946, Dublin, 22 June 1965

8 of 1965   Exchange of Notes between Ireland and Finland concerning Trade Agreement of 1 June 1951, Helsinki, 28 May 1965

9 of 1965	Agreement between Ireland and Finland on Recognition of Tonnage Certificates of Merchant Ships, Dublin, 15 Sept. 1965
10 of 1965	Free Trade Area Agreement and Related Agreements and Record of Understandings between Ireland and UK, London, 14 Dec. 1965
11 of 1965	Charter of the United Nations and Statute of the International Court of Justice, San Francisco, 26 June 1945
12 of 1965	Customs Convention on the ATA Carnet for the Temporary Admission of Goods, Brussels, 6 Dec. 1961
13 of 1965	Customs Convention on the Temporary Importation of Professional Equipment, Brussels, 8 June 1961
14 of 1965	Customs Convention concerning Facilities for the Importation of Goods for Display or Use at Exhibitions, Fairs, Meetings or similar events, Brussels, 8 June 1961
15 of 1965	Customs Convention on the Temporary Importation of Packings, Brussels, 6 Oct. 1960

1966

1 of 1966	Fisheries Convention Agreement as to Transitional Rights (Regarding Ireland). Agreement as to Transitional Rights (Regarding UK). Protocol of Provisional Application of the Fisheries Convention, London, 9 Mar. 1964
2 of 1966	Agreement on Social Security between Ireland and UK, Dublin, 28 Feb. 1966
3 of 1966	European Convention on Extradition, Paris, 13 Dec. 1957
4 of 1966	Convention supplementary to the Warsaw Convention for the Unification of Certain Rules relating to International Carriage by Air performed by a person other than the Contracting Carrier, Guadalajara, 18 Sept. 1961
5 of 1966	Exchange of Notes between Ireland and UK relating to Oceanic Area Control Centres at Shannon and Prestwick, Dublin, 28 Mar. 1966
6 of 1966	Exchange of Notes amending Annex C to Free Trade Area Agreement and Agreement on Trade in Cotton Textiles between Ireland and UK, London, 14 Dec. 1965 and Dublin, 6 June 1966
7 of 1966	Exchange of Notes between Ireland and Germany (FDR) concerning Air Transport Agreement of 12 June 1956, Dublin, 8 Feb. 1966
8 of 1966	Exchange of Notes between Ireland and UK modifying the Air Transport Agreement of 1946, Dublin, 30 June 1966
9 of 1966	Exchange of Notes between Ireland and UK amending the Agreement relating to trade in certain Agricultural and Fishery Products signed in London, 14 Dec. 1965, Dublin, 29 June 1966

10 of 1966   Exchange of Notes between Ireland and UK concerning Article XXII of Free Trade Area Agreement between the two Governments signed in London, 14 Dec. 1965, Dublin, 29 June 1966 and 14 July 1966

11 of 1966   Exchange of Notes between Ireland and Finland concerning Trade Agreement of 1 June 1951, Helsinki, 7 Dec. 1965

12 of 1966   Exchange of Notes between Ireland and Japan concerning Reciprocal Waiving of Passport Visas, Dublin, 1 Sept. 1966

13 of 1966   European Convention on Establishment, Paris, 13 Dec. 1955

14 of 1966   Protocol for the Extension of International Wheat Agreement, 1962, Washington, 22 Mar. 1965. Protocol for Further Extension of the International Wheat Agreement, 1962, Washington, 4 Apr. 1966

15 of 1966   Protocol for the Further Prolongation of International Sugar Agreement of 1958, London, 1 Nov. 1965

16 of 1966   Exchange of Notes between Ireland and Germany (FDR) concerning Trade Agreement of 2 Dec. 1953, Bonn, 1 Sept. 1966

17 of 1966   Exchange of Notes between Ireland and France concerning Trade Agreement of 10 Nov. 1959, Paris, 20 June 1966

18 of 1966   Agreement of Nice concerning International Classification of Goods and Services to which Trade Marks are applied, 15 June 1957

1967

1 of 1967   Convention on the Liability of Hotelkeepers concerning the Property of their Guests, Paris, 17 Dec. 1962

2 of 1967   Convention on the Privileges and Immunities of the United Nations, New York, 13 Feb. 1946

3 of 1967   Convention on the Privileges and Immunities of the Specialised Agencies of the United Nations, New York, 21 Nov. 1947

4 of 1967   Vienna Convention on Diplomatic Relations, Vienna, 18 Apr. 1961

5 of 1967   Vienna Convention on Consular Relations, Vienna, 4 Apr. 1963

6 of 1967   Final Act of the International Conference on Prevention of Pollution of the Sea by Oil and of the Conference of Contracting Governments to the Convention signed at London on 12 May 1954, London, 11 and 13 Apr. 1962

7 of 1967   Protocol for the Further Extension of International Wheat Agreement, 1962, Washington, 15 May 1967

8 of 1967   International Convention for the Protection of Industrial Property, Lisbon, 31 Oct. 1958

9 of 1967 International Agreement for Prevention of False or Misleading Indications of Origin on Goods, Lisbon, 31 Oct. 1958

10 of 1967 General Index to the Treaty Series 1961–5 in continuation of Treaty Series Nos 14 of 1954 and 4 of 1962 and List of Treaties 1961–5

11 of 1967 Protocol for the Further Prolongation of International Sugar Agreement of 1958, London, 14 Nov. 1966

12 of 1967 Exchange of Notes between Ireland and UK modifying the Air Transport Agreement of 1946, Dublin, 13 Apr. 1967 and 24 July 1967

13 of 1967 International Convention for Safety of Life at Sea, London, 17 June 1960

14 of 1967 Customs Convention on Containers and Protocol of Signature, Geneva, 18 May 1956

15 of 1967 Multilateral Agreement relating to Certificates of Airworthiness for Imported Aircraft, Paris, 22 Apr. 1960

16 of 1967 Customs Convention on the International Transport of Goods under Cover of TIR Carnets (TIR Convention) and Protocol of Signature, Geneva, 15 Jan. 1959

17 of 1967 Customs Convention on Temporary Importation of Commercial Road Vehicles and Protocol of Signature, Geneva, 18 May 1956

18 of 1967 Convention concerning Customs Facilities for Touring, New York, 4 June 1954

19 of 1967 Additional Protocol to the Convention concerning Customs Facilities for Touring, Relating to the Importation of Tourist Publicity Documents and Material, New York, 4 June 1954

20 of 1967 Customs Convention on the Temporary Importation of Private Road Vehicles, New York, 4 June 1954

21 of 1967 Agreement between the Member States of Council of Europe on the issue to Military and Civilian War-Disabled of International Book of Vouchers for Repair of Prosthetic and Orthopaedic Appliances, Paris, 17 Dec. 1962

22 of 1967 Convention on the Conflicts of Laws concerning Form of Testamentary Dispositions, The Hague, 5 Oct. 1961

23 of 1967 Agreement between Ireland and Canada for Avoidance of Double Taxation and Prevention of Fiscal Evasion concerning Taxes on Income, Ottawa, 23 Nov. 1966

24 of 1967 Cultural Agreement between Ireland and France, Paris, 4 Nov. 1967

25 of 1967 Exchange of Letters between Ireland and Canada concerning Trade Agreement of 20 Aug. 1932, Dublin, 21 Dec. 1967

26 of 1967 General Agreement on Privileges and Immunities of Council of Europe, Paris, 2 Sept. 1949. Protocol to General Agreement on Privileges and Immunities of the Council of Europe, Strasbourg, 6 Nov. 1952. Second Protocol to the General Agreement on Privileges and Immunities of Council of Europe, Paris, 15 Dec. 1956. Fourth Protocol to the General Agreement on Privileges and Immunities of Council of Europe, Paris, 16 Dec. 1961

27 of 1967 Protocol for the Accession of Ireland to General Agreement on Tariffs and Trade, Geneva, 30 June 1967

28 of 1967 Second Revisional Agreement between Minister for Agriculture and Fisheries of Ireland and Irish Sugar Company and Minister of Agriculture, Fisheries and Food for UK for Purchase and Sale of Sugar, 30 June 1967

29 of 1967 Exchange of Notes between Ireland and France concerning Trade Agreement of 10 Nov. 1959, Paris, 22 Dec. 1967

30 of 1967 Customs Convention concerning Welfare Material for Seafarers, Brussels, 1 Dec. 1964

1968

1 of 1968 Convention between Ireland and Austria for Avoidance of Double Taxation with respect to Taxes on Income, Vienna, 24 May 1966

2 of 1968 Convention between Ireland and Switzerland for Avoidance of Double Taxation with respect to Taxes on Income and Capital and Associated Exchange of Letters, Dublin, 8 Nov. 1966

3 of 1968 European Convention on the Adoption of Children, Strasbourg, 24 Apr. 1967

4 of 1968 Wheat Trade Convention, Washington, 29 Nov. 1967

5 of 1968 Agreement between Ireland and Finland for Avoidance of Double Taxation on Income derived from the Business of Sea and Air Transport, 1965, Dublin, 15 Sept. 1965

6 of 1968 Exchange of Notes between Ireland and UK amending Annex D of the Agreement between the two Governments establishing a Free Trade Area signed at London on 14 Dec. 1965, Dublin, 11 Mar. 1968

7 of 1968 Treaty on Principles governing the Activities of States in the Exploration and Use of Outer Space including the Moon and other Celestial Bodies, London, Moscow, Washington, 27 Jan. 1967

8 of 1968 Exchange of Notes between Ireland and USA establishing Agreement to permit Licensed Amateur Radio Operators of either Country to Operate Stations in the other Country, Dublin, 10 Oct. 1968

9 of 1968   Exchange of Notes between Ireland and Mexico concerning Reciprocal Waiving of Passport Visas, Washington, 19 June and 15 Aug. 1968

10 of 1968   Exchange of Notes between Ireland and UK regarding Guarantee by UK and Maintenance of the Minimum Sterling Proportion by Ireland, Dublin, 23 Sept. 1968

11 of 1968   Protocol No. 4 to the Convention for Protection of Human Rights and Fundamental Freedoms securing certain Rights and Freedoms other than those already included in Convention and in the First Protocol thereto. Strasbourg, 16 Sept. 1963

12 of 1968   Protocol relating to Status of Refugees, New York, 31 Jan. 1967

13 of 1968   Amendment of the Agreement for Co-operation between Ireland and USA concerning Civil Uses of Atomic Energy, Washington, 12 June 1968

14 of 1968   Amendment to Article 28 of the Convention on the Inter-Governmental Maritime Consultative Organisation, Geneva, 6 Mar. 1948, Paris, 28 Sept. 1965

15 of 1968   Exchange of Notes between Ireland and UK amending Annex C to Agreement Establishing a Free Trade Area, Dublin, 14 Dec. 1965, Dublin, 15 Oct. 1968

16 of 1968   Agreement on Rescue of Astronauts, Return of Astronauts and Return of Objects Launched into Outer Space, London, Moscow, Washington, 22 Apr. 1968

17 of 1968   Convention on the Political Rights of Women, New York, 31 Mar. 1953

18 of 1968   International Agreement on the Procedure for Establishment of Tariffs for Scheduled Air Services, Paris, 10 July 1967

19 of 1968   Revised Text of Annex XII to Convention on the Privileges and Immunities of the Specialised Agencies of United Nations, New York, 16 May 1968

20 of 1968   International Convention on Load Lines, 1966, London, 5 Apr. 1966

21 of 1968   Exchange of Notes between Ireland and Germany (FDR) concerning Trade Agreement of 2 Dec. 1953, Bonn, 23 and 30 Dec. 1968

1969

1 of 1969   European Agreement for the Prevention of Broadcasts Transmitted for Stations outside National Territories, Strasbourg, 22 Jan. 1965

2 of 1969   Memorandum of Understanding on the Supply of Bacon to UK Market with Exchange of Letters between Ireland and UK, London, 25 Feb. 1969

3 of 1969   Exchange of Letters between Ireland and UK amending Annex C to Agreement between the two Governments establishing a Free Trade Area, London, 14 Dec. 1965, Dublin, 17 June 1969

4 of 1969   International Sugar Agreement, 1968, New York, 3 to 24 Dec. 1968

5 of 1969   Amendment to the Articles of Agreement of International Monetary Fund, 31 May 1968

6 of 1969   Exchange of Letters between Ireland and France concerning Trade Agreement of 10 Nov. 1959, Paris, 2 July 1969

7 of 1969   European Agreement on the Abolition of Visas for Refugees, Strasbourg, 20 Apr. 1959

8 of 1969   Exchange of Notes between Ireland and Germany (FDR) concerning Trade Agreement of 2 Dec. 1953, Bonn, 16 Oct. 1969, 18 and 29 Dec. 1969

1970

1 of 1970   Trade Agreement between Ireland and Bulgaria, Dublin, 23 Apr. 1970

2 of 1970   Convention between Ireland and the Netherlands for Avoidance of Double Taxation and the Prevention of Fiscal Evasion with respect to Taxes on Income and Capital and associated Protocol, The Hague, 11 Feb. 1969

3 of 1970   Statute of the International Atomic Energy Agency, New York, 26 Oct. 1956

4 of 1970   Exchange of Letters between Ireland and France concerning Trade Agreement of 10 Nov. 1959, Paris, 18 Mar. 1970

5 of 1970   Agreement between Ireland and Belgium for Purpose of Avoiding Double Taxation of Income Derived from the Business of Sea and Air Transport, Brussels, 4 Dec. 1967

6 of 1970   Convention between Ireland and Finland for Avoidance of Double Taxation and Prevention of Fiscal Evasion with respect to Taxes on Income and Capital, Dublin, 21 Apr. 1969

7 of 1970   European Agreement on the Exchanges of Blood-Grouping Reagents, Strasbourg, 14 May 1962

8 of 1970   Treaty on the Non-Proliferation of Nuclear Weapons, London, Moscow and Washington, 1 July 1968

9 of 1970   Convention between Ireland and Norway for Avoidance of Double Taxation and Prevention of Fiscal Evasion with respect to Taxes on Income and Capital, Dublin, 21 Oct. 1969

10 of 1970   Exchange of Notes between Ireland and Germany (FDR) concerning Trade Agreement of 2 Dec. 1953, Bonn, 12 and 24 August, 1970

11 of 1970   Convention between Ireland and Cyprus for Avoidance of Double Taxation and Prevention of Fiscal Evasion with respect to Taxes on Income, London, 24 Sept. 1968

12 of 1970   Amendment to Statute of Council of Europe, Strasbourg, 14 Oct. 1970

1971

1 of 1971   Agreement between Ireland and Austria for the Abolition of Visa Requirements, Dublin, 10 Dec. 1970

2 of 1971   Convention between Ireland and France for Avoidance of Double Taxation and Prevention of Fiscal Evasion with respect to Taxes on Income, Paris, 21 Mar. 1968

3 of 1971   Amendment to Statute of Council of Europe, Strasbourg, 17 Feb. 1971

4 of 1971   Exchange of Letters between Ireland and France concerning Trade Agreement of 10 Nov. 1959, Paris, 15 Mar. 1971

5 of 1971   Convention on Facilitation of International Maritime Traffic, London, 9 Apr. 1965

6 of 1971   Exchange of Notes between Ireland and UK regarding guarantee by UK and Maintenance of the Minimum Sterling Proportion by Ireland, Dublin, 23 Sept. 1971

7 of 1971   Exchange of Notes between Ireland and UK modifying the Air Transport Agreement of 1946, Dublin, 23 Sept. 1971

8 of 1971   Multilateral Agreement relating to Collection of Route Charges, Brussels, 8 Sept. 1970. Bilateral Agreement relating to the Collection of Route Charges, Brussels, 8 Sept. 1970

9 of 1971   European Agreement relating to Persons participating in Proceedings of European Commission and Court of Human Rights, London, 6 May 1969

10 of 1971   Exchange of Notes between Ireland and Germany (FDR) concerning Trade Agreement of 2 Dec. 1953, Bonn, 3 and 7 May 1971

11 of 1971   Protocol No. 5 to Convention for Protection of Human Rights and Fundamental Freedoms, amending Arts 22 and 40 of Convention, Strasbourg, 20 Jan. 1966

12 of 1971   Wheat Trade Convention. Opened for signature on 29 Mar. 1971, Washington, 29 Mar. 1971

13 of 1971   Trade Agreement between Ireland and Romania, Dublin, 20 July 1971

14 of 1971   Protocol concerning Trade between Ireland and Bulgaria in 1972, Dublin, 19 Nov. 1971

1972

1 of 1972   European Code of Social Security, Strasbourg, 16 Apr. 1964

2 of 1972   European Agreement on the Instruction and Education of Nurses, Strasbourg, 25 Oct. 1967

3 of 1972   Agreement between Ireland and International Atomic Energy Agency for the Application of Safeguards in connection with the Treaty on Non-Proliferation of Nuclear Weapons, Vienna, 29 Feb. 1972

4 of 1972   Treaty on the Prohibition of Emplacement of Nuclear Weapons and other Weapons of Mass Destruction on Seabed and Ocean Floor and in Subsoil thereof, London, Moscow and Washington, 11 Feb. 1971

5 of 1972   Exchange of Letters between Ireland and UK concerning Trade in Cotton and other Textiles between Ireland and UK, Dublin, 31 Mar. 1972

6 of 1972   Trade Agreement between Ireland and Czechoslovakia, Dublin, 14 Dec. 1972

1973

1 of 1973   Protocol concerning Trade between Ireland and Bulgaria in 1973, Sofia, 14 Sept. 1972

2 of 1973   Exchange of Notes between Ireland and USA amending Air Transport Agreement of 3 Feb. 1945, Dublin, 11 June 1973

3 of 1973   Exchange of Notes between Ireland and USA with regard to Advance Booking Charter Flights, Washington, 28 and 29 June 1973

4 of 1973   Convention between Ireland and Zambia for Avoidance of Double Taxation and the Prevention of Fiscal Evasion with respect to Taxes on Income, London, 29 Mar. 1971

5 of 1973   Protocol relating to an Amendment to Convention on International Civil Aviation (Art. 56), Vienna, 7 July 1971

6 of 1973   Protocol to amend Agreement on North Atlantic Ocean Stations signed at Paris, 25 Feb. 1954, London, 13 May 1970

7 of 1973   Convention on Reduction of Cases of Multiple Nationality and Military Obligations in Cases of Multiple Nationality, Strasbourg, 6 May 1963

8 of 1973   Protocol to amend the Agreement on North Atlantic Ocean Stations signed at Paris on 25 Feb. 1954 as amended by Protocol signed at London on 13 May 1970, Montreal, 1 Dec. 1972

1974

1 of 1974   Trade Agreement between Ireland and USSR, Dublin, 28 Dec. 1973

2 of 1974   The Fourth International Tin Agreement, London 1 July 1970, 29 Jan. 1971 and 23 Sept. 1971

3 of 1974   Exchange of Notes between Ireland and Yugoslavia concerning Mutual Abolition of Visas, London, 10 Sept. 1974

4 of 1974   Convention between Ireland and Japan for Avoidance of Double Taxation and the Prevention of Fiscal Evasion with respect to Taxes on Income, Tokyo, 18 Jan. 1974

5 of 1974   Convention between Ireland and Belgium for Avoidance of Double Taxation and Prevention of Fiscal Evasion with respect to Taxes on Income, Brussels, 24 June 1970

1975

1 of 1975   Convention between Ireland and Italy for Avoidance of Double Taxation and Prevention of Fiscal Evasion with respect to Taxes on Income and Supplemental Protocol, Dublin, 11 June 1971

2 of 1975   Convention between Ireland and Pakistan for Avoidance of Double Taxation and Prevention of Fiscal Evasion with respect to Taxes on Income, Paris, 13 Apr. 1973

3 of 1975   Agreement between Ireland and UK providing for the Reciprocal Recognition and Enforcement of Maintenance Orders, London, 9 Dec. 1974

4 of 1975   Convention between Ireland and Luxembourg for Avoidance of Double Taxation and the Prevention of Fiscal Evasion with respect to Taxes on Income and on Capital, Luxembourg, 14 Jan. 1972

5 of 1975   General Index to the Treaty Series 1966–70 in continuation of Treaty Series No. 4 of 1962

6 of 1975   International Convention concerning Carriage of Goods by Rail (CIM) with Additional Protocol, Berne, 7 Feb. 1970

7 of 1975   International Convention concerning Carriage of Passengers and Luggage by Rail (CIV) with Additional Protocol, Berne, 7 Feb. 1970

8 of 1975   Protocol 2 drawn up by Diplomatic Conference convened with view to bringing into force International Conventions concerning the Carriage of Goods by Rail (CIM) and the Carriage of Passengers and Luggage by Rail (CIV) of 7 Feb. 1970 concerning the extension of period of validity of the Additional Convention to the CIV of 1961 relating to Liability of Railway for Death of and Personal Injury to Passengers, signed on 26 Feb. 1966, Berne, 9 Nov. 1973

9 of 1975   Protocol 3 drawn up by Diplomatic Conference convened with a view to bringing into force the International Conventions concerning the Carriage of Goods by Rail (CIM) and the

Carriage of Passengers and Luggage by Rail (CIV) of 7 Feb. 1970 concerning the Increase in Maximum Rates per kilometre of Contributions of Contracting States towards the Expenses of the Central Office, Berne, 9 Nov. 1973

10 of 1975   Additional Convention to International Convention concerning Carriage of Passengers and Luggage by Rail (CIV) of 25 Feb. 1961 relating to Liability of Railway for Death and Personal Injury to Passengers (with Protocol B), Berne, 26 Feb. 1966

11 of 1975   Protocol 1 drawn up by the Diplomatic Conference convened with a view to bringing into force International Conventions concerning the Carriage of Goods by Rail (CIM) and the Carriage of Passengers and Luggage by Rail (CIV) of 7 Feb. 1970, Berne, 9 Nov. 1973

12 of 1975   Agreement between Ireland and UK concerning Exemptions from Tax, London, 3 June 1975

13 of 1975   Convention establishing European Centre for Medium-Range Weather Forecasts, Brussels, 11 Oct. 1973

1976

1 of 1976   Exchange of Letters between Ireland and USA extending to 31 Mar. 1976 the Memorandum of Understanding between the Governments of 29 June 1976, concerning Advanced Booking Charter Flights, Dublin, 9 Jan. 1976

2 of 1976   Convention on Offences and Certain Other Acts Committed on Board Aircraft, Tokyo, 14 Sept. 1963

3 of 1976   Agreement between Ireland and France on International Carriage of Goods by Road, Dublin, 20 Jan. 1976

4 of 1976   Agreement on International Energy Programme, Paris, 18 Nov. 1974

5 of 1976   European Convention for Protection of Animals during International Transport, Paris, 13 Dec. 1968

6 of 1976   Convention for the Suppression of Unlawful Seizure of Aircraft, The Hague, 16 Dec. 1970

7 of 1976   Exchange of Notes between Ireland and USA concerning Air Passenger Charter Traffic, Dublin, 28 May 1976

1977

1 of 1977   Agreement between Ireland and European Space Agency, Paris, 29 Nov. 1976

2 of 1977   Agreement between Ireland and Germany (FDR) in respect of Regulations of Taxation of Road Vehicles in International Traffic, Dublin, 10 Dec. 1976

3 of 1977   Convention for the International Council for Exploration of Sea, Copenhagen, 12 Sept. 1964

4 of 1977   Protocol to Convention for International Council for Exploration of Sea, Copenhagen, 13 Aug. 1970

5 of 1977   Amendments to the International Convention on Load Lines, 1966. Adopted on 12 Oct. 1971

6 of 1977   Exchange of Notes between Ireland and USA terminating Agreement of 16 Apr. 1958 respecting Use of Counterpart for Establishment of an Agricultural Institute, Dublin, 5 Jan. 1975

7 of 1977   ACP–EEC Convention of Lomé and related Protocols, Declarations, Agreements and other Documents, Lomé, 28 Feb. 1975

8 of 1977   Internal Agreement on Measures and Procedures required for the Implementation of ACP–EEC Convention of Lomé Internal Agreement on the Financing and Administration of Community Aid, Brussels, 11 July 1975

9 of 1977   Agreement between Ireland and Belgium on International Carriage of Goods by Road, Brussels, 28 February 1977

10 of 1977   Agreement between Belgium, Denmark, Germany (FDR), Ireland, Italy, Luxembourg, the Netherlands, European Atomic Energy Community and International Atomic Energy Agency in Implementation of Article III(1) and (4) of Treaty on the Non-Proliferation of Nuclear Weapons, Brussels, 5 Apr. 1973

11 of 1977   Convention between Ireland and UK for Avoidance of Double Taxation and the Prevention of Fiscal Evasion, with respect to Taxes on Income and Capital Gains, Dublin, 2 June 1976

12 of 1977   Implementing Agreement for Programme of Research and Development on Application of Heat Pump Systems to Energy Conservation, Paris, 16 Mar. 1977

13 of 1977   Protocol between Ireland and UK amending Convention for Avoidance of Double Taxation and Prevention of Fiscal Evasion with respect to Taxes on Income and Capital Gains, Dublin, 28 Oct. 1976

14 of 1977   Agreement between Ireland and Belgium on Holding of Stocks of Crude Oil and/or Petroleum Products, Dublin, 28 Apr. 1977

15 of 1977   Exchange of Letters between Ireland and UK regarding Amendment of certain provisions relating to Rules of Origin contained in Anglo-Irish Free Trade Area Agreement, Dublin, 27 June 1977

16 of 1977   Agreement between Ireland and Germany (FDR) on International Carriage of Goods by Road, Dublin, 26 May 1977

17 of 1977   Agreement between Ireland and Poland on Development of Economic, Industrial, Scientific and Technological Co-operation, Poznan, 13 June 1977

18 of 1977   Convention on International Regulations for Preventing Collisions at Sea, London, 20 Oct. 1972

1978

1 of 1978   Convention on Prevention and Punishment of the Crime of Genocide, New York, 9 Dec. 1948

2 of 1978   General Index to the Treaty Series 1971–76 in continuation of Treaty Series 5 of 1975

3 of 1978   Agreement between Ireland and Poland concerning Civil Air Transport, Warsaw, 21 Apr. 1977

4 of 1978   Agreement between Ireland and UK for Avoidance of Double Taxation and Prevention of Fiscal Evasion with respect to Taxes on Estates of Deceased Persons and Inheritances and on Gifts, London, 7 Dec. 1977

1979

1 of 1979   Amendments (1974) to Intergovernmental Maritime Consultative Organisation (IMCO) Convention

2 of 1979   Memorandum of Understanding concerning Modification of the Air Services Agreement between Ireland and Italy of 1947, Rome, 17 Nov. 1978

1980

1 of 1980   Agreement between Ireland and USSR on Development of Economic, Industrial, Scientific and Technological Co-operation, Moscow, 16 Dec. 1976

2 of 1980   Agreement on Technical Co-operation between Ireland and Tanzania, Dar-es-Salaam, 3 Feb. 1980

3 of 1980   International Convention for Protection of Performers, Producers of Phonograms and Broadcasting Organisations, Rome, 26 Oct. 1961

4 of 1980   Agreement between Ireland and Spain for Avoidance of Double Taxation derived from Business of Sea or Air Transport Madrid, 25 Feb. 1975

5 of 1980   Agreement between Ireland and USSR relating to Transit Flights by Aeroflot between the USSR and Countries in the Western Hemisphere with Technical Landings at Shannon Airport, Dublin, 23 Jan. 1980

6 of 1980   Agreement between Ireland and UK on International Carriage of Goods by Road, Dublin, 9 Apr. 1980

1981

1 of 1981   Air Transport Agreement between Ireland and Malta, London, 21 Oct. 1980

2 of 1981   Agreement between Ireland and Denmark on the International Carriage of Goods by Road and Protocol drawn up under Article XV of Agreement, Dublin 26 Feb. 1981

3 of 1981   Convention setting up European University Institute, Florence, 19 Apr. 1972

4 of 1981   Agreement between Ireland and Italy on International Carriage of Goods by Road, Dublin, 22 Apr. 1981

5 of 1981   Convention on Reduction of Statelessness, New York, 30 Aug. 1961

6 of 1981   Convention on Recognition and Enforcement of Foreign Arbitral Awards, New York, 10 June 1958

1982

1 of 1982   Agreement on Technical Co-operation between Ireland and Zambia, Lusaka, 6 Jan. 1982

2 of 1982   Financial Protocol between Ireland and France, Dublin, 27 Apr. 1979

3 of 1982   Cultural Agreement between Ireland and Belgium, Dublin, 8 July 1980

4 of 1982   Agreement between Ireland and Greece on Cultural and Scientific Co-operation, Dublin, 17 July 1980

5 of 1982   Agreement between Ireland and Spain on Cultural Co-operation, Madrid, 27 May 1980

6 of 1982   Protocol between Ireland and Switzerland amending Convention signed at Dublin on 8 Nov. 1966 for Avoidance of Double Taxation with respect to Taxes on Income and Capital, Dublin, 24 Oct. 1980

7 of 1982   Agreement between Ireland and the Netherlands concerning Cultural Co-operation, The Hague, 21 July 1980

8 of 1982   Air Transport Agreement between Ireland and Turkey, Dublin, 24 Jan. 1980

9 of 1982   Agreement between Ireland and Finland on International Carriage of Goods by Road, Dublin, 19 May 1981

10 of 1982   Agreement between Ireland and Greece concerning International Carriage of Goods by Road, Athens, 15 July 1981

11 of 1982   Agreement between Ireland and Norway on International Carriage of Goods by Road, Dublin, 15 Sept. 1981

12 of 1982   Agreement between Ireland and Sweden on International Carriage of Goods by Road, Dublin, 19 May 1981

1983

1 of 1983   Agreement between Ireland and Australia for Avoidance of Double Taxation and Prevention of Fiscal Evasion with respect to Taxes on Income and Capital Gains, Canberra, 31 May 1983

2 of 1983   Agreement between Ireland and the Netherlands on the International Carriage of Goods by Road, Dublin, 30 May 1983

3 of 1983   Agreement between Minister for Transport of Ireland and Minister for Transport of Luxembourg on the International Carriage of Goods by Road, Luxembourg, 8 June 1983

4 of 1983   Agreement between Ireland and Germany (FDR) concerning Cultural Co-operation, Dublin, 10 Feb. 1983

1984

1 of 1984   Agreement between Ireland and UK on Reciprocal Holding of Stocks of Crude Oil and/or Petroleum Products, Dublin, 22 Oct. 1984

2 of 1984   Cultural Agreement between Ireland and Italy, Dublin, 9 Nov. 1984

1985

1 of 1985   Agreement on Technical Co-operation between Ireland and Tanzania, Dar-es-Salaam, 7 Mar. 1985

2 of 1985   Anglo-Irish Agreement 1985 between Ireland and UK, Hillsborough, 15 Nov. 1985

3 of 1985   Economic and Technical Co-operation Agreement between Ireland and Saudi Arabia, Dublin, 20 Oct. 1983

4 of 1985   Agreement between Ireland and Iraq on Economic, Scientific and Technological Co-operation, Baghdad, 7 Oct. 1981

5 of 1985   Agreement between Ireland and China on Cultural Co-operation, Dublin, 16 May 1985

1986

1 of 1986   Agreement between Ireland and China on Economic, Industrial, Scientific and Technological Co-operation, Dublin, 8 May 1986

2 of 1986   Agreement between Ireland and USA on Preinspection, Dublin, 25 June 1986

3 of 1986   The Wheat Trade Convention 1986, New York, 28 June 1986

4 of 1986   The Food Aid Convention 1986, New York, 28 June 1986

5 of 1986   Agreement Establishing an International Foot and Mouth Disease Vaccine Bank, London, 26 June 1985

6 of 1986   Agreement between Ireland and France on the Holding in French Territory of Reserve Stocks of Crude Oil and/or

Petroleum Products on behalf of Companies established in Ireland, Dublin, 10 Dec. 1985

7 of 1986   Convention concerning Medical Examination of Seafarers, Seattle, 29 June 1946

8 of 1986   Convention concerning Vocational Rehabilitation and Employment (Disabled Persons), Geneva, 20 June 1983

9 of 1986   Convention on the Elimination of All Forms of Discrimination against Women, New York, 18 Dec. 1979

10 of 1986   Agreement between Ireland and UK and USA concerning International Fund for Ireland, Washington, 26 Sept. 1986

11 of 1986   Chronological Index to the Treaty Series 1977–86 in continuation of Treaty Series No. 2 of 1978

1987

1 of 1987   Agreement between Ireland and UK concerning International Fund for Ireland, Dublin and London, 18 Sept. 1986

2 of 1987   European Convention for the Protection of Animals kept for Farming Purposes, Strasbourg, 10 Mar. 1976

3 of 1987   Treaty on Extradition between Ireland and USA, Washington, 13 July 1983

4 of 1987   Bilateral Agreement between Ireland and Nigeria on Rescheduling of Insured Trade Debts, Lagos, 11 Dec. 1987

5 of 1987   Air Transport Agreement between Ireland and USSR, Moscow, 29 Sept. 1987

6 of 1987   Exchange of Letters relating to Agreement of 1927 between Great Britain, the Irish Free State and Northern Ireland as to the Registration and Control of Dentists, Dublin, 13 Nov. 1987

7 of 1987   Convention on Long-Range Transboundary Air Pollution, Geneva, 13 Nov. 1979

1988

1 of 1988   Exchange of Letters on 26 May 1988 at London relating to the Agreement signed at London on 9 Dec. 1974 between Ireland and UK providing for Reciprocal Recognition and Enforcement of Maintenance Orders, London, 26 May 1988

2 of 1988   Memorandum of Understanding between Aeronautical Authorities of Ireland and UK, Dublin, 11 Mar. 1988

3 of 1988   Cultural Agreement between Ireland and Finland, Dublin, 3 Sept. 1985

4 of 1988   Additional Protocol to European Agreement on Exchanges of Blood-Grouping Reagents, Strasbourg, 29 Sept. 1982

5 of 1988   Convention between Ireland and New Zealand for Avoidance of Double Taxation and Prevention of Fiscal Evasion with respect to Taxes on Income and Capital Gains, Dublin, 19 Sept. 1986

6 of 1988   Convention between Ireland and Sweden for Avoidance of Double Taxation and Prevention of Fiscal Evasion with respect to Taxes on Income and Capital Gains, Stockholm, 8 Oct. 1986

7 of 1988   Additional Protocol to the Agreement on Temporary Importation Free of Duty Medical, Surgical and Laboratory Equipment for Use on Free Loan in Hospitals and other Medical Institutions for the Purpose of Diagnosis or Treatment, Strasbourg, 29 Sept. 1982

8 of 1988   Additional Protocol to European Agreement on the Exchange of Therapeutic Substances of Human Origin, Strasbourg, 29 Sept. 1982

9 of 1988   European Agreement on Transmission of Applications for Legal Aid, Strasbourg, 27 Jan. 1977

1989

1 of 1989   European Convention for Prevention of Torture and Inhuman or Degrading Treatment or Punishment, Strasbourg, 26 Nov. 1987

2 of 1989   Protocol between Ireland and Austria amending Convention for Avoidance of Double Taxation with respect to Taxes on Income, Dublin, 19 June 1987

3 of 1989   Agreement on Film and Video Relations between Ireland and Canada, Dublin, 4 Apr. 1989

4 of 1989   Agreement on International Carriage of Perishable Foodstuffs and on the Special Equipment to be used for such Carriage (ATP), Geneva, 1 Sept. 1970 (as amended to 6 July 1989)

5 of 1989   Agreement between Ireland and Austria on Social Security, Dublin, 30 Sept. 1988 (and Administrative Arrangement of 9 June 1989)

6 of 1989   European Convention on the Legal Status of Children born out of Wedlock, Strasbourg, 15 Oct. 1975

1990

1 of 1990   Agreement between Ireland and UK concerning Delimitation of Areas of Continental Shelf between the two Countries, Dublin, 7 Nov. 1988

2 of 1990   Protocol 8 to the Convention for Protection of Human Rights and Fundamental Freedoms, Vienna, 19 Mar. 1985

3 of 1990	European Convention on the Suppression of Terrorism, Strasbourg, 27 Jan. 1977
4 of 1990	Exchange of Notes between Ireland and USA relating to Air Transport Agreement of 3 Feb. 1945, Dublin, 29 Sept. 1989
5 of 1990	Agreement between Ireland and Yugoslavia on International Carriage of Goods by Road, Dublin, 8 June 1988
6 of 1990	Exchange of Notes between Ireland and UK amending and prolonging Agreement on International Carriage of Goods by Road, Dublin, 9 Apr. 1980. Exchange of Notes Amendment – 1985. Protocol done at London on 20 Feb. 1987
7 of 1990	Convention Establishing Multilateral Investment Guarantee Agency (MIGA), Seoul, 11 Oct. 1985
8 of 1990	Agreement between Ireland and UK concerning Veterinary Surgeons, London, 11 Apr. 1988
9 of 1990	International Covenant on Civil and Political Rights, New York, 16 Dec. 1966
10 of 1990	International Covenant on Economic, Social and Cultural Rights, New York, 16 Dec. 1966
11 of 1990	Optional Protocol to International Covenant of Civil and Political Rights, New York, 16 Dec. 1966

1991

1 of 1991	Convention for the Establishment of European Space Agency, Paris, 30 May 1975
2 of 1991	Memorandum of Understanding between Aeronautical Authorities of Ireland and UK, 5 May 1982
3 of 1991	Treaty on Extradition between Ireland and Australia, Dublin, 2 Sept. 1985
4 of 1991	European Convention on General Equivalence of Periods of University Study, Rome, 6 Nov. 1990
5 of 1991	Exchange of Notes between Ireland and USA amending Air Transport Agreement of 3 Feb. 1945
6 of 1991	Exchange of Notes between Ireland and UK relating to Oceanic Area Control Centres at Shannon and Prestwick, Dublin, 23 Apr. 1990
7 of 1991	Air Transport Agreement between Ireland and Greece, Dublin, 27 Mar. 1984
8 of 1991	Additional Protocol to European Convention for Protection of Animals during International Transport, Strasbourg, 10 May 1979
9 of 1991	Convention concerning International Carriage by Rail (COTIF), Berne, 9 May 1980

10 of 1991   Air Transport Agreement between Ireland and India, New Delhi, 20 Feb. 1991

11 of 1991   Exchange of Notes between Ireland and Hungary concerning Mutual Abolition of Visas, Dublin, 12 Apr. 1991

12 of 1991   Exchange of Notes between Ireland and Korea (South) in regard to Mutual Abolition of Visas, Dublin, 12 June 1989

13 of 1991   Agreement between Ireland and Austria on Air Transport, Vienna, 7 June 1991

14 of 1991   Exchange of Notes between Ireland and Czechoslovakia concerning Mutual Abolition of Visas, Prague, 12 Apr. 1991

15 of 1991   Agreement between Ireland and USSR on Cultural Co-operation, Moscow, 22 July 1991

16 of 1991   Cultural Agreement between Ireland and Portugal, Dublin, 11 Oct. 1990

17 of 1991   Protocol for Suppression of Unlawful Acts of Violence at Airports serving International Civil Aviation, Montreal, 24 Feb. 1988, supplementary to Convention for the Suppression of Unlawful Acts against Safety of Civil Aviation, Montreal, 23 Sept. 1971

1992

1 of 1992   Agreement on the Rules governing Carriage of Frozen and Deep-Frozen Foodstuffs by Equipment with Thin Side Walls to and from Italy, Paris, 24 June 1986

2 of 1992   Agreement for a Programme of Educational Exchange between Ireland and USA, Dublin, 27 Oct. 1988

3 of 1992   Convention for Prevention of Marine Pollution from Land-based Sources, Paris, 4 June 1974

4 of 1992   Protocol amending the Convention for Prevention of Marine Pollution from Land-based Sources, Paris, 26 Mar. 1986

5 of 1992   Double Taxation Agreement between Ireland and Korea (South), Dublin, 18 July 1990

6 of 1992   International Convention relating to Arrest of Seagoing Ships, Brussels 10 May 1952

7 of 1992   International Convention on Certain Rules concerning Civil Jurisdiction in Matters of Collision, Brussels, 10 May 1952

8 of 1992   European Convention for Protection of Animals for Slaughter, Strasbourg, 10 May 1979

9 of 1992   Agreement between Ireland and Spain on International Carriage of Goods by Road and Protocol, Dublin, 28 June 1992

10 of 1992   Vienna Convention for Protection of Ozone Layer, Vienna, 22 Mar. 1985

11 of 1992   Agreement between Ireland and Malaysia, Shannon, 17 Feb. 1992

12 of 1992   European Convention on Recognition and Enforcement of Decisions concerning Custody of Children and on Restoration of Custody of Children, Luxembourg, 20 May 1980

13 of 1992   Convention on Conservation of European Wildlife and Natural Habitats, Berne, 19 Sept. 1979

14 of 1992   Agreement on Social Security between Ireland and Canada, Ottawa, 29 Nov. 1990

1993

1 of 1993   Convention on Civil Aspects of International Child Abduction, The Hague, 25 Oct. 1980

2 of 1993   Protocol supplementary to Agreement between Ireland and UK concerning Delimitation of Areas of Continental Shelf between the Two Countries, signed at Dublin on 7 Nov. 1988. Protocol signed at Dublin on 8 Dec. 1992

3 of 1993   Agreement between Ireland and Australia on Social Security, Canberra, 8 Apr. 1991

4 of 1993   Protocol between Ireland and USA to Treaty of Friendship, Commerce and Navigation of 21 Jan. 1950. Protocol done at Washington on 24 June 1992

5 of 1993   Convention for Protection of Individuals with regard to Automatic Processing of Personal Data, Strasbourg, 28 Jan. 1981

6 of 1993   Protocol on Consultations between Ireland and USSR, Moscow, 22 July 1991

7 of 1993   Exchange of Notes between Ireland and UK concerning Reciprocal Recognition and Enforcement of Maintenance Orders, London, 6 July 1993

8 of 1993   Exchange of Notes between Ireland and Poland concerning Mutual Abolition of Visas, Dublin, 20 Nov. 1992

1994

1 of 1994   Agreement between Ireland and UK concerning Transmission of Natural Gas by Pipeline between Ireland and UK, Dublin, 30 April 1993

2 of 1994   International Convention on Maritime Search and Rescue, Hamburg, 27 Apr. 1979

3 of 1994   Convention on Rights of the Child, New York, 20 Nov. 1989

4 of 1994   Agreement between Ireland and USA on Social Security and Administrative Arrangement, Washington, 14 Apr. 1992

5 of 1994   Convention on Psychotropic Substances, Vienna, 21 Feb. 1971

6 of 1994   Convention between Ireland and Denmark for Avoidance of Double Taxation and Prevention of Fiscal Evasion with respect to Taxes on Income and Annexed Protocol, Dublin, 26 Mar. 1993

7 of 1994   Agreement between Ireland and Finland for Avoidance of Double Taxation and the Prevention of Fiscal Evasion with respect to Taxes and Capital Gains, Dublin, 27 Mar. 1992

8 of 1994   Agreement between Ireland and Cuba, and Annex, Havana, 8 June 1991

9 of 1994   Memorandum of Consultations, signed at Dublin on 23 Mar. 1994 and Exchange of Letters dated 23 and 24 Mar. 1994 extending Agreement between Ireland and USA on Preinspection of 25 June 1986

10 of 1994   Agreement between Ireland and Hungary, Budapest, 29 June 1992

11 of 1994   Agreement between Ireland and New Zealand on Social Security and Administrative Arrangement, Wellington, 20 May 1993

12 of 1994   Agreement between Ireland and Hungary on International Carriage of Passengers and Goods by Road, and accompanying Protocol, Budapest, 29 June 1992

13 of 1994   Agreement between the Romanian Committee for Adoptions and Minister for Health of Ireland on the Working Arrangements for Co-ordination of Intercountry Adoption, and Annex, Bucharest, 7 July 1954

14 of 1994   Framework Convention on Climate Change, and Annexes, New York, 9 May 1992

15 of 1994   Protocol amending 1986 Convention between Ireland and Sweden for Avoidance of Double Taxation and Prevention of Fiscal Evasion with respect to Taxes on Income and Capital Gains, Dublin, 1 July 1993

16 of 1994   Agreement on Economic, Industrial Scientific and Technical Co-operation between Ireland and Korea (South), Seoul, 10 Nov. 1994

17 of 1994   Convention on the Service Abroad of Judicial and Extrajudicial Documents in Civil and Commercial Matters, The Hague, 15 Nov. 1965

18 of 1994   Convention between Ireland and Portugal for Avoidance of Double Taxation and Prevention of Fiscal Evasion with respect to Taxes on Income and Protocol, Dublin, 1 June 1993

19 of 1994   Convention on the Control of Transboundary Movements of Hazardous Wastes and their Disposal, and Annexes, Basle, 22 Mar. 1989

20 of 1994   Understanding on Social Security between Ireland and Quebec, and Administrative Arrangement, Quebec, 6 Oct. 1993

21 of 1994 General Index to the Treaty Series 1977–94, in continuation of Treaty Series 2 of 1978

1995

1 of 1995 International Convention on Establishment of International Fund for Compensation for Oil Polluting Damage, Brussels, 18 Dec. 1971

2 of 1995 Protocol to International Convention on Establishment of International Fund for Compensation for Oil Pollution Damage, 1971, London, 19 Nov. 1976

3 of 1995 International Convention on Civil Liability for Oil Pollution Damage, 1969, London, 29 Nov. 1969

4 of 1995 Protocol to International Convention on Civil Liability for Oil Pollution Damage, 1969, London, 19 Nov. 1976

5 of 1995 International Convention Relating to Intervention on High Seas in cases of Oil Pollution Casualties and Annex, Brussels, 29 Nov. 1969

6 of 1995 Protocol concerning Intervention on High Seas in cases of Pollution by Substances other than Oil, with Annex, as amended, London, 2 Nov. 1973

7 of 1995 Agreement between Ireland and Georgia and Annex, Dublin, 2 Mar. 1995

8 of 1995 Agreement on Technical Co-operation between Ireland and Ethiopia, Dublin, 21 Feb. 1995

9 of 1995 Agreement on Technical Co-operation between Ireland and Uganda, Dublin, 7 Oct. 1994

10 of 1995 Agreement between Ireland and Russia, and Annex, and Memorandum of Understanding, Moscow, 31 Mar. 1993

1996

1 of 1996 Exchange of Notes relating to Abolition of Visas between Ireland and Israel, London, 8 Aug. 1985

2 of 1996 Convention between Ireland and Spain for Avoidance of Double Taxation and Prevention of Fiscal Evasion with respect to Taxes on Income and Capital Gains and Protocol, Madrid, 10 Feb. 1994

3 of 1996 Agreement between Ireland and Russia for Avoidance of Double Taxation with respect to Taxes on Income, Moscow, 29 Apr. 1994

4 of 1996 Agreement on the Future Direction of Co-operation in the area of Civil Aviation between the Minister for Transport, Energy and Communications of Ireland and the Minister for Transport of the Russian Federation, Dublin, 9 Dec. 1994

5 of 1996	Agreement between Ireland and Latvia on International Carriage of Passengers and Goods by Road, Vienna, 8 June 1995
6 of 1996	Agreement between Ireland and Poland for Avoidance of Double Taxation and the prevention of Fiscal Evasion with respect to Taxes on Income, and Protocol, Madrid, 13 Nov. 1995
7 of 1996	Convention between Ireland and Israel for Avoidance of Double Taxation and the prevention of Fiscal Evasion with respect to Taxes on Income, Dublin, 20 Nov. 1995
8 of 1996	Agreement between Ireland and Czech Republic on International Carriage of Goods by Road, Prague, 14 Nov. 1995
9 of 1996	Convention between Ireland and Czech Republic for Avoidance of Double Taxation and the prevention of Fiscal Evasion with respect to Taxes on Income and on Capital, Prague, 14 Nov. 1995
10 of 1996	Agreement between Ireland and Russia concerning International Road Transport, and Protocol on the Application of the Agreement, Dublin, 9 Dec. 1994
11 of 1996	Convention on the Service Abroad of Judicial and Extrajudicial Documents in Civil or Commercial Matters (concluded at The Hague, 15 Nov. 1965). A revised Notification in relation to Art. 3, a revised Objection in accordance with Art. 10 and a revised Declaration in accordance with Art. 15 of above Convention, deposited by Ireland pursuant to Art. 21 of the Convention with the Ministry of Foreign Affairs of the Netherlands
12 of 1996	Convention between Ireland and Hungary for Avoidance of Double Taxation and the Prevention of Fiscal Evasion with respect to Taxes on Income and Protocol, Dublin, 25 Apr. 1995

1997

1 of 1997	Convention on the Recovery Abroad of Maintenance
2 of 1997	Convention on Biological Diversity
3 of 1997	Convention on Nuclear Safety
4 of 1997	Convention against Illicit Traffic in Narcotic Drugs and Psychotropic Substances
5 of 1997	Exchange of Notes Constituting an Agreement between Ireland and USA concerning Employment of Dependants of Employees assigned to official duty in Territory of the Other Party
6 of 1997	European Convention on Mutual Assistance in Criminal Matters with Declarations and Reservations made by Ireland upon Ratification
7 of 1997	Additional Protocol to the European Convention on Mutual Assistance in Criminal Matters with Declaration made by Ireland upon Ratification

8 of 1997   Convention on Laundering, Search, Seizure and Confiscation of the Proceeds from Crime with Declaration and Reservations made by Ireland upon Ratification

9 of 1997   International Grains Agreement 1995, (A) Grains Trade Convention 1995 and (B) Food Aid Convention 1995

10 of 1997   Agreement between Ireland and Czech Republic for Promotion and Reciprocal Protection of Investments

11 of 1997   Agreement on Technical Co-operation between Ireland and Mozambique

12 of 1997   Convention Determining the State Responsible for Examining Applications for Asylum Lodged in One of the Member States of the European Communities

13 of 1997   United Nations Convention to Combat Desertification in those Countries Experiencing Serious Drought and/or Desertification, particularly in Africa

1998

1 of 1998   United Nations Convention on Law of Sea and Agreement concerning Implementation of Pt. XI of UN Convention on Law of the Sea of 10 Dec. 1982

2 of 1998   Protocol to 1979 Convention on Long-Range Transboundary Air Pollution on Long-term Financing of Co-operative Programme of Monitoring and Evaluation of Long-Range Transmission of Air Pollutants in Europe (EMEP)

3 of 1998   Protocol to the 1979 Convention on Long-Range Transboundary Air Pollution Concerning the Control of Emissions of Nitrogen Oxides or their Transboundary Fluxes

4 of 1998   European Convention on the Protection of Archaeological Heritage (Revised)

5 of 1998   Exchange of Notes constituting an Arrangement between Ireland and Canada for Employment of Dependants of Government Employees Assigned to Official Duties in Each Other's Country

6 of 1998   Co-operation Agreement signed on 19 Feb. 1998 between Minister of Health and Children of Ireland and Romanian Committee for Adoptions

1999

None printed

2000

1 of 2000   UN Convention on Prohibition of Development, Production, Stockpiling and Use of Chemical Weapons and on their

Destruction, done at Paris on 13 Jan. 1993. Entered into force 29 Apr. 1997

2 of 2000   Trademark Law Treaty, done at Geneva on 27 Oct. 1994. Entered into force 13 Oct. 1999

3 of 2000   Agreement between Ireland and USA concerning Mutual Assistance between their Customs Administrations, signed at Dublin, 16 Sept. 1996. Entered into force 21 May 1998

4 of 2000   Agreement between Ireland and USA for Promotion of Aviation Safety, done at Dublin on 5 Feb. 1997. Entered into force 5 Feb. 1997

5 of 2000   Agreement on Medical Treatment for Temporary Visitors between Ireland and Australia, done at Dublin on 12 Sept. 1997. Entered into force 25 May 1998

6 of 2000   Agreement between Ireland and Switzerland on Social Security, signed at Dublin on 11 Dec. 1997. Entered into force 1 July 1999

7 of 2000   Convention between Ireland and Mexico for Avoidance of Double Taxation and Prevention of Fiscal Evasion with respect to Taxes on Income and Capital Gains, signed at Dublin on 22 Oct. 1998. Entered into force 31 Dec. 1998

8 of 2000   Convention for Protection of Architectural Heritage of Europe, done at Grenada, 3 Oct. 1985. Entered into force 1 May 1997

9 of 2000   European Convention on Abolition of Legalisation of Documents executed by Diplomatic Agents or Consular Officers, signed at London on 7 June 1968. Entered into force 9 Mar. 1999

10 of 2000   Convention between Ireland and Slovak Republic for Avoidance of Double Taxation and Prevention of Fiscal Evasion with Respect to Taxes on Income and Capital Gains, signed at Dublin on 8 June 1999. Entered into force 30 Dec. 1999

11 of 2000   Budapest Treaty on International Recognition of Deposit of Micro-organisms for Purposes of Patent Procedure, done at Budapest on 28 Apr. 1977 and amended on 26 Sept. 1980. Entered into force 15 Dec. 1999

12 of 2000   Comprehensive Nuclear-Test-Ban Treaty adopted by General Assembly of UN on 10 Sept. 1996, opened for signature at New York on 24 Sept. 1996. Entered into force 15 July 1999

13 of 2000   Exchange of Letters between Ireland and NATO constituting an Agreement in relation to the Provision of a Contingent of the Permanent Defence Force for Service with UN Authorised International Security Presence in Kosovo (KFOR). Entered into force 27 Aug. 1999

14 of 2000   Exchange of Letters between Ireland and NATO constituting an Agreement in relation to Ireland's Financial Responsibilities

for Participation in the UN Authorised International Security Presence in Kosovo (KFOR). Entered into force 27 Aug. 1999

15 of 2000   Agreement between Ireland and UK establishing Independent International Commission on Decommissioning, done at Belfast on 26 Aug. 1997. Entered into force 24 Sept. 1997

16 of 2000   Convention between Ireland and USA for Avoidance of Double Taxation and Prevention of Fiscal Evasion with respect to Taxes on Income and Capital Gains and Protocol and Exchange of Letters constituting an Agreement of 28 July 1997 and Exchange of Letters of 24 Nov. 1997, signed at Dublin on 28 July 1997. Entered into force 17 Dec. 1997

17 of 2000   Protocol between Ireland and UK amending convention for Avoidance of Double Taxation and Prevention of Fiscal Evasion with respect to Taxes on Income and Capital Gains signed at Dublin on 2 June 1976, as amended by Protocols signed at Dublin on 28 Oct. 1976 and at London on 7 Nov. 1994, signed at London on 4 Nov. 1998. Entered into force 23 Dec. 1998

18 of 2000   Agreement between Ireland and UK (British–Irish Agreement), done at Belfast on 10 Apr. 1998. Entered into force 2 Dec. 1999

19 of 2000   Air Services Agreement between Ireland and New Zealand, signed at Dublin on 20 May 1999. Entered into force 9 Jan. 2000

20 of 2000   European Agreement relating to Persons Participating in Proceedings of European Court of Human Rights, done at Strasbourg on 5 Mar. 1996. Entered into force 1 July 1999

21 of 2000   Framework Convention for Protection of National Minorities, opened for signature at Strasbourg on 1 Feb. 1995. Entered into force 1 Sept. 1999

22 of 2000   Convention for Prohibition of Use of Stockpiling, Production and Transfer of Anti-Personnel Mines and their Destruction, concluded at Oslo on 18 Sept. 1997. Entered into force 1 Mar. 1999

23 of 2000   Exchange of Letters Constituting an Agreement between Ireland and the Netherlands on Privileges and Immunities Necessary for Proper Performance of Tasks of Liaison Officers at the European Police Office (EUROPOL). Entered into force 1 May 1999

24 of 2000   Convention signed at Washington on 24 Sept. 1999 amending Convention between Ireland and USA for Avoidance of Double Taxation and Prevention of Fiscal Evasion with respect of Taxes on Income and Capital Gains, signed at Dublin on 28 July 1997. Entered into force 13 July 2000

25 of 2000   Convention abolishing Requirements for Legalisation for Foreign Public Documents, done at The Hague on 5 Oct. 1961. Entered into force 9 Mar. 1999

26 of 2000   Agreement between Ireland and UK establishing a British–Irish Council, done at Dublin on 8 Mar. 1999. Entered into force 2 Dec. 1999

27 of 2000   Agreement between Ireland and UK establishing a British–Irish Intergovernmental Conference, done at Dublin on 8 Mar. 1999. Entered into force 2 Dec. 1999

28 of 2000   Agreement between Ireland and UK establishing Implementation Bodies, done at Dublin on 8 Mar. 1999. Entered into force 2 Dec. 1999

29 of 2000   Exchange of Letters Constituting a Supplementary Agreement concerning Interpretation of Certain Terms in Implementation Bodies Agreement. Entered into force 8 Mar. 1999

30 of 2000   Agreement between Ireland and UK establishing North–South Ministerial Council, done at Dublin on 8 Mar. 1999. Entered into force 2 Dec. 1999

31 of 2000   Agreement between Ireland and UK establishing Independent Commission for Location of Victims' Remains, signed at Dublin on 27 Apr. 1999. Entered into force 28 May 1999

32 of 2000   Exchange of Notes constituting an Agreement between Ireland and the Slovak Republic regarding the Agreement done at Prague on 12 Apr. 1991 between Ireland and the Czech and Slovak Republics concerning Mutual Abolition of Visas. Entered into force 14 Sept. 2000

Source: *Consolidated List of Government Publications: 1929–1931* (Dublin, The Stationery Office), External Relations, Section X. Department of Foreign Affairs.

BIOGRAPHIES

Abbreviations

CBS   Christian Brothers' School
CWC   Clongowes Wood College
IRA   Irish Republican Army
ITGWU Irish Transport and General Workers' Union
KC/QC King's Counsel/Queen's Counsel
NS   National School
QCB   Queen's College Belfast (to 1908)
QCC   Queen's College Cork (to 1908)
QCG   Queen's College Galway (to 1908)
QUB   Queen's University of Belfast (from 1908)
RBAI   Royal Belfast Academical Institution
RIA   Royal Irish Academy
TC   Trinity College
UCC   University College Cork (from 1908)
UCD   University College Dublin
UCG   University College Galway (from 1908)

Adams Gerry (1948–). Born in Belfast and educated at St Mary's CBS, he became a Republican activist, then president of Sinn Féin (1983–), MP for West Belfast (1983–92, 1997–), member of the Northern Ireland Assembly (1981) and member of the new Northern Ireland Assembly (1998–). Adams was a founder of the Provisional Republican movement in 1970 and interned in 1971. Between 1982 and 1983 he was responsible for dropping some traditional policies such as absentionism in Dáil Éireann (1986). In the late 1980s he began a series of talks with Social Democratic and Labour Party leader John Hume, culminating in 1993 in the Hume–Adams agreement, which played a key part in the adoption of the peace strategy by the Republican movement. He authored *Falls Memories* (1986).

Ahern Bertie (1951–). Born in Dublin and educated at St Aidan's CBS, Rathmines College of Commerce and UCD, he has been a TD (1977–), Minister for Labour (1987–91) and Minister of Finance (1991–4). He was Lord Mayor of Dublin (1986–7), leader of Fianna Fáil (1994–) and Taoiseach (1997–).

Aiken Frank T. (1898–1983). Born in Camlough, Co. Armagh, and educated at CBS, Newry, he joined the Irish Volunteers (1913) and the Gaelic League (1915). In 1917 he became a Sinn Féin organiser in South Armagh and was a commandant in the IRA during the Anglo-Irish War. He opposed the Treaty and was IRA Chief of Staff (1923). Elected a TD (1923–73) he did not take his seat until 1927. In 1926 Aiken became a member of Fianna Fáil. He served as Minister of Defence (1932–9), Minister of Lands and Fisheries (1936), Minister for the Co-ordination of Defensive Measures (1939–45), Minister of Finance (1945–8), Minister of External Affairs (1951–4; 1957–69), Minister of Agriculture (March–May 1957) and Tánaiste (1965–9) until his retirement to the back benches in 1969.

Aikenhead Mary (1787–1858). Born in Cork to parents of a mixed marriage, she became a Catholic in 1802. She established the Irish Sisters of Charity (1815) which was accorded papal recognition (1816) and served as its Superior-General for the remainder of her life. She also founded St Vincent's Hospital, Dublin.

Andrews John Miller (1871–1956). Born Comber, Co. Down, and educated at the RBAI, he was Unionist MP in the Northern Ireland parliament (1921–53), serving as Minister for Labour (1921–37) and Minister of Finance (1937–40), before succeeding Craigavon as Prime Minister (November 1940 – April 1943). Active in the Orange Order, Andrews was Grand Master of the All-Ireland Orange Institution (1948).

Armour Revd James Brown (1841–1928). Born at Lisboy, Ballymoney, Co. Antrim, and educated at Ballymoney Model School, RBAI, QCB and QCC, he was ordained as a Presbyterian minister (1869). Armour was a Liberal, supported tenant right, but became a Liberal Unionist (1886–92). On 15 March 1893 he announced his adhesion to home rule. Subsequently he supported a Catholic University and opposed the partition of Ireland.

Ball John Thomas (1815–98). Born Portmarnock, Co. Dublin, and educated at TC and the King's Inns, he was called to the bar (1840), becoming a QC (1854) and Bencher (1863–94). Ball was an MP (1868–75), Solicitor-General (1868), Attorney-General (1868, 1874–5), Lord Chancellor (1875–80), President of the Chancery Division of the High Court of Justice (1878–80) and Vice-Chancellor of the University of Dublin (1880–95).

Ball Sir Robert (1840–1913). Born in Dublin and educated at Tarvin Hall, Chester, and TC, he was a distinguished academic who held posts at TC and Cambridge. He was Royal Astronomer of Ireland (1847–92), President of the Royal Zoological Society of Ireland, and Fellow of the Royal Society (1873). Ball authored *The Story of the Heavens* (1886).

Barrie Hugh T. (1860–1922). An MP (1906–18, 1919–22), Barrie was Vice-President of the Department of Agricultural and Technical Instruction and High Sheriff of Londonderry (1918). He headed the Ulster delegation in the Irish Convention, 1917–18.

Barrington Sir Jonah (1760–1834) (knighted 1807). Born into a Protestant landowning family near Abbeyleix, Queen's Co. (Laois) and educated at TC, he was called to the bar (1788), an MP in the Irish parliament who opposed the Act of Union, and an Admiralty Court judge (1803–30) until removed from office for embezzlement. He authored the influential *The Rise and Fall of the Irish Nation* (1833), an account of the bribery employed by the government in order to secure passage of the Act of Union which was often cited by nationalist critics of the Union.

Barry Kevin (1902 – 1 November 1920, by hanging). Born in Dublin, he was a medical student at UCD who participated in a raid during the

Anglo-Irish War in which several people were killed. Because of his age, the execution occasioned widespread protests.

Barry General Tom (1897–1980). Born in Rosscarbery, Co. Cork, and educated at a local National School, he served in the British army during the First World War (1915–19). When he returned to Ireland (1919), Barry joined the IRA and commanded the West Cork Flying Columns. He opposed the Treaty. Barry was general superintendent with the Cork Harbour Commission (1927–65). In 1934 the de Valera government had him arrested; he broke with the IRA (1938) over the bombing campaign in Great Britain. He authored *Guerrilla Days in Ireland* (1949).

Barton Robert Childers (1861–1975). Born into an Irish Protestant family at Glendalough, Co. Wicklow, a cousin of Erskine Childers, and educated at Rugby and Oxford, he was an officer in the Irish Fusiliers (1914) and stationed in Dublin during the Easter Rising, after which he resigned his commission. Barton was elected as a Sinn Féin MP (1918) but sat instead in Dáil Éireann (1919–28; he did not take his seat after 1922), serving as Minister for Agriculture (April 1919 – August 1921). He was a member of the delegation which negotiated the Treaty, and though he signed it Barton subsequently supported the anti-Treaty forces during the Civil War. Later, he was chair of the Agricultural Credit Corporation (1934–54).

Béaslaí Piaras (1881–1965). Born in Liverpool and educated at a Jesuit college there, he was editor of the *Catholic Times* in England before migrating to Dublin (1904) where he joined the Gaelic League, and later the Irish Volunteers, and participated in the Easter Rising. He was founder and editor of the Gaelic League periodical, *An Fáinne* (1917–22), and elected a Sinn Féin MP (1918), but instead sat in the Dáil Éireann (1919–23). Béaslaí supported the Treaty but withdrew from politics (1923), thereafter concentrating on the revival of the Irish language. He authored *Michael Collins and the Making of the New Ireland* (1925).

Beckett Samuel Barclay (1906–89). Born in Foxrock, Co. Dublin, to a Protestant family and educated at Portora Royal School, Enniskillen and TC, he emigrated to France where he lived for all but brief periods thereafter. Following the fall of France (1940) he joined the French Resistance. Beckett became a leading force in the Theatre of the Absurd. He received the Nobel Prize for Literature in 1969. He authored many plays and novels, among which was *Waiting for Godot* (1952).

Behan Brendan (1923–64). Born in Dublin, he was educated by the Sisters of Charity, William St and North Brunswick St CBS. He joined the Irish Republican Army (1937) and after his arrest for possession of explosives (1939) he was detained in borstal until December 1941. Shortly after his return to Dublin (1942) he was imprisoned until 1946. His first book, *Borstal Boy* (1958), was followed by a string of successes in both Dublin and London.

Bennett Louie (1870–1956). Born in Temple Hill, Dublin, to a merchant family and educated at Alexandra College, in England and Bonn, she was general secretary of the Irish Women Workers' Union (1917–55). A co-founder of the Irish Women's Suffrage Federation (1911), she served as its first secretary and was the first woman president of the Irish Trade Union Congress (1932). Bennett was a member of the Commission on Vocational Organisation (1939–43) and stood unsuccessfully as a Labour Party candidate for Dáil Éireann (1944).

Beresford Lord John George de la Poer (1773–1862). Born in Waterford, younger son of the Marquess of Waterford, and educated at Eton and Oxford, he was Church of Ireland Bishop of Cork and Ross (1805–7), Raphoe (1807–19) and Clogher (1819–20), Archbishop of Dublin (1920–2) and Armagh and Primate of All Ireland (1822–62). In addition, he was Vice-Chancellor of the University of Dublin (1829) and Chancellor (1851). Beresford made major financial contributions to Trinity College and also paid for the restoration of Armagh cathedral.

Bergin Osborn Joseph (1872–1950). Born in Cork and educated at Cork Grammar School, QCC and Freiburg, Germany, where he took a PhD (1906), before taking up a post as lecturer at QCC (1897–1909). He was Professor of Old Irish at UCD (1909–40) and then the first director of the School of Celtic Studies in the Dublin Institute for Advance Studies (1940), though he resigned within a year. He authored *Stories from Keating* (1909).

Bernard John Henry (1860–1927). Born in India and educated at TC, he was ordained in the Church of Ireland (1886). He was Dean of St Patrick's Cathedral (1902), Bishop of Ossory, Ferns and Leighlin (1911–15) and Archbishop of Dublin (1915–19). Bernard was president of the RIA (1916–21), a key figure in the Irish Convention (1917–18) and Provost of TC (1919–23). A noted scholar, he edited *The Works of Bishop Butler* (2 vols, 1900).

Biggar Joseph Gillis (1828–1890). Born in Belfast and educated at the Belfast Academy, he entered the family provision business, becoming its chairman (1861–80). He was active in the Belfast Corporation (1868), serving as chairman of the Belfast Water Commission (1869–72). Biggar was a prominent Ulster Presbyterian home ruler who converted to Catholicism (1877). He took a major part in the National Conference in November 1873 and was an MP (1874–90). Biggar enlisted in the IRB (1875) and was a member of the Supreme Council (1874–7) until expelled from the organisation for refusing to give up his parliamentary seat. He was also a key participant in the obstruction struggles of the 1870s and a prominent figure in the Irish Party during the 1880s.

Blackburne Francis (1782–1867). Born at Footstown, Co. Meath, and educated at TC, he was called to the bar (1803), serving successively as Attorney-General (1831–5, 1842), Master of the Rolls (1842–6), Chief Justice of the Queen's Bench (1846–56), Lord Chancellor (1852, 1866–7) and Lord Justice of Appeal (1856–66). He presided over the trials of William Smith O'Brien and Thomas Francis Meagher (1848).

Blake Edward (1833–1912). Born into an Irish Protestant immigrant family at St Adelaide, Upper Canada (Ontario) and educated at Upper Canada College and the University of Toronto, he was called to the bar (1856), becoming Prime Minister of Ontario (1971–2), Minister for Justice (1975–7) in the Federal Parliament and leader of the Liberal Party (1880–8). Blake was induced to become an anti-Parnellite MP (1892–1907) and acted as an intimate political adviser to John Dillon.

Blythe Ernest (Earnán de Blaghd) (1889–1975). Born into a Protestant family in Magheagall near Lisburn, Co. Antrim, and educated at a local National School, he was active in the Gaelic League and the IRB (1909), subsequently joining the Irish Volunteers. He was elected to the Sinn Féin executive (25 October 1917) and returned as MP (1918) but instead he sat in Dáil Éireann (1919–33), where he was Minister for Trade and Commerce (April 1919 – September 1922). Blythe accepted the Treaty and was Minister for Local Government (1922–3), Minister for Local Government and Public Health (1922–3), Minister for Posts and Telegraphs (1927–32), Minister for Finance (1923–32), Vice-President of the Executive Council (1927–32) and Senator (1933–6). He was managing director of the Abbey Theatre (1941–67). He authored *Trasna Na Bóinne* (1957).

Boland Gerald (1883–1973). Born in Manchester but reared in Dublin and educated at O'Brien Institute, Fairview, he participated in the Easter Rising and played a prominent part in establishing Fianna Fáil (1926). He was a TD (1923–61; took seat 1927), serving as Minister for Posts and Telegraph (1933–6), Minister for Lands (1936–9), Minister for Justice (1939–48, 1951–4) and Senator (1961–9) but resigning from the party (1970) when his son Kevin left it as a consequence of the arms scandal.

Boland Harry (1887–1922). Born in Dublin and educated at Synge Street CBS and de la Salle College, Castletown, Queen's Co. (Laois), he joined the IRB (1904), the GAA and later the Irish Volunteers. Boland participated in the Easter Rising and was returned as a Sinn Féin MP (1918), instead sitting in Dáil Éireann (1919–22). He opposed the Treaty and was killed by the Free State forces (1922).

Boland Kevin (1917–2001). Born in Dublin, son of Gerald, and educated at St Joseph's CBS, Fairview, he was a Fianna Fáil TD (1957–70) and Minister for Defence (1957–61), Minister for Social Welfare (1961–5) and Minister for Local Government (1966–70). He resigned from the government and Dáil (1970) over the handling of the arms affair. Boland formed Aontacht Éireann (1971) and resigned its leadership in 1976.

Boycott Captain Hugh Cunningham (1832–97). Born in Norfolk and educated at Blackheath and Woolwich, Boycott, a former officer and agent for Lord Erne's estates in Co. Mayo (1873–86), achieved notoriety when he came into conflict with the Land League (1880) and was ostracised, or what subsequently became known as boycotted. He left Ireland in May 1886.

Breen   Dan (1894–1969). Born near Solohedbeg, Co. Tipperary, he joined the IRB and Irish Volunteers (1914). He was part of the gang that killed two policemen in Tipperary (21 January 1919), marking the first engagement since the Easter Rising of 1916 and known for his daring exploits during the Anglo-Irish War. Breen rejected the Treaty and fought for the republican side in the Civil War. He was elected a TD (1923–7, 1932–65). In April 1927 he became the first republican to take the Oath of Allegiance and served as a Fianna Fáil TD, but lost his seat later in the year. Breen authored *My Fight for Irish Freedom* (1924).

Brodrick   William St John (9th Viscount and 1st Earl of Midleton; succeeded 1907, created Viscount 1920) (1856–1942). Born in London and educated at Eton and Oxford where he was president of the Union (1878), Brodrick sat as a Conservative MP for English constituencies (1880–1906). He held office (1886–92, 1895–1900), becoming Secretary of State for War (1900–3) and Secretary of State for India (1903–5). As chairman of the Irish Unionist Alliance, Midleton was a key spokesman for southern Unionism after 1914, sitting in the Irish Convention in 1917–18. He authored *Records and Recollections 1856–1939* (1939).

Brookeborough   Viscount (created 1952) (Basil Brooke) (1888–1973). Born in Colebrook, Co. Fermanagh, and educated at Winchester College and Sandhurst, he served on the Western Front during the First World War. He was a member of the Northern Ireland Senate (1921–2) and was then returned as a Ulster Unionist MP (1929–68). After serving as Minister of Agriculture (1933–41) and Minister for Commerce and Production (1941–3), he succeeded John Miller Andrews as leader of the Unionist Party and Prime Minister of Northern Ireland (1943–63). He declined to have any contact with Catholics during his term as Prime Minister.

Browne   Dr Noël (1915–1997). Born in Waterford and educated by the Marist Brothers, Athlone, Ballinrobe CBS, a Jesuit school in England, Beaumont, and TC where he qualified in medicine, Browne was elected a Clann na Poblachta TD (1948–51), Independent (1951–4, 1957–8), National Progressive Democrat (1958–63) (a party he founded in 1963), Labour (1963–5, 1969–73), and Senator (1973–7). He was Minister for Health (1948–51). His greatest success was the eradication of tuberculosis and the setting up of a national system of blood transfusion. However, he is best remembered for his part in the Mother-and-Child controversy (1951). Browne resigned from the government and campaigned on health issues and against clerical power for the rest of his political career. His autobiography is *Against the Tide* (1986).

Brugha   Cathal (Charles William St John Burgess) (1874 – 7 July 1922, killed by Free State soldiers). Born in Dublin and educated at Belvedere

College, he joined the Gaelic League (1899), the GAA and the Irish Volunteers (1913). Injured in the Easter Rising, he was IRA Chief of Staff (1917–19). He was elected MP (1918) but sat in Dáil Éireann (1919–22), serving as President of the Assembly (1919) and Minister for National Defence (1919–21). An opponent of the Treaty, he fought on the republican side in the Civil War and was killed in Dublin.

Bruton John (1947–). Born in Dublin, he was educated at CWC, UCD and King's Inns. He was called to the bar (1972) and became a TD (1969–), serving as Minister for Industry and Commerce (1975–7), Minister for Finance (1981–2, 1986–7), Minister for Industry and Energy (1982–3), Minister for Industry, Trade, Commerce and Tourism (1983–6) and Minister of Finance (1986–7). Bruton became deputy leader of Fine Gael (1987), leader (1990–2001), and Taoiseach (1994–7).

Bryce James (Viscount Bryce, created 1913) (1841–1922). Born in Belfast and educated at Belfast Academy, the University of Glasgow, Oxford, Heidelberg and Lincoln's Inn, he was called to the bar (1867) and served as Regius Professor of Civil Law at Oxford (1870–93). Bryce was an English MP (1880–1907) until becoming ambassador to the United States (1907–13). An Ulster Presbyterian by background but a leading Liberal home ruler, Bryce served as Chief Secretary (December 1905 – February 1907). He authored *Modern Democracies* (1921).

Burke Thomas Henry (1829 – 6 May 1882 assassinated). Born in Knocknagur, Co. Galway, he became a clerk in the Irish Administration (1847), rising to Under-Secretary (1869–82). He and Lord Frederick Cavendish, the new Chief Secretary, were murdered in Phoenix Park by the Irish National Invincibles.

Bushe Charles Kendal (1767–1843). Born near Kilmurry, Co. Kilkenny, to a Church of Ireland cleric and educated at private schools and TC, he was called to the bar (1790). He was an MP in the Irish parliament and opposed the Union. Bushe was Solicitor-General (1805–22) and Lord Chief Justice (1822–41).

Butler Mary Lambert (Máire de Buitléir) (*c.* 1872–1920). Born in County Clare, a cousin of Sir Edward Carson, she was an active member of the Gaelic League. She authored a number of works including *The Ring of Day* (1903).

Butt Isaac (1813–79). Born at Glenfin, Co. Donegal, son of a Church of Ireland cleric and educated at Middleton College, Cork, Royal School, Raphoe, and TC, he was a founder (1833) and editor of the *Dublin University Magazine* (1834–8) and Watley Professor of Political Economy at TC (1836–41). Butt was called to the bar (1838). He was first returned as an MP for an English constituency (1852); he then sat for Youghal (1852–65) and Limerick City (1871–9) and was chairman of the Home Rule Party (1874–9). He was counsel for several Young Ireland prisoners in the late 1840s and defended a number of Fenians in the 1860s. He also served as the head of the Amnesty Association (1869) and Tenant League.

Byrne Alfred (Alfie) (1882–1956). Born in Dublin and educated there, he was MP (1914–18), TD (1923–8, 1931–56), a Senator (1928–31) and Lord Mayor of Dublin (1930–9, 1954–5).

Callan Nicholas Joseph (1799–1864). Born in Darver, Dromiskin, Co. Louth, and educated at the Dundalk Academy, Navan seminary and Maynooth, he was ordained (1823) and awarded a DD, Sapienza University, Rome (1826). He returned to Maynooth (1826). Callan was a pioneer in electrical science; among his inventions was the induction coil.

Campbell James Henry Mussen (1st Baron Glenavy; knighted 1917, created Baron 1921) (1851–1931). Born in Tenenure, Co. Dublin, and educated at Kingstown School and TC, he was called to the bar (1878) and was a QC (1890) and Unionist MP (1898–1900, 1903–16). Campbell served as Solicitor-General (1901–5), Attorney-General (1905, 1916), Lord Chief Justice (1916–18), Lord Chancellor (1918–21), Vice-Chancellor of TC (1919–31) and first chairman of the Free State Senate (1922–8).

Campbell Joseph (Seosamh MacCathmaoil) (1879–1944). Born and educated in Belfast, he was a poet associated with the Ulster Literary Theatre. He became secretary to the Irish Literary Society (1906), settling in Wicklow (1912). He took the anti-Treaty side in the Civil War and was interned for 18 months. He moved to New York where he founded the School of Irish Studies (1925), lecturing at Fordham University before returning to Wicklow. He collaborated with Herbert Hughes in setting words to folk melodies in *Songs of Uladh* (1904). Among his writings are *The Mountainy Singer* (1909) and *Earth of Culalann* (1917).

Carleton William (1794–1869). Born at Prillisk near Clogher, Co. Tyrone, to a Catholic tenant farmer, he was educated in a hedge school. He became a Protestant on his marriage and taught at the Erasmus schools in Dublin and Mullingar. He was awarded a civil list pension (1848) in recognition of his voluminous contributions to literature which included *Stories of the Irish Peasantry* (5 vols, 1830–3).

Carson Sir Edward (knighted 1900; Lord Carson of Duncairn, created 1921) (1854–1935). Born in Dublin and educated at Portarlington and he was called to the Irish bar (1877) and the English bar (1893), serving as Irish Solicitor-General (1892) and English Solicitor-General (1900–5). He was MP (1892–1921) and Ulster Unionist leader (1910–20). He made his name as a crown prosecutor in Ireland in the 1880s and gained a major reputation following his successful prosecution of Oscar Wilde (1895). During the unionist struggle against the third Home Rule bill, he argued for constitutional and extra-constitutional opposition to the bill. He was a minister during the First World War, briefly as Attorney-General (April–October 1915), then as First Lord of the Admiralty (January–July 1917) and a member of the war cabinet (July 1917 – January 1918) becoming a Lord of Appeal in Ordinary (1921).

Casement   Sir Roger David (knighted, 1911, annulled 30 June 1916) (1864 – 3 August 1916 by hanging at Pentonville Prison, London). Born into a Protestant family in Sandycove, Co. Dublin, but reared in Co. Antrim and educated at Ballymena Academy, he went to Africa, entering the Colonial Service (1892) where he earned a reputation for humanitarian work. His report (1904) on the treatment of natives in the Belgian Congo won him international acclaim. A similar report on the exploitation of natives in Peru (1912) confirmed his reputation. He joined the Gaelic League early in his career and, after retirement from government service (1912), the National Volunteers (1913). Having made his way to Berlin (November 1914), Casement recruited Irish prisoners of war to serve under the German flag. He was captured in Kerry where he was attempting to land with a shipment of German arms intended for use in the Easter Rising and he was subsequently tried and executed for high treason. In order to thwart the voluminous requests for clemency, the British government circulated to influential people extracts of Casement's diaries ('Black Diaries') that revealed homosexual proclivities. His remains were reinterred in Glasnevin cemetery following a state funeral (1 March 1965).

Castlereagh   Viscount and 2nd Marquess of Londonderry (Robert Stewart) (1769–12 August 1822, suicide). Born into a Protestant landed family in Co. Down, he was educated at the Royal School Armagh and Cambridge. Returned as an MP to the Irish parliament in 1790, he was Chief Secretary (1798–1801) and played a key role in the passage of the Act of Union (1800). Castlereagh was returned as an MP for Ireland (1801–5, 1812–21), becoming President of the Board of Control (1802) and translated to the War Department (1804–6). He returned to the War Department (1807–9) and became Secretary for Foreign Affairs (1812–14). As Minister Plenipotentiary (1814–15), Castlereagh played a key part in the negotiations at the Congress of Vienna. Succeeding as the 2nd Marquess of Londonderry in 1821, he committed suicide the following year.

Chichester-Clark   Major James Dawson (Lord Moyola, created 1971) (1923– 2002). Born at Castledawson, Co. Londonderry, and educated at Eton, he was commissioned in the Irish Guards. After retirement from the army (1960) he was elected to succeed his grandmother, Dame Debra Parker, as Unionist MP to the Northern Ireland parliament (1960–71), becoming his party's chief whip (1963), Leader of the House (1966–7) and Minister for Agriculture (1967–9), until his resignation over the pace of implementation of Captain Terence O'Neill's policies. In August 1969 he assumed the leadership of the Unionist Party and became Prime Minister of Northern Ireland until resigning (20 March 1970).

Childers   (Robert) Erskine (1870 – 24 November 1922, by firing squad). Born in England into a partly southern Irish Protestant family but reared at Glendalough, Co. Wicklow, and educated at Haileybury and Cambridge, he was a Clerk of the House of Commons (1895–1910) and served in the Boer

War (1899) where he was wounded. He became converted to home rule (1908) and his yacht was used for the Howth gun-running (1914). Childers was commissioned in the Royal Navy (1914) and was accorded the Distinguished Service Cross. After being demobbed (1919) he settled in Dublin, becoming publicity director for the IRA and a confidant of Eamon de Valera. Childers was Dáil Éireann's first Director of Propaganda, a TD (1921–2) and acted as First Secretary to the delegation sent to London to negotiate the Treaty in October 1921. Declining to support the Treaty, he was executed by the Irish Free State during the Civil War. He authored *The Riddle of the Sands* (1903).

Childers Erskine Hamilton (1905–74). Born in London, son of (Robert) Erskine Childers and educated at Gresham School, Norfolk, and Cambridge, he was first a businessman and then Fianna Fáil TD (1938–73), holding the posts of Minister for Local Government (1944–8), Posts and Telegraphs (1951–4), Lands, Forestry and Fisheries (1957–9), Transport and Power (1959–66), Posts and Telegraphs (1966–9). He then became Tánaiste and Minister for Health (1969–73). Childers succeeded Eamon de Valera as President of the Republic of Ireland (1973–4), an office he held until his death.

Clarke Austin (Augustine Joseph) (1896–1974). Born in Dublin and educated at Belvedere College and UCD, he taught at UCD and had a regular programme on Radio Éireann (1942–55). Clarke, a noted poet, playwright, novelist and scholar, authored *The Celtic Twilight and the Nineties* (1969).

Clarke Thomas James (1857 – 3 May 1916, by firing squad). Born on the Isle of Wight where his father was serving in the British army, he lived in South Africa and then Dungannon, Co. Tyrone, before emigrating to the United States (1880) where he joined Clan na Gael. Clarke was arrested and sentenced to imprisonment for life (1883) for his role in the dynamite campaign in England but released (1898), returning to America the following year. He settled in Dublin (1907) and was a member of the IRB military council (1915), then served as a leader of the Easter Rising at the General Post Office, for which he was executed.

Cluskey Frank (1930–89). Born in Dublin and educated at St Vincent's CBS, Glasnevin, and Harvard, Cluskey was a TD (1965–83), Lord Mayor of Dublin (1968) and leader of the Labour Party (1977–81). He resigned and then, as a member of Fine Gael, he became Minister for Trade, Commerce and Tourism (1982–3).

Cobbe Frances Power (1822–1904). Born at Newbridge House in Dublin to a strict evangelical Protestant family, she was educated at home, with two years' schooling in Brighton. Her religious scepticism led her father to throw her out of the family home. After his death in 1856 she travelled in Europe and became Italian correspondent of the *London Daily News*. Settling in

England, she involved herself in philanthropic work and wrote for her living on religious, educational and feminist themes. Among her books is *Essays on the Pursuits of Women* (1863).

Coffey Denis J. (1865–1945). Born in Tralee, Co., Kerry, and educated at Holy Cross School, Tralee, Cecilla St Medical School, the Catholic University of Louvain, Madrid and Leipzig, he was president of UCD (1908–40).

Collins Michael (1890 – 22 August 1922, assassinated). Born at Woodfield, Clonakilty, Co. Cork, and educated in Clonakilty National School, he went to London (1906) where he was a clerk in the post office and then worked for a stockbrokerage firm. There he joined the GAA and the IRA. He returned to Ireland (1915) in order to avoid conscription and served in the General Post Office during the Easter Rising. Collins was elected an MP (1918) but instead sat in Dáil Éireann (1919–22), serving as Minister for Home Affairs (1919) and Finance (1919–22). During the Anglo-Irish War he was a highly effective director of intelligence for the IRA. Collins was a signatory to the Anglo-Irish Treaty (December 1921) and his position as president of the IRB was a major reason for many in the IRA supporting the Treaty. Collins was Chairman of the Provisional Government and Commander in Chief of the new National Army when the Civil War commenced. He was killed in an IRA ambush at Béal na mBláth, near Macroom, Co. Cork.

Connolly James (1868 – 12 May 1916, by firing squad). Born in Edinburgh, he was a Marxist, trade union organiser and head of the Irish Citizen Army. Connolly came to Ireland (1896) and was in America (1903–10), then returned to be an organiser for the Irish Transport and General Workers Union (ITGWU). He was military commander of the republican forces in Dublin and had command at the General Post Office during the Easter Rising for which he was executed. Connolly remains a revered figure of the political left. He authored *Labour in Irish History* (1910).

Conway Cardinal William (created 1965) (1913–77). Born in Belfast and educated at the Barrack Street CBS, QUB and Maynooth, he was ordained (1937). He was awarded a DD by the Gregorian University (1938) while in Rome (1938–41). Conway was then on the faculty at Maynooth (1942–58) before becoming Auxiliary to Cardinal D'Alton whom he succeeded as Archbishop of Armagh and Primate of All Ireland (1963–77).

Cooke Revd Henry (1788–1868). Born in Grillagh, Co. Londonderry, he was educated locally, at Glasgow College, TC and the Royal College of Surgeons before being ordained into the Presbyterian ministry (1808). A vocal anti-Arian, Cooke was an ardent opponent of Daniel O'Connell's Repeal movement, Cooke was also a leader of the Orange Order.

Corish Brendan (1918–1990). Born in Wexford and educated at Wexford CBS, he was a TD (1945–82), serving as Minister for Social Welfare (1954–7) and Health and Social Welfare, as well as Tánaiste (1973–7) and leader of the Labour Party (1960–77).

693

Corkery Daniel (1878–1964). Born in Cork and educated there by the Presentation Brothers and at St Patrick's College, Drumcondra, where he trained as a National schoolteacher. Corkery, a TD (Fianna Fáil from 1926) (1921–32, 1933–7), opposed the Treaty. He was professor of English in UCC (1931–47) and then a Senator (1951–4), also publishing literary works including *The Hidden Ireland* (1924).

Cosgrave Liam (1920–). Born in Dublin, son of William T. Cosgrave, and educated at the CBS, Synge Street, Castleknock College and King's Inns, he became Senior Counsel (1958). He was a TD (1943–77), serving as Minster for Industry and Commerce (1954) and Minister for External Affairs (1954–7). He became leader of Fine Gael (1965–77) and Taoiseach (1973–7).

Cosgrave William T. (1880–1965). Born in Dublin and educated at a CBS, he was elected to the Dublin Corporation (1909) and joined the Irish Volunteers (1913). He was sentenced to death for participation in the Easter Rising. This was commuted to penal servitude for life, but he was released under the general amnesty in January 1917. Cosgrave was returned to the House of Commons in a by-election (August 1917) but declined to take his seat. After re-election (1918) he instead sat in Dáil Éireann (1919–44) and supported the Treaty. Cosgrave was Minister for Local Government (1919–1922), President of the Second Dáil (1922), President of the Executive Council (1922–32), Minister for Finance and Defence (1924) and leader of Cumann na nGaedheal (1922–33) and of Fine Gael (1934–44).

Costello John Aloysius (1891–1976). Born in Dublin and educated at O'Connell School, UCD and King's Inns, he was called to the bar (1914), the inner bar (1926) and became a bencher (1926). Costello was Attorney-General of the Free State (1926–32), Fine Gael TD (1933–69) and the compromise choice for Taoiseach (1948–51), serving again in 1954–7.

Craig Sir James (knighted 1918, 1st Viscount Craigavon, created 1927) (1871–1940). Born at Strandstown, Belfast, and educated privately and at Merchiston Castle, Edinburgh, he was a founder of the Belfast Stock Exchange and then served in the Boer War and again during the First World War (1914–16). Craig was Unionist MP (1906–21), leader of the Ulster Unionist Party (1921–40) and Northern Ireland Prime Minister (1921–40).

Craig William (1924–). Educated at the Dungannon Royal School, Larne Grammar School and QUB, he was an MP in the Northern Ireland parliament (1960–73) where he served as chief whip (1962–3) and Minister for Home Affairs (1966–8). In February 1972 he founded Ulster Vanguard and a year later the Vanguard Unionist Party. Craig was elected to the Northern Ireland Assembly (1973–4) and the Northern Ireland Constitutional Convention (1975–6). He lost influence (1975) when he suggested that under some circumstances power-sharing could be acceptable.

Crawford Frederick Hugh (1861–1952). Born in Belfast and educated at Methodist College and University College London, he was a Boer War veteran. Crawford created 'Young Ulster' (1892) and was a key figure in the

694

Larne gun-running (1914). He helped revive the Ulster Volunteer Force (1920–1).

Crawford William Sharman (1781–1861). Born in Co. Down, he was MP (1835–7) and held an English seat (1841–51), serving as High Sheriff of Down (1811). Crawford, a Protestant landlord in Co. Down, supported Catholic Emancipation but is best known for advocacy of legislation for tenant right, forming the Ulster Tenant Association (1846) and Tenant League (1850). He also favoured federalism.

Cregan Martin (1788–1870). Born in Co. Meath and educated at the Dublin Society's School of Art and in London, he returned to Dublin (1822). Cregan, a portrait painter, was an original member of the RHA (1823) and its president (1832–56).

Croke Thomas William (1824–1902). Born in Ballyclough, Co. Cork, and educated at Charleville, Co. Cork, the Irish Colleges in Paris and Rome, he was ordained (1846), becoming Bishop of Auckland, New Zealand, prior to translation to the Archbishopric of Cashel and Emly (1875–1902). Croke supported national causes, sometimes antagonising the papacy. He was patron to the Gaelic Athletic Association (GAA) (1884).

Cullen Cardinal Paul (created 1866) (1803–78). Born at Prospect, Co. Kildare, and educated at a Quaker school at Ballitore, Co. Kildare, Carlow College and the College of Propaganda, Rome, he was ordained in Rome (1829). Cullen was rector of the Irish College, Rome (1832–49), becoming Archbishop of Armagh (1849–52), and he was then translated to the Archbishopric of Dublin and became Primate of All Ireland (1852–78). Founder of Holy Cross College, Drumcondra (1859), he was Ireland's first cardinal. Cullen placed Catholic issues above the national question and was unsympathetic to movements that rivalled his influence. He kept his distance from the home rulers and they in turn mistrusted him.

Curran John Philpot (1750–1817). Born into a Protestant family at Newmarket, Co. Cork, and educated at Midleton School, TC and the Middle Temple (London), he was called to the bar (1775), becoming a KC (1782). Curran, an MP in the Irish parliament, was legal counsel for prominent United Irishmen but refused to defend Robert Emmet, whom he detested, though Emmet was engaged to his daughter Sarah. He was Master of the Rolls (1807–14).

Cusack Margaret Anne (Sister Mary Frances Clare, the Nun of Kenmare) (1832–99). Born in Dublin, she joined an Anglican sisterhood in London but became a Catholic (1858), enlisting in the Poor Clares in Newry (1860). She served her order in Kenmare, Co. Kerry, and then at Knock, Co. Mayo (1881), authoring, *The Nun of Kenmare* (1889).

Cusack Michael (1847–1906). Born in Carron, Co. Clare, he was a teacher at Blackrock College and CWC, becoming co-founder of the GAA (1884) and its secretary.

D'Alton Cardinal John Francis (created 1953) (1883–1963). Born in Claremorris, Co. Mayo, and educated at Blackrock College, the Royal University, Holy Cross College, Drumcondra, Oxford and Cambridge, he was awarded a DD from Rome (1908), later becoming President of Maynooth (1936–42), Bishop of Meath (1943–6) and Archbishop of Armagh and Primate of All Ireland (1946–63).

Daly Cardinal Cathal B. (created 1991) (1917–). Born in Belfast and educated at St Malachy's College there, QUB, Maynooth and the Institut Catholique, Paris, he was ordained (1941). Daly was Bishop of Ardagh and Clonmacnois (1967–82), Bishop of Down (1982–90) and Archbishop of Armagh and Primate of All Ireland (1990–6).

D'Arcy Revd Charles Frederick (1859–1938). Born in Dublin and educated at the High School and TC, he was ordained in the Church of Ireland (1885). He was Bishop successively of Clogher (1903–7), Ossory, Ferns and Leighlin (1907–11), Down and Conor (1911–19) and Archbishop of Dublin (1919–20) and then Archbishop of Armagh and Primate of All Ireland (1920–38). He was elected a Fellow of the RIA (1907).

Daunt William Joseph O'Neill (1801–85). Born at Tullamore, King's Co. (Offaly), into a prominent Protestant family, O'Neill Daunt was a convert to Catholicism. He was elected a Repeal MP for Mallow (1832) but was unseated on petition. Daunt supported the Repeal Association in the 1840s and for a short time in the early 1870s was the paid secretary of the Home Government Association. He authored *A Life Spent for Ireland* (1896).

Davis Thomas Osborne (1814–45). Born in Mallow, Co. Cork, and educated at a mixed preparatory school and TC, he was called to the bar (1838). Davis joined the Repeal Association (1839) but became a leader of Young Ireland and critic of Daniel O'Connell, co-founding the *Nation* (1842). An ardent advocate of national rights, he inspired later generations of nationalists. He died prematurely of scarlet fever in September 1845. Davis wrote the nationalist ballad, 'A Nation Once Again'.

Davitt Michael (1846–1906). Born in Straide, Co. Mayo, his family emigrated to Lancashire (1850) where he was educated at a Methodist school after losing his right arm in an industrial accident at the age of 11. Davitt joined the Fenians (1865) and was sentenced to 15 years' imprisonment (1870), being released on a ticket of leave in December 1877. He was a founder of the Land League (21 October 1879), remaining a prominent figure in the struggle against the Irish landlords. First elected an MP in February 1882, he was declared ineligible as an undischarged felon. He was then returned as an Anti-Parnellite in December 1892 but was unseated on petition. Davitt finally became an MP in February 1893 but resigned in May 1893 on being declared bankrupt. He again was elected in 1895 and sat until resigning in 1899. He authored *The Fall of Feudalism in Ireland* (1904).

De Rossa Prionsias (1940–). Born in Dublin and educated at the Marlborough Street NS and Kevin Street Technical College, he was a

Workers' Party TD (1982–92) when he left the party, becoming leader of the Democratic Left and TD (1992–). In 1999 the Democratic Left fused with the Labour Party.

De Valera Eamon (1882–1975). Born in New York, reared in Bruree, Co. Limerick, and educated at Blackrock College and UCD, he taught mathematics at several colleges. He was leader of Sinn Féin (1917–22), of anti-treaty Sinn Féin (1922–6), a founder of Fianna Fáil (1926) and its leader (1926–59). De Valera was elected an MP (1917) but declined to sit and was re-elected (1918) but sat instead in Dáil Éireann (1919–59; declining to sit 1922–7), serving as President of the Dáil (1919–22), President of the Executive Council (1932–7), Taoiseach (1937–48, 1951–4 and 1957–9) and then President of Ireland (1959–73). His significance lay in his opposition to the Treaty and in his decision (1926) to take most of the anti-Treaty Sinn Féin into constitutional politics. After gaining office (1932), he gradually withdrew Ireland from its links with the British Empire. In 1937 he was responsible for the writing of a new Constitution, and during the Second World War kept Ireland neutral. His Catholic and conservative policies dominated Ireland during these years to such an extent that people continue to refer to this period as de Valera's Ireland.

Devlin Joseph (1872–1934). Born in Belfast he received primary education at the Divis CBS. He was an MP (1902–22, 1929–35) and sat in the Northern Ireland parliament (1921–34) where he led the Nationalist bloc. Devlin was president of the Ancient Order of Hibernians (1905–34), an organisation he used to great effect politically. He was a close ally of John Dillon and succeeded him as Irish Party chairman when Dillon lost his seat (December 1918).

Devoy John (1842–1928). Born at Kill, Co. Kildare, and educated in Dublin and at evening classes at the Catholic University, he joined the Fenians and subsequently enlisted in the French Foreign Legion (1861), returning to Ireland (1862) and becoming an organiser for the IRB. Devoy was arrested (February 1866) and imprisoned until January 1871 when he was released on condition he left the British Isles until his 15-year sentence expired. He was one of the 'Cuba Five' who went to America and became a member of the Clan na Gael there. An architect of the New Departure (1879), Devoy was an ardent republican. During the Edwardian years he opposed the policies of the Irish Party and aided the republican movement during and after the First World War. He authored *Recollections of an Irish Rebel* (1929).

Dillon James Mathew (1902–86). Born in Dublin, the son of John Dillon and educated at Mount St Benedict, Gorey, Co. Wexford, UCD and King's Inns, he was called to the bar (1931). He was TD (1932–68) and co-founded the National Centre Party. When it became part of Fine Gael (1933) Dillon was selected as its vice-president. During the Emergency Dillon criticised the policy of neutrality and became an Independent (1942), rejoining Fine Gael

(1953). He was Minister for Agriculture (1948–51, 1954–7) and leader of Fine Gael (1959–65).

Dillon John Blake (1816–66). Born in Ballaghaderreen, Co. Mayo, and educated at Maynooth and TC, he was called to the bar (1841) and became a member of Young Ireland and the Irish Confederation. In 1842 he co-founded the *Nation*. He took part in the Rising of 1848 and fled to France, returning to Ireland (1855) and was an MP (1855–66). He was the father of John Dillon.

Dillon John (1851–1927), Born in Blackrock, Co. Dublin, the son of John Blake Dillon and educated at the Catholic University and the Royal College of Surgeons, he took an active part in the home rule movement in the 1870s and was an MP (1880–3), resigning his seat and settling in America until 1885. After returning to Ireland he again sat in the House of Commons (1885–1918). Though never personally close to Parnell, Dillon was among the most prominent members of the Irish Party, a major figure in the Land League and, along with William O'Brien and T. C. Harrington, the chief organiser of the Plan of Campaign. He became chairman of the anti-Parnellite majority in succession to Justin McCarthy (February 1896), resigning (1899) to make way for reunification of the national party. Following the death of John Redmond he succeeded to the party chairmanship (March 1918) but lost his seat the following December and gave up the leadership.

Doyle James Warren (1786–1834). Born near New Ross, Co. Wexford, and educated at the Augustinian College, New Ross, and the University of Coimbra, Portugal, he was ordained (1809), becoming Bishop of Kildare and Leighlin (1819–34). Doyle supported the Catholic Association, Daniel O'Connell and the National Education System.

Drennan William (1754–1820). Born in Belfast, the son of a Presbyterian minister, he was educated at the University of Glasgow and then Edinburgh where he received an MD (1778). He went to Dublin (1789), where he assisted Thomas Russell and Wolfe Tone in the organisation of the United Irishmen but had little contact with the movement after 1795. Following his marriage he returned to Belfast (1807) and was a founder of the RBAI. During his later years he authored a number of works critical of the British government.

Drummond Thomas (1797–1840). Born in Edinburgh and educated at the University of Edinburgh, he came to Ireland in 1824. As Under-Secretary (1835–40) he was a leading advocate of reforms until his early death.

Duffy Sir Charles Gavan (knighted 1873) (1816–1903). Born in Monaghan and educated at the RBAI, he was a co-founder of the *Nation* newspaper (1842) and was called to the bar (1845). Duffy was a leading member of Young Ireland. He was an MP (1852–5) but emigrated to Victoria, Australia (1855), where he became Prime Minister (1871–2) and Speaker of the Assembly (1876–80). Duffy returned to Europe (1880), living mainly in southern France, and promoted moderate self-government ideas. He authored *My Life in Two Hemispheres* (1898).

Duffy George Gavan (1882–1951). Born in France, son of Sir Charles Gavan Duffy, and educated in France and Stonyhurst College, Lancashire, he was a solicitor in London until 1917. Duffy prepared the defence of Sir Roger Casement (1916). He was called to the Irish bar (1917), joined Sinn Féin and was elected an MP (1918), but instead sat in Dáil Éireann (1919–23) and was a member of the negotiating team which signed the Treaty on 6 December 1921. Subsequently, he was called to the inner bar (1929) and became a judge of the High Court (1936) and its president (1946).

Duggan Eamon (Edmund) John (1874–1936). Born in Longwood, Co. Meath, and educated locally and in Dublin where he qualified as a solicitor (1914), he joined the Irish Volunteers and fought in the General Post Office during the Easter Rising. Duggan was elected an MP (1918) but instead sat in Dáil Éireann (1919–33). For a time he was IRA Director of Intelligence. Duggan was a member of the delegation sent to London in October 1921 to negotiate the Treaty, which he subsequently supported. He served as Minister for Justice (1922), Minister without Portfolio (1922–3) and Minister of Defence (1927–32) and as a Senator (1933).

Dukes Alan M. (1945–). Educated at Coláiste Mhuire, Parnell Street, Dublin, and UCD, he was chief economist for the National Farmers' Association (1967–72) and director of the Irish Farmers' Association, Brussels (1973–6), prior to being elected a Fine Gael TD (1981–). He served as Minister for Agriculture (1981–2), Finance (1982–6), Justice (1986–7) and Transport, Energy and Communications (1996–7), and was leader of Fine Gael (1987–90).

Dunraven 4th Earl of (succeeded 1871) (Wyndham Thomas Wyndham Quin) (1841–1926). Born in Adare, Co. Limerick, and educated privately in Rome and Oxford, he joined the Life Guards and was then a war correspondent. Dunraven was Under-Secretary for the Colonies (1885–6, 1886–7). A prominent southern landlord and Unionist, he represented landowners' interests at the land conference (December 1902), founded and was President of the Irish Reform Association (1903) and was a delegate to the Irish Convention (1917–18). In 1922 he became a member of the first Senate. He authored *Past Times and Pastimes* (1922).

Edgeworth Maria (1767–1849). Born daughter of Richard Lowell Edgeworth in Black Bourton, Oxfordshire, and educated in Derby and London, she came to Ireland (1782), residing on her father's estate in Longford. She published educational books and her novel *Castle Rackrent* (1800) earned her wide acclaim. During the Famine she worked to relieve starvation.

Edwards Robert Dudley (1909–88). Born in Dublin and educated at the Catholic University School, St Enda's, Synge Street CBS, UCD and the University of London (King's College). He was co-founder of *Irish Historical Studies* (1938) and joint editor (1938–77), being on the faculty at UCD (1939–77) and Chair in Irish History from 1945.

Egan Patrick (1841–1919). Born in Ballymahon, Co. Longford, and educated locally, he rose to become managing director of a Dublin bakery, serving as a member of the Supreme Council and treasurer of the IRB until 1877. Egan became treasurer of the Land League, subsequently emigrating to America (1883) where he was president of the National League of America (1884–6) and Minister to Chile (1888).

Emmet Robert (1778 – 20 September 1803, beheaded). Born in Dublin, brother of the United Irishman Thomas Addis Emmet, and educated at private schools and TC, he joined the United Irishmen for which he was expelled from Trinity (April 1798). On 23 July 1803 he led an assault on Dublin Castle but the rising collapsed within hours. Emmet fled but was apprehended on 25 August and subsequently executed.

Faulkner (Arthur) Brian Deane (Lord Faulkner of Downpatrick, created 1977) (1921–77). Born Co. Down and educated at St Columba's College, Rathfarnham, Dublin and TC, he was an MP in the Northern Ireland parliament (1949–72), serving as Minister for Home Affairs (1959–63) and Minister for Commerce (1963–9), resigning in protest at Prime Minister Terence O'Neill's decision to establish a commission to examine the causes of violence in October 1968. Following O'Neill's resignation, Faulkner became Minister of Development (1971–2) under James Chichester-Clark. Following Chichester-Clark's resignation he became Prime Minister (March 1971 – March 1972) until Stormont was prorogued and he then became Chief Executive of the power-sharing administration (1974). His acceptance of the Sunningdale Agreement (1973) proved too controversial for the Ulster Unionist Party which he headed (1971 – January 1974) and he resigned. The Executive was brought down by a loyalist general strike (May 1974). He later formed the Unionist Party of Northern Ireland. He retired from active politics (1976), dying in a riding accident near his home (March 1977).

Ferguson Harry George (1884–1960). Born in Dromore, Co. Down, and educated locally, he piloted the first air flight in Ireland (1909), began manufacturing vehicles (1911) and was most notable for the development of the Ferguson tractor. A supporter of the Ulster Volunteer Force, he participated in the Larne gun-running (April 1914).

Ferguson Sir Samuel (knighted 1878) (1810–86). Born in Belfast and educated at the RBAI and TC, he was called to the bar (1838) and became a QC (1859). Ferguson accepted the post of Deputy Keeper of Irish Records (1869) and President of the RIA (1882–6). In the 1840s he founded the Protestant Repeal Association. A promoter of the Gaelic revival in Irish literature, he was a noted author, poet and antiquarian. *Hibernian Night's Entertainment* (1887) was published posthumously.

Figgis Darrell (1892–1925, suicide). Born in Rathmines, Dublin, and taken to Ceylon as a child, he joined the Gaelic League and Sinn Féin after returning to Ireland. He purchased the arms in Hamburg that were landed

700

by the Irish Volunteers (1914), became secretary to the reorganised Sinn Féin (1917–19), supported the Treaty, was a TD (1922–5) and helped draft the Constitution of 1922. He authored *The Sinn Féin Catechism* (1918).

Fitt Gerald (Baron Fitt, created 1983) (1926–2000). Born in Belfast and at a local CBS, he was a councillor in the Belfast Corporation, then MP (1966–83) and leader of the SDLP (1970–9) as well as with serving as Stormont MP (1962–72) and subsequently a member of the Northern Ireland Assembly (1973–5). Fitt was Deputy Chief Executive of the short-lived Power-Sharing Executive (1974) and a member of the Convention (1975–6). Earlier he helped form the Republican Labour Party (1960). On entering Westminster (1966) he played a pivotal role in raising the issue of civil rights. A founding leader of the SDLP (1970), he resigned over the decision by the party not to attend a constitutional conference organised by the British government. From then until his defeat at the next general election (1983), he stood as an Independent Socialist MP. He became a life peer in that year and was subsequently critical of such policies as the Anglo-Irish Agreement (1985) because of the lack of consultation with the Unionists.

FitzGerald Garret (1926–). Born in Dublin and educated at Belevedere College, UCD and King's Inns, he was a lecturer in Political Economy at UCD (1959–73). He was a Fine Gael TD (1969–92), its leader (1977–87), Minister for Foreign Affairs (1973–7) and Taoiseach (1981–2, 1982–7). He wrote *Towards a New Ireland* (1972).

Foley John Henry (1818–74). Born in Dublin and educated in the art schools of the Royal Dublin Society and Royal Academy (London), he designed the Grattan monument on College Green, the O'Connell memorial on O'Connell Street, the statues of Edmund Burke and Oliver Goldsmith outside the main gate of TC in Dublin and part of the Albert Memorial in London. Foley was elected to the RA (1858) and the RIA (1861).

Ford Patrick (1837–1913). Born in Galway and educated locally, his parents emigrated to the United States (1841). His career in journalism began in Boston (1855). During the American Civil War he served in the Union forces. In 1870 Ford founded the *Irish World* in New York, a newspaper identified with labour and radical opinions, which he published until his death. Ford supported John Redmond after Parnell's death. After 1900 he opposed the Clan na Gael and remained faithful to the policy of the Irish Party.

Foster John (created Lord Oriel, 1821) (1740–1828). Born in Collon, Co. Louth, and educated at TC, he was called to the bar (1766). Foster was the last Speaker of the Irish House of Commons (1785–1800). He opposed the Act of Union but was subsequently Chancellor of the Irish Exchequer (1804–6, 1807–11).

Gandon James (1742–1823). Born in London and educated at Shipley's Academy, he came to Ireland (1781) to supervise the building of the Custom

House in Dublin (completed 1791) and supervised the extension to the Parliament House (1782). In 1785 he became architect of the Four Courts which was completed in 1802. He retired in 1808.

Gibson Edward (1st Baron Ashbourne, July 1885) (1837–1913). Born in Dublin and educated at TC, he was called to the bar (1860) and took silk (1872). He was Conservative MP for the University of Dublin (1875–85), serving as Attorney-General (1877–80) and Lord Chancellor (1885–6, 1886–92, 1895–1905). His views on Irish matters carried great weight among senior Conservatives. The land purchase legislation (1885) is known as the Ashbourne Act.

Gill Thomas Patrick (1868–1931). Born in Ballygraigue, Nenagh, Co. Tipperary, and educated at CBS Nenagh and TC, he was a journalist and MP (1885–92), supporting the anti-Parnellites (December 1890). Gill became involved with the Irish co-operative movement and other groups promoted by Sir Horace Plunkett. He was secretary to the Recess Committee (1896), held a similar position in the Department of Agriculture and Technical Instruction (1900–23) and served as president of the Irish Technical Education Association (1925–9).

Ginnell Laurence (1854–1923). Born in Co. Westmeath and self-educated, he was called to the Irish and English bars and was a founder of the Irish Literary Society. Ginnell was arrested several times. He was a leading advocate of 'cattle driving' during the ranch war (1907–9). An MP (1906–18), Ginnell was expelled from the Irish Party (1909) and thereafter sat as a National Independent. He was elected under the Sinn Féin banner (1918) but sat in Dáil Éireann (1919–23) and served as Director of Publicity in the first Dáil Éireann. He opposed the Treaty.

Gogarty Oliver St John (1878–1957). Born in Dublin and educated at CWC, TC and briefly Oxford, he was a surgeon by training and an author. Gogarty served in the Senate (1922–36) but became disillusioned with Ireland and passed his later years in the United States. His writings include *As I Was Going Down Sackville Street* (1937).

Gonne (MacBride), Maud (1866–1953). Born near Aldershot and educated by a governess in France. In the 1890s, though still living much of the time in Paris, Gonne belonged to the Amnesty Association, was a member of Cumann na nGaedheal, the Irish Transvaal Committee and the National Council, and founded the republican-suffragette Inghinidhe na hÉireann (1900). Gonne converted to Catholicism (1902) and married Major John MacBride (1903) whom she divorced after the birth of their son, Seán MacBride. After some years abroad, she returned to Ireland (1917) and was one of those incarcerated during the German plot (1918). Gonne rejected the Treaty and worked for republican causes thereafter. Her autobiography is *A Servant of the Queen* (1938). She is immortalised in the poetry of W. B. Yeats, whom she first met in 1889.

Goulding Cathal (1922–98). Born in Dublin into a republican family, at 15 he was apprenticed as a house painter and also joined the IRA. He was sentenced to eight years in prison in England (1953) and on his release (1961) moved to Navan, Co. Meath. He emerged as the IRA's Chief of Staff (1962). Goulding, a Marxist, devised the policy of political agitation which came to fruition in the later 1960s. In 1969 the IRA split into the Provisional and Official wings; he remained head of the Marxist Officials. Goulding retired from politics in 1980.

Grattan Henry (1746–1820). Born in Dublin and educated at Mr Ball's and Mr Young's Schools in Dublin, TC and the Middle Temple (London), he was called to the bar (1772) and elected an MP in the Irish parliament (1775). Grattan was the leader of the Irish parliament (1782) and after opposing the Act of Union also served in the Westminster House of Commons (1805–20), where he supported Catholic Emancipation. The eighteenth-century Irish parliament is often referred to as Grattan's parliament. His statue stands in College Green, Dublin.

Graves Charles (1812–99). Born in England and educated at a private school near Bristol and TC, he was a Church of Ireland cleric, a Fellow of TC, president of the RIA (1861–6), Dean of Clonfert (1864–6) and Bishop of Limerick, Ardfert and Aghadoes (1866–99). A mathematician and poet, he was elected Fellow of the Royal Society (1880).

Gray Edmond Dwyer (1845–88). Born in Dublin, son of Sir John Gray, on completion of his education in Dublin he took up employment with the *Freeman's Journal*, becoming proprietor following his father's death (1875). Like his father before him, the younger Gray took an active part in municipal life, entering the Dublin Corporation and serving as Lord Mayor (1879–80). Gray was an MP (1877–88) and High Sheriff of Dublin (1882). Although born a Protestant, Gray converted to Catholicism after his marriage. A political moderate, he was an influential figure in the Irish national movement and Irish Party.

Gray Sir John (knighted 1863) (1816–75). Born in Claremorris, Co. Mayo, into a Protestant family and the father of Edmond Dwyer Gray, he obtained a medical degree from the University of Glasgow. After settling in Dublin (1839) he became co-proprietor of the *Freeman's Journal* (1841) and sole owner (1850), also serving on Dublin City Council (1852). Gray, who had supported Repeal, was a Liberal and then home rule MP (1865–75). His statue stands in O'Connell Street, Dublin.

Gregory Lady Augusta Isabella (1852–1932). Born Augusta Persse at Roxborough, Co. Galway, and educated privately, she married Sir William Gregory (1880). Lady Gregory was nearly 50 when her literary career began. She co-founded the Irish Literary Theatre (1898) and subsequently became an active director of the Abbey Theatre from its formation in 1904 until 1928. She wrote more than 40 plays, including *The Rising of the Moon* (1907), and her home at Coole Park, Co. Galway, was a centre for Irish literary figures.

Griffith Arthur (1871–1922). Born in Dublin and educated at the CBS, Strand Street, he was a journalist, a founder of the Celtic Literary Society, and active in the Gaelic League and in the IRB until 1910. A founder and vice-president of Sinn Féin (1905), Griffith popularised the policy of economic self-reliance and abstention from the Westminster parliament while serving as editor of *Sinn Féin* (1906–15) and *Nationality* (1916). He joined the Irish Volunteers (1913) and participated in the Howth gun-running. Griffith did not take part in the Easter Rising. He was returned as an MP (1918), sitting instead in Dáil Éireann (1919–22), serving as Minister of Home Affairs (1919) and Minister of Foreign Affairs (1921), and while Eamon de Valera was in America he served as President of the Dáil (June 1919 – close 1920). He was the head of the Irish delegates to the conference in London (October–December 1921) and signed the Treaty. In January 1922 he became President of the Dáil; he died suddenly on 12 August 1922. His best-known work is *The Resurrection of Hungary* (1904).

Griffith Sir Richard John (1784–1878). Born in Dublin and educated in Dublin, London and Edinburgh, he was engineer to the Commission on Irish Bogs (1809–12), and supervised the valuation of Ireland, known as 'Griffith's Valuation', under the Act of 1852. He was chairman of the Board of Works (1850–64).

Guinness Sir Arthur Edward (became a knight on the death of his father, 1868; 1st Baron Ardilaun, created 1880) (1840–1915). Born in Clontarf, Dublin, son of Benjamin Lee, and educated at Eton and TC, he was head of the family brewery (1868–77), a Conservative MP (1868–9, 1874–80) and president of the Royal Dublin Society (1897–1913). Among his many bequests, he paid for the restoration of Marsh's Library and presented St Stephen's Green to the city of Dublin.

Guinness Sir Benjamin Lee (knighted 1867) (1798–1868). Born in Dublin and educated there, he was head of the family brewery (1855–65), Lord Mayor of Dublin (1851) and a Conservative MP (1865–8). His charitable bequests included paying for the restoration of St Patrick's Cathedral (1860).

Guinness Edmund Cecil (1st Earl of Inveagh, created 1891) (1847–1927). Born in Clontarf, Dublin, son of Sir Benjamin Lee Guinness, he was educated privately and at TC, becoming manager of the family brewery until it became a public company (1886). He was a philanthropist.

Gwynn Stephen Lucius (1864–1950). Educated at St Columba's College and Oxford, a grandson of William Smith O'Brien, he was born into the Protestant Ascendancy, but followed the family legacy of taking up patriotic causes. He was an Irish Party MP (1906–18), served in the British army during the First World War and was a member of the Irish Convention (1917–18). His numerous writings are within a nationalist tradition. He authored *The Fair Hills of Ireland* (1906).

704

Hamilton   Sir William Rowan (knighted 1835) (1805–65). Born in Dublin and educated by his uncle in Trim, Co. Meath, and TC, he was a mathematical prodigy, becoming a professor (1827), Astronomer Royal of Ireland and president of the RIA (1836–46).

Hanna   Revd Hugh 'Roaring' (1824–92). Born at Dromara, Co. Down, and educated in Belfast, he was ordained into the Presbyterian ministry (1852). His sermons incited violence against Catholics on several occasions. In 1857 his defiance of the ban on his preaching in Belfast led to days of rioting. Hanna was prominent in the Revival of 1859. He was appointed a Commissioner of National Education (1880).

Hannay   Revd James Owen (pen name George A. Birmingham) (1865–1950). Born in Belfast and educated at Haileybury and TC, he was ordained in the Church of Ireland. Active in the Gaelic League and a well-known author, he wrote *Up the Rebels* (1919).

Harland   Sir Edward James (knighted 1885) (1831–96). Born in Scarborough (England), he was apprenticed to the Robert Stevenson shipyard, Newcastle. He migrated to Belfast (1853), purchasing a shipyard (1858) and then forming the partnership of Harland & Wolff (1862). He was Chief Harbour Commissioner for Belfast (1875–87), Mayor (1885–7) and Unionist MP (1889–96).

Harney   Mary (1953–). Born in Galway and educated at a NS, Newcastle, Co. Dublin, the Convent of Mercy, Inchicore, the Presentation Convent, Clondalkin, and TC, where she was the first woman auditor of the College Historical Society, she was elected a Fianna Fáil member of the Senate (1977–81), a member of Dublin City Council (1979–91) and a TD (1981–), becoming co-founder of the Progressive Democrats (1985), Minister for Environmental Protection (1989–92), Minister for Enterprise, Trade and Employment and Tánaiste (1997–). Harney became the first woman to lead an Irish party when she took over the reins of the Progressive Democrats (1993–).

Harrington   Timothy C. (1851–1910). Born in Castletown, Berehaven, Co. Cork, he was educated at NS and TC. He founded the *Kerry Sentinel* (1977) and became secretary to first the Land League and subsequently the National League (1882), he was called to the bar (1887). Harrington was one of the chief figures in the Plan of Campaign (1886). He was an MP (1883–1910) and Lord Mayor of Dublin (1901–3). Harrington supported Parnell in December 1890.

Haslam   Anna (1829–1922). Born Anna Maria Fisher in Youghal, Cork, to a Quaker family that was active in the anti-slavery movement, she was active in the 1860s in the campaign to provide better access to education and training for women. She took part in the married women's property campaign, to afford married women control over their own property, and she spearheaded the Dublin section of the campaign against the Contagious Diseases Acts. In 1876 she and her husband (Thomas, 1825–1917) founded the Dublin

Women's Suffrage Association. She was also a co-founder of the Women's Liberal Unionist Association.

Haughey Charles James (1925–). Born in Castlebar, Co. Mayo, reared in Dublin and educated at St Joseph's CBS, Fairview, UCD and King's Inns, he was an accountant. After marrying a daughter of Seán Lemass, he became a member of Dublin City Council (1953–5), a Fianna Fáil TD (1957–92), Minister for Justice (1961–4), Minister of Agriculture and Fisheries (1964–6), Minister of Finance (1966–70), Minister of Health and Social Welfare (1977–9), Leader of Fianna Fail (1979–92) and Taoiseach (1979–81, 1982, 1987–92). Haughey was dismissed as Minister of Finance (1970) by Taoiseach Jack Lynch for his alleged involvement in the arms crisis (1970). He was cleared by the court of all charges of gun-running, but nevertheless the scandal remained with him for the rest of his political career. Haughey returned to the front bench (1977) and was the first Fianna Fáil leader to have to form a coalition government (1989).

Hayes Richard James (1902–76). Born in Abbeyfeale, Co. Limerick, and educated at CWC and TC, he joined the staff of the National Library (1926) becoming its director (1940–67). He compiled *Manuscript Sources for the History of Irish Civilisation* (11 vols., 1965).

Healy Timothy Michael (1855–1931). Born in Bantry, Co. Cork, and educated at the CBS Fermoy, Co. Cork, he emigrated to England in his teens. Healy was an ambitious young journalist who was initially mesmerised by Charles Stewart Parnell and briefly served as his private secretary. He was called to the Irish bar (1884), became a QC (1899) and was called to the English bar (1910). Healy was an MP (1881–6, 1887–1910, 1911–18). He took the lead against Parnell in December 1890 and played the largest role in the vitriolic attacks on him. Healy was closely connected with the Sullivan clan, to whom he was linked through marriage to T. D. Sullivan's daughter, but was widely mistrusted. His clashes with John Dillon were legendary. Healy defended the employers in the Dublin Lockout (1913) and was Governor-General of the Irish Free State (1922–8).

Heaney Seamus Justin (1939–). Born in Londonderry and educated there at St Columb's College and QUB, he was first a secondary school teacher (1962–3) and a lecturer at St Joseph's College of Education (1963–6) and then at QUB (1966–72). Subsequently, he devoted himself mainly to writing, though also being professor of poetry at the University of Oxford (1989–94) and holding a visiting appointment at Harvard University. Heaney was awarded the Nobel Prize for Literature (1995). He authored, among many other works, *Death of a Naturalist* (1969).

Henry Paul (1876–1958). Born in Belfast, son of a Baptist minister, he was educated at the RBAI, Belfast School of Art and in Paris. Henry lived in Achill (1912–19), painting many scenes during this period, and then came to Dublin (1920). Elected to the RHA (1929), his autobiography is *An Irish Portrait* (1951).

Hillery Patrick (1923–). Born in Miltown Malbay, Co. Clare, and educated at an NS, Rockwell College and UCD, from which he received an MD (1947), he was a Fianna Fáil TD (1951–73). Hillery was Minister for Education (1959–65), Minister for Industry and Commerce (1965–6), Minister of Labour (1966–9) and Minister of External Affairs (1969–72), leaving Irish politics to be the Irish Commissioner and a vice-president of the Commission of the European Economic Community (1973). Hillery was President of the Republic of Ireland (November 1976–90).

Hobson Bulmer (1883–1969). Born into a Quaker family in Holywood, Co. Down, and educated at Friends' School, Lisburn, he joined the Gaelic League (1901), founded Na Fianna Éireann (1903) and became a member of the IRB (1904). He was a founder of the Dungannon Clubs (1905), Vice-President of Sinn Féin (1907) and co-founder of the Irish Volunteers (1913). After 1916 he took little part in public life, holding the post of Chief Revenue Commissioner of the Stationary Department (1922–48).

Hume John (1937–). Born in Denned, Co. Londonderry, and educated at St Columba's College, Londonderry, and Maynooth, he was an MP in the Northern Ireland parliament (1969–72), a member of the Northern Ireland Assembly (1973–5), Minister for Commerce in the power-sharing executive (1974), member of the Northern Ireland Convention (1975–6), Social Democratic Labour Party member of the European Parliament (MEP) (1979–), member of the Northern Ireland Assembly (1982–6), a Westminster MP (1983–), a member of the Northern Ireland Forum (1996–7), a member of the new Northern Ireland Assembly (1998–), a founding member of the SDLP (1970) and party leader (1979–2001). One of the chief architects of the peace process, he was awarded the Nobel Peace Prize (1998).

Hussey Thomas (1746–1803). Born in Ballybogen, Co. Meath, and educated in Salamanca, Spain, he originally took vows as a Trappist monk and then left to be ordained. Hussey negotiated the establishment of the Maynooth Seminary and was its first president (1795–7) and Bishop of Waterford and Lismore (1797–1803). He was elected a Fellow of the Royal Society (1792).

Hyde Douglas (1860–1949). Born to a Church of Ireland cleric at Frenchpark, Co. Roscommon, and educated at TC, Hyde was an academic and member of the Society for the Preservation of the Language at Trinity and subsequently of the Gaelic Union. With W. B. Yeats he founded the Irish Literary Society in London (1891) and the National Literary Society in Dublin (May 1892) and was a leading force in the foundation of the Gaelic League and its first president (1893–1915). He was a member of the Senate (1925–38) and the first President of Ireland (1938–45). He authored *Literary History of Ireland* (1899).

Johnson Thomas (1872–1963). Born in Liverpool, he left school at 12, and went to Ireland (1900). Johnson served on the committee organised for the Belfast General Strike (1907), was a founder of the Labour Party (1912) and president of the Irish Trade Union Congress (1916–) and its secretary

(1920–8). He was a member of the Mansion House Conference which opposed conscription (1918). Johnson was co-author of the Democratic Programme adopted by the first Dáil Éireann, a TD (1922–7) and Irish Leader of the Labour Party (1922–8) and a Senator (1928–38), he became a member of the Labour Court (1946–55).

Johnston Francis (1762–1829). Born in Co. Armagh, he was an architect responsible for adapting the Parliament House for the Bank of Ireland (*c.* 1803), designing General Post Office, Dublin (1815–7), and making alterations to the Vice-Regal Lodge (1816). He was a founder of the RHA (1823) and its president (1824–9).

Johnston (William) Denis (1901–84). Born in Dublin and educated at St Andrew's School there, at Munchiston School, at the universities of Edinburgh and Cambridge and at Harvard Law School, he was director of the Gate Theatre (1932–6) and an author. His autobiography is *Nine Rivers from Jordan* (1953).

Joyce James Augustine Aloysius (1882–1941). Born in Dublin and educated at CWC, Belvedere College and UCD, he was one of literature's formative figures. He migrated to Paris (1920), living in France for the remainder of his life. *Ulysses* was published in 1922 and *Finnegan's Wake* in 1939. At the outbreak of the Second World War the family moved to Switzerland, where he died.

Kane Sir Robert John (knighted 1846) (1809–90). Born in Dublin, and educated at TC and Paris, he was the president of QCC (1845–73), president of the RIA (1877–82), Fellow of the Royal Society (1849) and Vice-Chancellor of the Royal University (1880–90). Kane was a member of the scientific commission established (1845) to discover a cure for potato blight and he established the Museum of Irish Industry (1846), serving as its first director.

Keating John (Seán) (1889–1977). Born in Limerick and educated at St Munchin's College there, Limerick Municipal School of Art, Metropolitan School of Art, Dublin, and in London, he returned to Ireland (1916), spending four years in the Aran Islands. He was elected to the RHA (1923) and was its president (1949–62). He is associated with nationalism in art. Among his paintings is *Men of the West* (1915).

Kennedy Hugh Boyle (1879–1936). Born in Dublin and educated privately, at UCD and King's Inns, he was called to the bar (1902) and became a KC (1920) and a member of the Gaelic League. During his period as Law Officer to the Provisional Government (January–December 1922), Kennedy was a member of the commission that drafted the Constitution of 1922. He was Attorney-General of the Free State (1922–4), a TD (1923–4), Chief Justice (1924–36) and a member of the RIA.

Keogh William Nicholas (1817 – 30 September 1878, suicide). Born in Galway and educated at Mountjoy School, Dublin, and TC, he was called to the bar (1840) and became a QC (1849) and an MP (1847–56). Keogh was a leading member of the Independent Irish Party and a founder of the Catholic Defence League, but accepted office as Solicitor-General (1853–5), becoming Attorney-General (1855–6). He became a judge of Common Pleas (1856–78), attracting controversy for his conduct of Fenian trials and also for the Galway Election Petition trial (1872).

Kettle Thomas M. (1880 – 9 September 1916, on the Western Front). Born in Dublin, son of Andrew Kettle, an associate of Charles Stewart Parnell, and educated at North Richmond St CBS, CWC and UCD, he was called to the bar (1905). Kettle was professor of economics in the National University (1909) and an MP (July 1906 – December 1910). He joined the Irish Volunteers (1913), being regarded as a leading intellectual and young turk.

Kickham Charles Joseph (1828–82). Born near Mullinahone, Co. Tipperary, he was successively a supporter of the Repeal movement, Young Ireland and a member of the IRB (1861), going to Dublin (1863) to work on the *Irish People* for which he was imprisoned (1865–9). He became a member of the Supreme Council of the IRB (1872) and then its president (*c.* 1873–82). Kickham found fame as a novelist, including *Knocknagow* (1879).

Lalor James Fintan (1807–1849). Born in Tinnakill, Queen's County (Laois), and educated at Carlow Lay College, he was a advocate of national principles in the 1840s but is chiefly known for his radical views on the land question. He contributed a series of articles to the *Nation* (1847) on land. Though fairly obscure in his lifetime, he was appropriated by later radical and nationalist figures, notably James Connolly and Patrick Pearse.

Lane Sir Hugh Percy (knighted 1909) (1875 – 7 May 1915, on the *Lusitania*). Born in Ballybrack House, Co. Cork, where his father was the Church of Ireland rector, he was a nephew of Lady Gregory, and was educated privately and on the continent. He was an art collector and dealer, being appointed director of the National Gallery of Ireland (1914). His will gave 39 pictures to the gallery, though it took many years to resolve the question of ownership of these paintings.

Lansdowne 5th Marquess of (succeeded 1866) (Henry Charles Keith Petty-Fitzmaurice) (1845–1927). Born in England and educated privately, at Eton and Oxford, he was a southern Irish Unionist who exerted immense influence, especially in the post-1912 years. Lansdowne held offices in the government (1869–74, 1880) before serving as Governor-General of Canada (1883–8) and Viceroy of India (1888–93). Subsequently he held major posts (1895–1905) and was leader of the Conservative opposition in the House of Lords (1906–16).

Larkin James (1876–1947). Born in Liverpool to an Irish family, he went to Belfast (1907) to organise workers in the docks and then to Dublin (1908). He founded the Irish Transport and General Workers Union (ITGWU) (1909) and led the employees' resistance to the Dublin Lockout (1913). He was in the United States from 1914 to 1923, including a period of imprisonment (1920–3). When Larkin returned to Ireland he attempted to regain control of the union. On losing his bid, he formed the Irish Workers' League (1923). He was a TD (1937–8, 1943–4). The bitter fight between him and William O'Brien led to the ITGWU disaffiliating from the Irish Congress of Trade Unions.

Lecky William Edward Hartpole (1838–1903). Born in Blackrock, Co. Dublin, and educated at Armagh School, Cheltenham College and TC, Lecky is known primarily as an intellectual and historian, though he was also a Unionist MP (1895–1902). His *The Leaders of Public Opinion in Ireland* (1861) exerted considerable influence. A fine statue of Lecky graces the front quadrangle of TC.

Lemass Seán Francis (1899–1971). Born in Ballybrack, Co. Dublin, and educated at O'Connell CBS, he joined the Irish Volunteers (1913) and fought in the General Post Office during the Easter Rising and later in the IRA during the Anglo-Irish War. He opposed the Treaty. Elected to Dáil Éireann in 1925, he declined to take his seat. He was a founder of Fianna Fáil (1926) and took his seat as TD (1927–69), serving as Minister of Industry and Commerce (1932–9, 1941–8, 1951, 1957–9), Minister of Supplies (1939–45), Tánaiste (1945–8, 1951–4, 1957–9) and Taoiseach (1959–66). His time as Taoiseach saw Ireland depart from protectionism and begin economic reform; also, relations with Northern Ireland softened.

Lester Seán (John Ernest) (1888–1959). Born in Woodburn, Carrickfergus, Co. Antrim, and educated at Methodist College Belfast, he was a journalist and active in the national movement. He accepted the Treaty. Lester joined the Department of External Affairs (1922), becoming Irish representative to the League of Nations (1929), League High Commissioner at Danzig (1934), and Secretary-General (1940–7).

Lever Charles James (1806–72). Born in Dublin and educated at private schools, TC, Gottingen and Louvain, he practised medicine in several places in Ireland. Lever settled in Florence (1847) and was British consul in various places. He was a prolific author, including *Charles O'Malley* (1841), and his writings were very popular for many years.

Londonderry 6th Marquess of (succeeded 1884) (Charles Stewart Vane-Tempest-Stewart) (1852–1915). Born in London and educated at Eton and Oxford, he was a Conservative MP (1878–84), Lord Lieutenant (1886–9) and held cabinet office (1900–5). Londonderry was among the most influential Irish Unionists.

Londonderry 7th Marquess of (succeeded 1915) (Charles Stewart Henry Vane-Tempest-Stewart) (1878–1949). Born in London and educated at Eton and Sandhurst, Londonderry's political career straddled Ireland and England, being the only person to serve in both the Northern Ireland and British cabinets, respectively as Minister of Education and Leader of the

Senate (1921–6), and as Secretary of State for Air (1931–5) and Lord Privy Seal (1935). In Ireland he was noted for his progressive Unionism.

Logue Cardinal Michael (created 1893) (1840–1924). Born in Carrigart, Co. Donegal, and educated at hedge school and private school at Buncrana and Maynooth, he was ordained (1866), becoming professor of dogmatic theology at the Irish College, Paris (1866–74), followed by a succession of posts at Maynooth (1874–8). Logue succeeded as Bishop of Raphoe (1879–87) and Archbishop of Armagh and Primate of All Ireland (1887–1924). He supported the Treaty.

Long Walter (Viscount Long of Wraxall, created 1921) (1854–1924). Born in Bath and educated at a private school, Harrow and Oxford, he was an MP (1880–1924; South Co. Dublin 1906–10). A Conservative with close ties to southern Irish landowners, Long was Chief Secretary (March–December 1905), chairman of the Irish Unionist Party (1906–10) and its vice-chairman (1910–21). Long founded the Union Defence League (1907) and chaired the committee (1919) charged with drawing up a plan for Irish self-government. He authored *My Memories* (1923).

Lover Samuel (1797–1868). Born in Dublin and educated privately, he was a painter elected to the RHA (1828) but forced to abandon this work because of failing eyesight. He was a founder of the *Dublin University Magazine.* Lover moved to London where he took up literature and also composed more than 300 songs. He authored *Rory O'Moore* (1836).

Luby Tomas Clarke (1821–1901). Born in Dublin to a Church of Ireland cleric and educated there at Mr Murphy's School and TC, he first supported the Repeal Association, then joined Young Ireland and subsequently belonged to the Irish Confederation before being a founder of the IRB (1856). He was sentenced to 20 years' imprisonment (1865) but released (1871). Luby settled in New York where he joined Clan na Gael and was a trustee of the Skirmishing Funds. He opposed the New Departure and the Land League. He authored *The Lives and Times of Illustrious and Representative Irishmen* (1878).

Lynch John (Jack) (1917–1999). Born in Cork and educated at North Monastery, Cork CBS, UCC and the King's Inns, he was called to the bar (1945) and joined the civil service (1936). A renown hurler, he was a TD (1948–81), Minister for the Gaeltacht (1957), Minister of Education (1957–9), Minister of Industry and Commerce (1959–65), Minister of Finance (1965–6), Taoiseach (1966–73, 1977–9) and leader of Fianna Fáil (1966–79). Lynch led his party to its largest majority ever in the Dáil (1977), but two years later was forced to step down after a mutiny of backbenchers masterminded by Charles Haughey.

Lynn Kathleen (1874–1955). Born at Mullafarry, near Killala, Co. Mayo, to a unionist family, she studied at Alexandra College and the Royal College of Surgeons. In 1909 she became a Fellow of the Royal College of Physicians in Ireland. An active feminist, nationalist and socialist, she founded St Ultan's

Hospital for infants (1919), a pioneering hospital that catered for Dublin's poor. In 1923 she was elected to the Dáil, but abstained.

Lyons Francis Stewart Leland (1923–83). Born in Londonderry and educated at St Stephen's School, Tonbridge Wells School, the High School, Dublin, and TC, he was a prolific historian, professor at the University of Kent (1964–74) and Provost of Trinity College (1974–81). He authored *Ireland Since the Famine* (1971).

McAleese Mary Patricia (1951–). Born in Belfast and educated at St Dominic's High School, Belfast, and QUB, she was called to the Northern Ireland bar (1974) and entered King's Inns (1978). She was professor at Trinity College (1975–9, 1981–7), before becoming director of the Institute of Legal Studies at QUB (1987) and Pro-Vice-Chancellor (1994). She was elected President of the Republic (1997–).

McAliskey (Josephine) Bernadette (Bernadette Devlin) (1947–). Born in Tyrone and educated at the St Patrick's Girls' Academy, Dungannon, and QUB, she was an MP (1969–74), and at the time of her election the youngest ever member of the House of Commons. She is chair of the Independent Socialist Party of Ireland and authored *The Price of My Soul* (1969).

MacArdle Dorothy (1869–1958). Born in Dundalk, MacArdle was educated at Alexandra College, where she later taught, and at UCD. Active in the Gaelic League and Sinn Féin, she supported the Easter Rising and opposed the Treaty. Between 1939 and 1945 she took a special interest in the refugee question and was president of the Irish Association of Civil Liberties (1951). MacArdle wrote numerous plays, though her best-known work is *The Irish Republic* (1937).

McAteer Eddie (1914–1986). Born in Coatbridge, Scotland, his family moved to Londonderry (1916) where he was educated at St Columb's College. He sat in the Northern Ireland parliament (1945–69), taking the initiative in founding the Anti-Partition League. McAteer was leader of the Nationalist Party (1953–69) and accepted the role of official opposition (1965–8).

McAuley Catherine (Mother) (1778–1841). Born in Glasnevin, Dublin, and raised as a Protestant, she opened her first school (1827) and took vows (1829), forming the Sisters of Mercy (1831), which received papal approval (1835) and confirmation (1841).

MacBride Major John (1865 – 5 May 1916, executed). Born in Westport, Co. Mayo, he briefly belonged to the IRB in the 1880s. Subsequently a member of the Gaelic League and the Celtic Literary Society, he played a significant part in the 1898 centenary celebrations. MacBride was an organiser of the Irish Brigade and served with it in the Boer War. In 1903 he married Maud Gonne. MacBride became vice-president of Cumann na nGaedheal, a member of the National Council, of Sinn Féin and of the IRB, of which he was on the Supreme Council. He was executed for his part in the Easter Rising.

MacBride Seán (1904–1988). Born in Normandy, son of Maud Gonne and Major John MacBride, he was educated at St Louis de Gonzaga, Paris, Mount St Benedict's, Gorey, Wexford, and UCD. He fought with the IRA during the Anglo-Irish War and as an opponent of the Treaty; he was on the republican side in the Civil War. MacBride was a prominent member of Comhairle na Poblachta, organised the first convention of Saor Éire (1931) and was IRA Chief of Staff (1936–8). Called to the bar (1937) and the inner bar (1943), he was a prominent advocate. He founded Clann na Poblachta (1946), was a TD (1947–57) and served as Minister for External Affairs (1948–51). In later years he was active in defence of human rights, being secretary-general of the International Commission of Jurists (1963–71), a founder of Amnesty International and its chairman (1961–74), president of the International Peace Bureau (1974), a member of the Council of Minorities' Rights Group, Irish representative to the Council of Europe Assembly and United Nations commissioner to Namibia (1974–6). He was awarded the Nobel Peace Prize (1977) and the Lenin Peace Prize (1978).

McCabe Cardinal Edward (created 1882) (1816–85). Born in Dublin and educated at Fr Doyle's School on the Quays and Maynooth, he was ordained (1838), becoming Archbishop of Dublin and Primate of Ireland (1879–85). He was cool to the Irish Party, especially when it fell under the chairmanship of Charles Stewart Parnell and had little sympathy for the Land League.

McCarthy Justin (1830–1912). Born near Cork and educated locally, he was a journalist on the *Cork Examiner* (1848–52) and then worked on various English newspapers, most especially the *Morning Star* (1860–8) and the *Daily News* after 1870. McCarthy's first novel was published in 1866 and he remained a prolific writer throughout his life. *A History of Our Own Times* was initially published in 1879 and went through numerous subsequent editions. He was an MP (1879–1900), becoming vice-chairman of the Irish Party (December 1880) and chairman of the anti-Parnellites (December 1890 – February 1896).

McCormack John (created Count by the Pope, 1928) (1884–1945). Born in Athlone and educated at Summerhill College, Sligo, he was a tenor who appeared widely. He became an American citizen (1919) and during the 1930s made appearances in films.

MacDonnell Sir Antony Patrick (knighted 1893) (1st Baron MacDonnell of Swinford, created 1908) (1844–1925). Born in Shragh, Co. Mayo, and educated at Summerhill College, Sligo, and the QCG, he entered the Indian Civil Service (1864–1901), was Lieutenant Governor of the United Provinces (1895–1901) and appointed Under-Secretary of the Irish Office (1902–8). A Catholic and brother of an Irish Party MP, MacDonnell was vested with unusual authority for an Under-Secretary. He was a member of the Irish Convention (1917–18) but declined a seat in the Free State Senate (1922).

MacEntee Seán (1889–1984). Born in Belfast, he was educated at St Malachy's College and Belfast Municipal College of Technology, training as

713

an electrical engineer. He joined the Irish Volunteers and participated in the Easter Rising for which he was sentenced to death but reprieved. Elected an MP (1918), he instead sat in Dáil Éireann (1919–22) but opposed the Treaty and was subsequently a founder of Fianna Fáil (1926), TD (1927–69), Minister for Finance (1932–9, 1951–4), Minister for Industry and Commerce (1939–47), Minister for Health and Social Welfare (1957–65) and Tánaiste (1959–65). He authored *Poems* (1918).

MacEoin General Seán (1894–1973). Born in Bunlahy, Granard, Co. Longford, he was educated at Ballinalae NS. MacEoin joined the Irish Volunteers, becoming a company commander (1914). During the Anglo-Irish War he was made a general. He accepted the Treaty and was Chief of Staff of the Free State army (1928–9), TD (1921–3, 1929–65), Minister for Justice (1948–51) and Minister for Defence (1951, 1954–7), standing unsuccessfully for President (1945 and 1959).

McGee Thomas D'Arcy (1825 – 7 April 1868, assassinated). Born at Carlingford, Co. Louth, and educated in Wexford, he was active in Young Ireland and the Irish Confederation. He founded Irish newspapers in New York and Boston, moving to Montreal in 1857. He played a prominent role in Canadian politics, serving as president of the Council of the Legislative Assembly (1862, 1864) and Minister for Agriculture and Emigration (1867). Following his denunciation of the Fenian raids on Canada he was assassinated in Ottawa.

McGill Patrick (1891–1963). Born in Mass, Co. Donegal, into an impoverished farming family, McGill grew up in Glenties, on which he based the 'Glenmornan' of his fiction. He was sent to a hiring fair at the age of 12 and at 14 he left to work on the potato fields in Scotland, then on railways and construction sites, spending some time as a tramp, experiences on which he based several of his novels. He became a poet and novelist and worked as a reporter for the *Daily Express* in London. Among his novels is *Children of the Dead End* (1914). In 1981 a Patrick McGill summer school was launched in Glenties.

MacGonigal Maurice (1900–79). Born in Dublin and educated at the Synge St CBS, Metropolitan School of Art, Dublin, and in the Netherlands, he joined the IRA and was interned before the Treaty. Noted as a landscape artist, he was Keeper of the RHA (1936–9, 1950–61), professor of painting (1947–78) and president of the RHA (1962–77).

McGuinness Martin (1950–). Born in Londonderry and educated at CBS Technical College, he was a member of the IRA delegation which met the British government (1972). He was elected as a Sinn Féin member of the Northern Ireland Assembly (1982–6), an MP (1997–) and a member of the Northern Ireland Assembly (1998–). Along with Gerry Adams, he became Sinn Féin's most prominent spokesperson in the development of his party's peace strategy in the 1990s. During the negotiations that led to the Good

Friday Agreement (April 1998), he was Sinn Féin's chief negotiator and Minister for Education in the power-sharing Executive (1999–2001).

MacHale John (1791–1881). Born in Tobbernavine, Tirawley, Co. Mayo, and educated at a hedge school and Maynooth, where he taught after his ordination (1814–25). He was appointed coadjutor Bishop of Killala, thus becoming the first prelate since the Reformation to be educated entirely in Ireland. He became Archbishop of Tuam (1834–81). MacHale supported Catholic Emancipation, repudiated the system of National Education (1831), endorsed the Repeal Association, and was opposed to Young Ireland and later the Land League.

MacNeill Eoin (1867–1945). Born at Glenarm, Co. Antrim, and educated at St Malachy's College, Belfast, and the Royal University. He became an authority on Old Irish and was a founder of the Gaelic League (1893) of which he was vice-president. MacNeill was appointed professor of early and medieval Irish history at UCD (1909). He helped found the Irish Volunteers (1913) and was its Chief of Staff. During the Easter Rising he countermanded the orders for mobilisation of the Irish Volunteers and was blamed for the resulting confusion. Elected an MP (1918), he instead sat in Dáil Éireann (1919–27), serving as Minister for Finance (1919) and Minister for Industries (1919–21). MacNeill supported the Treaty; he was Minster without Portfolio (January–August 1922), Minister for Education (1922–5) and represented the Free State on the Boundary Commission (1924–5), but resigned following the revelation published in the *Morning Post* (7 November 1925) that the boundary would remain substantially unaltered. He authored *Phases of Irish History* (1919).

MacNeill James (1869–1938). Born in Glenarm, Co. Antrim, a brother of Eoin MacNeill, and educated at Belvedere and Blackrock Colleges and Cambridge, he joined the Indian Civil Service (1890). Later MacNeill was chairman of the Dublin County Council (1922) and a member of the committee which drafted the Constitution of 1922. He was High Commissioner of the Free State (1923–8) and then Governor-General (1928–32).

MacNeill John Gordon Swift (1849–1926). Born in Dublin, son of a Church of Ireland cleric, and educated at TC and Oxford, he was called to the bar (1876), became a QC (1893) and held the posts of professor of criminal law, King's Inns (1882–8) and professor of constitutional law, UCD (1909–). He was an Irish Party MP (1887–1918), opposing Charles Stewart Parnell in December 1890. He authored *What I Have Seen and Heard* (1925).

McQuaid John Charles (1895–1973). Born in Cootehill, Co. Cavan, and educated at St Patrick's School, Cavan, Blackrock and CWC and UCD, he was ordained in the Holy Ghost order (1924) and was president of Blackrock College (1931–9). He was an extremely conservative Archbishop of Dublin (1940–72).

MacRory Cardinal Joseph (created 1929) (1861–1945). Born in Ballygawley, Co. Tyrone, and educated in St Patrick's Seminary, Armagh, and Maynooth where he was ordained (1885) and later vice-president (1909), MacRory was Bishop of Down and Connor (1915–28) and Archbishop of Armagh and Primate of All Ireland (1928–45).

MacSwiney Terence J. (1880 – 24 October 1920, on hunger strike). Born in Cork and educated at North Monastery, Cork CBS and UCC, he was a member of the Gaelic League and the Irish Volunteers. He was elected as a Sinn Féin MP (1918) but sat instead in Dáil Éireann (1919–20). MacSwiney was Lord Mayor of Cork (March 1920) when he died on hunger strike in Brixton Prison (London). He authored *Principles of Freedom* (1921).

Maguire John Francis (1815–72). Born in Cork and educated locally, he was a follower of Daniel O'Connell. Maguire founded the *Cork Examiner* (1841) to support O'Connellite views and was called to the bar (1843). He was an MP (1852–72) and Lord Mayor of Cork (1853, 1862, 1863 and 1864). He authored *The Irish in America* (1868).

Mahaffy Sir John Penland (knighted 1918) (1839–1919). Born in Vevey, Switzerland, of Irish parents and educated at home in Donegal and TC, he was ordained in the Church of Ireland (1864), becoming a Fellow of the College the same year and then Senior Fellow (1899). He was president of the RIA (1911–16) and Provost of Trinity College (1914–10). Mahaffy was a member of the Irish Convention (1917–18). He authored *History of Classical Greek Literature* (1880).

Markievicz Countess (Constance Gore-Booth) (1868–1927). Born in Lissadell House, Co. Sligo, she was educated privately and studied art at the Slade School and in Paris. She married Casimir Markievicz (1900) but they soon separated. She subscribed to Sinn Féin and founded Fianna Éireann (1909). Markievicz was active in the suffragette movement, supported the workers during the Dublin Lockout (1913) and joined the Irish Citizen Army. She was sentenced to death for her participation in the Easter Rising, but this was commuted and she was released in the general amnesty (January 1917). Countess Markievicz was elected a Sinn Féin MP (1918), the first woman returned to the House of Commons, but instead sat in Dáil Éireann (1919–22). She opposed the Treaty and was imprisoned for aiding republican forces during the Civil War. Though elected again (1923), she refused to take her seat.

Martin John (1812–75). Born Loughorne near Newry, Co. Down, and educated in Newry and TC, Martin, an Ulster Presbyterian, was a Young Irelander in the 1840s, being transported to Tasmania (1849–54) for his role in the Irish Confederation and then returned to Ireland (1856). He started the National League of Ireland (1864) to advance self-government ideas and was a founder of the Home Government Association (1870). He was an MP (1871–5) and secretary of the Home Rule League (1873–5). John Mitchel was his brother-in-law.

Martin Richard (1754–1834). Born in Dublin and educated at Harrow and Cambridge, he was called to the bar (1781), practising on the Connaught circuit. Martin owned around 200,000 acres in Connemara. He sat in the Irish House of Commons (1776–83, 1798–1800), supporting the Act of Union in 1800, then was an MP at Westminster (1801–26). Widely known as 'Humanity Dick', he was a founder of the Royal Society for the Prevention of Cruelty to Animals (1824).

Martin Violet Florence (Martin Ross) (1862–1915). Born at Ross House, Co. Galway, and educated at Alexandra College, Dublin, she co-authored numerous books with her cousin, Edith Ann Oenone Somerville, including *Some Experiences of an Irish R.M.* (1899).

Martyn Edward (1859–1924). Born at Masonbrook, Co. Galway, and educated at Belvedere College, Beaumont, Windsor and Oxford, he supported the Gaelic League, was a founder of the Irish Literary Theatre (1899), a member of the board of the Abbey Theatre, from which he withdrew in 1914, and president of Sinn Féin (1905–8). He authored *The Placehunter* (1902).

Mathew Revd Theobald (1790–1856). Born in Thomastown Castle, Cashel, Co. Tipperary, and educated at Maynooth before ordination as a Capuchin priest (1814). In 1833 he began a temperance crusade. In 1849 he took his campaign to the United States.

Maxwell Constantia Elizabeth (1886–1962). Born in Dublin and educated at St Leonard's School, TC, and Bedford College, University of London, she was successively lecturer in history (1909–39), professor of economic history (1939–45) and professor of modern history (1945–51). She was the first female professor in TC. Among her studies is *Dublin Under the Georges* (1936).

Mayo 6th Earl of (succeeded 1868) (Richard Southwell Bourke, Lord Naas, succeeded 1849) (1822 – 8 February 1872, assassinated in India). Born in Dublin and educated privately and at TC, he was a Conservative MP (1847–68), Chief Secretary (1852–3, 1858–9, 1866–8). He was Viceroy of India (1869–72) when he was killed.

Meagher Thomas Francis (1822–67). Born in Waterford and educated at CWC, he supported Young Ireland and helped found the Irish Confederation. For his part in the rising of 1848 he was transported to Tasmania from where he escaped (1852) and settled in the United States. During the American Civil War he was a brigadier general (subsequently lieutenant general) of the New York Irish Brigade and then (1865–6) acting governor of Montana when he was killed.

Mellows Liam (1892 – 8 December 1922, by firing squad). Born in Ashton-under-Lyme, Cheshire, and reared near Inch, Co. Wexford, he was educated at Portobello and the Royal Hibernian Military School. He joined the IRB (1912) and became a member of the Provisional Committee of the Irish Volunteers (1913). After the Easter Rising he fled to New York, returning to Ireland (1921) and becoming active in the IRA. He was elected an MP

(1918), but instead sat in Dáil Éireann (1919–22). He opposed the Treaty. He participated in the seizure of the Four Courts (June 1922), after which he was imprisoned. He was executed by the Provisional Government in reprisal for the assassination of Seán Hales.

Midgley Harry (1893–1957). He served in the army (1914–18) and was a trade union organiser (1919–42) and a Northern Ireland Labour Party MP in the Northern Ireland parliament (1933–8, 1941–57), breaking with the party (1942) and founding the Commonwealth Labour Party. He served as Minister for Public Security (1943–4). After joining the Ulster Unionist Party (1947) he became Minister for Labour (1944–5) and Minister for Education (1952–7). He was an active member of the Orange Order.

Mitchel John B. (1815–1875). Born in Dungiven, Co. Londonderry, son of a Presbyterian minister, and educated in Newry and TC, he joined the Repeal Association (1843) but seceded along with other members of Young Ireland and joined the Irish Confederation (1847). He was convicted (1848) and sentenced to 14 years' transportation to Tasmania from where he escaped (1853), thereafter living in the United States. Mitchel was revered in radical national circles. He stood and was twice elected MP for Tipperary (1875), but his return was declared invalid as an undischarged convict. His best-known publication is *Jail Journal* (1854).

Molyneaux James Henry (Baron Molyneaux of Killead, created 1997) (1920–). Born in Killead, Co. Antrim, and educated at Aldergrove School, Co. Antrim, he served in the Royal Air Force (1941–6). Molyneaux was deputy grand master of the Orange Order (1971), MP (1970–97) and leader of the Ulster Unionist Party (1974–95).

Montgomery Revd Henry (1788–1865). Born in Killead, Co. Antrim, and educated privately and at Glasgow College, he was ordained in the Presbyterian ministry (1809). Montgomery led the Arian secessionists in their withdrawal from the Synod of Ulster; the new Remonstrant Synod held its first meeting (May 1830).

Moody Theodore William (1907–84). Born in Belfast and educated at RBAI, QUB and King's College, University of London, he co-founded and served as joint editor of *Irish Historical Studies* (1938–77), also holding the Erasmus Smith chair in history, TC (1940–77). He was elected a member of the RIA (1940). His publications include *Davitt and Irish Revolution, 1848–82* (1981).

Moore George Augustus (1852–1933). Novelist and playwright, son of George Henry Moore. Born at Moore Hall, Co. Mayo, he was educated at Oscott College and trained as a painter in Paris before turning to writing. He was influenced by the literary realism of Zola, which he brought to Irish subjects in several of his works. He left Ireland in 1911 and in 1924 Moore Hall was burned down. Among his novels is *A Drama in Muslin* (1886).

Moore George Henry (1811–70). Born at Moore Hall, Co. Mayo, he was educated at Oscott College, Birmingham and Cambridge. As an MP

(1847–57, 1868–70) he supported tenant right, was a founder of the Catholic Defence Association and leader of the Irish Brigade. He participated in the formation of the Independent Irish Party. He was defeated (1857) but returned to the House of Commons (1868).

Moore Thomas (1779–1852). Born in Dublin and educated at Samuel White Academy, TC and the Middle Temple (London), he left Ireland (1799) and resided principally abroad. He was a successful author, composer and poet who supported Catholic Emancipation, and Daniel O'Connell generally, though he declined to stand for the House of Commons as a Repealer. He authored *Memoirs of Captain Rock* (1824).

Moran David Patrick (1872–1936). Born in Waterford and educated at Castleknock College, Dublin, he was active in the Gaelic League and Irish Literary Society in London where he lived (1888–99). On returning to Ireland (1898) he edited the *New Ireland Review* and then founded the *Leader* (1900). His *Philosophy of Irish Ireland* (1905) articulated the ideas of the more extreme Gaelic revivalists.

Moriarty David (1814–77). Born in Kilcaragh, Co. Kerry, and educated in France and Maynooth where he was ordained (1839), he was vice-president of the Irish College, Paris, and then president of All-Hallows, Drumcondra (1845–54), becoming coadjutor Bishop of Kerry (1854) and Bishop (1856–77). Moriarty was a renowned critic of Fenianism.

Mulcahy General Richard James (1886–1971). Born in Waterford and educated at Mount Sion CBS, he was a member of the Gaelic League and joined the Irish Volunteers (1913). He participated in the Easter Rising, was Chief of Staff of the IRA and elected an MP (1918), but instead sat in Dáil Éireann (1919–37, 1938–43, 1944–61), serving as Minster for Defence (1919, 1923–4), Minister for Local Government (1927–32), Minister for Education (1948–51, 1954–7) and a Senator (1943–4). A supporter of the Treaty, he was Chief of Staff of the National Army. Prominent in the Blueshirt movement, he was a founder of Fine Gael (1933), party leader (1944–59) and chairman of the Gaeltacht Commission (1925–6).

Murphy William Martin (1844–1919). Born in Bantry, Co. Cork, and educated at Belvedere College, he was an MP (1885–92) and a close ally of T. M. Healy. Owner of Clery's department store and Independent Newspapers (1905), Murphy as president of the Dublin Chamber of Commerce formed the Employers' Federation to oppose the Irish Transport and General Workers' Union led by James Larkin. His actions led to the Dublin Lockout (1913). During the First World War he promoted military recruitment.

Murray Daniel (1768–1852). Born in Arklow, Co. Wexford, and educated in Dublin and at Irish College, Salamanca, where he was ordained (1792), Murray became coadjutor Bishop of Dublin (1809), president of Maynooth (1812–13) and Archbishop of Dublin (1823–52).

719

Napier Sir Joseph (knighted 1867) (1804–82). Born in Belfast and educated at RBAI, TC and Gray's Inn (London), he was called to the bar (1831) and became a QC (1844) and an MP (1848–58), serving as Attorney-General (1852–3) and Lord Chancellor (1858–9, 1868). Napier was a member of the Judicial Committee of the Privy Council (1868–81), president of the Historical Society (TC) (1854–82) and vice-chancellor of the University of Dublin (1867–82).

Norbury 1st Earl of (created 1827) (John Toler) (1745–1831). Born in Co. Tipperary and educated at TC, he was called to the bar (1770) and sat in the Irish parliament. A supporter of the Act of Union, Toler was Chief Justice of Common Pleas (1800–27) before being removed. He presided at the trial of Robert Emmet (1803).

Norton William (1900–63). Born in Dublin and educated locally, he was secretary of the Post Office Workers' Union (1924–57), TD (1926–7, 1932–63), leader of the Labour Party (1932–60), Minister for Social Welfare (1948–51), Minister for Industry and Commerce (1954–7) and Tánaiste (1948–51, 1954–7).

Ó Briain Art (O'Brien) (1872–1949). Born in London and educated at St Charles College, London, he qualified as a civil engineer. He joined the Gaelic League (1899) and was president of the London branch (1914–35). Ó Briain joined the Irish Volunteers, becoming president of the Sinn Féin Council of Great Britain (1916–23) and was co-founder of the Irish Self-Determination League of Great Britain, which he served as vice-president (1919–22) and president (1922–4). An opponent of the Treaty, he was imprisoned in Britain (1922–4). He was Irish Minister Plenipotentiary to France and Belgium (1935–9).

O'Brien James ('Bronterre') (1805–64). Born in Co. Longford and educated at Edgeworthstown School, TC and Gray's Inn, London, he was a leading radical, being imprisoned in 1840–1, and a major figure in the Chartist movement.

O'Brien Peter (Baron, created 1900; knighted 1891) (alias 'Peter the Packer') (1842–1914). Born in Ballynalacken, Co. Clare, and educated at CWC and TC, he was called to the bar (1865) and became a QC (1880) and an effective Crown Counsel during the land agitation of the early 1880s for which he earned his nationalist-inspired appellation for skill in jury selection. O'Brien was Solicitor-General (1887–8), Attorney-General (1888–9) and Lord Chief Justice (1889–1913).

O'Brien Richard Barry (1847–1918). Born in Kilrush, Co. Clare, and educated at the Catholic University, he was called to the bar (1874) but worked mainly as a journalist, editing the *Speaker*. He belonged to the London branch of the Gaelic League, serving as its chairman (1892–1906) and president (1906–11) and was also president of the Irish Literary Society in London. He authored *The Life of Charles Stewart Parnell* (2 vols., 1898).

O'Brien William (1852–1928). Born in Mallow, Co. Cork, and though a Catholic educated at the Church of Ireland Cloyne Diocesan School and QCC, he was a journalist and author who took a vigorous role in the Land League and was editor of *United Ireland* at its inception in 1881. Along with John Dillon, he was the principal leader of the Plan of Campaign (1886). O'Brien was in and out of parliament several times (1883–6, 1887–95, 1900–18), founding the United Irish League (1898). O'Brien and Dillon were close associates and friends but fell out in the aftermath of the Wyndham land purchase legislation (1903), becoming bitter enemies subsequently. O'Brien became the leading nationalist advocate of conciliation of Unionists, founding the All-for-Ireland League (1910). He authored *The Downfall of Parliamentarianism* (1918).

O'Brien William (1881–1968). Born near Clonakilty, Co. Cork, and educated in CBS at Dungarvan and Carrick-on-Suir, he joined the Irish Socialist Republican Party (1898) founded by James Connelly, becoming its financial secretary and treasurer. He was a founder of the Irish Transport and General Workers Union (1909), a TD (1922–3, 1927 and 1937–8) and a key figure in the Labour Party, being financial secretary (1931–9) and chairman of its administrative council (1939–41). O'Brien was an ardent opponent first of James Larkin and then of Larkin's son's attempts to regain control over the ITGWU of which he was general secretary for 22 years. He was president of the Trade Union Congress (1913, 1918, 1925, 1941).

O'Brien William Smith (1803–64). Born Dromoland Castle, Co. Clare, into a Protestant landowning family and educated at Harrow and Cambridge, he was an MP (1828–31; 1835–49), supporting the Catholic Association, the fight against tithes and Daniel O'Connell's Anti-Tory Association (1835). After joining the Repeal Association (October 1843), his relationship with O'Connell cooled and he left it (1846). Smith O'Brien acted as parliamentary spokesman for Young Ireland and accepted the leadership of the Irish Confederation (1847). For his leadership of the rising of 1848, he was condemned to death, a sentence commuted to transportation to Tasmania where O'Brien remained until being released (1854). He returned to Ireland (1856) but took no further substantial part in politics.

O'Casey Seán (John Casey) (1880–1964). Born into a Dublin Protestant family, he was largely self-educated. He joined the Gaelic League, the labour movement, the Irish Citizen Army and the IRB. His trilogy, *The Shadow of a Gunman* (1923), *Juno and the Paycock* (1924) and *The Plough and the Stars* (1926) were first produced at the Abbey Theatre. He went to England (1926), writing many further but less successful plays.

O'Connell Daniel (1775–1847). Born Carhen, near Cahirciveen, Co. Kerry, and educated at St Omer and Douai in France and Lincoln's Inn, London, he was called to the bar (1798). He was at the forefront in the campaign for Catholic Emancipation, winning the Co. Clare parliamentary by-election (1828) which forced the issue upon the Conservative ministry and then held the seat (1829–47). His alliance with the Whigs and Radicals after 1835 was a key component of Westminster politics. He was the first Catholic Lord Mayor of Dublin (1841–2) in the modern era. On 15 April 1841 he launched the Repeal Association which was the last great cause of his career.

O'Connell John (1810–58). Born in Dublin, son of Daniel O'Connell, and educated at CWC, TC and King's Inns, he was called to the bar (1837). He was an MP (1832–57) and his father's chief aid.

O'Connell Thomas J. (1882–1969). Born in Bekan, Co. Mayo, and educated at Bekan NS and at St Patrick's College, Drumcondra, he taught in a National School (1902–16), becoming general secretary of the Irish National Teachers' Organisation (1916–48), Labour TD (1922–32) and party leader (1927–32). O'Connell was a member of the Senate (1941–4, 1948–51, 1954–7) and president of the Trade Union Congress (1929–30).

O'Connor Feargus (1794–1855). Born in Connorville, Co. Cork, and educated at Portarlington Grammar School, TC and Gray's Inn (London), he was a Repeal MP (1832–5), but soon quarrelled with Daniel O'Connell and lost his seat (1835) on the grounds that he lacked the necessary property to qualify for membership in the House of Commons, though he sat again for Nottingham (1847–52). O'Connor's newspaper, the *Northern Star* (1837), was a leading radical periodical and he was imprisoned (1841–2) as a consequence of its championship of advanced radical causes. He played a leading part in the Chartist movement.

O'Connor Frank (Michael O'Donovan) (1903–66). Born in Cork, he was educated at St Patrick's NS and the CBS there. After supporting the republicans during the Civil War, he spent many years as a librarian (1925–38). His writings began to be published in the early 1930s and in the ensuing years he received international acclaim and was a director of the Abbey Theatre. He was elected to the Irish Academy of Letters (1941). O'Connor authored *The Big Fellow* (1937).

O'Connor Thomas Power (T. P.) (1849–1929). Born in Athlone and educated at the College of the Immaculate Conception there and the QCG, he moved to London (1870), establishing himself as a journalist. He was an MP (1880–1929), initially as a supporter of Charles Stewart Parnell, but later siding with the anti-Parnellites (1890). O'Connor was president of Irish nationalist political organisations in Great Britain continuously from 1883 and for many years he was 'father of the House of Commons'. A close friend and supporter of John Dillon, O'Connor also was on good terms with Sir Henry Campbell-Bannerman and David Lloyd George. He authored *Memoirs of an Old Parliamentarian* (2 vols, 1929).

Ó Dálaigh Cearbhall (1911–77). Born in Bray, Co. Wicklow, and educated at Scoil na Leanbh, Ring, Waterford, Synge St CBS, UCD and King's Inns, he was called to the bar (1934) and to the inner bar (1945). He served as Attorney-General (1946–8, 1951–3) before becoming judge of the Supreme

Court (1953) and Chief Justice and President (1961–72). He was Irish representative at the European Court of Justice (1972) and president of the First Chamber (1973–4). Returned unopposed to be President of the Republic of Ireland (1974), he resigned in November 1976.

O'Donnell Cardinal Patrick (created 1925) (1856–1927). Born in Kilraine near Glenties, Co. Donegal, and educated at the local NS, at Letterkenny and Maynooth, he was ordained (1880), becoming Bishop of Raphoe (1888–1922), during which time he presided over the Irish Race Convention (1896) and the National Convention (1900). He was the chief clerical representative at the Irish Convention (1917–18), breaking with John Redmond on the question of Ireland's financial autonomy under home rule. He effectively forced Redmond to retreat on this question. O'Donnell became coadjutor of the Archbishopric of Armagh (1922–4) and then succeeded as Archbishop of Armagh and Primate of All Ireland (1924–7).

O'Donnell Peadar (1893–1986). Born in Meenmore, Dungloe, Co. Donegal, and educated at a NS and St Patrick's College, Drumcondra, he became a noted socialist republican and writer. He joined the IRA (1920) and was active during the Anglo-Irish War and the Civil War. Opposing the Treaty, O'Donnell served as a member of the IRA executive (1924–34). Elected a TD (1923–7), he did not take his seat. O'Donnell was a key figure in Saor Éire (1931) and the Republican Congress (1934). He edited the *Bell* (1946–54) and authored *There Will Be Another Day* (1963).

O'Duffy General Eoin (1892–1944). Born near Castleblayney, Co. Monaghan, and educated locally, he worked as an engineer and architect until becoming an auctioneer and valuer. Joining the IRA (1920), he was part of the headquarters staff during the Anglo-Irish War and Director of Organisation (1921). O'Duffy was a TD (1921–2), supporting the Treaty, and became Assistant Chief of Staff in the National Army (January 1922). In September 1922 he was chosen to command the Gárda Siochána. O'Duffy was dismissed by the Fianna Fáil government (1933) and soon took command of the Army Comrades Association (1933) (Blueshirts), an organisation declared illegal (August 1933). In September 1933 he became the first president of Fine Gael, resigning in August 1934 in order to form the National Corporate Party. In 1936 he led a small contingent to Spain in support of General Franco.

O'Dwyer Edward (1842–1917). Born in Holycross, Co. Tipperary, and educated at Maynooth where he was ordained (1867), he was Bishop of Limerick (1886–1917). A frequent critic of the Irish Party, O'Dwyer called for Ireland to remain neutral during the First World War. He was the first member of the Hierarchy to defend the action of the rebels after the Easter Rising.

O'Faolain Seán (born John Whelan) (1900–91). Born in Cork and educated at a NS, Presentation Brothers' College, UCC and Harvard, he joined the IRA during the Anglo-Irish War and after rejecting the Treaty he became involved on the republican side in the Civil War. O'Faolain was a founder of the Irish Academy of Letters (1933) and the *Bell*, which he edited (1940–6). He was director of the Arts Council (1956–9). A prolific writer, many of his works have been influential, including *King of the Beggars* (1938).

Ó Fiaich Cardinal Tomás (created 1979) (1923–1990). Born in Cullyhanna, near Crossmaglen, Co. Armagh, and educated at Cregganduff Public Element-ary School, St Patrick's College, Armagh, St Peter's College, Wexford, UCD, Maynooth and the Catholic University, Louvain, he was ordained (1948) and served in various posts at Maynooth (1953–77), including president (1974–7), until becoming Archbishop of Armagh and Primate of All Ireland (1977–90). He authored *Irish Cultural Influence in Europe* (1966).

O'Flaherty Liam (1896–1984). Born in the Aran Islands and educated at an NS, Rockwell College, Co. Tipperary, Blackrock College and UCD, he served in the British army (1915–17), then supported the IRA during the Anglo-Irish War and was a founder member of the Communist Party of Ireland (1922). His many writings include *The Informer* (1925).

O'Grady Standish James (1846–1928). Born son of Viscount Guillamore at Castletown, Berehaven, Co. Cork, and educated at Tipperary Grammar School and TC, he was called to the bar (1872) but devoted himself to the study of old Irish myths and legends, editing *All-Ireland Review* (1900–6). His works influenced the later Irish literary revival and include *Finn and His Companions* (1892).

O'Hagan Thomas (Baron, created 1870) (1812–85). Born in Belfast and educated at the RBAI, he was called to the bar (1836). He was Solicitor-General (1860–1), Attorney-General (1861–5) and an MP (1863–5), he be-came a judge in Common Pleas (1865–8). Subsequently he became the first Catholic to be appointed Lord Chancellor in the modern era (1868–74, 1880–1).

O'Higgins Kevin (1892 – 10 July 1927, assassinated). Born in Stradbally, Queen's Co. (Laois), he was educated at CWC, Maynooth and UCD and called to the bar (1923). He joined the Irish Volunteers and was elected an MP (1918) but instead sat in Dáil Éireann (1919–27). A supporter of the Treaty he was Minister for Economic Affairs (1922), Minister for Home Affairs (1922–7), Minister for Foreign Affairs (1927) and vice-president of the Executive Council (1922–7). As Minister for Home Affairs during the Civil War, he was closely associated with the strong security policies of the government, most controversially the executions of 77 IRA men. His assassi-nation by republicans in 1927 was retaliation for these security policies.

O'Kelly Seán Thomas (Seán T. Ó Ceallaigh) (1883–1966). Born in Dublin and educated at O'Connell CBS, he was employed in the National Library where he became a keen student of Irish, joining the Gaelic League (1898). He was a member of Sinn Féin (1905) and the Irish Volunteers, and sat on Dublin City Council (1906) for 26 years. During the Easter Rising he was a staff captain in the General Post Office. He was a republican envoy to the Paris Peace Conference. O'Kelly was elected an MP (1918) but instead sat in Dáil Éireann (1919–45), though refused to take his seat (1922–7). He rejected the Treaty and supported the republican side in the Civil War. A founder of Fianna Fáil (1926), he was Minister for Local Government and Public Heath (1932–9), vice-president of the Executive Council (1932–8), Minister for Finance (1939–45), Tánaiste (1937–45) and President of Éire/ Republic of Ireland (1945–59).

O'Leary John (1830–1907). Born in Tipperary and educated at Carlow College, QCC, QCG, TC and Paris, he took part in the rising of 1848 for which he was briefly imprisoned. He later joined the Fenian movement though refused to take the oath; at the request of James Stephens he edited the Fenian newspaper, the *Irish People* (1863–5). For this role he was imprisoned (1865–71). Until 1885 when O'Leary returned to Dublin he lived mainly in Paris. A supporter of Charles Stewart Parnell during the split in the Irish Party (1890), O'Leary was president of the Supreme Council of the Irish Republican Brotherhood (1885–1907) and was involved in the Gaelic revival. He wrote *Memories of Fenians and Fenianism* (2 vols, 1896).

O'Leary Michael (1936–). Born in Cork City and educated at Presentation College, Cork, UCD, Columbia University and King's Inns, he was called to the bar (1979). He was education officer in the Trades Union Congress (1962–5), TD for the Labour Party (1965–82), serving as Minister for Labour (1973–7), deputy leader of the Labour Party (1977–81), party leader (1981–2), Tánaiste and Minister for Industry and Energy (1981–2) and was a member of the European Parliament (1979–81). O'Leary resigned the Labour leadership in 1982 and joined Fine Gael, for whom he was a TD (1982–7).

O'Malley Ernest (Earnán) (1898–1957). Born in Castlebar, Co. Mayo, his family moved to Dublin (1906) where he was educated at O'Connell's Schools and UCD. He joined the Irish Volunteers and participated in the Easter Rising. During the Anglo-Irish War he was an IRA staff captain. The first divisional commander to reject the Treaty, O'Malley repudiated the Provisional Government, fighting for the anti-Treaty side in the Civil War. Though elected a TD (1923–7), he did not take his seat. Most of the following years were spent abroad until he returned to Ireland (1935). Elected to the Irish Academy of Letters (1947), he authored *On Another Man's Wound* (1936).

O'Neill Captain Terence (Lord O'Neill of the Maine, created 1970) (1914–1990). Born in Co. Antrim and educated at Eton, he was a captain in the Irish Guards (1939–45). O'Neill was an MP in the Northern Ireland parliament (1946–70), serving as Minister for Health (1948–52), Deputy Speaker (1953–6), Minister for Home Affairs (1956), Minister for Finance (1956–63) and Prime Minister (1963–9). In January 1965 he met the Taoiseach, Seán Lemass, an event that angered many Unionists, and despite his reforming style he was also faced by a civil rights movement demanding far greater action against discrimination than O'Neill contemplated.

O'Reilly John Boyle (1844–90). Born in Dowth Castle, Co. Louth, and educated privately, he spent several years in Preston (1858–63). He joined the IRB after returning to Ireland. For his efforts to recruit British soldiers into the Fenian movement he was sentenced to death (1866), but this was commuted to transportation to Western Australia for 20 years. He escaped to the United States (1869), where he became part-owner of the *Boston Pilot.* He supported the Clan na Gael but was a political moderate and perhaps best known as a poet. O'Reilly authored *Moondyne* (1879).

Orpen Sir William Newenham Montague (knighted 1918) (1878–1931). Born in Stillorgan, Co. Dublin, he studied at the Metropolitan School of Art, Dublin, and at the Slade School, London. He was elected to the RHA (1908) and to the Royal Academy (1921). He painted portraits of many well-known Irishmen and was the official war artist (1917–19). He authored *Stories of Old Ireland and Myself* (1924).

O'Shea Katharine (neé Wood) (1845–1921). Born in Rivenhall, Essex, she married Captain William Henry O'Shea (1867). Her liaison with Charles Stuart Parnell started at the beginning of the 1880s. After her divorce, she and Parnell married on 25 June 1891. Important elements in the relationship are divulged by her in *Charles Stewart Parnell: His Love Story and Political Life* (2 vols, 1914).

O'Shea Captain William Henry (1840–1905). Born in Dublin and educated at Mary's College, Oscott, and TC, he was the husband of Katharine O'Shea. O'Shea was elected MP (1880–5) when he narrowly lost his bid to be elected as a Liberal for a Liverpool constituency. Parnell then insisted that O'Shea be returned for the Galway borough by-election (10 February 1886). Capt. O'Shea declined to vote on the second reading of the Government of Ireland bill, walking out of the House of Commons. In December 1889 he filed for divorce, naming Parnell as co-respondent, and was granted a decree nisi on 17 November 1890, precipitating the crisis that split the Irish Party.

Paisley Revd Ian (1926–). Born in Armagh and educated at Sixmilesbridge and the Model School, Ballymena, he was ordained (1946) and became a co-founder of the Free Presbyterian Church of Ulster (1951). He has been an MP (1970–), a member of the European Parliament (1979–), an MP of the Northern Ireland parliament (1970–2), a member of the Northern Irish Assembly (1973–4), a member of the Northern Ireland Convention (1975–6), a member of the Northern Ireland Assembly (1982–6), a member of the Northern Ireland Forum (1996–8) and leader of the Democratic Unionist Party which he founded (1971–). Paisley came to prominence in the 1960s as the most outspoken critic of Terence O'Neill's reforming unionism. Since then he has been the most vocal and consistent advocate of hard-line unionism.

Palles Christopher (1831–1920). Born in Dublin and educated at CWC, TC and King's Inns, he was called to the bar (1853) and became a QC (1865), serving as Solicitor-General (1872) and Attorney-General (1872–4), before becoming Chief Baron of the Exchequer (1874–1916). He was also chairman of the Irish Board of Intermediate Education (1896–1910), Commissioner of National Education (1890–1913) and chairman of the Commission on Irish University Education (1908).

Parnell Anna Catherine (1852–1911). Born at Avondale, Rathdrum, Co. Wicklow, a sister of Charles Stewart Parnell, and educated at the Metropolitan School of Art, Dublin, she was a founder of the Ladies' Land League (January 1881). After his release from prison (May 1882) her brother suppressed the Ladies' Land League (August 1882), angering Anna who never spoke to him again. She moved to England where she lived thereafter. Her version of events is in *The Tale of a Great Sham* (ed. by Dana Hearne, 1986).

Parnell Charles Stewart (1846–1891). Born at Avondale, Rathdrum, Co. Wicklow, he was educated in several private schools in England and Cambridge. An MP (1875–91), he became Irish Party chairman (May 1880). As a consequence of the O'Shea divorce (17 November 1890), a majority of nationalist MPs joined Justin McCarthy in rejecting Parnell's leadership (6 December).

Pearse Patrick Henry (1879 – 3 May 1916, by firing squad). Born in Dublin of an English father and an Irish mother, he was educated at the Westland Row CBS and the Royal University. He joined the Gaelic League (1895), editing its journal, *An Claideamh Soluis* (1903–9). Pearse founded St Enda's School (1908) and was a member of the Irish Volunteers (1913), then became a member of the Military Council which planned the Easter Rising. He was the Provisional President of the Irish Republic (1916) and chief author of the Proclamation of the Irish Republic. Pearse was executed for his role in the Rising.

Pigott Richard (*c.* 1828 – 28 February 1889, suicide). Born in Co. Meath and educated locally, Pigott was a journalist who ran Fenian newspapers. These he sold to Charles Stewart Parnell and associates (1881) who converted them into *United Ireland.* Pigott was a shadowy figure on the fringes of national politics. In February 1889 he was exposed as the forger of the Parnell facsimile letters reproduced in *The Times* (1887) as 'Parnellism and Crime', whereupon he fled to Madrid and committed suicide.

Pirrie William James (1st Viscount Pirrie, created Baron 1906, Viscount 1921) (1847–1924). Born in Quebec of Ulster parents, he was raised in Co. Down and educated at the RBAI before being apprenticed as a draftsman (1862). He joined the board of directors as a partner in Harland & Wolffe (1874), becoming chairman (1904). Pirrie was Lord Mayor of Belfast (1896–7) and Controller-General of Merchant Shipbuilding (1918).

Plunkett George Noble (created Count by the Pope, 1884) (1851–1948). Born in Dublin and educated at CWC and TC, he stood unsuccessfully as an anti-Parnellite candidate for parliament (1892, 1895 and 1898) and was elected as a supporter of Sinn Féin (1917), but declined to take his seat, instead sitting in Dáil Éireann (1919–27). Opposing the Treaty, he declined to sit (1922–7). He was the father of Joseph Mary Plunkett who was executed for his part in the Easter Rising.

Plunkett Sir Horace Curzon (1854–1932). Born in Gloucestershire and educated at Eton, where he was a contemporary of Gerald Balfour, and at Oxford, Plunkett spent 10 years ranching in Wyoming, returning to Ireland in 1888. He was a Unionist MP (1892–1900), chairman of the Recess Committee (1896), vice-president of the Department of Agriculture and Technical Instruction (1899–1907) and chairman of the Irish Convention (1917–18). He was the founder of the Irish Agricultural Organisation Society. Plunkett authored *Ireland in the New Century* (1904).

Praeger Robert Lloyd (1865–1953). Born in Holywood, Co. Down, and educated at the RBAI and QCB, he was appointed to the National Library (1893), becoming librarian (1920–4) and president of the RIA (1931–4). He authored *Natural History of Ireland* (1951).

Redmond John Edward (1852–1918). Born in Ballytrant, Co. Wexford, and educated at CWC and TC, he was the eldest son of William Archer Redmond, MP, and brother of W. H. K. Redmond. Redmond was a clerk in the House of Commons in the late 1870s but gave up his post and became involved in home rule politics. He was an MP (1881–1918), supporting Charles Stewart Parnell in December 1890, and leader of the Parnellites (1891–1900) after Parnell's death, assuming the chairmanship of the united Irish Party (1900–18).

Redmond William Hoey Kearney (1861 – 9 June 1917, on the Western Front). Born in Wexford and educated at CWC, he was the younger brother and close confidant of John Redmond, MP, and the son of William Archer Redmond, MP, being an MP himself (1883–1917).

Reynolds Albert (1932–). Born in Rooskey, Co. Roscommon, and educated at Summerhill College, Sligo, he was president of the Chamber of Commerce (1974–8), member of the Longford County Council (1975–8), Fianna Fáil TD (1977–97), Minister for Posts and Telegraphs (1979–81), Minister for Industry and Energy (1982), Minister for Industry and Commerce (1987–8), Minister for Finance (1988–92), Taoiseach (1992–4) and party leader (1992–4).

Rice Edmund Ignatius (1762–1844). Born at Westcourt near Callan, Co. Kilkenny, he was educated locally. He moved to Waterford (1779) where he worked in a family exporting business. Rice established a school for the poor at Mount Sion (1803), then further ones at Clonmel (1806), Dungarvan (1806) and Cork (1811). He took religious vows (1808) and his Christian Brothers in Ireland received papal recognition (1820).

Robinson Esmé Stuart Lennox (1886–1958). Born in Douglas, Co. Cork, son of a Church of Ireland cleric, and educated at Bandon Grammar School, he was manager of the Abbey Theatre (1910–14, 1919–23) and wrote numerous plays and other works including *The Big House* (1926).

Robinson Mary (neé Bourke) (1944–). Born in Dublin and educated at TC, King's Inns and the Middle Temple (London), she was a Senator (1969–89), resigning from the Labour Party (1985) over its support for the Anglo-Irish Agreement (1985). A high-profile lawyer who had campaigned on women's and civil rights issues, Robinson was President of Ireland (1990–7), transforming the role of the head of state, most noticeably in its new proactive style. She resigned (1997) in order to take up the post of United Nations Commissioner for Human Rights.

Rossa Jeremiah O'Donovan (1831–1915). Born at Roscarbery, Co. Cork, and educated locally, he founded the Phoenix National Literary Society (1856) which merged into the IRB (1858). Business manager of the *Irish People* (1863–5), he was imprisoned as a consequence (1865–71), following which he went to America. There he was active in Clan na Gael and organised the Skirmishing Fund. His treatment in prison became a cause célèbre; he authored *Irish Rebels in English Prisons* (1882).

Russell Charles (1st Baron Russell of Killowen, created 1894) (1832–1900). Born in Killane, Co. Down, and educated at private school in Newry, Belfast Diocesan Seminary, Vincentian College, Castleknock, TC, King's Inns and Lincoln's Inn (London), he became a solicitor (1854). He was called to the English bar (1859) and became a QC (1872) and an MP (1880–5 in Ireland, 1885–94 in England), serving as Attorney-General (1886, 1892–4) in Liberal governments and was made Lord of Appeal (1894) and Chief Justice of England.

Russell George William (A. E.) (1867–1935). Born into a Quaker family in Lurgan, Co. Armagh, and educated at Rathmines School, he studied art at the Metropolitan School of Art, Dublin. Russell began publishing poetry in the early 1890s and joined the Irish Agricultural Organisation Society (1897), editing the *Irish Homestead* (1904–23) and *Irish Statesman* (1923–30). He authored *Collected Poems* (1913).

Russell Thomas (1767 – 21 October 1803, executed). Born at Bessborough, Co. Down, he served in the British army in India (1782) and was the first librarian of the Linen Hall Library, Belfast. He joined the United Irishmen and was deported to Scotland (1796–1802), where he was held without charge. Again in Ireland and learning of Robert Emmet's capture (1803), he came south to rescue him but was seized, found guilty of treason and hanged.

Russell Thomas Wallace (1841–1920). Born in Cupar, Fife, and educated locally he settled in Ireland (1859), becoming Unionist MP (1886–1910) and an Irish Party MP (1911–18). Russell was secretary to the Local Government Board (1895–1900) and vice-president of the Department of Agricultural and Technical Instruction (1907–18). An Ulster Protestant, he was a strong advocate of compulsory land purchase.

Ryan Frank (1902–44). Born near Elton, Co. Limerick, and educated at a local NS, St Colman's College, Fermoy, and UCD, he belonged to the IRA during the Anglo-Irish War. Rejecting the Treaty, he was a founder member of Comhairle na Poblachta and Saor Éire (1931). He served with the republican forces in Spain where he was wounded and imprisoned (1938), being released to Germany (August 1940) where he died.

Sadleir John (1815 – 17 February 1856, suicide). Born at Shrone Hill near Tipperary and educated at CWC, he was an MP (1847–53, 1853–6) and a key figure in the Irish Brigade in the House of Commons and Catholic Defence Association. Sadleir accepted the post of Lord of the Treasury (December 1852) which was believed to undermine the Independent Irish Party. His financial manipulations at the family-owned Tipperary Joint-Stock Bank brought about its ruin and he took his own life on Hampstead Heath.

Sands Bobby (1954–81). Born in Belfast, he left school at 15, joining the IRA (1973), and was imprisoned (1973–7). A few months after his release he was convicted again and sentenced to 14 years' imprisonment (1977). While on hunger strike he was elected an MP (9 April 1981), but died 5 May on the 66th day of his fast. His death was the occasion of extensive communal rioting in Northern Ireland.

Saunderson Colonel Edward (1837–1906). Born in Ballinamallard, Co. Fermanagh, and educated in Nice, France, where he spent his youth, Saunderson returned to Ireland (1858) and was a Liberal MP (1865–75) and a Conservative/Ulster Unionist (1885–1906). He was chairman of the Ulster Unionist Party (1886–1906).

Sexton Thomas (1848–1932). Born in Ballygannon, Co. Waterford, and educated at the local CBS, he was a journalist, an MP (1880–96), High Sheriff of Dublin (1887), Lord Mayor (1888, 1889) and chairman of the *Freeman's Journal* (1892–1912). Sexton had immense influence within the Irish Party and supported the anti-Parnellites in December 1890. Regarded as a financial expert, he was a member of the Royal Commission on the Financial Relations between Great Britain and Ireland (1894–6) and the Viceregal Commission on Irish Railways (1906–10).

Shaw George Bernard (1856–1950). Born in Dublin and educated at Wesley College, he moved to London (1876) where he joined the Fabian Society (1884). Shaw's first play was produced in 1892. During the First World War he was a pacifist. He received the Nobel Prize for Literature in 1925. With W. B. Yeats he founded the Irish Academy of Letters (1923). Though living his adult life in England, he declined British honours, turning down the Order of Merit and a peerage. Shaw was a major benefactor to the National Gallery, Dublin. He authored *Pygmalion* (1912) among many other works.

Shaw William (1823–95). Born in Cork and educated at TC and the theological seminary, Highbury, he was a minister in the Congregational Church in Cork (1850–4), then entered business there. Shaw was an MP (1868–85) and was elected chairman of the Irish Party following Butt's death (May 1879), but lost the leadership to Parnell (17 May 1880). He withdrew from the party (January 1881), thereafter generally supporting the Liberals. Shaw was chairman of the failed Muster Bank; he was declared bankrupt in 1886.

Sheehy Skeffington Hanna (1877–1946). Born in Loughmore Co. Tipperary, daughter of David Sheehy, MP, she was educated by the Dominican nuns and at UCD. She was co-founder of the Irish Women's Franchise League (1908) and was imprisoned (1912) for breaking windows in protest at the failure of the Home Rule bill to include female enfranchisement. During the Easter Rising she carried messages to the General Post Office. Her husband Francis was executed at the direction of Captain J. C. Bowen-Colthurst in the most infamous incident during the Easter Rising. Hanna supported Sinn Féin and Irish independence. She was a judge in the Dáil courts and sided with the republicans during the Civil War. She helped found the Women's Social and Progressive League.

Sheil Richard Lalor (1791–1851). Born in Drumdowney, Co. Kilkenny, and educated at Stonyhurst and TC, he was called to the bar (1814) and began writing plays while reading law at Lincoln's Inn. He supported Catholic Emancipation. He was among the first Catholics called to the inner bar (1830) and he was an English MP (1829–31), later taking up an Irish seat (1831–51). He authored *Adelaide* (1814).

Sheridan Richard Brinsley (1751–1816). Born in Dublin and educated at Harrow, he achieved literary success with *The Rivals* (1775) and *The School for Scandal* (1777). He entered politics in 1780, sitting as an English MP until 1812. He opposed the Act of Union.

Sloan Thomas Henry (1870–1941). Born in Belfast and educated locally, he was employed in Harland & Wolff's shipyard. After expulsion from the Orange Order for criticising Colonel Edward Saunderson, he co-founded the Independent Orange Order (1902). He was a Unionist MP (1902–10).

Somerville Edith Ann Oenone (1858–1949). Born in Corfu where her father was stationed in the British army, and educated in West Carbery, Co. Cork, and Alexandra College, Dublin, London and Düsseldorf, she studied art in Paris. She was a member of the Irish Academy of Letters from its foundation (1932). With her cousin Violet Martin, she wrote numerous books, including *Some Experiences of an Irish R.M.* (1899).

Spring Richard (Dick) (1950–). Born in Tralee, Kerry, and educated at the CBS, Tralee, Mount St Joseph's College, Roscrea, and TC, he was called to the bar (1975). After playing rugby for Ireland and dropping the ball, allowing a famous English victory, Spring was a Labour TD (1981–), serving as Minister for Justice (1981–2), Minister for the Environment (1982–3), Minister for Energy (1983–7), Minister for Foreign Affairs (1993–7), Tánaiste (1983–7, 1993–7) and leader of the Labour Party (1982–97).

Stack Austin (1880–1929). Born in Ballymullen, Tralee, and educated at the CBS Tralee, he joined the IRB (1908) and the Irish Volunteers in Kerry, holding the rank of Commandant during the Easter Rising. Elected a Sinn Féin MP (1918) he instead sat in Dáil Éireann (1919–27), though as an opponent of the Treaty he declined to sit (1922–7). Stack was Secretary for Home Affairs (1919–21). He was president of the Kerry GAA County Board (1918–29).

Stephens James (1824–1901). Born in Kilkenny and educated at St Kieran's College, Kilkenny, he was a civil engineer by training. Stephens supported Young Ireland and the Irish Confederation, taking part in the rebellion of 1848. He escaped to Paris and after returning to Ireland (1856) was a founder of the Fenian movement (1858). He was captured (1865) but escaped abroad, living (1866–85) in Paris and then in Switzerland until returning to Ireland (1891).

Stoker Abraham (Bram) (1847–1912). Born in Fairview, Dublin, and educated at the Revd W. Wood's private day school, Dublin, and TC, he entered the civil service but met Henry Irving (1876), becoming his manager (1878–1905). During this time he entered the Inner Temple (London) and was called to the English bar (1890). Stoker authored *Dracula* (1897).

Sullivan Alexander Martin (1830–84). Born in Bantry, Co. Cork, a brother of T. D. Sullivan, and educated at a local NS, he was a member of Young Ireland. He succeeded Charles Gavan Duffy as editor of the *Nation* (1855), handing over control to T. D. Sullivan (1876) when he was called to the English bar (1877). Sullivan was a pious Catholic who turned the newspaper into a voice of the Catholic Hierarchy as well as being an advocate of self-government principles. He was detested by Fenians. Sullivan attended the private meeting at the Bilton Hotel (19 May 1870) which founded the modern home rule movement. He was an MP (1874–81). Sullivan authored *New Ireland* (1877).

Sullivan Timothy Daniel (1827–1914). Born in Bantry, Co. Cork, older brother of A. M. Sullivan and later father-in-law to T. M. Healy (q.v.), and educated at a local NS, he supported Young Ireland and took over the *Nation* (1876). Sullivan was an MP (1880–1900), Lord Mayor of Dublin (1886–7) and, despite being a moderate, was imprisoned for a short period during the Plan of Campaign. Sullivan, a pious Catholic, devoted considerable energy to clerical interests, disliked Parnell and sided with his opponents in December 1890. He composed *God Save Ireland* (1867), the unofficial national anthem in the home rule era.

Synge John Millington (1871–1909). Born in Newtown Little, Rathfarnham, Dublin, and educated privately and at TC, he studied music for a time at the Royal Irish Academy of Music. He travelled widely on the continent and then spent summers on the Aran Islands (1899–1902). Synge was closely associated with the founding of the Abbey Theatre. His plays performed there proved controversial, leading to the famous riot over *The Playboy of the Western World* (1907).

Thompson William (1775–1835). Born in Cork to a wealthy Ascendancy family, he became one of the leading socialist theoreticians of his day and in some respects was a forerunner of Marx. A close friend of Jeremy Bentham, he was influenced by the ideas of Robert Owen and was an early champion of co-operative ideas. He wrote *An Inquiry into the Principles of the Distribution of Wealth most Conducive to Human Happiness, applied to the Newly Proposed System of Voluntary Equality of Wealth* (1824). He was also an advocate of the rights of women, co-writing with Anna Wheeler the *Appeal of One Half of the Human Race, Women, Against the Pretensions of the Other Half, Men, To Retain Them in Political, and Thence in Civil and Domestic Slavery* (1825).

Trimble (William) David (1944–). Born in Bangor, Co. Down, and educated at Bangor Grammar School and the QUB, he was called to the Northern Ireland bar (1969) and became a member of the law faculty at the QUB (1968–90). In the early 1970s he joined Ulster Vanguard which he represented in the Convention (1975). In 1977 Trimble shifted to the Official Unionist Party, becoming an MP (1990–) and then leader (1995–). A member of the North Ireland Assembly (1998–) he became First Minister of the new devolved assembly (1999–2001) and was also awarded the Nobel Peace Prize (1998).

Troy John Thomas (1739–1823). Born in Porterstown, Castleknock, Co. Dublin, and educated at Rome, he became a Dominican friar (1756). Made Bishop of Ossory (1776–84) he was translated to the Archbishopric of Dublin (1784–1823). He supported the Act of Union and Catholic Emancipation.

Ua Buachalla Domhnall (1866–1963). Born in Maynooth, Co. Kildare, he was educated at Belvedere College and Catholic University School, Dublin, being elected an MP (1918), but instead sat in Dáil Éireann (1919–22). He rejected the Treaty, was a founder of Fianna Fáil (1926), a TD (1927–32) and Governor-General (Seanascal) (1932–7).

Walker John (1768–1833). Born in Roscommon, son of a Church of Ireland cleric and educated at TC, he was ordained in the Church of Ireland. Walker, a Fellow of TC, seceded from the church (1804) and subsequently founded the Church of God.

Walker William M. (1871–1918). Born in Belfast and receiving a primary school education, he was apprenticed in Harland & Wolff. He became president of the Irish Trade Union Congress (1894).

Walsh William J. (1841–1921). Born in Dublin and educated at St Laurence O'Toole Seminary, Dublin, the Catholic University and Maynooth, he was professor of dogmatic and moral theology (1867–78), vice-president (1878–81) and president (1881–5), before becoming Archbishop of Dublin (1885–1921).

Walton Ernest T. S. (1903–95). Born in Dungarvan, Co. Waterford, son of a Methodist minister, he was educated at Methodist College, Belfast, and TC.

A physicist, he worked for several years in Cambridge but returned to Trinity (1934), being awarded the Nobel Prize in Physics (1951).

Webb   Alfred (1837–1908). Born in Dublin to a Quaker family and educated at the Quaker School there and at Dr Hodgson's High School, Manchester (England), he was a founder of the Home Government Association (1870) and remained part of all subsequent home rule organisations. He served most as treasurer. Webb was a founder of the Protestant Home Rule Association (1886) and wrote numerous pamphlets and articles on Irish questions, serving as an MP (1890–5) when he supported the anti-Parnellites (December 1890). Webb compiled *A Compendium of Irish Biography* (1878).

Wellington   1st Duke of (Arthur Wellesley) (1769–1852). Born in Dublin and educated at Eton, he was an MP in the Irish House of Commons (1790–5) and Lord Lieutenant (1788–94). After the Union he was Chief Secretary (1807–9). Best known for his military feats, Wellington was Prime Minister (1828–30), holding office during the Catholic Emancipation crisis.

Wheeler   Anna Doyle (1785– *c.* 1851). Born in Clonbeg, Co Tipperary, to a liberal Protestant home, she was introduced by tutors to the ideas of the *philosophes.* Wheeler left an unhappy marriage (1812), settling first in Guernsey, then in Caen, where she became the centre of a group of Saint-Simonians. In the 1820s she lived in London, where she befriended and worked with Robert Owen. Early in the 1820s she met William Thompson, with whom she co-wrote the *Appeal of One Half of the Human Race, Women, Against the Pretensions of the Other Half, Men, To Retain Them in Political, and Thence in Civil and Domestic Slavery* (1825).

Whitaker   Thomas Kenneth (1916–). Born at Rostrevor, Co. Down, and educated at the CBS, Drogheda, he took a University of London external degree before entering the civil service (1934–69), being attached to the Department of Finance (1938). After becoming secretary of the department (1956) he was instrumental in drafting *Economic Development,* which became the basis for the First Programme for Economic Expansion (1958). Whitaker was Governor of the Central Bank of Ireland (1969–76) and president of the RIA (1985–7).

Wilde   Oscar Fingal O'Flahertie Wills (1854–1900). Born in Dublin, the son of Sir William and Lady Jane Wilde, and educated at TC and Oxford, he authored numerous successful plays including *The Importance of Being Earnest* (1895). Wilde was incarcerated in Reading prison for sodomy (1895–7) and lived abroad, mainly in Paris, after his release.

Wilson   General Sir Henry (knighted 1919) (1864 – 22 June 1922, assassinated). Born in Currygrane, Edgeworthstown, Co. Longford, and educated at Marlborough College (England), he was commissioned into the Longford Militia. He was an adviser to David Lloyd George during the First World War and the Anglo-Irish War and Chief of the Imperial Staff (1918). Elected a Conservative MP (1922) he was shot dead in London by two republicans.

Wyse Sir Thomas (1791–1862). Born St John's Manor, Co. Waterford, and educated at Stonyhurst, TC and Lincoln's Inn (London), he was an early supporter of the Catholic Association. He was an MP (1830–2, 1835–47) and was made ambassador to Greece (1849).

Yeats John (Jack) Butler (1871–1957). Born in London, son of John Butler Yeats and brother of William Butler Yeats, he was educated privately and at art school in London. On his return from London (1900), he commenced painting watercolours and worked as an illustrator for the Cuala Press, a family business. He painted *The Tinker*.

Yeats John Butler (1839–1922). Born in Tullylish, Co. Down, and educated at TC, he studied art at Heatherleys Art School, the Royal Academy and the Slade School of Art in London. A painter of numerous portraits, he settled in New York (1907). Among his portraits is one of his son, William Butler Yeats.

Yeats William Butler (1865–1939). Born in Dublin the son of John Butler Yeats and brother of Jack Butler Yeats, he was educated at the High School in Dublin and studied art at the Dublin Metropolitan School of Art. He was a founder of the Irish Literary Society and the Irish National Literary Society, the Irish National Literary Theatre and the Abbey Theatre. In 1916 he proposed marriage to Maud Gonne McBride who refused him. He married Georgina Hyde-Less (1917). He became the first Irishman to be awarded the Nobel Prize for Literature (1923). He authored, among many other works, *Last Poems* (1940).

GLOSSARY

Abbey Theatre Opened on 27 December 1904, it was formed from a merger of the National Dramatic Company, owned by the brothers Frank and William Fay, and the Irish Literary Theatre Society founded in 1899 by, among others, W. B. Yeats, Lady Gregory and Edward Martyn. In 1924 a grant from the Irish government made this the first state-subsidised theatre in the anglophone world. Ernest Blythe long served as its head. The premises were destroyed by fire in 1951 and the company was accommodated at the Queen's Theatre until 1966, when it moved permanently to a new building in Lower Abbey Street.

abdication crisis (1936): Edward VIII's abdication had ramifications for the Irish Free State which was then part of the Commonwealth. On 11 December, the day Edward abdicated, Dáil Éireann convened to consider what became the Constitutional and the External Relations Acts. The first removed all references to the monarch, while the second recognised the throne only for the purposes of appointing diplomatic and consular representations and for the making of international agreements.

Act of Union Identical measures passed in 1800 by both the Westminster and Irish parliaments came into effect on 1 January 1801, creating the legislative unity of Great Britain and Ireland. It ceased to exist under provisions for the jurisdictions of the two parts of Ireland (1920–2).

Agricultural and Technical Instruction Act, 1899 Legislation dedicated to improving the quality of agricultural and technical instruction throughout Ireland. It arose from the report of the Recess Committee in 1896. In 1931 the Department of Agricultural and Technical Instruction created under the Act was dissolved in the Free State. The Technical Instruction Department was placed under the Department of Education and the Department of Agriculture was then formed for the remaining functions.

Agricultural Credit Corporation Established in 1927, it was the first of the Irish state-sponsored bodies, and had the purpose of advancing capital to farmers.

Ailtirí na hAiséirighe A nationalist organisation principally active during the 1940s, it fielded candidates in the general elections of 1943 and 1944. Some members were subsequently involved in Clann na Poblachta.

Aliens Act, 1935 Defined anyone who was not a citizen of the Irish Free State (including British subjects) as an alien.

All-for-Ireland League Founded by William O'Brien in 1910 to promote the doctrine of conference, conciliation and consent between Irish people on questions affecting Ireland. It had its base in Cork. It largely ceased to exist after 1918.

Alliance Party Founded in Northern Ireland in April 1970, it is a non-sectarian party which advocates co-operation between the communities in Northern Ireland and the pursuit of social justice. It held three seats in the

Northern Ireland parliament when the parliament was prorogued in March 1972. It advocated 'power-sharing' and accepted seats in the Executive formed by Brian Faulkner in 1974. It held six seats in the Northern Ireland Assembly elected in 1998 and 10 candidates stood under its banner in the general election to the Westminster House of Commons in June 2001.

All-Ireland Committee   Founded in February 1897 to secure implementation of the Report of the Royal Commission on the Financial Relations between Great Britain and Ireland (1896).

All-Party Anti-Partition Committee (Mansion House Committee)   Founded in January 1949 to seek the peaceful reunification of the island. It sponsored publications and meetings in Ireland and Great Britain.

American Association for the Recognition of the Irish Republic   Formed by Eamon de Valera on 16 November 1920, it enlisted Irish-American support for the aim of securing an Irish Republic. It was initiated after de Valera and the Clan na Gael split. By 1926 it had virtually ceased to function.

American Commission of Inquiry   Launched in August 1920 in the United States to inquire into the excesses of British troops and the police in Ireland. It released an interim report in 1921.

American Land League   Founded by Charles Stewart Parnell in March 1880 in New York as the North American arm of the Irish land movement.

American note   Delivered by the American government in February 1944 to the Free State regime demanding that German and Japanese diplomats be removed from the country. Eamon de Valera declined, reiterating the neutrality of the Free State.

American wake   Held for an emigrant to the United States on the night prior to his/her departure.

Amnesty Association   Founded in 1868, it agitated until 1872 for the release of imprisoned members of the Irish Republican Brotherhood (IRB or Fenians). Isaac Butt served as its president.

Amnesty Association of Great Britain   Founded by Dr Mark Ryan in London on 23 January 1892, it functioned until 1898, seeking the release of prisoners imprisoned for causing explosions in Britain in the 1880s.

Ancient Order of Hibernians (AOH)   First initiated in 1641, its modern form began as a Catholic association in 1836 in New York. It split in the United States in 1878 and in Ireland in 1884; in 1904 a reunion under the Board of Erin was achieved. In 1905 the AOH registered as a friendly society, after which membership mushroomed. In Belfast, under the presidency of Joseph Devlin (1905–14), it emerged as a nationalist political machine.

Anglo-Irish Agreement   (15 November 1985): Concord between the governments of the Republic of Ireland and the United Kingdom, allowing the first some voice in the internal affairs of Northern Ireland, while it recognised the right of Northern Ireland to exist and agreed to co-operation on security.

Anglo-Irish Agreements (1938): Three agreements signed between the United Kingdom and the Free State government (Éire) on 25 April 1938 brought the Economic War to an end. Under these the Free State made a payment to settle all British financial claims arising from the withholding of the land annuities, the British market was reopened to Irish Free State cattle, and the Treaty Ports were returned to the Dublin government.

Anglo-Irish Free Trade Area Agreement (AIFTAA) On coming into effect on 1 July 1966 there was a gradual removal of tariffs between the United Kingdom and Republic of Ireland.

Anglo-Irish Trade Agreement (1948): It linked the prices of Free State and British cattle and sheep.

Anglo-Irish War (1919–21): *see* War of Independence.

Anti-Coercion Association Founded by H. M. Hyndman in 1880, it was intended to muster support in Great Britain for the Irish Land League.

[new] Anti-Partition League Founded in 1947 for the purpose of protesting against the political division of Ireland.

Aontacht Éireann Political party formed in 1971 by Kevin Boland to oppose the Irish government's handling of the Northern Ireland question. It supported a united Ireland and proposed to aid republicans in Northern Ireland who sought to end partition. It had effectively ceased operations by 1976.

Apprentice Boys of Derry Founded in 1844 in Londonderry to commemorate the apprentice boys who locked the city gates against Catholic troops in 1688, it is a Protestant Unionist organisation closely associated with the Orange Order. It celebrates the shutting of the gates annually on 18 December and holds an annual march on 12 August.

arbitration courts First mooted by Daniel O'Connell, the courts, which operated briefly in 1843, were intended to frustrate the functioning of crown courts. The idea was revived during the War of Independence with the establishment of Sinn Féin arbitration courts. Land arbitration courts were also founded.

arms crisis (1970): Two ministers in the Fianna Fáil government, Neil Blaney and Charles Haughey, were dismissed for allegedly using government money to import arms for the IRA. The charges against Blaney were dropped; Haughey was acquitted.

Army Comrades Association Founded in February 1932 to uphold the Free State and for the commemoration of those who died during the War of Independence. In 1933 a remodelled organisation began wearing 'blue shirts'

741

and members became known as Blueshirts. In 1933 it was renamed the National Guard.

Army Mutiny (1924): A section of IRA veterans with the Free State Army on 6 March demanded an end to demobilisation, abolition of the Army Council and a declaration that the government was committed to the ideal of a Republic. It concluded in October with the resolution of some army grievances.

Arrears Act, 1882 Legislation allowing tenants in arrears of rent payment to utilise provisions of the Land Act of 1881.

Articles 2 and 3 (Constitution of 1937): Claim by the government of the Republic of Ireland to sovereignty over the whole island of Ireland.

Ascendancy Term attributed to John Gifford, applied to the Protestant landowning class which dominated Ireland's life in the eighteenth and nineteenth centuries.

Ashbourne Act, 1885 *See* Land Acts.

Aud A German ship carrying arms for the Easter Rising captured on the coast of Kerry on 22 April 1916.

Auxiliaries When the Royal Irish Constabulary (RIC) was targeted by the Irish Republican Army during the War of Independence, recruitment fell and the government filled the void in July 1920 by creating a new force in Britain from among demobilised soldiers which was intended to supplement the RIC. There was a shortage of RIC uniforms for the new force and accordingly they were issued with trousers (military) and dark tunics (police), hence the name 'Black and Tans'. Its members were stigmatised for their brutality and came to symbolise British actions during the conflict. The unit was disbanded in 1922.

Bachelor's Walk (26 July 1914): Following the Irish Volunteers' gunrunning at Howth, a regiment of the King's Own Scottish Borderers was subjected to abuse and retaliated by shooting at a crowd in Bachelor's Walk, Dublin. Three people were killed and at least 38 others were injured.

Ballot Act, 1872 It introduced the 'secret' ballot throughout the United Kingdom. Though sometimes credited with facilitating the rise of the Home Rule Party, it had only a marginal impact on the outcome of Irish elections.

Baptist Society Founded in London in 1814, it established schools in Connaught where it used Irish for teaching.

Belfast boycott (1920–2): The boycott of goods produced and distributed from Belfast was a reaction in the south of Ireland to the anti-Catholic rioting in Belfast during the summer of 1920. It began in August on unofficial lines when shopkeepers in Galway City refused to stock goods originating in Belfast and lasted until the Craig–Collins Agreement.

Belfast News-letter Founded on 1 September 1737, the *News-Letter* is the oldest daily in Ireland and is second only to *Lloyd's List* (1719) as the oldest newspaper in the British Isles.

Belfast Protestant Association A working-class anti-Catholic organisation founded in 1900 from Belfast lodges of the Orange Order.

Bell Based in Dublin, it was an influential monthly journal specialising in literary and social comment. It was published from 1940 until 1954. Seán O'Faolain and Peadar O'Donnell were two of its editors.

Bessborough Commission Royal Commission established on 29 July 1880 under the chairmanship of the 6th Earl of Bessborough to investigate the functioning of the Land Act of 1870. It reported in favour of granting the three Fs (fair rent, fixity of tenure and free sale) on 4 January 1871.

Better Government of Ireland Act, 1920 Repealed the Government of Ireland Act of 1914, granting home rule to most of the country while making the six north-eastern counties of Ulster (Londonderry, Tyrone, Fermanagh, Antrim, Down and Armagh) a separate state of Northern Ireland within the United Kingdom. This division is generally known as 'partition'.

Biblicals Evangelical clergymen active in Ireland among the Catholic population in the second decade of the nineteenth century, proselytising, preaching and distributing free Bibles (hence their name). They were also known as 'New Reformers' and were part of the 'Second Reformation'.

Black and Tans *see* Auxiliaries.

black diaries Journals describing homosexual activity were discovered among the belongings of Sir Roger Casement in 1916. Extracts were shown to certain journalists and to American officials in order to weaken appeals to spare Casement's life.

Blackfeet An agrarian secret society which operated during the 1820s and 1830s.

Bloody Sunday (21 November 1920) Members of Michael Collins's Special Intelligence Unit killed 13 men and injured six others, most of them British intelligence agents, known as the Cairo Gang. As a response, two Republican prisoners and Conor Clune in Dublin Castle were shot in an alleged attempt to escape. In a further reprisal Black and Tans (Auxiliaries) dispatched to Croke Park fired into a crowd attending a Gaelic football match, killing 12 and wounding 60 (others were injured in the resultant panic).

Bloody Sunday (10 July 1921) During the Belfast boycott, this Sunday saw concerted attacks by Orange factions and Special Constables upon Catholics and Catholic-owned properties in Belfast. Fifteen people were killed, 68 seriously injured and 161 Catholic-owned homes were razed to the ground.

743

Bloody Sunday (30 January 1972)   The shooting by British army paratroopers of 14 civilians during a civil rights demonstration in Londonderry. A massive anti-British demonstration ended with the burning of the British Embassy in Dublin. The incident remains highly controversial. An escalation of violence followed and Stormont was suspended in March.

Blueshirts   The popular name given to members of the Army Comrades Association (above). In July 1933 Eoin O'Duffy became leader of the organisation now titled the National Guard. It merged with Cumann na nGaedheal and the Centre Party in 1933 to form Fine Gael with O'Duffy as leader. He resigned in September 1934. The Blueshirts adopted new names – first the Young Ireland Association and later the League of Youth – before passing from the scene.

Board of Erin   Executive of the Irish branch of the Ancient Order of Hibernians created in 1902 in an attempt to resolve the dispute between the American and Irish branches. *See* Ancient Order of Hibernians.

Board of Works   (Office of Public Works): Created in the eighteenth century and re-constituted in 1831, it was responsible for administering public money for relief works to ease hardship through unemployment. During the first half of the nineteenth century it assumed responsibility for the upkeep of public buildings, drainage waterways and canals; subsequently it was empowered to cover the loans for improvement to land and the construction of labourers' cottages and working-class dwellings in towns. In 1922 it was placed under the authority of the Department of Finance; its functions became limited to the construction and maintenance of public buildings.

Bodenstown Sunday   (Co. Kildare): Annual commemoration for Theobald Wolfe Tone on the penultimate Sunday in June.

Boundary Commission   Established in 1924 in accordance with Article 12 of the Treaty, its purpose was to 'determine in accordance with the wishes of the inhabitants, so far as may be compatible with economic and geographic conditions, the boundaries between Northern Ireland and the rest of Ireland'. The Commission sat for most of 1925, but following a leak of its findings in the *Morning Post* in November 1925, Eoin MacNeill, the representative of the Free State, resigned in protest. The Commission's report was suppressed and not published until 1969.

bowler hat and sash   Traditional costume worn during marches by members of the Orange Order.

boycotting   The practice of ostracising, first directed at Captain Charles Boycott (1832–97), land agent for Lord Erne's estate at Lough Mask, Co. Mayo: hence the name. It was used frequently during Irish land agitations, mainly against tenants who took up farms from occupiers who had been evicted.

British Relief Association   Founded on 1 January 1847 for the purpose of 'alleviating distress caused by the potato failure in Ireland and Scotland'.

Broadcasting Act, 1960   The Act set up an authority to administer an Irish television service.

Brunswick Clubs   Protestant clubs with the object of opposing Catholic Emancipation founded in August 1828 as a replacement for the Orange Order, which had been suppressed.

Buckingham Palace Conference   (21–24 July 1914): Meeting of main political parties convened by King George V in order to break the impasse over the Better Government of Ireland act. It ended without an agreement.

Bunreacht na hÉireann   *see* Constitution of Ireland, 1937.

Cairo Gang   British intelligence officers during the War of Independence. On 21 November 1920 (Bloody Sunday) its agents were assassinated, provoking a reprisal in Croke Park.

Cameron Commission   Appointed by the government of Northern Ireland in 1969 to investigate clashes between loyalist and civil rights marchers, it was chaired by Lord Cameron.

Campaign for Democracy in Ulster   Founded in 1965 by a small contingent of Labour MPs in Britain to oppose gerrymandering and discrimination in Northern Ireland. It was associated with the Campaign for Social Justice in Northern Ireland.

Campaign for Social Justice in Northern Ireland   Founded in 1964 to combat social injustice in Northern Ireland and absorbed into the Northern Ireland Civil Rights Association on its formation in 1967.

Capuchin Annual   Published by the Capuchin Friary in Dublin from 1930 to 1977, it was a leading forum for fiction, verse, theology, history, literature and art.

Carders   Agrarian secret society active in Connaught in the early nineteenth century, taking its name from the mutilation inflicted by digging a steel comb used for carding wool through their victims' flesh.

Castle document   A forgery by Joseph Plunkett and Seán MacDiarmada published on 19 April 1916, purporting to give instructions for the suppression of the Irish Volunteers, ordering the occupation of key areas suspected of harbouring sedition, and calling for the arrest of certain individuals.

Catholic Association   Established in May 1824 by Daniel O'Connell and Richard Lalor Sheil to seek Catholic Emancipation. It was suppressed by the government in March 1825 under the Unlawful Societies Act but reorganised in July 1825 as the New Catholic Association.

Catholic Associations   (Belfast and Dublin): The Belfast Catholic Association was founded in 1896 by the Catholic Bishop of Down and Connor, Dr Henry Henry, as a local political machine. Henry opposed the United Irish League and his movement weakened to the point where it became inoperative in

1905. In Dublin the Catholic Association was founded in 1902 for the purpose of highlighting discrimination in employment against Catholics. It faded from the scene in 1904.

Catholic Board   A revival in 1812 of the Catholic Committee which had been harassed by the Irish government under the Convention Act of 1793. The Board continued the fight for Catholic Emancipation but was hampered by the provisions of the Veto scheme, which divided supporters, and was dissolved in June 1814.

Catholic Bulletin   A Catholic and nationalist periodical published between 1911 and 1939.

Catholic Committee   First founded in 1760 but dissolved in 1793; it was revived in May 1809 as the General Committee of the Catholics of Ireland, but was suppressed in 1811 under the Convention Act.

Catholic Defence Association   Founded in Dublin in August 1851, by prominent members of the 'Irish Brigade', it was intended to act as a permanent agency for the publication of Catholic grievances, but had only limited success.

Catholic Emancipation   (1829): Emancipation meant the right of Catholics to sit as MPs without having to subscribe to the Oath of Supremacy. Catholics had also been virtually excluded from a wide range of public offices, most of which were opened to them after Emancipation. Emancipationists sought equality between Catholics and Protestants in public life, the law and the army. The principal objectives were gained in the Catholic Relief Act, 13 April 1829.

Catholic rent   Sums of money collected from 1824 to support the Catholic Emancipation campaign through O'Connell's Catholic and New Catholic Associations. The 'rent' was collected by Catholic priests.

Catholic Union   Formed by Cardinal Paul Cullen in 1872 in an effort to counter growing support for the Home Government Association. Never very large, it ceased in 1876.

Catholic University of Ireland   Established under papal authority in 1854 to provide higher education for Catholics. John Henry Newman became rector of the new university. For most of its lifespan the university possessed little endowment and was unable to secure a charter enabling degrees to be awarded. The University Act of 1879 established a Royal University empowered to grant degrees to any students who attained the necessary standards, thereby permitting students at the Catholic University to receive awards. As University College, the Catholic University was administered by the Society of Jesus from 1883 until it became a college of the National University of Ireland under legislation enacted in 1908.

cattle driving   Term for the impoundment of cattle owned by an Irish tenant in arrears with his rent. His cattle were driven to the nearest town and held there until the arrears were paid off. During land agitation in the early twentieth century it referred to the practice of removing livestock from the lands of grazing farmers as part of the effort to break up 'ranches' and redistribute land to farmers.

Celtic Literary Society Founded in 1893 as an exclusively male society to promote the study of the Irish language, history, literature and music, it was merged into Cumann na nGaedheal in 1900.

Celtic Society Founded in 1845, it was devoted to the preservation and publication of early Irish manuscripts. It merged with the Irish Archaeological Society (founded in 1840) to become the Irish Archaeological and Celtic Society.

Censorship Board Appointed in 1930 under the Censorship of Publications Act (1926), it was empowered to recommend to the Minister of Justice works that ought to be prohibited from sale in Ireland, a task performed with notorious zeal. Amended in 1946 to allow for appeals, it gave authority to customs officers to seize any literature which they considered infringed the Act. A further amendment of 1967 allowed a reconsideration of all banned works, many of which were then allowed to be sold while others were subjected to a further ban. Under this amendment a book is banned for a maximum of 12 years.

Censorship of Films Act Passed in 1923, it established a censorship board to examine films offered for commercial distribution in Ireland. A Film Appeals Board was established in 1964.

centenary celebrations (1898): Held to mark the centenary of the rising of the United Irishmen in 1798.

Centre Title of the head of a Circle of the Irish Republican Brotherhood, the first being James Stephens.

Changedale It allowed for a rotation of individual portions of land to ensure that everyone shared both the good and poor holdings.

Charitable Bequests Act, 1844 Facilitated legacies for Catholic religious or charitable purposes hitherto subject to control by a predominantly Protestant board.

Chester Beatty Library Established in 1953 to house the collection of Islamic and Oriental art and manuscripts bequeathed to Ireland by the American-born Sir Alfred Chester Beatty (1875–1968).

Chief Secretary (to the Lord Lieutenant): From the creation of the Union until 1921, the political official responsible for the Irish Civil Service and spokesman for the conduct of Irish government in the House of Commons.

Children's Land League Established in 1881 by the Land League and the Ladies' Land League, it was outlawed in October 1881 in common with the movement as a whole.

Christian Brothers   Found by Edmund Rice to teach poor boys. In 1820 his community was confirmed by the Pope.

Christus Rex   Clerical organisation founded in 1941 to foster the study of social issues from a Catholic perspective.

Church Education Society   Church of Ireland association founded in 1839 because of dissatisfaction with the system of National Education. It implemented the free use of the Bible in class and made no distinction between religious and literary training. In 1870 it was dissolved and the remaining schools joined the National Education system.

Church Temporalities Act, 1833   It reduced the four archbishoprics of the Church of Ireland to two, and the 20 bishoprics were reduced to 10, along with other reforms.

Civil Authorities (Special Powers) Act (Northern Ireland), 1922   Generally known as the Special Powers Act, it granted the Minister for Home Affairs the powers to 'take all such steps and issue all such orders as may be necessary to preserve the peace', including authority to arrest without warrant and intern without trial, prohibit coroners' inquests, flog, execute, requisition land or property, ban any organisation and prohibit meetings, publications, and the like.

Civil War   (1922–3): Led by Eamon de Valera, those who rejected the Treaty constituted themselves as the legitimate Second Dáil. The anti-Treaty faction seized the Four Courts on 13 April 1922. This precipitated the Civil War, when on 28 June government troops moved against the occupants. Skirmishing continued until April 1923 when republican resistance effectively ended.

Clan na Gael   Irish-American republican revolutionary association founded by Jerome J. Collins in New York on 20 June 1867. It was a secret and oath-bound organisation recognising the Supreme Council of the Irish Republican Brotherhood as the government. It almost ceased to exist after 1940.

Clann Éireann   (Irish People's Party): Founded by William Magennisin in 1925 as a breakaway from Cumann na nGaedheal in protest at the settlement which shelved the Boundary Commission. It disappeared after a poor result in the general election of 1927.

Clann na Poblachta   Party founded on 6 July 1946 and led by Seán MacBride, it was supported by some members of the Irish Republican Army. It saw itself as a modernising force and attracted many who wished to see a wide range of social reforms implemented. The party was dissolved in 1969.

Clann na Talmhan   Party founded on 29 June 1939 at Athenry, Co. Galway, to defend the small western farmer. The party's strongholds were in counties Galway, Mayo and Roscommon. It had disappeared by 1965.

Clerkenwell explosion   (13 December 1867): A Fenian rescue attempt at the Clerkenwell House of Detention caused an explosion, killing 12 people and injuring more than 50 others. Michael Barrett was convicted of the crime and was hanged on 26 May 1868 in the last public execution in the United Kingdom.

Coal–Cattle Pact   Agreement between the Free State and British governments in 1935 allowing an increase of one-third in the quota of Irish cattle allowed into the United Kingdom, in return for which Ireland agreed to import coal only from the United Kingdom.

Coercion Acts   Legislation giving the Irish administration special emergency powers. One hundred and five Coercion Acts were passed between 1800 and December 1921.

coffin ships   Vessels carrying refugees from the Famine to the New World in the second half of the 1840s. Deaths from exposure, typhus and cholera on board or after arriving at North American ports were numerous.

Colwyn Committee   Established under the chairmanship of Lord Colwyn in 1923 to examine the question of Northern Ireland finances and contributions to be made to the Imperial Fund. The Committee suggested that the contribution to be made by Northern Ireland should be the residue after domestic expenditure had been met.

Comhairle na Poblachta   (Central Council of the Republic): Political party founded in 1929. It lasted for only a short period.

Comhaltas Ceoltóirí Éireann   Founded in 1951 for the promotion of Irish traditional music, song and dance with branches developing in Ireland, Great Britain, Australia, Canada and the United States.

Comhdháil Náisiúnta na Gaeilge   (National Congress of the Irish Language): Founded in 1943 as part of a movement to preserve and foster the language. It became a co-ordinating body for organisations involved in the presentation and promotion of the language.

Commonwealth Labour Party   Founded in December 1942 by Harry Midgley as a breakaway from the Northern Ireland Labour Party, it was pro-Unionist and supported the involvement of Northern Ireland in the war. After 1947, when Midgley joined the Ulster Unionist Party, it disintegrated.

Communist Party of Ireland   Founded in October 1921 it opposed the Treaty and promoted a republican-socialist programme. After the Comintern withdrew its recognition in 1923 and transferred it to the Irish Workers' League it dissolved in 1924. The Communist Party was re-established in 1933 by the Revolutionary Workers Group and the Workers' Party of Ireland, but was dissolved in 1941 and then revived as the Irish Workers' League in 1948. This last body founded another communist party, the Irish Workers' Party, in 1962, which united with the Communist Party of Northern Ireland on 15 March 1970 to become the Communist Party of Ireland.

749

Compensation for Disturbances bill, 1880 Designed to deal with the agrarian crisis, it empowered the courts in certain cases to order a landlord to compensate a tenant upon eviction even if the eviction was for non-payment of rent, provided that the tenant could prove that inability to pay was a direct result of agricultural and economic depression. The bill was to apply to designated areas in the west and south of the country and was for a period of 18 months only. The bill passed through the House of Commons but was defeated in the House of Lords.

conacre System of landholding by which a portion of land was rented for a season for the sowing of crops but without creating a contractual relationship between landlord and tenant. It was a common arrangement between tenants and subtenants. This system was most commonly encountered in Munster and Connaught.

Congested Districts Board Established in 1891, it consisted of a body of commissioners whose duty it was to dispense assistance to the 'congested' districts – Donegal, Sligo, Leitrim, Roscommon, Galway, Clare, Limerick, Kerry and Cork. Regions under the board's authority were areas in which the rateable valuation was less than 30 shillings per head, amounting to around 3.5 million acres, with a population of about half a million. The sums at its disposal were spent on building harbours, encouraging a fishing industry, fish-curing, cottage industries and attempting to modernise farming methods. It also bought estates, reorganised them and sold them back to tenants at low interest. The Board was dissolved in 1923 by the government of the Free State and its functions were handed over to the Land Commission.

Congress of Irish Unions (CIU): Founded in 1945 when the Irish Transport and General Workers Union disaffiliated itself from the Irish Trades Union Congress and the Labour Party. In 1959 it amalgamated with the Irish Trades Union Congress to form the Irish Congress of Trades Unions.

Connaught Rangers' Mutiny (28–30 June 1920): Refusal to perform duties by some members of the regiment stationed in India because of atrocities being committed in Ireland by the Black and Tans and Auxiliaries. One man was executed. The regiment was disbanded in 1922.

conscription crisis (1918): Following passage of an Act (16 April 1918) to extend conscription to Ireland, Irish Party members withdrew from the House of Commons and returned to Ireland where they joined forces with Sinn Féin, the Catholic Hierarchy, the trades unions and the Labour Party to oppose it. The threat of conscription was met with a series of mass meetings across Ireland.

Constitution Amendment Act, 1931 Established a military tribunal with power to deal with political crimes and to impose the death penalty. It empowered the government to outlaw associations and the police were given extensive powers of arrest and detention.

Constitution of Ireland, 1937 Replaced the Constitution of 1922. Important changes included recognition of the special position of the Catholic Church, prohibition of divorce and the assertion of a territorial claim for the whole island of Ireland. Gaelic was accorded status as the first official language. The Constitution created a Department of External Affairs and omitted all reference to the sovereign.

Constitution of the Irish Free State, 1922 Following three drafts, a document consisting of 79 articles and the Treaty was accepted by the British government. It was published on 16 June 1922 and on 6 December the Free State or Saorstát came into existence. It was replaced by the Constitution of 1937.

Constitution of Northern Ireland Act, 1973 Passed by the United Kingdom parliament after the closure of Stormont, it created a new 78-seat Assembly elected on the basis of proportional representation and with a power-sharing Executive. Elections took place in May 1973. *See* Sunningdale Agreement and Ulster Workers' Council Strike.

Co-operative Movement *See* Irish Agricultural Organisation Society (IAOS).

Córas Iompar Éireann (CIE): Established by the Transport Act (1944) and extended by the Transport Act (1986), CIE became a state-owned company with three autonomous subsidiaries, Iarnród Éireann, Bus Éireann and Bus Átha Cliath.

Córas na Poblachta Republican movement founded in 1940 by members of the Irish Republican Army anxious to secure a political footing for the movement. It was absorbed into Clann na Poblachta in 1946.

Cork Defence Union Established in October 1885 to oppose home rule and the Irish National League.

cottier One who rented a cabin and between one and one and a half acres of land upon which to grow potatoes, oats and possibly some flax. He held the ground on a year-to-year basis and his rent was often paid in labour.

Council for the Status of Women Founded in 1968 for the purpose of liaison between the government and women's groups in order to combat discrimination.

Council of Ireland Designated under the Better Government of Ireland Act (1920), it was intended as a body composed of 20 representatives equally divided between Northern and Southern Ireland. The Council's purpose was to consider questions of mutual concern and to be a possible bridge between the two parts of the island. The government of Northern Ireland withdrew from the Council but the idea was revived in the Sunningdale Agreement (December 1973).

Council of State Created under the Constitution of 1937 to aid and counsel the President.

751

Council of Three Hundred A proposal taken up by Daniel O'Connell for the 60 Irish nationalist MPs at Westminster to join with 240 others and form an independent Irish parliament under the crown. The Council never came into existence but a similar idea was floated later by Arthur Griffith.

Counsellor Popular name for Daniel O'Connell before 1829. It paid tribute to his success as a barrister. After 1829 he was known as the 'Liberator'.

Coventry explosion (25 August 1939): The Irish Republican Army declared war on Britain on 16 January 1939. This took the form of a series of bombings, some 120 in all. The campaign culminated in the explosion at Broadgate, Coventry, when five people were killed and 70 injured. The Coventry explosion caused outrage in Ireland and throughout the United Kingdom. Two men were executed for the incident.

Craig–Collins Agreements (January and March 1922): Agreements secured by Sir James Craig, Prime Minister of Northern Ireland, and Michael Collins, Chairman of the Provisional Government. In an attempt to end strife on both sides of the border, Craig and Collins met in London. The first agreement, published on 21 January, sought an end to the Belfast boycott, the reinstatement of Catholics dismissed from employment, and the appointment of a subcommittee to examine proposals for a mutual agreement on the boundary between the two states. On 30 March an agreement was reached that special police in mixed districts would be composed of half Catholics and half Protestants; an Advisory Committee composed of Catholics would be set up to assist in the selection of Catholic recruits for the special police; and searches for arms would be carried out by police forces, consisting equally of Catholics and Protestants (which was never achieved). A committee was to be established in Belfast with an equal number of Catholic and Protestant members to hear and investigate complaints of intimidation and outrages, and IRA activity was to cease within the six northern counties. The Northern signatories undertook to use every method to secure the restoration of expelled workers and if this was impracticable to have them employed on relief works. Both the Northern and Free State governments undertook to arrange the release of political prisoners imprisoned for acts committed before 31 March 1922.

Crime and Outrage Act (29 November 1847): Legislation giving the Lord Lieutenant power to draft police into a district, such a district immediately being required to repay the cost of the extra policing. Arms were to be borne only by persons already licensed or holding official positions. When a murder had been committed, all male persons in the district between the ages of 16 and 60 were liable to be called upon to assist in finding the criminal, and failure to assist was a misdemeanour, punishable by two years' imprisonment.

Cuba Five Fenians who sailed to New York in January 1871 on the SS *Cuba* following their release from imprisonment, including Jeremiah O'Donovan Rossa and John Devoy.

Cumann na mBan Women's organisation founded in Dublin in November 1913 at the same time as the Irish Volunteers, of which it became the women's division. In its constitution after the Rising, the Cumann declared itself 'an independent body of Irish women, pledged to work for the establishment of an Irish republic, by organising and training the women of Ireland to take their places by the side of those who are working for a free Ireland'. The Cumann continued to work for the republican movement during the War of Independence. The majority of its members opposed the Treaty.

Cumann na nGaedheal (1) Founded on 30 September 1900 by Arthur Griffith and William Rooney to provide a co-ordinating body for smaller societies whose aim was to oppose English influences in Ireland. Later Cumann na nGaedheal was absorbed into Sinn Féin.

Cumann na nGaedheal (2) Political party launched on 8 April 1923 by supporters of the Treaty. It was led by William T. Cosgrave and formed the government until 1932 when on 16 February it lost the general election to Fianna Fáil. It became part of Fine Gael in September 1933.

Cumann na Poblachta Party founded by Eamon de Valera in March 1922 and supported principally by opponents of the Treaty. Following the defeat of the republican cause in the Civil War the party was absorbed into Sinn Féin.

Cumann Poblachta na hÉireann Party founded in 1936 to be a forum for republicans opposed to the Republican Congress. It disappeared after a brief period.

Curragh incident or mutiny (20–24 March 1914): On 20 March 1914, 60 cavalry officers led by Brigadier General Hubert Gough at the Curragh Military Camp, County Kildare, offered their resignations rather than participate in an action against Ulster Protestants who resisted the imposition of home rule on the North. On 23 March the officers were informed that there had been a misunderstanding and that there was no intent on the part of the government to take offensive action against Ulster. The assurance was given without cabinet authority and both the Secretary of State for War and the Chief of the Imperial General Staff were obliged to resign.

Custom House On 25 May 1921 the Dublin Irish Republican Army brigade planned to burn down the Custom House in order to damage the operation of the civil service. They were interrupted by Black and Tans, but during the ensuing engagement a fire was started which burned for eight days.

Dáil courts Established during the War of Independence and operating under the jurisdiction of Dáil Éireann, the courts claimed the authority of the crown courts. In October 1922 the authority of the courts was rescinded.

Dáil Éireann (21 January 1919–December 1922): First assembled on 21 January 1919, consisting of 73 Sinn Féin MPs elected to the Westminster parliament but who refused to take their seats, it claimed to be the legitimate

753

legislative body of Ireland. In May 1920 Sinn Féin participated in the elections held for the parliaments of Northern and Southern Ireland respectively and the Second Dáil (August 1921 – June 1922) was enlarged to 125 seats. After 1922 the lower house of the legislative assembly of the state continued to be termed Dáil Éireann, the upper house being known as the Senate, or Seanad Éireann, and the two combined known as the Oneachtas.

Declaration of Independence   Read at the first meeting of the Dáil on 21 January 1919, it asserted the right of the Irish people to political independence.

Defence of the Realm Act, 1914   Enacted on 27 November 1914, it granted extensive powers of arrest and was employed after the Easter Rising of 1916 to suppress Irish revolutionary organisations and again during the War of Independence. It ceased on 31 August 1921.

Democratic Programme   Approved by the First Dáil Éireann on 21 January 1919. Declaration of the progressive social and economic aspirations of the revolutionary regime. It was drafted by William O'Brien and Thomas Johnson.

Democratic Unionist Party   Founded in 1971 by Ian Paisley among others to oppose the Ulster Unionist Party. A strongly Unionist body, it opposed power-sharing in 1974, stood against the Anglo-Irish Agreement (1985) and declined to endorse the Good Friday Agreement (1998).

Devolution Crisis   (1904–5): This arose out of a proposal by the Irish Reform Association in August 1904, which advocated devolved powers of local self-government. The proposal was repudiated in late September by the Chief Secretary George Wyndham, but the crisis brought about his resignation in the following year.

Devon Commission   (1843): Under the chairmanship of Lord Devon the Commission investigated relations between landlords and tenants, modes of occupation on the land, land cultivation, the need for improvement and the conditions of agricultural labourers. It reported in 1847.

Diplock Report   A committee chaired by Lord Diplock issued a report on 22 December 1972 recommending trial without jury in cases of scheduled offences in Northern Ireland.

direct rule   (1972–2001): Rule in Northern Ireland by the Westminster government and parliament without the tier of a province-wide elected legislative body with a responsible executive. On 24 March 1972 the Westminster government suspended devolved government in Northern Ireland and the office of Secretary of State for Northern Ireland was created. Under the Northern Ireland Constitution Act (July 1973) Stormont was abolished. In 1983 the number of MPs for Northern Ireland was increased from 12 to 17 and raised further to 18 in 1997. Direct rule was imposed twice during 2001.

disestablishment of the Church of Ireland   (1869): Legislation which became law on 26 July 1869 ending the status of the Church of Ireland as the established confession as of 1 January 1871, while also drawing to a close annual grants for Catholic and Presbyterian theological training.

Document No. 2   Proposal for an alternative Treaty between Great Britain and Ireland which was put forward by Eamon de Valera on 14 December 1921. It differed from the Treaty by deleting the Oath of Allegiance and the provision for a governor-general, while the defence facilities would be granted to Great Britain for five years only. It reproduced the clauses in the Treaty concerning Northern Ireland, but a subsequent version (Document No. 3) presented in January 1922 omitted these clauses. The Document was withdrawn prior to consideration in the Dáil.

Downing Street Declaration   (15 December 1993): Joint declaration by the Taoiseach and the Prime Minster on the principles for a future framework for peace and government in Northern Ireland.

Dublin Castle   The administrative headquarters of the Irish administration in Ireland (there was also an Irish Office in Whitehall).

Dublin Lockout   (1913): In August 1913 employers led by William Martin Murphy combined to compel workers to withdraw from the Irish Transport and General Workers Union or be dismissed. The action petered out, with most strikers returning to work by late January 1914 on terms dictated by the employers.

Dublin Metropolitan Police (DMP)   Founded in 1786, it remained distinct from the Royal Irish Constabulary. In 1836 the Dublin Metropolitan Police was created under central control. Under the Police Forces Amalgamation Act (1925) it became part of the Gárda Síochána in April 1925.

Dungannon Clubs   Founded by Bulmer Hobson and Denis McCullough in 1905 in commemoration of the 1782 Volunteer Convention at Dungannon, Co. Tyrone. The clubs were non-sectarian, republican and separatist and flourished mainly in Ulster. They were absorbed into the Sinn Féin League between 1906 and 1908.

Dynamiters   Campaign of violence in Great Britain between 1883 and 1885 instigated by Irish-Americans. A number of Fenians were captured and sentenced to long terms of imprisonment, inspiring the renewal of an amnesty movement in the 1890s. The last convict, Thomas Clarke, was released in 1898.

Easter Rising   (24 April – 1 May 1916): Rebellion commencing on Easter Monday 1916 with the aim of establishing a republic. Though it was quickly suppressed and the main leaders were executed, this marked the effective beginning of the armed struggle for Irish statehood.

Ecclesiastical Titles Act, 1851   Forbade Catholic clerics to assume ecclesiastical titles taken from anywhere in the United Kingdom. Its passage was vigorously opposed by the Catholic Defence Association.

Economic Development   (1958): An official report by T. K. Whitaker favouring a return to a more competitive free-trade economy. *See* Programmes for Economic Expansion.

Economic War   (1932–8): The 'war' began after the Fianna Fáil government withheld land annuities from the British Exchequer in 1932. Britain held that this was in breach of the financial agreements of 1925 and 1926 and imposed tariffs on Irish cattle and agricultural produce entering the United Kingdom. De Valera then imposed tariffs on British goods entering the Free State. The Anglo-Irish Agreements in 1938 ended the dispute.

Eighty-Two Club   Founded in 1845 in memory of the Volunteers of 1782 and the independent parliament of the late eighteenth century.

Éire   Official name for Ireland in the Constitution of 1937. Under the Republic of Ireland Act (1948) it was renamed the Republic of Ireland.

Electoral Amendment Act, 1927   Provided that a candidate for Dáil Éireann would have to sign an affidavit that if he were elected he would take his seat and the Oath of Allegiance within two months. The Act ended a policy of abstention adopted by Eamon de Valera and his followers.

Emergency   The period of the Second World War in Éire which retained its status as a neutral in the conflict.

emergency men   During the Land War (1879–82) an Emergency Committee of the Orange Order was established 'for the purpose of protecting loyal subjects in Ireland against the activities of the Land League'. Financed by the Committee, emergency men took over the farms from which tenants had been evicted, worked them in the landlords' interests and provided labour for landlords who were boycotted.

Emergency Powers Act, 1939   Supplemented the Treason Act and the Offences Against the State Act, both designed to deal with the Irish Republican Army, which, since January 1939, had been engaged in a campaign against Northern Ireland and Britain. The Emergency Powers Act was extended the next year, granting the Minister for Justice powers to intern known or suspected members of the IRA or those who aided them.

Emergency Powers Act, 1976   Empowered the Gardai to arrest without warrant and hold in custody for up to seven days persons suspected in connection with offences under the Offences Against the State Act (1939). It lapsed in October 1977.

Emmet Monument Association   Founded in New York in 1855, it was the precursor of the Irish Republican Brotherhood, having the object of gaining Irish independence by invading the country with an Irish-American army. Members of the Emmet Monument Association provided £80, which James Stephens used to found the Irish Republican Brotherhood in Dublin (17 March 1858). The Association was absorbed by the Fenians, the American counterpart to the IRB.

Encumbered Estates Acts, 1848, 1849   Legislation allowing the sale of Irish estates which had been mortgaged and whose owners, because of the Famine of 1845–9, were unable to meet their obligations. Under the Act of 1849 an Encumbered Estates Court was established with authority to sell estates on the application of the owner or encumbrancer (one who had a claim on the estate).

Evicted Tenants Act, 1907   Enabled the Land Commissioners to acquire untenanted land compulsorily for the purpose of providing holdings for tenants, who, or whose predecessors, had been evicted from their holdings since 1878, and who had applied to the Commissioners before 1 May 1907.

Executive Council   Governing body of the Free State from 6 December 1922 until 29 December 1937. The Prime Minister was known as the President of the Executive Council. Under the Constitution of 1937 the head of the government was known as the Taoiseach.

External Association   Devised by Eamon de Valera in 1921 as an attempt to bridge the gap between Dominion status and a republic. He called for free association with the British Commonwealth.

External Relations Act, 1936   Delimited the functions of the crown in the field of external relations of the Free State.

faction fighting   Common in the pre-Famine era, this usually took place at fairs, markets, races and other public occasions. The last recorded faction fighting was in Tipperary in 1887.

Fair Employment Act (1974 Northern Ireland)   Made it illegal to discriminate in employment on religious or political grounds and also established the Fair Employment Agency.

fairs   Markets held at traditional times of the year at established venues for the sale or interchange of goods. Labourers could also be hired at 'hiring fairs'.

Famine   (1846–9): Though Ireland experienced several famines, the use of the term Famine or Great Famine is identified with the disaster of the 1840s.

Farmers' Party   It represented the more substantial farmer in Dáil Éireann between 1922 and 1932. It supported the Cumann na nGaedheal governments. After 1932 the party disappeared and its supporters were absorbed by Cumann na nGaedheal and its successor, Fine Gael.

Fenians   Name given by John O'Mahony to the republican organisation founded in New York on 17 March 1858 at the same time that the Irish Republican Brotherhood (IRB) was formed in Dublin. Though they were separate groups, the term Fenian was employed for their collective identity.

Fianna Éireann, na   Republican youth movement founded in Dublin in August 1909.

757

Fianna Fáil Party founded on 16 May 1926 by Eamon de Valera with the aims of the reunification of Ireland, the preservation of the Irish language, the distribution of large farms among the small farmers and a policy of protection and self-sufficiency for the Irish economy. It broke with the Sinn Féin policy of abstention from Dáil Éireann and entered the Dáil on 11 August 1927. It won the general election in 1932 and formed the government.

Fianna Uladh Political wing of Saor Uladh founded in 1953 in Co. Tyrone. It was banned in 1956.

Fine Gael Originally called the United Ireland Party; founded in September 1933 from a merger of Cumann na nGaedheal, the National Guard and the National Centre Party.

Flags and Emblems Act (1954 Northern Ireland) Passed by the parliament of Northern Ireland, it gave the Minister for Justice the power to order the seizure of 'provocative emblems' and also made it an offence to interfere with the Union Jack in a public place.

Flying Column Principal unit used by the Irish Republican Army during the War of Independence, it consisted of a small, highly manoeuvrable group operating on an independent basis.

forty-shilling freeholders Those who held a lease for life of a house or land, in which the lessee had an interest worth 40 shillings a year, were granted the vote in 1793, but with the passage of the Catholic Relief Act (1829) the qualification for the franchise was raised from 40 shillings to £10.

Four Courts Located on the bank of the Liffey and the centre of the Irish judiciary. It was seized by a battalion of the Dublin Brigade of the Irish Republican Army on 14 April 1922. After prolonged negotiations the Provisional Government bombarded the building on 28 June, an action that marked the commencement of the Civil War.

Framework Document (February 1995): Blueprint for the future governing arrangements in Northern Ireland.

Free State The designation for the area of the 26 counties of Southern Ireland delimited in the Treaty. The name was altered to Éire in 1937.

Friends of Ireland Group Section of backbench British Labour MPs who came together in 1945 to express opposition to the methods of the Ulster Unionist Party in Northern Ireland. It ceased to exist after 1951.

Friends of Irish Freedom Republican organisation founded at the first Irish Race Convention, New York (4–5 March 1916). The aim of the organisation was 'to encourage and assist any movement that will bring about the national independence of Ireland'.

Friends of Religious Freedom and Equality Founded in October 1862, it was an ephemeral organisation for the purpose of seeking repeal of the Ecclesiastical Titles Act and disestablishment of the Church of Ireland.

Gaelic Athletic Association   (GAA) (Cumann Lúthchleas Gael): Amateur sporting association founded in November 1884 by Michael Cusack for the preservation and cultivation of national pastimes.

Gaelic League   (Conradh na Gaeilge): Founded on 1 July 1893 it was dedicated to the 'de-Anglicisation of Ireland' through the revival and preservation of Irish as a spoken language. Douglas Hyde, the first president, hoped that a non-political and non-sectarian league would offer common ground upon which all sections of Irish political and religious opinion could meet for a cultural purpose. Against Hyde's wishes the League had by 1915 taken a political stance. At the Ard Fheis of that year in Dundalk it was resolved that the political independence of Ireland was a primary aim. This led to Hyde's resignation.

Gaelic Society   Scholarly association founded in 1807, which during its brief existence was devoted to the discovery, translation and publication of early Irish manuscripts.

Gaeltacht   Areas of Ireland in which Irish is the vernacular of the majority of the people. Two types of Gaeltacht are distinguished; the Fior-Gaeltacht in which 80 per cent or more of the population speak Irish, and the Breac-Gaeltacht in which 25 to 79 per cent speak the language. By the Gaeltacht Areas Order (1956) Gaeltacht districts were declared in Counties Clare, Cork, Donegal, Galway, Kerry, Mayo and Waterford.

gale   The semi-annual payment of rent.

Gárda Siochána   Police force established in the autumn of 1922. Initially an all-male service, the Gárda Siochána Act of 1958 provided for the recruitment of women.

Gardiner Report   (30 January 1975): Under the chairmanship of Lord Gardiner a committee recommended that detention without trial be maintained but employed only under the authority of the Secretary of State for Northern Ireland and also that the 'special category' status of prisoners convicted of offences for a 'political' purpose be ended.

German plot   Dublin Castle announced in May 1918 that evidence had been found that 'certain subjects . . . domiciled in Ireland had entered into treasonable communication with the German enemy'. No evidence of such a plot was ever found.

Gibraltar shootings   On 6 March 1988 the British Special Air Services (SAS) shot dead three Irish Republican Army figures who were suspected of being about to plant an explosive. The incident led to a lengthy investigation and received wide publicity.

Gombeen men   They were generally shopkeepers and others, mainly in the west, who made loans at high interest rates.

Good Friday Agreement (1998): Proposals accepted by the Social Democratic and Labour Party, Sinn Féin, the Ulster Unionists and several smaller parties of a formula for the government of Northern Ireland.

Goulburn's Act, 1825 Legislation to suppress the Catholic Association. Political associations of more than 14 days' duration were outlawed. It expired in 1827.

Governor-General The post of Governor-General of the Irish Free State was created in December 1922. He represented the crown in Ireland and occupied the Viceregal Lodge in Phoenix Park. The office was abolished by Eamon de Valera upon the passage of the External Relations Act (December 1936).

grand jury Body responsible for the administration of the county unit. Peers were disqualified from service but members were generally the leading landowners. The upper limit of members was 23 and the position was honorary. They met at the assizes to assist the judges on circuit and their chief function was to strike the rate or 'cess' for the county. Under the Local Government Act (1898) a new system of elected county and district councils came into operation and took over the grand jury's functions.

Grattan's Parliament Popularly applied during the nineteenth century to the assembly that existed between the 1780s and the Union.

Green Knights Members of the Brunswick Clubs used the term when referring to Daniel O'Connell's supporters.

Griffith's Valuation Compiled under the supervision of Sir Richard Griffith, chairman of the Board of Works, under the Valuation Act (1852), this *Valuation of Ireland* assessed in detail the rental value of all Irish land. It became the standard reference for the relative movements in rentals.

Grosse Isle Islet on the St Lawrence River which is the burial place of thousands of Famine refugees. It was opened in 1832 as a quarantine station.

H-blocks, Maze Prison In February 1975 the government announced an intention to construct units in the Maze Prison, which became known as the H-blocks, to hold republican and loyalist prisoners.

Harland & Wolff The shipyard in east Belfast formed in 1861, noted both for its production of ships and also as a centre of Protestant working-class militancy.

Harp Society Founded in Belfast (1808) the principal aim of the Society was to enable blind children to earn a living by teaching them the harp. Another purpose was to promote the study of the Irish language, history and antiquities.

Hawarden Kite Disclosure by Herbert Gladstone on 16 December 1885 that his father had been converted to home rule.

hedge schools Schools which mushroomed during the eighteenth century to provide instruction for Catholics who otherwise had limited access to formal education. They were supplanted by the National Schools established under legislation passed in 1831.

hiring fair Place where men and women offered themselves for employment to substantial farmers for the agricultural season. Those who hired themselves out were known as 'spalpeens'.

Home Government Association Launched on 1 September 1870 its aim was to press for a federal system which would grant Ireland a domestic parliament responsible for internal affairs. It was succeeded in November 1873 by the Home Rule League.

home rule The term was first used in the 1860s, possibly by Revd J. A. Galbraith, and meant the creation of an Irish government with a legislature having responsibility for domestic affairs. It was variously interpreted until 1886 when the Government of Ireland bill introduced by W. E. Gladstone gave it a more precise definition.

Home Rule bills (1886, 1893, 1912): On each occasion Liberal governments introduced measures for the establishment of a legislature with a responsible executive for Irish affairs. The first two bills failed, while the third was passed in 1914 but was not implemented.

Home Rule Confederation of Great Britain Founded in 1872, its purpose was to elicit support, especially from the Irish population of Great Britain, for the self-government programme. It largely fell into abeyance during the Land War (1879–82) and was succeeded by the Irish National League of Great Britain when this was formed in October 1883.

Home Rule League Founded in November 1873 to replace the Home Government Association, it had the identical aim to seek self-government for Ireland based on a federal system. Whereas the Home Government Association was a private body, the new League was a public organisation which solicited a wide membership. The League disappeared during the Land War (1879–82) and was succeeded by the Irish National League in October 1882.

Home Rule Party Founded on 3 May 1874, its first chairman was Isaac Butt. Though associated with the Home Rule League, members were never responsible to the extra-parliamentary organisation and the linkage was informal. The new party had whips and members were to consult together. Following Butt's death in 1879, William Shaw was selected as sessional chairman. He was displaced by Charles Stewart Parnell in May 1880. Though the party came to be known as the Irish Parliamentary Party or Irish Party, it had continuity from 1873 until its demise after 1921.

Home Rule Union Organised by the British Liberal Party in 1886, it disseminated propagandist literature, much of it supplied by the Irish Press Agency, in an attempt to foster support for home rule. The Union provided lecturers (most of them members of the Irish Parliamentary Party) throughout Britain. It collapsed following the split in the Irish Party (1890–1).

Howth gun-running A landing by the Irish Volunteers of a shipment of weapons at Howth on 26 July 1914. Later in the day this led to the shooting at Bachelor's Walk. *See* Bachelor's Walk.

hunger strike Refusal by a prisoner to take food or water which, if prolonged, ends in the death of the inmate.

Hunt Commission Commission of inquiry appointed by the British government and chaired by Sir John Hunt. It was established in August 1969 to examine the recruitment, organisation, structure and composition of the Royal Ulster Constabulary, and the Special Constabulary in Northern Ireland. The report of the Commission, issued in October, recommended that the RUC should be relieved of all duties of a military nature and that its function should be restricted to intelligence-gathering, the protection of important persons and the enforcement of specified laws. It also proposed that there should be a Police Authority for Northern Ireland, whose membership should reflect the proportions of the different religions in the community, and that the Special Constabulary (B Specials) should be disbanded and replaced by a locally recruited, part-time force.

Iberno-Celtic Society A short-lived organisation founded in Dublin in 1818 as a scholarly society with the object of preserving venerable remains of Irish literature by collecting, transcribing, illustrating and publishing the numerous fragments of the law, history, topography, poetry and music of ancient Ireland. It issued only one publication (1820).

Independent Irish Party Founded in September 1852 from an alliance of the Irish Brigade and the Tenant League, the Independent Irish Party consisted of Irish MPs pledged to be 'independent of and in opposition to' all British governments that did not treat the demands of the Tenant League and commit themselves to repeal the Ecclesiastical Titles Act. The party ceased to exist after 1859.

Independent Orange Order A breakaway group from the Orange Order, it was founded in June 1903. Based on the militant Belfast Protestant Association, it was predominantly working class.

Industrial Credit Company (ICC) A state bank established in 1933 to provide capital for Irish industry.

Inghinidhe na hÉireann (Daughters of Ireland): Nationalist movement founded in 1900 by Maud Gonne to support Irish separatism and the Irish-Ireland movement, it also opposed the Irish Party. It was absorbed into Cumann na mBan in 1913.

internment Detention without trial. It was used under British rule and subsequently in both parts of post-1921 Ireland.

interparty government   A coalition of two or more parties sharing posts and agreeing on a common set of policies.

Invincibles   Founded in November 1881 and known as the Irish National Invincibles, it was a breakaway from the Irish Republican Brotherhood. It plotted a number of assassinations and was responsible for the Phoenix Park murders on 6 May 1882. Five members of the conspiracy were executed for the murders and the group disappeared.

Ireland Act, 1949   British legislation recognising the Republic of Ireland and also that Northern Ireland would remain part of the United Kingdom and would not have its status changed without the consent of the parliament of Northern Ireland.

Irish Academy of Letters   Founded in 1932 by William Butler Yeats and George Bernard Shaw to promote a bilingual creative literature in Ireland; to support work of intellectual and poetic quality by writers of Irish birth or descent; to counter any obstacle that hampered literary activity; and to develop a public appreciation for all work which should, in the Academy's opinion, contribute to the creation of a distinctive Irish literature. Membership of the Academy is limited to 35 at any one time.

Irish Agricultural Labourers' Union   Founded in 1873 to advance the interests of labourers, it collapsed within a few months.

Irish Agricultural Organisation Society (IAOS)   Founded in 1894 by Sir Horace Plunkett and others to co-ordinate the activities of the various Irish co-operative units in an effort to improve the state of the country's agriculture. It published *The Irish Homestead* edited by George W. Russell (A. E.).

Irish Amateur Athletic Association (IAAA)   Founded in 1885 to regulate and organise athletics in Ireland.

Irish Battalion of St Patrick   Eight companies of soldiers raised in Ireland in 1860 to serve Pope Pius IX in his resistance to Italian nationalists who desired to unify the country.

Irish Brigade   Irish MPs who banded together in order to oppose the Ecclesiastical Titles bill during the 1851 parliamentary session. They had the approval of the Archbishop of Dublin, Paul Cullen, when they founded the Catholic Defence Association to aid the cause outside parliament. Later the Brigade's critics termed it 'the Pope's Brass Band'. It entered into an alliance with the Tenant League in August 1852 to form the Independent Irish Party.

Irish Christian Front   Founded in 1935, it was a non-party organisation, closely associated with the Blueshirts and dedicated to resisting the alleged threat to Ireland of international communism. It had the tacit support of the Catholic Hierarchy in efforts to put pressure on the government to sever diplomatic relations with the Republican government in Spain and, shortly afterwards, to support General Franco's armed opposition to that government.

763

Irish Citizen Army   Founded on 23 November 1913 as a workers' defence corps during the Dublin Lockout, with the immediate purpose of protecting the workers from attacks by the Dublin Metropolitan Police and the employers' 'hired bullies'. After the lockout ended in the spring of 1914 the membership dwindled and the remaining 200 or so were taken over by James Connolly, who reorganised it. The Army under Connolly played a key role in the Easter Rising. Many members declined to accept the Treaty. It virtually ceased to exist after the close of the Civil War in May 1923.

Irish Confederation   Founded on 13 January 1847 by members of Young Ireland who had seceded from the Repeal Association. It began an armed rebellion at Ballingarry, Co. Tipperary, in July 1848, which was quickly suppressed. The leaders either fled abroad or were convicted of treason and transported to Tasmania. In the wake of the rebellion the movement collapsed.

Irish Congress of Trade Unions (ICTU)   Formed in 1959 from an amalgamation of the Irish Trades Union Congress (ITUC) and the Congress of Irish Unions (CIU) with the purpose of co-ordinating, advising and generally assisting member organisations.

Irish Convention   (25 July 1917 – 5 April 1918): An attempt by a 'representative' body of Irishmen under the chairmanship of Sir Horace Plunkett to secure a final settlement of the demand for home rule. The Convention ended in April 1918 with a report, signed by less than half of the members, which recommended self-government. A minority report to the government stated that it would be dangerous to extend conscription to Ireland.

Irish Council   Formed in 1847 it attempted to devise a system to alleviate famine distress, but as conditions deteriorated the Council disintegrated. Its achievement was an investigation into the prevailing social conditions.

Irish Council bill   (1907): Proposal to grant Ireland limited devolved powers of government through an appointed council. It was rejected by both the Irish Party and the Unionists. The government withdrew the measure in June 1907.

Irish Countrywomen's Association   (Bantracht na Tuaithe): Founded as the United Irishwomen by Anita Lett in 1911, it is dedicated to the general improvement of rural life and concentrates on home and farm management instruction, handicrafts and general social and cultural activities.

Irish Dominion League   Founded on 27 June 1919, it sought self-government for Ireland within the British Empire. It gained little support.

Irish Education Act, 1892   Made school attendance compulsory up to 13 and abolished fees for children at National Schools up to the leaving age.

Irish Farmers' Association (IFA)   Formed on 1 January 1970 from the National Farmers' Association and other bodies, its remit is to represent the interests of farmers in the Republic of Ireland.

Irish Federated Trade and Labour Union Founded in Cork in 1890, it was an effort to establish a trade union for agricultural labourers and sought universal suffrage, free education, land settlement, houses for workers and reduced working hours. It broke up as a result of the split in the Irish Parliamentary Party in 1890–1, although a remnant of it persisted into the 1920s.

Irish Fever Act (27 April 1847): Legislation to contain fever which accompanied the Famine. It gave local bodies wide preventative powers, including the erection of temporary fever hospitals and proper burials for the Famine dead; it remained in force until August 1850.

Irish Folklore Commission (Coimisiún Béaloideas Éireann): A state-funded body founded in 1927 for the purpose of collecting and preserving oral tradition. It maintains a library of manuscripts, assembled by collectors throughout the country.

Irish Free State Constitution Act Statute of 1922 which incorporated the Free State Constitution of 1922 giving it constitutional recognition in English law.

Irish Freedom Republican newspaper published by members of the Irish Republican Brotherhood from 1910 until December 1914, when it was suppressed by the authorities. Another paper of the same name was published by the republican movement in Dublin from 1939 to 1944 and in Belfast in 1951.

Irish Georgian Society Founded in 1958 for the preservation and protection of buildings of architectural merit.

Irish Historical Studies Academic periodical founded in 1938, it remains an important forum of historical scholarship on the Irish experience.

Irish Homestead Journal founded in 1895 to advance the views of the Co-operative Movement.

Irish Independence Party Founded in Northern Ireland in October 1977 to advocate a British withdrawal from the province.

Irish-Ireland Term for revivalists around the turn of the century who advocated cultural and economic independence.

Irish Labour Defence League Originally the Workers' Defence Corps, it was renamed on 7 July 1931. It consisted of the left-wing members of the Irish Republican Army and Dublin trades unionists. The League was outlawed by the government on 17 October 1931 and disappeared within a short time.

Irish Labour League Founded in 1891 by the Dublin branch of the National Union of Gasworkers and General Labourers. The League sought the nationalisation of transport. It failed within a short time through lack of support.

Irish Land and Labour Association Founded in Cork at the end of the nineteenth century, it sought to organise agricultural labourers and small tenants as a successor to the Irish Democratic Labour Federation. It lost impetus after 1912 and was absorbed into the new Labour Party.

Irish Literary Society Founded in London in 1891 from the Southwark Literary Club for the purpose of encouraging and stimulating literature which would be thoroughly and distinctively Irish.

Irish Literary Theatre Founded at the close of 1898 by W. B. Yeats for the purpose of promoting the production of Irish work, it became part of the Abbey Theatre in 1904.

Irish Loyal and Patriotic Union (ILPU) Founded in May 1885 for the purpose of resisting home rule, it concentrated on propaganda after 1885. It became part of the Irish Unionist Alliance in 1891.

Irish Manuscripts Commission (Coimisiún Láimhsinbhisi Éireann): Established in 1928 to investigate and report on existing manuscripts of literary, historical and general interest and importance, and to edit and publish them.

Irish Nation League Founded by nationalists in Ulster after the Rising of 1916, its purpose was to oppose any proposal for partition.

Irish National Aid Association Founded after the Easter Rising, its purpose was to raise funds for the dependants of the deceased and imprisoned Irish Volunteers. Within a short time it amalgamated with the Irish Volunteers Dependants' Fund.

Irish National Alliance Founded by members of Clan na Gael who regarded the Irish Republican Brotherhood as too conservative. Its support had declined to a handful by 1900.

Irish National Club Founded in London in January 1899 largely from among those who organised the 1898 centenary celebrations, its object was 'to promote a healthy spirit of nationality among London Irishmen and the study and encouragement of Irish history and literature'.

Irish National Federation Formed in March 1891 by anti-Parnellites who seceded from the National League. It was succeeded in 1900 by the United Irish League.

Irish National Foresters Founded in Dublin in 1877 as a benefit society. To qualify for membership one had to be Irish by birth or descent.

Irish National Land League Founded on 21 October 1879 with Charles Stewart Parnell as president, it was the organisational manifestation of the Land War. Many of the leaders were held in prison under the Protection of Person and Property Act (1881). It was proclaimed illegal after the issuance of the 'No Rent Manifesto' in October 1881.

Irish National Land League of Mayo   Found on 16 August 1879, it was the forerunner of the Land League, which absorbed it in October.

Irish National League   Inaugurated on 17 October 1882, it was an arm of the Irish Party. Membership dwindled after the party split in 1890. After party reunification in 1900, it was replaced by the United Irish League.

Irish National Liberation Army (INLA)   Formed in 1975 as a splinter group from the Official Irish Republican Army, it had earlier been known as the People's Liberation Army (1974).

Irish National Society   Founded in London in 1844 to bring Irishmen together, regardless of their political or religious beliefs. It did not survive the break-up of the Repeal Association.

Irish National Teachers' Organisation   Founded in 1868 for those employed within the National education system.

Irish Nationality and Citizenship Act, 1935   Under it Irish nationals ceased to be British subjects.

Irish Neutrality League   Founded in 1914 for the purpose of keeping Ireland from involvement on the side of Great Britain in the First World War. It was involved in activity to stop recruiting.

Irish News Agency   Established by Seán MacBride in 1949 to publicise Ireland abroad. It closed in 1957.

Irish Office   Established in 1801 for the transaction of business by the Chief Secretary while in London during the parliamentary session. It was abolished after the Treaty.

Irish Press Agency   Founded in 1886 to distribute information in Great Britain on Irish affairs. It collapsed in 1891 after the Irish Party split.

Irish race conventions   (1896, 1916, 1919): Irish-Americans organised the convention held in Dublin in 1896 in order to facilitate the reunion of the Irish national ranks. Only a section attended and it had merely a limited impact. On 3–4 March 1916 a convention was held in New York under the auspices of Clan na Gael. It founded the Friends of Irish Freedom. Another convention was held in Philadelphia in February 1919 to support an Irish Republic.

Irish Reform Association   Established in 1904 as a mainly reformist Unionist body, its programme was limited devolution of some power to an Irish body.

Irish Republican Army (IRA)   Founded when the first Dáil recognised the Irish Volunteers as the Army of the Irish Republic. One section refused to adhere to the Treaty and fought against the government during the Civil War. It was given fresh life during the 1960s in Northern Ireland.

Irish Republican Brotherhood   *See* Fenians, Phoenix National and Literary Societies.

Irish Republican Defence Association Founded in London in 1937 to organise Irish support in Great Britain for the Irish Republican Army and its aim of securing an all-Ireland republic. It supported the IRA campaign against Britain which started in January 1939.

Irish Republican Socialist Party Founded in December 1974, it was registered as a political party in May 1975. It sought a united Ireland organised on socialist lines. The party newspaper was titled the *Starry Plough*.

Irish Self-Determination League of Great Britain Founded in March 1919 to support Sinn Féin and the first Dáil Éireann in the fight for Irish independence. It split over the Treaty and became virtually defunct.

Irish Socialist Republican Party Founded in Dublin on 29 May 1896 as a successor to the Dublin Socialist Party. Following James Connolly's departure for the United States in 1903 the party was reorganised as the Socialist Party of Ireland.

Irish Society Formed by Anglicans in 1818 for the promotion of scriptural education and religious instruction for Catholics through the medium of their own language.

Irish Sugar Company (Comhlucht Siúicre Éireann Teoranta): Established in 1933 as a state-owned company for the production of home-grown sugar beet.

Irish Texts Society Founded in 1899 for the purpose of publishing texts in the Irish language.

Irish Trade and Labour Union An attempt in 1890 to form a trade union, which failed within a short time.

Irish Trades Union Congress (ITUC) Formed in Dublin 1894 to further the interests of the trades union movement. In 1912 Congress passed a motion by James Connolly calling for the formation of an Irish Labour Party, as a result of which the Irish Labour Party and Trades Union Congress was formed. In 1945 William O'Brien split Congress and the Labour Party when he withdrew the Irish Transport and General Workers Union from Congress and was followed by 14 other unions. They formed a rival Congress of Irish Unions. The two organisations were reunited in 1959.

Irish Transport and General Workers Union (ITGWU) Founded on 4 January 1909, in 1910 it affiliated to the Irish Trades Unions Congress. In 1945 it left the Congress but the two bodies were reunited in 1959.

Irish Unionist Alliance Founded in 1891 from the Irish Loyal and Patriotic Union it was principally an association of southern unionists with the remit to resist home rule. It disseminated anti-home rule propaganda in Ireland and throughout the United Kingdom.

Irish Universities Act, 1908 The Royal University was abolished and two new universities were constituted: Queen's University of Belfast and the

National University of Ireland, made up from the Queen's Colleges of Galway and Cork, with University College Dublin.

Irish Volunteers Founded on 25 November 1913 it came under the leadership of John Redmond in 1914. One section refused to follow his call for it to serve in the war. It played a prominent part in the War of Independence, becoming the backbone of the Irish Republican Army in 1919.

Irish Volunteers' Dependants' Fund Established in 1916 to aid the dependants of those involved in the Easter Rising.

Irish Women Workers' Union Established in 1911 as a sister organisation to the Irish Transport and General Workers Union. In 1984 it amalgamated with the Federated Workers' Union of Ireland.

Irish Women's Suffrage Federation Founded in 1875 as the Dublin Women's Suffrage Society, it subsequently became the Irish Women's Suffrage and Local Government Association. In 1911 it became the IWSF.

Irish Workers' and Farmers' Republican Party Founded in 1930 with the aim of severing the connection with Great Britain, to bring about co-operation between rural and urban workers and to end the exploitation of imperialism and capitalism. It was outlawed on 17 October 1933.

Irish Workers' League Founded by James Larkin in 1923 and then replaced by the Communist Party of Ireland as the Irish section of the Comintern.

Irish Working Farmers' Committee Founded in the west in the 1920s, it favoured co-operative farming and was banned by the government in October 1933.

Joint Committee of Unionist Associations Founded in 1907 as the co-ordinating arm of northern and southern Unionist organisations.

Kildare Place Society (Society for the Education of the Poor in Ireland): Founded in 1811 it was a Protestant organisation, providing interdenominational education in which the Bible could be read without comment or notes. By the early 1830s it operated 1,621 schools.

Kildare Street Club Founded in 1782, it was a centre of political life, especially for Protestants, for many decades. In 1975 it merged with the University Club.

Kilmainham 'Treaty' (1882): Informal compact between Charles Stewart Parnell and W. E. Gladstone which allowed the Land War to be brought to an end, the detainees under the Person and Property Act to be released and for further land legislation.

King's Inns Buildings, library and legal body in Dublin for the training and registration of barristers.

Kingstown Name for Dún Laoghaire between 1821 and 1922.

knee-capping The practice of shooting people in the knee, often associated with the Irish Republican Army and used principally on other Catholics who are suspected of passing information or engaging in criminal activity.

Knights of St Columbanus An association of Catholic laymen founded in 1915 by Canon James O'Neill.

Knock, Co. Mayo Scene of a reported apparition by the Virgin Mary on Thursday, 21 August 1879.

Labour Court Created by the Industrial Relations Act (1946) and granted revised powers under the Industrial Relations Acts (1969, 1975), its function is to allow Industrial Relations Officers to prevent or settle industrial disputes.

Labour Party Founded in 1912 it was titled the Irish Labour Party and Trade Union Congress until 1930.

Ladies' Land League Founded in January 1881, it played a vigorous role in the Land War, particularly after the detention of the male leaders of the Land League. It was dissolved in August 1882.

Land Acts (1860–1933): Legislation pertaining to the occupancy and ownership of Irish land was passed in 1860 (Landlord and Tenant Law), 1870 (Landlord and Tenant Act), 1881 (Land Law Act), 1882 (Amending Act), 1885 (Purchase of Land Act – Ashbourne Act), 1887 (Land Act), 1888 (Land Purchase Act), 1891 (Land Act), 1896 (Land Act), 1903 (Land Act – Wyndham Act), 1907 (Evicted Tenants Act), 1909 (Land Act); in the Free State, 1923 (Land Law Act), 1923 (Land Act – Hogan Act), 1927 (Land Law Act) and 1933 (Land Act).

land agent Local representative of the landlord, usually vested with responsibility for the practical management of an estate. A powerful figure, often hated by the tenants.

land annuities Money payable to the United Kingdom Exchequer by tenants who had purchased their land under one of the Land Acts. In 1933 these were withheld by the Irish government, precipitating the Economic War.

Land Commission Established under the Land Act of 1881, its purpose was to determine 'fair rents' for tenant holdings and it had responsibility for overseeing land purchase. In 1923 it absorbed the Congested Districts Board.

Land Conference (December 1902): Representatives of landlords and tenants convened to recommend a settlement of the land question. Legislation embodying its recommendations was passed in 1903 (Wyndham Act).

Land Court Established under the Land Act of 1881, it arbitrated between the landlord and tenant when the parties could not agree on a 'fair rent'.

Land League *See* Irish National Land League.

Land League of Mayo *See* Irish National Land League of Mayo.

Land War (1879–82): A campaign orchestrated by the Land League, it was brought to a halt by the Kilmainham Treaty in 1882. Further phases took place in the second half of the 1880s and at the turn of the century.

Landed Estates Court It was established in 1852 from the Encumbered Estates Court and had the function of guaranteeing the titles of estates being sold as a result of the bankruptcy of former owners. In 1877 its duties were passed to the Land Judges.

Landed Improvement Act, 1847 Empowering the state to advance money for agricultural use, it was administered by the Commissioners of Public Works.

Larne gun-running On the night of 24–25 April 1914 the Ulster Volunteers landed a shipment of German arms at Larne and also at Donaghadee.

law adviser Official in Dublin Castle responsible for advising the Irish government and magistracy on legal matters.

Legion of Mary An association of lay Catholics founded by Frank Duff in 1922.

Leinster House Designed by Richard Castle in 1745 for the Earl of Kildare, it has been home to Dáil Éireann and the Seanad since 1921.

Liberty League Founded by George Noble Plunkett in April 1917 in an effort to supersede both Sinn Féin and the Irish Nation League. It had disintegrated by mid-1917.

Lichfield House Compact Informal arrangement between Daniel O'Connell and Lord Melbourne reached in March 1935 under which the Repealers and Radicals would aid the Whigs in opposing the government of Sir Robert Peel. On returning to office, a Whig government would resolve the tithes question and reform municipal corporations to permit Catholic membership.

Limerick Declaration (1868): Petition signed by approximately 1,600 priests in 1868 urging Repeal of the Union.

Limerick Soviet Formed on 14 April 1919, it was extinguished by British troops on 24 April.

Linen Hall Library Created in 1788 as the Belfast Reading Society, in 1792 it became the Belfast Society for Promoting Knowledge. It has occupied its present site since 1892.

Local Defence Force (LDF) Established in September 1940 during the Emergency as a line of defence against any invasion of the country.

Local Government Act, 1898 Introduced a two-tier system of democratically elected county and district councils. Women were permitted to stand for election as district councillors and from 1911 as county councillors.

Local Government Act, 1919 Extended proportional representation to the 26 town and urban district councils and to 200 other local authorities.

Local Government Board Established in 1872, it assumed responsibility for the Poor Law Commissioners, supervised the dispensary system, adjudicated between local authorities, controlled hospitals, administered the Housing Acts and Public Health Acts, had responsibility for public hygiene and for the distressed; from 1908 it paid out old-age pensions.

Local Option Party Founded in 1929 in Northern Ireland to contest elections in the interest of prohibition. It was short-lived.

Local Security Force (LSF) Formed in May 1940 during the Emergency as a non-military auxiliary to the army.

Londonderry House Agreement (1911): Agreement reached on 6 April 1911 between the Union Defence League and the Joint Committee of the Unionist Association of Ireland where the first assumed responsibility for collecting funds and acting as a bureau in Great Britain in the fight against home rule.

Long-Term Recovery Programme (1949): Programme for economic development drawn up as part of the Republic of Ireland's application for Marshall Aid.

Lord Lieutenant Alternatively referred to as the Viceroy, he was the chief official in Ireland who acted as the surrogate of the crown.

Loyalist Association of Workers Founded in Belfast in 1971 from former supporters of the Workers' Committee for the Defence of the Constitution. It opposed power-sharing and engaged in the strike which brought down the Executive in Northern Ireland in May 1974.

Maamtrasna 'Massacre' (8 August 1882): A horrific murder of a family in a remote part of Co. Galway known as 'Joyce country' resulted in three men being executed. It became a *cause célèbre* because of the execution of Myles Joyce who was stated to be innocent by some of the gang who committed the crime. Joyce professed his innocence in the confessional. Nationalists took up the case as an illustration of the despotic rule of the Irish administration under Lord Spencer. They lost interest after 1886 when W. E. Gladstone adopted home rule and Spencer supported him.

Magheramore Manifesto Document in July 1905 emanating from the Independent Orange Order calling for all Orangemen to 'hold out the hand of friendship to those who, while worshipping at other shrines, are still your countrymen'. It also endorsed compulsory land purchase and a national university and criticised the Ulster Unionist Council.

Manchester Martyrs On 18 September 1867 the rescue of Fenians from a prison van resulted in the death of the guard, Sergeant Brett. Three men were refused clemency and publicly hanged on 23 November. The executions ignited demonstrations in Ireland and among the Irish in Great Britain. The three Fenians were commemorated annually as martyrs until after the Easter Rising.

Mansion House Committee Established in 1918 to co-ordinate the activities of various movements involved in Sinn Féin.

Mansion House Conference (8 April 1918): Called to discuss the proposal to introduce conscription. The delegates co-ordinated an anti-conscription campaign.

Marshall Aid An agreement signed with the United States in June 1948 whereby Éire would receive substantial financial assistance on condition of drawing up a programme outlining national import requirements for the next three years.

Maynooth, St Patrick's College Found in 1795 at Maynooth, Co. Kildare, it is the Catholic national seminary. In 1910 it became a 'recognised' college of the National University of Ireland of which it is now a constituent college. It consists of a seminary, a pontifical university (1899) and a lay college (1966). The lay college became a constituent college of the National University of Ireland in 1997.

Maynooth Grant Act of parliament in June 1845 which significantly increased state subsidy to the college, igniting a public controversy.

middleman Tenant of a landlord who in turn sublet land.

Military Council (IRB) Formed in 1915, a secret group within the Irish Volunteers, largely responsible for planning the Easter Rising.

Military Pensions Act, 1934 Legislation granting pensions to members of the Irish Republican Army who had fought for the republican cause during the Civil War.

Ministers and Secretaries Act, 1924 Reduced the number of departments in the Free State from over 40 to 11.

Mitchelstown 'Massacre' On 9 September 1887 police fired into a crowd gathered for a Plan of Campaign demonstration, killing three people, at Mitchelstown, Co. Cork.

Model Schools Established in 1846 to facilitate the training of teachers, they were administered by the Commissions of National Education.

Molly Maguires Anti-landlord secret society flourishing from 1835 to 1855, which subsequently spread to America where as an offshoot of the Ancient Order of Hibernians it was active in the unrest in the coalfields of Pennsylvania. The name came from the practice of dressing in women's clothing. It was disbanded in the United States in 1877.

Monetary Reform Political party with a brief existence founded in 1943 to advocate an increase in the money supply by printing more currency.

Mother and Child Scheme (1951): Proposal to provide a non-compulsory healthcare system for all mothers and children up to the age of 16, which would not be means-tested. Faced by opposition from the Irish Medical Association and the Church, it was dropped, being a *cause célèbre* for liberal opinion.

Municipal Corporations Act, 1840 Fifty-eight corporations were dissolved and the 10 remaining corporations were reconstituted. Catholics were allowed to enter the corporations for the first time.

National Agricultural Labourers' Union (NALU) British union which extended its activities to Ireland in 1873 in an attempt to defend the rights of Irish farm labourers and prevent migrant labourers strike-breaking in England. It disappeared after 1877.

National Association Founded on 29 December 1864, it advocated tenant right, disestablishment of the Church of Ireland and freedom of education. It had strong clerical backing but was short-lived.

National Centre Party Founded from the National Farmers' and Ratepayers' League in 1932–3, it merged with Fine Gael in 1933.

National Coalition Government Formed in 1973 from a coalition of Fine Gael and the Labour Party. It came to an end in June 1977.

National Corporative Party Founded in 1935, it was inspired by Mussolini, but quickly faded.

National Council Formed by members of Cumann na Gaedheal to protest against the visit to Ireland of King Edward VII in 1903. The Council remained in existence afterwards and ultimately merged with Sinn Féin.

National Farmers' Association (NFA) Formed in 1955 to advocate the interests of farmers, it merged with other organisations to form the Irish Farmers' Association on 1 January 1970.

National Farmers' and Ratepayers' Party Founded in October 1932, its purposes were the promotion of agriculture, stronger representation of farmers in the Dáil, an end to the Economic War and the end of partition by mutual consent.

National Guard Title of the Army Comrades Association from July 1933. In September 1933 it merged with Cumann na nGaedheal and the National Centre Party to become Fine Gael.

National Labour Party Founded in 1943 as a splinter from the Labour Party with which it was reunited in June 1950.

National Land League Founded in 1965 as an organisation for small farmers, it was opposed to the Republic of Ireland's entry into the European Economic Community and the purchase of land by foreigners. It also wanted the redistribution of large holdings.

National League   *See* Irish National League

National League of the North   Party founded in 1928 to support the unification of Ireland, it disappeared after the death of Joseph Devlin in 1934.

National League Party   Founded in September 1926, its programme was co-operation with Great Britain and Northern Ireland; it merged with Cumann na nGaedheal in the early 1930s.

National Party   Founded in 1924 as a result of the Army Mutiny, it demanded the reinstatement of the leaders of the Mutiny. The party disappeared during 1925.

National Party of Northern Ireland   A continuation of the Irish Parliamentary Party after partition, members did not take their seats in the parliament of Northern Ireland until 1924. In 1965 it agreed to become the official opposition. It was replaced by the Social Democratic and Labour Party, formed in 1970.

National Petition Movement   Founded in 1859 at the offices of the *Nation*, it secured 500,000 signatures asking for self-determination.

National Political Union   Founded and controlled by Daniel O'Connell in 1832.

National Progressive Democratic Party   Socialist Party founded in 1957 and dissolved in 1963.

National Schools   A system of education founded under legislation passed in 1831, the schools were transferred to the jurisdiction of the newly created Department of Education in 1924.

National Unity and the National Democratic Party   Founded in Northern Ireland in 1959, it advocated a United Ireland but recognised the constitution of Northern Ireland and opposed violence. In 1970 it joined the Social Democratic and Labour Party.

National University of Ireland   Established in 1908, its constituent parts are the National University of Ireland, Dublin; the National University of Ireland, Cork; the National University of Ireland, Galway; and the National University of Ireland, Maynooth.

National Volunteers   Founded in November 1913, the majority heeded John Redmond's call in 1914 to join the war effort; a minority declined and ultimately became the basis of the Irish Republican Army in 1919.

New Catholic Association   New title assumed in 1825 of the dissolved Catholic Association.

New Departure   (1879): Policy of co-operation between Fenians, land reformers and a wing of the Home Rule Party.

New Irish Library   A series of nationalist books issued by Sir Charles Gavan Duffy after he settled in London in 1880.

New Reformers   Evangelical clergymen active between 1822 and 1860.

New Tipperary   As part of the Plan of Campaign, an alternative town was constructed. It was opened on 12 April 1890 as a consequence of the landlord of Tipperary town evicting 146 tenants. The project collapsed after consuming substantial financial resources from the Plan's treasury.

Night of the Big Wind   (6–7 January 1839): The greatest gale in several centuries.

No Rent Manifesto   Issued by the leaders of the Land League on 18 October 1881 after the imprisonment of several of the most prominent figures, it called upon tenants to refuse to pay any rents. This enabled the government to suppress the Land League.

Northern Ireland   Legal name for the area brought into existence under the Better Government of Ireland Act (1920).

Northern Ireland Assembly   A 78-member body with a power-sharing Executive created in 1973 as part of limited devolution for the province. The Executive collapsed in May 1974 in the face of the Ulster Workers' Council strike. Legislation in 1998 brought into being a new Northern Ireland Assembly consisting of 108 members and a power-sharing Executive.

Northern Ireland Civil Rights Association (NICRA)   Founded in Belfast in February 1967, it was based on the Campaign for Social Justice and the National Council of Civil Liberties in Great Britain. Its goals included reform of local election procedures, an end of bias in the allocation of council housing and repeal of the Civil Authorities (Special Powers) Act. The first major public demonstration was on 24 August 1968. It had a predominant role in the early civil rights campaign in Northern Ireland.

Northern Ireland Labour Party (NILP)   Founded in 1923, it has remained a small party.

Northern Ireland Office   This office was created on 24 March 1972 as part of the arrangement to suspend the sitting of the parliament of Northern Ireland for one year and establish direct rule from Westminster.

Northern Resistance Movement   Founded in 1971, it was a bridge between radicals and republicans in the common front of opposition to government policies in Northern Ireland.

Northwest Loyalist Registration and Electoral Association   Founded in 1886 to thwart home rule by organising the Unionist vote in north-west Ulster.

Oath of Allegiance   (1919, 1922): Declaration administered to the members of Dáil Éireann in August 1919; declaration to recognise the authority of the Constitution of 1922. The latter was abolished under the Removal of Oath Act (1933).

Offences Against the State Act, 1939   Provided for the establishment of military tribunals which had the powers to arrest and intern suspects.

Oireachtas   Legislature of the Republic of Ireland, consisting of Dáil Éireann, Seanad Éireann and the President.

Orange Order   Organisation founded in 1795 with the aims of protecting Protestants from Catholics, supporting the Protestant religion and maintaining the monarchy and the Constitution. Its ruling body, the Grand Orange Lodge, was dissolved in 1825 but reconstituted in 1845. It holds processions annually on 12 July.

Order of Liberators   Founded in 1824 to pursue the struggle for Catholic Emancipation and to protect the 40-shilling freeholders who voted against their landlords.

Orders of Frightfulness   Instructions issued to the anti-Treaty Irish Republican Army on 30 November 1922, listing 14 categories of persons who were to be regarded as legitimate targets to shoot on sight and also to have their property destroyed.

outdoor relief   Term for poor relief outside the workhouse.

Pact Election   Agreement on 20 May 1922 between Michael Collins and Eamon de Valera to allow the general election (16 June) to be held in fair conditions and not on the basis of pro- and anti-Treaty.

Pale   Region around Dublin which in earlier times approximated the fortified area of English rule.

Pan-Celtic Society   Literary society founded in the 1880s and subsequently absorbed by the Irish National Literary Society.

Parliament Act, 1911   Reduced the power of the House of Lords to veto a bill to three parliamentary sessions; set the maximum term of parliaments at five years; and introduced payment for MPs.

Parliament House   Constructed between 1729 and 1739, it is one of the finest buildings in modern Dublin. It was sold to the Bank of Ireland after the Union and remains in the Bank's hands to the present day. Standing opposite Trinity College, Parliament House was a symbol of legislative independence in Ireland to later nationalists.

'Parnellism and Crime'   A series of articles published in *The Times* during March and April 1887 accusing Charles Stewart Parnell and other prominent members of the national movement of having supported criminal behaviour during the Land War (1879–82).

partition   Term applied to the division of Ireland in 1921.

Peace Movement   Founded in Northern Ireland in 1976, it strove to mobilise people across the sectarian divide in order to end the violence. Mairead Corrigan and Betty Williams shared the Nobel Peace Prize for 1976 for their roles.

Penal Laws Acts passed in the seventeenth and eighteenth centuries delimiting the rights and privileges of Catholics. These were popularly seen as the legal establishment of Protestant Ascendancy. The last legal vestiges were abolished under the Catholic Relief Act (1829).

People's Democracy Socialist movement founded on 9 October 1968 at Queen's University, Belfast, to pursue the campaign for civil rights in Northern Ireland. It faded in the early 1970s.

People's Rights Association Founded as a constituency organisation in 1897 by T. M. Healy after he had broken with the Irish National Federation.

Persico Mission Investigative tour by Monsignor Ignazio Persico in 1887, which led to the papal condemnation of the Plan of Campaign.

Phoenix National and Literary Societies Republican societies founded in Skibbereen, Co. Cork, in 1856. During 1858 and 1859 they integrated into the Irish Republican Brotherhood.

Phoenix Park murders On 6 May 1882 Lord Frederick Cavendish, the newly installed Chief Secretary, and the long-serving Under-Secretary, T. H. Burke, were assassinated by a party of Invincibles in Phoenix Park.

Pigott forgeries In March 1887 *The Times* published a letter alleged to have been written by Charles Stewart Parnell in 1882 expressing satisfaction over the assassination of T. H. Burke in Phoenix Park. This and other letters attributed to the Irish leader were exposed as the work of Richard Pigott in February 1889.

Plan of Campaign Proposed on 23 October 1886, it was a second phase of the Land War directed at securing reductions in rent. It was severely damaged by government measures, then weakened further by the split in the Irish Party (December 1890), grinding to a conclusion in 1893.

Poor Law Act, 1838 Under legislation passed in 1838, 130 partly elected Guardians of Poor Law Unions were made responsible for relief of the poor. They were replaced when the Free State came into existence.

Poor Law Valuation (PLV) Valuation of property for the assessment of rates which financed Poor Law Unions.

poteen Illicit, home-made whiskey.

Powis Commission (1869): Commission of Inquiry into Primary Education appointed under the chairmanship of Lord Powis in 1868 to examine the system of National Education. It recommended local contributions towards primary schooling and suggested provisions allowing convent and brothers' schools to enter the National system.

Precursor Society Founded in 1838 by Daniel O'Connell to seek reforming legislation.

Programmes for Economic Expansion (1958–72): Three programmes for economic expansion were drawn up in an attempt to transform the country's economy. The first ran from 1958 to 1963, the second 1963 to 1968, and the third 1969 to 1972.

Progressive Unionist Party Founded in Northern Ireland in 1938 to advocate a radical housing programme and an end to the high level of unemployment. It disappeared after the general election of that year. The modern Progressive Unionist Party was formed in 1977 as a Labour-oriented, working-class Unionist party.

Property Defence Association Founded in 1880 to aid landlords against tenants who belonged to the Land League. It ceased in 1883.

proportional representation System of election used in Ireland. It functioned briefly in Northern Ireland in the early 1920s and was revived there for the Assembly created in 1999.

Protection of Person and Property Act, 1881 Legislation to suspend portions of the common law, to detain persons as suspects without trial and to convict without juries.

Protestant Colonisation Society Formed in 1830 in order to ensure that lands vacated by Protestant tenants were relet to Protestants. It was abandoned a few years later.

Protestant Home Rule Association Founded in 1886 to propagandise for home rule.

Protestant Nationalist Party Founded in 1892 it advocated expropriation of the landlords. It disappeared at the turn of the century.

Provisional Government (16 January – 6 December 1922): Established under article 17 of the Treaty, it was the instrument of government until the Free State constitution came into existence.

Provisional Irish Republican Army *See* Sinn Féin.

Provisional Sinn Féin *See* Sinn Féin.

Public Safety Acts (1923, 1924, 1926, 1927, 1931): Series of legislative enactments granting special powers for the purpose of dealing with political threats to the state.

Quakers' Central Relief Committee Founded in Dublin on 13 November 1846, it established soup-kitchens and attempted to mitigate starvation during the Famine.

quarter-acre clause – 'Gregory clause' Clause in Poor Law Extension Act (1847) which disqualified occupiers of a quarter of an acre or more from receiving relief from the poor rates.

Queen's Colleges Founded under the Provincial Colleges Act (1945), non-denominational colleges were established in Belfast, Cork and Galway. The

779

Catholic Hierarchy came to denounce these as 'godless colleges'. They formed the collegiate part of the Royal University of Ireland in 1879; under the Act of 1908 the college in Belfast became a free-standing university while the colleges at Cork and Galway were joined with the Catholic University in Dublin to become the National University of Ireland.

Radio Telefís Éireann (RTE)   National broadcasting service initially opened in 1926; television service began in 1961.

Ranch War   (1906–9): Fourth phase of the land agitation. It was fostered by radical agrarians who wanted to break up large-scale ranches used for livestock rearing and redistribute the land to smallholders.

rebellion of 1848   A small-scale revolt by Confederates who were headed by William Smith O'Brien. On 29 July 1848 about 100 rebels engaged the police but quickly dispersed.

Recess Committee   Established in 1895 under the aegis of Horace Plunkett, its report advocated the establishment of a department of agriculture and industries, assistance for Irish agriculture and other measures to boost the Irish economy. The report was issued in August 1896.

Registrar-General   Office created in 1845 with its duties extended in 1863 to include the registration of births, deaths, marriages and successful vaccinations; the compilation of emigration statistics; an annual statistical report on criminal and judicial statistics; and superintendence of the decennial census.

regium donum   Dating from the reign of Charles II, it was the sum payable to the Presbyterian Church and from 1802 directly to ministers. It was commuted to a capital sum of £770,000 under the Irish Church Act (1869).

Remonstrant Synod   Formed in 1830 by Presbyterians who seceded from the Synod of Ulster.

Removal of the Oath Act, 1933   It amended the Constitution of 1922 to remove the Oath of Allegiance to the Monarch.

Repeal   *See* Repeal Association.

Repeal Association   Founded by Daniel O'Connell on 25 April 1840 to advocate Repeal of the Union between Great Britain and Ireland (the Act of Union), it held a series of mass or monster meetings, especially during 1843. It disintegrated shortly after O'Connell's death in 1847.

Representative Church Body   Established after the Irish Church Act came into effect (1 January 1871) to be responsible for churches and burial grounds and to oversee the finances available to the Church of Ireland.

Republic of Ireland Act, 1948   It repealed the External Relations Act and legislated for the creation of the Republic of Ireland, which came into existence on Easter Monday 1949.

Republican Congress   Socialist-republican movement formed in 1934 from Saor Éire, following a split in the Irish Republican Army. It was dissolved in 1935.

Republican Labour Party   Founded in Belfast in 1953 as a splinter of the Labour Party. It collapsed shortly after the creation of the Social Democratic and Labour Party in 1970.

resident magistrates   First appointed under legislation enacted in 1814, they replaced stipendiary magistrates and were a vital part of the machinery of justice and intelligence.

Restoration of Order in Ireland Act   (9 August 1920): Extended the Defence of the Realm Act, empowering the Commander-in-Chief to arrest and hold without trial anyone suspected of membership in Sinn Féin or the Irish Republican Army. Suspects could be tried by secret court martial and only have legal representation from a crown-appointed lawyer.

'Resurrection of Hungary'   A series of 27 articles by Arthur Griffith advocating emulation of the Hungarian example, including withdrawal of Irish MPs from the Westminster parliament.

Revival of 1859   Protestant, especially Presbyterian, movement of religious revival in Ulster.

Ribbonmen   Local groups which were an underground of agrarian secret societies noted for instigating violence.

Richmond Commission   Appointed in August 1879 by the Conservative government to investigate agricultural conditions in Great Britain and Ireland, it was chaired by the Duke of Richmond, reporting in January 1881.

Rotunda   A Dublin lying-in maternity hospital opened in 1745 as the first of its kind in the British Isles.

Royal Dublin Society (RDS)   Founded on 25 June 1731, it assumed the title 'Royal' in June 1820. It sought 'to improve husbandry, manufactures and other useful arts and sciences'.

Royal Hibernian Academy   Incorporated in 1823, it encouraged artists through an annual exhibition of their works. It was reorganised in 1861.

Royal Irish Academy (RIA)   Founded in 1785 to 'advance the studies of science, polite literature and antiquities'.

Royal Irish Constabulary (RIC)   Formed in 1836, it was granted the title 'Royal' in 1867. After the Treaty the force was disbanded in the Free State, while in Northern Ireland members were absorbed by the new Royal Ulster Constabulary.

Royal Ulster Constabulary (RUC)   Established on 1 June 1922 as the province-wide police service in Northern Ireland.

Royal University of Ireland   Examining body established under the University Education Act (1879). It was replaced by the National University under the Act of 1908.

St Enda's   Founded in 1908 at Cullenswood House, Dublin, by Patrick Pearse, it was a bilingual school which fostered the Irish language and provided an atmosphere steeped in the heroic tradition.

Saor Éire   Socialist-republican group of the Irish Republican Army founded in September 1931. It was outlawed on 17 October 1931.

Saor Uladh   Splinter group of the Irish Republican Army founded in Co. Tyrone in 1954.

Scarman Tribunal   Body chaired by Lord Scarman to examine the causes of the violence in the summer of 1969. A report was published on 6 April 1972. It concluded that the disturbances arose from a mixture of social, economic and political factors. It exonerated the Royal Ulster Constabulary from accusations that it co-operated with Protestants in attacks on Catholics, but found the force seriously at fault on a number of occasions.

School Attendance Act, 1926   Legislation for compulsory attendance for children between the ages of 6 and 14 with power for the Minister for Education to extend the leaving age to 16.

seanchaí   Storyteller, descending from the tradition of the old Irish bard.

Second Reformation   Evangelical campaign organised in the Church of Ireland in the 1820s which engaged in proselytising in the west. It disintegrated in the 1860s.

secret societies   Groups, usually local or regional in membership, engaged in agrarian violence and intimidation, including Blackfeet, Carders, Defenders, the Hearts of Oak (Oakboys), the Hearts of Steel (Steelboys), Peep O'Day Boys, the Terry Alts, the Thrashers and the Whitefeet.

shebeen   Illicit drinking house.

Sinn Féin   Founded in 1905 by Arthur Griffith, its policy was withdrawal from the Westminster parliament. After reorganisation in spring 1917, it was at the forefront of the political campaign against British rule during the War of Independence. Later, in the 1930s and 1940s, it advocated British withdrawal from Northern Ireland. It became a Marxist vehicle during the 1960s and in 1970 a split created two branches. The larger, provisional Sinn Féin, is associated with the Irish Republican Army with Gerry Adams as its president.

Sinn Féin League   Founded in April 1907 from a merger of the Dungannon Clubs and Cumann na nGaedheal. In September 1908 it merged with the National Council to become Sinn Féin.

Skirmishing Fund   Established by Fenians in the United States in 1875, its purpose was to finance activities directed at the harassment of British rule.

Social Democratic and Labour Party Founded in Northern Ireland in August 1970, it has been the largest party representing northern Catholics since then.

Socialist Labour Party Founded in Dublin in November 1977 to oppose coalition government, capitalism and imperialism, it also called for withdrawal of the British presence in any part of Ireland.

Socialist Party of Ireland Formerly the Irish Socialist Republican Party, it became the Communist Party of Ireland in 1921.

Society for Irish Church Missions to Roman Catholics Founded on 28 March 1849 to resist Evangelical campaigning in Ireland.

Solemn League and Covenant Signed on 28 September 1912, it was a pledge by Unionists to resist home rule.

souperism Term applied to Catholics who changed their religion in return for food and drink.

Southern Ireland Area (26 counties) designated under the Better Government of Ireland Act (1920). A parliament for Southern Ireland met briefly in 1920 but was suspended.

Southern Unionist Committee Founded on 20 February 1918 to represent southern Unionists dissatisfied with the Irish Unionist Alliance. It dissolved after the Treaty.

Southwark Literary Club Founded in London on 4 January 1883, its purposes were the cultivation and promotion of Irish history, art and literature and to provide a venue where Irish people might meet.

spalpeen A wandering labourer who hired out his labour to farmers.

Special Branch Established in 1925, its main preoccupation has been to monitor and combat political crime, unrest and subversion.

Special Powers Act (Civil Authorities (Special Powers) Act (Northern Ireland), 1922) It replaced the Restoration of Order in Ireland Act (1920), granting power to ministers to proscribe organisations, ban and reroute marches and arrest and detain suspects. It was made permanent in 1933 and constituted the legal basis of interment in 1972. It was repealed in 1973, being replaced by the Emergency Provisions Act (Northern Ireland) (1973) and the Prevention of Terrorism Act (UK) (1974).

Statute of Westminster, 1930 No law made by the parliament of a Dominion should be inoperative because it was repugnant to the law of England. It largely ceded legislative autonomy to the Dominions.

Stormont (Castle) Home of the parliament of Northern Ireland (1932–72) located outside Belfast. Previously the parliament met in the Council Chamber of Belfast City Hall and in the Assembly College, Belfast.

783

Subletting Act, 1826 Attempted prohibition of subletting of property by tenants except with the consent of the proprietor.

Sunningdale Agreement Reached on 9 December 1973 between the governments of the United Kingdom and the Republic of Ireland along with the incoming Executive of Northern Ireland. The two governments agreed that there should be no alteration in the status of Northern Ireland until a majority of the people expressed support for change, to revive the Council of Ireland, and that there should be co-operation between the two countries on law and order. The Executive fell as a consequence of the Ulster Workers' Council strike in May 1974.

Supreme Council (of the Irish Republican Brotherhood) Directing body of the Irish Republican Brotherhood, consisting of 11 members.

Synod of Thurles (22 August – 9 September 1850): First national synod of the Catholic Hierarchy held in Ireland since the Middle Ages.

Synod of Ulster Supreme body of Irish Presbyterians until union with the Secession Synod in 1840 created the General Assembly.

Tánaiste Deputy Taoiseach or deputy Prime Minister since December 1937.

Taoiseach Title of Prime Minster since December 1937.

TD Teachtaí dála, or member of the Dáil.

Temporalities Commission Established after the Irish Church Act in 1869 to administer the revenues of the Church of Ireland.

Tenant League Founded in August 1850 in Dublin, also known as 'The League of North and South', to seek the three Fs (fair rent, fixity of tenure and free sale) for tenant farmers. In 1852 it came into alliance with the Irish Brigade to form the Independent Irish Party.

tenant right Known as the Ulster Custom, it allowed a tenant to sell occupancy of his holding to the highest bidder.

Tenants' Defence Association Founded on 15 October 1889 to aid tenants who participated in the Plan of Campaign. It collapsed after the Irish Party split (December 1890).

Thrashers Agrarian secret society active in the 1820s and 1830s.

three Fs Fixity of tenure, fair rent and free sale. They were substantially obtained in the Land Act (1881).

tinkers (travellers) Traditional term for itinerants who although natives of Ireland are akin to Roma. They prefer to be called travellers, which is the term now more commonly used.

Tithe War (1830–8): Resistance by Catholics to the collection of tithes for the Church of Ireland. The dispute was resolved by the Tithe Commutation Act (1838).

tithes Sum of money gathered from the population for the support of the Church of Ireland. Its collection sparked the Tithe War by Catholics. The Tithe Commutation Act (1838) made the sum a semi-annual rent charge at three-quarters of the old composition payable by the head landlord.

townland A unit of land of different extent (1 to 7,012 acres).

transportation Removal of prisoners and dangerous persons to penal servitude abroad. It was abolished in 1868.

Treason-Felony Act, 1848 Allowed prosecution of a person who by open and advised speaking compassed the intimidation of the crown or parliament.

Treaty Agreement signed between plenipotentiaries of the United Kingdom government and Dáil Éireann on 6 December 1921.

Treaty Ports Great Britain retained rights over four ports including three in the Free State along with aviation and storage facilities under an annex to the Treaty. In time of war other facilities were to be granted. These were handed back to Éire in 1938.

Triangle Triumvirate which dominated the Clan na Gael in the 1880s (Alexander Sullivan, Michael Boland and Denis Feeley).

tricolour National flag of the Republic of Ireland. It is sometimes employed by republicans to display opposition to the status of Northern Ireland.

Trinity College Dublin (University of Dublin): Created in 1592 as a Church of Ireland foundation, it possesses some of the finest university architecture and a distinguished academic reputation.

Truce Came into effect on 11 July 1921 between the United Kingdom and Dáil Éireann.

turbary-right Ancient right to cut turf in a bog.

Ulster Constitutional Defence Committee Founded in 1966 in protest against republican commemoration of the Easter Rising of 1916.

Ulster Custom *See* tenant right.

Ulster Defence Association Paramilitary organisation founded in Northern Ireland in August 1971.

Ulster Defence Regiment (UDR) Military force established in Northern Ireland in 1970 to replace the Ulster Special Constabulary ('B' Specials).

Ulster Defence Union Founded in 1894 to organise resistance to home rule.

Ulster Loyalist Anti-Repeal Union Founded in Belfast on 8 January 1886 for the purpose of resistance to home rule.

Ulster Protestant Action Loyalist-Protestant movement in the 1950s.

Ulster Protestant League Founded in 1931 it called on Protestant employers not to employ Catholics and urged Protestants not to work or do business with Catholics.

Ulster Protestant Volunteers Founded in 1966, it was supported by Ian Paisley and initially had a connection with the Ulster Volunteer Force.

Ulster Special Constabulary Known as 'B' Specials, it was a part-time force which came into existence in 1921 and was disbanded in April 1970.

Ulster Tenant Right Association Founded in 1847 by William Sharman Crawford and others, it promoted tenant right.

Ulster Unionist Council Founded on 3 March 1905 in Belfast, it served as an umbrella for opposition to home rule. It adopted a new constitution in 1946, 'to maintain Northern Ireland as an integral part of the United Kingdom and to uphold and defend the Constitution and Parliament of Northern Ireland'.

Ulster Unionist Party Created in 1886, it remains the largest political party in Northern Ireland.

Ulster Volunteer Force (UVF) Founded in January 1913 for the purpose of resisting home rule, it suffered heavy casualties during the First World War and was disbanded after 1921. It was revived in 1966 and proscribed in 1974.

Ulster Womens' Unionist Council Founded on 23 January 1911 for the purpose of maintaining the legislative Union between Great Britain and Ireland.

Ulster Workers' Council Formed in 1974, it opposed the power-sharing Executive, which it was instrumental in bringing to an end through a province-wide strike in May 1974.

ultramontanism Recognition of the absolute authority of the Pope in matters of faith and morals.

Under-Secretary Permanent head of the civil service in Ireland under the Union.

Union Defence League Founded in 1907 to resist home rule.

Unionist Anti-Partition League Formed by southern Unionists in 1919 to prevent the division of Ireland.

Unionist Clubs Founded in 1893 to organise opposition to home rule.

Unionist Party of Northern Ireland Founded by Brian Faulkner on 24 June 1974 to support his policy of power-sharing after the Ulster Workers' Council strike brought the Executive to an end.

United Irish League Founded on 23 January 1898, it became the recognised organisation of the reunited Irish Party in June 1900. The United Irish

League of Great Britain was formed later in the year and the United Irish League of America was created in December 1901.

United Irishmen   The Society of United Irishmen was founded in Belfast in October 1791. Its last manifestation was Robert Emmet's abortive rebellion in 1803.

United Trades Association   Formed in 1863, it sought to protect labour and encourage native manufactures.

United Ulster Unionist Council (UUUC)   Founded in 1974 to oppose the power-sharing Executive. It disappeared during 1976.

Unity Proposals   (May 1922): An attempt by officers in the Irish Republican Army to resolve the differences between pro- and anti-Treaty factions.

urban and rural district councils   Created under legislation in 1898 they were elected bodies replacing grand juries and had some authority for raising revenue for local purposes.

Vanguard   Ulster Unionist organisation founded by William Craig in February 1972 to oppose reforms. It had largely disappeared by late 1975.

Veto   Proposal to link Catholic Emancipation to the British government's right to veto the appointment of Catholic prelates in Ireland.

Volunteer Political Party   Founded in April 1974 as a political branch of the Ulster Volunteer Force. The UVF was proscribed in October 1974 and the party disappeared soon afterwards.

wake   Custom of remaining with a corpse until its removal to the church. After the body was prepared, relatives would be brought formally into its presence and a lament, known as a keen, was then performed. Chief mourners provided food, drink, snuff and tobacco for those in attendance. Drink, dancing and merrymaking were traditionally part of a wake, as was the playing of special wake games, the origins of which are pre-Christian.

War of Independence   (21 January 1919 to 9 July 1921): The period when republicans struggled by armed means to secure an Irish state.

White Cross   Founded on 1 February 1921 as a Sinn Féin organisation to assist in the distribution of the American-based White Cross Fund. Proceeds were used to assist republicans and their families who were suffering financial hardship through involvement in the War of Independence and also to aid Catholic workers expelled from employment in Northern Ireland.

Whiteboys   Agrarian secret society founded in Tipperary in 1761, it remained a model for similar groups in the nineteenth century.

Widgery Report   Committee established under the chairmanship of Lord Widgery to investigate the events in Londonderry on 'Bloody Sunday'. It reported on 18 April 1972 that the organisers of the protest 'created a highly dangerous situation', that the soldiers present showed 'a high degree of responsibility' but that 'none of the deceased or wounded is proved to have been shot whilst handling a firearm or bomb'. It remained highly controversial, leading in 1999 to the establishment of a new body sitting in Londonderry to investigate the events of 'Bloody Sunday'.

Wolfe Tone Society Founded in 1963 'to work out a synthesis between traditional republican populism and socialism'.

Workers' Party of Ireland Founded in May 1926 it sought and failed to secure affiliation to the Comintern. It ceased to function in the following year.

Workers' Revolutionary Party Socialist organisation founded on 13 March 1930, it was banned on 17 October 1931.

Workers' Union of Ireland Syndicalist trade union founded in June 1924 by James Larkin and others.

Wyndham Act, 1903 *See* Land Acts.

Young Ireland Nationalist movement centred on the *Nation* newspaper, it had a strong Protestant element. Key figures included Thomas Davis, Charles Gavan Duffy and John Blake Dillon. It broke with Daniel O'Connell and the Repeal Movement, and in 1848, following a split in Young Ireland, a section known as the Irish Confederation started an unsuccessful rebellion at Ballingarry, Co. Tipperary.

INDEX

Note: Irish Free State/Éire/Republic of Ireland is abbreviated as IFS/É/ROI in the index.

789

797